This book discusses the political and economic history of the port of Bushehr, which by the end of the eighteenth century had become the gateway to southern Persia (Iran). It offers a detailed analysis of Bushehr's demography, industry, health care, education, and standard of living; as well as its trade, and how politics impacted its well-being. Throughout this period Bushehr had to ward off the growing competition from other Persian Gulf ports such as Bandar Abbas. It did so successfully, enjoying growing trade and wealth, despite internal and external political problems. Because of its important commercial position Bushehr was also twice attacked and occupied by the British (1856, 1915-18). What brought the port city down finally, however, was not the British attacks and occupations, nor the occupation and looting of the city by Tangestani tribesmen (purported protectors of the constitution) in 1909; it was the expansion of the ports, roads, and railroads of the oil-rich province of Khuzestan. This caused economic decline for Bushehr, which resulted in a loss of trade and much of its population between 1920 and 1940. The World War II years did not bring much improvement to its situation either. The economic malaise contributed to a tribal uprising in Fars in 1946, in which Bushehr played an important role. However, the uprising failed, and as such was but a last spasm of a bygone era.

پست ممالک محروسه ایران
POSTES PERSANES
Under British
Occupation
Ch

THE PERSIAN GULF

BUSHEHR

CITY, SOCIETY & TRADE 1797–1947

WILLEM FLOOR

MAGE PUBLISHERS

Library of Congress Cataloging-in-Publication Data
Available in detail at the Library of Congress

ISBN
1-933823-86-0
978-1-933823-86-7

Printed and Manufactured in the United States

MAGE PUBLISHERS
Washington DC
202-342-1642 • as@mage.com
Visit Mage Publishers online at
www.mage.com

Contents

Images

Note

Most of the photos in this book were made available by Dr. Iraj Nabipour; the other images are from Dubeux 1841, Flandin 1851, Vilmorin 1895; Moore 1914; Braunagel 1925; Hinz 1936; Roknzadeh 1352 ; India Office; *Illustrated London News* (18 April 1857) and photos from my own collection. The stamps are courtesy of Mehdi Stamps. The tile image from the Tavakkoli House on page xxii, and the cover page, which is a tile section from an old house in Shiraz (Seif 2014), depicting the British naval attack on Bushehr in 1857, were kindly provided by Hamid Kooros.

Tables

FOREWORD

This is my eighth book in the series *The Persian Gulf* in which I discuss the vicissitudes of Bushehr, Persia's most important sea port in the Persian Gulf, during its rise in the nineteenth century as well as its decline during the end of the Qajar period, which continued during the Reza Shah period (1800-1941). Ideally, the scope of this book should go beyond 1947, but data are scant for the post-1947 period and so I leave this remaining period to other scholars. This book completes the discussion of the role of and developments in the major Persian ports in the Gulf (Bandar Abbas and Lengeh are the two others). Logically, I should continue this series with the history of Mohammerah. However, I have discussed its early history in another publication in this series,[1] while its rise as a modern major port has been competently dealt with by Shahbaz Shahnavaz.[2] I intend to write at least another book in this series, dealing with Khark, a book that is in *statu nascendi*, but there may yet be others, as you never know where your fancy takes you.

In chapter one, of this book about Bushehr, I provide a description of the location, morphology and characteristics of the district and town of Bushehr, including its population, water supply, health, education, and living conditions. In chapter two, I discuss the port and its facilities and analyze the nature and structure of the trade of Bushehr and the reasons for the changes therein. In chapter three, I discuss the political developments of the town, in particular of the interaction between the Arab Al Mazkur dynasty that ruled the port and the government of Fars, as well as the town's vicissitudes under a parliamentary Persia and of the new centralizing Pahlavi state. In chapter four, the government and civic institutions that were present in Bushehr are discussed, including the many new institutions that were created in the twentieth century as well as the foreign consulates present in the port.

Finally, I want to thank those who have been helpful, while I wrote this study. First, thanks are due to my friends Sayyed Qasem Ya Hoseyni and Iraj Nabipour from Bushehr, who provided me with photographs of Bushehr as well as Mojtaba Tabrizniya, co-editor of the *Pazhuheshnameh-ye Khalij-e Fars* and Parisa Mohammadi who provided me with electronic copies of some relevant Persian sources. Last, but most certainly not least, I owe great thanks to my good friend Keith Openshaw for editing my English, and to my son Guus for making the map of Bushehr ca. 1920 on p. 30.

The system of transliteration of Persian words used is simple and as follows:

Long and short a= a
Long u = u
Short u= o
Long i= i
Short i= e

---

1. 1 Floor 2011 b, chapter four.
2. 2 Shahnavaz 2005.

Present-day map of Bushehr and vicinity

INTRODUCTION

Bushehr was the gateway to much of Southern Persia from the 1750s until the 1920s. It took over this function from Bandar Abbas in the 1750s, but lost the race for economic primacy against the fast rising modern port of Mohammerah (later called Khorramshahr) in the 1920s. During that period Bushehr had a varied and sometimes violent history, including occupation by British troops (1857; 1915-18), while changing its character from a port ruled by a hereditary Arab Sheikh (until 1850) to one that was ruled by central government bureaucrats who came from other parts of Persia. Trade increased during that period, a trend that was sustained until the 1920s, while its contacts with Europe also grew. All these and other events and developments to which Bushehr was exposed, of course, left its imprint on the port. However, unlike other port cities in Asia and elsewhere, Bushehr did not display any of the characteristics that such 'colonial ports' are supposed to acquire.

Port cities and their hinterland have attracted the attention of many scholars of varying disciplines. Scholars such as Basu, Murphy, Broeze, Driesen and Nas have drawn attention to various characteristics of port cities.[1] They stress that port cities are places where different cultures and diverse environments meet and interact and through which people, goods, services, and ideas flow. While all this may be true, these characteristics are not necessarily ones peculiar to port cities. The same arguments can be made for land-based 'ports', such as caravan cities and rural market towns.[2] Therefore, some scholars stress that these cities were more than an extension of a port, because the economic policies of port cities are maritime in nature. For example, according to Broeze, a port city is "a city where goods and/or passengers are physically transferred between two modes of transport, of which at least one is maritime (transfer from ship to ship can of course also occur ...)." Leaving aside the 'maritime' part in this definition, which is inherent to the function of any sea port, this description is also characteristic for any urban settlement that has a nodal marketing function.

A few years ago[3] I submitted that urban areas in Persia, or for that matter in any post-industiral country, constituted the main market for the disposal of the agricultural surplus by the rural population (both sedentary and non-sedentary) as well as the provider of various services necessary to rural consumers and producers. Many urban trades and crafts conducted activities that for the greater part were directly related to the agricultural (rural) sector of their hinterland. These included the collection, storage, trading, and simple processing of agricultural commodities; the distribution of some agricultural inputs; and the production of agricultural implements and equipment. These trades and crafts also produced and traded a substantial part of the goods and services bought in the market by peasants. The

1. Basu 1985; Murphy 1989, Bird 1971; Broeze 1989; Driessen 2005; Nas 2005.
2. Ironically, in Persian, the word for port or *bandar*, also means a trading town, an emporium.
3. Floor 2003 a, p. 13.

incomes of these trades and crafts therefore fluctuated in consonance with farm incomes (and certainly with the level of agricultural production) rather than with urban incomes. Roughly the rural-urban relationship is as follows:

1.1 Rural-Urban Sector Relationship

Sector	Location	Product/subsector
Agriculture	Rural	- Grains - Vegetables, fruit - Vegetable oils - Meat, animal products - Non-food: wood, cotton, wool, silk, tobacco
Agricultural processing	Rural	- of grains
	Urban/Rural	- of animal products - of non-food products
Current input production	Urban/Rural	- fertilizers - irrigation - water
Capital input production	Rural	- small implements
	Urban	- on-farm construction - other equipment - civil works construction
Other manufacturing	Urban	- intermediates
	Urban/Rural	- capital goods - consumer goods
Other services	Urban	- public services - private services

As may be clear from the above, a market town is as much a place where goods and services are transferred between two different economic spheres, one rural and agricultural and the other urban and manufacturing.

Murphy, who agrees with Broeze, added another dimension to urban-hinterland relationship by submitting "that a city cannot exist without providing a *range* of goods and services to a wider area tributary to it, to which it is tied by virtue of its superior access."[4] I agree with that statement, but, as is clear from the above, it applies to any primary city and large rural market towns as well, thus weakening the argument of the usefulness of the concept of port city. Towns such as Isfahan, Shiraz, Yazd and Kerman were and still are many times larger than the largest settlement in their region. This is due to the difficulty of life outside the irrigated rural environment. Before 1930, there was no integrated national Persian market, and secondary cities were the economic center for their hinterland. There was certainly extraction of part of the surplus to the capital city, but because

4. Murphey 1989, p. 228.

of the decentralized nature of government, the underdeveloped communication and transportation system, less was siphoned off to Tehran than was the case after 1930. This was certainly the case in the nineteenth century when the provinces were slow and/or delinquent in paying their full revenue share to Tehran, so that customs duties and indirect taxation became the most important sources of revenue for the central government.[5]

In Persia there were many small market towns. There were 80 such towns with a population in the 5,000 to 20,000 category in 1900.[6] These market towns held a traditional position as point of extraction, distribution center and central place of dominance for their hinterland.[7] This even held for the largest villages in most districts, which also had the distributive function. "Burazjan is the only trade centre in Dashtistan and its trade is consequently an epitome of the trade of that district. The exports all go to Bushehr town and the imports in the contrary direction."[8] Despite this essential urban-rural relationship nobody is calling these rural market-towns port cities.

Nevertheless, Rhoads Murphy argued that generalizations could be made. "However much individual cases may resist being squeezed into one or even several large categories, the validity of the port concept as a centre of land sea exchange is undeniable, as is the generalization that this process has been and remains a major source of livelihood, and a major force for culture mixing."[9] I disagree, for the Persian Gulf ports do not fit the conceptual framework that these various theoretical studies have produced. To bring home his point, Murphy further argues that "where maritime trade seeks to connect with productive land areas, it develops an entrance. The port thus created is a powerful magnet for improvements in land transport, focused on the port like the spokes of a wheel."[10] However, nothing was farther from the truth in the case of Persia. Whether we take the situation of Bandar Abbas, Bandar-e Lengeh or Bushehr, - the three major ports on the Persian littoral, - no effort was ever made to improve land transport, there was no wheeled transportation, and as a result commercial traffic was subject to delays, pilfering, robberies and blackmail, thus increasing its cost and reliability. Moreover, having studied the situation in the major Persian ports in the Persian Gulf, I can only conclude that there was no development of additional functions in manufacturing, administration and other services, which, according to Murphy, was also one of the characteristics of port cities.[11] Another vaunted characteristic of ports is the meeting of peoples and cultures. However, in Persian ports there was no "highly varied mix of peoples and cultures reflecting their widespread connections."[12]

Murphy finally notes that there was a transformation of the port cities in that there was a "progressive reversal of the traditional Asian pattern of inward-centredness in each country. Traditionally the largest Asian cities, including the national capitals, were inland. By 1900, the largest cities in each country were instead all ports, in the smallest countries

---

5. Floor 1998 b.
6. Bharier 1972, pp. 51-61.
7. For the twentieth century see e.g. (Arak, Bam, Dezful, Malayer, Semnan, Tabas). Ehlers 1975, pp. 38-452; Idem, 1971, pp. 6-33; Bonine 1980. See, for example, the sketch map of the provinces of Ispahan and Yezd in *DCR* 4838 Ispahan and Yezd (1911).
8. Lorimer 1915, vol. 2, pp. 328-29.
9. Murphy 1989, p. 225.
10. Murphy 1989, p. 234.
11. Murphy 1989, p. 234; for Persian ports, see Shahnavaz 2005; Floor 2010; Idem 2011 a.
12. Murphy 1989, p. 236.

the only big cities."[13] The urban population of Persia was about 7 percent at the beginning of the nineteenth century. This percentage had been higher in the seventeenth century, but due to anarchy and warfare during most of the eighteenth century de-urbanization had taken place on a significant scale. In 1869, it is estimated that Persia had 30 towns with a population higher than 10,000, with a total population of 850,000 inhabitants. There were 58 such towns, with a population of 1.8 million, in the early twentieth century. Of these, three towns had more than 100,000 inhabitants: Tehran about 280,000, Tabriz 200,000 and Isfahan 100,000. Four other towns each had 50,000 inhabitants or more.[14] Contrariwise, Persian port cities in the Persian Gulf had a population that only in the early twentieth century reached the 20,000 level. There were differences between the large towns, which even now persist. Apart from the capital city, Tehran, there were ancient handicraft centers (Isfahan, Tabriz, Kashan, and Yazd), religious centers (Mashhad, Qom), ports (Bushehr, Enzeli) and an array of market towns, which mainly had an administrative and distributive function. The difference between these towns was not so much in wealth as in natural endowment, often determining the nature of its economic activity.

However, more importantly, then as now, there was city primacy, combined with a relative large number of secondary primate towns. Ehlers and others have remarked that although all secondary towns served as a central place of dominance *vis à vis* their hinterland, these in turn, were all dominated by Tehran. This held in particular, of course, for luxury goods, but even for many daily necessities.[15] Invariably, the primate city was the capital city. Not only was there the concentration of all political and economic power, but also, it tended to be the largest city in terms of population size and growth. Whether Isfahan in the seventeenth century, or Shiraz in the eighteenth century, these capital cities were the home of the country's political, bureaucratic, military and economic elite. Isfahan also housed the religious elite, but this function, other cities, or later Tehran did not acquire. This primate role was also evident in the downfall of these cities, when they lost not only a major chunk of their population, but also the other functions, although Isfahan held on to its religious function till about 1850.[16]

In fact, the flow of people, ideas, services, and goods that sustained the cultural, social, and political development of commercial nodal points, such as colonial port cities was characteristic of cities in the interior in nineteenth century Persia, in particular the cities of Tabriz and Tehran. It was these two cities rather than the Persian Gulf port cities that were centers for the reception and transfer of culture and knowledge. It was from these cities that political, social, economic and cultural change spread to the rest of the country, including to the port cities. Not surprisingly, they were and remained the largest cities in the country, although they are inland!

The various studies cited above also stress that the so-called hinterland influences its port city and vice-versa. They make the point that the functions of the port city are determined by its relationship and the nature therefore, with its hinterland and its foreland, i.e. the countries and places with which it trades. Studies of modern port cities have led to the conclusion that there is more than one hinterland. There is the immediate hinterland

---

13. Murphy 1989, p. 242.
14. Gilbar 1976, pp. 147-49
15. Ehlers 1992, pp. 168-169.
16. Ehlers 1992, see in particular fig. 1, p. 157.

(the port area), the primary hinterland (the area where the port city has a commanding role), the commodity hinterland (areas that supplies or receives particular types of commodities), and the inferred hinterland (the area that the port city controls, i.e. that satisfies the demand of imports in the area it serves). Of course, the nature and intensity of the relative importance of each of these various segmented hinterlands changes over time and that depends on the socio-economic and political context in which the port city functions.[17] It may be that these various characteristics are true for so-called colonial port cities in S.E. Asia and in the Mediterranean as compared with other non-colonial cities in other areas and/or countries.[18] However, they are not distinctive to the Persian port cities on the northern coast of the Persian Gulf.

Why is it that Persian port cities do not fit the generalizations that seem to match Asian port cities? Unlike their Asian counterparts, they were not at the crossroads of socio-economic, cultural and political encounters and of cosmopolitism; Persian ports were just caravan termini, with a small population that hardly grew over the centuries. There was no important local market to speak of, and no important port-related elite (who mostly lived in the interior). The foreigners who lived in these ports were only a handful and there was relatively little communication between them and the society at large in which they lived. The population of these port cities was ethnically not uniform and there was a regular influx of newcomers from the hinterlands. There was some cultural mixing and hybridization, but not with foreigners, but only among the groups from the hinterland. This was facilitated by similarity in culture, religion (in most cases), and to a certain extent in language. The mercantile elite was influenced by their interaction with Western counterparts and over time most of them were transformed from importers into agents for foreign importing firms. However, this was in and by itself no major and absolute shift, but only one of degree. Most of these agents of foreign firms had been agents of Persian importing firms, mainly based inland. In short, Bushehr was unlike Asian port cities, although like them its economic well-being clearly was connected to its role as a port.

17. Bird 1971.
18. Broeze 1989, p. 35.

Tile from the Tavakkoli House in Shiraz depicting defense of Bushehr from the British invasion in 1857

1

The Town and Peninsula

Location

Bushehr is situated at the northern end of a cigar-shaped peninsula of quaterny sandstone. It is about 19 km (12 miles) long from its north-western tip, on which stands Bushehr town, to Ras Halileh at the opposite end, by 6.5 km (4 miles) wide at its widest part. It ran parallel to the main land and was joined in the middle to it by a sandy plain about 33 km (21 miles) wide, known as the Mashilah, which in winter more resembled a marsh. Therefore, sometimes the peninsula was referred to as Rishahr Island (*jazireh-ye Rishahr*).[1] The town is situated a little above sea level because it was built on a rocky ridge and, according to some, until the early nineteenth century, it was frequently "from the rise of the tides, an island."[2] However, this was a rare occurrence, because in 1809, Morier observed this had happened only once during the last decade and then only for three days,[3] so that in reality it had become a peninsula.[4]

The town of Bushehr was not the only settlement on the peninsula for it shared this area with about 30 villages of which Rishahr was the largest. Sadid al-Saltaneh distinguished three groups, to wit: the eastern, western and central villages.

The eastern villages included Jabrabad, Zolmabad and Setamabad that by 1910 had become part of the town of Bushehr. Previously its inhabitants had lived in Bushehr in date branch huts or *kapars*. In 1856 when the British attacked and took Bushehr, the then governor Hasan `Ali Khan Daryabegi, son of Mirza `Ali Akbar Khan Qavam al-Molk, was afraid that British gunfire would set fire to these huts and thus threaten the entire town of Bushehr. Therefore, he forced these hut dwellers to take up abodes outside the town,

1. Waring 1973, p. 2; Kinneir 1970, p. 69; Trade Report 1913-14, p. 1; Trade Report 1910-11, p. 1; Binning 1857, vol. 1, p. 140; Lorimer 1915, vol. 2, p. 330; Brittlebank 1873, p. 92; Sa`adat 1390, p. 50; Sadid al-Saltaneh 1371, p. 52; Government of India 1924, p. 24. Halileh "has a trifling square fort, with a tower at each angle, but without any guns." Morier 1812, p. 59.
2. Waring 1973, p. 2; Kinneir 1970, p. 69; Sani` al-Dowleh 1294, vol. 1, p. 300; Sa`adat 1390, p. 50; Government of India 1924, p. 25. There also were low cliffs south-west of the town and south of Rishahr. "One hollow called Ander-i-Buneh Dareh or Andar Bandar runs down the middle of the peninsula to its east side; and parallel to this, on its south side, is a Qanat which taps a subterranean water-supply." Lorimer 1915, vol. 2, p. 330. According to the editors of Sa`adat 1390, p. 221, the term is pronounced *ondor bondor*; see also Hamidi 1380, p. 91 (with a suggestion for the origin of this term).
3. Morier 1812, p. 56.
4. Curzon 1892, vol. 1, p. 231; Sa`adat 1390, p. 18.

hence, allegedly, the names of the villages, which all express the memory of their forced relocation that was perceived to be an act of injustice. Other eastern villages were Pudar, (Bagh-e) Shekeri, Bagh-e Zahra that previously had many date groves, Bagh-e Helali, Lul-e Bahrainiha, Lul-e Hasan Ahmadi, and many others.

The western villages included: Gonbad-e Sayyed, the Bushehr cemetery; Mahmudabad, where the Russians had a residence, while it also housed the German consulate, the town of (*qasabeh-ye*) Rishahr, and the port of Halileh. There even was an area where one could hunt gazelles.

The central villages included: Khal`ati, Askani, Bon Mane`, Neydi, Bahmani, Emamzadeh, and Sabzabad: the latter housed the summer quarters of most Europeans and wealthy Bushehris. For example, at Sabzabad the British Resident had a house on the highest part of the island. North-east of Jofreh a.k.a. Hofreh, the Dutch consul built his residence called *Holandarabad*, which was later purchased by the French. These central villages bordered on Halileh.[5] In the 1970s, Roger Stevens found the area quite pleasing. He wrote:

> The interior of the Bushire peninsula, too, has a certain wistful charm. It is dotted with large white country houses in, I suppose, an Anglo-Iranian style, with deep balconies and columns on their flat roofs which presumably carry awnings in the hot weather. There are gardens with stone parapets, banyan and acacia trees, and well built stone walls. At least in winter, when the undulating wasteland is green, it is a park-like landscape, a mildly tropical version of Wimbledon Common.[6]

Farming/market gardening

The inhabitants of these villages were mostly engaged in agriculture and/or animal husbandry as well as fishing and some weaving. In 1802, Waring saw "some castor-oil shrubs, and found, upon enquiry, the oil was only used for lamps."[7] However, the peasants mostly tilled wheat, barley, cotton, dates, fruits and vegetables, although even observant reporters such as Morier and Fraser often saw no more than "a few cotton-bushes, here and there date-trees, now and then a konar-tree, with water-melons, berinjaus, cucumbers, [being] the only verdant objects."[8] The cultivation of vegetables was neither large nor of a great variety.[9] Because of its climatological condition some cultivation was done differently than elsewhere in Persia, such as in the case of cotton.

> The cultivation of cotton in the environs of Bushire is somewhat peculiar as compared with the system existing in the interior where the plants are

5. Sadid al-Saltaneh 1371, pp. 51-52 (with a complete list of all villages); Lorimer 1915, vol. 2, pp. 334-38; Sa`adat 1390, pp. 50-54; Hamidi 1380, pp. 222, 224. About other possible origins of the names of Zolmabad, Solhabad and Jabri, see Kanin 1391, p. 218.
6. Stevens 1979, p. 258.
7. Waring 1973, p. 8. On the use of oil and other products as a source of illumination, see Floor 2003 b, pp. 112-85.
8. Morier 1812, p. 68; Fraser 1984, p. 58; Government of India 1924, p. 25, 107.
9. Anonymous 1828, p. 57.

View of Bushehr and its environs

annuals and grown by irrigation, whereas it is grown here without any irrigation and the plant lives up to twenty-five and thirty years without diminishing in yield. A plot of ground is plowed several, at least three, times, during the rainy season, with the object of rendering te soil as soft as possible; then, just after the *last* rains, seeds, first cleaned of all vestiges of the cotton, are soaked in water (in casks or vessels) for two or three days and then sown in furrows of 8 to 10 inches deep in rows 5 or 7 feet apart. The seeds are thickly sown (about 40 or 50 seeds going to the span) and covered over with earth. The young plants are entirely left to the mercy of the elements; the only precaution taken is to prevent their being destroyed by cattle. With a heavy fall of rain after the sowing, as a rule, the seeds die or come up very sparsely, and fresh seeds have to be put down immediately. If the soil is rich and soft the plants grow thickly, forming a sort of hedge, but generally only two or three plants survive in a space of one yard. The plants, if in good soil, begin to bear in the first year, otherwise in the following, and continue increasing in yield up to their fifth or sixth year, when they may have said to have arrived at development. During the successive rainy seasons the intervening space between the rows is carefully plowed up and grain sown, with double advantage, the plowing being considered highly beneficial to the cotton., and its dead leaves in turn serving as manure for the grain. Cattle are allowed to enter the cotton fields in the end of autumn, they doing the work of pruning. A healthy plant will give cotton to the value of 8 *d.* [pence], but the average may be taken as 1 *s.* [shilling] for every six plants. The plants blossom first in May and the cotton is collected in June, when they blossom immediately a second time, ripening in September.[10]

10. Malcolm 1887, p. 273 (italics in original).

All this land was government property and the peasants paid taxes on how much land they had under cultivation, based on a unit referred to a *gav* (cow) or *khish* (plow). A *gav* is a piece of land that one bullock can plow during a period of 35 to 55 days sowing a quantity of each of wheat and barley. Peasants used a light plow drawn mostly by one ox only in the early nineteenth century. If a horse was pulling the plow the unit was equal to 1.5 *gav* of land and taxed accordingly. However, by the end of the nineteenth century, generally two donkeys were used to pull the plough and which were calculated as one *gav*. Usually 2/3 of wheat and 1/3 of barley was sown per *gav*. There was already cultivation of wheat and barley 1.5 km beyond the town. The soil was sandy, here and there rocky, and in summer it looked as if nothing would grow there. The soil selected for cultivation was "*cheety*" or "*narmeh*", i.e. sandy or soft and "*masheel*" or muddy and hard. The seeds were scattered on the surface of the unprepared soil and because the soil was so light it was turned over with very little labor. Plowing '*cheety*' land was easier and thus a larger area was used and seeds were sparingly sown. It was also more rewarding when the rainfall was inadequate. Contrariwise, more seeds were sown of *masheel* soil, which produced a higher output, if rains were abundant. The season started around 25 October and some 3,500 *gav* were ploughed ("*khoshk kaur*"). More seed was sown than necessary to compensate for losses due to decay and birds. The land was not manured, because peasants used dung as a fuel. However, it was generally believed that the scorching heat acted as a kind of soil fertilizer. Wet plowing started immediately after the first abundant rains began, which in normal years was during the second or third week of November. In good years the seed/yield ratio was 8 to 15 and even 20 fold, while the average yield was 5 to 8 fold. This included the yield of chopped straw (*kah*), which formed an important part of the revenue obtained from cultivation. In 1905, the major cost elements for a peasant were as follows:

Table 1.1: Cost structure of a Bushehri peninsula peasant's land preparation

Cost element	Cost (*Qrans*)
Average cost of wheat seed	48.00
Average cost of barley seed	30.00
2.5 *man* of barley to feed the cow	25.00
Cost of plough	4.50
Wages of the plower	20.00
Government tax	80.00
Hire of cow	20.00
Sundry petty expenses	2.50
Total	230.00

Source: NA, FO 248/1024, "Note by an Armenian merchant in 1905."

The cost of harvesting, threshing and winnowing was about 20% of the tenant's outlay. The duration of the period between harvesting and final storage was 60 to 90

Irrigation using the Persian wheel

days, and in case of a bumper crop even 120 days.[11] Morier reported cotton was sown more systematically at Halileh than at Bushehr.[12] In 1802, Waring reported that "From some cotton bushes near Bushire, they [merchants] fabricate a kind of cloth nearly equal to the China nankeen."[13] Around 1910, each year the peninsula produced about 400 *man-e hashem* (16 *man-e Tabriz* or 46.4 kg) of cotton. At that time, one *man-e Tabriz* cost 8,000 dinars, mostly bought by Halileh inhabitants, who spun and dyed it and used it to weave their fabrics. In good years the peninsula had an output of 500 *fard*, and not less than 250 *fard*.[14]

Also, there were some scattered date groves, but they were not very thriving. By 1910, the date palms numbered 15-20,000.[15] In the past there were more groves, because in 1856, when the British took Bushehr they cut down about 4,000 date trees to make room for their military camp. Although they paid an enormous sum to the owners, it meant the end of Bagh-e Zahra.[16] However, in the twentieth century there no longer appears to have been any date cultivation on the peninsula. In the 1930s, Bushehr satisfied its date needs from Khorramshahr. Its price was uncontrolled and in 1939 was about 6.25 rials

---

11. NA, FO 248/1024, "Note by an Armenian merchant in 1905;" Morier 1812, p. 60; Lorimer 1915, vol. 2, p. 331; Fogg 1875, p. 176; Government of India 1924, p. 107; Pelly 1865 a, p. 45.
12. Morier 1812, p. 59.
13. Waring 1973, p. 8. According to Sani` al-Dowleh 1294, vol. 1, p. 300, the rural population wove a silken fabric.
14. Sadid al-Saltaneh 1371, p. 52; Government of India 1924, p. 25.
15. Lorimer 1915, vol. 2, pp. 331-32; Government of India 1924, p. 107; for details on date cultivation, see Appendix II.
16. Sadid al-Saltaneh 1371, pp. 55-56 (also for the names of the types of dates on the peninsula).

per 12 lbs. Bushehris did not want to eat the dates from Borazjan, whose production, although small, was nevertheless mostly sent inland. The same held for dates grown in Dashti, known as *qasb*, which were not popular in Bushehr, but were exported to India where they were liked.[17]

Fruit on the peninsula was produced in orchards and gardens, which around 1910, numbered 19. Their output included: grapes, apples, figs, oranges, and lemons. The crops were partly watered from wells and partly rain fed. Most of the wells only had brackish water and just sufficient water to irrigate small plots of vegetables such as beans, lettuce, carrots, beets, tomatoes and spinach during winter, and during the hot season melons, ladies gingers, eggplants, onions and cucumbers. Every year, around 1910, watermelons, were irrigated usually from 500, but not less than 300 wells.[18] These wells (*gav chah tarkari*) were characteristic for Bushehr and some other locations on the Persian littoral and e.g. on Kish Island, and were a peculiar feature of the peninsular viticulture.

> On a declivity a well of 4 feet in diameter is dug to a depth of 16 feet, and a space of 5 feet is filled with fresh soil well manured; then a healthy layer of the vine is put down early in March. For the first month it is watered four times, and gradually less frequently, about twice a month, till the autumn. The reason of planting the vine in wells and in slopes is to prevent the scorching heat of the sun striking at the roots and to permit of rain-water to collect therein during the winter months, which is the only means of watering the plant. The vine begins to bear from the first year, but the bunches are plucked off for the first three years. The plaint attains its maturity in six years, when its yield varies, according to the soil and the attention it receives, from 130 to 700 pounds and more. The vine in the interior is is grown partly by artificial irrigation and partly by rain only, the yields varying from 20 to 80 pounds, and, very rarely, about 200 pounds.[19]

The vines were trained over rockeries of loose stones. Each vine-pit and mound was surrounded by a low dry-stone wall and formed a circular enclosure with an average diameter of about 20 meters (66 feet). The vines of Rishahr were particularly prolific. To outsiders these vine-pits looked like small oases. The grapes were sold in Bushehr.[20] The British Residency had a field of potatoes some 5.5 km distance from Bushehr. Around 1850 it was destroyed by Tangestani bandits as were other crops raised by the British. "It is said that they threw the roots away, and boiled and ate the green tops, which I hope they relished."[21]

There was some animal husbandry on the peninsula. Around 1910, there were about 1,000 sheep at Halileh; 500 at Sar-tel; 300 at Tangak-e thalatheh; and 200 at Bagh-e Sheikh

---

17. Administration Report 1939, p. 7; Administration Report 1940, p. 7.
18. Sadid al-Saltaneh 1371, pp. 52, 54-56; Fogg 1875, p. 176; Lorimer 1915, vol. 2, pp. 331-32; Government of India 1924, p. 107; Sa`adat 1390, p. 22. In Ahram (Tangestan) there was cultivation of citrus fruits. NA, FO 371/15473.
19. Malcolm 1887, p. 273 (italics in original).
20. Lorimer 1915, vol. 2, pp. 331-32; Fogg 1875, p. 176; Bradley-Birt 1910, p. 46; Government of India 1924, pp. 25, 107.
21. Binning 1857, vol. 1, pp. 143, 149.

View of Bushehr, 1890

Abul, etc., for a total of 2,340 on the peninsula.[22] However, there was no grazing ground for pack animals, although the brackish water was fit for the animals. Therefore, mules and donkeys graze at Ahmadi, 16 km (10 miles) away.[23] The fowl of Bushehr were much appreciated and often, even taken to India to improve the local breed there.[24]

Despite these agricultural activities, visitors invariably opined that "dreariness, solitude and heat, are indeed the chief characteristics" of Bushehr and all Persian Gulf ports.[25] This even held for the road to Sabzabad, the location of the British residency and others who wanted to escape the heat of Bushehr, which was considered to be a long and sandy drive.[26] However, it all depended on the season. In 1934, Mrs. Merritt-Hawkes opined that driving from Bushehr to Sabzabad in spring was lovely. "The corn was unbelievably green, and among it, in some fields, were dainty blue lilies which had the fairy-like qualities of our bluebells but a finer shape, there were quantities of small reddish gladioli, and yet other pieces of land were covered with a wild lavender stock which was a misty veil by day and a delicious perfume by night."[27]

22. Sadid al-Saltaneh 1371, p. 54; Hamidi 1380, p. 119 (it was well-known for its stone quarry).
23. Government of India 1924, p. 45.
24. Anonymous 1828, p. 57; Binning 1857, vol. 1, p. 150 ("Fowls are large and fine").
25. Morier 1812, p. 38; Alexander 2000, p. 92; Mignan 1839, vol. 2, p. 137.
26. Bradley-Birt 1910, p. 46.
27. Merritt-Hawkes 1935, p. 2. For a similar observation, see Stevens 1979, p. 259.

The population of the peninsula consisted of two groups, the original inhabitants (*ra`iyat*) and landless migrants (*khoshneshin*), who were known as Alvar (Lors). The latter paid for each *fard* of cultivated land, 15,000 dinars to the government and 10 *shahis* to the village chief's assistant (*pakar*). A *ra`iyat* paid for each *fard* of cultivated land 3 *tumans* to the government and 10 *shahis* to the *pakar*. Each loom in Halileh paid 5,000 dinars to the government, which also collected per date tree 1,000 dinars, per vine 1,400 dinars, per *gav chah* one *tuman* and 10 *shahis*. A *ra`iyat* paid per 3 sheep, 1,000 dinars, the Alvar for each sheep 10 *shahis*. Moreover, at New Year (*Nowruz*) the owner of a herd had to give one copper kettle to the district chief (*zabet*). The tax per cow and donkey was 30 *shahis*. The head tax (*saraneh*) for a *ra`iyat* was 10 *tumans* per household; in addition, both the Alvar and *ra`iyat* had to pay an annual contribution (*a`aneh*) that amounted to 12,000 dinars and 10 *shahis* per person. The levy per *gav chah* of cotton was 6,000 dinars and per *dalv dast* of cotton was 5,000 dinars and 10 *shahis*. A *dalv dast* of vegetables was exempt of taxes. The properties belonging to some sayyeds, the Imam Jom`eh and some local officials were exempt from taxes owed to the government of Bushehr.[28]

General Aspect of the Port of Bushehr

The reaction of seeing Bushehr for the first time from the sea varied among the different visitors ranging from interesting, a floating spectacle, to miserable. However, when coming ashore these nuances disappeared when the visitors experienced the town first hand and the general opinion was that it was an unattractive place. Being miles away at sea, the first thing that an observer saw was the Kuh-e Khormaz that looked "like a guardian standing watch and ward over the Shah's good city of Bushire."[29] Also, when viewed from a distance, the town looked to most observers interesting and picturesque, promising more than it found afterwards to contain.[30] There were also those who opined that even from afar the town's appearance was far from inviting, and Waring even cites a sailor who "swore very bluntly that we were going ashore to a burying ground."[31] Because Bushehr was so low that before observing the land on which the town was built, the tops of the houses were first seen, which seemed to rise out of the sea. To Capt. Ellis it looked like "a city half built."[32] As you got closer, people saw different things that stood out. Cursetjee mentioned "the tall melon-shaped dome of the Imambara [sic; Imamzadeh], white as a wedding cake, standing amidst a rare grove of trees."[33] Others singled out the square buildings with their wind towers that stood as minarets, or just saw "a mass of dingy yellow."[34] However, most people when approaching Bushehr, either from land or sea, only saw its arid and dirty appearance, an impression that was further reinforced by many houses that

---

28. Sadid al-Saltaneh 1371, p. 52-54. A *dalv dast* is a unit of area that was watered from a well from which water was hauled by hand (*dast*) with a bucket (*dalv*) tied to a rope, which was fastened around the peasant's waist with which he hauled water from the well.
29. Cursetjee 2001, p. 107.
30. Kinneir 1973, pp. 69-70; Brittlebank 1873, p. 93; Buckingham 1971, p. 346; Mignan 1839, vol. 2, p. 137.
31. Alexander 2000, p. 92; Waring 1973, 10; Wellstead 1840, pp. 130-31.
32. Ellis 1866, p. 95; Milburn 1813, vol. 1, p. 128; Buckingham 1971, pp. 346-47; von Tzschirner-Tzschirne 1918, p. 158; Geary 1878, vol. 1, p. 62.
33. Cursetjee 2001, p. 108 (the Imamzadeh of `Abdol-Moheyman is located 800 m north of the village of Sabzabad).
34. Kempthorne 1835, p. 283; Norden 1928, p. 44.

were partly or wholly in ruins.[35] From the roadstead Bushehr "is merely something very flat, brownish with bits of green, that has only just managed to land."[36] As a result, most visitors found Bushehr after their first encounter "an eminently uninteresting place."[37] In fact, due to "a total absence of trees, gardens, or verdure, the whole picture is of a dull grey, sandy hue, particularly uninviting, and even fatiguing to the view under a sultry sky"[38]

City wall and gate in 1856

The town wall

The town of Bushehr was 3.2 km (two miles) in circumference in the early nineteenth century. The town occupied the very point of the peninsula, and formed a triangle. The longest sides were those on each sea bank, which were entirely open. The base of the triangle, i.e. towards the South, on the land side, was alone fortified. However, the mud wall built from the bay to the sea, 1.2 km in length, was not kept in good repair.[39] The town had 12 towers at unequal distances along the walls, according to Morier. Kempthorne stated that at every two hundred meters there was a round tower. Each

35. Binning 1857, vol. 1, pp. 139, 141; Buckingham 1971, p. 346; Brittlebank 1873, p. 93.

36. Merritt-Hawkes 1935, p. 1.

37. MacGregor 1879, vol. 1, p. 10; Buckingham 1971, p. 346; Binning 1857, vol. 1, p. 139; Wellstead 1840, p. 132.

38. Buckingham 1971, pp. 346-47.

39. Morier 1812, p. 56 (2 miles); Milburn 1813, vol. 1, p. 128 (3 miles); Hollingberry 1976, p. 14; Buckingham 1971, p. 348; Kempthorne 1835, p. 283; Wellstead 1840, p. 132.

tower chequered at the top by loopholes for musketry. Two of these towers formed the town gate, of which there were two on the land side, one on each side.[40]

Whereas Morier opined that the fortifications might possibly be a safeguard against "the predatory incursions of the horse," others believed that these were wholly insufficient for the purposes of defense.[41] At each of the two town gates there was a "very large brass cannon, the diameter of the bore of which is 11.5 inches: they were brought from Ormus in 1622, and though they bear the date of 1502, appear as if new." Some considered them still serviceable around 1810, while Johnson held that they "might as likely destroy the defenders as the assailants."[42] According to Buckingham, Bushehr's only and very questionable defenses were:

> A few dismounted guns, without this gate; a battery of 6 or 8 nearly abreast of the factory, in the SW quarter of the town; and half a dozen others, placed before the Custom-house, in the NE quarter and facing the inner harbor - all of them of different calibre, and mounted on carriages of such a crazy kind, as would certainly fall to pieces on a second or third discharge."[43]

On the sea side, Bushehr's only defenses were its many "war galliots" and a dozen long guns placed on the Custom's pier in the early nineteenth century.[44]

Mohammad Shah (r. 1834-1848) ordered the town's fortifications to be repaired and reinforced in 1841 after his conflict with Great Britain about Herat that resulted in the British occupation of Khark in 1839 (see chapter three). In June 1841 the works started, which were aimed to protect the town against any future British attack, which meant erecting fortifications on the sea side. The British Resident reported that Sheikh Naser, the governor of the port, was erecting a fort at the flanks of the town walls of Bushehr close to the backwater. He considered that the site was:

> well chosen as it command a shore where it is easy to land, but a small vessel drawing less than 10 feet could come to within half a pistol shot of this building and thus, could soon be made untenable, if need be. He is believed to wish to live there, probably to have easy access to the sea and facilitate flight if arrest by Shiraz is threatening or a danger from his own people. He also erected a breast work, 5 feet high and 2 feet wide, along the coast covering the whole front of the Residency, thus commanding the landing places and cutting off communication between the Residency and the sea.[45]

---

40. Morier 1812, p. 56; Kempthorne 1835, p. 283; Milburn 1813, vol. 1, p. 128.
41. Morier 1812, p. 56; Heude 1819, p 43; Buckingham 1971, p. 348.
42. Milburn 1813, vol. 1, p. 128; Kinneir 1973, p. 69; Johnson 1818, p. 19; Wellstead 1840, p. 132; Morier 1812, p. 66 (a large brass Portuguese gun, a sixty-eight pounder, on a very uncertain carriage). According to Milburn 1813, vol. 1, p. 128, "there is neither castle nor battery in or near the town belonging to it," which clearly is not borne out by other sources.
43. Buckingham 1971, p. 348.
44. Milburn 1813, vol. 1, p. 128; Alexander 2000, p. 92.
45. NA, FO 248/99, Hennell/Residency to Sheil/Erzerum 09/06/1841; Idem, John Bird to Commodore G.B. Brucks, 07/06/1841; "the fort is situated at the end of the wall behind the bazaar, it is square, with one tower at the corner that commands the landing place, well built; 4 feet thick and each side 100 feet; not finished yet; they are working fast, the wall is now 5 feet high."

The town walls ca. 1870

The works continued until 1844, and were supervised by `Abdollah Khan the king's engineer (*me`mar-bashi*). The British Resident was not happy with the new corner breast work on the sea that ran 50 or 60 meters in the front of the Residency. He argued that the Residency always had "uninterrupted right of access to the sea and camels could go there to the gate of the Residency. This would be cut off by a completely continuous breastwork." Therefore, he wanted a small gateway in the wall to allow access to the sea. This would not weaken the walls defensive capability, because in case of danger it could easily be closed by a couple of masons in a few hours.[46] In September 1844, the foundation for the new so-called *Borj-e Mobarak* opposite the Residency gateway was excavated. The Resident both petitioned the governor-general of Fars and the government in Tehran for this work to be halted.[47] In December 1844, orders arrived from Tehran instructing `Abdollah Khan "not to construct the increased number of bastions as ordered by the Amir [governor-general of Fars] and not to build them so high that they overlook the Residency premises." As a result, `Abdollah Khan removed the foundation of the *Borj-e Mobarak*. He "closed up the gorge of the new angle formed by the new alteration of the breastwork in front of the site of the projected tower with loopholes and an embrasure that points directly at our gateway this forming a small triangular redoubt at the same elevation as the breastworks for the four guns seaward and towards the Residency buildings. As a work of any strength, this redoubt is below contempt."[48] In March 1844, `Abdollah Khan had already left an opening in the breastwork at the British Resident's request, so that both local people as well as those in the Residency would continue to have free access to the sea.[49]

46. NA,FO 248/263, Hennell to J.P. Willoughby, Secretary Bombay Govt. 04/03/1844.
47. NA, FO 248/263, Hennell to Sheil 24/09/1844.
48. NA, FO 248/263, Hennell to Sheil 11/12/1844.
49. NA, FO 248/263, Hennell to royal engineer 08/03/1844; Idem, `Abdullah Khan royal engineer to Hennell, received 09/03/1844; Idem, Persian originals; Idem, Hennell to Sheil 26/03/1844.

The result of the reinforced fortification was more the appearance than the reality of an effective defense. It was a wall with small towers at intervals and three or four bastions with a few old guns. One redeeming feature was that one gate exhibited some architectural taste. In front of the gate there was a small breastwork, "with embrasures for guns; and six large rusty cannon, mounted on old crazy carriages, are there planted," to keep the shah's forces out.[50] This last qualification was a reference to the defensive stance adopted by the last Al Mazkur hereditary governor of Bushehr (see chapter three). As of April 1852 additional work was done. Bastions were erected, others were marked out and their foundations laid and material collected to start work, which progresses very slowly. In particular the erection of a bastion of the usual size was raised at 80 paces on the right front of the Residency. The British protested and for a while the work was stopped. However, in May 1854 the Resident reported that the foundation of a new bastion was dug right in front of the Residency's gate. He pointed out to the town's governor that the two structures already existing were at a distance of a musket shot and therefore, this new bastion was not necessary and showed disrespect towards a friend.[51] The governor replied that the government had ordered that "bastions had to be constructed on the side of the sea and in the same manner as those erected on the land side, so that in the entire cirumference of the city there is room to reside for the men of the garrison." The governor added that he did not understand why walling the city with bastions and curtain walls between them would be unfriendly and disprectful to the British. A total of 14 bastions had to be built on the sea side in a regular continuous line, of which 13 had been completed. The site of the last one was between the *Borj-e Bahri* and the new bastions and was of the same type and dimension as the other ones and at the same distance from the Residency. "Not building it at this site would not be in line with the others, unconnected with them and all expense made for nothing. However, I will order construction to be stopped and Tehran will discuss this matter and let us know its decision."[52] The Resident countered that:

> The interval of 60-70 paces of the new bastion to the right front of the residency and the Borj-e Bahri within short musket range of its gate to the left does not exceed 250 yards. This space is covered with a redoubt for four guns with a running curtain wall and these works mutually flank each other and together have complete command of the sea; the new structure seems to be superfluous. ... Moreover, if your argument is valid for the building in question then this means that the connecting wall with corresponding height would bar the residency from access to the sea and exclude it from the breeze and make it uninhabitable.[53]

---

50. Binning 1857, vol. 1, p. 143. Cherikof 1358, p. 8 writes that in 1850 Bushehr had a strong wall, on which guard-houses were situated.

51. NA, FO 248/180, Capt. Kemball, Resident to Sheil, 18/08/1852; Idem, Kemball to Mirza Hassan Ali Khan, 09/05/1854/11 Sha`ban 1270 (Persian text); Idem, A. Kemball to W.T. Thomson 13/05/1854; Heravi 1372, p. 72.

52. NA, FO 248/180, Mirza Hossem Ali Khan to A. Kemball, 11/05/1854/13 Sha`ban 1270 (in Persian); see also Hamidi 1380, p. 133, who is incorrect as far as the builder is concerned.

53. NA, FO 248/180, A. Kemball to Mirza Hassan Ali Khan, 13/05/1854/15 Sha`ban 1270 (Persian text).

The work was not stopped, however, and Captain Kemball, the Resident, asked the British Envoy in Tehran to obtain orders to stop the construction.[54]

The result of the new fortifications was that the town became 3.2 km (2 miles) in circumference, protected on the land side by a wall and various towers.[55] However, despite all the money and effort spent, this result was not very good. In the mid-1850s Shepherd reported that "The walls are composed of a white sandstone, worn so thin in places that a bullet would penetrate them,"[56] and they were easily breached by British artillery when the town was taken in 1856. In that same year, the Rishahr fort was repaired and occupied by Persian troops who defended it against the British.[57] Thereafter, the government of Persia did not spend any more money on the maintenance of the walls. Every traveler who visited the town after 1860 reported that its walls were falling to pieces, and its bastions at intervals also were dilapidated.[58] Therefore, those wishing to avoid being detained at the town's gate, for whatever reason, could "ride out upon the plain through a gap made by British shot and shell."[59] By 1880, the walls, which had disappeared on the sea side, were falling apart on the land side.[60] However, towers, mostly ruined, were still commanding the beach.[61] By the beginning of the twentieth century, the wall on the landward south side, was "almost concealed amidst the recent extensions of the town in that direction, and only traces are visible here and there."[62]

Although the walls did not really serve an effective defensive purpose, the gates were still standing and were more or less maintained, which allowed the government to keep some control over those who entered and left the town enabling it to tax certain people and products. Until 1874, one *qran* was levied per three mules from the muleteer, but not from the merchants. In 1876, this amount was reduced to 0.25 *qran* per head after the muleteers had petitioned for a reduction. The only gate tax that was levied at that time was an unspecified amount per 20 sheep from butchers.[63] At night the gate was closed and travelers had to wait till the next day. This happened to Buckingham in 1816, who had to sleep outside and had to wait till sunrise to enter Bushehr.[64] Staff of the British Residency was allowed to enter and leave town after the gate had been closed, although

---

54. NA, FO 248/180, Kemball to Mirza Hasan Khan Daryabegi, 15/11/1854/23 Safar 1271 (Persian text; "I refer you to my letter of 15 instant where I have given definite answer on this issue."); Idem, Mirza Hasan Khan to Kemball, 24 Safar 1271/16/11/1854 (Persian text).

55. Shepherd 1857, p. 139. By 1947, the town covered an area of about 0.74 sq km (1.75 square miles), an indication that like its population it had decreased in size. NA, FO 371/15473.

56. Shepherd 1857, p. 136.

57. Curzon 1892, vol. 1, p. 235; Stack 1882, vol. 1, p. 26 ("Some embankments remain as memorials to our temporary occupation").

58. Fogg 1875, p. 173; Stack 1882, vol. 1, p. 27; Geary 1878, vol. 1, p. 62; de Rivoyre 1883, p. 135; de Vilmorin 1895, p. 356; Curzon 1892, vol. 1, p. 234; Sani` al-Dowleh 1294, vol. 1, p. 298.

59. Fogg 1875, p. 173.

60. Stack 1881, vol. 1, p. 27.

61. Geary 1878, vol. 1, p. 62.

62. Lorimer 1915, vol. 2, p. 341; by 1914, only one tower was still left, Sa`adat 1390, p. 18.

63. NA, FO 248/318, Asst. *kargozar* to Prideaux, 21 Rajab 1293 - 13/08/1876; Idem, Kerbela'i Evaz to Malek al-Tojjar, no date (Persian text); de Rivoyre, p. 135. See also Saldanha 1986, vol. 7/2, p. 165.

64. Buckingham 1971, p. 344.

at times, depending on the political situation, the guard would not cooperate and refuse to open the wicket.[65]

Houses

Bushehr stood "partly on a slight eminence, which is greatest in the centre, and is not more than one hundred feet at its highest elevation from the sea."[66] The houses were literally built upon the sand, and the houses came down to the water's edge.[67] The houses were low, small, flat roofed, and without windows.[68] Each house, with walls that usually were no higher than 5 meters (16 feet), was built in the form of a square, having an open courtyard in the center, which had no air circulation. In this court yard there was usually a well with brackish water, and around it all the household refuse was deposited. When water was drawn some of it was spilt and moistened the nearby refuse, which the sun heated up resulting in an awful smell. As the building materials contained much salt, the walls got soaked through during the rains, so that after the rain they were so moist that the rooms remained damp for a long time.[69]

The square tower-like houses were terraced, two or three stories in height, and the larger ones "laid out in central courts and small apartments, badly lighted, and often as badly aired."[70] The servant's quarters in the wealthy households were on the ground floor, the master's was above that, because it caught more of the sea breeze.[71] The houses may have been without windows in the early nineteenth century, although that seems unlikely, but in the twentieth century they, "unlike those of central Persia, are built of stone with two stories and many outward-facing windows."[72] The impression of not having windows probably was caused by the use of very small windows towards the street that appeared to be closed by shutters that nevertheless allowed the wind through by way of slatters.[73] In fact, the French traveler de Vilmorin and 80 years later the British traveler Stevens liked the houses of Bushehr, especially their magnificent green shutters, which provided protection against the sun. Some houses even had small wooden balconies, called *shenashir*.[74] The houses were of stone and nearly all had an upper storey: none had two stories and few had only a ground floor.

65. NA, FO 248/108, Hon. Lt. Campbell, Steam vessel Nimrod/Bushire to Robertson, 14/10/1842; NA, FO 248/263, Hennell to Sheil, 19/07/1844.
66. Buckingham 1971, p. 347; Lorimer 1915, vol. 2, p. 341 (40 feet); "Bushire is built on a ridge that is not higher than 12.1 m." Norden 1928, p. 49.
67. Buckingham 1971, p. 347; Alexander 2000, p. 92; Brittlebank 1873, p. 92.
68. Morier 1812, p. 57; Waring 1973, p. 2; Alexander 2000, p. 92.
69. NA, FO 248/232, A.N. Hojel asst. surgeon to Lewis Pelly, 13/05/1868.
70. Buckingham 1971, pp. 346-47; Kempthorne 1835, p. 283; Geary 1878, vol. 1, p. 62; Sadid al-Saltaneh 1371, p. 39; Sa`adat 1390, p. 22.
71. Norden 1928, p. 50.
72. Government of Great Britain 1945, p. 503; "with latticed windows and often with projecting upper stories." Weeks 1895, p. 129; "Countless windows, mere bare slits, close-barred and shuttered," Bradley-Birt 1910, p. 22; "slit-like windows and closed shutters, and heavily barred doors" Norden 1928, p. 49.
73. Locher 1889, p. 50; Bradley-Birt 1910, p. 37; the windowless houses, Böhme 1977, p. 250.
74. de Vilmorin 1895, p. 351; Stevens 1979, p. 258 (who mentions blue shutters, however); Hamidi 1380, pp. 424-25 (with photo).

Traditional houses

Most of the dwellings have on the terraced roofs a kind of kiask [sic; kiosk], constructed from the branches of the palm tree, or the green grass of the desert, in which the natives shelter themselves during the summer nights, from the burning winds and the drenching dews of the sea. Those who sleep without this shelter, generally rise covered with sand and soaked with dew, which gives them a most comical and muddy appearance.[75]

75. Stern 1854, p. 89; "In the summer the richer inhabitants build Tchardaks [*chahartaq*], or booths, to live in, on the roofs of their houses, for coolness." Rich 1839, p. 202; Mignan 1839, vol. 2, p. 140; Pfeiffer 1852, p. 239.

House with balcony

All the houses of the wealthy were equipped with tall, square towers, called *badgir* or wind-catcher, that were 15-20 feet high, according to some, while others again gave figures of 60 to 100 feet, which seems highly unlikely. They were closed during the winter.[76] There were two kinds: *Arab* or *Luleh*. The *Arab* wind-catcher was only opened towards the south, i.e., the sea-side, because during the hot season usually there was a landward wind. It stood at a height of 3 meters (10 feet) above the roof. The room connected to the wind-catcher was larger than any other room in the house to accommodate a considerable number of people. The *luleh* wind-catcher was open on all four sides and thus, might capture the breeze coming from any direction. People only made use of the wind-catchers during day as they slept on the roof at night taking all their necessaries (carpet, lights, pots, water pipe, charcoal brazier, etc.) with them. Some people could not be bothered to go down in the morning and installed themselves on the roof during the entire hot season.[77]

The *badgirs* at Bushehr seem to have been of the *luleh* type, as they were said to be open at each side. They "arrest every current of air, no matter from which direction it may blow, and send it through flues into the rooms below to enable the inmates below to exist during the summer heats."[78] According to Dubeux, the *badgirs* were mainly used to cool female apartments, because they were restricted in their movements.[79] It seems

76. MacGregor 1879, vol. 1, p. 11; Geary 1878, vol. 1, p. 62; Alexander 2000, p. 92; Dubeux 1841, p. 50; Shepherd 1857, p. 139; Wellstead 1840, p. 132; Pfeiffer 1852, p. 239.

77. Floyer 1882, p. 140.

78. Geary 1878, vol. 1, p. 62; Kinneir 1973, pp. 69-70.

79. Dubeux 1841, p. 50.

that the number of *badgirs* increased during the late nineteenth century, because visitors in that period mention that they were more common than did the visitors in the early nineteenth century.[80] Although very comfortable during the summer heat, *badgirs* were not without risk, because when an earthquake occurred they might cause damage to neighboring buildings.[81] By the beginning of the twentieth century the *badgirs* that had been so common before were being abandoned. According to Lorimer, "The lofty badgirs, which were once a distinctive feature, have now all but 2 or 3 disappeared. It is considered unlucky to build new ones."[82] However, by the 1940s it is reported that Bushehr had numerous *badgirs*.[83]

The ordinary building material is described differently by various authors, but mud and grey sandstone are the ones most often mentioned.[84] The small island of Moharraq situated between the island of `Abbasak and Pudar (2.5 km above Bushehr), which was covered at high tide, supplied mud for construction activities in the eastern part of Bushehr.[85] However, it appears that most houses were constructed with a soft friable conglomerate of sand and shells (called madrapore, or coraline) from the ruins of Rishahr or from adjacent quarries in the peninsula. Most of the adjacent villages were built of the same stone, which in Bushehr was called *gassar*. It was rapidly eroded by the weather and older houses, therefore, look decayed.[86] As a result, foreign observers such as Kinneir (ca. 1810) opined that Bushehr did not have more than five or six decent houses, built of sun-dried bricks. The best of these sun-burnt bricks were imported from Basra.[87] Those few houses built of brick were plastered with mud, or imperfectly whitewashed.[88] This soft stone made the town look white and clean, but on landing "it is then seen to be but a mean and dirty place."[89] Nevertheless, there were visitors who considered that the houses of the town were "not bad looking for Persian habitations, some of them indeed are well-built." In any case they were better built than those at Bandar Abbas.[90] In fact, one visitor in 1881 considered Bushehr to be "the best-built town on the Persian coast, and shows some signs of care and improvement. A good sea-wall runs along a great part of its seaward face."[91] Apparently, the sea-wall was not as good as people thought, because when Malek al-Tojjar returned from Europe in 1884 he undertook to build a new sea

---

80. Buckingham 1971, pp. 346-47; Stirling 1991, p. 8; Sani` al-Dowleh 1294, vol. 1, 298; Binning 1857, vol. 1, pp. 140-41; Fogg 1875, p. 174; Curzon 1892, vol. 1, p. 233; Collins 1896, p. 25; Morier 1812, p. 57; Shepherd 1857, p. 139.

81. Morier 1812, p. 57; Dubeux 1841, p. 50.

82. Lorimer 1915, vol. 2, p. 341; Sadid al-Saltaneh 1371, p. 39.

83. Government of Great Britain 1945, p. 503.

84. Hollingberry 1976, p. 14; Kinneir 1973, pp. 69-70; Alexander 2000, p. 92; Brittlebank 1873, p. 93; Geary 1878, vol. 1, p. 62; Locher 1889, p. 49.

85. Lorimer 1915, vol. 2, pp. 340-41.

86. Morier 1812, pp. 66-67; Waring 1973, p. 3; Buckingham 1971, p. 346; Binning 1857, vol. 1, p. 140; Mignan 1839, vol. 2, p. 137; Shepherd 1857, p. 138; Stirling 1991, p. 8; Lorimer 1915, vol. 2, p. 341; Hamidi 1380, pp. 542-43. The stone was quarried with a crow-bar called *mantil*, after which the stone was cut into the shape of a *nim-shams* or a rectangle. Sa`adat 1390, pp. 23, 220.

87. Kinneir 1973, pp. 69-70; Buckingham 1971, p. 347; Heude 1819, p. 43 ("only twelve or fifteen houses of any consequence").

88. Binning 1857, vol. 1, p. 140; Shepherd 1857, p. 138; MacGregor 1879, vol. 1, p. 11; Ballantine 1879, p. 58.

89. Waring 1973, p. 2; Hollingberry 1976, p. 15; Kempthorne 1835, p. 283.

90. Locher 1875, p. 50; De Rivoyre 1883, p. 131.

91. Stack 1882, vol. 1, p. 24.

wall, "to prevent the sea from flooding the plain outside the walls of Bushire."[92] By the turn of the twentieth century, Bushehr was a mix of old and new houses, of those built with gypsum (*gach*) or sandstone. The gypsum came from Tangestan and Dashti, while the (mangrove) beams for the ceilings, called *chandal* (rafters), came from Zanzibar.[93]

Bushehr was a compact town, and houses were built close to one another and tall to catch the wind.[94] Sometimes, this was an opportunity to raise problems such as in 1852. In that year, an Armenian agent of the British, Mr. Malcolm, complained to the British Resident stating that Mirza Hasan `Ali Khan, the governor of Bushehr had raised objection to the construction of his house that already he had started some years ago. His neighbor had "built his in front of it and so high that it totally cut off the wind and thus rendered it inhabitable during the very hot summer months." Although the governor had passed it many times, even asking to see it when finished, he never had complained about it. Malcolm believed that, as he was wont to, the governor tried to

> find an excuse to make trouble from those who depend on the British. ... The house is not high, it is on one side high and the other low by 12 feet. So from one side it looks somewhat high, but on the other rather low. There are other houses in my neighborhood that are so high that they entirely command mine and is a source of inconvenience. There are many houses of Christians and Jews in this town that command those of Moslems without anyone protesting. What makes it even more surprising, I was short of building materials and a few days ago I applied to the Daryabegi [i.e. the governor] permission to get them which he gave (for some time this had not been permitted, these materials needed for the construction of the towers).[95]

Around 1810-30, the town boasted of 400 to 600 houses.[96] In mid-nineteenth century the number was estimated to be 700 to 800.[97] By the turn of the twentieth century, the number of houses was about 1,400 and a decade later 1,569.[98] In view of the size of its population (see below Table 1.2) this number seems to be inadequate. And, indeed the population was dense and out of proportion to the number of fixed dwellings.[99] However, the town had more than greystone and mud dwellings. In fact, the larger part of Bushehr's population lived in so-called *kapar*s "or mere hovels constructed of date-sticks and leaves, covered with mats made of the date-leaf, or of a long bulrush called *peezur*, which grows in swampy soil. The *kappar* is so small and low, that one cannot stand upright in it, except

---

92. Administration Report 1884-85, p. 8.

93. Sadid al-Saltaneh 1371, pp. 39, 99 (*chandal*s were imported in units called *krvjh* [?] which contained 20 beams and were sold in 1913 for 30 rupees); Report 1912-13, p. 19; Sa`adat 1390, p. 23; Hamidi 1380, p. 248.

94. Lorimer 1915, vol. 2, p. 341; Weeks 1896, p. 129.

95. NA, FO 248/85, Statement signed by James McAlister Cdr. concerning Malcolm's house n.d. ("it does not stand out compared with others.")

96. Morier 1812, p. 57 (400); Heude 1819, p. 43 (500); Kempthorne 1835, p. 283 (600). Buckingham 1971, p. 347 estimates a higher number, about 800 to 1,000.

97. Shepherd 1857, p. 138.

98. Lorimer 1915, vol. 2, p. 341; Sadid al-Saltaneh 1371, p. 44.

99. Lorimer 1915, vol. 2, p. 341.

A 1950s *kapar* inside the city

in the centre; and a family huddled together in such a wretchedly close domicile, can have but little notion of comfort or cleanliness."[100] Morier mentions that there were many reed huts forming several alleys on entering the gates "which may add an equal number to the whole."[101] By 1816, according to Buckingham, there were at least 500 "reed enclosures scarcely deserving even the name of huts, as most of them are unroofed, and are inhabited by none but the slaves and the very lowest order of people."[102] By mid-century there were 1,000 to 1,200 so-called *cajan* huts, built of date-fronds and occupied by the lower classes and soldiers.[103] These *kapar* or *cajan* huts formed encampments everywhere, ranging from the open shore line to even, for a time, around the British Residency.[104]

I have already mentioned above that there were hardly any buildings of note in Bushehr. Buckingham's comments made in 1816 are an adequate description for much of the nineteenth century. He wrote: "Except for the East India Company's factory, the residence of the governor and a few good dwellings of merchants, in particular Armenians,

100. Binning 1857, vol. 1, p. 140; Rich 1839, p. 202 ("mat and reed hovels"); Curzon 1892, vol. 1, p. 234 ("kapars or huts made of date-stocks and leaves, the nauseous domicile of the lower classes"); Hamidi 1380, p. 500 (*kapar*; in standard literary Persian *chapar*). Ael 1931, p. 99 (with a photo of a *kapar*).

101. Morier 1812, p. 57; Heude 1819, p. 43.

102. Buckingham 1971, p. 347; Rich 1839, p. 202 ("A considerable portion of the houses are mere mat and reed hovels"); Kempthorne 1835, p. 283 ("perhaps four hundred Cajan huts").

103. Shepherd 1857, p. 139. In the 1670s, Fryer, 1909, vol. 1, pp. 60, 136, 144, described *cajan* as a palm leaf or as boughs of a Toddy tree. The term *cajan* huts refers to the use of *Cajanus cajan* (L.) or the pigeon pea, like in Senegal, where the branches of *Cajanus kerstingii* are used for making temporary hut walls.

104. Curzon 1892, vol. 1, p. 234.

The promenade with Amiriyeh building

there is scarcely one comfortable, let alone handsome edifice in the place."[105] I discuss the British Residency in chapter four, but I only mention here that it was a Persian owned and built edifice that, according to Binning, was the only "really good and comfortable house in Bushire."[106] Persians also agreed with the opinion that the British Residency was one of the best buildings in town.[107]

However, there were other buildings that stood out, in particular towards the end of the nineteenth century. First, after as the governor's residence, then followed trading and consular buildings, and finally the residences of wealthy merchants. In 1816, the fort inhabited by the Sheikh of Bushehr was situated on the east side of the town.[108] Sheikh `Abdol-Rasul (1814-32) built a new fort or government house in the center of town, which was large and commodious, "some of the sitting-rooms being fitted up with a degree of eastern splendor and elegance."[109] In 1851, the fort itself was considered to be "small, and poorly fitted up; containing apparently a few habitable rooms, with little appearance of comfort."[110] The governor's residence was known as *Chahar Borj* and by the 1880s was described as a large, square dilapidated stone building, with many outhouses,

105. Buckingham 1971, p. 347.

106. Binning 1857, vol. 1, p. 140.

107. Sani` al-Dowleh 1294, vol. 1, p. 299.

108. Binning 1857, vol. 1, p. 141. This probably was the building known as *Arg* in the Shanbadi quarter. Hamidi 1380, pp. 73-74 (with photo).

109. Kempthorne 1835, p. 284; Sadid al-Saltaneh 1371, p. 37. In 1850, according to Cherikov, Sheikh Naser constructed a fort, known as *Naseriyreh*, which was used as a stable for the horses brought to the port. Cherikof 1358, p. 129.

110. Binning 1857, vol. 2, pp. 419-20.

the latter probably occupied by servants. In the middle of the courtyard there was a flag-staff. It was situated at the extremity of the port. In front there was a small square which separated it from the sea. The mansion was flanked by two cannons and a guard.[111] These were so-called time-guns which were fired at Ramazan and daily at dawn and sunset as well as for saluting purposes. They stood on the *Meydan*, which extended to the village of Jabri, which was situated at a distance of about 0.7 km.[112] E`temad al-Saltaneh opined that the *Chahar Borj* was not that bad of a building. He may have written this, because under Naser al-Din Shah (r. 1848-1896) the governors of Bushehr received more than 60,000 *tumans* for repairing the *Chahar Borj*. However, not all of the money seems to have been spent, or at least not well spent, because, according to Sadid al-Saltaneh, the building was falling apart by about 1910.[113] However, by that time it had been replaced by another building. At the seafront, on the narrow and crumbling esplanade "stand most of the better sort of residences and offices with the Governor's palace, an unimposing building in bad repair."[114]

The western promenade, facing the open sea, stretched some 9 km to Sabzabad. This was the most pretentious part of town, for the British Residency, the principal European residencies and consulates as well as places of business were all located along it.[115] First you saw the British Residence at Sabzabad, then the large buildings of the Telegraph office at Rishahr. Nearer the city were the German and Russian consulates, "the latter a handsome building flanked by a tower at either end, with a flag." Further, in the city itself was the British Consulate-General.[116] Starting from northern end of the seafront there was the *Amiriyeh* built by Daryabegi in 1899 at a cost of 18,000 *tumans*, which, in 1901, the Jamshidiyan bought for a small amount. In 1905 it housed the most important Customs officials, but later it was transformed into the governor's residence, who, in 1913, rented it for 30 *tumans* per month. To the east there was the Arab quarter, to the north the Jewish quarter and to the south the Kuti quarter.[117] To the south-east of the town was a building erected by the brothers Nezam al-Saltaneh and Sa`d al-Molk, when they were governors, who financed its construction. The government later spent 300,000 rupees to demolish it and build a customs house there.[118]

Next were two blocks of buildings occupied by the Russian Steam Navigation and Trading Company, after which the British Residency was situated. Close to the Residency was the *Ab-anbar* or the water reservoir for the public benefit built by the Qavam al-Molk when governor in 1864. Beyond the *Ab-anbar* was the Turkish vice-consulate, and there the town ended. On the other side of the island there was the customs-yard along the Khur Soltani quays, the bazaar and then you finally emerged at the *Chahar Borj* or Government House, where one rejoined the Khur Soltani in the extreme south-west corner of town. At the northern end of the town there was an open space called *Basidun*,

111. Locher 1889, p. 50; De Rivoyre 1883, p. 132.
112. Lorimer 1915, vol. 2, p. 342.
113. Sani` al-Dowleh 1294, vol. 1, p. 299; Sadid al-Saltaneh 1371, p. 37; Idem 1362, p. 15.
114. Curzon 1892, vol. 1, p. 233; Cursetjee 2001, p. 113; Lorimer 1915, vol. 2, p. 342.
115. Cursetjee 2001, p. 114.
116. Bradley-Birt 1910, pp. 22-23; Stack 1882, vol. 1, p. 27.
117. Lorimer 195, vol. 2, p. 342; Sadid al-Saltaneh 1371, p. 38. For a short biography of Ahmad Khan Daryabegi, see Hamidi 1380, pp. 303-06.
118. Sadid al-Saltaneh 1362, p. 15; Idem 1371, pp. 37-38; Hamidi 1380, p. 90.

A villa in Bahmani

where there was a block of buildings with the Customs-house and the Post Office.[119] In 1888, the New Oriental Bank was housed in a three-storied building with a garden. The other bank was a Persian bank, which was less formal.[120] The Imperial Bank of Persia (IBP) opened offices as of 1889; the building was in the north-east part of town and belonged to the bank's translator Mirza Mohammad Javad. A residential building for the IBP manager was constructed outside town in Neydi at a cost of 250,000 rupees.[121]

The houses, even of the rich merchants, were not that good or impressive, according to E`temad al-Saltaneh.[122] However, some of the old mansions were very big such as the *Malek* in Bahmani, the *Golshan* (now *Bank-e Melli*), that of Haji Ra'is, which could house up to 100 people, and the *Kazeruni*, which allegedly had room for more than 2,000 people.[123] Even now their remains are testimony to their owners' ambitions.

Summer-houses

During the summer, most inhabitants left for Chahkutah, a large village 27 km inland (15 miles S.W. of Borazjun and 18 miles east of Bushehr), where they lived in tents, or in large airy houses, both "cooled through evaporation by 'tatteis', which consists of a

119. Lorimer 1915, vol. 2, p. 342; Hamidi 1380, pp. 96 (with a photo of the *Ab-anbar*), 118 (Basidun from the French word *bastion*, initially denoted a bulwark built in the time of Nader Shah, but which was demolished in the second half of the nineteenth century), 174 (Basidun was situated at the end of the Behbahani quarter), 483 (details about the *ab-anbar*).

120. de Vilmorin 1895, p. 352.

121. Sadid al-Saltaneh 1371, p. 37.

122. Sani` al-Dowleh 1294, vol. 1, p. 299.

123. Afshar Sistani 1369, vol. 1, p. 491; Kanin 1391, p. 217; Hamidi 1380, pp. 455-58 (with photos). In the 1930s the Malek residence was rented by the military. Political Diaries, vol. 10, p.212.

light framework of date-wood filled in with camel-thorn, and kept constantly wet."[124] The British also moved there in the 1830s, because prior to that date they usually stayed at Halileh or Rishahr. When in 1845, Major Hennell, the Resident and some other British staff built some small cottages in Choghadak this was brought to the attention of Mohammad Shah. He instructed Mirza `Abdol-Hoseyn Khan, the governor-general of Fars to order Hennell put an immediate stop to construction. The governor added "If you need to be cool go to the nearby hills, or otherwise come here." Hennell was not pleased with this as he had summered there for the last ten years. He, of course, stopped any further construction and wrote to Sheil that the shah had been misinformed. Hennell therefore, invited Hedayatollah Khan, the acting governor of Bushehr and `Abdollah Khan, the royal architect to show them that the constructions were simple cottages and asked them to report this to Tehran. Hennell also offered to send the building plans to Tehran. To the governor-general of Fars he wrote a similar letter, further thanking him for his invitation, but pointing out that "I cannot leave my district without permission of my government."[125]

Mohammad Shah relented and gave permission for the cottages to be built and the British continued to spend the summer there. However, due to the war of 1856, the summer residences of British citizens at Choghadak were almost entirely destroyed by Persian troops. The Resident, Capt. Felix Jones, whose summer house had to be totally rebuilt intended "to build in its place an entire wooden summer house or an improved chahar tak" but closer to Bushehr.[126] In November 1857, he asked the governor of Bushehr permission to build a temporary summer house closer to town rather than rebuilding his old house at Choghadak. The governor's reaction was not encouraging, and therefore, Jones asked the British Legation in Tehran to see whether permission might be obtained from the authorities in Tehran.[127] He submitted that if he could rent a summer-house he would do so, but living in tents he considered not a feasible option. Fortunately for Jones, Tehran gave permission to build a modest dwelling.[128] However, the prime-minister, who had given permission, died shortly afterwards and the Minister of Foreign Affairs, alerted by local well-wishers that Jones was constructing a large building, ordered construction to be halted. Jones replied that he would do so, of course, but it had already been completed. Moreover, his family lived there due to an epidemic in the town and environs. He further pointed out that he did not understand why such a fuss was made as he had sent a sketch of the dwelling with precise measurements to Tehran. It was constructed with the same dimensions as his field tent and the roof was of mats. When he had received permission to construct, only the canvas walls and roof were removed and replaced with rubble and mortar. The outhouses for the cook and servants and the stable were all made of rubble, mud and straw. In short, it was smaller than his previous destroyed house at Choghadak.

---

124. Shepherd 1857, p. 154; Binning 1857, vol. 1, pp. 148-49; Lorimer 1915, vol.2, p. 351.

125. NA, FO 248/263, Resident to Shah, 09/07/1845; Idem, Governor Shiraz to Resident; Idem, Resident to Governor Shiraz, 08/07/1845 (drawing of the buildings at Choghadak). Sayyah 1346, p. 12 (Rishar was the *yeylaq* or summer quarters of Bushehr in the 1870s); Cherikof 1358, p. 9 (Choghadak, which the translator misread as Aligarh). For a description of Choghadak, meaning dry, barren hill, see Hamidi 1380, pp. 244-45.

126. NA,FO 248/168, Cmdr Felix Jones to C.A. Murray envoy-extraordinary, 14/11/1857.

127. NA, FO 248/183, Jones to Murray, 12/01/1858.

128. NA, FO 248/183, Jones to Ahmad Khan 22 Jomadi I 1274/09/01/1858; Idem, Ahmad Khan to Felix Jones, 24 Jomadi I 1274 - 11/01/1858.

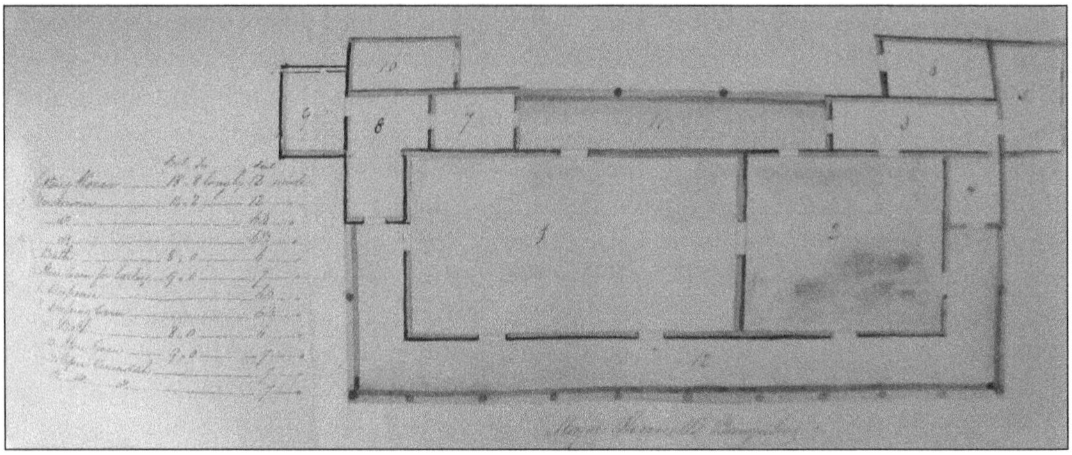

Major Hennell's (British Resident) summer house plan

He suspected that the accusation came from some person inimical to Ahmad Khan, the governor and himself who wanted to stir up trouble locally and in Tehran. Ahmad Khan had never raised any problems after permission to construct had been received; he even settled some minor dispute with claimants concerning the ground. He in person inspected the house and when negative rumors from Tehran reached Bushehr he publicly commented "a fisherman or a cowherd in Europe would have a better dwelling." If suspicion still existed let the Minister of Foreign Affairs send competent and impartial men to investigate, Capt. Jones suggested.[129] He further reported that:

> A few months later it became clear that Mirza Saeed Khan's charge was in relation to the erection of a small building for the accommodation of Dr. Wood of the Residency, whose summer quarter at Chaghudak were destroyed at the same time as mine. When I applied for permission to transfer the summer place to this current location I had never thought that it only applied to me. We do not occupy more than the original premises assigned. Dr. Wood's building is 12 feet square stands 90 paces from the construction that is my domain. The whole platform of barren rock is 400 paces to the south and east to west is egg-shaped. The space is just what is necessary for privacy, as the doctor supplies medicines to all comers. The charge that I have chosen for myself another piece of soil is incorrect. The prince-governor nor any high official has raised any objection to these constructions and when visiting me never stated that I was in contravention of the agreement with the Prime Minister.[130]

However, the Minister was adamant and in January orders were received that Jones had to destroy the summer residence near Rishahr. He laconically replied that it was raised through the favor of the Minister of Foreign Affairs and it could be demolished through his disfavor.[131]

---

129. NA, FO 248/183, Jones to William Doria, charge d'affaires, 09/12/1858; Lorimer 1915, vol. 1, p. 2103.
130. NA, FO 248/189, Jones to Alison, 28/09/1860.
131. NA, FO 248/206, Jones to Mirza Syed Khalil, 10 Rajab 1278 - 11/01/1862; Geary 1878, vol. 1, p. 56.

House of the manager of the Imperial Bank of Persia in Sabzabad

After Jones' departure, the government of Persia was less reluctant to allow the British to have summer homes, because by the 1870s, Europeans changed their place of residence every six months and lived during the cold season in the town itself, but in the hot season in "large substantial structures built isolated, on a low sandy plain, two and three miles away from the city, coming in to business on horseback early in the morning, and returning late at night."[132] Clearly this was an option only available to the wealthier town dwellers (Persians and Europeans), who had gardens and country houses at Sabzabad, which was situated in the northern part of the peninsula, about 9 km from Bushehr itself. Here they lived, "driving or riding every day to their business in town."[133] Apart from cooler and breezier surroundings Sabzabad also offered other amenities. Doctor Waters in the 1870s wrote, "on returning to the house [at Sabzabad] we plunged into a small circular tank of fresh water at the back of the house."[134] As of the beginning of the twentieth century, in addition to Sabzabad, Europeans and the more wealthy Persian families also resided at Neydi 4 km (2,25 miles) from the town or in rural Bushehr 10 km (6 miles) of the town itself. "These residential areas are comparatively clean and healthy and most of the houses contain a second storey to catch cool breezes from the sea in the summer."[135]

In short, visitors did not consider Bushehr a beautiful town, and it did not have any monuments or relics of antiquity.[136] There were no trees in the city itself, nowhere a patch

132. Ballantine 1879, p. 53; Collins 1896, p. 24.
133. Lorimer 1915, vol. 2, p. 330; De Rivoyre 1883, p. 131.
134. Waters n.d., p. 26.
135. Trade Report 1923-24, p. 1.
136. Trade Report 1913-14, p. 1.

of green. "For this is the first dominant impression of Bushire, that one has run one's head against the wall."[137] Everything was grey, the windowless houses, the soil, and streets were all sandy grey. Even the natives were walking around in dusty clothes grey like the sand. Only at the seafront were some buildings that looked like European commercial establishments, otherwise one only saw bare walls that here and there were topped by crowns of dust-covered palms.[138] This negative view irked Stevens, a mid-twentieth century visitor. He opined that Bushehr was much maligned, and it had obviously fallen on evil days. But in the city itself, he opined, there were a number of fine eighteenth- and early nineteenth-century buildings, with balconies whose blue shutters rattled in the wind. He liked the shell-coral material from which the houses were made.[139]

Hotels and Restaurants

Travelers usually spent the night in one of the caravanserais in Bushehr or stayed with friends. In the late 1820s, Rabbi Beth Hillel wrote that Bushehr was "a miserable place with narrow streets and markets; but there are good houses for travellers and keeping of merchants goods called caravanseras."[140] Europeans usually slept in their consul's residence, with a European residing in Bushehr, or with an Armenian family,[141] there being no hotel. In 1816, Buckingham rode to the British factory, and then to the Resident's house "where we found a room and many of my countrymen staying there."[142] In 1874, Fogg lodged with an English merchant whose house was "three miles outside the walls, to which we ride out every night and return in the early morning."[143] In 1906, the Dutch traveler Maurits Wagenvoort slept in a building next to the Armenian church being too tired to go to *Holandarabad*, the French consulate.[144] In 1927, the German traveler Hermann Norden learned that Bushehr had no hotel. He hoped that the British residency would take him in, which it did. It had a guest-house where he was given a room plus kitchen. He had to go into town to buy provisions and have his servant prepare his meal.[145]

By 1930 the hotel accommodation situation changed. The *Imperial Airways* rest house offered the best accommodation; in addition there were the *Shimkhani* and the *Akbar Brothers* hotel as well as the *Kazeruni* guest-house (3 km out of town near the airfield; daily rate about 50 rials) and *Apcar* (near the Customs; daily rate about 35 rials).[146] However, this

---

137. Bradley-Birt 1910, p. 22. Here and there was a lote tree (*sadr, konar*) in Bushehr, one of which was known as *konar-e Mohanna*, which the people of Bushehr considered a holy site. Hamidi 1360, pp. 132-33; Idem 1380, p. 522.

138. Böhme 1977, p. 250.

139. Stevens 1979, p. 285.

140. Beth Hillel 1832, p. 107; Sa`adat 1390, pp. 20-21 (five are mentioned in 1914); Sayyah 1346, p. 12.

141. Stern 1854, p. 85; Sargent 1820, part 2, p. 344.

142. Buckingham 1971, p. 344; Rich 1839, p. 196. Binning stayed "in lodgings for strangers" that was available in the Residency compound. Binning 1857, vol. 1, p. 142.

143. Fogg 1875,p. 172; and so did Ballantine 1879, p. 52.

144. Wagenvoort 1926, p. 82.

145. Norden 1928, p. 47. Ael 1931, p. 98 also reports that there was no hotel.

146. Ebtehaj 1932, p. 184; Simmonds 1935, p. ix; Gray 1937, p. ix.

Kazeruni guest-house

information provided by the *Guide to Persia* was too optimistic in its favorable appreciation. For, according to Mrs. Merrit-Hawkes referring to the situation in 1934, "There is no hotel in Bushire and the local substitute is both odiferous and insectiferous. I believe missionaries have stayed there, but that's all right for them as they are spending eternity in heavenly mansions."[147] By 1940, there was in addition to the above hotels, the Hotel *Eqtesad*.[148]

The various lodging accommodations did not necessarily include food arrangements. The British Residency rest-house did not, for example, and thus, guests usually had their servant prepare meals. However, not everybody had a servant to cook for him, which was the case of Böhme, a German Junker's pilot, who in 1930, in search of an alternative to his own cooking found no restaurant in Bushehr.[149] He must have had a rather European idea of a restaurant (it seems that this was the first time he was abroad), because in 1934, according to a Mrs. Merrit-Hawkes, "The innumerable small restaurants all had Western meat choppers but an Eastern supply of flies. ... There was a great variety of restaurants, some selling fish, some only fish-heads, some providing good meat, and others, for the porters, the poorest of all the workers, who bought only heads and feet of sheep."[150]

---

147. Merritt-Hawkes 1935, pp. 1-2.
148. Political Diaries, vol. 14, p. 292.
149. Böhme 1977, p. 250. Around that time, Ael 1931, p. 98 also writes that there was no restaurant in Bushehr and he had to buy canned food in what he called a British shop, presumably one that sold mainly British goods.
150. Merritt-Hawkes 1935, p. 8.

Those who did not want to eat, but just wanted a place to stretch their legs and drink something in a public establishment were disappointed for much of the nineteenth century. In 1816, Buckingham noted that in Bushehr "Coffee-houses there are none, as this beverage is not much in use among the inhabitants."[151] This situation changed over time. By 1930, "There were lots of tea-shops, decorated with ladies in semi-European clothes, drinking wine and showing a great deal of leg, or European prima donnas in the architectural hairdressing of the gay nineties. ... The gramophone produced Persian music."[152]

Streets

Bushehr was larger than the other Persian Gulf towns, but otherwise similar in its general features. The streets, or rather lanes, formed a narrow, tortuous, irregular, unpaved, undrained labyrinth. They were also exceedingly dusty, but when it rained they turned into sewers of mud. The lanes were only 2-2.5 m wide, and hemmed in on each side by inhospitable mud walls of the courts that surrounded the overhanging houses, revealing only a thread of blue sky to the bewildered pedestrian. It was not unusual that people from opposite houses spanned a cover (*taq*) between their houses, which were known to people by their names, such as *taq-e golshan*. This provided the only advantage that the narrow streets possessed, viz. that the walls sheltered the passers-by from the sun, which therefore, were cooler for the passers-by and for the occupants of the houses. Some of the lanes were so narrow that a man with outstretched arms could touch the houses on either side of the street. The lanes were also filled with filth, household refuse, dead animals, mangy dogs, and an oppressive stench, and until the 1920s were not swept. The lanes were also busy with long lines of mules and donkeys passing through. As a result, they were worn into deep channels in the center by the mule traffic, and the pedestrians had to pick their way along the higher ground on either side.[153] The town had hardly any open spaces.[154] The only road in the peninsula fit for strongly built vehicles was 9 km long from Bushehr to Sabzabad, with a branch to Rishahr. It was maintained by private subscribers under the supervision of the British Residency.[155] By 1928, there were some new paved streets and electric lighting.[156] By 1945, "a broad lane leads from the east to the west shore, and there is an esplanade of sorts on the seaward side."[157] However, at that time, the streets were still mostly narrow and winding, but some had been paved and most of these were lit by electricity.[158] Therefore, in the early twentieth century there were

---

151. Buckingham 1971, p. 348.
152. Merritt-Hawkes 1935, p. 8; Hamidi 1380, p. 477.
153. Morier 1818, pp. 13, 41; Morier 1812, pp. 57, 67; Alexander 2000, p. 93; Buckingham 1971, pp. 347-48; Kempthorne 1835, p. 283; Binning 1857, vol. 1, p. 141; Shepherd 1857, p. 138; Locher 1889, p. 50; MacGregor 1879, vol. 1, p. 11; Geary 1878, vol. 1, p. 63; Stack 1882, vol. 1, p. 27; Curzon 1892, vol. 1, p. 233; Lorimer 1915, vol. 2, p. 332; Trade Report 1913-14, p. 1; Norden 1928, p. 49; Sa`adat 1390, p. 23; Pfeiffer 1852, p. 239.
154. Lorimer 1915, vol. 2, p. 341; Hamidi 1380, pp. 439-40 (*taq*).
155. Lorimer 1915, vol. 2, p. 332.
156. Mahrad 1978, p. 88; Norden 1928, p. 49.
157. Government of Great Britain 1945, p. 503. Prior to World War II, the Armenian merchant Abkar constructed a *meydan* and a building as part of the urban renewal plan. Hamidi 1380, p. 66.
158. NA, FO 371/15473.

Typical street in Bushehr

only a few carts of the four-wheel fourgon type in Bushehr, because they were difficult to use because of the bad and narrow streets.[159]

Town quarters

Bushehr was divided into four quarters, in addition to smaller ones such as that of the Jews, Kazerunis and others that were components of the four main ones. Around 1916, Sadid al-Saltaneh described the four quarters as follows:

(1) Mahalleh-ye Behbahani. To the east and north it bordered on the sea and to the prayer direction to the Qabri bath-house; to the south it bordered on the Shabeh'i quarter and Jews Street (*kucheh-e yahudan*). This quarter had five mosques, viz. Gharib, Kufa, Dashti, Qabri, and Haji Bab. It had three bathhouses: Khan, Tala and Qabri. The latter was for the exclusive use by women. The quarter had a *qadamgah* a.k.a. Khvajeh Khezr. It had 360 houses and 15 shops, and there were 50 street lamps installed by the municipality. Its notables in 1916 were: Soleyman Mirza, the *ra'is-e maliyeh*; the `Alam al-Huda family; Haji Gholam `Ali Tajer Behbahani; Haji Baqer A`la; Haji Yahya a.k.a. Haji Baba; Haji Mirza Gholam Hoseyn Tajer Kazeruni; Haji Abu'l-Qasem Tajer-e Shirazi a.k.a. Gangugar; Haji `Abdol-Molk Tajer-e Behbahani a.k.a. Rowghani; Aqa Mohammad Dehdashti; Haji Mohammad Saleh a.k.a. Kholaseh; Sayyed Taher Taraz; Sayyed Hoseyn *ra'is-e baladiyeh*; Haji Akbar Bazzaz; Mahmud Tajer-e Kazeruni as well as the office of the *Mozaffari* newspaper.

---

159. Government of India 1924, p. 113. A fourgon is a covered wagon for carrying baggage.

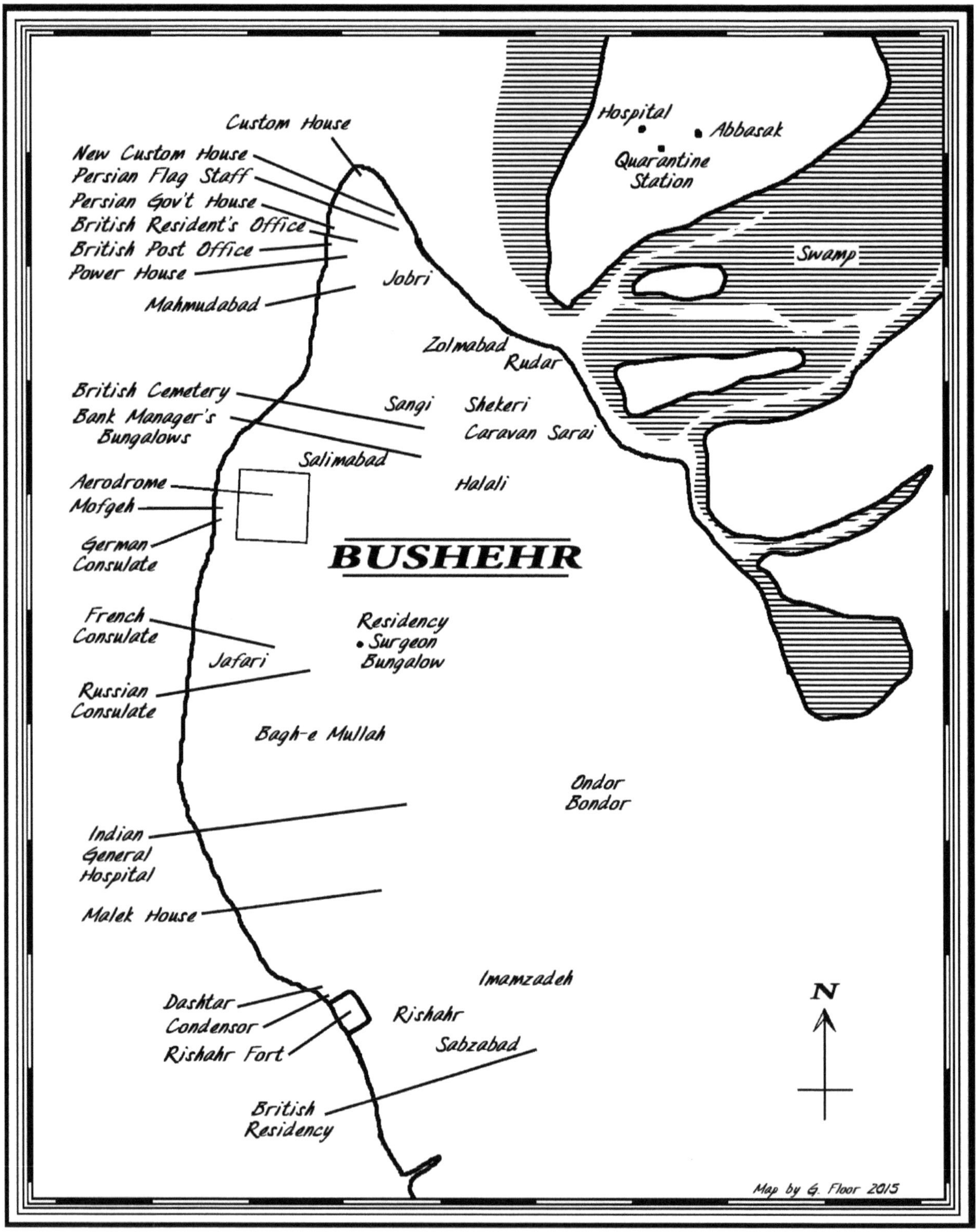

Plan of Bushehr ca. 1920

(2) Mahalleh-ye Kuti. In Bushehr they called the British Residence *kuti* or fort. It was the first building erected in that quarter and hence its name. To the north it bordered on Yahudan street and to the east on Mirza Soleyman street, to the west the barracks

Hoseyniyeh-ye Kazeruni and courtyard of the Arab mosque: Kuti quarter

(*sarbaz-khaneh*) and to the east the sea. It had three mosques: Fil, Sheikh Sa`dun, and Sunniha. There was one bathhouse a.k.a. Delgosha and two *qadamgahs* a.k.a. Maqam-e `Ali and Pesar-e Zeyd. There were 440 houses and 11 shops such as a *gomaj-forush* (sweet bread seller), a grocer and a tailor; it had 30 municipal street lights. The notables were: Sayyed

`Abdol-Reza Hafez al-Sehhat; the Haji Taher family; the Al Safar; Abu'l-Qasem, son of Haji Mohammad Hasan Tajer-e Borazjani; Nakhoda Ebrahim, captain of the *Persepolis*; Haji Yusof Abu'l-Hasan Kalantar; Abdol-Reza Khan and Abdol-Rasul Khan, sons of Haji Bashir Khan; Hayki, son of Makardich, an Armenian merchant, Andrus, the engineer of the *Persepolis*, the sons of Ya`qub Tajer, Osama Satur Maghazehchi, Andubi, the customs clerk, and the French physician. In this quarter were also situated the English Residency and the Russian commercial agency.

(3) Mahalleh-ye Shanbeh'i, which was also called Khashavi. This quarter was situated higher than the other quarters and, therefore, the place of residence of the notables and the wealthy.[160] To the east was the sea and to the north the Qabri mosque, to the south *kucheh-ye Kazemi* and to its south the house of Haji Hoseyn Khashavi and the Baraheh-ye Kazeruni. It had four mosques: Nur, Malek, Qassabha, and Jom`eh, and one Armenian church. The Christian cemetery was in that church. The old Armenian church was situated there and its dome and church were still there by 1917. The concentration of houses inhabited by Armenians and of Armenian religious buildings in this quarter was referred to as *Tell-e Armaniha*, because it stood on an elevated surface, overlooking the old bazaar and the New Mosque.[161] The quarter had five Hoseyniyehs, viz. Sokuncheh, Baraheh-ye Mir `Abdu, Baraheh-ye Kazeruni, Baraheh-ye Sayyed `Abdol-Reza and Taq Sayyed Ne`matollah. It had two bathhouses: Haji Mohammad Ja`far Safar and Sheikh Hasan; and one *qadamgah* a.k.a. `Abbas `Ali. There were 469 houses, 53 shops such as a dried-fruit seller (*ajilforush*), a gold-smith, a tailor, a shoe-maker, one watch-maker and a blind rope-maker (*bandbaf*); there were 24 municipal street lamps. Its notables were: Haji `Abdol-Rasul *ra'is al-tojjar*; Haji Sayyed Mohammad Reza Tajer-e Kazeruni; the Imam Jom`eh family; Molla Hoseyn Jadid al-Eslam; Tegram Malkom; Ahmad Shelesh; Hosam al-Sadat; Sadid al-Saltaneh; the Sadr al-Eslam family; Sayyed Mohammad `Ali Mojtahed; Sheikh Mohammad `Ali *moqaddam-e gomroki*; Sorush al-Molk; Haji Mullah Ahmad Khan Saheb; and Sheikh al-Hokama.

(4) Mahalleh-ye Dehdasht. The Jews had two quarters. One was here and the other in between the Behbahani and Kuti quarters, while the Jewish synagogue was in the Behbahani quarter; the Jewish quarter was locally known as Yowdya. To the north was the bazaar, to the east the sea, to the south the gate and to the west to Kucheh-ye `Ali `Abdu. The Dehdasht quarter had four mosques and one *hoseyniyeh*. The Dehdashti and the Sheikh Jaber mosque, which after its destruction and becoming a stable, was rebuilt around 1914 by Haji Mohammad Hoseyn Dehdashti. The Dovvani mosque was build recently and belonged to the Sheykhis. Further, the Namaki mosque and the Pir-e Zan *hoseyniyeh*, which was a new building, were constructed by the mother of Zar Khedr Khan Tangestani. There was one bathhouse a.k.a. Namaki; 300 houses and 60 shops such as a smith, a grocer, a confectioner, and a turner; there were 15 municipal lights. Its notables were: Sheikh Mohammad `Ali Mojtahed Behbahani; Haji Mohammad Hoseyn Tajer-e Dehdashti, son of Haji Abu'l-Qasem Asghar; Mansur-e Divan; Hosam al-Re`aya; Haji

160. Lorimer 1915, vol. 2, p. 341, has Khashshabi, while Sa`adat 1390, p. 19 and Nezam al-Saltaneh Mafi 1391 (throughout) both have Shanbadi. Sa`adat 1390, p. 19, n. explains that the term is a contraction of *shanbeh* and that the quarter was thus called because its inhabitants did not eat fish on *shanbeh* or Saturday. Anonymous 1367, p. 72 further submits that the original inhabitants of this quarter were a group of Arabs known as Shanbandi. Kanin 1391, p. 210 and Hamidi 1380, p. 425, submit that the Shanbeh'i quarter was named after Shanbeh, the eleventh forefather of the Al Osfur clan.

161. Hamdidi 1380, p. 207.

Aqa, *monshi* (clerk) of the Russian consulate; the Dovvaniha family; the Haji Abu'l-Fazl-e `Ali family; and the Chuk Behbahani family.[162] There was also an Arab quarter, which was to the east of the *Amiriyeh* building.[163] In 1932, a Sangi quarter is mentioned, which was situated 3 km from the town on the road to the British Residency. It is likely that this quarter was a new development to house some of Bushehr's growing population. This is also suggested by the names of the new peripheric quarters that came into being after 1950, which all bear names of former villages such as Solhabad, Shekeri, Pudar, Bagh-e Zahra and Dastak.[164]

There was strong enmity between the four quarters of Bushehr, which sometimes led to hostile acts, mostly during the Moharram-Safar period, resulting in blood-feuds between them. According to the British consul, "The basis of these feuds is merely hostility between the four quarters of the city, fomented by the action of the Mullahs, who endeavour in each case to protect the offenders inhabiting their own Mohallahs." The mutual hostility may be traced back to the tribal origins of the original settlers of these quarters. This is clear from the opposition of the Behbahani quarter against the Al Mazkur in 1815 (see chapter 3). This enmity often led to fights between the quarters and even to murder. One such event occurred during Moharram (April 1906), when one person was killed unprovoked, due to the ill-feeling that prevailed between the Behbahani and Kuti quarters. The murderer was tried in religious court; although 300 *tumans* was offered as blood money, the Behbahani residents refused the offer and demand his execution. Another event occurred on 2 February 1907, when a youth from the Kuti quarter was killed by a gang from the Behbahani quarter in retaliation of a killed Behbahani young man. When finally a culprit was identified the governor ordered the *kalantar* to produce him on pain of the bastinado.[165] At the 40th day of `Ashura (30 Safar 1326/3 April 1908) serious fights broke out between residents of Shamadi (sic; Shanbadi) and Dehdashti quarters, one man was seriously wounded. This led to a fight between the deputy and the *kargozar* how to deal with the aftermath and who was to blame for it.[166]

Population

Population diversity

Although Bushehr originally was Arab in character, already at the beginning of the nineteenth century, its population was a mixture of Arabic-Persian speakers and both languages were used.[167] In the 1830s, the majority of the population was still Arabic, but through intermarriage the Arabs had lost their distinctive characteristics. Because of this

162. Sadid al-Saltaneh 1371, pp. 41-42; Lorimer 1915, vol. 2, p. 342; Kanin 1391, pp. 204-15; Hamidi 1380, pp. 168, 174, 332, 425, 695.
163. Sadid al-Saltaneh 1371, p. 38.
164. Political Diaries, vol. 10, p. 56. For the names of the new quarters, see Hamidi 1380, p. 168.
165. Political Diaries, vol. 1, pp. 336, 376, vol. 2, p. 49.
166. Political Diaries, vol. 3, p. 120. It may also a local variant of the rivalry between the so-called Heydaris and Ne`matollahis, who would regular clash with one another at various times of the years in towns and large villages in Persia see John Perry, "The Haydari-Ni`mati Conflicts," *Iranian Studies* 12 (1979), 135-62.
167. Buckingham 1971, p. 349; Beth Hillel 1832, p. 107; Stern 1854, p. 85; De Rivoyre 1883, p. 131.

Persian and Arab inhabitants of Bushehr in 1856 (from a photograph)

and the influx of new migrants, the population was not homogenous. Enmity existed between the various 'ethnic' groups. For example, the Behbahanis were opponents of the Al Mazkur family, and both sides sometimes fought each other such as during the 1815 siege.[168] In 1836, there were in fact, six different 'ethnic' groups or 'tribes.' Of these, the most important were the Kazerunis, Derisis, Behbahanis and the Dehdashtis, who each had their own chief or *kadkhoda*. The other two 'tribes', the Shirazis and the Shushtaris did not have a separate chief.[169] Bushehr retained its predominant Arab character at least until the 1850s, though by then the majority of the population had become Shiite.[170]

Although both Arabic and Persian were spoken in Bushehr, it was thought that its people pronounced both languages with little elegance. For example, they spoke "a corrupted form of Persian, which the Sirazis pronounce to be unintelligible." However, Europeans found that they never had any difficulty in understanding it.[171] English was the commercial means of communication, which allegedly sometimes even locals, one must assume highly educated ones, used amongst themselves.[172] The situation changed over time and by 1900 the Arabic element was clearly on the wane. According to Lorimer,

168. NA, FO 248/38, Bruce to Sir Evan Nepean, Governor Bombay, 03/09/1815.

169. Anonymous 1367, p. 72. Derisis probably were migrants from Deris, a rural district in Kazerun or were Darazis, from the Darazi district some 30 km n.e. of Tangestan. Hamidi 1380, p. 299.

170. Binning 1857, vol. 1, p. 144.

171. Buckingham 1971, pp. 349-50; Binning 1857, vol. 1, p. 148. For the Bushehri dialect, see Farid Mirshakar, *Farhang-e Vazhegan-e Mahalli-ye Bushehr* (Daneshnameh-ye Ostan-e Bushehr), vol. 1 (alef-ba). Tehran, 1389.

172. De Rivoyre 1883, p. 131; Aubin 1908, p. 191.

though the Bushehr population was heterogeneous, mostly Persian was heard in the streets. One-third of the population still spoke Arabic, but few spoke it habitually. In addition to this permanent population, there was a large floating population of traders, travelers, and temporary laborers.[173]

Because of the increased trade there was a continuous influx of Persian speaking migrants from Behbahan, Kazerun, Dehdasht and Shiraz. Also, tribesmen from Tangistan provided the labor class and fishermen, not only in Bushehr, but also elsewhere in the Persian Gulf. However, the town still kept its mainly Arab character, though the Persian contingent was considerable and Persian was spoken by all.[174] Apart from linguistic, religious, or other distinctions, the Bushehris were divided according to whether you were 'a native' or not. That is, the 'original' inhabitants of the peninsula were called *ra`iyat*, undoubtedly reflecting that they constituted the early and main group of immigrants, while the immigrants or *khoshneshin* were not, who were called *Alvar*, i.e. Lurs.[175]

An element that was prominent in the population mix, but receives rather little attention in contemporary reports, was intermarriage with Africans. This mixture of Arabs, Persians and Africans was quite strong all along the Arab and Persian littoral due to slavery, of which Bushehr was one of the major importing ports.[176]

Apart from Moslems there were some Christians and Jews in Bushehr. In 1816, there were several Armenian families and a priest, while around 1828, there were allegedly 500 Armenian families, some of whom were rich merchants and the rest were craftsmen. In the 1870s there were 60-80 Armenians.[177] By 1890, there were some 100 Armenians, all engaged in trade, but by 1900 there were only 35 Armenians and 18 Iraqi Christians left.[178] Although there were no Jews of any note in 1816, as a group they were much larger than that of the Christians. Around 1828, there were allegedly 200 Jewish families, most of whom were goldsmiths. By 1850 there were 70 Jewish families, who were better treated than their co-religionists in the interior of Persia. By 1900, there were 600 Jews who lived in two separate sub-quarters.[179]

Until about 1856, in addition to Persian subjects of various ethnic and religious affilitiation, there were also a number of Indians (Hindus and Khojas) living in Bushehr.[180] However, by 1864 all Hindus had left, for Col. Pelly observed that there was not a single Banyan at Bushehr, which he ascribed to a downturn in the local economy. "The fact is, a Banyan will stand any tyranny, any misery, anything you please, except *permanent* loss of profits; when this last calamity arrives, he goes away, as he has done from Bushire."[181] A decade later they had returned, because in 1876, there were six Moslem Indians or Khojas

173. Lorimer 1915, vol. 2, pp. 343-44; Sani` al-Dowleh 1294, vol. 1, p. 299.

174. Report 1910-11, p. 1.

175. Sadid al-Saltaneh 1371, p. 53.

176. Merritt-Hawkes 1935, p. 7; on slavery, see Floor 2013 b.

177. Johnson 1818, p. 23; Beth Hillel 1832, p. 108; De Rivoyre 1883, p. 166.

178. Curzon 1892, vol. 2, p. 233; Lorimer 1915, vol. 2, pp. 343-44.

179. Buckingham 1971, p. 350; Beth Hillel 1832, p. 108; Benjamin 1859, p. 182; Lorimer 1915, vol. 2, pp. 343-44.

180. Waring 1973, pp. 3-4; Stern 1854, p. 85; Sani` al-Dowleh 1294, vol. 1, p. 299. The term Banyan is derived from *vaniya* (pl. *vaniye*) a Gujarati word meaning 'trader.' The Portuguese used this word, in the form of Banyan or Banian or some other similar form, to refer to any Indian trader, and this appellation was later adopted by other Europeans. Khoja is a term derived from the Persian honorific *khvajeh*, meaning 'lord, master,' referred to those converted to Nizari Ismaili Islam in the Indian sub-continent.

181. Pelly 1865 a, p. 61, note.

Musicians in Bushehr, ca.1810

in Bushehr. According to Sani` al-Dowleh, 60 years earlier the population consisted of Arabs and Hindus, but by 1880 they were mostly Persian, while by then the Hindus were mostly in Lengeh, where they had a special bazaar. The number of Indians increased to some 40 by 1900, amongst whom there were some Hindus.[182] As a result, by 1930, the population was allegedly "conversant with English and Indian languages,"[183] which may have been true for a few people.

Finally, there were a few Europeans in Bushehr, who were mainly diplomatic and commercial staff. Initially, there was only a handful, growing to some 50 Europeans by 1900. Ten years later their number had dropped to some 30-40, and this number would fall further thereafter, until there was only a handful again.[184]

Population size

Table 1.2 gives the estimated population size of Bushehr from 1809 to 1956. As can be seen, the estimates vary considerably. The size of the population of Bushehr grew during the nineteenth century and thereafter. The available data are not based on a census, but are estimates made by travelers, which they most likely obtained from local Persian and/or British officials, who had lived for a considerable time in the port. The low estimate by Kinneir of 5,000 is not shared by his contemporaries such as Morier, Heude and Buckingham. Milburn's estimate probably was not based on his own knowledge of Bushehr and may be discounted. The drop in population size in the 1820s may be ascribed

182. Administration Report 1876-77, p. 5; E`temad al-Saltaneh 1294, vol. 1, p. 299; Lorimer 1915, vol. 2, pp. 343-44. FO 248/271, Table of (35) British subjects in Bushehr in 1871.

183. Ebtehaj 1932, p. 184.

184. Lorimer 1915, vol. 2, pp. 343-44; Trade Report 1910-11, p. 1; Mahrad 1978, p. 88.

to the internal political problems in Bushehr, as discussed in the next chapter. The figure for 1828 appears to be on the high side (Table 1.2) as it would have meant a more than doubling of the population in a short period, which is unlikely. Also, Rabbi Beth Hillel's figures for the number of Jews (200 families) and Armenians (500 families) are clearly much too high (see below) and, therefore, quite likely his number for Moslems (5,000 families) is too high as well. For the same reason the figure given by Stern for 1845 of 2,000 people is much too low, even though the population had shrunk by one-third after the 1832 plague and in 1836 there continued to be daily migration of people from Bushehr to Basra and Khark.[185] In 1851 the estimated population was 11,000, but not even 20% of that number still lived in the town and only the poor remained,[186] which was due to the 'regime change' in Bushehr (see chapter two). According to Shepherd, in 1858 the population included 3,000 militia, which was a temporary phenomenon. Thereafter, the population grew to some 20,000 or 25,000 by the early twentieth century. This number increased even more after 1910, and despite Bushehr's diminishing role as a port after 1925, its population continued to grow. However, by the late 1930s its population had shrunk by half, remaining at about 8,000 people. Leaving aside the question whether the figures for 1930 and 1938 are correct, a fact is that Bushehr lost population from all classes. This was partly due to the demand for labor elsewhere in the Persian Gulf as well as, in particular, the fact that in past a large number of coolies worked in the date groves during harvest time, but thereafter were replaced by Iraqi seasonal laborers.[187] But most importantly, the migration was due to the growing importance of the oil industry in Khuzestan and the ports serving it. A considerable number of people migrated from Bushehr district to Mohammerah, Abadan and towns in the interior, Bahrain and the Arab coast.[188] Due to famine conditions in Bushehr's hinter land in 1941 its population grew from 6,000 to 11,000.[189] This trend continued in 1942, but this time in addition due to more positive developments. For there was a high demand for labor, because of the opening of the UKCC car assembly plant and increased shipping of war suppies. As a result, Busher's population grew to almost 25,000.[190] However, after 1943, because of the closure of the car assembly plant and trade coming to almost a standstill labor started to migrate from Bushehr, and this trend continued in the years thereafter.[191] As a result of these developments and further decline of the port, by 1956, once prosperous Bushehr, only had 16,000 inhabitants, i.e. at the level of the 1880s.[192]

---

185. Anonymous 1367, p. 73.
186. Binning 1857, vol. 1, p. 144
187. Mahrad 1978, p. 88. "Iranian census authorities state that a considerable amount of unauthorized migration to the Arab side of the Gulf took place during the year." Administration Report 1937, p. 4.
188. Administration Report 1934, p. 4; Administration Report 1937, p. 10.
189. Administration Report 1941, p. 14.
190. Administration Report 1942, p. 21.
191. Administration Report 1945, p. 9.
192. Stevens 1979, p. 284.

1.2: Estimated population size of Bushehr 1809-1958

Population	Year	Source
5,000	1809	Kinneir 1973, p. 70
10,000	1809	Morier 1812, p. 57; Milburn 1813, vol. 1, p. 128
10,000	1811	Rich 1839, p. 202
8,000	1815	NA, FO 248/38, Bruce to Bombay, 03/09/1815
11,000	1816	Heude 1819, p. 43
10,000	1816	Buckingham 1971, p. 349
10,000	1821	Fraser 1984, p. 66; Rich 1839, p. 202
5,000	1820-30	Sani` al-Dowleh 1294, vol. 1, p. 299
20,000	1828	Kempthorne, 1835 p. 283; Mignan 1839, vol. 2, p. 138
28,500	1828	Beth Hillel 1832, p. 108 (5,000 Moslem families)
4,000	1836	Anonymous 1367, p. 72 (800 households)
2,000	1845	Stern 1854, p. 85
15,000	1848	Pfeiffer 1852, p. 239
11,000/2,000	1851	Binning 1857, vol. 1, p. 144
4,000	1858	Shepherd 1857, p. 138 (800 houses)
20,000	1870	Waters n.d. p. 20
20,000	1874	Fogg 1889, p. 173
12,000	1875	Ballantine 1879, p. 58
12,000 - 15,000	1885	Stolze & Andreas (1885); Sani` al-Dowleh 1294, vol. 1, p. 299
15,000	1890	Curzon 1892, vol. 1, p. 231
25,000	1905	Gleadowe-Newcomen 1905, p. 60
22-25,000	1910	Kuss 1911, p. 10
20-22,000; 30,000	1912	Sadid al-Saltaneh 1371, p. 37; Sa`adat 1390, pp. 18, 21
18,000	1914	Report 1913-14, p. 1; Military Report 1924, p. 25 (ca. 16,000)
20,000	1930	Administration Report 1937, p. 10; Ebtehaj 1932, p. 183 (40,000)
8,000	1939	Administration Report 1939, p. 14
6,000	1940	Administration Report 1941, p. 14
11,000	1941	Administration Report 1941, p. 14
25,000	1942	Administration Report 1942, p. 21
16,000	1956	Stevens 1979, p. 284

Around 1900, Lorimer estimated the popuation at 15,000, which, by ethnic composition, was mainly Persian of a very heterogenous origin, as shown in the table below. These were all permanent residents; among the large floating population (temporary labor, travelers, sailors, etc.) there were about 200 Kazerunis and 100 Behbahanis.

1.3: Estimated ethnic composition of the population of Bushehr (ca. 1905)

Persians		*Other Orientals*	
Bushehris	5,000	Jews	600
Shambadis	2,500	Armenians	35
Behbahanis	1,000	Goanese	20
Kazerunis	1,000	Baghdad Moslems	20
Khanasiris	300	Baghdad Christians	18
Shirazis	200	Memons*	4
Tangasiris	200	Bohrahs*	3
Dovvanis	200	Other British Indians	10
Dehdashtis	150		
		Europeans	
Dashtis	100	British	24
Samghunis	40	Eurasians	10
Kharagis	30	French	5
Esfahanis	10	Russians	5
Tehranis	10	Belgians	5
Gabrs	5	Germans	2
Lingavis	5	Greek	1
Arabs			
Local	200		
Bahrainis	20		
Kuwaitis	10		
Hasawis	10		

Source: Lorimer 1915, vol. 2, pp. 343-44. * = Moslem Indians.

In 1908, the population of Bushehr governorate was estimated at 94,000 people, of which some 22,000 lived in town and the peninsula.[193] In 1947, it was estimated that this last number was only 15,000 and the population of the *shahrestan* likewise had dropped significantly to only 43,000. It was expected that the drop in population would continue as people left for areas with better opportunities.

1.4: Estimated population of the Bushehr governorate

Location	1908	1947
Bandar Rig	15,000	5,000
Bandar Delam	12,000	4,000
Borazjan	15,000	10,000
Ahram	10,000	3,000

193. Sa`adat 1390, p. 54 has 30,000 for the entire peninsula and 20,000 for the people outside the town.

Khormuj	20,000	5,000
Bushehr town	22,000	15,000
Total	94,000	43,000

Source: NA, FO 371/15473.

Dress

The dress worn by the Bushehri men reflected the fact that the town's population was a melting pot and hence their clothes likewise were a mixture. "The shirt, trowsers, and zuboon, or outer garment, are Persian; but the turban and the abba, or cloak, are Arabic, - the one is formed of the blue checked cloth of Muscat, or the brown cloth of Shooster; and the other of the manufacture of Lahsa, Kateef, and Coete, on the opposite shore. The black sheepskin cap, the most peculiar feature of the Persian dress, is worn only by such as come down from the higher country, and is in no instance used by a native of Bushire."[194] In the 1880s, the male inhabitants of Bushehr still dressed very much like the Persian merchants in Masqat, but now nearly all of them wore the high Persian sugar-loaf shaped hat, or the black dyed lamb's fleece. They further dressed in tight fitting coats, closed in front, and of black, green blue or brown color, with a white, or colored scarf round their loins, in which they generally carry a fine, silver-mounted, curved dagger, or a pair of long, single-barreled pistols. Also, some of them wear a short broad, double-edge sword, dangling from a leather belt. Nearly all of them had their finger nails painted crimson, and the palm of their hands dyed with henna."[195]

According to Sadid al-Saltaneh, in the early twentieth century, Bushehri males wore a short shirt that was closed at the neck. It was made of *karbas* or *chalvar*. Under it they wore a wide under coat (*zir-e jameh*) made from *chalvar* or from a black fabric, called *meysuni*. The *band-e zir jameh* was woven by their wives. Their overcoat (*qab*) was short and made of *qadak* or *qadak-e chalvar*, which at Bushehr were dyed in various colors. Under the *qaba* they wore an *arkhaleq* or waist coat, which was the same size as the *qaba* and made of chintz or nankin (*qalamkar*). Their waist shawl was of *chalvar* and they fastened it very wide to which they attach a string (*qatar*) and bandolier. In summer they wore a thin cotton *qaba* that was domestically woven, and in winter a short felt one, which they called *gordik*. Also, of course, they carried a gun or if they could not afford one then a mace and sword.[196]

However, Lorimer and other contemporary reporters give a different picture of the ordinary male dress, at least for those belonging to the middle and upper class. Elderly and religious persons still wore the robe confined at the waist by a shawl, the loose drawers, the white Shiraz socks and the broadcloth cloak which was universal as late as the 1880s. By 1900, instead of the *qaba*, "a long garment like a light overcoat, but reaching nearly to the heels, called a *sardari*, is worn, and is made quite plain of dark material either suitings or Black Italians, or of Broad cloth among the chiefs and people of wealth. There is also

194. Buckingham 1971, p. 349; Binning 1857, vol. 1, p. 144.

195. Locher 1889, p. 51. However, de Windt 1891, p. 217 writes that the Bushehris wore "bright-coloured garments, white 'bournouses,' and green turbans ... in striking contrast to the sombre, rook-like garments affected by the natives of Iran."

196. Sadid al-Saltaneh 1371, p. 28.

another kind, corresponding with the European frock-coat, but with pleats below the waist at the back, called a *sardari-e nezami*. Under the *sardari*, they wore a waist coat, pantaloons, woolen socks and imported shoes. On their head they had the *kolah-e namadi* (black, grey or white), or the *kolah-e mahuti*, or an *araqchin* worn with a Masqati turban."[197] After the Constitutional Revolution of 1906, the younger generation preferred ready-made cotton and woolen vests, particularly zephyrs: thin soft white shirts of the style known as tennis shirts, ready-made white drill trousers, drawers, socks and shoes (white canvas uppers and leather soles). Most vests were imported from Bombay, but were mainly of Japanese manufacture. The zephyrs were mainly worn by the working class in the Gulf Ports in the summer months instead of a shirt; and the nomad tribes were reported to start using these garments.[198] In 1930, only some merchants and officials wore European dress.[199]

Women's dress was different, of course. In the early nineteenth century, "They do not wear shoes; their dress consists of a very ample shirt, a pair of loose trowsers, and the veil which goes over all. Their appearance is most doleful." When the originally brown color became dirty it was dyed dark-blue or black. "Their blue linen baggy trousers are tied tight round their ankles, and their feet encased in the clumsy low-heeled *pa-poush* so common in Persia. They all look like professional mourners."[200] Women wore arm and neck bands embellished with artificial foreign beads, in its midst hung a copper coin (*ashrafi*). Some armlets were of glass and were known as *alangu*, and others were of silver. Women wore trousers (*shalvar*) made from Madras nankin (*Sadras qalamkar*) and an *arkhaleq* made of cheap multi-colored silk. Over it they wore a red-striped *aba*, which was woven in Dashti and Dashtestan and known as *nahmani*. Some pierced the ears of their children and put ear hangers there with a bead, called *khazzameh*. They also tattooed their brow.[201] The *chador* and mask (*ruband*) were common for wives of the wealthy. However, poorer women were less confined.[202] Women generally veiled in the streets. Some wore a Persian dark-blue mantle and white veil, but most wear a "striped or variegated Arab mantle and black veil for the face. This latter is often thrown back over the head, for the sake of coolness," but they put it back when a stranger approached.[203]

197. Lorimer 1915, vol. 2, p. 345; Trade Report 1911-12, p. 11.

198. Report 1912-13, p, 18.

199. Böhme 1977, p. 251.

200. Morier 1812, pp. 61-62; Cursetjee 2001, p. 114.

201. Sadid al-Saltaneh 1371, p. 27; Pfeiffer 1852, p. 239. On the history of tattooing in Persia and the technique used, see Floor, "Khalkubi," [iranica.com].

202. Sadid al-Saltaneh 1371, p. 27; Morier 1812, p. 61.

203. Binning 1857, vol. 1, p. 144; Pfeiffer 1852, p. 239; Cursetjee 2001, p. 114.

A street in the old bazaar

Employment, Trade and Industry

Employment

Bushehr did not boast of a leisured class, most inhabitants were engaged in trade (merchants, brokers, shopkeepers), seafaring and fishing (mostly Arabs), portering, some boat builders (*gallaf*) the usual craftsmen (see Table 1.5.) and various minor occupations.[204] As trade is discussed in chapter two, I only mention the presence of merchants in Bushehr and limit myself here to retail traders and craftsmen operating in the bazaar.

The bazaar of Bushehr did not make a great impression on visitors, although it was here that all trade was transacted. The bazaar was situated on the east side of the town adjoining the Khur Soltani. It was described as a row of little open sheds that served as shops. In it was a little platform, raised about 60 cm above the footpath, where the artisan displayed his wares on simple benches. In between the row of parallel arranged shops was a passageway that served as a street, which was covered with matted rafters, palm leaves, and later also with corrugated metal. Although wretched in appearance this roof provided protection against the sun.[205] In 1828, Kempthorne opined that the bazaar was "large, and well supplied with almost every kind of article," as well as close to the landing place.[206] In 1856, Shepherd described the bazaar as follows:

> The bazaar, which extends from the Custom-house quay for some eighty yards, takes a sharp turn to the right, gradually twists again to the left, and terminates in a long straight piece, but very scantily occupied by general dealers, who sell anything, from tin-plates with the alphabet round their edge, balls of sewing cotton, Manchester and Birmingham ware, Persian carpets, Shiraz tobacco, senna, coffee, tea, sugar, Grecian coins, gun-flints, almonds, raisins, dates, to turquoise and diamonds, the former set in rings of silver, and worn on their fingers, the latter stowed away in some small strong box, folded in dirty paper, unset, and rascally cut. The middle or twisted part of the bazaar is principally in the possession of gun-smiths and workers in tin, who make as much noise as they possibly can, and the whole is roofed in, altogether forming a most crowded and anomalous combination.[207]

---

204. Buckingham 1971, p. 349; Trade Report 1913-14, p. 1; Hamidi 1380, p. 544. E.g., there was the *aluch va lakkeh'i* or *aluchi*, a rag collector, who went around town to buy people's rags, which he sold in Borazjan and Kazerun as raw material for the making of so-called *maleki* shoes. Also, the peripatetic gypsy or *khalifeh*, who made, among other things, iron implements. Hamidi 1380, pp. 84, 287.

205. Heude 1819, p. 43; Morier 1812, pp. 41-42; Buckingham 1971, p. 348; Binning 1857, vol. 1, p. 142; MacGregor 1879, vol. 1, p. 11, Merritt-Hawkes 1935, p. 9. For some details about the bazaar, see Hamidi 1380, p. 117.

206. Kempthorne 1835, p. 284.

207. Shepherd 1857, pp. 144-45.

Trade

The bazaar consisted of a number constructions. One was the so-called *bazar-e bala*, which was a big, long and covered bazaar, which began from the *bazar-e morghi* and ended next to the old pier (*askeleh*), where it merged with the straight section (*rasteh*) of another bazaar. In its own *rasteh*, the Namaki mosque and the Namaki bathhouse were situated. In this bazaar, which does not exist anymore, various guilds (*asnaf*) were found. Another covered bazaar, which does not exist anymore, was the *bazar-e Hajj-e Ra'is*, named after its builder Hajj `Abdol-Rasul Talebi Ra'is al-Tojjar Bushehri. It had one peculiarity in that the level on which the shops were situated was higher than the surface of the bazaar lane. Another covered bazaar was that of Sayyed Mohammad Reza, which had two *rastehs* and was built by Hajj Mohammad Reza Kazeruni and still exists. The *bazar-e morghi* was built by Hajj Mohjammad Sadeq Esfahani in 1872 and does not exist anymore. The new covered bazaar is called *bazar-e safa* and was partly built by Mohammad Dovvani. [208]

The bazaar complex was only open at certain hours; from November till May it was closed from 12.00 till 15.00 because of the heat, while throughout the year, it was closed the entire day on Fridays as in the rest of Persia.[209] In 1887, Fogg considered that "the bazaars here are quite interesting; there are many stalls where 'lollipops' are sold. ..... The carpet bazaar, too, is very attractive," but Curzon found them extensive, given the size of the town, though narrow and confined.[210] According to Lorimer, by 1900, the principal bazaar was "clean, lofty, and roofed over, and some 200 yards in length; it somewhat winding and at its south-eastern end breaks up into several smaller bazaars chiefly occupied by dealers in food. In all, the bazaar contains some 600 shops."[211] One of these shops, - owned by an Armenian, had European goods, amongst which "tinned meats and other conveniences for the road."[212] Around 1910, there were 441 shops in the bazaar as well as some warehouses (*anbar*).[213]

Although generally not offering an attractive view, the bazaar looked totally different two weeks prior to *Nowruz*, when the shops were festively decorated. In the shops "bunches of wild pink gladioli and red poppies stood in vases among the sweet, vegetables, meat and flies. ... Long strings of dried yellow dates were festooned across the shops, and there were especially large quantities of dried prawns and shrimps, which looked awful, smelt worse, but actually tasted very good. Everywhere there were pomegranates, symbols of fruitfulness throughout the East, on account of their red colour and many seeds. They were always decorated, and sometimes entirely covered, with bits of gold paper."[214] But even during the rest of the year some shops looked more festive than others. For example, in 1934, "Every barber's shop at Bushire and a great many of the *droschas* at Shiraz had mirrors with an advertisement of Ansell's brewery and Tennant's beer and stout. Those

---

208. Hamidi 1380, p. 117.
209. de Vilmorin 1895, p. 353.
210. Fogg 1875, p. 175; Curzon 1892, vol. 1, p. 233.
211. Lorimer 1915, vol. 2, p. 345.
212. Collins 1896, p. 26.
213. Sadid al-Saltaneh 1371, pp. 43, 55.
214. Merritt-Hawkes 1935, p. 19.

firms must have sent out boat-loads of mirrors, but now their advertisements were simply annoying, for beer was on the list of prohibited imports and so almost unobtainable."[215]

The old bazaar was dirtier than the new one, because it was so narrow and therefore, there was little room to sweep. However, also here an attempt was made to make things look cleaner. Some shopkeepers covered the dates with paper to keep the flies away and in one big sweet shop a little boy was fanning the confectionary trays. It was here that various craftsmen were engaged. There were cotton carders, and the whining noise of the bow used to beat the wool was heard in that part of the bazaar where bed covers (*lehaf*) were made.[216] The bazaar was otherwise mostly occupied by sellers of all kinds of goods, because the only manufacture at Bushehr was "of copper coffee-pots which find a market at various places in the Persian Gulf."[217] The carpenters of Bushehr were quite competent and hence they were used in all ports.[218] There was a good watchmaker at Bushehr, but it is not clear whether he worked at home or in the bazaar.[219] In all events, Bushehr numbered 33 guilds or *asnaf* (see Table 1.5).[220] The members of the guilds had to pay guild taxes and as of July 1893, foreign retailers also had to pay a business tax, when "a scheme for the taxation of foreigners engaged in retail trade and industries was announced by the Persian Government, and has since come into force."[221]

By 1915, Bushehr had three flour mills, which did not produce more than local demand. The bazaar was well-stocked and had a meat and a large vegetable market; grain and grocers were spread throughout the bazaar. The bulk grain stores were at the southern end near the wharves.[222] Outside the town proper, but on the peninsula, in Halileh village people wove *abas* and *chador-shabs* of cotton and wool.[223] Fruit was available in the bazaar in great quantities all the year round; in the 1850s it was brought mainly from Shiraz.[224] By 1915, except for vegetables, all fresh food for Bushehr was brought by sea, either from the Angali district via Shif or from Hayat Da'ud via Rig or Ganaveh. Firewood came from Tangestan mainly by boat via Dayyer and by donkey via the Mashilah.[225]

1.5: The Main Guilds or *Asnaf* in Bushehr

Hucksters (*khordeh-forush*)	90	Kebab sellers (*kebab-forush*)	90
Herbalists (*attar*)	30	Grocers (*baqqal*)	30
Green-grocers (*sabzi-forush*)	24	Fish sellers (*mahi-forush*)	14
Butchers (*qassab*)	6	Biscuit sellers (*qaki-forush*)	21

215. Merritt-Hawkes 1935, p. 7.
216. Merritt-Hawkes 1935, p. 9.
217. Lorimer 1915, vol. 2, p. 345.
218. Sadid al-Saltaneh 1371, p. 39.
219. Sadid al-Saltaneh 1362, p. 12.
220. Sadid al-Saltaneh 1371, p. 44.
221. Administration Report 1893-94, p. 11. On this issue, which held for the whole of Persia, see Floor 2009 c.
222. Government of India 1924, p. 107. On the flour mills (*kargeh-ye ardeh'i*), see Hamidi 1380, p. 489
223. Sadid al-Saltaneh 1371, p. 37.
224. Kempthorne 1835, p. 284.
225. Government of India 1924, p. 107.

Tailors (*khayyat*)	15	Coffehouses/opium dens (*qahvehkhaneh/ vafurkhaneh*)	15
Saddlecloth sellers (*jol-duz*)	3	Soup-kitchens (*kalleh-paz* and *ash-paz*)	12
Farriers (*na`l-band*)	2	Saddlers (*sarraj*)	2
Tin-smiths (*halabi-saz*)	9	Shoemakers (*kaffash*)	6
Dyers (*sabbagh*)	15	Sweet bread sellers (*komaj-forush*)	4
White-smiths (*safidgar*)	6	Bakers (*khabbaz*)	6
Makers and sellers of the *maleki* shoe (*maleki-duz* and *-forush*)	6	Donkey renters	6
Money-changers (*sarraf*)	20	Storage of firewood sellers (*heymeh-forush*) and date sellers (*khorma-forush*)	35
Warehouses of grain sellers (*jens-forush*)	20	Karavanserai	n.a.

Source: Sadid al-Saltaneh 1371, pp. 42-43.

There was production of alcohol from dates in Bushehr, which was in great demand. As a result, drunkenness was "a very prevalent vice among all classes; but it is, of course, privately indulged in. The consumption of date-brandy is said to be very great, in proportion to the population."[226]

Apart from the tax collectors and other government officials, who helped people to reduce the burden of their wealth, there was another group of people, viz. the whining beggars at every corner, who "were an unmitigated nuisance."[227] They were in particular active at *Nowruz*.

> Beggars developed a special trade at this season; in one hand they held a little tray on which a tiny dish of sprouting barley or wheat, and in the other hand a vase of rose-water which they sprinkled over passers-by, saying, 'Allah is one God, Mahomet is his prophet.' This salutation, together with the sprouting corn, brought good luck, so in return the pedestrian put money, dates, herbs, sweets, cakes upon the tray. I was nearly drenched by the time I reached the end of the bazaar and did not smell very nice, for rose-water is not always as sweet as roses.[228]

Bushehr's main economic activity was trade, especially maritime trade. Therefore, many of its inhabitants worked on ships as crew or as pilots.[229] By 1800, there were at Bushehr a small number of vessels belonging to those who traded to and from Masqat, Bandar Abbas and Basra.[230] The 500 ton *Rahmani* was owned by the Sheikh of Bushehr `Abdol-Rasul Khan and was armed to deal with pirates. The *nakhoda* or captain had no

226. Binning 1857, vol. 1, p. 145.
227. Geary 1878, vol. 1, p. 63.
228. Merritt-Hawkes 1935, p. 19. *Nowruz* was the time when people gave each other gifts.
229. Buckingham 19171, p. 349.
230. Milburn 1813, vol. 1, p. 128.

Bushehr sea front in 1840

idea of navigation and relied on his first mate. In addition, it had one gunner, 21 Indian sailors (*classies*), 91 Arab sailors (*classies*) and African slaves with passengers for a total of 240 souls on board. It was old and leaky and needed pumping. A dhow accompanied it for protection.[231] By 1900, Bushehr had some 50-60 *mashuwahs* or lighters of 10-15 tons and each manned by 6-7 men, which only ran between the harbor and the town; about 50 *sambuks*, *bums* and large *mashuwahs* of 30-40 tons, which made voyages to all principal Gulf ports; 4 *baghlahs* of 50-60 tons, and about 20 still larger vessels which visited Karachi, Bombay and Zanzibar. Besides these, there were 350 fishing boats, because the inhabitants of the small coastal villages were mostly engaged in fishing.[232] The working class mostly was composed of immigrants from Dashti (known as Khanasiris), the remainder were Tangestanis and Dovvanis.[233]

By the 1930s, when Bushehr had become a minor port, it boasted of two launches, one belonging to the British Indian Steam Navigation Company (BISNC) (1.5 m deep) with a capacity for 80 persons, and the other to the Quarantine station with a smoke apparatus with a capacity of 60 persons. Also, there were a number of motor dhows: one owned by the British Residency of 50 ton; further there were 2 motor dhows one of 20 ton and one of 30 ton capacity. There were still 19 sail dhows of 20 ton, 6 of 16 ton, 5 of 20 ton (the latter belonging to the BISNC). In addition there are some trading dhows of over 30 tons and many fishing vessels.[234]

---

231. Lumsden 2010, pp. 23, 25.

232. Lorimer 1915, vol. 2, p. 346; Trade Report 1910-11, pp. 1-2; Buckingham 1971, p. 349. For an overview of the variety of boats and their names, see Sadid al-Saltaneh 1371, p. 114. "The kind of boat or coasting-vessel called in India a Trankey, is here called a Bateel." Rich 1839, p. 202.

233. Lorimer 1915, vol. 2, p. 344.

234. Mahrad 1978, p. 88.

Daryabegi power and ice-making plant ca. 1930

In 1947, the following vessels were available at Bushehr: one Anglo-Iranian Oil Company (AIOC) launch for 60 persons; one Quarantine launch for about 80 persons, one motor dhow of 15 tons for the British consulate for 25 persons and 11 locally owned motor dhows of 15-18 tons. Usually, there were 20 sailing dhows in the harbor with an average capacity of about 20 tons, although there were also larger ones. Finally, there were numerous fishing boats, some 200 or 300.[235]

Modern factories

Although the small handicraft sector in Bushehr remained traditional in nature, there was some movement to introduce modern technology. In 1913, there were two ice-making plants in Bushehr that were owned by Golzar and Haji `Abdol-Nabi. Its price fluctuated and around 1914, the price per ice blocks had dropped from 2,000 dinars to 35 *shahis*. The ice blocks were not only sold in the local market, but each week ice was transported to Bahrain.[236] Also, at that time, an effort was made to start a small power company to supply electricity to those who could afford it. However, after some time it must have failed, because in 1921 it was reported that a defunct Electric Light Company had recently been resuscitated with the aid of the British military authorities. "It is now entirely controlled by a committee of directors, who are assisted by the manager of Ziegler & Co. Thus, life was enhanced with some electric lights and fans for those who could afford the expense."[237] The electric company continued to be operational, but due to lack of funds and proper supervision, its finances were in a very precarious position; the income barely covered the expenditure. Therefore, no new parts were bought though some were urgently needed. "It is doubtful whether the company will last much longer. Its loss will be felt, even though its

235. NA, FO 371/15471.

236. Sadid al-Saltaneh 1371, p. 95. One *shahi* equaled 20 dinars.

237. Trade Report 1920-21, p. 1; Sa`adat 1390, p. 46.

Power plant in the 1930s

service was not continuous. By the end of the year, the advisor of Ziegler resigned due to the un-businesslike methods used and the unlikely chance to improve the situation."[238] In 1923, the electric company worked throughout the year, but in spite of the purchase of a considerable amount of new machinery, the service remained extremely unreliable, mainly due to dissensions and intrigues among the directors of the company.[239] In early 1925, it looked as if the electric company would go bankrupt, mainly because the government departments did not pay their bills. Therefore, in April 1925, the Municipality gave the company a trial run for a few days to establish whether it would be able to at least break-even in the future. One month later, a proposal by Dr. Neuhaus, a German national, to manage the company, provided the governor would collect the user charges, was declined.[240] Apparently, there was no change in this precarious financial and operational situation for some time, but in 1937 an order was placed in Great Britain for a new power plant.[241] In July 1937, the town suffered a lack of ice, because the ice factories stopped production, due to a lack of ammonia. Moreover, the military commandeered all ice and put guards at the ice factories to make sure that nobody else would get any. To keep the crowd at a distance the soldiers stood guard with fixed bayonets. After much toing and froing

238. Trade Report 1921-22, p. 1.

239. Trade Report 1923-24, p. 5.

240. Political Diaries vol. 7, pp. 279, 288, 290 ("Neuhaus has received permission from the German embassy to take over the archives of the German consulate").

241. Administration Report 1937, p. 6; Political Diaries, vol. 13, p. 59. For the cost of maintenance of the ice, electric and condensing plants between 1920 and 1934, see IOR/L/PS/10/893 (file 3237/1920), IOR/T 161/553/6 and IOR/T 161/553/7.

Customs released two bottles of ammonia after payment of £12 security.[242] One year later the governor held a meeting with influential merchants concerning the electricity situation. The owner of the new plant agreed to supply 24 hours current as well as ice to the town. Therefore, one million rials were raised, which was to be included in the mill's capital. The owner also asked that government sell him £5,000 in foreign exchange to buy extra parts. It was not given and the owner went to Tehran to try and get it; he returned having received the money in German marks. However, when the plant arrived in May 1940, it was a second-hand plant bought in Tehran, because it was not certain that the German plant would arrive.[243] As a result, by 1941 there was, apart from the water condensors, one 50 kW plant that supplied light to the town. Also, there were two 40 kW and two 8 kW engins that belonged to the British Residency and the British Consulate.[244] In April 1942, the power plant was down for a few weeks. With the help of APOC, the Residency arranged for repairs to be carried out. Because of this problem the shareholders held a meeting, where the majority voted to dissolve the company, because they were not prepared to put up additional funds. It was only in October 1943 that power supply was restored to Bushehr.[245] As of 16 June 1944, the Bushehr Ice and Electric Company began producing ice; the whole-sale price was Rls. 2/kg and shopkeepers had to sell it at Rls. 2.5/kg.[246] In May 1946, a new power and ice company was created in Bushehr with a capital of Rls. 2 million. Mr. Hoseyn Agar (ایگر) (E`temad al-Tojjar) was managing director and arranged for the import of the machinery from Great Britain. The machines arrived in February 1947, but some cases were dropped in the sea from the lighter. The cases were lying in 5-meter deep water, but it was not immediately possible to raise the cases.[247] However, eventually the machinery was salvaged and in 1947, the new private company provided electricity, 24 hours/day during the hot season and a limited number of nightly hours during the cold season. The plant was about 0.4 km s.e. from the town on the sea-front. It had two diesels engins of 200 kW and 135 kW; there was also a two ton/day ice plant in the same building.[248]

All of the above activities were for non-productive end-uses (lighting, water, ice) and were not used significantly for productive economic uses. This situation seemed to experience a change, for in 1933 the building of a Spinning-Weaving-Bleaching and Finishing plant was considered, but it was dropped as being futile; instead in November it was decided to erect a gunny factory. Apparently some raw material was available at Kazerun and Behbahan.[249] However, the governor continued to try inducing the local business community to engage in the funding of modern industrial development, just as this was happening elsewhere in Persia. In 1936, several ideas were discussed for new economic activities amongst which the formation of a Steam Navigation Company. At the first meeting merchants offered to invest 1,550,000 rials (£15,500). Its potential other

242. Political Diaries, vol. 12, p. 511.

243. Administration Report 1938, p. 6; Political Diaries, vol. 13, pp. 159, 287; vol. 14, pp. 96, 121.

244. Mahrad 1978, p. 90; Government of Great Britain 1945, p. 503 (3 small plants supply electricity).

245. Political Diaries, vol. 15, pp. 93, 612; Administration Report 1942, p. 7.

246. Political Diaries, vol. 16, p. 125.

247. Political Diaries, vol. 17, pp. 107, 351; Administration Report 1946, p. 5. Mr. Hoseyn Agar, formerly a merchant of Manchester also was chairman of the board of directors of the Shiraz Cotton Spimming Mill and its moving spirit. Administration Report 1934, p. 18.

248. NA, FO 371/15473.

249. Administration Report 1933, p. 3; Political Diaries, vol. 10, pp. 266-67 (with details).

E`temadiyeh spinning mill in the 1950s

activity was to form a Company for the sale of motor vehicles. None of these companies materialized.[250] At that time, the central government considered establishing a fishing plant dealing with 'fillets' in Bushehr, like the one that had been studied for Bandar Abbas. In 1938, Blegvad, the Danish conSoltant, submitted his final report. However, the project never materialized.[251]

However, in July 1936, what did materialize was the creation of the *Sharekat-e sehami-ye risandegi va bafandegi E`temad* (E`temadiyeh Weaving and Spinning Company), as suggested to local merchants by Messrs. Agar and Hoseyn Aqa E`temad of the firm Haji `Ali Akbar Shirazi and Sons Ltd. of Manchester. The then governor, Mr. Sadri and the merchants liked this better than the Steamship Company, over which they would have no control. They received permission from Tehran to import a weaving and spinning plant and another one for dyeing. The spinning machinery and most of the power plant were imported from England. In December 1936 all material arrived and construction of a building to house the plant outside the town was accelerated.[252] Because of the humidity the Bushehr climate was very suitable for this activity, so no expensive humidifying equipment had to be installed.[253] "The spinning section of the local mill came into operation in January this year [1938]. It produces 10-count and 20-count yards. A master weaver was engaged from Great Britain. He arrived in June and some cloth (unbleached shirtings and coloured prints) was put on the market in September. The prices charged,

250. Administration Report 1936, pp. 4-5.

251. Administration Report 1938, p. 3. For the Bandar Abbas cannery, see Floor 2011 a, p. 32.

252. Administration Report 1936, pp. 4-5; Political Diaries, vol. 12, pp. 188-89, 227, 281, 344, 377; FO 371/40222 f. 44. For the political and economic reasons behind the establishment of modern factories, see Floor 2009 b.

253. NA, FO 371/15473.

however, were too high for local acceptance."The owner, Mr. Agar, held a shareholders' meeting in September 1938 in Shiraz and a managing committee of seven merchants, mostly from Bushehr, was appointed. The distribution of profits was agreed upon: 5% for Agar, 4% for members of the committee, and 1% for the auditor, the remainding 90% was for the shareholders.[254]

A serious crisis broke out at the *E`temadiyeh* spinning mill in May 1939, when the manager, Mr. E`temadiyeh was unable to fulfill orders, although he had already received 1.2 million rials through advance sales to merchants in Shiraz. An audit showed that the manager had embezzled funds and the managing committee turned against him. In June 1939 the mill stopped working due to lack of inputs and in July most of the workers were laid off. In September work was resumed, it was said that committee members each had lent 20,000 rials to the company, and the manager repaid a considerable sum. He was able to overcome various problems and prospects looked good for the mill. "It is producing to full capacity and has been working day and night shifts."The chief problem was the sustained supply of cotton as it was rumored that large quantities had been sold to Germany. The mill's products were sold in Shiraz, because they were too expensive for the local Bushehri market. The employment of foreign experts was only one factor that led to the high cost of its final output. "Four English experts have been in charge of the technical working of the mill throughout the year. The other employees number about 450."[255]

The situation of the *E`temadiyeh* mill improved; debts were paid off, dividends ranging from 4-12% were paid to the shareholders in March, June and October 1940. After a long wait the new power plant finally arrived from Germany; however, its efficiency was not optimal due to the loss of a piston en route. Two British experts left at the end of their contract; the two remaining ones were in charge of the plant's technical management. Other employees numbered 600 in 1940 and for part of the year the mill was working at full capacity producing 40,000 meters of cloth a week. Its price averaged 4 rials per meter, for which good markets existed in the larger cities. In 1941, the *E`temadiyeh* Mill worked 24 hours/p.d. and this much improved its financial situation. Its major markets were especially in Shiraz and Isfahan. In October 1941, the Company paid a 30% interim dividend, with the promise of a further payment of 40-50% in March 1942. As a result, its shares rose in value; a Rls. 5,000 share tripled in value. The British experts who had left in 1940, were replaced by a Hungarian and a Czech specialist. Although the prices of the mill's output doubled, workers were given only a small raise and clerical staff a raise of 10-20%. However, towards the end of 1941 output was reduced because of irregular supplies of raw cotton.[256] In 1942, the *E`temadiyeh* mill continued to have good financial results. Although the price of its cloth rose by 75% compared with 1941 sales were so good that an interim dividend of 75% was paid. The rest of the profits were used to buy an auxiliary electricity plant and increase the Company's capital. A share of Rls. 5,000 rose in value to Rls. 20,000. This time workers also shared in the profits, because their wages rose by 50%, while the clerical staff got a 25% raise. In November 1942, the plant stopped working for three days due to lack of cotton. The problem was resolved

254. Administration Report 1938, p. 6.

255. Administration Report 1939, pp. 6-7.

256. Administration Report 1940, pp. 6-7; Administration Report 1941, p. 12; Political Diaries, vol. 14, pp. 96, 538.

when Mr. Agar imported 200 tons of cotton from Basra.[257] In February 1943, a conflict broke out between Messrs. Agar (manager) and Mr. Dashti (managing director) about the former's plan to give a larger dividend. He also announced that by increasing the price of cotton cloth by 1% he had made Rls. 200,000 extra profit, which he would give to charity. In February 1943, a shareholders meeting took place. It was announced that profits during 1321 (1942-43) had been 200% and that an interim dividend of 75% had already been paid. It was decided that half of the net profit would be paid as dividend and the other half to be paid in the form of shares. In this way the company's capital rose to one million *tumans*. However, there was great dismay over Millspaugh's new tax law of 80% on incomes of Rls. 50,000 and above, because the tax was charged to the mill and not to individual shareholders; this hurt smaller shareholders. Also, its shares dropped in value from 7 *tumans* to 1 *tuman*, when the government announced that it would establish a monopoly of piece-goods, sugar and tea.[258] In March 1944, the *E`temadiyeh* Mill started a new scheme by issuing cloth coupons to its shareholders at the rate of 1,000 meters per share of Rls. 5,000. The coupon allowed the shareholders to buy cloth at a reduced price, be it that this amount would be deducted from their dividend. The paper profit would be less as would be the taxable amount. Shareholders sold their coupons of Rls. 5,000 for double that amount.[259]

Report on labour and industry in Bushire Consular area (1943)

1. Industrial development in this area has been confined to Bushire where the Etemadieh Spinning and Weaving Mill has been established since 1936. Statistics of wages, working hours, numbers employed and general conditions are given below:

(a) Working hours start at 6.30 a.m. and consist of three shifts of 8 hours in the cotton and thread section, and two shifts of 9 hours each in the weaving section.

(b) The numbers employed in the spinning and weaving section are at present 800 and 228 respectively and the following wages are given:

Girls under 15 on the bobbing section. Rls. 12-13 per day.

Boys under 15 on the weaving section. Rls. 13-19 per day.

Women employed on cotton Rls. 17-19 per day.

Wages for labour vary from Rials 17-35 per day, depending on the qualifications of the individuals concerned. Those in [the] weaving section are are paid on piece work and may earn from Rias 10-20 per day.

(c) No housing is given to the labour employed but free bread is issued, medical attendance is provided and working dress is also supplied. Conditions are generally satisfactory judged by Persian standard.

Source: FO 371/40222, f. 44

In 1943, it was decided to increase the number of spindles. In May 1944, new Mirrlees engines were received at the *E`temadiyeh* plant. However, because the MWT company refused to send a ship to Bushehr the 5-tons cases were shipped to Khorramshahr, from

257. Administration Report 1942, p.18; Political Diaries, vol. 15, p. 318.
258. Political Diaries, vol. 15, p. 404-05, 410; Administration Report 1943, p. 16.
259. Political Diaries, vol. 16, p. 54.

E`temadiyeh spinning mill's showroom - 1950s

there by train to Tehran and then by truck to Bushehr. The total cost from Khorramshahr to Bushehr was higher than the cost of transportation from Great Britain to Khorramshahr.[260] In October 1944, due to a slump in the Persian market the *E`temadiyeh* Mill could not sell most of its product. It held 800,000 meters of cloth in stock, the number of shifts was reduced and 250 workers were laid off. In November 1944, Mr. Agar convened a meeting of the cloth coupon holders. He gave them a 40% discount and thus, succeeded in selling part of his stock and obtain payment "of all drafts outstanding against merchants in favour of the mill."[261] In June 1945, Mr. Agar announced an interim dividend of 40% for 1323 (1944-45) and a bonus of 1,000 meters of cloth per share. Total profits were Rls. one million of which Rls. 800,000 had to be paid as income tax. In February 1945 the factory received a powerful new British electric engine. In June 1947, the *E`temadiyeh* Mill announced an interim dividend of 15% and a coupon for 100 meters of cloth per share, although the Company had suffered a loss of Rls. 15 million.[262]

In April 1947, there was trouble again at the *E`temadiyeh* Mill concerning the right of management to fire workers. The manager, Riyazi, invited representatives of the Ministry of Labor, who, sweetened by the manager, ruled in his favor. The workers then went on strike, while the manager called the police to arrest the ringleaders. When the Tehran representatives wanted to interfere they were beaten up and kicked out of the mill. The police began firing wildly into the air wounding an old woman and waking up people

260. Political Diaries, vol. 16, p. 100; FO 371/40222 f. 44.

261. Political Diaries, vol. 16, pp. 223, 247.

262. Political Diaries, vol. 16, p. 423; vol. 17, p. 451; Administration Report 1945, p. 17.

from their siesta. By the end of April the mill operated again, but the conflict had not yet been settled. Mr. Agar resigned from the mill's management in May, due to ill health.[263]

Although the *E`temadiyeh* mill started in November 1937, and changed hands several times between its start in November 1937 and 1947, the principal shareholders still lived in Bushehr or in Shiraz. In 1947, the managing director was D. Aryan, a prominent Shiraz businessman. The *E`temadiyeh* plant was built when the Shabankareh irrigation project was planned to cultivate cotton and ensure a steady and reliable supply of this vital input. However, the war broke out when the irrigation scheme was ready, but before the development plans were operational.[264] As a result, the project was put on hold. Several governors, such as Hesabi in 1944, tried to revive the plan, but it remained talk only. During the war, cotton was expensive and thus it was cost-effective to bring cotton from Central Persia, but after the war, due to low cotton prices and international competition, the future of *E`temadiyeh* plant was not bright, unless the cost of its raw material input could be lowered. Its machinery was from the British Mather & Platt Ltd. powered by 2 Mirrlees Bikerton & Day diesel engines, generating 200 and 135 kW each, and one Deutz plant of 160 kW. It employed 2,000 workers with a 6-day workweek in two 8-hour shifts, under technical supervision of a British spinning master. The mill had 140 looms with a daily output of 70-75 meters of cloth; its quality ranged from medium to inferior.

In December 1946, despite the gloomy outlook for the *E`temadiyeh* plant, a Company was registered in Tehran, financed by Shirazi and Bushehri merchants, with a capital of Rls. 35 million to build a second cotton mill on the Bushehr peninsula. In 1947, this second cotton spinning and weaving mill was erected. It was the *Sharekat-e risandegi va bafandagi* which was expected to be operational by the end of 1947. The machinery was imported from Italy, and it would employ 1,000 to 1,200 workers; its output would be higher than that of the *E`temadiyeh* factory as its equipment was more modern. During the first two years Italian technical supervisors would be in charge of production, which aimed to make a higher-priced class of piece-goods. The owners were a group of mainly Bushehri shareholders, and the driving force was Haji Reza Hafteh, a prominent local businessman.[265]

During the WWII, the United Kingdom Commercial Cooperation (UKCC) operated a truck-assembly plant with some American supervision and advice, while the assembly was done by Persian labor. Here American lend-lease vehicles from India were assembled to enable the UKCC to carry out its motor transport mission. In December 1941, considerable progress had been made in establishing a workshop for the assembly of trucks, so that by the end of that month it was ready to start production. In mid-January 1942 news was received that 1,700 trucks would arrive at Bushehr in February to be assembled at the UKCC plant, which expanded its existing capacity to its limits. In April 1942, the last batch of the 1,700 trucks was received and the plant's layout was revised. To improve security most of its Tangestani security force was dismissed and more trustworthy guards were hired. By mid-May 1942 the assembly of all trucks received had been completed,

---

263. Political Diaries, vol. 17, p. 404.

264. In 1941, small bridges had been built and the lining of the water distribution channnels had been completed, according to the British consul, the only positive news item to report from Bushehr. Administration Report 1941, p. 4; Political Diaries, vol. 14, p. 435; vol. 15, p. 33 (five irrigation water channels had been completed by January 1942 and made available to peasants).

265. Political Diaries, vol. 17, p. 293; Administration Report 1945, p. 16; NA, FO 371/15473.

which left in convoy with Persian drivers, because only once 80 Russian drivers had come to Bushehr. However, the output of the Bushehr and the other truck-assembly plant at Rafadiyah was insufficient to supply the number of trucks promised to the Soviet Union. At the end of 1941, these needs were estimated at 2,000 trucks per month. Therefore, in 1942 a large GM truck-assembly plant at Andimeshk was built, while an American officer was added to the Bushehr plant, who provided technical advice and supervision. In August 1942, it was decided that Persian drivers would drive the assembled trucks to Tehran. The trucks suffered from the bad road, attacks by bandits, and bad driving by the less experienced Persian drivers. Therefore, once they had arrived at Tehran, the trucks were inspected, repaired and serviced and then were transferred to the Soviet authorities.

In July 1942, there was a small strike at the plant, after some workers had been fired for having struck an Armenian clerk. About 80 fitters laid down tools and were fired. Their ringleader was let go with a warning by the police. In August 1942, work at the plant slowed down, because the bodies and chassis were delivered a few days before the driver's cabs arrived. This held up the assembly line and output dropped. Also, due to lack of drivers some trucks were not moved. It was understood that many drivers did not return from Tehran out of fear of the insecurity on the road. In October 1942 the assembly line for the new 'Delta pack' trucks was completed, expecting that this would boost output with 20-25 trucks/day. In December 1942, a doubling of output had been achieved by small but important reorganizations in the assembly yard. This was probably due to the fact that in August 1942 the single supervising US officer was replaced by a small US team that stayed more than one year. There continued to be limited pilferage of spare parts in the plant despite strict supervision.

In December 1942, 444 trucks were assembled and 295 were dispatched. Output fell in January 1943 due to lack of battery acid. At the end of February 1943, daily output was 44 trucks/day which equalled that of the modern Andimeshk plant. Many trucks were still waiting in Bushehr due to lack of drivers; in March 1943 this was as many as 750 trucks. In April 1943 output fell again due to lack of battery acid. Between 2 February 1942 and 18 March 1943, a total of 1,263 trucks were assembled at Bushehr and driven to to Tehran at a total cost of $275,000, which came down to $218 per truck. This was much too high as compared with cost ($28/truck) at the US Army operated plants in 1944 at Khorramshahr. Because there was still insufficient capacity it was decided to continue operation the Bushehr plant for a while. The British disagreed with the negative view of the Bushehr plant, but they had troubles with the Russians about this. During a discussion in Moscow in the summer of 1943, Grigori M. Polyansky, a commercial representative of the USSR embassy at Tehran exclaimed: "God protect us from Bushire assembly!" Therefore, it was decided to close the Bushehr plant, which during its lifetime had delivered 2,628 trucks, practically all of which were handed over to the Russians. The assembly line was closed down on 3 June, while on the previous day 60 trucks had been assembled. In the second half of July 1943 the remaining 500 assembled trucks were driven to Shiraz.[266] Then the assembly plant was closed and this meant a loss of remunerative employment and thus more poverty in Bushehr.

---

266. Vail Motter 1952, pp. 34-35, 84, 143-49, 275, 494 (Table 7); Political Diaries, vol. 14, p. 588 (December 1941); vol. 15, p. 4, 94, 118, 190 (strike), 223, 288, 316, 348, 352, 380, 407-08, 432, 460, 463-4, 512, 538, 541, 563, 565. In 1942, there were two American officers and 9 ranks in Bushehr. Administration Report 1942, p. 7.

Truck assembly plant, 1942

The British Resident was rather miffed about this decision. He was very proud of the record and output by the Bushehr plant, a result due to Mr. Bode, who had been lent by the AIOC. Because of his management skills by mid-1943 the plant produced 50 cars/p.d. a figure only just met by the new Khorramshahr plant. However, the Resident had to admit that the performance of the other UKCC plants was dismal and had left "a reputation of incompetence and petulance." The Resident also indirectly blamed the Americans for their lack of cooperation and understanding. Visiting US officers neither consulted their British counterpart nor cooperated with them. They electrified the fence around the factory without consultation and as result the first victim was a US soldier. To get back at the Americans the Resident could not help himself but report some instances of their deplorable misbehavior. When he gave a party for them at Sabzabad they were drunk and stole spoons etc. from adjacent houses.[267]

267. Administration Report 1943, pp. 4, 11.

Moharram procession in Bushehr

Moharram procession in Bushehr

Religion

Religious affiliations

By 1800, there were about as many Shiite as Sunni Moslems, who each had respectively four and three mosques.[268] The two groups usually lived along side each other without too many problems, but sometimes, they, "like other sectaries fight about shadows. One of the chief bones of contention between these parties being, that the latter [Sunnis], like spiteful wicked boys, will make the tops of their graves convex instead of flat-which the former insist ought to be their shape-according to tradition."[269] But already by 1850 the majority of the population was Shiite and the majority followed the Akhbari school of thought. Fifty years later almost the entire Moslem population was Shiite, who by then mostly followed Osuli olama. By 1910, there were only some 50 Sunni families left, all adherents of the Shafi`i school.[270] Whereas the Sunni majority did not seem to have been hostile to the Shiite minority in the early nineteenth century, the Shiites, when they overtook the Sunnis in number behaved in a rather hostile manner towards their fellow Sunni townsmen. During the months of Moharram and Safar, Shiites cursed Sunnis in the streets and on 9 Rabi` I, the day when they commemorate the Kerbela tragedy, they burnt the caliph Omar in effigy. Prior to 1907, Daryabegi always had taken steps to prevent these excesses out of respect for the Sunnis, but under his successor the custom was revived and the British Resident feared that Sunnis in Basra would retaliate against

268. Morier 1812, p. 57.

269. Shepherd 1857, p. 139. On 1 July 1811, "A salute from a vessel belonging to the governor of the town announced the feast of the Beiram, which is not celebrated with much splendour here." Rich 1839, p. 198.

270. Sadid al-Saltaneh 1371, p. 37; Sa`adat 1390, p. 43.

Shiites there, which did not happen. In February 1911, to please the Ottoman Sunni consul, the local mullahs in Bushehr had posters displayed on the walls of the coffee shops banning the use of firecrackers during the festival of *Omar-koshan* "on the ground that as Islam is suffering oppression all expressions of joy are out of place."[271]

By 1932, it was forbidden to engage in breast-beating in public during Moharram. Each *rowzeh-khvan* had to pass an examination and had to get a pass from the police before he could mount the pulpit. A policeman was present to ensure that no political remarks were made or that unauthorized persons preached.[272] A peculiarity of the peninsula was that: "Here and there over the plain are some little spots sacred to the dead, and defended by small works of stones."[273] This probably was a remnant of an earlier religion adhered to in the region.

Whereas in 1809 Morier reported a total of seven mosques, in 1816 Heude only reported six, while in 1828 Kempthorne only saw two.[274] This confusion about the number of mosques may have been due to the fact that "The mosque of Bushire is excessively mean,"[275] and thus, some may not have been noticed. The mosques were described as being "all open buildings, without domes or minarets, and inferior in appearance and neatness to the smallest village of Arabia."[276] This situation had not changed by 1850, when "The chief mosque is a low shabby mud and brick edifice, which I should never have guessed to be a mosque."[277] By about 1910, there were 16 mosques, 7 *takiyeh*s, and 4 *qadamgah*s.[278]

Apart from Moslems there were Christians, of which the largest group was formed by Armenians, who had one church and a priest.[279] The Armenian St. George church, which was situated near the gate, was a somewhat more respectable building than the chief mosque.[280] It would appear that at the end of the nineteenth century a new Armenian church was built. This is implied by Sadid al-Saltaneh when he mentions that in 1916 the Armenian church was in the Shanbeh'i quarter, while a few lines later stating that "the old Armenian temple was also situated near there and its dome and church were still there by 1917."[281] The grant of the Constitution, which was strongly supported by the Christians as it held out the promise of equal treatment, also made its impact felt on the church itself. In May 1907 the Armenian community acquired a church bell, which was rung, because it

271. Political Diaries, vol. 2, p. 157; Political Diaries vol. 4, p. 509. On cursing and the *Omar-koshan* activities, see Floor 2005 a and Idem 2015 b.

272. Political Diaries, vol. 10, p. 69; vol. 12, p. 100.

273. Morier 1812, p. 59.

274. Morier 1812, p. 57; Heude 1819, 43; Kempthorne 1835, p. 283.

275. Waring 1973, p. 10.

276. Buckingham 1971, p. 348.

277. Binning 1857, vol. 1, p. 141.

278. Sadid al-Saltaneh 1371, p. 44. For the names of mosques, tombs and cemeteries on the peninsula, see Sadid al-Saltaneh 1371, p. 53; Sa`adat 1390, pp. 19-20 (21 mosques) and Hamidi 1380, pp. 600-01. In 1827, the number of *takiyeh*s may have been fewer, because Ellis saw "one of the takiehs or large tents, fitted up for the performce of the Moharrem." Ellis 1866, p.95; Hamidi 1380, p. 134 (with a photo of a Hoseyniyeh).

279. Johnson 1818, p. 23; Kempthorne 1835, p. 283; Mignan 1839, vol. 2, p. 142; Shepherd 1857, p. 143; Sadid al-Saltaneh 1371, p. 44. According to Beth Hillel 1832, p. 108 they had more than one church; he also reports that they were ill-treated.

280. Binning 1857, vol. 1, p. 141; for pictures, see Hamidi 1380, pp. 513-14.

281. Sadid al-Saltaneh 1371, p. 42. On the history of Christians in Bushehr, see Mashayekhi 1382.

The Armenian St. George Church with bells

believed the old rule suppressing this custom was illegal under the Constitution. However, Moslems in the bazaars were upset about this and talked about reprisals. Mr. Miller, the Russian consul-general, who sometimes worshipped at this church, asked the governor to take action to prevent disturbances. The governor took this very seriously and in person supervised nightly patrols of 50 soldiers, when an outbreak was expected. `Alam al-Huda, a local mullah, contacted the British Resident about this issue, who informed him that the governor had already stopped the ringing of the bell. However, Tigrane Malcolm, the US vice-consul complained to the US Minister in Tehran. In early June 1907, he received a telegram from the Minister of the Interior that the Armenians were allowed to hang their bell and ring it. However, this apparently did not happen, for in January 1908 the Bishop of Isfahan sent a telegram to the local council and the governor asking that the bell be allowed to be hung and rung "as is done in other towns of Persia." The local council did not reply and it is likely that the bell remained silent.[282]

The Christian community had another place of worship, viz., the Anglican church of the Epiphany. Due to Dr. Sharp's endeavors, funds were collected to build this church, whose construction began in February 1943 in the presence of of the governor, the Imam Jom`eh and other local notables. It was situated behind the British Residency, where its British staff worshipped in a chapel; which was closed in 1947.[283] Only some of the

282. Political Diaries, vol. 2, pp. 178, 215-16; vol. 3, p. 41. As to the affairs of the St. George Church in 1952, see FO 248/1550.

283. Administration Report 1943, pp. 11; Stevens 1979, p. 285; Stern 1854, p. 85; IOR/L/PS/12/1341. In December 1914 it was reported that Father Bernard, a French Catholic priest was in charge of a Roman Catholic chapel, where he intended to open a free French school. Political Diaries, vol. 5, p. 569; Hamidi 1380, p. 515.

Anglican Epiphany Church

Jewish Synagogue

surviving church's lead-lights are a reminder of its existence, which are preserved by the Bushehr historical society as I observed in 2000.[284]

The Jews, who numbered 200 families and allegedly had three synagogues around 1828, only had 70 families around 1850, with one synagogue in the Behbahani quarter and one rabbi, who in 1848 was Mullah Eliyahu, the British Residency's *sarraf*.[285] He was probably succeeded by Rabbi Murad Nassim who put his entire savings into the hands of David Sassoon, who made his fortune in Bombay.[286] The Jews invariably were ill-treated and despised and relegated to the margin of society. For example, in 1915, when most groups were invited to an official party at Government House to celebrate the anniversary of Ahmad Shah's enthronement, they were not. However, the governor sent them a few sheep, some rice and money to celebrate this joyous event in their own synagogue.[287] There were occasional flare-ups of anti-Jewish agitation, such as in 1906, when in mid-November 1906, some 70 Jews from Shiraz left Persia to settle in Jerusalem, because of the ill-treatment by officials and the population. They were joined by some Bushehri Jews.[288] The ill-treatment continued under Reza Shah's rule. In February 1923 orders were received from Tehran prohibiting the emigration of Jews; only those leaving on pilgrimage or business were allowed to leave the country, provided they arranged for an appropriate guarantee for their return. On 21 February 1936, at orders from Tehran

284. See Mashayekhi 1382, p. 193 for a photo.

285. Beth Hillel 1832, p. 108; Stern 1854, p. 86; Sadid al-Saltaneh 1371, pp. 42, 44. On the situation of the Jews, see Geary 1878, vol. 1, pp. 79-80; Benjamin 1859, p. 182.

286. Waters n.d., p. 20.

287. Nura'i 1385, p. 252.

288. Political Diaries, vol. 1, p. 536. For the treatment of Jews in Persia in general, see Yeroushalmi 2009.

British cemetery in the 1970s

to the heads of local departments throughout the country, the Customs Department dismissed its Jewish employees. The reason for this measure was not reported. Later they were given a function in the interior of the country, but without recognizing their past service.[289] This hostile local attitude towards Jews also influenced British decision making. When in 1944, the Jewish Council in Persia wanted to show a Jewish propaganda film to counter German propaganda that "Jewish influence provoked the Allies into war," it asked the British consul T.E. Rogers for the use of the Consulate's Reading Room and the loan of its projector, which was denied. This decision was based on the consul's sounding of local opinion, which was not very sympathetic to Jews and local opinion approved of his decision to advise the Jewish Council to show the the film only in the synagogue or in a private home.[290] The remains of the synagoge are still to be seen in the Yowdya (the Jewish quarter), but all Jews have departed for Israel.[291]

It seems that only the Hindus did not have a temple, at least it is not mentioned anywhere. Nevertheless, the Hindus lived unmolested in Bushehr, and in the early 1800s it was reported that they were "neither insulted nor oppressed by the government." Given

289. Political Diaries vol. 7, p. 165; Political Diaries, vol. 12, pp. 43, 161.
290. Political Diaries, vol. 16, pp. 289-90; see further IOR/L/PS/12/3455.
291. Hamidi 1380. p. 695.

the fact that they continued to live there, it seems that there was no change in this manner of treatment, nor are there any reports to the contrary.[292]

Apart from houses of worship the various groups also had cemeteries, although there was no *ghossal-khaneh* (a house where the bodies of the dead are washed) in 1877, when a simple tent on the beach served that purpose.[293] In 1851, "In one quarter of the town, the graveyard encroaches on the thoroughfare, and many of the flat tombstones lie in the way of all passers by."[294] In 1866, there were two burial grounds, one outside the wall on the space that was not flooded during spring tide and the other in the town itself. The dead were buried 1.20 (4 feet) deep, and sometimes less. During a sickly season, such as in 1865, it was said that 5-6 persons were buried there daily. In 1868, on three sides of the British Residency there were cemeteries and there were daily burials and the smell was awful and sickening.[295] However, this was not the only place where graves were to be found. In fact, Moslem burial grounds seem to have been dispersed throughout the town. "All over town graveyards are stumbled upon. When the plague was last here, in 1868, and during the frightful famine [1871-72] which desolated Persia a little after, these shallow graveyards were full to bursting; the corpses scarcely found earth to hide them."[296] By 1900, at the end of the town there was a native cemetery on a cliff.[297]

In the veranda behind the Armenian church there was a burial ground, where all Christians were buried.[298] After the war of 1857, the British buried their soldiers in a new cemetery, which was desecrated in December 1857, "to the disgust of those [Britishers] living and still serving here. A public meeting has been held to see how the tombs can be cared for and maintained and public subscription by all those who are friendly to the British people."[299] The necessary repairs concerned the inner wall that had been partly damaged; this wall was barely one meter high, but the British Resident also wanted to build a lower exterior wall to keep out the sand. However, the governor of Bushehr said that he needed instructions from Tehran before he could allow this. Because no reply was forthcoming the Resident raised the issue with the governor-general of Fars and the British envoy in Tehran, which at the end of 1859 finally resulted in the permission being granted.[300] In May 1862, despite the walls around it were being topped with broken glass, the British burial ground at Bushehr was again desecrated as people used it for cultivation. The authorities at Bushehr were reluctant to take action against the perpetrators. After British pressure in Tehran, one of the perpetrators was fined 38 Mohammad Shahi *qrans*, being the cost of the repair of the burial ground. However, the Persian authorities were

---

292. Waring 1973, p. 3-4.

293. Sayyah 1346, p. 12. In 1872, Hajj Mohammad Sadeq Tajer-e Esfahani built the karavansara-ye Ahmadi and a public *ghossal-khaneh*. Hamidi 1380, p. 117.

294. Binning 1857, vol. 1, pp. 141-42.

295. NA, FO 248/232, A.N. Hojel asst. surgeon to Lewis Pelly, 13/05/1868.

296. Geary 1878, vol. 1, p. 64

297. Lorimer 1915, vol. 2, p. 342. This had been established after 1872 and measured about 2,000 sq. *zar*. By 1914 it was getting too full; there also was a small shed to wash the dead. The municipality moved it to the sea-side for health reasons. It is not clear whether it is the same as the one built in 1872. Sa`adat 1390, pp. 26-27.

298. Morier 1812, p. 47; Mignan 1839, vol. 2, p. 143; Stocqueler 1832, vol. 1, pp. 13-4; Binning 1857, vol. 1, p. 141; De Rivoyre 1883, p. 166.

299. NA, FO 248/168, Cmdr Felix Jones to C.A. Murray envoy-extraordinary, 31/12/1857.

300. NA, FO 248/176, Jones to William Doria charge d'affaires, 12/11/1859; Idem, Jones to William Doria charge d'affaires, 12/11/1859.

not willing to go beyond that in the punishment, because the piece of land concerned was privately owned and its owner had never been asked for permission as to the use of his land. Despite the fact that a watchman had been appointed another desecration took place in October 1862. Thereafter the British obtained a decree from the government to exclusively occupy the terrain and compensated "Aghayee," the owner of the land.[301] In 1979, so-called 'revolutionaries' once again desecrated the grave stones of the British or the General cemetery, which in 2005 was looked after by the Bushehr historical society.[302]

Also, there seems to have been a Roman Catholic cemetery. Mrs. Constant, who was killed by an assailant on 8 March 1913, was buried the next day in the Roman Catholic cemetery. However, I have not been able to ascertain where this cemetery was located and whether it was separate from the general Christian cemetery, which seems unlikely.[303] In fact, in 1916, Sadid al-Saltaneh states that all Europeans were buried in the cemetery of the Armenian church.[304]

Drinking and Irrigation Water

Water supply

The principal rivers of the Bushehr district are the Rudhilleh (formed by the junction of the Shapur and the Daleki river), flowing into the sea 24 km north of Bushehr and the Mund river, which appears at Shiraz as Qara Aghaj and flows out into the Khur-e Ziyarat in Dashti some 100 km north of Bushehr.[305] According to Sadid al-Saltaneh, in the past there had been 70 subterraneous canals (*qanats*) of which the traces could still be seen at various locations around 1914. In 1892, a new one was built, but it was not maintained thereafter. There also were two *qanats* in the villages of Madani and Moqam that were built with funds from Haji Mohammad Ja`far Safar and Sheikh Mohammad Imam Jom`eh, but after their death they fell into disuse.[306]

In consequence, apart from the occasional floods after heavy rains, there was no source of open water near Bushehr and, therefore, for its fresh water, the town was dependent on wells and on reservoirs. Both depended for their replenishment on rain. The problem was, and still is, that the rainfall pattern was rather erratic and unpredictable. In a good year, early and sufficient rains would fall in December and January and then once again in March. However, that was not always the case. Fortunately, the British installed a meteorological observatory at Bushehr in 1877, which collected data on precipitation since that time.[307]

---

301. NA, FO 248/206, Capt. Disbrowe, officiating Resident to Alison, 24/03/1862; Idem, Capt. Disbrowe to Alison, 16/05/1862; Saldanha 1986, vol. 7/2, pp. 149-50.
302. Mashayakhi 1382, p. 197-210 (with photos). For British arrangements, drawn up up in the late 1960s, for the maintenance of the Christian cemetery, see FCO 47/413
303. Administration Report 1913, p. 14
304. Sadid al-Saltaneh 1371, p. 42.
305. Trade Report 1910-11, p. 1.
306. Sadid al-Saltaneh 1371, pp. 38, 53.
307. Administration Report 1877-78, p. 8.

1.6: Observations of the rainfall at Bushehr for the winter season October-May (1877 - 1940)

Year	Rainfall in cm (inch)	Year	Rainfall in cm (inch)	Year	Rainfall in cm (inch)
1877-78	39.1 (15.41)	1900-01	22.5 (8.88)	1923	38.7 (15.25)
1878-79	13.1 (5.16)	1901-02	7.9 (3.10)	1924	59.90 (23.60)
1879-80	16.1 (6.34)	1902-03	27.6 (10.85)	1925	21.2 (8.34)
1880-81	50.3 (19.88)	1903-04	13.3 (5.25)	1926	37.2 (14.64)
1881-82	24.3 (9.57)	1904-05	22.9 (9.05)	1927	17.7 (6.97)
1882-83	36.7 (14.1)	1905-06	18.7 (7.36)	1928	21.7 (8.54)
1883-84	54.5 (21.46)	1906-07	22.7 (8.94)	1929	41.6 (16.37)
1884-85	75.5 (28.95)	1907-08	17.6 (6.92)	1930	22.8 (8.99)
1885-86	39.6 (15.62)	1908-09	16.3 (6.41)	1931	18.0 (7.10)
1886-87	14.8 (5.26)	1909-10	41.5 (16.32)	1932	13.2 (5.20)
1887-88	41.9 (16.50)	1910-11	51.5 (20.29)	1933	14.0 (5.53)
1888-89	25.2 (9.95)	1911-12	23.3 (9.20)	1934	31.8 (12.51)
1889-90	20.0 (7.89)	1912-13	15.4 (6.07)	1935	37.3 (14.69)
1890-91	52.6 (20.70)	1913-14	29.3 (11.55)	1936	24.3 (9.60)
1891-92	19.5 (7.68)	1914-15	27.6 (10.99)	1937	17.7 (7.0)
1892-93	28.6 (11.26)	1915-16	22.2 (8.75)	1938	33 (13.0)
1893-94	44.9 (17.66)	1916-17	19.2 (7.58)	1939	40.6 (16.0)
1894-95	60.0 (23.63)	1917-18	17.7 (5.95)	1940	43.1 (17.0)
1895-96	12.4 (4.90)	1918-19	20.4 (8.60)	1941	9.65
1896-97	20.3 (7.99)	1919-20	18.6 (7.34)	1942	2.63
1897-98	17.8 (7.0)	1921	33.8 (13.34)	1943	5.59
1898-99	18.4 (7.26)	1922	7.4 (2.92)	1944	10.49
1899-1900	36.0 (14.21)	-	-	1945	14.22

Source: Administration Report 1884-85, p. 11; Administration Report 1889-90, p. 20; Report 1910-11, p. 6; 1911-12, p. 6; Report 1912-13, p. 12; Report 1913-14, p. 6; Report 1915-16, p. 4; Report 1917-18, p. 4; Report 1918-19, p. 2; Report 1919-20, p. 2; Report 1920-21, p. 2; Report 1922-23, p. 3; Report 1923-24, p. 3; Administration Report 1936, p. 14 (1921-35); Administration Report 1937, p. 14 (1922-37); Administration Report 1940, p. 13; Administration Report 1945, p. 20.

It was not total rainfall, however, that determined the good or bad outcome of the harvest, but rather its geographical and temporal distribution. That is, some rain, locally well distributed over an extended period, was much better than a lot of rain at a few locations. Such excess rainfall caused considerable damage, as it washed away the seeds, while the land might also remain under water for a long period. Contrariwise, "a late rain in December could result in good harvest if rains also fell in March and April. If they did not, the harvest was considerably reduced as a consequence."[308] Because agriculture was rainfed, lack of rain or a bad rainy season (e.g., an uneven rain due to its distribution pattern) held out the terrible specter of famine and people, therefore, were constantly worried about the rains, when they would come and how much would fall. For example, in the winters of 1932 and 1933 there had been no rain to speak of, which led to threat of food, fodder and water famine. Local authorities took steps to import grain as well as water from Mohammerah and Bombay, and drinking water had to be brought in skins from Bahmani, a distance of 10 km.[309]

As a result, as in the rest of Persia, there were rain-making ceremonies that dated from pre-historic times, but since then had acquired an Islamic sheen.[310] These beliefs also included the avoidance of anything that was perceived to lessen precipitation or that was perceived to negatively interfere with it. A nice example is the occurrence on 5 January 1897, when an armed mob of a few hundred attacked the installation of the Indo-European Telegraph Department (IETD) at Rishahr, 8 km from Bushehr. They destroyed "the bench marks of the recently completed longitude operations" and later also "the tidal level record. ... The outrage was instigated by the Syeds was in pursuance of a vulgar superstition, that these record marks had been the cause of the deficient rainfall. At the close of the year the mutilated scientific records were formally replaced." Although a few ignorant villagers were punished by the authorities, the real culprit, the sayyed ringleaders, went scot-free, of course.[311]

Wells

In view of the above the water supply situation of Bushehr was not ideal. On the peninsula people sank wells to a depth of 54 meters (30 fathoms) "and before they could reach the spring they have been obliged to perforate three layers of a soft stone composed of sand and shells."[312] However, the quality of the water in many wells was bad, being brackish. For this reason, there were no drinking wells inside the town itself.[313] The only drinkable water came from some wells several kms from the town.[314] Even water from these wells was usually dirty, i.e. it contained much sediment.[315] Therefore, even for daily needs, such water was barely potable. It tasted very much like a dose of Epsom salts, even when

---

308. Trade Report 1920-21, p. 2; Trade Report 1910-11, p. 6. For a graphic description of the damage caused by heavy rains and storms, see Hamidi 1378, pp. 58, 196.

309. Administration Report 1932, pp. 5, 11; Sa`adat 1390, p. 53.

310. Rishahri 1382, vol. 1, pp. 93-99; Hamidi 1380, pp. 405 (*shahsherifak*), 548 (*geli daravardan*). On the subject of rainmaking, see Floor 2003 a, pp. 202-03.

311. Administration Report 1896-97, p. 10; Saldanha 1986, vol. 7/2, p. 160. Naser al-Din Shah agreed to the establishment of a tidal observatory at Bushehr and excavations started. Administration Report 1891-92, p. 11. The tidal basin operating since a few months. Administration Report 1892-93, p. 13. On the role of Sayyeds in Persia, see Floor, "Sayyeds in Qajar Iran according to European Sources," *Studia Iranica* 2016 (forthcoming).

312. Morier 1812, p. 56; Binning 1857, vol. 1, p. 149; Sani` al-Dowleh 1294, vol. 1, p. 299 (depth of at least 30 ells or *arj* or some 15 m).

313. Milburn 1813, vol. 1, p. 130.

314. Collins 1896, p. 25; Shepherd 1857, p. 139; Sayyah 1346, p. 12; Cherikof 1358, pp. 7-8.

315. Government of Great Britain 1945, p. 503.

A traditional well near Bushehr

obtained 15 km from the town and it had a similar effect on strangers.[316] This appreciation of the brackish water was shared by all those contemporaries who cared to write about its quality. Ice blocks to cool drinks did not have that problem, because they were brought from the mountains near Kazerun.[317]

Because good drinking water was scarce, people, had it brought from outlying places.[318] The nearest water well with sweet water was at 10 km distance at Bahmani S.E. of the town. "At a short distance from the old fort of Reeshire, lies the well, from which the best fresh water used in Bushehr, is drawn. It is very deep, and extremely narrow. They said that this well was dug by prince Bahman, who ascended the throne" as Ardashir.[319] From there some of the best water came as well as from the wells at Bagh-e Mullah 10 km away.[320] There was a well at Neydi, from where the cooking water for Bushehr came.[321] Halileh, which was situated south of Bahmani at the end of peninsula, according to Lorimer,

316. Milburn 1813, vol. 1, p. 130; Binning 1857, vol. 1, p. 149; Waring 1973, p. 10. Epsom salt is an inorganic salt containing magnesium, sulfur and oxygen.

317. Sargent 1820, part 2, p. 352.

318. Milburn 1813, vol. 1, p. 130; Sani` al-Dowleh 1294, vol. 1, p. 299; De Vilmorin 1895, p. 34 (well at 10 km distance); Sa`adat 1390, p. 21.

319. Binning 1857, vol. 2, pp. 421-22 ("the fort is called Selim"); Hollingberry 1976, p. 16; Kinneir 1973, p. 70; Government of India 1924, p. 25; Sadid al-Saltaneh 1371, p. 52; Sa`adat 1390, p. 227.

320. Ballantine 1879, p. 59. This was the residence of Mullah `Abdol-Khaleq Mohammadi, a well-known *rowzeh-khvan*. Hamidi 1380, p. 119.

321. Sadid al-Saltaneh 1371, p. 52; Sa`adat 1390, p. 121, n. (at about 2 km from the town; the proper name was Najdi, but it was pronounced as Neydi).

had the best water on the island at a well that was only one meter deep.[322] At the British Residency they drank water brought from Rishahr, although even this water was slightly brackish.[323] This is probably the same well to which E`temad al-Saltaneh refer to when he writes that people fetched their good water from a village called Bati Shaji at 18 km (3 *farsakh*) from Bushehr. Those who were poor obtained it from wells at some 3 km from town, at depth of at least 30 ell (*arj*), while the taste was not that good.[324] According to Kinneir, the best water on the peninsula came from `Ali Changi, a distance of 25 km (near Choghadak).[325] However, by the early twentieth century the wells of the village of Bahmani had run dry. At that time, good water came from a well (Ondor Bondor) in the village of (Bagh) Moqam at 5 km north-east of Rishahr fort. There were also other wells, but their water was not so good.[326] However, it seems that a decade or so later, the Bahmani wells were producing water once again.[327]

Therefore, most of the water used in the town came from these wells. It was brought into town in goatskins, either carried by women or on donkeys, driven by boys or men, and this water was used by all those who could afford it.[328] I wrote most water, because, in addition to water from wells, some houses had rain water tanks, which was the only form of water supply inside the town itself.[329] Because water supply was so individual, there were rarely destructive epidemics which would be the case if there had been a central supply. Rain "is collected from the roofs in deep cement pits, the ab-anbar, made in the courtyards, where it may be stored for years. If one ab-anbar gets infected it does not spread to the neighbours."[330] Moreover, in 1857 a large reservoir to collect rainwater was built on the sea front by a local merchant. It was built of cement and stone, was very strong, and had a capacity of 450,000 liters of water. It was open for public use in April-May, but it was found that it was infested with Guinea worm (*reshteh*). By the mid-1870s, according to Hajj Sayyah, it was dilapidated due to lack of maintenance.[331]

Poorer women went in groups to draw water. "I have seen the elder ones sitting and chatting at the well, and spinning the coarse cotton of the country, while the young girls filled the skin which contains the water, and which they all carry on their backs into the town."[332] Every day you could see long processions of women carrying goatskins filled with water, across the plain. These skins, weighing 60-80 pounds (27-36 kg; twelve or

322. Lorimer 1915, vol. 2, pp. 334,335, 337; Curzon 1892, vol. 1, p. 234.
323. Binning 1857, vol. 1, p. 149; Lorimer 1915, vol. 2, p. 346.
324. Sani` al-Dowleh 1294, vol. 1, 299 (1 *arj* = 52 cm); Kinnier 1973, p. 70.
325. Kinnier 1973, p. 70.
326. Sadid al-Saltaneh 1371, p. 38 (see note 2).
327. Government of India 1924, p. 25.
328. Kinnier 1973, p. 70; Ballantine 1879, p. 59; Binning 1857, vol. 1, p. 149. It took 6 to 8 hours to transport this water, according to Cherikof 1358, p. 7.
329. Binning 1857, vol. 1, p. 149; Trade Report 1921-2, pp. 1-2.
330. Merritt-Hawkes 1935, p. 6. By the 1930s, most large houses had an *ab-anbar*, "from which the poorer members of the population are also allowed to draw." IOR/L/PS/12/3595, Biscoe/Bushire to Legation/Tehran, 18/02/1932.
331. Curzon 1892, vol. 1, p. 234; Sadid al-Saltaneh 1271, p. 117; Government of India 1924, p. 48. According to Sa`adat 1390, p. 26 and Sayyah 1346, p. 12, the reservoir was built by Qavam al-Molk.
332. Morier 1812, p. 61.

Women carrying water

fourteen gallons) were either carried on their head, their back, or were strapped to their shoulders. They walked with the greatest ease and agility.[333]

> They have small buckets to which hairy ropes are tied and with it they fill mushuks, made of skins of goats or sheep, tanned whole, after cutting off the head and feet. The skin is left open at the neck as a funnel for the water, and the holes remaining, on detaching the feet, are tied up and turned inwards. The whole skin, thus prepared, forms a bag for water, which is denominated a mushuk. This vessel, when filled with water, being of considerable weight, is raised and fastened to the back, a little above the loins, by means of a flexible rope, or flat band of hair, about six feet long, carried for the purpose along with the empty mushuk. In preparing for the burden, the rope is doubled and laid on the ground, with the ends twelve inches asunder. The mushuk is laid across, midway between the noose end of this bended rope and its extremities, and it is then filled with water, which is secured by doubling back the skin of the neck, and then tying it with a narrow thong of leather. The woman to whom it belongs seats herself before it on the ground between the ends of the rope; she then passes the band or noose over her head, so as when tightened, to reach the pit of her stomach. Then drawing the two ends of the rope under her arms, she passes them through the loop and pulls them downwards as tight as she can. In this recumbent posture, attaching herself to the mushuk, she draws up her legs so as to obtain a footing on the ground; then, holding the ropes with one hand, she gives the other one to one of her companions,

333. Stern 1854, p. 89; Fogg 1875, p. 177. "Good women" did not leave their house. Ya Hoseyni 1394, p. 23.

> who standing with her feet asunder draws her up; and in this manner they mutually raise each other, and afterwards return together to the town.[334]

Contrarisewise, men and boys went to the wells to get water with a number of donkeys each with a pair of water skins (*mashuks*). However, they never went to the same wells that were used by women. As a result, there was also a constant procession of donkeys and mules carrying skins of water going between them.[335] Wealthy families or large establishments such as the British Residency had their own water transporters, who saw to it that they were supplied with fresh water on a daily basis. By 1890, if not earlier, water supplies were transported from Basra and Mohammerah, for those who could afford it, because of the occurrence of Guinea worm in the Bushehr water.[336]

Ships calling on Bushehr took in brackish water, which was considered wholesome, by an anonymous author. Unless you were a pure water drinker, he opined you didn't need lime juice or spirits as Capt. Horsburgh recommended. He further added that more expeditiously, better and cheaper water was available at Rishahr, where men-of-war sometimes went to get it. However, for merchant ships this option was too much of a hassle and therefore, they mostly took in water at Khark after leaving Bushehr.[337] With the arrival of steam ships this would change as these ships would take their own sweeter water from India.

The greater the distance from the town the purer, better and more expensive the water. The water brought by donkeys had to be paid for at prices that varied per season. Prices quoted by contemporary sources reflect this. In 1878, it was a few bits of copper coins,[338] while Curzon in 1890 noted that the price was 5-6 *puls* (3/4 *d.*) for the ordinary quality and 16 *puls* (2.25 *d.*) for the better quality per donkey load.[339] De Vilmorin, for the same year reported an amount of 1 *qran* per goatskin home delivered.[340] In 1907, the ordinary Bushiri paid 2 pence (*d.*) per donkey load.[341] Some seven years later, two skins or one donkey load cost 15 *shahis*.[342]

The brackish water also had its use. I have already noted that it was used for irrigation. Furthermore, Europeans used it for washing their clothes, whereas the women of Bushehr usually washed their clothes in salt water on the sea-shore, "beating them on large flat stones with a sort of wooden bat."[343]

---

334. Johnson 1818, pp. 20-21.
335. Johnson 1818, p. 21; Alexander 2000, p. 96; Collins 1896, p. 25.
336. de Windt 1891, p. 216.
337. Anonymous 1828, p. 57; Mignan 1839, vol. 2, p. 139; den Tex 1871, p. 26. Native vessels would also make use of "a sinking vessel called Tanasa, made of a certain kind of red earth, the aperture of which is stopped. The vessel takes in a quantity of sea-water; of which, when the vessel is again drawn on board, the water oozes out, while the salt remains behind. In this manner a tolerably drinking water can be obtained." Benjamin 1859, p. 177, n. 1.
338. Ballantine 1879, p. 59
339. Curzon 1892, vol. 1, p. 234.
340. De Vilmorin 1895, p. 347.
341. Bradley-Birt 1910, p. 46
342. Sadid al-Saltaneh 1371, p. 38.
343. Collins 1896, p. 25; Government of India 1924, p. 96; Mahrad 1978, p. 89.

At the beginning of the twentieth century nothing much had changed, despite the establishment of a Company in August 1911, by the leading Persian merchants of Bushehr to acquire a plant that would make sweet water from salt water, a plan that never materialized.[344] In 1919, the British Strike Force installed soda water machines in Bushehr, Kazerun and Shiraz, which yielded a handsome profit of Rs10,000 during the first nine months. Soda water was supplied at no cost to hospitals and at a small charge to the troops. The latter also received fresh water from India, because the supply of the condensed water was insufficient for drinking and other uses at Bushehr. However, importing water was very expensive as was condensing it. Therefore, as of 1 August 1919, the import of water from India was discontinued and water was brought by train from Borazjan.[345] By 1920, the water supply situation in Bushehr was as follows. The water was still bad, but by then almost every house had a well. In addition, about 10% of the houses had rain water reservoirs. However, Europeans and wealthy Persians still obtained their water from Bahmani, Ondor Bondor, or Gonjeshkdan. Because the government of India chemist has declared all water on the peninsula unfit for human consumption, the British Residency obtained its water from Basra or Karachi by vessel.[346] Since 1917, in addition to wells and rain water tanks, there was one new big water reservoir in the town and two condensers built by the British military at Dastak. The output of the condensers, which was stored in a large reservoir, was for the British at Rishahr. They also used water of the wells at Ondor Bondor, which was distributed by donkeys.[347] This meant that the water supply situation of the Bushehr peninsula had quantitatively and qualitatively improved. The total water supply was estimated to be:

1.7: Drinking water supplies in Bushehr ca. 1920

I. **Fresh and distilled water**		
Two condensers at Dastak with a capacity of 15,000 gallons per day (p.d.)	Storage tanks at Rishar with a capacity of 80,000 gallons p.d. This is continuous capacity, normally are respectively 14,000 and 5,000 gallons for the 2 condensers.	A 1.6 km 3-inch underground pipe connects the Dastak condenser with the Rishahr storage tank in the Telegraph compound.
- 1 Imperial gallon = 4.56 liter		A cattle trough and stand pipe for filling water tanks are on the road near the reservoir. Also a pipeline to the HQ buildings and the military hospital.

344. Hamidi 1378, pp. 36-37. Moses Khan had proposed to buy a condensor to be paid in installments. By July 1911, to that end, the governor had already collected 9,000 *tumans*. The Municipality borrowed 16,000 *tumans* from the IBP with security from local merchants to finance the remainder.It is not clear why the plan fell through. FO 248/11033. Political Diary July 1911, p. 13 (item 713). In early August 1909, when drinking water was scarce and of bad quality, some boatmen imported water from the Shatt al-Arab for sale in Bushehr. Although reasonable profits were made there was no follow-up. Political Diaries, vol. 3, pp. 706.

345. FO 248/1229, Report Bushire Field Force, 28/11/1919 (the condensors produced 10,000 gallons/day requiring 5 tons of coal. Therefore, to reduce cost, the use of oil instead of coal was considered as well as more supply from Borazjan, and to use the condensors only in case of emergency).

346. Lorimer 1915, vol. 2, pp. 346-47; Bradley-Birt 1910, p. 46; Sa`adat 1390, p. 21.

347. Government of India 1924, p. 52.

I. **Fresh and distilled water**		
-	A stone-cement covered storage reservoir 40 m from the eastern-most jetty of customs house with a capacity of 120,000 gallons.	This capacity is not included in the quantity of fresh water available at Bushehr
II. **Well water**	-	-
Bandar Andar group of wells	4,000 gallons p.d.	-
Zangina group of wells	6,700 gallons p.d.	-
Gharibu wells	600 gallons p.d.	-
Sangi wells	1,200 gallons p.d.	-
Total II	12,500 gallons p.d.	-
III. **Wells at Rishar and Zangina**	Capacity of respectively 1,600 and 800 gallons	Used by local people; could be used in an emergency by the military
IV. **Drinking water for animals**		-
Bushire group of wells	12,000 gallons p.d.	-
Andar Bandar group	13,000 gallons p.d.	-
Other scattered sources	4,000 gallons p.d.	-
Total IV.	29,000 gallons p.d.	-

Source: Military Report 1924, pp. 94-95.

Thus, the British-Indian troops used well and condensed water. The well water was sweet enough, but contained salt and adversely affected *dhal* preparation. Soldiers, therefore, were given 2.25 liters of fresh water as an extra ration to well water. The storage reservoir near the easternmost jetty of customs house was used for the British Strike Force in 1918 and from water brought by steamers. By 1920 it was no longer used and the British government tried in vain to sell it.[348]

There was no change in the water supply situation during the next two decades. In August 1934 water had become very scarce, because most of wells outside town had dried up. Therefore, brackish water was brought in small sailing boats from Halileh and sold at 23 *shahis* per tin. The governor asked Tehran to send an engineer to study the possibility of bringing drinking water to Bushehr from the Mund and Shahpur rivers.[349] In 1938, two engineers investigated the possibility of this project as well as the possibility of damming them for irrigation. They concluded that damming was possible, while one of them hoped to bring water from Khaviz or from Halileh. However, nothing

348. Government of India 1924, p. 95. According to Russian reports, the old condenser had a capacity of 18,160 liters per day. The new one 1,362 liters, Mahrad 1978, p. 89.

349. Political Diaries, vol. 11, p. 243. In March 1929, a Belgian engineer investigated a water supply project for Bushehr drawing water from a spring near Ahram. He recommended "to build a pipe line direct to the vicinity of Sabzabad, erect a reservoir there and by a smaller pipe bring the water into town more or less along the main road. He proposes charging 5 krans for 200 gallons of sweet water. It seems very doubtful whether the money for this scheme will be forthcoming." Political Diaries, vol. 8, p. 307.

The water reservoir (the Qavam ol-Molk *Ab-anbar*) - in the background the British consulate.

came of these plans.[350] Because 1942 was going to be a year with a shortage of water the municipality took steps in December 1941 to import water at cheap rates. In December 1941, the price of water had risen from Rls.1.25 for two skins to 4 Rls.[351] With funds from the Anglo-Persian Relief and Reconstruction Fund (APRRF) a dam was built at Ondor Bondor to collect rainwater. In December 1942, in the valley behind the dam a 4.5 million liters of water was stored.[352]

At the end of 1942 work at `Ali Changi, about 25 km from Bushehr, was started. The objective was to tap an underground water reservoir and to supply 818,000 liters of drinking water per day to the town. In January 1944, the workers were mainly busy with the *qanats* to access the water resources. The construction of the pipeline to supply Bushehr had to wait for a shipment of iron and glazed clay pipes from abroad. The funding for the project was from Reza Shah's estate. In 1944, lack of rain was a cause of concern not only for the harvest, but also for the drinking water situation, because the water reservoirs had little water in them. Work on the `Ali Changi water project was continuing and it was hoped that by June 1944 the pipe would reach Borj-e Moqam, the first gendarmerie post on the Bushehr peninsula. The pipeline that would cross the Mashilah was to be made of local clay pipes surrounded by asphalt. The need for this project to be finished was desperate. By April 1944, some 10 km of the pipeline was complete and another 7 km needed completion. At that time the rainwater tanks (*ab-anbars*) in Bushehr were almost empty and water carriers in Bushehr sold their water at Rls. 10 per two skins. Even when the `Ali Changi pipeline would reach Borj-e Moqam by summer its water still needed to be transported to town. Therefore, the governor requested two tanker

---

350. Administration Report 1938, p. 5. On 25 March 1937, the Shah and the crown prince were in Bushehr; the Shah was mainly concerned with the decrease of the port's population and the bringing of sweet water to Bushehr from Ab-e Shapur. Administration Report 1937, p. 1.

351. Political Diaries, vol. 14, p. 593; vol. 15, p. 6.

352. Political Diaries, vol. 15, p. 349.

trucks with a capacity of 10,000 liters. By May 1944 it was clear that the project would be delayed because of the non-arrival of 25 tons of tar to coat the clay pipes. Also, the iron pipes had not arrived yet. It was only in October 1944 that work at the `Ali Changi project started up again and it was estimated that the remaining 8 km of clay pipes would be laid in 6 weeks time to link up with the water-bearing area with the first pumping station. From there iron pipes, supplied by the British military, would be used. After that it still would take another 6 months to lay the iron pipes; also suitable pumping-engines still had not been found. As of that month, Eng. Farzaneh was assisted by a Russian engineer (earlier two Yugoslav engineers had assisted him).[353]

At the request of the governor, the British army decided to release 9.5 km of iron piping and two tanker trucks until the completion of the project; the trucks from the Road Department arrived in the second half of July 1944. The need for this project was highlighted by the high price of water. A committee saw no choice but to organize the free distribution of water to the poor; water sellers were forced to sell water at Rls. 7 per two skins. In September 1944, the two promised British army tanker trucks arrived at Bushehr. As a result, the price of water dropped to Rls. 3.50. In December-January 1945, two km of iron piping was laid, while a water reservoir was constructed on top of the Imamzadeh ridge, so that 5 km remained to be done at a pace of 100-200 meters/day. Because of heavy rains the laying of the clay pipe across the Mashilah was suspended. The good news was that the ordered pumps had arrived. In May 1945, the project still was not finished. All funds had been spent, but an additional 50,000 *tumans* were needed to buy two power-driven pumps to complete the project. These funds were made available by the Shah. Due to high tide in the Mashilah in June 1945, the 3-km clay pipe along the causeway connecting Bushehr was flooded with sea water. In November 1945, it was said that the project would be completed in two months, which was indeed the case. However, the water coming from the pipe was slightly brackish. Therefore, it was not connected with any water reservoir in town and was left running into the sand outside the town. Eng. Farzaneh officially transferred the project to the Municipality on 24 February 1946. A local committee was formed that would finance the connection of households to the water supply system on a commercial basis. However, it would take another two years before the water from the `Ali Changi project would benefit the people of Bushehr.[354]

As a result, even as late as 1947, Bushehr still relied on wells and rain water tanks for its water needs. There were additional potential sources of supply, whch were not made use of, however. These included two condensers of which one was beyond repair, while the other one could be repaired and used again. The water storage tank at the telegraph concession at Rishahr with a capacity of 308,000 liter still existed and was still in good condition. In the past it was connected with a pipe to the condensers, but the pipe had been removed. There was a small condenser with a capacity of 1,350 liters/p. d. (300 gallons) that supplied water to Europeans.[355]

By 1947, municipal water was supplied by *qanat* from `Ali Changi. At the *qanat*'s collection head water was piped by gravity flow to a pumping station, then to the peninsula

353. Political Diaries, vol. 16, pp. 16, 48, 51, 76, 96, 227.

354. Political Diaries, vol. 16, p. 148, 151, 290, 397, 446, 448, 551; vol. 17, pp. 4, 32.

355. Mahrad 1978, p. 89; Government of Great Britain 1945, p. 503; Merritt-Hawkes 1935, p. 6. Until mid-August 1932, when the money ran out, the Municipality with funds from the Red Lion and Sun Society distributed free water to the poor. Political Diaries, vol. 10, p. 112.

where it was pumped into a water reservoir with a capacity of 50,000 gallons or 227,000 liters. This reservoir was 40 m above sea level and from there by gravity, fed the town through a 15 cm pipe. This new system was completed in 1947 at a cost of Rls. 12 million, a gift from the Shah. However, the project was implemented too hurriedly. Rather than wait for the availability of non-porous earthenware pipes from Central Persia, pipes were made on the spot from local clay. These were baked in specially built kilns. A few months after they had been laid it was found that they were porous; salt water seeped through and contaminated the sweet water. This effect was worst when the Mashilah through which the pipe ran was inundated by seawater. The governor, Lotf `Ali Ghavami, took steps to correct this error at a cost of Rls. 1.5 million to the municipality.[356]

The Climate

Although water supply might be a problem for the population of Bushehr and its environs this did not mean that it was an arid environment. On the contrary, both the temperature and the humidity were high, which combination made the weather very unpleasant. Because of the damp and heat during summer, "even the water is tepid, and requires to be cooled in deep brackish wells, with which every house is provided."[357] The hottest month was August and the coldest months were January-February. The temperature in summer might even rise as high as 115.5 Fahrenheit or 46.4 Celsius in the shade. People used fly whisks made of horse tails to chase away bugs and get some cooling. The period from 20 July to 15 September was the worst due to the high humidity, and the only relief was the north-west breeze during that period. Dr. Hojel reported that especially a day or two about 23 August 1867, the temperature was so intense and oppressive that the entire population refused to move. Nobody was seen in the streets and the shops were closed, for "the whole population are under water," as they said in Bushehr.[358] According to Rich, "the heat of Bussora is less in degree, but more oppressive and relaxing, than that of Baghdad-and by the same rule that of Bushire than Bussora."[359]

In the local dialect many different winds and gales are distinguished such as the *shamal* (north), *sohaili* (east), *barri* (land wind), *lahimar*, *lachizab*, *qus*, *ghoyub*, *tariyeh*, *pir-e zan* and *sah`eh*," in addition to a normal generic hurricane (*tufan*).[360] The wind was not only unpleasant from its parching quality, but also because during July-September, "it is often loaded with a quantity of fine sand, which, covering ourselves and everything about us with dust, quite banished all personal comfort." [361]

The period from November to February was the rainy season, which also might be intermittently stormy and cold. Although freezing temperatures seldom occurred, it happened that it sometimes was almost zero degree Celcius (32 degrees Fahrenheit). Europeans considered heating necessary between December and February, when, according to Binning, "the principal rooms in the houses, are furnished with fireplaces, and in

356. NA, FO 371/15473
357. Stern 1854, p. 88; Mignan 1839, vol. 2, pp. 139-40.
358. NA, FO 248/232, A.N. Hojel asst. surgeon to Lewis Pelly, 13/05/1868.
359. Rich 1839, p. 201.
360. For details, see Afshar Sistani 1369, vol. 1, pp. 44-47; Lorimer 1915, vol. 1, pp. 2206-07; Kanin 1391, pp. 37-42; Vadala 2536, p. 120; Hamidi 1380, pp. 112-16.
361. Fraser 1984, p. 67.

January and February, fires are often maintained all day." But even after sundown till the end March "it was sufficiently chilly in the evenings to allow of our enjoying a fire."[362]

Sanitary Conditions, Public Health and Medical Care

Public Hygiene

Although prior to 1850 Bushehr seems to have been a healthy place, this positive outlook soon and drastically changed thereafter. In 1870, the British Residency Surgeon Hojel drew up a report concerning the sanitary situation of Bushehr, which town he described as mostly "a collection of ruined houses, stagnant cesspools, dirt heaps of the foulest description and devoid of drainage of any kind whatsoever."[363] Except for those on the grounds of the British Residency, there were only two drains in Bushehr. One led from the slaughterhouse and one from the tanning works that were open and, "not being made with a fall towards the sea, they are full of noxious matter." According to Dr. Colvill in 1866, such a situation was to be expected in a town "where refuse is thrown into the court yard, privies are pits in the ground, cleaned out once in 6 years, and where the urinals on top of the houses open by spouts into the streets below, there is no need for drains."[364] The shoreline was "the public necessary of the town." In 1856, Dr. McAlister wrote that at the beach to the S.W. of the town, "a host of impurities accumulate, and the almost unapproachable place emits a deadly sickening stench along, with eddying bubbles of noisome gas, and the mid-day breeze coming from the west carries the noxious elements through and over the town." [365] The shoreline was not the only place where people dumped their refuse. Three hundred meters south-east from the British Residency was a large open cesspool where refuse and the night sewage of the barracks, containing 400 men, accumulated.[366] People also dumped their refuse at other places outside the walls such as the neck of land immediately outside the town that during the spring tide was inundated and made Bushehr almost an island. Here people also threw their dead animals, emptied privies, which, unfortunately, the tide did not carry away, but only moistened it. Moreover, "Here is a grave yard where bodies are buried some two or three feet deep. Here dying and dead animals of every kind are thrown to rot, and vegetable refuse to decay."[367] To the north-east corner of the town, outside the walls, was the slaughter-house, which being below the water level had no drainage. As a result, impurities were "accumulated on a gigantic scale and the morning breeze coming from the eastward conveys the noxious particles to the lungs of the inhabitants."[368] In short, both within and without Bushehr was a town filled with rotting and reeking human and animal refuse to which daily more was added.

362. Binning 1857, vol. 1, p. 148; Collins 1896, p. 25; Government of India 1924, p. 93; Böhme 1977, p. 251.
363. NA, FO 248/271, Ass. Surgeon A. N. Hojel Residency Surgeon to Pelly, Bushehr 10/04/1870.
364. Report Colvill, quoted in NA, FO 248/232, A.N. Hojel asst. surgeon to Lewis Pelly, 13/05/1868.
365. Report McAlister quoted in NA, FO 248/232, A.N. Hojel asst. surgeon to Lewis Pelly, 13/05/1868.
366. NA, FO 248/232, A.N. Hojel asst. surgeon to Lewis Pelly, 13/05/1868.
367. Colvill report quoted in NA, FO 248/232, A.N. Hojel asst. surgeon to Lewis Pelly, 13/05/1868. The refuse heap outside the city was known called *telagdun*. Hamdidi 1380, p. 208.
368. NA, FO 248/232, A.N. Hojel asst. surgeon to Lewis Pelly, 13/05/1868.

In the years thereafter there was no change. In 1875, the then Residency Surgeon Waters wrote in his annual medical report:

> The bane of Bushire consists in the fact of its being built on a labyrinth of choked up sewers interspersed with sewage pits, of which these sewers were supposed to be the outflow, but of which instead they are but tortuous continuations fraught with pestiferous matters of such concentrated virulence as the ultimate products of the uninterrupted process of 25 years or upwards of organic decomposition would be likely to acquire.
>
> Can we wonder, then, that Bushire, 30 years ago, so free from sickness, that it was the health resort of the inhabitants of all districts bordering on the Gulf, is now the endemic home of a fever which nothing but a change of residence is effectual of shaking off, and which but for the well selected position of the town and the almost universal prevalence of a seabreeze might in a short space of time more than decimate the population?[369]

The town remained filthy, crowded, badly built, devoid of roads other than gaps between the houses, which made ventilation of any kind impossible. During the hot season, the air was heavy with a smelly and damp stench, caused by the poisonous effluvia of many stagnant pools, so that even breathing was difficult. This was because refuse, excreta, both human and animal, were deposited or thrown indiscriminately into the mud lanes that separated the houses from each other. These were generously distributed over the town by the traffic that passed through these lanes. Many of the houses had their drains opening up to the lanes; in others, pits in the houses were used for this purpose and their putrefying contents was often the accumulated filth of years. Apart from drainage into some wells, drainage was non-existent and "during the rains each street is a conduit unto itself."[370] Geary, a visiting journalist, commented that, given "its crooked lanes and stone-blinded alleys, ... it would be a wonder if the plague, once it got in, could find its way out."[371] Although the sea breeze brought relief to the inhabitants of Bushehr, this was not the case with north-western winds. According to Alexander, "the whole air was filled with minute particles of sand, and at dinner in the evening it was excessively annoying: our heads were completely powdered, as were all the viands." After sleeping on the terrace, the following morning "my eyes [were] completely filled with sand, but which was not half so annoying as the innumerable flies and mosquitoes which swarmed about our faces immediately after sunrise."[372]

Although in 1854 Dr. John Snow showed that there was a link between cholera and contaminated drinking water and that human sewage contamination was the most probable disease vector, his ideas of combating the disease were only slowly accepted and applied. The British Residency surgeon, Dr. Hojel was one of those physicians who was an

---

369. IOR/V/24/2639, Medical Report on Bushire for the year ending 21/03/1875, pp. 2-3.

370. Trade Report 1921-22, pp. 1-2; Trade Report 1913-14, p. 1; Johnson 1818, p. 19; Geary 1878, vol. 1, p. 64; Ballantine 1879, p. 50; Stern 1854, p. 89; Merritt-Hawkes 1935, p. 5; Hamidi 1378, pp. 33, 117, 164; de Rivoyre 1883, p. 135.

371. Geary 1878, vol. 1, p. 64.

372. Alexander 2000, pp. 94-95.

early 'convert' to these new ideas, which he wanted to introduce to public health practice in Bushehr. On 14 October 1869 he met with with the *kargozar* (agent for foreign affairs) and the *hakim-bashi* (chief traditional Persian physician), who recently had been appointed in Bushehr. He pointed out to them the means modern science had for checking the spread of or modifying the type of epidemic for densely populated and filthy areas such as Bushehr. Therefore, Dr. Hojel suggested the following:

> i. house to house inspection and measures proposed which the dwellers should take;
>
> ii. general conservancy of the town and its neighborhood;
>
> iii. fires in the streets at night on which sulfur, frankincense and other disinfecting substances should be thrown;
>
> iv. fumigation and general use of disinfectants of the houses;
>
> v. regulation of diet, clothing, general habits etc.;
>
> vi. intra-mural internment, i.e. in walled cemeteries;
>
> vii. the fumigation of the persons entering and leaving town;
>
> viii. the quarantine of the villages in the vicinity of Bushire;
>
> ix. the prevention of large numbers of people congregating together;
>
> x. the necessity for great particularity in regard to the water supply;
>
> xi. as to the most judicious treatment; and the advisability of making known to the people, the greater benefits to be expected from an early resort to medical treatment in case of an attack;
>
> xii. the clothes, bedding, and all clothes soiled by the evacuation of the sick, should at once be burned, and the evacuation collected in utensils and immediately disinfected; and
>
> xiii. that the practice now prevalent in Bushire of the priests and their employees calling out from the roofs of the Musjeds and other places, that a scourge has fallen upon the town, etc. should be stopped, as it is calculated to create a panic and so favor the spread of the disease.

Both the *kargozar* and the *hakim-bashi* agreed with Hojel that the suggested measures should be taken, but said it would take time and required instructions from Tehran. As a result, nothing changed, and Hojel had to conclude that nothing was done and that the town remained a reeking and filthy place; ironically, the vicinity of the *kargozar*'s house was filthier than anywhere else in town. Therefore, he suggested to Col. Pelly, the British Resident to use his "authority to awaken the Persian authorities from their lethargy concerning sanitation, for delay may mean thousands of deaths. I also ask you to inform them about the baneful effect of washing the dead in their houses or anywhere in the town, a practice which is still continued despite my remonstations against it."[373]

Another indication of the lack of government interest in public health with a view to establish more sanitary conditions in Bushehr was the practice of storing corpses. There was a constant flow of coffins coming from the interior, each containing two corpses

---

373. NA, FO 248/232, Ass. surgeon Hojel to Pelly, 15/10/1869.

and in varying stages of decompostion, which were stored in the landing zone (*bandar*) awaiting shipping to Kerbela for burial. In particular in 1870, this was a matter of concern to the British Residency physician, when famine ravaged Bushehr and much of the rest of Persia and the danger of another outbreak of cholera was high and much feared after the devastating outbreak of 1869. Dr. Hojel reported that:

> Awaiting transportation to Kerbella and other Shrines, in different parts of the town and especially in the European quarter still obtains. The bodies of those who have died in Bushire, and some of the suburbs, during the past two months have been concealed, I cannot say buried, in shallow trenches, with but a slight covering of dry sand, and no attempt at disinfection, and this within two hundred yards, or so, of the Residency. The presence of such a cemetery in the European quarter and especially the Residency that stands next to it, may have baneful influence on health.[374]

In response to British demand for action the *kargozar* sent the Residency physician a note informing him that he had taken care of his concerns. However, when Dr. Hojel went into town to see for himself he observed that the *kargozar* had been misinformed by his servants, for nothing useful had been done.

> Stones of the size of a fist have been placed around some of the graves, and a few basketful of earth scraped from the sides has been thrown in the middle of it. There is no ban on the storing of bodies in town for transportation to Karbala. On the contrary their number is daily increasing. They are all kept above ground merely covered with a slight structure of stonework held together with some chunam which when it dries, cracks and opens into various directions, thus becoming utterly useless. Some have been replastered as the FO agent states, but 2 days of sun has them reduced to their former condition and it will always be like that with this system. I had hoped that repeated representations would led to a ban in intra-mural burial, but astounding as it may sound with 2 epidemics (cholera, small-pox, vying which each other this dangerous method has been recommended). Yesterday 2 bodies were placed near the Residency on a bier; in the evening one had been placed in the yard in a nearby mosque, the other was untouched and only a shallow grave had been scraped in the soil; this in the heart of the European quarter we have 2 corpses lying around only covered with a thin sheet. In the evening one was out in a shallow grave with one one foot of loose sand over it; the other is still unburied. I also measured the open grave, it was only 2 feet deep.[375]

Personal hygiene was also deficient and people's clothes were filled with vermin.[376] This was because people wore their clothes unwashed for a long time (a shirt for 4 weeks,

374. NA, FO 248/271, Ass. Surgeon A. N. Hojel Residency Surgeon to Pelly, Bushehr, 10/04/1870.

375. NA, FO 248/271, Hojel, surgeon to Pelly, 27/04/1871. *Chunam*, from the Hindi word *chuna*, meaning dust, means quicklime, also plaster or mortar.

376. Merritt-Hawkes 1935, p. 7.

trousers for 6 months). Although people regularly went to the public baths this did not necessarily mean that people became clean after having taken a bath.[377] Moreover, in 1816, according to Buckingham, there was only one bath, which he described as "small, mean, filthy, and badly attended."[378] However, other travelers who were in Bushehr at that time and somewhat later report that there were three bathhouses in the town.[379] These baths were nearly underground and despite their sub-optimal hygienic condition, Europeans also took a bath there, as their understanding of hygiene at that time was not much better than that of the Bushehris.[380] By the turn of the twentieth century, Bushehr boasted seven bathhouses (see Table 1.8).[381] Around 10 November 1908, the governor wanted to collect a special tax on bathhouses. Its keepers went to Imam Jom`eh, who then asked the governor to refrain from doing so.[382]

1.8: Bathhouses in Bushehr ca. 1912

Name	**Annual rent in *tumans***	**Owner/Observations**
Haji Mohammad Ja`far	50	Hajj `Abdol-Karim Roghani
Delgosha	130	Sayyed Sadeq owner/ Mir Ahmad Rishahri leaser
Tala	66	Vaqf heirs of Sayyed Mohammad `Ali
Khan	120	Vaqf heirs of Mullah Sayyed Nesa/ women only
Shur or Namaki	40	Heirs of Haji Abu'l-Qasem Asghar
Sheikh Hasan	140	Haji Ebrahim Rowghani/ at bazaar entrance
Aqa Hasan Madul	*	Heirs of Aqa Hasan Madul
Arg	-	In ruins outside town/ new bathhouse being built

Source: Sadid al-Saltaneh 1371, pp. 44, 98-99, 100.
*was idle; renovated by Ostad Mosib and rented for seven years.

In 1934, despite some efforts to clean the streets, Bushehr was still a fairly smelly town[383] and this continued to be the case for at least another two decades.

Public Health

From the above it is clear that sanitation in Bushehr was practically non-existent, although it was desperately needed. What was needed was a Persian institution to deal with public health. However, there was none, and as a result, public health was left to fend for itself. It would appear that in Bushehr, like the rest of Persia, no records of births and deaths

377. Shepherd 1857, p. 143. The dirty bath water itself often was a source of disease, see Floor 2004 a, p. 62 and Sa`adat 1390, p. 20.
378. Buckingham 1971, p. 348.
379. Heude 1819, p. 43; Kempthorne 1835, p. 283; Shepherd 1857, p. 143. Morier 1812, p. 57 (two bathhouses).
380. Lumsden 2010, p. 30.
381. Sadid al-Saltaneh 1371, p. 44 (with data re characteristics, cost, fuel, etc); Sa`adat 1390, p. 20. In November 1938, the governor stopped "the use in the public baths or reservoirs for bathing and has arranged that Turkish baths should be made in place of the reservoirs." Political Diaries, vol. 13, p. 203.
382. Political Diaries, vol. 3, p. 337.
383. Merritt-Hawkes 1935, p. 5.

were kept, which would have allowed the authorities to assess the state of public health in the town.[384] According to a report by Dr. Hojel in April 1870,

> I would be happy if I could report that the Persian authorities have taken any step to remedy this situation, but unfortunately they have not. It rather looks as if they wanted to make Bushire a nursery for diseases by ignoring even the simplest rules of sanitation, and it looks like they have been successful. The local authoritiers in what I call criminal apathy cannot claim ignorance on the means they should adopt to halt the spread of disease in this town and make it a pleasant and healthy place. I have on several occasions made suggestions what they could do, but the government had presented the Persian head physician with a robe of honor for entirely ignoring them. The disease goes on and makes Bushire into a pestilential charnel-house in which it is hazardous to enter.[385]

Malek al-Tojjar returning from Europe in 1884 initiated some unspecified sanitary measures, which had no discernible impact on the existing unsanitary situation.[386] Given these unsanitary conditions and the fact that many people did not wear shoes,[387] it was no surprise that the population of Bushehr was afflicted by endemic diseases as well as occasional outbreak of the plague, cholera and other diseases, most of which were imported by passengers and crews coming from India by ship. The most prevailing endemic diseases included malaria (due to the *ab-anbars* or water reservoirs), rheumatic affections, skin, eye, and diseases of the digestive organs (worms), venereal diseases, and diseases of the respiratory system.[388]

The traditional water supply from wells at Bushehr was linked to the frequent occurrence of typhoid fever and dysentery.[389] On the other hand, the higher use of *ab-anbars* (i.e. very small rain-water reservoirs) in the courtyards of the houses after 1900 contributed to the drop in these epidemics, which would not be the case if there had been a central supply. Because if "one ab-anbar gets infected it does not spread to the neighbours."[390] However, these water tanks had a major drawback, because they teemed with mosquitos and householders were reluctant to permit any preventive measures.[391] Mosquitos and flies were not only found at water sources, but were literally everywhere. Just walking in the streets or bazaar, a casual observer would see "myriads of black flees were battening on it, and imparted to fruit and bread their own dark hue."[392] Therefore, the wetter the rainy season the more people suffered from malaria. Visits to the dispensary were down

384. Report 1921-22, pp. 1-2.
385. NA, FO 248/271, Ass. Surgeon A. N. Hojel Residency Surgeon to Pelly, 10/04/1870.
386. Administration Report 1884-85, p. 8.
387. Sani` al-Dowleh 1294, vol. 1, p. 299
388. Administration Report 1900-01, pp. 9-13; Idem, 1914, p. 12; Idem, 1913, p. 34; Trade Report 1913-14, pp. 6-7 (trachoma is the major epidemic eye disease); Report 1915-16, p. 5; Trade Report 1920-21, pp. 1-2 (venereal disease is rampant); Cursetjee 2001, p. 114 ("The common complaints appeared to be eye-troubles, fever and cough."); Government of India 1924, pp. 94, 99; NA, FO 371/15473; NA, FO 248/232, A.N. Hojel asst. surgeon to Lewis Pelly, 13/05/1868; Hamidi 1378, p. 33.
389. Collins 1896, p. 25.
390. Merritt-Hawkes 1935, p. 6.
391. Trade Report 1920-21, pp. 1-2.
392. Brittlebank 1873, p. 96.

Aerial view of compact and crowded Bushehr mid-1930s

during a period of milder weather, but "in normal years this season is a 'rush' one for hospital staff."[393]

It is possible that the occurrence of malaria may have been a later development, because in 1850 Binning submitted that "the bad fevers that at that time [hot season] prevail so extensively in the interior of Persia, are not common here."[394] This was at a time when Bushehr was still considered to be a healthy place. In 1934, however, Merritt-Hawkes commented:

> Malaria is the curse of Bushire, but the natives prefer treatment to prophylaxis; they will swallow tons of quinine, and enjoy hundreds of injections, but they won't cover up the little pool in every courtyard where mosquito larvae gambol undisturbed. Enlarged stomachs, produced by enlarged spleens, are

393. Administration Report 1932, p. 11. Malaria was known as *tebb-e nowbeh*. Hamdidi 1380, pp. 215-16 (also gives traditional method of treatment).

394. Binning 1857, vol. 1, p. 148.

> everywhere, and when a woman isn't having a baby, a constant occupation unless they have a venereal disease, they look as if they were.[395]

Those visiting the dispensary for treatment of malaria numbered 5,720 (1918), 4,940 (1919), 4,892 (1920), 1,200 (1932) and 3,619 (1933); at that time Bushehr had a population of some 20,000 people.[396] In general, malaria represented between 25% and 30% of patients seen at the dispensary. The relatively low number in 1932 was due to a drought, but malaria cases increased in very rainy seasons.[397]

Lapuk-mazzeh amulet

Waring, in 1802, reported that "at least one-third of the inhabitants of the Dushtistan have something the matter with their eyes," whilst others reported it to be a general phenomenon.[398] To prevent that children would be affected by eye disease parents had their children wear an amulet, called *lapuk-mazzeh*, a white or blue seal in various forms, on the back or neck.[399]

In 1894, dengue fever made its reappearance after an absence of many years.[400] According to Sadid al-Saltaneh, the Guinea worm made its appearance in Bushehr in 1856, because prior to that time it was unknown there. He alleges that the worm was introduced by the British-Indian troops that invaded Bushehr, who might have been infected with it in India. The occurrence of the Guinea worm coincided with the construction of the large water reservoir built by Mirza `Ali Akbar Qavam al-Molk in that same year, which was found to be infested with it.[401] However, it would seem that the Guinea worm was already present in the water before 1800. According to a report from the late 1700s, the Bushehr bazaar well supplied with fruits and vegetables, but the water was very bad. "It will breed worms in the people's flesh several fathoms in length; when it is mixed with a spirituous liquor, or lime-juice, its quality is not so pernicious, for they have observed that it has a more malignant effect on the Lascars, who do not use strong liquors, than on the Europeans who drink them."[402] In 1890, de Windt still mentions its presence, but by 1920, the Guinea worm was not mentioned as a problem for Bushehr by the British military.[403] Even if it still had been

395. Merritt-Hawkes 1935, p. 6; "Malaria was this town's scourge and many fever-stricken people with chills were lying in shade spots in the streets." Böhme 1977, p. 251.

396. Administration Report 1933, p. 11; Trade Report 1920-21, pp. 1-2.

397. Administration Report 1936, p. 11; Idem, 1938, p. 11; Idem, 1939, p. 11.

398. Waring 1973, p. 10; Hollingberry 1976, p. 15; Rich 1839, p. 199; Mignan 1839, vol. 2, p. 140; Binning 1857, vol. 1, p. 148; Sa`adat 1390, p. 22.

399. Hamidi 1380, p. 565.

400. Administration Report 1894-95, p. 10.

401. Sadid al-Saltaneh 1371, p. 117. The water reservoir was built by a native merchant, according to Curzon 1892, vol. 1, p. 234. In 1889, the worm still infested the drinking water of Bushehr. De Vilmorin 1895, p. 347. The disease was locally known as *(reshteh-ye) peyuk*. Hamidi 1380, pp. 199-200.

402. Anonymous 1801, p. 174.

403. de Windt 1891, p. 216; Sa`adat 1390, pp. 22 (a problem in the past), 254; Government of India 1924, p. 99.

at that time, by 1940 the worm was certainly no longer present in Bushehr. However, it reappeared in August 1944; it was thought because the rainwater reservoirs had "never properly been filled with fresh water."[404]

Small-pox was endemic usually in early spring. People in general were not in favor of vaccination, even during an epidemic.[405] In 1902-03, small pox broke out during winter and many died.[406] In March 1906, there was a small outbreak of small-pox,[407] while in 1914 small pox affected nine persons. Quarantine was enforced and many children were vaccinated by the British Residency dispensary, where services were offered once a week to the public. There were 525 deaths, of which 262 were children.[408]

Cholera was another disease that occasionally ravaged the population of Bushehr. In 1821, there was a serious outbreak in many parts of Persia including in Bushehr. According to Fraser, some 10-12 persons died daily in August and many persons fled the town. The death rate increased to 20-30 daily in September. It was reported that more than 400 had died by mid-September when the epidemic stopped.[409] In 1851 and 1852, cholera was epidemic all over S. Persia; in August 1851 there were 30 deaths daily in Bushehr.[410] The epidemic disappeared in October leaving about 500 dead in its wake. Bushehr was again hit in 1869 as was the rest of Persia. The journalist Geary wrote, "The plague nearly emptied the town on its last visitation."[411] In 1870, Hojel, the physician of the British Residency blamed the lack of sanitation in Bushehr that it was "the home of one epidemic of the other like that of cholera in the fall of 1869 succeeded by a malignant form of small-pox, which killed as many as its predecessor. And before its ravages ceased, we are again visited by cholera and worse, there is a rumor that plague has broken on the coast 60 miles from here."[412] There was another outbreak of cholera, be it a small one, during 14-19 April and the last week of July 1871, when also there was an outbreak of small-pox in Bushehr. The maximum number of deaths reported per day was 45 and the daily average was 14-15.[413] In the summer of 1892 there was an outbreak of cholera on the Persian Gulf littoral, but Bushehr only had a few cases, although surrounded on all sides by cholera for a few months. This positive result was due to the fact that the local authorities in collaboration with Mr. Lobo, the apothecary of the British Residency took steps to (i) keep the Neydi and Bahman wells clean and protected; (ii) enforce quarantine

404. Lindberg 1955, p. 26; Political Diaries, vol. 16, p. 180.

405. Report 1920-21, pp. 1-2. In 1874, Dr. G. Waters, the Residency physician wrote: "My greatest disappointment in matters medical, since assuming charge of my present office,has been my inability to re-introduce vaccination in Bushire and its neighbourhood." FO 248/302, Annual Medical Report 1874, p. 8 (with details on his past and ongoing efforts to do so).

406. Administration Report 1902-1903, p. 1.

407. Administration Report 1905-1906, p. 18.

408. Trade Report 1913-14, pp. 6-7 ("About 80 corpses were moved to Kerbala after temporary burial for a minimum period of three years"). In 1906, sanitation authorities urged the governor-general of Fars to insist that cholera victims be not exhumed for at least one year and be transported for burial in Karbala. Administration Report 1905-1906, p. 19.

409. Fraser 1984, pp. 58, 65.

410. Lorimer 1915, vol. 1, p. 2052.

411. Geary 1878, vol. 1, p. 64.

412. NA, FO 248/271, Ass. Surgeon A. N. Hojel, Residency Surgeon to Pelly, 10/04/1870.

413. Administration Report 1889-90, pp.15, 17; Saldanha 1986, vol. 7/2, p. 7.

by sea and land; and (iii) establish a quarantine station on the "Jazira."[414] In August 1889, an outbreak of the disease was prevented by imposing a quarantine after a few cases had been identified.[415] Bushehr was again threatened by cholera in 1893 and at the urging of the British Residency the Persian government imposed a quarantine. Haji `Ali Dubashi, a port official, was most helpful in executing the quarantine.[416] In 1923 there was no cholera or other infectious diseases nor are any major outbreak reported thereafter.[417]

In 1911, the British consul reported that due to strict quarantine procedures in Bushehr, plague was unknown until then.[418] Unfortunately this positive statement is not borne out by the facts. For example, in 1832 the plague raged with such violence in Bushehr that over two months more than one-third of the inhabitants died. The plague lasted three months and many other Persian Gulf ports were depopulated.[419] When the plague broke out in March 1832 many inhabitants fled to neighboring villages such as Borazjan and Rudhilleh. Sheikh Naser, the acting governor, fled to one of his boats and it remained lying in the roads. Likewise, M. D. Blane, the British Resident fled to the island of Khark. On 10 May Mr. Blane received information from Mr. C.A.H. Tracy in Bushehr, who reported that at a certain time 100-200 persons per day had died. In the neighboring villages of Bushehr where its population had fled the same level of mortality was seen. Tracy estimated the total number of dead in Bushehr was half the population, although he reported that locals said that it amounted to 65%. On 13 April 1832, the governor of Bushehr, Sheikh Naser wrote to Blane that the plague was at an end and at his request people were returning. Those who were a little sick recovered after 2-3 days. Sheikh Naser estimated the number of corpses at 2,000, so that the stench in the streets was great; in each house there were one to four corpses. Therefore, he hired 100 men at 4 *tuman* each per day to bury the dead and to fumigate all houses. He expected that this would take two to three days. These men were not from Bushehr as the whole town was empty. Mr. Blane remarked that he thought that Sheikh Naser was a bit too optimistic, because the disease was spreading towards Shiraz and other parts of the Persian Gulf having already reached Kangan. On 10 May, Mr. C.A.H. Tracy reported that Sheikh Naser had done much to clean up town. However, many corpses were still unburied; of the 100 men hired on or about 12 April to bury them, all but four had died by that time. The six persons who had been left to guard the Residency all had died. As a result, it had been looted and all valuables were taken. Tracy wrote that Bushehr was a dying town; there were fresh cases of plague, but people recovered "as it seems to be now a milder form of the disease."[420]

Plague appeared again at the end of May 1899. At the end of August 1899 Bushehr was plague-free again. The plague was discovered on 29 May by the British Residency surgeon. His diagnosis was confirmed by the Russian physician. The Resident asked the government of India for medical assistance to put a plan in action to prevent its further

414. NA, FO 248/567, J.A. Crawford, Resident to Kargozar Bushehr, 15/12/1893. The *jazira* or island refers to the `Abbasak Island (see below).

415. Administration Report 1889-90, p. 9. For the history of "Cholera in Persia," see Idem, pp. 15-18.

416. Administration Report 1893-94, p. 11.

417. Trade Report 1922-23, p. 3.

418. Trade Report 1910-11, p. 6.

419. Kempthorne 1835, p. 283; Saldanha 1986, vol. 2, p. 308 (between about 10 March and about 26 June 1832).

420. Anonymous 1833, p. 34; Idem 1832-1833, p. 797. Both sources state that Blane stayed at Corgu, a small uninhabited island next to Khark, which is the more likely place for a refuge.

spread, if agreed to by the Persian authorities. Tehran was also informed, which authorized the acting governor of Bushehr to implement the proposed plan, which consisted of burning old clothes, exposing goods, detention in quarantine. Instead of doing so, he asked the local olama for their opinion, who rejected the plan. Stories circulated in town that the European doctors wanted to poison the natives. The acting governor informed Tehran that after examination it was found that there was no plague. This impending plan was opposed by the Moslem population that rioted against it at the end of July and he wanted clear orders from Tehran on this subject. The acting governor told a group of merchants at a prayer meeting that the government was pressured by foreign doctors and therefore, they should appeal to the Shah. Then, on 24 July the rabble started rioting. The alleged reason was the fact that the British physician had visited the house of a sayyed, whose wife had been infected by the disease. This examination of a disease in a Moslem household was unacceptable and the olama demanded that the authorities put a stop to this. Some unsavory characters demonstrated in front of the British Residency where they cut and destroyed some trees. "The people closed their shops, and assembled daily in the mosques, while they were harangued by the Mollas." The rioters were given food and supplies by the olama and Mohammad Sharif, a merchant, who spread the rumor that the Europeans wanted to examine the women and burn the dead. The reason for Mohammad Sharif's agitation was that his Trading Company had issued bank notes. Because this was an infringement of the rights of the Imperial Bank of Persia the British Minister pressured the Persian government to have these illegal notes withdrawn. Moreover, he had already a history with the British, who earlier had asked the governor to fine and imprison him, because of fraud. He had a good relationship with Prince Dabija, the Russian consul at Isfahan, who had instructed him to build a Russian Consulate at Bushehr. At the time of the plague, Prince Dabija visited Bushehr and refused to respect the quarantine procedure, claiming that there was no plague. By 3 August 1900 the tensions were reduced, helped by the threat of the governor to use force, if need be. As a result, the bazaar was open for business the next day. A disinfection machine was sent from India, which was only operational by the end of September. The governor only agreed to its use if there was not further unrest. It would be put in use on the quarantine island and it was expected to be operational in 1900. In October 1900 some of the ringleaders of the riots were bastinadoed at the demand of the British Resident, while others were expelled from the city.

To establish to truth of the matter, Tehran sent a Persian physician, Zeyn al-`Abedin Khan to Bushehr. After investigation he drew five conclusions: (i) the quarantine for arrivals by sea was selective, only Persians were detained, but neither Europeans nor ships' crews; (ii) several people died in quarantine (of diarrhea, broken ribs) and one man, also having died of diarrhea, was buried by his friends, who substituted another for him, without the quarantine physician finding out; (iii) one of the suspected cases of plague was probaby syphilis; (iv) the Russian physician considered the quarantine procedures inadequate; and (v) the Persians feared the European physicians because of the sanitary plan and therefore, brought them only ordinary cases of the not very ill. The British reacted to the first point by stating that they simply had followed the Venice Convention rules, whereby quarantine was relaxed for first and second-class passengers. It was agreed that these rules needed to be improved for Persian circumstances and that everybody should be treated alike.[421]

Table 1.9: Number of deaths due to the plague in Bushehr in 1899

In June 1899 there were	53 deaths
July	37
August	31
September	40
October	41
November	49
December	36
January	20
February	18

Source: Administration Report 1899-1900, pp. 2-3.

In 1904-05, due to strict quarantine procedures, Bushehr remained free of plague, while in the adjacent areas the disease raged and ravaged the population.[422] In April 1910, despite preventive measures, Bushehr was struck again by the plague, followed by a more severe outbreak in the spring of 1911. This led to the flight of people and thus had a depressing effect on trade. In 1910, 66 people died of the plague and 98 in 1911. The total mortality rate was 637 in 1910-11 as against 965 in the previous year, of which almost 25% were children. Containment of the disease was constrained by the refusal of householders to have their home inspected, when it was reported that there was an infected person in it.[423] The plague appeared again in February 1912 and spread as far as Kamarej and led to large scale flight of some 6,000 of Bushehr's inhabitants to Mohammerah, Basra and elsewhere. Entire families died of the plague. The authorities urged the inhabitants to inoculate themselves and 4,048 inoculations took place, which was much better than in the past (411 in 1911) and it was mostly very effective for that group. The epidemic lasted till June 1912, and the number of deaths was 729 or 75% of the reported cases, or a mortality of 3-4% of the total population.[424] Given the estimated population of Bushehr of 20,000 (25,000 for the island) such a mortality rate brought business to a standstill and over 8,000 people left between February-June. From April to May the bazaars were closed, and only life necessities were sold. Manual labor was unavailable and ships could hardly be unloaded. Plague also penetrated the villages 50 km inland. The general mortality was

421. Lorimer 1915, vol. 1, p. 2548; Administration Report 1899-1900, pp. 2-3; Hamidi 1378, pp. 52-56; Heravi 1372, p. 133; Sa`adat 1390, pp. 136-37 (writes that it was not a Russian, but Zeyn al-`Abedin Khan, a physician sent by the government, who disagreed with the British physician. His conclusion was contrary to unstated British objectives and as a result, the Persian physician was dismissed). According to the French traveler de Vilmorin, when in 1889 the British enforced the quarantine they allowed British ships to enter. De Vilmorin 1895, p. 350. For the relevant decision by the Public Health Committee in Tehran, see Appendix XIII. 5. For a detailed discussion of this issue, see Elgood 1951, pp. 524-26..

422. Administration Report 1904-1905, p. 2.

423. Trade Report 1910-11, p. 6; Political Diaries vol. 4, p. 95. For other mortality figures due to the 1911 plague as well as the number of deaths by location, see Sadid al-Saltaneh 1371, pp. 115-16 and Sa`adat 1390, pp. 173-74.

424. Trade Report 1911-12, p. 6; Administration Report 1912, p. 17, 34; Sa`adat 1390, p. 174.

398 adults and 201 children as against a total of 637 (1910-11) and 965 (1909-10).[425] The plague reappeared in April 1913, but in a mild form only, and there were only 30 cases of which 25 died.[426] These figures are only indicative of the gravity of the situation, because, as British physicians commented, there were "no statistics that would be of value are available to show the extent of the ravages of the diseases."[427]

1.10: Estimated total mortality and due to the plage in Bushehr (1899-1916)

Year	Plague	Other causes	Total deaths
1899-1900	-	408	408
1909-10	66	899	965
1910-11	98	539	637
1911-12	729	599	1328
1912-13	678	518	1196
1913-14	25	500	525
1914-15	-	436	436
1915-16	3	571	574
1916-17	-	1,149	1,149

At that time, the average death rate of Bushehr was estimated at 34 per month or 408 per year, given a population of about 20,000, or a death rate of 20 per mille. As there had been no census and not all deaths were reported this is, of course, an estimate. Administration Report 1899-1900, p. 2; Trade Report 1914-15, p. 4; Trade Report 1915-16, p. 5. The higher figure for 1916-17 is due to the heat that prevailed and the 5,000 temporary workers (poor peasants) that migrated to Bushehr for the unloading of ships at Basra. Trade Report 1916-17, p. 5; Trade Report 1917-18, p. 4.

There was no plague in 1914-15 and 1915-16, apart from a small outbreak on 5 April 1916, which was imported by five coolies who arrived by ship on 1 April. There were in total 10 cases and 3 deaths.[428] Thereafter, no cases of the plague occurring in Bushehr were reported. It was difficult to carry out preventive work, because when alerted that there was a case of plague, which could not be ignored, "householders strongly resented their houses being visited."[429]

In 1918-19, the population of Bushehr was also infested by the worldwide influenza pandemic, which was a disease unknown before. The epidemic started on 4 September in Bushehr and from there moved northwards (Shiraz 3 October). It led to great mortality, with whole families being wiped out. About 15,000 cases were reported of which some 2,000 died. Thousands fled the city in panic.[430]

In addition, at Bushehr, like in other parts of the Persian Gulf, people were afflicted by a psychic illness (*zar*) that was ascribed to spirit possession. Those possessed were locally known as *ahl-e hava*. This particular belief and its cure had been brought from East Africa

425. Trade Report 1911-12, p. 6; Sa`adat 1390, p. 174 (for different mortality figures).
426. Trade Report 1912-13, p. 12; Administration Report 1913, p. 34.
427. Trade Report 1920-21, p. 2.
428. Administration Report 1916 p. 10.
429. Administration Report 1910, p. 20.
430. Administration Report 1918, p. 9; Trade Report 1918-19, p. 2; George C. Kohn, *Encyclopedia of Plague and Pestilence*, New York, 2008, p. 299.

as an unintended side-effect of the importation of African slaves. The British refer to this practice in 1914, when they report that "Female superstition still requires the presence of the medicine-man, expert in casting out malicious Jinns."[431]

Quarantine service

Although epidemics such as cholera had regularly wrought havoc along the Persian littoral and its hinterland, it was not until 1893 that the Persian authorities for the first time instituted quarantine measures at Bushehr by sea in June and by land in August, according to Lorimer.[432] There had been cases of incidental quarantines such as on 10 July 1811, when the governor of Bushehr took the precaution to forbid any communication which two ships on the road, one of which, the *Malabar*, had come from Bahrain where cholera raged. When the ship, with its sick crew, sailed to Basra the governor banned any contact between his town and Basra, and later also with Masqat.[433] Another case occurred in 1876, when Captain Prideaux, the British Resident reported that at that time 15 days of quarantine had to be observed in case of passengers and cargo landing at Bushehr. However, the rules were not very well known, even to the British Resident. He had been under the impression that when a ship had received a bill of clean health from the Persian quarantine officers at "the quarantine station of Kusbah ul-Nussar" (Basra), that there was no need for further precaution. Since May 1876 a strict quarantine was maintained at Bushehr for any passengers and cargo coming from Basra. However, when on 18 June Prideaux asked the Persian authorities whether he might place cargo on the mail boat they said that he could to his great surprise. [434] Another case of an early quarantine occurred on 28 July 1890, when it became known that cholera had broken out in Basra. Sa`d al-Molk had made quarantine arrangements "on an island at 3 to 4 *farsakh* from the town," which remained in force for the time being.[435]

These early attempts were not applied systematically, as is clear from the discussion of the occurrence of cholera and plague in Bushehr (see above). However, all this changed as of June 1893. Also, at that time the wells were secured, and, as a result there were no deaths in Bushehr that year due to the cholera epidemic, while there were many on the Bushehr-Shiraz road. A next step was that on 20 June 1898, when Persia ratified the Convention of the 1894 Paris International Sanitary Conference. However, like Great Britain, Persia made a reservation with regard to the provisions concerning the Persian Gulf. On this and subsequent Sanitary Conferences there were differences of opinion in particular between Great Britain and France, whose differences later would also manifest themselves in the Persian Gulf. In 1904, for example, the French, on their own behalf, sent Dr. Faivre to study the sanitary and quarantine conditions in the Persian Gulf. As a result, the British felt that they should do a similar study. In February 1905, Dr. Theodore Thomson arrived, and thus, the two studies were but a continuation of the discussions held in 1903 at the Cholera Conference in Paris, and failed to bring agreement between the two sides.[436]

431. Report 1913-14, p. 1. For more information of *zar*, see Floor 2004 a, p. 57.
432. Lorimer 1915, vol. 1, p. 2525.
433. Rich 1839, pp. 199-201.
434. NA, FO 248/318, Captain W.J. Prideaux to Thomson, 08/06/1876.
435. Abbasi and Badi`i 1372, pp. 34-35.
436. Lorimer 1915, vol. 1, pp. 2525, 2528, 2542-43.

In 1896, the Persian government realized that it had to take serious steps with regard to quarantine regulations. First, a Persian agency was charged to apply these regulations. After lengthy discussions with the British it was decided to impose a 5-days quarantine for healthy ships arriving at Bushehr. Plague infected ships could neither land passenger nor goods, but an exception was made for the mail. Because the Persian agency was unable to satisfactory implement the quarantine rules, the Persian government delegated this task to the British Residency physician at Bushehr on 23 October 1896. At first, this caused some friction with the local authorities, who did not want to lose this important source of revenue.[437]

Under this new arrangement the Persian government was responsible for all sanitary matters along the littoral, while the medical officers implementing Persian policy were British, on loan from the government of India. There were sanitary stations at Mohammerah, Lengeh, Bandar Abbas, and Jask, while at Bushehr there was a large lazaret. The sanitary staff consisted of the British Residency surgeon as Chief Sanitary Officer, with one assistant and six assistant-surgeons. As of 1899, a Persian physician, Zeyn al-`Abedin Khan, was appointed to monitor the British sanitary authorities in the littoral. In 1900 he was replaced by Sadr al-Atibba, but in May 1901 he was withdrawn.[438] Whether successors were appointed has not been reported, but this seems likely.

Quarantine inspection took place on land or at sea on board of vessels wishing to enter the port. On land the quarantine post was outside the city. Ships with the plague had to carry a yellow flag; it took one hour to travel from the anchorage to Bushehr.[439] The British Residency surgeon was the port health officer, but enforcement of the quarantine rules was the responsibility of the Persian customs authorities. The quarantine station was on the `Abbasak island in Bushehr bay, as well as the 'hospital.'[440] Formerly, 10 days of quarantine were required for a ship coming from Karachi, but in early 1907 this period was cut in half. However, Bradley-Birt reported that for ships coming from Masqat, the passengers had to stay only 1.5 days on the quarantine island.[441] A German traveler characterized the quarantine island, where he had to stay for two days, as a desolate place.[442] According to Bradley-Birt, `Abbasabak, the quarantine island was Purgatory; it was a bare, desolate, and wind-swept piece of sand, with "a long, low bungalow, a group of huts, and a single palm-tree." It was not easy to get to the island, especially when the sea was choppy. Passengers had to jump from the steamer into a small sailing boat or *baghlah* at the right moment when the waves pushed it up. Arrived at the island passengers had to transfer from the *baghlah* to a very small rowing boat, which only had room for one passenger in addition to the two sailors. Arriving on the island, "one has to submit to be carried ashore clinging in an altogether uncertain and undignified manner round the necks of two sturdy Arab sailors." The quarantine station was a rough, hastily finished building and its staff consisted of two persons. For the Asian travelers there were huts and for Europeans the bungalow; there were no other buildings but an incinerator to destroy the clothes of the plague-stricken. During the cold season passengers suffered from bitter cold on the island and had to put on all their clothes to get some warmth. Finally, when the quarantine

437. Lorimer 1915, vol. 1, p. 2547; see appendix XIV.
438. Administration Report 1907-1908, p. 18; Lorimer 1915, vol. 1, pp. 2548-49.
439. Norden 1928, p. 45.
440. Lorimer 1915, vol. 2, pp. 349, 341.
441. Bradley-Birt 1910, p. 28.
442. von Tzschirner-Tzschirne 1918, p. 158.

period ended the ferry-boat arrived and took passengers to Bushehr for final inspection, where some were more equal than others. "For the white man the doctor's examination is a mere formality; for the Asiatic it is a little less perfunctory."[443]

Although the Persian authorities were satisfied with the manner in which the British Residency surgeon managed the quarantine regulations in his capacity as Chief Sanitary Officer on their behalf, foreign representatives in Tehran were not, or acted as if they were not. The cost borne by the Persian government was quite low and did not amount to more than £100 per month. This critical attitude by foreign powers the British ascribed to jealousy and it certainly seems that this was an aspect of the jockeying for power and influence in which European diplomats were engaged. This was part of the so-called Great Game that in actual reality was often a small-minded one. In 1903, Russia proposed that control of sanitary operations be transferred to the Customs Department. The latter already collected the sanitary fees and disbursed the funds allocated for sanitation by the Persian government. When some Customs officials actually tried to interfere with sanitary matters the British government lodged a complaint in Tehran. The Persian government replied that it did not want to change the existing arrangement, be it that it wanted to see an end to the differential treatment at Bushehr, real or perceived. Despite this, the French physician Dr. Brussière, who arrived in Bushehr in 1904, and who was in the employ of the Customs department, tried to interfere in sanitary matters. The director of the Customs department, among other intrusions, even went so far as to order vessels to be detained that the British sanitary official had given permission to leave. Although this interference clearly had been ordered by Tehran, after a strong protest from the British the Persian government instructed the Customs department not to interfere in sanitary matters.

However, because there was a difference of opinion in particular between France and Great Britain about the sanitary strategy to be followed, the differences aired in Europe were also played out in the Persian Gulf and the interference by Russia and the Customs department were but symptoms of those European differences of opinion. For example, every month, the Chief Sanitary Officer sent a report about the health situation in Bushehr to Tehran. The Sanitary Board, presided by the Shah's French physician Schneider tended to ignore or suppress recommendations made in this report, while pushing those submitted by the Bushehr-based French physician Dr. J.A. Bussière, which his British colleague considered to be irresponsible ones. The French were not the only ones who felt they had to challenge the British position, but of course, so did the Russians. Whereas France was an insignificant player, Russia and Great Britain were vying for control over Persia in all sectors of life, even though neither France nor Russia had any significant economic interests in the Persian Gulf. Nevertheless, on 21 November 1905, the Russian Consul-General Passek, accompanied by his Cossacks, went to visit the mail steamer, which was always in quarantine when in port, while it flew the quarantine flag. The British Residency surgeon, therefore, put the Russian consulate under quarantine, while Daryabegi, the governor asked Passek to explain himself. Meanwhile, passengers aboard complained about the unequal treatment, because they had to spend time on quarantine island, whereas the Russians went to Bushehr.[444]

---

443. Bradley 1910, pp. 28-34.

444. Administration Report 1905-1906, pp. 18-19; Lorimer 1915, vol. 1, p. 2550; Political Diaries, vol. 1, p. 219.

Quarantine and hospital building in 1939. Now the Abu'l-Fazl private health clinic.

On 6 March 1907, the Persian government adopted the 1903 Paris rules, reducing the quarantine period from 10 to 5 days. An international campaign waged against the quarantine system as practiced by British physicians on behalf of the Persian government induced the British government to make some concessions. The British, of course, ascribed this campaign as being due to jealousy by foreign governments and Persian nationalists. Henceforth, the British quarantine officers would fly the Persian instead of the British flag, while all correspondence and communication would be in Persian or French, instead of English. Finally, the Chief Sanitary Officer would report via the local Persian official to the President of the Sanitary Council in Tehran. The British hoped that this would steal some of their critics' thunder.[445]

In 1907, to strengthen the quarantine system, extra staff was added as well as the latest steam pressure disinfecting stoves. A Clayton apparatus for 'deritisation,' i.e. extermination of all rats aboard a vessel, was ordered. However, the quarantine buildings on Persian soil were all in a very bad condition. The Sanitary Council in Tehran was aware of this and promised to do something about it as soon as the country's financial situation permitted.[446] In 1908, the Germans also joined the chorus of critics when an agent of Wonckhaus visited a ship in the roads before the Health Officer's inspection, which was against the rules. Listemann, the German consul engaged in a useless letter writing campaign when informed of this error.[447] In 1915, Bushehr's quarantine station was thoroughly repaired. Nevertheless, by 1926, all quarantine buildings were considered to be generally unsuitable and in particular lacked the means of isolating and treating cases of sickness that might

445. Administration Report 1906-1907, p. 14.
446. Administration Report 1907-1908, p. 19.
447. Administration Report 1908, p. 8.

occur among those quarantined. Also, the Bowman disinfector at Bushehr needed to be overhauled and made operational again, which was done at British expense in 1927.[448]

1.11: Quarantine inspections at Bushehr 1907-1924

Year	Number of steamers	Number of crew aboard	Number of passengers aboard	Number of passengers for port	Total number of people inspected
1907/08	469 (incl. sail)	-	-	-	43,155
1908	281	20,145	11,643	-	31,788
1909	305	18,697	23,101	-	-
1910	323	23,715	21,551	4,398	-
1911	345	25,666	26,840	6,828	-
1912	386	28,296	43,941	3,096	-
1913	370	29,356	44,976	7,951	-
1914	317	25,396	29,112	5,705	-
1915	259	24,151	9,225	3,124	-
1916	212	18,120	15,582	2,368	-
1917	n.a.	n.a.	n.a.	n.a.	n.a.
1918	170	13,208	15,171	3,393	-
1920	293	26,341	71,881	13,514	-
1921	331	32,421	88,540	5,580	-
1922	319	38,921	95,195	5,721	-
1923	341	-	-	5,175	-
1924	355	34,553	41,043	3,661	-

Source: Administration Report 1906-1907, p. 14; Administration Report 1908, p. 12 (Aprl-Dec); Administration Report 1909, p. 17; Administration Report 1910, p. 20; Administration Report 1911, p. 28; Administration Report 1912, p. 34; Administration Report 1913, p. 35; Administration Report 1914, p. 13; Administration Report 1915, p. 10; Administration Report 1916 p. 10; Administration Report 1918, p. 9. Administration Report 1920, p. 8. Administration Report 1921, p. 9. Administration Report 1922, p. 9; Administration Report 1923, p. 14; Administration Report 1924, p. 10.

On 4 August 1928, the quarantine service was handed over to the Persian government, including the Persian staff and all material. The Persian staff consisted of: 1 chief quarantine medical officer, 2 quarantine medical officers and 12 quarantine *farrash*es; they had a motor dhow given by the Customs department to inspect vessels. Later that same year the staff was reduced to 1 chief quarantine medical officer, 1 quarantine medical officer and 6 quarantine *farrash*es.[449] In 1943 it was decided to build a new jetty for the quarantine station. In May 1945 it became clear that the cement and other materials that had been placed on `Abbasak island had been ruined by water. New funds had to be

448. Administration Report 1915, p. 10; Administration Report 1926, p. 6; Administration Report 1927, p. 8.

449. Administration Report 1928, p. 12. For a detailed discussion about the to and fros that led to the handing over of the quarantine service, see Elgood 1951, pp. 538-83.

requested to complete the jetty.[450] By 1947, quarantine regulations were still overseen by the port and quarantine medical officer appointed by the Ministry of Health.[451]

Medical capacity in Bushehr

In 1922, the British Resident reported that apart from the Residency dispensary maintained by the Indian government, "there is no government medical aid of any kind. The Residency surgeon and his staff therefore performed practically the whole of the medical work of Bushire."[452] This statement was not entirely true, because one could argue that the existence of a government public health official (*hafez al-sehhat*) constituted governmental medical aid. The function of such Persian public health officials was created in 1870. They were appointed in all major towns, where, applying the guidelines given to them, they had to prevent the import of cholera; they reported to the national board of public health (*majles-e hefz-e sehhat*). However, the practical impact of this unofficial institution whose members only occasionally met was more formal than real and served as a reporting agency rather than one that dispensed medical care.[453] This also held for the individual public health officials who often were not paid, and if they were it was irregular. Therefore, if they practiced medicine it was on a personal title rather than that of a public medical officer. For completeness' sake the arrival in 1897 of Drs. Marc and Oust, two Russian physicians, who came to Bushehr to study the plague has to be mentioned. Apart from sending reports to their government they treated patients free of charge during their short stay. In 1898, two other Russian doctors (Rodzewitz and Kornajevski) paid a visit to Bushehr and in December 1898 a Dr. Poschkowski arrived there. These visits, which according to the British were politically inspired fact-finding missions, were short and incidental and thus failed to have a lasting effect on the Bushehr public health situation.[454]

In addition to the Persian public health officers, there was between 1903 and 1913 a French army physician, who looked after the health of the French and Russian consuls and their staff as well as that of the staff of the Customs Department.[455] The first French physician was Dr. J.A. Bussière, who in 1908 left after five years of service; his successor was Dr. Abel Combier who arrived at the beginning of 1909.[456] In 1910 or thereabouts, he was replaced by Dr. Major Marzin, who left at the end of 1913. As he was not replaced a British physician henceforth took care of the staff of Russian and French consulates and that of the Customs Department.[457]

In addition to foreign governmental medical aid, there existed some private sector medical capacity in Bushehr. First and foremost, of course, there were the practioners of folk medicine such as herbalists (*`attar*), blood letters (*bad-keshi*; *salmani*) and bone-setters (*shekasteh-band*). Finally, there were a few Persian *hakims* or traditional physicians who

450. Political Diaries, vol. 16, p. 397.
451. NA, FO 371/15473.
452. Trade Report 1921-22, pp. 1-2.
453. Afkhami 2003, p. 200. In 1862, the government had appointed a *hakim-bashi* to Bushehr. However, no details are available about his status and tasks (see above Public Hygiene section).
454. Saldanha 1986, vol. 8/III, p. 2
455. Administration Report 1908, p. 7.
456. Administration Report 1909, p. 10.
457. Administration Report 1913, p. 6; Vadala 2536, p. 171 also only mentions these three physicians.

Sayyed `Abdol-Reza Hafez *al-Sehhat*

were trained in Galenic-based medical practice.[458] It is unknown how many of them there were, but their number must have been small. One of them was Sayyed `Abdol-Reza, who studied with Mir Sayyed `Ali and after his death succeeded him. Also, in 1896, he was the public health official of Bushehr, although the government had not fixed or paid him a salary as yet. According to Sadid al-Saltaneh, he treated most people free of charge. He knew English and was knowledgeable in literature.[459] Another traditional physician practicing in the first decade of the twentieth century was Mirza Mohammad `Ali Sadr al-Atebba.[460] In 1914, there were a "few medical practitioners, of whom only three employ European methods and drugs, the remainder remaining faithful to Avicenna and Galen."[461] In April 1925, at the governor' recommendation, a certain Haji Mirza Mohammad Javad was licensed to practice as "a Vaccinator. His qualification seems to be that he has worked for three years in Bombay as a dresser in a hospital and with Dr. Banaji, an ohpthalmist."[462] In the 1930s there were still a number of traditionally trained physicians working in Bushehr. In 1934, Merritt-Hawkes was invited to a family outing in Bushehr.

> The men were doctors and Sayids, a very paying combination I judged from the expensive carpet, the splendid gramophone and the whole silver ingot used to make each tea-glass holder. They belonged to a family that had been doctors for generations and were qualified for their job by heredity and not

---

458. On the various traditional medical practioners, see Floor 2004 a.
459. Sadid al-Saltaneh 1362, p. 12; Hamidi 1378, pp. 58, 238; Hamidi 1380, pp. 440-41.
460. Rusta'i 1382, vol. 2, p. 331; see further, Hamidi 1380, pp. 440-41.
461. Report 1913-14, p. 1. One of them was Dr. Bahrami, who, in 1910, had established a small laboratory in Bushehr. Hamidi 1378, p. 73.
462. Political Diaries vol. 7, p. 285.

> by usual academic training, but they were men of ability and knew how to wield the hypodermic needle as well as anyone who had returned from Europe.[463]

Apart from traditional Persian physicians, there was, until March 1931, the modern Indo-European Telegraph Department (IETD) dispensary at Rishahr where a British company physician only treated IETD staff, their families and dependents.[464] Finally, there were non-Persian physicians in private practice, one of whom was "Sub-Assistant Surgeon Jemadar Mohammad `Ali Najmi, I.M.D. (Retired)."[465] It has not been reported who dealt with dental issues in Bushehr. One may assume that traditional surgeons offered dental services, but there may have been a modern trained dentist by the 1930s, because in 1934, many people with teeth all covered with gold were seen in the streets.[466]

Prior to the opening of the British Residency dispensary, the population of Bushehr had no choice but to have recourse to the Galenic-trained physicians and to folk-medicine. The latter was similar to the kind of superstitious methods that also prevailed in the rest of the country.[467]

British Residency Dispensary

For many decades, the British Residency's physician had issued medical advice and medicines free of charge to the people of Bushehr and environs as part of official British policy. This policy came under fire in May/June 1862, when the *kargozar* or agent for foreign affairs, Mirza Mehdi, who had an adversarial attitude towards the British, prohibited all classes, rich and poor, to consult for medical assistance anybody but the local *hakim-bashi*, who had recently been appointed by Tehran. The British Resident was unable to obtain a copy of the document that spelled out this prohibition, but he learnt that it allegedly had been issued by the shah, was dated Ramadan 1278 (March 1862), and was addressed to the late prince-governor of Bushehr. It prohibited the application for medicine in general terms, but did not mention the Residency. The Resident was baffled by this measure, because everybody in Bushehr and environs was grateful for the medical care offered by the Residency. Whether officers, merchants, or leaders of both the Sunni and Shiite communities, they all owed their recovery from illness to the Residency physician. Especially in 1861, when there was an epidemic in town, the demand for medical services had been huge. The Resident learnt that the cause of this prohibition was the thwarting of Persian plans to interfere in Bahrain, for which Mirza Mehdi had been the point man, as well as his personal avarice. The ban created much irritation among the entire population. Towards the end of May 1862, when the Resident heard about the

---

463. Merritt-Hawkes 1935, p. 28.

464. Administration Report 1932, p. 11.

465. Administration Report 1931, p. 14. IMD is Indian Medical Department. There also was the Persian nurse Zayer Mohammad Najafi a.k.a Zar Mahad or Manu Hakim, who, after he had left his employment with the British hospital, established himself as a physician in town. For his and others like him, see Hamidi 1380, p. 617.

466. Merritt-Hawkes 1935, p. 7. The presence of a dentist in Bushehr is certain for 1945, see NA, FO 371/15473.

467. On the practice of medicine in nineteenth century Persia, see Floor 2004 a.

prohibition, he and Dr. Wood decided to treat it with contempt and continued offering gratis medical service. However, as of the beginning of June, spies were placed at the Residency and patients coming to the dispensary or to the house of Mr. Hayward, the medical assistant to Dr. Wood, were insulted and maltreated. After a formal protest and pressure from Tehran, the prohibition was ended some time in July 1862, which after all was not supported or sanctioned by the government in Tehran.[468]

However, before that happened patients and British Residency staff were harassed and molested. In early June 1862, Mr. Hayward, reported that Esma'il Zeylu, the *darugheh* (police chief) had come to tell him that it would be better not to give medicines anymore. Hayward told him that he only listened to his superiors. However, the next day the *darugheh* and two *farrash*es threatened people coming to the dispensary and forced them to go to the *hakim-bashi*. Fewer people came to the dispensary thereafter; those that came were arrested and taken by soldiers to Mirza Mehdi; others were threatened with a beating.[469] The harassment continued throughout the month of June, and visitors, whether male or female, were insulted, threatened with violence, and even sometimes were the victim of money extortion.[470]

As of 1873, the British had what they classified as a second-class dispensary at Bushehr.[471] The Residency physician was not very pleased with his working conditions. He wrote:

> The want of a place properly adapted for the systematic treatment of the seriously sick indoor daily thwarts my endeavours to put in practice those restorative measures which the nature of may ailments imperatively requires. At present there isonly a small apartment available for medical purposes, in which there is scarcely room enough to move about when half a dozen people are present awaiting their turn to be examined with a view to treatment, and as regards operative operative interference it is utterly impossible from want of space excepting very minor operations indeed, such as the extracting of a tooth or the opening of an abcess.
>
> Now to obviate the difficulty above described I would suggest that a small hospital capable of accommodating six inmates be built with the requite appurtenances. A small institution of this sort could, I have been advised, be maintained at an expenditure of one hundred rupees per mensem, and for this trifling consideration, taking fourteen days as the average period of residence in hospital, medical aid of the most material and important nature might thus be accorded to no less than one hundred and fifty-six individuals in the course of one year, who under existing circumstances are entirely excluded from a surgical operation. The persons I refer to are generally residents of huts

---

468. NA, FO 248/206, Capt. Disbrowe, officiating Resident to Alison, 12/06/1862.

469. NA, FO 248/206, Mr. Hayward's diary (Persian text).

470. NA, FO 248/206, Mr. Hayward's diary.

471. This classification of dispensaries was administrative and financial in nature. The first two classes were funded and managed by the government of India. Whereas the first class dispensary was open to all comers, those of the second class only served a special section of the public, in this particular case the staff of the British Residency and the population of Bushehr. Government of India, *Statistics of British India, Part V. Public Health*. Calcutta, 1906, p. 36.

of very limited compass, while some have no roof to shelter them whatever, and all have not the necessary to attendance at command.[472]

Despite the cramped working conditions, the dispensary was a great success among the population, not only because it was the only modern medical facility in town, but its services were also gratis to the poor. "This boon is much prized by the natives, and if there was an arrangement for treatment of indoor patients, the results would be still more satisfactory than at present."[473] As a result, be it after initial reluctance about the Ferangis bearing gifts, the number of patients increased steadily (see Table 1.12). The statistics show that the largest daily attendance took place during the height of the hottest weather, i.e., June, July, and August.[474] Many of the patients were and continued to be women as well as children, whose numbers were also on the rise as indicated by the data available.[475] Bushehr, with 24,000 inhabitants around 1920,[476] had a much higher attendance at its dispensary that those in Bandar Abbas or Lengeh with a similar population size, probably due to the fact that people were longer accustomed to its service.[477]

1.12: Out- and in-patients and operations in the Bushehr dispensary-hospital (1873-1928).

Year	Total	Out-pa-tients	In-patients	In-patients operations	Total operations
1873-74	19,056	19,056	-	-	-
1874-75	13,672	13,672	-	-	-
1879-80	7,022	7,022	-	-	-
1898-99	6,418	6,418	-	-	395
1899-1900	5,026	5,026	-	-	315
1900-01	8,050	8,050	-	-	525
1907-08	13,393	13,254	139	69	609
1908	8,821	8,734	87	-	476
1909	16,581	16,422	59	-	589
1910	13,094	13,045	49	-	389
1911	13,470	13,397	73	-	599
1912	13,747	13,716	31	-	589
1913	15,155	15,009	146	-	552
1914	13,295	13,190	105	-	636
1915	14,667	14,537	140	-	n.a.
1916	15,575	15,520	55	-	639
1918	14,759	14,696	63	63	583

472. FO 248/ 302, Annual Medical Report 1874 by Dr. G. Waters, p. 5.

473. "It is the only place for free treatment in Bushire," Administration Report 1914, p. 12; Administration Report 1873-74, p. 7; Sadid al-Saltaneh 1371, p. 38.

474. Administration Report 1907-08, p. 19.

475. Administration Report 1914, p. 12; Idem, 1913, p. 34. "We found the doctor busy considering prescribing for and dosing a number of patients, among whom were a great many women and children." Cursetjee 2001, p. 114.

476. Administration Report 1919, p. 10.

477. Also, the service there had begun in 1907, see Floor 2010, p. 23 and 2011 a, p. 43.

Year	Total	Out-patients	In-patients	In-patients operations	Total operations
1919	12,764	12,711	53	n.a.	n.a.
1920	12,374	12,302	72	69	709
1921	11,453	11,365	88	-	614
1922	13,571	13,461	110	-	945
1923	10,912	10,766	148	146	664
1924	18,852	18,747	105	94	1,169
1925	42,177	42,030	147	119	1,649
1926	59,198	59,056	142	135	2,263
1927	47,454	47,298	156	87	1,828
1928	40,308	40,160	148	n.a.	n.a.

Source: IOR/V/24/2639, Medical Report on Bushire ending 21 March 1875, p. 1 (in 1873-74 of the total 3,432 admissions were from fever, one year later that figure was 2,591); Government of India, Report on the Administration of the Bombay Presidency for the year 1879-80, pp. cclx-cclxi; Administration Report 1898-99, p. 15; Idem, 1899-1900, p. 11; Idem, 1900-1901, p. 11; Idem, 1907-08, p. 19; Idem, 1908, p. 12; Idem, 1909, p. 17; Idem, 1910, p. 20; Idem, 1912, p. 43; Idem, 1913, p. 34; Idem, 1914, p. 12; Idem, 1915, p. 10; Idem, 1916, p. 10; Idem, 1918, p. 8; Idem, 1919, p. 10; Idem, 1920, p. 7; Idem, 1921, p. 9; Idem, 1922, p. 9; Idem, 1923, p. 14; Idem, 1924, p. 8; Idem, 1925, p. 10; Idem, 1926, p. 6; Ibid, 1927, p. 7; Ibid, p.10.

In 1907, the dispensary was referred to as a hospital for the first time,[478] and usually thereafter as the hospital-dispensary and as of 1922 as the Bushehr Civil Hospital or Bushehr Residency Dispensary and Charitable Hospital.[479] The qualification of hospital was determined by the fact that as of 1907 in-patients were treated and what was qualified as major operations could be and were performed (e.g. lithotomy, removal of urethral calculus -i.e., removal of stones). Minor operations were mainly the extraction of the teeth, evacuation of abscess and removal of wax.[480] The most modern methods and treatments were introduced as soon as these became available. For example, with some pride, the Political Agent reported the "Successful treatment of leprosy cases by means of the new Nastine treatment inaugurated by Professor Deycke Pasha."[481]

1.13: Male, female and child patients visiting the Bushehr dispensary (1899-1901).

Year	Total	Daily attendance	Men	Women	Children
1898-99	6,418	58.5	2,849	1,959	1,610
1899-1900	5,026	27.7	2,266	1,652	1,108
1900-01	9,050	43.7	3,465	3,470	2,115

Source: Administration Report 1898-99, p. 15; Idem, 1899-1900, p. 11; Idem, 1900-1901, p. 9.

478. Administration Report 1907-08, p. 19; Sa`adat 1390, p. 23. It was situated on the eastern shore of the island of `Abbasak. Lorimer 1915, vol. 2, p. 341.

479. Administration Report 1922, p. 9; Idem, 1925, p. 10; Nura'i 1385, p. 163 (*mariz-khaneh* in June 1914). Locally, people referred to the hospital as *espital*. Hamidi 1380, p. 75.

480. Administration Report 1898-99, pp. 15-20.

481. Administration Report 1908, p. 12.

The Bushehr dispensary had so much success that in 1908 it was reported that "The hospital has been open the whole twelve months under report. Owing to the gradually increasing attendance the rooms hitherto occupied by the dispensary in the Residency building having become too small for requirements, and the congregation of patients in the Residency court-yard a source of considerable inconvenience, the Government of India were pleased to sanction the renting of a capacious house next door to the town Residency and the hospital and dispensary were moved in."[482] The move made in 1912 to other premises was in hindsight not a good one, for although the building was well situated it "was poorly adapted for taking-in patients," which made the work for the medical staff difficult. Also, after complaints about subordinate staff these were all changed. Such a move was also important as the number of Moslem and Jewish women coming to the dispensary was large.[483] In 1917, Cursetjee visited "Dr. Hudson in his dispensary which is located on the first floor of a rickety house on the sea-face, and which we had to climb up over a flight of narrow, portentously steep and dirty steps."[484] Given this description of the dispensary, it is understandable that the British Resident wrote: "The provision for a decent hospital for Bushire is much to be desired and had been mooted by a few leading members of the community, but it seems desirable it take the form of a development of the existing Residency Dispensary rather than that the latter should suffer or be eclipsed in any way by an independently conducted institution."[485] One of the main problems of the new location was that the building, located next to the Residency, was owned by Mo`in al-Tojjar, who did not maintain it and therefore, it being old, dirty and in disrepair and only having small rooms, which made operations difficult, the medical staff considered that they needed better housing soon.

> A small fund, accumulated by contributions of some of the chief habitants of Bushire, has for some time been destined by them to go towards the provision of a good hospital, and until recently it appeared as if the intention was that the new hospital should be run by Persians. A counter-proposal with some considerable authority to back it is to effect that funds raised locally to assist in the building of a new hospital on a site to be granted free by its proprietor. The hope has been expressed that the Government of India would be good enough to permit the Staff of the Residency Dispensary to run the new Hospital intended to replace it, and that further the Government of India might possibly assist in the expense of building the hospital. There is little

482. Administration Report 1907-08, p. 19.

483. Administration Report 1913, p. 34; Trade Report 1921-22, p. 1. In July 1911, Moses Khan, the Armenian deputy-chief of Customs in Bushehr proposed to the governor, with the support of the local merchants, to levy 2 *shahis* per imported package. He estimated that this would yield 300 *tumans* per month, which amount was to be used for the maintainance of a hospital which Sayyed Mohammad Reza, a wealthy local merchant, had promised to build. Moses Khan also suggested to buy a condensor for the quarantine service, which responsibility this Persian hospital also could assume. The governor collected 9,000 *tumans* to that end and the municipality borrowed 16,000 *tumans* from the IBP on condition that local merchants would guarantee the balance needed. The hospital was not built, but the financing arrangement was retained and used to support the British dispensary. Political Diaries vol. 4, p. 410.

484. Cursetjee 2001, p. 114.

485. Administration Report 1913, p. 34.

> doubt that it will be a considerable time before the local efforts, if united, will suffice to build and maintain a good hospital.[486]

Dispensary Becomes Charitable Hospital

According to Denis Wright, a new hospital was established in 1916 with financial help from local merchants,[487] which is incorrect. Indeed such a plan for a hospital and a free dispensary was initiated many years ago, but its realization was delayed by the Great War.[488] He may have referred to the activities in that year by Mr. Chick, vice-consul and Major McPherson, the Residency Surgeon to start collecting funds from Persian and British sources for the construction of the hospital. Major McPherson proposed to buy the building from Mo`in al-Tojjar and to build a proper hospital, where he could safely operate patients and keep them in wards. Chick then proposed to collect money from British companies trading with Persia and from Persian merchants, because the main beneficiaries would be the people of Bushehr. He drafted an appeal (see appendix VIII) which had the following result:

1.14: Contributors to the cost of the construction of the hospital

Name contributor	*Tumans*	£	Rupees
BISNC, Bombay			4,500
Turner, Morrison & Co. Bombay-Persia Line			1,500
Turner, Morrison & Co. Arabian Steamers Company			1,000
Persian Gulf Steam Navigation Company, Bombay			1,000
Sir P. Z. Cox, Political Resident			500
Colonel Trevor, Deputy Political Resident			500
Sir P. M. Sykes			400
Some 20 other British individuals, Bushehr, India			1,826
Ziegler and Company, Manchester			1,000
E.D. Sassoon and Company, Bombay			1,000
Gray Paul and Company, Basra and Bushehr			1,000
Haji `Ali Akbar and Sons, Manchester			1,000
A. A. and A. Gorji, Bombay			1,000
Other merchants in India, Indians and Iraqis	470		1,200

486. Administration Report 1914, p. 12. For a short bio of Mo`in al-Tojjar, see Hamidi 1380, p. 170.

487. Wright 2001, p. 127. Merchants had already started to contribute from May/June 1913 by collecting from all goods coming from the interior 1 *shahi* per package (*naqleh*) and 1 *qran* per weight difference. By October they had already collected 1,000 *tumans*. Sadid al-Saltaneh 1371, p. 113. This was done at the suggestion of Moses Khan and the permission of the governor. It was expected to amount to 300 *tumans* per year and to serve to pay for the maintenance of the hospital that Sayyed Mohammad Reza wanted to build. FO 248/1033, Political Diary for July 1911, p. 12 (item 712).

488. In 1915, a house was rented and transformed into a British General Hospital with 66 beds (officers 23; ranks 41); another house was rented and turned into an Indian General Hospital with 182 beds. Huts and tents were erected nearby to accommodate resp. 50 and 404 patients. Two additional houses accommodated physicians and nurses. Government of India 1924, p. 51.

Name contributor	*Tumans*	£	Rupees
H.C. Dixon, Manchester		200	
Anglo-Persian Oil Company, London		100	
David Sassoon and Company, London		50	
Imperial Bank of Persia	750		
Assigned by the dept. Pol. Resident with approval of Govt. of India			11,700
Total	1,220	350	29,126

Source: IOR/L/PS/11/182

From Persian merchants 7,793 *tumans* was collected by Messrs. Chick, McPherson, the Residency's dragoman and the chief of the Municipality, who, night after night, called on the merchants to ask them to contribute. Daryabegi supported the activity, called several meetings and sent out a circular appeal asking merchants to give money to this initiative. Sheikh Khaz`al of Mohammerah donated 1,000 *tumans* and two Persian notables from Bandar Abbas and Lengeh gave Rs2,000. The merchant community of Bushehr further contributed 429 *tumans* and Rs13,500, the total collected by the voluntary 1 *shahi* fee per package imported between 1913 and 1915 with a view to build a hospital with the proceeds. By the end of 1918, an additional amount of 1,075 *tumans* and Rs200 had been collected, so that total sum collected from local Persian sources amounted to 10,297 *tumans* and Rs15,700. The Rs11,700 contributed by the government of India was a fund made available to the deputy Resident for charitable purposes.[489]

In 1917/18, a founding committee was established, which bought the land and premises from Mo`in al-Tojjar for 5,000 *tumans*, of which he donated 1,000 *tumans* for the construction of the hospital. On 30 January 1918, both Persian and British founders and contributors had a general meeting, which decided that the deed of sale of the land bought for the hospital would be transferred to a committe of two Persians and two Brits, as follows:

> In accordance with a Power of Attorney executed by Haji Mu`in-ut-Tujjar, Haji Muhammad Baqir Behbehani is to draw up a legal deed of sale of the two houses known as 'Kuzeh-Kanani' in the name of sale of the founders of the hospital, and the founders of the hospital are then to transfer the deed of sale to four persons, of whom is one the British Consul-General and the second the Residency Surgeon and (the other) two chosen from two of the founders deemed suitable (by the founders).

The four-man committee (two Persians, two Brits) formally was in charge of the construction and management of the hospital, although it hardly functioned after the completion of the hospital, while the IBP manager was appointed honorary treasurer of the hospital.[490]

---

489. IOR/L/PS/11/182.

490. IOR/L/PS/11/182; Elgood 1951, p. 548.

The deputy Resident further asked the government of India to give a grant of Rs30,000 for the hospital building and a grant of medical equipment of Rs16,000. In January 1920, already some Rs97,000 had been collected in Bushehr to finance the initial cost, while a continuation of a voluntary 1-*shahi* fee per imported package, paid by Persian and British merchants, was expected to yield Rs500/month. With these funds it was proposed to build a hospital with two small rooms for European patients, 35 beds for Persian male patients, a good operating theater, a good dispensary, and quarters for a nurse. It was suggested to start construction with the available funds and to add the upper storey when additional funds came available. Funds permitting, it was also intended to build "a separate women's ward under strict purdah conditions." Further that the existing dispensary and its staff would form the nucleus of the new hospital and that the annual grant of Rs3,400 to the Bushehr dispensary would be continued, given rising cost. On 9 September 1920, the government of India decided to give a grant of Rs15,000 to the building fund, a Rs15,000 grant for medical equipment and an annual grant of Rs1,500 for the hospital's maintenance, provided that the remaining funds to build the hosptal were raised locally within a resonable time. Also, it was expected that the hospital accommodation would be made available to its servants. The annual grant of Rs3,400 for the separately operating dispensary was continued. The funding was not without self-interest, for the government of India saw the hospital as a means to maintain influence among the population, while the annual maintenance grant gave it the means to ensure that the Residency Surgeon would be in charge of the hospital.[491]

It was only by the end of 1920 that "work had started by the residency mason and under the supervision of the British Executive Engineer for the Gulf Ports."[492] It was expected that in 1922, the dispensary would move to better place; therefore, the old place was "demolished and is being reconstructed on a better and more sanitary basis."[493] The first storey was almost complete by September 1921.[494] It was quite an improvement on the present building where the Residency surgeon carried on his work under adverse conditions.[495] In 1922 it was reported that "The work on the new Charitable Hospital, built by public subscription, was practically complete by the end of the year. The equipment still remains to be purchased. It is hoped that it may be opened during the next year,"[496] which indeed it was.

> The new hospital was occupied in April 1923. Its design is a compromise between what is needed for a hospital on the one hand and local Persian ideas of architecture coupled with insufficiency of funds on the other. As a result, when occupied, it lacked electric light, a water-supply, cookhouses, quarters for staff, and a sanitary and drainage system. Electric light has been installed, two engines purchased and, thanks to the Anglo-Persian Oil Company, a free supply of kerosene oil and petrol for power. A proper drain has been made into the sea, latrines constructed and a water-tank on the roof for finishing

491. IOR/L/PS/11/182, Finance Department to Secretary of State for India, Simla, 09/09/1921.
492. Trade Report 1920-21, p. 1.
493. Administration Report 1920, p. 7.
494. Trade Report 1920-21, p. ii.
495. Trade Report 1921-22, p. 1; also Trade Report 1922-23, p. 3.
496. Administration Report 1922, p. 9.

> purposes supplied by an automatic electric pump from a well, is in course of erection. A large 'Ab-ambar' has been constructed to be connected by a semi-rotary hand pump to another tank on the roof for the supply of water to the operation theatre and dispensary. But until the quarters of the staff have been built the hospital can only be considered to be an 'outdoor' dispensary.[497]

The facilities were still insufficient to receive in-patients. The hospital, therefore, continued to operate as dispensary, because much equipment was still lacking as was the chief medical officer.[498] By the end of 1925, shortages were overcome and the Bushehr Residency Dispensary and Charitable Hospital was fully operational. Nevertheless, there were still problems, because the great demand by outpatients hampered the extension of in-patient work.[499] The work was still not optimal, because facilities for proper in-patient care were lacking, in particular suitable accommodation for nursing staff, if such personnel were available, which they were not.[500]

It was not easy to run a hospital, for apart from the medical problems there were financial ones, because expenses tended to be higher than receipts, at least for the years that published data are available. In 1926, the budget deficit was due to the expansion of the out-patient attendances, despite the fact that in that March the hospital benefited from the stores transferred from the Indian Military Hospital that was closed when the Punjab regiment departed from Bushehr and was not replaced. This was not the only subsidy that the hospital received, for what is not shown in the tables is "the Contract Block Grant of the Residency Budget, being accounted for by the Residency and expended on salaries, and medicines and dressings received from the Medical Store Depot Bombay."[501]

1.15: Hospital Receipts (1925-28)

	1925		**1926**		**1927**	**1928**
	Qrans	Rupees	*Qrans*	Rupees	*Qrans*	*Qrans*
Contributions from Govt. of India and Residency	-	1,485	2,015	1,860	7,801	5,698
Contribution of APOC and Customs Dept.	4,750	-	6,600	-	6,500	5,999
Proceeds of voluntary one *shahi* tax	16,098	-	14,587	-	12,798	10,339
Sale of medicines	550	152	545	9	1,229	66
Miscellaneous	1,946	500	2,574	-	2,042	-
Total	23,324	2,137	26,321	1,669	30,730	22,302

Source: Administration Report 1926, p. 5; Administration Report 1927, p. 6; Administration Report 1928, p. 11.

497. Administration Report 1923, p. 14. It was nevertheless, considered to be "quite an improvement on the present building where the residency surgeon carried on his work under adverse conditions." Report 1921-22, p. 1
498. Administration Report 1924, p. 8.
499. Administration Report 1925, p. 10.
500. Administration Report 1926, p. 5.
501. Administration Report 1926, p. 5.

The most important source of income was that of the voluntary 1-*shahi* fee, which was an uncertain source of income, because this not only depended on the goodwill of the merchants, but also on how well their business and trade in general performed. This is clear from the downward trend of this revenue, which in 1925 still represented some 69% of total receipts, but only 46% in 1928 (Table 1.15). Most of the expenditures was represented by the salaries of the European medical staff (ca. 30-40%) and medicines (ca. 30%), which were imported from Europe and bought in the bazaar.[502] It was the hospital's intention to have a balanced budget in the future.

1.16: Hospital Expenditures (1925-28)

	1925		**1926**		**1927**	**1928**
	Qrans	Rupees	*Qrans*	Rupees	*Qrans*	*Qrans*
On medicine and dressings	21,744	402	22,029	28	15,210	11,512
On equipment	12,702	2,020	623	-	-	-
On electric light and telephone	2,092	206	952	556	1,903	3,246
Petty expenses	7,065	228	5,357	-	3,872	-
On stationary	1,092	-	463	-	45	-
On salaries	2,878	1,750	4,159	1680	12,918	13,202
Miscellaneous	1,944	-	389	-	1,023	1,887
Dieting of patients	2,371	-	5,985	-	2,432	1,644
Repairs and maintenance	50	-	263	-	394	1,529
Contingencies	-	-	-	-	-	2,971
Total	51,938	4,606	40,220	2,264	37,797	35,991

Source: Administration Report 1926, p. 5; Administration Report 1927, p. 6; Administration Report 1928, p. 11.

In 1927, the hospital faced a larger number of in-patients, but it was still constrained by inadequate facilities. Expenditures (37,797 *qrans*) were still higher than receipts (30,370 *qrans*), but the objective remained to cut cost and assure a stable financial position.[503] In 1929, expenditures again exceeded receipts which was due to the fact that in September the Customs Department cancelled its contribution, the 1-*shahi* voluntary tax, which was three months in arrears, averaging about 110 *tumans* per month. Also, there was a slight drop in the number of patients treated, because as of September the medical care of the Customs Department, Post & Telegraph Department, and the Finance Department was taken over by the Persian chief quarantine medical officer.[504]

502. Administration Report 1899-1900, p. 15.
503. Administration Report 1927, p. 6.
504. Administration Report 1928, pp. 10-11.

Hospital Becomes Persian

In 1929, as indicated above, significant changes took place as to the status of the Charitable Hospital. On 9 February the British Residency Dispensary was removed from the hospital to the Residency compound. This move was due to the fact that in September 1928, `Abdollah Khan Monajjami, the head of the finance department (*ra'is-e maliyeh*), who was acting governor of Bushehr at that time, informed the Residency Surgeon that the Charitable Hospital had to be handed over to the Persian authorities.[505] The British authorities pointed out that the funding for the establishment and maintenance of the hospital had mainly come from British sources, while "in addition to this contribution the Government of India allows the hospital to benefit gratis by the services of the Residency Surgeon, the Sub-assistant surgeon, compounder, dressers, sweepers, etc. whose salaries are all paid by that Government." At the same time the Persian government had contributed nothing. Also, the deed of the hospital was held in trust by the 4-man committee created by the hospital founders, so that legally the British government could not change the status of the hospital.[506] On 2 December 1928, the Resident reported to New Delhi that according to the Residency Surgeon continuation of the hospital was unimportant from a professional point of view. The cases he and his staff saw were insufficient to keep their professional know-how up-to-date. Also, 90% of the patients were Persians, while the remaining 10% (mostly Indians) would be better served by the re-establishment of a small hospital in the old Residency building. Because the cavalry guard had left their barracks were empty where at little cost a dispensary and a four-bed ward could be prepared. Moreover, with the expected withdrawal of the contributions of the various Persian government institutions the hospital would be unable to continue to function anyway. Therefore, it was better to each party go separate ways, which was a better and financially viable alternative. Therefore, the Resident proposed to inform the Persian government immediately of the British withdrawal from the hospital.[507]

And indeed, the Persian authorities were not interested in legalistic and other arguments to maintain the status quo. After all, the decision to demand the transfer of the hospital was a political one, based on national pride and the desire to rely as little as possible on foreigners, in particular the British. As the Resident expected, to put some pressure behind Persian government's 'suggestion', the Customs Department shortly thereafter withdrew its financial contribution to the hospital. It further instructed its employees henceforth to go to a dispensary that had been opened within the Customs Department and which was operated by Persian physicians. Soon thereafter the Post Office and the Finance Department likewise withdrew their financial contributions and their sick. The collection of the so-called one *shahi* voluntary fee, which represented some 50 per cent. of the Hospital's income (see above), had systematically been underperforming for some time and it was not paid at all during the last quarter of 1928. It was clear to the British authorities that all these measures were aimed at bankrupting the hospital and thus embarrass the British. As a result, the British government decided to sever its relationship with the Charitable Hospital on 9 February 1929, a relationship that had lasted some 60 years. The medical responsibility was immediately transferred to Dr. Bahrami, the Persian chief quarantine medical officer, who, assisted by Dr. `Ali Khan carried out the medical work.

505. Administration Report 1929, p. 8. For a detailed discussion of this issue, see Elgood 1951, chapter XIX.
506. IOR/L/PS/11/182, R.C. Parr, Britsh Legation to Taqi Esfandiary, Tehran, 12/10/1923.
507. IOR/L/PS/11/182. Johnston to New Delhi, 02/12/1928.

The British government divided all medical supplies and surgical equipment in half, one part of which was moved to the Residency dispensary. As a result the dispensary's operating room equipment was incomplete and serious cases could not be dealt with.[508]

Despite the separation of the two medical establishments, there was a concern among the Persian authorities about the capacity of the now Persian hospital to sustain its level of previous quality service. During a visit made in January 1930 at the request of the governor of Bushehr, the British Residency surgeon noted that "the Hospital was not conspiciously clean and that Dr. `Ali Khan's learning was not of a very high order, in fact not even of mediocre standards."[509] The same held for his chief, Dr. `Abol-Qasem Bahrami, who was described as a pleasant person, but his medical qualifications were not immediately apparent. He was more interested in bacteriology than in operations, which he seldom did, and in serious cases he referred people to the British Residency or the IETD doctors.[510]

Despite this reduced level of service at the hospital, the Persian authorities expanded the capacity of medical services at Bushehr via the *Red Lion and Sun Society*, which had been established in 1928 by the governor and was managed by Dr. Bahrami, the Health and Chief Quarantine Medical Officer. In 1930, the Society bought the old Turkish consulate and turned it into a maternity hospital. It was also active outside Bushehr in that the Society gave 5,000 francs to France for people in the inundated areas of the Seine and another sum to earthquake victims of the ruined Demavand villages.[511]

Meanwhile, the British received negative reports about the medical service offered at the hospital. A Persian patient, who came to the British Residency Dispensary, who had been to the hospital for treatment, "reported that there are no medicines available with the exception of Eno's fruit salts locally purchased which is issued to all and sundry, one teaspoonful at a time."[512] Another reported that if any more elaborate treatment was required, "a prescription is written which, on presentation at a local pharmacy, is made up on payment of a sum of money. It is also stated that Bahrami, the head of the Charitable dispensary staff, is more than part owner of this pharmacy. He and his staff are genuine apostles of the hypodermic syringe and cheap German ampoule, with which the bazaar is flooded." This led to misuse where patients even died (after repeated injections with strychnine and caffeine) or suffered bad side effects (ruptured spleen, acute arthritis).[513] In 1931 there were persistent complaints about the hospital, and the inadequacy of treatment by the new physician, Dr. Muniri and his staff. "The municipality are so dissatisfied that they have debated opening a municipal dispensary on the grounds that no medicines are to be had at the Charitable Hospital." The municipality also considered hiring part-time "Sub-Assistant Surgeon Jemadar Mohammad `Ali Najmi, I.M.D. (Retired),"

---

508. Administration Report 1929, p. 8; IOR/L/PS/11/182.

509. Administration Report 1929, p. 8.

510. Administration Report 1929, p. 3.

511. Administration Report 1930, p. 4.

512. Invented in the 1850s by James Crossley Eno of Newcastle, Fruit Salt sold like hotcakes to sailors looking for something to keep them healthy on long journeys. The product is still available today; it sells in vast quantities worldwide as a popular anti-acid and a reliever of bloatedness, upset stomach, indigestion and heartburn that provides immediate relief from gas and acidity and is without known side effects. It is much used in Indian cooking. It contains sodium bicarbonate, citric acid and sodium carbonate.

513. Administration Report 1930, p. 12.

who had begun a private practice in Bushehr. However, the anti-foreign elements in the municipal council were against hiring a foreigner. "Considering the present conditions of medical education in Persia it is not understood from where the nationalist elements in the Baladieh [municipality] consider they would get anyone more satisfactory than Muniri and it is probable that the proposal will come to nought."[514]

The replacement of Dr. Bahrami by Dr. Muniri as Quarantine and Health officer on 18 February 1931 did not bring the hoped for change in the hospital's performance. One potentially positive change was that Dr. Muniri's wife held a French diploma in midwifery. She took charge of the *Shahdokht Maternity Hospital* for some time at 80 *tumans* per month. In April 1931, she began a glass of ten girls with an elementary school diploma training them in "midwivery and treatment of female cases."[515] However, in 1932, "General Coulonger, the French Director-General of the Persian Medical Service, visited Bushire in the early summer and was shewn around the Dispensary. For the period of his visit, the twenty beds of the Bushire Charitable Hospital were filled by twenty reluctant 'patients' who were paid Rials 3 per diem. It has been reported that after one or two days incarceration the 'patients' struck and demand Rials 5 per diem and were paid their demands. Normally the beds are empty, or occupied by members of the hospital staff."[516] Following the shah's visit and the report of General Coulonger, the Bushehr hospital began "to give free treatment and also actually to admit patients and treat them."[517] However, it would seem that these changes did not last long, because in 1933 the municipal council considered the services offered at the hospital inadequate. Therefore, in April 1933 new municipal taxes were levied with a view to provide 10 beds for a lying-in ward for poor persons in the municipal infirmary. Moreover, the municipality also funded a local physician "to look after them and to treat other poor patients free of charge."[518] It seems that thereafter the situation changed somewhat for the better, although problems remained. In 1934, when Merritt-Hawkes visited to hospital, she reported:

> Although it was scrupulously clean-there were even puddles on the floor after the morning wash-up – there were very few patients, and much of the apparatus and the instruments looked as if they were more ornamental than useful. There was so much obvious illness that the empty beds seemed odd; the doctor said no one would come into the hospital at No-Ruz, the great yearly holiday which was just due, but the out-patient department was very busy. There was a small maternity hospital in a good position on the front, but after a year of being in the hands of an entirely unqualified person, it had been shut up.[519]

---

514. Administration Report 1931, p. 14. In January 1930, Dr. Habib Rezapour was appointed health officer. "He condemned some meat and threw it into the sea. The butchers went on a strike and no meat could be had for a week." Political Diaries, vol. 9, p. 4.
515. Administration Report 1931, p. 5; Political Diaries, vol. 9, p. 483.
516. Administration Report 1932, p. 11.
517. Administration Report 1932, p. 4.
518. Administration Report 1933, p. 4; Idem, 1935, p. 5; Political Diaries, vol. 11, p. 280.
519. Merritt-Hawkes 1935, p. 6.

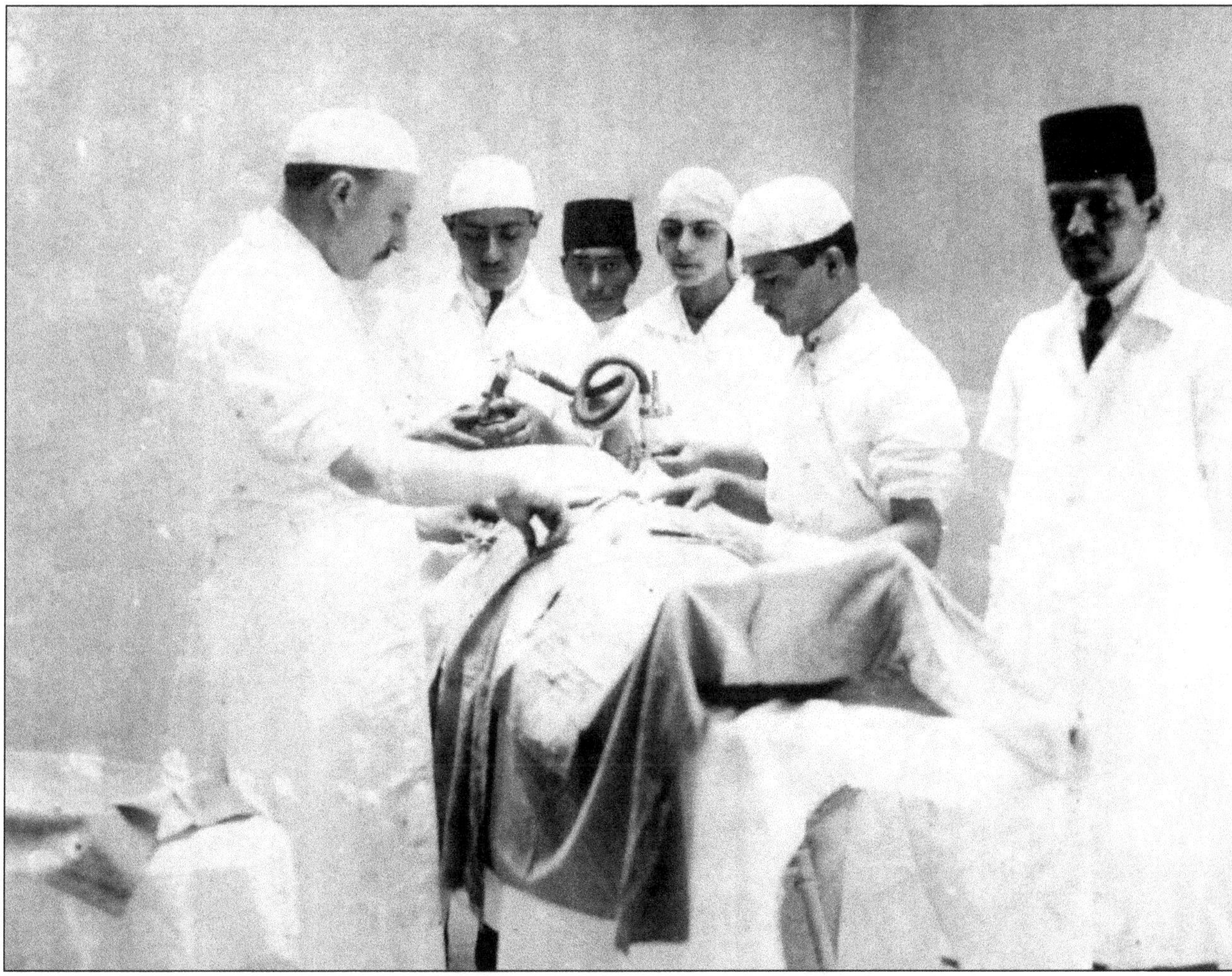

Dr. Nasir Sina'i in the operating room of the Government Hospital (January 1936)

In 1936, the municipality continued to fund the same medical service initiated in 1933, while as of that year it also provided funds for "a small asylum for a few lunatics and an isolated house for accommodating some 20 lepers."[520] The same municipal medical service was funded during 1937-1939 with the difference that the number of beds for the infirmary had been reduced to eight. In October 1938, the municipal infirmary was merged with the hospital to reduce the latter's deficit.[521] In October 1938, the existence of a military hospital in Bushehr is mentioned, without stating when it was established and where it was located, although presumably at Bahmani, where the barracks were.[522] In 1940, there is no information about the municipal-funded medical infrastructure. However, it seems that Bushehr hospital still existed, because it was reported that it maintained 20 beds for indoor patients.[523] In December 1941, there was a small pox epidemic. Only in Bushehr and in accessible villages vaccinations took place. The only hospital with room for 20 inpatients, was miserably equiped and had insufficient medicines

520. Administration Report 1936, p. 5.

521. Administration Report 1937, p. 11; Administration Report 1938, p. 3; Administration Report 1939, p. 3; Political Diaries, vol. 13, p. 180.

522. Political Diaries, vol. 12, p. 179,

523. Administration Report 1940, p. 3.

Bushehr polyclinic 1930s

even for the needs of the town. A small hospital was built in Borazjan, but so far it was used by the Head of Economics Department as his residence.[524] In September 1943, Dr. Siadat, the public health officer, opened a sanatorium outside town at Shekeri, where poor people suffering from malnutrition and tropical ulcers were received. The Anglo-Persian Reconstruction Relief Fund (APRRF) contributed with medicines and dressings. However, Dr. Siadat had difficulty finding money to keep his patients there. Merchants had promised to contribute 2,000 *tumans*, but the money had not been given to him so far. Fortunately, the APRRF helped by assuming the responsibility for the patients' food, while the Health Department promised to provide adequate staff and maintain quality of medical service in the sanatorium.[525]

In 1947, the hospital had a nominal capacity of 40 in-patients, but due to a shortage of linen, nurses, etc. the actual capacity was only 15-20 in-patients. Its staff was able to perform minor surgeries, but the standard of medical care was low, which also held for the

524. Administration Report 1941, p. 7.
525. Political Diaries, vol. 15, pp. 586-87, 615; vol. 16, p. 224.

two dispensaries that existed in Bushehr at that time. This was partly due to the climate, which made it "very difficult to keep hospital equipment and surgical instruments in good condition; the latter seem to be only fit for post-mortem needs." Moreover, although the hospital was given a good supply of medicines and food for patients, much of these were sold on the black market. By 1947, in addition to the ailments mentioned above, VD and TB were on the rise; 7% of the population had VD and the incidence of TB was even higher.

However, the public health situation of Bushehr was not as gloomy as in the past, for progress had been made. For example, between 1945-47, Dr. `Ataollah, the Medical Officer (MO) for the governorate, was able to practically eliminate malaria from the Bushehr peninsula and Borazjan Town. He was assisted by three physicians, one of whom was a dentist. Outside Bushehr there were six dispensaries in Khormuj, Ahram, Borazjan, Delam, Ganaveh and Kangan. In each of them a medical aid, trained in the Bushehr hospital, ran the dispensary. The MO or his assistants regularly visited these dispensaries to supervise their work.

Moreover, mortality of mothers or children in child birth was lower in Bushehr than in the rest of the governorate due to the presence of these physicians, who could take care of complicated cases. Outside Bushehr traditional midwives still performed this task, with often dire consequences. However, mortality of children up to 1 year in Bushehr was higher than elsewhere in Persia, probably due to the climate, when for part of the year goat and cow milk were not available.

Also, the government wanted to further improve the public health situation in the governorate. Thus, in 1947, the Ministry of Health purchased the old British Persian Gulf Residency at Sabzabad, 10 km from the town. There, in 1947, it intended to open a new hospital with 100 beds. However, given the supply-demand situation for health care workers and better living conditions elsewhere, it was expected to be very difficult to find sufficient qualified staff, thus endangering the opening of the hospital. The Health Department further considered developing the hot springs at Ahram and Khormuj for the treatment of rheumatism and related ailments.[526]

British Residency Dispensary Continues

After the transfer of the Charitable Hospital to the Persian authorities in February 1929, the British Residency Dispensary continued its work as before. It served "Residency Staff and the families, the employees and their families of the Imperial Bank of Persia and the three European firms, the Mesopotamia Persia Corporation, Messrs. Ziegler and Company and Messrs. A. and T. J. Malcolm."[527] However, because of rising cost of medical supplies the British Residency Dispensary ran into financial difficulties. Therefore, the Resident requested the government of India to continue to fund the annual grant of Rs4,000. Originally, since 1912, this amount was divided over Bushehr (3,050), Lengeh (650) and Jask (300). In 1921, an additional Rs200 was made available for the Lengeh dispensary, which, however, was closed in 1929. Because the Rs3,050 were insufficient the Resident asked New Delhi to continue to finance the annual grant of Rs1,500, which had been

526. NA, FO 371/15473.
527. Administration Report 1929, p. 8.

assigned to the Charitable Hospital. With these two amounts plus the Rs850 for Lengeh the Bushehr Residency Dispensary would have sufficient funds to cover its cost.[528]

Despite the reduced number of organizations whose sick the British had treated until 1929 the number of out-patients increased, but stabilized at between ten and eleven thousand per year until 1940, then it increased substantially, reaching over 38,000 in 1945 as discussed below. Initially, the number of in-patients also grew, but dropped by 50% in 1932 and by 90% in 1935 compared to 1929. (see Table 1.17). The initial increase in operations was made possible by the purchase of new instruments imported from Great Britain so that most emergencies could be dealt with. "However, the waiting list is long as capacity is limited. In fact, anybody that needed an operation either has to come to the Dispensary or go to Basra, Bahrain or India."[529] Probably, the drop in operations after 1932 was due to the reduced number of Europeans living in Bushehr as a result of the worldwide economic depression.

1.17: Number of patients and operations in the British Residency dispensary (1929-1940)

Year/Activities	In-patients	Out-patients	Operations
1929	54	9,320	86
1930	67	9,346	235
1931	49	13,136	279
1932	27	10,119	127
1933	24	10,873	181
1934	22	11,353	214
1935	6	11,580	245
1936	1	10,990	168
1937	6	11,339	207
1938	15	13,069	261
1939	5	10,104	198
1940	8	11,237	117
1941	14	16,754	361
1942	18	35,486	385
1943	14	37,455	407
1944	7	35,876	369
1945	-	38,122	391
1946	-	35,166	323

Source: Administration Report 1929, p. 8; Idem, 1931, p. 14; Idem, 1932, p. 11; Idem, 1933, p. 11; Idem, 1934, p. 11; Idem, 1935, p. 13; Idem, 1936, p. 11; Idem, 1937, p. 11; Idem, 1938, p. 11; Idem, 1939, p. 11; Idem, 1940, p. 11; Idem 1941, p. 15; Idem 1942, p. 22; Idem 1945, p. 18; Idem 1946, appendix I.

528. IOR/L/PS/11/182, Foreign Secretary India, New Delhi to Under-secretary for India, London. 07/01/1930.

529. Administration Report 1929, p. 8. The pharmacist of the British dispensary was Mirza Esma`il Mojeb. Hamidi 1380, p. 172.

Malaria remained the main illness seen. In 1931, there was an increase in patients, due to the increase in malaria and non-malaria fever patients, in particular the influenza outbreak during the last six weeks of the year. Further, this was also due to attending the staff and families of the Public Works Department, E&M Section at Dastak. Prior to March 1931 they attended the IETD dispensary at Rishahr, but from then on, they were seen to by the Residency surgeon. The number of operations had dropped because the surgeon was absent for two months. In November and December 1931 there were no winter rains, but instead very cold weather for a few days with a biting north wind. This contributed to an influenza outbreak with attendant cases of pneumonia that lasted till February 1932. This caused alarm in Bushehr as several hundreds of the aged and infirm died of pneumonia, due to weakness from endemic malaria and were not properly warmly dressed, while they lived "in buildings more fitted to let in air than to keep out piercing north winds." Because there was less rain in 1932, there was less malaria, which also applied to other ailments, because in general there was lower attendance in milder weather. This was the case in 1932, when "The autumn and early winter were remarkable for the paucity of attendances. In normal years this season is a 'rush' one for hospital staff."[530] In 1933, the weather was mild and the rains were good and well distributed. Moreover, they were not followed by the north wind that caused so many respiratory diseases. In addition, the hot season was one of the mildest. Because the water cisterns in each house were filled up this meant an increase in malaria cases (a rise from 1,200 to 3,619).[531] The same weather type prevailed in 1934, and as in the previous year it caused malaria to increase (1/3 of all cases). Despite this worrying trend, "The Health Authorities [did] not undertake any anti-malarial work, and it would be difficult to deal with the private reservoirs, as the inhabitants depend almost entirely on these for drinking water."[532] In 1935, the weather was mild and rains average, but the summer was one of the hottest and longest, and natives suffered almost as much as foreigners. Malaria cases continued to represent 1/3 of total cases seen.[533] In 1936, there was a slight fall in attendances due to the dwindling of Bushehr's population, but malaria continued to maintain its position, representing 1/3 of all patients, a situation that also held for 1937.[534] In December 1938 there was a mild epidemic of measles, while the summer was one of the hottest on record. There were 26 heat-strokes deaths among the local population, a cause of death that prior to 1938 was very rare. The share of malaria in total cases seen dropped to somewhat more than 25%.[535] In 1939, the hot season was mild, in fact, one of the best on record. There was also a decrease in attendances, not due to the mild weather, but because the British Residency assistant-surgeon was forbidden to engage in private practice. "Since the end of 1937, the Persian Government have refused the issue of further licenses to practice to foreign practioners, but the Assistant-Surgeon was unofficially permitted to practice until June." Malaria continued to hold its position at higher than 25% of total cases seen.[536]

530. Administration Report 1931, p. 14; Administration Report 1932, p. 11. E&M means 'electrical and mechanical.' Perhaps this refers to a disease known in Bushehr as *agar-magar*, or *barq*, because it spread so fast, which was thought to be the plague or cholera, but whose occurrence is not reported at that time. Hamidi 1380, p. 83.

531. Administration Report 1933, p. 11.

532. Administration Report 1934, p. 11.

533. Administration Report 1935, p. 13.

534. Administration Report 1936, p. 11; Administration Report 1937, p. 11.

535. Administration Report 1938, p. 11.

536. Administration Report 1939, p. 11.

In March-April 1940, there was a severe epidemic of small-pox at Borazjan, and consequently there were some imported cases in Bushehr. General vaccination was carried out and the town escaped the threat. "A small branch dispensary was opened at Sabzabad in April 1940. This is attended by the Residency employees, their families and others from the nearby villages. The Assistant Surgeon sees cases there daily."[537] Malaria remained the main disease throughout the 1940s, while in 1942 dysentery, due to water supply problems was on the increase.[538] In December 1944, the British Residency went to Choghadak with a new mobile dispensary. Because no Persian physician had ever been there the people flocked to the dispensary to have their festering sores, ulcers and burns treated. The village had suffered terribly during the drought and many men had left to Abadan for work. Because of heavy rains the mobile dispensary only visited Khoshab and Halileh in early January 1945. In the second half of that month the dispensary visited Khesht and Konartakhteh and treated 300 patients. In February the mobile dispensary went to Borazjan, Ahmadi and Choghadak where in total some 400 patients were treated. In February the British dispensary visited Hoseyniki, Sural, Choghadak and Khark island. In March 1945, Ahram was visited, where many children were affected by trachoma. It was arranged that for two weeks a trained practitioner would be lent to the village chief to give free eye-drops to those affected. Also, follow-up visits were made to villages previously visited.[539] Again, there were many malaria cases in the fall and winter of 1945. In that year, the APRRF supported the Caravanserai Shakeran containing 85 paupers; distributed free medicines to the poor in Bushehr and villages, where neither government nor private persons provided medical services. In 1945, the mobile dispensary treated a total of 9,000 patients.[540] It is likely that the Residency Dispensary ceased its activities at the end of 1946 or in mid-1947, when the British consulate was closed down

The Persian government also started a mobile dispensary, which arrived on 2 February 1945. It was led by Drs. Nur al-Din Pezeshki and Basirian, who had two assistants. Its purpose was to visit all parts of the governorate. The unit was to stay in the Bushehr area for four months, and was one of the six that had been established to tour the country. It was financed by the Public Health Department and by a gift from the Shah.[541]

Education and Modern Social Activities

Schools

Until 1899, there was no modern educational institution in Bushehr apart from the traditional *maktab* or Koran school.[542] According to Sadid al-Saltaneh, children (he meant boys, of course) were sent to the *maktab* when they were eight years old, where half of

537. Administration Report 1940, pp. 3, 11; Administration Report 1942, p. 15; Mahrad 1979, p. 89.
538. Administration Report 1941, p. 15; Administration Report 1942, p. 22.
539. Political Diaries, vol. 16, p. 271, 292, 295, 329, 349, 352-53, 375; vol. 17, p. 5.
540. Administration Report 1945, pp. 15, 18; see also IOR/L/PS/12/3542.
541. Political Diaries, vol. 16, p. 323.
542. Sani` al-Dowleh 1294, vol. 1, p. 300 states that "*az 'elm va honar bahreh nadarad*" (they are neither endowed with knowledge nor with excellence"). Afshar Sistani 1369, vol. 1, p. 446.

the time they were used as servants of the teacher. First they learnt the Koran without understanding the text. Then they read Obeyd-e Zakani's *Cat and Mouse* and *Khalu Suskeh* and the like. Once having mastered those works they proceeded to read Hafez's *Divan*. If the teacher saw fit they might also read parts of Ferdowsi's *Shahnameh*, which teachers tended to like. If he was a preacher then the children also read *Ketab-e Mokhtar* and *Jowhari*, which they had to memorize. If the child's father liked poetry Sa`di's *Kolliyat* was read, and if he liked history the *Nasekh al-Tavarikh*, or also the beginnings of the *Roba`iyat* were read. Those children who were not interested in education, or rather whose parents were not due to financial or any other reason, were not sent to school, but started to learn their father's craft or trade.[543] The presence of these Koran schools was noticeable even to a casual visitor of the port.

> When moving about the narrow lanes of Bushire in the mornings, we could hear the boys reciting out aloud their lessons in the schools attached to every mosque. Almost every child in Persia is taught to read and write. The instruction is not, indeed of the best; so long as the boy can read a little of the Koran, and can write his name, he passes muster as a fair scholar; and of higher education there is little.[544]

It was not only at the Koran schools that the recitation of the *Shahnameh* was popular, but it would seem among the population at large. In 1864, Col. Pelly, the British Resident, reported:

> In Bushire there is a man who daily in the afternoon takes his high arm-chair out and places it against the wall of a terraced tea and coffee shop. Women come and sit like crows immediately above along the edge of the flat roof, and male auditors crowd round and squat in the street below. Then he commences his recitative [of the Shahnameh] in a loud and authoritative voice. All sit rapt in interest, and will sit so for hours scarcely moving a limb. Surely one should in part judge a literary or poetical work by the effect it produces on the nation in general to which it was addressed.[545]

The first attempt to establish a modern school in Bushehr took place around 1830, when, during his brief stay in that port, the British missionary Joseph Wolff, with the assistance of the local British and the Armenian community founded a small school for the Armenians. British residents in Persia subscribed 700 pounds. According to the British journalist Stocqueler, who visited the school in 1832, Wolff lost interest in the school after his departure. As a result, "none of the fair promises he made have yet been realized. The school possessed, while I was at Bushire, no more than thirteen pupils, who were struggling through the rudiments of the Persian and Armenian languages, under the guidance of a sleepy old Armenian."[546] In subsequent years the school ceased to exist, but in 1851

543. Sadid al-Saltaneh 1371, p. 26.
544. Geary 1878, vol. 1, p. 82.
545. Pelly 1865 b, p. 156, note. On the popularity of *shahnameh-khvani*, see Floor 2005, pp. 90f.
546. Stocqueler 1832, vol. 1, pp. 13-14; Mignan 1839, vol. 2, p. 143; Wolf 1860, p. 208.

Binning reported that there were "some hopes of its being shortly re-established,"[547] hopes that proved to be in vain.

The second attempt was made by Sheikh Ahmad, who founded the *Ahmadiyeh* school in 1890 or thereabouts, which was not really a modern school, because only religious subjects, the Koran and Hafez's *Divan* were taught. The school had one teacher, Sayyed Morteza. After the founder's death in 1898, the school was continued by Sheikh Mohammad Baqer Behbahani, who modernized the curriculum. When in 1898, Ahmad Khan Daryabegi was appointed governor of Bushehr he supported Behbahani materially and otherwise in his drive for educational modernization. The students were children of poor families and were taught in two rooms in a house rented in the center of the town. In 1899, the *kargozar* Mirza `Ali Khan proposed to establish a really modern school. With the support of Daryabegi a meeting was held of notables and merchants in Government House and almost 1,500 *tumans* were pledged for that purpose. To get a competent principal, Daryabegi wrote to the Minister of Education for assistance in finding one. The latter sent Sheikh Mohammad Hoseyn Sa`adat, who, accompanied by his brother, arrived in Bushehr on 30 May 1900 and took charge of the school. Since then the school was known as the *Sa`adat-e Mozaffari* or just the *Sa`adat* school. Although people were reluctant to send their children to such a modern school they gradually did so. In 1900 there were more than 350 students and four teachers, including the principal. Although the school began its life in the center of Busher, it was soon decided to move to a larger building outside the town. At the request of the trustees, a new funding meeting was convened on 22 January 1901, which raised 2,000 *tumans* for the construction of a new school building at Neydi. It was built in two months time on land given by Haji Mohammad Mehdi Malek al-Tojjar. The new school had six rooms, one hall, four corridors and a storage space. This was the result of cooperation between merchants and school supporters. Daryabegi asked the shah for financial support, who assigned 1,000 *tumans* of the Bushehr customs dues for the construction of the school. The school had not been finished when Daryabegi was recalled to Tehran. Matin al-Saltaneh and Mirza Yanes, the Armenian translator of the Customs Department, appealed to the merchant community to complete and support the school, who pledged 3,000 *tumans* for the schools expenditures for a period of three years. At the suggestion of Mirza Yanes, one *shahi* per bale of imports and 0.5 *shahi* per bale of exports would be levied to pay for the school. A school committee was formed that consisted of: Ra'is al-Tojjar, Mirza Gholam Hoseyn, Haji Yahya, Sorush al-Molk, Moses Khan, Mirza Mohammad Javad Bang, Haji Mohamad Hoseyn Dehdashti, and Mirza *Monshi*. It met weekly on Wednesdays in the school or in the house of one of the board members. The school moved to its new location at the end of March 1902.[548] On 13 October 1906, the British Assistant Resident attended the annual examinations (held from 6-16 October) and gave a silver watch to the best student in English. He thought that it was a well-run school and that the teacher of English was a capable man. He also saw some Russian maps and two globes with Russian texts, about which he was not worried as no Russian was taught at the school.[549]

---

547. Binning 1857, vol. 1, p. 148; Curzon 1892, vol. 1, p. 233.

548. Mashayekhi 1377, pp. 21-30, 60-66; Afshar Sistani 1369, vol. 1, pp. 447-60; Sadid al-Saltaneh 1371, pp. 110-11; Hamidi 1378, pp. 57-58, 250 (short biography of Sheikh Mohammad Hoseyn Sa`adat); Sa`adat 1390, pp. 138-39; Mashayekhi 1382, p. 156 (list of contributors); Hamidi 1380, pp. 369-73.

549. Political Diaries, vol. 1, p. 500.

The 1907 Constitution stated (art. 19 of the Supplementary Laws) that education was compulsory and that all schools were to be established at the expense of the state and regulated by the Minister of Education (Minister of Sciences, Religious Endowments and Fine Arts). However, the government lacked the funds to establish schools. Therefore, the *Sa`adat* school remained a private school for Moslem children. Pupils paid 5,000 dinars up to 1 *tuman* per month. It was still supported by private contributions, taking the form of a voluntary tax of one *shahi* on every bale of merchandise (*naqleh*) imported by Persian merchants. In this way, merchants contributed about 250 *tumans* monthly; the school's monthly expenses were about 230 *tumans*.[550]

In 1907, Daryabegi was re-appointed governor, and he remained for two years in office. He exerted himself to support the school. The Khans of the districts wanted to send their sons for education to Bushehr, but were afraid that they would be held hostage by the government in case of disputes. A request to Mohammad `Ali Shah resulted in a royal command banning the taking of the Khan's sons as hostages for good behavior.[551] The students also had to pass an exam at the end of the school year. The students were examined in the following subjects: Koran, Persian, Arabic, English, history, Islamic rules, geography, geometry, arithmetic and accounting (*siyaq*). In 1914, one of the examinators for Arabic and English was the British Resident, who was fluent in Arabic; he donated a cash prize and some pens for the best students. By 1913, the *Sa`adat* school had seven grades and 286 pupils. In the beginners' grade there were 80 pupils, 1st 50; 2nd 50; 3rd 40; 4th 30; 5th 20; 6th 16 pupils. English was taught by an Armenian educated in Calcutta, and the three upper classes spent one hour daily learning the language. The children also practiced singing, because in July 1915 the school boys sang at Government House on the occasion of the anniversary of Ahmad Shah's coronation. The school staff included the principal Sheikh Mohammad Hoseyn, Magardich, who taught English and Mirza `Ali Akbar, who taught the other subjects.[552]

There was also an Armenian school founded in October 1907 by Moses Khan and likewise maintained by private subscription. In this school Armenian, English, and Persian were taught. Pupils paid 4 rupees/month if English was part of the curriculum, and 3 rupees when they were not taught English. Poor Armenian pupils attended without payment. The school raised about 40 rupees per month in this manner, the rest of the necessary funds, Musa Khan collected from the local Armenian community. In 1913, the school had a reserve fund of 500 *tumans*, which it deposited in the bank at 4% interest.[553] In July 1908, there was also a small French school whose purpose was to teach French, about which nothing else is known.[554]

There also was a Jewish school, which was financially supported by the Finance Department with a small amount and supervised by the Persian government. I don't

---

550. Sadid al-Saltaneh 1371, p. 111; Hamidi 1378, pp. 60-61, 106-09 (with list of donors), 113-16 (more donors), 122, 130-34, 161-62.

551. Afshar Sistani 1369, vol. 1, pp. 447-60.

552. Mashayekhi 1377, pp. 28-34, 69-75, 93-100, 129ff (44 pages with photographs and facsimiles of the *Sa`adat* school related documents); Sadid al-Saltaneh 1371, p. 111; Report 1913-14, p. 1; Hamidi 1378, pp. 78-89, 118-19, 189-90; Nura'i 1385, p. 252 (8 Siyam= Ramazan 1333/July 1915).

553. Sadid al-Saltaneh 1371, p. 101 (Annually school expenses were the wages: English teacher 70 rupees; Armenian teacher 20 *tumans*; Persian teacher 10 *tumans*; further for renting the building 8 *tumans* and 5,000; and the wages of the servants 3 *tumans*); Trade Report 1913-14, p. 1; Hamidi 1378, pp. 162-63.

554. Lorimer 1915, vol. 2, p. 350; Political Diaries, vol. 3, p. 222.

know when this school was established, but the small fund was first decreased and in 1929 totally stopped. The school had about 70 pupils, both boys and girls, "many of whom pay little or nothing." However, the salaries paid to the teachers were so low that these "were of the worst class of people in Bushire and were almost uneducated. Thus all the parents, who wished their sons to have good character, had to stop them of attending the school." Therefore, on 5 March 1929, the Jewish community asked the British Resident to ask "the Jew merchants in England, or the Palestine Government to build a school for us here," because they were too poor to finance this themselves. Because of bureaucratic procedures, only on 18 July 1933 the Colonial Office forwarded the request to the Anglo-Jewish Association, which on 24 October 1933 replied that regretfully it was unable to finance the school "in consequence of demands on the funds of the Association."[555] As there is no report that mentions the continued operation of this school and given the poverty of the Jewish community it must be assumed that this school closed in 1929.

It was only towards the end of the 1920s that modern state schools would be started in Bushehr. These were four elementary schools financed by the government, but the only high school was the *Sa`adat* school that still was supported by private contributions. Pursuant to the Civil Service Law of 1922, the staff of the Educational Department of the governorate was selected by the Minister based on the recommendations from the local department heads. Therefore, to oversee and manage the development of the educational capacity in Bushehr, the government appointed a chief of the Education Department (*ra'is-e ma`aref*). In 1929, this was Mohammad Nurbakhsh who in May was recalled to Tehran because of corruption. "He was openly selling appointments." The position remained vacant till 16 September 1929 when Mr. Fakhr-e Dai arrived.[556] It is not known when he left, but in 1931, Sheikh Mohammad Hoseyn, the acting director of education, was found guilty of embezzlement and was dismissed. At the end of the year, he was replaced by Sayyed Mohammad Farzan. During this period no new schools were opened due to the lack of funds. The *Madraseh-ye Sa`adat*, which was still a private high school, also had financial difficulties at year's end. Its headmaster was accused of having misappropriated school funds that were raised by subscription.[557] In 1933, the Education Department was separated from that of Shiraz and henceforth functioned directly under the Ministry of Education in Tehran.[558]

By 1934, the Education Department of Bushehr was in charge of 15 schools in Bushehr town, district and in the sub-ports. Despite the growth of schools, there was no simultaneous improvement in their working or efficiency, according to the British Resident.[559] May be it was too much to be expected given the constraints under which these schools had to operate, of which even the lack of funds may not have been the major one. Fortunately, Mrs. Merritt-Hawkes who visited Bushehr in 1934 has left a description of some of the schools in Bushehr that gives us some idea how the schools were

---

555. IOR/L/PS/12/86.

556. Administration Report 1929, p. 3. The schools were placed under the director of public education in Shiraz. Political Diaries, vol. 9, p. 4. One of these four schools was the *Ferdowsi* school. Political Diaries vol. 7, p. 184; see further Mashayekhi 1377, pp. 103-11.

557. Administration Report 1931, p. 4.

558. Administration Report 1933, p. 3. In that year the *madraseh-ye Okhuvvat* was built by the government and opened. Hamidi 1380, p. 72.

559. Administration Report 1934, p. 4.

operated. She noted that there were schools for boys and girls, schools in some villages, as well as Koran schools which continued to operate. As to the girls school she reported: "Six years ago two girls schools for 200 pupils were opened. ... The girls learn to read, to write, to do a few sums, to see maps and know how small Persia is in the big world."[560] Also, they were taught history; moreover, there were sewing-machines with which they "make mechanical European embroideries, terribles *appliqués* of bad pink cotton on bad pink net, *brodererie anglaise a la Singer*." They were proud of their work and the machine. When asked why they did not make embroidery the traditional way, the teacher and girls greatly surprised pointed to the machine and the things they had made and said: "*Chic, chic*."[561] As to the school buildings, Merritt-Hawkes wrote, "The schools were old houses in narrow lanes, now kept clean with a broom, a pan, and a brush. ... The girls were nearly all dressed in European-shaped frocks, badly cut, made by their mothers on machines at home. They sat two by two at a desk, and rose when I came in, giving a military salute."[562] Some of the girls had bobbed hair, "a symbol to them of some strange influence out of the West that produced women like me who had traveled far."[563] There was yet another girls' school that was somewhat different from the first one.

> The second school, run by the central Government, was free and more modern than the other, for the Koran was taught for only half an hour three times a week. There were 120 girls, some of them in a uniform of black and white check cotton, a strong and cheap material woven in Persia. Parents who sent their daughters here were advanced. Besides the subjects taught at the other school they had some natural history and a little hygiene. ... The school had once been a magnificent building belonging to a rich merchant, who now preferred to live out of town as he had a good car. It was decorated with complicated glass windows, fine 'gatch' work on the walls, and paintings on the ceiling, where the classic but unhappy Persian lovers, Mejnun and Leila, had gazed at one another for three hundred years.[564]

Merritt-Hawkes also visited a large boys primary school, which was a show school.

> When I entered, they were all busy saying the mid-afternoon prayers; but that didn't prevent them turning their heads, and whilst in the attitude of prayer, looking backwards through their legs at the stranger. The boys were all dressed in regulation khaki, so looked very pleasantly tidy. ... The whole school, like most in Persia, was in the grip of the 'Programme', a hard and fast syllabus that came from Tehran quite regardless of the local needs, of local conditions, and, most important, the capacity of local teachers. The pupils were learning far too much by memory and very little by thinking and reasoning. They were doing practical chemistry entirely out of a book: there weren't any test tubes, and nobody saw that a cup or a glass might be used as a substitute. The office

560. Merritt-Hawkes 1935, p. 9. On attitudes in Bushehr about girls' education and women's role, see Ya Hoseyni 1394.
561. Merritt-Hawkes 1935, p. 10.
562. Merritt-Hawkes 1935, p. 10.
563. Merritt-Hawkes 1935, p. 11.
564. Merritt-Hawkes 1935, p. 11.

> of the director had a number of natural history charts in French, but nobody knew either French or natural history.[565]

Merritt-Hawkes further commented that the teachers were doing their best and that this kind of education was an improvement over the Koran school. As to the latter, she noted that "One school was run locally and studied the Koran every day, the children paying a small fee, which increased as they went into higher classes."[566] Merritt-Hawkes also made a visit to "a tiny country school, in a village of two hundred, which was so popular that in the lower classes four sat on a bench made for two. Many of the boys here were also in khaki uniform." She further observed that the boys were all intelligent and knew poetry that they recited. They received training in military drill that was taught by a young soldier.[567]

What is clear from Merritt-Hawkes' description was that not everything was ideal, school- and teaching-wise, but that there was a great deal of pride and enthusiasm both among the teachers and their pupils. The latter, therefore, also worked hard to graduate from school. To that end school exams were held, which in 1935 took place on 1 March, which was two months earlier than usual. The number of boys sitting for the exam was 50 instead of 60 in 1934. On that occasion 33 government certificates were handed out to those students who had passed. There was a further educational innovation in that at one government school, co-education was introduced. The Education Department now oversaw 16 schools that were operated as in the past, indicating that no improvements were introduced. To increase the revenues of his administration, the director of the Education Department took steps to determine which houses and shops were *vaqf* or endowment property and allocated 5% of their rents to aid the schools.[568] On 1 March 1936, 57 pupils sat for the school exam. At that time the Education Department's budget had increased and amounted to 200,000 rials (£2,500), which permitted construction to start two new schools, one in Lengeh and the other in Chabahar. The Education Department had made arrangements with the local schools in Bushehr and other Gulf ports to teach 3,000 illiterates to read and write in night classes. They helped by encouraging the discarding of the veil and in November introduced 'public speaking' as an educational subject. It had some success in collecting 5% from the rents of endowments (*vaqf*).[569] In 1937, the construction of a new office building for the Endowments and Education Department (*Owqaf va Ma`aref*) was begun, but by the end of 1939 it was still not completed.[570] By 1940, there were more than 50 elementary and secondary schools in Bushehr and districts with a total of 250 teachers. The standard of education was considered to be low and the British Resident, always willing to see a glass half empty, doubted whether the children learned anything.[571] The town itself had 14 elementary and 2 secondory schools for boys and 2 elementary and 1 secondary school for girls. However, the teachers were not motivated

565. Merritt-Hawkes 1935, pp. 12-13.
566. Merritt-Hawkes 1935, p. 10.
567. Merritt-Hawkes 1935, pp. 13-14.
568. Administration Report 1935, p. 5.
569. Administration Report 1936, p. 5; Political Diaries, vol. 12, pp. 280-81.
570. Administration Report 1937, p. 3; Idem, 1938, p. 3; Idem, 1939, p. 3.
571. Administration Report 1940, p. 3.

`Abbas `Ali Samadi, physical education teacher with class at the Shahdokht School

because of low pay and lack of supervision and therefore, the quality of education suffered. Those who could afford it sent their children to Shiraz, where schools were better.[572]

Over time the number of schools in the Bushehr district grew, but the challenge was to induce all children of peasant families to attend. As children were an important part of the rural workforce, parents did not send their children to school unless encouraged to do so. By 1947, two of the seven schools in Bushehr town were secondary schools, one for boys (157) and one for girls (152). Admittance was conditional on having an elementary school leaving certificate; also a small fee had to be paid. In addition to those subjects taught at elementary schools, English, Arabic, elementary science, and astronomy were studied. Courses were for 3, 5, and 6 years, and at the end of each course a certificate was given if the course was completed satisfactorily.

1.18: Location and number of schools and attendance in the Bushehr governorate (1947)

Locaility	Boys	Girls	Attending Boys	Attending Girls
Bushehr Town	5	2	615	257
Bushehr Peninsula	3	1	374	53
Borazjan Town	2	1	305	46
Borazjan District	5	-	272	-
Khormuj Town	1	-	64	-
Khormuj District	3	-	151	-
Ahram Town	1	-	67	-

572. Administration Report 1941, p. 7.

Locaility	Boys	Girls	Attending Boys	Attending Girls
Ahram District	1	-	28	-
Kangan Town	1	-	66	-
Kanga District	2	-	118	-
Delam Town	1	-	114	-
Delam District	1	-	8	-
Total	22	4	2,182	356

Source: NA, FO 371/15473

The above data show that boys were given more opportunity than girls to get educated. However, once girls were allowed to study they were as eager, if not more so, than boys to continue their studies as is clear from the attendance figures for the secondary schools in Bushehr. The data further show that indeed peasants did not send their children to school and that government officials failed to change that situation by pressuring traditional leaders not to discourage, or even prevent, peasant children to attend school. Probably, the reason for non-attendance of rural children was due to a variety of factors. Income per se was not an obstacle, because attendance was gratis for children

Nurse Shah Ebrahim Moheyman's room in the Shahdokht girls school

of poor parents, but better-off parents had to pay 10 rials/month/child. School books were the responsibility of the parents, however. Here charitable organization helped poor children to get these books.

In Bushehr and Borazjan night schools were available for adult education in the three 'Rs' at the elementary school level. It was an experiment of the education department. For illiterate conscripts, the vast majority, received training in reading and writing. However, as this was not compulsory and given mostly during their leisure time attendance was very low. Most of the attendees were those who wanted an army career.[573]

In January 1935, the governor called on local officials, young merchants and traders to start a Sports Club in Bushehr. A subscription collected 370 *tumans* with which it was proposed to build a tennis court and a football field. However, these funds were insufficient, for in April 1936 the governor had the merchants subscribe Rls. 8,000 for the Sports Club. In December 1938, the authorities still had not found a building for the Sports Club.[574] The club finally found a home in 1939, but it soon turned into a gambling den for government officials. In December 1941, the acting governor wanted to change that,

573. NA, FO 371/15473.

574. Political Diaries, vol. 11, p. 372; vol. 12, p. 102; vol. 13, pp. 58-59 (drill and games by school children), 225.

School sports team

but whether that happened is unknown. I have found no further report on the activities in and by the Sport Club.[575]

Libraries and Reading Rooms

In October 1906, an Islamic Reading Room or *qara'at-khaneh-e eslamiyeh* was established in Bushehr; at that time the establishment of the *Sa`adat* school was not yet finalized. Initially it had 20 members. By about 1915 it had 280 books in Persian, 40 in Arabic, 70 in English, and 60 in French. I don't know how long this reading room existed, but in 1944, a public library was founded by Bushehri well-wishers.[576] After the Allied invasion of Persia in August 1941, the British consul made great efforts to to promote a better image for Great Britain. To that end he not only participated in all kinds of social events and dinners, but also he organized sport events (hockey and football), while some Persians joined the consulate's library and sport club. At the end of 1942, the British Residency opened a Reading Room, which operated as a club to attact influential Persians. It had a radio, a library with Persian books, many Persian newspapers and periodicals, light refreshments and propaganda materials. A committee consisting of Persians managed the club, of which the governor, all department heads and many merchants were members. As of July 1943, the Reading Room experienced competition from a Persian club, where drinks and gambling drew visitors like flies to a lamp. However, the Reading Room remained popular and the social center for the educated class in the months thereafter. The more so, since as of February 1944, the Room was also open to members during the daytime on holidays. In March 1944, the club had 220 members and some 70 were on the waiting list for election. It was intended to expand the library with more Persian publications and indoor games on a larger scale. Many high Persian officials frequented the Room in the evening, reading or playing bridge.[577] The Anglo-Persian Reading Room Club remained popular; however, given budget cuts due to the end of the war, the committee decided to put the club on self-financing basis. All cost by end 1945, except electricity, were met by subscriptions of members. They also paid half of cost of the repairs and the white-washing of the club in the summer.[578]

Newspapers

In 1900, the first printing press was established in Bushehr by Mirza `Abdol-Hamid Khan Matin al-Saltaneh Thaqafi and Mirza `Ali Aqa Labib al-Molk Shirazi. The lithograph press (*sangi*) was imported from India, erected in the Behbahani quarter and known as *Mozaffari*. Six Indian professionals trained local staff over 16 months. In 1904, Labib al-Molk went to India to buy a modern moveable type press (*sorbi*) and returned with the press and six

575. Political Diaries, vol. 14, p. 594. In 1950, the wrestling club *Shahin* was founded. Hamidi 1380, p.

576. Sadid al-Saltaneh 1371, p. 111; Sa`adat 1390, p. 34; Afshar Sistani 1369, vol. 1, p. 478; Hamidi 1378, pp. 60, 62-63, 194-95, 198, 204-06. The library belonged to Haji Sheikh Mohammad Imam Jom`eh, son of the late Sheikh Ibrahim Al Onsur. He was a wealthy man, who owned one house in Bushehr and two outside the town as well as land, gardens and *qanat*s in the villages of Bushehr. Sadid al-Saltaneh 1362, p. 11.

577. Political Diaries, vol. 15, p. 538; vol. 16, pp. 24, 29, 53; Administration Report 1942, pp.12-13.

578. Administration Report 1945, p. 14.

Indian printers. The latter suffered from the hot climate during the summer and, as a result, the press was sometimes idle for a few weeks. Therefore, Labib al-Molk wanted to use Persian workers. However, these were not skillful enough and he had to continue using Indian printers. It was this press where Bushehr's first comic and illustrated newspaper *Tolu`* was printed. This newspaper was published soon after the arrival of the first printing press in 1900 and was discontinued in 1901. However, avid readers were not deprived of their printed news, because in that same year, the (bi-) weekly newspaper, *Mozaffari* (1901-08) was published. This newspaper, with interruptions, due to its being occassionally banned, appeared until 1908, when because of political problems its editor left Persia.[579] The newspaper *Aslah* was published by Mohammad Reza Aslah who was very anti-British. This paper may also have been printed by the *Mozaffari* press; by mid-1923 this newspaper was discontinued.[580]

The *Mozaffari* printing press also published books, amongst which, as the first, *Twenty Thousand Leagues under Sea* by Jules Verne, the *Decamerone* by Boccaccio translated by Ahmad Khan Daryabegi, as well as other translations by Daryabegi and a book by him on the Persian Gulf. Further an abridged translation of E.G. Browne's book *The Persian Revolution* and the works by Talibof. The market for books in Bushehr was not very large, because even years later the press still had many first prints in stock. This may have been not only due to lack of interest or to the small market of readers, but also because many of these books were serialized in the newspaper *Mozaffari*.[581] One of these serialized books was *Ehya al-Millat* (Renaissance of the People), written by Sheikh Hasan Ahrami Bushehri a.k.a. Mo`taqed-e Ahrami. In it he argued that the rule by assembly, which he called *Majles-e dar al-shura*, instead of just rule by one ruler was Islamic and sanctioned by the Koran, the more so, since its members were all upstanding people.[582]

In 1911, a group of four persons (including, Labib al-Molk, Sayyed `Abdollah Alavi, and Mirza `Ali Aqa) established the second printing press in Bushehr under the name of *Ahmadiyeh*. The press only lasted two to three years and nothing is further known about it.[583] Some time later Sayyed `Abdollah `Alavi bought the equipment of the *Ahmadiyeh* press and with financial help from Sayyed Hoseyn Baladiyeh (the first head of the municipality) he imported a modern press from India. On 28 June 1915, he established the *Alavi* press, which still exists. It printed a number of newspapers such as *Nur-e Afshan*, *Neda-ye Jonub* and others (after 1947).[584] *Nur Afshan* (Radiant) was published Mrs. Showlat-Salami as of August 1930 as a moderate right weekly. Its editors were M. Afghami, Sayyed Abu'l-Hasan Alavi. Since October 1911, the *Neda-ye Jonub* (Call of the South) was published by Mohammad Baqer Tangestani in Tehran. As of the summer of 1946 it was published in Bushehr.[585]

---

579. On the rise of modern institutions in Bushehr in general, see Sa`adat 1390, pp. 31-32, 34. On the role and influence of the *Mozaffari* newspaper, see Martin 2000, pp. 182, 185, 187, 189-95, 199, 202.

580. Political Diaries vol. 7, p. 197.

581. Ya Hoseyni 1390, pp. 24-87. This author is mistaken when he conjectures that there was a printing-press among the publication materials brought by the Carmelites to Bandar-e Rig in 1665, see Ya Hoseyni 1390, pp. 17-18. For the Carmelites of Basra, see Gollancz 1927.

582. Ya Hoseyni 1390, p. 66; Martin 2000, pp. 190-93, who, mistakenly, ascribes its authorship to Sayyed Morteza Ahrami.

583. Ya Hoseyni 1390, pp. 89-90.

584. Ya Hoseyni 1390, pp. 91-98.

585. Elwell-Sutton 1968, p. 101; Hamidi 1380, p. 645.

۳۳۳

مظفری

نمرهٔ پنجاه و هشتم

عنوان مراسلات
ادارهٔ جریدهٔ مظفری در بوشهر
جریده ایست آزاد
ماهی دو مرتبه طبع و توزیع میشود
غرهٔ شهر ذیحجة الحرام
مطابق ۱ برج حوت
۱۳۲۰ هجری
مصادف با غرهٔ مارس
۱۹۰۳ میلادی
وجه اشتراک پیشکی باید داده شود
قیمت اعلانات سطری دو قران
درصورت تکرار باید باداره گفتگو شود

قیمه اشتراک
سالیانه — شش ماهه
بوشهر
دو تومان — سیزده قران
در سایر بلاد ممالک محروسهٔ ایران
بیست شش قران — پانزده قران
هندوستان
هشت روپیه — پنج روپیه
در سایر بلاد اروپا
دوازده فرانک — هشت فرانک
روسیه
پنج منات — سه منات

وجه پست هر جا بعهدهٔ اداره است

در این جریده از هر گونه وقایع و اتفاقات و مطالب مفیده راجع بصنعت و تجارت و مقالات علمیه و ادبیات بحث میشود و نوشتجات
مفید و عام المنفعه که منافی با دین و دولت نباشد پذیرفته و درج خواهد شد

فهرست مندرجات

مراکش — متمهدی سومالی — یاغی‌های مفتون — تولد و تناسل حیوانات
حیرت — شیراز — مظفری — تعرفهٔ جدید — اعلان دولتی
اعلان گمرکخانه — تعیین مال التجاره که از محصولات ایران بوده و بروسیه
حمل میشود — بقیهٔ مقالات علمی از دریای کبیر نمرهٔ ۲۶ — گفتگوی
صفاخانه بقیه از نمرهٔ ۲۷ — [illegible] — اعلان — ایضاً اعلان
ایضاً اعلان و اعتذار — ایضاً اعلان مخصوص — [illegible]

مراکش

جریدهٔ خلاصة الحوادث مینگارد — از قرار اخبار دیگر از مراکش تازه انقلاب و شورشی در آن مملکت روی داده و سلطان آن
همراهی قشون و قوهٔ عسکریه معتنابه روانهٔ ناحیه [illegible] شده که شورشیان را
تنبیه نماید از همین خبر معلوم میشود که قشون سلطانی شکست فاحش
خورده و چندین هزار تن از ایشان کشته شده —
سلطان مراکش که برای دفاع شورشیان همراهی قشونی
کامل بوده بواسطه شکست مجبور شده که توپها و قسمتی از خیمه‌های خود را
از دست داده بشهر فاز مراجعت نماید و از قرار معلوم عما قریب شهر
مزبور محاصره خواهد شد وضع دولتی سخت پریشان و مشوش است
علاوه بر شورش اعیان بسیاری از رعایا از حکومت ناراضی میباشند —
در انقلاب [illegible] که قشون سلطان مراکش با شورشیان نموده بود
دوازده عراده توپ بتصرف شورشیان افتاده —
قشون دولت فرانسه در سرحدات

Mozaffar, the first newspaper of Bushehr

In 1923, Yusef Okhuvvat, a local merchant, established the *Khalij-e Fars* press, which, apart from some general noticces, only published the newspaper *Anjoman-e Okhuvvat*. As of December 1929, this newspaper appeared as *Khalij-e Fars*. This newspaper was apparently established in July 1923 with assistance of the Soviet consul. He arranged that one Ebrahim, the teacher of the *Ferdowsi* school was to write under the pseudonym of Sadeq. However, the Soviet consul's lack of funds led to postponement of its publication. As of

1929, it was published twice per week; its editor was Abdol-Hoseyn Okhuvvat. This press, about which nothing else is known probably lasted until 1941, when it was discontinued.[586]

Cinema

As of 1891, the first motion picture or rather the pre-cinema presentation was shown in Bushehr, This probably was the so-called zoetrope (*shahr-e ferang*), which showed a rapid sequence of photographs by rotating a drum in which a sequence of pictures were mounted. The spectator looked through slits in the side of the drum and the rapid succession of imgages created the illusion of motion. Those interested in this experience went to the Sara-ye Mohammadiyan, which situated in one of the city quarters east of the old barracks. In 1920, Hajj Yahya Firuzi Shirazi, a local owner of a photography shop (*Firuzi*), imported a Pathé film projector. For a short while he operated the first cinema in Bushehr until it was burnt down by religious fundamentalists, who considered this to be an invention of the devil. It was a few years later that Dr. Mulabakhsh, an Indian physician and photographer, living in Bushehr, wanted to open a cinema with financial backing from local Persian and Indian merchants. However, he did not receive any encouragement from the governor and therefore, dropped his plan. It was only in mid-1933 that Hajj Mohammad Ghowth Ahmadiyeh, a British-Indian employee of the British Residency constructed a building in the Kuti quarter, where he opened a cinema called *Khayyam*. It had a capacity of 300 persons, but no seats, and in the middle was a pond with fish. The *Khayyam* cinema showed Indian and other movies, including, just prior to its closing, the first talking movie. It closed in 1937, when Hajj Mohammad Ghowth went bankrupt.[587] In 1936, the governor of Bushehr intended to project films in mosques during Ramadan, but it is unknown whether he realized this plan.[588] It was only from November 1942 that films were regularly shown in Bushehr, which were generally well received. In April 1943 the first full-length film was shown (*Pimpernel Smith*) in Bushehr.[589] The British consulate continued to show movies regularly during the war years as part of its program to counter German propaganda. In early 1945 it received a 16 mm projector with which bi-weekly shows were given at schools. The 35 mm projector was used for showing movies in the rural areas. In that year, the projector also went to Ganaveh by sea, which was the first ever that a move was shown there. Also, once per week a film was shown for the reading club members, except during Moharram. The British cinema shows were discontinued in 1945, after the end of second World War.[590]

586. Ya Hoseyni 1390, p 99; Political Diaries vol. 7, pp. 184, 189, 248; Elwell-Sutton 1968, p.85.

587. Mo'azzeni 1389, pp. 37-49.

588. Administration Report 1936, p. 5; Political Diaries, vol. 12, pp. 280-81. This may refer to a plan to open a cinema in the sport club in that year, an initiative of Mr. Sehhatzadeh, the chief of education, see Mo'azzeni 1989, p. 54

589. Political Diaries, vol. 15, p. 317, 461.

590. Administration Report 1945, p. 15; Mo'azzeni 1389, pp. 50-54.

Modern Theater

Whereas in other parts of Persia modern theater already made its entry in the 1880s,[591] it was only in 1941 that the performance of a modern play in Bushehr is reported. In January 1941, at the *Sa`adat* School the sixth anniversary of the discarding of the veil was celebrated with music, and a play (a comedy) performed by the teachers and school boys and girls.[592] There is neither a report on earlier nor on later performances either at this school or elsewhere in Bushehr. Apparently, by about 1950 in the house of the Forutan family in the Kuti quarter plays were performed. Thereafter, theatrical performances became more common in Bushehr.[593]

Cost of Living

When reading Milburn's and an anonymous description of food availability in Bushehr during the first decades of the nineteenth century one gets the impression that there was no supply problem. "Provisions and refreshments are all brought from the interior by caravans, and the town is well supplied with fruits, vegetables, and meat, which are both good and cheap. A full grown sheep cost from 1,5 to 2 rupees each. Oxen which weigh from 4 to 5 cwt. Each from 6 to 8 rupees. The fruits are good, such as apples, pears, peaches, nectarines, apricots, plums, and grapes. Bread, butter, milk and vegetables are excellent, and reasonable. There are fish of various kinds in great plenty."[594] And indeed, food availability was not the problem (unless there was political turmoil),[595] but people's purchasing power was low. Although we have no description of what constituted a normal average diet for a Bushehri worker, in the rival port of Lengeh a typical meal for a day laborer was "a lump of dates before going to work, some bread (unleavened) and salt fish for dinner [sic; i.e., lunch], and some boiled rice for supper. The men who earn higher wages possibly wear a better shirt and turban, but nothing more; whatever they save is usually converted into ornaments for their women."[596] Probably, this diet was typical for day laborers in Bushehr as well. Anyway, the dietary situation of most families was not ideal. In 1851, Binning observed that, in particular, children in Bushehr were ill-looking. None were cheerful. "Such little wizened, squalid, peevish countenances, I think I never saw before." However, Armenian children "looked fair and good," probably because they belonged to merchant families, who were better off.[597] As is clear from what follows, the food situation in Bushehr was determined by people's financial situation (work or unemployed, well-paid or not) and the weather.

---

591. See Floor 2005 b.
592. Political Diaries, vol. 14, p. 295.
593. Dehqani 1389.
594. Milburn 1813, vol. 1, p. 130; Anonymous 1828, p. 57; den Tex 1871, p. 26.
595. "Provisions are scarce, and nothing is brought from the country." Binning 1857, vol. 1, p. 150.
596. Smith 1871, p. 402.
597. Binning 1857, vol. 1, p. 145.

The Great Famine

One constant of the Persian littoral was the frequency of droughts, followed by a large or small famine, followed by bans of grain export (see Chapter 2). Unfortunately, for the grain merchants, the people of Bushehr demanded such bans, because they feared grain shortages of which they had already experienced many and suffered the consequences. Therefore, they were very sensitive to rumors about anything that pertained to the general food situation, and understandably so. In particular, the period of 1870-72 stands out in the history of Persia when a persistent drought savaged the entire country and ravaged its people, and Bushehr was not spared either.[598]

In April 1870, the streets of Bushehr were full "of famine-stricken people. Many in the last pangs of starvation, and not a few dead. Those that are still able to move about busy themselves turning over the various collections of refuse to be found in every corner, and consider they have found a prize should they succeed coming across a fowl's entrails, or a dry fishbone. Those who are not so fortunate, deaded the cravings of hunger by eating the droppings of the donkeys in the street."[599] At that time, Bushehr had for some time been without a governor, which did not improve the situation. Driven by famine a mob prevented the export of grain by British merchants in Bushehr. Col. Pelly, the British Resident, was willing to hand over all grain in the granaries of British merchants to the local authorities, but there was no one. Therefore, he induced British merchants to sell their grain at low prices to the population. This lasted for one month when a new governor arrived and the remaining stock of grain was handed over to him. After the famine had ended, the merchants asked compensation for their loss; they got some, but not as much as they demanded.[600]

However, the drought and consequently the famine did not end in 1870, but continued in 1871, and its effects were also felt in 1872. Things got worse when in February 1871 there was an outbreak of cholera in Bushehr. In March 1871, Col. Pelly wrote: "For the past two months Bushire has been crowded with mendicants from all parts since the outbreak of the cholera in the middle of February; many of the absolute poor have succumbed to starvation. The local authorities have attempted to induce the poor to leave the place by the bestowal of money and dates, but without success. The destitute have either returned or others have taken their place."[601]

Given that Bushehr was a port where much trade was carried on, its situation was relatively better than in other parts of drought-stricken Persia, because supplies could be more easily shipped there. Nevertheless, as Brittlebank, who traveled through Persia in

598. Shoko Okazaki, "The great Persian famine of 1870-71," *BSOAS* 49/1 (1986), pp. 183-92. The situation was bad in most areas of Persia, such as in Shiraz, about which Dr. Cumming reported the following: "Have been over the plain; all springs dried up except at Karaja. Very little wheat sown. Crop sparse; opium almost a total failure. No cholera, people are dying from famine; not one eighth of the population left as calculated by the Moolahs, almost daily robberies both in town and outside supposed by Eliots who drive off whole flocks of sheep and cattle or beasts of burden. No bread is made in the bazaars which are all closed, have just returned from visiting the town." NA, FO 248/271, Dr. S. Mc. Cumming, Shiraz to Sydney Smith, ass. Resident. For the situation in Qom, see D. J. Gurney and M. Sefatgol, *Qom dar Qahti-ye Bozorg*. Qom: Mar`ashi Library, 1387/2008.

599. NA, FO 248/271, Ass. Surgeon A. N. Hojel, Residency Surgeon to Pelly, 10/04/1870.

600. Saldanha 1986, vol. 7/2, p. 6, 8; NA,FO 248/281, Persian receipt from Nasir al-Molk of the wheat sold in 1870 to the FO agent by Haji Musa.

601. Saldanha 1986, vol. 7/2, p. 7.

1872, observed, "Still the sights that were to be met with in the streets were so horrible that even now the bare thought of them makes the blood run cold."[602] Pelly who raised much money in London (from Sir Moses Montefiore, the Lord Mayor), Bombay and Calcutta where Relief Committees to aid hungry Persians had been established, together with a number of Europeans, managed the Relief Committee in Bushehr.[603] Among the major contributors were mentioned "Khoja Abdul Ghanny Meah, C.S.I., and his son Asad Oolah of Decce, [who] have merited the thanks of the Relief Committee at Bushire and the gratitude of the poor in this place for being the first to extend charity to the unfortunate famine-stricken of these regions. Mr. Vurjeevundass Mahdoudass and three others have also contributed liberally."[604] In addition, there were funds given by Sir Joseph Montefiore separately for the Jews of Bushehr, which were "distributed among the poor who deserve it while the merchant sarrafs [bankers] and other Jews who don't need it received none."[605] Dr. Waters, the surgeon of the Residency, who was in charge of implementing the relief effort, indicated that "well-to-do Persians made little effort for saving the life of their unfortunate fellows."[606]

Having the money, in total 148,507 *qran*s between July 1871 and February 1872, was only part of the solution, because the major challenge for the Relief Committee was how to most effectively use it to combat the effects of the famine. The problem was made more difficult, because those in need were not only those people who lived in Bushehr itself. In fact, all those in need from its hinterland came to the port city in an emaciated state, barely able to walk due to hunger and sore feet. Some of those who were able to reach the British Residency never got further, as they dropped dead on arrival!

> At first the money was given in small doles to the people assembled on the sea beach. But this system appealed to the acquisitiveness of the well-to-do Persians. As many as four thousand people paraded for relief. I suggested to Sir Lewis Pelly that the starving people should be picked in the streets and put in an empty house with large grounds, and fed there with food purchased in the bazaar. To this he agreed, and appointed me chairman of a committee to see to the care of the famine stricken. ... By this arrangement now we found that the actually starving people numbered only some few hundreds, and of these not a few contributed to their livelihood by basket making.[607]

---

602. Brittlebank 1873, p. 96; Lorimer 1915, vol. 1, p. 2052. For a description of the emaciated people, children and mothers, lying almost too weak to move on the ground in the bazaar, see Brittlebank 1873, p. 97; Waters n.d., p. 23.

603. Waters n.d., p. 20; Saldanha 1986, vol. 7/2, p. 7.

604. Saldanha 1986, vol. 7/2, p. 7; Lorimer vol. 1, p. 2080 (Khvajeh Abdol-Ghani Miyan and Asadollah of Dacca). C.S.I. stands for 'Companion of the Order of the Star of India,' an award given to British and Indian officials serving in India.

605. In total 1,175 *qran*s were distributed among 42 poor Jews, a list of them with the allotted amounts is included in NA, FO 248/281, Statement made on 29/08/1872 by Rahim Amran, Moshee Amran, Yakub Benjamin and Ahroun Awaz.

606. Waters n.d., p. 24. He was assisted by Mr. George MacKenzie of Grey, Paul & Co, the local representative of Grey, Dawes & Co., the agents of the British India Steam Navigation Co.

607. Waters n.d., p. 21.

However, it was found that distributing food in cooked form was not the best way to reach the needy. Therefore, it was decided to give them some copper coins, so that they themselves could best decide what they needed to address their wants. Unfortunately, it was soon clear that this plan did not work well in practice, because "of vast assemblages, the confusion and the consequent abuse of the charity." It was then decided to start a food-for-work program by employing the needy for road construction, street cleaning, and the establishment of an orphanage and infirmaries for the aged and the helpless men and women. This indeed has the desired result. Furthermore, daily bread was given to the poor in Sabzabad, where the women and children from most of the villages gathered. In addition, relief in cash was given to "many persons of respectability, whom the famine had reduced to poverty." As the Relief Committee had ample funds to cope with the situation in Bushehr it also extended its relief activities to Isfahan, Shiraz, and Kazerun.[608]

Fortunately, in the winter of 1871-72 the rains were good and despite the fact that a rather reduced area of land had been tilled, prospects for a bumper harvest in 1872 looked good. Of course, funds were still needed to tide people over to the post-harvest period, but "on 15 August 1872 the famine relief was practically closed, with some money (7,260 *qrans*) left for orphans." The balance of the relief fund (9,713 *qrans*) was sent to Bengal with approval of Lord Mayor of London.[609] Among the survivors of the famine at Bushehr there were not only many family bereavements, but the shared fate also had created intimacy resulting in a desire to marry. Dr. Waters took it upon himself to help this beginning of a new life by employing "A Moolah to perform the marriage ceremony, and paid him a small fee for each marriage, and gave each bride a small wedding present, and so the famine ended."[610]

Famine never far away

In 1874, again there was fear for famine in Bushehr, but at last the rains arrived.[611] For a decade thereafter the situation remained normal until 1886, when many small traders failed, because people could not buy their goods due to high food prices caused by a bad harvest.[612] This bad harvest had a disastrous impact on the food situation in 1887, when prices rose in Bushehr to "nearly famine pitch and the outlying districts were in an unprosperous and consequently unsettled conditions." Export of grain was again banned and grain had to be imported.[613] After this mini-famine almost another decade passed before another similar event took place. The harvest of 1896-97 was a failure, only 20 cm of rain fell. As a result, there was insufficient grain to feed people and rice had to be imported, mainly from Burma. Meanwhile, food prices sky-rocketed. The British Resident wrote: "It is a proof of the increase in property of Bushire during the last 25 years that in spite of these high rates there has not been actual famine and it has been unnecessary to provide public relief." Failure of the winter rains made famine look imminent

608. Saldanha 1986, vol. 7/2, p. 7; Lorimer vol. 1, p. 2080.
609. Waters n.d., p. 22; Saldanha 1986, vol. 7/2, p. 7.
610. Waters n.d., p. 21.
611. Saldanha 1986, vol. 7/2, p. 8.
612. Administration Report 1886-87, p. 22.
613. Saldanha 1986, vol. 7/2, p. 12; Administration Report 1887-88, pp. 11, 32.

and many starving people came to Bushehr from the interior. In November 1897, the British Resident received permission in case of need to use the surplus (Rs.14,000) of the Famine Relief Funds. Moreover, the shipwreck of many date vessels that had gone to Basra to buy dates there caused a loss of many lives. This loss of labor reduced the area of land under cultivation. Fortunately, in March 1898 there were good rains and famine was averted. But there was a great deal of crime in Bushehr and surrounding area due to high food prices.[614] The year 1898 was a quiet year; there were few violent crimes, due to good rainfall and a good harvest that provided work for everyone and lower prices. Also, arms traffic was stopped and action was taken against the Tangestanis. Initially, food prices remained high, but after the harvest prices dropped by 50% in June. However, in July they rose 60% above ordinary prices, because producers did not want to sell fearing another bad year. [615] In 1899, food prices were 30-40% lower compared with 1898, fortunately, which was good for everybody.[616] In 1901 there was yet another bad harvest, no less than half the crop had been lost. The poor population on the littoral would have been in really dire straits were it not for the abundance of fish in the Persian Gulf and of dates in Basra the poor would have been in a disastrous situation.[617]

A change of governor, a weakening of the authority of the local or central government was seen as an opportunity by all kinds of local actors to make a profit. For example, following the political unrest after the announcement of the grant of a Constitution in September 1906, the butchers in Bushehr bribed the *kalantar* ("the Bazaar master") and then raised prices of meat from the beginning of Ramazan (17 October) from 4 to 5 *qrans* per *man*. The *kargozar*, as acting governor, torpedoed this action by taking a number of sheep destined for export to Bahrain and opened a few shops where meat was sold at 4 *qrans*.[618] In October 1908, the lower classes of Bushehr were suffering because the dates that at this time of the year came from Tangestan did not come due to tribal feuds.[619]

1.19: Prices of foodstuffs at Bushehr for the years 1893 to 1897

Article	1893		1894		1895		1896		1897		Weight of *man* in lbs
	Qran	Cts	*Qran*	Cts	*Qran*	Cts	*Qran*	Cts	*Qran*	Cts	
Wheat	8	-	8	25	10	50	22	50	25	-	Per 124 lbs
Barley	4	50	4	50	5	50	12	-	16	-	"
Dates 1st quality	10	-	11	-	15	50	24	-	26	-	"
Dates 2nd quality	10	-	11	-	13	-	24	-	22	-	"

614. Saldanha 1986, vol. 7/2, p. 16; Administration Report 1897-98, pp. 9 18-19; Sirjani 1361, p. 526.
615. Administration Report 1898-99, pp. 6, 31-33.
616. Administration Report 1899-1900, p. 41-42.
617. Administration Report 1901-1902, p. 12. For a list of prices in 1900, see Hamidi 1378, p. 59; for price lists from 29 July 1902 until 9 March 1904, see Nezam al-Saltaneh Mafi 1391, vol. 2, appendix 5, pp. 703-72.
618. Political Diaries, vol. 1, p. 528.
619. Political Diaries, vol. 3, p. 269.

Article	**1893**		**1894**		**1895**		**1896**		**1897**		**Weight of *man* in lbs**
Dates 3rd quality	9	-	10	-	12	-	20	-	20	-	"
Rice (Shahri)	20	-	22	-	22	-	24	-	32	-	"
Rice (Indian)	26	-	26	-	n.a		n.a.		41	-	"
Rice (Kazeruni)	22	-	24	-	26	-	28	-	32	-	"
Rice (Firuzabadi)	28	-	28	-	29	-	32	-	40		"
Ghee	5	75	6	25	6	25	7	-	7	25	7.5 lbs
Dhall	17	-	20	-	22	-	28	-	36	-	124 lbs
Peas	11	-	12	-	13	-	20	-	40	-	"

Source: NA, FO 248/651.

In 1911, according to the British consul, the inhabitants of the littoral were well-off. They ate well, and only a few heads of families spent less than the value of 1 pound in money or kind per month. Nevertheless, the primitive conditions of the area were an obstacle to trade development. Also, the purchasing power of the townspeople was generally higher reflecting their higher cost of living. Wages paid for house boys at that time were at a minimum £1 per month and usually £1.25 to £1.5. Office messengers and servants were paid higher wages.[620]

1.20: Prices of foodstuffs at Bushehr for the year 1911-12

Food product	From *s. d.*	To *s. d.*	Observations
Eggs	0 0.5		Each
Fowls	1 1	1 5	Each
Mutton or goat	0 3.25	0 4.25	Per lb
Flour	0 14	-	Per lb. of 7.75 lbs.
Persian Bread	0 9	-	Idem
Charcoal	5 3	7 10	Per 124 lbs.
Firewood	2 7	3 4	Idem
Tea	5 3	8 3	Per 7.75 lbs.
Milk	11 14	-	Per *man* of 7.75 lbs.
Rice	0 10	1 2	Idem

Source: Trade Report 1911-12, p. 7. s. = shilling; d. = pence.

However, conditions changed thereafter. In both 1915 and 1916 the rains started at the end of December rather than in the beginning of November, which was necessary for a good ploughing and sowing season. Despite the short sowing period plants came up very well, but the prospects for harvesting were completely ruined by the rains holding off in March 1917. Thus, the stalks dried up before reaching maturity. Therefore, for the

620. Trade Report 1911-12, pp. 2, 7.

third year in succession there was a great shortage of grain throughout the producing Persian Gulf regions. The effect was already considerable by March 1917. The inhabitants of the littoral could import flour from India, but the nomads and villagers from across the mountains suffered a partial famine, and large numbers migrated. In Shiraz the need was so high that 750 tons of flour were imported via Bandar Abbas and Lengeh. "In fact, the inhabitants of the Gulf region, and such centres as Shiraz, have relied on India to provide them with food."[621] In 1917-18 the harvest was a moderately good one, because the rains were late once again (December). However in the interior (Shiraz, Firuzabad), famine conditions prevailed, partly due to a plague by locusts.[622] In 1919 the harvest was not a good one, but the 1920 harvest was good, although in many parts it was spoilt by locusts.[623] When locusts arrived people (men, women, and children) came out of their houses and started making an enormous noise with their pots and pans and ran around their farm land. They also had straw warning-sticks that were lit and smoking which they waved around. Others lit fires on the ground. When it was clear that this was in vain, they collected the locusts on the ground and took of their legs and wings and ate them raw, which was considered to be a delicacy.[624]

In 1927, the harvest was bad due to locusts in Dashti and Dashtestan, but not in Ma`shur and Hendiyan and therefore, the supplies of Bushehr were assured.[625] The following year the harvest was rather good, despite the lack of rain in February-March, but there was no shortage of grain. However, the high tariffs on tea and sugar, which especially were a burden for the poor, caused much economic hardship.[626] In 1929, partly due bad harvest, partly due to the changing economic circumstances and diminishing competitiveness of Bushehr compared to ports at the head of the Persian Gulf, poverty was on the rise among the population at large.[627] In November 1931, the Municipality opened a bakery to improve the quality of bread. In February 1932, both the failure of rain and consequently of the crops caused serious problems for the population. According to the Resident, "This year not a single acre had been sown and not only that but the rains have also failed in the mainland and I understand there is a shortage at Shiraz and elsewhere." Prices started to rise and barley and bhoosa were not even unobtainable in February/March 1932. Livestock was being killed and sold at nearly nominal prices and robberies were on the rise.

Product	**Year**	**Year (in *qran*s/per Hashem *man* of 128 lbs.)**
	1931	1932
Barley	15	40
Wheat	24	50

621. Trade Report 1916-17, pp. 4-5.
622. Trade Report 1917-18, p. 4. On the food situation in Persia at that time, see Floor 2015 a.
623. Trade Report 1918-19, p. 2; Trade Report 1919-20, p. 2.
624. Böhme 1977, pp. 257, 259; Locusts could interfere with what otherwise would have been a good harvest such as in 1921. Trade Report 1920-21, p. 2. Also, birds ate two-thirds of all the seeds. Sani` al-Dowleh 1294, vol. 1, p. 300. On this problem, see Floor 2003 a, pp. 321-37.
625. Administration Report 1927, p. 5.
626. Administration Report 1928, pp. 7-8.
627. Administration Report 1929, p. 5.

Product	Year	Year (in *qrans*/per Hashem *man* of 128 lbs.)
Bhoosa	4	16

Moreover, there was a severe shortage of water, and many of the *ab-anbars* were not completely filled. The whole peninsula had to draw water from the wells at Bahmani, 12 km from Bushehr. However, their output was insufficient to satisfy local demand, while deepening the wells was not an option, because the water then became brackish. The governor estimated that the town's water needs would rise from 18,000 liters/day (4,000 gallons) in March to 36,000 liters in May and 54,000 liters/day (12,000 gallons) in mid-summer, when the wells would have completely dried up. At the governor's request APOC sent a tug with 130,000 liters (29,000 gallons) of water. However, APOC informed the governor it would have to charge £300/month if he would ask the Company to tow sailing boats to and from the Shatt al-Arab to import water, money which the governor did not have. However, the governor had no alternative but to import water from Mohammerah and Bombay. Via an arrangement with the BISNC this Company imported 100 tons of water per week, at a much lower rate. Wheat and barley prices soared, until the municipality imposed price controls; wheat straw was unobtainable. The governor of Bushehr made real efforts to help the sufferers and after a month of hard work was able to overcome Tehran's apathy by convincing it to exempt wheat and fodder import from trade monopoly restrictions. To reduce the stress in the local food market, the British Residency asked the British Legation in Tehran to get permission from the Persian government to import foodstuffs for its staff and their dependents, totalling 300 persons, and more than 50 animals, whose monthly food requirements were:

1.21: Food requirements of the staff of the British Residency (1932)

Requirement	Weight in lbs.	Weight in Tabriz *mans*
Wheat	13,000	2,000
Atta (white wheat flour)	5,950	900
Flour white	1,300	200
Barley	16,150	2,500
Rice	10,400	1,600
Ghee (clarified butter)	1,625	250
Butter	195	30
Lentils	1,710	260
Bhoosa (chopped wheat straw)	26,000	4,000
Buji	65	10
Gram (small dried peas)	195	30
Hay	650	100
Tinned milk	33.5	5

Source: IOR/L/PS/12/3595, Castrell/Bushire to Legation/Tehran 06/03/1932.

Although Tehran finally reacted to the many urgent pleas from the governor, wheat from Kerman and aid did not reach Bushehr until October 1932. Drought and famine affected the tribes, who lost almost all their animals and also many people died. There was not enough pasture near Shiraz for additional herds. "The Government had sent 5,000 tons of grain from Mohammerah to be used as food and seed, the Governor of Bushire had requisitioned money from the few wealthy of Bushire and had brought 2,000 tons of wheat from Basra, 2,000 from Kermanshah, and from other places had come 2,000 tons of wheat and 1,600 tons of barley. Water, too, had been brought down from Mohammerah to be distributed to the people in skins." Nobody died of starvation, but there were many thin people. The Resident commented that "it was pitiful to see the old people and the animals." Some 1,000 persons from Dashti, Dashtestan and Tangestan and Hayat Da'ud came to Bushehr and were helped by funds raised by merchants. Relief measure work started on a road from Bushehr to Lengeh, which really mostly consisted of clearing the surface of the most important obstructions. Unfortunately, there was not enough money for the construction of the road to Lengeh and to hire more men. In the execution of the work there was mishandling and underpayment of workers, which led to discontent and protests to governor. By the end of 1932, when funds were exhausted the workers went on strike when the road had passed Kangan. The work was discontinued and thereafter the rain wiped out most of the work done. "Advances of seed-grain were made to the peasantry who had been for many months destitute and entirely dependent on the Bushire Municipality for food and lodging." At Christmas rain fell and next year's crop prospects looked good.[628]

In 1933, economic conditions were better as there had been a good harvest, but most people were still very poor. There was no improvement in this situation in 1934. In the beginning of that year steps were taken to ensure that there were sufficient supplies to tide the town over till the next harvest; 50 *tumans* of wheat were bought and stored for sale to bakers. However, the majority of people in the port's hinterland remained dirt poor and made ends meet by providing guides to smugglers or by enlisting as road guards and for a fee warning the smugglers about preventive patrols. However, these options only could provide an income to a limited number of people. Therefore, in January 1934, very poor peasants poured into town and the municipality housed their families in a caravanserai outside the town. To improve this situation and provide a living for the needy, local officials obtained permission to restart work on the coast road between Bushehr and Lengeh. To that end, the Finance Department gave the municipality 40,000 *tumans*. Work started in September 1934 and employed 500 men, most of them poor migrant peasants.[629] In that same year, Mrs. Merritt-Hawkes observed what peasants ate in one village near Bushehr. Dinner in one village consisted of rice, lentils, peas and a herbs mixture "with bread, a white curd cheese and immense quantities of a very hard and tough lettuce, and also radishes, leaves. Meat is not for every day, but, unless the people are very poor, it is Friday (the Islamic Sunday) treat. All the people who are lucky enough to have a milk-giving animal eat mast [yoghurt]."[630] She further observed that peasants visiting Bushehr were eating salad while walking in the streets.[631]

In 1935, at the suggestion of the governor, the Finance Department, which held the monopoly of the trade in grains, advanced wheat seed and money to peasants; many

628. IOR/L/PS/12/3595, Biscoe/Bushire to Legation/Tehran 18/02/1932; Idem, Castrell/Bushire to Legation/Tehran 06/03/1932; Administration Report 1932, pp. 4-6, 9; Merritt-Hawkes 1935, p. 4.

629. Administration Report 1933, p. 3; Administration Report 1934, p. 4; Political Diaries, vol. 11, p. 5.

630. Merritt-Hawkes 1935, p. 17.

631. Merritt-Hawkes 1935, p. 9.

availed themselves of this opportunity and more land was brought under cultivation. Rainfall was good (37.3 cm) and consequently the harvest was good and peasants were better off than in 1933. Nevertheless, some people continued to act as guides for smugglers as this paid good money.[632] In 1936, peasants recovered somewhat from the losses suffered during 1931-33 due to a bumper crop. However, because of the higher customs tariff and the government monopolies this also meant higher costs for food stuffs. Despite their poverty, the population remained passive, and there were no signs of unrest. Moreover, if there was a protest the ringleaders were immediately 'liquidated' as the authorities did not tolerate any form of popular show of discontent.[633] The middle class was not doing much better, because merchants and small traders lost much of their business, because of the monopolies of wheat, piece goods, sugar, and tea. Therefore, merchants, having lost both foreign and forwarding trade, invested part of their capital in recently created companies in Tehran, Isfahan and Shiraz. Shopkeepers and small traders were worst off, because of smuggling and the lack of purchasing power of the peasantry, who hardly made any purchases in town. Consequently, many closed their shops and left for Khorramshahr or other towns in the interior. Consumers did not fare any better, because, despite their higher expenditures, Bushehr did not benefit from the collected revenues. As a result, "nothing but articles of immediate necessity and a very few primitive comforts are to be bought in the bazaar."[634]

1.22: Cost of life necessities in Bushehr in rials (1936-39)
Units: rial per 7.75 lb unless otherwise stated

Commodity	Jan. 1936	Dec. 1936	Jan. 1937	Dec. 1937	Feb. 1938	June 1938	1939
Local bread	-	-	2.00	2.45	4.50	3.50	3.00-3.50
Flour	-	-	2.40	2.40	4.00	3.50	2.20
Ghee per 7.75 lbs	23.00	35.00	35.00	42.00	38.00	34.50	38.50
Meat per 7.75 lbs	7.20	8.25	8.25	11.20	8.00	9.60	9.60
Tomatoes	-	-	1.60	1.20	4.10	4.50	4.00-4.50
Potatoes	-	-	3.00	4.00	4.00	4.00	3.10-6.00
Rice bread/ Shiraz rice	-	-	7.00	7.50	8.25	10.00	11.50
Tea: per 500 gr.	15.50	20.00	20.00	18.00	20.00	22.00	22.00
Loaf: each	-	-	1.25	2.00	2.50	3.00	3.00
Water: per skin	-	-	1.00	1.00	1.25	1.50	n.a.
Crystal sugar: per 3kg. (6.6 lb)	-	-	-	-	-	8.75	9.25

Source: Administration Report 1936, p. 8; Idem, 1937, p. 9; Idem 1938, p. 9 (Flour and bread mentioned in the table are of the most inferior quality); Idem 1939, p. 7.

Although the municipal council occasionally tried to cap prices of food necessities, these efforts often proved to be ineffective. For example, in 1937 the council tried

632. Administration Report 1935, p. 5.
633. Administration Report 1936, pp. 8, 10.
634. IOR/L/PS/12/3595, Extract from Bushire Diary for June 1936; Administration Report 1937, p. 9.

to lower the price of meat, but this failed due to opposition by the butchers, while the reduction of the bread price "was inherently unsuitable and the price fixed was never applied." Therefore, three bread shops were opened to curtail price fluctuations and possible exploitation by bakers. Bread was sold at 2.40 rials per *man*, while the bakers' price had been 3 rials per *man* of 2.9 kg.[635] Jobs in the construction of the barracks as well as activities by the Municipality such as the desultory work on the roads, offered poor people some financial relief.[636] Taxation of goods in common use hit the poor in particular, who spent a relatively high percentage of their income on them. Municipal rates were 6-7%, and there was a local tax of 3% ad valorem on merchandise brought into town. Wages remained low in 1937, though employment for laborers was good, due to road work and the construction of the new barracks.[637]

1.23: Representative daily wage rates in Bushehr in rials (1937-39)

	1937	1938	1939
Customs coolie	2-3	3	5.5
Labourer	3 ½ - 4	4.5	4.5 to 6
Cotton operative	2 ½ - 5	2.5 to 6	7
Semi-skilled builder	6	7	12
Skilled builder	12	15 to 20	30
Carpenter	12	12 to 15	14-20
Builders' foreman or mechanic	20	30	48[?]

Source: Administration Report 1937, p. 10; Idem 1938, p. 9; Idem 1939, p. 7.

The effect of this was that all classes of people left Bushehr for places that offered employment and more economic opportunities. In 1931 the town had 20,000 inhabitants, but only 8,000 in 1937, a drop of 60% in six years! Another effect was rather successful smuggling, for which the government's economic policy provided a powerful incentive.[638] Living conditions for most people of Bushehr did not improve; taxes remained high, while a number of shops in the bazaar closed because it was difficult to obtain goods for sale; those few shops still open sold mostly inferior goods bought in and imported from Tehran. Wages improved somewhat in 1938 (Table 1.23) as there was steady work at the *E`temadiyeh* mill and the construction of the barracks.[639] Fortunately, sufficient stocks for the town were kept, plus some wheat that the peasants had hidden was smuggled into town and sold at prices lower than that fixed by the government. Although there was an increase in average wages this was offset by a rise in the cost of living (Table 1.22). There were some price reductions in 1938, but in 1939 the price of goods, other than food-stuffs, rose by 50% and some items such as cement and iron were unavailable. There was

635. Administration Report 1937, pp. 6, 9; Political Diaries, vol. 12, p. 512.
636. Administration Report 1937, p. 6.
637. Administration Report 1937, p. 10.
638. Administration Report 1937, pp. 4, 10.
639. Administration Report 1938, p. 9.

a rise in the cost of monopoly sugar, which was probably due to lack of smuggling.[640] In that year wheat and barley crops were good; the price of wheat was controlled; grain of inferior quality was as usual bought by the government with discounts of 15% in weight for adulteration at 140 rials per 300 kg and sold at 200 rials. Because the quality was bad, bakers mixed it with better wheat bought secretly from private traders. The price of barley was not controlled and was only exported and used locally as animal feed.[641]

Adequate wheat supplies were held for local consumption, and in 1940, monthly supplies were sent to Lengeh, Bandar Abbas, Jask and Chabahar. Wheat was bought at Rls.400 per ton and sold at Rls.500. Tobacco was bought at 2-4 rials per *man* of 7.5 lbs. and sold at 80 and 70 cents per 100 grams respectively for category 1 and 2. The price of piece goods was raised by about 25% for British and 15% for Japanese articles. The sugar and tea monopoly, which were under separate control, raised the prices of soft sugar by 123%, loaf sugar 133% and for tea by 10%.[642] The wheat and barley crops were satisfactory in 1940; free export of barley was allowed till August, when government control was imposed again. All stocks were bought by the Economic Department and bakers were forced to buy barley with every purchase of wheat. In 1940, wages hardly increased despite an increase in the cost of living, which at year's end became very noticeable combined with a shortage of ghee and rice. The price of food and piece-goods rose as well as those of tobacco and matches. This had a negative impact on many Bushehris, because there was less work as fewer ships came to Bushehr.[643] In March 1940, the metric system for weights and measures was officially introduced in the bazaar, which was imperfectly understood by some of the public. "It provided the shopkeepers occasionally with the opportunity for a little extra profit."[644]

In January 1940, the government made more land available for cultivation and relaxed the control of grain prices, which improved life for the peasants. There was export of wheat to Germany in early 1940, which caused a shortage of wheat in Bushehr and other ports, the more so as rains had not been good. However, the government allowed the free export of fruit. In December 1940, a system of rationing of grain was imposed at Bushehr. In January 1941, it was further ordered that wheat had to be mixed with at least 30% barley. Unfortunately, the 1941 harvest was not as good as the previous year, although it would have been sufficient for local needs. In May 1941, there was a bread shortage in Bushehr, which was relieved by the sale of recently imported wheat. However, the local authorities complained that it was unfit for consumption. By August 1941, it became clear that there was a wheat shortage and bakeries did not have enough supplies; this development coincided with the British and Soviet invasion of Persia in that same month. The government shop in Bushehr that retailed wheat was closed and instead limited supplies were made available to the bakeries. The local situation worsened by sending wheat to other Gulf Ports (Lengeh, Bandar Abbas, Jask and Chabahar). The result was that the poor sometimes could not get bread for a number of days. The already troublesome food situation worsened because of the departure of Reza Shah. For it became more difficult to collect grain than in the past due to fear of the shah's despotic power. Because this fear and

640. Administration Report 1939, p. 2, 7.
641. Administration Report 1939, p. 7.
642. Administration Report 1940, p. 2.
643. Administration Report 1940, pp. 4, 7.
644. Administration Report 1940, p. 8.

power was gone, the political and administrative system was in disarray, and therefore, it became much more difficult to supply the cities, the more so because transportation had been disrupted because of the occupation. Moreover, the food situation was worsened due to hoarding and an inefficient distribution system.[645] Until August the Economic Department bought wheat at 1,000 rials selling it at 1,150. In September higher prices were offered, but landowners preferred to wait for even higher prices. In September 1941 the situation improved, although wheat was still rationed. By the end of the same month, sugar was in short supply and by year's end the price was Rls. 22.5 (soft sugar) and Rls. 35.5 (loaf sugar) per 30 kg. Sugar remained scarce and cigarettes had the same problem.

The World War II Years

By October 1941, local stocks of wheat were almost exhausted when a ship from India arrived with 1,000 tons of wheat, which averted a renewed bread shortage. Thereafter Great Britain continued to deliver wheat for the next two years to alleviate the local food situation. For example, the British landed 13,500 tons of wheat at the Persian Gulf ports in November 1941, while another 15,000 tons were en route.[646] These imports were insufficient to restore stocks to a safe level, while prospect for next year's harvest were not good, because of disappointing rainfall. Although wages for workers increased (since Reza Shah's abdication, wages of government officials rose by 25% to 100% depending on the function), but the cost of living rose, as most prices rose far more than the wage increase. Prices for sugar and tea were raised by some 10%, while fabrics prices rose by 75% by year's end. Also, taxes were increased. In December 1941, the bread situation improved after the governor took steps against profiteering bakers. However, there were still too few bakeries with too little wheat, which sold bread at a high price. Therefore, wheat and sugar were transported from Shiraz. Because of a lack of rain, a drought seemed to be imminent and very few peasants had tilled their fields around Bushehr. Consequently, the price of fodder had risen.[647]

In 1942, the bread situation remained one of great concern. In January 1942, the bakeries were always crowded, but the poor could not afford to buy bread. The quality of bread was reduced through adulteration. Wheat supply to the bakeries was rationed, but the bread situation did not improve. The government closed the Monopoly sugar shops and in February introduced a system of ration cards, so that people could buy sugar directly from the Economic Department. But large stocks were available in Customs, which was held there to drive up prices, as a result of inducements provided by importers to Customs officials.[648] As feared, the crops failed in 1942, due to lack of rain. Only in Liravi and some parts of Tangestan and Dashti was there sufficient supply for local needs. The rest of the governorate suffered a shortage, which was relieved by imports from India and Canada. In addition, the government banned the exports of dates. By April 1942, the food situation had become desperate for a great many people in the Gulf

645. For a discussion of this 1941-42 famine, see Floor 2015 a.

646. Azimi 1989, pp. 41, 45; Skrine 1962, pp. 94-96, 117; Political Diaries, vol. 15, pp. 93, 118, 152, 156, 465, 487, 491, 517.

647. Political Diaries, vol. 14, pp. 5, 265, 403, 436, 492, 511, 535, 560, 589; Administration Report 1941, pp. 5, 13-14.

648. Political Diaries, vol. 15, pp. 33, 65; Administration Report 1942, p. 14.

1.24: End month prices of foodstuffs at Bushehr for the period between November 1942 and January 1945 (in rials/kg)

Item/ year	Nov 42	Dec 42	Apr 43	May 43	Jun 43	Aug 43	Oct 43	Nov 43	Dec 43	Jan 44	Feb 44	Mar 44	Apr 44	Jun 44	Jul 44	Sep 44	Oct 44	Jan 45
Mutton	-	7	12	-	12	18	18	19	20	20	22	25	25	21	21	21	21	22
Ghee	37	42	50	-	58.5	63	62	67.5	57.5	67.5	70	79	79	67	77	80	80	110
Rice	-	10	20	-	-	20	22.5	32.5	20	22.5	19	20	22	18	18	21	20	15
Tea	110	125	96	-														
Tea open market	-	-	200	-	180	160	160	180	160	160	180	300	320	300	300	270	240	240
Sugar monopoly	10	-	19	-	-	-	-	-	-	-	-	-	-	-	-	-	-	-
Sugar commer-cial	30	40	90	-	65	85	100	100	95	85	110	110	120	90	90	50	60	70
Flour	7	-	7	7	6.75	9	9	8	8	8	8	8	8	10	10	10	8	12
Barley	-	-	3.5	3.2	4	4.25	4	4.5	4.5	4.5	4.5	4.5	4.5	4.5	4.5	4.5	4.5	6
Potatoes	-	9	-	9	6.75	Un.	10	10	6	6	4.5	5	7	9	18	10	9	8
Milk	-	-	-	6.75	4.5	4.5	4.6	4.6	4.6	4.6	4.6	4.6	4.6	4.6	4.6	4.6	4.6	6
Charcoal	-	-	-	-	-	4	5.5	6.5	7	5.5	5	3.5	3.5	4	3.5	3.5	3.5	4.5
Wheat	-	7	-	-	-	-	-	-	7.75	7.75	7.75	7.75	7.75	7.75	7.75	7.75	7.75	7.75
Wheat black market	-	-	-	-	-	-	-	-	-	-	-	-	10	8.5	8.5	9	8.5	10
Wheat mixed-govt. price	-	-	-	-	-	-	-	-	-	-	-	-	5	5	5	5	5	5
Dhal	-	-	-	-	-	-	-	27	27	27	27	27	27	27	27	27	27	13
Onions	-	-	-	-	-	-	-	-	3	4	3	6.5	4	3.5	3.5	4	5	5
Beef	6	-	-	-	-	-	-	-	18	18	20	20	20	20	20	20	20	n.a.
Firewood	-	-	-	1.5	1	-	2.5	3	2.5	2	1.5	1.5	1.5	1.5	1.5	1.5	1.5	6
Dates	-	-	4	-	-	-	-	-	5.25	4.5	9	5	7	3	3.5	3	3.5	3
Coffee	-	-	-	-	-	-	-	-	45	45	45	45	45	45	45	45	45	45
Butter	-	-	-	-	-	-	-	-	Un.	72	72	80	80	80	80	82	80	100
Fish				-					9.5	8	9	9	7	9	12	12	10	11.9

Source: Political Diaries, vol. 15, pp. 318, 353, 465, 487, 491, 513, 517, 539, 564, 566, 614, 616, 631, 635, 651, 655; Idem, vol. 16, pp. 5, 10, 26, 30, 46, 54, 73, 78, 96, 98, 102, 123, 128,150, 153, 177, 199, 203, 226, 229, 249, 253, 271, 292.

Un. = unobtainable; n.a. = not available. Dhal = a dried pulse which has been split, or stews made from it, and an important ingredient of Indian food.

The sources also provide available mid-month price data, such as for the last available price data in the last column, which are valid for the first half of January 1945.

Ports, in particular in Dayyer, where some people died of starvation. Many poor peasants came to Bushehr to try and find food. The merchants of Bushehr started a subscription and by mid-April had collected Rls. 54,000 to feed the poor with dates and bread. The governor was persuaded to confiscate all local stocks of dates and to fix an appropriate

کوپن دی ۱۳۲۱ سه ۳ خزانه‌داری کل	کوپن دی ۱۳۲۱ دو ۲ خزانه‌داری کل	کوپن دی ۱۳۲۱ یک ۱ خزانه‌داری کل	کوپن مهر ۱۳۲۱ سه ۳ خزانه‌داری کل	کوپن مهر ۱۳۲۱ دو ۲ خزانه‌داری کل	کوپن مهر ۱۳۲۱ یک ۱ خزانه‌داری کل
کوپن بهمن ۱۳۲۱ سه ۳ خزانه‌داری کل	کوپن بهمن ۱۳۲۱ دو ۲ خزانه‌داری کل	کوپن بهمن ۱۳۲۱ یک ۱ خزانه‌داری کل	کوپن آبان ۱۳۲۱ سه ۳ خزانه‌داری کل	کوپن آبان ۱۳۲۱ دو ۲ خزانه‌داری کل	کوپن آبان ۱۳۲۱ یک ۱ خزانه‌داری کل
کوپن اسفند ۱۳۲۱ سه ۳ خزانه‌داری کل	کوپن اسفند ۱۳۲۱ دو ۲ خزانه‌داری کل	کوپن اسفند ۱۳۲۱ یک ۱ خزانه‌داری کل	کوپن آذر ۱۳۲۱ سه ۳ خزانه‌داری کل	کوپن آذر ۱۳۲۱ دو ۲ خزانه‌داری کل	کوپن آذر ۱۳۲۱ یک ۱ خزانه‌داری کل
کوپن اسفند ۱۳۲۱ شش ۶ خزانه‌داری کل	کوپن اسفند ۱۳۲۱ پنج ۵ خزانه‌داری کل	کوپن اسفند ۱۳۲۱ چهار ۴ خزانه‌داری کل	کوپن آذر ۱۳۲۱ شش ۶ خزانه‌داری کل	کوپن آذر ۱۳۲۱ پنج ۵ خزانه‌داری کل	کوپن آذر ۱۳۲۱ چهار ۴ خزانه‌داری کل
کوپن بهمن ۱۳۲۱ شش ۶ خزانه‌داری کل	کوپن بهمن ۱۳۲۱ پنج ۵ خزانه‌داری کل	کوپن بهمن ۱۳۲۱ چهار ۴ خزانه‌داری کل	کوپن آبان ۱۳۲۱ شش ۶ خزانه‌داری کل	کوپن آبان ۱۳۲۱ پنج ۵ خزانه‌داری کل	کوپن آبان ۱۳۲۱ چهار ۴ خزانه‌داری کل
کوپن دی ۱۳۲۱ شش ۶ خزانه‌داری کل	کوپن دی ۱۳۲۱ پنج ۵ خزانه‌داری کل	کوپن دی ۱۳۲۱ چهار ۴ خزانه‌داری کل	کوپن مهر ۱۳۲۱ شش ۶ خزانه‌داری کل	کوپن مهر ۱۳۲۱ پنج ۵ خزانه‌داری کل	کوپن مهر ۱۳۲۱ چهار ۴ خزانه‌داری کل

Monthly food ration coupons for the entire family 1942

price. However, the merchants bribed the governor, retook control over their stocks and raised the price of dates, which cost them Rls. 32 to Rls. 110-120 per Hashem *man* (ca. 60 kg). Some merchants withdrew their contributions and complained about the governor's behavior in Shiraz. The governor in his turn took bribes to allow the export of ghee and vegetables. To address the desperate situation, the governor-general of Fars ordered an extra 1,000 kg of wheat to be given to the bakeries in Bushehr, which he placed under the control of the police chief, who exercised strict control. The Jewish community, which in March 1942 had not received its 600 kg of wheat allotment this time received 700 kg. All these measures eased the bread situation in Bushehr.[649]

By April 1942, sugar, tea, and matches were all rationed and the same was planned for wheat. Despite the issue of an additional 500 kg of wheat to the bakers and the construction of another bakery by the Municipality there were still long lines at the bakery shops. In particular, the poor suffered and therefore, the *Khalij-e Iran*, Bushehr's daily, ran a series of articles accusing the governor of procrastination in distributing the Rls. 60,000 allotted to the poor from Rls. 68 million from the ex-Shah's estate. In vain, the governor tried to have the paper stop publication, but pressured by the merchants, the Chamber of Commerce and the police authorities he gave in and agreed to distribute the funds as follows: (i) Rls. 20,000 to the local poor identified by the merchants; (ii) Rls. 6,000 for the upkeep of the Municipality's Poor House; (iii) Rls. 5,000 to the poor of Borazjan; and (iv) Rls. 23,000 to buy dates and bread to feed the poor. The merchants of Bushehr raised another Rls. 60,000, while on 15 April, the British consulate fed 700 people and distributed cloth to poor women.[650]

649. Political Diaries, vol. 15, p. 92 (in Borazjan the governor-general of Fars also increased the daily allotment from 400 kg to 1,200 kg); Administration Report 1942, pp.19.

650. Political Diaries, vol. 15, pp. 88-89.

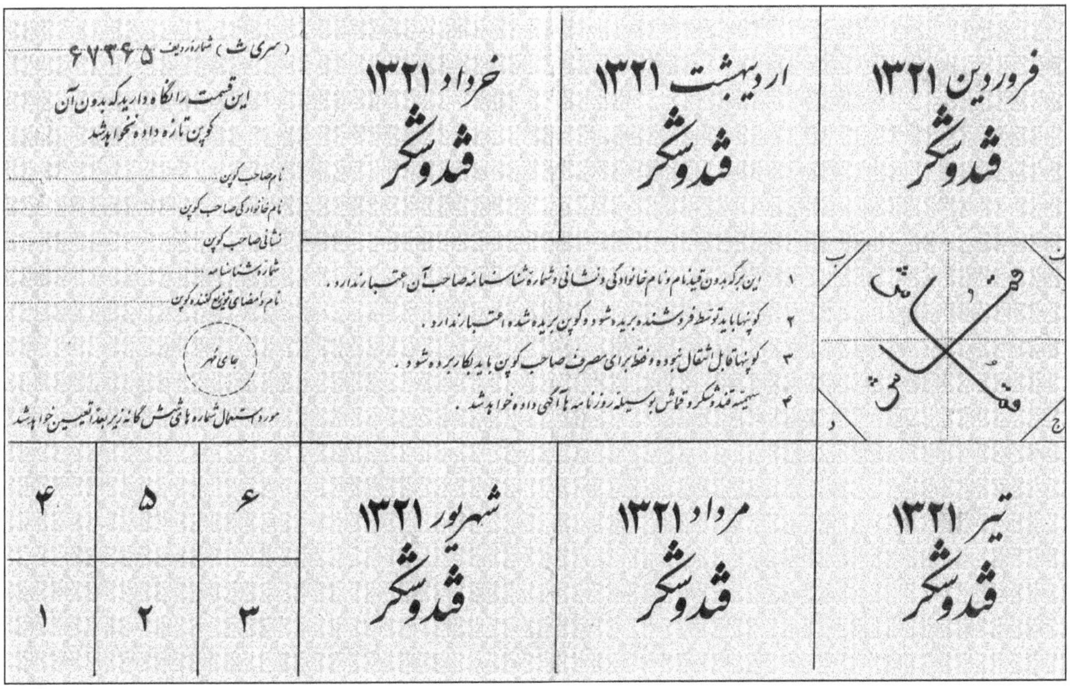
فروردین ۱۳۲۱ قند و شکر
اردیبهشت ۱۳۲۱ قند و شکر
خرداد ۱۳۲۱ قند و شکر
تیر ۱۳۲۱ قند و شکر
مرداد ۱۳۲۱ قند و شکر
شهریور ۱۳۲۱ قند و شکر
۶۷۳۶۵
۴ ۵ ۶
۱ ۲ ۳

Monthly ration coupons for sugar, tea and fabrics, per family, 1942

Prices of other products such as sugar, tea, and piece-goods further increased due to export restrictions by the government of India. This led to an increased sale of locally produced cotton fabrics. The sugar situation was aggravated by mismanagement of 55 tons of sugar by the Economic Department. As a result, sugar rationing was stopped and people had to buy sugar on the black market at double the price. Although sugar rationing was resumed in the first week of May 1942, but immediately too many ration cards were issued, for a price, of course. As a result, two-thirds of the population still had to buy sugar at Rls. 64 per *man* (2.9 kg) on the black market. Therefore, Shiraz began a census to determine how many cards should be issued. The bread situation worsened as poor people continue to come into town in search of food. To better address this problem, the governor wanted to build a model bakery and plans to that effect were studied. Rice was not rationed as the importing merchant agreed to sell his product at only 10% profit. Rice was mainly consumed by the wealthy, who then ate less bread, thus making more bread available to the poor.[651]

In the second half of May 1942, the leading merchants of Bushehr sent a complaint to Tehran about the dire situation of food, medicines, water and the lack of electricity due to the power plant breakdown. The census of Bushehr was completed and concluded that within a radius of 6 km of the town there were 20,000 people. The British consul suspected that this figure was higher than the real number of inhabitants as the census was done in a slipshod manner and the desire to please certain merchants to show that Bushehr was entitled to a larger share of sugar imports and wheat stocks. By order from Tehran, the sugar ration of 1 kg/p.p. was halved.[652] Again, because of famine conditions

651. Political Diaries, vol. 15, pp. 93-94, 117-18 (sugar price further rose; also of tea to Rls.50 per packet), 122.

652. Political Diaries, vol. 15, pp. 151, 157.

in the rural areas many poor came to town in large numbers. Therefore, the governor convened the merchants and asked them to resolve the problem. In June they contributed 6,000 *tumans* for the poor. But this was insuficient and the committee of merchants then raised money to repair and old caravanserai out of town, where they provided lodging for 500 men, women and children. Plans were also made to provide food, clothes and medical help for the sick among them. In July, the Economic Department sold rice cheaply, but only for one month. Also, the Rls. 60,000 of rice and Rls. 100,000 of sugar, tea and fabrics sent to Tangestan and Dashti was misappropriated by the local chiefs. The food situation in Bushehr remained bad; at one time in August 1942 there were only stocks left for 3 days' supply; fortunately help from Shiraz and the timely arrival of a British ship with 2,000 tons of wheat brought much needed relief. The situation was unnecessarily made worse by smuggling and bad distribution, enabled by payment to the chief of police and chief of the gendarmerie, whose organizations were to prevent smuggling on alternate nights. Moreover, even when stocks were large and sufficient there was profiteering by delaying distribution.[653] In November 1942, food supply in Bushehr was insufficient to feed the town until the next harvest let alone the surrounding districts. The town's bread situation was serious; the bread ration was 170 grams (6 ounces)/head/p.d. As result, bakeries were besieged by crowds and many deaths occurred due to malnourishment. Some individual cases were heart-rending such of a Dashti man who sold his two children. They were bought not to be used as slaves, but to help out the father. Meat and dates also increased in price, respectively from Rls. 5.5 to Rls. 7 per kg, due the fodder shortage, and from Rls. 80 to Rls. 190 per Hashem *man*, due to purchases by the Bank. The food situation was also used for local politicking. On 24 November 1942, the staff of the Post Office and the Economic Department rushed to the bakeries for bread. This was done to embarrass the acting governor, who had placed an unpopular man in charge of the bazaar control.[654] In November 1942, the British Residency regularly distributed dates among the poor of Bushehr, while in November 1942 it also sent 270 baskets of dates to Hayat Da'ud and other Gulf ports. In December 1942, the merchants of Bushehr raised 10,000 *tumans* to help the poor; half of this was supplied by Mr. Agar of the *E`temadiyeh* Cotton Mill. The butchers threatened to close their shops, because the army had not paid its bill of 500 *tumans*; the garrison commander Nuri was known to make a hefty profit from the shopkeepers at Bahmani.[655] In December 1942, the local Charitable Committee began to distribute daily meals, fuel, lighting and clothes. By the end of the month 500 people had been helped, who had been housed in a caravanserai rented for that purpose for a few months. The continuation of this scheme depended on the availability of additional funds. Meanwhile prices of food continued to rise, while the Committee of Price Control did not interfere at all.[656] By the end of 1942, staple food prices had risen 200% compared to 1941 and 400% compared with 1936. The rise in the cost of living was due to a variety of factors, most importantly by: i. increase in population; ii. hoarding by merchants; iii. ineffective control by the Municipality over bazaar prices. Therefore, the governor appointed a committee to fix prices of foodstuffs and appointed a municipal market inspector. It is not known how effective these measures were, but they could only

653. Political Diaries, vol. 15, pp. 223, 261; Administration Report 1942, pp. 7-8.
654. Political Diaries, vol. 15, pp. 315-16; Administration Report 1942, pp. 15-16.
655. Political Diaries, vol. 15, pp. 317-18, 347. A basket of dates (*qowsarah*) weighed 31.6 kg.
656. Political Diaries, vol. 15, pp. 352-353 (price list).

have had a temporary PR impact. The government of India made seed available, of which Bushehr only received 350 tons, half of what was needed for the governorate. Of this quantity 100 tons were made available to the Shabankareh project. A local committee decided on the best distribution of the remaining 250 tons, while sub-committees were set up in districts to do the same at their level. The result were considered satisfactory, while fine rains promised a good harvest.[657]

In January 1943, Tehran informed the merchants of Bushehr that Shiraz had been ordered to send extra rice and maize to Bushehr, but there was no extra wheat available. The Ministry of Foodstuffs finally began issuing ration cards in Bushehr town for sugar (500 g/p.p./m), tea (50 g/p.p./m) and bread, for which the amount was to be announced later. However, due to inertia in the system, it took a while before shopkeepers were able to comply with the new rations.[658] In February 1943, the British Residency gave 50 baskets of dates, two bags of rice and 1,000 *tumans* for distribution to the Commission for the Poor (*Komisiyun-e Mostamandan*). Food stocks were low in Bushehr in that month. Barley was mixed with wheat to alleviate the situation until 100 tons released from the British Army would arrive, which measures improved the situation considerably. While people paid 8 *tumans* for 450 g of tea and 6 *tumans* for 1 kg of sugar, 5,000 tons of sugar and 500 tons of tea were held in the Customs. Meat and fish were scarce and some days not even available, which was partly due to a butchers' strike protesting against price control measures taken by the Municipality. All this made life for the population of the littoral very harsh, the more so when officials of the Foodstuffs Department misappropriated food allotments. In Bushehr in February 1943, the Department began selling 20,000 baskets of dates at Rls. 120, which was Rls. 30 below the market price. Initially, sales took place through some trusted shopkeepers, but the Department soon took sales into its own hands when it was found that the traders were not to be trusted after all. By March 1943, barley supplies were ample and harvest prospects looked very good. Subscription were held to buy clothes for the poor for New Year. Mr. Agar offered to match the amount subscribed.[659]

In the second half of April 1943 food supplies arrived from the districts. Wheat was sold at Rls. 32 per 3.5 kg and barley at Rls. 18 per 3.5 kg. Sugar prices rose from Rls. 55 to Rls. 110 on the black market, later its price dropped to Rls. 90. Government sugar rose from Rls. 11 to Rls. 19/kg. There was no longer shortage of meat. The British Residency distributed date baskets at Delam and Shabankareh. Although there were imports of flour and grains, the price of wheat rose on the black market to Rls. 8.5/kg. The new harvest was processed by June 1943, but the problem was its collection. Moreover, troubles in Dashti and Tangestan made it unlikely that supplies might be coming from there.[660] In June it was expected that 183 tons of wheat would be collected from the districts. Prices went slightly down, but meat was in short supply. In early July 1943, the Supply Department threw 1,000 baskets of dates and 80 tons of potatoes into the sea as they had become unfit for human consumption, due to the fact that its director, Mr. Navvab, had stored

657. Administration Report 1942, pp. 14-15 (only 25% of land in the Shabankareh project had been brought under irrigation. Also, better cement was needed to prevent leakage in the irrigation channels), 20.

658. Political Diaries, vol. 15, pp. 381-82.

659. Political Diaries, vol. 15, pp. 404, 409, 433, 461 (food situation at Lengeh is serious).

660. Political Diaries, vol. 15, pp. 465, 487, 480-91, 512-13.

them too long and refused to give them to the public. He also gave permits to anyone who wanted to buy wheat. As a result, peasants held back stocks and the price of wheat rose to 500 *tuman*/ton in Borazjan as compared to the government price of 350 *tumans*/ton. After an intervention by the British in Tehran the issuance of such permits was withdrawn. The remaining dates in stock were sold by the *Khvarbar* or Foodstuffs Department, while prices remained unchanged.[661] Unfortunately, the commitments made by major landlords as to the wheat supply were not honored and the supply estimates were reduced. What also did not help this situation was that the transport situation was bad and that during the last year the head of the Foodstuffs Department had been changed five times, which made the functioning of this Department even more disorganized than previously. The collection of food was carried under three different schemes: "(i) in the northern ports area, on a contract between Fathullah Khan [Hayat Da'ud] and H.M. Consul; (ii) in Dashtistan and the Southern Ports area, on contracts granted by the Shiraz Supply Department; (iii) in Dashtistan and Tangistan, under the Bushire Supply Department, with (formerly) the assistance of the military column." However, by September 1943, Fathollah Khan Hayat Da'udi had difficulty meeting his contractual obligation due to the lack of transport inland. Supplies from other contractors and local purchases hardly amounted to anything noteworthy. Because some of the contractors fell under Shiraz it was difficult to put pressure on them to honor their obligations.[662] It was decided not to copy the ration sale system of Tehran (sale of wheat instead of bread), but to permit the sale of a limited quantity of grain (60% wheat, 40% barley) at the Supply Department's rate of Rls. 5/kg. The grain sold to the bakers was reduced by the quantity that was sold via a Municipal shop, which resulted in a market price of Rls. 6/kg, much below the black market price of Rls. 7.5/kg. The government made a profit by selling the grain mixture at Rls. 5.5/kg, which it bought at Rls. 3.6/kg. This profit was used to subsidize the remaining share of the daily supply taken care of by the bakers, who sold this subsidized bread at Rls. 3/kg with a reasonable profit for themselves. If a baker would buy 400 kg of grain from the Supply Department and sell it to the public at the official price, it was calculated he would suffer a loss of Rls. 225/day. Therefore, bakers sold each flap of bread for Rls.1, on average there were five flaps per kg. However, with the new system, the subsidized price was enforced. There was still uncertainty whether the monthly supplies for the Gulf Ports (304 tons) would be secured. The Customs authorities were also ordered to forward 4,000 tons of sugar to Tehran and to make room for future imports.[663]

In October 1943, the Supply Department began a census for the issue of new coupons for sugar, tea, and cloth. The bread ration scheme had not yet been put into effect and supplies to the bakeries were insufficient. Also, two trucks for the collection of grain only became available in November 1943. The Foodstuffs Department asked the government that the rations for Bushehr be fixed at the same level as that of Tehran at 250 g/day/pp.[664] After Fathollah Khan Hayat Da'udi had supplied the town with 1,500 tons of grain, thus averting a disaster in Bushehr during the critical period, the British consul wanted to transfer his contract to the Supply Department. However, because the latter was slow

---

661. Political Diaries, vol. 15, pp. 516-17, 538-39 ('Ali Chahpiri Tangestani offered his peasants only 266 *tumans*/ton, while in Dashti the chiefs paid 333 *tumans*/ton), 541-42.

662. Political Diaries, vol. 15, pp. 563-64, 566, 588, 613.

663. Political Diaries, vol. 15, pp. 612-14.

664. Political Diaries, vol. 15, pp. 616, 631, 634-35, 651.

and unclear about the precise terms of the contract, the delivery of supplies from Hayat Da'ud slowed down. As a result, the town's food situation became critical, because the other contractors did not live up to their obligations. People were afraid for a new famine, because the rains had not started yet by December 1943. Fortunately, the terms of the contract with Fathollah Khan were resolved. However, one of the other contractors was unable to supply the promised wheat, which in January 1944, caused a serious problem that temporarily was stop-gapped by taking wheat from a shipment for Shiraz. Steps were taken to speed up deliveries from Dashti with help of the military.[665] The wheat situation remained precarious and there was barely enough to cover daily needs. Ironically, because of the rains, supplies were difficult to transport. Fortunately, the sugar situation in January 1944 improved, for the *Khvarbar* (Foodstuffs) Department raised the monthly sugar ration from 400 g to 600 g. In February 1944, a baker who was short-selling bread was given 50 lashes.[666] In March 1944, the `*Adalat* Party complained to Tehran about the percentage of millet and barley mixed with wheat, while it also protested against sending supplies from Bushehr to other Gulf ports. Also, the *Khvarbar* Department was renamed *Edareh-ye Ghalleh* and took over from the Finance Department (*dara'i*) as of 24 March 1944.[667]

In mid-April 1944, the Bushehr Cereal and Bread Department had no supplies for the bakeries and announced that it permitted the free import of wheat and its sale in town. The reason was that most of the contractors had failed to supply the promised quantities of wheat for 1943-44. The only contractor who had done reasonably well (51%) was Fathollah Khan, the *ra'is-e entezamat* of Liravi, Hayat Da'ud and Rudhilleh; the other contractor, Hekmat only supplied 7% of what he had promised to deliver. The drought and crop failure (except in the irrigated part at Shabankareh) made deliveries of grain more difficult. The situation looked dire for the Gulf Ports, because without new supplies famine threatened again. A supply from Shiraz of 100 tons of wheat and 400 tons of barley provided temporary relief. Bread in Bushehr at that time consisted of 80% barley.[668] Despite this worrisome situation, the public contributed Rls. 130,000 to the victims of the Gorgan earthquake in April as well as in March more than Rls. 160,000 to the APRRF, which by May had risen to Rls. 200,000. In 1944, the APRRF included the maintenance of 160 poor in a caravanserai at Shekeri, arrangements for the burial of the poor, and a monthly grant to the Public Health Department to maintain a number of sick poor. Clothes for 150 people were distributed to the poor, while the APRRF was also instrumental in arranging the two tanker trucks for water distribution (see above).[669]

The precarious food situation also affected the British Residency and its staff; because of transportation problems even the British in Bushehr had great trouble in getting food supplies, which, moreover, had to be bought at very high prices. Therefore, in early 1944 the Resident requested that Army rations be made available for a few months. On 21 June 1944, the Army Council approved this request, becauwe of the exception circumstances prevailing at Bushehr.[670] In May 1944, the *Edareh-ye Ghalleh* allowed the import and sale of wheat in Bushehr with special permits. This led to a price drop on the black

---

665. Political Diaries, vol. 15, pp. 654-55; vol. 16, pp. 5, 9-10.
666. Political Diaries, vol. 16, pp. 25-26, 29-30.
667. Political Diaries, vol. 16, pp. 46, 49
668. Political Diaries, vol. 16, pp. 73, 77-78.
669. Political Diaries, vol. 16, pp. 75. 96, 98, 224. For the caravanserai at Shekeri, see Hamidi 1380, p. 420.
670. IOR/L/PS/12/3595, War Office to Foreign Office 21/06/1944.

market for wheat to Rls. 7,150/ton (the government price was Rls. 5,000) and barley to Rls.5,140 (the government price was Rls. 3,750). Two so-called 'free' bakeries sold bread with a high percentage of wheat at Rls. 2 per flap, while the government shops still sold bread with 80% barley. This mixture remained in use at explicit government orders until further notice. Fathollah Khan delivered more wheat and was expected to deliver another 500 tons from Liravi.[671]

The sale of rationed cloth in early March 1944, detailed below, is a case in point how corrupt the distribution system was.

671. Political Diaries, vol. 16, pp. 101-02, 122-23, 127-28, 150, 153, 177, 181, 199.

The Kharbar Department recently received order from Tehran permitting them to proceed with the sale of cloth to the public at the scale of 3 metres per ration ticket holder. The news soon spread round the town, and those who had not already done so hastily registered their own ration tickets in addition to any others they could lay their hands on. All waited expectantly for the opening of the one of the Government cloth distribution shop in which two assistants were apparently preparing themselves to deal with a situation which would clearly be similar to a summer sale at a London store.

This Government cloth shop has been open for the past nine months but if anyone ventured inside, the assistant in charge would point to a notice hung up by the door which informed the public briefly 'Tatil', and explained that no cloth could be sold from the year 1322 [1943/44] as orders had not been received from the Capital. On March 6th the sales were started, prices averaging Rials 60/- a meter for silk and Rials 12/- for cotton, and when one considers that the open market rates for cloth are still in the neighbourhood of Riuals 250/- for silk and Rials 45/- for cotton per metre, in addition to the fact that no Government cloth ration has been issued to the public for the past year, it is not surprising that enormous crowds collected to purchase the Government material. It was soon found out that no special arrangement had been made to deal with the situation and chaos reigned. Certain officials in the Kharbar Department however, were quick of the mark and made large purchases in the name of various people in the town, including apparently the recently deceased. They are now believed to hold large stocks in their houses for more convenient disposal.

If some unfortunate customer in the crowd did eventually, by a miracle, reach the counter and secure attention he was invariably told that the cloth of his choice was earmarked for a Government official, or if he received his 3 metre ration, he then saw several more metres being cut off the arms roll and stowed behind the scenes, 'for Officers of Government Departments', as the attendant would explain. In the case of more attractive rolls they would be informed that the piece had been received a metre short from Tehran and could not be sold until the discrepancy had been cleared up. At the end of each day hundreds of disappointed customers would be turned away, some unfortunates having been waiting since dawn. The chaos still continues more or less unabated.

Source: Political Diaries, vol. 16, pp. 45-46.

Bread and cloth were not the only products that were the object of corruptive practices, but so were sugar and tea of which each person was supposed to receive 500 g (sugar) and 50 g (tea) per month, at the official government price of Rls. 18 and Rls. 80/kg. The black market price for sugar fluctuated between Rls. 80-110 and for tea Rls. 250-300/kg. The distribution officials claimed larger quantities than they actually distributed and sold the difference in the black market. Although this was known to the government it took no action, despite continuing scandals about its implementation.[672]

672. Political Diaries, vol. 16,p. 179-80, 201.

In September 1944, the *Edareh-ye Ghalleh* announced that henceforth it would issue a mixture of wheat and barley in equal proportion, which news was welcomed by the consumers. In October 1944, the bakeries were put under the control of the *Edareh-ye Ghalleh*, which caused a storm of protest of those who stood to lose illicit gain. Because the 1944 local harvest had been a failure the authorities wanted to make sure that peasants had seeds to sow in November. To that end 800 tons of wheat seed was shipped from India, while 400 tons of barley seed came from Shiraz. The seed was distributed (2/3 wheat and 1/3 barley) to Liravi, Hayat Da'ud, Rudhilleh, Angali (450 tons), Bushehr, Borazjan (450 tons), Tangestan, Dashti and the Bandar-e Thalatheh (300 tons). Farmers wanting seed needed to ask the *Edareh-ye Ghalleh* and give a guarantee (with security) that they would repay the government. By November 1944 the distribution of seed had succeeded well and good harvest prospects were supported by excellent rainfall. Farmers were pleased with the seed, the more so because it had a higher yield than the local variety. Even fallow land near Bushehr and land that had not been cultivated for years had been seeded and tilled, even waste land along the road to Sabzabad. Only in Tangestan the Indian seed was not distributed as the main landowner distributed his own seed there.[673]

In March 1945, the food situation had much improved. More ghee was sold in the market, while its price had dropped to Rls. 280/kg. Some 20 additional poor persons were sent by the police to Shekeri, where in March 1945 some 160 persons were living. Of these 20 persons 10 left, because they were professional beggars. In that month it was clear that there was enough food in the governorate. The expected quantity available after the harvest was 4,400 tons, of which the governorate consumed 4,000 tons. On Nowruz the APRRF distributed a free meal (rice, vegetables and meat) to about 1,000 poor in the different quarters of the town. The support to the poor at Shekeri also continued.[674] When a swarm of locusts landed at `Ali Changi and Bunehgaz, peasants brought about five tons of them for sale to Bushehr in early March, which was a welcome additional source of protein.[675] In that same month, the Finance Department began selling cloth at 3 m/p.p./per coupon. However, the cloth was expensive and of bad quality and only suitable for women's wear. Therefore, people complained to the governor saying that good government cloth had been substituted by cheap bazaar cloth. The APRRF allotted 5,000 m of white calico and distributed 5 tons of *gur* (sugar made of cane and date juice) from India. To prevent corruption the calico was distributed as 1 meter strips throughout the governorate. The *gur* was distributed over the 15 different areas of the town.[676] In 1945, the British consul distributed the balance of the cloth from India in Borazjan, Ahram, Ganaveh, Saadabad, Darwahen and Dehkohneh. Because the poor had been unable to buy cloth during the last five years the APRRF activity was greatly appreciated.[677] But for the APRRF, little of the government cloth, tea and sugar reached the villagers. Whereas in Bushehr these articles were only distributed on coupon, outside the town these were

---

673. Political Diaries, vol. 16, pp. 202-03, 224-26, 228-29, 249, 253, 271, 292. Poor people not only had trouble paying for food. In December 1944 it was reported that recently a committee of merchants and a *mojtahed* had been formed to collect regular funds for the burial of paupers and repair of houses in Bushehr. Monthly subscriptions were asked but, according to the British consul, "it is likely that it will not achieve much due to mistrust in it." Political Diaries, vol. 16, p. 274.

674. Political Diaries, vol. 16, pp. 324, 347, 352-53; Administration Report 1945, p. 15.

675. Political Diaries, vol. 16, p. 348.

676. Political Diaries, vol. 16, pp. 347, 349.

677. Administration Report 1945, pp. 15, 17.

given to the various *ro'asa-ye entezamat.* These sold most of the allotment of their villagers on the black market.[678]

The 1944-45 harvest was the best in 23 years, so that in April 1945 there was a labor shortage and harvest time lasted one month longer than usual. The date crop was also excellent and prices of dates were lower than at any time since 1939. The government announced that henceforth the grain market was free, and indeed, grain was offered at much lower and even at moderate prices. Bakeries were told to buy their needs in the free market, but refused. After a meeting between all parties concerned it was decided that the government would continue to supply the bakeries. The share of barley was reduced from 50% to 25%. The meeting also decided that five bakeries would be sufficient for the town (one at Bahmani, one at Sangi and three in town). The British consul disagreed with this last decision; he held the view that to prevent overcrowding there should be at least 10 bakeries. In May 1945, as an indication that the food situation had become normal and under control, Shiraz informed the Bushehr authorities that all sub-branches of the *Edareh-ye Ghalleh* would be closed per 22 May 1945 and that no more wheat would be sent and that the bakeries had to buy their wheat in the free market. This they did, despite their earlier opposition.[679] In June 1945, the APRRF sold the *gur* (sugar) imported from India to the poor of Bushehr and suburbs at cost; 600 m of calico was sent to Lengeh for sale to the poor there. In February 1946 the British consul distributed 56 khaki suits, presented by the government of India to the APRRF, for poor school boys.[680]

In April 1946, the wheat harvest was looking good as well. Therefore, the Bushehr committee decided to lower the price of bread from Rls. 4 to Rls. 3.5 per kg. The bakers, supported by Hoseyn Shabankareh, the mayor, went on strike. The governor broke the strike by giving permits to other bakers and revoking those of the striking bakers. Fathollah Khan Hayat Da'udi promised to supply wheat to Bushehr at a fixed rate of Rls. 140 per 56 kg.[681] In August 1946 the Finance Department lifted the restriction on the movement of wheat and allowed wheat to be sold freely, except for the 1946 crop, which had to be sold to the government.[682] Despite the good supply situation of grains, prices of foodstuffs rose sharply in November-December 1946, probably because shopkeepers took advantage of the change of administration and the weakness of the governor. In July 1947, prices of wheat rose and caused a shortage of bread; it was believed that this was the result of hoarders hoping that rains would be late.[683] Because of the rise in prices wages also had to rise, such that the cost of living allowance for government employees almost equalled their pay. This situation was made worse by "the corruption and inefficiency of the local Administration (especially the Central Government Departments) is only equalled by the apathy of almost all the local inhabitants and their inability to complain against misgovernment."[684]

From the above, it is clear that the war years were not kind to the people of Bushehr as most port development, and thus employment, took place in the upper Persian Gulf

678. Administration Report 1945, p. 16-17
679. Political Diaries, vol. 16, pp. 378-79, 397-98, 401; Administration Report 1945, pp. 16-17.
680. Political Diaries, vol. 16, p. 426; vol. 17, p. 33.
681. Political Diaries, vol. 17, pp. 82, 107.
682. Political Diaries, vol. 17, p. 182.
683. Political Diaries, vol. 17, p. 293, 491.
684. Administration Report 1946, p. 2.

area. Moreover, landlords, shopkeepers, and government officials misused their control over the supply and distribution chain to misappropriate goods as well as to create artificial shortages, thus securing their own benefits, but hurting that of the majority of the population. It was these corruptive practices and low purchasing power of the poor more than anything else that caused hunger and malnutrition among them. By 1947, most of the governorate's inhabitants were dirt poor. The workers of the modern factories were an exception to this rule. Those living on the coast, as before, made ends meet with smuggling and given the ample availability of fish they could satisfy their daily intake of the staple food, viz. fish. The rest of the population was engaged in agriculture, mainly wheat and barley, while date production was poor.[685]

685. NA, FO 371/15473; Binning 1857, vol. 1, p. 150 ("Fish abound; the best are halva-mahi or Pomflet fish and biyah a species of mullet."). For the fish available in the Persian Gulf, see the article "Fish," *EIr*. For other lists of fish in the Gulf see Lorimer 1915, vol. 2, Appendix E, "Fisheries of the Persian Gulf," pp. 2308-2218, Vadala 2536, p. 110 and Sadid al-Saltaneh 1342, pp. 111-115 (local names and weights), annex pp. XIX-XXI (local names). For a detailed list of all fish occurring in the Persian Gulf, accompanied by pictures, see Hoseyn Nurbakhsh, *Abizan-e Khalij-e Fars*. Tehran: Amir Kabir, 1370/1991.

2

The Trade of Bushehr

Although Bushehr remained the most important Persian port in the Persian Gulf during the Qajar period (1794-1925) the reason for this was not obvious nor did it go unchallenged and in the end Bushehr lost its leading position.[1] Bushehr was not a better port than its competitors, in fact in some ways it was worse. Thus, Bandar Abbas in the early part of the nineteenth century and Mohammerah in the early part of the twentieth century tried to dislodge Bushehr from its leading position. However, a combination of political, institutional, logistical and commercial factors enabled Bushehr to stave off its competitors until the 1920s, when new modern ports with better facilities and roads took over and reduced Bushehr to a minor port.

Four competing ports

During the nineteenth and the early part of the twentieth century four ports on the northern shores of the Persian Gulf dominated the caravan trade routes to Persia's interior, to wit: Bandar Abbas, Bushehr, Mohammerah and Basra. Lengeh was but a minor irritant for the other ports and mainly played a local role, its trade being for the most part with the Arabian coast.[2] Of these ports Basra and Bushehr were by far the most important, but Basra was an Ottoman, not a Persian port, although at least 65% of Basra imports around 1900 were destined for the Baghdad Kermanshah route.[3] There were a number of reasons why Bushehr remained the most important port of southern Persia. It was not because it was better situated or more convenient than the other ports. In fact, none of the Persian ports were very attractive. Apart from Mohammerah, no other Persian port had a harbor. "Bushire, Lingah and Bundar Abbas are merely open roadsteads, where a landing can sometimes be effected only with great difficulty, and for days it may be impossible to work cargo."[4]

Why then had Bushehr become the most important Persian port? There were three factors that favored Bushehr over the other ports: (i) a commercial community that was more numerous and influential than in any other southern port; (ii) the presence of the British Residency as well as about 10 Consulates of foreign nations; and (iii) relatively

1. For the situation before 1800, see Floor 2007 a.
2. See Floor 2010.
3. Whigham 1903, p. 147.
4. Whigham 1903, p. 156.

large markets in its hinterland. I will discuss these three factors in what follows, but first I discuss the less favorable characteristics of Bushehr as a port in comparison with its competitors.

Bandar Abbas had a shallow anchorage of some three km from shore, which was protected to some degree from the winds by the three islands of Hormuz, Larak, and Qeshm.[5] Some observers, therefore, held that Bandar Abbas was the better harbor, although admitting it needed much improvement. However, as in the case of other Persian ports, there was very little public investment in port upgrading.[6] Therefore, as a result, by 1900, there was only "a dilapidated stone pier at Bandar [Abbas], which is left high and dry at low water."[7] The situation at Lengeh was not much better. Its roadstead was sheltered from the north-west winds, but was dangerous when winds blew from other directions. In the 1850s, a small masonry breakwater provided some protection to small vessels.[8] When Whigham visited the port 50 years later he noted that "There is a diminutive dock, which, when I visited the port, was mainly occupied by a small sailing-ship that had got inside on an abnormally high tide, but could not be removed."[9] Mohammerah (now Khorramshahr), located on the confluence of the Shatt al-Arab and Karun rivers, had the advantage of a river anchorage on the Shatt al-Arab, but it lacked storage capacity and to become more attractive would require opening up a new caravan route to the interior of Persia, along a more arduous, less safe and not shorter road.[10] Sailing to Basra and then clearing Turkish customs was another option, which entailed changing to river craft, then breaking up bulk goods, followed by crossing an unsafe route between Baghdad and Kermanshah, where Persian duties had to be paid. Therefore, this route was only used for consumption along the Tigris, in Kermanshah and Hamadan.[11]

Anchorage

According to a British commercial commission, Bushehr was neither the best situated nor the most convenient of Persian ports.[12] Binning went even further and wrote that given Bushehr's anchorage it was "a poor apology for a great commercial seaport."[13] The port of Bushehr consisted of an open roadstead and lighter quays along the shore. In fact, it had two poor anchorages, which were only partly protected against the prevailing winds from the NW. The inner one was 4 to 4.5 km offshore with minimum depths of 6 meters (m); the outer one was 10 km distant from the shore with minimum depths of 12 m. The

5. Trade Report 1912-13, p. 6.
6. Gleadow-Newcomen 1905, p. 33.
7. Whigham 1903, p. 156. For a detailed discussion of the anchorage situation at Bandar Abbas, see Floor 2011 a, p. 125.
8. Pelly 1864, p. 251.
9. Whigham 1903, p. 156. For a detailed discussion of the anchorage situation at Lengeh, see Floor 2010, p. 75.
10. Trade Report 1912-13, p. 7; Pelly 1865 a, p. 59.
11. Pelly 1865 a, p. 59.
12. Gleadowe-Newcomen 1905, p. 59; see also Pelly 1865 a, p. 49.
13. Binning 1857, vol. 1, p. 139.

The Bushehr Dock (1914)

approaches were narrow and shallow.[14] The tides in the inner harbor rose by 1.8 meter (6 feet) and in the outer harbor by 1.20 meter (4 feet).[15]

Sailing ships exceeding three hundred tons burden, as well as steam ships after 1860, had to lie in the roads where the holding ground of mud was good. Here steamers dropped anchor and waited to be relieved of their mails and cargo and to receive fresh shipments. However, the outer anchorage was only partly protected especially in winter, as tides were strong when breezes prevailed, such as strong prevailing winds from the north-west (*shamal*) and east (*sharqi*), then it became unusable due to high swells, which made landing of goods and maintenance of communications difficult.[16] In the first part of the nineteenth century, especially, "during the fury of the N.W. winds, ships were frequently forced to cut their cables and bear up for Karak."[17] In the Halileh bight the beach was low and sandy with 3.6 – 5.5 m of water; it was used by small vessels to anchor when the *shamal* blew.[18] The outer anchorage had room for large number of steamers of up to 5,000 tons gross in water of 4-5 fathoms.[19]

In about 1863, to facilitate entering the roads, `Abdol-`Aziz of the Bani Hajer erected the 10 m high Aziz Lighthouse (*Manareh-ye `Aziz*) in the southwest of Bushehr, which for 15 years served as a beacon for ships. Each year the British-Indian Steam Navigation Company (BISNC) paid him 60 *tuman* and 24 tins of coconut oil; one year before his death the beacon was discontinued because 3 to 4 bulbs broke.[20] Thereafter the outer

14. Pelly 1865 a, p. 49; Buckingham 1971, p. 356; Trade Report 1912-13, p. 7; NA, FO 371/15471; Sa`adat 1390, pp. 29-30. Before steamers were used in the Persian Gulf the roadstead was more accessible, because sailing ships drew less water.
15. Anonymous 1828, p. 57.
16. Wellstead 1840, p. 132; Kinneir 1973, p. 70; Government of India 1924, p. 44; Pelly 1865 a, p. 49; Lorimer 1915, vol. 1, pp. 339-40; Ebtehaj 1932, p. 183; Stevens 1979, p. 284.
17. Kinneir 1973, p. 70; Kempthorne 1835, pp. 283-84; Sani` al-Dowleh 1294, vol. 1, 298; Buckingham 1971, p. 356.
18. Mahrad 1978, p. 91.
19. Government of India 1924, p. 43.
20. Sadid al-Saltaneh 1371, p. 56.

anchorage was marked by a buoy with an automatic white flashing light and another with a red flashing light near the inner anchorage, presumably installed by the British. From the British town Residency, on a flag mast at 22 meter (72 feet), a white light and a red light at 16.5 meter (54 feet) could be seen respectively from a distance of 24 km and 18 km (15 and 11 miles).[21] In January 1912, the Russian consul of Bushehr, Dmitriev, hoisted two powerful acetylene lamps high on the Russian consulate's flag mast to help ships to navigate at night. The shipping community very much appreciated this beacon as it could be seen far out to sea. However, by mid-1912 the lamps worked irregularly and during high winds they did not work at all, so that by year's end both were mainly out of order and were illuminated very irregularly.[22] Because, the Russian consulate was more or less moribund, thereafter the beacon likewise was discontinued. In 1936, the construction of a lighthouse and a small house began 5 km (3 miles) south of Bushehr was begun by an Italian engineer in Persian service.[23] In October 1940, the new Bushehr Lighthouse was inaugurated, which was operated by the Persian Navy.[24]

The inner anchorage provided better shelter during bad weather than the outer anchorage.[25] Moving from the outer to inner anchorage was done via a channel that was marked by red-flashing buoys; the actual anchorage was marked by a black-painted buoy. The two anchorages were separated by a distance of 8 km (5 miles) consisting of mudflats with only 5 meters of water at low tide.[26] Thus, it was only accessible to ships drawing less than 5 meter (15 feet), "and as the entrance is over a bar across a channel of less than half a mile [800 m] wide, such vessels can only go in with favorable wind, and at the top of high water in spring tides. The depth within increases to three and a quarter and three and a half fathoms [5.8 to 6.3 m], and the holding ground is good."[27] The inner anchorage was situated "at the head of a channel called Khur Deyreh and is situated in the middle of the bay," at about 5 km (3 miles) from Bushehr. It was sheltered on the NW side by a sand bank called *raq`at al-`ali*. The holding ground in the channel was good and the soundings 3 to 4 fathoms [5.4 to 7.2 m], but the approach in many parts had only 4.5 to 5.1 m [15 to 17 feet] of water and the inner anchorage was a rough one in a *shamal* or northern wind. "The bottom being very soft, steamers drawing 15 feet can enter Khur Deyreh in any state of the tide" when the wind was favorable. This was the case when the south wind was blowing, but not the north wind, which mainly prevailed, in which case it was necessary to wait for high tide. Six to seven steamers of 3,500-5,000 gross tons drawing 6 to 6.5 meter (19 to 20 feet) could generally be brought in during the highest water. Because the channel between the inner anchorage and wharves only had 1.5 meter (5 feet) of water at low water, vessels had to unload their goods on lighters. Moreover, these lighters could not draw more than 1.4 meter (4.6 feet), and only more when there was a favorable tide.[28] The stretch between the roads and the shore of some 9.5-14.5 km (6-9 miles) could "be so tough that strong men have been turned back to

---

21. Government of India 1924, p. 43; Administration Report 1913, p. 3.
22. Administration Report 1912, p. 30.
23. Administration Report 1936, p. 6.
24. Administration Report 1940, p. 4.
25. Kinneir 1973, p. 70; Kempthorne 1835, pp. 283-84.
26. Government of India 1924, p. 43.
27. Buckingham 1971, p. 356; Heude 1819, p. 43.
28. Lorimer 1915, vol. 2, pp. 339-40; Government of India 1924, p. 43; Geary 1878, vol. 1, p. 62.

the land. Passengers have been dropped into the dhows by cranes, and one woman, for safety had been deposited among bags of sugar when the waves tossed the dhow up to a level with the deck."[29] It usually took about one hour in the pilot's boat to reach Bushehr from the inner harbor.[30]

Passengers packed on a boat (1935)

From the inner anchorage to the 120 meter (360 feet) wide creek known as Khur Soltani was 5 km (3 miles). Here the customs jetty was located. In 1816, vessels could no longer anchor close to the north-eastern side of the town, because the narrow channel leading up to the Khur Soltani "now scarcely admits of small dows, except when they are lightened. There are anchorage-births for native boats behind some small islands, to the NE extremity of the inner harbor, or in the deepest part of the bight which it forms."[31] The situation did not change during the nineteenth century, for as late as 1940 the same limiting conditions existed. Only small vessels such as tugs, gun-boats, and small tankers that were able to cross this bank could lie on a flat sandy bottom in the Khur Soltani when the tide was out.[32] Even as late as the 1950s, modern vessels still had to anchor at 10 km (6 miles) from Bushehr and discharge their cargo and passengers by lighter.[33]

29. Merritt-Hawkes 1935, p. 1.
30. Cursetjee 2001, p. 113.
31. Buckingham 1971, p. 356; Wellsted 1840, p. 132 (here vessels could "land or receive their cargoes close to the houses."); Milburn 1813, vol. 1, p. 128.
32. Government of Great Britain 1945, p. 502; Lorimer 1915, vol. 2, p. 340; Government of India 1924, p. 44.
33. Stevens 1979, p. 284.

To make access to Bushehr easier a tender was offered in the mid-1870s to dredge the channel, but nothing came of it, despite the fact that it had been estimated that the cost would not be prohibitive.[34] In 1906, it was again suggested to improve the harbor of Bushehr "by dredging, at a small cost, enabling ships to anchor in a safe harbor, at a short distance for town."[35] But, once again, nothing was done to implement this harbor improvement. On 26 January 1931, Col. E.V. Collier, engineer of the Anglo-Persian Oil Company (APOC) came to advise the Persian authorities concerning the feasibility of constructing a new port at Bushehr. He said that the charts were out of date and, therefore, a new survey had to be made, costing £5-6,000. He estimated the total cost of the harbor project at £150,000 and recommended to contact a specialized firm in this field. The governor reported this to Tehran, but there was no follow-up, which was understandable given that the government had already opted to develop Bandar Shahpur, Ahvaz and Khorramshahr.[36] However, this meant that Bushehr was definitely out of the race to remain an important port.

Because of the difficult access to the landing jetty, in the early nineteenth century "strange ships signal to the town for a pilot, as all ships bound for Basra do, while those coming from Basra put their pilots ashore at Bushire."[37] This remained the pattern for the next 100 years and was a source of income for the governor of the port. Therefore, local government insisted that ships made use of a pilot (*robban*) on entering and leaving, which by the twentieth century was an imposition as the captains of the steamers knew "every square inch of both harbours." If it happened that the pilot came too late as the captain had already entered, then he could only excuse himself for his late arrival. The pilot went with departing ships as far as the bar of the Shatt al-Arab.[38] Because vessels were lying 10 km offshore, a departing ship fired a signal-gun to alert passengers ashore.[39]

Shipping & Handling

On arrival at Bushehr, apart from the unattractiveness of its harbor, reception, handling and forwarding of goods was done in an inefficient, cumbersome, and therefore, in an unnecessarily expensive way. First, lighters had to ship goods from the roadstead to the Customs wharf, during which process damage occurred, but this system also held for other Persian ports. The same inconveniences existed for the export of goods. The great distance, coming from the outer anchorage, involved greater risk of lightering and delays due to inadequate transport capacity and overloading of the lighters.

The capacity of handling goods was limited by the number of lighters (*teshaleh*) and coolies available. The lighters were "large row-boats, their crews sitting on the thwarts facing inward and rowing with the heart-shaped blades on their long sweeps almost parallel with the thwarts. This appeared an ingenious way of shirking a hard pull, but later

34. Stack 1882, vol. 1, p. 24.
35. Gleadow-Newcomen 1905, p. 33.
36. Administration Report 1931, pp. 6-7.
37. Milburn 1813, vol. 1, pp. 128-29.
38. Cursetjee 2001, pp. 109, 118; Nura'i 1385, p. 17; Government of India 1924, p. 43-44.
39. Ballantine 1879, p. 51.

Bushehr sailing ships

I discovered that all boats on the Persian Gulf are rowed in the same awkward manner."[40] Actually, the lighters had both sails and sweeps to make trips between ships and shore. The loading and unloading was done by coolies, a gang consisting of 20 men working at each hatch. Separate gangs were used for loading and unloading.[41] In the 1920-30s, there were no steam lighters, only those with engines and sails.[42] In the 1940s, about 40 lighters with 15-20 ton deadweight capacity, and dhows of 15-20 tons were available for unloading. The maximum monthly capacity with this equipment was about 6,000 tons of heavy cargo or 10,000 of light cargo, "allowing for bad weather, but with night work."[43] By 1947, the capacity of handling goods under difficult conditions amounted to:

> 1. For heavy cargo; i.e. using ship derricks and jetty cranes, only 100 tons per 24 hours, taking into account rough weather 5-7 months per year. This figure was doubled in calm weather.
>
> 2. For light cargo. i.e., packages of 3 cwt, which could be mostly manhandled, the capacity was 200 tons in rough and 400 tons in calm weather. In practice these volumes are higher.[44]

---

40. Cresson 1908, p. 254 (a sweep is a long oar used to propel a boat); Nura'i 1385, p. 9, n. 3; Hamidi 1380, p. 205.
41. NA, FO 371/15471.
42. Mahrad 1970, p. 88.
43. Government of Great Britain 1945, p. 503.
44. NA, FO 371/15471.

Bushehr Docks in the late-Qajar period.

The boatmen and coolies worked for a maritime transporter or *hammal-bashi*, who held the monopoly for landing and embarking goods at Bushehr. In about 1850, to ensure better handling of cargo arriving from sea, this function was created by Bushehri merchants, with the consent of the governor.[45] The *hammal-bashi* was not a government official, but a person in the service of the merchants. Initially, he does not seem to have paid anything for his monopoly, but he soon had to farm the right to do so from the governor. Initially, he paid 2,000 *qrans* per year an amount that rose to 9,000 *qrans* towards the end of the nineteenth century.The *hammal-bashi* had to buy the right to operate each year, and his appointment was subject to the approval of the director of the Customs Department and the local consuls. In 1903, he paid a lump sum to the governor and the Customs. Moreover, he had to pay 2,500 *qrans* monthly, of which 300 *qrans* were for the governor. However, according to others he had to pay 220,000 *qrans* per year or seven

45. NA, FO 60/658, letter 12/05/1902; Pelly, p. 49; Nura'i 1385, pp. 2, 53 (*ra'is-e hammal-bashiha*).

times more.[46] This amount may include the lump sum mentioned. Anyway, the amount did not depress the *hammal-bashi* very much, because he "still wore a prosperous look, and was supposed to pay more to the governor than he could pay considering the official fees he may charge."[47]

There were several disadvantages to this monopoly. First, the boatmen tried to take advantage by demanding high rates, so that sometimes a ship refused to pay these and went to Basra.[48] Second, boats could "not depart after sunset, nor move cargo ashore until the Manifest has been seen by the governor to ensure that the goods are moved by the *hammal-bashi*."[49] Third, the *hammal-bashi* could not guarantee a regular service, because he did not have enough boats and men. It happened that during a busy period, such as the grain export season, not more than 5 to 6 boats were available. Because he was not a government official he could not force other available vessels to unload waiting merchantmen.[50] The problem of the lack of lighters became worse, when a rival landing company tried to usurp the *hammal-bashi*'s position.[51] In 1872, attempts by the business community in Bushehr to buy steam barges and replace the lighters of the *hammal-bashi* came to nought. Initially, Tehran favored this plan. However, the plan had to be approved by the Bushehri authorities and the British firm of Gray, Paul & Co. who initiated the plan, feared that this would result in failure. They wrote: "It is our experience that local officials are callous to and rather obstruct any progressive measure if they don't gain by it personally, due to the farming of the revenues and the short and uncertain tenure of office." Gray, Paul & Co., therefore, tried to have the principal merchants of Bushehr sign the official request to Tehran, hoping that this would be sufficient to obtain permission to launch the scheme. However, Tehran refused to go along and thus, the old monopoly system was continued.[52]

There continued to be problems with the discharge of cargo, despite complaints by either the shipping agents or jointly by British firms.[53] By 1900, there was not only an insufficient number of lighters, causing confusion and inconvenience to ships that had to wait longer, but moreover, the crews of the lighters were untrustworthy and helped themselves to goods that they transported.[54] In 1904, losses had increased from 20 to 30% compared with 1903. Furthermore, the *hammal-bashi* or transport agent rather than behaving as the employee of the merchants, acted as if he was employed by the Customs house.[55] Therefore, British, Persian, Indian, German and Russian merchants proposed to establish a landing company that would be in charge of a systematic transport service to Shiraz. The Customs authorities at Bushehr refused to agree to this, because they believed it would be a smuggling organization. They would only allow a private transportation

46. NA, FO 60/658, letter 12/05/1902; Gleadow-Newcomen 1905, p. 44; MacLean 1903, p. 53; Sadid al-Saltaneh 1343, p. 195.
47. Gleadow-Newcomen 1905, p. 44.
48. Geary 1878, vol. 1, p. 63.
49. Pelly 1865 a, p. 49.
50. Gleadowe-Newcomen 1905, p. 44.
51. NA, 2.05.38 (old B 93), Verslag van bevindingen omtrent den Staat van Zaken te Bender Bouchir by Ltz. J.W. van Oorschot. Ternate, 30/12/1877.
52. NA, FO 248/281, Gray, Paul & Co. to Pelly, 25/07/1872.
53. Administration Report 1896-97, p. 10.
54. Administration Report 1900-1901, p. 25
55. Administration Report 1904-1905, p. 21.

company, when "goods are landed in decked boats, with sealed hatches, every package being also sealed, and a fee paid, of course, for each seal and stamp."[56] Apart from the control issue, the fact was that a strong relationship existed between the customs authorities and the *hammal-bashi*.This reationship was mutually beneficial, for each would blame the other in case of losses or thefts, so that it was almost impossible to recover one's money in such cases. Moreover, the *hammal-bashi* paid *modakhel* (unofficial emoluments) to the customs officials, which they did not want to forgo.[57]

The year 1907, with its political upheaval due to the granting of a constitutional form of government, was also a troubled one for the office of the *hammal-bashi* at Bushehr. On 29 April 1907, the president of the local council, Haji `Abdol-Rasul tried to induce a badly attended council to help Shokrollah Davvani, the *hammal-bashi*, who has been sacked by the Customs Department for dishonesty, regain his old function. The governor supported this move. However, as the *hammal-bashi* was appointed by a committee, of which the head of the Customs Department and the British vice-consul were members, there was no chance that this plan would be realized. However, Shokrollah Davvani did not give up and showed that he was willing to go to any end to achieve his goal. On 19 June 1907, he had employees of a Persian merchant beat up Mr. Lucas, an Armenian and the *hammal-bashi* at that time. The assailants then had the nerve to go to a mullah complaining that Mr. Lucas had cursed Islam and therefore, deserved to be stoned to death. Although this attempt did not have the desired result, three weeks later Mr. Lucas ended his own career. On 31 July 1907, the lightermen refused to go to the mail steamer as they had not been paid. On 6 August, therefore, Mr. Lucas resigned and refused to supply labor to sort the goods in the Customs House. The merchants had to manage this themselves. It was expected that `Abdol-Reza, the assistant of the former *hammal-bashi*, would jointly assume the function.[58] Despite improvements, there continued to be problems such as in 1910, when the *hammal-bashi* refused "to accommodate steamers that were unable to come into the inner roadstead and pay for the difference. Heavily loaded steamers cannot make the shallow inner anchorage. The greater distance not only involved greater risk of lightering, but also greater delay and over-carriage. Exports were cleared and lightered directly by the interested exporters."[59]

The problems with the number and quality of lighter crews seem to improve after the first decade of the twentieth century. At that time, there were sufficient coolies available for the loading and unloading of the merchandise. In 1920, there were some 1,000 to 1,500 coolies, but during harvest time (spring; August-September) only 500 or so.[60] Therefore, the availability of labor affected trade in Bushehr. If the wheat harvest had been good many men were needed for the wheat cleaning machines of the export firms during the rest of the year. In 1911, ten wheat-cleaning and separating machines were at work in Bushehr and new machines arrived that year. Further demand came from construction activities in town, while the growing number of vessels calling at Bushehr

---

56. Gleadowe-Newcomen 1905, p. 64.
57. Gleadowe-Newcomen 1905, p. 44; MacLean 1903, p. 53.
58. Political Diaries, vol. 2, pp. 167, 230, 285, 294.
59. Trade Report 1910-11, p. 7 (with a table indicating the cost of lighterage and wharfage handling and delivery for a large number of commodities).
60. Government of India 1924, p. 49. There is no mention of further complaints about the *hammal-bashi*, who still existed as late as 1923, see Floor 1998 b, p. 376, n. 342.

required more Bushehri men to work cargo at Mohammerah and Basra. The Arabs at these last two towns were less productive and/or unwilling to work, a reason why it had become the custom for all vessels with the cargo to be discharged and loaded at Basra to take on Persian laborers at Bushehr and use them at Mohammerah and Basra. This led to an upward pressure on labor cost. Other problems also resulted, such as work-gang bosses hiring their rival's workers which led to fights. Also, less savory types were engaged which increased pilfering of the goods.[61] Because of the lack of coolies elsewhere in the Persian Gulf, departing ship took "a large posse of majuries, to help unload and load cargo at Koweyt, Mahomereh and Basra, as great difficulty is experienced in obtaining proper hands at these ports."[62]

The warf's coolies

In the 1850s, according to Pelly, in Bandar Abbas, handling, landing and the processing of goods was done more efficiently and without damage to the goods. In addition, dues were moderate and were levied without needless delay or damage to goods. Moreover, no local tax or octroi was levied, while there were no subsequent government demands, apart from a moderate charge at Yazd, whereas with trade at Bushehr octroi was levied en route as well as a heavy demand and delay at Shiraz, while goods coming from both routes had to pay customs duties at Isfahan.[63] Lengeh's attraction was that goods could be dropped off more quickly than at Bushehr and with less interference and cost. Also, goods were sometimes smuggled through the dilapidated walls of Shiraz without paying, because only the caravan from Bushehr was announced to the Shirazi authorities.[64] However, similar disadvantages held for Bandar Abbas where likewise lighters had to be used and where later in the century the formal system of *hammal-bashigari* also operated. In fact,

61. Trade Report 1911-12, pp. 7, 14.
62. Cursetjee 2001, p. 118.
63. Pelly 1865 a, p. 61.
64. Pelly 1865 a, p. 52.

according to Whigham, the situation at Bushehr was better, because "cargo can be brought alongside the Custom House in boats in almost any weather, provided the boats can get to the steamers, which cannot come nearer than 3.5-5 km (2.5-3 miles).[65]

However, even when a merchant's goods had been landed, cleared by customs and were ready to be transported up-country his troubles were not over. This was because at Bushehr the unfortunate shipper had to risk two trans-shipments, one between the ship and the Customs wharf and the other between Bushehr and Shif. At Shif, for example, goods coming for Bushehr from up-country "had to lie on the beach, exposed to the weather, waiting, often for weeks. When the boatmen finally picked up the goods, they caused much damage through overloading and inadequate covering, and often pilfered cargo confined to their care."[66] The subsequent late arrival of goods sometimes required re-shipping to another port or might result in a loss due to a rise in price. All this unnecessarily increased the cost of trade.

It appears that for at least one decade or so, the shipping agents had control over loading and unloading of steamers. This situation changed in April 1941, when it was announced that henceforth *Iranbar*, a government agency, would assume control. The fear that this would result in an increase of cost, loss of efficiency and thus a delay became already evident one month later.[67] In mid-1942 shipping and handling at the Customs became a bottleneck. Lighter men refused to unload steamers, because then they had to wait 2-3 days before they could discharge the goods at the Customs wharf. Part of the problem was that there were less coolies available, who were employed as agricultural labor at that time. Also, the work was hard and for bread they had to stand in line for a long time. Moreover, the two new cranes were reserved for the landing of trucks. After much pressure the Customs Department finally hired more coolies which improved the situation considerably. The situation improved further by the arrival of an additional tug; this meant that two tugs and five barges were able to relieve the lighters.[68] In 1943, the British consul wanted to improve S&H at Bushehr. He suggested that the Americans not only operate the ports of Khorramshahr and Bandar Shahpur, but also that of Bushehr to relieve the pressure on these other ports as well as on Basra. The consul submitted that despite the millions spent on Bushehr it still had only one 39-year old tug with 3 barges, which only recently had been improved by another tug and 3 barges. If additional cranes were added, he argued, Bushehr could easily handle 10 times more tonnage. Moreover, the road to the interior was underutilized. However, it was decided that given "the port's shallow offshore roadstead, the execrable highway inland, the distance of the port from Tehran, and the lack of truckable cargoes for inland carriage by vehicles assembled at the UKCC plant made improvement of Bushire less desirable than expenditure of equal effort at more promising locations."[69]

---

65. Whigham 1903, p. 156. For the text of the *hammal-bashi* contract at Bandar Abbas see Sadid al-Saltaneh 1342, pp. 195-99; in general for the situation at Bandar Abbas, see Floor 2011 a, pp. 130-33.
66. Gleadowe-Newcomen 1906, pp. 60, 64. For a description of Shif, see Hamidi 1380, pp. 431-33.
67. Political Diaries, vol. 14, pp. 379, 403; vol. 15, p. 408 (pilfering continued in March 1943 and thereafter).
68. Political Diaries, vol. 15, pp. 226, 316.
69. Political Diaries, vol. 15, p. 380; Vail Motter 1952, pp. 205 n, 414.

Customs Warf

WHARF FACILITIES AND STORAGE CAPACITY

What was definitely better at Bushehr than at other ports was its quay, although this did not mean that given the needs of trade it was a good one. In 1816, the north-eastern part of Bushehr, which "faces the inner harbor, has a wharf or two for landing goods on, and is better sheltered; but it is not accessible even in boats due the sand bank, unless you know the shoals."[70] Alexander, describing the same situation 10 years later, did not mention a wharf but rather a pier.[71] In 1851, Binning described it as "an apology for a quay."[72] Shepherd, five years later was more detailed in his description of the quay-pier, which he called a jetty. "The Custom-house Jetty, a long strip stolen from the sea, built upon date-tree trunks, and boasting a very primitive crane, rather like a gallows, and near to which is a brass nine-pounder."[73] In 1875, Ballantine, wrote that he landed "at the ebb of the tide in a lot of mud and sand, the rudely constructed pier being high and dry, some yards off!"[74] In 1881, this landing facility consisted of "small stone quays where a buggalow of sixty or eighty tons can lie and discharge cargo."[75] In short, the actual port consisted of a quay facing Khur Soltani, which was mostly dry at low water.

Not only was the capacity of the quay insufficient, so was that of the Customs premises. In the 1850s, "The Custom-house, [was] a large building with a large gateway, surmounted by a square tower with Venetian windows opening each side, where sit and watch the tax-takers."[76] In the 1870s, the custom-house was "a sort of open shed."[77] According to the Dutch consul, Charles Keun, there was no proper customs office, only halfway the quay a small room where the customs officials sat with a small warehouse

70. Buckingham 1971, p. 348.
71. Alexander 2000, p. 92.
72. Binning 1857, vol. 1, p. 141.
73. Shepherd 1857, p. 125.
74. Ballantine 1879, p. 51.
75. Stack 1882, vol. 1, p. 24.
76. Shepherd 1857, p. 126.
77. Ballantine 1879, p. 51.

in the back. Therefore, it was not unusual that large cargoes were unloaded elsewhere, but to avoid trouble, it was advisable to warn and gift the governor beforehand.[78] The Customs wharf and premises remained cramped and inconvenient, thus, proving to be an obstacle to efficient handling and storage. As a result, goods were often damaged during handling and from exposure to sun, rain and damp. Moreover, the number of customs staff was insufficient.[79] This situation also led to theft of goods at the Customs House such as in 1898, when goods were stolen from a lighter at night by Persian merchants, who were in cahoots with some staff of the Customs Department and of the *hammal-bashi*. It soon became clear who had stolen the goods and 15,000 *tumans* was recovered from the culprits. As a result, frauds and robberies diminished after this severe punishment of the culprits.[80]

The Customs building, which was owned by Mo`in al-Tojjar, was not weather tight. There was no drainage on the piece of land the building stood and, despite minor repairs, goods stored there were wetted and flooded, whenever there was heavy rainfall. Art. 5 of the Anglo-Persian Commercial Convention of 1903 stipulated that suitable customs premises had to be built. In January 1910, Tehran informed Daryabegi that the Customs premises, for which Mo'in al-Tojjar charged 450 tumans/month, had been placed under attachment because he had failed to implement certain repairs. This meant that the buildings had become government property. Therefore, in 1911, it was decided to reconstruct the Customs-House with a quay and small piers, permitting lighters to discharge alongside.[81] It took a while before the new Customs buildings were completed and many of the new warehouses were only ready by the end of 1921. The new buildings were opened early 1922; they were further up the creek and slightly further from the main bazaar. Some merchants agitated to return to the old building, especially those whose offices were close by the latter. "The new buildings cost several lakhs to build and are on Government land; the owner of the old customs was demanding a rent of 700 tomans per month, so there was little chance for the agitation to succeed." When completed, there were 12-15 warehouses between the old and the new customs house along the wharf with 12 x 5 m (36 x 15 feet) average dimension, adequate to store 2 million bags of grain. Also, they needed to be covered in case of wet weather with tarpaulin because roofs were lacking. In addition, there were 8 warehouses available in the rear of the wharf with an average size of 27.3 x 10.6 x 4.5 m at the new Customs wharf. They had a concrete floor, tin roofs with air vents, but the roofs were not water proof; thus, tarpaulins were needed. As yet, there were no cranes and cargo was transported by handcarts from the quay to warehouses. There were also some small warehouses in town as well as the APOC warehouses at Pudar.[82]

---

78. NA, B 149, Keun to van der Does. 6 January 1876; Keun to van der Does. 13 May 1876.
79. Gleadowe-Newcomen 1905, pp. 25, 60, 64; Trade Report 1910-11, p. 7; Lorimer 1915, vol. 2, pp. 339-40; Mahrad 1970, p. 91; Trade Report 1911-12, p. 8.
80. Administration Report 1898-99, p. 33; Administration Report 1899-1900, p. 41.
81. Gleadowe-Newcomen 1905, pp. 25, 60, 64; Trade Report 1910-11, p. 7; Lorimer 1915, vol. 2, pp. 339-40; Mahrad 1970, p. 91; Report 1911-12, p. 8; Government of Great Britain 1914, pp. 9-12 (nr. 20), 51 (nrs. 128-29); Political Diaries vol. 4, p. 10.
82. Trade Report 1920-21, p. ii; Trade Report 1921-22, p. 1 (M. Delcorde, the provincial director of Customs, was the moving spirit behind the construction of the new Customs building); Government of India 1924, p. 45, 48; Mahrad 1979, p. 89

By 1947, there were 8 modern warehouses (90 x 35 x 25 feet) at the new Customs jetty, which were in good condition. They had concrete floors and ventilated corrugated roofs.[83]

By 1940, the Bushehr peninsula had four small jetties. The total length of the Customs quay at the Khur Soltani was about 800 m. The Khur was dry at low tide, except at the new Customs jetty at it southern end for about 180 m to the old customs building at its northern end, where stood the old Customs jetty. The quay was built of mud and sand, surfaced with large rocks, except at the new customs house, where a wood and concrete wharf was built. This quay was almost level with the sea at normal high tide, but it was about 30 cm under water, when there was a strong northwest wind. The new customs jetty had a length of 73 m; its depth at ebb was 1.5 to 2.1 m. By 1935, despite all improvements, the landing facilities were still inadequate. Goods still had to be brought in by dhows from ships anchored several miles off shore. It was only then that a new fixed 7-ton manually operated crane with a 2.4 m long jib was installed on the new Customs jetty to replace the old hand operated crane on the old Customs jetty; it was repaired in 1942 by the British military. In March 1938, in addition, a 10-ton power crane mounted on tractors was erected, which became operational in November when a quay extension was opened. However, the British consul opined that the new quay was unsatisfactory, because "some beam-ends and store-blocks [were] protruding from it." He feared that when the sea was rough the lighters risked damage when lying close to the wall, as happened with one that sank. There was a light railway to speed up handling of goods with hand trolleys, which covered the entire Customs terrain.[84]

The third jetty was that of the British Residency, which was about 135 m distance, situated south of the new customs quay, with a length at the end of ca. 9 m and a depth at ebb of 60 cm. The fourth jetty was the APOC one at Pudar, about 2.4 km south of the new Customs wharf. In Dastak, 11 km from Bushehr, below the Rishahr cable station, was a stone and concrete wharf built by British troops in WWI for the sea-water distillation plant. In 1921 the British government offered it to the Persian government for a nominal sum, but it declined. Then it was blown up. With good weather and a calm sea, the wharf's surface of about 372 m^2 and a 6 m (18 feet) T piece jutting out into the Khur was functional; it was still in good condition by 1947. Two 'dolphins' 24 m (70 feet) apart were placed at the end of either side of the T piece. The depth was 3.5 m (10.5 feet) at high tide and 1 m (3 feet) at low tide. It was fit for landing in fair weather only. But "with a stiff breeze there is a strong ground swell, in particular with southern wind that endangers any ship, because the quay is built in shallow water."[85]

Once goods had been landed or had cleared customs they needed to be stored. Near the wharf were the serais or warehouses of the major merchants. In 1800, there were three serais "for the accommodation of merchants, out of repair, and old: indeed the only building of any note belongs to Mehdee Ulee Khan, the British Resident at this place."[86] In 1816, there were one or two good caravanserais near the landing-place for

83. Government of Great Britain 1945, p. 503; NA, FO 371/15471.

84. Trade Report 1935-36, p. 3; Administration Report 1938, p. 6; NA, FO 371/15471. According to Government of Great Britain 1945, p. 503, there were two 10-ton tractor-cranes on the quay (1942) and a 7-ton hand-crane on the new Customs jetty (1938).

85. Government of India 1924, p. 45; Mahrad 1978, p. 87; Government of Great Britain 1945, p. 503; NA, FO 371/15471

86. Waring 1973, p. 2.

Merchandise landing place

boats, occupied by and belonging to Armenian merchants; but those belonging to the Mohammadans hardly deserve the name."[87] Visitors differed in opinion about the number of caravanserais, and Heude in 1816 counted four.[88] In 1851, Binning only mentions one large caravanserai, where goods might be stored.[89] However, there was more than one in the mid-1850s. Next to the customs-house was the larger of the two caravanserais that Bushehr boasted. It was "a large square surrounded by high walls, with long rows of stabling for the mules and horses (the camels may lie about outside), and arched recesses in the walls, for the accommodation of the merchants and their goods; with a large square platform in the middle raised some five or six feet from the ground, on which they sleep in the hot weather." To the left were two towers where all the accumulated filth of the town was thrown, which emitted a horrible stench. To the right, after 7 m (20 feet), was the beginning of the bazaar.[90] In 1882, these serais were described as being large buildings with large courtyards, surrounded by galleries. The offices were on the first level, the goods at ground level. During the day the merchants did business there, at night they returned to their homes.[91]

There was no fuel storage (coal or oil) at Bushehr. The British Residency kept a store of steam coal for its own use as did the Customs Department for its vessels.[92] This changed

87. Buckingham 1971, p. 348.
88. Heude 1819, 43; Kempthorne 1835, p. 283 (one); Sadid al-Saltaneh 1371, p. 44 (number not mentioned).
89. Binning 1857, vol. 1, p. 141.
90. Shepherd 1857, pp. 127-28.
91. De Rivoyre 1883, p. 131; see also Sa`adat 1390, pp. 20-21.
92. Lorimer 1915, vol. 2, pp. 346-7; Mahrad 1970, p. 90.

by the late 1930s or early 1940s, when the AIOC oil depot at Pudar had 13 large storage tanks with total capacity of 1.4 million gallons. In addition it had three packed-oil stores with maximum capacity of 63,000 four-gallon tins and served the province of Fars and part of Isfahan. Every three days, the oil was transported by three vessels (3,000 tons, 500 tons; and a barge towed by a tug) from Abadan to Bushehr. The largest tanker could not enter the port. Once landed, the oil was transported upcountry in 28 Leyland 10-ton trucks; each day about six trucks left for Shiraz. [93]

ROUTES FROM BUSHEHR TO SHIRAZ

Once the difficulties of handling goods were overcome the other, perhaps more challenging problems started, i.e., that of transportation and its logistics. From Bushehr the distance to Shiraz was some 283 km (175 miles), and then onwards to Isfahan another 450 km (280 miles), for a total of 733 km (455 miles).[94] There were three ways for goods to leave Bushehr: (i) on pack-animals by the town gate and land route via Ahmadi and Borazjun to Kazerun and Shiraz; (ii) by lighter to Shif and from there for consumption in the three neighboring districts and to a large extent for dispatch to Shiraz; and (iii) by transshipment to other ports of the coast.[95] I only discuss the first two routes, because the maritime route did not constitute a problem and was used to distribute goods to neighboring, mostly smaller ports.

(I) THE LAND ROUTE TO AHMADI/CHOGHADAK

The first halting place after Bushehr was Ahmadi, a distance of about 32 km, by following the eastern edge of the peninsula for about 6.5 km and then crossing the Mashilah.[96] As discussed in chapter one, between Bushehr and Ahmadi (Choghadak), the first stage, there was a salt marsh, called Mashilah, of some 32 km (20 miles) wide. It was a wide expanse of dried mud, often dusty, and not even a blade of grass. The soil was clay mixed with gypsum, and thus in principle it would be easy to make a road over it. However, because of its wet nature such a road was expensive to maintain especially in case of heavy traffic. From March to November the route over the Mashilah was excellent to travel. However, during the wet season it was in large part impassable, certainly if you left the beaten track. When raining it might happen that your horse sunk over the hoofs. In such cases, the muleteers were forced to walk barefoot, to avoid that they would lose their shoes in the wet soil. Therefore, for three months trade used the alternative route via Shif by boat.[97] On arrival at Ahmadi, the landscape changed; there were different plants as well as palms. In 1828, Ahmadi was a village of 200 inhabitants, who lived in "dwellings made of [the]

93. NA, FO 371/15471.
94. For various descriptions of the road from Bushehr to Shiraz, see Kinneir 1973, pp. 363-66; Monteith 1857; Mahrad 1970, p. 90.
95. Report 1915-16, p. 6.
96. Stirling 1991, p. 9; Curzon 1892, vol. 1, p. 229; Lorimer 1915, vol. 2, p. 347.
97. Arnold 1877, pp. 403-05; Weeks 1895, p. 128; Government of India 1924, p. 24. For a short description of Shif, see Hamidi 1380, pp. 431-32.

coarsest material, being merely mats supported on sticks and very low."[98] A new, well-built caravanserai welcomed caravans around 1870.[99] The next stage was Borazjan, where the road coming from Shif merged with the one from Bushehr.

(II) The route via Shif

The alternative route to Shiraz was by boat from Sheikh Sa`d, a small fishing village on the Khur Soltani to Shif, on the northern coast of the bay, at three hours sailing from Bushehr. Shif was described as a small landing place with three tumble-down houses. Nevertheless, in the first two decades of the twentieth century, the Shif route was favored by muleteers; Borazjun could be reached in one stage, while via Bushehr it took two.[100] Passengers and merchandise traveled by sail-boat, or as of the 1870s often by motor-launch, if they could afford it. Those who could would send a telegram from Borazjan to Bushehr to assure that the motor-launch would be ready at Shif. Passengers and their luggage were carried on the shoulders of the porters from the shore to the boat. The facilities at Shif were not optimal as there was only a dilapidated, square and roofless caravanserai. It was occupied by two road guards, who operated a coffee-shop. Goods coming from Shiraz and from Bushehr were dumped at this caravanserai, as a result of which heaps of merchandise were piled up outside it walls and often were left lying there for weeks. The goods landed at Shif were forwarded to Borazjun, then via Kazerun to Shiraz. "There was no water at the place for man or beast, and mules coming down from the interior after having unloaded immediately hurried back 20 miles or so to water at Khoshab or other villages on the higher plain." However, appearances deceived, for the *tofangchi-bashi* of Shif farmed the place for 5,000 *tumans* in 1905, which indicates that it was a much used and profitable transit station.[101] Later, the station fell under the municipality of Bushehr.[102] Merchants did not favor the Shif route, because of the careless behavior of the muleteers. "Sometimes a muleteer will contract unknown to his individual clients, for the conveyance of two or three consignments at a time and having gort the loads to Shief by boat he starts up the road with a modicum of each consignment and repeats this process until he accumulates all the loads at Kazeroon, where he carries out the same procedure again between there and Shiraz,"[103] a practice referred to as *do-kesh*. Also, there was a lot of pilfering and after 1906, the use of this road varied according to the level of exactions imposed on the alternative route.

Because no fodder or pasturage was available at Bushehr, pack animals were raised and grazed in its hinterland (see Table 2.1) as well as upcountry such as around Kazerun. Usually at Bushehr, in the beginning of the twentieth century, 300 mules, 400 camels and 1,000 donkeys would be available for transportation. During the grazing season (15 March-15 May) many came down to Chahkutah, when not more than 40 mules could

---

98. Stirling 1991, pp. 9-10 (The chief was called Sher Lall, descended from Hindus, but already for 6-7 generations his family was in possession of the village).

99. Arnold 1877, p. 403; Weeks 1895, p. 128.

100. Lorimer 1915, vol. 2, p. 347; Trade Report 1913-14, p. 8.

101. Curzon 1915, vol. 2, pp. 229-30; Weeks 1895, pp. 127-28; Moore 1915, p. 440; Wagenvoort 1926, p. 81; Gleadow-Newcomen 1905, p. 65; see also McLean 1903, p. 56; Lorimer 1915, vol. 2, p. 347.

102. For taxes levied at Shif, see Hamidi 1378, p. 72.

103. Administration Report 1907-1908, pp. 9-10.

be obtained.[104] This was an insufficient number of animals. In 1865, Col. Pelly reported that "It takes 3,000 mules to carry the cargo of a 500 ton vessel."[105] Because of the lack of fodder near Bushehr and paucity of supplies along the trade road, the caravans usually only numbered 50 to 60 mules. This transport reality could play havoc with transportation rates. Col. Pelly reported that when around 1860 the Bandar Abbas road was blockaded, its trade was diverted through Bushehr. As a result, the price of transportation from Bushehr to Shiraz, a distance of 180 miles, rose from 15 or 17 *qrans* to 80 *qrans*. He commented, "Of course, a sudden demand for additional transport capacity will temporary increase rates, but the shortness of the distance and the 5-fold rise shows that the response function of the market is rather inelastic in the short-run."[106] By 1911, not more than 2,500 to 3,000 mules per month were leaving Bushehr to transport goods in-land, which caused transport rates to rise. Other reasons included the collection of illegal duties (*rahdari*) en route and the

> Jealousy between Persian forwarding agents at Bushire as to who should do the largest forwarding business, and secure the most mules. This was encouraged by mule-brokers. In this way, instead of competing to forward at lower prices than his neighbours, each merchant used to cap the prices which he was told they were offering. As the goods generally belong to merchants up country, not to themselves, and the Bushire forwarding agents took commission on their disbursements, many Bushire merchants had no inducement to cut rates, while the British merchants were forced to pay the same rates as Persians in order to secure mules at all.[107]

2.1: Estimated number of pack animals in the Bushehr's governorate ca. 1920

District	Horses	Camels	Donkeys	Mules
Liravi	200	100	200	-
Hayat Da'ud	350	250	2,000	150
Rudhilleh	250	400	1,300	200
Shabankareh	200	-	3,000	100
Angali	100	-	500	-
Dashti	100	350	1,600	50
Dashtestan	200	500	2,500	350
Tangestan	30	100	1,000	20

Source: Government of India 1924, pp. 114-15.

---

104. Government of India 1924, p. 115; Sa`adat 1390, pp. 30-31.
105. Pelly 1865 a, p. 48.
106. Pelly 1865 a, p. 49. "Three respectable merchants (Malek al-Tojjar, Nabi and Nilforush) all declare that the Bushehr weight is always used in calculating hire of the muleteers. The place of hiring is the place where the packages are weighed and this weight is the basis on which all is calculated." NA, FO 248/271, Lewis Pelly to Charles Alison, Minister Plenipotentiary and Envoy Extraordinary, 22/07/1871.
107. Government of Great Britain 1914, p. 18.

The two routes merge

From Choghadak/Ahmadi caravans traveled via Khoshab to Borazjan over an alluvial plain, where it was so hot during the summer months that people were known to have fallen dead in traversing it. From Borazjan, where the roads from Ahmadi and Shif merged, the road was stony and broken until Daleki, the location of the first caravanserai. The most arduous stage was that from Daleki to the plain of Khesht, a distance of 26 km (16 mile). There was no road, but only steep mountain passes or *kotals*, which Pelly described as "a corkscrew stamped into a steeply inclined plain." This route was so bad and steep that "camels scarcely ever attempt it, whilst it kills the best mules in from two to three years."[108] Here, the *do-kesh* system was also used, i.e., "A portion of the consignment is taken forward a stage or two, and is then dumped down by the side of the road, whilst the mules return for another supply, the whole being gradually worked forward in this manner."[109]

The villages on the road to Shiraz had brackish wells. However, drinkable water was to be found just below the ground surface and the people were expert in digging temporary wells. Food and fodder were also available in sufficient quantities along the trade route.[110] Because there was no proper paved road, only a camel track, no carts could be used and consequently, the cost of transport was high, making products costly. Other factors that increased transport rates included the high mortality of pack-animals, as referred to above.[111] When in 1913 transportation rates were higher than people liked they blamed this on the recently created transport (*naqliyeh*) department. However, the British Resident rightly pointed out that the real problem was the shortage of mules. Moreover, he, in a very prescient observation, submitted:

> It is hard to see the remedy for this trouble, as the mules are no longer bred. Persia has too many crying needs to permit her to think of such luxuries as encouraging mule breeding and it will take years of security to bring back the old state of affairs, when 6,000 mules per month went up and down the Bushire-Ispahan road, loaded with merchandise. It is even doubtful whether it would be worth while making serious efforts in this direction, were such possible, as is seems that before long mechanical means of transport must abolish the antiquated 'caravan.'[112]

Another factor was the outbreak of an epidemic such as of cholera in 1904, when at one time transport to Shiraz was three times the normal rate of 90 *qrans* per *kharvar*.[113]

---

108. Pelly 1865 a, pp. 143-44; Gleadowe-Newcomen 1905, p. 42; Trade Report 1912-13, p. 7. Indeed, the first caravanserai was only in Daleki, until a new one was built in Borazjan in 1872. Stirling 1991, p. 15; Floor 2011 b, p. 41.
109. Gleadowe-Newcomen 1905, p. 59.
110. Pelly 1865 a, p. 143.
111. Gleadowe-Newcomen 1905, p. 42. On this road an often recurring scene was "An incident typically Persian; we came upon a poor donkey lying beside the road, its back one mass of bleeding sores, and its impotent legs folded under the body. ... Its owners were walking off, about to leave it to a death of slow agony, since it could no longer take one more tortured step." Moore 1915, pp. 407, 418.
112. Administration Report 1913, p. 33.
113. Gleadowe-Newcomen 1905, p. 65.

The Caravanserai at Borazjan

Therefore, in the mid-1870s, "Messrs. Gray and Paul proposed to make a road with English money from Bushire to Shiraz, and to charge a toll on all vehicles." The Persian authorities were only interested in their share and when none was offered refused permission. "It never entered into their head to make the road themselves and charge a toll. The same happened to its Basra Branch, Gray and MacKenzie, which offered to open the Karun with steam vessels, was refused for the same reason."[114]

Comparison of the trade roads of competing ports

In 1905, the British commercial mission opined that "It is astonishing how Bushire, ever came to surpass Bandar Abbas as a trade-distributing centre. The latter stands at the mouth of one of Persia's natural gates, the former at the foot of a wall."[115] Indeed, the Bandar Abbas-Isfahan route was a much easier and more level road than the Bushehr-Isfahan axis. Also, there was an abundant supply of camels instead of a limited supply of mules - each camel load being 450 lbs against a mule's 340 lbs and costing one-third less.[116] The disadvantages of this route were that it was much longer than the Bushehr-Isfahan one. Moreover, the town and road were considered less safe, although this was mitigated by the size of the caravans, which numbered from 1,000 to 2,000 camels. In Bushehr it was rare to see 100 mules in one caravan. Also, on the stretch from Shiraz to Bandar Abbas, supplies were obtainable as far as Lar, from there onwards caravans had to carry their own food and fodder, and even water.[117] This was due to the fact that there was no major cultivated area apart from Minab in the hinterland of Bandar Abbas.[118] Similar problems bedeviled Lengeh. The route to Shiraz was arduous, ill-supplied, and unsafe; it took ten days from Lengeh to Lar alone.[119] Although Mohammerah had the advantage of being a river anchorage on the Shatt al-Arab and of very extensive production of grain in Khuzestan

114. Geary 1878, vol. 1, p. 67.
115. Gleadowe-Newcomen 1905, p. 42.
116. Pelly 1865 a, p. 61.
117. Pelly 1865 a, p. 62; Idem, 1865 b, p. 153.
118. Trade Report 1912-13, p. 6.
119. Pelly 1865 a, p. 52; Idem, 1865 b, p. 153.

province, it was only after 1888 that river transport to Ahvaz (120 km) was possible. Moreover, it was only as of 1900 that caravans could travel via the Lynch-Bakhtiyari road to Isfahan, which was a distance of 310 km through very mountainous terrain, which was worse than the Shiraz-Isfahan route. Moreover, unlike in the case of Bushehr, there were no towns of importance between Ahvaz and Isfahan.[120] The advantages of the Bushehr-Shiraz road were that water and fodder was available everywhere along the route. There was a very fertile plain of grain producing country for about 160 km (100 miles) both south and north of Bushehr. There were also important townships and trade feeders on the road between Bushehr and Shiraz and Shiraz and Isfahan.[121]

Of course, the figures in Table 2.2 are averages for normal periods. Mule caravans ordinarily took from 20 to 30 days to accomplish the journey to Shiraz, but in the grazing season (the spring months), when the animals fed as they traveled, doing short stages, the entire journey lasted 40 to 50 days.[122] But even during normal times, it might happen that, e.g., on the Bushehr-Shiraz road transport was scarce, while at the same time (after 1900) it was cheap and in abundance on the Ahvaz-Isfahan route. In these instances part of piece goods were reshipped and diverted to Mohammerah.[123] Camel caravans covered the distance between Bandar Abbas and Kerman, about 482 km (300 miles), from 18 to 25 days, and were less costly. However, the availability of pack-animals was a problem and the country was sparsely populated. Moreover, the road suffered from attacks by marauding tribes.[124] Despite the problems with port and handling facilities as well as the difficult road to Shiraz, there were other reasons that led Bushehr to maintain its position as the leading Persian port in the Persian Gulf.

2.2: Commercial routes from the Persian Gulf (1910)

Route	Average duration-days	Transport medium	Weight (kg)	Price (*Marks*)	Remarks
I. Mohammerah-Tehran					
A. *Via Isfahan*	60	Ship, then mule	297	144	-
Stages					
a. Mohammareh-Ahvaz	2 upstream 1 downstream	River steamer idem	1,000	12.80	Transshipment from sea to river steamer
b. Ahvaz-Isfahan	26	Mule, donkey	5.94	1.20-2.0	Very difficult in winter
c. Isfahan-Tehran (Lynch or Bakhtiyari road)	20 25	Camel Mule	297	ca. 60	-
B. *via Baghdad*	60	Steamer, caravan	297	160-200	-

120. Trade Report 1912-13, p. 7.
121. Trade Report 1912-13, p. 7.
122. Gleadowe-Newcomen 1905, p. 42.
123. Trade Report 1913-14, p. 9.
124. Gleadowe-Newcomen 1905, p. 42; Trade Report 1912-13, p. 6.

Route	Average duration-days	Transport medium	Weight (kg)	Price (*Marks*)	Remarks
Stages					
a. Mohammerah-Basra	2-8 hours	Steamer	1,000	25	If no connection, up to 14 days
b. Basra-Baghdad	5 upstream 3.5 downstream	Steamer	1,000	25	If no connection, up to 14 days
c. Baghdad-Qasr-e Shirin	6	Camel and mule	198.5	25-44	In exceptional cases higher
d. Qasr-e Shirin-Kermanshah	7	Camel and mule	198.5	25-44	In exceptional cases higher
e. Kermanshah-Tehran	20-25	Camel	297	144-160	-
II. Bushehr-Tehran	60-90	Camel	297	144-160	-
Stages					
a. Bushehr-Shiraz	14-16 30-35	Camel	334 334	80* 72*	Yek-kash Do-kash
b. Shiraz-Isfahan	14	Camel	334	60	-
c. Isfahan-Tehran	20 25	Mule Camel	5.94 5.94	1.40 1	-
III. Routes via Bandar Abbas					
1. Bandar Abbas-Kerman	30-35 20-25	Camel Donkey	297 297	64-80	In winter, longer duration and cheaper; in summer the reverse
2. Bandar Abbas-Yazd	35-40 30-35	Camel Donkey	297 297	112-180	Idem
Yazd-Isfahan	18	Mule	594	16-32	-
3. Bandar Abbas-Narmashır-Sistan-Berjand, 1,052 km	50	Camel, donkey	ca. 180	36-44 (donkey) 60-80 (v.v.)	Heavily traveled route; pasturage
4. Bandar Abbas-Rafsanjan-Kerman-Mashhad	90	Camel	297	160-200	-

Source: Küss 1911, p. 57. * = these prices concern bales. Other packing pays special rates such that, e.g., one pays for the same quantity of copper 84 *Mark*, sugar 88 *Mark*, tea 84 *Mark*, haberdashery 88 *Mark*. One *Mark* was 4 *tumans*.

The unsafe and blocked trade road (1907-18)

Although in the nineteenth century the trade road from Bushehr to Shiraz had always suffered from attacks by bandits these were not a major obstacle for trade, because the

Fars government usually maintained good security on the road.[125] In 1905 the trade road to Shiraz became unsafe due to attacks by local chiefs and therefore, for some time, the less convenient Firuzabad road was used. Measures were taken to strengthen security, but its effect was only temporary. In early 1906, the situation was totally out of control and the Shiraz government claimed it could do nothing due to the disturbed situation of Fars after the dismissal of its governor-general.[126] From the very beginning of the political troubles in Persia in 1906, the local chiefs along the trade road from Bushehr via Borazjan, Daleki, and Kazerun to Shiraz, smelled financial and political opportunities. As a result, these local chiefs behaved as if they were independent of the governor-general of Fars and were constantly fighting with each other and preying on commercial traffic. To provide themselves with additional cash income, they imposed and levied illegal fees on travelers and caravans passing through their territory.[127]

Already, the problem started at the gate of Bushehr where 1 *qran* was collected by the *kalantar*, despite protests from the British government. The local governor justified its collection by referring to the fact that the Minister of Finance included this fee in the *kalantar*'s revenue schedule. The gate revenues amounted to about 18,000 *tuman*s per year, which was quite a substantial sum. Once outside Bushehr, the Khan of Angali wanted caravans to pass through his territory. He, when he could, collected fees or detained mules, to force caravans to use the Daleki-Shif road. The Bushehr-Borazjan, Daleki-Kazerun road was blocked for two months because of a feud between the Khan of Kamarej and the headman of Daleki and the Khan of Borazjan. The cause of the feud was the control over the road and there was heavy fighting in the narrow mountain passes.[128] By December 1906, travelers preferred to take the Ahmadi route from Borazjan to Bushehr.[129] Another important source of insecurity was the chaotic situation in Kazerun in 1907-08, due to "intestine feuds and the absence of all authority, and the standing quarrel between Hyder Khan of Kamarij and Nur Muhammad Khan of Daliki, each of whom had his candidate for the post of Kadkhuda of Konartakhteh."[130] As stated above. the feud between Daleki and Kamarej, which had been dormant in 1907, exploded in January 1908, when a small war broke out about and at Konar Takhteh. Many people were killed and the road was closed between mid-January and mid-February 1908. Also, there were the usual robberies, while raiders plundered a caravan; seven more were waiting in Daleki for the violence to subside and relative safety to return.[131]

During the summer of 1909, traders took the Firuzabad road, which was controlled by Sowlat al-Dowleh, the chief of the Qashqa'i tribe. It was rather safe, but unfit for anything

---

125. Floor 2011 b, pp. 132ff; Geary 1878, vol. 1, p. 65; Saldanha 1986, vol. 7/2, p. 10. Nevertheless, the drivers of the pack animals tried to make a martial impression on would-be robbers. In 1856, a camel driver in Bushehr had "pistols in his belt in company with three daggers and a sabre, together with a variety of cartouch boxes and several ramrods." Shepherd 1857, p. 127.

126. Administration Report 1905-06, pp. 21-22.

127. Trade Report 1909-10, p. 1; Political Diaries, vol. 3, p. 52. For a more detailed discussion for the insecurity of the trade route to Shiraz, see Floor 1911 b, pp. 135ff.

128. Government of Great Britain 1910, pp. 87; Sa`adat 1390, p. 39. On the Khan of Angali, see Hamidi 1380, pp. 93-95.

129. Administration Report 1906-07, pp. 15, 19.

130. Administration Report 1907-08, p. 23. For a photo of Sheikh Ahmad Angali, see Roknzadeh 1352, p. 204.

131. Administration Report 1907-08, pp. 23-24.

but summer travel, due to lack of any accommodation. However, Sowlet al-Dowleh had tasted money and was unlikely to let this morsel drop from his mouth. Robberies were still numerous that year,[132] while also there was fighting to control stretches of the trade road, such as the part that was controlled by Kazerun. These continuous fights and robberies had their impact on the direction of commercial traffic, because in 1909 no less than five different routes were used to travel from Bushehr to Shiraz:

(i)via Kazerun;

(ii)Firuzabad;

(iii) via Jirreh, Haft Mellah-Myan-Menzil-Jirreh;

(iv) via Jirreh (Borazjun, Tang-e Ram Jirreh);

(v) via Jirreh (Borazjan, Daleki, Sar Mashhad, Jirreh).[133]

The endemic feuding, raiding and plundering not only had its impact on which route trade took, but also on its volume. Trade via the Bushehr-Shiraz route had declined since 1907 due to fighting between the Arab, Lor, and Qashqa'i tribes. Because of the resulting insecurity, goods could not be shipped and this led to congestion. Because Persian merchants mainly depended on British credit, bills were not paid as merchants either could not sell or had to sell goods at a loss. This led to bankruptcies among Persian traders, while British firms had large sums outstanding which they were unable to settle. Imports via the trade road dropped from £439,937 in 1907-08 to £328,375 in 1908-09, or a reduction of about 25%. Prospects for the next year looked even worse. What made matters worse was that the local khans along the trade route acted totally independent of the governor-general of Fars. Their constant fighting caused the road to be unsafe or entirely blocked for months, while they also exacted illegal imposts. Moreover, because of ill-treatment by the 'road guards' many muleteers refused to travel this route causing a shortage of transport capacity and thus higher rates. In 1905, some 5-7,000 mules traveled the road, while in 1909, their number was estimated to be only 2-3,000. Transportation rates per 737 lbs. for the Bushehr-Shiraz route rose from 80-90 *qrans* during 1900-05, to double that rate in 1909, and even to 200-300 *qrans* in 1909-10. As a result, insurance premiums also rose from 15s. per £100 in 1905, to 30s. in 1907, 40s. in 1908, while in 1909 hardly any insurance was offered at all, unless at war risk premiums (£5 per £100), or 250% higher.[134]

Meanwhile, the route between Kazerun and Daleki was unsafe, and numerous robberies occurred. The Jirreh route remained open under Sowlat al-Dowleh's protection, but it lacked accommodation at various stages. Moreover, the muleteers resented Sowlet al-Dowleh's recent agreement with the Khans of Daleki and Borazjun to divert the trade through their territories. This meant that caravans had to make two long marches on a bad

132. Administration Report 1909, p. 26.

133. Trade Report 1909-10, p. 1

134. Government of Great Britain 1910, pp. 87-89, 90 (list of imposts collected and where); Idem 1911, pp. 23, 38.

road without supplies being available. Meanwhile, the khans of Tangestan and Chahkuteh also tried to have trade pass through their territory, thus creating more uncertainty and insecurity.[135] In September 1910, the road from Kazerun to Bushehr remained closed, and caravans continued to use the Firuzabad road.[136] However, towards the end of the year that road also became unsafe, for by that time, "The roads in Fars are all unsafe, and traffic is almost entirely suspended."[137]

In mid-1911 the road became unsafe again due to troubles in Shiraz. Trade came to a total standstill, for although the road was open, goods could not be distributed from the market towns, due to anarchy in their hinterland. In October and November 1911, the Bushehr-Shiraz road was partially and then entirely closed.[138] In 1912, traffic on the road was interrupted for prolonged periods and was forcibly diverted "to execrable and little used tracks" to avoid infighting by the various khans.[139] By June 1912, the unauthorized Shif route had been brought in use again.[140] In October 1912, Mokhber al-Saltaneh, the governor-general of Fars decided to put the Shiraz-Kazerun road under the control of a force consisting of 150 gendarmes and 110 local riflemen, who would be paid by the gendarmerie. Henceforth no road-tax (*rahdari*) would be collected.[141] The result was a somewhat safer road near Kazerun, but the fire was not put out, for it remained smoldering. Transportation rates had risen to 500 *qrans* in 1912, but in March 1913 they had already been reduced to 300 *qrans*; for certain commodities they even went down to 225 (piece-goods) and 270 *qrans* (sugar).[142] In 1914, the gendarmerie took control over Kazerun and the Shiraz-Bushehr road.[143] After a poor start in 1913, the gendarmerie became quite effective in bringing security to the trade road in 1914, according to the British. "Rahdari had ceased, caravans and travelers have passed practically unmolested and credit must be given to the Gendarmerie for having brought about, for the moment, this satisfactory state of affairs."[144] Although by 1913 the Shif route was not authorized for goods destined for places beyond Borazjun, people used it anyway even if this meant having to smuggle goods.[145] As a result, by 1916 this route competed with the land route via Ahmadi.[146]

---

135. Government of Great Britain 1911, p. 38 (February 1910)
136. Government of Great Britain 1911, p. 101.
137. Government of Great Britain 1911, p. 111.
138. Administration Report 1911, pp. 20-23.
139. Administration Report 1912, pp. 17-18.
140. Government of Great Britain 1913, pp. 78-79 (Smart to Townley 08/06/1912, p. 78-79).
141. Government of Great Britain 1912, p. 195 (22/10/1912); Mokhber al-Saltaneh 1344, pp. 248, 254 (he was not convinced that Swedish officers were needed).
142. Administration Report 1913, pp. 23, 32; O'Connor 1931, p. 200. For the proposal submitted in December 1912 by Mr. H. G. Chick, the Residency's commercial adviser, which, among other things, aimed to bring down transporation rates, abolish the *do-kesh* system, provide incentives to muleteers to perform better and take strong measures to prevent mule-brokers to torpedo the plan, was accepted by all merchants and successfully implemented. The governor employed a clerk, who received applications for mules, who allotted the daily number of mules in proportion. Some merchants did not like the way this part of the plan worked and therefore, henceforth, the division of mules was made on the basis of the number of packages a merchant had on hand in Bushehr. For the plan, see Government of Great Britain 1914, p. 17 (nr. 38).
143. O'Connor 1931, p. 209; *The Times* (25/03/1914), p. 7; Oberling 1974, p. 123; Sa`adat 1390, p. 47.
144. Administration Report 1914, p. 9; Cronin 1996, p. 111.
145. Trade Report 1913-14, p. 8.
146. Trade Report 1915-16, p. 5.

The outbreak of World War I in July 1914 changed the dynamics on the trade route. Persia had declared itself neutral, but willy-nilly it was drawn into the war by the warring parties. In August 1915, Great Britain occupied Bushehr and Russia started operations in northern Persia. The existing anti-British and anti-Russian feelings were reinforced by a number of factors. German agents inside Persia wanted to harass and damage British interests in the south, "by embarrassing us and drawing off troops from the more important theatre."[147] By distributing money and propaganda they found fertile ground, in particular among those who were hurt by British efforts to curb their illegal exactions and raiding of caravans and/or who were anti-British, or all of the above.[148] Many of those were found among the members of the Democratic Party that stood for a nationalist policy and complete independence of Persia; one free from foreign influence. What helped these currents in political life was the issuance of *fatwa*s by leading ulama in Najaf and elsewhere declaring holy war or *jihad* against Russia and Great Britain. It was this argument that, e.g. Sowlat al-Dowleh and others used to maintain their innocence of rebellion and the illegal use of violence by claiming they had just followed the orders of the ulama and the government of Persia. The problem with this argument is that on many occasions Sowlat al-Dowleh and others chose to ignore the orders of that same government of Persia, when it did not suit their own particular personal agenda.[149] On 10 November 1915, the Democrats in Shiraz, supported by the gendarmerie under the command of Major `Ali Qoli Khan Pesiyan, arrested all British subjects and took the males to Ahram in Tangestan; the females were released and sent to Bushehr where they arrived on 20 November 1915. The Democrats were assured of strong support from Kazerun, which had been surrendered by the gendarmerie to local forces.[150]

Despite these changes, what did not change was the continued usual infighting on the lower part of the road, which was disputed between the *kalantar*s of Khesht (pro-British, or so they believed), Nur Mohammad Khan of Daleki (originally anti-British, later chastened, or so they believed) and the rival league of Tangestan on the one hand and that of the Hayat Da'ud confederacy on the other hand. The main news item was the expulsion of Nur Mohammad Khan from the Konar Takhteh plain and the occupation of the Kotal-e Malu by a loyal *kadkhoda* of Konar Takhteh. These events were followed by a serious quarrel between Borazjun and Daleki in September 1917. In consequence, Nur Mohammad Khan of Daleki started to divert traffic via the Shabankarch-Shif route; he finally made an agreement with the Khans of Shabankareh and Angali to oppose the Tangestan league and protect trade on the Shif-Daleki stretch. This was a serious blow to the rebel confederates.[151] Meanwhile, in 1916, Great Britain established the South Persian Rifles, a Persian force led by British officers, which established control over Bandar Abbas, Kerman, Yazd and Shiraz, but was stopped at Kazerun.

---

147. Douglas 1923, p. 105. Anticipating the outbreak of World War I, Great Britain sent a brigade from India to Bushehr, which was a violation of Persia's neutrality. When a few days later war was declared this force was moved immediately to Basra. One battalion was left behind in Bushire as a garrison.

148. Cronin 1996, p. 117.

149. For Sowlat al-Dowleh's reasons, see Oberling 1974, p. 139.

150. Administration Report 1915, pp. 7-8; O'Connor 1931, pp. 223, 231-33; Oberling 1974, pp. 135-36. For a description of Ahram, see Hamidi 1380, pp. 99-101 (with photo).

151. Administration Report 1917, pp. 2-3.

Improvement of the trade road

Because of the insecurity in Bushehr's hinterland and in particular the road to Shiraz the British reinforced their garrison in Bushehr. To reach Shiraz it was decided that it would be best to construct a light-gauge railway to Daleki. The reason was that camels could be used until Daleki, but only mules could traverse the difficult passes thereafter. However, the number of mules available was small and therefore, the decision to construct a railway was taken. In September 1918, a British Strike Force left Bushehr and established control over the entire trade route by January 1919. Originally, the intention was to construct the railway as far as Daleki, but given greater than expected terrain difficulties and to avoid delays it only went as far as Borazjan, about 64 km (40 miles) in length. Instead a cart road was made between Borazjan and Daleki, while goods were transported by light Ford trucks from the railhead to the foothills. This freed up the pack animals for use beyond Daleki, after completion of the road and railway. A light Indian single mule-cart was also considered very useful, because it easily climbed the mountains' steep slopes.[152]

As a result, a considerable portion of the Bushehr-Shiraz road (from Borazjun to Rudak, 10 km from Kamarej) was made passable for car traffic. The rest remained unfinished as the Army's Labor Corps departed, because of the end of World War I. The unfinished part was a well-graded camel path over which a car could travel and actually had done so all the way to Shiraz. However, in the following years there was no road maintenance and thus the road deteriorated. It took a number of years before a new motor road was constructed. However, by the end of 1918 this road was safe and trade boomed.[153]

The Bushehr-Borazjan railway was opened to civil traffic in May 1919 and helped to boost trade to Shiraz, but it was too short to make a real difference; however, the new safety on the roads did. One advantage of the railway was that the muleteers could leave their donkeys at Borazjan, rather than go to Bushehr, which had no grazing, and they then went back to Borazjan where they could graze.[154] Even the well-built railway to Borazjan experienced great difficulty in the winter of 1919-20 when it was twice washed away.[155] On 21 March 1921, the railway ceased to carry passengers and public goods, because there was no buyer for it. The railway was dismantled and shipped to India before the end of August 1921.[156]

After the departure of the Strike Force, the trade road was taken over by the South Persian Rifles (SPR), which, for a short while, were assisted by Indian troops.[157] By 1922, practically the whole trade from Bushehr to Shiraz went via the usual trade road. Since the railway was dismantled in March 1921, all goods went up by caravan, though the road up to Daleki, some 88 km (55 miles) from Bushehr, was passable for motor cars during the dry season. During the rainy season (November-April) the road was impassible except for the pack animals due to the deep mud and slush of the Mashilah.[158] However, when the

---

152. Douglas 1923, p. 108; Government of India 1924, pp. 113-14; IOR/L/PS/10/783 Pt. 3; FO 248/1229, Report Bushire Field Force, 28/11/1919.
153. Floor 2011 b, p. 170; FO 248/1229, Report Bushire Field Force, 28/11/1919.
154. Trade Report 1919-20, pp. 1-2; FO 248/1229, Report Bushire Field Force, 28/11/1919.
155. Government of India 1924, p. 24.
156. Trade Report 1920-21," page ii.
157. Floor 2011 b, p. 171; Administration Report 1920, p. 4.
158. Trade Report 1921-22, p. 2.

SPR, which had maintained and secured the road, was disbanded in 1921 it was allowed to go into disrepair, while exactions on the roads increased. By 1923, the road condition became so bad that no wheeled traffic used it anymore. Because the government of Persia wanted to use the road for trucks and other heavy military transport, it was expected that repairs would be carried out. Also, the Parsi Syndicate intended to start operating a motorized passenger service. The heavy winter rains of 1922-23 further damaged the road surface and repairs were costly, in particular "as the existing alignment, which was never meant for motor traffic" was very poor.[159] And indeed, in 1923, at considerable cost, two European engineers improved the bad corners of the Kazerun-Bushehr road to allow the heavy military material to pass.[160] However, heavy rains during November-April made it impassable for cars. A positive sign was that security on the road improved due to the stationing of Persian soldiers along its route.[161] In 1925, for most of the year the road was only fit for animals. Nevertheless, repairs to the road were being made, including improving its surface and making parapets outside the edge of the road in the passes. Also, 5 km of the former railway embankment across the Mashilah was remade under the Italian engineer Argenti. As a result, car traffic between Bushehr-Shiraz though limited was on the increase. In 1924-25, no less than 135 cars, inclusive military ones, left for Bushehr and places in between, while 112 arrived from Bushehr. In the 11 months ending on 20 February 1926 a total of 387 cars left for Bushehr and in between, and 375 arrived from Bushehr. A British contractor from Tehran made the trip with heavy trucks to transport military equipment, but he said he would not brave the passes a second time with trucks. It was clear that given the condition of the road at that time, commercial traffic with trucks was not practicable; 4-5 vehicles were lost in the passes that year.[162]

In 1926, the road remained open throughout the year for car traffic. Its surface was improved somewhat and at the Kotal-e Pir-e Zan culverts were made to drain rain water. But there was not enough money for proper maintenance and repairs.[163] Nevertheless, in 1927, more cars used the trade road, including in the carrying trade. Transportation rates dropped and cars started competing with mule transport, which, as a result, suffered. The British Resident was worried whether Persian car owners, when calculating their rates, would take into account depreciation. If not he expected that they would have problems financing news cars out of their capital instead of profits. In 1928, the carrying trade by car continued to increase, while transportation rates fell to almost one rupee (= 16 annas) per ton/mile as opposed to about nine and a half annas for animal transport.[164]

Although in 1928, the road was kept in reasonable repair, while some of the worst passes were widened and protected by parapets, nevertheless the winter snow did much damage and repairs were costly. Because only loose earth was spread over bad portions of the road and "no ramming or rolling in of stones is done," it was expected that this would be a recurrent problem. Also, little was done to the track across the Mashilah, which meant

159. Trade Report 1922-23, p. 1; Administration Report 1923, p. 10; for details see p. 21.

160. Administration Report 1923, p. 22.

161. Administration Report 1924, p. 7. For a detailed description, illustrated with photos, of the difficulties traveling with trucks on this road, see Braunagel 1925.

162. Administration Report 1925, pp. 9, 20.

163. Administration Report 1926, p. 4.

164. Administration Report 1927, p. 5; Administration Report 1928, p. 8.

that transport had to face interruptions after every rain.[165] Although there were several instances of robberies on the trade road,[166] it remained safe until about 1929, when it was raided by Boir Ahmadis, Qashqa'is, and Banauis. The *Amniyeh* (the force that replaced the Gendarmerie) was incapable of suppressing the banditry and initially, even the military, despite very costly operations, had little success. Although in 1929 the road still had to be closed for 3-4 months due to the Qashqa'i rebellion, by 1930 the road became safe and few robberies occurred.[167]

In 1929, due to overcapacity of motor transport in Bushehr rates fell to 130 *tumans* per *kharvar*. Animal transport was trying carry on and it competed well in December when the rains made the road impassable for cars. However, animal transport would be a relic of the past if the roads were well maintained. Unfortunately, this was not the case, while the track over the Mashilah remained as bad as ever. According to the British Resident, it took then 2-3 days by car to reach Shiraz, but this could be 12 hours shorter if "a real attempt were made to metal and regrade the kotals," which he considered unlikely.[168] Car transport decreased (there were also restrictions on the import on motor vehicles), but in relation to reduced traffic, supply exceeded demand and thus rates were low, despite a new tax on motor vehicles. The firm of H.S.M.R. Kazerooni started a transport service in mid-1930 and by the end operated a fleet of some 30 trucks of 1.5 to 3 tons. Although trade was depressed, so far the firm was successful, partly due to the fact that Kazerooni transported many of its own goods as well by the efficiency of its operation. Despite the new vehicle tax, no work was done to the road, the surface in the passes was bad and becoming worse. In January-February the Mashilah was impassible for wheeled traffic, but otherwise the road was open the whole year. A positive point was that there was only some minor brigandage.[169] In 1931, because of the boggy condition of the Mashilah, the trade road, apart from February, was open the whole year. The road in some of the passes was widened and its surface improved. Kazeruni increase his service to some 40 trucks, but he was in trouble due to heavy capital outlay for purchase trucks and plant, which suffered heavy operating losses, because transportation rates were lower than in the previous year.[170] Although in 1932 the government spent much money to build a permanent track over the Mashilah this effort failed due to the use of unsuitable materials. As a result, as in the past, when it rained wheeled traffic stopped. However, other parts of the road were improved such as the widening of certain parts and the erection of low parapets along the most dangerous stretches. Shale was used to make the road surface leveler, but this did not improve the grip for cars.[171]

In 1933, work started on a new car road from Shiraz via Firuzabad to Bushehr (rather than via Kazerun) and 10 km (6 miles) from Shiraz was ready at the end of 1933. Gradually road conditions improved, but not that of the Mashilah. Ironically there was less car transport due to the fall in trade and transport rates were so low that "sometimes it

---

165. Administration Report 1928, p. 8.
166. Administration Report 1925, p. 13.
167. Administration Report 1926, p. 4; Administration Report 1927, pp. 2, 5; Administration Report 1928, pp. 18-19; Administration Report 1929, p. 6; Administration Report 1930, p. 9.
168. Administration Report 1929, p. 6.
169. Administration Report 1930, p. 9.
170. Administration Report 1931, p. 11.
171. Administration Report 1932, p. 8.

Modern road to Shiraz in 1922

did not pay even the cost of petrol and oil consumed."[172] In Bushehr taxis could be hired to drive to Shiraz in 7-9 hours or to Tehran in four days, which was quite an improvement compared with the situation in 1930.[173] Mrs. Merritt-Hawkes who took such a taxi in 1934, wrote that at a certain point of the road the driver said to crouch down and he would drive faster because it was favorable spot for shooting, which seems odd as otherwise security on the road was good.[174]

The arrival of the taxi service was a clear sign that "The cheapness and speed of motor transport has practically killed the animal transport services, although considerable quantities of Anglo-Persian Oil Company's products were sent up country on camels."[175] Nevertheless, because the Mashilah was still an obstacle for traffic during the

172. Administration Report 1933, p. 18; Administration Report 1934, p. 10.
173. Ebtehaj 1932, p. 184.
174. Merritt-Hawkes 1935, p. 4.
175. Administration Report 1933, p. 10.

rainy season, donkeys took care of transportation needs. However, by 1935 motorized transport had totally replaced animal transport, because donkeys were only used on narrow tracks where cars could not pass. Although construction of an all-weather road had begun, the road to Shiraz continued to deteriorate and no attempt was made to improve it. As a result, in 1935, the Shiraz road, the coastal road to Lengeh and the Bushehr-Abadan road were washed away by each rain and each time traffic had to wait 2 weeks. Fortuitously, Davar, the Minister of Finance was also caught in this mess, but he said that the government did not have the money to maintain the roads, but it would repair the Bushehr-Firuzabad-Shiraz road, which did not go through the mountains and precipices as the Kazerun road did.[176]

In November 1936, the Deka Company was given the contract to build the Bushehr-Borazjan stretch. Transportation rates to Shiraz by lorry were 90 rials per *kharvar* or 654 lbs in spring, 60 rials in summer and 90 rials in the fall and winter. Camel transport averaged 45-50 rials but took 2-3 weeks. Although due to lack of inundation of the Mashilah there was no transport problem, but finally construction of an all-weather causeway over it was started.[177] The Bushehr-Borazjan road was repaired and embankments and bridges completed, but it was not yet open in 1937; traffic had to use the old road. The new road was built to guarantee uninterrupted traffic during the winter. The Shiraz-Firuzabad section was open, but not the stretch to Bushehr. Although it was ready, it had not yet been transferred to the authorities. To Shiraz, lorry rates per *kharvar* were in rials: 65 (May) to 110-120 (December), to Isfahan resp. 140 and 230-250, and to Tehran 170 and 300-320. The rates were influenced by demand, road conditions, and externalities such as the military commandeering trucks. Attempts by the governor of Bushehr to fix rates for transport of government goods failed, because there was strong demand for truck capacity.[178] Despite having been repaired twice in 1938 the road to Shiraz was impassible for two weeks in December after heavy rain. The Bushehr-Firuzabad road was still not complete, while progress was slow.[179]

2.3: Transport cost from Bushehr to Tehran in 1939 (in rials per *kharvar* of 665 lbs.)

	Average	Lowest	Highest
To Shiraz	60	30/February	95/October
To Isfahan	135	75/March	200/June
To Tehran	200	120/March	290/December

Source: Administration Report 1939, p. 8.

In 1938, truck owners did not do well, because due to a fall in the volume of trade traffic diminished, while their overhead remained the same. Although the Shiraz road was maintained, it was still impassible in December for a few days. The Bushehr-Firuzabad stretch was still not completed, while at the end of 1938 preparations were made to restart

176. Trade Report 1935-36, p. 3; Administration Report 1935, pp. 4, 11.
177. Administration Report 1936, pp. 4, 9.
178. Administration Report 1937, pp. 3, 9.
179. Administration Report 1938, p. 3.

work on the Lengeh road.[180] In 1939, there were five garages in Bushehr that supplied trucks and cars for hire, but they were not doing well, in fact one closed in 1940. Car rates varied depending on the amount of traffic and the chance of return freight, but were lower than in 1939. The Shiraz road was being repaired by road gangs, but there were serious doubts about its lasting effect, give past experience. The Bushehr-Firuzabad road was still unfinished, although the section to Shiraz was said to be good. The Lengeh road was still in a bad state of repair and seldom used, except by military and civil authorities.[181] As of 1940 the road to Shiraz became unsafe. Robbers killed and disarmed road guards, some of whom actually joined the robbers. Many cars were attacked and looted, inparticular between Daleki and Kazerun and less so between Bushehr and Borazjan. Therefore, by the end November 1941 cars and trucks left in convoy with military escorts. This situation also badly affected road maintenance.[182] Thereafter so-called *cheriks* or local levies were hired, who, in March 1942, started robbing passing car traffic when they were not paid. They threatened to leave altogether if they were not paid soon.[183] The completed Bushehr-Shiraz route, although an improvement, was still a bumpy ride, due to lack of maintenance. In particular, trucks needed to be regularly repaired. Therefore, in 1947, the government decided to build a road via Ahram, Farrashband and Firuzabad, which had an easier gradient and caused less wear and tear on trucks.[184]

Bushehr's Comparative Advantage

Based on the above, it may be surprising that Bushehr remained Persia's major port in the Persian Gulf until the 1920s. This was also the conclusion drawn by the British Commercial Mission, which wrote in 1905 that Bushehr was the most important and most convenient, though not the best situated Persian port. In fact, it wrote that Bandar Abbas was the better port.[185] Indeed, its anchorage was not ideal, shipping and handling were costly and time-consuming, the road linking it to its markets was a challenge and rates were high. The other ports had many better points as to anchorage, shipping and handling, and road conditions, but all was not ideal in these other ports either, as discussed above. As a matter of fact, by the 1870s, Bushehr had become the uncontested "chief port for the general import trade of Persia."[186] As a result European firms, mainly British, established permanent offices there.[187]

As mentioned previously, there were basically three additional factors that made Bushehr a more attractive port than its competitors. These factors, which all its competitors lacked, were the presence of: (i) a commercial community that was more numerous

180. Administration Report 1938, pp. 2, 9.

181. Administration Report 1939, p. 8; Administration Report 1940, p. 3, 7. For a traveler's description of part of this road, see Lindberg 1955 (Bushehr until `Asalu).

182. Political Diaries, vol. 14, pp. 561-62; Administration Report 1941, pp. 5-6.

183. Political Diaries, vol. 15, p. 63; Administration Report 1945, p. 10.

184. NA,FO 371/15471.

185. Gleadowe-Newcomen 1905, pp. 33, 59.

186. Dickson 1884, p. 4.

187. Administration Report 1878-79, p. 29.

and influential than in any other southern port; (ii) the British Residency as well as of about 10 Consulates of foreign nations; and (iii) relatively large markets in its hinterland.[188]

Bushehr's Commercial Community

The nature and the causes of the growth of Bushehr's economic activities as well as its political situation were reflected in both the size and composition of the mercantile community as well as of the population, which changed over time. The most important change was that unlike during the eighteenth century no merchants came to Bushehr anymore from the interior during the October-April trading season. This was because ships came year-round to Bushehr since the beginning of the nineteenth century. Most Bushehri merchants still remained forwarding agents, like in 1828, when they were characterized as "being traders on the capital of others and in most transactions are only agents."[189] In 1860, most merchants still were agents for merchants up country (Shiraz, Isfahan, Yazd).[190] What facilitated this development was that Persian merchants settled in India (Bombay, Calcutta), who preferred to do business with fellow countrymen and/or townsmen, with whom they often had family ties. Living in India, these merchants often became British subject or British-protected persons and therefore, their goods and vessels could and did claim British protection against piracy and other forms of violent interference with their business.[191]

Like Bushehr's population at large, the mercantile community was not a homogenous group, for there were ethnic, language, and religious differences. Nevertheless, it would seem that the differences between these traders from different backgrounds were no major obstacle in their social and commercial relations.[192] Around 1828, the merchants of Bushehr were equally composed of Persian Moslems and Armenians. The latter had more connections with India, and were wealthier and thus more influential, because of wine making and their export monopoly as well as due to their contacts with the English India Company Resident.[193] The well-known and influential Armenian Malkam (Malcolm) family was the repository of much of the wealth of the Moslem population of Bushehr, because of their reliability and their protected British status.[194]

This also implies that the merchant community was a tight one, where religion played a lesser role in personal relations than in society in general. When an Armenian merchant, who was employed by the British Residency was harassed by Sheikh Naser in 1841, he went to Haji `Abdollah, the Malek al-Tojjar, to discuss the problem, who then resolved it by discussing it with the Sheikh. Haji `Abdollah was a trusted advisor of Sheikh Naser at that time, because of his financial and economic power. According to the British Resident: "The Mullik-o-Tujar, having available a large sum of ready money, has

---

188. Administration 1873-74, p. 5 mentions two of these factors.
189. Grummon 1985, pp. 227-29, 254-55.
190. Brugsch 1865, vol. 2, p. 244.
191. Grummon 1985, pp. 232-35.
192. Sadid al-Saltaneh 1362, pp. 2-12.
193. Buckingham 1971, p. 350; Alexander 2000, p. 94.
194. Sadid al-Saltaneh 1362, p. 6. Despite their wealth, J.A. Malcolm was agent for, among others, Messrs Alexander Hector & Co of Baghdad. NA, FO 248/157, J.A. Malcolm to Kemball and J.A. Malcolm to Kemball, 06/11/1854. On the different Armenian merchants, see Mashayekhi 1382, pp. 131-49.

been enabled to command the markets, and consequently to exercise a degree of control over his less rich brethren...." Because merchants were the repository of wealth and cash, they were in great demand by politicians and officials as a source of loans, information, and mediation. Both the Al Mazkur and the British used merchants as intermediaries to discuss sensitive issues, which allowed arms-length negotiations and emphasized their importance.[195] By the 1870s, the composition of the merchant community in Bushehr had changed, for it was composed of Persian Moslems, Armenians, Arabs, Jews, Khojahs, Hindus, and Europeans.[196]

However by that time, according to the British Resident, "In Persia, the merchants who have acquired great wealth are few, and with increased competition the number would scarcely increase. The famine of 1871 caused the failure of many cloth merchants of Bushire."[197] Nevertheless, Bushehr had its share of wealthy merchants. Sadid al-Saltaneh distinguished three categories of merchants in Bushehr without defining them, although the ranking was linked to their wealth. Among the first category we find Aqa Mohammad `Ali Malek al-Tojjar, who died in 1877 and was said to be the richest man in Persia. Because he died childless his property was inherited by his elder brother Haji Baba, a naturalized British Indian subject who resided in Bushehr at that time.[198] Moreover, Mohammad `Ali Malek al-Tojjar had excellent ties with government circles in Tehran and even became governor of Bushehr. He was not the only wealthy merchant, because after his death Haji Baba was the richest man in Bushehr. He died in May 1883 and his grandson and heir Haji Mohammad Mehdi received the titles of Malek al-Tojjar and Ra'is al-Tojjar,[199] who like other wealthy Bushehri merchants continued to have influence in Tehran and played a leading role in local affairs. Haji Mohammad Mehdi was one of the first category merchants and so was Aqa Mohammad Sadeq, son of the late Haji `Abdol-Nabi. The former had an estimated wealth of more than 100,000 *tumans*. He made his money in the cotton years (1862-65) when many went broke, while others became rich. Tegran Malcolm was one of Armenian merchants in this category, who also was the honorary US consul. The second category merchants included Mirza Gholam Hoseyn, while Aqa Gholam `Ali, son of the late Haji Ja`far Behbahani was one of the third category merchants.[200]

Until the late 1870s, most British commercial transactions were done through Armenian merchants. However, Hotz & Sons opened shop in Bushehr as of 1876 with its own representatives and Ziegler & Co. did likewise in 1890s. In 1883, Hotz and other Europeans firms in Bushehr opened branches at Shiraz and Isfahan to supply the large consuming hinterland of these cities, instead of through native agents. This decision led to the retirement of some Persian merchants and the closing of many agency houses at Bushehr.[201] In 1895, a German firm Joh. Werth & Co. tried to start a business in Bushehr,

---

195. In general, see Floor 2009 a, chapter 2; NA, FO 248/99, letter Mr. Essai, 26/09/1841; Grummon 1985, pp. 243-44, 246, 255-56. For a short biography of the malek al-tojjar, see Hamidi 1380, p. 170.
196. Administration 1873-74, p. 10. An early European merchant house was that of Mr. Paul of Gray & Paul was in Bushire. Geary 1878, vol. 1, p. 65.
197. Administration 1873-74, p. 11.
198. Administration Report 1877-78, p. 5. The *malek al-tojjar* was also very avaricious. Sayyah 1346, p. 12.
199. Administration Report 1883-84, p. 8. For a short biography, see Hamidi 1380, pp. 171-72.
200. Sadid al-Saltaneh 1362, pp. 6, 15. About the Malcom family, see Hamidi 1380, pp. 614-15.
201. Administration Report 1883-84, p. 38.

but failed due its methods which did not appeal to Persian merchants. From its ashes arose a new German firm, with the same management, under the name of *Deutsch-Persische Handels Gesellschaft.* In 1897 it opened agencies in Shiraz and in two small ports and mostly traded in German sugar. It used most of its capital, but due to failure to obtain payments it was liquidated. British firm suffered more competition from Dutch goods imported by Hotz & Sons.[202] However, that came to an end when in 1903 Hotz & Sons went into voluntary bankruptcy.[203]

By 1900 there were several European firms and agents in place, among which were a Russian and German one. Moreover, important Persian Moslem merchants by then also held agencies for Manchester firms.[204] By 1912, the European official and mercantile community numbered some 40 persons.[205] The most important foreign merchants included: H.R. Dixon; Gray Paul & Co; the Imperial Bank of Persia; Livingstone Zeitun & Co (Armenian); A & T Malcolm (Armenian); Leo Malcolm (Armenian); the Russian-Persian Company; Shaul Morad Hayim & Son (Jewish); Woenckhaus & Co; Ziegler & Co. There were some 21 important Persian merchants: Abdol-Majid, Abdol-Rasul Khovak, Aqa `Ali Dehdashti, Haji `Abdol-Karim and Haji `Abdol-Reza Dehdashti, Haji `Abdol-Khalil Dehdashti, Haji `Abdol-Nabi Kazeruni, Haji `Abdol-Rasul Bushehri Ra'is al-Tojjar (agent for David Sassoon & Co), Haji `Abdol-Qasem Shirazi, Haji Aqa Behbahani, Haji Akbar Kazeruni, Haji Gholam `Ali and Haji Mohammad Baqer Behbahani and Sons (agents for the Bombay Persia Steam Navigation and E.D. Sassoon, London), Haji Yusof and Haji Mohammad Taqi Kazeruni, Mashhadi Mohammad `Ali Dehdashti, Haji Mohammad Hasan and Haji Baqer Borazjani, Haji Mohammad Hasan Dovvani, Haji Mohammad Hoseyn Dehdashti, Haji Sayyed Mohammad Reza Kazeruni (agent for Haji `Ali Akbar & Sons, London), Mahmud Bushehri, Mashhadi Reza & Company, Mirza Gholam Hoseyn and Haji Reza Kazeruni, Mirza Mahmud Kazeruni, Sayyed Bashi Behbahani, and Sayyed Hoseyn Behbahani.[206]

In contrast to the situation in Bushehr, in Bandar Abbas there were no European businessmen and very few Persian merchants of importance. There were some Indian merchants, which was due to the fact that the principal merchants at Yazd were Zoroastrians, some Moltani Hindus, and a few Isfahanis.[207] This composition of the mercantile community reflects the nature of the trade of Bandar Abbas and its links with foreign capital. By 1900, this situation had not really changed in Bandar Abbas a town of 12,000 inhabitants, where there were at least four European residents, the British and Russian consuls, the agent of the British India Company, and a Belgian Customs official.[208] Even as late as 1912, the Persian commercial communities at Mohammerah and Bandar Abbas were not large either, although they were growing.[209] Lengeh, which had some rich pearl

202. Administration Report 1895-96, p. 17; Administration Report 1896-97, p. 5; Administration Report 1897-98, p. 18. Administration Report 1898-99, p. 31.

203. Floor 2007 b, p. 192.

204. Gleadowe-Newcomen 1905, p. 60. Ra'is al-Tojjar was agent for PGN Co. Cursetjee 2001, p. 116.

205. Trade Report 1913-14, p. 1.

206. Küss 1911, part III, p. 12; Sa`adat 1390, pp. 24, 43-44. Merchants worked in an office, which in Bushehri dialect became *hafis* or *hafiz*. Hamdidi 1380, p. 225.

207. Pelly 1863, p. 61, note.

208. Trade Report 1912-13, p. 6; Fogg 1875, p. 167. There was also a *na'eb-e kargozar* as of 1902. Lorimer 1915, vol. 2, p. 14.

209. Government of India, *Report* 1912-13, p. 7.

2.4: Distribution of imported goods at Bushehr (1912/13 - 1915/16) in tons.

Product	Total import 1912-1913	1913-1914	1915-1916	For. to Shiraz 1912-1913	1913-1914	1915-1916	Trans shipped to coast ports 1912-1913	1913-1914	1915-1916	(half year only) sent inland via Shif 1912-1913	1913-1914	1915-1916
Loaf sugar	6,039	8,634	4,717	2,518	2,565	3,256	1,761	2,846	1,348	326	1,053	149
Crystal sugar	3,704	2,925	2,914	726	938	1,047	723	1,087	1,348	116	303	182
Tea	220	170	600	234	293	761	-	54	180	-	3	105
Spices	145	174	315	127	158	301	63	54	180	32	27	53
Rice	1,405	2,716	1,778	-	-	-	213	576	501	140	480	183
Flour	183	1,402	366	-	10	17	-	11	-	-	125	-
Wheat	24	391	43	-	115	19					78	
Barley	-	68	284	-	-	-					521	
Cotton piece goods	3,064	1,861	1,617	1,780	1,920	1,095	634	487	116	48	80	154
Cotton yarn and thread	130	181	195	63	146	122	34	22	116	-	1	22
Jute tissues and yarn	80	-	-	9	63	27	-	9	5	-	1	-
Matches	40	130	62	43	85	28	8	4	14	-	1	3
Candles	199	51	98	194	84	89	-	8	19	-	1	3
Kerosene	772	229	424	129	112	125	77	178	180	110	129	67
Metals block tin 33	254	453	462	117	195	139	4	9	23	1	9	2
Chinaware, earthenware	120	99	34	76	48	23	-	21	9	-	-	-
Glassware	32	24	10	9	14	3	-	-	-	-	-	-
Window glass	9	18	8	2	16	3	-	-	-	-	-	-
Chemical products	64	66	26	48	93	22	-	16	-	-	1	-
Paper	37	38	26	23	25	17	-	-	1	-	1	-
Haberdashery	-	-	-	-	-	-	-	30	-		7	
Indigo	12	14	5	10	16	6	-			-	7	2
Forage (military)	82	53	11	-			-			-		
Coal, charcoal	302	446	453	-	-	-	-	-	-	-	-	-
Timber. Wood	1,762	1,623	1,890	-	-	-	-	-	-	-	-	-
Miscellaneous	965	1,632	2,088	141	269	233	-	-	20	63	62	216
Total Tons	19,712	23,614	18,041	6,249	7,185	7,333	3,517	5,365	4,959	866	2,881	1,141

Source: Trade Report 1912-13, p. 15; Trade Report 1914-15, p. 6; Trade Report 1915-16, p. 6. The totals do not always add up, because some digits were very difficult or impossible to read and had to be guessed.

merchants, had otherwise a small mercantile community, whose trade was focused on the Arabian coast, not the domestic Persian market.

Political and Administrative advantages

Trade developments as well as political changes further enhanced the role of Bushehr over other ports. Until the mid-nineteenth century Bushehr and the other Persian ports were ports-of-call. Such a port served as a marketing and transit center for long distance trade where two distinct sets of merchants (importers and exporters) met and exchanged goods. This exchange took place under market conditions, i.e., prices were determined by supply and demand. Merchants came looking for buyers or sellers, and would move on to another port if they could not find a ready sale or purchase.[210] In 1750, Plaisted reported that "Here [in Bandar Abbas] Capt. Robinson meeting with a good Market for his Cargo, was under no Necessity to go up as far as Bisheer, or Bowchier [Bushire] to dispose of it here."[211] This situation was determined by the fact that the Persian Gulf was one single market, where goods could be landed at many ports. The availability of buyers and a positive reception (including low customs rates) by local governors determined the place where merchants would land their goods. The governors of the ports concerned, therefore, tried to induce merchants to land their goods in their port by offering competing and more attractive customs duties as well as to reduce hassle and maintain a safe and predictable environment. The market was dependent on the presence of merchants, who would come from upcountry to the ports to buy what merchants calling on the port were offering. Also, these merchants came to these ports during the trading season only, which was during the fall and winter. In summertime there was no trade to speak of.[212] In 1836, Hennell gave a perfect example of such port-of-call behavior by arriving ships. "Coming from Basra they say that they will sail in a few days, but usually it is from 2 to 6 weeks that they leave. The report that a caravan or a batch of horses is about to start from Shiraz, will sometimes detain a vessel that has really made every preparation for sailing on a fixed day, for a fortnight longer."[213]

The advent of mercantile steamships in the Persian Gulf in the 1860s, which were not dependent on the monsoon for sailing conditions, meant that the seasonal nature of trade changed to one where trade could be carried on throughout the year. Moreover, because of the regular schedule of the steamships as well as the establishment of the telegraph in 1863 trade became more predictable. I.e., merchants could let exporters know what they wanted and when, almost in real-time. As a consequence, the itinerant behavior of merchants came to an end, while vertical integration was slowly established throughout the market supply chain and predictability of the behavior of customs authorities increased, thus reducing commercial uncertainty. As a result of these various developments, Bushehr gradually became a port-of-transit, or a caravan terminus for the interior. This meant

---

210. For a detailed discussion of this subject, see Grummon 1985, pp. 206-41.

211. Plaisted 1757, p. 7. This situation also existed upcountry for land-based trade. Connolly in the early 1830s, referring to the situation in Mashhad, reports "Thus, for want of a regular understanding many [merchants] bring goods at a complete venture, and if they do not suit the market, send them east or west, to any place at which there is a change of their selling." Connolly 1834, vol. 1, p. 347; see also Buckingham 1971, pp. 354-55.

212. From April to October no native vessel leaves the Gulf the opportunity is one in 6-8 weeks. NA, FO 248/85, Hennell, Residency to McNeill, 15/12/1836. For the same situation in the Safavid period see Floor 2000 and Floor 2006 a.

213. NA, FO 248/85, Hennell to McNeill, 15/12/1836.

that henceforth Bushehr was a point of transfer between long-distance maritime trade and long-distance caravan trade. Goods bought in, for example from India, were landed in Bushehr and forwarded immediately upcountry for distribution. The same owner managed all this. The shipper at Bushehr need not necessarily be the owner, but usually was an agent. Consequently, the merchant class of Bushehr consisted mainly of forwarding agents for merchants inland (Shiraz, Isfahan, and Yazd) rather than merchants trading on their own account. Of course, this did not mean that if prices were higher in Basra than in Bushehr, contrary to earlier expectations, that captains would not continue their voyage to Basra instead. However, this became a much less frequent occurrence, mostly concerned sailing ships, and was the exception rather than the rule.[214]

Bushehr had suffered much as a port from the grasping behavior of its ruling local dynasty of Al Mazkur Sheikhs, and its hostilities with the governor of Shiraz and neighboring chiefs. This situation was resolved when in 1850, the Al Mazkurs were ousted from their position of hereditary governors and henceforth only outsiders functioned as governors of Bushehr.[215] Thus, as of 1850, the territory of Bushehr remained under a governor and local officers appointed by the central government in Tehran. Customs and revenues were either contracted for by the governor or accounted for in detail to the royal treasury.[216] What further helped the development of Bushehr was that in 1888, the prime-minister Amin al-Soltan created the governorship of the Gulf Ports (*mamlaket-e Banader-e Khalij-e Fars*). The jurisdiction of governor, who had the title of *daryabegi* and was based in Bushehr, was in charge of the littoral and islands from Bandar Delam to Jask, including Bandar Abbas. The town of Bandar Abbas was under the Persian Gulf Ports governor as well as the three islands opposite to it and the districts of Shamil, Minab, Biyaban, and Jask. The Lengeh district, under a deputy-governor, was also subordinate to Bushehr.[217]

With the change in the nature of the governorship of Bushehr, and subordination of its rival ports, there were changes in other administrative functions. In addition to being the seat of the governor of the Persian Gulf Ports, Bushehr was the location where the customs farmer (*shahbandar*) of the Gulf Ports was established. For example, in 1887-88, Malek al-Tojjar Bushiri farmed the customs of Shiraz, Bushehr, Lengeh and Bandar Abbas. Later farmers were notables, who were merchants themselves or had close links with them, ensuring that customs policy favored their own business dealings and thus, the ports where they controlled the customs department.[218] Also, in 1888 a branch of the New Oriental Bank Corporation was established in Bushehr, which was bought by the Imperial Bank of Persia one year later, thus bringing modern banking to the port and made doing business easier.[219] Another important administration official who established himself in Bushehr as of 1856 was the *kargozar*, the agent of the Ministry of Foreign Affairs, whose task it was to manage the conflicts between Persian and foreign subjects in collaboration with foreign consuls. Although there were *kargozars* in Lengeh and Bandar Abbas, they were subordinates of the one in Bushehr, who formally was responsible for all the Gulf Ports.

---

214. Floor 1988 c, pp. 59-77 and 179-182.

215. See Grummon 1985, pp. 120-69; Floor 2011 b, pp. 12ff.

216. Pelly 1865 a, p. 33. Sometimes the governor depended directly from the governor-general of Fars.

217. Lorimer 1915, vol. 2, p. 582; Trade Report 1910-11, p. 1; Curzon 1892, vol. 2, pp. 401-06. Also, Kong, `Asalu, Naband, Nakhilu, Shiru, and Khark. Busse 1972, pp. 340, 343, 352, 397, 399, 417, 419.

218. Administration Report 1887-88, p. 33.

219. Administration Report 1888-89, p. 29.

The presence of the British Residency for the Persian Gulf in Bushehr also was an important support for Bushehr's continuing role. For example, even though by 1830, Bushehr had "lost a considerable portion of its commercial importance of late years. It still, however, continues a useful channel of communication between the British authorities in India and their delegates in Persia, at the same time that it furnishes a convenient resort to the vessels of war, constantly cruising about the gulph to prevent the regeneration of piracy."[220] Because of Bushehr being the unofficial headquarters of British activities in the Persian Gulf, its head, the Resident, acquired considerable influence in the port. This influence increased during the second half of the nineteenth century due to the weakening of the Persian government. As a result by the 1870s and thereafter, foreign travelers dignified the Resident as being, if not the king of the Persian Gulf, certainly the real governor of Bushehr.[221] Other foreign representatives also established themselves in Bushehr due to its growing economic and administrative importance, which further enhanced its prominence as a trading port. By about 1900, there were 10 countries represented in Bushehr.

Unlike the other ports, Bushehr also boasted other modern developments such as having more than one printing-press and a comic illustrated newspaper *Tolu`* (1900-01) and a (bi-) weekly newspaper, *Mozaffari* (1901-08).[222]

All these various developments gave Bushehr a comparative advantage, which, as we have seen, translated into a concentration of administrative, political, and commercial capacity and influence in the port. Moreover, all this was either lacking in other ports or present at a later date in a minor and subordinate form.

Distribution port

Trade in Bushehr was mainly due to its function as an entrepôt for markets in the interior, and thus, the security on the road to Shiraz determined its volume, as is clear from the above section on this road. Its importance rose and fell in consonance with the level of economic activity in its hinterland, in particular Isfahan and Shiraz, and on the quantities of transport available.[223] This also explains why there was so little interest in Bushehr of what was happening in the rest of Persia. According to the British consul, "there is little connection between Bushehr and northern Persia and Tehran; the interests of the population is mainly limited to the local province and the towns along the caravan routes."[224] From a port-of-transit, Bushehr became the major distribution center for much of Fars province. This included (i) the towns along the main caravan routes (Kazerun, Abadeh), including Shiraz, which was the main upcountry distribution center, up to and including Isfahan and Fars province as well as (ii) the coast littoral, south of the mountain range towards Shiraz, for a distance of more than 240 km (150 miles), including Behbahan town

---

220. Stocqueler 1832, vol. 1, pp. 12-13.

221. Geary 1878, vol. 1, pp. 55-56 ("The Resident at Bushire has exercised a sort of informal dictatorship wherever the Persian, or the Turkish, or the Omani power, was not able to assert itself decisively."); Rivoyre 1883, p. 136; Vilmorin 1895, pp. 349-50; Cresson 1908, p. 255.

222. On the rise of modern institutions in Bushehr in general, see Sa`adat 1390, pp. 31-32, 34. On the role and influence of the *Mozaffari* newspaper, see Martin 2000, pp. 182, 185, 187, 189-95, 199, 202.

223. Trade Report 1910-11, pp. 3-4; Trade Report 1913-14, p. 1; Administration Report 1923, p. 11; Mahrad 1978, p. 88; Rich 1839, p. 265.

224. Trade Report 1911-12, p. 2. This was not an exceptional situation and also held for other regions, see Floor 2003, pp. 68-69.

and district. Around 1910, the population of Bushehr district and the towns of Behbahan, Kazerun and Firuzabad (also all commercially dependent on Bushehr) were estimated at 150,000 and of Fars at 750,000, a sizeable market, which partly explains the attractiveness of Bushehr as a port-of-transit.[225]

Bushehr's distributive role had always been larger than that of Bandar Abbas. In 1863, Pelly reported that "The general opinion at Shirauz seemed to be, that the trade passing though Abbass is greater than that passing through Bushire, but that the consumption of Bushire and its neighbourhood being larger than that of Abbass, Bushire is the better known port."[226] Nevertheless, at that time it only had a small part of imports that were re-exported "to other Gulf ports in a smaller class of sea-going vessels. The bulk, however, is taken to the interior of Persia. After reaching Shiraz it is divided into destination Yazd and Isfahan, a sprinkling round these cities."[227] This distributive role grew in importance, such that by the late 1870s, the role of transit trade at Bushehr started to decrease. Bushehr's hinterland, including its neighboring minor ports (Delam, Mash`ur, Rig, Hendiyan, Liravi, Taheri, `Asalu, and Ganaveh) became almost as important as markets for its imported goods as Shiraz. This held in particular for consumer goods such as tea, sugar, kerosene, and rice. The latter that traditionally had been imported from Shiraz, now came from India. The trend towards increased business ties with its nearby hinterland was reinforced by the growing insecurity in Fars after 1906 as well as by the greater security and purchasing power on the littoral. As a result, by 1913 the distribution of goods imported into Bushehr was almost evenly shared between Bushehr's immediate hinterland and Shiraz.[228] Bushehr's local trade was of no great importance, however.[229]

Bushehr and its immediate hinterland

Table 2.5 shows the importance of traffic between Bushehr and the outlying ports as a means of distribution during 1912-13/1915-16. In 1912-13, traffic to Shiraz represented only one-third of total imports (in weight), though in value its share was higher. However, the trend was for local trade to increase. One of the reasons was the increased purchase of goods, especially sugar, by nomads who between September-March sent special caravans to the ports to purchase their needs and visited less and less the Shiraz bazaar. Tea is missing from the table for the year 1912-13, which indicates that the smaller ports were already amply supplied with smuggled tea. In the years thereafter, due to the presence of British warships in connection with World War I, smuggling became temporarily unimportant, and therefore, the distribution of tea to the other ports also took place.[230] Goods for the immediate Bushehr hinterland were sent via Shif.[231] In 1913-14, the pattern was the same. Of total imports of 23,614 tons, 7,185 went to Shiraz, 5,365 were transshipped to other coast ports and 2,881 tons, via Shif, were consumed in Bushehr's immediate hinterland.[232]

225. Trade Report 1911-12, p. 1.
226. Pelly 1865 b, p. 153.
227. Pelly 1865 a, p. 48.
228. Trade Report 1911-12, p. 1; Trade Report 1912-13, p. 14; Trade Report 1913-14, pp. 8-9.
229. Gleadowe-Newcomen 1905, p. 61.
230. Trade Report 1912-13, p. 15.
231. Trade Report 1913-14, p. 8.
232. Trade Report 1913-14, p. 8.

What is further noteworthy is that transshipments of all goods (except for cottons) to other Persian ports were as important for Bushehr as Shiraz. Given that the road to Shiraz was often blocked during those years (see above) this meant that these other ports were vital for the prosperity of Bushehr.

The shipments to other Persian ports represented between 55% and 75% of the goods in weight sent to Shiraz during 1912-15, which is an indication of the increased importance of demand in the other ports. However, these percentages are in fact lower, because the largest destination port was Mohammerah and the sixth one was Bandar Abbas (Table 2.5). The shipments to these two ports were not for local consumption, but represented an overflow of goods at Bushehr (due to the closure of the trade road) that were destined for Isfahan. The other ports were of more interest as they were not competing with Bushehr, but were distribution centers for their local hinterland. For example, Buzi, Ma`shur and Hendiyan supplied parts of the interior of Khuzestan up river, while to some extent Hendiyan also supplied Behbahan. Delam was the main port for Behbahan, the chief seat of the Kuhgilu tribe. Rig supplied several of the Qashqa'i groups, except in summer, while Lawar was the main port for Dashti.[233] As is clear from what follows in the section of Trade Development, when Bushehr lost the race with Mohammerah and its hinterland a decade later, it was the beginning of its inevitable decline.

2.5: Export from Bushehr to various Persian ports in 1915-16 (in tons)

Port	Loaf sugar	Crystal sugar	Piece goods	Yarns	Rice	Spices	Kerosene	Tea	Misc.	Total
Mohammerah	43	258	323	34	25	50	-	688	38	1,459
Buzi	11	54	-	-	17	-	-	-	6	88
Mashur	132	138	83	18	16	38	7	60	6	498
Hendiyan	55	71	9	3	36	4	21	-	4	203
Deylam	96	195	213	53	33	28	48	119	23	808
Ganaveh	32	49	19	-	39	8	13	1	1	162
Rig	140	224	74	3	201	34	160	33	9	878
Rudhilleh	6	29	30	2	40	8	23	28	-	166
Khark	-	5	-	-	16	-	2	-	1	24
Karri	-	9	-	-	5	-	-	-	1	15
Lawar	11	156	8	-	57	4	9	-	1	246
Dayyer	3	35	4	1	-	1	2	-	1	47
Kangan	-	13	1	-	1	1	2	-	-	18
Taheri	18	47	9	-	6	4	2	6	2	94
`Asalu	1	18	-	-	-	-	-	-	-	19
Bandar Abbas	63	42	21	-	7	2	-	72	10	217
Total	611	1,343	794	114	499	182	289	1,007	103	4,942

Source: Trade Report 1915-16, p. 7.

233. Trade Report 1915-16, p. 7.

The other leading Persian Gulf ports also played a similar distributive role, but much less so, because there were no major population centers in their hinterland.[234] Taking into account their location, we note that from the mouth of the Persian Gulf, where Bandar Abbas is situated (population 5,000), the next major port was Lengeh (population 8,000) at 174 km (108 miles), from there it was another 484 km (301 miles) to Bushehr (population 18,000) and from there, 278 km (173 miles) to Mohammerah (population 15,000). What this means is that due to the distances between the ports there was little overlap in terms of distribution to the interior markets in Persia, mainly Yazd and Isfahan. The hinterland for Bandar Abbas was Kerman province, from which Yazd province was also partly supplied, and beyond that Mashhad. Lengeh mainly served its immediate hinterland, of which Lar and Jahrom were the outer limit. Beyond these towns there were no major caravan routes and there was little commerce between Lengeh and central Persia. The Bushehr distribution area extended 160 km to the north and 240 km to the south near the littoral. Inland it covered Kuhgilu country and the Qashqa'i summer quarters on the west, and on the east it followed the border of Fars towards the province of Yazd. Isfahan was the main terminus of caravan traffic from Bushehr, and the town of Yazd was also partly supplied from Shiraz. The Mohammerah area included Khuzestan with the towns of Ahvaz and Dezful, and to some extent Lurestan and by the Ahvaz-Isfahan road the Bakhtiyari country and partly the town and province of Isfahan.[235]

As a result of the above described developments, each port supplied its 'own' market, the location of which was determined by its geographical position and that of the markets upcountry. This meant that each port had a certain captive market, which determined that part of the imports into the Persian Gulf would become its share, as it would be less attractive or even uneconomical to import these goods for particular markets via another port. As a result, there was a certain ranking of ports, indicated by their volume of trade, the order of which changed, of course, over time. In 1902, for example, of the whole trade of the Persian Gulf, Basra was responsible for 32%, Bushehr for 23%, Bandar Abbas for 6% and Mohammerah for not more than 4.5%. All these places were really ports for the interior of Persia, since of the Basra imports at least two-thirds were destined for the Baghdad-Kermanshah route.[236] However, the ranking had totally changed 12 years later,[237] when Mohammerah became the number two port. Despite its success at maintaining its position as the gateway to Southern Persia, Bushehr was not the most important Persian port. In 1914-15, for example, Bushehr was the second most important customs port in Persia, the gross receipts amounting to 5,458,508 *qrans* as against 7,693,982 *qrans* collected at Enzeli and smaller ports in Gilan.[238]

Bandar Abbas and Lengeh had a special role. The former supplied the Yazd-Mashhad market (tea, piece-goods) and the latter the Arab coast. This function came to an end for a combination of factors. Due to the construction of the Trans-Caspian railway and the opening of the Batoum-Ashkabad route, Russian sugar and piece-goods practically

234. See Floor 2010 and Idem, 2011 a.

235. Trade Report 1912-13, p. 6.

236. Whigham 1903, p. 147.

237. Trade Report 1912-13, p. 6 (Bushire 1.75 mln; Mohammerah 1.03 mln; Bandar Abbas 0.68 mln; and Lengeh 0.39 mln). Sani` al-Dowleh 1294, vol. 1, p. 298 stated that Bushehr was the most important port followed by Bandar and trailed by Lengeh.

238. Trade Report 1914-15, p. 3.

flooded the market of Mashhad, thus greatly reducing the role of Lengeh and Bandar Abbas. This trend was further reinforced by the 1903 Customs treaty, which favored Russian goods. As of 1906, the little trade in British and Indian goods that still went to Khorasan had to compete with similar imports from the Quetta-Nuskhi-Sistan road. In addition, the establishment of a uniform customs department all over Persia as of 1903 with the application of higher tariffs meant that goods destined for the Arab coast henceforth went directly to these markets rather than via Lengeh. These developments hardly affected the ports of Bushehr and Mohammerah.[239]

Until 1925, while Lengeh did not recover from these blows, Bandar Abbas still continued to play a busy role as distributing center for Kerman, Yazd, Lar and other towns in its hinterland. However, thereafter this role gradually diminished, so that in 1934 its annual trade was half of that in 1925. Moreover, the trend of its dwindling trade continued due to worsening economic conditions in Persia as well as to the increased commercial role of Mohammerah, Bandar Shahpur and Ahvaz. In the 1930s, it still had no wharves, still the same old pier and inadequate storage facilities, although the latter were enlarged in 1934.[240]

This shift in ranking, where Mohammerah was increasing its role at the expense of Bushehr was unexpected. Certainly, Messrs. Lynch had hoped that their road connecting Ahvaz with Isfahan would attract merchants from Bushehr to Mohammerah, but many doubted that this would happen.[241] What boosted the role of Mohammerah, and what nobody could have planned for, was the discovery of oil in Khuzestan and the building of the refinery at Abadan, just opposite Mohammerah. Its position, and that of Bandar-e Shahpur and Ahvaz, was further reinforced by the construction of the Trans-Iranian Railway, the creation of the city of Madar-e Soleyman and the construction of new roads that made lorry traffic competitive with that of Bushehr. As a result, it was soon very clear that Bushehr suffered from the rise of Mohammerah, Bandar-e Shahpur and Ahvaz, and only maintained some of its position, mainly its entrepot trade as a distributing center for Kazerun and Shiraz. Furthermore, what did not help its position either, was the fact that its landing and storage facilities remained inadequate. At the end of the 1920s, Mohammerah had taken over the role of the gateway to Southern Persia and did not, as was initially feared, lose its ranking to Bandar Shahpur, situated 60 km to the east on the Khur Musa. The latter due to its as yet inadequate landing and shipping facilities was mainly used for importing government material and stores, while all general cargo continued to pass through Mohammerah.[242]

Bushehr did not regain its position when during World War II Persian ports played a major role in supplying Russia, by then also most traffic went to Khorramshahr and other ports at the head of the Persian Gulf. Bushehr received no major investments, for in the 1950s, modern vessels calling at Bushehr still were lying at some 10 km and discharged cargo and passengers by lighter. The once prosperous port of some 40,000 inhabitants

---

239. Administration Report 1901-02, pp. 13-14; Administration Report 1903-04, pp. 23-24; Administration Report 1905-06, p. 16; Floor 2004 b, pp. 82-96; 2009 a (it also meant the loss as clearing house of pearls).

240. Forester 1929, p. 14; Gamble 1935, p. 14; Todd 1937, p. 5.

241. Whigham 1903, pp. 148-49.

242. Forester 1929, p. 11; Gamble 1935, pp. 11-13; Ebtehaj 1932, p. 183; Government of Great Britain 1945, pp. 502-03; Shahnavaz 2005.

was reduced to 14,000 by 1958. "Ten foreign consulates were once established there, in 1957 there was one foreign resident, a Russian maid servant."[243]

The Development of Trade at Bushehr

Introduction

The annual turnover of trade in Bushehr, as elsewhere in the world, depended on a number of conditions, both exogenous and endogenous. Of the former, the weather was of vital importance. Persia was a subsistence economy based on agriculture and therefore, incomes rose and fell in harmony with the harvest. The British Commercial Mission rightly observed in 1905, "In years of scanty rainfall and failing crops the people, whose 'margin of solvency' is even smaller than that of similar classes in India (owing to their wants being greater and to the uncertainty of the pecuniary demands that may be made on them), have perforce to reduce expenditures to its lowest limits, contenting themselves with the barest necessities of life."[244] As a consequence, trade fluctuations in Bushehr were in particular influenced by the amount of rainfall "as a good rainfall stimulates export of cereals and the consequent import of foreign goods."[245] This not only held for the grain producing areas in the littoral, but also for the markets upcountry served by Bushehr. Because poverty in Fars and Isfahan, for whatever reason was not good for trade as people would not be able to buy imported goods.[246]

But it was not only the weather that determined a peasant's income, but also his encouragement and protection by the state, meaning being protected from oppression by governors, officials, landlords and brigands, which presumed a competent, enabling and responsible government, one that was sorely lacking. Similarly, security on the roads and a positive business climate, when it existed, had an upward effect on trade, or a downward trend when it did not. Further, the cost and availability of labor and transport affected the cost and the rapidity by which the market might be served.[247] Other factors that had a great impact on the volume of trade at Bushehr was the outbreak of the Turco-Russian war in 1877, which permanently led to a partial trade shift via the north of Persia to the Persian Gulf. What sustained this shift was the coincidental establishment of a more frequent service of steamships to Persian Gulf ports. Overstocking, either locally, or in importing countries also had a depressing effect on trade as did the depreciation of the Persian currency, or the fall in price of important export products such as opium. The occurrence of the plague in Bombay and Karachi, two major destinations for Bushehri exports, also meant that trade in Bushehr would suffer.[248]

---

243. Stevens 1979, pp. 284-85 (the British Resident was the last of the consuls to depart in 1947).

244. Gleadowe-Newcomen 1905, p. 9.

245. Administration Report 1899-1900, p. 41.

246. Administration Report 1882-83, p. 30; Administration Report 1895-96, p. 17.

247. See Floor 2003 a, pp. 17-21; Idem 2014 b, chapter eight.

248. Administration Report 1877-78, p. 25; Administration Report 1878-79, p. 28; Administration Report 1881-82, p. 21; Administration Report 1882-83, p. 30; Administration Report 1891-92, p. 19; Administration Report 1894-95, p. 21; Administration Report 1895-96, p. 17; Administration Report 1896-97, p. 5.

The growth of trade

Despite all the above mentioned real obstacles, trade increased with extraordinary rapidity during the early part of the reign of Fath `Ali Shah (1797-1834), because of the greater security upcountry and greater attention paid by the Persian government to the Persian Gulf trade, the maritime security provided by the British fleet to small vessels as well as the continued economic growth in Persia itself.[249]

2.6: Imports and Exports at Bushehr (1788-1810) in Rupees

Year	Imports	Exports	Total Trade	Source/Observations
1788-89	11.3 lac	-	-	Grummon 1985, pp. 174-75 (Charles Watkins)
1799	23,00,000	9,60,000	-	Grummon 1985, p. 175 (Maister/Fawcett Report)
1800	17,50,000	-	1,60,00,000	Grummon 1985, p. 175 (Malcolm)
1802	-	12,00,000	-	Waring 1973, p. 8
1809		36.7 lac	-	Morier 1812, p. 239
1809	30-40 lac	30-40 lac	-	Grummon 1985, p. 176 (Bruce)
1810			20 lac	Kinneir 1971, p. 177

1 lac = 100,000 ; 1 *tuman* = 104.8 rupees.

The data presented in Table 2.6 provide conflicting information. On the one hand the data suggest that the growth of trade tapered off (Waring, Kinneir) between 1800-1810, while on the other hand (Malcolm, Bruce) indicate that there was solid growth. Given the fact that Kinneir reported that "the trade of Bushire is very considerable" and a long time local trader (Hardford-Jones) explicitly wrote that trade had increased, we may assume that this indeed was the trend.[250] This is further borne out by data for the second decade of the nineteenth century, which show a steady growth of trade (see Table 2.7). Imports at Bushehr in 1817 were estimated to be £300,000 and by 1823 already £670,000. However, in 1824, imports fell to £467,000.[251]

2.7: Total Imports and Exports through Bushehr with British vessels (1816-23) or all vessels (1829-33) in Persian Rls.

Year	Total Imports	Total Imports	Total Exports	Total Exports
	All vessels	British vessels only	All vessels	British vessels only
1816	-	36,81,415		6,00,309*
1817	-	30,03,947	-	29,27,767
1819	-	32,06,085	-	36,77,313*
1820	-	66,52,274	-	36,97,449
1821	-	54,35,711	-	35,54,429

249. Lorimer 1915, vol. 1, p. 1955; Issawi 1971, pp. 90-91.
250. Kinneir 1973, p. 70; Lorimer 1915, vol. 1, p. 1955.
251. NA, FO 60/25 (30/12/1825).

Year	Total Imports	Total Imports	Total Exports	Total Exports
1822	-	77,69,538	-	24,94,657
1823	-	32,15,806	-	26,85,056
1829-30	106,78,611	-	40,85,293	-
1832-33	52,45,856	-	24,93,879	-
1833-34	17,79,733 (89,27,636)+	-	8,74,132 (47,32,986)+	-

Source: Grummon 1985, p. 179.

* data obtained between 25 October and 31 December.

+ Figures in parenthesis represent total trade figures obtained from the Bushehr customs house.

Grummon argues that trade did not fall in the mid-1820s, because there was an upsurge of trade in 1829. He argues that the decline in trade only began in 1832/33.[252] However, it probably started earlier, for in 1831, Stocqueler observed that "Bushire has lost a considerable portion of its commercial importance of later years."[253] This observation was confirmed by Whitelock who in 1835 visited Bandar Abbas and observed: "When Bushire, a few years ago, remained for some time in a disturbed state, commerce found its way again into this channel [Bandar Abbas]."[254] This is probably what Wellsted referred to in 1827, viz. that trade in Bandar Abbas was increasing and he thought that this port "would very soon recover a considerable portion of its former importance."[255]

There appear to have been two developments working at the same time namely the loss of trade to other ports and the general decline of trade in the Persian Gulf. Bushehr was losing trade to Bandar Abbas. This was a reverse of the trend begun in the mid-eighteenth century, when Bushehr replaced Bandar Abbas as the premier Persian port in the Persian Gulf. In 1809, Pottinger submitted that the resort of merchants "to the sea-port of Abooshuhr or Bushire, gains daily ground, to the prejudice of Bunder Abbass, and, of consequence, Kirman."[256] Bushehr continued to hold the predominant position as the major port for Persia in the Persian Gulf. In 1800, some 87% of Persian trade went via Bushehr and about 50% of total imports in the early 1820s. The other smaller ports absorbed the remainder of imported goods.[257] As a result, contemporary travelers note that "This [Bushehr] is a place of considerable mercantile importance, the commerce of the Gulf centres here."[258] The trade of Bushehr represented about two-thirds of the Perso-Indian trade in the 1820s, according to Astelt the EIC agent in Bushehr.[259] According to British data, in the years 1845-46 and 1846-47, Persian merchants in India consigned goods three times as often to Bandar Abbas than to Bushehr. This shift was also to be

252. Grummon 1985, p. 180.
253. Stocqueler 1832, vol. 1, p. 12.
254. Whitelock 1836-38, p. 117.
255. Wellsted 1840, vol. 1, p. 74.
256. Pottinger 1816, p. 225.
257. Grummon 1985, p. 176; Issawi 1971, pp. 90-91; Lorimer 1915, vol. 1, p. 1955.
258. Stirling 1991, p. 8; Buckingham 1971, p. 351 ("Bushire is the best port of the Gulf apart from Basra."); Kempthorne 1835, p. 283.
259. NA, FO 60/24, Astelt to Gore (07/07/1824), unfoliated.

noted in the increased role that Bandar Abbas played in supplying Eastern Persia, where it sent most of the goods.[260]

Although Bushehr was the most important Persian port it was not the largest one in the Persian Gulf. Morier remarked that "The whole of its trade is closely connected with that of Bussorah, as almost every ship which navigates the Gulf touches at both places, either to receive or discharge merchandise; but it does not employ annually more than eight ships under English colours, and about six under Muscat, making on average about 4500 tons of shipping."[261] As a result, there were "a number of small merchantmen belonging to those who trade to and from Muscat, Gombroon and Bussorah."[262]

The manner in which these merchants conducted their business had not greatly changed over the centuries. In 1842, Robertson, the acting Resident, made an effort to find out how business relations might be improved to which end he performed an informal survey among the local merchants. The result was not surprising. British merchants liked to be paid in cash, while local merchants wanted to have credit for a number of months. This was due to the way they did business. It was rare that a merchant made a direct large purchase. Rather they used middlemen or brokers, who found other merchants who would buy smaller amounts. Ideally, the purchasing merchant wanted to pay his creditors after he had sold all his goods, which required time. In fact, he demanded a longer period of credit, because he had to give credit to his purchasers, who either resold their goods to merchant inland or retailed it. Therefore, merchants did not like to buy large quantities of goods out of fear of not being able to sell in case of a contrary market.[263]

Bushehr maintained its predominant commercial position as the main port for goods destined for Persia, which it had assumed as of 1760, until the late 1820s. It was only then that Bandar Abbas again started to challenge Bushehr's position. This phenomenon was reinforced by the fact that since the early 1790s until 1868, Bandar Abbas was outsourced to the Soltan of Oman, who, of course, wanted to get a good return on his investment.[264]

At Bushehr, in the early part of the nineteenth century, the customs rate was basically held constantly at 3-4% (see Table 4.1), while at Lengeh and Mohammerah none were levied.[265] Unfortunately, no data are available on the customs rate levied at Bandar Abbas. They were said to be low. But more than possibly lower customs duties, the local political situation was the main reason for the decline in trade at Bushehr. The high-handed behavior of Sheikh `Abdol-Rasul, the internal domestic troubles as well as those with Shiraz had created an environment that was not conducive to undisturbed trade and merchants therefore, began to take their business elsewhere. Sheikh `Abdol-Rasul levied many exactions on merchants, forcing them to buy his goods at prices fixed by him, but

---

260. Issawi 1971, pp. 92-103; Idem 1970, p. 19f; Grummon 1985, p. 268.

261. Morier 1812, p. 38; see also Heude 1819, p. 42.

262. Milburn 1813, vol. 1, p. 128; Morier 1812, p. 38 ("There is none of the bustle and movement which indicates the activity of commerce." Only here and there a boat).

263. NA, FO 248/108, Robertson to Sheil 23/07/1842. For the situation in the seventeenth and eighteenth centuries, see Floor 2000 and Idem 2007 a.

264. Floor 2011 a. On Masqat's aggressive policy to control the carrying trade in the Persian Gulf, see Idem 2014 b and literature quoted.

265. Grummon 1985, pp. 275-76; the Dutch who arrived in 1824 with one ship paid 1.5%, probably to induce them to make more voyages in the future.

all admit that after the Persian governors, he was better suited to rule the Bushehris.[266] From 1824 to 1827, each year a Dutch ship called on Bushehr. One of the reasons that they did not return after 1827 was Sheikh `Abdol-Rasul's interference with trade. The Dutch could not sell their sugar in 1826 and 1827, because he wanted to buy it, but only offered 1.6 *qran* per *man-e Tabriz* (3 kg). Other merchants did not dare to buy the sugar as the Sheikh had forbidden them to bid. At first he only offered 1 *qran* and after a long delay and after having taken many samples he finally bought only the best chests with sugar. However, he did not pay and when urged to do so he deducted an arbitrary amount for tare, which he claimed was not adequate enough. He might not even have paid at all if the Dutch agent did not have the Sheikh's IOU. To circumvent the Sheikh's tyranny the Dutch sent samples to their agent in Shiraz, but the Sheikh confiscated the samples, because he did not allow any messengers to leave Bushehr without his permission. As a result of the Sheikh's greed, merchants only bought small lots to avoid creating the impression that they had lots of money, because otherwise the Sheikh might pay them a visit to make them share some of that money with him.[267]

Another contemporary observer noted that the Sheikh of Bushehr "only thinks about filling his own coffers, without regard for the welfare of his subjects. He has ships of his own trading with Bombay, Calcutta etc. and though it may take months before one of these ships is available he does not allow any of his subjects to send their goods with an earlier of cheaper conveyance. One man was ruined because he could not send them to the market in the right season and had to pay high storage rent in a caravanserai."[268] Finally, the conflict between the Sheikh of Bushehr and the governor-general of Fars as well as that between Persia and Great Britain about Herat and the British withdrawal of its Residency from Bushehr to Khark (1839-42) also depressed trade in the port (see Chapter 3).

2.8: Imports and Exports between the Persian Gulf and Bombay 1835-39 (in Bombay Rupees)

Trade	1835-36	1836-37	1837-38	1838-39	1839-40
Imports	36,67,586	35,00,241	37,33,125	24,13,961	28,60,817
Exports	40,03,835	35,59,589	36,02,274	29,97,490	28,95,719

Source: Grummon 1985, p. 181.

There was a second development, viz. that of a very modest growth in the overall trade in the Persian Gulf, which seems to have begun in 1831; this did not work in Bushehr's favor either. Bombay's trade with the Persian Gulf between 1821-28 to 1844-45 rose only from 7.2 million to 7.9 million Rupees.[269] During the 1840s, according to the available information, imports and export increased respectively 1.8% and 1.5% per year.[270] This development was the result of the growing insecurity in Bushehr and on the trade

266. Wellstead 1840, p. 133.
267. den Tex 1871, p. 29.
268. Anonymous 1830, p. 2. According to den Tex 1871, p. 26, the Sheikh had five merchant ships.
269. AP 1831-32, 10, part 2; Issawi 1971, p. 83.
270. AP 1867, lxxii, pp. 48-49, 54-55.

route to Shiraz, which resulted in the increased use of the northern import route via Trabzon and Tabriz, in particular for British goods. This shift in trade routes established the dominance of this northern route for the next 40 years. This not only held for textiles, but also for sugar. A further reinforcing factor for this shift was the introduction of steam navigation between Istanbul and Trabzon in 1826, which was expanded thereafter and reduced transportation cost significantly.[271]

The competitive customs duties, greater security, and other inducements offered had indeed a positive impact on the trade of Bandar Abbas and Lengeh to the detriment of Bushehr. However, Bushehr began its comeback in the mid-1840s, when relations with Great Britain were normalized and there was local political stability as well as in the relationship with the governor-general of Fars.[272] In 1850, consul Abbott noted that "a portion of the Indian trade having latterly been diverted to the port of Bandar [Abbas] where the customs duties have been reduced, whilst they are maintained at Bushire at their former rate,"[273] but this diversion probably was due to the troubles in Bushehr connected with the expulsion of the Al Mazkur in that year. Bushehr, notwithstanding its decline in the 1830-40s, was still the principal port of Fars in the early 1860s, Bandar Abbas having about 75% of Bushehr's turnover.[274] The smaller ports had some trifling traffic, according to Abbott.[275] These smaller ports included Lengeh. It had been rather unimportant, but in the decade or so prior to 1863, its trade had grown and in that year it was estimated that its annual trade was about one-third of that of Bushehr. However, Lengeh's hinterland was the Arabian coast and therefore, was not a competitor for the trade of Bushehr.[276] Apart from Bandar Abbas there was Mohammerah (now Khorramshahr), located on the confluence of the Shatt al-Arab and Karun rivers and just opposite Basra. As of the 1830s, its attraction was the result of an aggressive trade policy by the Bani Ka`b Sheikhs by charging no customs duties. This meant that many goods for Basra were landed in Mohammerah and also some destined for Bushehr. However, since its hinterland was limited it could as yet not really challenge Bushehr. Not surprisingly, it was the Pasha of Baghdad who sacked Mohammerah in 1839 for commercial reasons. However, the setback was only temporary and the port regained a flourishing state later in the nineteenth century.[277]

In 1851, the trade of Bushehr, though considerable, was in utter stagnation,[278] because of the troubles related to the expulsion of the Al Mazkur from the port (Chapter 3). However, thereafter trade increased significantly. Certain trade developments helped bolster Bushehr's pre-eminent position. By the 1860s, there was an upswing in Bushehr trade in particular, and of the Persian Gulf in general. In fact, trade with India between 1845-1865 quintupled, while between 1861-65 it tripled. This was amongst other things due to the cotton crisis in Bombay (there were no American supplies because of the US civil war), which led to a 100-fold export of cotton from Persia. Also, the export of opium gained in importance via Batavia to China. With the end of the US civil-war trade

---

271. Issawi 1971, pp. 92-103; Idem 1970, p. 19f; Floor 2003 b, pp. 334-35.
272. Grummon 1985, p. 187.
273. Amanat 1983, p. 86.
274. Amanat 1983, pp. 86-87 (Bushehr imported £500,000 from India); Pelly 1865 b, p. 153.
275. Amanat 1983, p. 87.
276. Pelly 1865 a, p. 52; Floor 2010.
277. Grummon 1985, pp. 269-71; Floor 2011 b, pp. 212-17.
278. Binning 1857, vol. 1, p. 150.

fell by 50% and then stabilized over the next two years at more than 20 million rupees/year.[279] Col. Pelly, the Resident wrote in 1866, that the last three years had brought much prosperity due to peace and high cotton prices. As a result, the peasants demanded more comfort that they could usually afford due to sale of cotton; also steam navigation was more secure and reliable than sail ships, which was good for trade.[280] Another change was that the role of Java sugar increased significantly in the 1850s and thereafter, a trend enhanced by the export of opium by these same sugar entrepreneurs. This was due to the Armenian connection in that Armenian merchants in Java sent sugar to family members and/or co-religionists in Bushehr. This development gained such momentum that the Dutch government even established a consulate in Bushehr in 1868.[281]

Various Routes and Distances, in Day's Marching, by which Merchandise arrives in Persia.

From Trebizond to Tabreez, from 32 days in winter to 70 days in summer, when the beasts of burden are permitted to pasture along the route.

Tabreez to Teheran, 14 days to 18 days.

Baghdad to Teheran, via Khanakhin, Kermanshah, and Hamadan, about 28 days, according to the season.

Bushire to Teheran, about 46 days, including stoppages.

Bushire to Shiraz, 10 days.

Shiraz to Ispahan, 14 days.

Ispahan to Teheran, 14 days.

Teheran to Tabreez, 18 days.

Source: *DCR* 1440 (Azerbaijan, 1893-94), p. 6.

Up to 1870, the Trabzon-Tabriz trade route was the main channel for imported goods to Persia. Tabriz supplied most of northern and western Persia throughout the entire period. However, after 1866, the trade of Tabriz declined due to a number of factors, such as the outbreak of the silk disease in Gilan, which reduced purchasing power significantly. This disaster was followed by the general famine of 1871-73 in Persia, which caused the death of tens of thousands, both human and animal life, resulting in reduced demand for imports and higher transportation cost due to lack of transport animals and high cost of fodder. The routing of trade via northern Persia had come to a stop due to the Russo-Turkish war of 1877-78 and the abolition of the exemption on goods in transit through the Caucasus. Major importers therefore, were forced to import goods via

279. Lorimer 1915, vol. 1, p. 258 quoting Pelly's letter of 12/05/1866; italics in the original; Pelly 1865 a, pp. 49-51; Issawi 1971, pp. 83, 91; Brugsch 1865, vol. 2, p. 244 (trade in 1860 was estimated at 2.8 million thaler export and 5 million thaler in imports).

280. NA, FO 248/232, Lewis Pelly to C. Gunne, secr. of government of India, 29/09/1866.

281. Floor 1988 c, pp. 59f; Idem, 2003 b, pp. 333-34.

the Bushehr-Isfahan and the Baghdad-Kermanshah-Hamadan trade routes,[282] a development further reinforced and helped by the opening of the Suez Canal in 1869, cheaper transportation cost in the Persian Gulf due to the use of steamers.[283]

After the 1880s there was further a significant increase in trade, due, among other things, to the export of opium and the advent of steam navigation. By 1885, trade had doubled from 10 million to 20 million rupees for Bushehr during 1873-88, and that of Bandar Abbas between 1878 and 1888 had increased from 3 to 8 million rupees.[284] In 1873, the tonnage of British shipping in the Gulf was only 37,000 tons and in 1883 it had risen to 219,000 tons, representing 99% of all steamers in that year. In 1870, only one monthly steamer visited the Persian Gulf from Bombay and 3 to 4 sailing ships direct from Great Britain. By 1890, there were weekly and fortnightly services (see Table 2.33).[285] By the 1880s, Bushehr had become the uncontested "chief port for the general import trade of Persia."[286] As a result European firms, mainly British established permanent offices there.[287]

Since the 1873, when the British started to regularly collecting and publishing trade statistics of the main ports in the Persian Gulf, Bushehr's trade showed an upward trend, be it with annual fluctuations (see Appendix VI). Above all, what influenced the ups and down in trade for the next 40 years were good or bad harvests and/or a fall of the prices of export products, which impoverished the population and led to bankruptcy of small traders and large merchants alike. Furthermore, gluts in the market due to overstocking, depressed demand of opium in China, high transportation rates, and as of 1890 the depreciation of silver also impacted the volume of trade.[288]

The breakdown of authority in Persia in 1908 and subsequent years resulted in a period of economic decline in Bushehr's main markets, the provinces of Fars and Isfahan. Moreover, the outbreak of banditry made the trade road unsafe. Caravans were plundered or, if they were lucky, only had to pay all kinds of illegal taxes. But even when goods arrived at Shiraz these could not always be distributed to the rural market towns and beyond by small merchants and peddlers, because of safety issues. Fighting and rebellion had broken out in Lar, Fasa, Kazerun and Behbahan, resulting in lawlessness. Goods could not be moved and this had a dampening impact on trade in the following year, the more so, because the alternative route from Mohammerah to Isfahan had similar problems for a while.[289] As noted above, given Bushehr's role as entrepôt for markets in the interior, the volume of its trade was determined by the security on the road to Shiraz. Up to 1907, the Bushehr-Shiraz-Isfahan trade route had been the principal caravan road for

282. *AP* 68 Tabreez (1867), p. 500; *AP* 66 Tabreez (1870), p. 961; *AP* 58 Tabreez (1872), p. 1190; *AP* 65 Azerbaijan (1872), p. 968; *AP* 75 Tabreez (1873), p. 205; *AP* 75 Tabreez (1877-78), p. 1696; MacLean 1904, p. 46; *AP* 68, Ghilan 1867-68, p. 297; Küss 1911, p. 91; Issawi 1971, p. 84; Idem, "The Tabriz-Trabzon Trade," pp. 22-27; NA, FO 60/463, Report on the Trade (1884), not foliated. Küss 1911, p. 91; Issawi 1971, p. 84; Idem, "The Tabriz-Trabzon Trade," pp. 22-27; NA, FO 60/463, Report on the Trade (1884), not foliated.

283. Administration Report 1877-78, p. 25-26; Administration Report 1878-79, p. 28; Issawi 1971, pp. 84, 97-104.

284. Administration Report 1878-79, p. 29; Idem, Administration Report 1889-90, p. 30.

285. Curzon 1892, vol. 2, p. 557.

286. Dickson 1884, p. 4.

287. Administration Report 1878-79, p. 29.

288. Administration Report 1873-1909.

289. Floor 2011 b, pp. 135f; Trade Report 1910-11, p. 3; Trade Report 1911-12, p. 4.

all trade entering Persia via the Persian Gulf (piece-goods, sugar and other commodities) for the important Isfahan market. After that year increased traffic on the Lynch road from Ahvaz to Isfahan eliminated, to a large extent, trade between Bushehr and Isfahan, both in imports and exports. Although increased demand in Fars and the coastal region shored up Bushehr's position for the time being, the continued disorder upcountry and the insecurity/blockage of the trade road were the main reasons for the lack of further growth of trade at Bushehr. As a result, trade with Shiraz fluctuated widely and declined. Also, there was a shortage of vessels, because due to WWI there was hardly any direct shipments between the Persian Gulf and Europe, while shipping between India and the Persian Gulf was almost entirely seen to by British vessels, which for some of the time were required for military needs in connection with the 1915 Mesopotamia Expedition.[290] Moreover, transport capacity on the Bushehr-Isfahan road was already overtaxed before the outbreak of WWI. This situation became worse due to the commandeering of pack animals by the military. Transportation charges on the Isfahan-Tehran route doubled and on the Mohammerah-Isfahan route even quadrupled. Because the Western routes via Trabson and Baghdad-Kermanshah were closed due to WWI, while imports from Russia were restricted and imports from other countries through Russia had ceased altogether, it became increasingly difficult to supply the markets upcountry. The only access road to Central Persia was via the Persian Gulf.[291] In 1916, the rebellion in Shiraz and Kazerun and the attacks by Tangestani chiefs of Bushehr did not help trade either, because due to these events the road to Shiraz was closed for most of the year.[292] Therefore, even though sometimes imports seemed high, merchants had to keep large stocks of unsold goods in some years. Export also suffered, because of transport and security problems on the Isfahan-Shiraz-Bushehr trade road.[293]

2.9: Comparison of imports and exports (1908-1921).

Units: in £ and in tons

Year	Imports/tons	Imports £	Exports/tons	Exports £
1900	-	1,323,478	-	710,338
1901	-	1,631,478	-	573,649
1902	-	1,179,996	-	348,202
1903	-	870,803	-	366,666
1904	-	889,825	-	454,981
1905	-	761,932	-	469,980
1906-07	-	863,842	-	598,421
1907-08	-	1,052,465	-	497,990
1908-09	16,981	793,465	6,400	432,596
1909-10	16,404	651,901	6,016	364,446

290. Trade Report 1914-15, p. 1.
291. Bader 1919, p. 1.
292. Floor 2011 b, pp. 160-69; Administration Report 1916 p. 2.
293. Trade Report 1915-16, p. 2.

Year	Imports/tons	Imports £	Exports/tons	Exports £
1910-11	13,879	623,286	9,339	317,227
1911-12	16,597	847,756	28,034	608,200
1912-13	19,712	951,720	13,776	637,091
1913-14	23,614	825,767	6,609	601,765
1914-15	18,041	609,339	5,723	719,171
1915-16	14,029	717,317	3,863	583,056
1916-17	21,467	1,299,562	3,001	443,434
1917-18	39,258	2,439,179	2,746	920,951
1918-19	26,830	2,946,450	2,777	395,150
1919-20	23,212	2,723,357	3,837	917,655
1920-21	21,154	2,462,797	3,496	898,571
1921-22	19,473	1,526,594	3,962	680,097

Source: Trade Report 1900-1921. Data on the weight of total trade for the years prior to 1908 and after 1921 are not available.

Although trade at Bushehr seemed to have increased since 1900, judging by its nominal value, it was in fact going down. Allowing for inflation (unfortunately its rate is unknown) and for the fluctuations (first up and then downwards) in the rate of exchange (*qran* to the £ and to the Rs) meant that the value of trade in real terms was declining. This trend is quite clear when we ignore the value of trade, but examine the tonnage of trade. In particular exports decreased significantly (see Table 2.9). After a surge during 1911-12 exports declined. In 1913 exports were at the same weight level as in 1908 and in 1921 they were 40% lower than in 1908! At the same time imports by weight showed an increase (with a dip during two of the WWI years). The result, as in the previous centuries, was a deficit of the current account.

2.10: Average rate of exchange at Bushehr 1900-1924

Year	*Qrans* per £	*Qrans* per 100 Rls.
1900-01	52.82	352.87
1901-02	54.36	362.58
1902-03	57.51	387.19
1903-04	57.25	379.62
1904-05	60.20	406.62
1905-06	60.12	400.59
1906-07	55.50	374.45
1907-08	51.25	343.18
1908-09	54.54	362.93
1909-10	56.15	376.87
1910-11	54.80	367.75
1911-12	54.10	302.92

Year	*Qrans* per £	*Qrans* per 100 Rls.
1912-13	56.18	377.42
1913-14	56.76	379.62
1914-15	62.50	411.65
1915-16	63.09	420.61
1916-17	43.81	195.69
1917-18	23.12	232.46
1918-19	30.40	222.82
1919-20	28.83	261.28
1920-21	37.00	300.62
1921-22	52.00	347.37
1922-23	56.18	361.99
1923-24	48.63	324.98

Source: Trade Report 1907-23.

Trade increased after WWI, but business was not good for everybody, because it came as a great shock when in 1920 the Qasemiyeh Company in Shiraz (with a branch in Bushehr) went bankrupt. As a result, many smaller traders also failed.[294] Because of the world trade depression in 1921 trade did not improve. Bushehr firms felt its impact and suffered losses. The good news for buyers was that German goods made their reappearance in the market as did Wonckhaus, who opened agencies in all ports, thus increasing the likelihood of competitive prices.[295] Trade remained constrained in the following year because of the insecurity on the road as well as by the government's new fiscal policy that threatened to hurt trade. Because silver coins (*qrans*, rupees) had a higher metal value than their exchange value, much silver was exported. Therefore, the government first banned the export of silver and then towards the end of the year declared cabotage invalid, i.e. the export of *qrans* from one Persian port to another, thus hurting intra-port trade. This law was passed by the *Majles* in December 1922 and had negative consequences for the people of the coasts and islands of the Persian Gulf. The export ban included rupees, against which the British protested, because this would result in the immobilization of a large amount of rupees in the ports and in particular Bushehr where the Imperial Bank of Persia (IBP) was the depository of the funds of the Indian government treasury. Finally the export of rupees was allowed, but under conditions and at a price to the exporter that it was hardly worthwhile doing so.[296] As expected legal trade was hurt and that led to smuggling. The government's decision to ban the export of specie strangled trade between Bushehr and its customary coastal distribution outlets. The government did not even allow the transport of coin from Bushehr to Ganaveh to pay Anglo-Persian Oil Company (APOC) workers. As a result, the men had no wages, the contractors could not import food and stores in Bushehr gave no credit when it was not allowed to send money. There was almost a famine; finally the APOC risked transporting coin overland.

---

294. Administration Report 1920, p. 6.
295. Administration Report 1921, p. 6 (his agent in Bushehr was Konoff).
296. Administration Report 1922, p. 5.

After many protests from British merchants, the ban on cabotage of *qrans* and the export of rupees was lifted. In 1923, the trade route to Shiraz was well protected by the Persian military, which was much appreciated by traders and muleteers alike. However, at the same time, a large military force was collecting tax arrears in Dashti and Dashtestan, which commandeered animals for their official and private use. This became such a huge problem that muleteers refused to transport goods or only at higher rates, which increased the cost of goods and reduced demand. This was not the only problem that year. As a sign of what was in store for other merchants, Messrs. Dixon & Co. from Manchester went into voluntary bankruptcy; the Mesopotamia Persia Corporation undertook to sell its remaining goods at Bushehr.[297]

Trade did not improve in the following years constrained as it was by the lack of money due to the system of monopolies, high customs duties on tea and sugar, the continued ban on export of grain, lambskins, silver, etc. Moreover money supply became even tighter, when in 1926 the government declared that rupees were no longer legal tender. This was a significant political as well as economic step, because in trade, the rupee had always been more readily accepted than the *qran*. Also, occasionally large importers had difficulty selling their goods because peasants had no money until their opium and other products were bought. An additional factor that impeded trade was that the customs revenues were in their entirety spent elsewhere in Persia, which resulted in a reduction of purchasing power of Bushehr and its hinterland, thus demand was weak. "This has had considerable effect on Bushehr which is the distributing entrepot for a wide area." The new 1928 Autonomous Customs tariff that increased customs on most goods further depressed trade.[298]

In 1928, what the British feared happened, viz. the Russian commercial invasion of the Persian Gulf took place when three ships entered Bushehr (*Tobolsk*, *Michael Frunze*, *Kommunist*). The result was a serious challenge to British-Indian trade, because the Russians dumped their sugar and piece-goods, which were cost-competitive with British ones. However, despite their low prices and attractive credit (2-3 months) the Russians were unpopular, because they undercut the small traders. This situation did not change in the following year, when five Russian vessels came to Bushehr.[299] Nevertheless, according to the British Resident, 1929 was a black year for trade, despite a good harvest and low grain prices. For trade had almost come to a standstill in that year, because Bushehr's lifeline, the trade route to Shiraz was closed due to the Qashqa'i rebellion. Merchants could not forward their goods upcountry and lost money by having to store it. The higher tobacco and opium monopoly tax, the fall of the silver price, resulting in a depreciation of the *qran*, and the Wall Street crash also hurt trade. Merchants refused either bills or were forced to sacrifice profits.[300]

Trade conditions in the 1930s were not much better for Bushehr. To stop the depreciation of the *qran*, the government decided to fix the rate of exchange and decreed that all foreign exchange transactions had to go via the government's Exchange Commission.

---

297. Administration Report 1923, pp. 10-11. Cabotage is the right to transport goods or passengers between two points in the same country by a vessel registered in another country.

298. Administration Report 1924, p. 7; Administration Report 1925, p. 9; Administration Report 1926, p. 4; Administration Report 1927, p. 5; Administration Report 1928, p. 8; Curzon 1892, vol. 1, p. 236.

299. Administration Report 1928, p. 8; Administration Report 1929, p. 6.

300. Administration Report 1929, p. 5.

However, this proved to be impossible to realize in practice, and the government had to allow merchants a certain flexibility to meet their obligations to foreign exporters. Although this brought some relief it had the effect to drive up prices, while the value of the *qran* fell from £65 in January to £120 in December 1930. As a result, the market of Bushehr remained depressed. Small traders had to abandon foreign trade, which fell more and more into the hands of large merchants with foreign exchange assets abroad. They focused on tea and sugar import, whose price at the end of the year were respectively 90% and 40% above the January levels, which led to speculation by mid-year.[301]

In 1930, no less than eight Russian ships visited Bushehr, importing large quantities of sugar and piece goods. They had adapted their sales practice, sometimes selling "for sterling only, sometimes for krans, now extending credit, now withholding it, their chief policy seemed to be to upset the market as much as possible." The Russians were keen to get their hands on foreign exchange and only sold goods for *qrans* to the extent that they needed them to finance their exports of gum arabica, almonds, etc. The British consul was worried about this development, because if the Russians would continue doing business in this manner their position would improve considerably. Moreover, Russia, "thanks mainly to their system of barter, were from the first exempt from selling any exchange on account of their exports in the North." Also, it seemed they did not pay with any foreign exchange in the Persian Gulf. Another disturbing development for trade was that people's purchasing power was decreasing daily due to new and increased taxation, which because of its regressive nature mainly impacted the poor. It was feared that shrinking of "all but the most inelastic market" would be inevitable. Only when prosperity would return did the British consul expect that the British position might be recoverable. However, that would not necessarily be enough, because the Russians were aggressively increasing their market share in the Persian Gulf, while the Japanese were waiting for the right moment to join in the fight to increase market share as well given their recent success on the Arab coast.[302]

In 1931, domestic market prices were rising and the price of silver was rock bottom and thus, also that of the *qran*, while the government's attempt to control the rate of exchange had failed. To deal with many, if not all, of the problems, the Trade Monopolies Act of 25 February 1930 was passed and ratified on 11 March 1931 by the *Majles*. The new law created government monopolies over sugar, opium, tobacco, tea, matches, cotton piece goods, wheat and rice. Later, the rules were relaxed for the last three products, but traders had to get a special and expensive license to trade in them. Henceforth, all foreign trade of the other products was done by the Ministry of Commerce. The law's objective was to remedy foreign exchange problems and to cushion the economy of Persia against the world depression, to reduce the alleged margin between imports and exports, secure greater exchange stability, increase Persia's bargaining power (especially vis-à-vis the Soviet Union) and to stimulate domestic production and industrial development. In theory, the entire foreign trade of Persia had become a government monopoly, but in actual practice imports were subjected to a system of quotas and import licenses and in

301. Administration Report 1930, pp. 6-8 (here a detailed discussion of the foreign exchange policy).
302. Administration Report 1930, pp. 8-9.

most cases, made dependent on prior export of Persian goods. The immediate effect was to disturb trade conditions.[303]

In Bushehr prices of all goods rose, money was tighter than ever, and more merchants abandoned foreign trade, so that the bazaar remained dull. Moreover in February 1931, the market was jolted by the new 60% surtax on customs duty, introduced without warning, and in March, as noted above, foreign trade was replaced by the Trade Monopoly Law. After August things became somewhat better when merchants had adapted to the new rules. The consequences for British trade were immediately obvious. British ships, the main carriers of imports and exports to Bushehr, only imported 8,000 tons in 1931, half of the 1930 imports, and in particular British/Indian piece goods were replaced by Russian ones. At the same time, in 1931, nine Russian ships called on Bushehr and the Russians imposed a virtual monopoly over trade. In most cases they made the sale of their goods and the giving of credit, subject to the buyer's agreement to also buy old stocks of samovars, tinned fish, etc. The Russian position was strengthened by the signing of a Russo-Persian Commercial Treaty on 27 October 1931, which ceded 52% of all import trade (including a monopoly of sugar, matches, and oil, and 55% of all imports of cottons). As a result, Russian commercial prospects at Bushehr (despite a bad harvest in 1931) looked good, while those of British-Indian trade looked definitely bad.[304]

In 1932, "Trade restrictions, monopolies, exchange control, high customs tariffs," and the "almost monthly variations in the customs surcharge and the continual amendment of laws and regulations" left merchants and customs officials alike bewildered, but also made trade almost impossible. Therefore, merchants had to make a living somehow, thus smuggling thrived, which the Customs department was incapable to curb. Also, foreign merchants found it very difficult to trade with Persia, because Bushehri merchants paid up to 25% with the order and the rest with bills on the sellers at 30 to 150 days' sight, depending on how quickly they believed they could sell the goods. Again, the high customs duties, road and other taxes on foreign goods put them beyond the capacity of most to buy. Meanwhile, the Soviet *Sharq* company was renamed *Vneshtorg*, while a Russian bank was also opened. However, because of the control given to Russia over the Persian market as well as Russian trade practices, Persian merchants began to boycott Russian goods, demanding the Commercial Treaty's cancellation. The Persian merchants were not the only ones who assailed the Russian position, but so did the Japanese.[305]

It was difficult for merchants, whether local or foreign, to stay in business. In 1932, Messrs. Ziegler & Co., the oldest and last British firm in Bushehr, was only able to continue operating by cutting staff, but in 1933 the company decided to close its Persian operations by the end of that year.[306] The Mesopotamia Persia Corporation Ltd. only had as business the agency for the British-Indian Steam Navigation Company (BISNC) and as of 1934 also for City Hall Lines. However, it suffered like all firms from the declining

303. Simmonds 1935, p. 1; Administration Report 1931, pp. 9-10 (with details about the working of the law and problems with its implementation).

304. Administration Report 1931, p. 11.

305. Administration Report 1932, pp. 2, 7-8.

306. Administration Report 1932, p. 3; Administration Report 1933, p. 2.

trade. In 1937, it restructured and became Gray, Mackenzie and Company Ltd.[307] Not only British merchants, small and large, felt the pinch of the crippling government trade and currency regulations, but also the declining commercial role of Bushehr. In 1934, `Abdol-Rasul Kazeruni went bankrupt, later followed by two *sarrafs*.[308]

In 1933 trade was not improving, because of the above-mentioned reasons. The quota system and the monopoly of certain goods further limited the number of merchants that could enter the market, which meant that most trade, and increasingly so during the 1930s, was in the hands of a few wealthy merchants. To survive, smaller traders, made a living smuggling, including gold, by buying it at the fictitious government value and selling it abroad at market value. The Japanese made further inroads, because people were poor and therefore, could only afford to buy the cheap Japanese goods. So far, Persian merchants ordered Japanese goods from Bombay, but as of 1933 one established Tehran firm (*Sankoyu*) had `Abdol-Qasem Tavakkol as agent in Bushehr. Russian goods had almost disappeared from the market. *Vneshtorg* had sold its stock and then closed shop in March 1933. Although the embargo on trade with Russians was lifted in August, there was no longer Russian trade worthy of mention.[309]

The year 1934 was a very bad trade year for Bushehr and its hinterland, which was due to targeted government policy. "The decision of Government to develop the port of Bandar Shahpur and the Ahvaz and Mohammerah routes to the North at the expense of the port of Bushire and the route of Shiraz became apparent in the allocation of the Customs import quotas. It is realized that if the project can be carried through, the port of Bushire will serve solely to feed Shiraz and the district, whilst the Isfahan and other northern market will be lost." As a result in 1933, for example, trade at Shiraz had fallen to one-third of its past level.[310] Moreover, trade was either a government monopoly or a limited number of merchants were allowed to form a syndicate for goods such as opium, piece-goods and vehicles. This limited the import trade considerably, while Bushehr still continued as an entrepôt for its much reduced hinterland, but now it was being mostly supplied from Tehran! British trade felt increasing competition from Japanese goods, because of their cheapness.[311]

As of 1935, the foreign trade monopoly became more comprehensive due to the establishment of several companies that were awarded exclusive import-export rights for specific goods, such as sugar. At the end of March 1935, another company was formed to sell piece goods to drapers in Bushehr and Lengeh. With less reluctance than for the sugar company, merchants provided its capital of 600,000 rials. This development helped to reduce the sale of smuggled sugar and piece goods in Bushehr and perhaps in Lengeh, but all other goods were still smuggled.[312]

In September 1936, the Finance department announced that the sale and purchase of wheat supplies was a government monopoly and started buying at the following prices:

---

307. Administration Report 1932, p. 3; Administration Report 1934, p. 2 (here called Mesopotamia Iraq Corporation Ltd.); Administration Report 1935, p. 3; Administration Report 1936, p. 2; Administration Report 1937, p. 2.
308. Administration Report 1934, p. 17.
309. Administration Report 1933, pp. 6-9.
310. Administration Report 1934, p. 18; Administration Report 1933, p. 18.
311. Administration Report 1934, pp. 4, 7-9.
312. Administration Report 1935, p. 4.

1st class at Rials 130 per 315 kilos	£1 12s. 6d. per 6 cwts of 98 lbs
2nd class at 120 Rials per 315 kilos	£1 10s. 0d. per 6 cwts of 98 lbs
3rd class at Rials 110 per 315 kilos	£1 7s. 6d. 6 cwts 8 of lbs
4th class at Rials 100 per 315 kilos	£1 5s. 0d. per 6 cwts of 98 lbs

The Finance Department classified wheat as 1st and 2nd class and sold it at 145 and 125 rials per 315 kg. In January 1937, the wheat monopoly bought wheat in Bushehr district at 60 rials, minus 20% for dust and adulteration. The Finance department at first sold wheat to the public, but later allowed merchants to do so "to prevent delay in purchase and destruction by weevil." There was a slight shortage at end year due to large export to Germany.[313] In 1936, the Finance department also established an araq monopoly. It took all available stocks of araq and began selling it at 6 rials (1sh. 6d.) per bottle as against 9 rials sold before by the Jews. Early December 1936, the sale and purchase of tobacco also became a government monopoly and the Finance department began buying from stock-holders and opened two shops selling tobacco at 2.5 rials per 4.5 kg.[314] In the following years, the tobacco monopoly bought stocks in 3 classes and offered cigars, cigarettes and tobacco for sale in two shops at respectively, 16, 15 and 14 rials per 3 kg. Cigarettes from Tehran were also sold in Bushehr. Because of the high prices there was much smuggling. Nevertheless, in 1939 the Tobacco monopoly allegedly made an estimated profit of 750%.[315]

In 1935, the impact of the creation of a government monopoly for piece-goods had a downward effect on British and Indian trade. Also, the import of Indian yarns was banned, and even with tea, India lost market share to Japan and Java.[316] The government Piece-Good Company had a short and not very active life. In 1936 it was unable to function, because it did not receive any piece-goods, while two years later it was abolished as a private entity because its agents were selling monopoly goods above the fixed rate. Therefore, in May 1938, the government took business into its own hands and opened a branch office of the monopoly of piece-goods in Bushehr. After initial heavy demand local shopkeepers were allowed to buy a limited quantity of piece-goods and retailed it at prices fixed by government.[317] Because the monopoly sold these at reasonable prices there was no smuggling of piece-goods.[318] Everything else was smuggled, in particular considerable quantities of wheat, tobacco and carpets as well as sheep and cattle. Sometimes bribery failed, which led to fights with the road guards. On one occasion such a fight resulted in

313. Administration Report 1936, p. 3; Administration Report 1937, p. 2-3.

314. Administration Report 1936, p. 3; however, the tobacco monopoly was established in 1929. Simmonds 1935, p. 25. Perhaps it had been temporarily suspended for some time in connection with ongoing negotiations to find a foreign investment partner.

315. Administration Report 1937, p. 3; Administration Report 1939, p. 2.

316. Administration Report 1935, pp. 9-10 (Italian imports were under an embargo after the Italian invasion of Ethiopia. This embargo did not last as Persia had a trade deficit with Italy).

317. Administration Report 1936, p. 3; Administration Report 1938, p. 5 (The sugar and tea companies respectively paid a dividend 28%; the one for piece goods even paid 30%.).

318. Administration Report 1939, p. 2. In 1939, the price of piece goods rose leading to smuggling. The piece goods monopoly was transferred in December of that year from the Bank-e Melli to the Finance department. The piece goods monopoly did not pay in the first year, but in 1937 paid 15% dividend. The Tobacco Monopoly in Bushehr continued to make 100% profit on purchases of local stocks. Administration Report 1938, p. 3.

16 of them killed.[319] In 1940, the sugar-tea monopoly did not pay any dividend. Their high prices diminished sales, while the quantity of sugar made available by the government was also smaller.[320] In the early 1940s little trade was done in Bushehr, because merchants were waiting for Tehran to ease foreign exchange restrictions. Moreover, due to the lack of trucks, which were comandeered by the police for food distribution or by the army for troop movements, little or no trade was possible with upcountry.[321]

What the above shows is that merchants in Bushehr had given up trying to operate as independent private operators and became mere forwarding agents for the government monopoly companies. Also, the bulk of imports were in transit for markets upcountry and very little was consumed in Bushehr and its environs. The growing imports stood in sharp contrast to the worsening situation of the people in the port and its hinterland. Moreover, the Customs quay was so overloaded with bales and cases that the Customs department had to find additional space to avoid making the congestion worse. Every arriving ship added more goods, which situation was not so much due to increased imports, but due to a lack of foreign exchange. Importers had to wait for the Exchange Commission in Tehran to make funds available so that they might pay their accepted bills. The effect of the growing poverty in Bushehr and environs was that of all classes people left to find work elsewhere in the Gulf area, despite successful smuggling activities that eased their situation somewhat. In 1931, the town had 20,000 inhabitants, but by 1937 there were only 8,000 left. The other effect was rather successful smuggling, against which preventive action was ineffective.[322] The departure of 60% of the population did not go unnoticed, for in 1938 Tehran sent a committee of high officials from the Ministry of the Interior to examine the conditions of peasants in Bushehr's hinterland and the underlying reasons for continued emigration to the Arab side. Although a report was prepared the results remain unknown.[323] Meanwhile, the further penetration of Japanese goods in the market continued as did those of Germany, the result of the Persian-German clearing agreement of 1935. Russia only brought sugar and matches and less so than in previous years; all this was detrimental to the market share of British-Indian goods.[324]

By 1937, it was clear that Bushehr as a port was of no longer of great importance. According to the British consul, "Bushire has, in the past two years, ceased to exists as an independent trading centre of any importance, and no longer offers openings for foreign trade, as local demand, except for staple goods such as, sugar and piece goods, which are already the object of monopoly, is insufficient to justify trading for the local market." The port was a simple channel to serve market upcountry and no longer constituted a market of its own. The changed situation was also reflected in its economic activity. The bazaaris only served local consumers and all other trading activities were in the hands of monopoly branches. Consequently, employment in commercial firms was dropping, "the population becoming increasingly dependent on the official departments, Customs, Malieh, municipality, etc."[325]

---

319. Administration Report 1940, p. 2.
320. Administration Report 1940, p. 7.
321. Political Diaries, vol. 15, p. 125.
322. Administration Report 1936, pp. 7, 9; Administration Report 1937, p. 10.
323. Administration Report 1938, p. 5.
324. Administration Report 1936, pp. 8-9.
325. Administration Report 1937, p. 5.

Whereas the town was inactive, the port was not, as foreign trade remained exceptionally active. In early 1937 there was substantial congestion on the customs quay, so that ships even had to over-carry cargo due to lack of space on the wharves and warehouses. Customs clearances stopped in April and June when the Exchange Commission had no foreign exchange. In the last three months of 1937, things were better due to the internal reorganization of the customs facilities and the greater regularity of the Exchange Commission.[326] However, this surge in imports was a fluke, for there was no improvement in trade in 1938; one or two merchants were still engaged in the import of general goods for local consumption; all others were forwarding agents. In fact, forwarding was all that kept the port alive. All the important merchants had moved to Tehran and Shiraz leaving a small capacity behind for customs clearance. The latter remained very slow due to restrictions by the Exchange Control Commission which had no foreign exchange. In January 1938, the government required that exporters "account for only 50 per cent of the sale proceeds of their goods to the Control Committee and were allowed to import goods against the remaining 50 per cent." This did not help much as the staple goods were in the hands of the Monopolies.[327] As of March 1938, the barter agreement with Germany was cancelled resulting in the rise of prices of German goods and cancellation of orders that had not yet arrived. Trade-wise, Bushehr just held its own, but it was feared that Bandar Shahpur would take over its entire trade in another two to three years.[328] The feared take-over seemed a bit further away in 1939, because Bandar Shahpur still had storage accommodation and other facilities problems and thus, Bushehr was actually somewhat busier than in 1938. Despite the increase in the volume of trade the usual congestion at Customs was not as problematic as in previous years, because by the end 1938, it was announced that a special import permit was no longer needed, just a sanction document (*movafeqat-nameh*) was sufficient. At the end of 1939 importers were also helped by the "removal of the ban on the purchase of foreign exchange except at official rates." As the ban had never been effective its revocation also had limited impact, although now banks could be asked to find sellers of foreign exchange. Freight rates rose by 30-50% after the outbreak of World War II.[329]

In 1940, Bushehr's trade situation was where it had been during the entire decade, i.e., there was hardly any trade for Bushehr itself, which acquiesced in merely being a forwarding center. Also, the shortage of ships and war conditions led to a drop in commercial activity. Imports declined by 24% compared with 1939 and exports by 33%.[330] In January 1940, merchants grumbled about the the lack of prospects for business, but they were careful not say this too loud. Their discontent and consternation grew when in February it was announced that Tehran Chamber of Commerce had decided that henceforth all imports and exports via the Persian Gulf had to pass through Bandar-e Shahpur by railway. For this meant that effectively trade at Bushehr would come to an end. Moreover, the visiting assistant-director of Agriculture of Fars gave a series of talks in Bushehr in February 1940, stating "that Bushire, from the point of view of trade, was dead and that for their future prosperity the people must depend on agriculture." Given

---

326. Administration Report 1937, p. 5.
327. Administration Report 1938, p. 5.
328. Administration Report 1938, p. 6.
329. Administration Report 1939, pp. 4-5.b
330. Administration Report 1940, p. 5, 8 (there also was a slight increase in some Customs fees).

these negative signals from the central and provincial government the governor asked Tehran for additional information. In March 1940, the Director-General of the Customs Department arrived in Bushehr and was able to allay the fears of the Bushehr merchants, because he stated that, while it was desirable to ship all goods via Bandar-e Shahpur it, as yet, did not have the capacity to do so. In fact, in many respects Bushehr's facilities were better. The municipality, therefore, asked Tehran to allow Bushehr to export goods to avalue of Rls. 1,000 in exchange for foreign imports without the need to obtain import-export permits; further that for import permits Bushehr should not have to apply for every single one to Tehran. Despite the good intentions, by August 1940, many people whose work was related to the Customs and shipping trade were out of work due to the drop in steamers calling on Bushehr. In February 1941, Germany informed merchants in Bushehr that due to problems of shipping goods via Russia it would no longer buy Persian goods. In June 1941, the price of imitiation silk fabrics and tea were increased by respectively 50% and 44% at instructions from Tehran.[331]

Because of the above reasons trade at Bushehr was and remained in a slump during WWII. For the Allies favored Khorramshahr, Bandar Shahpur and Basra to Bushehr. There was very little trade and fewer ships called on Bushehr. Until mid-1943 there were steamers that regularly called on Bushehr to supply its truck assembly plant. What did not help was that in July 1943 the Allies decided that henceforth Bushehr would be no longer used as a port for war supplies to Russia, which had serious consequences for the situation on the local labor market. Local trade also suffered from unclear rules as well as the lack of trucks to haul goods upcountry.[332] In 1945, trade continued to be at a standstill due to trade restrictions on export and because the government maintained the monopoly of sale of tea and sugar. Also, the exodus of labor contined, and despite end of the war there was no end to the very high cost of living in Bushehr. Even when in November 1945 the government abolished the monopoly and told merchants they were free to trade, this did not boost Bushehr's commercial community's business.[333] The situation did not improve in 1946. Most active merchants had already left a long time ago, while the older ones preferred to live off the rents of their capital until the end of their life rather than risking it in trade deals in uncertain times. Consequently, money was expensive, trade was hampered by government controls and sometimes no steamer called on Bushehr for as many as six weeks, all an indication that trade at Bushehr had come to a standstill.[334]

Structure of Trade

Although Bushehr had commercial relations with many countries and ports (Masqat, Basra, Bahrain, Red Sea, China, and Java after 1824, and the small Persian Gulf ports) its major trading partner was India, more in particular, as in the eighteenth century, with Masulipatnam (or Machilipatnam in Andhra Pradesh). It also imported goods from other parts of India (Gujarat, Bengal, Coromandel, and Malabar), but these were less important.

331. Political Diaries, vol. 14, pp. 5, 29, 32, 59, 91-92, 95, 181, 324, 438.
332. Political Diaries, vol. 15, pp. 541, 563, 616.
333. Administration Report 1945, pp. 9, 16.
334. Administration Report 1946, p. 5.

Around 1800, about 33% of all imports and 60% of specie exports came from or were sent to Masulipatnam. However, this pattern changed totally 30 years later, when Masulipatnam imports represented only 5% of Bushehr's imports. This was due to the growing competition from British fabrics and the growing role of Bombay (Gujarat).[335] Until the 1870s, trade was dominated by Indian commodities. It was only in 1873, that the British resident observed that the "import trade here has become more British."[336] It was not until the arrival of other European nations (Germany, France, Belgium, and Austria) that Britain's market share sank, although India remained its most important competitor. Together, British-Indian trade far outstripped any other of Bushehr's trading partners and usually it held a market share fluctuating between 60-85%. Because of World War I, most other European nations were absent from the Persian Gulf, so that the British-Indian market share even reached 98% in 1917-1918 (Tables 2.11, 2.12 and appendix VI). After that year, the British-Indian market share slowly started to diminish. This was not yet due to the arrival of Japanese goods in the market in relative substantial quantities as of 1917. Moreover, ironically in the statistics, Japanese goods were not separated from those from India as they were imported via agents in Bombay. Also, there were no Japanese agents in Bushehr and therefore, no estimate could be made of its volume.[337] However, all other W. European competitors returned after 1919 and eroded the British-Indian position. However, the greatest drop in the British-Indian market share occurred in the 1930s when first the Russians successfully drove British-Indian piece-goods from the market, followed by the Japanese who did the same to the Russian ones. Java also became a small player as did Egypt and the USA. Nevertheless, the British-Indian market share remained just above 50% for imports, which was not always the case for exports. Trade with other ports in the Persian Gulf (Masqat, Bahrain, Basra) remained limited and only that with Basra and its hinterland at times reached some level of significance. Sailing vessels coming from the ports on the Arabian coast, were usually "laden with coarse linen for turbans, earthen pots, mats, &c. for which they carry away dates."[338]

2.11: Origin of Imports into Bushehr during 1873-1923 (in %)

Unit: percentage & last column, rupee to 1903, £ from 1904

Year/ Country	Great Britain	Other W. Europe	Persian ports	India	Arabian Coast Bahrain	Kuwait, Basra, Baghdad	Muscat	Java	China	Total valur in Rupee to 1903
1873	16	-	4	51	1	11	<1	15	-	46,02,925
1874	15	-	5	56	1	3	<1	18	-	35,97,700
1875	30	-	3	56	<1	2	<1	8	-	51,58,825
1876	38	-	5	39	1	5	<1	12	-	45,96,999
1877	20	-	6	50	1	2	<1	19	-	33,67,115
1878	28	-	9	46	<1	5	<1	8	-	73,95,600
1879	38	-	3	55	<1	<1	<1	3	-	1,87,76,900

335. Grummon 1985, p. 183-86
336. Administration Report 1878-79, p. 28.
337. Trade Report 1917-18, p. 2.
338. Morier 1812, p. 58.

Year/ Country	Great Britain	Other W. Europe	Persian ports	India	Arabian Coast Bahrain	Kuwait, Basra, Baghdad	Muscat	Java	China	Total valur in Rupee to 1903
1880	37	-	1	49	1	2	<1	8	<1	1,68,66,050
1881	32	4	7	36	<1	2	<1	13	4	70,33,800
1882	53	3	4	37	<1	4	<1	2	3	1,01,88,980
1883	46	-	3	40	<1	2	<1	3	-	1,37,39,200
1884	43	-	2	39	<1	1	<1	3	-	1,00,97,950
1885	49	5	<1	42	<1	<1	<1	2	<1	99,62,170
1886	46	4	-	-	<1	2	<1	-	<1	82,73,230
1887	37	3	-	n.a.	<1	<1	<1	-	1	1,16,03,570
1888	53	<1	-	44	<1	<1	<1	-	1	80,68,310
1889	52	4	-	41	<1	<1	<1	-	<1	1,15,65,770
1890	53	5	-	34	<1	<1	<1	-	-	1,64,87,800
1891	70	2	-	27	<1	<1	<1	-	1	1,71,43,390
1892	55	7	-	36	<1	<1	<1	-	<1	1,63,86,310
1893	50	8	-	40	<1	<1	<1	-	<1	1,55,31,970
1894	53	5	-	39	<1	1	<1	-	1	1,80,64,430
1895	68	3	-	25	<1	2	<1	-	<1	1,79,78,760
1896	50	13	2	29	-	3	1	-	<1	1,34,01,080
1897	68	5	2	18	-	2	1	-	1	1,83,25,270
1898	47	6	11	27	1	4	<1	-	2	1,34,95,390
1899	48	8	14	24	<1	3	<1	-	1	1,37,47,920
1900	54	11	9	21	<1	1	<1	-	1	1,98,45,947
1901	55	10	7	19	<1	5	<1	-	1	2,44,72,172
1902	50	24	4	24	<1	3	<1	-	2	1,65,09,101
1903	49	6	4	33	<1	3	<1	-	5	1,42,55,457
1904	44	22	-	23	<1	2	<1	<1	2	889,825
1905	42	17	-	23	<1	7	<1	1	2	761,932
1906	38	23	-	30	<1	1	<1	2	1	863,842
1907	54	6	-	34	<1	3	<1	<1	<1	1,052,043
1908	48	10	-	37	<1	3	<1	<1	<1	793,465
1909	28	16	-	50	<1	1	<1	<1	<1	717,091
1910	42	17	-	36	<1	1	<1	1	<1	675,614
1911	55	15	-	31	<1	3	<1	2	<1	932,531
1912	48	21	-	23	<1	4	<1	1	1	951,720
1913	30	30	-	32	<1	4	<1	1	<1	825,767
1914	29	16	-	50	2	1	<1	<1	<1	669,339
1915	10	<1	-	86	-	<1	-	1	<1	777,317
1916	15	<1	-	80	-	1	-	<1	-	1,299,562
1917	5	<1	-	93	-	<1	-	-	-	2,439,179
1918	16	<1	-	77	<1	<1	-	2	1	2,946,450

Year/ Country	Great Britain	Other W. Europe	Persian ports	India	Arabian Coast Bah-rain	Kuwait, Basra, Baghdad	Muscat	Java	China	Total valur in Rupee to 1903
1919	26	2	-	47	<1	2	<1	<1	<1	2,723,357
1920	28	5	-	44	<1	1	<1	7	2	2,462,797
1921	24	9	-	51	<1	<1	<1	7	2	1,526,594
1922	36	14	-	39	<1	<1	-	4	<1	1,382,961
1923	30	18	-	39	<1	<1	<1	4	1	2,011,772

Source: Administration Report 1873-1905; Trade Report 1906-1923.
Because the import data of some countries have not been listed, the sum of the listed entries is less than 100% in that same year.

2.12: Direction of Exports from Bushehr 1873-1923 (in %)

Unit: percentage & last column, rupee to 1903, £ from 1904

Year Country	Great Britain	Persian ports	India	Arabian Coast and Bahrain	Turkey and Turkish Arabia	Muscat	Java	China	Red Sea	Total value in Rupee to 1903
1873	8	9	33	7	13	<1	1	25	3	39,20,729
1874	15	8	22	6	5	<1	5	32	5	30,91,775
1875	16	10	28	7	10	<1	4	30	1	18,62,230
1876	11	7	40	5	3	-	2	27	5	60,04,806
1877	10	3	39	1	6	-	-	39 Incl. Java	<1	77,35,640
1878	8	1	46	3	1	<1	<1	36	<1	1,37,41,300
1879	3	<1	28	4	2	<1	<1	62	<1	80,94,900
1880	9	<1	23	5	5	<1	<1	54	<1	1,00,17,850
1881	6	1	12	1	1	<1	1	72	1	79,83,800
1882	19	2	22	1	9	1	-	42	2	65,66,220
1883	23	2	23	1	7	<1	-	35	4	73,72,300
1884	15	1	27	<1	5	<1	-	41	5	67,34,570
1885	9	1	24	<1	3	<1	-	51	9	74,45,170
1886	16	-	23	1	5	<1	-	45	4	71,89,990
1887	22	-	36	1	6	<1	-	30	4	59,64,680
1888	13	-	34	<1	9	<1	-	36	-	57,60,350
1889	16	-	31	<1	6	<1	-	40		78,25,490
1890	10	-	31	<1	6	<1	-	48	4	93,60,460
1891	19	-	26	<1	7	<1	-	44	3	93,51,690
1892	11	-	21	<1	11	<1	-	50	-	98,51,570
1893	34	-	29	1	4	<1	-	36		80,22,730
1894	18	-	20	1	12	<1	-	43		95,35,580
1895	31	-	14	1	8	<1	-	35		89,41,360
1896	24	5	17	2	5	3	-	36		74,85,289

Year Country	Great Britain	Persian ports	India	Arabian Coast and Bahrain	Turkey and Turkish Arabia	Muscat	Java	China	Red Sea	Total value in Rupee to 1903
1897	25	4	19	1	2	3	-	41		62,80,526
1898	27	2	17	-	3	<1	-	41		68,27,550
1899	15	2	18	<1	3	<1	-	55	-	79,40,220
1900	22	1	19	-	3	<1	-	44	-	1,06,55,066
1901	19	5	16	2	4	<1	-	46		86,04,732
1902	26	4	24	<1	4	<1	-	34	4	52,23,025
1903	12	3	21	<1	6	<1	<1	43	6	64,55,630
1904	16	-	27	2	6	<1		40	<1	454,981
1905	20	-	32	3	9	<1	<1	22	3	469,941
1906	29	-	25	2	7	<1	<1	18	<1	598,421
1907	49	-	17	2	8	<1	<1	9	3	497,990
1908	33	-	22	1	9	<1	-	25	<1	432,596
1909	32	-	24	3	9	<1	-	17	2	400,892
1910	33	-	28	4	10	<1	-	8	<1	348,950
1911	41	-	13	2	6	<1	<1	18	<1	669,020
1912	43	-	19	2	8	<1	6	10	<1	637,091
1913	16	-	16	3	3	<1	41	3	<1	601,765
1914	50	-	20	1	6	<1	5	3	<1	719,171
1915	49	-	23	1	8	<1	-	4	-	583,056
1916	36	-	25	-	2	-	-	4	<1	443,434
1917	35	-	19	-	2	-	-	8	-	820,951
1918	7	-	28	<1	12	-	-	10	-	395,150
1919	7	-	44	4	4	-	-	19	-	917,655
1920	10	-	27	1	2	-	-	42	-	898,571
1921	10	-	29	<1	1	<1	-	42	-	680.097
1922	8	-	20	2	<1		-	13	-	1,079,780
1923	7	-	18	2	<1	<1	-	12	<1	2,057,078

Source: Administration Report 1873-1905; Trade Report 1906-1923.
Because the export data of some countries have not been listed, the sum of the listed entries is less than 100% in that same year.

Imports

Around 1800, Bushehr imported from India: chintzes (Coromandel-Masulipatnam), piece-goods (Bengal, Gujarat, Malabar). Further it imported indigo, rice, spices, leather, sugar and sugar candy, wooden planks, shawls, cotton cloths, yarns (India) and coffee from the Red Sea. Imports from Europe and Bombay were: woolens, cloth, iron, steel, tin and lead as well as chinaware from China and sugar (China, Java). In 1789, of the total goods almost 70% were of Indian origin and European goods little more than 3%. Malcolm estimated the latter at 13% in 1801. During the first half of the nineteenth century, Bushehr's main imports were piece-goods (45-55%), sugar (10-20%), grains (5-10%) and metals. Furthermore, indigo, spices, woolen goods and in minor quantities various luxury products. After 1850, the import of cotton-twists and yarns increased in importance as did a new commodity, tea, whose import constituted <1% of total imports in the 1870s, but grew thereafter, be it, percentagewise, usually in the lower digits.[339]

Piece goods

Many fine cotton fabrics, white or prints from Coromandel, Bengal muslins, and Cashmere shawls were imported via Bushehr. Part of the textiles imported from India was re-exported to the Ottoman Empire and the Arabian Coast. Olivier noted a caravan leaving Kermanshah for Baghdad loaded with, amongst other things, muslins, Indian textiles and Cashmere shawls.[340] According to Waring, who was in Persia in 1804, there was a considerable domestic production of textiles, "but speaking generally, they rely almost entirely on foreigners for furnishing them with articles of dress and luxury."[341] According to Brydges-Jones, in 1810, Bushehr imported 500 to 600 bales of chintzes per year.[342]

During the first two decades of the nineteenth century, above all "a large quantity of British goods, particularly cottons, are imported *via* Bushire, from whence they are conveyed to all the Southern cities of Persia, such as Shiraz, Yezd, Kerman, Ispahan; from whence they find their way still further inland, supplying Irak, Khorasan, and even the further regions of Tartary."[343] There was also importation of European chintz for clothing and Indian and European muslins via Bushehr and Shiraz.[344] By 1829, British piece goods represented 34% of cloth imports as against 13% for Indian piece goods.[345] The importance of British piece goods continued to grown thereafter. In the first two decades of the twentieth century, Indian piece goods only represented some 1-3% of the import of British piece goods at Bushehr.

In 1873, the imports of piece goods at Bushehr were estimated at 1.78 million rupees, 668,000 from Great Britain and 1,090,000 from India. At that time, the Bushehr route had become more important than the one via Trabzon-Tabriz and those goods that formerly reached Central Persia via Tabriz were now preferably served by Bushehr.[346] The diversion of trade from Tabriz to the southern route was due to the virtual ban on the transit of foreign goods through Russia, and the cheaper transportation cost from Europe to the Persian Gulf. At the same time there was a difficult trade in Mexicans (a kind of coarse calico) and shirtings, while there was an increased import of chintzes. This resulted in a

339. Waring 1973, p. 8; Hollingberry 1976, p. 15; Milburn 1813, vol. 1, pp. 122-23; Amanat 1983, pp. 101-03; 112-13; O'Connor 1884/85, p. 815; Issawi 1971, p. 83; Buckingham 1971, p. 353; Hollingberry 1976, p. 15; Kinneir 1973, p. 70; Heude 1819, p. 43.

340. Olivier 1802, vol. 5, p. 323; vol. 6, pp. 269, 321; Milburn 1813, vol. 1, p. 120.

341. Waring 1973, p. 76.

342. Brydges-Jones 1976, p. 433 (he added that in the 1760s Bushehr imported only 70 bales of chintz per year).

343. Fraser 1826, pp. 380, 373, 376; Idem 1984, Appendix, p. 94; Elphinstone 1998, p. 295; Heude 1819, p. 43l; Issawi 1971, p. 90.

344. Stirling 1991, pp. 129-30 (there was a lot of local manufacturing and use Idem, 171-76); Conolly 1834, vol. 1, pp. 349-50; Bélanger 1838, vol. 2, p. 437.

345. Grummon 1985, p. 186.

346. Administration Report 1873-74, p. 13.

fall of indigo imports, because peasants preferred the fancier imported fabrics over the stout T-cloth dyed domestically with indigo.[347] The import of British piece-goods was faster than those from India; in 1879-80, imports from Great Britain were 6.5 million and from India only 2.2 million rupees, or respectively five times more than of Indian goods in 1873. Piece-goods trade was mostly in the hands of British merchants.[348]

In 1885, initially trade boded well, and substantial quantities of cottons were contracted. However, then the bread price rose, leading to a fall in demand and resulted in overstocking. The fall in the value of silver and copper also contributed to losses by importers.[349] In 1887, imports were consequently lower, but trade was resuscitated by the end of the year, which trend persisted into 1888. Good harvests also stimulated trade, but due to the higher rate of exchange some losses were sustained. Trade was brisk till "the hot weather, when the usual slackness returned and demands for goods fell off considerably. In August, however, improvement set in."[350] However, despite good demand in C. Persia, the southern market was down and results were bad, compounded by continued large imports of cottons. "The advance in silver caused stocks to be pressed heavily for sale, and the Persian dealers, who thought they had bought at cheap rates, found goods offered at still lower rates falling week by week. The result in a market where credit is the rule and where native buyers are in general without reserves was inevitable, that is to say, cancellation of engagements became frequent and in many instances native dealers became insolvent."[351] The next year was not much different, despite a good beginning to trade, due to the losses suffered in 1890 and tightness of credit.[352] The year 1893 was a bad one for cottons despite initial strong demand. However, the fall of the *qran*, crop failure due to locusts in Fars and cholera led to a serious fall in demand and hence a drop in imports of £90,000.[353] In 1894, there was increased import of cottons, despite the fact that locusts, insecurity and epidemic reigned in Fars that year. Imports increased from £471,781 in 1893 to £592,962 in 1894, or almost an increase of 25%.[354] Despite difficulties, imports continued to increase in 1895 and thereafter. In 1898, the poverty of the peasants depressed the market. However, later, expecting a better crop, sales revived. In 1898, there was some competition from Dutch cotton goods. They were marked 'made in Holland' and also imported via Baghdad. "These Dutch goods are transshipped either at Manchester or London into British bottoms... why are Dutch competitors able to send these goods to Persia and find sale for them, notwithstanding that they have to pay extra freight?"[355] However, after the bankruptcy of Hotz & Sons in 1903, Dutch piece-goods disappeared from the market. What did not change was the solid share of piece-goods in total imports, which continued to oscillate around the 40% mark. Most of these were British-Indian in origin, be it that in the 1930s this market position was seriously and successfully challenged, first by Russian imports (as of 1928) and from 1935 by Japanese

347. Administration Report 1884-85, p. 41.
348. Administration Report 1873-74, p. 13; Floor 2009 a.
349. Administration Report 1885-86, p. 29.
350. Administration Report 1888-89, p. 28.
351. Administration Report 1890-91, p. 17.
352. Administration Report 1891-92, p. 19.
353. Administration Report 1893-94, p. 24.
354. Administration Report 1894-95, pp. 11, 22.
355. Administration Report 1898-99, pp. 31-32.

imports. Russian piece-goods were equal in price and quality to the British product and therefore, these made serious inroads into this market segment. However, Russian piece goods although cheap, were not imported in such large quantities that they totally ousted the British and Indian cottons.[356] The 1931 Russo-Persian Commercial Treaty further helped increase the market share of Russian piece-goods. However, as of 1932, the Russian position in piece-goods was seriously challenged by the Japanese who, with their cheap products, now in their turn drove Russian piece-goods from the Bushehr market.[357] In 1935, Japanese piece-goods pushed out British ones. The creation of a monopoly for piece-goods reinforced this trend. Moreover, after the monopoly was taken over by the government it sold piece-goods at reasonable prices[358]

2.13: Value of import of piece-goods into Bushehr (1873-1923)

Units: Percentage of piece goods compared to total. Value: Rupee to 1902, £ from 1903

Year	Piece-goods	Total	%	Year	Piece-goods	Total	%
1873	18,08,000	46,02,925	39	1898	60, 91, 470	1,34,95,390	45
1874	15,25,000	35,97,700	42	1899	56,08,380	1,37,47,920	41
1875	20,67,800	51,58,823	40	1900	74,27,470	1,98,45,947	37
1876	20,94,000	45,96,999	46	1901	1,12,65,475	2,44,72,172	46
1877	4,74,000	83,67,115	5	1902	63,30,585	1,65,09,101	38
1878	30,00,000	73,95,560	36	1903	301,500	870,803	35
1879	87,40,000	1,87,76,900	46	1904	312,611	889,825	35
1880	70,37,500	1,68,66,050	42	1905	306,671	761,932	40
1881	20,60,000	70,33,800	29	1906	364,039	863,842	42
1882	51,15,500	1,01,88,980	50	1907	526,847	1,052,043	50
1883	70,62,500	1,37,39,200	51	1908	396,788	793,465	50
1884	49,66,000	1,00,97,500	49	1909	280,051	717,091	39
1885	51,22,320	99,62,170	51	1910	301,080	675,614	45
1886	37,60,900	82,73,230	45	1911	460,434	932,531	45
1887	46,46,900	87,15,680	53	1912	520,308	951,720	55
1888	47,14,950	81,35,360	58	1913	320,559	825,767	42
1889	61,51,200	1,16,03,570	53	1914	262,958	669,339	39
1890	95,66,200	1,65,48,710	58	1915	280,472	777,317	36
1891	1,13,12,000	1,72,80,870	65	1916	453,485	1,299,562	35
1892	1,00,63,530	1,64,58,850	61	1917	861,537	2,439,179	35
1893	76,66,430	1,56,97,950	49	1918	1,118,547	2,946,450	38
1894	1,06,73,320	1,83,51,110	58	1919	1,067,927	2,723,357	39
1895	1,13,97,600	1,83,04,490	62	1920	677,287	2,462,797	28

356. Administration Report 1928, p. 8; Administration Report 1929, p. 6.
357. Administration Report 1932, pp. 2, 7-8.
358. Administration Report 1935, pp. 9-10; Administration Report 1939, p. 2. For total national import of piece goods, see Gray 1937, p. 33.

Year	Piece-goods	Total	%	Year	Piece-goods	Total	%
1896	61,59,000	1,34,01,080	46	1921	632,245	1,526,594	41
1897	1,08,57,560	1,83,25,270	59	1922	695,740	1,382,961	50
				1923	851,376	2,011,772	32

Source: Administration Report 1873-1905; Trade Report 1905-1923.
All figures have been rounded up or down.

Indigo

Although indigo was an important import during the Safavid period, it seems to have played no significant role in Persian imports during the eighteenth century. In 1801, John Malcom mentions that indigo from Bengal had been imported over the last four years and was much appreciated and he had high hopes for its growing demand. This seems indeed to have been the case, as indigo is mentioned as one of the Bengali imported goods, but no quantities are mentioned. However, in 1822/23, it was the most important commodity imported from India, representing about 60% of total imports (see Table 4.1). Unfortunately, no quantitative data are available for the period until 1873, but it seems that although indigo continued to be imported it was at a much lower level.[359]

After an initial decrease, indigo continued to show a strong demand and imports consequently rose. In 1893 the level of import was above average, but in 1894 there was a further increase.[360] However, in 1895 there was a drop in imports due to depreciation of the *qran*.[361] Calcutta indigo fell out of favor, and cheaper qualities were imported, more suitable to market conditions. Trade rebounded, after the end of a famine in India, and imports increased considerably.[362] Calcutta indigo continued to be ignored and only the cheaper qualities were imported. Oudh (or Awadh, in central Utar Pradesh) indigo was the preferred kind. Because there was a revival in the weaving industry and hence in dyeing operations, larger quantities of indigo were imported. But large stocks were said to have been left unsold at the end of the year.[363] The famine in India accounted for the falling-off in the import of indigo of about £19,444.[364] "Calcutta indigo is said to be getting into disfavour, and cheaper sorts, more suitable for supplying the wants of the country, are being sought after. The trade, however, has revived considerably from the depression caused in the previous year by the Indian famine, and the imports show an increase of 17,006*l.* over 1896."[365] Calcutta samples of indigo continued to be neglected and transactions have been limited to the cheaper sorts. Oudh indigo is reportedly preferred in Persia. "The revival of the weaving industry and dyeing operations in the interior caused a greater quantity of the dye to be used this year [1898], thereby improving the imports

359. Grummon 1985, pp. 186-88; for a discussion of the trade and use of indigo in Persia, see Floor 2006 b.
360. Administration Report 1894-95, p. 23.
361. Administration Report 1895-96, p. 18.
362. Administration Report 1897-98, p. 19.
363. Administration Report 1898-99, p. 33.
364. *DCR* 2018, Bushire 1896, p. 3.
365. *DCR* 2186, Bushire 1897, p. 5.

by about 1,20,428 Rs. (7,527*l*.). It is, however, reported that large stocks remained unsold at the close of the year."[366]

Import of Indian indigo dropped from £21,164 to £15,833 due to competition from Europe. This was due to the import of the synthetic product, which was sent in tins to Isfahan, one of the great dyeing centers. Consequently, in India there was "fear that imports will decrease because piece goods are increasingly dyed at Bombay, whereas formerly it was almost all done in Persia."[367] In 1907-08, indigo imports increased to 2,160 cwt against 1,444 cwt in the previous year. However, this gain was threatened by German synthetic indigo, which showed an increase from 71 cwt to 264 cwt. during the second year of its introduction. "Two separate companies have been competing in Shiraz, one of which had sent up a representative in 1906, but its sales are reported to be limited to that district." Madras and Khairpur indigo should be able to keep their market share if due diligence is applied. There was, however, a complaint from Isfahan that indigo there was often of poor quality and that the Madras dealers were unwilling to send good quality on consignment.[368]

In some years (1903-07), the data on indigo also include a small volume of cochineal (*qermez*), which typically represented about 1 percent of the total figure of indigo imports. Given its insignificance no attempt had been made to separate the two products. In 1907, the British consul reported that the import of *qermez* had practically ceased, which means that for the years after 1907 the data only refer to indigo.[369]

The consumption of indigo was directly linked to the level of activity of the Persian textile industry, in particular more to the extent in which the craftsmen still dyed their yarns and fabrics. Given the fact that there was a downward trend in the dyeing of yarns and fabrics in Persia, indigo imports likewise were decreasing. This trend was accelerated after 1909, when synthetic indigo was vigorously marketed in Persia, whose importation had not been banned as other synthetic aniline dyes had. Because of its ease of use and higher profits, the Persian dyeing crafts increasingly abandoned indigo in favor of its synthetic alternative. The only region which seems not to have been affected by the synthetic indigo bug was Khorasan where it was not used. The much-awaited inevitable demise of natural indigo was not realized, because the outbreak of World War I put a stop to German exports to Persia. However, soon after the end of the war (1921) synthetic indigo found its way back onto the market and by the end of the Qajar period (1925) it was fast making up for lost time to replace natural indigo.

2.14: Value of imports of indigo through Bushehr compared to total imports (1873-1923)

Units: Percentage of indigo to the total value. Value: Rupee to 1902, £ from 1903

Year	Indigo value	Total value	%	Year	Indigo value	Total value	%
1873	5,20,750	46,02,925	11	1899	2,98,380	1,37,47,920	2

366. *DCR* 2346, Persian Gulf 1898, p. 6.
367. *DCR* 3951, Bushire 1906-07, p. 12.
368. *DCR* 4179, Bushire 1907-08, p. 18.
369. *DCR* 3951, Bushire 1906-07, p. 12.

Year	Indigo value	Total value	%	Year	Indigo value	Total value	%
1874	4,02,400	35,97,700	11	1900	5,35,750	1,98,45,947	3
1875	7,38,600	51,58,823	14	1901	3,33,790	2,44,72,172	1
1876	2,16,000	45,96,999	5	1902	93,870	1,65,09,101	0.1
1877	3,50,000	83,67,115	4	1903	18,786	870,803	0.2
1878	4,80,000	73,95,560	6	1904	27,181	889,825	0.3
1879	10,16,000	1,87,76,900	5	1905	21,164	761,932	0.3
1880	8,40,000	1,68,66,050	5	1906	16,657	863,842	0.2
1881	3,90,000	70,33,800	5	1907	30,500	1,052,043	0.2
1882	2,80,000	1,01,88,980	3	1908	13,028	793,465	0.1
1883	4,47,700	1,37,39,200	3	1909	19,974	717,091	0.2
1884	1,84,500	1,00,97,500	2	1910	5,576	675,614	-
1885	6,67,600	99,62,170	7	1911	5,844	932,531	-
1886	5,38,400	82,73,230	7	1912	4,117	951,720	-
1887	5,19,300	87,15,680	6	1913	4,575	825,767	-
1888	3,84,900	81,35,360	5	1914	1,290	669,339	-
1889	7,31,500	1,16,03,570	6	1915	40	777,317	-
1890	5,96,250	1,65,48,710	4	1916	15,818	1,299,562	-
1891	3,96,500	1,72,80,870	2	1917	27,741	2,439,179	-
1892	5,19,500	1,64,58,850	3	1918	37,891	2,946,450	-
1893	7,63,150	1,56,97,950	5	1919	9,480	2,723,357	-
1894	9,51,830	1,83,51,110	5	1920	21,021	2,462,797	-
1895	6,89,300	1,83,04,490	4	1921	23,240	1,526,594	-
1896	3,88,470	1,34,01,080	3	1922	26,739	1,382,961	-
1897	4,23,060	1,83,25,270	2	1923	32,299	2,011,772	-
1898	4,94,520	1,34,95,390	4	-	-	-	-

Source: Administration Report 1873-1905; Trade Report 1905-1923.
All figures have been rounded up or down. Total imports are in Rupees; from 1904 in £.

Metals

Among the metals that were imported at Bushehr copper was the most important, followed by iron, tin and brass; they were imported in sheets, rods and ingots. Persia had always been an importer of these metals despite the fact that its subsoil is rich in metals. However, various reasons (low technology, lack of energy sources, water, and labor) made it unprofitable to mine this mineral wealth.[370] Copper in particular was important, because all household utensils were made from it. Moreover, copperware also served as a kind of piggy-bank, because in times of poverty peasants would sell their pots and pans to survive. This function of copper, therefore, affected the volume of trade in this and other metals. For example, in 1900, the import of all metals increased, because "people

370. Floor 2000, pp. 303-08; Idem 2003 b, pp. 186-210.

now being in a position to replace their wares which they had to part with during the previous years of scarcity."[371] The metal trade was also influenced by factors such as the price level as well as the exchange rate of the Persian currency and, because metals are heavy, transportation rates.[372]

2.15: Value of import of metals through Bushehr compared to total value (1873-1923)

Units: Percentage of metals to the total. Value: Rupee to 1920, £ from 1903

Year	Metals value	Total value	%	Year	Metals value	Total value	%
1873	1,49,400	46,02,925	3	1898	6,81,350	1,34,95,390	5
1874	1,44,900	35,97,700	4	1899	10,35,540	1,37,47,920	8
1875	4,27,875	51,58,823	8	1900	8,45,540	1,98,45,947	4
1876	4,69,600	45,96,999	10	1901	5,71,005	2,44,72,172	2
1877	3,91,300	83,67,115	5	1902	5,11,279	1,65,09,101	3
1878	4,92,300	73,95,560	7	1903	213,610	870,803	26
1879	5,22,000	1,87,76,900	3	1904	112,794	889,825	13
1880	21,08,500	1,68,66,050	13	1905	21,165	761,932	2
1881	12,80,100	70,33,800	18	1906	22,881	863,842	3
1882	21,07,200	1,01,88,980	21	1907	33,494	1,052,043	3
1883	25,41,700	1,37,39,200	18	1908	34,210	793,465	4
1884	9,95,300	1,00,97,500	10	1909	22,570	717,091	3
1885	9,03,200	99,62,170	9	1910	24,811	675,614	4
1886	5,88,070	82,73,230	7	1911	22,534	932,531	2
1887	7,41,580	87,15,680	9	1912	10,389	951,720	1
1888	3,46,900	81,35,360	4	1913	29,249	825,767	3
1889	11,78,970	1,16,03,570	10	1914	26,383	669,339	4
1890	15,81,800	1,65,48,710	10	1915	9,961	777,317	1
1891	19,14,000	1,72,80,870	11	1916	15,364	1,299,562	1
1892	8,76,140	1,64,58,850	5	1917	15,106	2,439,179	0.5
1893	11,19,010	1,56,97,950	7	1918	13,427	2,946,450	-
1894	6,80,090	1,83,51,110	4	1919	108,726	2,723,357	-
1895	2,74,370	1,83,04,490	1	1920	34,362	2,462,797	1
1896	5,02,275	1,34,01080	4	1921	16,306	1,526,594	1
1897	4,05,450	1,83,25,270	2	1922	9,125	1,382,961	-
				1923	25,610	2,011,772	1

Source: Administration Report 1873-1905; Trade Report 1905-1923.
All figures have been rounded up or down.

371. Administration Report 1900-1901, p. 27; see also Administration Report 1882-83, p. 30; Mignan 1839, vol. 2, p. 138 (copper imports valued at £30,000 in 1830).

372. Administration Report 1885-86, p. 29; Administration Report 1894-95, p. 22; Administration Report 1895-96, p. 17.

SPECIE[373]

Although usually ignored in discussions about trade, Bushehr also imported specie, thus enabling it to sustain the sometimes large amounts of export of specie. As is clear from Table 2.16 the inflow of specie in some years was quite significant, in 1879 even reaching 34% of total imports. However, usually the import was in the single digits, even being as low as a fraction of one percent in some years. The major sources of this specie were India and Turkey.

2.16: Value of import of specie into Bushehr compared to the total value (1873-1923)

Units: Percentage of specie compared to the total. Value: in Rupees, in £ from 1903

Year	Specie value	Total value	%	Year	Specie value	Total value	%
1873	6,17,405	46,02,925	13	1898	9,66,660	1,34,95,390	7
1874	1,25,000	35,97,700	3	1899	12,97,665	1,37,47,920	9
1875	76,800	51,58,823	1	1900	28,77,654	1,98,45,947	14
1876	1,80,000	45,96,999	4	1901	43,01,661	2,44,72,172	17
1877	1,40,000	83,67,115	2	1902	25,36,505	1,65,09,101	15
1878	12,10,000	73,95,560	16	1903	33,703	870,803	4
1879	64,90,000	1,87,76,900	34	1904	101,598	889,825	11
1880	19,15,000	1,68,66,050	11	1905	63,390	761,932	8
1881	4,33,000	70,33,800	6	1906	8,659	863,842	1
1882	4,48,000	1,01,88,980	4	1907	69,095	1,052,043	6
1883	2,32,000	1,37,39,200	2	1908	23,187	793,465	3
1884	1,07,650	1,00,97,500	<1	1909	82,349	717,091	11
1885	55,420	99,62,170	<1	1910	55,778	675,614	8
1886	2,11,570	82,73,230	2	1911	89,710	932,531	10
1887	1,30,200	87,15,680	1	1912	38,066	951,720	4
1888	3,25,670	81,35,360	4	1913	26,261	825,767	3
1889	23,160	1,16,03,570	<1	1914	10,559	669,339	1
1890	1,03,120	1,65,48,710	<1	1915	6,844	777,317	<1
1891	1,61,350	1,72,80,870	<1	1916	103,655	1,299,562	8
1892	1,03,120	1,64,58,850	<1	1917	51,676	2,439,179	2
1893	2,08,340	1,56,97,950	1	1918	9,553	2,946,450	<1
1894	3,43,900	1,83,51,110	2	1919	15,711	2,723,357	<1

373. Qajar Persia did not produce enough exportable wares to compensate for the huge quantities of spices and manufactured goods, mainly fabrics, imported from India. Therefore, it had a trade deficit with that country, its main trading partner. Consequently, the difference between imports and exports had to be paid in specie or coin. Because Persia had a positive trade balance with the Ottoman Empire and Russia the specie it obtained from these two sources served to finance the trade deficit with India and other trading nations. This situation long predates the Safavid period. A pattern of precious metal moving from Europe to Asia in return for luxury goods, reflecting an imbalance of payments between West and East, can be traced as far back as the early medieval period and well before the advent of Islam.

Year	Specie value	Total value	%	Year	Specie value	Total value	%
1895	5,81,610	1,83,04,490	3	1920	9,679	2,462,797	<1
1896	4,73,531	1,34,01080	3	1921	?	1,526,594	
1897	4,52,860	1,83,25,270	<1	1922	?	1,382,961	
				1923	?	2,011,772	

Source: Administration Report 1873-1905; Trade Report 1906-1923.
All figures have been rounded up or down.

SPICES

Most spices were imported from India and some from China. The most important were: (1) tamarind (*tamar*), of which there were three kinds: (i) without seeds; (ii) with a few seeds, and (iii) with many seeds; (2) pepper (*felfel*); (3) ginger (*zanjabin*); (4) turmeric (*zardchubeh*); (5) cinnamon (*darchini*); (6) cardamom (*hel*); and (7) cassia (*folus*). After 1904, because of the high import duty (15%) there was much smuggling of this group of products.[374]

2.17: Value of import of spices through Bushehr compared to total import value (1873-1923)

Units: Percentage of spices compared to the total. Value: in Rupee to 1902, £ from 1903

Year	Spices value	Total value	%	Year	Spices value	Total value	%
1873	98,640	46,02,925	2	1898	97,730	1,34,95,390	<1
1874	66,150	35,97,700	2	1899	1,79,525	1,37,47,920	1
1875	45,800	51,58,823	-	1900	1,48,929	1,98,45,947	<1
1876	1,19,500	45,96,999	3	1901	1,90,201	2,44,72,172	<1
1877	1,32,000	83,67,115	2	1902	1,18,966	1,65,09,101	<1
1878	1,04,000	73,95,560	1	1903	14,485	870,803	2
1879	44,300	1,87,76,900	<1	1904	9,939	889,825	1
1880	1,87,000	1,68,66,050	1	1905	8,259	761,932	1
1881	1,03,500	70,33,800	1	1906	11,407	863,842	<1
1882	1,06,200	1,01,88,980	1	1907	13,541	1,052,043	<1
1883	1,33,100	1,37,39,200	1	1908	12,200	793,465	2
1884	1,31,820	1,00,97,500	1	1909	7,709	717,091	1
1885	1,58,000	99,62,170	2	1910	3,219	675,614	<1
1886	1,33,980	82,73,230	2	1911	7,416	932,531	<1
1887	1,31,380	87,15,680	2	1912	7,172	951,720	<1
1888	1,06,290	81,35,360	1	1913	8,909	825,767	1
1889	1,37,910	1,16,03,570	1	1914	17,505	669,339	3
1890	1,45,200	1,65,48,710	<1	1915	24,908	777,317	3
1891	1,89,920	1,72,80,870	1	1916	13,946	1,299,562	1

374. DCR 3951 (Bushire, 1906-07), p. 9; DCR 4179 (Bushire, 1907-08), p. 16.

Year	Spices value	Total value	%	Year	Spices value	Total value	%
1892	2,19,040	1,64,58,850	1	1917	31,598	2,439,179	1
1893	2,13,950	1,56,97,950	1	1918	45,629	2,946,450	1
1894	1,93,160	1,83,51,110	1	1919	15,342	2,723,357	<1
1895	63,500	1,83,04,490	<1	1920	12,581	2,462,797	<1
1896	40,910	1,34,01,080	<1	1921	8,352	1,526,594	<1
1897	75,640	1,83,25,270	<1	1922	12,420	1,382,961	<1
				1923	23,422	2,011,772	1

Source: Administration Report 1873-1905; Trade Report 1905-1923.
All figures have been rounded up or down.

SUGAR

Sugar and sugar candy were important imports during the preceding centuries. It was mainly Java and Bengal sugar (both candy and loaf) that was imported into Persia in the early nineteenth century.[375] With the disappearance of the Dutch from the Persian Gulf at the end of the eighteenth century (the last direct voyage from Java was in 1796),[376] sugar from India dominated the Persian sugar market again in the nineteenth century, although some of it may have been Java sugar, which was marketed by the Dutch in Surat and Bombay. In 1805, the Persian Gulf, imported 3.1 million sicca rupees in goods from India, of which 0.382 million rupees (12%) was represented by sugar. This made sugar the second most important import article for the Persian market and this ranking would not change during the entire Qajar period, although its relative size doubled.[377]

In 1824, Java sugar was directly imported into Persia for the first time since 1796 (the last time Java sugar was shipped there) when a Dutch ship called at Bushehr with 5,000 picols of sugar. Thereafter, other Dutch ships followed on an annual basis with smaller quantities of Java sugar. The Persians wanted white sugar, and Java sugar was darker than that of Bengal. However, it was also rather sweet and a liking for this product was developed.[378] By the end of the 1840s, the British consul Keith Abbott concluded, after his extensive commercial intelligence gathering tour through Persia, that:

> The manufacture of coarse loaf sugar from the raw article of India, Java, and Siam is calculated to require a daily supply of about 2,500 Tabreez Mens, or 53,000 Cwt. in the year and the number of small factories in which it is consumed for this purpose is 96. This article is sent to almost every part of the Country, and is used by many people in preference to that of Europe, from religious scruples.[379]

375. Olivier 1807, vol. 5, p. 323.
376. Floor 2007 a, pp. 218-22.
377. Milburn 1813, vol. 1, p. 123. Import of sugar from India. Kinneir 1813, p. 37.
378. Den Tex 1871, pp. 23, 28.
379. Amanat 1983, p. 104. "It [raw sugar] sells at Kerans 4/15 per Men, and the value of the above quantity would therefore be Toms. 216,000 (=£ 98,000). Sugar candy. From 18,000 to 35,000 Mens in the year, believed to be of the produce of China; the price was 6 Kerans on credit." Idem, p. 107. In Isfahan "there are 55 small factories where the raw article of India and Java is converted into Loaves." Idem, p. 99.

He further observed that Fars imported considerable quantity of raw sugar from Java, Siam and Bengal and sugar candy from China. Furthermore, that while raw sugar in Isfahan came mainly from Java, its sugar candy was mainly from China and Bengal.[380] In 1844-45, Bushehr imported 4,000 bags of soft sugar and 800 bags of cane-sugar for a total amount of 40,000 *tumans*.[381]

By the early 1860, sugar imports from Java increased 10-fold at the expense of that from India, Siam and Mauritius. "The refiners find that the Java sugar yields a larger quantity of loaf sugar per *man* than the other sugars."[382] In fact, by the 1860s, Java sugar had slowly ousted Bengal sugar from the southern market. In 1864, Bushehr imported a total of value of 950,000 rupees in sugar, and 40,000 rupees in sugar-candy. "The sugar trade with Java has increased during the past 20 years from 5,000 Peculs (17 Tabreez maunds each) to 50,000 Peculs. This sugar drives those of Mysore, Bengal, Mauritius, and Siam out of the market. The refiners find that the Java sugar yields a larger quantity of loaf sugar per maund than the other sugars."[383] By the 1870s, Java sugar had become so dominant that Höltzer rather matter-of-factly reported that "the craft of sugar workers [in Isfahan] is mainly to refine the sugar imported from Java."[384]

After 1880 in Southern Persia, various countries competed for the Persian market. As in the North, Java sugar, which had once again dominated the market in the south, was driven out by Marseilles sugar, which was first marketed in the Gulf area around 1865. Although of inferior quality, as compared with the Java sugar, it was cheaper. Most of it came from Mauritius or Marseilles, which was appreciated because of its higher sugar content. In Isfahan there were 12 sugar-works, which refined Mauritius and Marseilles sugar, and the refined final product was the most sought after by the consumer.[385] French sugar, or rather Marseilles loaf sugar (Mediterranean and St. Louis Refineries), was both sweeter and more quickly soluble than the other kinds, and dominated the market northwards from Shiraz. It was superior in quality, white, fine-grained, floury and easily soluble.[386]

Although Java sugar had been ousted from the market by Marseilles sugar in Southern Persia, this did not mean that Marseilles sugar held a monopoly situation. In fact, it had to compete with, for example, with Austrian-Hungarian soft or crystal sugar, which, though less successful than the French variety, was able to create a niche for itself. It was a very sweet sugar in clear, white, large crystals and packed in bags of 2 cwt. net. There was also another Austrian-Hungarian sugar, but its crystals were not so large and white.[387] Another competitor was Germany, which also tried to obtain a market share. One German sugar variety was only appreciated in the [Persian Gulf] coast districts. It was a particularly hard kind of lump sugar, which was marketed as of about 1900. "It is moist and yellow-tinged,

---

380. Amanat 1983, p. 101, 112-3.

381. Nateq 1368, p. 223.

382. Pelly 1865 a, p. 51.

383. Pelly 1865 a, pp. 47, 51. See also "Report by Mr. Thomson," *AP* 61 (1864), pp. 193-194, who estimated imports of Java sugar at £100,000 in the early 1860s.

384. Höltzer 2535, p. 50. Batavia, the capital of Java, was called 'Patoua' by the Bushehris. Floyer 1882, p. 151.

385. DCR 1662, Ispahan, 1894-95, p. 19; Ministerie van Buitenlandsche Zaken 1896, p. 593.

386. Trade Report 1915-1916, pp. 9-10.

387. DCR 3951, Bushire 1906-07, p. 11.

almost dirty in colour, and not nearly so sweet as the crystal sugar."[388] Because of its limited market attraction, this sugar disappeared for some time, but by 1910, it made its reappearance.[389]

Austrian and Marseilles sugar was driven from the market by Belgian sugar, which was marketed as of 1900 in the Persian Gulf. Belgian loaf sugar (*Raffineries Tirlemontoises*, or RT) was less bright and harder than the Marseilles variety, but commended itself to the consumer of the littoral, "who likes to stir his sugar long in his glass; it is far less quickly soluble in water than either the French or Hungarian sugars, and is not too sweet, but the principal attraction lies in its cheapness."[390]

After piece-goods, sugar was the most important import commodity, and was estimated to represent 19% of total imports in 1910. "The rapid increase in the demand for loaf sugar is attributed partly to the spreading use of tea among nomads and other tribesmen and partly to a change in the fashion which now demands the use of quick dissolving loaf sugar for purposes, notably in tea, for which crystal sugar was used in the past. The Persian is a great tea-drinker and likes his tea turned into a sort of syrup."[391]

Consequently, many countries competed for this market; in the first fifteen years of the twentieth century, mainly Russia, France, Belgium, Germany and Austria dominated it. Of loaf-sugar, which constituted 85% of sugar imports, Russia had an 80% market share or 71 million *qrans* in 1907-08. As is the case of other commodities, the common border, the transport routes and access to the best markets in Persia (towns in the North) favored Russia. In addition, there was a Russian export premium of 1.75 ruble per *pud*. Therefore, the non-Russian exporters found it difficult to compete, in particular France and Austria, who saw their market share diminish. An additional handicap was the growing insecurity of the trade routes in the South, in particular from Bushehr to Shiraz and beyond. The central zone, where the other exporters had been able to oust Russian sugar, lost ground and was therefore more and more supplied with Russian sugar from the north. The only disadvantage of Russian sugar was that it was hard and had a low saccharine content. Belgian and French sugar was well liked, which were better than German sugar. In 1910-11, total imports in the Persian littoral were 45,000 tons.[392]

In 1915, loaf sugar imports were at a real low level (<10% of the usual) level, because the usual sources of supply (Austria, Belgium, France and Germany) were at war and trade with these countries was discontinued. Other exporters made up the difference. This held in particular for Egyptian loaf sugar (*Raffinerie le Cairo* [sic]). The local merchants and community however did not like it very much. They considered it to be inferior to all the sugars that had been imported before the war. The advantage of Egyptian sugar was that it could be conveniently obtained from Bombay and so, when the supply of RT and other brands failed, it stepped in and took over. The loaf weighed 1.60 kg, thus conforming to

388. DCR 3951, Bushire 1906-07, pp. 10-12.

389. Trade Report 1909-1910, p. 5. Another German sugar (Belgian made for German consigners) was known as UTO. It had the same quality and weight as the Belgian RT. Trade Report 1915-1916, p. 9.

390. DCR 3951, Bushire 1906-07, p. 11; Trade Report 1915-1916, p. 9.

391. Trade Report 1913-1914, p. 11.

392. Trade Report 1911-1912, p. 12; Entner 1965, p. 72, table 13.

the demand of the Persian market. In addition to Egyptian sugar, Persia also imported refined sugar from Hong Kong as well as from Mauritius and Java.[393]

Trade in sugar in the 1920s did not improve, because merchants suffered from lack of money due to the system of monopolies and as of 1925, high customs duties on sugar. In 1928, there was a serious challenge to British-Indian trade, because the Russians dumped their sugar and by year's end had a virtual sugar monopoly.[394] The Russians continued to export large quantities of sugar in the following years.[395] In 1930, the Persian government established many trade monopolies, including one for sugar. At the urging of Mohammad `Ali Mirza Rokni, the governor of Bushehr, local merchants formed a company to buy sugar for local consumption in Bushehr and environs from the Customs department. Half of the capital of 150,000 rials was provided by the merchants, the other half by the government. `Ali Akbar Davar, the Minister of Finance, during his stay in Bushehr from 28 January till 4 February 1934, arranged that "the Company would get loaf sugar at 8 rials per *batman* or 7 lbs and crystal sugar at 7 rials a *batman*. The Company added 40 Cts and sold it to retailers, who could add 75 Cts to fix the consumer price." Because the Bushehr market was small Lengeh was included.[396] The Sugar Company continued selling sugar, but as of May 1936, the Tangestanis did not buy anymore from it. Therefore, the company was unable to compete with smugglers who supplied Tangestan.[397] In 1940, the sugar-tea monopoly did not pay any dividend. Their high prices diminished sales, while the quantity of sugar made available by the government was also smaller.[398]

2.18: Value of import of sugar through Bushehr compared to total import value (1873-1923)

Units: Percentage of sugar compared to the total. Value: Rupee to 1902, £ from 1903

Year	Sugar	Total	%	Year	Sugar	Total	%
1873	6,29,000	46,02,925	14	1898	11,19,540	1,34,95,390	8
1874	6,28,800	35,97,700	17	1899	13,14,245	1,37,47,920	10
1875	7,98,650	51,58,823	15	1900	23,88,019	1,98,45,947	10
1876	7,04,875	45,96,999	15	1901	21,35,564	2,44,72,172	8
1877	10,69,700	83,67,115	13	1902	26,85,474	1,65,09,101	16
1878	9,40,000	73,95,560	13	1903	86,318	870,803	10
1879	8,18,500	1,87,76,900	4	1904	197,988	889,825	22
1880	20,70,000	1,68,66,050	12	1905	126,810	761,932	17
1881	11,41,500	70,33,800	16	1906	178,802	863,842	21
1882	6,84,200	1,01,88,980	7	1907	118,087	1,052,043	11
1883	13,13,000	1,37,39,200	10	1908	96,679	793,465	12

393. Trade Report 1915-1916, p. 9. Egyptian sugar appeared for the first time on the market in 1908, with a market share of only 100,000 *qrans*. Government of France 1914, p. 38.

394. Administration Report 1928, p. 8; Administration Report 1929, p. 6.

395. Administration Report 1930, p. 8; for national import data, see Gray 1937, p. 33.

396. Administration Report 1935, p. 4.

397. Administration Report 1936, p. 3; Administration Report 1937, p. 5 (the Sugar monopoly, which included tea as of 1938, paid a dividend of 25% compared with 22% net in 1936-37).

398. Administration Report 1940, p. 7.

Year	Sugar	Total	%	Year	Sugar	Total	%
1884	17,14,370	1,00,97,500	17	1909	136,036	717,091	19
1885	12,28,880	99,62,170	12	1910	127,933	675,614	19
1886	12,41,450	82,73,230	15	1911	142,973	932,531	15
1887	6,37,320	87,15,680	7	1912	194,434	951,720	20
1888	5,10,750	81,35,360	6	1913	221,612	825,767	27
1889	11,27,740	1,16,03,570	10	1914	145,437	669,339	22
1890	17,98,570	1,65,48,710	11	1915	77,874	777,317	10
1891	7,08,960	1,72,80,870	4	1916	288,799	1,299,562	22
1892	22,02,790	1,64,58,850	13	1917	691,556	2,439,179	28
1893	24,58,110	1,56,97,950	16	1918	572,126	2,946,450	19
1894	13,70,600	1,83,51,110	7	1919	603,374	2,723,357	22
1895	8,75,930	1,83,04,490	5	1920	565,336	2,462,797	23
1896	12,11,973	1,34,01,080	9	1921	386,510	1,526,594	25
1897	11,89,790	1,83,25,270	6	1922	189,035	1,382,961	14
				1923	509,711	2,011,772	25

Source: Administration Report 1873-1905; Trade Report 1905-1923.
All figures have been rounded up or down.

Tea

Because tea consumption in southern Persia was still rather limited in the first half of the nineteenth century, tea imports were unimportant. The earliest quantitative data are from 1849, when it was reported that Isfahan imported chiefly Pekoe and black tea via Bushehr, (price in 1849, respectively 20-25 *qrans* and 14 *qrans* per *man-e shah*). In the same year, Yazd imported 1,500 to 2,000 cases of 474 *man* each, at a price of 90 *qrans* per case, of mainly of Pekoe tea. Probably, most of this was for re-export. Shiraz also imported an unknown quantity of tea.[399] It would seem that the consumption of tea in southern Persia did not grow very much, because in 1865 only 2,500 cases with a value 1,00,000 Rs. were imported via Bushehr. This level of imports does not show a major increase over the import estimates supplied by Abbot for 1849.[400] Although there was a quadrupling of total tea imports in the 1870s, the real important increase only took place in the 1880s, due to the fact that tea had now become popular in the south of Persia.

Tea imports in 1893 continued to increase, and more improvement was expected. Tea was almost exclusively from India and Java.[401] In 1894, tea imports in Bandar Abbas more than doubled. Also, India and Java tea were ousting Chinese tea. India tea in particular sold well. Bandar Abbas saw the highest growth due to demand in Khorasan. However, in 1895 there was a drop in imports due to the depreciation of the *qran*[402] and the lack of purchasing power among the poor. However, at the same time "the use of coffee is said to

399. Amanat 1983, pp. 101 (coffee was also imported at the same time), 107, 113.
400. Pelly 1865 a, p. 69.
401. Administration Report 1893-94, p. 25.
402. Administration Report 1894-95, p. 23; Administration Report 1895-96, p. 18.

be dying out in Persia, and the little trade done in it resulted in a loss."[403] Tea imports at the same time grew by 50% although it had not as yet regained the level of imports of 1896.[404]

The import of tea in Bushehr had its ups and downs due to the changes in the purchasing power among the poor, the principal purchasers.[405] But the general trend was upwards. The other trend was that Indian tea took over the market and reduced the role of China and Java tea to a minor one.[406] During WWI tea imports in Bushehr increased significantly, because the main Dardanelles-Batoum supply route was closed.[407] Thereafter, Indian maintained its dominant position, with Ceylon tea, and later Java tea, playing a minor role.[408] On 1 October 1936, at the urging of the governor of Bushehr, the Tea Company was formed. It had a capital of 500,000 rials of which 25% was paid by the Sugar Company and the rest by merchants, who formerly traded in tea; however, the Company only received tea by the end of the year. In 1938, the tea and sugar monopoly were merged.[409]

2.19: Value of import of tea through Bushehr compared to total import value (1873-1923)

Units: Percentage of tea compared to the total import. Value: Rupee until 1902, £ from 1903

Year	Tea value	Total value	%	Year	Tea value	Total value	%
1873	48,000	46,02,925	1	1898	8,43,200	1,34,95,390	6
1874	36,000	35,97,700	1	1899	9,59,205	1,37,47,920	7
1875	1,06,750	51,58,823	2	1900	9,58,945	1,98,45,947	5
1876	27,850	45,96,999	<1	1901	1,97,424	2,44,72,172	<1
1877	14,000	83,67,115	<1	1902	21,77,816	1,65,09,101	13
1878	50,000	73,95,560	<1	1903	62,119	870,803	7
1879	1,00,000	1,87,76,900	<1	1904	59,172	889,825	7
1880	1,60,000	1,68,66,050	<1	1905	64,489	761,932	8
1881	2,60,000	70,33,800	4	1906	56,376	863,842	6
1882	2,08,000	1,01,88,980	2	1907	79,582	1,052,043	7
1883	2,15,950	1,37,39,200	2	1908	69,645	793,465	9
1884	2,24,400	1,00,97,500	2	1909	38,609	717,091	5
1885	2,81,460	99,62,170	3	1910	31,963	675,614	5
1886	1,34,640	82,73,230	2	1911	36,722	932,531	4
1887	2,48,450	87,15,680	3	1912	26,287	951,720	3

403. Administration Report 1897-98, p. 19, 20.

404. Administration Report 1898-99, pp. 32, 34. On the introduction of the habit of tea drinking in Iran and the various kinds of teas imported, see Floor 2004 b.

405. *DCR* 2186, p. 6.

406. *DCR* 2346, p. 7.

407. Report 1915-16, p. 2.

408. Lingeman 1928, p.35; Idem 1930,, p. 41; Simmonds 1935, p. 44; Gray 1937, p. 33.

409. Administration Report 1936, p. 3; Administration Report 1937, p. 5 (the Sugar monopoly, which included tea as of 1938, paid a dividend of 25% compared with 22% net in 1936-37.

Year	Tea value	Total value	%	Year	Tea value	Total value	%
1888	2,11,050	81,35,360	3	1913	23,738	825,767	3
1889	3,77,930	1,16,03,570	3	1914	70,171	669,339	10
1890	4,26,510	1,65,48,710	2	1915	264,540	777,317	34
1891	9,53,400	1,72,80,870	6	1916	62,438	1,299,562	5
1892	7,94,710	1,64,58,850	5	1917	145,501	2,439,179	6
1893	12,27,590	1,56,97,950	8	1918	576,159	2,946,450	20
1894	13,44,020	1,83,51,110	7	1919	212,360	2,723,357	8
1895	7,62,720	1,83,04,490	7	1920	188,748	2,462,797	8
1896	7,32,975	1,34,01080	4	1921	46,512	1,526,594	3
1897	5,40,900	1,83,25,270	3	1922	114,512	1,382,961	8
				1923	132,931	2,011,772	7

Source: Administration Report 1873-1905; Trade Report 1905-1923.
All figures have been rounded up or down.

Woolen goods

Traditionally, much European woolen cloth had been imported via the Persian Gulf and it still was at the beginning of the nineteenth century. These imports from the south always had to compete with imports via Turkey and later also via Russia.[410] By the 1820s, if not earlier, European woolens were no longer imported via Bushehr, although Cashmere shawls continued to be imported. Most European cloth and woolens were imported via Russia (Tiflis), and as of 1831 via Turkey (Trabson). In 1834, Brant, the British consul estimated the annual consumption of woolens in Persia at 50,000 yards. Printed brightly colored shalloons were widely used, but camlets were preferred. Thin cloth or *shalli* was less used.[411] The import of woolen goods via Bushehr was determined by two main factors. One, the competition of imports via northern Persia (where the major markets were), as is clear when in the late 1890s broadcloth and woolens were imported via the Trabson-Tabriz route to avoid higher tariffs in the Persian Gulf.[412] The other factor was the severity of the winter. When a winter upcountry was not very cold this translated into less demand for woolen goods, because "the people found little need for warm clothing."[413] Imports rarely exceeded one percent of total imports, indicating that it was an article for the monied class.

---

410. Floor 2000, pp. 156-59; Amin 1967, pp. 117-27; Milburn 1813, vol. 1, pp. 122, 129.
411. NA/FO 78/241, f. 235 b-236.
412. *DCR* 2291, Tabreez (1898-99), p. 6.
413. Administration Report 1896-97, p. 6. On the subject of woolen goods in Persia in general, see Floor 2009 a, pp. 92-99.

2.20: Value of import of woolen goods through Bushehr compared to total value (1873-1923)

Units: Percentage of woolen goods compared to total imports. Value: Rupee to 1902, £ from 1903

Year	Woolen goods	Total	%	Year	Woolen goods	Total	%
1873	52,000	46,02,925	1	1898	2,18,020	1,34,95,390	2
1874	21,000	35,97,700	<1	1899	40,195	1,37,47,920	<1
1875	1,20,050	51,58,823	2	1900	3,35,503	1,98,45,947	2
1876	1,41,400	45,96,999	3	1901	2,34,900	2,44,72,172	1
1877	76,000	83,67,115	1	1902	1,14,850	1,65,09,101	<1
1878	84,000	73,95,560	1	1903	26,740	870,803	3
1879	67,500	1,87,76,900	<1	1904	16,322	889,825	2
1880	4,75,000	1,68,66,050	3	1905	19,292	761,932	3
1881	1,62,500	70,33,800	2	1906	27,498	863,842	3
1882	1,31,200	1,01,88,980	1	1907	26,808	1,052,043	3
1883	2,14,700	1,37,39,200	2	1908	14,225	793,465	2
1884	2,35,000	1,00,97,500	2	1909	10,726	717,091	1
1885	2,78,570	99,62,170	3	1910	13,677	675,614	2
1886	4,10,670	82,73,230	5	1911	11,027	932,531	1
1887	2,78,120	87,15,680	4	1912	15,873	951,720	2
1888	2,61,120	81,35,360	3	1913	8,066	825,767	1
1889	2,58,270	1,16,03,570	2	1914	8,634	669,339	1
1890	5,11,410	1,65,48,710	3	1915	4,161	777,317	<1
1891	2,54,010	1,72,80,870	1	1916	32,276	1,299,562	2
1892	77,310	1,64,58,850	<1	1917	81,518	2,439,179	3
1893	4,13,450	1,56,97,950	3	1918	95,948	2,946,450	3
1894	4,23,150	1,83,51,110	2	1919	57,661	2,723,357	2
1895	2,84,620	1,83,04,490	15	1920	113,785	2,462,797	5
1896	1,49,644	1,34,01080	1	1921	16,707	1,526,594	1
1897	1,82,730	1,83,25,270	1	1922	1,320	1,382,961	<1
				1923	2,634	2,011,772	<1

Source: Administration Report 1873-1905; Trade Report 1905-1923.
All figures have been rounded up or down.

Exports

During the first half of the nineteenth century, exports mainly consisted of dried fruits, dates, raw silk, and horses. In particular, raw silk export, but also that of horses diminished much in importance after the 1860s, while the export of dried fruit and dates fluctuated as a function of market conditions. Grain was exported in good years, although in financial terms of total exports it was insignificant except for a few years (e.g. 1870, 1879). After 1863, the export of cotton and woolen goods acquired some importance, in particular after 1873 when the demand for Persian carpets grew substantially. Until the 1860s, specie was the main export item, when it decreased in importance. There were two other new export products that acquired an important share in total exports. The first was opium, which dominated Bushehri exports, even when its share started to decline in the twentieth century. The other new export product was gums, which grew in importance after 1900.[414]

SPECIE

Persia always had been a major exporter of specie to India, and goods only played a minor role. As in previous centuries Persian Gulf trade had a deficit on the current account and paid for imports with merchandise and above all with specie. In the second half of the eighteenth century this was as high as 80 to 90%.[415] The latter consisted of a great variety of metals, but in general consisted of "Persian and Turkish coins, Venetian sequins, German crowns, gold and silver bars."[416] However, in the early years of the nineteenth century, copper continued to be part of the bullion export just as it had been in the eighteenth century. In 1816, old copper, which was collected in the interior in the form of domestic utensils was still sent to Bengal.[417] Estimates vary as to the relative share of specie in export, but all sources agree that it was more than 50% of total exports. In 1802, according to Waring, as much as 87.5% of exports consisted of specie.[418] Milburn stated that in 1811 this figure was 80% of total exports.[419] In 1816, Buckingham reported that "The exports equal do not equal one-third of the imports so the residue is made up in money," i.e. about 70%.[420] This figure tallies with British data produced by William Bruce, the Bushehr Resident. He reported that during 1816-23 the annual average export of specie was about 83% of total exports, whereas this figure was about 66% during 1829-33. There are no similar data available for the period after 1833 until the 1850s.[421] During the 1850s and 1860s gold and silver still represented about 40% of exports to India, although the yearly amounts fluctuated widely. For example, in 1856 it was 56%, while in 1865 only 15%, but it was back to 51% in 1869.[422] In the remainder of the period under study, the role of specie was much reduced, because of the raw cotton exports in the early 1860s. When these declined, the deficit was made up in particular, by increased export of opium and to a lesser extent by other commodities such as carpets. As is clear from Table 2.21, during 1884-1923 the share of specie compared to total exports varied, but usually was below

414. Hollingberry 1976, 15; Waring 1973, p. 8; Milburn 1813, vol. 1, p. 122-3; Buckingham 1971, p. 353; Brugsch 1865, vol. 2, p. 244; Amanat 1983, pp. 101-03; 112-13; O'Connor 1884/85, p.815; Issawi 1971, p. 83

415. On this issue, see Matthee, Floor and Clawson 2013, pp. 55-98, 175, 237-43; Amin 1967, p. 130, n. 2; Grummon 1985, p. 191; Kinneir 1971, p. 70; AP 1831-32 XB, pp. 632-36.

416. Milburn 1813, vol. 1, p. 130; Buckingham 1971, p. 353; Hollingberry 1976, 15; Kempthorne 1835, p. 283.

417. Buckingham 1971, p. 353. For the situation in the eighteenth century, see Matthee, Floor, Clawson 2013, chapter 5.

418. Waring 1973, p. 8, n.

419. Milburn 1813, vol. 1, p. 130.

420. Buckingham 1971, p. 353.

421. Grummon 1985, p. 192. For the period 1821-27 it was estimated that gold and silver only represented 52% of the trade with India. AP 1831-32 XB pp. 632-36.

422. AP 1860 lxv; 1861 lxi; 1862 lvii; 1863 lxix; 1864 lx; 1866 lxxiii; 1867 lxxii; 1868-69 lxii (not paginated).

10% toward the end of the century. The available information after 1923 indicates that although specie was still exported it remained a minor share of total exports.

2.21: Value of export of specie through Bushehr compared to total value (1873-1923)

Units: Percentage of specie compared to the total. Rupees until 1902, £ from 1903

Year	Specie value	Total value	%	Year	Specie value	Total value	%
1873	10,53,396	39,20,729	27	1898	3,06,860	68,27,550	4
1874	4,46,000	30,91,775	14	1899	4,67,220	79,40,220	6
1875	2,89,500	18,62,230	15	1900	11,12,885	1,06,55,066	10
1876	19,30,000	60,04,806	30	1901	4,67,220	86,04,732	5
1877	7,30,000	77,35,640	9	1902	1,99,542	52,23,025	4
1878	10,80,000	1,37,41,300	8	1903	17,922	366,666	5
1879	16,50,000	80,94,900	20	1904	31,436	454,981	6
1880	13,50,500	1,00,17,850	13	1905	60,572	469,941	13
1881	2,65,000	79,83,800	3	1906	45,542	598,421	7
1882	20,62,500	65,66,220	31	1907	24,042	497,990	5
1883	8,82,000	73,72,300	12	1908	31,809	432,596	7
1884	5,64,720	67,34,570	8	1909	4,118	400,892	1
1885	3,88,250	74,45,170	5	1910	25,210	348,950	7
1886	5,98,860	71,89,990	8	1911	8,941	669,020	7
1887	4,29,860	62,49,550	7	1912	20,625	637,091	3
1888	3,63,320	59,64,680	6	1913	17,732	601,765	3
1889	5,06,470	81,51,620	6	1914	79,337	719,171	11
1890	9,55,200	95,49,670	10	1915	49,458	583,056	8
1891	7,01,200	93,51,690	7	1916	103,655	443,434	23
1892	9,44,860	1,00,93,910	9	1917	51,676	820,951	6
1893	8,18,240	84,81,940	10	1918	2,929	395,150	<1
1894	12,54,850	1,01,13,050	12	1919	20,546	917,655	2
1895	4,49,160	95,18,880	5	1920	-	898,571	
1896	7,72,327	74,85,289	10	1921	-	680,097	
1897	5,80,732	62,80,526	9	1922	-	1,079,780	
				1923	-	2,057,078	

Source: Administration Report 1873-1905; Trade Report 1905-1923.
All figures have been rounded up or down.

HORSES

The export of horses (and to a lesser extent of mules) from the Persian Gulf, which played such an important role during the sixteenth century, hardly played a role until 1814. From that time, this export took off significantly to satisfy the British Indian army demand. In 1814, Bruce reported that Persia might supply some 2,000 horses per year.

Although no quantitative data are available it would seem that thereafter the export of horses increased, be it that there were ups and downs.[423] In 1821, Fraser reported that "at this time the place has been drained of its best [horses] by purchases for mounting our cavalry in India."[424] In 1837, the British Resident reported that during the last years some 400 horses/year were exported, and a large number were exported from Basra, Baghdad and Mohammerah.[425] By 1840, in addition to specie, horses were said to be most important Persian export to India.[426] In 1848, horses accounted for 48% of total exports (almost 5,550 horses), but by 1864 only some 232 horses were still exported with a value of £1,630. In 1851, Binning opined that "the value of horses imported annually from the Persian Gulf to Bombay has been reckoned at not less than 40,000£."[427] After 1880, the export of horses from Bushehr declined and was usually lower than one percent or of total exports.[428] This did not necessarily mean that in some years their number were not high, such as in 1885 when 605 horses were exported as compared to 177 in 1889 and only 10 in 1897.[429] This last low number was due to plague and famine in India and therefore, exceptional. In 1892, Weeks observed that "As the exportation of Persian and Arab horses is the principal business of the Gulf ports, the decks of the steamers are like floating stables."[430] Horses continued to be exported from Bushehr in numbers ranging from 200 to 400 well into the twentieth century, but by then in ever declining numbers, to low two-digit and finally to single-digit numbers (see Table 2.22).

The horse trade was in the hands of Persian merchants, who mostly purchased them upcountry and gathered them at Shiraz. From there they were sent to Bushehr for export, which sometimes led to problems about the level of duty to be paid. It was the rule that when horses were bought and left the gate of Shiraz that the customs officials demanded a fixed sum per horse. However, horses bought in Dashtestan and places depending on Bushehr that did not pass through Shiraz, paid not even one dinar to Shiraz.[431] According the British Resident, writing in 1837, some 20 years ago the export duty was one Persian rupee per horse, which later was increased to 10 *sahib qrans*, and thereafter to 15 *qrans*, which rate still applied at that time.[432]

However, in March 1837, Fereydun Mirza Farmanfarma, the governor-general of Fars issued orders to Sheikh Naser of Bushehr that henceforth no horses were allowed to be exported to India. Captain Hennell, the British Resident who received this news on 31 May 1837, was greatly surprised, because the ban not only applied to Persians but also to British subjects and thus also to British gentlemen "returning to India, or those traveling from Europe through Persia cannot take their horses with them. Such interference with private property is contrary to all customs and rules that when you present it to the shah

423. Grummon 1985, p. 196.

424. Fraser 1984, p. 80.

425. FO 248/85, Hennell to McNeill, 01/06/1837.

426. Grummon 1985, p. 197.

427. Binning 1857, vol. 2, pp. 256-57.

428. In 1860, a member of the Prussian ambassador still mentioned horses among Bushehr's exports horses. Brugsch 1865, vol. 2, p. 244.

429. Administration Report 1897-98, p. 20.

430. Weeks 1896, p. 129. In that year 487 horses were exported from Bushehr. Administration Report 1892-93, p. 28.

431. NA, FO 248/263, Petition of merchants of Bushire to the P.M. n.d. (September 1844).

432. NA, FO 248/85, Hennell to McNeill, 14/10/1837.

he will either rescind the prince's order or adjust it so that members of the Residency or British officers leaving Persia are excluded."[433] The British Minister in Tehran submitted a request to the shah, who gave a decree granting the freedom to British gentlemen to export horses and that no taxes be collected on their horses and baggage.[434]

Fereydun Mirza applied the *farman* as follows. He informed the governor of Bushehr and Hennell that the export of horses to India was allowed, but whoever wanted to do so from Shiraz had to pay 2 two *tumans* per horse export duty. Horses for export bearing the king's brand or those belonging to Hoseyn `Ali Mirza, the previous and rebel Farmanfarma, had to be seized and brought to the authorities. `Ali Akbar Khan, his *ishik-aghasi bashi* had farmed the collection of the duties of horse export and appointed Haji Musa Shirazi as his agent. Therefore, horse dealers when shipping horses needed to have a document from `Ali Akbar Khan.[435] Captain Hennell, the British Resident assessed the impact of the new regulations. He noted that the increased new rate of 2 *tumans* only applied to horses coming from Shiraz and north of it. The duty levied on horses bought in the lowlands and shipped from Bushehr was 1 *tuman*. Everybody paid the same tax, the property of British officers excepted. The effect of the princely order (*raqam*) was that the duty was increased by 5 *sahib qrans* on horses from the area north of Shiraz and 20 *qrans* on those from the low lands. Because most horses bought for the Indian market had already been shipped the immediate impact on British interests was limited to some 100 horses. Undoubtedly, in the future, he commented, schemes would be devised to avoid paying the duty. However, what worried Hennell more than just the increase in the export duty on horses was that the innovation indicated a willingness to interfere with established custom and that implied that other commodities might be interfered with as well, which might harm trade with India.[436]

In late September 1840, the horse dealers in Shiraz were told to pay 10 *tumans* for each horse before they were allowed to leave. This amounted to a substantial sum, because there were 1,200 horses in Shiraz at that time.[437] The British feared that this delay would result in losses and that this experience would deter merchants from investing in the future export of horses. The more so, since the horse dealers, who paid heavily for the permission to export horses, were detained in Shiraz at that time.[438] One week later the horse dealers were allowed to leave with their horses to Bushehr, but not before they had paid an additional 6 Mohammad Shah rupees or 67.5 in total. The British Residency believed that the treatment of horse dealers "is bound to have negative effect on trade given that this affects Persia's two most important exports, specie and horses."[439]

---

433. NA, FO 248/85, Decree Fath Ali Shah to Hoseyn Ali Mirza Farmanfarma; Idem, Sheikh Nasr to Hennell, 31/05/1837; Idem, Hennell to McNeill, 01/06/1837.

434. NA, FO 248/85, Decree Fath Ali Shah to Hoseyn Ali Mirza Farmanfarma; Idem, Persian text of Fath Ali Shah's decree.

435. NA, FO 248/85, *Raqam* Fereydun Mirza, Governor-general of Fars - Rabi` II or July 1837; Idem, *Ta`liqa* Mirza Ahmad Khan, his vizier.

436. NA, FO 248/85, Hennell to McNeill, 14/10/1837.

437. NA, FO 248/99, News writer's report, 03/10/1840. Despite the political conflict between Persia and Great Britain, or perhaps because of it, in September 1840 the heavy tax on horse export was withdrawn. NA, FO 248/99, Residency/Khark to Reid/Bombay, 11/09/1840.

438. NA, FO 248/99, T. MackKenzie acting ass. resident/Khark to Reid/Bombay, 07/10/1840.

439. NA, FO 248/99, T. MackKenzie acting ass. resident /Khark to Sheil 17/10/1840 (horses finally allowed to leave, but only after payment of an additional 8.5 Mohammad Shah rupees per horse or a total of 67.5). Idem, Residency/Karrak to Reed/Bombay 23/10/1840.

However, all the feared negative consequences did not materialize. Since 1840, during the horse export season, a man from the collector of horse duties came down from Shiraz to Bushehr to count the horses. If there were more horses than in the document that showed how many had left Shiraz, and thus without paying duty there, then he demanded that the Shiraz duty be paid on those horses, i.e. horses from Dashtestan and elsewhere had to pay this fixed Shiraz fee, and he insisted very much on this. The horse dealers therefore, petitioned the prime minister "to order to ban this innovation and that the old rule be re-established."[440] To support the horse dealers' petition they organized the issuance of a testimony (*esteshhad-nameh*) from leading merchants of Bushehr, who stated that "it has never been the rule to demand the Shiraz tax from merchants, Persian and British, exporting horses," except once when Farhad Mirza was acting governor. At that time a British merchant bought horses, paid Bushehr customs, boarded them and left. The prince demanded payment of Shiraz duty of the ship's agent, but when he came to Bushehr it was explained to him that this was an innovation and he ordered it to be cancelled.[441]

There was another problem that was raised on 19 September 1844. Sheikh `Abdollah, the acting governor of Bushehr, sent Hennell a note informing him that he had been instructed by the governor-general of Fars to increase the duty under the title of the Shiraz Customs on the mules bought by a British merchant, Mr. Lacouforque and embarked on his vessel. Hennell protested against this, because the merchant was a British subject and the mules were shipped in a British flagged ship and had been shipped to a British port. He further pointed out that since the establishment of the Residency at Bushehr never more than one old *tuman* per horse or mule was asked from a British subject when exported from Bushehr. Mr. Lacouforque paid this on his 104 mules before embarking them. Article 3 of the commercial treaty of Torkomanchay (1828), stipulates that no more than 5% may be collected from a Russian. Article 1 of the Treaty of Commerce of October 1841 states that this rule also applies to British subjects. The mules were not bought by the Armenian merchant Mr. Malcolm, who acted only as interpreter, but by the owner of the mules Mr. Lacouforque. Mr. Malcolm only acted as interpreter as the owner did not know Persian. Given these facts Hennell assumed that the governor would give orders to apply the old rate.[442] The vizier of the governor-general of Fars replied that if Mr. Malcolm had an order from the Prime Minister or the governor-general then no duty would be levied, if he did not have such a document then he had to pay the new rate.[443] In 1847, more duties were collected from the horse dealers than customary. Because the customs house master did not give a voucher for any monies paid on account of duties, the British Resident persuaded the merchants of Bushehr and some revenue officers to sign an *esteshhad-nameh* to that effect to be presented to the governor-general during his expected visit to Bushehr.[444]

In August 1853, Sheikh Hoseyn, acting governor of Bushehr, tried to impose an extra tax on the export of horses. Capt. Kemball, the British Resident asked W.J. Thomson, the

---

440. NA, FO 248/263, Petition of merchants of Bushire to the P.M. n.d. (September 1844). For the text see Appendix XIII. 3

441. NA, FO 248/263, English and Persian text of the *eshteshhad-nameh* concerning the horse and mule tax, September 1844. For the text, see Appendix XIII. 4

442. NA, FO 248/263, Hennell to Amir, 19/09/1844.

443. NA, FO 248/263, Mirza Hedayat, vizier of the Saheb Ekhtiyar to Sheikh Hoseyn (October 1844).

444. NA, FO 248/129, Hennell to Sheil, 15/01/1847.

British charge d'affaires to obtain exemption of this duty, because "our naval squadron guarantees the peace in Gulf and ports justifies British vessels to be exempted from it."[445] This request did not result in the requested exemption. In 1861, a new problem arose with the export duty on horses. Until then, Persian merchandise and animals came under the same category for export duty at Bushehr and 5% was paid on the prime cost of the latter, either certified to, or sworn to by oath. Since his arrival, Mirza Sayyed Khalil, the *kargozar*, wanted to change the procedure, although he admitted that he could not introduce new customs dues. However, he tried to change the custom of appraising horses shipped by appointing a man selected by him. Captain Jones, the British Resident, protested against this as an innovation and one shipment by Ebrahim Khan Qandahari was done in a manner that he protested against. Then Jones was told that British subjects and dependents had to pay the same amount as Persian subjects for the sealing of the appraisal document, i.e. 72.5 Mohammad Shahi *qrans* per animal. Jones protested against this, as being contrary to treaty rights and for some time his wish was respected. However, in early April 1861, the Resident was informed that henceforth 90 *qrans* per horse would be levied. Moreover, he was held responsible for the payment of the unadjusted balance. The problem with this was that Jones did not know what the traditional rate was on the *kargozar*'s ever rising scale. Moreover, his letter was so vague that Jones did not understand what it meant.[446] It seems that this was the last major problem with the export of horses; at least none are reported in the following decades.

2.22: Value of export of horses through Bushehr compared to total value (1873-1923)

Units: Percentage of horses compared to the total. Value: Rupee to 1902, £ from 1903

Year	Horses	Total	%	Year	Horses	Total	%
1873	1,35,00	39,20,729	<1	1898	11,700	68,27,550	<1
1874	92,000	30,91,775	3	1899	61,290	79,40,220	<1
1875	75,000	18,62,230	4	1900	25,280	1,06,55,066	<1
1876	1,21,600	60,04,806	2	1901	25,500	86,04,732	<1
1877	64,800	77,35,640	<1	1902	6,300	52,23,025	<1
1878	6,11,000	1,37,41,300	4	1903	4,333	366,666	<
1879	79,250	80,94,900	1	1904	8,645	454,981	2
1880	2,50,000	1,00,17,850	2	1905	6,560	469,941	1
1881	16,000	79,83,800	<1	1906	4,120	598,421	<1
1882	60,000	65,66,220	1	1907	2,332	497,990	<1
1883	78,050	73,72,300	1	1908	1,117	432,596	<1
1884	54,150	67,34,570	<1	1909	2,489	400,892	<1
1885	96,400	74,45,170	1	1910	4,279	348,950	1
1886	58,900	71,89,990	<1	1911	1,561	669,020	<1
1887	54,900	62,49,550	<1	1912	319	637,091	<1
1888	60,300	59,64,680	1	1913	265	601,765	<1

445. NA, FO 248/180, Capt. Kemball, Resident to W.J. Thomson, charge d'affaires 15/08/ 1853.
446. NA, FO 248/198, Jones to Alison, 05/04/1861; Idem, Jones to Alison, 19/07/1861.

Year	Horses	Total	%	Year	Horses	Total	%
1889	26,550	81,51,620	<1	1914	55	719,171	<1
1890	54,100	95,49,670	<1	1915	305	583,056	<1
1891	51,950	93,51,690	<1	1916	195	443,434	<1
1892	73,050	1,00,93,910	<1	1917	420	820,951	<1
1893	72,000	84,81,940	<1	1918	300	395,150	<1
1894	70,800	1,01,13,050	<1	1919	400	917,655	<1
1895	60,300	95,18,880	<1	1920	35	898,571	<1
1896	44,370	74,85,289	<1	1921	-	680,097	<1
1897	4,800	62,80,526	<1	1922	17	1,079,780	<1
				1923	-	2,057,078	<1

Source: Administration Report 1873-1905; Trade Report 1905-1923.
All figures have been rounded up or down.

Raw Cotton

Cotton only became a major Persian export commodity due to the 'cotton famine' created by the US civil war. Because American cotton exports dropped precipitously while prices sky-rocketed, Europe looked for alternative sources of supply, which led to increased production of cotton in Egypt, Turkey and Syria, as well as in Persia. Before that time, the role of Persian cotton as an export commodity had been insignificant, but as of 1863 cotton played an increasingly important role in Persia's exports. Before 1860 there had been no export of cotton via the Gulf, but by 1860-61, there was some export of cotton with a value of 19,200 rupees. Because of the 700 percent rise in the price of cotton in 1863, many landowners decided to grow cotton. "The cotton trade at Bushire has, as elsewhere, received a considerable impetus by the American Civil War. 60,000 Tabriz maunds (7¾ lbs. each) have been shipped, and it is said during the coming season ten times that quantity may be thrown on the market. Prices rose so high, that it would have paid to bring Cotton from Tabreez, some 12 or 13 hundred miles, on mules, and export it at Bushire."[447] In Fars province, cotton cultivation was rapidly expanded, so that the export via Bushehr in 1862-63 of 660,000 kg (1.6 million rupees) increased to 3.3 million kg (6.7 million rupees) in 1864-65 (6.7 million rupees), or 500 percent higher.[448] After the end of the US civil war cotton exports via Bushehr dropped and from 1866 cotton was no longer exported from Isfahan to India for some time.[449]

Exports via the Persian Gulf would remain insignificant throughout the remainder of the Qajar period. After the end of the US Civil War, cotton exports declined significantly due to transit difficulties and high duties, which rendered cotton exports less profitable.[450] In 1873, cotton with a value of Rs. 188,300 was only exported. In 1879, cotton was exported again in considerable quantity and there was an increase in value,

---

447. Pelly 1865 a, p. 50.

448. *AP* 72 (1866), p. 211; Idem, *AP* 70 (1866), p. 476; Idem, Thomson *AP* 61 (1864, Persia), p. 2; Idem, Dickson *AP* 72 (1866, Persia), pp. 207, 211.

449. Issawi 1971, p. 245, notes 5-6.

450. Administration Report 1873-74, p. 12.

a total of Rs. 624,000. However, the next year was disappointing due to both climatic (drought, death among pack animals) and political factors (purchase of mules by India and requisitioning by the Persian government).[451] This trend persisted and exports in 1882 were only Rs. 297,400 and in 1883 only Rs. 395,000.[452] One of the reasons for the relative slow development of the market were the high transportation cost which made cotton too expensive for transport to Europe; also its fiber was relatively short. In addition, the volume of the Indian cotton crop and prices in Europe determined the demand in India for Persian cotton. If these were respectively low and high Indian factory owners showed little interest to buy expensive low-quality Persian cotton. Because US cotton exports to Europe increased significantly in the 1880s and low prices prevailed, there was a diminishing demand for Persian cotton.[453]

In the 1880s, yearly exports to India oscillated between 15,000 and 20,000 bales each of 3.5 cwt, which usually represented around 12 percent of total exports via Bushehr.[454] Persian cotton, which once had seemed so promising, never reached these levels again. The export of cotton via Bushehr declined both in relative and financial terms. The highest amount was in 1880 (36 percent of total exports), but most of the time it was of marginal importance not even exceeding single digit figures. The Bombay mills only bought when Indian cotton was insufficient or the price too high. "When there are large crops in India and prices in the European markets are comparatively low, Bombay mill owners have little inducement to buy cotton from Persia."[455] What is further worthy of note was the growing importance of Bandar Abbas as port for the export for cotton. As of 1887, it started to compete with Bushehr and in 1895 for the first time exported more cotton than Bushehr. An additional point of interest is the export of small quantities of cotton from Mohammerah, starting in 1890, due to the opening up of the Karun River to commercial navigation. Finally, Lengeh started to export occasionally minor quantities of cotton.[456]

By 1894, the Russian market had become so attractive that cotton, which previously had been exported to Bombay, via Bushehr, was now exported to Russia.[457] In 1898 it was noted that there was a further decline of cotton export via Bushehr due to greater domestic consumption, partial failure of the crops, and export to Russia where better prices were obtained.[458] Thereafter, the export of cotton via Bushehr was and remained a minor affair.

---

451. *AP* 74 (1876); Idem, *AP* 75 (1880), pp. 1745, 1758; Idem, *AP* 70 (1872), p. 113; Schneider 1990, p. 171. Tahvildar 1342, p. 56, stated that, for some years, peasants had benefited from the export of cotton, referring to the cotton famine period, but that since then the situation had changed.

452. *AP* 74 (1883), pp. 2003, 2021; Idem, *AP* 77 (1884-85), p. 1880.

453. *AP* 78 (1884-85), p. 1145; Idem, *AP* 83 (1892), p. 3; O'Connor 1884/85, p. 815.

454. Curzon 1892, vol. 2, p. 496; Schneider 1990, pp. 183-84.

455. O'Connor 1884/85, p. 815.

456. Floor 2003 a, p. 423.

457. *AP* 99 (1895), p. 5; also DCR 1376 (1894, Report of a Journey), p. 18. See also DCR 1662, Ispahan 1897-99, p. 67.

458. DCR 2346, Persian Gulf 1899, p. 7.

2.23: Value of export of raw cotton through Bushehr compared to total value (1873-1923)

Units: Percentage of raw cotton compared to the total. Vale: Rupee to 1902, £ from 1903

Year	Raw cotton value	Total value	%	Year	Raw cotton value	Total value	%
1873	1,85,600	39,20,729	5	1898	7,650	68,27,550	<1
1874	82,750	30,91,775	2	1899	54,575	79,40,220	<1
1875	1,59,600	18,62,230	9	1900	3,51,800	1,06,55,066	3
1876	30,518	60,04,806	<1	1901	53,970	86,04,732	<1
1877	13,83,370	77,35,640	18	1902	1,01,622	52,23,025	2
1878	17,00,000	1,37,41,300	12	1903	4,216	366,666	1
1879	6,20,000	80,94,900	8	1904	11,704	454,981	2
1880	9,05,000	1,00,17,850	9	1905	11,741	469,941	2
1881	2,83,000	79,83,800	3	1906	13,872	598,421	2
1882	2,92,500	65,66,220	4	1907	7,936	497,990	2
1883	3,35,000	73,72,300	4	1908	4,122	432,596	<1
1884	7,87,500	67,34,570	12	1909	8,858	400,892	2
1885	9,32,800	74,45,170	12	1910	5,430	348,950	1
1886	2,26,250	71,89,990	3	1911	7,807	669,020	1
1887	10,09,200	62,49,550	16	1912	4,034	637,091	<1
1888	6,13,340	59,64,680	10	1913	2,219	601,765	<1
1889	11,60,750	81,51,620	14	1914	228	719,171	<1
1890	15,99,720	95,49,670	17	1915	308	583,056	<1
1891	7,76,870	93,51,690	8	1916	236	443,434	<1
1892	6,97,000	1,00,93,910	7	1917	4,153	820,951	<1
1893	3,14,190	84,81,940	4	1918	18,018	395,150	5
1894	1,74,610	1,01,13,050	1	1919	25,656	917,655	3
1895	22,070	95,18,880	<1	1920	12,751	898,571	1
1896	68,115	74,85,289	<1	1921	773	680,097	<1
1897	17,604	62,80,526	<1	1922	8,195	1,079,780	<1
				1923	36,998	2,057,078	2

Source: Administration Report 1873-1905; Trade Report 1905-1923.
All figures have been rounded up or down.

Fruit

Under this heading various kinds of dried fruit are included. The most important were sweet almonds and pistachios, which were exported to Bombay and Europe. The volume of export fluctuated due to a variety of factors such as increased almond demand in Russia, high transport cost, rain or other natural causes that resulted in a poor almond harvest, increased local demand, bumper almonds crops in Europe, and decreased export demand. The other important fruits included under this heading were raisins and dates.[459] Nevertheless, the share in total exports of dried fruit, usually 1-3%, steadily increased in the twentieth century and sometimes even reached double digit numbers in percents of total export. The following varieties of dates were exported: "hallawees, long golden; khadrawees, short and dark; and sayers, long chestnut colored. The date picking season was from mid-August until mid-November and dates were shipped in three waves, referred to as first (end August), second (end September) and third tide (end of October). Dates were packed at make-shift packing stations called *chardagh (chahar taq)*, and put in boxes containing either 50-56 lbs. or 64-70 lbs. net weight of pressed-down dates. Dates were also packed in fancy cardboard boxes of which 50-60 fit in one wooden box. To withstand rough handling these boxes were covered with gunny.[460]

2.24: Value of export of fruit and vegetables through Bushehr compared to total value (1873-1923)

Units: Percentage of fruit & vegetables compared to the total. Value: Rupee to 1902, £ from 1903

Year	Fruits + veg.	Total value	%	Year	Fruits + veg.	Total value	%
1873	99,299	39,20,729	2	1898	2,58,040	68,27,550	4
1874	52,470	30,91,775	2	1899	2,83,030	79,40,220	4
1875	32,730	18,62,230	2	1900	7,38,614	1,06,55,066	7
1876	1,79,700	60,04,806	3	1901	3,60,630	86,04,732	4
1877	1,25,620	77,35,640	2	1902	3,98,260	52,23,025	7
1878	36,800	1,37,41,300	<1	1903	16,546	366,666	4
1879	22,800	80,94,900	<1	1904	32,741	454,981	7
1880	1,30,700	1,00,17,850	1	1905	53,276	469,941	11
1881	71,050	79,83,800	<1	1906	55,415	598,421	9
1882	76,200	65,66,220	1	1907	32,216	497,990	6
1883	1,86,150	73,72,300	2	1908	22,681	432,596	5
1884	1,24,550	67,34,570	2	1909	45,702	400,892	11
1885	1,52,700	74,45,170	2	1910	36,241	348,950	10
1886	1,38,340	71,89,990	2	1911	54,046	669,020	8
1887	1,81,490	62,49,550	3	1912	47,828	637,091	7
1888	1,79,000	59,64,680	3	1913	51,106	601,765	8
1889	2,39,300	81,51,620	3	1914	31,556	719,171	4
1890	2,48,690	95,49,670	2	1915	17,919	583,056	3
1891	4,45,770	93,51,690	5	1916	12,697	443,434	3
1892	4,28,120	1,00,93,910	4	1917	24,361	820,951	3
1893	1,27,770	84,81,940	1	1918	27,783	395,150	7
1894	2,05,250	1,01,13,050	2	1919	51,107	917,655	6
1895	3,00,860	95,18,880	3	1920	39,173	898,571	4

459. Administration Report 1878-79, p. 28; Administration Report 1893-94, p. 25; Administration Report 1894-95, p. 24; Administration Report 1895-96, p. 18; Administration Report 1896-97, p. 7.

460. Forester 1929, pp. 9-10.

Year	Fruits + veg.	Total value	%	Year	Fruits + veg.	Total value	%
1896	1,86,793	74,85,289	2	1921	62,666	680,097	9
1897	60,124	62,80,526	1	1922	81,033	1,079,780	7
				1923	69,657	2,057,078	3

Source: Administration Report 1873-1905; Trade Report 1905-1923.
All figures have been rounded up or down.

Opium

Until the 1860s, opium was of marginal economic importance and was mainly produced for local consumption. It was only in the 1830s, when there was increased demand for opium on the world market, that some export of Persian opium took place, but this remained unimportant. The main reason for the sudden change in fortune for Persia was the fact that India, the traditional supplier of opium to China, had reduced opium cultivation in favor of cotton to profit from the cotton famine caused by the US civil war, and later to supply its own growing cotton manufacturing industry. At the same time, Chinese demand for opium grew due to increased exports of tea and silk. As a result, Persian opium export rose 750% between 1858-1870.[461] Apart from growing demand on the world market and the need for an alternative to silk in Khorasan, the increase in opium production was due to supportive measures by the government.

Most of the opium was purchased through middlemen from the cultivators directly. Opium was harvested in May-June and most of it, after processing, was transported to the ports between September and January. The main export ports for Isfahan and Fars opium were Bushehr and Bandar Abbas. Khorasan and Kerman opium was taken to Yazd, which, including its own produce, exported part of the opium via Bushehr and part via Bandar Abbas. Opium export was mainly to China (80%), Great Britain, Turkey and Russia.[462] In 1880, some 65 percent of opium was exported via Bushehr and 35 percent via Bandar Abbas. In particular in the winter, Yazd opium went via Bandar Abbas.[463]

The export of opium decreased significantly in the early twentieth century. Between 1900 and 1908 there was a loss of 80 percent in export earnings, both the result of reduced production and exports, and lower prices in export markets.[464] The decline in export due to loss of markets to Japan and reduced demand in China was partly and temporarily compensated by the drop in output of Anatolian opium. Another factor, which constrained the export of opium, was the change in the customs regime in Persia between 1898 and 1904 that led to a sharp rise in the tariff, from 5 percent *ad valorem* in 1898 to 20 percent *ad valorem* in 1904. Also, smuggling had become more difficult due to the better and more efficiently functioning Customs department.[465] The export of opium had been in decline during the first decade of the twentieth century, in 1911-12 only 106 tons of opium

461. Gilbar 1978, p. 32; Administration Report 1878-79, p. 31; "Of late a considerable trade in opium has developed. Though there are rumors of adulterated goods." Pelly 1865, p. 51.
462. Floor 2003 a, p. 456.
463. Floor 2003 a, pp. 451-52.
464. Gilbar 1978, p. 331.
465. Gleadowe-Newcomen 1905, p. 89.

(value £246,036) was exported via Bushehr, but a considerable improvement compared with 1910-11 when only 37 tons were exported (value £53,732).[466]

More disturbing for opium growers was the fact that Persia had signed the Hague Convention of 1913. As a result, the production, trade and manufacturing of opiates was restricted by a new law (*Nezamnameh-ye Tahdid-e Taryak*), which had been adopted by the *Majles* in 1913. This law led to regulation and supervision of cultivation and of the export of opium in all its stages with the intent to reduce opium consumption in Persia itself.[467] Despite implementation problems, the new opium laws hampered export trade, although there was considerable smuggling. The export of opium nevertheless remained considerable, despite the losses incurred during the first decade of the twentieth century. By 1912, exports were at the level where they had been in 1905 and would firmly remain so in the years thereafter. With the outbreak of WWI exports suffered, because of transport and security problems on the Isfahan-Shiraz-Bushehr trade road.[468] However, in 1917, opium exports did very well, in fact they trebled in value, due to the destruction of the Turkish supply.[469] However, as of 1918 exports, in financial terms, returned to normal annually fluctuating levels.

2.25: Value of export of opium through Bushehr compared to total value (1873-1923)

Units: Percentage of opium compared to the total. Value: Rupee to 1902, £ from 1903

Year	Opium value	Total value	%	Year	Opium value	Total value	%
1873	12,57,520	39,20,729	32	1898	33,68,120	68,27,550	49
1874	14,52,800	30,91,775	47	1899	45,87,000	79,40,220	58
1875	7,90,500	18,62,230	42	1900	51,57,900	1,06,55,066	48
1876	20,57,000	60,04,806	34	1901	45,87,000	86,04,732	53
1877	33,46,000	77,35,640	43	1902	26,28,400	52,23,025	50
1878	51,00,000	1,37,41,300	37	1903	178,032	366,666	48
1879	51,52,200	80,94,900	64	1904	199,136	454,981	44
1880	62,12,000	1,00,17,850	62	1905	124,156	469,941	26
1881	57,45,000	79,83,800	72	1906	157,777	598,421	26
1882	36,55,000	65,66,220	72	1907	238,405	497,990	48
1883	33,68,200	73,72,300	51	1908	196,044	432,596	45
1884	33,06,000	67,34,570	49	1909	117,320	400,892	29
1885	42,53,000	74,45,170	57	1910	53,732	348,950	15
1886	42,43,000	71,89,990	59	1911	246,036	669,020	37
1887	29,39,500	62,49,550	47	1912	293,861	637,091	46
1888	22,00,000	59,64,680	37	1913	295,687	601,765	49
1889	33,86,000	81,51,620	51	1914	454,093	719,171	63
1890	48,05,000	95,49,670	50	1915	347,498	583,056	60

466. Trade Report 1911-1912, p. 15.
467. Trade Report 1912-13, p. 20.
468. Trade Report 1915-16, p. 2.
469. Trade Report 1917-18, p. 1.

Year	Opium value	Total value	%	Year	Opium value	Total value	%
1891	47,22,000	93,51,690	50	1916	236,338	443,434	53
1892	54,17,500	1,00,93,910	54	1917	622,188	820,951	76
1893	33,46,000	84,81,940	39	1918	189,039	395,150	48
1894	45,62,290	1,01,13,050	45	1919	337,340	917,655	37
1895	33,06,200	95,18,880	35	1920	498,405	898,571	55
1896	37,70,479	74,85,289	50	1921	285,389	680,097	42
1897	31,10,520	62,80,526	49	1922	664,340	1,079,780	62
				1923	1,246,433	2,057,078	60

Source: Administration Report 1873-1905; Trade Report 1905-1923.
All figures have been rounded up or down.

After World War I opium export decreased toward the end of the 1920s, which trend was reinforced by the high export duty imposed by the government of Persia. The Opium Monopoly in 1930 was mainly held by the Namazi family (20%), Behbahani (30%) and the Pahlavi Bank (8%), the remainder of the shares was held by smaller private investors.[470] In 1937, because the export tax and increased competition from Anatolian opium hurt Persia's opium exports, the government discontinued the high export duty.[471] This policy was at odds with its domestic policy which aimed to eliminate opium consumption. In 1936, the Finance Department posted an announcement that henceforth it was prohibited to cultivate poppies for the production of opium and raised the banderole tax on opium, making the price 2 rials per *methqal* (4.6 g) in order to make it prohibitive for opium smokers and eaters and so force them to abandon the habit.[472] Opium exports indeed increased in the following years only to decline again in 1940 due to the outbreak of WWII. What was new that the USA became a major market for Persian opium in 1942 representing 25% of exports.

2.26: Export of opium 1930-1940 (in number of cases)

Year	No. cases	Illicit	Year	No. cases	Illicit
1924	4,961	-	1935	2,638	-
1925	6,227	-	1933	830	3,787
1926	7,894	-	1934	1,346	600
1927	6,369	-	1935	2,638	-
1928	4,730	-	1936	1,350	-
1929	6,812	-	1937	1,980	1500
1930	3,374	-	1938	4,755	-
1931	2,456	-	1939	7,356	-

470. Administration Report 1931, p. 12.
471. Administration Report 1933, p. 7; Administration Report 1934, p. 8; Administration Report 1935, p. 10-11; Administration Report 1936, p. 10; Administration Report 1937, p. 8.
472. Administration Report 1936, p. 3.

Year	No. cases	Illicit	Year	No. cases	Illicit
1932	1,350	-	1940	2,712	-
1933	830	3,787	1941	1,816	-
1934	1,346	600	1942	1,170	

Source: Administration Report 1925, p. 9; Administration Report 1926, p. 4; Administration Report 1927, p. 6; Administration Report 1928, p. 9; Administration Report 1929, p. 7; Administration Report 1931, pp. 12-13; Administration Report 1932, p. 9; Administration Report 1933, p. 7; Administration Report 1934, p. 8; Administration Report 1935, pp. 10-11; Administration Report 1936, p. 10; Administration Report 1937, p. 8; Administration Report 1938, p. 8; Administration Report 1939, p. 6; Administration Report 1940, p. 6; Administration Report 1941, p. 12; Administration Report 1942, p. 17.

Raw Silk

Although there are no quantitative data about the export of silks, both woven silks and brocades (from Kashan and Yazd), red silks from Gilan as well as raw silk, were exported via Bushehr.[473] In fact, during the early part of the nineteenth century, raw silk and bullion were the principal returns from Bushehr.[474] As far as raw silk is concerned the bulk of Persia's production was exported via Northern Persia and the same is likely true for woven silks.[475] Silk that once had been one of the main items among the commodities that were exported via Bushehr declined considerably in the 1880s, dropping from 3-4% to 1% and lower, and finally as of 1903 to zero. Initially, this decrease was due to the drop in silk production caused by the silk disease that had broken out in the main silk producing province of Gilan. However, later increased domestic demand and a less attractive market in India resulted in decreasing and finally in zero silk exports (Table 2.27).[476]

2.27: Value of export of raw silk through Bushehr compared to the total value (1873-1923)

Units: Percentage of raw silk compared to the total. Value: Rupee to 1902, £ from 1903

Year	Silk raw value	Total value	%	Year	Silk raw value	Total value	%
1873	1,73,880	39,20,729	4	1898	47,450	68,27,550	<1
1874	1,25,400	30,91,775	4	1899	67,635	79,40,220	<1
1875	89,500	18,62,230	4	1900	61,300	1,06,55,066	<1
1876	2,00,000	60,04,806	3	1901	67,635	86,04,732	<1
1877	1,20,000	77,35,640	1	1902	9,400	52,23,025	<1
1878	1,50,000	1,37,41,300	1	1903	-	366,666	
1879	2,30,000	80,94,900	3	1904	-	454,981	
1880	1,63,000	1,00,17,850	2	1905	-	469,941	
1881	3,28,500	79,83,800	4	1906	-	598,421	
1882	2,76,500	65,66,220	4	1907	-	497,990	

473. Milburn 1813, vol. 1, pp. 122-3; Heude 1819, p. 43; Brugsch vol. 2, p. 244.
474. Kinneir 1971, p. 70; Kempthorne 1835, p. 283; Mignan 1839, vol. 2, p. 138.
475. Floor 2003 a, chapter 17; Idem 2009 a.
476. Administration Report 1894-95, p. 21; Administration Report 1895-96, p. 19. Administration Report 1896-97, p. 7; Administration Report 1897-98, p. 21; Administration Report 1898-99, p. 35; Administration Report 1900-1901, p. 28. For the production of raw silk, see Floor 2003 a, pp. chapter 17.

Year	Silk raw value	Total value	%	Year	Silk raw value	Total value	%
1883	3,45,300	73,72,300	5	1908	-	432,596	
1884	1,42,900	67,34,570	2	1909	-	400,892	
1885	86,870	74,45,170	1	1910	-	348,950	
1886	1,19,560	71,89,990	2	1911	-	669,020	
1887	1,70,200	62,49,550	3	1912	-	637,091	
1888	1,07,010	59,64,680	2	1913	-	601,765	
1889	43,810	81,51,620	<1	1914	-	719,171	
1890	31,150	95,49,670	<1	1915	-	583,056	
1891	1,57,750	93,51,690	2	1916	-	443,434	
1892	91,550	1,00,93,910	1	1917	-	820,951	
1893	4,25,050	84,81,940	5	1918	-	395,150	
1894	82,100	1,01,13,050	<1	1919	-	917,655	
1895	78,600	95,18,880	<1	1920	-	898,571	
1896	96,237	74,85,289	1	1921	-	680,097	
1897	80,000	62,80,526	1	1922	-	1,079,780	
				1923	-	2,057,078	

Source: Administration Report 1873-1905; Trade Report 1905-1923.
All figures have been rounded up or down.

Wool

Around 1805, Jaubert, referring to exports, mentioned wool among the products exported by Persia to India and Turkey. However, Milburn in his list of possible export commodities from the Persian Gulf did not mention wool at all.[477] In 1851, Binning did not mention wool either as an export product to India and neither did Polak, who, in fact, remarked that wool was little and irregularly exploited, partly because of the low market price, partly because of its quality which permitted it to be used only for coarse fabrics.[478] By the early 1860s, some 10,000 Tabriz *man* of wool were exported, partly brought in from other and minor ports. Pelly commented that more could be exported, if there were incentives to do so.[479] It would seem that starting in the 1860s, the export of wool was mainly via Bushehr to India rather than via the Northern or Western trade routes. The wool trade was organized by urban merchant capital, as in previous centuries, through pre-clip sales, cash advances, and barter, and/or a combination of these methods. In 1862 there was 200 tons of wool exported via Bushehr to India with a value of Rs. 150,000. However, the following year only Rs. 30,000 was exported because the "dealers prefer sinking their capital in cotton, as it gives hope of larger profits and speedier sale."[480] Wool

477. Jaubert 1821, p. 253; Dupré 1819, vol. 1, p. 443, vol. 2, pp. 374-75; Milburn 1813, vol. 1, pp. 132-42.

478. Binning 1857, vol. 2, p. 298; Polak 1865, vol. 2, p. 101; Idem 1862, p. 111. The export of wool with a value of 88,390 rupees in 1841 must therefore have been an exception. Schneider 1990, p. 189, table 43.

479. Pelly 1865 a, p. 51.

480. *AP* 61 (1864), p. 194; *AP* 72 (1866), p. 211; Schneider 1990, p. 188. The data in Idem, p. 189, table 43 contradicts the level of the 1862 export given in an earlier British report.

produced in northern Persia rather than being exported to Russia went to the Gulf. "The wool of Khorasan commands a higher price in India than that of India and Sindh. Price is 2 krans per 7 lbs. 3 shahis per 7 lbs. customs. Exported is about 1 million lbs. but more could be imported from Torkoman country."[481] There was hardly any export via Tabriz during the 1860s. In 1872, there was a trial export of wool via Tabriz to Great Britain.[482] This situation did not a change in the 1870s and 1880s either. It would seem that the bulk of the wool that was exported went via Bushehr, and later above all via Bandar Abbas and Mohammerah, to India and Europe, and some via Bandar-e Gaz to Russia.[483] Wool processing in Persia, like that of so many other products, was not done in an efficient manner, while no effort was made to increase its quality. Therefore, most wool was first exported to Basra "where there are facilities for cleaning, sorting, and pressing it. It is not thought high of, then shipped mostly to London."[484]

This trend would soon be reversed, however. In 1891, only 102,000 kg of the total Khorasan clip of 7.37 million kg were exported via the Persian Gulf, whereas 2.17 million kg went to Russia.[485] Less wool was exported via the Persian Gulf, where Bandar Abbas (the conduit for Khorasan wool) and Mohammerah played a more important role than Bushehr. This pattern did not change much despite the sudden increase of export, due to demand from Europe, in 1893-94.[486] Because after 1873, there was a rise in the export of carpets, the export of wool decreased as more of it was used for carpet weaving.[487] It also happened that the export of wool suffered due to mortality among the sheep in the preceding year.[488] The export of wool via Bushehr decreased in importance over time, because of the growing demand in Russia for this commodity. In fact, only from 1888 to 1898, were wool exports 2-3% of total exports. However, Bushehr remained an important port for the export of carpets, although it suffered from competition from export via Basra and Baghdad.[489] The fact that in 1906 two wool presses had been installed at Bushehr to facilitate the development of the wool trade shows the intent to boost wool trade, which nevertheless remained at a level of less than one percent of total exports.[490] Carpet export suffered from the use of aniline instead of natural dyes as well as from the occasional overstocking abroad.[491] However, this was a temporary effect, because exports increased, be it with the normal ups and downs, due to market conditions (see Table 2.26).

---

481. Government of Great Britain, Eastwick 1864, Report on the Trade of Khurasan, p. 266; see also Schneider 1990, p. 189, table 43.
482. *AP* 65 (1873), p. 971.
483. For a summary of the available information concerning this period, see Schneider 1990, pp. 190-92.
484. Administration Report 1891-92, p. 20; Administration Report 1893-94, p. 26.
485. *AP* 83 (1892), p. 7.
486. *AP* 99 (1895), pp. 7, 15, 24; Schneider 1990, p. 195. In that year, wool export via Bushehr was less than one percent of total epxorts.
487. Administration 1873-74, p. 13.
488. Administration Report 1900-1901, p. 29.
489. Administration Report 1891-92, p. 21.
490. DCR 3951 (Bushire 1906-07), p. 18.
491. Administration Report 1901-1902, p. 15.

2.28: Value of export of woolen goods (carpets) through Bushehr compared to the total (1873-1923)

Units: Percentage of woolen goods compared to the total. Value: Rupee to 1902, £ from 1903

Year	Wool goods val.	Total value	%	Year	Wool goods val.	Total value	%
1873	1,24,000	39,20,729	3	1898	5,23,570	68,27,550	8
1874	96,400	30,91,775	<1	1899	4,87,810	79,40,220	6
1875	19,600	18,62,230	<1	1900	8,89,176	1,06,55,066	8
1876	1,46,530	60,04,806	2	1901	4,86,810	86,04,732	6
1877	33,700	77,35,640	<1	1902	2,60,110	52,23,025	5
1878	32,000	1,37,41,300	<1	1903	42,317	366,666	11
1879	27,500	80,94,900	<1	1904	31,431	454,981	7
1880	60,800	1,00,17,850	<1	1905	70,450	469,941	15
1881	55,000	79,83,800	<1	1906	63,414	598,421	11
1882	74,700	65,66,220	<1	1907	36,826	497,990	7
1883	3,93,000	73,72,300	5	1908	39,070	432,596	9
1884	1,96,800	67,34,570	3	1909	63,948	400,892	16
1885	1,39,800	74,45,170	2	1910	55,329	348,950	16
1886	4,19,700	71,89,990	6	1911	62,032	669,020	9
1887	2,00,400	62,49,550	3	1912	78,949	637,091	12
1888	2,20,800	59,64,680	4	1913	64,588	601,765	11
1889	3,08,750	81,51,620	4	1914	27,024	719,171	4
1890	1,43,120	95,49,670	1	1915	51,151	583,056	9
1891	1,59,150	93,51,690	2	1916	18,093	443,434	4
1892	2,83,370	1,00,93,910	3	1917	12,244	820,951	1
1893	11,87,230	84,81,940	14	1918	24,675	395,150	6
1894	14,18,070	1,01,13,050	14	1919	128,169	917,655	2
1895	19,25,900	95,18,880	15	1920	144,630	898,571	16
1896	4,53,898	74,85,289	6	1921	151,868	680,097	22
1897	3,60,340	62,80,526	6	1922	119,775	1,079,780	11
				1923	160,460	2,057,078	8

Source: Administration Report 1873-1905; Trade Report 1905-1923.
All figures have been rounded up or down.

GRAINS

Writing in 1865, Col. Pelly, the British Resident wrote that "The export of grain had never been of importance in the past, although there had always been some export."[492] However, its export was of local importance and had considerable impact on rural incomes. Moreover, in the nineteenth century there was a growing demand for it, mainly in India and Mauritius. Grain (mainly wheat and barley), of good quality and in considerable quantities, was grown in all the districts bordering the sea (Dashtestan, Tangestan, Delam,

492. Pelly 1865 a, p. 45.

Hayat Da'ud, Shabankareh).[493] Although output was dependent on rainfall and other climatic conditions, in 1910, these districts yielded some 40,000 tons of which 15,000 tons was available for export, although only 2,570 tons were exported via Bushehr. Of the 40,000 tons, the four districts north, south and east of Bushehr produced 22,000 tons. Barley was commonly mixed with wheat by wheat brokers, up to 25%. In the Rudhilleh district due to the flooding of the river, the sown seeds of barley and wheat naturally mixed. In the northern districts clean wheat could be had at a slightly higher price.[494]

2.29: Amount of wheat raised in the coastal districts in 1910 and 1911

Units: Indian maunds

District	Amount grown in 1910	Amount available in 1910	Amount grown in 1911	Amount avail. in 1911
Liravi	1,68,000	84,000	2,17,952	1,68,000
Hayat Da'ud	2,45,000	1,12,000	1,75,924	1,12,000
Rudhilleh	77,000	56,000	2,00,000	84,000
Shabankareh	73,360	56,000	2,00,000	84,000
Angali	30,800	Absorbed	No data	..
Ahmadi+Chahkutah	56,000	By	51,156	28,000
Khushab +Ziyarat	92,400	Bushehr	No data	..
Zira	23,240	8,400	No data	..
Dashestan	No data	..	Do.	..
Dashti	Do.	..	3,30,400	1,96,000
Tangestan	Do.	..	1,73,600	1,45,000
Shibkuh	Do.	..	No data	..

Source: Government of India 1924, p. 105

In 1912/13, wheat production in the four districts north (12,000 tons), south and east (18,000 tons) of Bushehr was down due to poor rainfall, except for Dashti, which produced 10,000 of the 18,000 tons of the eastern districts.[495] The data in Table 2.30 for the period between 1914 and 1921 concerns the four districts environing Bushehr. It shows that 1914 was an average year and the following period of 1915-21 suffered a fall in output due to declining rainfall, which also explains why little or no grain was available for export.

493. Administration Report 1873-74, p. 12; Government of India 1924, p. 107. "The seed was of several kinds: white, yellow, red, kuleh (a large hard grain, not liked for export trade)." Trade Report 1910-11, p. 13.

494. Trade Report 1910-11, p. 13.

495. Trade Report 1912-13, pp. 19-20.

2.30: Amount of wheat raised and available in coastal districts in 1914 and 1915-21

Units: Indian maunds

District	Amount grown in 1914	Amount available in 1914	Amount grown 1915-21	Amount avail. 1914-21
Tangestan	20,000	Nil	14,000*	Nil
Dashti	60,000	4,000	30,000	Nil
Dashtestan	60,000	3,000	20,000	Nil
Chahkutah+Ahmadi	6,000	1,000	3,000	Nil

Source: Government of India 1924, p. 106
* More than 3/4 of that quantity came from Ahram vicinity which has irrigated land independent of rainfall.

Merchants bought the grain from the Khans and shipped it over land to Bushehr as well as via the smaller Persian ports. Later in the century European merchants started to play a major role in this trade, although they were induced to limit their business to Bushehr. In 1878, the BISNC wanted to call on Rig regularly. The Persian government opposed this as it would reduce the revenues of Bushehr. Therefore, in various ways it impeded the development of trade in Rig, and levied, e.g., extra duty at Bushehr on exports from Rig. In June 1878, the governor of Bushehr seized wheat-cleaning machines of Gray, Paul & Co. that had been placed in vessels to be taken to Rig; as a result, one of the machines was broken when taken ashore and 50 *tumans* damages were paid.[496]

One constant of the Persian littoral was the frequency of droughts, followed by a large or small famine (see chapter one). Unfortunately, this negatively impacted on trade due to the large mortality among the people and their animals as well as the related government grain export bans. Such bans were imposed in 1851, 1863, 1866, 1868, 1871, 1874, 1877, 1878, 1883, 1885, 1888, 1889, 1890, 1893, 1894, and 1905. The bans were vigorously applied to foreigners, but with laxity in case of locals.[497] The sudden ban on grain export could have a negative impact on trade. Ships that had declined other cargos, suddenly would find themselves without any. Sometimes they had to buy stone ballast to leave. In 1864, Pelly, the British Resident, commented that "a few years ago 6 to 7 square-rigged vessels came from Mauritius annually in ballast to return with corn. This trade has ceased and now goes to Karachi."[498] Therefore, foreign merchants were very much upset by the subjective, arbitrary and mercurial nature of decision making that played havoc with the planning and finances of grain merchants. This situation was made worse by local politicians and religious leaders taking advantage of these situations for their own political and financial gain by invoking mob rule, thereby increasing the already insecure and unstable situation. Furthermore, they were upset by the different treatment of Persian merchants, who were friendly with the governor and were allowed to export

496. Saldanha 1986, vol. 7/2, p. 166.
497. Saldanha 1986, vol. 7/2, pp. 1, 166-69; Lorimer 1915, vol. 1, pp. 2092-95; NA, FO 248/157, J.A. Malcolm to Kemball 06/11/1854; Idem, Mirza Hasan Ali Khan, governor Bushehr to Mirza Ahmad, *monshi* of the Residency, 12/09/1851 received.
498. Pelly 1865 a, p. 50.

grain during the embargo. However, "Europeans are absolutely forbidden to buy or even remove grain from one place in Persia to another."[499]

In April 1877, for example, the government cancelled the embargo on grain export based on the expectation that the harvest would be good that year. When by June of that year there was certainty about the favorable nature of the harvest, Aqa Sayyed Soleyman, a local religious leader started to agitate against the export of grain. His lackeys incited the mob to beat wheat brokers, while others threatened traders and brokers not to buy or export grain. To give their agitation a sheen of respectability, a mullah-led mob went to the Telegraph Office and sent a telegram to the governor of Fars asking him to declare a grain export embargo. The latter asked Tehran for advice, but at the same time the governor of Fars ordered the customs master of Bushehr not to allow any export of grain pending a final decision by Tehran. The local authorities in Bushehr received orders from Tehran to report on the grain situation in Bushehr. These consulted merchants who were not in the grain business and not familiar with market conditions. They gave a pessimistic outlook, forecasting that the price of wheat might rise to 8 *qrans* per *Hashem man*. The grain merchants pointed out that this was ridiculous, because prices of grain of the quality that the poor bought were at 6 and 6.5 *qrans* at that time. Furthermore, they pointed out that since 1856, even in years of plenty, the price of wheat had never been below 8 *qrans*. In fact, wheat was allowed even to be exported when prices were higher, such as in:

1867	the cost of wheat was 10 *qrans* per Hashem *man*
1868	9.25, 10.5 and 11.1 *qrans*
1869	9.25 *qrans*
1875	9 *qrans*

Given the fact that they had already paid for their grain, had chartered vessels to transport this grain, and often had already paid export customs duties on it, they asked the British authorities to intervene with the government in Tehran, as they would suffer heavy losses, while they had acted in good faith. Also, it often meant that when finally the ban was lifted less grain would be exported than was possible and for which had been originally transacted. In 1905, for example, £22,000 less grain was exported than would have been possible, which meant a serious economic loss for peasants and other stake-holders involved.[500] What really upset merchants was that grain embargos were imposed when the authorities feared a bad harvest or famine in Shiraz or even further away. A ban in Bushehr would not make any difference to the situation upcountry as it was almost impossible to send grain there.[501] Also, the grain embargo was not enforced if merchants were willing to pay the local authorities. In 1889, merchants were banned from exporting wheat, unless they paid 7% rather than the usual 5%. This they refused and it showed that

499. Administration Report 1899-1900, p. 41. For such an arbitrary case of grain embargo and the favoring of the wealthiest merchant of Bushehr, see NA, FO 248/157, J. Malcolm to Kemball 28/07/1854; NA, Idem, J.A. Malcolm to Kemball 06/11/1854 ("P.S. Haji Abdol Mohamad has at least 6 godowns in Bushire filled with wheat with 2,000 *Hashem man* of wheat and daily is being added to it receiving wheat from the villages. I have 340 *Hashem man* on which 5% had already been paid").

500. NA, FO 248/229, Malcolm and A.V. J.J. Malcolm/Bushire to Prideaux 04/06/1877; Idem, Gray & Paul/Bushire to Prideaux 04/06/1877; Administration Report 1894-95, p. 10.

501. Administration Report 1894-95, p. 10; in general see Floor 2015 a, ch. 8.

the ban was but an excuse to obtain money.[502] This was also the case in June 1891 when a grain embargo was imposed despite an excellent harvest as well as in 1895 when there was an embargo most of the year, but export was allowed with a view to levy the higher fees.[503] Imposing grain export embargos remained a constant problem for grain merchants and a contentious issue between the British and the Persian government. During all that time, sometimes large quantities of wheat and barley were surreptitiously exported; other times the ban was strictly enforced. Some bans lasted as short as a month, some lasted seven months.[504] It would seem that after WWI, bans on the export of grain were rarely imposed by the government, with the exception, of course, of the shortage years of 1942-44 (see chapter one). This experience had made the Persian government very skittish on this issue, for, in May 1947, it issued an export ban of cereals to the Arabian coast, when there was no shortage in the Bushehr area.[505]

Gums

Bushehr's immediate hinterland produced a variety of agricultural products, most of which were of no interest to those engaged in foreign trade. However, one product was the exception, because there was a demand in foreign parts for various gums. Fortunately, gum insoluble and gum tragacanth (*katira - Astragalus sp*) were available in large quantities near Bushehr and beyond in Fars province.[506]

2. 31: Gum insoluble was mainly produced by:

Town	quantity (in tons)
Maimand	100
Firuzabad	150
Burazjun	110
Shiraz (from various parts of Fars)	300
Kazerun	225
Kumarij	45
Khesht	75
Bandar Rig	130
Behbahan	350
Shustar, Ram Hormuz	175
Total	1,660

Source: Trade Report 1911-12, p. 15.

502. NA, FO 248/484, Muir of Hotz & Sons to Lucas, ass. res. 16/08/1889.
503. Administration Report 1895-96, p. 8; Administration Report 1891-92, p. 10.
504. Administration Report 1878-79, p. 9; Administration Report 1883-84, p. 8; Administration Report 1885-86, p. 7; Administration Report 1888-89, p. 12; Administration Report 1890-91, p. 9; Administration Report 1893-94, p. 10; Administration Report 1894-95, p. 10; Administration Report 1905-1906, p. 16.
505. Political Diaries, vol. 17, p. 428.
506. On the various gums growing in Persia, see Floor 2003 a, pp. 494-504.

At the turn of the twentieth century, the British Resident opined that gum tragacanth (*katira*) might become an important export commodity, given that there were vast tracts of the plant in Fars. However, he warned that "it appears that the peasantry employed in the collection of the tragacanth work in a reckless manner, causing much damage to the plants, which are burnt down after incision to such an extent as to render the same field unproductive for some years to come."[507] The fear, that the cutting of the bushes would have negative consequences for the supply and prices of charcoal in Bushehr, proved to be unwarranted. Charcoal import from Karachi had increased by 1906. Formerly, little had been imported, "but since the peasants have learnt that there is a price on gum-bearing trees the reckless burning of wood has largely diminished."[508] There is no further report that the fields indeed became unproductive, but the Resident's other prediction became true, for gums, and in particular gum tragacanth, which constituted the bulk of gum exports, became a major export product for Bushehr (Table 2.32)

2.32: Export of gums from Bushehr (1903-1923)

Value in £ and % of total export value

Year	Export value	In %	Year	Export value	In %
1903	38,046	10	1913/14	89,997	15
1904	64,869	14	1914/15	59,618	8
1905	70,949	15	1915/16	51,351	8
1906/07	168,031	28	1916/17	55,196	12
1907/08	81,992	16	1917/18	75,166	9
1908/09	76,722	17	1918/19	47,945	12
1909/10	77,473	19	1919/20	210,449	23
1910/11	96,490	14	1920/21	87,822	10
1911/12	113,316	17	1921/22	116,403	17
1912/13	95,520	15	1922/23	70,850	6
			1923/24	72,741	3

Source: Trade Report 1906/07-1923/23.

Shipping

The nature of the shipping trade changed significantly during the nineteenth century. Whereas for the first two decades of that century merchants preferred to ship their goods with British ships, this changed completely after 1820. The reasons for this change were twofold. First, because of the insecurity in the Persian Gulf, due to the raiding activities by the Qavasem, Hulas, and Utbis, merchants preferred to pay the higher freight cost of British ships, because of the greater security, and thus, the certainty that their goods would safely arrive at their destination. In 1817, according to William Bruce, two-third's

507. Administration Report 1900-1901, p. 23.
508. DCR 3951 (1906-07), p. 8.

of the ships calling on Bushehr were British.[509] Native ships sailing into the Persian Gulf came as a group in convoy. On 2 November 1808, Morier observed that "a large fleet of boats came to Bushehr from the coast, which kept together out of fear of the Qavasem pirates.[510] However, the number of ships calling on Bushehr was small, for the roads of Bushehr were not filled with the masts and sails of hundreds of vessels at anchor and neither innumerable boats plying between them and the port. Usually, there was hardly one at the time.[511] According to Morier, Bushehr "does not employ annually more than eight ships under English colours, and about six under Muscat, making on average about 4,500 tons of shipping."[512] In 1816, Buckingham observed that "on average 12-15 merchant ships arrive from Bengal and Bombay" to Bushehr,[513] which agrees with the Heude's findings who writes: "besides cruizers, men of war, inferior Arab dhows, and country craft, it is usually visited by ten or twelve vessels from India of a considerable size which trade within the Gulf under the protection of our flag; seven or eight of these making a double trip within the year."[514]

In 1819, after the British pacification operation of the Arabian Coast leading to the suppression of these sea raids, merchants preferred to ships their goods with the smaller native vessels, because that was much cheaper. In 1800, according to John Malcolm, the cost of shipping with a native vessel was one-third of the cost if shipped with a European square-rigged vessel. These lower cost were due to lower wages (in particular when slave labor was used) and because native shippers did not pay insurance premiums. The security reigning in the Persian Gulf after 1820 was due to the continued presence of a British naval squadron that enforced the maritime peace that the various Arab Sheikhs had agreed to by treaty with the British-Indian government. However, the cost of maintaining this peace was not borne by the inhabitants of the Persian Gulf or its merchants and ship owners, but by the Indian tax payers.[515] In 1828, Kempthorne noted that "ships from all parts of India thus come here, and I have seen as many as fourteen merchant-vessels in its haven at one time."[516] In 1836, Hennell wrote: "Much of the trade of Bushire has been carried by native boats and the number of ships visiting Bushire and Basra from India has been much reduced."[517] Even as late as 1865, the bulk of imports to Bushehr were transported in native vessels of 100, 200 to 300 tons burden, which could not sail during the S.W monsoon. Also, there were a few square-rigged vessels, mostly European that came to Bushehr.[518]

Native ship owners enjoyed this cost advantage until the arrival of steamships in the Persian Gulf in 1862.[519] Since then a regular steam service was in operation between Bombay and the Gulf ports. Already in 1836, there had been expectation of their use in

509. Grummon 1985, pp. 202-03.
510. Morier 1812, p. 58.
511. Dubeux 1841, p. 50.
512. Morier 1812, p. 38.
513. Buckingham 1971, p. 352.
514. Heude 1819, p. 42.
515. Grummon 1985, pp. 202-05.
516. Kempthorne 1835, p. 283.
517. NA, FO 248/85, Hennell, Residency to McNeill, 15/12/1836.
518. Pelly 1875 a, p. 48.
519. On the beginning of steam navigation in the Persian Gulf, see Issawi 1971, pp. 166, 168-70.

Bushehri ship masters ca. 1810

the Gulf when Hennell wrote: "If the two expected steamers are appropriated for the Gulf, the communications will become much more regular."[520] However, Bushehr had to wait for another quarter century, when hesitatingly the steamship service started with vessels of 500 tons every six weeks, which became a fortnightly service around 1870, and a weekly service of ships of 1,100 up to 1,200 tons around 1877. Also, as of 1870, there was a one-monthly communication with London via the Suez Canal.[521] In 1885, the British-India Steam Navigation Company's (BISNC) steamers called on Bushehr every second Wednesday en route to Basra and by 1900 the roadsteads were seldom without a steamer two days in succession. "Twice a week the steamers of the BISNC do a fast mail call at Bushehr as do the slow steamers. Also, direct boats from London also call."[522] Because there was a bad harvest in 1879 and 1880 this led to fewer steamships arriving at Bushehr.[523] However, this was a temporary effect, because in 1881 more steamers came, so that freight rates dropped.[524] Not only did more steamers, but also a greater number of steamship companies have a downward effect of rates. In 1894, the Clan Line started a direct service London-Persian Gulf, which resulted in a 40% drop of rates during that

520. NA, FO 248/85, Hennell to McNeill, 15/12/1836. There were steamships in the Persian Gulf, even calling on Bushehr in, e.g., 1836 and 1838, but these were naval ships that mapped the Euphrates in 1836 and in 1838 participated in the occupation of Khark. Issawi 1971, p. 165.

521. Geary 1878, vol. 1, pp. 58-59; Administration 1873-74, p. 10; Issawi 1971, p. 170.

522. Gleadowe-Newcomen 1905, p. 60; Curzon 1892, vol. 1, p. 557. For the schedule and cost of tickets of steamers, see Sadid al-Saltaneh 1371, pp. 39-40. In 1904, the BISNC received an annual subsidy of 426,000 rupees to operate the fast mail between Karachi and the Persian Gulf in a 12-day round trip and the slow mail in three weeks time. Lorimer 1915, vol. 1, p. 2442.

523. Administration Report 1879-80, p. 62.

524. Administration Report 1881-82, p. 21.

year. Apparently, this was not what the Clan Line wanted, because it discontinued its service in the following year.[525]

From the very beginning, British steamships dominated, and among those BISNC was and remained the main carrier. Other steamers had no regular schedule and occasionally called on Bushehr. Among those carriers other British companies such as the Persian Gulf Steam Navigation and British-flagged steamers owned by Persian and Indian Bombay-based merchants dominated. The few Turkish pilgrim steamers visiting Bushehr only sailed to Turkish territory. Later, the French company Mesnier & Co. would occasionally call on Bushehr for a number of years (1882-86, 1890, 1897) as did vessels from Norway (1894-95, 1898-99), the Netherlands (1895), Germany (1895-96), and Austria (1897, 1899-1900).[526] In 1896, two new steamship companies entered the market. One was British, the Colonial Steam Navigation Company and the other Messageries Maritimes, which was supported by the French state and did not even try to make their voyage pay commercially. Therefore, it was no surprise that the French company did not return the next year.[527] In 1897, the British India-, Bombay-, and Persia-, Anglo-Arabian Persian Gulf Steamship companies had the field to themselves, but in 1889, the British and Colonial Steam Navigation Company once again returned to the Persian Gulf.[528]

In 1873 the tonnage of British steam shipping in the Gulf was 36,000 tons. In 1899, this amounted to 119,000 tons in Bushehr out of a total of 126,000 tons (see Table 2.33) However, the role of sailing ships was not played out yet, although inexorably they were losing market share. From 100% tonnage in 1850 the share for sailing vessels had fallen to 27% in 1873. Its market share fell further to 15% in 1899 and to 10% in 1917, the last year for which we have quantitative data on sailing vessels for Bushehr. The most significant change was the reduction in the number of square rigged European vessels, which had become rare in the second half of the nineteenth century. After 1885, there were no more British vessels of this type sailing to Bushehr. However, there were yearly voyages of square-rigged vessels from Java and Mauritius until respectively 1886 and 1878. Throughout the second half of the nineteenth century the annual number of native sailing vessels entering the port of Bushehr remained at about 230, with occasional dips and crests, carrying between 15,000 to 25,000 tons annually. But, with a few exceptions, their role was limited to the distribution of goods to all parts of the Persian Gulf. These included vessels from India, the Persian Coast, the Arab Coast, Basra, Kuwait, Masqat, and occasionally from Aden and Zanzibar. The average tonnage of these sailing vessels differed; those from India and Masqat were about 100 tons, from Zanzibar and Basra 75 tons, while those from the Persian and Arab coast generally were in the 30-40 tons range. Of course, there were also many smaller and the occasional larger sailing vessels.[529]

525. Administration Report 1894-95, p. 22, 25; Administration Report 1895-96, p. 17.

526. See Appendix VII; Administration 1873-74, p. 10.

527. Administration Report 1895-96, p. 17. Administration Report 1896-97, p. 5.

528. Administration Report 1897-98, p. 18; Administration Report 1898-99, p. 31.

529. See Appendix VII; Administration 1873-74, p. 10.

2.33: Number of steamers and sailing ships and their tonnage (1873-1940)

Year	Total Steam-ships	Tonnage steamers	British steam-ships in %	Total sailing ships	Tonnage sailing ships	Total ships	Total tonnage	British steam-ers in % of to-tal tonnage
1873	36	37,000	99.5	221	13,715	257	50,715	73
1874	53	54,550	-	220	14,845	273	69,395	79
1875	64	48,100	-	218	12,843	282	60,943	79
1876	62	52,600	-	229	13,511	291	66,111	80
1877	72	98,602	-	255	17,185	327	115,787	85
1878	90	84,590	-	324	17,440	414	102,030	83
1879	101	73,910	-	276	13,340	377	87,250	85
1880	98	80,025	-	334	15,880	432	95,905	83
1881	184	138,470	-	606	24,981	790	163,451	85
1882	211	171,894	-	545	17,684	756	189,578	91
1883	243	218,837	-	286	7,490	529	226,327	97
1884	226	202,985	-	348	9,294	574	212,283	92
1885	163	143,356	-	1,049	59,837	1,212	203,193	93
1886	111	100,821	96	235	5,890	348	106,711	94
1887	96	90,543	98	222	9,100	318	99,543	91
1888	100	91,894	100	135	5,881	235	97,775	94
1889	111	112,784	99	159	5,768	270	118,570	95
1890	110	106,396	100	90	7,668	200	114,064	93
1891	142	145,801	100	84	6,100	226	151,901	96
1892	127	132,390	99	222	13,440	349	145,830	91
1893	111	119,566	96	220	15,475	331	135,041	89
1894	121	140,509	92	315	26,800	436	167,309	84
1895	138	170,706	96	252	12,650	390	189,356	90
1896	111	131,065	94	232	12,460	343	143,526	91
1897	94	100,453	96	253	10,945	347	111,398	90
1898	78	85,822	97	297	11,410	375	97,232	88
1899	106	126,016	95	402	22,640	508	148,766	85
1900	113	135,564	98	448	25,500	561	161,064	84
1901	112	130,273	97	515	16,000	627	146,273	89
1902	97	155,392	98	605	19,400	748	174,792	82
1903	77	195,292	96	535	15,700	694	210,992	91
1904	66	72,600	97	354	20,590	420	93,190	78
1905	158	198,278	97	522	15,260	680	213,538	93
1906	172	245,238	99	291	6,575	463	251,813	93
1907	192	259,730	91	181	5,179	373	264,909	98
1908	190	245,139	92	237	7,402	427	252,541	97
1909	178	235,703	92	594	15,911	772	251,614	94
1910	180	261,035	92	400	10,777	580	271,812	96

Year	Total Steam-ships	Tonnage steamers	British steam-ships in %	Total sailing ships	Tonnage sailing ships	Total ships	Total tonnage	British steam-ers in % of to-tal tonnage
1911	200	319,234	73	549	13,735	749	332,969	-
1912	201	325,650	73	515	12,239	716	337,889	-
1913	192	325,495	84	393	10,224	585	335,719	-
1914	137	244,180	95	611	17,683	748	261,863	-
1915	126	197,370	99	525	12,682	651	210,052	-
1916	108	152,290	89	403	10,349	511	162,639	-
1917	92	133,343	82	618	15,241	710	148,584	-
1918	73	96,728	80	-	-	-	-	-
1919	104	299,164	98	-	-	-	-	-
1920	103	220,450	95	-	-	-	-	-
1921	177	396,889	100	-	-	-	-	-
1922	161	324,766	97	-	-	-	-	-
1923	169	622,915	97	-	-	-	-	-
1924	-	-	-	-	-	-	-	-
1932	228	-	-	-	-	-	-	-
1933	217	-	-	-	-	-	-	-
1936	301	-						-
1937	291	-	78	-	-	-	-	-
1938	186 +	-	-	-	-	-	-	-
1939	219	-	68	-	-	-	-	-
1940	161	-	70	-	-	-	-	-
1941	>10	-	-	-	-	-	-	-
1942	64	-	-	-	-	-	-	-
1943	32	-	-	-	-	-	-	-
1944	46	-	-	>198	-	-	-	-
1945	39	-		-	-	-	-	-
1946	14	-	-	>270	-	-	-	-
1947	?	-	-	-	-	-	-	-

Source: Administration Report 1873-1940; Trade Report 1905-1934; Political Diaries, vols. 14-17.

Even in the twentieth century, the dominance of British shipping was really never challenged, although there was a sizeable and growing dent in its market share during the period of 1911-13 and after the mid-1930s. Although some ships from foreign nations visited Bushehr in the nineteenth century, their number never exceeded the single digit status. This would change in the twentieth century, first by the advent of Russian steamships as of 1904, and in particular by German (1906) and later by Japanese vessels (1916). This was good news for merchants, because due to fierce competition between these shipping lines, freight rates dropped,[530] in particular between 1900 and 1910, with very lows in 1902 and 1908-09. In 1913-14 there was a significant rise in rates due to the outbreak of WWI (and the Mesopotamia campaign) resulting in shortage of tonnage, higher insurance rates and other war related circumstances.[531] Rates remained high and stabilized. After 1914, the available data are only given for a few main commodities using different freight measures and thus, allow no comparison with the preceding period. Also, for the period after 1923, I have been unable to find any data on freight rates.

2.34: Rates for general cargo, Bushehr to Great Britain, per 40 cubic feet (1899-1913)

Year	£. *s*. *d*. to	£. *s*. *d*.
1899	-	1 6 0
1900	1 7 6	1 10 0
1901	1 5 0	0 19 0
1902	1 0 0	0 14 0 (a result of keen competition)
1904	1 7 6	1 10 0
1905	-	1 10 0
1906-07	1 10 0	1 0 0
1907-08	1 0 0	1 0 0
1908-09	0 15 0	0 17 6
1909-10	0 17 6	1 0 0
1910-11	1 0 0	1 5 0
1911-12	1 2 6	1 7 0
1912-13	-	1 5 6
1913-14	1 5 6	1 0 6

Source: DCR 4179 (1907-08 Bushire), p. 9; there were 12 pence (*d*) to the shilling and 20 shillings (*s*) to the pound.

The Russian Odessa Line was never really a commercially viable operation and the continued visits of its vessels were the result of Russian policy to challenge Great Britain's influence in the Persian Gulf. Invariably, they brought kerosene, oil and vermicelli, and on the return trip loaded tobacco for Aden.[532] However, the number of Russian ships remained limited to 4 or 5 ships that came at irregular intervals. Moreover, the ships seldom had any significant cargo. In fact, in 1907, the agent of the Odessa Line, Mishtolt said that he had practically no business at all, and therefore, intended to leave, although he did not leave. In 1908, there were rumors that because the Russian vessels had no real business, the Odessa Line would suspend its voyages to Gulf. However, by then it still had

530. Administration 1901-02, p. 13. In 1904, the three British shipping lines operating in the Persian Gulf formed a combine to fix freight at a remunerative rate, which appeared to be effective apart from 1908-09 when a fall in the rate occurred. Issawi 1971, p. 167.

531. Trade Report 1914-15, p. 7; Trade Report 1915-16, p. 7.

532. Administration Report 1909-1910, p. 27; Administration Report 1912, p. 40. According to the British government, the Russian subsidy was £4,000 per voyage plus a refund for the Suez Canal dues. Gleadowe-Newcomen 1905, p. 17.

18 months to go contractually. In 1909, the Odessa Line continued its operations and Mishtolt still was its agent. His job was but a sinecure, because the Russian vessels only brought glassware, earthen-ware teapots and 101 tins kerosene in that year. Although the Duma had voted not to renew the contract, it was overruled by the imperial council. In 1910, the Odessa Line did so little business that its agent was sent as consul to Egypt and the French dragoman became its new acting agent. In September 1910 a new agent came, Wram, a well-known arms dealer in Masqat, who disappeared after one month after the acting Consul-General had informed the shipping company that he was unfit to represent it and would bring it in disrepute. Strick & Co. made an offer for the tobacco contract, but the Russian Line rate was so low that nobody could compete with it. In 1911, the Odessa Line still did not do much business, but in 1912 had more trade due to its new agent Kouneff. What also helped was that it still had the contract for shipping tobacco of the Societé de Tambaku monopoly to Turkish ports. The outbreak of WWI meant that no Russian ships returned to Bushehr until 1928.

The German Hamburg-Amerika Shipping Company (HASC) was a successful and active enterprise. It was the first foreign shipping company to have a regular schedule with a number of ships that exceeded the double digits. The company began regular sailings in August 1906. The Wonckhaus firm was its chief agent and commercial patron. Moreover, the Germans were doing fine, fortuitously "facilitated by the extremely irregular sailing of our British Lines," which apparently waited until they had a full cargo before they sailed, whereas the Germans had sufficient wealth to be regular. Of course, as in the case of the Russian ships, the British suspected the Germans of having all kinds of ulterior motives to challenge the British position in the Persian Gulf and Iraq. In 1907, HASC continued its activities unabated and, according to the British, due the heavy subsidy it received. However, these subsidies were not as deep as the British said they were, because in 1908 the British Resident reported that although HASC was very active, it seemed to be working at a loss as Mr. Ballin, the managing director approached various British lines to form a combination. In 1909, due to crop failure and thus a fall in trade, the number of German ships calling fell somewhat from 12 and 13 in 1907 and 1908 to only nine. However, like British vessels, the German ones had direct sailing to Europe. The Germans maintained their regular monthly schedule until 1914. It was only in 1912 that a German vessel that was not a HASC steamer, but one from the German-Austrian Line called on Bushehr. Its main cargo was dates from Basra destined for Australia. Finally, there was the incidental visit by ships from Norway, Sweden, Austria and France as well as by local sailing vessels from Iraq, Kuwait, Masqat (no more after 1906) and the Arab Coast during that period.[533]

Of course, shipping shrunk during WWI and vessels from some nations (Russia, Germany, Turkey, France) disappeared completely from the Persian Gulf. After the war, shipping gradually increased, although in 1921 the mail service was not as yet up to its pre-war speed, but increasingly faster mail steamers called on Bushehr, be it still on an irregular schedule. Unfortunately, information on shipping (number of vessels, tonnage, nationality) is absent, spotty and/or incomplete after 1923. One thing is clear, after WWI, the major shipping line calling on Bushehr remained the BISNC, which still had

---

533. Administration Report 1904-1905, p. 22; Administration Report 1905-1906, p. 23; Administration Report 1906-1907, pp. 12-13; Administration Report 1907-1908, p. 10; Administration Report 1908, p. 7; Administration Report 1909, pp. 15-16; Administration Report 1910, pp. 17-18; Administration Report 1911, pp. 25-26; Administration Report 1912, p. 30.

the virtual monopoly of the mail service and together with other British lines (Strick, Bucknall and, since 1935, Ellerman) it took the majority of export goods. As late as 1940, British vessels still carried 50% of all of Bushehr's exports. From 1940, a British newcomer, City Line entered the race with two ships. However, BISNC did better than the other British steamship companies, of which in the 1930s Bucknall and Ellerman only maintained an irregular service. There were two shipping developments. The first was that Bushehr's volume of trade was decreasing and so was shipping. Secondly, competition was on the increase and market share of British shipping was declining. The decrease in shipping was also noticeable by the decrease in the frequency of service. As of 1937, BISNC only operated a fortnightly instead of a weekly service of mail steamers and as of March 1939 no more fast mail ships visited Bushehr, although the slow service continued. Also, although more shipping lines sent vessels to Bushehr they increasingly did so on an irregular basis, while some discontinued their service altogether.

As of about 1920, the German Hansa Line operated a monthly service to the Gulf, although German trade was diminishing towards the end of the 1920s. Messrs. Unduch closed the Bushehr office in February and handed over the Hansa Line to Mirza Hasan `Ali Kazeruni (Golshan) & Sons. A visit by a certain Mr. Walden to Bushehr in 1925 was rumored to be connected with the possible opening of (i) a Russian bank branch; (ii) an agency of the Russian shipping company, and (iii) a wireless station in Bushehr.[534] As of 1936, the Hansa Line operated a fortnightly service from Hamburg to the Persian Gulf and one steamer per 3 weeks in the opposite direction instead of monthly, which was the result of the new Persian-German trade agreement of 1935. In 1937, the Hansa Line continued its fortnightly service and brought more cargo than any other line. In total 37 German steamers called on Bushehr that year. In 1939, 34 Hansa ships called, but then World War II broke out, which meant the end of German ships visiting the Persian Gulf.

Russia also wanted a larger share of Bushehr's trade and three vessels of the Russian Steamship Service called on Bushehr in 1928. In 1929, the Russian Steamship Company had an irregular service of 5 ships calling on Bushehr. In 1930, eight Russian ships and in 1931 nine Russian ships called. In 1937 only four chartered Russian ships called and in 1938 not more than two charters with Russian goods visited. As of 1939 no more Russian ships called on Bushehr.

As of 1931 US vessels arrived; three ships of the American Silver Line called on Bushehr in that year, and in 1932 only one and none in 1933. In 1938, when only one US ship visited Bushehr, the American Silver Line and other US lines discontinued their service. But in 1939, three US steamers of the Ishmian Steamship line called and in 1940, ten US steamers called (of the Isthmian, Ker, and Isbrandsen Moller Lines) mostly with general merchandise and cars.

A relative newcomer was Japan. From 1916, ten to eleven Japanese vessels called on Bushehr every year. In 1932 only one and in 1933 three Japanese ships arrived in Bushehr. In 1934, the Bombay-Japan Conference Lines, i.e. P&O, NYK and OSK maintained a monthly service between Japan and Gulf ports. From the beginning of 1935, a new service began by Osaka Shosen Kaisha Line with a monthly service between the Far East and the Gulf. In 1936, there were as many as four Japanese shipping companies operating in the Persian Gulf, viz. Mitsui Bussan Kaisha, Yamashita Line, Osaka Shosen Kaisha and

534. Administration Report 1925, p. 9.

Nippon Yusen Kaisha, which together in 1937 sent 16 Japanese steamers. However, as of 1938 two Japanese lines discontinued their service, so that in 1938 only two Japanese lines remained, Mitsui and Yamashita, which sent 23 Japanese steamers to Bushehr in 1939. In 1940, 20 Japanese ships called though they carried more imports than in the previous year.

In addition to these shipping companies, there were others who maintained an irregular service or only occasionally came to Bushehr. In 1935, the Italian Lloyd Triestinio Company ran a service of cargo vessels every two months, but in 1936 its service became irregular and in 1937 only one Italian steamer visited. However, in 1939 this changed, when five Italian Lloyd Triestino vessels called, followed by seven Lloyd Triestino in 1940. Other nations also entered the Persian Gulf to obtain a market share. At the end of 1936 the Dutch Java Silver Pacific Line began a monthly service between Java and the Gulf, but in 1937 only two Dutch ships (with tea) and in 1938 one Dutch steamer came to Bushehr. This changed in 1939, when three Dutch steamers of the Java-Pacific Line called and in 1940, ten Dutch Java-Pacific Line ships brought tea and sugar. For a three year period (1919-23) an annual average of two Chinese ships entered Bushehr. Finally, during 1919-20 a Norwegian ship visited and again in 1938, one Norwegian and two Greek vessels with Russian goods visited Bushehr. In 1932 and 1940, one Belgian ship called, and in 1940 one Egyptian ship. Moreover, during this entire period, local sailing vessels both from the Arab and Persian coast called on Bushehr, although no quantitative data are available.[535] Of course, freight rates rose by 30-50% after the outbreak of the WWII further driving up consumer prices.[536]

Although the mail steamers connecting Basra with India continued to call on Bushehr there was very little trade in the first half year of 1940. Some consignment for Germany and Italy were actually returned or diverted to Iraq and Russia. Exports declined by 50% and imports by some 20%. Trade by sailing vessels increased due to the reduced number of steamships coming to the port. In 1939, 151 steamers came, but in 1940 113, and in 1941 only 69 (43 British, 14 Amercian, 4 Japanese, 3 Norwegian, 3 Greek, 1 Dutch, and 1 Russian). Despite the negative prospects for trade in December 1941, the American steamer company Isbrandtsen Mollar opened a sub-agency at Bushehr that was managed by Mirza Khalil Kazeruni. Trade was slack in December 1941, partly due to lack of security on the road to Shiraz, partly due to the political uncertainty. Moreover, all trucks were gathered to transport goods to Russia.[537] In 1942, trade remained dull, because merchants were waiting for government decisions to relax import-export regulations. Moreover, practically all trucks were commandeered by the army and by the Economic Department for wheat transport. Although there was an increase in ships calling on Bushehr, most of them landed war supplies, trucks and foodstuffs. In total 106 ships: 81 British, 19 American, 3 Dutch, 2 Norwegian and 1 Russian, while there was in increase of sailing vessels calling on Bushehr. There were also some exports, mostly small quantities of lambskins, gums, goat hair, asafetida, and rosewater.[538] The situation in 1943 brought

535. Trade Report 1920-21, p. 5; Administration Report 1928, pp. 8-9; Administration Report 1929, pp. 6-7; Administration Report 1930, p. 8, 10; Administration Report 1931, pp. 10, 12; Administration Report 1934, pp. 9; Administration Report 1935, p. 11; Administration Report 1936, p. 9; Administration Report 1937, pp. 8-9; Administration Report 1938, pp. 7-8, 10; Administration Report 1939, pp. 5-6, 9-10; Administration Report 1940, pp. 5-6, 9; Gamble 1935, p. 9.

536. Administration Report 1939, p. 5.

537. Political Diaries, vol. 14, pp. 181-82, 237, 538, 588; Administration Report 1941, pp. 11-12.

538. Political Diaries, vol. 15, pp. 125; Administration Report 1942, pp. 16-17.

no improvement. Trade remained slack, for there was no commercial cargo, due to lack of shipping and trucks. Also, often, there was an embargo on the release of goods from Customs. Moreover, when Customs finally released goods then there were no trucks, as these were used for transport of monopoly goods. Given this situation, towards the end of 1943, merchants were more and more turning to speculation, because even imported goods could not be forwarded.[539] After July 1943, Bushehr was no longer used to land war supplies the volume of shipping went down. In total, 30 British ships and 9 foreign came to Bushehr that year. At the same time, there was a surge in the number of mostly sailing dhows (20-30 tons mostly) coming from various Persian and Arabian ports, generally carrying raw cotton, dates, empty bottles, while exporting various local Persian products including *attari*, roots, rosebuds and cereals (when allowed). However, trade in 1944 and 1945 was not vibrant at all. In 1944-45, ships often called on Bushehr two or three days apart coming from different directions (i.e. one coming from India, the other returning from Basra). This so-called bunching of ships was unfortunate as it limited trade opportunities for merchants. A further indication of the low level of trade was that ships called and left on the same day, because there was either little to unload and/or to load.[540] In 1945, steamer service was worse than ever. Because three steamers were withdrawn from service in the Persian Gulf on average only a slow steamer called on Bushehr once a month. The regular AIOC tugs compensated somewhat for this drop in maritime communication by ensuring regular contact with Khorramshahr. Because the number of steamers was reduced the owners of country crafts experienced a boom in shipping rice, potatoes, dried fruits, walnuts, ghee, etc. to the Arabian coast where these were bartered for sugar, tea and piece-goods. Despite these activities, trade was at standstill, the more so because of continuing export restrictions. As a result, labor continued to migrate from Bushehr, while the cost of living continued to rise.[541] In February 1947, Khorramshahr and Bandar-e Shahpur were closed for repairs and improvements. Therefore, vessels were told to unload their cargo at Bushehr. However, the shipping companies BISNC and Messrs. Strick refused to unload heavy cargo at Bushehr, because its port facilities were in a poor state.[542] How slow trade remained, even after the war, is clear from the fact that in March 1947, one ship unloaded 7,000 packages in 17 hours, which, as the British consul noted "was the largest consignment since the war."[543] It is unlikely that the commercial situation of Bushehr improved greatly thereafter, given the development of Khorramshahr and Bandar Shahpur. Nevertheless, as of 1947, the British-Indian slow mail steamers called fairly regularly on Bushehr.[544]

---

539. Political Diaries, vol. 15, pp. 564, 586, 588, 616, 635, 650, 654-55.
540. Political Diaries, vol. 16, pp. 379, 401-02; Administration Report 1943, p. 15.
541. Administration Report 1945, pp. 10, 17.
542. Political Diaries, vol. 17, p. 251.
543. Political Diaries, vol. 17, p. 376.
544. Political Diaries, vol. 17, p. 473.

3

Bushehr under the Qajars

In this chapter I discuss the political events that transformed Bushehr from a traditional Arab Sheikhdom into a regular governorship, one that after the Constitutional Revolution developed into an extension of the centrally governed and modernizing state. Bushehr's position is discussed within the context of political events that played out at the national level, but that directly impacted the situation in the port itself (e.g. 1838 and 1856). Also, Bushehr's interaction with its hinterland is highlighted, given the importance its environs had on the political and economic situation of the city. I first delineate the development of the jurisdiction of the Sheikhdom and governorate of Bushehr. Then I provide background on the port's immediate hinterland, viz. the district of Bushehr and discuss those elements that were of importance to its functioning. Finally, the political developments of the port are discussed, in which various periods are distinguished that mark them off from other periods.

Bushehr's Jurisdiction

Before discussing the various political events that took place in Bushehr, it is necessary and useful to describe the appellation Bushehr, because this term encompassed more than just the port of that name. The jurisdiction of the governor of Bushehr changed over time, although it seems that it remained mostly unchanged under the hereditary Al Mazkur Sheikhs. In the first decade of the nineteenth century the Sheikh of Bushehr's jurisdiction was "not confined to the town, which contains about five thousand souls, but extends along the coast, from Reshir to Bunder Deelum, a distance of near seventy miles."[1] This did not mean that the Sheikh's authority was always respected throughout his jurisdiction (see below). But even when the Sheikh's authority was respected throughout his jurisdiction there were always some problems, sometimes of his own making. In 1825, the area around Borazjun was unsettled due to "the grasping disposition of the Sheik of Bushire, who in endeavoring to get under his jurisdiction the whole of the low country."[2]

1. Kinneir 1971, p. 70. In 1802, the Sheikh of Bushehr lost control over Daleki, which up to then had been part of his jurisdiction. Lorimer 1915, vol. 1, p. 1911. Borazjan, Angali and perhaps Hayat Da'ud also were included in Bushehr's jurisdiction.
2. Alexander 2000, p. 100.

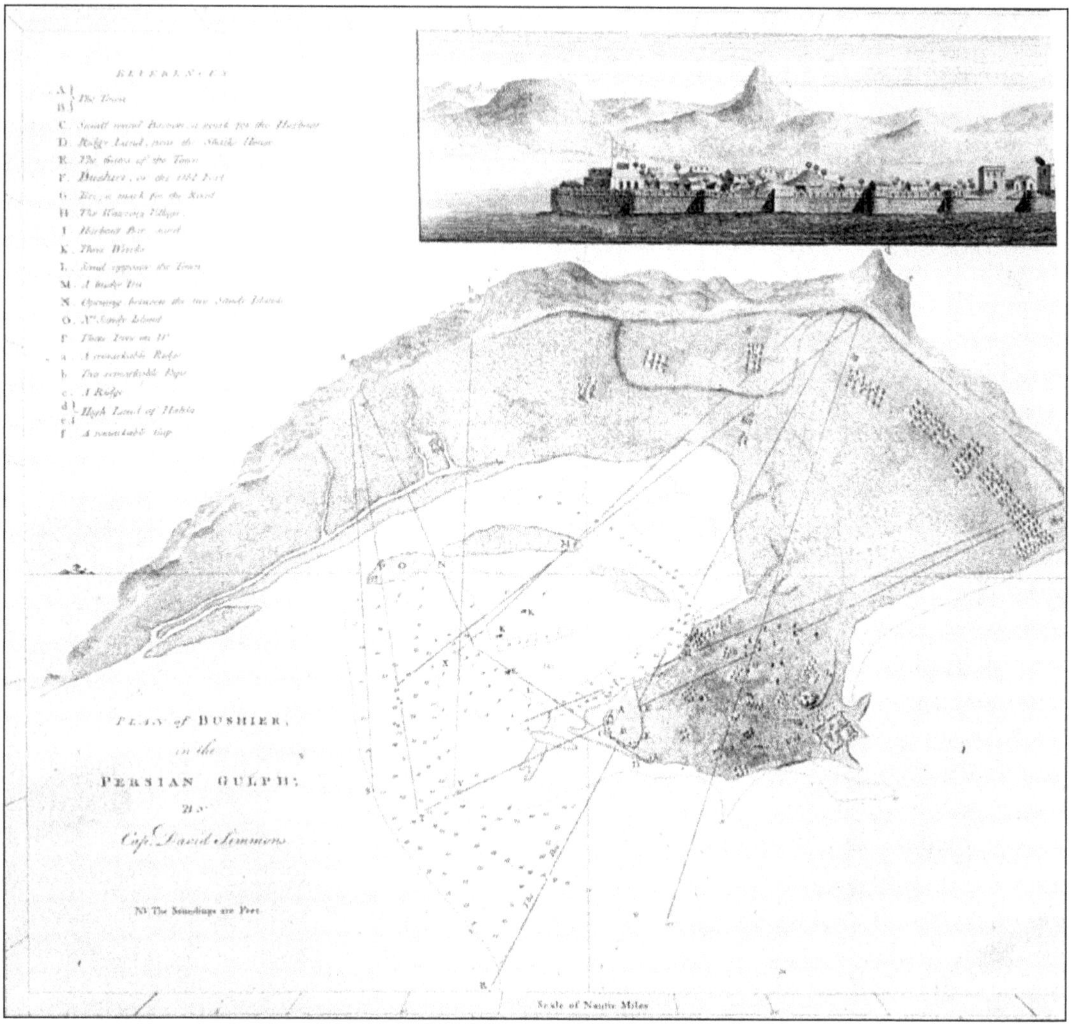

Map of Bushehr, 1774

After 1850, the Persian governor of Bushehr's jurisdiction included Bushehr, Hayat Da'ud, Angali, Dashtestan, Tangestan, and Dashti.[3] The Persian governors sometimes also had problems in asserting their authority; sometimes it was restricted to the town itself in times of unrest. For example, in 1857, the governor of Bushehr had no control over his district beyond 30 km from the town.[4] In 1860, Tahmasp Mirza Mo'eyyed al-Dowleh was appointed governor-general of Fars and he appointed his son Abdol-Baqi Mirza as governor of Bushehr, Dashti, Dashtestan, Gallehdar, Asir, Alamervdasht, Kangan, and `Asuliyeh.[5]

Until 1840, Delam, the port of Liravi, was part of Bushehr. Thereafter it was part of Behbahan. In 1862, Delam was added again to Bushehr's administration.[6] However, it seems to have been returned to Behbahan at some unknown later date, because in 1887

3. Pelly 1863 a, p. 33; Administration Report 1875-76, p. 8.
4. NA, FO 248/168, Cmdr Felix Jones to C.A. Murrat envoy-extraordinary, 26/11/1857.
5. Fasa'i 1378, vol. 1, p. 823.
6. Anonymous 1367, p. 77 (in 1836, Hayat Da'ud was under Sheikh Ahmad Khan, a nephew of Sheikh `Abdol-Rasul Khan and was part of Sheikh Naser III's jurisdiction); Pelly 1865 a, p. 41.

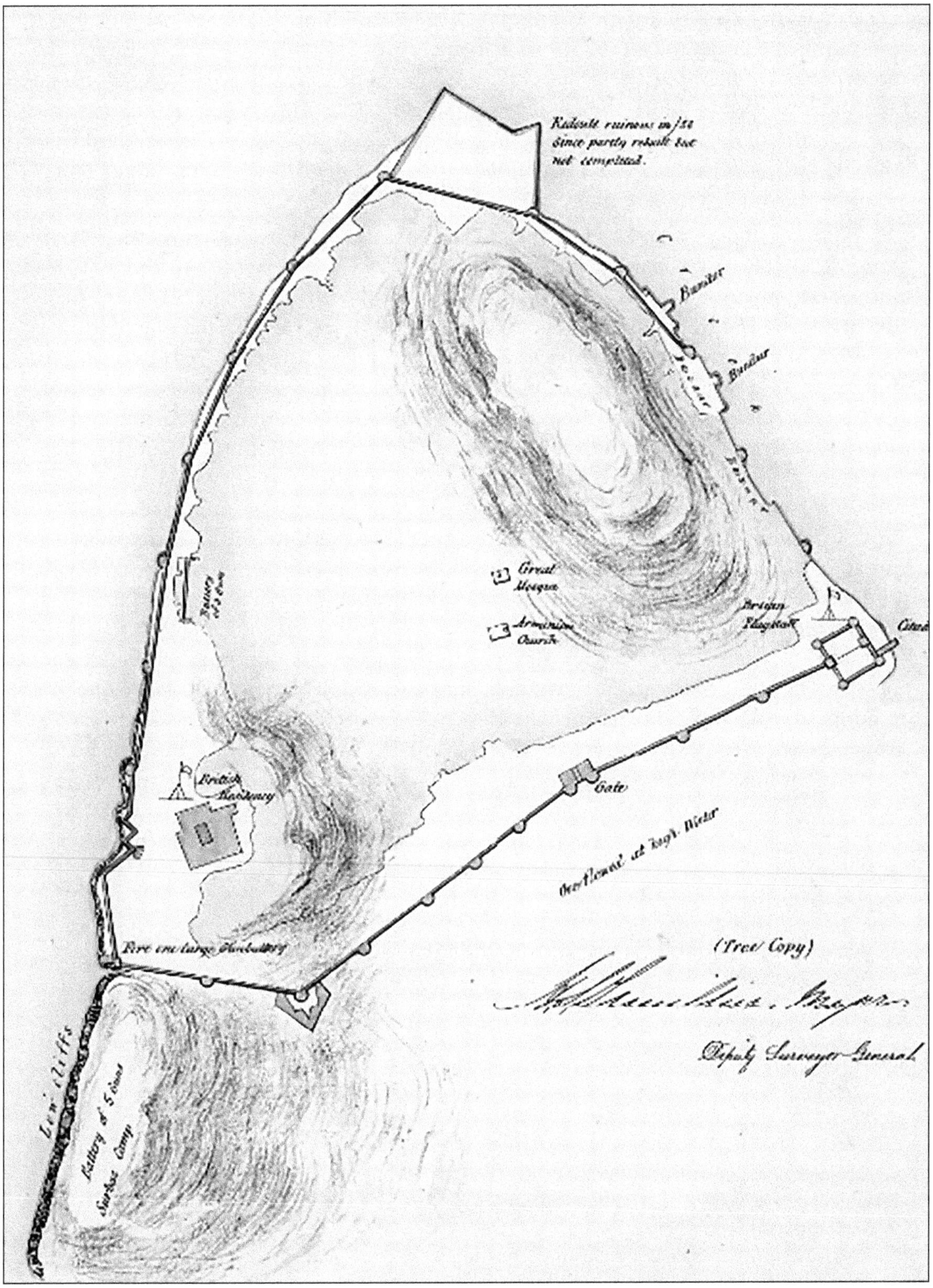

Plan of Bushehr showing the forts, 1853

Delam was put again under the Gulf Ports.[7] The relationship with Delam was not always a smooth one. In January 1892, Ja`far Khan, *zabet* of Delam evaded payment and the governor of Bushehr sent 30 soldiers to arrest him. "The townspeople rose in his favour and a fight ensued in which the soldiers were worsted. Jafar Khan was afterwards replaced by the Zabit of Reshire."[8] Apparently, the sub-district of Liravi had been removed from the jurisdiction of Bushehr (Gulf Ports), because in 1914 the Khans of Liravi urged Tehran to place the district under Gulf Ports.[9]

The area under the Al Mazkur Sheikhs and later under their rotating non-hereditary Persian successors was part of the province of Fars, whose governor-general was the immediate superior of whoever was in charge of Bushehr. Although Bushehr usually fell under the Fars government, its governor-general sometimes charged one of his sons as supervisor of the southerly districts. For example, on 16 January 1877, Oweys Mirza, Ehtesham al-Dowleh, the governor of Behbahan and the governor-general's oldest son, had the overall supervision of these districts.[10] However, "At some periods Bushire and attached districts have been administered by a Governor holding office directly under the Central Government at Teheran and independent Governor of Fars."[11] This was the case, for example, in 1862-63 when the Bushehr jurisdiction was temporarily separated from Fars when `Amid al-Molk became governor.[12] At that time, the extent of Bushehr's jurisdiction included Bushehr, Kong, `Asalu, Naband, Nakhilu, Shiru, Khakat, Khark, and Lengeh and some hamlets.[13] In 1873, Bushehr once again was separated from Fars and placed directly under the responsibility of the government in Tehran. At that time, Asadollah Mirza, Nayeb al-Eyaleh was governor of Bushehr, who jurisdiction "extends northwards of the town about thirty miles and towards the south along the coast about a hundred miles. Inland it reaches the hills."[14] This situation was normalized again in 1875, for when Hoseyn Qoli Khan Sa`d al-Molk became governor of Bushehr he was again subordinate to the Shiraz government. "The authority of this Governor extends over a tract reaching the sea side from about thirty miles north of the town of Bushehr to the port of Deyyer to the south. The Government of Bushire is divided into districts as follows:

1. Bushire with Heyat Daood and Angalee.
2. Dashtistan.
3. Tengistan.
4. Dashtee."[15]

7. Administration Report 1913, p. 31.
8. Saldanha 1986, vol. 7/2, p. 13; Lorimer 1915, vol. 1, p. 2061.
9. Administration Report 1914, p. 10.
10. NA, FO 248/329, Captain W.J. Prideaux to Thomson, 12/02/1877; Administration Report 1877-78, p. 5.
11. Administration Report 1875-76, p. 8.
12. Busse 1972, p. 347; Fasa'i 1378, vol. 1, p. 824
13. Pelly 1865 a, p. 33.
14. Administration 1873-74, p. 5.
15. Administration Report 1875-76, pp. 7-8. For a short biography of Sa`d al-Molk, see Hamidi 1380, pp. 378-80.

In some years, Dashti and Dashtestan were removed from Bushehr's jurisdiction and were governed by a separate governor. This remained the normal situation in much of the second half of the nineteenth century and thereafter, for in 1923 it is reported that for years the British Residency had suggested to include Dashti and Dashtestan in Bushehr province, which, apart from 1912-14 when this was the case, but was not accepted by Tehran.[16]

In 1888, Amin al-Soltan created the governorate of the Gulf Ports (*mamlekat-e Banadar*). The jurisdiction of the governor (*hokmran*), who still retained the old title of *daryabegi* and had his seat of government in Bushehr, extended 85 miles north (with the exception of the town of Delam).

> Further, an area from the middle of the Kuh-e Bang mountains about 55 miles north of Bushehr, to the borders of Tangistan about 12 miles south of the town. The extent of the province in this part is not more than miles inland, though about 32 miles behind the peninsula. All the districts outside the peninsula are administered by local chiefs, independent of the Government officials. Henceforth he was also in charge of the ports of Lengeh (under a deputy-governor), Khamir, Bandar Abbas, part of the districts of Shamil and Minab, and Jask as well as and the islands of Qeshm, Hormuz, Larak, Henjam and Sirri. In the various small ports the governor leased the customs for a stipulated sum as a rule to an enterprising merchant, usually an Indian; in larger places he puts subordinate officials.[17]

This meant that Dashti and Tangestan were removed from Bushehr's jurisdiction and became subject to the governor-general of Fars. Dashtestan was split between Bushehr and Shiraz.[18] The governor of the Gulf Ports was appointed by the central government at Tehran. Normally he was independent of the governor of Fars. However, if that individual was a prince he sometimes made his influence felt in the affairs of the Gulf Ports.[19]

In 1923, Bandar Abbas plus Minab were no longer under Bushehr's jurisdiction, but were placed directly under the Minister of Interior in Tehran.[20] The previous situation was restored at the end of November 1924.[21] In July 1931, the Gulf Ports were separated from Fars.[22] In 1936, the governorate (henceforth called *shahrestan*) of the Ports (Banader) was created, which depended directly from Tehran. Therefore, the authority of the governor was greatly reduced. It still included the entire littoral from Bandar-e Delam until Jask.[23] In 1938, another reorganization took place, which led to the creation of a governorate (*shahrestan*) of Bushehr, which was much smaller in size and for administrative purposes it was placed under Fars. As of then, it covered the area from Delam in the north to Kangan in the south, and as far Borazjan in the interior; inland its extent varied between 15 to 40

16. Administration Report 1923, p. 9.
17. Lorimer 1915, vol. 2, pp. 1460-63, note; Trade Report 1910-11, p. 1.
18. Lorimer 1915, vol. 1, pp. 2054-55.
19. Trade Report 1920-21, p. 1.
20. Administration Report 1923, pp. 26-27.
21. Administration Report 1924, p. 13.
22. Administration Report 1931, p. 3.
23. NA, FO 371/15473.

miles, a total area of 6,000 sq. miles. The separated part was added to the province of Fars. The new Bushehr *shahrestan* was divided into six districts or *bakhsh* (Borazjan, Ganaveh, Delam, Ahram, Khormuj, and Kangan), each of which was under a *bakhshdar*. Each district was subdivided into sub-districts or *dehestan* under a *dehdar* or controller. Small townships, large villages or groups of small villages were under a *kadkhoda* or village chief. At the head of the *shahrestan* was the governor or *farmandar*. He was appointed by royal decree at the recommendation of the Minister of Interior and the governor-general of Fars (*ostandar*), selected from among regular government officials. *Bakhshdars* were selected from among government officials, usually from the governorate. They were appointed by the governor (agreed to by the *ostandar*) and approved by a decree from the Minister of Interior. The governor appointed the *dehdars* and *kadkhodas* in consultations with the *bakhshdars*, usually from among the permanent inhabitants of the village.[24] In September 1945, the Bushehr governorate was separated from Fars and came directly under Tehran.[25]

The Governorate of Bushehr

Bushehr's immediate hinterland was entirely tribal in character with an ethnically very mixed population. As stated in the previous section the districts that were dependent on Bushehr were: Chahkutah and Tul-e Siyah (7-9 villages), Dashtestan/Borazjan (24-31 villages), Tangestan (41 villages), Dashti (55-75 villages), Angali (8 villages), Rudhilleh (15 villages), Shabankareh (33 villages), Zireh (15 villages), Hayat Da'ud (28 villages) and Liravi (25 villages). The borders between these districts had been defined and accepted over time by the traditional chiefs and usually were formed by natural features such as a water course, a low range of hills or a river in the case of Rudhilleh.[26] The Bushehr district stretched from Bandar Rig to Halileh Bay and included the coastal districts of Hayat Da'ud and Angali to the north of the town. The district of Dashtestan included the low-lying plain between the sea and the mountains from the village of Daleki to about Chahkutah. Its principal town was Borazjan. Next to Dashtestan, to the south, is Tangestan, which is partly mountainous and borders on the sea. Its chief resided in Ahram; its heterogeneous tribal population spoke a dialect peculiar to themselves. Dashti was a bigger and more populous district than Dashtestan and Tangestan. It is situated south of Tangestan, to the west it borders on the sea and to the south flanked by the Kangan and Jam districts and to the east by Bushkan in the mountains. The various districts were under local, mostly hereditary chiefs, who farmed their district. The chiefs, various called Sheikh, Khan, *Ra'is*, *Zabet*, *Zayer* or *Zar*, had to pay a lump sum of revenue per year to the

24. Administration Report 1938, p. 2; NA, FO 371/15471.

25. Administration Report 1945, p. 9.

26. Trade Report 1911-12, p. 1. Ganaveh, Khark, Bandar-e Rig were under Khan Ali; Tangestan under Ali Khan Tangestani, Dashti under Heydar Khan Dashti (Dayyer, Kangan). Saldanha 1986, vol. 7/2, pp. 1-3. The chief (*zabet*) of Rishahr was called *kadkhoda*; around 1900 he paid 1,500 *tumans* to the governor of the Gulf Ports, but by about 1913 only 850 *tumans*. At Rishahr, the government had posted 30 *tofangchis* at 3 *tumans*/p.p./month headed by one chief at 10 *tumans*/month, but usually there were only 12 *tofangchis* who were paid 2 *tumans*/pp/month. The ports of Dashti around 1880, when they had 700 households and 2,000 people, paid three different taxes: (i) head tax (*saraneh*), which was paid in three installments with an annual total of 420 *tumans*; (ii) a tax on the date groves (*nakhlestan*) of 190 *tumans*; and (iii) the government's share in agricultural output (*manal*) of 260 *tumans*. The Dashti chief at that time was Saleh Soltan. The taxes for the various different localities are detailed in Sadid al-Saltaneh 1371, pp. 55, 57-58.

governor of Bushehr or that of Fars and to provide military levies when called upon. If the revenues were not paid punctually, the governor would send a tax collector (*mohassel*) or usually an armed force. In particular, in the aftermath of the constitutional revolution, payment of taxes fell into arrears, although this was also a common occurrence in the nineteenth century. Therefore, these chiefs were often imprisoned in Shiraz and/or had their sons taken as hostage for their good fiscal behavior. The governor could remove the local chief at his discretion. Due to smuggling, the tribesmen were mostly well armed. The district's population owed feudal service to their khan, who took care of judicial matters, although usually criminals would be sent to Bushehr. The population of Bushehr and its main surrounding districts was about:

Bushehr peninsula	23,000
Dashti	20,000
Dashtestan	20,000
Hayat Da'ud and Liravi	20,000

The Persian villages (except Dashti, which could defend itself) were more under control of Bushehr than the Arab villages.[27]

After the 1880s, the districts dependent on Bushehr were not peaceful and quiet places, with the possible exception of Hayat Da'ud and Rudhilleh. Around 1900, these two districts were under chiefs belonging to one family. Under the leadership of the oldest brother, Heydar Khan of Bandar Rig, the Khans of Hayat Da'ud, Rudhilleh and Liravi collaborated closely. Through marriage ties the Khan of Angali (a former foe) was allied with Heydar Khan and followed his guidance. Heydar Khan also had good relations with the Khan of Shabankareh. Heydar Khan and family paid their taxes regularly and kept good order and security apart from giving some support to Customs officials by preventing smuggling and maintaining good relations with the government. Thus, they gave no pretext for the governor to interfere with them and were allowed to manage their own affairs. Although the Hayat Da'ud allies kept the peace at home that did not mean that they had no conflict with their neighbors. However, unlike the chiefs of the other districts they were not constantly engaged in intrigues against one another and formed combinations and counter-combinations among themselves for the promotion of their own interests. Because of the weak central government in Tehran and Fars as well as a weak local Bushehri government, the Khans of Borazjan, Tangestan and Dashti did not pay their taxes regularly and often just refused to pay. Chahkutah did likewise. The Khans of Shabankareh and Zireh were feuding with the chief of Borazjan; while the Khans of Dashti supported their ally of Borazjan. The chief of Angali had a standing feud with Chahkutah, while Tangestan, which was internally divided was a long-standing enemy of Hayat Da'ud, while the Dashtis were mostly on bad terms with the Tangestani

27. Administration 1873-74, p. 6; Administration Report 1875-76, pp. 7-8; Pelly 1865 a, p. 42; Trade Report 1911-12, p. 1; Government of India 1924, p. 70. For a description of Ahram, see Hamidi 1380, pp. 99-101. The population figures differ per source. Around 1900, the inhabitants of the peninsula numbered 8,500 (Lorimer 1915, vol. 2, p. 330), but in 1912, the peninsula's population was 30,000 (Sadid al-Saltaneh 1371, p. 37). The honorific *Zar* or *Zayer* indicated that the person had made the pilgrimage to Kerbela. Hamidi 1380, p. 351.

headmen. All Khans of the littoral, even his allies of necessity, disliked and distrusted the Khan of Borazjan, while in 1914-18, only the Borazjan, Dashti and Tangestani chiefs were anti-British, all the others chiefs were friendly. The Khans had one thing in common; they resented any outside interference, in particular with the control over their subjects. Not only were the district chiefs feuding with one another, but so was the population among themselves, village against village. Lorimer submitted that "Cattle raids and thefts occur which are followed by military altercations, every man having a modern rifle and a cartridge-loading machine."[28] This was not a recent development, for already in 1817, Johnson observed that Dashtestan etc. were mostly inhabited by "tribes of Arabs, who have formed themselves into petty states. They are often at war with each other; and the inhabitants of each settlement not only enclose their towns, but in their journeys from one place to another go armed."[29] Likewise in 1879, the British Resident noted that in these abovementioned districts, where feuding was a way of life, "the peasant ordinarily prepares himself for his night's repose by arming himself to the teeth."[30]

Although the various districts were dependent on Bushehr that did not mean that its governor always had full control over them. Like other things in life this varied. A case in point was the situation in Tangestan. Until mid-1807, the Qa`ed lineage controlled Ahram, the chief settlement in Tangestan. However, when in that year the Tangestani chief Sheikh `Abdol-Rasul succeeded his father, he dismissed the Qa'eds and appointed his own man, a certain Aqa Shafi`, who held this function until 1836. Sheikh Naser of Bushehr then farmed Ahram to Mohammad Baqer Khan of the Bani Hadhil, the *zabet* of Tangestan for 3,000 *tumans*, who appointed his brother Mohammad `Ali as chief of Ahram. He was killed in Bushehr at the instigation of Haji Khan, the *zabet* of Dashti. Thereafter, Mohammad Baqer Khan gave Ahram to his son Ahmad Khan, who was killed together with Ahmad Shah Khan, son of Mohammad `Ali Khan, when fighting against the British at Bushehr in 1857. Then Hasan Khan, another son of Mohammad Baqer Khan, received Ahram, who held it for 16 years. However, in 1858 Ahram was for one year in the hands of Mohammad Khan, the *zabet* of Dashti. After Hasan Khan's death in 1871, his son `Ali Khan received Ahram, but he was a weakling for the real power was in the hands of Zar Soleyman, a local petty chief. As of then the influence of the hereditary Tangestani Khans of the Bani Hadhil declined. While their authority waned that of the lower chiefs increased. During the rule of Zar Soleyman, Ahram was for one year again in the hands of Mohammad Khan, *zabet* of Dashti. In 1886, when Malek al-Tojjar was governor of Bushehr, he summoned `Ali Khan and Zar Soleyman to Bushehr and imprisoned them and entrusted Ahram and Tangestan to Heydar Khan, son of Ahmad Khan. In 1897, there was a conflict among the chiefs resulting in casualties, as a result of which there was a bloodfeud between them. In 1900, Daryabegi gave Tangestan to Zar Khedr and in 1901, when Salar-e Mo`azzam was governor, he once again gave Ahram to Heydar Khan, be it under the supervision of Zar Gholam `Ali, while he mortgaged his property. In 1906, Daryabegi gave Ahram to Hoseyn Khan, son of `Ali Khan and the sons of Zar Gholam `Ali and took the mortgage document of Hoseyn Khan's property as

---

28. Government of India 1924, pp. 69-70; Lorimer 1915, vol. 1, p. 1465; Sadid al-Saltaneh 1371, pp. 6, 61; see also Appendices III, IV and V. For the fiscal burden of the various districts, see Sadid al-Saltaneh 1371, pp. 57-58, 62, 66, 69, 71-72, 76, 79. For the Khans of Shabankareh, see Hamidi 1380, pp. 406-09.

29. Johnson 1818, p. 19.

30. Administration Report 1878-79, p. 30.

security.[31] The situation was different, for example with Dashti, whose Khans had always been able to resist control by Bushehr and being encroached upon by their neighbors.[32]

Despite the disarmament and pacification drives that the army engaged in since 1923, by the late 1940, the Tangestanis, Dashtis and Dashtestanis were still a source of trouble. Although a rather disparate population, they were united in their desire "to be free from Persian officials, who might, amongst other things, seriously interfere with their smuggling activities." Nevertheless, the military operations had left their mark on the district. The old influential chiefs no longer existed and under Reza Shah they all had been banished with their families. In 1947, the chiefs in the three regions, although not lacking in influence, were merely landowners. Moreover, unless they were appointed *dehdar* or *kadkhoda* they were not involved with the administration of their district. Moreover, they all hated each other, and thus by a 'divide and rule' policy, boosted by the strong presence of army and gendarmery, the government increased its authority.[33]

The tribal population

The needs of the tribesmen of Tangestan, Dashti and Dashtestan were limited to food and clothing, which were supplied by Bushehr. They lived mostly in simple huts made with mud and plaster, sometimes whitewashed. The roof consisted of date tree beams over which date branches had been laid. Only the houses of Khans had window glass and teak doors; they also might have chairs and a table. For ground cover, people used locally made mats. Otherwise the worldly possessions of most people consisted of: bedding, metal trays for food, a little crockery e.g., basic earthenware and enamelware, also teapots, generally of Russian manufacture, earthenware plates, a metal copper cauldron for cooking, wooden or sometimes tin chests as receptacles.[34]

> The dress of the S. Persian tribesman is almost entirely dependent on imported cotton-goods. The only item manufactured locally is the *kolah*, a high stiff hat of black or brown felt, which was sold in the bazaars for 4-8 qrans. His aba or outer-cloak is made of camel-hair or wool, and his *maleki* or footwear of rough canvass uppers, with soles of old cottons or cloth folded, macerated and beaten into layers, reinforced by stripes of hide and with horn or hide plates under the heels and pointed toes. These are often home made or otherwise sold at 10 *qrans* per pair.

---

31. Sadid al-Saltaneh 1371, pp. 6, 61, 68-69; Appendices III, IV and V. For a history of the Khans of Tangestan, see Farrashbandi 2535 and Ya Hoseyni 1387; Hamidi 1380, p. 211-14. For a description of a journey to Ahram and Haviz, with detailed description of some localities en route, see Sadid al-Saltaneh 1371, pp. 58ff, 67-72 (description of Ahram), 72-79 (description of Haviz). For a short bio of Zayer or Zar Khedr, see Hamidi 1380, pp. 102-04.

32. For a detailed discussion of Dashti, see Lorimer 1915, vol. 2, pp. 366-79; Adamec 1989, vol. 3, pp. 194-96; in 1809, Hasan Khan was chief of Dashti. Morier 1812, p. 65. In 1844, the chief was Haji Khan, who was succeeded by his son Hoseyn Khan. In 1856, the chief was Heydar Khan, but Jamal Khan and Hoseyn Khan are also mentioned. In 1886, Haji Salem was chief of Dashti and during the first two decades of the twentieth century it was Jamal Khan, see Floor 2014 a; Hamidi 1380, p. 226 (with photo), pp. 314-23 (with family tree); for Angali, see Lorimer 1915, vol. 2, pp. 79-82; Adamec 1989, vol. 3, pp. 47-48; Hamidi 1380, pp. 93-95; for the other districts, see Appendices III, IV and V.

33. NA, FO 371/15471.

34. Trade Report 1911-12, p. 2.

Tangestanis

The Persian tribesmen wears:

(i) A long undershirt (Jameh-Juma or Pirahan) made of nainsooks (whit or dyed black), or white Mulls, 20 yrads, or dyed black in Bombay. Nomads also use coloured drills. In winter, white Shirtings are used: and an inferior kind is made of mexicans (48 yards).

(ii) Drawers reaching to the ankle (Zir Jameh) and very wide. For summer wear in the littoral, white Mulls, or dyed in Bombay, are used: for winter White Shirtings, or the same dyed blue in Bombay and then known as kasawari. The proper classes also wear Mexicans.

Arkhaluq (often pronounced Alkhuluq), a long garment reaching below the knees, low at the neck and not low over the chest. Asteri, Lamseh and "Ursi"prints, Black and white Discharge, Purple and Chocolate Dubahrs, Crimps, are commonly used. The better class also wear Kalamkars and 'Shamis'.

Qaba (a long outer garment open at the neck). For quality, this depends on the wealth of the wearer. The lowest class wear "Abreh", i.e., pieces of five yards of Liepmann's shirting, given to local dyers, and dyed in various colours.

> Shal-i Kamar. Among the tribesmen universally, and among the majority of townspeople, a heavy thick roll, usually consisting of an entire piece of Mulls (22 yards long) or Drill, coloured, or of purple Twills for mourning, is wound around the waist over items of dress (i), (ii), and (iii).
>
> Shalwar (Trousers). When worn by the better class over the Zir-i Jameh, these are commonly made of black Italians and Twills."
>
> A rifle cartridge belt and a cheap telescope in a sling make up the rest of the outfit.[35]

The Tangestani women, and most likely also those of the other districts surrounding Bushehr, wore a thin yellow-blackish cloak (*aba*), woven in Dashti and Tangestan, instead of a *chador*. In case of death or visiting a bereaved home both men and women wore a black fabric (*dastmal*) around their waist. The wives of the elite, however, instead of the *dastmal* wore a black veil (*charqad*) over their *aba*.[36]

Agricultural activities

The environs of Bushehr, a 65 km (40 miles) plain up to the mountains as well as along the littoral, was flat, sandy, lacking vegetation, and deficient in good water. The greater part was unproductive, being little better than a desert, covered with particles of salt and, in the first half of the nineteenth century, abounding in antelopes. The smaller productive part was green when cultivated in winter and spring, but parched during the rest of the year. There were many streams coming from the mountains, which, during the rainy season, flooded the plain and then could be difficult to cross, but were otherwise dry. This held in particular for Rudhilleh and Shabankareh, which, because such streams passed through and flooded their land during spring, were more fertile than the other districts. Contrariwise, Tangestan was not very fertile; its date groves at Ahram and Khaviz were not very productive, although the villages around Gurak produced a large quantity of vegetables. The principal revenue of the chiefs was the fruit gardens of Khaviz in the hills and the Ahram date gardens. Dashti was in a better condition, because it was a grain-growing district, due to a river that passed through it. It also had extensive date groves. The land was dotted with villages that were situated about 8 km (5 miles) from each other; each had some 100-500 dwellings, but most had around 100. The houses were made of mud bricks, but many were just simple mat huts. In 1821 Fraser, therefore, described their habitation as follows: "The towns and villages, built of the materials afforded by the soil, are scarcely to be discerned from its surface, and resemble rather irregularities thereon, than inhabitations for men." The village heads usually lived in a mud fort. The villages had no markets and were supplied from the coast and a few towns such as Borazjun, mostly by peddlers. Most villages had date groves for their own consumption, but only the plantations at Ahram, `Ali Changi, Khaviz, Gurak (Tangestan) and Zireh exported most of their production. Otherwise people cultivated wheat and barley on plots of two gavs

35. Trade Report 1911-12, pp. 2, 11.
36. Sadid al-Saltaneh 1371, pp. 61-62.

of land. However, this was an uncertain occupation as cultivation was rain-fed (*deymi*). This meant that, for example, after a number of bad years peasants did not have enough seed; they often had to borrow seed, and as a result, large tracts of arable land remained half-sown. Only narrow, light plough-shares were used which barely scratched the soil. Sowing had to take place immediately after the first heavy rains; reaping took 40 days and threshing even longer. This was because labor was a limiting factor that negatively influenced agricultural output, as able-bodied men migrated to the ports and towns as well as to non-wheat growing districts to earn money. Those that remained behind worked as share-croppers, receiving one-third of the crop. In a normal year, this was enough to ensure survival. Only vegetables and dates were irrigated from wells with brackish water, which also supplied people's drinking water. The wells at certain places did not produce enough water, such as at Ahmadi, so that animals had to walk 7 km to Choghadak to get water. To lift the water, a water-wheel or *charkh-e chahab* was used that was turned by a bullock. The grain and vegetables (mostly from Gurak) were transported to Bushehr and other ports. Other crops included tobacco, cotton, and millet. Around Choghadak very good, but expensive, oats were cultivated as a fodder crop, which locally was known as *zangol*. At Khushab and surrounding villages, straw and husks from the threshing floor was obtainable.[37] Borazjan had ample food supplies, including dates as well good tobacco and firewood from the Gisakan hill.[38]

The districts close to the mountains or in the valleys farther away produced much gum insoluble, wild berries, oil-seeds, and wild almond kernels and were supplied with *rowghan* or clarified butter by pastoral villages at higher altitudes. *Ahluk* or small bitter almonds were produced by the same wild tree as gum insoluble and before the gum season, i.e., in late spring and summer. The ones from Kazerun arrived unshelled. There also were "*kulkhung*" berries, which grew in clusters from large trees with a green husk and were full of oil and of an agreeable pungent odor (which is is said to lose on being crushed) and with a tiny kernel. *Bannak* were similar berries, but larger, without the odor and less oil. Cotton-silk, a silk-like substance, with very fine strands, was extracted from large pods on bushes growing in some districts of the hinterland. There was no demand for these products in Bushehr itself and therefore, no incentive for the peasants to market them.[39]

The Al Mazkur Governorship of Bushehr

The governor (*hakem*) was the most important government official in Bushehr. The governors usually limited themselves to (a) the maintenance of law and order and (b) the collection of revenue, and often they only did the latter.[40] I discuss the various people

37. Kinnier 1971, p. 70; also Sani` al-Dowleh 1294, vol. 1, p. 299; Buckingham 1971, p. 346; Fraser 1984, p. 54; Sadid al-Saltaneh 1371, pp. 54-55; Government of India 1924, pp. 70, 108; Trade Report 1910-11, p. 2; Trade Report 1911-12, p. 2; Lorimer 1915, vol. 2, p. 370.

38. For a detailed description of Borazjan's situation, see Floor 2011 b, chapter 2.

39. Trade Report 1911-12, pp. 1, 16. For *ahluk*, properly *aluk*, see Hamidi 1380, p.84.

40. de Rivoyre 1883, p. 135 (the only role of the government is the collection of taxes). For an itemized list of the revenues of Bushehr, see Administration Report 1875-76, p. 26; Administration Report 1884-85, p. 46; Administration Report 1888-89, p. 35.

that governed Bushehr as well as the changing nature of the governor's authority.[41] Under Qajar rule, the governor's freedom to act was increasingly curtailed and by the end of the period under study, he was merely the highest bureaucrat with a circumscribed task, carrying out policies formulated in Tehran. In this task he was assisted by specialized departments of the centralizing and modernizing Persian state. These various new central government departments curtailed the scope of the governor's authority, who, before the establishment of the telegraph, was a rather independent official. The governor sometimes was given the title of *daryabegi*, a vestige from the days that Sheikh Naser Al Mazkur in 1748 was referred to by this title, because of his command of the remnants of the royal fleet in Bushehr, the then naval port of Persia. One of the governors, Mirza Ahmad Khan, was always referred to as Daryabegi rather than by his name or other titles.[42]

Sheikh Naser II Al Mazkur Administration

The Al Mazkur family that had held sway in Bushehr since 1748 had cooperated with the Zand regime since the uncontested establishment of its rule in 1763. However, in 1792, for various reasons, Sheikh Naser I decided to transfer his allegiance to the rising star of the Qajars. He helped defeat pro-Zand forces in the littoral and for his trouble was confirmed as governor of Bushehr by the new ruler, Aqa Mohammad Qajar (r. 1794-1797).[43] Since April 1789, Sheikh Naser II, son of Sheikh Naser I was governor of Bushehr.[44] Grummon has argued that because the Qajars did not need naval power, they were less interested in developing a special relationship with the Al Mazkur than the Zand rulers. They had less interest in what happened in the Persian Gulf and, therefore, considered the Al Mazkur as a cash cow. According to Grummon, the Al Mazkur's reaction to this was a policy of avoidance, i.e. they tried as much as possible to avoid any personal contact with the governor-general of Fars. Although, I agree with his characterization of the Qajar side's view of the relationship, I am less convinced by the so-called 'avoidance policy' allegedly pursued by the Al Mazkur Sheikhs. In my view, Grummon makes too much of the 'special' relationship between the Al Mazkur and the Zands, who needed their naval power. While the latter is true, the Al Mazkur Sheikhs did not have much choice in the matter, nor did they like to go to Shiraz, whether it was during the Zand or the Qajar period, as such visits were costly affairs. Moreover, Sheikh Naser II's thwarting of the combined Omani-Persian operation against Bahrain in 1799 was not exactly the behavior of somebody pursing an avoidance policy! The same holds for the pattern of less than prompt payment of taxes to Shiraz by the Al Mazkur, which finally resulted in the loss of their hereditary rule. Also, during the Qajar period the Al Mazkur were just simply unable to avoid the governor-general of Fars. True, it was only in 1802 that Sheikh Naser II went for the first time to Shiraz, but that did not mean he was beyond the grasping

41. For a list of all governors of Bushehr and the Gulf Ports (Banader), see Appendix I.
42. Shepherd 1857, 145; Binning 1857, vol. 2, p. 419; Floor 2007, pp. 243, 280.
43. For a discussion of this period, see Floor 2007, pp. 223-314.
44. Waring 1973, p. 7; Sani` al-Dowleh 1294, vol. 1, p. 300. The name of the three Al Mazkur Sheikhs, who bore the name of Naser, was either written as Naser (ناصر) or as Nasr (نصر). However, in 1838, both the Arabic *monshi* of the British Residency and Col. Robertson, the officiating Resident, in 1843 explictily state that the name of Naser I should be written as نوصر, i.e. "Nawsir, not Nassir or Nasir," see NA, FO 248/99, An Account of the Island of Karrak 01/1838; FO 248/108, Robertson to Sheil 04/01/1843.

hand of its governor, even though he had been appointed by Fath `Ali Shah and unlike his successors, not by the governor-general. Finally, avoidance behavior was not something new, it was a knee-jerk reaction of all Arab and Persian petty chiefs along the Persian littoral; none of them wanted interference from the Persian government. This avoidance, or rather aversion, went even so far that Sheikh Naser II asked the East-India Company (EIC) to replace their agent, Mirza Mehdi `Ali Khan, who was a Persian, because he did not want a Persian spy in his town.[45]

Moreover, even if the Al Mazkur was unable or reluctant to pay a visit to Shiraz that would not have stopped, and in fact did not stop the governor-general from making monetary and other demands from them. Moreover, how much actual avoidance was there? We don't know, because not enough information is available about Sheikh Naser II's movements. However, his son Sheikh `Abdol-Rasul spent almost seven years in Shiraz as a virtual prisoner from 1808 to 1815. When he was restored to power in 1815, he was well-known in the Shiraz court circles, so much so that he got himself into trouble in 1826 when his intrigue with one of the governor-general's wives backfired (see below). In short, there was no avoiding the Persians from Shiraz as is clear from the vicissitudes of Al Mazkur rule. There were good reasons for the Al Mazkur to suspect Persian interest in their affairs. This interest was not merely a financial one, but the Qajars, be it in a haphazard manner, also clearly signaled that they wanted to end Arab rule over their southern littoral. We really cannot call it a policy as it was not one that was publicized or even consistently pursued, but gradually the Qajars were able to reduce or eliminate Arab influence in Khuzestan (1840), Bushehr (1850), Bandar Abbas (1868) and Lengeh (1879), although they failed to do so in the Shibkuh coast (1880).[46]

Even though the new Qajar government was pre-occupied with challenges to its rule in northern Persia, this did not mean that it had lost interest in Bushehr or the Persian Gulf. Already, in 1796, when a conflict broke out between Persia and Oman, Sheikh Naser II received orders from Agha Mohammad Shah to prepare a land force to attack Masqat. Mills and Lorimer surmised that this attack was not implemented, but according to Bastaki it was. Matters clearly were amiably resolved, because in 1797 an Omani fleet poised to attack Basra was lying peacefully on the roadstead of Bushehr.[47] More upsetting were the events that took place in April 1798, when Hoseynqoli Khan, the governor-general of Fars rebelled against Fath `Ali Shah. He marched on Bushehr, deposed Sheikh Naser II and appointed the latter's cousin Sheikh Ghanem as governor. However, Hoseynqoli Khan was defeated in August 1798, north of Bushehr, while a land force led by Sheikh Mohammad, Sheikh Naser II's brother, and a naval force led by Sheikh Naser II himself, retook the city after a five days' siege, during which the inhabitants had only "water little better than the sea." On arrival of the `Otubi fleet, probably 16 September 1798, Mr. Hankey Smith, the British Resident hired a vessel to ship his and the East India Company's (EIC) goods to Khark. The first `Otubi vessel entering the harbor immediately started plundering the hired vessel. Mr. Smith complained to Sheikh Salem, the `Otubi commander, who ordered that all goods had to be restituted. The order was complied with and all goods were returned, except for two bags of tin and a few bags of rice that had been accidentally dropped into the sea. However, Sheikh Naser II refused to allow Mr.

45. Grummon 1985, pp. 126-30. On Mirza Mehdi, see Lorimer 1915, vol. 1, pp. 1884-86, 1921.

46. Floor 2010; Idem 2011 a; Idem 2011 b, chapter 4; Idem 2014 a.

47. Bastaki 1339, p. 190; Mills 1966, p. 287; Lorimer 1915, vol. 1, p. 421.

Smith to leave to Khark, who then had to return to Bushehr and become part of the besieged population. In the evening of 20 September 1798, Sheikh Ghanem led a sortie, which failed. The besiegers pursued the sortie party when it withdrew and were able to enter the town with them. The defenders panicked and Sheikh Ghanem, having failed to rally his men, fled, forgetting to pay 300 piasters that he owed Mr. Smith. The victors spent the night plundering and looting the town until the next morning. It was with great difficulty that Mr. Smith was able to prevent the EIC building, which at that time was in the center of Bushehr, from being plundered as well. However, his servants were not so lucky, as they "were robbed of even the shirts on their backs." It is of interest to note here that the `Otubis of Bahrain supported Naser II with ships and men. It took Sheikh Naser's force five days to retake his own city, which further indicates that Sheikh Ghanem had strong local support. His defection, moreover, was the beginning of family factionalism, which undermined the family's ability to resist outside forces.[48]

In 1799, the governor-general of Fars and the ruler of Oman, Soltan b. Ahmad, planned a joint attack Bahrain. The `Otubis of Bahrain informed their ally Sheikh Naser II that they wanted to pay tribute to Persia and become Persian subjects, or, according to Lorimer, it was Sheikh Naser who suggested this ploy. Sheikh Naser went secretly to Bahrain to receive the tribute, which angered the Soltan b. Ahmad who had already arrived at Bushehr to initiate the operations. Allegedly, Persian troops had already arrived outside Bushehr.[49] Despite having to swallow his pride and refrain from attacking Bahrain in 1799 the financial attraction of its rich pearl banks was irresistible. Therefore, in 1801, Soltan b. Ahmad attacked Bahrain again and invaded the island. This time he was victorious; the Omanis expelled the `Otubis from the island which they occupied. However, already a few months later the `Otubis were able to retake the island and expel the Omanis. In reaction, Soltan b. Ahmad sent a new invasion force, which was able to occupy part of the island, but unable to expel the `Otubis. Frustrated in his attempt and not being strong enough to overcome the `Otubis, who received help from the Wahhabis, Soltan b. Ahmad turned to Persia for assistance. In August 1802, the prince-governor of Fars reacted positively to Soltan b. Ahmad's request and sent 200 horse and 2,000 foot soldiers to Bushehr who boarded the Masqat fleet. This time the Omanis were able to expel the `Otubis and take control over the island for a while.[50]

Although the governor-general of Fars was able to send troops to Bahrain, he was unable, or not greatly interested, to establish security on the trade route connecting Bushehr and Shiraz, because in that same year of 1802, caravans from Bushehr to Shiraz were regularly plundered.[51] The same held for the security in the Persian littoral and its offshore area. In August 1803, when two British ships stranded on the island of Bu Sho`eyb they were plundered by the local sheikh. The British complained in Shiraz and the governor-general ordered Sheikh Naser to mount an expedition against Nakhilu. He dragged his feet and only did so after two years, which expedition cost him 100,000 piasters.[52] Despite this delay, there continued to be good relations between the British and the Al Mazkur. In fact, in 1807, the Bombay government paid Rs3,000 to Sheikh

48. Grummon 1985, pp. 128-29; Lorimer 1915, vol. 1, pp. 1910, 1920-21.
49. Lorimer 1915, vol. 1, p. 1911; Grummon 1985, p. 131.
50. Mills 1966, pp. 294-98; Lorimer 1915, vol. 2, p. 434; Risso 1986, pp. 176-78.
51. Grummon 1985, p. 124.
52. Saldanha 1986, vol. 2, p. 65; Grummon 1985, pp. 132-33; Lorimer 1915, vol. 1, pp. 1921-23.

Naser II for his assistance in a case of piracy against a British vessel and as compensation for the loss of a vessel. On 23 January 1807, Sheikh Naser left per *Sooliman Shahee* to Mecca leaving his son `Abdol-Rasul as acting governor.[53] Shortly thereafter, in May 1807, Sheikh Naser II died during his pilgrimage.

Sheikh Abdol-Rasul Al Mazkur's First Administration

As a result, a succession struggle developed between Sheikh `Abdol-Rasul and Sheikh Ghanem. Despite the latter's presence in Shiraz, the Fars governor-general confirmed `Abdol-Rasul only one week later, for a fee of course. This fee probably was higher than the 10,000 piasters that the Sheikh wanted to borrow from the East India Company (EIC). The Company lent him 5,000 piasters on condition that it would be exempt of customs duty until he had repaid the loan.[54]

Sheikh `Abdol-Rasul did not appear to be the ideal candidate for governor of Bushehr. In 1808, Morier described him as a "young Arab, of sluggish, dissolute, and unwarlike habits. ... his body bent double with excessive debauch." More importantly, he could not count on the same loyalty as his grandfather.[55] However, he was able to pay the price that the governor-general of Fars demanded and this was all that mattered, as the new governor found out one year later. In 1808, the Fars government insisted on the repayment of a loan of 28,000 *tuman*s that `Abdol-Rasul had contracted in Shiraz to settle his tax obligations to the Fars governor-general. Now, on behalf of his creditors the latter demanded its repayment.[56] The driving force behind this demand was not so much the government of Fars, but rather Mohammad Nabi Khan, a wealthy merchant and former ambassador to India (Calcutta). On his return to Persia, Mohammad Nabi Khan using his wealth and influence immediately started buying the governorships of several districts, such as that of Jahrom. He also had his eyes on Bushehr and Mohammad Nabi Khan and his brother Mohammad Ja`far intrigued in Shiraz against Sheikh Abdol-Rasul, which led to the demand of the repayment of the loan.[57] For an alleged sum of 40,000 *tumans* Mohammad Nabi Khan procured the governorship of Bushehr and Dashtestan. He himself stayed in Shiraz, while his brother Mohammad Ja`far was appointed deputy-governor.[58]

---

53. Saldanha 1986, vol. 2, p. 61.
54. Grummon 1985, pp. 133-34; Morier 1812, p. 18; Brydges-Jones 1976, pp. 39ff; Heude 1819, p. p. 41. In 1802, the Sheikh of Bushehr had to pay 4,000 *tumans* in annual taxes in addition to unspecified presents Lorimer 1915, vol. 1, p. 1911.
55. Morier 1812, pp. 12, 18.
56. Morier 1812, pp. 20-21.
57. Hardford Jones Brydges 1976, pp. 39; Saldanha 1986, vol. 2, p. 63; Lorimer 1915, vol. 1, p. 1912.
58. Busse 1972, p. 132; Lorimer 1915, vol. 1, p. 1912; Brydges 1976, p. 46.

Mohammad Nabi Khan's mother was a Parsi woman who was the concubine of Mr. Douglas, one time chief of the EIC factory at Bandar Abbas and later of the one at Basra. They had a daughter who inherited her father's wealth and married an English gentleman. After Douglas's death her mother married Aqa Kuchek, a very respectable merchant in Bushehr and bore him a son, Mohammad Nabi and a daughter who married Haji Khalil, the Persian envoy to India who was killed in Bombay in 1802, and several other children. Aqa Kuchek suffered a setback and was in precarious circumstances; the family was mainly supported by the mother's daughter remittances from England. Mohammad Nabi worked for sometime as clerk (*monshi*) for Hardford Jones, the EIC agent at Basra and to make ends meet, he also acted there as commercial agent for Haji Khalil, his brother-in-law. By 1794, he had become one of the first merchants of Basra and was respected by the Ottoman government. The richer he got the more he became interested in political intrigue and interference in government matters. In 1798, in Baghdad he increased his wealth and reputation and was involved in "politico-mercantile speculations." Meanwhile, Haji Khalil had become the largest merchant at Bushehr, mainly trading with India. After Haji Khalil was killed in Bombay, Mohammad Nabi became the guardian of his sister's son and executor of Haji Khalil's estate. Mohammad Nabi intrigued in Tehran to be appointed ambassador to India instead of his brother-in-law. He was successful in doing so, became a Khan and served as ambassador from 1805 to 1807 with the same charge as Haji Khalil. His stay in Calcutta was very remunerative, because he made 700,000 rupees as ambassador there. Source: Hardford Jones Brydges 1976, pp. 33-37, 48; Lorimer 1915, vol. 1, pp. 1889-94, 1912.

On 26 October 1808, the vizier of Fars, Nasrollah Khan sent Mohammad Hoseyn Khan, his *nasaqchi-bashi* to Bushehr to force Sheikh `Abdol-Rasul to pay the borrowed amount.[59] When news arrived that a body of horse was approaching from Shiraz, Sheikh `Abdol-Rasul put guards on the walls and kept himself watch at the gates. He had already put all his property aboard ships.[60] Sheikh `Abdol-Rasul offered to pay 5,000 *tumans* immediately and promised to pay the rest in installments. This was refused, and the Sheikh gave orders to auction off "his effects, his horses, mules, and asses; and in the course of a few days raised fifty thousand piastres." The British Resident then drew up a statement with British claims from `Abdol-Rasul for a total of Rs25,787 (incl. grain supplied to alleviate the 1806 famine), which was not very helpful. But, it was to no avail because on 26 October 1808 Mohammad Hoseyn Khan arrested him while both were on their way to pay a visit to Sir Harford Jones, the British Envoy, and took him to Shiraz.[61] The Sheikh's wives and servants embarked on his boats as did his vizier Haji Soleyman.

> The shops were shut, the streets crowded with men transporting their households to the sea shore, and their wives and daughters were beating their breasts and crying in loud lamentation. Nor was there a shew of resistance,

59. Saldanha 1986, vol. 2, pp. 62-63; Morier 1812, p. 19.
60. Morier 1812, p. 18; Brydges 1976, p. 39.
61. Morier 1812, p. 21; Saldanha 1986, vol. 2, pp. 62-63; Lorimer 1915, vol. 1, p. 1912.

> except on the walls; or a thought of defence: the only hope and the only thought of very man was the preservation of his little fortunes and the honour of his women. The same alarm prevailed in the country; all the poor date-hut villagers flocked for protection into the Factory, and trusted to its walls the security of their families and their scanty wealth.

Mohammad Hoseyn Khan said his orders were only to arrest the Sheikh, his cousin and his vizier and not to molest the inhabitants. However, he would not spare Bushehr if the Sheikh's vizier was not given to him and therefore, the people intercepted him during his flight to his boat and handed him over (however, see below). The Sheikh's cousin escaped.[62] Sheikh Darvish, a brother of Sheikh `Abdol-Rasul, fled with one or more ships to Oman, to his original tribe, and carried out piratical raids against Bushehri vessels and killed any Persian he found on board. However, his actions were at best pin-pricks and neither inconvenienced Mohammad Nabi Khan nor his successors.[63]

First Non-Al Mazkur Administration

One day after Sheikh `Abdol-Rasul's arrest, Mohammad Hoseyn Khan took control over the port and announced that security and peace would be guaranteed and that everybody could return. To show that he meant business, he severely punished a soldier who took a turban from a Jew. The bazaar was opened again and the town was quiet. However, soon thereafter he began extorting donations from the merchants, who wanted to flee. The bastinado was freely applied. He tried the same with Mohammad Ja`far, the acting governor, who refused to pay and "wrote to the townsmen to arm in revenge, and defend themselves against such requisitions." A few days later Mohamad Ja`far was invested as acting governor "by the girding of a sword on his thigh." On 7 November 1808, Mohammad Hoseyn Khan threw him in chains in prison; the reason was that he allegedly had instigated the flight of the vizier by sea; he either had to deliver the fugitive or pay 20,000 *tumans*. As Mohamad Ja`far could not he remained in prison. Later he offered to find him, but Mohammad Hoseyn Khan deemed the security offered to return too uncertain. Although Mohammad Nabi Khan was not on the best terms with his brother he could not tolerate this insult to his family and he was able to have his brother released and restored as acting governor. Mohammad Nabi Khan went in person to Bushehr, where, after his entry on 4 December 1808, he received a robe of honor from the governor-general of Fars making his appointment official. Meanwhile, in Shiraz, Sheikh `Abdol-Rasul was threatened with beheading or blinding, but due to Mohammad Nabi Khan's intercession the prince relented and just kept him imprisoned.[64]

On or about 20 November 1811, Mohammad Nabi Khan was suddenly summoned to Shiraz; on his arrival Nasrollah Khan, the vizier of Fars was dismissed and imprisoned.

62. Morier 1812, pp. 22-23.

63. Grummon 1985, pp. 137-38.

64. Morier 1812, pp. 23-27; Lorimer 1915, vol. 1, p. 1912 has as date 19 December 1808. There also was a rumor that Mohammad Nabi Khan had been so upset by the enmity of the people of Bushehr towards him that he asked permission to resign as governor, offering 2,000 *tumans* for the privilege. Given the prince's thirst for money it seems unlikely that he would have declined such an offer. The governor would receive the robe of honor at the *tell-e khel`at-pushan*. Hamidi 1380, p. 208.

He had been accused of having collected extra revenues and keeping them for himself; that people complained about these higher taxes was not helpful either to the vizier. Mohammad Nabi Khan, who was on bad terms with him, produced the evidence against the vizier. Hoseyn `Ali Mirza Farmanfarma, the governor-general now made Mohammad Nabi Khan his vizier, who, in his turn, appointed his brother Mohammad Ja`far Khan as acting governor of Bushehr.[65] However, Mohammad Nabi Khan had many enemies, who were intriguing against him and who eventually, were the cause of the loss of his life and fortune. But for the time being he was collecting additional wealth from Al Mazkur's supporters. Some of the close supporters of the Al Mazkurs were among his first victims. The Demukh tribe, immigrants from Arabia, had settled at Chahkutah and were a close supporter of Bushehr and formed the first landward line of defense of the town. They were also richer than the other tribes and therefore, attracted Mohammad Nabi Khan's interest; this almost led to their extirpation in 1809. Mohammad Nabi Khan made use of Tangestani levies to enforce his rule and bring the Demukh down.[66] However, the Demukh were not the only ones to suffer from the governor's greed, for due to his grasping hand and misgovernment the governorate was greatly impoverished resulting in lower tax revenues.[67]

In 1811, Mohammad Nabi Khan fell from power. He was summoned to Tehran, where he was blamed for the revenue shortfall of Fars province of 70,000 *tumans*. He received the bastinado together with another official suspected of having embezzled funds and almost suffered defenestration at the Shah's orders. However, he was received back in royal favor and then he received treatment for his wounds and a robe of honor as an incentive to produce the missing funds. In 1815, he apparently was still alive, for he sought refuge in a sanctuary in Shiraz. Farmanfarma wrote, when it was rumored that he intended to reappoint him as governor of Bushehr, that this was a preposterous idea. "When he was prosperous he was unfit for public service, why would I reappoint him? He is not fit to be a *kadkhoda* let alone a governor of Bushire." It would appear that thereafter he lost his life in a cruel manner.[68]

His brother Mohammad Ja`far Khan, who succeeded him as governor of Bushehr and Dashtestan, did not do a better job and was removed in March 1813. In his stead Mehdiqoli Khan Qajar was appointed, whose administration did not improve matters. He was inept and raised taxes to pay for the fortification of Bushehr's walls. This led to local disorder and as a result, much of the littoral was insecure and the various Sheikhs were fighting against each other. Therefore, Mehdiqoli Khan Qajar willingly agreed in November 1814 that Sheikh `Abdol-Rasul take over as governor of Bushehr, although he remained governor of Dashtestan. The appointment of the Al Mazkur Sheikh was an acknowledgement that the family had always been able to collect the revenue.[69]

In early 1815, Fath `Ali Shah (r. 1797-1834) sent a decree of indemnity to Sheikh Mohammad, Sheikh Naser II's brother, who had taken refuge on Khark Island. Being

65. Saldanha 1986, vol. 2, p. 63; Sa`adat 1390, p. 66.

66. Brydges 1976, p. 46; Ouseley 1819-23, vol. 1, p. 255; Lorimer 1915, vol. 1, p. 1913; Grummon 1985, pp. 138-39; Grummon 1985, pp. 138-39.

67. Saldanha 1986, vol. 2, p. 77.

68. Morier 1818, p. 95; Lorimer 1915, vol. 1, p. 1913; NA, FO 248/38, *Farman* governor-general of Fars to Bruce rec. 11/08/1815; Brydges-Jones 1976, p. 46.

69. Lorimer 1915, vol. 1, p. 1913; Grummon 1985, pp. 122, 136.

welcomed back into the Qajar fold must have been a relief for the Al Mazkur, because during the 6-year period of exile and powerlessness the family had no access to its assets and was aided by its supporters to make ends meet.[70] Because Sheikh `Abdol-Rasul was still in prison, his uncle, Sheikh Mohammad b. Naser I became acting governor of Bushehr. However, the honeymoon between the Persian government and the Al Mazkur did not last long. Already in July 1815, Sheikh Mohammad believed that Mirza Hasan Khan, the bearer of a decree from the governor-general of Fars to William Bruce, the British Resident, had been appointed the new governor of Bushehr and had secret orders to arrest him, his family and his tribe and to take them as prisoners to Shiraz. Therefore, he refused him entry and collected a large force from people to the north of Bushehr. If the governor-general did not want to keep him as govenor he intended to oppose entry of the Shiraz officials until he could obtain vessels to sail away to the Arabian shore. Sheikh Mohammad complained that the Al Mazkur had already suffered much by their ouster in 1808 and would never have returned to their native country again, if the Shah had not sent a *farman* inviting them back from various places in Arabia, where they had scattered. Despite assurances given in the royal decree, they had barely settled when again a similar hostile act was undertaken against them. Therefore, he had to take measures to protect the interests of the Al Mazkur. Sheikh Mohammad asked Bruce to inform Mirza Hasan Khan of his determination. Bruce sent a message to Mirza Hasan Khan and the vizier in Shiraz, but the messenger missed him en route. However, on 28 July, Mirza Hasan Khan sent a horseman with a note for Sheikh Mohammad and Bruce that he would enter the town on 30 July. Sheikh Mohammad told the horseman what he thought about that and Bruce wrote Mirza Hasan Khan advising him to come only with a few men and stop under a large Banyan tree about 2.5 km outside Bushehr, where Bruce would wait for him to try and mediate. Mirza Hasan Khan came with the *farman* and Bruce told him how matters stood in town. The Khan swore that the Sheikh was mistaken, there were no secret orders. Mirza Hasan Khan asked Bruce to arrange that he would be allowed into the town, he was willing to come all alone and that the Sheikh might keep his force and occupy the towers. Bruce then sent a message to Sheikh Mohammad to ask him to come in person or send a confidante.

After several hours Sheikh Rahma, first cousin of the Sheikh arrived with 100 matchlockmen. Long discussions followed during which Mirza Hasan Khan took oaths of every kind to dissuade them of the idea that he had secret orders. Finally, Sheikh Rahma said that nothing would convince them unless Bruce pledged that they would not be molested and would stand security for their safety. Bruce declined, saying that he was not allowed to interfere in local matters. Sheikh Rahma repeated that unless Bruce stood security in person Sheikh Mohammad would not change his mind and "would repel force by force." Mirza Hasan Khan then tried to convince Bruce to do so, but he "had learnt that promises made by government officials could not be trusted, and I had reliable private information" that the Khan had orders to arrest the Al Mazkurs. Sheikh Rahma left and Mirza Hasan Khan asked what he should do. Bruce told him to return to Tangestan and await further orders from Shiraz that would reach him in 5-6 days. Mirza Hasan Khan said he would return to gather a force and attack. Bruce said that surely his orders did not include that the population of Bushehr had to suffer as they would be if he attacked. He then asked Bruce to return to Bushehr and ask Sheikh Mohammad to

70. Lorimer 1915, vol. 1, p. 1913; Grummon 1985, pp. 137-38.

give in and let him know the reply. If not, the next morning he would cut off all water supplies, except for Bruce's own use. Sheikh Mohammad did not change his position and Bruce informed Mirza Hasan Khan accordingly. On the first of August 1815, Mirza Hasan Khan came to the Banyan tree with a large force of Tangestanis. Bruce went there to ask what his intentions were. He replied, to cut off water and storm the town. Bruce said there was nothing in his orders that stated that he had to cut off water or storm the town. Mirza Hasan Khan said Sheikh Mohammad had thrown off allegiance and was now a rebel. Bruce then asked him to give orders that the Residency's watermen would not be molested and would be accompanied by a sepoy.

Nothing happened until the 3rd of August, when the Residency's watermen, their donkeys and skins were seized and were kept for most of the day. The Residency staff suffered much as there was not a drop of fresh water in the town and the heat in that season was excessive. The watermen returned in the evening having been beaten and several of their water skins taken. Bruce wrote Mirza Hasan Khan a note, who replied with frivolous apologies and did not promise that it would not happen again. The distress of the inhabitants of Bushehr was shocking and several people died from thirst. The merchants appealed to Mirza Hasan Khan who then allowed 50 donkeys per day to enter and this for a town of 8,000 people. Therefore, as soon as the donkeys entered a mob rushed towards them so that only a little of the water reached the Residency. Bruce had almost 300 people there, all under British protection and their families, and thus all of them were under great distress. Therefore, Bruce asked the commander of the *FyzelKarim*, to make preparations to receive him and his dependents. He intended to move to Khark, when forced to by lack of water, and stay there until calm returned. In his opinion, the troops of both parties consisted of rabble and were prone to plunder.[71]

Mirza Hasan Khan allowed water to come in again. On 11 August 1815, orders arrived with Yasavol Khan to try and reach an agreement with Sheikh Mohammad. If this failed he had to get more men and storm the town. Mirza Hasan Khan sent Bruce a note wishing to see him at the Banyan tree. He said that the governor-general did not intend to do anything to the Al Mazkur family and therefore, he urged Bruce to pledge his word. Bruce said that he could not do that, but he was willing to point out to Sheikh Mohammad the ruinous consequences of his behavior. Bruce asked the Khan to send his confidante Mirza Kazem with him. The prince-governor's decree intimated that Bruce had the power and means to arrest Sheikh Mohammad and ought to do so. Bruce commented that if he would do so, there would be bloodshed on both sides, as in 1808, when the governor-general asked Bruce to invite and then arrest Sheikh Abdol-Rasul and send him bound to Shiraz. At that time Bruce had the means not only to take the Sheikh, but the whole town.[72] Of course, he had declined and he considered this second attempt a sign of disrespect for the British. From 11 to 13 August 1815, Mirza Kazem and Bruce did everything possible to change Sheikh Mohammad's mind and have him agree to admit the prince-governor's officers. He refused; it was his town and his family's hereditary function already for several generations. He would, however, continue to pay the revenues to whomever the governor-general assigned. He would not be deposed, 6-7 years wandering as beggars had been enough. He would hold out as long as possible, and

71. NA, FO 248/38, Bruce to Sir Evan Nepean, Governor Bombay, 05/08/1815.

72. For the British force (some 450 men plus artillery) at Bushehr that accompanied General John Malcolm, the Envoy to the Persian court in 1808, see Lorimer 1915, vol. 1, p. 1895.

if he had to yield he would board his dhows and *batils* and batter the town to the ground, except of course the British factory and then go to Khark or some other place and sent boats to constantly harass the town. Yasavol Khan collected some more men, but did not attack as yet. However, on 15 August all the watermen were returned, including those of the British factory. Yasavol Khan informed Bruce not to take offense, but to send a vessel to Halileh and get there as much water as he wanted, because cutting off water by land was the only way to force the Sheikh and his men to give in. Bruce replied that he agreed to do so, but only when the weather allowed this. On the morning of 16 August, Yasavol Khan allowed normal water transport again. Meanwhile, business in the town was at total standstill and people were alarmed. Sheikh Mohammad received reinforcements and had 1,000-1,200 men with much ammunition. Kangan was also besieged by Persian forces. Captain William Bruce, the British Agent in Bushehr commented on both these events, as follows: "It would therefore appear that the policy of the Persian Government is to withdraw the Arab tribes from the Coast and transplant them into the interior, a plan, however, they will not be able to carry into effect."[73]

On 19 August 1815, Yasavol Khan again banned the supply of water. Because of a strong south wind Bruce could not send vessels to Halilah. He informed Yasavol Khan about this and asked him to allow his watermen to the wells; also that it might be better for him and his people to move to a place assigned by Yasavol Khan outside Bushehr and reside there in tents. Bruce's messenger was shot at by his musketmen and despite the fact that he yelled who he was they continued firing and he returned. Bruce then asked a beggar boy to bring the note to the musketmen and ask them to give it to Yasavol Khan. They beat the boy but forwarded the note. Late in the evening Yasavol Khan sent a note saying the water ban stayed and nobody including Bruce was allowed to leave town. Because there was no water, Bruce therefore, hired a *baghlah* to take his family, guards and dependents and whatever they could carry to go to Khark, intending to return when things were calm again. He left some sepoys to guard the factory with three day's water supply.

From 19 to 22 August 1815, he was busy making preparations for his departure. On the morning of 22 August, Bruce wrote Yasavol Khan that he was on the eve of leaving Bushehr. He blamed him for this inconvenience, informing Yasavol Khan that he left all public and private British property behind, which now was his reponsibility. Yasavol Khan immediately reacted and wrote that Bruce was allowed to go to Rishahr or Halileh. Bruce then decided to go to Halileh as it was close to Khark. Because Sheikh Mohammad had a garrison on the island, his last resort and refuge, Bruce realized that his going there might be interpreted as support for Sheikh Mohammad's position. The next morning Bruce and party went to Halileh and pitched tents; the nearby villagers were very friendly to the influx of about 500 people. Before leaving Bushehr, Bruce told Sheikh Mohammad that although having thrown off Persian allegiance, he expected him to consider British property sacred, which he promised. Most inhabitants and merchants had already left town. On 25 August, five Qavasem vessels anchored at Halileh. One man came ashore to Bruce's camp, who said that Soltan Saqr (Sugger) had sent them from Sharjah to assist Sheikh Mohammad. They had left on 19 August and had a force of 800 men. He asked how the situation was and to indicate which houses contained British property and were

73. NA, FO 248/38, Bruce to Sir Evan Nepean, Governor Bombay, 16/08/1815.

under British protection. His Sheikh, Mohammad b. Qadib (Ghutheab) would place persons over it to protect them to prevent plunder, as it was their intention to plunder the town, especially the quarter where the Behbahani tribe lived, who were enemies of Sheikh Mohammad. Bruce gave him the information and the man said that they would leave at midnight when the land wind was good. Bruce immediately sent a messenger to Yasavol Khan with news about the arrival and intention of this force. On 27 August, in the morning, the Qavasem landed at Bushehr and asked Sheikh Mohammad to allow them to attack the Persian troops. There was also news that Aqa Baba Khan with many troops was soon to arrive from Shiraz; he was said to be at one day's distance. The Qavasem put white flags on the houses Bruce had indicated.

On 28 August 1815, in the morning, Bruce went by sea to the factory in Bushehr. Sheikh Mohammad came and told him that he had been forced to take strong measures against the Behbahanis because since the previous night and that morning they had incessantly fired on his men from their rooftops. Several had been shot, two men of the Qavasem were killed. Therefore, he ordered their houses and caravanserais to be plundered before the evening. Several of their women, children and slaves had been carried off. Many were wounded in the fight. While Bruce and Sheikh Mohammad were talking, Sheikh `Abdollah, a relative of his, arrived. He said that Aqa Baba Khan had arrived with a large force; therefore, he intended to embark that night or the next morning with his family, his plunder, and his possessions.

At sunset Bruce returned to Halileh. Sheikh Mohammad and his men left at midnight and the Persian troops scaled the walls and entered the town without opposition. The only shots fired were from the dhows, which wounded four men. Aqa Baba Khan would not have dared to attack if a messenger had not alerted him, because he was not yet ready, having only arrived in the morning. The Persian troops immediately started plundering in a manner worse than Sheikh Mohammad and the Qavasem. The latter had concentrated on the Behbahani quarter, which they plundered for one day only, whereas the Persians were still doing it on 3 September, six days later. "The main plunderers are Tangestanis. No redress is to be obtained and all is in great confusion." Bruce talked to Mirza Hasan Khan, who has been named governor, but said he could not control the troops. Those people still remaining in town were leaving and Bruce expected that soon there would be nobody left. Bruce and his staff returned on 30 August and Sheikh Mohammad and his 32 small and large vessels sailed that same morning for Khark. Bruce wrote to Shiraz saying that during Sheikh Mohammad's and the Qavasem's presence no British property was taken, but since the prince-governor's men had entered, houses and warehouses had been emptied, and if they were to stay longer Bruce would not be surprised if they attacked the Factory. Bruce estimated the damage due to plunder at about one million piasters and he opined that it would take a long time for Bushehr to recover from this shock. "The only thing one sees is empty houses without doors and windows, all taken by the Persian troops."[74]

Mirza Hasan Khan was only the acting governor, for Farmanfarma had appointed his son, Anushirvan Mirza, governor or *beglerbegi* of Bushehr. Given his age, his father had appointed his steward (*nazer*) as deputy-governor. Farmanfarma further asked Bruce for

74. NA, FO 248/38, Bruce to Sir Evan Nepean, Governor Bombay, 3 September 1815. Sheikh Mohammad b. Qadib, was the Qavasem chief of Lengeh. Therefore, the men came from that port and not from Sharjah, where the chief of the Qavasem resided.

cavalry sabers, muskets, ordinance, shot and vessels to carry troops to Khark. Bruce replied that such equipment was not available in Bushehr, moreover such a request had to be made in Tehran. He commented: "As a result, Shiraz let it be rumoured that they suspect us to favor Sheikh Mohammad for his disloyalty and therefore, I am being difficult."[75] In another letter, Farmanfarma rhetorically asked Bruce: "how could you allow matters come to such a pitch," as if it was Bruce's business. The prince continued that Sheikh Mohammad had nothing to fear as he had done nothing wrong. Sheikh `Abdol-Rasul has been sent to the Shah and Farmanfarma expected him to be sent back with honor. Mirza Hasan Khan only had been sent to collect the revenues during Sheikh Abdol-Rasul's absence and would remain there until his return.[76]

Sheikh Abdol-Rasul Al Mazkur's Second Administration

Anushirvan Mirza was not a great success as governor, and therefore, the governor-general of Fars appointed Sheikh `Abdol-Rasul in his stead. This did not stop the rivalry between him and Sheikh Naser I's other grandson, Sheikh Mohammad Rasul. However, their competition for control of Bushehr was without violence. "They appeared, indeed, content that the one or the other should reign (as it has of late happened) each in his turn."[77] Sheikh `Abdol-Rasul prevailed and resumed his position as governor. He was a hands-on administrator, who often was seen going about town in public with his uncle Sheikh Mohammad, to whom he always accorded the greatest honors. When walking about, the two men always had a guard of about 20 and servants. Before noon and in the afternoon, after the *al-`asr* prayer, it was their daily practice to come to the harbor, where they sat on a bench in a matted hut, -

> erected for that purpose, and derive great pleasure from the salutes of passengers, and from observing what may be doing among the shipping. When Sheik Mohammed, who is the eldest, but not the actual Governor, happens to be there, his nephew first stands at a respectful distance, with his hands folded beneath his cloak. He then desired to seat himself, which he does frequently on the ground, and in the humblest and most obscure place that he can find behind his uncle. After some time he is desired to advance forward, and he ventures to change his first seat for a better one; and this farce continues, until, after repeated invitations, he becomes seated in front of his superior, while all the rest stand; but he never shares the same bench with his relative.[78]

After Sheikh `Abdol-Rasul's reinstatement, for a number of years Bushehr was left more or less in peace by Shiraz and each year the Sheikh received his robe of honor confirming his investiture, such as on 26 April 1820, which, as required by custom, was

75. NA, FO 248/38, Farman of the governor-general of Fars to Bruce rec. 30/07/1815; Idem, Bruce to Morier, Minister Plenipotentiary, September 1815.

76. NA, FO 248/38, Farman of the governor-general of to Bruce rec. 11/08/1815.

77. Heude 1819, p. 42.

78. Buckingham 1971, pp. 350-51; see also Heude 1819, p. 42.

accompanied by the necessary ceremony.[79] A serious dissonant was the outbreak of cholera in Fars in the fall of 1821, when "the road between Bushehr and Burazjan was strewn with corpses."[80] Another event was a renewed attempt by Farmanfarma to shake down Sheikh `Abdol-Rasul. On 6 August 1822, in his presence, the prince-governor announced his intention to attack Bahrain that winter and the Sheikh pledged "to furnish his ships and buggalows for his service, which, if he performs, the other ports will readily supply such vessels as they possess."[81] The invasion did not happen, after the governor of Bombay, on learning about this plan, wrote to the Shah and the prince to warn them of the consequences. These might include an end to the peace in the Persian Gulf and a resumption of maritime violence, in which case the British government would be forced to establish a military force there. Although the invasion was shelved, in 1824, Sheikh `Abdol-Rasul bought off the prince-governor who wanted to come to Bushehr as a launching pad for the reconquest of Bahrain. However, it would seem that these invasion intentions were repeated regularly as a means to milk the Sheikh and deduct the inflated cost of such expeditions (or rather their alleged preparations) from his annual remittances to Tehran. In 1825 in his turn, the Sheikh, clearly no stranger to extortion, was trying to do the same to the area around Borazjun, which was unsettled due to "the grasping disposition of the Sheik of Bushire."[82]

However, perhaps the biggest reverse in his life Sheikh `Abdol-Rasul suffered, was against the Soltan of Masqat, with whom he found himself at war. The reasons for the conflict are not entirely clear. The simple explanation is that the Soltan of Masqat wanted to marry a Qajar princess, a daughter of the prince-governor of Fars to improve relations with the prince-governor, which lately had become strained over Bandar Abbas. Sheikh `Abdol-Rasul allegedly intrigued to prevent this and was able to delay the marriage.[83] However that does not seem to be the whole story. For if that was the case why would `Abdol-Rasul maltreat some servants of the Soltan who had come to trade in Bushehr?[84] Also, both men had been busy building up support among the coastal tribes. The Soltan had support from those living between Qeshm and `Asalu, while `Abdol-Rasul had cultivated good relations with the Qavasem (the Soltan 's enemies) and the Al Nasur of Kangan. One does not drum up such support to influence a royal marriage, and therefore, other elements (trade, politics) must have played some role. The fact that the Soltan also attacked and seized Kangani vessels at that time, is telling in this context.[85] Furthermore, it is not entirely clear how Sheikh `Abdol-Rasul could have played such a role at the court of Shiraz, given that, allegedly, he was not a regular member and only visited Shiraz occasionally. Nevertheless, it is reported that in the Shiraz court intrigue he supported one of Hoseyn `Ali Mirza's wives, whom he escorted to Mecca in early 1826. The Soltan

79. Lumsden 2010, pp. 29-30.

80. Lorimer 1915, vol. 1, p. 1913.

81. Saldanha 1986, vol. 2, p. 143.

82. Grummon 1985, pp. 124-25; Kelly 1968, pp. 190-91; Alexander 2000, p. 100; Lorimer 1915, vol. 1, p. 1934.

83. Kelly 1968, p. 220; Lorimer 1915, vol. 1, p. 1914; Miles 1966, p. 328; Alexander 2000, p. 93. For the troubles concerning Bandar Abbas, see Floor 2011 a, p. 73.

84. Alexander 2000, p. 93.

85. Floor 2014 a, pp. 56-57.

supported another wife, Hajijah, who asked him to arrest `Abdol-Rasul on his return from Mecca. As his reward he would get her daughter as wife.[86]

Whatever the cause(s) of the conflict between Masqat and Bushehr, naval action was felt to be imminent. In April 1826, Soltan Sa`id was threatening to take Khark or Bushehr itself, claiming that Shiraz supported this. Sheikh Mohammad, `Abdol-Rasul's uncle, sent two merchants to Masqat to placate the Soltan. It did not help. According to the British traveler Alexander, who was in Bushehr at the end of May 1826, when the Omani fleet would arrive at Bushehr it was expected that Sheikh Abdol-Rasul would flee to the mountains. It was also expected that the Shiraz governor might attack and plunder Bushehr. Therefore, Sheikh `Abdol-Rasul employed Baluchis, who guarded the town's gates and walls. When he wanted to bastinado five Baluchi guards, they refused to submit and fought and were killed, after which the rest left Bushehr.[87]

This implies that Sheikh `Abdol-Rasul must have left Bushehr in early July 1826 for Mecca. However, given the fact that the prince's wife went on the hajj, which started that year on 14 July 1826, he must have left probably already in March, the more so, since his uncle Sheikh Mohammad and not he himself contacted Soltan Sa`id in April. The Soltan's flotilla of two ships and one brig arrived on the roadstead of Bushehr on 26 July 1826. The flotilla's orders were clearly aimed against Sheikh `Abdol-Rasul not against Bushehr. For with them was the *Nosrat Shah*, a ship returning from Bengal and belonging to the Sheikh, but captured by the Omanis. It had been refitted as a warship and had come along to disembark goods consigned to Bushehri merchants; those belonging to the Sheikh had been taken out at Masqat. Furthermore, the flotilla had orders to seize any ship belonging to or carrying goods for the Sheikh, but not to interfere with Bushehr's trade or the port itself.

The commander of the flotilla, Mohammad b. Soleyman, via the British Resident, informed the merchants of Bushehr of his intentions to unload their goods, provided they paid him the normal duties owed at Bushehr. The Resident was able to induce Mohammad b. Soleyman to land the goods free-of-charge, else the merchants would have to pay twice. Because Sayyed Sa`id took no action against Bushehr, people considered the entire affair as a private feud between the two rulers, like those between the chiefs in Dashtestan and Tangestan. However, the Resident feared that this feud might blow out of proportion and kindle other feuds all over the Persian Gulf. If the Sheikh would return via the land route it might be a signal to start hostilities. The Omani flotilla moved to Basra to enforce some of the Soltan's private and public claims there. Bombay ordered the Resident to remain neutral and let the Soltan resolve his quarrels with Basra and Bushehr, which was at odds with its warning to Persia in 1822 not to attack Bahrain! British officials increasingly were in the habit of abandoning their alleged neutrality if it suited British ends, and it was not the last time. In the same vein, Bombay further argued that, once the Basra quarrel was amiably settled Sayyed Sa`id could concentrate on Sheikh `Abdol-Rasul.[88]

86. Fasa'i 1376, vol. 1, pp. 745-47; for other versions, see Wellstead 1840, vol. 2, pp. 133-36; Sa`adat 1390, pp. 74-75.

87. Alexander 2000, p. 94.

88. Saldanha 1986, vol. 1, pp. 249; Lorimer 1915, vol. 1, pp. 1914-15; Busse, p. 147.

Things came to a head in Bushehr when Sheikh `Abdol-Rasul was seized by the Omanis. In September 1826, the Omani flotilla moved to Qeshm to intercept the returning Sheikh, whom they captured on 13 September together with two of his ships.[89] There were two developments. One was that the governor-general of Fars wrote to Bombay, expressing his displeasure about Lt. Col. Stannus, the British Resident because he had neither prevented the arrest nor brought about the release of Sheikh `Abdol-Rasul and his ships. Bombay replied in October 1826 that the Resident's instructions were only to prevent the renewal of piracy of piracy in the Gulf, but in no way to intervene in legitimate warfare between independent states. Bombay reiterated this message again in November of that year.[90]

The other development was the change of governor in Bushehr. In August 1826, Sheikh Mohammad, the acting governor of Bushehr asked an estranged distant relative, Sheikh Ahmad b. Khamis, to help defend the port against the Omani fleet. He had been a favorite of the Arab part of the population for a long time and the extreme dislike for Sheikh `Abdol-Rasul's rule helped him. Sheikh Ahmad endeared himself to the merchants and other inhabitants by promising better rule and less oppressive commercial policies.[91] When Sheikh `Abdol-Rasul's capture became known, support for his son, Sheikh Naser III and Sheikh Mohammad evaporated and Sheikh Ahmad took over the administration of the town without the "slightest disturbance." Although the governor-general of Fars had received Rs1,400 from Sheikh Ahmad on his assumption of power, it it is unclear whether the takeover was officially sanctioned by Shiraz. In the night of 27 November 1826, Sheikh Naser III, the oldest son of Sheikh `Abdol-Rasul fled from the house of his grand uncle, Sheikh Ahmad, where he had been kept since his grab of power and asked for British protection. Sheikh Hoseyn, Sheikh `Abdol-Rasul's younger brother, also fled to the Residency and likewise asked for asylum. This was granted after they stated that they would not undertake any violent actions against Sheikh Ahmad. Col. Stannus, the British Resident, did not want to interfere in the internal affairs of Bushehr and informed Sheikh Ahmad about Sheikh's Naser's and Sheikh Hoseyn's flight as well as that he felt honor bound to grant asylum to them in the Residency. Sheikh Ahmad expressed surprise as he had always treated Sheikh Naser well and had not threatened his safety, but he was glad that his relative was received in such a friendly manner. Stannus hoped that Shiraz would not be offended by this and misconstrue his intentions. Bombay approved of the grant of asylum, but insisted that all parties (uncle and nephew) be informed of the conditions of the asylum.[92]

When it became known that the prince-governor would arrive in Bushehr in February 1827, Sheikh Ahmad intended to take hostages from each tribe in Bushehr and send them to Khark as security of support prior to the prince's arrival. However, because of this, Sheikh Ahmad's supporters deserted him.[93] In the night of 2 February 1827, at half past ten, alarm was given that there was a disturbance in the town. Stannus found that

89. Saldanha 1986, vol. 1, pp. 249-50; Sa`adat 1390, p. 75.

90. NA, FO 248/52, 16/10/1826, Mountstuart, governor of Bombay to governor-general of Fars; Idem, Mountstuart to governor-general of Fars, November 1826.

91. NA, FO 248/52,Stannus to MacDonald, Tehran, 28/11/1826.

92. NA, FO 248/52,Stannus to MacDonald, Tehran, 28/11/1826; Saldanha vol. 2, p. 251.

93. Busse 149; NA, FO 248/52, Stannus to William Newham, chief secr. government Bombay, 07/02/1827; Lorimer 1915, vol. 1, p. 1915.

Sheikh Hoseyn had left his asylum, while Sheikh Naser III had armed men with him, who had entered the Residency without the Resident's knowledge. Stannus told Sheikh Naser that his behavior was at odds with his being under British protection. Moreover, the moment he left the gate he would be on his own. He then decided to stay, promising to have no contact with the insurgents without the Resident's knowledge.[94]

During that night, Sheikh Hoseyn led a counter revolution supported by 150 men of the Bani Hajer (Bani Hadgee) who lived in the Rudhilleh district. During the night they surprised the only two towers of the fort occupied by Sheikh Ahmad's followers; at day light they surrounded the Sheikh's house.[95] In the morning of 3 February 1827, some of Sheikh Hoseyn's wounded men were brought to the Residency, they told that their party had taken the tower and the gate of the fort. Everything else was in the hands of the people of Bushehr and the Bani Hajer tribe, who the previous day had switched sides. Sheikh Ahmad still controlled his house and even tried to regain the magazine tower, but was repulsed. At 11 a.m. he sent a message asking that Dr. Riach, the Residency's physician, come and see him. Thinking he needed medical help this was agreed to; one half hour later Dr. Riach sent note that Sheikh Ahmad and his 6-year old son wanted asylum, he also asked protection for Aqa Jamal, the treasurer. Stannus agreed to this request, except for Aqa Jamal, who was Sheikh `Abdol-Rasul's servant. Moreover, Sheikh Ahmad wanted to come to terms with Sheikh Naser III. Lt. Strong who accompanied Dr. Riach reported that Sheikh Ahmad's position was desperate; he only had 100 fighters left and his ammunition was almost finished. His house was surrounded and his opponents were preparing to undermine it, while a *baghla* was incessantly firing from 50 m distance.

Stannus persuaded Sheikh Naser III to come to an agreement with Sheikh Ahmad to which end Stannus drew up a draft text. The agreement spelled out that Sheikh Ahmad stepped down as governor, would receive asylum in the Residency until such time the surrender of Khark was confirmed, in which case "he was to be furnished with the means of proceeding by sea beyond the limits of the Bushire territory." The agreement was sent to Sheikh Ahmad who insisted that Aqa Jamal also was given asylum. Sheikh Naser agreed to that until he would be claimed on the return of his father, which Sheikh Ahmad accepted and then signed the agreement. However, Sheikh Hoseyn demanded the articles to be altered or else he refused to cease hostilities. The fighting continued till the evening and fearing for the lives of the defenders the alteration was made. Sheikh Ahmad and his men were allowed to go to the Residency. The next day, early in the morning, Stannus told Sheikh Naser about the changes, which he refused to accept; he wanted to stick to the first agreement. The Demukh, Aqa Jamal and Mirza Baqer, who talked with Sheikh Naser, also agreed but wanted to wait till Sheikh Naser had become governor. Then, thanking Stannus for the asylum, Sheikh Naser left.

At that time, news was received that a large group of Tangestanis had arrived near Bushehr to assist Sheikh Ahmad. Stannus was suspicious of the conversations between him and two chiefs of that tribe who had taken refuge with him. His suspicions were confirmed when a delegation of merchants sent by Sheikh Mohammad came to see Stannus informing him that there was a plot by Tangestani horsemen supported by Sheikh Ahmad's men from the Residency to take the fort. Stannus then ordered the members

94. NA, FO 248/52, Stannus to William Newham, 07/02/1827, chief secr. government Bombay.
95. NA, FO 248/52, Stannus to William Newham, chief secr. government Bombay, 07/02/1827.

of the Demukh tribe and the two chiefs to leave the Residency immediately. Sheikh Ahmad admitted that the plot existed, but that he would abandon it and would respect the rules of asylum and the signed agreement. To ensure this, Stannus saw to it that the Demukh left Bushehr, which took time as it was difficult to find transport for them, their families and followers. The two chiefs accompanied them and before sunset the Tangestani horsemen had returned.

In the morning of 6 February 1827, news arrived that the Farmanfarma was at Ganaveh and would come to Bushehr. Sheikh Ahmad asked Stannus to help him submit his case to the prince-governor. Stannus agreed and asked Sheikh Mohammad, who was very ill, to induce his two relatives to agree to convey this message. Mr. Aratun Constantine, an Armenian merchant, went to Sheikh Hoseyn, who came to the Residency. However, he stopped Constantine from going to see Sheikh Naser, saying he knew his nephew's mind and he could decide for them both. However, when Stannus expressed his surprise about this he sent for him.

On arrival, Sheikh Naser immediately said since Stannus was the mediator, presentations to the authorities could only be made through him. As he had been removed by force he wanted to go himself to the prince as he had appointed him and was his superior, but he had no problem if Sheikh Ahmad did the same. Sheikh Hoseyn then said only the people of Bushehr should decide this matter, because they had revolted. The heads of the tribes would give an account of what had occurred and only they had to decide. He wanted adherence to the agreement, especially the clauses concerning Khark and the return of the *Mansuri* and that Sheikh Ahmad only then would be allowed to leave by sea. Stannus pointed out that the agreement did not require the return of the *Mansuri* prior to his departure, only a commitment to do so, which already had been made. As soon as Khark had surrendered Sheikh Ahmad could leave.

Sheikh Hoseyn then became furious and in this tone asked those present whether this was the correct interpretation. Stannus told him that he expected matters to be discussed calmly. He then became silent, but Sheikh Naser then said that Stannus should behave with impartiality, but now seemed to espouse Sheikh Ahmad's cause to the detriment of the other side. Stannus replied that he was not allowed to interfere in local politics and had never done so. However, they had asked for his protection and thus, had implicated him in their affairs, even though he did not want to. He was the channel of their agreement and thus, who else would act as mediator and see to it that it was implemented?

Sheikh Hoseyn admitted that Stannus was right, but asked whether it was not his interference that had spared the lives of Sheikh Ahmad and his men, and due to their gratitude they had followed his advice and suggestions? Stannus then said: "this was not certainly the case on your part, like that of Sheikhs Mohammad and Naser who acted with civility and were willing to listen, while he had interfered with Stannus's attempts to restore tranquility." Sheikh Hoseyn then stood up and left with his followers; thereafter the war cry was soon heard all over town. Sheikh Naser followed his uncle to appease him, but returned after a few minutes. Stannus then returned to the Residency. Some 15 minutes later reports came in that the guards at the towers overlooking the house were being considerably reinforced. Parties of armed men from all parts of town manned the walls, within a pistol shot of the Residency. At first Stannus did not believe that Sheikh Hoseyn wanted to take violent action against the Residency, but all doubts disappeared when a large cannon was placed against the building within 100 m of the walls. Parties of armed men were working up a frenzy by dancing in front of the Residency and made their hostile intentions clear. Stannus then put the place in state of defense and sent a note to Sheikh Naser asking him what the meaning of this was. Although the defenses were ready the Residency was short of water and provisions; also ammunition was in short supply. A Residency servant was seized within 20 m of the gate and all that he had taken from him. Khachatur Johannes returned with Sheikh Naser's reply, which expressed surprise about "who might have done that?" After all, "both I and the inhabitants of Bushehr are friendly toward you and have shown kindness. Nevertheless, they hope that nothing will be done by you contrary to the agreement. We are all obliged to you." This reply did not satisfy Stannus, because despite assurances that no hostilities were intended, outside the Residency it looked differently. Therefore, he wrote to Sheikh Naser: "The English are not in the habit of violating their engagements and you above all should know that. Your note does not explain the reason for these warlike preparations and therefore, I have prepared our defense. I ask you to withdraw the armed men and the guns aimed at us. For the insult given to the British government I shall seek redress elsewhere. Those in charge of the government of Bushire should know that we are desirous to keep our engagement and ready to defend ourselves, if attacked." To this note a non-committal reply only came late in the evening. At half past four several parties were stationed in the streets leading to the Residency to search all people for ammunition. The large cannon however, had been withdrawn. Khachatur came with a verbal reply that nothing was to be feared; he also confirmed that the fervor among the people had died down. Nevertheless, the Residency staff maintained a defensive posture. The next morning, on 7 February, Sheikh Naser came and tried to explain that no hostile action had been intended. The people had only wanted to prevent Sheikh Ahmad from escaping. Stannus told him he better stop as they would never agree about this.[96]

To Stannus it looked as there would be no security in sight as long as Sheikh Hoseyn kept his influence over the armed inhabitants. On 10 February 1827, he sent a servant with letters for Farmanfarma and his vizier, Mohammad Zaki Khan to which he received a reply the next evening, confirming his approach and a promise to redress the injuries suffered. Meanwhile, things became more orderly in Bushehr, due to the arrival of Anushirvan Mirza. He immediately took charge of government and appointed Shokrollah Khan as his vizier, in accordance with his father's orders. He insisted that Sheikh Ahmad to be delivered to him, but at Stannus's suggestion he allowed him to remain in the Residency. On that same day, Stannus went to meet the Farmanfarma outside Bushehr. The prince assured him that he would deal with British complaints and said that the offense offered by the rabble of Bushehr would be atoned for.

He was still willing to be lenient and even favorable to Sheikh Ahmad depending how he would handle the matter of the treasury `Abdol-Rasul had left behind. He was willing to make allowances for the necessary expenses Sheikh Ahmad had to make, and if he made a correct accounting of all that he had nothing to fear. Stannus was pleased with this reaction, but asked that Zaki Khan would go to him and tell him the same in person.

96. NA, FO 248/52, Stannus report, 07/02/1827; Idem, Text Proposal agreement between Sheikh Ahmad and Sheikh Naser; Idem, agreement between Sheikh Ahmad, Sheikh Naser and Sheikh Hasan [sic] under mediation of Resident, 05/02/1827; Idem, Note to Sheikh Naser from Col. Stannus 07/02/1827 and reply from Sheikh Naser on the same day; Idem, Stannus to Naser 06/02/1827 ("they brought an agreement to you to authenticate"); Idem, Naser to Stannus 07/02/1827; Saldanha 1986, vol. 2, p. 253; Lorimer 1915, vol. 2, pp. 1915-16.

This was granted and the next morning Zaki Khan came and later he left the Residency with Sheikh Ahmad. For several days Stannus heard nothing about Sheikh Ahmad, only that Sheikhs Naser and Hoseyn were treated with much distinction. Therefore, on 16 February, Stannus sent a note to Zaki Khan asking what steps were taken to redress the insults given. The same evening he received a reply stating that his complaint had been found to be unfounded and that the local government, alerted by alarmed people, had been justified in taking steps to prevent the escape of a traitor (i.e. Sheikh Ahmad), who had taken refuge at the Residency. Stannus replied that he was disappointed and that he would address higher authorities.

From the moment Bushehr was occupied by Persian troops great irregularities took place. The supply of water was repeatedly intercepted by the guards stationed at the gate of the fort. For several days this had been protested by word and writing to Shokrollah Khan and Zaki Khan. The troops were not under control of the ministers; the water carriers were beaten despite precautions taken by the two ministers. On 16 February, Stannus sent Lt. Hennell to Farmanfarma to inform him that he could not remain, when he and his servants were subjected to violence and that he was unable to ensure the water supply to the Residency. Therefore, he had no choice but to withdraw into the interior till such time that the army had gone and with them the cause of the grievances. The prince-governor immediately sent a messenger asking Stannus to stay and that orders would be given to punish the offenders. Stannus decided to stay and the next day there was no problem, but the morning of the 18th the water carriers again were stopped and plundered.

Stannus then sent a note to Farmanfarma telling him that he would board the *Bengal* in the forenoon. This resulted in a note from Zaki Khan, asking Stannus to see him at his house the next day, to meet Sheikhs Naser and Hoseyn, whom he hoped Stannus would support. The Resident was upset about this, given the way he had been treated by these two young men, as he called them. Sheikh Naser III was about 21 years at that time. Moreover, the preceding day it had been decided that they would be entrusted with the government of Bushehr after the Farmanfarma's departure. Stannus replied that he was unable to comply with his request and opposed that Sheikh Hoseyn had any share in the government. Zaki Khan was so upset by this refusal of a counter visit that he sent many messengers urging Stannus to change his mind; the prince-governor did the same. Stannus finally agreed to come the next morning of 19 February 1827, on condition that Sheikh Hoseyn would not be present. This was immediately agreed and at 8 a.m. that morning he left the *Benares* and sent a message that he was coming to Zaki Khan's house. Stannus waited at the Residency till 11 a.m. Because he received no reply and the weather was getting threatening rapidly, which might make it impossible for him to return aboard for several days, he wrote to Zaki Khan to send his apologies to Farmanfarma. He had to leave Bushehr and would remain in a village beyond its limits, where he would establish the Residency and carry out his normal duties, unless conciliatory measures were taken. Meanwhile, Farmanfarma wanted to leave his son in charge of Bushehr and take all the Sheikhs' relations to Shiraz. However, this plan met with much local opposition. "The Arab population found his professed anxiety concerning the release of Sheikh `Abdol-Rasul difficult to reconcile with his total disregard of the rights of that family. Therefore, he had to adopt a different strategy, and after having drained the treasury, seizing all of `Abdol-Rasul's property and increasing the tribute equal to the tax revenues he decided to reinstate the young Sheikhs and leaving them to govern without credit or resources for expenses. Thus the state of finances and the oppressive system that ensues might lead to such disorders that the Arabs find it justified if he placed the government in other hands." His son Anushirvan Mirza was proclaimed as honorary governor during the absence of Sheikh `Abdol-Rasul; later he could take over to 'redress' the abuses perpetrated by his deputies.[97] On 22 February 1827, Stannus sent Mr. Arrathoon Constantine:

> to inform Nowshirvan Mirza, governor Bushehr that I will return to Bushehr on condition that Sheikh Naser be excluded from all share of government until higher powers have decided in this matter concerning his violent and offensive behavior towards the Residency on 6 February. That this assurance be given under seal of the prince governor of Bushire and the Il Khan to that effect and that it is publicly announced to the merchants and inhabitants that Sheikh Hoseyn is not permitted to execise any authority. Sheikh Naser gave me a written engagement that he would restore the property of the Demukh tribe, on condition that they leave town. I considered this engagement fulfilled when I take the property that they have left behind. I further request that Sheikh Naser gets written orders to that effect and to comply with any requisition I may make for boats, qaseds or carriage of any description and that he be ordered to refrain from any interference with matters concerning the Residency and persons under its protection. When these reasonable demands are complied with I will return and await the pleasure of both governments concerning the indignity given to the Residency at the instigation of Sheikh Hoseyn, about which I in vain complained earlier to Shiraz.[98]

This letter had no immediate result. On 24 March 1827, Capt. Wilson took over as Resident from Col. Stannus, who remained at his camp near Halileh Bay. Wilson was on Her Company's Cruizer *Clive*, and was reluctantly received young Sheikh Naser III, who came to congratulate him. He urged the Resident to return to Bushehr. He was very obsequious and tried to convince him that his regrets were unfeigned.[99]

On 25 March 1827, Wilson received a haughty formulated letter from Shiraz which basically met Stannus's stipulations. Both he and Stannus decided to lift the temporary suspension of the Residency that same day. He informed Shiraz that the continuation of the Residency on the same footing would depend on orders from his superiors. Nowshirvan Mirza also wrote a letter, but in a more friendly and conciliatory tone. On 28 March another friendlier worded letter came from Shiraz, which Hennell attributed

---

97. NA, FO 248/38, Stannus to William Newham, pol. secr. Bombay 19/02/1827; NA, FO 248/52, Journal Col. Wilson; Idem, Statement Haji Jasun, chief pilot Bushire, 18/02/1827; Idem, Statement Cachatoor Johannes 18/02/1827; Idem, Stannus to governor-general of Fars and to Zaki Khan and their replies (in Persian), 09/02/1827.

98. NA, FO 248/52, Resident in Casnh Khore Khonine (sic), 22/02/1827.

99. NA, FO 248/52, Hennel to Lt. Col. MacDonald, 24/03/1827; Saldanha 1986, vol. 2, p. 253.

to the decline of the influence of minister Zaki Khan and rise of Mohammad `Ali Khan, the *Il Khan*. Indeed shortly thereafter he was replaced as vizier by Mirza Mohammad `Ali.[100]

Bombay approved that Wilson accepted this 'apology', but insisted that Sheikh Hoseyn would never be allowed a role in Bushehr's government. Also, it supported Stannus proposal to remove the Residency and construct a new one at a more favorable location, if approved by the local authorities. Bombay also insisted that the granting of asylum should be limited as much as possible, although it understood given local customs it could not always be avoided. The royal court gave assurances to MacDonald, the British Minister that reparations would be made and that Mohammad Zaki Khan was fined 40,000 *tumans* for his conduct on that occasion. Moreover, Sheikh Hoseyn was banned from "the exercise of any authority in the Government of Bushire." MacDonald further commented that the construction of "a defensible Residency beyond the walls of Bushire," would most likely be objected to by Tehran. When Capt. Bruce built a mansion its walls were totally destroyed. Tehran was very sensitive on this point as it believed "that our vast Empire in India grew out of a like establishment." Therefore, MacDonald advised to drop this matter. He suggested that the Residency should be ordered to maintain absolute neutrality in local quarrels and be banned from granting asylum, which only led to trouble.[101]

At the end of April 1827, Farmanfarma asked Wilson to mediate with the Soltan of Masqat, who was the prince's servant and get Sheikh `Abdol-Rasul released as Stannus had intimated he would do for the late Sheikh Mohammad Khan.[102] Due to the intercession of the governor-general of Fars, Sheikh `Abdol-Rasul was released in May 1827 after signing an IOU for 80,000 German crowns. He had a friendly meeting and made peace with the Soltan, but Sheikh `Abdol-Rasul's two vessels remained in Masqat until his arrival in Shiraz and the transfer of money to the governor-general. On 23 May 1827, Sheikh `Abdol-Rasul left Masqat to Shiraz via Bandar Abbas. Because through intrigues of Hajijah, the mother of Reza Qoli Mirza and Timur Mirza, he was imprisoned by Soltan Masqat for 8 months, he allegedly insulted Hajijah on his return and neglected to cultivate relations with her sons.[103]

Fath `Ali Shah sent `Ali Morad Khan, a *gholam-pishkhedmat* to hear British grievances, who talked with Wilson on 1 August 1827. Wilson reminded him of the insult offered by the rabble of Bushehr and raised the question of what protection might the Residency count on? `Ali Morad Khan said that he would talk to Sheikh `Abdol-Rasul in the presence of Wilson and the prince-governor and admonish him concerning his future conduct. Also, the Shah had made Farmanfarma answerable for any misconduct.

---

100. NA, FO 248/52 Hennell to Lt. Col. MacDonald, 30/03/1827; Saldanha 253; NA, FO 248/52, text *raqam*; March 1827. Anushirvan Mirza's letter was friendlier because he received a pair of shawls, a fowling piece and two cut glass shades, all without pair; Idem, second letter to governor-general of Fars; Idem, Proposal Anushirvan Mirza (basically agreeing to the four demands by Stannus); Idem, Wilson to MacDonald, Envoy Tehran 01/06/1827, transferring 28/04/1827 letter from Newham, Bombay; Idem, D. Wilson to Newham, Bombay, 14/06/1827.

101. Saldanha 1986, vol. 2, pp. 254-56. Stannus and Wilson did not insist on the permanent exclusion of Sheikh Hoseyn from the government of Bushehr, provided there was no risk of a repeat performance of his offensive behavior. Lorimer 1915, vol. 1, p. 1917.

102. NA, FO 248/52, Governor-general of Fars to Wilson, end of April 1827.

103. NA, FO 248/52, Abdol-Rasul Khan to Resident 18/05/1827; Busse 1972, p. 202; Saldanha 1986, vol. 1, pp. 249-50; Lorimer 1915, vol. 1, p. 1917; Miles 1966, p. 328 (agreed to surrender a Persian princess, who had been promised to him, but whom the governor of Bushire had delayed because he wanted to marry her himself); Fasa'i 1376, vol. 1, p. 746; Busse 1972, pp. 203-04; Sa`adat 1390, p. 74.

Wilson preferred that `Ali Morad Khan spoke in private with the Sheikh, who had been very friendly towards the Residency since his return.[104]

Wilson further asked that no *rahdari* be collected from British merchants and those connected with them as had been the case recently. `Ali Morad Khan agreed and stated that he would take a written undertaking from Mirza `Ali Akbar *kalantar*, the chief of customs and superior of all *rahdars* declaring the exemption in very precise terms. He also promised to have Sheikh `Abdol-Rasul issue a document stating that he had no intention "of interfering in any way with the merchants of Bushire, in the disposal or lading of their cargo upon any vessel, whether the English or not," and not compelling them to use his vessels. However, Wilson opined that the statement was not very precise "no radharee or gomcie [sic; *rahdari* and *gushi*] or duties of any kind shall be levied on article being conveyed through that country for the use of the English."[105]

On 28 August 1827, when it was learnt that a deserter form the *Amherst* was on board a *baghlah* in the harbor, a cutter was sent to retrieve the man. The lascars were beaten off by the crew of the *baghlah*. Capt. John Betham then went ashore to see Sheikh Naser III, but he was told that he was not at home. He then learnt where the deserter was hiding in town and therefore, sent his interpreter to Sheikh Naser to ask him to return the deserter. The Sheikh had the interpreter beaten almost to death and threw one of the *Amherst*'s lascars in prison and threatened to punish him. Betham then told the Sheikh to hand over the deserter, a British subject, else he would consider him an enemy. This was refused. Betham, who had three ships, then promised to sink the *Romani* [sic; *Rahmani*], a Persian ship as well as destroy all the Sheikh's ships. Seeing that the Captain meant business, the Sheikh handed over the interpreter as well as a lascar in lieu of the deserter until he could be found. Sheikh Naser also promised to recompense the interpreter. Wilson asked Betham to have no further contact with the Sheikh, but address all problems to him.[106]

Despite having been reinstated as governor of Bushehr, Sheikh `Abdol-Rasul was anxious about his position, feeling threatened by Shiraz and Masqat, although the Resident felt that this was because of his fear that Russia would acquire a definite influence over Persia. At that time, at the end of the Perso-Russian war (1826-28) Russian troops occupied much of Azerbaijan, including Tabriz. Therefore, on 8 January 1828, Sheikh `Abdol-Rasul informed the Resident that he wanted Great Britain's protection and that he considered "himself in future as belonging to it, and to be looked upon by it as one of its dependents." The Resident replied that since there existed ancient friendship and a treaty between Great Britain and Persia, of which he was a loyal ally, there was no need for him to express new assurances of his friendship for Great Britain. The Sheikh replied that of course he was a faithful ally of Persia and he never wanted to change that, he only wanted to show how devoted he was to Great Britain. Capt. Wilson opined that `Abdol-Rasul considered it "safe policy to be recognized as on a friendly footing with the British Government." Bombay refused to open the Sheikh's letter and sent it back unopened,

104. Saldanha 1986, vol. 1, pp. 256-57.

105. Saldanha 1986, vol. 1, p. 257; Lorimer 1915, vol. 1, pp. 1950-51.

106. Saldanha 1986, vol. 1, pp. 258-60; Lorimer 1915, vol. 1, pp. 1951-52.

not wanting to create the impression that they countenanced something that might be inconsistent with the Sheikh's duty towards his monarch, a British ally.[107]

Sheikh `Abdol-Rasul felt that he needed to bolster his rule against Shiraz, the Tangestanis and Masqat. The Al Mazkur were weakened as a family, while the Tangestanis and Shiraz were only waiting for the right moment to interfere with Bushehr. Finally, Sayyed Sa`id had gotten his way and married the daughter of Hajijah, while once again in 1828 he had tried to capture Bahrain. Unfortunately, for the Sheikh, there was no local or outside power that wanted to provide support or protection. Sheikh `Abdol-Rasul's fears became reality when in November 1828, the sons of Hajijah, Rezaqoli Mirza and Timur Mirza allied themselves with the Khans of Dashtestan, Tangestan and Dashti and laid siege to Bushehr with several thousands of musketeers. After a two days' siege they occupied the town. Sheikh `Abdol-Rasul fled on board his ship and watched from the sea the plundering of Bushehr. All the goods of native and foreign merchants were carried off. Two months later the invaders left. The merchants complained to the shah who ordered the Farmanfarma to restitute the plundered goods. When the people of Dashtestan refused to return the goods the Farmanfarma tried to come to agreement with Sheikh `Abdol-Rasul to settle matters. The latter wrote: "render me the enemy chiefs and I will compensate the merchants." Farmanfarma moved to Dashtestan to win over the Khans. Sheikh `Abdol-Rasul boarded his ship, when Farmanfarma entered Bushehr and took lodging's in the Sheikh's house known as the *Ark*. The prince arrested all the Khans, arrested Sheikh `Abdol-Rasul on his ship, but then released all the Khans to him, who after having paraded them in the bazaar, took them to Khark, where he drowned them all save one who fled.[108]

During his stay in Bushehr, Timur Mirza had asked Sayyed Sa`id, his brother-in-law, to seize two vessels that belonged to Sheikh `Abdol-Rasul. In January 1829, Sayyed Sa`id sent the frigate *Mozaffar* that peaceably accompanied the *Harriet*, belonging to the Sheikh, to Bushehr. The captain of the *Mozaffar* found that Farmanfama was in the port and that Sheikh `Abdol-Rasul stood high in his favor, who was given the jurisdiction over all the districts between Kazerun and the sea. This was neither to the liking of Timur Mirza nor that of Sayyed Sa`id, thus trouble was expected between Sheikh `Abdol-Rasul and Timur Mirza and that the latter would ask the Soltan of Masqat for naval support. Major Wilson informed Sayyed Sa`id that the governor-general of Fars had given all the land between Kazerun and Bushehr to the Sheikh and "Ickland, Izardwhost and Bowanat" to Timur Mirza and that the vizier of Fars, Mirza Mohammad `Ali was right then in Bushehr to arrange all that. Wilson further suggested that such naval support would not be in Sayyed Sa`id's best interest and would only create confusion, as Timur Mirza was but a governor, not the ruler of a country. However, Sayyed Sa`id could not let a chance pass by to harm

---

107. Saldanha 1986, vol. 1, pp. 261-62; Lorimer 1915, vol. 1, pp. 1953-54; Grummon 1985, p. 152. Mignan who visit Bushehr in 1830 reported that "During the period we remained here, the all-engrossing topic of conversation turned towards the coming of the Russians. The Armenians devoutly wished for the annexation of the whole country to Russia, as they would then be thought more of than they even can be under a Mahommedan government. They well know that the Muscovites have supplanted us in the favour of the shah, and that they contemplate the occupation of every town of Persia, and are determined by every means in their power to expel, not only our public officers, but every man bearing the name of an Englishman, from that country." Mignan 1839, vol. 2, pp. 144-45.

108. Busse 1972, pp. 202f; Fasa'i 1378, vol. 2, pp. 745-47 (who incorrectly has 1246/1830-31); Sa`adat 1390, pp. 74-75.

`Abdol-Rasul and he wrote to Farmanfarma that the Sheikh should not be appointed governor of Bushehr, but rather one of the prince's own sons. Farmanfarma was interested in this proposal, but informed Sayyed Sa`id that he needed his navy to achieve this objective. When the Resident learnt of this meddling in Persia's affairs, he pointed out to Sayyed Sa`id that only recently he had "recovered the dues from the Sheikh of Bushire (20,000 krans.)" Bombay also wrote to Sayyed Sa`id and strongly dissuaded him from interfering "with the affairs of Fars or of any province of Persia. Peace is important and the Sheikh has satisfied all your demands and there is no need to wage war on him."[109]

The next two years were fraught with problems, but Sheikh `Abdol-Rasul placated the prince-governor and tried to bolster his rule in the littoral. However, by the end of 1831, Farmanfarma was again in Bushehr to squeeze him or replace him as governor. Sheikh `Abdol-Rasul promised to pay annually 20,000 *tumans* more in taxes. Despite knowing that in Persia the promises in the mouths of princes "are frail as the breath in their nostrils," Sheikh `Abdol-Rasul allowed himself to be lured to Shiraz in February 1832; allegedly he had been promised marriage to a princess. The moment he arrived he was arrested, and it was considered to kill him. However, funds would not be then be forthcoming and so he paid a huge ransom after which he was released with the intention to seize him again in future for a new bleeding.[110] On his return from Shiraz, "he received a warning at Daliki, about the intentions of the Borazjanis. He ignored the warning and stayed the night in the fortress of Borazjan. The fort was surrounded by armed Borazjanis who offered bakht or free quarter to the Sheikh's followers, who accepted that. The sheikh withdrew to a small narrow tower of the fort where he could sell his life most dearly. After he had killed seven or eight of his assailants they set fire to the tower; he had to exit and was killed immediately. His corpse was burnt to ashes and scattered to the wind."[111] However, according to another version, the sons of the drowned men cornered Sheikh `Abdol-Rasul at Borazjun. After all his retainers but one were killed he fled into a tower, and from there with a gun shot one by one at his opponents. His last bullet he kept for himself.[112] The murderer presumably had been hired by the prince of Shiraz.[113]

Sheikh `Abdol-Rasul was not mourned by many. According to Mignan, who was in Bushehr in 1830, he was of "a cruel, crafty, and avaricious disposition, and his only aim was that of filling his treasury, no matter how." Another British traveler, Kempthorne, who knew him as well, described him as being "a despotic tyrant, and guilty of every kind of excess and cruelty towards his subjects. For a most trivial offence he would order offenders' eyes to be put out, or their tongues or ears to be cut off, and in some cases they were even blown from a gun. He was so feared that the inhabitants trembled at his approach."[114] Instead of respected he was feared and despised. This held in particular for the merchants, who had suffered for many years from his various schemes to benefit his own pocket rather than to promote trade. One of such wiles, according to Mignan, was that "The ships trading to this port are compelled to load with his goods, and convey them to India at a lower rate than they can possibly afford, and when any of the stock

---

109. Saldanha 1986, vol. 2, 263; Lorimer 1915, vol. 1, pp. 1917-18.
110. Wellstead 1840, pp. 135-36.
111. Binning 1857, vol. 1, pp. 158-59.
112. Busse 1972, p. 211; Grummon 1985, p. 154; Fasa'i 1376, vol. 2, p. 753; Sa`adat 1390, p. 76.
113. Busse 1972, p. 216.
114. Kempthorne 1835, pp. 283-85; Wellstead 1840, p. 133.

he has laid by in his granaries is scarce and dear in the bazaar, he forces the merchants to puchase from him at *his* own price, which is never less than fifty per cent above what they may produce it elsewhere."[115]

Princely Qajar Administration

His young 26-year old son, Sheikh Naser III, took over as governor. Sheikh `Abdol-Rasul was rather dismissive of his son, according to Mignan. "He has a son about four-and-twenty years old, of whom he is most lavish in his abuse. 'Look at that poor miserable animal;' he would exclaim; 'when my eyes are put out, the 'kulb' [sic; *kalb* or dog] will be sheikh.'[116] Although Sheikh Naser had succeeded his father, the British did not expect him to last long, even though the population looked upon him as a guardian against tyranny.[117] By the summer of 1832, Rezaqoli Mirza (a son of Hajijah), supported by Tangestanis marched on Bushehr. The inhabitants of Bushehr fearing another plundering of their town boarded their ships with as many of their goods as possible. Sheikh Naser Khan III fled to a British ship on the roads at Qavi. The prince took Bushehr and was appointed by his father as governor. He invited Sheikh Naser to come back, who sent his deputy. The prince remained at Bushehr to settle local affairs.[118] Sheikh `Abdol-Rasul's murderer presumably had been hired by the prince of Shiraz and, perhaps, therefore, his son Rezaqoli Mirza took no action to catch the killers of Sheikh `Abdol-Rasul. Sheikh Naser III, who had fled to Khark, then went to Bahrain, Qatif and Ras al-Khaima to ask his old allies, the `Otubis and Qavasem for support. In October 1832, he returned to Bushehr to claim his inheritance and avenge his father. Despite opposition from the Persian troops and their Tangestani allies, he took the town except for the prince's residence. However, when the leader of the attacking `Otubi force was killed and his head hung from the wall of the prince's residence, the Arab attack faltered and Sheik Naser III withdrew to his vessels.[119] Assisted by the `Otubis, he then blockaded Bushehr, but this did not have the desired effect. Trade was hurt, but not the land force that could easily hold out for a long time. Therefore, by November 1832 Sheikh Naser sailed to Kuwait. A few days later Sheikh Soltan b. Saqr arrived with a fleet and a force of 1,000 to 1,500 men. Their arrival did not much to enamor Sheikh Naser III to the people of Bushehr, especially its merchants, because the Qavasem, as in 1815, were not only there to reinstate the Sheikh, but also to plunder the town. However, Captain Blane, the Resident, induced the Qavasem by threat of force to return home, thus abandoning the principle of non-interference in local affairs.[120] He may have felt justified in doing so, as Lorimer argued, however, his interference is at odds with the position he took one month later. On 26 December 1832, Capt. Blane reported that he had received a letter from the governor-general Fars asking

115. Mignan 1839, vol. 2, p. 141; Kempthorne 1835, pp. 283-85; Wellstead 1840, p. 133; Lorimer 1915, vol. p. 1951.

116. Mignan 1839, vol. 2, p. 142.

117. Kempthorne 1835, pp. 284-85.

118. Busse 1972, p. 211; Lorimer 1915, vol. 1, p. 1918; Grummon 1985, pp. 154-55; Fasa'i 1376, vol. 1, pp. 749-50; Sa`adat 1390, p. 76.

119. Busse 1972, pp. 216-8. `Abdollah b. Ahmad after the failed attack began pirating and was then called to account by the British government and was for some time imprisoned on a British man-of-war. FO 248/150, Capt. Kemball, Resident to W.J. Thomson, charge d'affaires, 30/09/1853.

120. Lorimer 1915, vol. 1, p. 1918; Grummon 1985, p. 155; Sa`adat 1390, pp. 76-77.

him "to co-operate in the settlement of the affairs of the port and to take upon himself the prevention of any aggression by sea." Blane wrote the prince that he had orders to maintain absolute neutrality and not to interfere in the affairs of Persia.[121]

The Bushehris resented Rezaqoli Mirza's harsh fiscal policy, while the Tangestanis did not like his interference in their affairs. As a result, Aqa Jamal Khan, an Al Mazkur ally, engineered a coup against the prince, supported by Heydar Khan Dashti, with whom he had strong economic ties and the chief of Tangestan.[122] On 15 April 1833, Rezaqoli Mirza was expelled from Bushehr and authority over the town was given to Jamal Khan Bushehri. The cause for the uprising seems to have been prince's mother's behavior during a recent visit, who, by her demand to increase revenues, had introduced unpopular measures as well as by the arrest of the chief of Borazjan as part of these measures. On the evening of 14 April 1833 a large group of armed followers of the chief of Borazjan surrounded the prince's palace and engineered the release of their chief. They then threatened to take violent action against him if he did not depart the next morning. Attempts to placate them failed as there was nobody who supported him; therefore, he left accompanied by a few personal retainers. His womenfolk left a few days later after having organized enough palanquins (*takht-ravans*) for their transport and their luggage. The merchants and peaceful people of Bushehr were very much alarmed at what happened next.

In May 1833, the governor-general of Fars wrote to Blane, the Resident that the offenders had expressed their regrets and sorrow about their behavior and had asked that Timur Mirza be appointed. Timur Mirza was admitted to the town "on the alleged condition of his bringing few attendants and his retiring after a short stay and leaving the government in the hands of his infant son or some other nominal representative." However, he gradually increased the number of his followers, while the natural hostility existing between the various Khans slowly whittled away their power. As he had promised, Timur Mirza left Bushehr on 29 June 1833 leaving Mirza `Ali Khan and Tahmaspqoli Khan as his representatives. However, the power that Jamal Khan had previously assumed remained unchanged as was that of his supporters, the various tribal chiefs. But the coalition did not hold. The behavior of the chief of Tangestan looked suspect in the eyes of his associates. On the morning of 1 August 1833, Heydar Khan killed his Tangistani counterpart as well as Hoseynqoli Khan of Angali, one of his adherents, while another Khan was severely wounded. The rest sought refuge in the Residency, which got the opposing side to agree that they might return home by sea or land. The result was a blood feud, which did not promise well for the peace in the area. Shortly thereafter, Mirza `Ali Khan, the prince's agent feared so much for his life that he took refuge in the qazi's house, but on 19 August he fled to a safer place, the British Residency. The Resident had him smuggled out via sea to avoid problems. On 20 August 1833, the prince's troops appeared before Bushehr. The opposing party had not negotiated and thus fled by sea, despite their public statements of defending the walls. However, they were surprised by the size of the prince's force. There was some shooting from the towers which prevented them from entering during the day, but shortly after sunset they took the town and marched to the beach hoping to capture the chief opponents. However, they already had all gone. The three princes, Rezaqoli Mirza, Timur Mirza and Nasrollah Mirza marched into the town and took successful steps

121. Saldanha 1986, vol. 2, p. 264.

122. Lorimer 1915, vol. 1, p. 1918; Grummon 1985, p. 157.

to prevent it being sacked, the only exception being the houses of the rebel chiefs. The only loss of life occurred when some Tangestanis looking for loot in Jamal Khan's house put light into some jars of gunpowder and eight of them were killed. Jamal Khan had put his family and property aboard the *Feyzraban*, an Omani ship that was in the roads; he intended to follow a few days later. However, the Dashti chief allegedly caught him, to use him as a negotiating subject to get better terms for himself, as the princes were really very mad at him. But others said that he was able to get on the ship and reach Masqat, which was indeed what happened. In the hurry of the flight some Dashtis sought refuge at the British Residency, while throughout the town the Tangestanis were looking for them to take revenge give their blood feud.[123]

Although Rezaqoli Mirza had retaken the town he was unable to re-establish the same control over it as before. There was still opposition in Bushehr's environs. In the fall of 1834 the prince made a punitive expedition into Dashti, but he returned to Bushehr on 8 November 1834, because of the news that his grandfather, Fath `Ali Shah had died. He told Hennell, the British Resident that his father had been publicly proclaimed as Shah and he asked for British support "to the establishment of authority, most opposed to the Russians." Hennell told the prince "that the Resident was accredited to Shiraz only for the maintenance of the security in the Gulf, and that the British envoy in Tabriz was the sole authority authorized and competent to discuss such matters and engage in treaties that related to British-Russian relations."[124]

Shortly thereafter, Rezaqoli Mirza left for Shiraz and appointed Mirza `Ali Khan as his successor. That he and his father needed support was clear, when in that same month of November several chiefs of the Garmsir agreed to oppose Rezaqoli Mirza's government. They sent a letter to Sheikh Naser III inviting him to leave to Kuwait and join them in which case they would expel Mirza `Ali Khan and establish him as governor of Bushehr. Sheikh Naser III accompanied by Sheikh Sabah, son of the Sheikh of Kuwait arrived in eight vessels off Khark from where he sent a letter to Mirza `Ali Khan announcing that he had returned to assume his hereditary position. With this news the Khan immediately summoned Baqer Khan, chief of Tangestan and the only one who had not signed the letter of the Garmsir chiefs. Baqer Khan came the next day to Bushehr accompanied by 400-500 followers and Haji Mohammad Khan of Borazjan with a few men; later appeared the chiefs of Rudhilleh and Shabankareh, the main actors of the letter to Sheikh Naser III. Mirza `Ali Khan was able to play the chiefs against each other such that they decided to support Mirza `Ali Khan and sent a letter to Sheikh Naser that they had changed their mind and would oppose him if he came. The only answer was the appearance on 23 December of the Kuwaiti fleet consisting of light vessels. They entered the inner harbor and took up position at about 5 km from the town. The same day Hennell received a letter from Sheikh Sabah saying that he would cut off communication by sea. "As I considered Sheikh Naser a substantive power, I declined to recognize the blockade for British flagged vessels, the more so as Kuwait is nominally a Turkish dependency and is distinguished by the Turkish flag. As far as foreign vessels was concerned I did not feel necessary to interfere as long as they were not plundered." No acts of violence were committed and the shipping was not interfered with. Although some of the chiefs in town favored Sheikh Naser, all of

---

123. Saldanha vol. 2, pp. 265-66; Lorimer 1915, vol. 1, pp. 1918-20.

124. NA, FO 248/76, S. Hennell, ass. in charge of the Residency to Charles Norris, Chief Secretary Government Bombay, 10/11/1834; Grummon 1985, p. 158.

them together were united to oppose any attempt to land. Since the Kuwaiti force had only 300 men it was unlikely that an attack would take place, unless the chiefs in town would start quarreling. However, Mirza `Ali Khan did not strengthen his own position, when, forced by the Garmsir chiefs, he imposed a contribution on the merchants and other inhabitants to defray their men.[125]

Given these conflicting interests among the fair weather allies, the alliance started to fall apart in January 1835. Farmanfarma's bid for the throne in 1834 was in trouble and consequently, so was the Khan of Tangestan who supported him. In January 1835, forces from Shabankareh and Rudhilleh attacked Borazjun and renounced their allegiance to Shiraz. Mirza `Ali Khan realized that his position was untenable and fled Bushehr on 5 March 1835, after he had learnt "from Baqer Khan the chief of Tangestan that the chiefs of Tangestan had once again entered into a united force to re-establish Sheikh Nasr as governor of Bushire and due to the divisions among his own people who could no longer afford to oppose this combine." His flight was none too soon, because Sheikh Sa`dun, Sheikh Naser III's uncle entered Bushehr the next morning without meeting any opposition. He convened the notables of the town in the qadi's house, who agreed that he should be acting governor until Sheikh Naser's arrival from Kangan. The tension in the town was still high, because the chiefs of Tangestan and Borazjan were unwillingly forced by circumstances to accept the current change in government and there was no love lost between them and Sheikh Naser. Hennell commented that "The permanent substitution of the Arab for the Persian authority in Bushehr will be a serious blow for the prince in Shiraz engaged as he is for the crown of Persia. He always looked upon having Bushehr as a secure place of refuge in case of reverses through which he could escape with his treasure if fate is against him. Therefore it is most likely that the Shiraz government will make some attempt to undo this change of government in Bushire, which the Arab faction will oppose."[126]

Sheikh Naser III Al Mazkur's Administration

The first year of Sheikh Naser III's administration was without major problems. Hennell, the British Resident, however, was greatly upset when Mirza Masih the *mojtahed* responsible for the death of Alexander Griboyedov, the Russian ambassador received a hero's welcome in Bushehr.[127] Mirza Masih was en route to Mecca and on his arrival:

> The whole city poured out to meet him on his entrance and he was treated more like an inspired saint than a contemptible moolah. Since his arrival the intolerant feeling of the population, but more particularly the dependents and connections of Sheikh Hasan the qadi, has been greatly augmented. The first exhibition was made on the night of the illumination when a figure

125. NA, FO 248/76, Hennell, Ass. Resident to Charles Norris, Chief Secretary Government Bombay, 31/12/1834.

126. NA, FO 248/76, S. Hennell, ass. in charge of the Residency to Charles Norris, Chief Secretary Government Bombay, 06/03/1835; Grummon 1985, pp. 158-60; Lorimer 1915, vol. 1, p. 1918.

127. Mirza Masih roused the populace of Tehran to attack the Russian mission. During the attack ambassador Griboyedov was killed. The Russians demanded that Mirza Masih was exiled to Najaf and from there he went to Mecca; Hoseyni 1391, pp. 82-84.

> dressed in European clothes was suspended from a sort of gibbet by a chain round its waist in the public bazaar, although the circumstance did not come to my knowledge until some days afterwards. I did not choose to pass it over without notice.

Hennell lodged a formal complaint with Sheikh Naser about this effigy burning incident. The Sheikh offered to punish anyone that could be pointed out as being involved in the affair. However, Hennell was only able to learn that the effigy has been exposed in the so-called Shiraz bazaar. The dust had barely settled over this incident when another happened. At the end of December 1836, Elias, the Jewish Residency *sarraf*, when supervising some work made for Hennell in a gold-smith's shop, was struck hard without provocation, with a large stone by the nephew of the qazi, "a disreputable loose going character by name Sheikh Salman," so that he fainted. The Moslem goldsmith confirmed the unprovoked attack and Hennell sought redress from Sheikh Naser. However, Elias begged Hennell to drop the matter as a favor to him. Hennell did so realizing that: "As far as the qazi and his relatives are concerned the Sheikh is utterly powerless and really a mere cypher." However, the day thereafter "Sheikh Salman and a dependent known as Syed Ali met the shroff in the street and threatened him that they would leave no stone unturned to revenge both in life and property, because he had complained about it. The same language was repeated the day after." Hennell's immediate inclination was to demand Sheikh Salman's expulsion and the bastinado of Sayyed `Ali, and if Sheikh Naser would refuse to do so, to close the Residency and embark on one of the men-of-war in the roads. Also, if an attempt would be made to plunder the Residency or molest its dependents who would remain behind he would destroy any vessel belonging to Bushehr. However, he did not want to take an action that would result in the breaking of relations with Persia, and therefore, he wrote to the British Envoy in Tehran, asking him to take whatever action he considered appropriate under the current political circumstances. However, he added, foreseeing what indeed happened later,

> I fear we will have to take these measures in the future unless some check is imposed on the qazi and his dependents. This check would be effective if you could engineer the expulsion of Sheikh Salman and the punishment of Syed Ali, or to have them summoned to court to explain their conduct. I write to you to learn whether you wish these cases to be reported officially to you for your settlement, or that you wish us to take our own steps to obtain satisfaction for any future similar occurrence. The Persian court cannot have grounds for complaint, if we decline to reside in a place where the authorities are either too imbecile or too feeble to protect the accredited agent of a foreign power from insult from a portion of their own subjects.[128]

After Sheikh Naser's return to Bushehr matters returned to their normal state of affairs, i.e. yet another problem arose, this time of a commercial nature. In early February 1837, Mirza `Ali Akbar, the town's *vaqaye`-negar* or news writer claimed the right to

128. NA, FO 248/85, Hennell to McNeil (private letter) 30/12/1836; the name of Sheikh Salman is also found as Soleyman. Sa`adat 1390, p. 77.

appoint which person would be agent for the collection of freight of British vessels. Hennell protested against this, because it was "contrary to the established customs and rules of Bushire that allows any ship to select their own agent paying this person a fixed established percentage." Because there was no commercial treaty between Persia and Great Britain, all trade was carried out based on established custom. In his reply Sheikh Naser argued that the news writer was only doing his job, because he had received orders to collect all data on import and export of both money and merchandise and to make a monthly report for the Shah. He added that if there was more than one agent collecting the freight it would cause confusion and surely, "the Resident will not allow that the affairs of his government be disordered." Because Sheikh Naser did not offer to show the royal order and because he did not want to get involved in a long and fruitless correspondence with the governor, Hennell asked the British Envoy in Tehran to take up the matter with the Shah's government. He wrote:

> You could ask yourself why worry about such a minor issue, but if such a minor official as the news writer is allowed to overturn those old rules and customs that are the guide in commercial relations with this port, which not only will lead to confusion and embarrassment, but also to misunderstanding and disputes. If you agree it might be a good idea to get a royal order to Mirza Ali Akbar defining with greater exactitude the degree of interference that a person is allowed to undertake in the commercial affairs of the port. If such an order is issued may I get a copy so that I know what to do, as now the smooth operation of trade here threatens to be thrown in total confusion and disorder.[129]

Shortly thereafter, in May 1837, a royal order as well as one from the prime minister and the minister of foreign affairs arrived ordering Mirza `Ali Akbar to abstain from interfering in the future with trade of British subjects. At that time, Mirza `Ali Akbar was in Shiraz and Hennell kept the documents until his return.[130]

Sheikh Naser III had been reinstated as governor, because he "was better adapted for collecting and paying the revenues than the Persians."[131] However, he found that increasingly difficult to do, the reason why Sheikh Naser was in Shiraz in March-April. By May 1837 he was back in Bushehr. Presumably, he had been able to successfully discuss outstanding financial issues.[132] However, when back taxes were owed in the fall of 1837 Shiraz threatened to remove him. Therefore, on 22 September 1837, Sheikh Naser again went to Shiraz to convince the governor-general to grant him a delay in paying his arrears and obtain a reduction of his fiscal assessment. However, it did not work. On 1 November 1837, Mirza Mohammad Reza arrived in Bushehr as the new governor of Bushehr with authority to investigate Sheikh Naser's affairs, the treatment of his 'people' and to call on the tribes if opposition was offered. He was supported by Tangestanis and the remaining Demukh. Sheikh Naser III was absent and his uncle `Abdollah wanted to

---

129. NA, FO 248/85, Hennell to McNeill, 22/02/1837; Idem, draft note officiating Resident to Sheikh Nasr, 20/02/1837; Idem, Reply by Nasr, 21/02/1837. For the text of the notes, see Appendix XIII. 6 A.

130. NA, FO 248/85, Hennell to McNeill, 12/05/1837.

131. Wellstead 1840, p. 133.

132. NA, FO 248/85, Hennell to McNeill, 12/05/1837.

resist the invading force, because prior to his arrival the new governor's powers were not well known. Because ostensibly Mirza Mohammad Reza's mission was to bestow a robe of honor on Sheikh `Abdollah, the acting governor, he and other relatives considered this a stratagem to arrest him and send him to Shiraz. Learning of Mirza Mohammad Reza's approach he called on the Bani Hajer and the people of Rudhilleh, who were the best disposed towards the Al Mazkur, to prevent him from entering the town. However, they did not show, possibly being afraid of the Tangestanis and the Demukh tribe. Whereas previously, the Al Mazkur commanded respect and support, now this was no longer the case. Moreover, the Tangestanis and the Demukh were hostile if not inimical to the Al Mazkur, and thus, resistance melted like snow in the sun.[133]

On 1 November 1837, Sheikh `Abdollah, his brother Sheikh Hoseyn and a few retainers boarded two *batils*, one *baghla* and one *baqareh* with 50 men that were lying in the roads. Their families had already been shipped earlier to Khark. Sheikh Naser being a prisoner in Shiraz, his uncles believed that they might regain their position and the release of their nephew by putting pressure on Shiraz. The only means available to them was to impose a tax on vessels wishing to enter Bushehr's roads thus making this source of income for Shiraz less remunerative. The first ship that they wanted to target was the British-flagged *Colonel Newell* that was approaching. The Resident wrote to Sheikh `Abdollah as a friend that this would not be permitted and further advised him to release some other vessels that he had already detained. He also requested the British naval ship to watch Sheikh `Abdollah's moves, despite his wish to remain neutral in this event, but British interests were involved. Sheikh `Abdollah replied he had no such intention, but possibly realized that the planned action would be taken out on Sheikh Naser. On 4 November, he left for Khark, also may be because their water was running out. On 7 November, Sheikh `Abdollah asked the Resident's protection for Sheikh Naser's vessel the *Nasrat Shah* arriving from Bombay to be allowed to deliver the goods to the consignees. The Resident replied that he had the means to do so himself. Moreover, it seemed it was not necessary as that same day news arrived that Sheikh Naser had been reinstated as governor. The Tangestani and Demukh chiefs left on 8 November and Sheikh `Abdollah was invited to return from Khark and resume his task as acting governor. The reasons for the change of heart in Shiraz were mysterious and several opinions were offered. Did the governor-general want to use Sheikh Naser's ships against Bahrain, to retake Mohammerah from the Pasha of Baghdad and against possible further actions by Farmanfarma's sons in Baghdad?[134]

Barely back from Shiraz, Sheikh Naser III had to deal with a difficult and potentially explosive situation. In the evening of 17 December 1837, Mr. Gerald, the Residency's apothecary had gone to a small tomb erected near the Residency over the remains of a relative of Sheikh Naser, which had been kept in repair for a number of years by contributions from Mr. Gerald and the sepoys. He found it occupied by an Indian dervish who was a sayyed. This man, who was under the influence of bhang, used insulting language to Mr. Gerald and knocked of his cap, who then kicked the dervish. Hennell told Mr. Gerald to settle this affair to prevent all kinds of trouble and to come to an arrangement with the

133. Saldanha 1986, vol. 2, p. 267.

134. NA, FO 248/85, J. Mackenzie acting ass. res. in charge to J.P. Willoughby, Chief Secretary Government Bombay, 09/11/1837; Lorimer 1915, vol. 1, p. 1977; Saldanha, vol. 2, pp. 267-68; Grummon 1985, pp. 160-61, 165.

sayyed, given the influence this class of people had. Therefore, he sent a note to Sheikh Naser asking him for time so that Mr. Gerald could settle the matter quietly. The next day Hennell learnt that the sayyed had not suffered much injury and that there was no outcry in the town. In the afternoon, Sheikh Naser happened to meet Mr. Gerald during a stroll. He used the occasion to take his statement, with which he said he was satisfied. On 19 December a man from Sheikh Naser came to give Hennell a note about the incident in the course of the conversation he "made a point that sayyeds were highly venerated, the seriousness of the deed in the eyes of the olama, and he made an allusion to what had happened to the Russian ambassador [Griboyedov]. I replied that that was an event that he should not boast but be ashamed of. I asked him whether he mentioned it to terrify in which case he had failed to do so." Sheikh Naser's note stated that Mr. Gerald had to be handed over so that justice might have its course or there would be a general assault on the Residency, about which he could not do anything. Hennell replied that although Mr. Gerald had beaten the sayyed, that his demand could not be complied with and that since he was the governor, he was responsible to ensure that anyone connected with the British government would not be molested. Because there was no reaction in town, the sayyed continued to make a nuisance of himself and with a hatchet tried to assault some people attached to the Residency. Although nobody was hurt, Hennell immediately wrote to Sheikh Naser asking him to take steps to put a stop to such events. He replied that he would do so, but asked whether something might be given to the sayyed, which Hennell did not intend to do. He also reported that the persons behind all this were Sheikh Zeyn al-`Abedin and the *qadi* of Bushehr. Hennell did not understand the motives of the former as nobody of the Residency staff had ever been in contact with him. The qadi's role was clear, as his nephew had already started to make trouble in 1836 by beating the Residency's *sarraf*. Hennell did not think that there was ever a danger of an attack, but he found it disturbing that Sheikh Naser had no trouble to be the spokesperson for bigoted sentiments, which only heralded future trouble.[135]

At that time relations between Persia and Great Britain had soured. Ever since the early 1800s, Great Britain was worried about Russian designs on India. Therefore, it preferred that Persia and Afghanistan remained sovereign states, be it under British influence, to act as a buffer against the Russian threat. This threat was not considered hypothetical by British politicians, certainly not after the Russian conquest of the Caucasus and the occupation of Tabriz in 1828. Therefore, when in the late summer of 1837, Mohammad Shah marched to conquer Herat, which he considered to be part of his realm, McNeill, the British Envoy protested against this, because his government feared that Persian control over Herat would give Russia access to the road to Kabul and Kandahar, and thus, to the Indian border to cause mischief. Given the fact that Russia had given the Shah a loan of 50,000 *tumans* and promised to forgive the remainder of the war reparations it owed to Russia, if he took Herat, the Shah's action caused great misgivings in Britain and India. In March 1838, McNeill went to the Shah's camp, where he arrived one month later, to try

135. NA, FO 248/271, J. MacKenzie to McNeil 27/12/1837 and Sheikh Naser's reply. Sheikh Hasan Bushehri was a member of a well-known Shiite family of Bahraini olama, the Al Osfur. He was the second son of Sheikh Hoseyn b. Mohammad, who was Qadi and Imam Jom`eh of Bahrain. After his father's death, who was succeeded in his functions by his eldest son, Sheikh Hasan went to Bushehr in 1805, where he was active as Qadi and Imam Jom`eh of that port city; he died in 1845. Oshkuri 1990, vol. 2, p. 73; Afshari Sistani 1369, vol. 2, pp. 558-59. The family remained very prominent and influential, see Sadid al-Saltaneh 1362, p. 11.

to convince the Shah to abandon the siege of Herat. Before leaving he advised London that it might be a good idea to occupy Khark and keep it until the Shah had acceded to British demands. Sheil, the secretary of the British Legation in Tehran and at that time on leave in Britain, supported this proposal and even went farther by also recommending the occupation of Bushehr and keeping either or both. London liked the proposal and, on 1 May 1838, gave orders to Bombay to send a strong naval force with troops to the Persian Gulf to execute any service that McNeill might demand. Meanwhile, McNeill was unable to convince Mohammad Shah to abandon the siege of Herat, emboldened by the arrival of the Russian ambassador in his camp.[136]

The strained relations at the national diplomatic level also played out at the local level. At the end of March 1838, a man called `Ali Zaman struck the Residency *sarraf* in a public street. MacKenzie, the assistant Resident, asked Sheikh Naser to investigate and if the complaint was well founded to punish the man. Sheikh Naser was in a bind, because punishing a Moslem because he had struck a Jew would be incomprehensible and unacceptable to Moslems and might lead to disturbances. MacKenzie was in a bind as well, because complaining to Tehran would have little success given the strained relations. However, he could not allow people to think that persons connected with the Residency could be molested with impunity and unpunished, as some were already thinking. "I preferred to make it clear that those unfavourably disposed towards the Residency would become convinced that this would not be the case, either at Sheikh Salman's instigation or trusting that he might support them." Sheikh Naser replied that he had called `Ali Zaman to account and wanted to punish him, but as he was an old man others interceded for him and he was allowed to go away. Moreover, he said that `Ali Zaman had a claim against the *sarraf*; he would bring the document and then Sheikh Naser would establish the truth of the matter. MacKenzie pointed out that despite that both men had been in Bushehr for the last five years this claim had never earlier been made. Nevertheless, `Ali Zaman made an effort to make the *sarraf* appear before Sheikh Salman, for a decision of a claim that he said he had against him. In the meantime, a letter arrived from the British Envoy that he had informed the government that he could not be responsible for any disturbance that might occur in Bushehr and that any violence would be met by force. MacKenzie interpreted this as permission to protect the Residency and those connected with it. Therefore, he wrote to Sheikh Naser that satisfactory redress had not been offered and if this was not done, he considered moving from Bushehr and enforce compliance by blockading the port. This had the desired result; the man was immediately imprisoned and on 29 March he was sent to the Residency for whatever punishment MacKenzie decided upon. Given the fact that Sheikh Naser had given in and that the entire town by then knew that you could not molest Residency staff unpunished, MacKenzie did not want to add to the existing resentment and because of `Ali Zaman's age excused him from punishment.[137]

136. Kelly 1968, pp. 293-95.

137. NA, FO 248/85, MacKenzie to Willoughby/Bombay, 29/03/1838; Idem, draft note MacKenzie to Sheikh Nasr, 28/03/1838; Idem, Reply Sheikh Nasr 28/03/1838; Idem, MacKenzie to Sheikh Nasr, 28/03/1838.

Persian Governors again

Shortly after this incident, Sheikh Naser III fled from Bushehr. He had been dismissed as governor, because he could not meet his fiscal obligations and the governor-general of Fars appointed Mirza `Abbas as his successor. When the latter approached Bushehr, Sheikh Naser fled to Khark on 30 May 1838, where he felt safe, because the Fars authorities had neither the means nor the energy to pursue him and take the island. Mirza `Abbas to show his good-will did not quarter his troops in town.[138]

By mid-May 1838, McNeill came to the conclusion that only a show of force would make the Shah abandon the siege of Herat and show respect for British concerns. He felt strengthened in this view by the attack of a courier in the employ of the British Legation by Persian officials and soldiers in the summer of 1837, for which no satisfaction was offered. Furthermore, the case of the apothecary Mr. Gerald so upset McNeill when he learnt about it that he lodged a strong protest with Mirza Aghasi, the Prime Minister, accusing the Persian authorities of supporting the reprehensible behavior of the governor of Bushehr. He warned that any threat of violence would be met by force and London, which agreed, informed Mirza Aghasi that it would hold the government of Persia responsible in such event. On 16 May 1838, McNeill submitted British demands to Mohammad Shah, which included punishment of those who attacked the courier, the conclusion of a commercial agreement giving British commercial agents the same standing as consuls of other states, dismissal of the governor of Bushehr and punishment of those who had insulted and threatened the British Resident. McNeill only received an evasive reply and therefore, he left the Shah's camp on 7 June 1838 and left Tehran and stayed in Tabriz. Ten days later the British force arrived in the roads of Bushehr.[139]

Great Britain had decided to send a naval and military Field Force to the Persian Gulf to be able to "maintain its interests in Persia." Although the occupation of Southern Persia had been seriously contemplated by London, it was finally decided not to do so. It left the use of the Field Force to the governor-general of India. The government of India left the operational details to Bombay, which sent the armed steamer *Semiramis*, the sloop of war *Coote* and the brig of war *Tigris* with 387 sepoys and two six-pounders. The Field Force was commanded by Lt. Col. Sherriff subject to political control by Capt. Hennell. Bombay preferred the force to be stationed on Khark and Hennell was to inform the authorities at Bushehr that the force had been sent for special services in the Persian Gulf.[140] Bombay even wanted him to ask the governor of Bushehr permission to land troops on the island, but Hennell pointed out that this was futile as the governor would have to contact Shiraz. He proposed just to land the troops, then ask permission, and then receive a refusal. Hennell left Bushehr for Khark on 19 June 1838 with the H.C. Steamer *Semiramis*. He tried to contact Sheikh Naser, but he was not on the island and his uncle, Sheikh `Abdollah did not dare to make a decision. Therefore, Hennell ordered the troops to land, while he went to see Sheikh `Abdollah. "I told him that the Government had decided to send troops to perform a specific service and chosen to place them on Khark because of the salubrity of its climate. The sheikh replied that the island, people and all were at our disposal." He made coolies and boats available to help unloading the vessels.

---

138. Grummon 1985, p. 165; Lorimer 1915, vol. 1, p. 1977-78.
139. Kelly 1968, pp. 295-96.
140. Lorimer 1915, vol. 1, p. 1985.

There were not enough tents for the troops so the Residency tents were made available to Lt. Col. Sherriff so that all were comfortable lodged until the *Tamerlane* would bring the rest of the tents. Khark had water, but few supplies, which were obtained from Ganaveh, Rig and Bushehr. Steps were also taken to keep an eye what happened in Bushehr. "As the *Hugh Lindsay* will be the only man-of-war here after the departure of *Semiramis*, Sherriff agrees with me that it should be stationed at Bushire at least until we know how Shiraz looks at the stationing of troops on Khark. Both steamers will leave tomorrow to Bushire and *Semiramis* will return to India as soon as possible thereafter."[141]

Sheikh Naser III, who had gone to Bushehr to ask Hennell's permission to take action against Persian interests, returned the next day to Khark. He told Hennell that he "would be delighted to be under our protection." Hennell replied that "we are not at enmity with Persia and hoped that there would be no change in our friendship with that country. The troops were here for a special service, and Khark was chosen for its climate. Therefore, it was advisable for the Sheikh not to start any hostilities, because then it would be believed that we were the instigators." Sheikh Naser agreed and said he would wait for a few months; he claimed that he could easily raise 3,000-4,000 men in a short time and attack the coast. Hennell made it clear that the British troops would only protect their own boats and coal depot stores, assuming that Sheikh Naser had his own forces to defend the town on Khark. However, Hennell was interested in renting the former Dutch citadel. Sheikh Naser said that this was impossible, because all the wives and female relatives were living there.[142]

Hennell did not know how the Persian authorities would react to the landing of British troops on Khark. If they considered the landing on Khark a hostile act, they might use Baqer Khan Tangestani, who could easily raise 600 men, to attack the Residency. Therefore, he laid in stores of water, provisions and ammunition as well as added eight marines to his escort, thus having 39 bayonets. Hennell considered this not enough given the extent of the buildings and therefore, asked for 150 sepoys from the Khark Field Force. Relations with the governor had remained friendly and to keep it that way Hennell distributed some presents. Meanwhile, he was worried about the "non-arrival of *Tamerlane*, for unless firewood can be obtained from the southern part, *Hugh Lindsay* is dependent on this place for coal. The wood available is better than coal. I would suggest given the situation that the field force be reinforced by 5, but at least 3 companies of Europeans and further guns, ammunition and stores."[143]

On 21 June 1838, Hennell informed Mirza `Abbas, the governor that British troops had landed at Khark as being the best place, Basidu being unhealthy. He requested assistance, especially in allowing boats to carry supplies from Bushehr. Mirza `Abbas replied he would forward the request, but that there was no problem to ferry supplies. The governor-general of Fars asked for explanation and Hennell sent a conciliatory reply with the same earlier explanation on 11 July 1838. He asked McNeil, the British Envoy what to do when he left Persia. McNeill replied on 10 July 1838 that London did not wish the

141. NA, FO 248/85, S. Hennell, Residency on board H.C. Steamer Semiramis off Khark to J.P. Willoughby, Secretary Government Bombay, 20/06/1838.

142. NA, FO 248/85, Hennell a/b Semiramis off Karreek to J.P. Willoughby, Secretary Government Bombay, 20/06/1838; Saldanha 1986, vol. 2, p. 278.

143. NA, FO 248/85, Hennell to Willoughby/Bombay 25/06/1838. For an embellished and fictional account of the events leading to the departure of the British, see Sa`adat 1390, p. 77.

Residency to be moved to Khark, but if Shiraz threatened, reinforce Bushehr and place a garrison there, and if Hennell thought that with the troops on Khark he had sufficient strength to occupy and defend Bushehr he was authorized in such event to inform the governor that he would occupy and defend the port. If there was no threat it would be better to leave the troops at Khark.[144] To Hennell's great relief on 26 June, the arrival of the brig of war *Tigris* and the sloop *Elphinstone* occurred and on 29 June the transport *Tamerlane* arrived. On 28 June the governor of Bushehr received the prince-governor's reaction, who did not want to take hostile action, but waited for the shah's instructions. Therefore, Hennell did not consider it necessary to keep the detachments of the steamer *Hugh Lindsay* any longer, the more so as there were now two men of war in the roads that could help in case of demonstrations.[145]

Meanwhile, Mohammad Shah had decided to abandon the siege of Herat after an assault on 23 June 1838 had failed miserably. However, this was not known to Great Britain. In mid-July 1838, London instructed McNeill to inform the Shah, if he did not raise the siege that Great Britain assumed that the Shah had conceived the Herat campaign jointly with Russia with hostile intent toward Great Britain. In that case, the friendly relations with Great Britain would cease to exist and London would take such steps as it deemed necessary to secure its possessions. McNeill, who was in Erzerum at that time, sent Col. Stoddart to Herat to convey this message. Mohammad Shah was aware that the British had landed a force on Khark, while another force had been mobilized in India to march into Afghanistan. In August, Mohammad Shah, given his defeat at Herat and the threatening British movements, agreed to all British demands. On 9 September 1838, the Persian army began to withdraw from Herat.[146]

To be aware what transpired in Shiraz, Hennell hired a local man to write intelligence reports on that part of Persia.[147] Hennell wrote that "In the south great dissatisfaction prevails in consequence of oppressive conduct of the Prince Regent of Shiraz and his favorite Minister Mirza Ahmad Khan. Still no part of that province is in open rebellion, altho a general spirit of passive resistance to the payment of revenues would appear to exist. The unpopularity of the present Government of Shiraz is greatly augmented by the circumstance of all the authority being in the hands of the Northern Persians to the exclusion of Fars Nobles many of whom are leaving under various pretexts." Because of this the prince-governor abandoned his plan to tour the south to collect revenues. Contacts between Mirza `Abbas and the British Residency continued to be polite and even had a friendly character. Neither he nor Shiraz ever mentioned the Field Force on Khark. No sign of hostility was displayed, no reinforcements of the garrison or the fortifications of Khark were made, though the latter were in a dilapidated condition. However, in October 1838, the governor imposed a strict ban on the export of rice and wheat to Khark from Bushehr, which was a very unpopular measure among the local mercantile community.[148] Therefore, Hennell felt that it might be necessary to reinforce the exisiting defenses and

---

144. Saldanha 1986, vol. 2, pp. 277-78.
145. NA, FO 248/85, Hennell, Residency to J.P. Willoughby, Bombay, 01/07/1838.
146. Kelley 1968, pp. 299-300.
147. NA, FO 248/85, Hennell, Residency to J.P. Willoughby, Bombay, 25/09/1838.
148. NA, FO 248/85, Hennell to the Secret Committee of the Court of Directors, London, 26/10/1838.

make new ones so that the Field Force could defend itself without the support of the naval force, if the Shah would not agree to British demands.[149]

On 16 November 1838, a dispute broke out between the merchants of Bushehr and the governor, Mirza `Abbas, about the payment of certain duties that they claimed had been already paid to Sheikh Naser III, who was said to have taken a large sum with him "filched from the revenues of the place."[150] The bazaars were closed, but Mirza Abbas sent his *farrash*es on the morning of 17 November to force people to open their shops. Sheikh Hoseyn, the qadi, then ordered them to ignore this order and to gather at his house in arms. Under the pretext that one the governor's *farrash*es was drunk the qadi ordered all wine under the roofs of Jews to be destroyed. Then a crowd led by the qadi's slaves and a certain Sayyed `Ali, known for his past troubles, went to the Jewish quarter and forced their way into the house of the Residency's *sarraf*, where they destroyed wine and spirits packed for export with a value of 40-50 *tuman*s. They also beat and illtreated the owner himself such that he sought refuge in the Residency as he feared for his life. Mirza `Abbas was unable to take action against this, as requested by Hennell, as the qadi and merchants wanted to expel him from the town. He begged Hennell to write to the prince-governor who was at Kazerun at that time. Because Hennell had instructions to avoid the outbreak of hostilities, he decided not to punish the culprits himself. Therefore, he wrote to the prince-governor asking him to take action, although he expected no result from this. Hennell also intended to ask for the removal from Bushehr of the qadi Sheikh Hoseyn, his nephew Sheikh Salman and their dependents and the punishment in person and property of those involved in the attack, because the qadi's insult had to be punished.[151] Mirza `Abbas's life became even more complicated when a vessel from Qeshm was detained in Bushehr. This vessel was sent to Bushehr with a small portion of salvaged goods of the wreck of the *Fathol-Rahman* that Sheikh `Abdol-Rahman of Qeshm (which at that time was administered by the Soltan of Masqat) returned to the owners. Mirza `Abbas reacted immediately claiming Persian merchants had suffered in the wrecking of the vessel. He took hold of the vessel and would not allow it to leave without payment of a sum. Sheikh `Abdol-Rahman threatening consequences, immediately sent four vessels that arrived about 20 November. Shortly thereafter Mohammad `Ali Kebabi, a Persian, but for a long time a merchant of considerable consequence in Masqat, landed from his own vessel ostensibly to settle accounts with local merchants although it was said he had been charged with a secret mission concerning the governorship of Bushehr. He was arrested, which Hennell feared would cause a conflict with Sayyed Thuwayni, the Soltan of Masqat.[152]

---

149. NA, FO 248/85, Hennell to Willoughby 29/10/1838.

150. Anonymous 1838, p. 20.

151. NA, FO 248/85, Hennell to McNeil, 21/11/1838; Saldanha 1986, vol. 2, p. 280; Government of Great Britain 1841, pp. 4-5. NA, FO 248/99, unfoliated, "Persons involved on the attack of the shroff's house prior to removal of the Residency to Khark n.d.; Mahomed Ibrahim, servant of Haji Agha Dehdashty Nowruz Dullal; 10 or 12 slaves of the qadi one named Yacouth; Seyed Ally Reshebaff Behbehanee; Ghooloom servant of Hoossein Marifee, merchant; Gholloom of Kazem Hajjee Nezam, merchant; Kerbala Baker Shumbuddee Rusigree; Mahomad Baker rang-reez Behbahanee; Moollah Abbas, schoolmaster Masjid Reza; Ghooloom Hajee Agha Behbehanee; Mad Ally Bukkal Cazeroonee; Ibrahim son of Mahomed Ally Mesgar; Hajee Ally Shirazee; Jowher and Mobareek, slaves of the cazee; Syad Ally."

152. NA, FO 248/85, Hennell to Willoughby, Bombay 28/11/1838.

On 6 December 1838, Mirza Asadollah, the tutor of the prince of Shiraz entered Bushehr with orders for Mirza `Abbas to hand over the government and settle his accounts immediately and then return to Shiraz. On his entry the new governor was accompanied by the qadi, merchants and shopkeepers, who had gone to Kazerun, to complain about Mirza `Abbas's behavior. The triumph over a close relative of the vizier of Fars, Mirza Ahmad Khan, who was a favorite of the prince, was attributed to the payment of a large sum and the influence of merchants in Persia when they formed a united force. Mirza `Abbas, however, said that all his letters explaining the state of affairs and Hennell's letter complaining about the attack and destruction of the *sarraf*'s property had been intercepted en route. Therefore, Hennell sent a copy of his complaint to the prince. On 8 December, while refusing to settle his accounts or to give any of the money collected, Mirza `Abbas left Bushehr and went to Tangestan to await the prince's instructions.[153]

Some time after the new governor's arrival, Hennell received a reply from the prince-governor about his complaint. It simply stated that the *sarraf* was not a Residency dependent and was retailing wine, which was untrue. Given the tone and contents of the reply Hennell had no hope that Shiraz would give him any satisfaction. In fact, the prince's unfriendly attitude towards British subjects and their interests had only increased since the arrival of Mirza Asadollah as governor of Bushehr. Under Mirza `Abbas, apart from wheat and flour, all other products were allowed to be sent to Khark upon show of a pass from Hennell. The same procedure was sufficient to allow artisans needed to go to Khark. However, Mirza Asadollah banned any person or any product going to Khark. He first informed Hennell that the ban was because export would cause a scarcity. Later, he did not even use this flimsy pretext and only stated that it was at orders from Shiraz. Asadollah even went further by prohibiting the buying of the usual supplies by the British vessels lying in the roads, but gave in after an appeal was made. Nevertheless, to Hennell this was a sign on the wall. Therefore, he informed the British Envoy that given Asadollah's hostile actions against supplying British ships in the roads, he saw no other option than to strike the British flag and move to one of the ships or to Khark, depending on McNeill's rely, or the removal of the restrictions placed on the supplying of ships and Khark. There was no real supply problem, because wheat and barley were transported from Bushehr in any quantity to other parts of the Persian Gulf. However, he was worried that "This petty spite and annoyance will result in the lowering of our respect and influence here." Personally, Hennell saw in this unfriendly attitude justification to retaliate and blockade Bushehr and prevent supplies to enter it. If the governor knew that he was allowed to do so he would change his behavior, Hennell believed, because he depended of the collection of customs duties to meet the constant demand for money from Shiraz and he knew very well that no excuses would be accepted there.[154]

On 28 December 1838, Hennell again sent a request (*`arizeh*) to the prince-governor to get satisfaction for the attack on the *sarraf*. At the same time he pointed out that the local authorities in Bushehr were acting in an unfriendly manner. To his great surprise the prince's reply was conciliatory, stating that punishment according to the law of the land would be inflicted on the individuals involved. Further, that the ban on the export

153. NA, FO248/85, Hennell to Willougbhy, Bombay 12/12/1838; Government of Great Britain 1841, pp. 7-9, 66. The name in British sources is mostly written as Mirza Asad, but a few times as Asadoollah. Therefore, I have decided to render his name as Asadollah.

154. NA, FO 248/85, Hennell to McNeill, 28/12/1838; Government of Great Britain 1841, pp. 82, 84.

of supplies should not have been given without his instructions; in the spirit of friendship he had given orders to lift those prohibitions. However, Hennell did not trust this change of heart, the more so since a private letter from a trustworthy source informed him that secret letters had been sent to the chiefs of the Garmsirat and Lar directing them to raise troops with the purpose of assembling an army near Kangan. Hennell's source said that the ostensible reason was an invasion of Bahrain because of the oppression of descendants of Persian subjects by the `Otubis. The governor of Bushehr had been instructed to keep this a secret and not let it be known to the British. Hennell commented that it was possible, given the fact that the prince-goveror and his ministers had less influence at court and had to fear replacement by the Shah and that mounting an expedition against Bahrain would only be done for the purpose of avoiding a summons to come to Tehran. Also, given that so far the Persians always had great maritime problems in launching such undertakings, he believed that they did not intend to attack Khark or Bahrain. The only ports that had vessels adequate to transport troops were Bushehr, Kangan, `Asalu, Charak and Lengeh. Almost all the *baghla*s of Bushehr carried a British flag and their use, therefore, was out of the question. Of the remaining ports only `Asalu would give voluntary assistance in attacking Bahrain; all the others had friendly relations with the Qavasem and the `Otubis and would do everything to torpedo such a project. Therefore, Hennell suggested not to interfere with any such preparations. It was "better that they do this and waste the shah's resources than to have them available to march to Herat, given their almost certain defeat if they intended to attack Khark, which if executed would teach that government a lesson and would bolster our reputation here more than ever before."[155]

Meanwhile, relations between Great Britain and Persia remained strained. On his return to Tehran, Mohammad Shah did not make haste to honor the undertaking he had agreed to in August 1838 at Herat. In fact, the Shah sent a personal envoy, Hoseyn Khan, to London to plead his case with the British government. In reaction, in early 1839, McNeill broke off diplomatic relations and withdrew to Erzerum and returned to London. It was decided not to withdraw from Bushehr, because McNeill considered it useful for Hennell to remain there. The result was that Hennell became the target of the Shah's anger about his defeat at Herat, for which he blamed the British. The first sign of this hostility was the attack on the Residency's *sarraf*, which was followed by the ban on sending supplies to Khark. Hennell proposed to blockade the port of Bushehr, but London and the government of India did not agree, because this might hurt the interests of British and Indian merchants in Persia and of Persian merchants who remained friendly toward Great Britain. Moreover, it might induce the Shah to ban import of British goods via the north, while, moreover, it was unlikely that a blockade would change Persian attitude. However, if the supply embargo would endanger the force on Khark, Hennell was authorized to take the necessary steps to ensure continued supply. Although such an action was unnecessary, the letter came also after Hennell was once again confronted by a dispute with the Bushehr governor.[156]

---

155. NA, FO 248/85, Hennell to Willoughby, Bombay, 19/01/1839.

156. Kelly 1968, pp. 306-07; Saldanha 1986, vol. 2, pp. 281, 284. On the mission of Hoseyn Khan, its course, results and implementation, see Government of Great Britain 1841, pp. 18-84, 88-114.

British Residency moves to Khark

On Saturday 23 March 1839, Rear-Admiral Sir Frederick L. Maitland called on the governor of Bushehr. He informed him that supplies to his ship had stopped that day and asked whether he had done something wrong, and if so he would correct it. The governor said it was customary to send a list; Hennell said this was not true for men-of-war. The governor said it was irregular and contrary to the rules that boats landed at the Residency and that all boats should come to the landing place at the town. Hennell said the rule was that those landing at the Residency were shipped off at the same place and he could land his personal baggage and stopping this would be considered an insult to the Admiral personally as such a thing had never been done before. He would land on Monday and asked the governor whether he would try to stop him, which he refused to answer. After the admiral had left, a troop of soldiers was stationed in the sea tower near the Residency and a guard placed at the landing place; they had orders to prevent any boats from landing. When on 25 March boats from the *Wellesley*, commanded by Capt. Thomas Maitland, the admiral's brother, were about to beach to embark the admiral and his party, the guard cocked his musket and warned that he would shoot. Capt. Thomas Maitland grabbed the soldier's musket and threw up the muzzle. A waiting mob then attacked with sticks and stones, but were driven away by the British landing party. Other boats arrived from the British ships and shots were fired at them from a breastwork that had been thrown up during the night. The British returned fire but nobody was wounded. The admiral ordered to cease fire and sent a messenger to the governor to tell him that he should order his people to cease fire else he would be responsible for the consequences. Shortly thereafter the shooting stopped and the embarkation continued. It was then decided that in light of this insult to move the Residency to Khark. On Friday morning, Hennell moved from the Residency under protection of 10 gunboats lying off-shore. Baqer Khan Tangestani with about 400 of his tribesmen paraded on the left of the Residency, on the cliffs above the landing place. A landing part of British marines and the sepoy guard of the Residency immediately took up position in front of the gates to counter any attack or interference with the evacuation of Hennell's furniture and effects. However, Baqer Khan made no such attempt. On 27 March, Baqer Khan entered Bushehr and in the evening 200 of his armed men paraded in front of the Residency. Capt. Ellis once again drew up his marines and sepoys in front of the gates, but the Tangestanis dispersed. In the evening Capt. Ellis had some of his men make and fill flannel cartridges and bags of bullets. Also, two swivel guns were mounted on the Residency. In the morning the British saw that during the night the Persians had mounted two guns in a aquare tower left to the Residency. At that time they were busy making a breastwork of sandbags and entrenching themselves, while more tribesmen were entering Bushehr. To neutralize the Persian guns, Capt. Ellis had a four-pounder brass gun removed from a low bastion and placed on the roof of a high building. Only once a shot was fired from a distance and nobody was hurt. Hennell protested and demanded an explanation from the governor, who replied that he would try to find out who had fired, and if, successful would punish the man. That same evening a large party of Persians gathered in their fortified position, and, because there were still British vessels on the beach, Capt. Ellis had his troops take up position in front of the gates. During that night the Persians added a third gun to their position. In the morning of 29 March more armed were coming to the town. Because of heavy seas no vessels could come to the Residency, but a deputation of merchants left in a large boat to see Adm. Maitland and bring about a reconciliation with the governor. Maitland told the merchants unless the governor allowed the Resident and his servants to land and embark at the Residency, Capt. Hennell could not continue as Resident in Bushehr. Ironically, at that same time, the governor and Baqer Khan accompanied by a large armed force paraded in front of the Residency and the disputed landing place, and erected there a round tower to command it. On 29 March 1839, the ships left the roads for Khark where they anchored in the morning of 30 March, when the weather was beautiful. The remaining staff and luggage were all aboard by 9 o'clock and then the sepoys left and embarked in the boat. Finally, Capt. Ellis and his 30 marines left, marching through an armed crowd of some 400 to 500 armed Persians, who did not interfere. Then, together with Hennell and Capt. Maitland, accompanied by Ellis, they left to board the *Wellesley*. Hennell informed the governor of Bushehr and Bombay that this decision to depart was not because of the incident with Admiral Maitland, but because Mirza Asadollah's refusal to allow boats to land at the Residency and was the last of many insults during the preceding months. The *Clive* remained as guard ship in the roadstead of Bushehr to "look after British interests and shipping." The government of India approved of the move to Khark, although it regretted the incident and wondered whether it might have been avoided. The Residency buildings were not harmed, and, according to Hennell, there seemed to have been good feeling in Bushehr towards the British, because the merchants appealed to Hennell to remain.[157]

On Khark news was a received that Shiraz had sent an official to investigate Mirza Asadollah's behavior. Therefore, to learn more about this, Hennell sailed to Bushehr and anchored in the road on 16 April 1839. One hour later, the unnamed Khan from Shiraz and Baqer Khan with a party came aboard. The Khan asked Hennell to return and promised that all matters would be resolved to his satisfaction. Hennell replied that this would only be possible after Mirza Asadollah had been removed as governor, who denied that he had interfered with Adm. Maitland's landing and that shots had been fired. After inspection of the ships and its arms, the Persian party returned to Bushehr.[158]

In reaction to Hennell's departure, the Persian government made it known that Sheikh Hasan, the qadi with his nephew and Baqer Khan of Tangestan had expelled the British consul and his soldiers from Bushehr, during which operation there had been casualties on both sides. The British had withdrawn on their ship and had taken the island of Khark, where they had stored much wheat and fodder, which they had bought at four times the market price, which piece of information was supposed to brighten the hearts of the Bushehris and other Persians.[159]

---

157. Saldanha 1986, vol. 2, pp. 281-83; Ellis 1866, pp. 96-105; Government of Great Britain 1841, pp. 10-16, 43-44; (London's reaction was more forceful. Palmerstone told the Shah's envoy that Admiral Maitland would have been justified to bombard the town), 66-74; Kelly 1968, pp. 308-11. More than one year later, MacKenzie the asst. Resident, wrote that "I know that the treatment of the Admiral and the Residency by the authorities in Bushire was approved by the central government, when robes of honor were sent to them (the qadi and his nephew Sheikh Salman)." NA, FO 248/99, Residency T. MacKenzie acting ass. resident /Khark to Sheil/Erzerum, 17/10/1840; Hoseyni 1391, pp. 78-80.

158. Ellis 1866, pp. 107-08.

159. Busse 1972, p. 260; Martin 2005, p. 37; Sa`adat 1390, p. 77; Hoseyni 1391, pp. 75-78 (according to this author Sheikh Hasan, the qadi issued a fatva declaring jihad against the British, which, if true, was met with little enthusiam by the local population, judging by their behavior).

Col. Sherriff wanted Sheikh Naser III to leave Khark as his continued presence there constituted a source of embarrassment to Great Britain. Hennell disagreed, arguing that even when the Sheikh was peaceful and quite, the Persian government would say that his attitude was instigated by the British. Initially, Sherriff gave in, but he later changed his mind and overrode Hennell's opposition. Therefore, given that the Sheikh claimed the island as his hereditary property, while its meagre revenues were almost his only source of income, Hennell argued that he should be given a pecuniary compensation. The reasons given to Sheikh Naser for his removal were that he was not on friendly terms with the Persians and since the removal of the Residency it was believed in Bushehr that Sheikh Naser was in league with the British to attack Persia. "As these rumors may endanger the friendly relations between our two kingdoms it is best that you and those connected with you leave the island. As this means a cost to you I am willing to supply you with what is necessary for you to leave."[160] The government of India disapproved of Sheikh Naser's removal. It instructed the Resident to "make suitable reparation" to Sheikh Naser and help him settle comfortably wherever he had retired to. His house in Khark should be kept in the same condition and at a later date he might be invited back to Khark. Hennell reported that the Sheikh's house in Khark "only consisted of an upper storey of three rooms and was now used as a guard room by the British garrison." The government of India further decided that Khark, except for the Resident's establishments, would be under military administration. Some Baluch guards, hired by Sheikh Naser and whom he had left behind, were to be employed by the British government.[161] Meanwhile, the British maintained correspondence with Baqer Khan and other khans, which made Mirza Asadollah's position untenable.[162]

On 5 June 1839, Mirza Asadollah, the governor and Baqer Khan Tangestani, "military commandant of Bushehr," were given robes of honor sent by the Shah.[163] On 8 June, however, Mirza Asadollah received information from the vizier of Fars that he was removed as governor and replaced by Mirza Mohammad Hoseyn, the vizier's son-in-law. Mirza Asadollah was removed, according to the newswriter in Shiraz, because the Fars authorities wanted to signal to Hennell that they were sincere in wishing to have cordial relations with the British. This may indeed have been the case, because on 11 July 1839, Persia accepted all British demands to restore good relations and the return of McNeill. Mirza Asadollah left Bushehr, but waited in a village nearby, because the chief mullah and merchants had petitioned the governor-general of Fars to have him reinstated. Meanwhile Baqer Khan was acting governor.[164] On 26 August 1839, Hennell received a report that Sheikh Hoseyn, uncle of Sheikh Naser III, together with Baqer Khan Tangestani had expelled Mirza Mohammad Hoseyn the Persian governor of Bushehr, and had assumed the government. It was well-known when he was at Shiraz that Sheikh Hoseyn had intrigued to be appointed governor to the exclusion of his nephew. It was believed he

160. NA, FO 248/85, Hennell to McNeill 17/02/1839; NA, FO 248/108, Draft note from Hennell to Sheikh Nasr, 11/04/1839; Lorimer 1915, vol. 1, p. 1992.

161. Saldanha 1986, vol. 2, pp. 284, 286; Lorimer 1915, vol. 1, pp.1992-93.

162. Grummon 1985, p. 166.

163. Government of Great Britain 1841, pp. 84-85.

164. Saldanha 1986, vol. 2, p. 288; Lorimer 1915, vol. 1, p. 1978. However, more than one year later, MacKenzie, the asst. Resident, wrote that Mirza Assad was deprived of his appointment as governor as a rebuke to the British government. NA, FO 248/99, Residency T. MacKenzie acting ass. resident/Khark to Sheil/Erzerum, 17/10/1840.

would oppose the latter's return as he was said to have received a royal *farman* appointing him governor of Bushehr and that Baqer Khan would support him. The latter had interfered in the hope that he would be appointed governor "as the only person who possesses the means of maintaining any sort of tranquility in that town and its vicinity."[165]

Sheikh Naser III Al Mazkur reappointed as governor

Hennell sent the *Wellesley* to meet with Hoseyn Khan, who had been sent by the governor-general of Fars to discuss the move of the Residency. On 24 August 1839, Hennell reported that Manuchehr Khan Mo`tamed al-Dowleh, governor of Isfahan, Lorestan and Khuzestan and a favorite of Mohammad Shah, had invited Sheikh Naser and received him graciously. It was reported that he wanted to become governor-general of Fars and thought that the Sheikh might be helpful in that. Through his good offices Sheikh Naser III had been reappointed as "Lord High Admiral and Governor of Bushire." Hennell further reported that a clash had taken place between the prince-governor of Shiraz and his troops and the population, some lives were lost, and that the former had withdrawn into the citadel (*naranj-qal`eh*), while the city was in the hands of the insurgents.[166]

In December 1839, it looked as if Shiraz had second thoughts about Sheikh Naser III's appointment, when troops from Shiraz arrived and the Al Mazkur in Bushehr fled.[167] However, these probably were the 1,000 regular troops commanded by Haji Mohammad `Ali Khan that stayed in Tangestan and its neighborhood to quell troubles there. On 25 January 1840, Hennell received news from Shiraz that the Bani Hajer and the Demukh had buried the axe in November 1839 and would accompany Sheikh Naser to Bushehr. On 4 February 1840, one hour before sunset Sheikh Naser entered the town with the greatest pomp. He had promised to pay 3,000 *tuman*s from the Bushehr revenues within five days to the tax collectors (*mohassel*s) that came with him. He was visited by Nurollah Khan and by the commander of the regular troops followed by 180 soldiers.[168]

Despite the presence of a military force in Bushehr's environs, the situation was dangerous. The *Ilbegi* was with a substantial force in Dashtestan. After he had arrested Baqer Khan Tangestani and Haji Khan Dashti he sent them to Shiraz and returned to his own place. Haji Mohammad `Ali Khan styled *Sartip* destroyed the strong point near Borazjan occupied by Mirza `Ali Akbar, who was sent to Shiraz and thrown into prison. Haji Mohammad `Ali Khan also tried to take `Abbas Khan of Zireh with a force supported by two cannons and 60 artillerymen. He entered Zireh with 30 horsemen but `Abbas Khan knew his intention and laid an ambush, he rushed and took them all, then stripped them and put them in gunny bags; the other soldiers seeing this, all fled to Shiraz and took sanctuary. `Abbas Khan was said to have fled afterwards. Despite the presence of the military force, it was reported that many people wanted to leave Bushehr. It was also rumored that the Shah wanted to occupy Khark. Aqa Jamal, presumably the leader of the revolt against Rezaqoli Mirza in 1833, returned to Bushehr in December 1839. He may

165. Saldanha 1986, vol. 2, p. 286; Lorimer 1915, vol. 1, p. 1978.
166. Saldanha 1986, vol. 2, pp. 285-86; Lorimer 1915, vol. 1, p. 1979.
167. Grummon 1985, p. 166.
168. NA, FO 248/99, Substance of a letter by M.A. Malcolm to Hennell, 05/02/1840.

have carried a message from the Soltan of Masqat, because he first went to the Shah, who gave him a horse for his master as mark of his favor. On his return to Bushehr, Aqa Jamal was killed by Baqer Khan Tangestani. The reason for the murder seems to have been Aqa Jamal's interest to become governor of Bushehr. The governor-general of Fars bought the horse and sword, added something to it and sent it to Sheikh Seyf, the Omani governor Bandar Abbas to bring it to the Soltan of Masqat. The latter was furious about the murder, after all Aqa Jamal had gone to Persia under his guarantee. He demanded and eventually obtained a promise from the Shah that his murderer would be punished. As is clear from what follows this was an empty promise.[169]

After Sheikh Naser III left for Shiraz in mid-May 1840, the acting authorities of Bushehr prevented the transportation of any kind of supplies to Khark. The customs officers were very strict inspecting all goods destined for Khark and apparently spies were sent to find out who in Bushehr sent these supplies to Khark under the pretext that they were being shipped to Basra. Although Khark was amply supplied from other ports, what worried the British Resident was that apparently the implementation of the ban was done at the orders of higher authorities. Also, it was detrimental to the merchants of Bushehr.[170] Sheikh Naser was severely reprimanded by the governor-general of Fars, who accused him of having hired out the *Nosrat Shah* to the British to ensure the supply channel between Bushehr and Khark and that he did nothing to stop the supply from other ports. The Sheikh vehemently denied this, saying his vessel was taken up in Bengal to go to China and that no supplies were sent. The result was that the Sheikh had to sign a bond to station men at all those supply ports and to make sure that no wheat, barley, rice, even a single fowl or egg was leaving the coast. Meanwhile, Hennell instructed Lt. Col. Hughes to lie in a few months of supplies of provisions for the troops, although he did not believe that the application of the ban would be strict.[171]

During Sheikh Naser III's absence nobody was appointed governor of Bushehr, but `Abdollah Khan, who in June 1840 arrived at Bushehr with 300 men, was said to have been given full authority over the lowlands. His arrival had not yet resulted in a change in attitude towards communications with Khark; meanwhile there continued to be a free flow of cheap and plentiful supplies.[172] In July 1840, Sheikh Naser's family left Bushehr for Shiraz to remain there as security for his good behavior, therefore, his early arrival as governor at the port was soon expected.[173] Because the governor-general (*Saheb Ekhtiyar*) died this resulted in unsafe roads; caravans were robbed, while petty chiefs attacked each other. Sheikh Naser was still in Shiraz, while no governor of Bushehr had as yet been appointed. In early October 1840, a messenger arrived in Bushehr with an order banning

169. NA, FO 248/99, Mirza Mohammad Reza to Resident 8 Zu'l-hijja - 12/02/1840; Lorimer 1915, vol. 1, p. 1979. Hennell wrote: "I don't think that the Imam of Muscat wants to attack Bushire because of the murder of ex-governor Jomaal Khan. His reason was not only because he was an ex-governor, but I think he was the Imam's accredited agent with the shah with overture to matrimonial alliance with a member of the shah's family, and that Jomaal Khan's nomination as governor of Bushehr was due to the influence and funds of the Imam, whose objective seems to have been to place that port at the same footing as that of Bandar Abbas, in respect to himself." NA, FO 248/99, Hennell/Khark to Sheil/Erzeroom 12/06/1840.

170. NA, FO 248/99, Hennell/Khark to Sheil/Erzeroom, 25/05/1840.

171. NA, FO 248/99, Residency/Khark to Sheil/Erzeroom 13/06/1840.

172. NA, FO 248/99, MacKenzie acting assistant Resident/Khark 13/06/1840. Sheikh Hoseyn, Naser III's uncle had left town and went to Guseer (?) on the Persian coast. Idem, Hennell to Sheil, 25/05/1840.

173. NA, FO 248/99, Residency/Khark to Reid/Bombay 11/09/1840.

the export of old coins, because of the re-coining of the currency. The British commented that although this would cause problems for trade, it would not stop their outflow. None of the new currency had as yet reached Bushehr.[174]

Meanwhile, Shiraz interfered with the horse trade and imposed a higher export fee (see chapter 2). The ban on export of specie was ignored, but in October 1840, a messenger from Shiraz arrived to prevent merchants from exporting it to India. MacKenzie expected that as usual some deal would be struck and he learnt that this almost immediately happened. However, both these measures were feared to have a negative effect on trade given that this impacted on Persia's two most important exports: specie and horses. Another event that worried the British was that Sheikh Salman, nephew of Sheikh Hasan, the qadi, was received by the Shah with much respect and was honored with several private audiences in which the Shah referred to his good services regarding the admiral's affair and the removal of the Residency from Bushehr. He was given an expensive robe of honor and six horses. Moreover, a *farman* was issued not only confirming his family's pension but increasing it from 500 to 1,000; 600 *tumans* for Sheikh Hasan and 400 for himself. He was given another *farman* "enjoining every respect and obedience to Shaikh Hassan." On his return on 11 October in Bushehr, Sheikh Salman was treated everywhere as a person of rank and high favor and he was escorted by the regular troops and a host of people as a mark of great respect. The Shah also bestowed his favor on Baqer Khan Tangestani, who was in prison in Shiraz, because of the murder of Aqa Jamal. He was expected to be sent to the Shah's camp for execution, but his representations of the important role he and his tribe played in protecting Bushehr saved his life.[175]

In October 1840, Farhad Mirza was appointed as governor-general of Fars; Sheikh Naser III and Baqer Khan Tangestani received orders to pay last year's arrears to him forthwith; they had already paid all they could, but they were unable to borrow more.[176] The feud between the Dashtis and the Tangestanis was suspended for the moment. On 18 December the Resident received a letter from Sheikh Hoseyn, Sheikh Naser III's uncle, who announced his arrival in Delam, intending to march against Bushehr with troops of the self-styled governor of Behbahan, Mirza Kuma. However, the latter decided first to postpone and then to deny support to Sheikh Hoseyn.[177] On 22 December 1840, Farhad Mirza publicly told Sheikh Naser that the only thing that the Shah required from Fars was that the borders were secure, especially in Bushehr, and therefore, 200 regular troops were sent there. On 23 December 1840, the vizier called Baqer Khan Tangestani and said that he was in the Shah's favor because he had fought the British; however, there also were negative reports about him, viz. that from his place, limestone and corn were sent to Khark and that it would not be good for him if that was the case.[178] By January 1841, Sheikh Naser III and Baqer Khan had settled their debts and were permitted to leave. The Sheikh left Shiraz but waited at the first halt for Baqer Khan, who had remained behind. The reason was that Baqer Khan had supported Mirza `Ali Akbar after he had killed `Ali Khan, the chief of Borazjan, which caused the people of Borazjan much trouble. Shiraz

174. NA, FO 248/99, Residency T. MackKenzie acting ass. resident/Khark to Reid/Bombay 07/10/1840.

175. NA, FO 248/99, Residency T. MacKenzie acting ass. resident /Khark to Sheil/? 17/10/1840.

176. NA, FO 248/99, Newswriter Shiraz to Resident. 7 Ramazan - 05/11/1840.

177. NA, FO 248/99, Residency/Khark to Sheil/Erzerum, 18/12/1840. NA, FO248/99, News writer report 07/12/1840.

178. NA, FO 248/99, Report news writer, 24/12/1840.

demanded that Baqer Khan produce Mirza `Ali Akbar, who was promised security. He came and Baqer Khan decided to wait for him to settle his affairs in Shiraz before returning. Naser al-Molk, the vizier told Baqer Khan that he would send 40 horsemen with him who had to take care of some business in Dashtestan.[179]

On his return to Bushehr in February 1841, Sheikh Naser III, to comply with the promises made to Shiraz, imposed heavy taxes on the population, which those of the neighboring districts refused to pay. In Bushehr feelings of officials towards the British did not improve. Since Sheikh Naser's return all vessels leaving Bushehr were strictly watched and searched whether they had goods for Khark. This new practice was mainly due to the Persians, who had come with the Sheikh and who appeared to exercise some independent control over the Customs House. Meanwhile plenty and cheap supplies came from all other Persian ports to Khark.[180]

At the end of February 1841, Nurollah Khan Sarhang was supposed to leave Shiraz with 200 men to garrison Bushehr. However, he did not leave, because he did not get the means to properly outfit the troops. When the discussion became heated with the government officials, he took off his sword, threw it down, and said he would no longer serve and left the city. He was induced to return as the prince promised to treat him well. Meanwhile, the troops started stealing to feed themselves, one of them was caught and the prince had his ears cut off and then paraded him through the bazaar. Meanwhile, Sheikh Naser seized Haji Ja`far Behbahani, from whom he demanded 400 *tumans* or be expelled from Bushehr, who then hired a *baghla* to take him to Basra. It was said `Abdol-Mohammad, one of the wealthy merchants of Bushehr, interceded for him; he was on good terms with Sheikh Naser, who was guided by his advice. The Shiraz revenue collectors demanded 8,000 *tumans* from Sheikh Naser who was perplexed. To help him, `Abdol Mohammad lent him cloth and sugar to the value of 1,000 *tumans*.[181]

The governor-general of Fars sent a robe of honor from Borazjan to Sheikh Naser, who was embarrassed being unable to pay the revenue or to send an expensive present in return, let alone to afford the expense of a princely visit. It was unknown whether the governor-general would come to Bushehr. Sheikh Naser lifted the restrictions on sending supplies to Khark, probably after having learnt the news of an imminent renewal of relations between Great Britain and Persia.[182] When Farhad Mirza arrived in Bushehr's environs, he was supposed to visit the EIC sloop, but did not. However, his courtiers and second vizier, Mirza Sadeq visited it when lying in the roads off Chaef (?). The prince was persuaded not to do so by Sheikh Naser and the people of Bushehr, who feared that he then would land in Bushehr rather than in Chaef. The contacts with prince's staff were very friendly and civil in contrast to that of the authorities of Bushehr. Farhad Mirza arrived at Chaef on the morning of the 10th and returned in the evening to Chahkutah. After hunting in the hills of Halileh for two days the prince returned to Borazjan en route to Shiraz; he had 500 men with him.[183]

---

179. NA, FO 248/544, Report news writer, 14/01/1841.

180. NA, FO 248/99, Residency/Khark to Sheil/Erzerum, 18/02/1841; Idem, Residency/Khark to Sheil/Erzerum, 26/02/1841 (he made the success of British arms in Afghanistan and Baluchistan known; most believed it); NA, FO 248/99, Report news writer, 03/02/1841.

181. NA, FO 248/99, Report newswriter 7 Moharram - 01/03/1841; Idem, Keith Jopp, ass. acting resident Khark, 20/03/1841.

182. NA, FO 248/99, J. Hennell/Khark to Sheil/Erzerum 03/04/1841.

183. NA, FO 248/99, Commodore Geo B. Brucks/warship Coote to Hennell/Khark, 12/04/1841; Idem, Hennell/Khark to Sheil/Erzerum, 12/04/1841.

Despite these friendly overtures the authorities continued to make life for the British unpleasant. Moreover, some of the demands for reparations to British subjects who had suffered insults at the hands of the local authorities were never satisfied, despite solemn promises to do so. Neither Admiral Maitland or Hennell nor the Residency *sarraf* were given reperations or compensation for respectively, the insults and attack suffered by them.[184]

In June 1841, Sheikh Naser III began erecting a fort at the flanks of the town walls of Bushehr (see chapter one). Sheikh Naser lost no opportunity to show his enmity to the British government and those belonging to it. In Hennell's absence Sheikh Naser informed Col. Davies not to let any officers from Khark visit Bushehr. Hennell, on his return, informed Sheikh Naser that he did not acknowledge any oral information and therefore, he had better put it in writing. Sheikh Naser declined to do so until he received further orders from Shiraz.[185] Because of his money trouble, Sheikh Naser had not paid the arrears to the regular troops, which led to a fracas. His Arab followers fired on the troops, three of whom were seriously wounded. In view of this enmity the commander of the regular troops withdrew his men from the town and wrote to Shiraz. Sheikh Naser tried to induce him to return and to forget about the whole affair, however, he was not willing to pay the large sum that the commanding *yavar* was asking.[186]

Sheikh Naser's hostile attitude toward the British was most likely due to his resentment about having been removed from Khark. When Hennell appointed Mr. Essai Johannes as treasurer to negotiate government bills to be able to pay the troops, he was told by Aqa Shafi, the Customs master that he had to pay 300 Mohammad Shah rupees. When he told `Abdol-Mohammad about this, while visiting him in his counting house, the latter told him not to press the issue as he would talk to Sheikh Naser. The latter told him that Essai was neither merchant nor farmer and was sent by Hennell as a government agent to Bushehr to do the British government's business. Sheikh Naser also said: "what good has Hennell been to me? When he came to Khark he turned me out of the island and if he returns to Bushire he will do likewise." After more discussion the matter was dropped. Hennell considered this a harassment of a British dependent and told Commodore Brucks, who was going to Bushehr to refit the rigging, to ascertain from the governor whether this had occurred at his orders. Sheikh Naser refused to talk to the officer sent ashore by Brucks. Although the pressure on Mr. Essai had stopped, Hennell nevertheless reported Sheikh Naser's malicious and unfriendly attitude towards those linked to British government. He treated British officers sent to Bushehr with great discourtesy if he could do so without seriously committing himself.[187] Also, there were problems in the environs of Bushehr, this time in Dashti. In January 1842, Mostafa Khan was sent there with two cannons and 500 regulars, supported by the troops of Mohammad Baqer Khan Tangestani. There was a battle, which resulted in 50 dead and 50 wounded on both sides; also some forts were taken and villages plundered.[188]

---

184. Kelly 1986, pp. 350-51.
185. NA, FO 248/99, Residency to Sheil 14/06/1841.
186. NA, FO 248/99, Hennell, Residency to Sheil, 24/07/1841.
187. NA, FO 248/99, Hennell to Sheil 07/10/1841; Idem, Hennell to Sheil, 07/10/1841; Idem, letter Mr. Essai to Hennell, 26/09/1841; Idem, Brucks to Sheikh Naser, n.d..
188. NA, FO 248/99, Mirza Mohammad Reza to Col. Robertson, 23 Zi'l-Hijjah 1257 - 05/02/1842.

British Residency returns to Bushehr

In early May 1842, Col. Robertson sent Lt. Kemball to Bushehr to assess the state of the Residency buildings. Because the local merchants still had doubts whether Persia and Great Britain had re-established friendly relations and because the British flag still had not been hoisted, he had to convene some of the leading inhabitants such as Malcolm, Constatine, Satour, Haji Mohammad Baqer, `Abdol-Mohammad, Khvajeh Morad and Ya`qub and formally announce that although the Resident was not yet back, friendship between the two states has been re-established.[189] It became clear that all kinds of stories circulated in Bushehr, which made the merchants doubt that this was the case. They asked, "if McNeill has returned to Tehran, why has not the Resident returned, and why has the flag not been hoisted?" Also, Sheikh Naser III was sulky and did not talk about the peace. He refused to meet with Kemball unless he was accompanied by Mirza `Ali, the revenue collector left behind by the prince. He was afraid that this person would make false reports about him to the prince-governor. Although a meeting had been set up, the Sheikh did not come. Kemball reported to Robertson that he himself had to return to Bushehr to have the merchants believe that peace really had been concluded. He further reported that the Residency and adjacent buildings needed repairs, which would take 4-6 weeks.[190]

Robertson decided to go to Bushehr and hoist the flag, which he announced in a note to Sheikh Naser. The Sheikh acted as if was very pleased about this and asked the merchants to come with him on board to welcome Robertson, but they refused to accord him the customary welcoming (*esteqbal*) at sea. Therefore, Sheikh Naser decided to come to the Residency and welcome Robertson there. Essai, the Residency's accountant, further reported that Sheikh Naser did not have much authority, being under obligation to the merchants Haji Mohammad Baqer, Aqa `Abdol-Mohammad and Aqa Mir Baqer from who he had received money to pay the prince's men. There was also the *yavar* or head of the troops over whom the Sheikh had no authority and who did whatever he liked. Finally, there was Mirza `Ali, the prince's revenue collector, waiting to get 1,000 *tumans* from the governor. Because of all these circumstances, Sheikh Naser was quite powerless.[191]

At 3 p.m., on 10 May 1842, Robertson arrived in Bushehr. When the British flag was hoisted, a royal salute was given by the schooner *Maki*. There was no welcoming committee, despite the fact that the prince-governor had given Hoseyn `Ali Khan, the *mehmendar* instructions to organize a honorable reception of the Resident. Mr. Satoor, an old Armenian merchant of great respectability and Mr. Avit, a second rate merchant were the only ones who welcomed Robertson. They and Essai believe that it was not Sheikh Naser, but rather `Abdol-Mohammad, a wealthy Persian merchant, Haji Mohammad, a banker and merchant, and Mirza `Ali, the prince-governor of Shiraz's revenue collector who had plotted the entire affair of intended disrespect. Robertson ascribed this to the attitude of some disgruntled individuals. Therefore, he landed near the Residency. After he had arrived there, Sheikh Naser asked to be received. However, Robertson refused to do so, because he had not been there to welcome him and ignoring this slight would

---

189. NA, FO 248/108, Robertson officiating res. to Kemball ass. resident/Khark, 02/05/1842.

190. NA, FO 248/108, Kemball/Bushire to Col. Robertson/Khark, 03/05/1842; Idem, Kemball/Bushire to Col. Robertson/Khark, 04/05/1842.

191. NA, FO 248/108, Essai Johannes/Bushire to Robertson/Khark, 08/05/1842; Idem, Essai/Bushire to Robertson/Khark, 09/05/1842.

lower his position. Sheikh Naser then wrote a humble letter to the Residency *monshi* making an apology for not having met Robertson on board and begged him to arrange a meeting. He also sent a note, stating: "When I heard the guns I prepared with my uncle Sheikh Sadoon and my cousin Sheikh `Ali, son of Sheikh Mahometh Khan to welcome Resident to go to the boat for the estekbal. I was just stepping aboard that I was told the Resident had already arrived ashore close to the Residency. I am now in the upper room of your house, in which Sheikh `Ali lives, but which he will vacate for your own reception. I do not know whether to go home or to wait to see the Resident."[192] Robertson immediately granted him an interview, because when he was at the gate everybody had noticed his refusal to receive the governor and because he had apologized. Robertson also announced the signing of the Anglo-Persian treaty of 23 October 1841 to the mercantile community, although he had no Persian version. On 11 May 1842, the merchants requested to visit Robertson, but he said he had no time. During the day many individual applications were made, but he refused them all, except Messrs. Satoor and Avit. Robertson explained the reason for his actions as follows:

> One may question whether the resident is entitled to an estekbal at the anchoring ground, the residency is only 3 miles from the port and I myself thought that people having to go through all this trouble was uncalled for, but the propriety of such a welcome were established by the presence of Hoseyn Ali Khan having ordered it, by its having been proposed by sheikh Nasr and discussed, and by the apology later by Nasr, and by the custom of the country which prescribes an estekbal beyond the towns limits on land and at the port where the houses are built on the shore, the determined position is the anchoring ground. The weather and sea was calm and it was a perfect day for such an event.

In particular, Robertson was angry with the contemptible attitude by the Armenian merchants "who more than others have benefited from our former connection with Bushire is a remarkable as the exceptions to it, in particular Satoor who after the departure of the Residency in 1839 received any gentlemen traveling through Bushire in his house." The Residency was in such a state that it could not be lived in and therefore, on 12 May, Robertson returned to Khark without having spoken to anyone but the two merchants mentioned above and without having paid a return visit to Sheikh Naser III. Nevertheless, to show that the British were back, he made the Residency his official headquarters. Therefore, he and his assistant Kemball occasionally stayed there. Moreover, he kept his treasure chest there and the principal part of his escort.[193]

Robertson wrote to the prince-governor announcing the hoisting of the flag and that he would permanently move there once the repairs were completed.[194] He further complained about the fact that there had been no welcoming committee (*esteqbal*) despite the orders to organize one. Hoseyn `Ali Khan replied that Mirza Sadeq, the revenue collector had told him that Mirza `Ali had written that they had welcomed the Resident

192. FO 248/108, Sheikh Nasr to Residency *Monshi*, 10/05/1842.

193. NA, FO 248/99, Robertson/Bushire to Sir John McNeil, 10/05/1842; Idem, Resident/Bushire to Sir John McNeil, 11/05/1842; NA, FO 248/108, Resident/Khark to Sir John McNeil, 13/05/1842.

194. NA, FO 248/108, Robertson to prince governor, 10/05/1842.

with an *esteqbal* at the door of customs house and then had taken him to the Residency buildings; moreover, the Resident was not angry. Given the reported lack of respect shown to Robertson, Hoseyn `Ali Khan wrote to the Farmanfarma, who ordered Naser al-Molk to write a reprimand to Sheikh Naser III and that he had to change his conduct and show respect.[195]

The Fars and Bushehr authorities were very worried that Robertson remained on Khark rather than at Bushehr. Because Sheil had instructed him to write to the prince why he had not moved to Bushehr, he explained to Sheil that due to his duties on the coast of Arabia he had temporarily chosen to remain in Khark. Furthermore, he pointed out that whatever he might say Sheikh Naser and the prince would never forgive him for thwarting their plans to oppress the people of Khark. And indeed, the prince-governor wrote Robertson that he did not think his arguments for not living in a crumbling house in Bushehr were valid and that perhaps he remained in Khark for other reasons.[196] Robertson had written on 20 May 1842 to Bombay that on political grounds it would be better to remove the Residency from Bushehr, some miles in-land or on the coast, before spending any money repairing the Residency buildings. Because he only received an answer on 10 October, he had not made any repairs as this would have defeated the purpose of his request. As the Residency was uninhabitable, there were not even servants, the assistant Resident and the surgeon were given the option to stay privately at Khormuj, Khark or elsewhere and they chose Khark. Both he and Kemball went to Bushehr and stayed sometimes a week or more, and one occasion Kemball stayed for three weeks. He kept few guards at Bushehr, because the doctor believed that it was healthier for them to remain at Khark. The flagstaff, treasurer, accountant department with all the records and half the guard were sent to Bushehr. Robertson finally pointed out that even if he had gone to Khormuj, as had been permitted by the Shah, his assistant and surgeon would have stayed at Khark.[197]

Whether because of being miffed at the British or not, but on 3 June 1842, when Lt. Kemball was about to leave the gate of the town wall for an evening ride, one of the soldiers stationed there seized his bridle and did not want him to pass. His groom arrived immediately and stood security that his master would return. This had never before happened, British gentlemen and respectable natives always had the privilege to leave and enter the gate at all hours whatever the circumstances. Therefore, Robertson asked the governor for an explanation of the soldier's behavior and wrote to the prince-governor

---

195. NA, FO 248/108, Robertson to Hoseyn Ali Khan, 10/05/1842; Idem, Mirza Mohammad Reza news writer Shiraz to Robertson, 02/06/1842 ("concerning the disrespect shown to you, please send me the list of names so that they may be punished. Don't be annoyed at these blockheads for you will get satisfaction.") NA, FO 248/108, Hoseyn Ali Khan to Robertson n.d.

196. NA, FO 248/108, Robertson/Khark to Sheil, 11/08/1842; Idem, Mirza Mohammad Reza news writer to Robertson, 29/06/1842. The official worry may also have been partially due to the fact that the prince-governor expected a present. "Hasan Ali Khan pishkhedmat of the prince who went to Khark for you as mehmendar came to see me and said that on the island you had told him that you wanted to send a present to the prince, but not having a fit one for him that you would send it later. The prince wants to have a horse and a carriage. He said he had written to you about this." NA, FO 248/108, Mirza Mohammad Reza news writer to Robertson, 29/06/1842.

197. NA, FO 248/108, Robertson/Bushire to Sheil, 03/11/1842; Saldanha 1986, vol. 2, p. 291.

in Shiraz to inform him with the request that British residency staff and those under their protection would not to be treated with disrespect anymore.[198]

On 1 July 1842, Sheikh Naser had a private talk with Essai, the Residency treasurer and told him that he had learnt that Col. Sheil had been complaining about him at Court and argued for his removal and to send him to Tehran. He then gave Essai a letter for Robertson and verbally said if this was true, to please write him and to intercede for him that he may remain here. In his letter to Robertson, Essai gave as his opinion that "the Sheikh as governor is better than having a Persian as one, as most inhabitants are Arabs, and having the experience of some Persians here as governor they treated the inhabitants barbarously."[199] According to James Edwards, Residency accountant, Sheikh Naser's worry might have been caused by the arrival of four horsemen from Shiraz. They had to collect 1,600 *tumans* from Sheikh Naser, being the salary of Sheikh Hasan and Sheikh Salman, the qadis of Bushehr, which had not been paid and about which they had complained.[200] Whatever the reason may have been, Sheikh Naser was summoned by the Shah in August 1842. He appointed Sheikh `Abdollah as acting governor. He was still very worried about what Sheil might have said about him, because he asked Robertson to recommend him to the British ambassador. He ended his letter with "I am helpless and trust in God."[201] Robertson replied that there was no need for him to write to Sheil, because he was fully informed about the situation in Bushehr. At the same time, he reminded Sheikh Naser that he should not only ask, but also give service. Therefore, Robertson noted that it was not because of the heat that he didn't reside in Bushehr, but because of the vexations British dependents were exposed to at the hands of the soldiers and others, which lead to complaints and ill-feeling.[202] These added remarks were not superfluous, because on 14 October 1842, Lt. Kemball was again obstructed by Persian soldiers, this time when he wanted to leave with a boat that he had hired. Sheikh `Abdollah was much vexed at the interference, but he had no authority to punish anyone let alone a soldier, and therefore, Robertson had to seek redress from the prince-governor.[203]

This was not the only irritation and annoyance that upset the British. There was also the matter of the small city gate in the wall near the Residency. Since the re-establishment of friendly relations with the city government, Robertson had asked it to be re-opened. When part of the wall was built in the mid-1830s, Hennell asked that a small gate be made right opposite the Residency, "where there was an open space and a road between a few houses, sufficiently wide for a carriage, up to the projected opening." This was agreed to on condition that Hennell paid for the upkeep of a doorman, one of the governor's

---

198. NA, FO 248/108, Robertson/Karrack to Sheil, 08/06/1842; Idem, three Persian letters to Sheikh Nasr and replies; Idem, Essai/Bushire to Robertson/Karrack, 07/06/1842; Idem, *Raqam* Farmanfarma to Robertson n.d. However, in October 1842, the same incident happened twice, although the commander of the soldiers later apologized and promised punishing the soldier concerned. FO 248/108, Hon. Lt. Campbell Steam vessel Nimrod/Bushire to Robertson/Khark, 14 October 1842; Idem, Robertson to Sheil, n.d. (December 1842).

199. NA, FO 248/108, Essai/Bushire to Robertson/Karrack, 01/07/1842.

200. NA, FO 248/108, James Edwards, Residency accountant/Bushire to Robertson/Khark, 20/06/1842.

201. NA, FO 248/108, Letter from Sheikh Nasr n.d. rec. from Bandar Rig.

202. NA, FO 248/108, Robertson/Khark to Sheikh Nasr, 12/08/1842.

203. NA, FO 248/108, Robertson/Bushire to Sheil, 15/10/1842. It was only in December 1842, that the soldiers who refused to open the gate for Lt. Campbell and Selby were punished. NA, FO 248/108, Robertson to Sheil n.d.

dependents, whose duty it was to allow members of the Residency to come and go and no one else. The door was locked and its key was kept by the governor's man servant. When Hennell left in 1839, the gateway was built up with stones and lime, but the gate still was there. Robertson wanted it opened based on the old arrangement, even though the path was now blocked by hundreds of huts from poor weaver-migrants from Bahrain, who had erected their huts close to the Residency. He believed that paying them a little money to put their huts elsewhere would make it possible to open the road again and a wheel-carriage to pass. This was not possible through the public gate as the streets were too narrow. The acting governor declined as he had no power to decide and referred Robertson to write to Shiraz. Robertson informed Sheil about this issue, because he feared that it would be presented at court as if he asked for a new gateway.[204]

As to the Bahrainis, Kemball pressured Sheikh `Abdollah to remove them, because they encroached terrain that by custom was within the Residency. He also informed Sheil about the problem. He reminded Sheikh `Abdollah that after an altercation had taken place between Robertson's horse keeper and some Bahrainis, he had promised that he would remove the weavers from the spot where they had erected their huts within a few paces of the Residency's stable, contrary to former custom. Moreover, they also caused great inconvenience to the inmates of the Residency, because they threw their excreta and filth near and under the wall. Sheikh `Abdollah promised to comply with the request, but he did nothing because Sheikh Hasan, the qadi and fellow-Bahraini, said it was contrary to religious law. Kemball wrote to Sheikh `Abdollah that Sheikh Hasan was the judge, but not governor of the town and had no right to interfere between the government and the British authorities. Therefore, Kemball wrote to the governor-general of Fars hoping that he would re-establish the old custom. The latter replied that, since the Bahrainis had come without permission of the Shah he should write to Sheil, while he would write to Minister Foreign Affairs that orders for their removal be issued.[205]

The Bahrainis probably had come with Sheikh `Abdollah b. Ahmad, the ex-chief of Bahrain. He had come to Bushehr to have a safe asylum and to prepare his plans to regain Bahrain. Sheikh Salman's magnificent promises had made a great impression on him and it was only much later that he realized that these promises were empty ones. On 20 March 1843, Sheikh `Abdollah b. Ahmad paid a farewell visit to Hennell; he tried to convince him that he had never placed any faith in the promise of the Persian authorities of assisting him with troops to regain his authority on Bahrain. He left Bushehr on 26 March in a *batil* accompanied by another. Hennell believed that he would go to the Arabian Coast to force the blockade of Dammam his only remaining stronghold and bring supplies. If he were to succeed Hennell expected him back to rejoin his family in Naband.[206]

Sheikh Naser's stay in Tehran was the subject of much speculation in Bushehr. When he left he made it known that he was going to Tehran to be consulted on naval matters, which everybody believed. Also, that he would receive a more general title and obtain more control than ever before as Daryabegi. Later it was said the Shah wanted to name

---

204. NA, FO 248/108, Robertson/Busire to Sheil, 23/11/1842.

205. NA, FO 248/263, Kemball to Sheil, 27/09/1843; Idem, Kemball to Sheikh Abdollah, 25/09/1843; Idem, Kemball to Amir Nabi Khan, 25/09/1843; Idem, Reply by Kemball to Sheikh Abdollah, 26/09/1843; Idem, Amir to Kemball, Ramazan.

206. NA, FO 248/263, Hennell to Sheil, 26/03/1844; on the Dammam issue, see Kelly 1968, p. 381.

him *Amir al-Bahr* (admiral of the sea) and to restore all the lands of his ancestors.[207] Although the punishment of the soldiers had been dealt with there still continued to be incidents involving insults to British subjects or protected persons, one in which Sheikh `Abdollah, the acting governor played an active part, another where soldiers had interfered with the water supply to the British Residency.[208] On 20 November 1843, Musa Khan arrived from Shiraz to see to it that satisfaction was given to the British by punishing several individuals who had given insult. He showed orders that gave him the authority to remove the huts near the Residency and to punish several individuals, including Sheikh `Abdollah, who have given insult. The huts were immediately removed, while concerning the punishments, Sheikh `Abdollah even offered to submit to the same punishment, because his servant had grabbed the Residency's doctor's servant. Hennell told Musa Khan that it would give him little satisfaction to punish subordinates who probably had acted on orders of their superiors. The subordinates only modeled their behavior after that of their superiors, who were the real problem. If the *yavar*'s conduct was overlooked his mission had little significance and he asked for implementation of the orders to remove him. The Khan replied that the punishment of the subordinates was Robertson's affair; his orders were to assemble the culprits and deliver them for punishment by Robertson. As to the removal of the *yavar*, the Amir clearly considered that this reprimand was sufficient else he would have given different orders.[209] Musa Khan left on 30 March 1844 to join the Amir's camp. Except for the garrison commander, there has been a constant misunderstanding between the local authorities and the Amir, about a large share of the profits to be made from the new breastworks that Sheikh Salman had approved. Musa Khan left without any sign of respect or attention from his colleagues.[210] On 7 April 1844, the Amir made his entry into Bushehr. On 9 April Hennell went to visit him. Prior to his visit the Amir had informed Hennell that he agreed to his wish to dismiss the *yavar* and take him to Shiraz. Therefore, Hennell was very much surprised that the Amir early on 11 April accompanied by 75 horsemen had left Bushehr, without taking the *yavar* with him, who had asked for a delay to take care of business and settle his accounts.[211]

On 19 May 1844, Sheikh `Abdollah, the acting governor and Sheikh Sa`dun, the governor of Rudhilleh were arrested at the orders of the garrison commander, Hoseyn `Ali Khan and together with their *mirza*s they were placed under guard of soldiers, due to their inability to pay 800 *tuman*s to the town's garrison. On the same day several merchants

207. NA, FO 248/108, Robertson to Sheil, 23/01/1843.

208. For details on these events and the correspondence, see NA, FO 248/108, Robertson to Sheil, 14/04/1843; Idem, Kemball ass. resident in charge to Sheikh Abdollah, 04/05/1843; NA, FO 248/263, Kemball to Sheil, 27/09/1843; Idem, Kemball to Sheikh Abdollah, 25/09/1843; Idem, Kemball to Amir Nabi Khan 25/09/1843; Idem, Reply Sheikh Abdollah, 27 Sha`ban; Idem, Reply Kemball to Sheikh Abdollah, 26/09/1843; Idem, Kemball to Amir Nabi Khan, 25/09/1843; Idem, Kemball to Sheil, 25/09/1843; Idem, Kemball to Sheil, 21/10/1843; Idem, Persian letter from the Amir and replies; Idem, Amir to Kemball, Ramazan; Idem, Reply to Amir from Kemball n.d.; Idem, Kemball to Sheikh Abdollah and the Yavar, 13/10/1843; Idem, Amir to Sheikh Abdollah, Ramazan; Idem, Sheikh Abdollah's reaction to the Amir's letter, 17/10/1843;Idem, Amir to the Yavar, Ramazan; Idem, Reply Yavar to Kemball about the Amir's order, 04/10/1843.

209. NA, FO 248/263, Hennell to Sheil, 04/12/1843; Idem, Persian letter Amir; Persian letter to the garrison commander from the Amir; commander's reply. Sheil disapproved that the soldiers were not punished. Hennel promised that in the future "I'll see to it that punishment is meted out." NA, FO 248/263, Hennell to Sheil, 02/02/1844.

210. NA, FO 248/263, Hennell to Sheil, 02/04/1844.

211. NA, FO 248/263, Hennell to Sheil, 11/04/1844.

came forward and became security for the settlement of the claim on the acting governor and his relative.[212] Six weeks later, Sheikh `Abdollah suffered another embarrassment. At day break on 9 July 1844, his brother Sheikh Hoseyn arrived with 10 men at the town gate and entered alone through the wicket and passed unmolested to the house of the Qadi Sheikh Hasan, where he remained. The acting governor, who was well aware of the unscrupulous character of his brother, was in a state of considerable alarm because he had been able to enter despite all precautions. Several unsuccessful attempts were made to induce him to return to Shiraz and the matter was referred to Tehran.[213]

Local and hinterland problems

When Sheikh Naser III resumed his function as governor of Bushehr he was faced with many local problems, mainly with Baqer Khan Tangestani, who in 1845 had taken Borazjun, the most important settlement in Dashtestan. This was the lay of the land when the reconfirmed Sheikh Naser arrived on the morning of 7 September 1845.[214] However Baqer Khan was not Sheikh Naser's only problem, so was the Soltan of Masqat, who in 1846 threatened to blockade Bushehr if he did not get his way. Hennell was upset about this and argued that an amicable agreement was preferable. Therefore, the Soltan should have submitted his complaint to the Shah and tell him what kind of redress he sought, rather than threatening to destroy Persia's major port. Sheikh Naser's greatest fear was that the Soltan would seize Khark, "which under the present circumstances he could do without." Once he would have lost his island refuge, the Persian government would be able to dislodge Sheikh Naser.[215] Moreover, again there was a problem with the British. Some 20-30 armed followers of Sheikh Hoseyn, Sheikh Naser's uncle, and at his instigation, attacked a British subject, Sheikh Yusef b. Saqr on 2 August 1846, when he landed. "His left arm had been broken by a blow from an iron-headed club; his right hand was deeply wounded by a dagger and he was so severely beaten that he dropped senseless into the water. Some of his lascars were also cruelly treated." He fled to the Residency and on his way he ran into Sheykh Hoseyn, who did not ask what had happened, but told his men to let Sheikh Yusef go and more precisely, told him to go to hell. The previous day Sheikh Yusef had entertained Sheikh Naser and his wife, the princess on board his ship. Hennell asked Sheikh Naser III to arrest the perpetrators. The Sheikh expressing his regrets about the incident wrote that he would so. However, he could neither find his uncle nor his men as they had gone in hiding in the town. According to Hennell, this meant that "he and the whole town live in terror for the unscrupulous Sheikh Hoseyn and his followers, so that no one dared to take effective measures to arrest them." Therefore, Hennell wrote to Shiraz hoping that proper punishment of the perpetrators would be the

212. NA, FO 248/263, Hennell to Sheil, 20/03/1844.
213. NA, FO 248/263, Hennell to Sheil, 19/07/1844.
214. NA, FO 248/263, Hennell to Sheil, 09/09/1845; Saldanha 1986, vol. 2, p. 296.
215. NA, FO 248/263, Hennell to Sheil, 12/06/1846.

result.[216] In August 1846, Hoseyn `Ali Khan, the *mohassel*, sent by Shiraz arrived to take the culprits to Shiraz. His mission was delayed as Sheikh Hoseyn and the five individuals most involved in the attack of the commander of the *Feyz al-Bahr* escaped to Tangestan. Five other men were kept in chains since July 28 and Sheikh Naser told Hennell that it was not worthwhile to send them to Shiraz, because the Shiraz orders allowed him to punish them. Hennell agreed and they were brought to the gate of the Residency and given the bastinado and then let go.[217]

Shortly thereafter, Sheikh Naser learnt that on the evening of 9 September 1846, Sheikh Sa`dun, governor of Rudhilleh was treacherously murdered by two cousins, Sheikh `Abdollah and Sheikh Mohammad and three men of the Bani Hajer. The murderers immediately fled to the mainland. Sheikh Sa`dun's death was universally regretted as he was much liked and respected as the most able, intelligent and upright of the Al Mazkur family. He was on bad terms with Sheikh Naser III and Sheikh Hoseyn, who were jealous about his influence in all districts connected with Bushehr and therefore, Sheikh Naser, despite his arrest of Sheikh Mohammad, one of the killers, was suspected of being involved. The immediate result of the murder was an attack of the Rudhilleh people on the Bani Hajer in their district. Baqer Khan Tangestani who was connected by marriage to Sheikh Sa`dun was very indignant. He assembled troops and people thought that he might march on Bushehr and expel Sheikh Naser.[218] However, it was Sheikh Naser who had asked Baqer Khan to assemble troops and apprehend the murderers of his uncle Sheikh Sa`dun. Instead of seizing them, Baqer Khan destroyed some districts belonging to Bushehr such as Angali, after which he returned. Baqer Khan later arranged a meeting with Haji Khan of Dashti with the objective to unite forces and rebel against an unnamed head of the government to force him to agree to their terms. Sheikh Naser was invited to join their undertaking, but he refused. They wanted to come to Bushehr but Sheikh Naser nixed that idea. On 4 October 1846, the two Khans sent a man with a written and verbal communication asking him to join and if he refused they would do everything to destroy him. Sheikh Naser replied that he neither had the strength nor the power to rise up against the government. Therefore, he asked Hennell to contact them and convince them to abandon their planned rebellion.[219]

---

216. After his role in the revolt of 1827 and the British insistence that Sheikh Hoseyn should not be allowed any involvement in the administration of Bushehr, for a long time thereafter they had no contact with him, given his lawless behavior in attacking and plundering *baghlas* flying British colors at Basra. This finally led to his seizure by a British ship of war and his confinement until Sheikh Naser made himself responsible for the payment of a large sum for the compensation of this outrage. From the date of the Khark occupation until 1846 Sheikh Hoseyn was on friendly terms with British subjects and he refrained from any offensive conduct towards them. "I think that the attack had nothing to do with Yusuf being a British subject, but that it is entirely personal, although Hoseyn knew very well that Yusuf's ship flew British flag. People in town are in indignation about this attack of Yusuf and his sailors, which was confirmed by some leading merchants. I hope Shiraz takes firm action and subject him to proper punishment." NA, FO 248/263, Hennell, Resident to Sheil, 04/08/1846.

217. NA, FO 248/263, Hennell to Sheil, 08/09/1846.

218. For the population of Rudhilleh, see Lorimer 1915, vol. 2, p. 1595. "Sheikh Abdollah the principal character was a man of indifferent character who was expelled last year from Rudhilla for the murder of a young lad, who had incurred his displeasure by reporting some of his misdeeds. I understand that ever since the death of his father Sheikh Rahma he and his brother Mohammad were indebted to Sadoon for their support, which was always given until forfeited by their own behavior." NA, FO 248/263, Hennel to Sheil, 14/09/1846.

219. NA, FO 248/263, Sheikh Nasr to Hennell, 06/10/1846; Grummon 1985, p. 167.

The planned rebellion by the Garmsir chiefs probably had to do with the movements by Sarhang Samad Aqa who had been strongly urged by his uncle, the governor-general of Fars, to apprehend Sheikh Hoseyn. When he failed to do so, he decided to negotiate a solution via his wife. Having been assured that he would suffer no corporal punishment, and being tired of wandering, Sheikh Hoseyn returned to town to the house of Haji `Abdol-Mohammad and asked his intermediation to satisfy the British authorities. Hennell agreed to a 2-year period to settle a payment of 500 *tumans* claimed on account of the detention of Yusef's ship in Bushehr. As security for 300 *tumans* a deed of mortgage was made for one-fourth of the Residency buildings, which was his property and produced an annual income of 60 *tumans*. For the remaining 2,100 *tumans* he had to give a personal bond, for which `Abdol-Mohammad stood security. On 4 July 1846, Sarhang Samad Aqa told Hennell that the next day the five culprits would be brought to the gate of the Residency for punishment, as Hennell considered adequate. Previously he had discussed prison time for the Sheikh, and given that he spent four months of his miserable life as a wanderer, a period of two months was agreed upon. Two days passed and no culprits arrived at the gate. The day thereafter the *Sarhang* sent Hennell a note that the five men had placed themselves under the protection of the principal chiefs in Bushehr and he was unable to seize them. Moreover, he had to leave Bushehr to deal with the assembling of the Khans of Dashtestan; he hoped to return in which case all three of Hennell's demands with regards to the punishment of Yusef's culprits would be satisfied. Sheikh Hoseyn wanted to put an end to the entire affair and seemed to be willing to give up his five followers for punishment, if they had not left him. He was willing to submit to imprisonment, but Sheikh Naser was too afraid of his uncle to take the responsibility of imprisoning him. The chiefs of Dashtestan broke off discussions with Samad Aqa accusing him of putting them off with promises, while he was urging the dispatch of a larger force from Shiraz. Also, they insisted that Sheikh Hoseyn should not remain in Bushehr and urged him to leave Bushehr offering him asylum in their districts. He refused however, which Hennell considered a sign of his sincerity to settle his affairs with the British.[220] Because by January 1847, Sheikh Hoseyn had paid the imposed penalty and that those involved in the killing had all been punished, Hennell no longer insisted on the Sheikh's two months imprisonment, the more so since he had asked in that case to be confined in the Residency, which Hennell had refused.[221]

The positive attitude of the Fars governor-general in satisfying British requests may have been caused by his intention to pacify and bring the coastal districts under his control. He proposed to Hennell that when he would make a tour of the various "pirate ports" in January 1847, the British naval vessel *Hawkins* be instructed "to move along the coast with his vessel pari passu with his camp. Ostensibly this tour aims to suppress piracy, but in reality is to show the various chiefs of Dashtestan their retreat is cut off by our ships and that they have no choice but to submit to the Fars government." Hennell did not think that this tour would happen due to the difficulty of carrying it out, but if the governor-general continued to insist he would need authorization from the British ambassador in Tehran. Personally he was willing to agree to the request, because the Sheikhs of `Asalu and Charak still had to implement financial undertakings they had

220. NA, FO 248/263, Hennell to Sheil, 07/12/1846.
221. NA, FO 248/129, Hennell to Sheil, 13/01/1847,

made to the British.[222] As Hennell expected, Hoseyn Khan put off his plans to come to the coast and sent for Sarhang Samad Aqa. Meanwhile, he sent `Abdollah Khan, the architect (*me`mar-bashi*) to persuade the Dashtestan chief to pay their arrears. It was said that he collected 1,000 *tumans* from Borazjan and Tangestan.[223]

In March 1847, Samad Aqa was sent to the Garmsir with two regiments of infantry (1,000 men), 400 horse and four cannons. When he reached Kazerun he wrote to the various chiefs to honor the agreement reached with him when in Bushehr. All chiefs refused, being determined not to pay more than the amounts listed in the revenue books and they would not even do this unless the force returned to Shiraz. However, Hennell believed that this meant that they would make their own estimate of this normal amount. It was unlikely that Samad Aqa would march to the coast, because due to lack of rain there was every chance of a crop failure in the lowlands and thus, forage for his cavalry would be difficult to obtain. Moreover, if he would march to their area the chiefs would oppose him as long as possible and, if defeated, would avoid him by fleeing to safe places. Also, it was rumored that the mountain passes below Kazerun were secured by Lor tribes, supporting Mohammad Hashem Khan of Khesht. Baqer Khan of Tangestan had assembled 1,200 men and he expected Haji Khan of Dashti to join him with a large force. Sheikh Naser the governor of Bushehr was stalling both parties, but Hennell believed that he was collecting 400 troops, ostensibly to join the confederated chiefs.[224]

Therefore, Sarhang Samad Aga chose to negotiate with the lowland chiefs rather than use force. He came with only a small escort to meet them at Borazjan and from there would accompany them to Ahram (Tangestan). But after fruitless attempts to revive old feuds and thus create discord among the chiefs and after a failed attempt to make them pay at least part of the sum demanded, he was happy (hearing the recall of the Saheb Ekhtiyar to Tehran that was long expected) to be able to depart safely and unharmed. Baqer Khan the Tangestani chief arrived at Bushehr on 11 April having been invited by Sheikh Naser, who was in dire financial straits and consequently in serious dispute with the merchants of Bushehr. He was so desperate that his servants behaved in an insulting manner to the merchants when demanding money in the form of loans and payment of duties on goods that they expected from India. Moreover, their complaints fell on deaf ears. The situation had become so intolerable that on 9 April 1847, the merchants moved in one body, headed by the current and previous Malek al-Tojjar, 5 km out of the town and pitched tents there. This finally got Sheikh Naser's attention. Each day he rode to their camp and, allegedly with tears in his eyes, asked them to return with solemn promises of better treatment. However, it was only due to Baqer Khan's mediation that the merchants were induced to return to their homes in the evening of 12 April. However, Sheikh Naser had to sign a document that showed how much he already had collected and undertook not to demand any further loans. Finally, to dismiss at least one of his servants who in particular had displayed an obnoxious behavior.[225]

Sheikh Naser's situation did not improve thereafter. On 15 December 1848, he told Hennell that after his father's death he only had been able to pay his annual fiscal quota,

---

222. NA, FO 248/129, Hennell to Sheil, 11/01/1847; for these undertakings by `Asalu and Charak, see Floor 2014 a, pp. 66-68.
223. NA, FO 248/129, Hennell to Sheil, 13/02/1847.
224. NA, FO 248/129, Hennell to Sheil, 15/03/1847.
225. NA, FO 248/129, Lt. Kemball to Sheil, 14/04/1847.

officially assessed at 17,798 *tumans*, by making up the difference from private property left to him by his father. In the time of Mo`tamed al-Dowleh, his most lucrative dependency Ahram was taken from him, even though his quota was reduced by 2,000 *tumans*. However, when Fereydun Mirza became governor-general of Fars his assessment was increased to 20,020 *tumans* per year. Moreover, the prince added a sum of 2,512 *tumans*. When Hoseyn Khan became governor-general of Fars, his assessment was increased to 26,000 *tumans*, or an increase of 10,000 *tumans* since the death of Mo`tamed al-Dowleh. In this amount was not included an annual amount of 4,000 *tumans* in the form of presents, defrayment of *mohassels* and others as was customary. In addition to these heavy payments, he had to maintain a police force for the protection of the inhabitants and a garrison for the protection against external enemies. These increased demands were made even when it was well-known that the revenues of Bushehr had diminished. This also had personal consequences for Sheikh Naser. He complained to Hennell "that as hereditary governor of Bushire and as Darya Begi he should at least have sufficient income for the upkeep of his rank and dignity, but in reality he had barely a shawl for his waist or a respectable coat for his back, while any petty *zabet* of a village had a few mounted followers, he had great difficulty keeping one mare and a few yaboos. This while his father had owned ships and vessels, he had not even the means to buy a few planks and material to finish a small bughlah he was building." Meanwhile, the inhabitants of Bushehr were more prosperous and flourishing than anywhere else in Persia. He could only continue as governor if a considerable reduction was made in his annual tribute. Therefore, he asked Hennell, who "as a long resident could give an unbiased statement as to the truth of this, and given our long friendship," to use his influence at court to bring this about by a royal command to the governor of Shiraz to reduce the amount to 16,000 *tumans* where it had been formerly. Hennell told the Sheikh that he would do so, but warned him not to have high hopes. Hennell commented to Sheil that the Sheikh's "declarations concerning his straightened domestic situation is correct and the drop in revenue due to diversion of trade to other channels is obvious to all. Nasr's behavior to British subjects is satisfactory. I therefore support his request; he deserves some kindness from us while if successful would increase our influence here."[226]

On 10 May 1849, Haji `Abdol-Mohammad Malek al-Tojjar wrote to Kemball, the assistant Resident asking him for asylum or assure him safe departure from the town, or to intervene and check Sheikh Hoseyn Nasr[227] (uncle of Sheikh Naser who was in Shiraz at that time) as he was organizing a strong opposition against his nephew and he, Malek al-Tojjar felt his life was in danger. Kemball already knew that Sheikh Hoseyn Nasr had spread the word that he had received a letter from his nephew in which the latter complained about the double dealing by his old trusted adviser and ally, the Malek al-Tojjar. He uttered threats against him, so that the Malek al-Tojjar called a meeting of the main merchants, who remained in his house until the quarrel might be settled. Sheikh Hoseyn Nasr had been able to convince the acting governor Sheikh Hoseyn Saleh that

---

226. NA, FO 248/129, Hennell to Lt. Col. Farrant, charge d'affaires Tehran, 15/12/1848. In 1807, Sheikh Naser II paid 4,000 *tumans* per year plus a larger sum in the form of presents to the governor-general. Lorimer 1915, vol. 1, p. 1911.

227. It is only in the letters in 1848 and 1849 that the name Nasr is added to that of Sheikh Hoseyn. I have not been able to find out why this was done and what its meaning is.

the Malek al-Tojjar was working against Sheikh Naser and poisoning the mind of the prince governor against him to reduce the chance of his being reappointed governor.

Kemball could not interfere in such a hot local issue, the more so since the parties had hated each other for years. They had been opponents "on the proceedings connected with the attack upon the late Sheikh Yusuf ben Saggar in the summer of 1846" and it was clear that Sheikh Hoseyn Nasr mainly acted because of this enmity rather than to defend his nephew's interests. Nevertheless, to protect the Malek al-Tojjar he had his Mirza write Sheikh Hoseyn and Sheikh Hoseyn Saleh a note warning them that he knew what they were up to, and if this led to disturbances he would report this to Tehran. Moreover, if they were serious about ensuring Sheikh Naser III return, this would not be helpful. The next day and the day thereafter, Sheikh Hoseyn Nasr and the Malek al-Tojjar came to the Residency. Kemball did not discuss local police or fiscal rules, which were part of the conflict, but urged them to maintain calm in the interest of Sheikh Naser. To Sheikh Hoseyn and Sheikh Hoseyn Saleh he said that Hennell had made a favorable presentation to Tehran and an outbreak of violence in Bushehr would be counterproductive to what they wanted. Each promised not to take action against the Malek al-Tojjar. The latter assured Kemball that there was no truth in the charges brought against him. As proof, he showed Kemball the letters from the prince-governor, "commanding him to give notice to the merchants to suspend payment of Custom House duties until further orders; but that he had declined to act upon them." He preferred Sheikh Naser to return as governor. As proof he offered to write "an Istishad Nameh," addressed to Bahram Mirza requesting that the Sheikh be invested with the usual robe of honor and be reappointed as governor. On 14 May 1849, the merchants left the house of the Malek al-Tojjar, which calmed the mood in town.

On 26 May 1849, Kemball reported that despite his promise Sheikh Hoseyn had not stopped his intrigues against the Malek al-Tojjar. He made open threats of violence, even going so far as writing him that he had better leave town as soon as possible. At the same time, he took steps to prevent his departure by sea "suborning his boatmen, and as the event proved, had laid his plans to intercept his exit also by the town gate." On 22 May 1849, the Malek al-Tojjar in panic came to the Residency fearing for his life and asked protection. Kemball quieted him down and asked for an argued request in writing. That same evening the note arrived in which he stated that Sheikh Hoseyn Saleh had written him that he had received a note from Sheikh Naser in Shiraz in which he had agreed that the Malek al-Tojjar would depart from Bushehr. Further, that Sheikh Hoseyn had strongly hinted that he should leave. He asked Kemball what to do. Kemball replied his interest was public calm and he would therefore address Sheikh Hoseyn on this point as to his personal safety he knew best what measures to take. Malek al-Tojjar then wrote that he wanted to leave via Tangestan, whose acting governor Ahmad Khan (his father Baqer Khan was absent in Shiraz) had invited him and he showed Kemball the invitation letter. Sheikh Hoseyn Nasr used this as proof that the Malek al-Tojjar wanted to incite the Tangestan chief to attack Bushehr. Sheikh Hoseyn therefore, summoned armed groups from Ras Sheho (?) and held other followers in readiness in town to put down any opposition on the day that the Malek al-Tojjar would leave. The latter was met by a party of Tangestanis 10 km from town. As there were already Tangestanis in town Kemball believed that if the Malek al-Tojjar would leave fighting would break out. Therefore, Kemball invited the acting governor to the Residency and impressed upon him the importance of preventing any disorder. But so great was his fear for Sheikh Hoseyn, a fear shared by most inhabitants that he dared not to give a definite reply until he had consulted his uncle Haji Mohammad. It had been proposed that the Malek al-Tojjar would leave on 24 May. Because his departure was delayed by another day, which time Sheikh Hoseyn Nasr used to lay further plans to cut off the escape route of his enemy and to induce Sheikh Hoseyn Saleh to fail to perform his duty at the appointed time. He did not give the promised reply to Kemball and it was only in the afternoon of 25 May, prompted by a note from Kemball that he "engaged formally to supply an escort" for the departure of the Malek al-Tojjar beyond the reach of danger. Kemball deputized two persons to accompany the escort. This he justified by referring to the "cowardly attack upon the late Sheikh Eusuf ben Saggar in 1846," a repetition of which he wanted to prevent. The Residency involvement was really needed., because the town gate had been occupied by the Gutni (?) tribe from Ras Sheho and the followers of Sheikh Hoseyn Nasr had all come armed at his call. The two Residency servants found the Malek al-Tojjar scared to death, but the problem at the gate was solved, when Kemball sent the Residency Mirza to the acting governor reminding him that he had committed himself and that it was now too late to withdraw, otherwise the Malek al-Tojjar would be taken to the Residency and he would send a report to Shiraz. This had an impact and the acting governor told Sheikh Hoseyn Nasr that he had committed himself and had to keep his word. He rode with his men to the gate, which he cleared so that the party could leave unmolested; the escort went with him to Tangestan where it left him with the group that awaited him. Although it was rumored that as admiral `Isa (Esau) Khan had been appointed to go to Bushehr and to take command of the port, the prince confirmed Naser Khan.[228]

Al Mazkur's final act

Sheikh Naser III owed money to Mohammad `Ali Khan, Nazem al-Molk, vizier of Fars, but had not paid it back. Then the latter asked the court to be appointed governor of Bushehr, to which it agreed.[229] On 2 October 1849, Mohammad Hashem Khan, a nephew of Qavam al-Molk, unexpectedly entered the town and went immediately to the Residency and asked to speak to Hennell. He gave him a letter from Bahram Mirza, governor-general of Fars in which he stated that he was displeased about the irregular and dilatory way Sheikh Naser had dealt with the payment of arrears. Therefore, he had appointed Nazem al-Molk governor of Bushehr, Khesht and Kumarej, who had deputized his younger brother Mirza Mehdi Khan to act as governor. Moreover, Sheikh Naser had to go to Shiraz to settle his accounts. Mohammad Hashem Khan said that he was sent ahead to prepare the reception of the new governor and to induce Sheikh Naser to comply with Bahram Mirza's demands. It was clear the purpose of his visit was to prevent Sheikh Naser leaving by sea and possibly to occupy Khark, but Hennell told Mirza Hashem that he could not help him. That same day the Sheikh asked to speak Hennell; he came in the afternoon accompanied by Sheikh Mohammad, head of the Demukh tribe. He mainly talked about Shiraz's ungrateful treatment of him after all his sacrifices –"that the attack and capture ofTulisia [Tul-e Siyah], and the foray into the Rudhilla districts, which

228. Saldanha 1986, vol. 2, pp. 296-99; Lorimer 1915, vol. 1, p. 2051; Busse 1972, pp. 288-90 (has the date of appointment as on 1256 or 21/03/1849, the first day of the new year, which is the formal and normal starting date of any governorship, not necessarily the actual one, as in this case).

229. Busse 1972, pp. 288-90.

had been stripped of flocks, herds, camels and everything the unfortunate inhabitants possessed, had been executed by the Tungistanis at the instigation of the Nizam-ul-Mulk, Mahomed `Ali Khan, whose enmity to him was such that nothing but his (the Sheikh's) entire ruin would satisfy him." They had done so to prevent the collection of revenue to embarrass him with the prince as he could not pay the quotas due. They had been successful. He asked for advice; should he flee and resist? Hennell told him to do neither; it would be better go to Shiraz where he thought it likely that the prince would deal with him favorably. The Sheikh refused absolutely to do so because he would fall into the hands of Nezam al-Molk. He would one more time try to conciliate the prince, if that failed, he would depart. He asked Hennell if the prince asked for him would the Residency intervene? To which Hennell replied that he would not. The Demukh chief was in favor of fighting. He said that the new governor Mirza Mehdi Khan was accompanied by Baqer Khan, the Tangestani chief, as a kind of vizier. As they had recently been defeated at Ahmadi, losing 50 men, a deed never to be forgotten by the Tangestani chief, he would use his new position to get hold of every man of consequence with whom he had a blood feud and kill them. The fact that the Tangestanis had killed the chief of Ahmadi after having promised him quarter showed how much they were to be trusted. He'd rather die, weapons in hand, than believe the pledges of the Tangestani chief. Sheikh Naser was relieved by his ally's statement and although he said he would leave Hennell thought that he would oppose the new governor's entrance.[230]

After Nazem al-Molk had appointed his brother as deputy governor the two agreed that Mirza Mehdi Khan should arrest Sheikh Naser III after his arrival in Bushehr. When the Sheikh learnt about this he put his belonging on vessels and sent them to Khark, while he put cannons on the town's towers. When approaching the town, Mirza Mehdi Khan learnt about these defensive measures and contacted Baqer Khan Tangestani, Sheikh Naser's nemesis. Baqer Khan with 1,000 musketeers joined Mirza Mehdi Khan at Borazjan and together they marched to Bushehr. En route they were joined by additional Tangestani musketeers, so that on arrival they had 4,000 men. The day after their arrival the Tangestanis attacked, but the cannons prevented the musketeers from getting close and within shooting range. Therefore, Baqer Khan asked Mohammad Khan, governor of Behbahan to assist him. He arrived with two cannons and 2,000 horsemen at Rishahr and joined the besiegers. However, the government in Tehran through British sources learnt about the siege and ordered to end it and leave Sheikh Naser III in charge of Bushehr. Nazem al-Molk obeyed and recalled his brother and the auxiliaries all returned.[231]

Although Sheikh Naser III was able to resist this challenge to his rule in 1849 and even received a robe of honor from Shiraz in January 1850, he was unable to pay his taxes. On the night of 4 June 1850, at the Sheikh's orders, Mohammad Hashem Khan with three attendants and their horses were taken to Shif and told to go the Shiraz. Sheikh Naser was persuaded to come to Shiraz, where, in the beginning of October 1850, he

230. Saldanha 1986, vol. 2, p. 300; Sa`adat 1390, pp. 85-86

231. Busse 1972, pp. 288-90. Fifteen years later, Col. Pelly rationalized Persian decision-making rather than recognizing that it was a less rational and messy process, when he wrote: "When the Bushiris fell out with the neighboring tribes of Dashtistan and Tangestan the Shah used this dissension and establish his own governor at Bushire and reduce the tribes of Dashtestan and Tangestan, together with some minor tribes such as the Rohillas." Pelly 1865 a, p. 41. Pelly was right that with the unifying and rallying force of the Al Mazkur gone from the equation it was easier for the central government to impose its will on the Garmsir tribes.

was finally dismissed as governor and sent to Tehran, due to a large deficit in revenue over two years owed to Shiraz. Sheikh Naser was summoned to Tehran and Mirza Hasan `Ali Khan, Qavam al-Molk's son, was appointed governor of Bushehr with the title of *daryabegi*. The new governor sent his brother as deputy governor to Bushehr. When Hoseyn Khan, uncle of Sheikh Naser heard this he gathered his levies and put Bushehr in state of defense. He further made his ships ready to flee if need be. As a result, Bushehr was half deserted. Most inhabitants fled to Basra or Khark; merchants sent their effects and families to *baghla*s ready to leave in case of a siege. The Nazem al-Molk's brother gathered Tangestanis, mortal enemies of Sheikh Hoseyn, who with 4,000 men unsuccessfully attacked Bushehr, because of the guns on its walls. Thereafter, the Tangestanis pillaged the environs of Bushehr. At that time, Sheikh Hoseyn was an elderly man, but because he, like everybody else, dyed his beard he did not look more than forty. According to Binning, "He was dressed in a plain green cotton vest, a striped turban, with a white Arab mantle." Sheikh Hoseyn appointed himself governor and did not allow "the Shirazi interloper to enter. He only will yield to the prince. He has more than 300 fighting men, but he hopes to be joined by Arab clans who hate the Persians." Binning doubted that Sheikh Hoseyn's vagabond followers would oppose the new governor's force.[232] The new governor asked for reinforcements, which arrived in the form of two detachments with two cannons. Its commander Mostafaqoli Khan E`temad al-Saltaneh sent a letter to the inhabitants of Bushehr telling them to leave town, or else they might be killed and plundered. If they stayed they would not be entitled to indemnification. Sheikh Hoseyn seeing the worry that this caused the people of Bushehr then told the notables that he would depart that night. "He put his guns, military stores, and other valuables [including the customs revenues] on board a buggala, and sailed for the island of Carrack, where he now resides, with such of his followers as still adhere to him." Mirza Hasan `Ali Khan and E`temad al-Saltaneh entered Bushehr the next day and thus ended Al Mazkur rule.[233]

Hennell opined that Sheikh Naser III's rule in general had been mild and just and that he maintained tranquility during the late interregnum, and the flourishing state of Bushehr stood in stark contrast to the distress and misery in other towns in Persia, due to the state of anarchy prevailing after the late shah's death.[234] Hennell further had the impression that because of the 100 year relationship between the British and Al Mazkur that the Persian government believed it better to have a governor in Bushehr unrelated to that family and unconnected to the British. The Sheikh had some cause in claiming that the depredations by Baqer Khan Tangestani had deprived him of the revenues of the outlying districts, interrupting the trade of Bushehr and forcing him to keep a garrison at great cost, which led to arrears. On the other hand, a governor not of the Al Mazkur family "being free from all bias, and having no local interests, would not, like the Sheikh, be perpetually engaged in feuds and quarrels with his neighbours," which led to interruption in revenue collection.[235]

There were also some peculiarities about Sheikh Naser III, at least according to Richard Burton. He wrote that:

---

232. Fasa' 1376, vol. 1, p. 791; Busse 1972, pp. 288-90; Binning 1857, vol. 1, pp. 146-47, 153; Saldanha 1986, vol. 2, pp. 300-01; Lorimer 1915, vol. 1, p. 2050.

233. Binning 1857, vol. 1, pp. 146, 153, 330; Grummon 1985, pp. 167-69; Sa`adat 1290, p. 86; Fasa' 1376, vol. 1, pp. 794-95; Busse 1972, pp. 294-95.

234. NA, FO 248/129, Hennell to Lt. Col. Farrant, charge d'affaires Tehran, 15/12/1848.

235. Saldanha 1986, vol. 2, p. 301.

> Some Eastern 'Scrogin' [Sheikh Naser III] would ask his guests if they had ever seen a man cannon (Adami-top); and, on their replying in the negative, a greybeard slave was dragged in blaspheming and struggling with all his strength. He was presently placed on all fours and firmly held by the extremities; his bag-trousers were let down and a dozen peppercorns were inserted ano suo: the target was a sheet of paper held at a reasonable distance; the match was applied by a pinch of cayenne in the nostrils; the sneeze started the grapeshot and the number of hits on the butt decided the bets. We can hardly wonder at the loose conduct of Persian women perpetually mortified by marital pederasty. During the unhappy campaign of 1856-7 in which, with the exception of a few brilliant skirmishes, we gained no glory, Sir James Outram and the Bombay army showing how badly they could work, there was a formal outburst of the Harems; and even women of princely birth could not be kept out of the officers' quarters.[236]

Although Sheikh Hoseyn still tried to make a come-back for the Al Mazkur it was not to be. In the fall of 1852, an attempt was made to arrest Sheikh Hoseyn and the family of Sheikh Naser III on Khark, but they escaped to Basra, except for the mother and wives of Sheikh Naser who were made prisoner and were stripped of everything they possessed. Later they were allowed to go to Hendiyan. Sheikh Hoseyn's cannons and military stores were also captured.[237] Sheikh Naser's descendants continued to live in Bushehr, but were impoverished and did not regain their former status. In 1877, the Dutch consul bought a nice old door of the former Sheikh's harem to be put as the main door of the new residence that he was building in Bushehr. Because of local problems at the time, the chief of the telegraph office caused quite some mischief by sending a telegram to the governor of Shiraz claiming that the door was that of the telegraph office. After some time this calumny was set aright.[238] On 5 August 1908, the last of the Al Mazkur, Bibi Fatimah died without any near relatives. The Imam Jom`eh and Sheikh `Ali Dashti claimed to have documents giving them ownership of her property, which was considerable. There were, however, also other claimants.[239]

Persian Administration

The son of Mirza `Ali Akbar Khan Qavam al-Molk was the governor of Bushehr at the beginning of a new phase in its history, i.e. henceforth it was a Persian instead of an Arab administration that was in charge of the port and its environs. Despite efforts to maintain its Arab character, the Al Mazkur failed to do so. There probably was not much that they could have done to avoid this, because, be it in a haphazard and not in a concerted or even in a sustained manner, the Qajar government was reducing the power of not only Arab, but all local hereditary rulers, who tried to maintain their quasi-autonomy. In some cases the Qajars were more successful than others, and in some cases they actually failed

236. Burton 1885-88, p. 40(http://www.fordham.edu/halsall/pwh/burton-te.asp).
237. NA, FO 248/146, Hennell to Sheil, 13/11/1851; Idem, Hennell to Sheil, 17/11/1851; Binning 1857, vol. 2, p. 419; Lorimer 1915, vol. 1, p. 2052.
238. NA, 2.05.38, Keun to van der Does 02/08/1876 and appendices.
239. Political Diaries, vol. 3, p. 705.

despite trying hard. In any case, having rotating Persian officials in charge of the port meant, as Hennell pointed out, having governors with less local baggage. This did not necessarily mean that they were better governors, because often they were not. But it made the local administration less personal and therefore, there was less trouble with the tribal groups in Bushehr's environs. Having troops at his disposal, made it also easier for the governor to deal with them, and if that did not help, playing them off against one another usually worked as well.

The new governor, Mirza Hasan `Ali Khan, was "a sallow, sickly-looking young man; and his countenance indicates no sign of genius or talents of any kind." Given their collaboration in ousting the Al Mazkur, the Tangestanis promised to keep quiet, which augured a good start for the new and non-Arab administration.[240] In early March 1851, it became known that Firuz Mirza, governor-general of Fars would come to Bushehr. Therefore, Haji Qavam built a room in the citadel for his accommodation. Although all was quiet in Bushehr and trade was improving, the inhabitants complained greatly about the annoying behavior of the soldiers; apparently neither Haji Qavam nor the Daryabegi had much control over them.[241] In the afternoon of 26 March, Firuz Mirza made his public entry into Bushehr.[242]

Despite his visit, as in other parts of S. Persia (e.g., Lar), Bushehr's neighboring districts were in turmoil due to the feud between Hoseyn Khan and Heydar Khan, sons of the chief of Dashti, while Baqer Khan Tangestani was inclined to resist the authority of the governor of Bushehr. Baqer Khan took Ahmad Shah Khan, the nephew of the present and the son of the former head of the Tangestan tribe under his patronage. To counter this move, the governor of Bushehr wanted to rebuild Fort Tul-e Siyah near Tangestan and to place his new protégé there. Therefore, the son of the Tangestan chief declared that he would oppose this by force.[243] Apparently, the parties only engaged in posturing, for the only other noteworthy event in that year occurred in September 1851, when the first of many grain export bans was imposed (see chapter 2). The governor informed the Residency that the price of wheat had risen by 2 *qran*s per *man* and that people feared that there would be a famine.[244]

In early 1852, Firuz Mirza ostensibly pacified the Lar districts and the Garmsir and returned to Shiraz. He was joined by Haji Qavam, whom he had summoned, accompanied by a few *zabet*s (Baqer Khan Tangestani, `Abbas Khan of Zirah and Mohammad Hasan Khan of Borazjan). At first, Baqer Khan was kept under surveillance for some time in the Chahar Borj, because he was mistrusted in Shiraz and to make him pay his arrears. His son Ahmad Khan tried to collect the balance of the revenue owed.[245] Baqer Khan and Mohammad Hasan Khan, the hereditary chiefs of Tangestan and Borazjan were later kept in Shiraz. The former did everything to have his territory separated from that farmed by Haji Qavam and now administered by his son, the Daryabegi and to have it placed directly under Shiraz. But it seems Haji Qavam's influence was greater. In fact, the Daryabegi

240. Binning 1857, vol. 2, p. 419.

241. NA, FO 248/146, Hennell to Sheil, 15/03/1851.

242. NA, FO 248/146, Lt. Col. Hennell to Sheil, 29/03/1851; Sa`adat 1290, p. 87.

243. NA, FO 248/146, Hennell to Lt. Col. Sheil Tehran, 15/08/1851.

244. NA, FO 248/146, Mirza Hasan Ali Khan, governor Bushire to Mirza Ahmad *monshi* Residency, 12/09/1851 received.

245. NA, FO 248/150, Capt. Kemball, Resident to Sheil, 15/05/1852.

An 1856 illustration from photographs of a Persian diplomat, commander, and governor of Bushehr

intended to appoint his own *zabets* to the villages of Daleki (Dalkee), Behbera (Beybera), Sarkeverdun (Sirkaveran) plus Samal and Abad, two villages in Northern Tangestan, based on a decree that he said to have received, but this was rejected by Ahmad Khan, who threatened to oppose his appointees by force. Both appealed to the Shiraz government.[246] Around 20 July 1852, Daryabegi left Bushehr with 300 foot soldiers and two cannons to impose his will on Ahmad Khan, the chief of Tangestan. He was joined by a large body of retainers and others from his own district. He took up position at Gurak. Ahmad Khan thought resistance was futile and availed himself of mediation by Ja`farqoli Khan, the *yavar* of the government troops, to reach a compromise. This meant that he conceded the control of Daleki, Sarkeverdun and Behbera. He also gave a present (*pishkesh*) on account of Ahram, Samal, Abad, etc. of about 1,000 *tumans* and gave horses to the military commanders. In this way he avoided the dismemberment of his entire territory, pending further appeal to Shiraz. Daryabegi then released his irregulars and returned to Bushehr on 30 July.[247]

The jurisdictional problem was not resolved, while by December 1852 it was also time to collect tax arrears from the Tangestan chiefs. Therefore, Bushehr and environs were in uproar and disorder. Ahmad Khan was told to pay immediately the full amount of 1,500 *tumans* with an advance for the ongoing year or to vacate the major part of his districts farmed by him in favor of Haji `Abdol-Hoseyn, the head of another branch of the Tangestan tribe, who had offered a higher *pishkesh*. Because Ahmad Khan rejected this proposal, the Daryabegi waited for the arrival of a new detachment of soldiers to replace the old garrison and on 16 December he marched with 450 soldiers and two cannons into Tangestan. Ahmad Khan's counter-proposal to pay in installments was rejected,

246. NA, FO 248/150, Capt. Kemball, Resident to Sheil, 14/07/1852.
247. NA, FO 248/150, Capt. Kemball, Resident to Sheil, 18/08/1852.

because the Daryabegi believed that by just making a show of strength would get him the desired result, without any hostilities. In the meantime, Ahmad Khan had news that his father Baqer Khan had allegedly escaped from Haji Qavam's imprisonment. Moreover, he doubted that the threatened use of force by Darybegi was authorized by Shiraz and therefore, he prepared to oppose him. He was supported by Mohammad Khan, one of the Dashti chiefs with 600-700 men. Daryabegi seeing that he was outnumbered and that his opponents occupied a better position withdrew to his camp after some skirmishes, having suffered three dead and three wounded. He then waited for orders from Shiraz to be allowed to recruit peasants from neighboring districts. Apart from capturing some of Daryabegi's personal baggage the Tangestanis did not interfere with his retreat and, as in the previous fight, they were careful not to direct their fire too precisely at the royal troops. A second attack by Daryabegi, this time with the help of the auxiliaries failed as well. The auxiliaries suffered from lack of provisions and above all feared future reprisals by the Tangestanis, and therefore, were dismissed. A mediation effort by the Malek al-Tojjar and other merchants failed. Daryabegi finally retreated to Chahkutah, 18 km from Tangestan where he awaited reinforcements from Shiraz to be sent by his father. Kemball commented that this hasty and abortive action by Daryabegi would result in loss of influence and reputation, while the practice to set up one tribe against the other would only lead to further disorder. Fortunately, the Tangestanis had adopted a defensive strategy, but they might start occupying the roads to embarrass Daryabegi by cutting off trade between Bushehr and Shiraz.[248]

In September 1853, Hoseyn Khan, one of the Dashti chiefs arrived in Bushehr with a large body of retainers, probably connected with the imprisonment of Baqer Khan of Tangestan. Negotiations were underway with Daryabegi, but the fear that once freed he would try and take revenge on Haji Qavam's family for insults suffered made talks difficult.[249] At the end of September 1853, Sheikh Hoseyn Al Mazkur made a flying visit to Bushehr accompanied by two *ghonchas* of about 30 tons each and one small *baqara*. Sheikh Hoseyn lived near Basra, in one and then another village on either bank of the river. The Daryabegi was really alarmed and it looked as if Sheikh Hoseyn had chosen that exact moment to show up, because Firuz Mirza had been recalled. He apparently counted on the usual outbreak of troubles when a provincial governor was removed. Sheikh Hoseyn clearly had come to see whether he might reclaim power, but found that he had not really been invited by the chief of Tangestan and only found temporary refuge at the small port of Baraki, in the territory of Ahmad Khan. Kemball advised the governor to ignore Sheikh Hoseyn, which he did. As a result of the lack of support, Sheikh Hoseyn peaceably returned to Basra.[250] Thereafter, all was quiet in the Garmsir, even though Baqer Khan Tangestani was released and had resumed his post as chief of Tangestan.[251]

In August 1853, Mirza Reza, the *vaqaye`-negar* all of a sudden imposed harbor duties or an anchorage fee. The Persian consul in Bombay, where such a tax was levied, had suggested its application as a means to increase revenues for the Shah. Not only the British opposed this new tax, but so did local owners of vessels as well as the governor, be it

---

248. NA, FO 248/150, Capt. Kemball, Resident to Sheil, 15/01/1853.

249. NA, FO 248/150, Capt. Kemball, Resident to W.J. Thomson, charge d'affaires, 15/09/1853.

250. NA, FO 248/129, Kemball to Sheil, 09/04/1847; NA, FO 248/150, Daryabegi to Kemball (and seven other letters between them).

251. NA, FO 248/157, A. Kemball to W.T. Thomson, 15/02/1854.

each for different reasons. The British opposed it because it was in contravention of treaty obligations, because these stated: "that only facilities afforded to navigation are attended with expence that a state should levy toll and other duties equitably proportioned to indemnify itself for its disbursement." They made additional objections, such as that the proposer of the new tax could not explain its provisions. The governor (and his father) both were against it, because they were not involved in the scheme. Moreover, its revenues would remain under control of the *vaqaye`-negar*, who would transfer them directly to Tehran, which meant less income for the governor. In addition, a worry the governor shared with the British, was the possible negative impact this might have on the volume of trade. Vessels might prefer to call on Lengeh and Bandar Abbas rather than Bushehr, which would translate in lower revenues for the governor. Also, vessels from Masqat, Basra and the Arab coast would react negatively. Vessels from the Arabian Coast whose boats were solely engaged in transport and whose ports were rarely visited by foreign vessels might react to this impost by aggression at sea. The Omani authorities would recover the tax from Persian vessels calling on its ports as they had done when Sheikh Hoseyn, the acting governor of Bushehr tried to impose extra tax on the export of horses. The owners of vessels, especially those sailing to India, opposed the tax, because in Indian ports, where a similar tax was collected, this was done to pay for harbor improvements such as buoys, light-houses, etc., improvements that were totally lacking in Bushehr. Given the broad agreement of those opposing the new tax, the governor agreed to postpone its application until clear instructions arrived from Tehran. Because of the British complaint and arguments, supported by those submitted by the governor, the tax scheme was abandoned.[252]

There was some friction between the governor and the Residency concerning the construction of a wall on the seaside (see chapter one), while the conflict between Persia and Oman about Bandar Abbas also affected Bushehr. In July 1854, the Soltan of Masqat sent the Resident a letter announcing his intention to blockade Bushehr, provided Great Britain did not object.[253] Despite the Omani threat, the governor did not make an effort to accommodate the British, who were trying to defuse the situation with Oman. On 26 July 1854, the governor even threatened grain buyers of J. Malcolm, a British subject, imposing a wheat export or storage embargo, while allowing his client and wealthiest merchant of Bushehr, Haji `Abdol-Mohammad to buy and store wheat.[254]

252. NA, FO 248/150,Capt. Kemball to W.J. Thomson, charge d'affaires, 15/08/1853; Idem, Capt. Kemball to governor Bushire, 08/08/1853 (protesting imposition of the new tax without prior notice and discussion); Idem, Complaint about new tax by Haji Adam nakhoda; Idem, reply Daryabegi re Kemball's complaint; Idem, reply Kemball to Daryabegi; Idem, Daryabegi agrees to postpone collection of the tax, 09/08/1853. For the text of the complaint, see Appendix XIII. 6

253. NA, FO 248/157, A. Kemball to W.T. Thomson, 26/07/1854; Idem, Imam of Muscat to Resident ("he vaguely suggests that his problems with the Persians be mediated by us or failing that he'll be allowed to take his own measures and retaliate, although for the moment he prefers defensive measures"): NA, FO 248/157, Kemball to Thomson, 16/11/1854 (Sarem al-Dowleh is marching on Bandar Abbas; therefore, I have sent my son Thuvayni with troops there. I will not take further action until I receive your reply); Idem, letter to Imam; Idem, letter from Sarem al-Dowleh.

254. NA, FO 248/157, J.A. Malcolm to Kemball, 06/11/1854.

Captain Felix Jones, the British Resident in Bushehr (on the horse on the right).

British occupation of Bushehr

The wound that Persian pride had suffered as a result of the failed Herat affair (1837-41) was a festering one. As is clear from above, relations, although friendly on the surface, sometimes were strained due to persistent resentment. In 1847, Mohammad Shah once again allegedly pondered about launching another attack on Herat, which sent tongues wagging and hands writing memoranda. But it was a false alarm. Nevertheless, even though British-Russian relations were amicable at that time, anything that even seemed to threaten India immediately provoked a knee-jerk reaction in British political circles. When Naser al-Din Shah acceded to the throne in 1848, Mohammad Khan, the ruler of Herat asked him for protection. He feared that the forceful rulers of Kabul and Kandahar would oust him from his city. London instructed Sheil to get the Shah to agree not to send troops to Herat to prop up Mohammad Khan's rule, unless he was attacked, which the Shah did on 25 January 1853. However, things changed when war broke out between Turkey and Russia in July 1853. The Shah, who expected a Russian victory, made it known that he wanted to take advantage of this situation to extend his own borders. Great Britain and France had taken the side of Turkey and therefore, took exception to the Shah's declaration. In fact, London instructed the government of India to prepare a naval and a land force for operations in the Persian Gulf. Although diplomatic relations were restored with Persia, the British naval force carried out various exercises in February-May 1854 and then returned to Bombay, where it remained on standby. Also, London instructed Thomson, the new Envoy in Tehran, to alert London immediately if the Shah favored Russia or had designs on Herat. Meanwhile, Great Britain was so occupied with the Crimean War that it did not have much time for Persian affairs. In fact, it gave a non-committal reply to the Shah's question whether Great Britain would support Persia against Russian retaliation, if it maintained its neutrality. Therefore, the Shah looked for support among other powers and slowly a widening gap between the two countries came into being. On 19 October 1854, Naser al-Din Shah told Murray, the new British Envoy, that Persia could no longer remain neutral in the Crimea War unless it received an inducement to do so. He did not intend to side with Russia, but rather looked eastward for compensation. Dost Mohammad Khan, the ruler of Kabul, aimed to unify Afghanistan, which meant conquering Herat. Naser al-Din Shah wanted to take preventive action and annex Herat himself. He felt that whereas he was constrained from doing so by the agreement of January 1853, the British had given Dost Mohammad Khan the green light when the government of India concluded a treaty of peace and friendship with the latter.[255]

When on 4 November 1855, the government of Persia refused to allow Murray to appoint Mirza Hashem as newswriter in Shiraz, because the man was a government official, Murray protested. Then, on 16 November 1855, the government carried off the man's wife (whose sister was of one of the Shah's wives) and informed Murray that unless Mirza Hashem left British service, his wife would divorce him. Murray demanded the release of the wife, referring to existing treaty stipulations, which gave him the right to protect the British mission's employees. If not, he would leave the country, which he did. The government of Persia retaliated by circulating the news that the wife in question had been first Thomson's and later Murray's mistress. The diplomatic rupture was entirely unexpected in London, which was totally absorbed by the end phase of the Crimea War. Matters came quickly to a head due to developments in Afghanistan. Dost Mohammad Khan had taken Kandahar in December 1855 and was soon expected to march on Herat. The ruler of Herat asked Naser al-Din Shah for protection, who in February 1856 sent troops in his support. However, the inhabitants of Herat were suspicious of Persian intentions. When Soltan Morad Mirza, the commander of the Persian troops, asked them to agree to allow a Persian garrison into the city, read the Shah's name in the *khotbeh* and strike coins in the Shah's name, they revolted and ousted their ruler. The leader of the revolt sent messages to Murray and the government of India asking for help. London considered the Shah's action a violation of his undertaking of 1853 and a declaration of war. On 11 July 1856, Great Britain gave Persia an ultimatum, unless it withdrew its troops London would do whatever it deemed necessary to protect its interests. On 21 July 1856, London instructed Bombay to prepare a force to occupy Khark and the district of Bushehr.[256]

Part of the naval force was already in the Persian Gulf. Whether intentional or not, on 15 February 1856, the British naval flotilla of four ships that was lying near Bushehr held a firing practice, which greatly alarmed the people of Bushehr and environs. People from the villages came to town asking what happened and people feared a British attack on the town. The Resident, Capt. Felix Jones explained matters to the governor, while he asked the commander of the flotilla to hold firing practice in the future at such a distance so that it would cause no alarm, so as not to endanger the ongoing negotiations.[257] It was a tense period, because war was in the air. Jones reported that:

---

255. Kelly 1968. pp. 452-59.
256. Kelly 1968, pp. 459-69.
257. NA, FO 248/168, Felix Jones Resident to Commander squadron, 16/02/1856.

Persian plan of the fortifications of Bushehr prior to the British bombardment in 1856

> Indian traders expecting war have gone to the coast for safety. Christian and Mohammedan families under British protection have secured a retreat through my agency. Mohammedan families are more terrified of their own troops rather than any British ones coming and also wanted to leave, but this was interdicted by the local authorities, although since then some women and children were allowed to leave. The wealthy class is fearful for war as they see this as a license to plunder them and then will flee.[258]

On 7 September 1856, the grand vizier sent a reply to the British ultimatum, which did not address British demands and only announced that an envoy would be sent to

258. NA, FO 248/168, Felix Jones to Court of Directors, London, 17/11/1856.

Istanbul. On 26 September, London decided to instruct Bombay to send the expeditionary force. Also, it ordered its consuls to leave Persia immediately.[259]

At the end of October 1856, Ahmad Khan arrived in Bushehr, who was sent by Tehran to promote friendly relations between the two countries.[260] He was the first *kargozar* appointed to Bushehr, but he had little to do. For on 7 November 1856, Capt. Jones received news from Tehran indicating that relations between the two countries had unfortunately not improved. Therefore, he informed the governor that he vacated the Residency and would go aboard one of the British ships. He hoped that his departure would be temporary and that soon things would improve. He ended his letter with, "At least we both have not contributed to the existing problems. I recommend the Residency and all in it to your protection."[261] On 16 November, Jones and his staff embarked on the British vessel. In the preceding days he had moved most property from the Residency leaving some in the building with local servants. He wrote: "I was glad to leave, because if all was known to the populace things might get hot. Everybody hopes that negotiations will prevail, but nobody is aware that a force is coming from Bombay. During the last six weeks I was actively supporting the staff officers preparing that arrival of the force. Any advance news of its arrival I felt would render our situation within the walls precarious." It was ironic that on that day the British flag was displayed in town, followed by a salute of 50 guns, that on the same evening an illumination took place to celebrate the (false) news of the assault or capture of Herat.[262]

On 29 November 1856, the first ships of the invasion fleet arrived at Bushehr. Mirza Hasan `Ali Khan, the governor wrote to Jones asking the reason for their arrival. On 3 December, Jones replied stating that he was no longer Resident. Attached to the letter was a copy of the declaration of war, issued in India on 1 November 1856. On 4 December 1856, the British force of 5,720 men, eight steamers and 30 sailing vessels under general Outram took Khark. Outram arrived on 27 January 1857 at Bushehr.[263] On 3 February 1857 he attacked the Persian force at Borazjan and took it on 5 February. He returned to Bushehr on 7 February and routed the Persian army of 6,000 at the village of Khoshab, leaving 700 dead and two guns. Among the dead was Baqer Khan, whose oldest son, like the Persian soldiers, was so disgusted with the behavior of the officers of the Persian army that he told the British "that the next time British troops came into Persia, he should join them boldly with every efficient man, without even waiting for a guarantee for the future."[264] Meanwhile, negotiations were underway in Paris to resolve the conflict between the two countries. Finally, the two sides signed the so-called Treaty of Paris on 4 March 1857, whereby, among other things, Naser al-Din Shah promised to withdraw his troops, relinquish all claims on Afghan territory, allow more British consuls on a most-favored nation basis, give the British mission on its return an honorable reception, and made the withdrawal of British troops conditional on the withdrawal of Persian troops from

259. Kelly 1968, pp. 469-70.

260. FO 248/168, Daryabegi to Jones rec. 28/10/1856.

261. Felix Jones to Mirza Hasan Ali Khan Daryabegi, 10/11/1856 - 11 Rabi I 1273.

262. NA, FO 248/168, Felix Jones to Court of Directors, London 17/11/1856.

263. For the text of Outram's proclamation, see Busse 1972, p. 380.

264. Lorimer 1915, vol. 1, p. 2029. When he was alive, Baqer Khan was seen as a murderous ruffian by the Persian government, but because of his death in battle against the British he acquired quasi mythical hero status in Persian historiography, see, e.g., Fotuvvat 1383; Ya Hoseyni 1387.

Depiction of the British naval attack on Bushehr in 1857.

Herat. On 18 March, Outram went to Mohammerah and left General Jacob in charge of Bushehr. The attack on Mohammerah was only to take place if the Shah did not withdraw from Herat, but the news of the signing of the Treaty of Paris was not yet known in Persia. It was only on 5 April 1857 that Outram received this news and therefore, he immediately halted his operations. Because the treaty stipulated that the British troops would only leave after the government of Persia had implemented its conditions, Outram induced the Persian commanders to accept a cease-fire. After the treaty had been ratified on 2 May, Outram left Mohammerah more than two weeks later and sailed to Bushehr. He returned to India on 18 June, leaving the remaining troops under General Jacob. On 18 July 1857, Murray returned to Tehran and was received with suitable ceremony. The Persian troops left Herat in September. In October 1857, when it was reported that the Persian troops had withdrawn from Herat, the British troops withdrew from Bushehr and sailed to India. One battalion with artillery remained on Khark due to lack of transport.[265]

265. Saldanha 1986, vol. 7/2, p. 51. I have not given a description of the hostilities that took place between the two opposing forces, as these have been amply described in a number of detailed studies such as: English 1971, chapters 5 and 6 in particular; Sa`adat 1390, pp. 94-104; Fotuvvat 1383; Ya Hoseyni 1387, chapters 3 and 4; Busse pp. 319-35; Kelly 1986, pp. 472-99; Lorimer vol. 1, pp. 2070-77. For the Persian text of the agreement between the two governments, see Sani` al-Dowleh 1294, vol. 1, pp. 303-05.

THE PRICKLY YEARS

Although, Great Britain had won the war it had not made friends. The Persians mistrusted British intentions even more than before, a suspicion that was reinforced by strong resentment. This became clear from the moment the British transferred Bushehr to the Persian authorities and the occurrence of all kinds of petty incidents. On 27 or 28 October 1857, the new governor of Bushehr, Ahmad Khan Nava'i `Amid al-Molk, sent Mirza Hasan, his most inferior civil official ahead to receive provisional charge of the town pending his arrival. Mirza Hasan discussed the handing over of civil authority with Capt. Jones, who had resumed his function of Resident. It was agreed that the police, which were paid by the British, would withdraw at sunset when Persian officers and troops who intended to garrison Bushehr would approach the town. On 29 October, Jones sent his assistant, who during the occupation had been the superintendent of police, to the city gate with the Residency's *monshi*, who gave a handover letter to Mirza Hasan.[266] On 18 November 1857, Ahmad Khan Nava'i Daryabegi arrived in Bushehr. He made his entry with more than the usual display and was not satisfied with a simple congratulatory letter from the British Resident and a royal salute when the Shah's flag was hoisted. As Ahmad Khan wanted to needle the British, who in their turn did not want to be treated as a pin cushion, there were consequently hurt egos, harassments (real or perceived) and subtle

266. NA, FO 248/168, Felix Jones to Lt. H.T. Disbrowe ass. res. and off. superintendent of police 28/10/1857; Idem, Captain Felix Jones to Mirza Hasan, 28/10/1857 - 19 Rabi I 1274; Sa`adat 1390, p. 113.

insults, all resulting in a spate of correspondence. Jones wrote Murray, the British envoy, that: "Therefore, until I hear different from you I will not have contacts with the governor on matters concerning the Gulf unless they concern his district, but, if necessary and as before, address the prince governor of Fars. Otherwise, I see a loss of old established prestige and sacrifice of interests that will be to our detriment in Persia, Arabia and India. If the Persian government wants to promote its trade interests it should cooperate with British officers to whom these interests are confided in this quarter."[267]

Soon after his arrival Ahmad Khan raised the legitimate question why British troops had not left Khark, while Persian troops had left Afghanistan? This was not true, but the British did not know that at that time. Capt. Jones truthfully replied that this was due to the late arrival of transport vessels from India and that the troops would leave the moment these arrived.[268] On 11 January 1858, Ahmad Khan again asked why contrary to the treaty, British troops one month and four days after he raised this issue, were still on Khark. Moreover, the commander of the British troops was involved in the internal administration of the island. Also, while the Persian flag should be hoisted, the British one was. Although Ahmad Khan accepted Jones's apology, he reminded the Resident that the British "should realize they are living in somebody else's house, not their own," and therefore, should neither interfere in the island's internal affairs nor fly their own flag, but rather that of the owner.[269] Jones had to acknowledge that although most troops had left there were still some left waiting for vessels from India. He further noted that he was unable to "change the administration of the flag until I have received special instructions on this point. I shall alert the British Minister in Tehran about this matter, just in case there would be further delay."[270] To Jones's relief three weeks later he was able to report that the evacuation of the troops was complete. One warship was remaining to transfer the island to an officer appointed by Ahmad Khan. Also, some coal and stores still remained for future removal as soon as he would be able to engage a vessel to do so. Jones appointed Haji Mohammad Bushehri to be in charge of them and requested the governor's protection for this and their later transport.[271]

The departure of the troops did not resolve all outstanding issues related to the British occupation, but before Jones had to deal with these, there was an incident that involved the Residency's mail carried by the Residency's staff and a Persian customs official, who behaved disrespectfully towards Cdr. Griffith, the flotilla commander, who accompanied the mail carriers. The official did not want the Residency staff to board a boat without the governor's permission and thus, Griffith and his companions returned to the Residency.[272] Jones lodged a formal complaint, pointing out that the rank of commander was equal

267. NA, FO 248/168, Cmdr Felix Jones to C.A. Murray, envoy-extraordinary, 26/11/1857; Idem, Jones to Ahmad Khan; Idem, Ahmad Khan to Felix Jones, 16/11/1857 - 27 Rabi I 1274 (your letter reached me in Borazjan; I have deputed Mirza Hasan to look after certain matters in Bushire. etc.)

268. NA, FO 248/168, Ahmad Khan to Felix Jones, 09/12/1857-21 Rabi II 1274; Idem, Cmdr Felix Jones to C.A. Murray envoy-extraordinary 09/12/1857; Idem, NA, FO 248/168, Felix Jones to Daryabegi 09/12/1857-21 Rabi II 1274. It was only in March 1858 that the last Persian troops reluctantly left Afghan territory and only because Col. Taylor, a British officer had been sent there to check whether the agreed upon withdrawal had actually been implemented. Kelly 1968, p. 498. For an interesting case of hurt ego, see Appendix XIII.7.

269. NA, FO 248/183, Ahmad Khan Daryabegi to Felix Jones. 24 Jomadi I 1274-11/01/1858.

270. NA, FO 248/183, Felix Jones to Ahmad Khan 24 Jomadi I 1274 - 11/01/1858.

271. NA, FO 248/183, Felix Jones to Ahmad Khan 20 Jomadi II 1274 - 05/02/1858.

272. NA, FO 248/183, Cdr Griffith Jenkins to Felix Jones, 31/12/1857.

to that of a general or *sartip* 1st class. Furthermore, even if the customs official had been acting on the governor's orders there was no need to be loud and insolent; a civil tongue would have achieved the same result. Jones asked that the governor instruct his staff to be civil toward British officers and prevent further obstruction to the Residency's mail.[273] The governor replied that he had convened the customs staff and informed them not to behave in such a manner. The customs official in question pointed out they were not allowed to let vessels depart after the gun was fired without the governor's permission. Moreover, he had been very polite as nearby soldiers confirmed. The governor finally pointed out that "from sunset till sunrise when the second gun signal is fired no communication with the sea is allowed."[274] Jones immediately replied pointing out that he did not complain about the customs house official doing his job, only the manner in which he did it. Also, the man lied as the gun had not been fired yet.[275] The governor replied that the event must have been due to a misunderstanding, "because the Persian accompanying the Cdr had mistranslated what he said." However, to maintain friendly relations he had the customs official punished in the presence of the Residency's Persian clerk.[276]

After this incident was resolved another issue arose about double taxation. During the occupation, the British had collected the regular taxes from the inhabitants of Bushehr, Rishahr, Khark and Halileh. Even before Ahmad Khan assumed his post of governor there were rumors that he intended to collect taxes from these inhabitants. This caused great alarm and it was feared that entire villages and even the town itself would become depopulated. Jones told the inhabitants that the governor would not do so, the more so when he explained to them the purpose of art. 4 of the recent agreement, which calmed their fears. However, in December 1857 the governor sent tax collectors to collect the dues from the peasants of Rishahr for the period that it was under British administration. Jones protested against this as it was contrary to the spirit of art 4 of the peace treaty. Although both Jones and Ahmad Khan wanted to avoid to disturbing the good relations between their two countries, Jones was informed that the tax collection still continued (he had more than 90 notes of proof of payment of taxes), which he assumed was the doings of officials acting on their own. Nevertheless, he now protested officially against the levy of any dues of the population of Bushehr, Khark, Halileh and Rishahr for the period under British occupation. He noted that "I am not interfering in relations between you and the subjects, but about the respect of the seals affixed to an agreement by both our governments."[277] Ahmad Khan replied that he had not reneged on their agreement and gave a detailed explanation of what had been done. Jones disagreed with the time period that Ahmad Khan had adopted as well as the manner in which the tax quota was calculated. Because Jones did not want to continue the exchange as he considered it to

273. NA, FO 248/183,Felix Jones to Ahmad Khan 14 Rabi I 1274 - 01/01/1858

274. NA, FO 248/183,Ahmad Khan to Felix Jones, 16 Jomadi I 1274 03/01/1858.

275. NA, FO 248/183, Felix Jones to Ahmad Khan 16 Jomadi I 1274 - 03/01/1858.

276. NA, FO 248/183, Ahmad Khan to Felix Jones, 21 Jomadi I 1274 - 08/01/1858 (I'm glad re the solution and am sorry that I misunderstood you. It could all have been avoided by confronting accuser and accused); NA, FO 248/183, Felix Jones to Ahmad Khan 22 Jomadi I 1274- 09/01/1858.

277. NA, FO 248/183, Felix Jones to Ahmad Khan 5 Rajab 1274- 20/02/1858; Idem, Jones to Murray, 27/02/1858.

fruitless and had sufficient evidence for his protest, he wrote to Murray in Tehran for instructions.[278]

Because of the prickly situation between Ahmad Khan and Jones, Murray suggested to arrange an amiable meeting. This was arranged through intermediaries and on 30 March 1858, Jones and all his officers were received by Ahmad Khan and Persian officials "under the salute due to my rank and with every display that could mark the occasion. We were pleased and it was good that the misunderstanding which kept us apart for so long has been resolved and will now be followed by an amiable intercourse."[279] Thereafter, there were no major issues with Ahmad Khan, who in 1858-59, was replaced by Hasan Khan Qarachadaghi Azerbaijani as governor of Dashti, Dashtestan and Bushehr.[280] In 1859, Soleyman Mirza was appointed in that function after Hosam al-Saltaneh Morad Mirza, the governor-general of Fars, marched to the Garmsir to put down troubles. Jones wrote to him about the prevailing disorders on the Persian coast, which negatively affected trade and revenues. He proposed that the prince cooperate with Jones and the British naval squadron to deal with the coastal trouble makers. The prince gave a non-committal reply, probably because he had to return to Shiraz to deal with trouble there [281]

Asadollah Mirza, nephew of Hosam al-Saltaneh Soltan Morad Mirza, became the next governor of Bushehr, Dashtestan and Dashti. On 26 February 1860, he entered Bushehr. Jones interpreted from his nomination and of the previous one, Soleyman Mirza, that the governor-general, if not the government in Tehran, took a greater interest in the Persian Gulf. "The object surely is better government of the unruly tribes on shore, but as the country near Bushire is impoverished, which itself is simple an entrepot, it is more likely that a deterioration of the situation is the result as they are accompanied by high officers and a host of strangers."[282] However, in October1861, Asadollah Mirza, i.e. after less than one year, was replaced by Mehr `Ali Khan Shoja` al-Molk Nuri, who likewise was only governor for less than a year.[283]

This was also the year that the difficult relationship between the British and "the very corrupt" Mirza Mehdi, the *kargozar* began. It all started with the erection of a small building for the accommodation of Dr. Wood of the Residency, which was misrepresented by the *kargozar*, who promoted the interests of Kerbela'i `Evaz (Eyweth), a master mason from Bushehr. During the last war, Kerbela'i Evaz had risen to prominence in Bushehr through the appropriation of government property. He had been able to farm some of the monopolies of the town, and in mid-1860s tried to obtain the monopoly of all building activities in Bushehr in league with his partner Sayyed Reza, whom Jones described as a

278. NA, FO 248/183, Ahmad Khan to Felix Jones, 6 Rajab 1274- 21/02/1858; Idem, Felix Jones to Ahmad Khan 10 Rajab 1274 -25/02/1858; Idem, Ahmad Khan to Felix Jones, 16 Rajab 1274 -03/03/1858; Idem, Jones to Murray, 08/03/1858. Art. 4 reads: "His Majesty the Shah of Persia engages, immediately on the exchange of the ratifications of this Treaty, to publish a full and complete amnesty, absolving all Persian subjects who may have been in any way been compromised by their intercourse with the British forces during the war from any responsibiity for their conduct in that respect, so that no persons, of whatever degree, shall be exposed to vexation, persecution, or punishment on that account."

279. NA, FO 248/183, Commander Jones to Murray, 01/04/1858.

280. Busse 1972, p. 340.

281. NA, FO 248/189, Jones to Soltan Morad Mirza Ehtesham al-Saltaneh, governor of Dashtestan, 10 Jomadi II 1276- 02/01/1860; Sa`adat 1390, p. 113; Busse 1972, p. 343.

282. NA, FO 248/189, Jones to Alison, 06/07/1860; Sa`adat 1390, p. 115.

283. Busse 1972, p. 345.

notorious mischief maker. They needed the support of Mirza Mehdi, because all masons in the service of Residency and British protected subjects refused to cooperate with this trio, although at that time Jones was not aware of this. In September 1860, Mr. Seth Essai, a British dependent and purveyor (*dabbash*) to the HMS sloop the *Falklands*, was accused of encroaching on a road by 0.5 m in building a wall. The *kargozar* should have referred the case to the proper tribunal, but then he would have forgone his *modakhel*. Instead he summoned Mr. Essai to his house, and there, based on suborned evidence he was bastinadoed. Mirza Mehdi even himself kicked the prostrated Essai, because he invoked British protection. He then was thrown into prison. Never before had a high official behaved in such a manner toward a British protected subject. Mirza Mehdi had not referred the matter to Resident or the governor, who immediately ordered Essai's release and intimated that he would bring Mirza Mehdi's reckless conduct to the governor-general's attention. He then went in person into town and remedied as much as possible the negative impact on the public interest by the coalition against the masons. Jones complained about this to Alison, the British envoy, as a result of which Mirza Mehdi was recalled and left on a mission to Bahrain, where he intrigued to advance Persian interests.[284]

In 1861, Tahmasp Mirza, the governor-general of Fars appointed his son `Abdol-Baqi Mirza governor of Bushehr, Dashtestan, Dashti, Banader-e Thalatheh and Gallehdari. On 18 January 1861, he made his entry in Bushehr with more than usual pageantry. Jones was invited by the *kargozar* to be part of the welcoming committee. This apparently was not to the liking of the new governor, because he abruptly dismissed Jones and the British officers accompanying him. Jones was offended by this behavior and sent a 'friendly protest" to the *kargozar* about the prince's personal behavior to him and his suite. Jones wrote that in his entire career he had "never seen a reception designed to humiliate him."[285] The friendly protest did not have the expected result. `Abdol-Baqi Mirza made it a habit to annoy or harass British merchants and agents of British firms who had been under British protection for decades. Jones mentioned the firm of Messrs Malcom, whose principal Mr. Joseph Malcolm was the chief complainant and chief of the Armenian community. The governor had selected him for unfriendly demands, threatening to demolish his house. Jones thought that the governor's "real reason is for Mr. Malcolm to buy his goodwill and he feels that he has enough influence in Tehran. If he succeeds in this, things will get worse here. People are already concerned about him."[286]

In 1862, the Bushehr jurisdiction was separated from Fars and Mirza Ahmad Khan `Amid al-Molk became governor. He made his entry in Bushehr on 31 October 1862. Ahmad Khan informed Capt. Disbrowe, the assistant Resident that he had supreme authority on land and sea in the district. His vizier was Sheikh Hoseyn Chahkutahi a.k.a. Sheikh al-Vazir. The latter was a Sunni and he was offended when the *monshi* of Khan `Ali of Hayat Da'ud cursed the first three caliphs. Surprisingly, he was allowed to punish the Khan and marched with Dashtestan levies against him and took him prisoner; the

---

284. NA, FO 248/189, Jones to Alison, 23/09/1860; NA, FO 248/189, Jones to Alison, 28/09/1860; NA, FO 248/189, Jones to Alison, 06/10/1860; Idem, Letter from Chief Naval Officer commanding the Persian Gulf squadron to Jones 26/10/1860; Hamidi 1380, p. 299.

285. NA, FO 248/198, Jones to C. Alison, 03/02/1861; Idem, Note to the Governor. 24 Rajab 1277-22/01/1861; Sa`adat 1390, pp. 113-14.

286. NA, FO 248/198, Jones to Alison, 12/02/1861.

monshi's hands were cut off.[287] Apparently, relations with the governor remained friendly, but not so much with Mirza Mehdi, the *kargozar*. Capt. Disbrowe found Mirza Mehdi to be most unfriendly and disposed "to carry slight and insult to the utmost limit." Not only did he prohibit people going the British dispensary (see chapter one), but his insult during Queen Victoria's birthday, his insult to Dr Wood, his slight to the Commodore and the British flag, all these in a few weeks, showed that he tried to "insult and annoy us in every possible way." Therefore, the Resident submitted that a change of *kargozar* was needed.[288]

In March 1865, Ahmad Khan was replaced by Asadollah Mirza, the nephew of Hosam al-Saltaneh, the new governor-general of Fars. Three years later, in 1868 the latter was replaced his cousin by Hasan `Ali Khan Nasir al-Molk.[289] According to Sa`adat, writing in 1915, Asadollah Mirza's administration was so harsh that 50 years later people in Bushehr still talked about it. In 1870, Fars and the Gulf Ports came under Zell al-Soltan, governor of Isfahan and Iraq. He re-appointed Nasir al-Molk as governor of Bushehr, Dashtestan and Dashti as well as of Lar.[290] The relationship between Nasir al-Molk and the British was not a smooth one. He made trouble for the Residency and made allegedly groundless complaints against British subjects. Not only the British were the butt of his antagonism and intimidation, so was the foreign agent. Nasir al-Molk also interfered in matters concerning the *kargozar*'s court.[291] The contractor for the supply of stores to government shipping had gone to Masqat and left his cousin Humad in charge in case any government ship would call on Bushehr. On the day the contractor left the authorities seized Humad claiming that he had a house mortgaged to a Persian merchant. Because the stipulated period had passed he should make it over immediately. Edwards, the assistant Resident, requested the *kargozar* to let the Law courts take care of the matter. During the hearing Humad asked the complainant to give him time till the contractor returned from Masqat as he knew his affairs and was the main witness in the matter. The complainant refused saying that even if he gave time the governor would not allow it, showing that the real complainant was Naser al-Molk.[292]

The Great Famine

The year 1870 was the year that the Great Famine began. The winter of 1869-70 had very little snow and rain and consequently the harvest was bad. Although the real famine hit the people of Bushehr by the end of 1870, they felt it coming by June. In that month, Edwards, the assistant Resident, reported that the *kargozar* (who officiated in the absence

---

287. Busse 1972, p. 347; Sa`adat 1390, p. 114; NA, FO 248/206, Capt. Disbrowe, officiating Resident to Alison, 20/11/1862; Idem, Ahmad Khan to Disbrowe; Sa`adat 1390, p. 115.

288. NA, FO 248/206, Appointment farman of Mirza Mehdi Khan, Jomadi I 1278; Idem, Capt. Disbrowe, officiating Resident to Alison, 12/06/1862; Idem, Capt. Disbrowe, officiating Resident to Alison, 12/06/1862. His appointment letter showed that he had served in Tiflis and St. Petersburg, and had been promoted to Khan that year, and was charged with *kargozari* duties at Bushehr, all ports and islands, duties that are mercantile, passport office, and the suppression of slavery.

289. Busse 1972, p. 364.

290. Sa`adat 1390, p. 115; for a short biography of Nasir al-Molk, see Hamidi 1380, pp. 306-07.

291. NA, FO 248/263, From uncovenanted assistant Charles E. Edwards at Bushire to Thomson, 20/01/1870.

292. NA, FO 248/263, From uncovenanted assistant Charles E. Edwards to Thomson - 22/01/1870; Idem, Abdol Mohammad 2nd *monshi* to uncovenanted ass. resident, 17 Shavval 1286- 20/01/1870; Idem, Mirza Mohammad Khan, NA, FO Agent to uncovenanted ass. resident 21 Shavval 1286- 24/01/1870; Idem, uncovenanted ass. resident to Mirza Mohammad Khan, FO Agent, 21 Shavval 1286- 24/01/1870.

of a governor) refused to give permission for the export of wheat. On the morning of 27 June about 1,000 people surrounded the house of the British-protected exporter house to stop export. The mob entered his premises and wounded two men. Thereafter, the leaders of the mob, one of whom was a blacksmith called Nabi, took refuge in the house of a *mojtahed*. Other exporters were also threatened. Many of members of the mob came from a village, where Mirza Mehdi Khan, the nemesis of the British, was residing. The *kargozar* feared an uprising if he would try to arrest them, the more so since there was no civil authority in Bushehr. He admitted that he had not received orders for an export ban from Tehran, but the dangerous and volatile situation in Bushehr left him no choice as he was powerless to do anything.[293] Col. Pelly's suspicion that Mirza Mehdi Khan was inciting the population was confirmed, for he had returned to Bushehr to continue his intriguing. Because the *kargozar* told Pelly that there was nobody in Bushehr to control the mob, Pelly intended "to stop the mailboat or any other British steamer if, as of Monday evening, there is no assurance of order, to protect life and property."[294]

Pelly's worry was understandable, because total anarchy reigned, for Bushehr "is still at the mercy of the mob. ... If the mob wants to raise again the cry that they are thousands and the Christians are fifty my only recourse is to collect the Europeans of the Residency and defend ourselves here." On 26 June 1870, Mirza Mehdi Khan let it be known that he would return in 40 days as governor of Bushehr. Pelly suggested to Alison, the British envoy, that the Persian government buy all the wheat at a fair price and appoint the foreign agent to receive it. He had received a request from an unnamed Arab chief to get his permission to attack Bushehr. Pelly blamed the Persian government and its agent Mirza Mehdi Khan for the mess in Bushehr. On the same day, by telegram, Pelly learnt that on 21 June, Tehran had given peremptory orders to the governor-general of Fars to appoint a governor, restore order, take over the wheat and protect British citizens.[295]

By mid-July 1870, Bushehr had a new governor, Naser al-Molk who had not changed his manner. After his return he agreed with the new *kargozar*, Mirza Mohammad Khan that all their business communications would be in writing so that there would be a record of what had passed. On 27 July, the *kargozar* sent Pelly's letter with a complaint that the authorities dragged their feet in investigating a theft from the Residency's pharmacy to the governor together with the suspect "Ally Durwayee." After reading Pelly's letter the governor threw the letters away and cursed the *kargozar*. This was the last straw that broke the camel's back and the *kargozar* took his bedding to the flagstaff and stayed there. "Having positioned himself across from the governor's house he abused him and accused him of having offended the government and paid no attention to the FO agent's request and that he would send a telegram next morning to Tehran and remain sitting under the flagstaff until he received a reply. The governor then came outside and spoke to Mirza Mohammad Khan. The *yavar* of the regiment, the news writer of Bushehr, Mirza Rahim and some leading merchants, unsuccessfully tried to persuade him to return to his own

293. NA, FO 248/263, uncovenanted ass. resident Charles Edwards to Charles Alison, Minister Plenipot. and Envy Extraord, 27/06/1870; Idem, Lewis Pelly to Charles Alison, Minister Plenipot. and Envy Extraord., 27/06/1870.

294. NA, FO 248/263 Lewis Pelly to Charles Alison, Minister Plenipot. and Envy Extraord., 27/06/1870.

295. NA, FO 248/263 Lewis Pelly to Charles Alison, Minister Plenipot. and Envy Extraord. 27/06/1870; Idem, Lewis Pelly to Charles Alison, Minister Plenipot. and Envy Extraord. 27/06/1870.

house. The governor then entreated him to go, promising to visit him in the morning and give him satisfaction; he then returned home."[296]

At the end of August 1870, to help the people of Bushehr, the wheat merchants sold some 2,000 Hashem *man* of wheat to them at 12 *qran*s per *man* and 2,887 *man* was handed over to the governor. However, the governor refused to honor the merchants' claim and proposed an assembly of merchants to decide on its correctness. Because the merchants excused themselves, Edwards was forced to postpone the settlement until the three principal merchants were available or until Col. Pelly returned. Meanwhile the governor refused even to pay the stipulated value of 12 *qran*s on some frivolous pretext about the receipts.[297] The sale of grain did not prevent scores of people dying during the famine that lasted until 1872, despite the relief measures taken (see chapter 1).

The uneventful years

Although the famine ended in 1872 many people still suffered from its consequences and life necessities were nevertheless in short supply. Therefore, in 1873 the Bushehr governorate was and remained infested with robbers as in all of S. Persia. The government was unable to suppress them and bring them to justice. For example, there was an organized gang of robbers infesting the roads near Rishahr. The gang consisted of 10-15 men of different tribes, but mainly of Tangestanis, who normally lived in Kolol. The leader of the gang was Ewaz Al Ewaz, a well-known Tangestani, while Jamal Hoseyn Jamal, his deputy and a relative, was in charge during the leader's absence. In the fall of 1873, the gang was staying at Rishahr, where they had a haunt in the Bagh-e Sheikh Abul and Khasang Tangi, containing stone quarries. There was yet another gang of some 20 men, whose chief was Mohammad Haji, a Dashti who lived in Kolol. On 20 July 1873, some 15 well-armed men of the first gang attacked Capt. Guthrie, the commander of a Bombay Marine vessel and some of the Residency servants. Capt. Guthrie received a near fatal stab and the servants were stripped and robbed. The robbers evaded capture and got away with property of considerable value. The governor immediately send out some 100 soldiers. It was believed that the villagers of Imamzadeh and the *kadkhoda* of Rishahr knew the identity of the robbers, but nobody dared give information about the gangs, because informants were killed and therefore, the culprits were not found.[298]

In 1874, Naser al-Molk was succeeded by Asadollah Mirza as governor, who, during the summer went to the cooler clime of Shiraz, leaving his son in charge. When towards the end of 1874 it looked as if drought would cause another famine, an export ban of grain was issued. Fortunately the rains came at last. In January 1875, Asadollah Mirza went

---

296. NA, FO 248/263, Mirza Mohamad Hoseyn, head *monshi* Residency to Sydney Smith, 28/07/1870/26 Rabi II; Idem, Major Sydney Smith, Ass. Res. to Charles Alison, Minister Plenipot. and Envy Extraord. 29/07/1870; Idem, Report FO agent in Persian.

297. NA, FO 248/263, uncovenanted ass. resident Charles Edwards to Charles Alison, Minister Plenipot. and Envy Extraord. 26/08/1870; Idem, Mirza Mohammad Khan to Resident 13 Jomadi I 1287- 11/08/1870; Idem, uncovenanted ass. resident Charles Edwards to FO Agent 25 Jomadi I 1287 -23/08/1870; Idem, reply to the above; Idem, uncovenanted ass. resident Charles Edwards to FO Agent, 27 Jomadi I 1287 - 25/08/1870. The three merchants were Agha Mohammad Ali, Malek al-Tojjar; Haji Abdol-Nabi' and Haji Mohammad Nilforush.

298. NA, FO 248/290, Col. E.C. Ross to Ronald J. Thomson, Minister, 21/07/1873; Idem, Memorandum 24/10/1873; Administration 1873-74, p. 6. For the imamzadeh, see Hamidi 1380, p. 86.

with troops into the sub-districts to collect the revenue from the chiefs who would not pay anything unless force was used.[299] In 1875, Hosam al-Saltaneh was dismissed as governor-general of Fars; he was replaced by Yahya Khan, Mo`tamed al-Molk, Farmanfarma. Therefore, the former's cousin Asadollah Mirza was recalled and replaced as governor of Bushehr by `Abdol-Hoseyn Khan Sartip, who proved to be a failure and was removed and replaced by Sa`d al-Molk, who collected revenue with "a force of infantry and artillery." Although there was some unrest in Bushehr when there was no governor, the situation was satisfactory.[300]

On 11 May 1876, Sa`d al-Molk left to Shiraz; in his absence the Farmanfarma's *abdar-bashi* was acting governor. From then the state of town and environs was very unsatisfactory. On 27 June 1876, the acting governor was summoned to Shiraz and he left the same day. From 30 June 1876, the government was entrusted to Aqa Mohammad `Ali Malek al-Tojjar of Bushehr. However, due to his illness he was unable to carry out his functions, which he entrusted to one of his slaves, Kerbela'i `Evaz, *me`mar-bashi*, who was up till then the keeper of the gate, as deputy-governor (*na'eb al-hokumah*). Kerbela'i `Evaz, being inexperienced and guided by designing people, was unable to keep proper control and as a result the subordinate authorities did whatever they liked, because there was no check on their irregularities. Fortunately, they did not know the extent of the Malek al-Tojjar 's illness otherwise even more disorders would have been committed. Because his situation daily deteriorated it was feared, in case of his death, that things would get out of hand, unless immediately an able governor would be appointed. Therefore, Col. Ross expressed the hope to Tehran that the Shah would very soon appoint somebody of respectability and position as governor.

There were regular robberies on the road from Bushehr to Shiraz and frequently disputes occurred between the town's people and soldiers, whom the authorities were unable to control. E.g., on the night of 29 May 1876, a night-watch was wounded by a soldier who was prowling in the town with intent of robbery. On 8 June thieves were going about town with crowbars intending to force their way into homes, but watchful people chased them off. On 2 June, an Arab going home was wounded by a drunken soldier. On 25 June, a woman was wounded by a drunken artillerist. On 26 June, soldiers took all the water melons that came into town and forced people to pay any price they demanded. The governor was unable to do anything. On 27 June, when the *abdar-bashi* left soldiers took all water melons for nothing or at a low price and resold them to the town's people at high prices. On 28 June, soldiers levied a tax of 0.5 *qran* on every load of water melon entering town; their commanding officer had no control over them. On 17 July, soldiers again tried to take charge of the water melons and the commanding officer came with other soldiers to stop them and enforce his authority; a fight ensued, many were wounded and finally the unruly soldiers were expelled from the town and sent to Behbahan. The *yavar* and his adjutant were first ordered to go to Shiraz, but then were allowed to remain. On 28 July, soldiers surrounded the house of the Malek al-Tojjar and refused to leave until they received their pay and rations; finally they were given money

299. Nasir al-Molk was governor of Bushehr, Dashtestan and Dashti as well as of Lar. Sa`adat 1390, p. 115; Busse 1972, p. 364; Administration Report 1874-75, p. 5; Saldanha 1986, vol. 7/2, p. 8; Busse 1972, p. 364.

300. Administration Report 1875-76, pp. 4-5. In 1875-76, he was replaced by `Abdol-Hoseyn Khan, son of Khan Baba Khan. Busse 1972, p. 384; Sa`adat 1390, p. 115 (who does not mention Asadollah Mirza); Sirjani 1361, p.44.

and left. On that same day, a gang of robbers from Tangestan came to a melon field 3.5 km from Bushehr and stripped the owner's wife of her ornaments and clothes to a value of 150 *qrans* and threatened to kill her unless she told them where the money from the sale of melons was hidden; they dug it up and took 273 *qrans*. When they left they tried to take a bullock but then the gardener awoke and grabbed one of the robbers, who called for aid. His mates killed the gardener. In the morning a complaint was made to the Malek al-Tojjar, who telegraphed to Ehtesham al-Dowleh in Shiraz, who ordered better protection but nothing was done to arrest the culprits, compensate the robbed or provide compensation to the widow and children of the killed man. On 10 August 1876, soldiers were again clamoring for pay and rations; the *yavar* ordered them to be flogged and one soldier almost died; the rest fled and sought asylum under the flagstaff of the Turkish consul. Many other robberies were traced to soldiers who were driven to crime by desperation. They did not know to whom to apply for pay and rations and without it they could not exist; it was feared that they might even plunder the bazaar.[301] There was no change in this situation; in fact, there were highway robberies all over Fars in 1876-77.[302]

Oweys Mirza Ehtesham al-Dowleh, son of Farhad Mirza Mo`tamed al-Dowleh, governor-general of Fars was appointed governor of Behbahan, Kuhgilu'i and Bushehr, where Haji Esma`il Khan deputized for him. Ehtesham al-Dowleh visited Bushehr at the end of January 1877 (tax revenue collection time) and remained about 50 days. Ehtesham al-Dowleh was a tough and harsh administrator, just like his father Farhad Mirza, whose administration of Fars was so tough and oppressive that people in despair cried: "Fars is done for" (*Fars tamam shod*). Therefore, during his stay Heydar Khan of Dashti who had not visited Bushehr for many years thought it advisable to do during the time when Ehtesham al-Dowleh had a large force with him with the proven determination to use it to put down a rebellion. When the governor left he intended to make a tour of the littoral, but he was detained too long at Dashti and he left for Shiraz before it became too hot.[303] In 1877, a grain riot instigated by the olama occurred; some grain belonging to a British Indian subject was plundered. The Resident demanded action and the ring leaders were arrested, punished and forced to pay the full value of the stolen grain. Ironically, the ban on export of grain was mostly evaded.[304]

In 1877, Agha Mohammad `Ali Malek al-Tojjar and reputedly the richest man in Persia died. As he had no children his older brother Haji Baba, a naturalized British-Indian subject, was his sole heir. He died in 1883 and his estate was passed on to his grandson, Haji Mohammad Mehdi, who was appointed Malek al-Tojjar.[305] Also in 1877, deputy-governor Haji Esma`il Khan was replaced by Aqa Mohammad Baqer Khan. Ehtesham al-Dowleh, who had the overall supervision of the southern districts and visited Bushehr in February 1878 with a large force, but Bushehr and environs were peaceful.[306] There was one problem, however. In February 1878, Heydar Khan of Dashti, who had expelled his cousin `Ali Khan and was a frequent source of annoyance to the authorities, refused

301. NA, FO 248/318, J.C. Edwards, Ass. Resident, 12/08/1876; Idem, Captain W.J. Prideaux to Thomson, 05/07/1876; Idem, Captain W.J. Prideaux to Thomson, 15/08/1876; Saldanha 1986, vol. 7/2, pp. 8-9.

302. Busse, p. 385; Sirjani 1361, pp. 52, 61, 74-75. About safety in the countryside, see NA, FO 248/318, Prideaux to Superintendent Persian Gulf Telegraph Dept. 1876.

303. Administration Report 1876-77, p. 4; Sa`adat 1390, p. 115; Busse 1972, p. 388; Sirjani 1361, pp. 82-84.

304. Administration Report 1877-78, p. 5.

305. Lorimer 1915, vol. 1, pp. 2058-59.

306. Administration Report 1877-78, p. 5; Saldanha 1986, vol. 7/2, p. 10; Sa`adat 1390, p. 115.

to come to Bushehr and meet Ehtesham al-Dowleh, but went to Shiraz under promise of forgiveness of past mistakes. His brother Mohammad Khan came to see Ehtesham al-Dowleh and suggested that he replace Heydar Khan, who thereafter conveniently died in Shiraz and it was, of course suggested that he had partaken of the *shorbeh-ye Qajar.*[307] Also, the following year of 1878, Ehtesham al-Dowleh, governor of Behbahan made his usual tour through Bushehr and neighboring districts in February and fortunately, it was again peaceful in the district.[308] Haji Mohamad Baqer Khan remained governor with whom the British Resident had somewhat strained relations because of his unwillingness to resolve issues concerning British subjects. Therefore, Col. Ross appealed to Tehran, which instructed the governor to give satisfaction and since then there were cordial relations between the two officials.[309]

Mo`tamed al-Dowleh (in office since August 1876) remained in power until *Nowruz* 1882 and so did his agent Haji Mohammad Baqer Khan as governor of Bushehr. However, in March 1882, Zell al-Soltan became governor-general of Fars, who appointed his son Jalal al-Dowleh as his deputy. Mo`tamed al-Soltan, Mirza Mohammad Khan Mostowfi Nezam, a protégé of Zell al-Soltan, became the new governor of Bushehr. In the interim, the *kargozar* Mirza `Ali Akbar officiated, but he was so obstructive that the British engineered his recall. His successor was Haji Mirza `Abdollah Khan, the *kargozar* of Bandar Abbas.[310] In June 1881, Mohammad Khan, chief of Dashti died in Bushehr, having been imprisoned for arrears of revenue. His nephew Jamal Khan, son of Heydar Khan succeeded him.[311]

In 1882, Nasir al-Molk was appointed governor of Bushehr, who left for Shiraz in February 1883, leaving *kargozar* Haji Mirza `Abdollah Khan in charge.[312] In 1884, Mirza Mohammad Hoseyn Khan, son of the Saheb Divan was appointed governor of Bushehr succeeding Nasir al-Molk. He arrived in Bushehr in June 1884, but left in January 1885, because he was summoned by Zell al-Soltan to accompany him to Tehran. In the interim, Haji Abu'l-Fath Khan, his son-in-law came as deputy governor. In that same year, Mohammad Hoseyn Khan received the title of Mo`taman al-Molk.[313]

On 2 July 1884, there was some scuffle near Bushehr between soldiers and some Dashtis. The reason for this ruckus was that in 1881 Mohammad Khan, the chief of Dashti had died in prison in Bushehr. His widow, who was of Turkish origin, had considerable influence in the district and a large part of its population wanted her two sons, the eldest son was seven years old, to be the nominal chiefs. Jamal Khan, the chief of Dashti at that time was in Shiraz and the widow received encouragement to go there as well. With

307. Administration Report 1877-78, p. 6; Administration Report 1878-79, p. 9; Saldanha 1986, vol. 7/2, p. 10; Sa`adat 1390, p. 116.

308. Administration Report 1878-79, p. 8; Saldanha 1986, vol. 7/2, p. 10.

309. Administration Report 1878-79, p. 9; Busse 1972, pp. 397, 399 (in 1878-79, Haji Mohammad Baqer Khan was governor of Bushehr); de Rivoyre 1883, pp. 131, 133; Sa`adat 1390, p. 116.

310. Administration Report 1880-81, pp. 7, 9-10; Sa`adat 1390, p. 116; Administration Report 1881-82, p. 6; Busse 417 (In 1881-82, Mirza Mohammad Mostowfi-ye Nezam was the governor of Bushehr); Saldanha 1986, vol. 7/2, p. 31 (he arrived in Bushehr in January 1882).

311. Administration Report 1881-82, p. 6.

312. Administration Report 1882-83, p. 5; in 1882-83 he was replaced by Nasir al-Molk. Busse 1972, p. 419; Sirjani 1361, pp. 160-61.

313. Administration Report 1883-84, p. 8; Administration Report 1884-85, p. 8; Sa`adat 1390, p. 116; Sirjani 1361, pp. 182, 202, 206-08, 217 (in December 1883 the governor was summoned to Tehran; during his absence Fazlollah Khan officiated).

considerable presents she came to Bushehr in June/July 1884, with her brother `Evaz Khan and a numerous escort and she took residence in a country-house near Bushehr. To derail the widow's plans, Jamal Khan sent orders to the authorities in Bushehr to arrest certain Dashtis among whom was `Evaz Khan. The acting deputy governor then sent up to 100 men after dark to arrest them. The Dashtis were surprised and fire was exchanged resulting in three deaths and several wounded. The widow and her two sons sought asylum at Sabzabad, where she stayed one day and then left. The soldiers plundered the house and took all her property; she remained calm and restrained her men to avoid worse things to happen.[314] However, Jamal Khan achieved his goal and remained chief of Dashti.

In June 1885, Mo`taman al-Molk, Mostowfi 1st class, resigned due to bad health. It was then announced that Nowzar Mirza (grandson of Hoseyn `Ali Mirza Farmanfarma) was appointed deputy governor of Bushehr and Dashtestan. However, Haji Mohammad Mehdi Malek al-Tojjar requested that Abu'l-Fath Khan would continue to serve as deputy governor. In that case, Malek al-Tojjar promised to be responsible for the governorate's revenues and their proper management. Jalal al-Dowleh then decided to cancel Nowzar Mirza's appointment and confirmed Abu'l-Fath Khan as deputy governor except for Dashti. Because Malek al-Tojjar was responsible for the revenues and good government, Abu'l-Fath Khan and the Khans of Dashtestan had to obey his instructions. If they acted contrary to his orders, he was authorized to dismiss them and appoint others in their place. In short, Malek al-Tojjar was de-facto governor of Bushehr and its districts and he is mentioned as such by contemporary sources.[315] However, it seems that there were problems with this construction, because in September 1885 the British Resident reported that apparently the Malek al-Tojjar was not recognized as governor by the Persian authorities.[316] However, at that same time, to dispel any doubt, Zell al-Soltan sent a formal message to Malek al-Tojjar informing him that Bushehr was formally and actually entrusted to him. "All officials and zabets are under your orders. All have to obey you."[317] In May 1886, Malek al-Tojjar resigned as governor and was replaced by Haji Fath `Ali Khan, who, in his turn, was replaced by Haji Nasir al-Molk.[318]

Nasir al-Molk remained in office until July 1887. Because of a bad harvest, prices in Bushehr rose to near famine level; its outlying districts also were in bad shape and therefore unsettled. Matters were made worse by intrigues in Shiraz aiming to have Nasir al-Molk dismissed as governor. As a result, several *zabet*s were replaced. In April 1887, he returned to Shiraz and left Heydarqoli Khan as his deputy. Very soon, the latter was appointed deputy governor of Behbahan and in May 1887, Haji Ahmad Khan Sartip succeeded him as deputy governor of Bushehr. In July 1887, Nasir al-Molk came to

---

314. NA, FO 248/412, Lt. Col. E.C. Ross to Thomson, 07/07/1884; Administration Report 1884-85, p. 8; Lorimer 1915, vol. 1, p. 2062.

315. NA, FO 248/424, Jalal al-Dowleh to Malek al-Tojjar (Mo`tamad al-Soltan), Shavval 1302; Idem, similar letter by Saheb Divan Shavval 1302; Idem, telegram Saheb Divan to Malek al-Tojjar, 30/07/1885; Sirjani 1361, pp. 242-43; Administration Report 1885-86, p. 7; Sa`adat 1390, p. 116; Lorimer 1915, vol. 1, p. 2059 writes that Safar Ali Khan replaced Nowzar Mirza as deputy governor.

316. NA, FO 248/424, Lt. Col. E.C. Ross to Ronald Thomson, 08/09/1885.

317. NA, FO 248/424, *Raqam* Zell al-Soltan to Haji Mohamad Memed, Sartip 1st class and malek al-tojjar, Zi'lqa`deh 1302.

318. Administration Report 1886-87, pp. 8-10; Sa`adat 1390, p. 117; Lorimer 1915, vol. 1, p. 2059; Sirjani 1361, p. 287. Malek al-Tojjar's political role was not yet finished because he was instructed to consider himself admiral and was charged with a mission in Lengeh and Jask. NA, FO 248/448, Extract report Head *Monshi* Residency, 30/09/1887.

Bushehr via Firuzabad, accompanied by Jamal Khan, chief of Dashti with a force of 400 cavalry and 200 infantry. He stayed for a short period, and had to return to Shiraz due to intrigues by his family and resigned as governor. He was succeeded by Nowzar Mirza, who arrived in August, and intrigues against him started immediately. Because in 1885, he had torpedoed Nowzar Mirza's appointment as governor of Bushehr there was some bad feeling between Nowzar Mirza and Malek al-Tojjar. Therefore, in October 1887, Mirza Mohammad Khan, the *kargozar* of Bushehr arranged a meeting to reconcile the two men.[319] Nowzar Mirza left in October and resigned because of a censorious telegram from Amin al-Soltan. He was persuaded to stay and remained in office until February 1888. For in that month Zell al-Soltan was dismissed as governor-general of Fars and Amin al-Soltan took charge of Fars, who appointed Mohammad Hasan Khan Sa`d al-Molk, who like his brother, Hoseyn Qoli Khan Mafi Nezam al-Salteneh, had been henchmen for Hosam al-Saltaneh Morad Mirza. Later Sa`d al-Molk served the same function for Ehtesham al-Saltaneh Oveys Mirza, according to Sa`adat a local Bushehri historian. However, both brothers switched to Amin al-Soltan's camp after Sa`d al-Molk had been severely bastinadoed by Ehtesham al-Saltaneh.[320]

In 1887, the Malek al-Tojjar tried the make life for the British Resident difficult by, among other things, fabricating false accusations against the Residency Agent at Lengeh, which Col. Ross countered.[321] The British were not the only target of Malek al-Tojjar's designs, so was the *kargozar*. At the end of November 1887, the commander (*Sarhang*) of the *Persepolis* starved Mo`tamed al-Vezareh, the *kargozar* for two days, depriving him of food and drink to make him pay customs arrears. On 30 November, he escaped to the Residency asking asylum. When the Malek al-Tojjar's people and Haji Ahmad learnt this, the latter, in full uniform and drawn sword, led Malek al-Tojjar's men to the *kargozar*'s house. They opened all doors, took all the property in it, beat the *kargozar*'s younger son and took him and the servants to the Malek al-Tojjar's office. Haji Ahmad promised 100 *tumans* to whoever brought him the *kargozar* and 50 *tumans* for his older son. The wives of the *kargozar*'s servants were dragged out of the house by their hair and thrown uncovered into the street. At 4.30, half hour before sunset Malek al-Tojjar went to Haji Ahmad's house and after making inquiries dismissed the *kargozar*'s son, but the others remained confined in fetters and stocks. To provide justification for his action, Haji Ahmad Khan obtained a testimony (*esteshhad-nameh*) stating that he was asleep when he was informed that the *kargozar* had strangled the *sarhang* of the *Persepolis*. He put on his uniform to verify it and found it to be true; he released him from the clutches of the *kargozar*'s servants, did not touch any of the *kargozar*'s belongings, but only sealed off the house. The Malek al-Tojjar intended to get the merchants to sign this one by one. The governor had another *esteshhad-nameh* that stated the Ahmad Khan was drunk when he entered the *kargozar*'s house, threw out all his things and took away some. After much correspondence Mo`tamed al-Vezareh was allowed to leave for Tehran for examination

---

319. NA, FO 248/448, Extract report Head *Monshi* Residency, 18/10/1887; Sirjani 1361, pp. 289-90; for short biography of Sa`d al-Molk, see Hamidi 1380, p. 380.

320. Administration Report 1887-88, p. 10-11; Sa`adat 1390, p. 119; Sirjani 1361, pp. 292 (Nowzar Mirza was appointed in July 1887), 313-14 (Sa`d al-Molk was appointed in May 1888).

321. NA, FO 248/484, Ross to John Kennedy, charge d'affaires 19/05/1889.

of his case. He was dismissed and succeeded by Najafqoli Khan, "a person of no standing nor of much experience," according to the British Resident.[322]

In 1888, Sa`d al-Molk began to insult and annoy British authorities, such as in August, when he and the customs master refused to recognize the *javaz* or certificate for clearance at the 5% rate issued by the British Residency for goods imported from Manchester. He even informed the Resident that he intended to open packages destined for the British Legation, which were exempt of customs duty. Drummond Wolff, the British Minister reported the case to Amin al-Soltan who put a stop to it.[323] In 1889, Sa`d al-Molk remained in function, while Nowzar Mirza resigned as governor of Dashtistan, Tangistan and Dashti. Mohammad Hasan Khan Sartip succeeded him. Bushehr's neighboring districts were much disturbed due to feuds between local chiefs, mainly those of Borazjan and Angali.[324] On 29 June 1889, Mirza Hoseyn Khan, the chief of Borazjan, went to Isavand, near Khoshab. Mohammad Khan, the chief of Angali, learning about this sent men there to ambush the Borazjan chief. To entrap him the Angali chief sent another group to raid some shepherds near Khoshab to drive some of the animals off. Hearing this, Mirza Hoseyn Khan immediately pursued the raiders, overtook and engaged them. The raiders, while fighting, slowly led their opponents to the ambush. When the trap was sprung Mirza Hoseyn Khan's horse was shot from under him; he suffered 15 casualties among his men, while the other side only suffered two deaths. Sa`d al-Molk wanted Shiraz to replace Mirza Hoseyn Khan, but seems to have supported the Angali chief. On 1 July 1889, some 300 Tangestani *tofangchi*s came to support Mirza Hoseyn Khan and engaged Mohammad Khan's men. The fighting happened from 10 a.m. to 2 p.m. during which three hamlets were taken by the joint Borazjani-Tangestani force. Jamal Khan of Dashti with 600 horse and foot was preparing to support Mirza Hoseyn Khan. Mohammad Khan wrote Heydar `Ali Khan, a Tangestani chief not to support Mirza Hoseyn Khan. Heydar `Ali Khan replied he would remain neutral as long as Khan `Ali Khan also did. Sa`d al-Molk wrote to Amin al-Soltan accusing Malek al-Tojjar, Mo`tamed al-Dowleh of fomenting this trouble. At the end of June 1889, Sa`d al-Molk sent a sword and a shawl to both Khan `Ali Khan and Mohammad Khan Angali. Two days later Sa`d al-Molk sent his treasurer, Safar `Ali Beg to try and reconcile the two men, if they agreed his son Rezaqoli Khan would go to Shiraz, if they did not there would be no intercession in Shiraz. The Borazjanis threatened to kill Rezaqoli Khan if he would leave Bushehr. Sa`d al-Molk encouraged Mohammad Hasan Khan to continue the fight with the Borazjan chief, intimating that he was busy trying to get Nowzar Mirza dismissed to be replaced by himself.[325]

Sa`d al-Molk continued to be governor of the Gulf Ports, while Mohammad Hasan Khan Sartip remained governor of Dashtestan etc., but in 1891 Sa`d al-Molk was replaced

322. NA, FO 248/448, Extract report Head *Monshi* Residency, 01/12/1887; Idem, Extract report Head *Monshi* Residency, 11/12/1887; Administration Report 1886-87, p. 11.

323. Administration Report 1888-89, p. 11; NA, FO 248/484, Ross to John Kennedy, charge d'affaires, 19/05/1889; Lorimer vol. 1, pp. 2088-89.

324. Administration Report 1889-90, pp. 8-9.

325. NA, FO 248/484, news report Head *Monshi* Residency, 02/07/1889; Idem, news report Head *Monshi* Residency, 01/07/1889; Idem, news report Head *Monshi* Residency, 06/07/1889.

Nezam al-Saltaneh inner court Chahar Borj

by his brother Nezam al-Saltaneh.[326] The latter remained governor of the Gulf Ports until early September 1892, when he became governor-general of Fars; his nephew Rezaqoli Khan then served as deputy governor for the rest of the year. Thereafter, in March 1893, Sa`d al-Molk was again appointed as governor of the Gulf Ports.[327] In 1892, there were disturbances in the Bushehr governorate due to feuds between Khan `Ali Khan of Bandar Rig and Mohammad Khan of Rudhilleh; both were also unhappy with the governor of Bushehr, whose policy it was to play them off against each other. Mohammad Khan of Angali was murdered in blood feud, but his rival made peace with the government.[328]

Although Sa`d al-Molk continued to be governor of the Gulf Ports in 1893, he spent most of his time in Shiraz and only returned in January 1894. According to Sa`adat, for unspecified reasons, Nezam al-Saltaneh and his family were banned from the governorship of Bushehr for seven years, allegedly due to complaints about their misrule or to British pressure. In March 1894, Sa`d al-Molk was replaced by Mohammad Reza Khan Qavam al-Molk, who did not come immediately, but sent Haji Mirza `Abdollah Khan as his deputy [329] Khan `Ali Khan farmed Angali and other villages in Dashtestan, but its

326. Administration Report 1890-91, p. 9; Administration Report 1891-92, p. 9; Sa`adat 1390, p. 120 (at that time Nezam al-Saltaneh at a cheap price bought from the government the districts of Daleki, Zirah, and BiBara. The author also attributes the plan to sell the crown lands of *khaleseh* to him). On the sale of crown lands, see Floor 1998 a, pp. 340-46.

327. Administration Report 1892-93, p. 12; Sa`adat 1390, p. 120.

328. Saldanha 1986, vol. 7/2, p. 13; Administration Report 1892-93, p. 13.

329. Administration Report 1893-94, p. 10; Sa`adat 1390, p. 121.

people opposed this and Angali that held out was attacked with support of a cannon from Bushehr. In Tangestan a more serious conflict broke out, when Heydar Khan, assisted by Persian soldiers and a cannon, failed against the Tangesiri tribe, who armed with Martini-Henry rifles forced them to retreat.[330] In July 1894, Qavam al-Molk finally arrived in Bushehr. In 1895, the Malek al-Tojjar of Bushehr wanted to be governor and he began opposing Qavam al-Molk. The latter engineered the issuing of an order from Tehran that suggested that it would be better that the Malek al-Tojjar be temporarily removed from Bushehr. Qavam al-Molk then wanted to expel the Malek al-Tojjar, who took refuge in the Imamzadeh shrine. His supporters organized 'popular' demonstrations, while the bazaar, shops and offices were closed. Large crowds then occupied the telegraph office and remained there for many days and nights. Tehran did not react immediately to the popular demand for the dismissal of the governor. Of the latter's supporters the *hammal-bashi*, who had amassed many functions and much power, was the first to flee. In early March 1895, two weeks before the end of his term, Qavam al-Molk resigned. The only ones who still stuck with Qavam al-Molk were the Imam Jom`eh, `Alam al-Huda, Haji Ahmad Khan Kebabi, and Sayyed `Abdol-Reza Tabib. Their opponents then focused all their attention on these four, who then moved away, except for the Imam Jom`eh who was vilified by everybody. After the governor's departure, "Temporary and imperfect arrangements for the divided control of public affairs were somewhat tardily made, but these nevertheless, owing to the fact that the popular party was in the ascendant, sufficed to maintain order."[331] Also, the situation in the districts under Bushehr were turbulent. In Dashtestan, when one Sheikh wanted to transfer a piece of land that until then he had shared with Ahmad Sheikh, the latter killed the former. Tehran ordered a punitive expedition and a small force with a naval gun was sent. Ahmad Khan was joined by those of Tangestan and Shabankareh and was able to resist and reinforcements were sent with orders to reach an amicable solution. Ahmad Sheikh was induced to go to Bushehr with a strong force and received a royal order from the governor investing him with authority over the disputed land.[332]

Abu'l-Nasr Mirza Hosam al-Saltaneh was appointed governor of the Gulf Ports in March 1895, but he only arrived there in the middle of June 1895. His earliest problem was the transfer of certain coastal villages from Khan `Ali Khan to that of Heydar Khan, which the former resisted, but his death a few weeks later made it easier. In the fall of 1895, Heydar Khan received troop support with guns from the *Persepolis* to force his people to pay revenues; later more reinforcements followed. There was a fight and then the people sent a deputation to negotiate and a deal was reached with the authorities, which included that Heydar Khan also had to pay taxes. One month later the troops left. However, Heydar Khan had an odd way to show his appreciation for government support, because when the governor's agent came to ask for the revenues due, his mode of payment was holding a pistol to the agent's head. According to the British Resident, Hosam al-Saltaneh's administration, "was marked by an utter neglect of all duties and obligations of his office." The central government was only interested in the payment of revenues, which was taken care of by the mercantile coalition that had ousted Qavam al-Molk. Therefore,

330. Administration Report 1893-94, p. 11; Saldanha 1986, vol. 7/2, p. 14.

331. Sadid al-Saltaneh 1362, p. 11; Administration Report 1894-95, p. 10; Administration Report 1895-96, pp. 6-7.; Saldanha 1986, vol. 7/2, p. 14; Sa`adat 1390, p. 121. For the imamzadeh shrine of `Abd al-Moheyman, see Hamidi 1380, p.88.

332. Administration Report 1895-96, pp. 7-8; Saldanha 1986, vol. 7/2, p. 14-15.

the only incentive for the governor to be interested in public affairs disappeared. Power was wielded by others, with all the resulting abuses. His tenure was moreover uncertain, the result of financial difficulties with the government and in December 1896 he resigned and refused to do any further business.[333]

During this period there was a bitter fight between Haji Mohammad Mehdi Malek al-Tojjar, who was in charge of the supervision of arms imports and Haji Mo`in al-Tojjar about who would become the customs farmer. The conflict became so serious that Mo`in al-Tojjar was summoned to Tehran.[334] At the instigation of Malek al-Tojjar and Mo`in al-Tojjar, Ahmad Khan Daryabegi was appointed deputy governor. He was the son of Nazem-e Darbar *qapuchi-bashi*, who was originally from Azerbaijan, but lived in Tehran. He was then about 40 years old. He was rich and allegedly his expenditures amounted to more than 200 *tumans* per month, when later he became governor of Bushehr. Then he built a house outside of Bushehr. During his short 2.5 months period as deputy-governor he allegedly made more than 3,000 *tumans*.[335]

Mohammad Kazem Mirza, Eqtedar al-Soltan, son of `Alamshah Mirza, son of Timur Mirza, succeeded Hosam al-Saltaneh in March 1897; he was sacked in September and the *Amir Panj*, the garrison commander officiated. The latter died during an operation in Baluchistan, so that Rezaqoli Khan Mojir al-Saltaneh, a nephew of Nezam al-Saltaneh was appointed, but it was annulled and he returned to Tehran. According to Sa`adat, this was due to British pressure as the 7-year period that members of Nezam al-Salteneh's family were banned from the governorship of Bushehr had still two years to run. Then Qavam al-Molk became governor, who sent his son E`temad al-Soltan a.k.a. *beglerbegi*; he arrived in November 1897 and already resigned in February 1898. Thereafter, Malek al-Tojjar officiated, and in March 1898 Emad-e Nezam, a servant of Farmanfarma (who since October 1897 was governor-general of Fars) came as governor. In May 1898, he was succeeded by Sa`id al-Soltan and then by Mozaffar-e Nezam, who has just been removed.[336]

There continued to be much crime in Bushehr and environs due to high prices and the resulting distress, which was made use of by local rivals for power to discredit each other. But this was not the only trouble that confronted Bushehr authorities. "Another source of danger to Bushire is the neighbourhood of the Tangistanis, a tribe inhabiting the hilly broken country which lies between the lofty tableland of Persia, and the flat strip of sandy shore between the foot of the hills and the sea. Tangistan, as its name implies, consists of a succession of 'Tangs' or defiles, and is an almost impossible country for regular troops to enter." The Tangestanis were armed with breech-loaders and were used by government of Persia as irregular troops; the Malek al-Tojjar had several of them in his pay. At the end of 1897, Heydar Khan, the Tangestani chief, was deputized to punish

333. Administration Report 1896-97, p. 7; Saldanha 1986, vol. 7/2, p. 15; Sa`adat 1390, pp. 121-22; Sirjani 1361, pp. 501, 504.

334. Sa`adat 1390, p. 122. For a short biography of Mo`in al-Tojjar, see Hamidi 1380, p. 170. On the ban of arm imports, which was not established at British request as Sa`adat has it, but rather at Naser al-Din Shah's orders, see Floor 2011 a, p. 207.

335. Sa`adat 1390, pp. 125.

336. Administration Report 1897-98, p. 6; thus no less than 8 changes in one year!; Sadid al-Saltaneh 1362, p. 15; Sa`adat 1390, pp. 122-23; Sirjani 1361, pp. 517 (Hosam al-Saltaneh was replaced by Moshar al-Dowleh in November 1896), 524 (Jamshid Khan Mir Panj Eqtedar al-Soltan as of April 1897), 534 (Eqtedar al-Soltan dismissed in September 1897), 536 (replaced by Mas`ud al-Dowleh, nephew of Qavam al-Molk), 543 (replaced by Sa`id al-Soltan in April 1898), 548 (Mojir al-Saltaneh as of June 1898).

another chief `Ali Khan for non-payment of taxes. Heydar Khan being too strong, `Ali Khan took refuge at the Imamzadeh shrine at Rishahr and many followers were with him. They allegedly committed many of the crimes perpetrated in early 1898. Because it was feared that they might attack the Residency some marines were landed awaiting the arrival of 25 sepoys from Bombay. The garrison of Bushehr had been reduced by the dispatching of 150 men to Makran, and the governor-general sent 800 troops with one field gun under Sa`id al-Soltan from Shiraz to punish the Tangestanis. The troops ravaged the district, a few men, who may have been innocent, were executed, and monies were collected or extorted from whomever was solvent and was caught. At the conclusion of the campaign, Sa`id al-Soltan was appointed governor and he apparently acknowledged Heydar Khan as the sole chief of Tangestan.[337]

The situation in 1898-99 was an improvement in that Bushehr had only five governors that year: `Emad-e Nezam; Sa`id al-Soltan; Mozaffar-e Nezam; Mo`ezz al-Mamalek and Daryabegi. The first four were deputies of Farmanfarma, who was then governor-general of Fars. But later when the Gulf Ports were taken from him and given to Mojir al-Saltaneh, the nephew of Sa`d al-Molk and Nezam al-Saltaneh, Mo`ezz al-Mamalek was kept on as his deputy. However, Mojir al-Saltaneh's appointment was unacceptable to the British, because he was a nephew of Nezam al-Saltaneh. Therefore, Mirza Ahmad Khan, usually referred to by his title of Daryabegi, who at that time was commander of the *Persepolis*, became deputy-governor (*na'eb al-hokumeh*) in September 1898 and remained in that function until March 1899.[338]

On 20 May 1898, Sa`id al-Soltan accompanied by a force of 800 infantry and cavalry arrived in Bushehr and became governor. Apart from harassing the people of Tangestan and enforcing payment of revenues, he did not do much. He was recalled by the governor-general and returned with his force. "A few men were executed, but the popular opinion was that they were not the real criminals, and ransoms were taken from wealthy persons who fell into the hands of the 'Army'. The expedition was believed to have been financially a success." Whether his action had a lasting effect on the Tangestanis was doubtful. `Ali Khan was believed to have been responsible for the attack on the Residency and on Mahmud, the *jamadar* of the Telegraph Department, whose relatives were killed and whose house was looted in March 1898. Immediately thereafter `Ali Khan fled from his place of asylum and returned to Tangestan. His enemy Heydar Khan joined Sa`id al-Soltan and was confirmed as governor of Tangestan. `Ali Khan then fled further away and intended to go to Basra. But as no attempt was made to catch him he returned. He wrote to Mahmud and the Residency claiming his innocence and threatening that if he were not left alone he would take asylum (*bast*, or in Indian pronunciation, 'bust') with Mahmud. "It should here be explained that this custom of taking 'bust' is carried out in Persia to such a length that an accused person can enter the house of his accuser, who is bound to receive him,

337. Administration Report 1897-98, p. 9; Saldanha 1986, vol. 7/2, p. 16; Sa`adat 1390, p. 123; Lorimer 1915, vol. 1, p. 2133.

338. Sadid al-Saltaneh 1362, p. 12; Administration Report 1898-99, pp. 5-6; Lorimer vol. 1, p. 2130; Sa`adat 1390, pp. 125, 132-33 (however, Daryabegi and Malek al-Tojjar were rivals and in February/March 1901 the governor accused his rival of masterminding a theft of 8,000 *tumans* from the office of a Persian merchant. As a result, Malek al-Tojjar was summoned to Tehran. Later he left to Bombay where he remained). On the person of the Malek al-Tojjar, see Sa`adat 1390, pp. 134-36. According to Sa`adat 1390, p. 153, Azizollah Khan, an army officer officiated for three months, but he had to seek asylum in the British Residency for not paying his soldiers. He was replaced by Mirza Khalil Shirazi Mo`ezz al-Mamalek (later Moghith al-Dowleh) for three months on behalf of Mojir al-Saltaneh (Salar-e Mo`azzam).

and unable to take any steps against him, while he is in 'bust.'" He did not come but wrote to the Residency that he would come and surrender provided he got a fair trial and was promised that he would not be handed over to the Persians. This was agreed to; the investigation showed that there was a strong case of his connection to all the crimes. Claims of 4,000 *tumans* were submitted; he probably would have paid, provided that he received assurances that later the Persian authorities would not bother him. This was not feasible and thus as he had a safe-conduct he was allowed to leave after a six months' stay, but the Resident promised him that he would now demand compensation via the Persian authorities, since he had much landed property on the Bushehr peninsula.[339]

In 1900, Daryabegi became governor. He received a sword of honor from the Government of India because of his support to deal with the murder of Mr. Graves in Baluchistan. He also received a Russian decoration.[340] In May 1900, a Persian employee of the IETD was murdered, while during the night of 30 August the British Residency at Sabzabad was sprayed with gunfire, but fortunately only a horse was killed. Daryabegi stated that the Tangstanis had done it instigated by Nazem al-Tojjar, a nephew of Mo`in al-Tojjar who was at odds with Daryabegi at that time. The British considered Nazem al-Tojjar to be a notorious intriguer. They arranged that he was forced to leave Bushehr at the orders of Moshir al-Dowleh, the Minister of Foreign Affairs. Daryabegi collected a large force of Persian infantry and local levies supported by three of four cannons and moved to Tangestan, where most of the tribe submitted to him. He killed a few men, destroyed some forts, pillaged and laid waste to the land and returned. However, `Ali Khan was not caught, while Heydar Khan evaded Daryabegi's force and took refuge at the Imamzadeh. How long the resulting quiet would last was a question mark, the more so, since the Bushehri merchants imported and sold large quantities of rifles and the tribes were well armed with breach-loaders, which 10 years earlier were hardly seen. "Now, even in the town of Bushire itself, armed men are constantly seen, and in the adjacent villages there can hardly be a man who does not possess a Martini-Henry rifle."[341]

Daryabegi resigned and left for Tehran on 7 April 1901. He was succeeded by Mirza Khalil Shirazi Salar-e Mo`azzam, a nephew of Nezam al-Saltaneh, who was appointed on 18 August and only arrived in Bushehr on 23 December 1901. His deputy, Mo`ezz al-Mamalek, preceded him and arrived on 21 September. Despite the short 'interregnum' the situation in Bushehr was relatively quiet. The same could not be said of Tangestan, which was in its usual lawless state.[342] Salar-e Mo`azzam maintained good order, which was greatly appreciated by Bushehr's inhabitants. He also established a customs post at Rig, which the Khan of Rig had strongly opposed. Earlier, without his knowledge, the Belgian customs authorities had intended to do the same by force. In early May 1902, some 1,000 Tangestani and Dashti musketeers showed up in Bushehr. In mid-May the

339. Administration Report 1898-99, p. 6; Saldanha 1986, vol. 7/2, p. 17. For a negative appreciation of Heydar Khan, see Faramarzi 1390, p. 28.

340. Administration Report 1900-1901, p. 1; Lorimer vol. 1, p. 2131; Sirjani 1361, p. 619 (Daryabegi had not much authority and no perquisites or *madakhel*).

341. Administration Report 1899-1900, p. 1; Administration Report 1900-1901, pp. 1-2; Saldanha 1986, vol. 7/2, p. 160; Lorimer 1915, vol. 1, pp. 2134, 2140-41; Sa`adat 1390, pp. 132, 149-53 (who argues that his enemy Mo`in al-Tojjar was behind his dismissal). Mo`in al-Tojjar returned to Bushehr after a trip to Europe and was welcomed by the population, but not by the governor. Despite a closure of the bazaar in his support he was forced to leave Bushehr and settle in Tehran.

342. Administration Report 1901-1902, p. 1; Sa`adat 1390, pp. 153, 155 (Daryabegi was imprisoned in Tehran for 3 months, but payments in the right amounts to the right people set him free).

Khan of Angali also arrived with an additional group of armed men. The men had been enlisted by the Customs authorities without telling anyone their purpose. After the governor alerted Tehran about this unauthorized activity, Tehran prohibited the action and the musketeers were quietly disbanded. Later, Salar-e Mo`azzam arranged for a negotiated establishment of the customs post. He further tried to bring some control over Tangestan, where new trouble had broken out between Zayer Khedr and Zayer Gholam `Ali. In May 1902, they were reconciled, but shortly thereafter Zayer Gholam `Ali was killed by one of Zayer Khedr's followers. In January 1903, to put a stop to the feuding, the governor summoned Zayer Khedr to Bushehr and gave assurances as to his freedom of movement. However, on 3 February after leaving governor's residence Zayer Khedr was arrested. His men resisted and three of the governor's men were killed. Zayer Khedr remained in custody, however. His followers, who came to the Imamzadeh at Rishahr, wrote letters to the foreign consuls threatening violence, but nothing happened.[343] At the end of March 1904, Salar-e Mo`azzam left and was succeeded by Daryabegi, who had patched up his differences with Mo`in al-Tojjar; this enabled him to purchase the governorship of Bushehr. The *kargozar*, Mirza `Ali Mohammad Khan Movaqqer al-Dowleh ably served as governor pro-tem.[344]

343. Administration Report 1902-1903, p. 1; Sa`adat 1390, pp. 155-56.

344. Trade Report 1903-1904, p. 1; Sa`adat 1390, p. 156; Lorimer vol. 1, pp. 2131, 2134. For a photo of Movaqqer al-Dowleh, see Roknzadeh 1352, p. 90.

Ahmad Khan Daryabegi

Daryabegi arrived in Bushehr at the end of April 1904. As a result of the killing of Zayer Gholam `Ali, the whole district was in turmoil. At the orders of Tehran, Daryabegi left in October 1904 with 100 *tofangchi*s to assist the governor of Dashti against the

Tangestani troublemakers. Zayer Khedr fled, who apparently had been freed earlier. After looting and burning the village of Ahmadi Daryabegi returned to Bushehr.[345] Daryabegi, "though bereft of most of his power under the existing regime," made many promises that he seldom could fulfill. Despite the flight of Zayer Khedr, there were many petty robberies by Tangestanis in the outskirts of Bushehr. According to the British, Daryabegi was behind these robberies in order to have an excuse to launch a lucrative punitive expedition to Tangestan. There also was a robbery of a Kuwaiti by Persian artillerymen, but the authorities did nothing, even when pressed and promised to take action. Because of the continued frequent raids on the trade route by petty chiefs, merchants used the less convenient Firuzabad route. The governor-general of Fars, Sho`a al-Saltaneh, after pressure punished some road guards and things improved for a while, but in September 1905 it was blackmailing business as usual, in particular on the stretch between Kazerun and Borazjan.[346] Daryabegi also had other ideas to make money. On 30 April 1906, the governor issued a proclamation stating that all "inhabitants [need] to arrange to have the portions of the public roads, which adjoin their houses, paved with stones and cement, within 10 days, and stating that if they failed to do so, he will himself have the work done and recover the cost from the defaulters. No one has undertaken the work, and it is practically impossible to carry out the order as the required labour and materials are unobtainable."[347]

The Constitutional Period

The next 20 years or so was a period during which the governors were even less influential than they had been before. This was not just a local issue, but one that reflected the failure of the central government at the national level to assert itself. The hope for a new Persia after the granting of the Constitution was soon smothered due to a combination of factors such as the inability of Persian politicians, at both the national and local level, to lead the nation to a new and better future. They were not the only ones to blame. The growing influence of imperialist Russia and Great Britain was another factor. Prior to 1907, Persian politicians had been able to benefit from the rivalry that existed between the two powers, thus creating a kind a balance between the two. However, this also created 'pro' or 'anti' groups of politicians aligning them with one or the other power. This situation became worse after the signing of the Russian-British Convention by which Persia was divided into two spheres of influence and one neutral zone. This basically meant the end of Persia's independence, which so far Great Britain had pursued as a goal. However, the growing Russian influence over northern Persia made an independent Persia a 'threat' to India, and therefore, Persia had to be divided into spheres of influence, with a neutral zone as a buffer. This meant that the rivalry between the two powers somewhat subsided, but it made it impossible for any well-intentioned Persian government to carry out a

345. Administration Report 1904-1905, p. 1; Lorimer 1915, vol. 1, p. 2134. 2134; Faramarzi 1390, pp. 28-30 (with more details); Sa`adat 1390, p. 157 (Daryabegi made a trip to the dentist in Bombay, which led to the belief that he was in cahoots with the British concerning the status of Henjam, which was claimed by the Arabs). On the Henjam issue, see Floor 2011 a, p. 196.

346. Administration Report 1905-1906, pp. 19-20; for a detailed discussion of the lack of security on the trade road, see Floor 2011 b, pp. 135ff.

347. Political Diaries, vol. 1, p. 348.

uniform national policy, because either the one or the other, or both powers would protest if some measure was not to their liking. It also meant that Bushehr was firmly within the British zone of influence thus giving the British Resident even more clout than he had already. This clout was reinforced by the fact that the bankrupt government of Fars was subsidized by Great Britain after 1912, that Bushehr was occupied by Great Britain from 1915 to 1918, that Russia as a power to reckon with had ceased to exist after October 1917, leaving the field to Great Britain, a field over which the government in Tehran had already lost control by 1914.

Furthermore, at the local level, there was a change in the financial arrangement of the governorate. Prior to 1901, the governor was in charge of his governorate's revenues, often including that of the customs revenues. However, after that date, all revenues were managed and also (partly) collected by the Customs Department, which paid the governor's salary. Instead of being the holder of an office that he had bought to 'farm' as he liked, from that date, the governor had become a salaried employee with narrowly circumscribed authority and powers. Such a situation was not necessarily a bad or unworkable one, as the situation after 1922 shows. However, the difference was that prior to 1922, Persia had a very weak central government, whose authority after 1914, was but a nominal one. To a certain extent that also held for the governor of Bushehr, whose authority was constantly challenged by the well-armed tribesmen in the port's environs. It is within this context that the developments within Bushehr have to be seen.

Endeavors to have a functioning local assembly

On 11 August 1906, Mo`in al-Tojjar, the wealthy and influential Bushehri capitalist, sent a telegram to his agents (Shabankareh Brothers) informing them that Mozaffar al-Din Shah had granted a Legislative Assembly (*Majles*), including the right to elect representatives of all classes. He urged his agents to encourage the notables of Bushehr to send a congratulatory message to the Shah via him. It was clear that Mo`in al-Tojjar wanted to be elected by Bushehr, whose notables did not react to his 'encouragement.' On 15 August 1906, the Daryabegi held a meeting for the leading mullahs and merchants and read them the text of the government's telegram announcing the establishment of a *Majles*. He asked them to send a telegram of thanks to the shah, but the merchants had problems with the Customs Department. As a result, there was no unanimity and so nothing was done. At the same time, the captains (*nakhodas*) of native boats, who had to land their goods at the Customs House rather than elsewhere, as had been customary, sought support for their grievance. Two mullahs, Sadr al-Eslam and Sayyed Morteza Ahrami took up their cause, which resulted in a strike. Because the boatmen of the lighters supported the strike it was uncertain whether ships would be loaded and unloaded. The boatmen demonstrated against the Customs officials and mobbed Mr. Heynssens, who closed the Customs House on 20 August due to people's threatening attitude. On 19 and 20 August 1906, at the instigation of the two mullahs, the bazaars were closed. The next day, the Customs re-opened, after the demands of the mullahs were temporarily accepted. The town became quiet and the governor convened a meeting of religious leaders, merchants and boatmen on 25 August to discuss the situation. The governor read a message from the government stating that if there were grievances these had to be submitted to the Shah. In reaction, Sayyed Morteza Ahrami tabled a statement for submission to Tehran, while the merchants stated that they would do the same, but separately. The meeting unanimously asked the government to dismiss Messrs. Heynssens and Constant and two other Customs officials. Heynssens demanded punishment of those who had mobbed him on 20 August. A telegram from Moshir al-Dowleh to the leading *mojtaheds* of Bushehr asked them to intervene and restrain people from violent action. One of them replied that Heynssens had to be recalled, because people did not want him, while promising that the people's grievances would be sent via the governor.[348]

Meanwhile, Daryabegi tried to convince the mullahs that it was useless to ask for the dismissal of an individual as he would be replaced by another, without changing the reality on the ground. At the same time, Heynssens was obstinate and refused to leave his house until the persons who had assailed him were punished, which exasperated the governor, because Heynssens knew fully well that this was impossible. In early September 1906, the Imam Jom`eh and `Alam al-Huda sent messages to Tehran in support of Heynssens, who had received a present from the Customs department for his good work. Moses Khan, Heynssens' deputy was trying to persuade the mullahs to write that they had been instigated to oppose the Customs chief by interested parties. At that time, the grand vizier sent Daryabegi a telegram instructing him to escort Mr. Heynssens to the Customs House, "with fitting respect." However, Sayyed Morteza Ahrami and the merchants told the governor that if he did they would restart the agitation and, therefore, Daryabegi did nothing. The grand vizier also sent a telegram to Sayyed Morteza Ahrami making it clear that he expected him and other religious leaders to restrain people rather than inciting them to agitate. In reaction, Sayyed Morteza Ahrami circulated an open letter, in which he, referring to Koranic verses, stated that "believers should not tolerate oppression of Mohammedans by foreigners," hoping for renewed agitation to recall Mr. Heynssens.[349] When it became known that Tehran had instructed Daryabegi to suppress any agitation against the Customs Department or Heynssens, Sadr al-Eslam and Sayyed Morteza Ahrami jointly sent a protest telegram to Tehran urging the government to dismiss Heynssens, if only for his own protection, as he might by molested or even killed, if he returned to work. Also, he had defrauded 10,000 *tumans*. As a result, the people demanded that all Belgians be removed form the Customs Department. The governor did nothing and also remained silent when, in reaction, the people of Borazjan refused to pay their normal taxes. On 21 September 1906, Moshir al-Dowleh replied to Sayyed Morteza Ahrami saying that if he had proof of the alleged fraud that the government gladly would recover the 10,000 *tumans*. On that same day Daryabegi received orders to escort Mr. Heynssens to his work, which he did.[350] Sayyed Morteza Ahrami continued to make a name for himself and thus gained more influence, when Customs officials inspected the luggage of some pilgrims returning from Kerbela. Sayyed Morteza Ahrami wrote to Heynssens on 29 November that, as part of the settlement to end the recent agitation, it had been agreed that this inspection would be abolished. He also asked Heynssens to pay compensation to the boatmen, pay the arrears of a certain Sheikh Shahab, and threatened to launch demonstrations if his demands were not met. Heynssens asked the Daryabegi to take care of the matter, which he did.[351]

348. Political Diaries, vol. 1, pp. 438, 444, 451.
349. Political Diaries, vol. 1, pp. 458, 464.
350. Political Diaries, vol. 1, p. 469.
351. Political Diaries, vol. 1, p. 528.

On 7 October 1906, Mozaffar al-Din opened the constitutional assembly in Tehran and for three days Bushehr was decorated and illuminated.[352] A few days later Daryabegi convened a meeting on 22 October 1906 to arrange for the nomination of a deputy from Bushehr to the *Majles*. Two groups manifested themselves in the meeting; one favoring Mo`in al-Tojjar's nomination, the other opposing it. The meeting decided to postpone its decision until after Ramazan (17 November 1906). Therefore, it was only on 29 November 1906 that Daryabegi again held a meeting at Government House to read the royal edict granting the right of a national assembly (*Majles*) with branches in provincial towns. Daryabegi informed the meeting that three *Majles* members would be chosen from the Gulf Ports who each would receive 1,000 *tumans* per year. Further, that a local council of 'class' representatives should be formed and meet once a week at Government House to advise on local matters and complaints and that he had to act in harmony with their views. On 17 December another meeting was held, which failed to make any decision. There was no great interest to participate in this local council, in particular by the commercial community, while the guilds were not even invited. Moreover, people thought that the local council had to hear complaints, decide on them, or refer them to the religious court. Therefore, after the local council was formed it behaved as if the governor was subordinate to it and therefore, Daryabegi took advantage of their disagreements to do nothing. As a result, innumerable simple matters were not decided upon and accumulated "and Bushire may be said to have existed without a Government." To resolve this confusion the government in Tehran sent instructions on 7 February, how, as of 21 March 1907, the local councils had to operate. The mullahs who earlier had shown little interest, now feared that if the council functioned as it was intended it would take away half of their livelihood and perquisites and therefore, demanded to be made members as well. In April 1907, local elections were held and 15 representatives of four groups (clergy, merchants, landlords, and guilds) were chosen; merchants dominated the council. As of January 1907, the local newspaper *Mozaffari* was allowed to resume publication and the paper as well as its editor, Mirza `Ali Shirazi took an active part in political life. In 1903 he was bastinadoed and his paper suspended for printing articles against the British viceroy and advocating reforms. His writings, after the lifting of the ban, brought him into conflict with Sadr al-Eslam, the local Osuli *mojtahed*, who accused him of printing lies against a political opponent Haji `Abdol-Rasul, a leading merchant. Mirza `Ali Shirazi was maltreated by the clerics' followers and the right to publish his paper was suspended. He protested to Tehran and the Minister of the Interior had to give orders twice to lift the suspension and release its editor. Local political differences were not helped by the illness of Mozaffar al-Din Shah or by his death in early January 1907, the news of which was received calmly in Bushehr without the normal disturbances.

Experience with the Bushehr council was not promising. There was constant bickering in the meetings, fed by scurrilous pamphleteering and intrigues, which did not promote general peace and prosperity in the port. Daryabegi complained about the humiliating position he was in and the impossibility of exercising any effective authority. The British understood that he would bear the brunt of the nationalist criticism and pamphleteering, which they believed were encouraged by both German and Russian agents, despite their entente and the fact that these states had neither subjects nor much

352. Sa`adat 1390, p. 158; Political Diaries, vol. 1, pp. 492, 542-43 (Mo`in al-Tojjar arranged for his election from Tehran), 564.

trade in the Persian Gulf. Also, Great Britain was unpopular because of its strict enforcement of quarantine rules, suppression of slavery and arms traffic and the protection of Arab subjects of the Arab Sheikhdoms against Persian oppression and extortion.[353]

As expected there came some changes at the top of the local administration. Heynssens, the Belgian director of Customs in Bushehr, who was somewhat austere in his methods in dealing with locals, had caused much local enmity. In August 1906, a dispute between his staff and local lighter-men (see above) resulted in the transfer of Daryabegi and Heynssens a few months later. Heynssens believed that Daryabegi was the driving force against him, as his arrival made the governor's position subservient and undignified, but that does not seem to have been the case, at least according to the British Resident. Nevertheless, their relations became so strained that one had to go. In early December 1906, Daryabegi was recalled and Heynssens was transferred in February 1907. Daryabegi was replaced by Haji Sa`id al-Saltaneh, chief of police of Tehran, a friendly young man from Northern Persia with no experience with government or Persian Gulf conditions and policies. Daryabegi was able to convince the leading mullahs and merchants to send telegrams to Tehran expressing their satisfaction with his administration. He also, via his friend Mo`in al-Tojjar, sent 3,000 *tumans pishkesh* to Moshir al-Dowleh, which resulted in the cancellation of his recall. However, he was not sure whether he would be allowed to stay for long and therefore, sold his horses and much of his moveable property. On 13 December, Daryabegi was informed that the Shah had died and that he had keep to the town secure and keep watch on the tribes in the town's environs. Therefore, he moved to Moqam (9 km from Bushehr) with two field guns and 200 riflemen. However, shortly thereafter a telegram arrived making his recall final. Daryabegi, after many to's and fro's with Tehran, left on 30 January 1907.[354]

Sa`id al-Saltaneh arrived on 5 February. On arrival he made it known that (i) he was very rich and had no need for bribes; (ii) he hated lies and lying; and (iii) he wished all matters to be handled with perfect justice and the local council to continue its meetings. In a meeting with the clergy he informed them of his own religious qualifications as a sayyed and Haji.[355]

On 7 January 1907, a meeting was held of the local representative council at the *Chahar Borj*. The council consisted mostly of merchants and clergy; neither the artisan nor other classes were represented. Tigrane Malcolm having been invited by the governor to have the Armenian community appoint a councilmember declined to do so. A similar meeting of mullahs to select one of their number as a councilmember degenerated in discussing their personal animosities and the meeting dissolved. Certain mullahs also

353. Administration Report 1907-1908, p. 13; Political Diaries, vol. 1, p. 507.

354. Administration Report 1906-1907, p. 11; according to one source, Daryabegi had imported some rifles for himself, on which he did not want to pay customs duties. Therefore, he incited the lighter-men and a mullah to create trouble for Heynssens; he also once paid street boys and rowdies to threaten to beat up Heynssens when he was riding home on his bike, see Sa`adat 1390, p. 159. Political Diaries, vol. 1, pp. 551,559-60; vol. 2, p. 13-14, 31-32, 39 (Daryabegi could have stayed as governor if he would have paid 15,000 *tumans pishkesh*, 1,000 *tumans* more than his successor, but he did not have the money. He sold his house for 5,700 *tumans* to Tigrane Malcolm).

355. Political Diaries, vol. 2, p. 48. Despite his so-called 'religious qualifications' Sa`id al-Saltaneh seemed to have been an alcoholic. For at the end of August 1907, a man found 1,150 empty beer and wine bottles in the empty house of the former governor. During his five months in office he had invited neither Persians nor Europeans to his house. Political Diaries, vol. 2, p. 321.

combined their efforts to reduce Sadr al-Eslam's standing, because of his influence with the governor. "The fact being that if all claims are referred to the latter for decision, their own dignity will suffer and their incomes be reduced." After the meeting, on the morning of 17 January 1907, placards were found on the doors of coffeehouses and other places denouncing `Alam al-Huda and other minor mullahs. The governor had them removed. On 23 January the Daryabegi brought about a reconciliation between the Sadr al-Eslam and the Imam Jom`eh (respectively, leaders of the Osuli and Akhbari groups). He then suggested that they become members of the local council, which they refused given their age. He then asked them to appoint somebody, which was not acceptable to the other mullahs. Sayyed Morteza Ahrami protested and Daryabegi threatened to expel him if he incited people to riot. On 29 January 1907, the local council met at the house of Haji `Abdol-Rasul, which meeting Daryabegi attended. During the meeting a message from `Alam al-Huda, a dissenting mullah, arrived asking whether the meeting discussed the appointment of a representative of the clergy or other matters? When the council replied that its membership was complete he sent a protest to Tehran. On 30 January 1907, placards were found on the door of Haji `Abdol-Rasul's office, coffee-shops and other places warning him that if other council meetings were held in his house, he would be killed. The council's constitution was illegal and the people had not been able to vote and had protested in Tehran. Therefore, immediately a council meeting was held in Sadr al-Eslam's house. The *kargozar*, as acting governor, warned Sayyed Morteza Ahrami not to stir up trouble, who, in the knowledge of Tangestani support, remained defiant. A meeting held in mid-February in Haji `Abdol-Rasul's house to amiably settle the conflict about the selection of Sadr al-Eslam and Imam Jom`eh as council members failed. Although the two were popular, they were too old, while `Alam al-Huda was eligible, but not popular.[356] On 11 February 1907, a council meeting was held at the *Chahar Borj*, which, among other things decided that arrangements should be made for street cleaning and public lighting of the streets. The cost should be paid for out of a tax on the boatmen. No meetings were held during the month of Moharram (14 February-15 March 1907). Despite the quasi irrelevance of and general lack of public interest in the local council, it is interesting to note that when the governor had a butcher bastinadoed who had slaughtered a diseased goat, many people said that the governor should have referred the matter to the council.[357]

In the first week of March 1907, Haji `Abdol-Rasul (representative of the merchants) was slandered in abusive placards by his political opponents, among whom were Haji Sayyed Mohammad Reza and the editor of the newspaper *Mozaffari*. Sadr al-Eslam summoned the latter and berated him for publishing lies about `Abdol-Rasul. When he failed to give a satisfying answer Sadr al-Eslam struck him and the editor complained to the governor. Haji `Abdol-Rasul threatened to resign and after a meeting between him, Sadr al-Eslam and the governor made peace with this powerful group and promised to recall a close collaborator of `Abdol-Rasul, whom he had bastinadoed and then banished. The governor further imprisoned the editor of *Mozaffari* and suspended his newspaper; the next meeting of the council took place on 28 February. During a council meeting on 4 March 1907, the governor refused to release the editor at `Alam al-Huda's request. In a follow-up meeting `Alam al-Huda showed a telegram, allegedly from Tehran, ordering

356. Political Diaries, vol. 2, pp. 13-14, 20, 38-39, 49. For a description of one coffee-house, see Hamidi 1380, p. 477.

357. Political Diaries, vol. 2, pp. 60, 67.

the editor's release. Sadr al-Eslam tore up the telegram and accused `Alam al-Huda of supporting the editor in his scurrilous attacks. The governor said that he would take a decision after having consulted Tehran. On 9 March he released the editor, after the latter had apologized to Sadr al-Eslam.[358] Meanwhile, abusive placards were still thrown into the houses of certain political figures. The governor told Haji `Abdol-Rasul to ignore them, telling him that this was a common occurrence in Tehran, where even ministers were targeted that way. The council, fearing that the placards might have a negative impact on the *Majles*, sent a testimony (*esteshhad-nameh*) to Tehran denouncing the authors of the placards.[359]

On 24 March 1907, during a local council meeting, `Alam al-Huda protested against its constitution. After much discussion, six members were added to the council among whom was `Alam al-Huda, so that it now had 12 instead of the regulatory six members. Because of the constant bickering and conflicts the council had been unable to deal with matters of public justice and there was a considerable backlog of cases. On 25 March the governor invited the dissenting mullahs for lunch and made peace with them, so that their opposition against the addition of six members to the local council was dropped. Thereafter, all council meeting were indefinitely postponed by the governor. It was speculated that this was at the instructions from Tehran, which wanted the governor to foment dissent among the council members so that any form of local government would fail. Also, because its purpose was only to elect deputies for the *Majles*, not to concern itself with the administration of justice. In early April 1907, in imitation of the establishment of a so-called volunteer corps in other cities, some people in Bushehr decided to do the same. Some forty persons from the merchants class, including relatives of the principal merchants, were drilled by Nakhoda Ebrahim, the captain of the *Persepolis*. At first, the drill began indoors and with sticks only instead of rifles. Although the purpose of these National Volunteers, as they called themselves, was unclear it seemed that their interest was only to be used for local purposes. The governor complimenting the Volunteers said now Bushehr could also be called upon by Tehran to supply recruits, from which duty it was exempt so far. He received the five chiefs of the 130 men strong Volunteers force on 7 April and called them *mojahedin fi sabil ollah* (warriors in the path of god) and asked Tehran for permission to form this corps. Meanwhile, the distribution of anonymous fly-sheets continued, threatening to murder Haji `Abdol-Rasul if he attended the council and denouncing the Volunteer corps. The governor was said to have informed Tehran that he had suspended council meetings for one month, but on 10 April 1907 the council met, be it without the governor's approval. During this meeting Sadr al-Eslam and `Alam al-Huda agreed to withdraw from the council and appoint substitutes.[360]

On 18 April 1907, the local council met at the *Chahar Borj* and resolved the election of the representative of the clergy. The council members were the following:

> For the clergy: Sayyed Mohammad `Ali, Sayyed Morteza (Sadr al-Eslam's brother), Sayyed Mohammad Shafi`, Sayyed Morteza (`Alam al-Huda's brother). Sadr al-Eslam and Imam Jom`eh served as their advisors.

---

358. Political Diaries, vol. 2, pp. 76, 84.

359. Political Diaries, vol. 2, p. 94.

360. Political Diaries, vol. 2, pp. 105, 115, 124, 135; *Habl al-Matin* no. 31 (28 March 1907), p. 22 with an accurate report on the situation in Bushehr.

For the merchants: Haji `Abdol-Rasul.
For the notables: Sayyed Mohammad Reza, Haji Mirza Gholam Kazeruni, Haji Mohammad Hasan Borazjani, and Haji Mohammad Shafi`.
For the landed proprietors: Haji Mahmud, Haji Mohammad Ja`far, and Haji Mohammad `Ali Dashti.
For the artisans: Mirza `Ali Kazeruni, Haji Mohammad Taqi, and `Abdol-Reza.

Because Tehran had sent a strongly worded telegram urging the governor to sent a deputy to the *Majles* the local council elected Sayyed `Abdol-Reza Hakim, a local physician and a partisan of Mo`in al-Tojjar.

On 28 April 1907, `Alam al-Huda proposed in the weekly meeting of the local council that Persians should be warned not to take up service with foreigners and those not heeding this advice should be punished. However, neither the governor nor the local council agreed with him. The council also discussed the remuneration of its chosen deputy, but as no money was made available Sayyed `Abdol-Reza Hakim did not leave Bushehr. When at the end of April, Haji `Abdol-Rasul received the title of Ra'is al-Tojjar, mullahs who were hostile to him held a meeting and concluded that they would not recognize him as chairman of the local council, because he was now beholden to the government in Tehran.[361]

On 2 May 1907, the governor informed the council that at Tehran's instruction he would no longer attend the meeting, as the council had to be able to freely select representatives (no deputy had as yet been elected) or other matters. In case of need his deputy would attend. In the night of 6 May anonymous letters were thrown into people's homes abusing those council members who had not been popularly elected and sarcastic remarks were made about the mullahs. On 8 May 1907, placards lambasting `Alam al-Huda and Sayyed Morteza Ahrami were produced in a coffee shop. It was said that these had been made by followers of the Imam Jom`eh.[362]

On 7 May 1907, the local council met and the meeting was spent in acrimony, as usual. The governor was present, despite his earlier statement not to do so, which led to trouble. At the instigation of Sayyed Morteza Ahrami, he said that henceforth the participation of the representatives of the guilds was no longer needed. This led to a separate meeting at the Sadr al-Eslam's house on 9 May, attended by boatmen and the *nakhoda* class in large numbers, guild representatives and some merchants. The attending boatmen, who were about to be taxed to pay for local street cleaning measures, were in particular incensed and therefore, demanded to be present in the assembly. It was decided to insist on the independence of the council and support it "even to death." The governor was cursed and the boatmen threatened to strike and not serve the steamers, unless the governor allowed their representatives to take their place in the council.[363]

Because of the acrimonious relations nothing came of plans for street cleaning and lighting (see chapter 4) or of any other plans. On 2 May 1907, the local council met (present were 3 mullahs, 5 merchants and the governor) and discussed street lighting and

---

361. Political Diaries, vol. 2, pp. 146, 156-57.
362. Political Diaries, vol. 2, pp. 167, 178.
363. Political Diaries, vol. 2, p. 179.

the usurious practices by the soldiers. Also, around 20 June 1907, a meeting was held to discuss the water supply of Bushehr. There were three possible projects: (i) to bring water from Haviz at 40 km distance through pipes; (ii) to sink an artesian well at Rishahr; and (iii) to invest in a sea water condenser.[364]

As a result of the continuing animosity two 'parties' emerged. One led by Sadr al-Eslam, the other led by `Alam al-Huda and Sayyed Morteza Ahrami. The Imam Jom`eh remained neutral. As a result, the governor ordered Sayyed Morteza Ahrami to leave the council.[365] On 21 May 1907, the governor read a long telegram from the *Majles* addressed to all local councils that they should stop airing grievances through local agitation, but rather chose to contact the *Majles* for that purpose. Still no election had taken place, but at a subsequent meeting of merchants, three members were elected, viz. Haji `Abdol-Rasul, Sayyed Mohammad Reza and Haji Mohammad Shafi`, whose choice was accepted by the governor. Nevertheless, Mohammad Esma`il al-Musavi from Shiraz published a letter in the 30 April issue of the newspaper *Majles* calling the Bushehr local council "a plaything for the young and an object of ridicule for the old."[366]

Thereafter it appeared as if the council had ceased to exist as no weekly meetings were held. The governor proposed that instead of the council a commercial council be formed. On 5 June 1907, some merchants attended a meeting convened by the governor, who said that the continuous acrimonious debates had finished the local council and that henceforth, he intended to hold weekly meetings of merchants to discuss local commercial matters. However, the merchants were not interested in this kind of meeting and only two were present at the meeting of 12 May.[367] In June 1907, the circulation of anonymous abusive leaflets increased against which the governor took no steps at all. On 23 June a leaflet was distributed with caricatures of the governor, the *kalantar*, a chief adherent of a mullah, and a disreputable woman who had taken refuge in the mullah's house.[368]

Around 20 June 1907, a meeting was held in the *kargozar*'s office with the principal merchants. They discussed the local council, but Haji Mirza Gholam Hoseyn Kazeruni, the agent of Arbab Jamshid, said that as long as Haji `Abdol-Rasul and Haji Mohammad Reza remained enemies no deputy from Bushehr would be elected. It was decided to hold a meeting on 21 June at Mohammad Shafi`'s house to appoint 12 members of a council of merchants that would arrange for the election for the local council. Tehran also informed Haji `Abdol-Rasul that a new council had to be chosen, which led him to resign his claim to its presidency. A meeting of merchants on 28 June elected as their representatives: Haji `Abdol-Rasul and Haji Mohammad Shafi`, both as *ra'is al-tojjar*. The former refused the post, but his refusal was not accepted. On 5 July 1907, the guilds held a meeting to elect their representative to the local council. Mirza `Ali Kazeruni was chosen by the petty traders (*khordeh-forush*), drapers (*bazzaz*) and most grocers (*baqqal*), but Haji Sayyed Mohammad Reza objected arguing that one man could not represent all guilds.[369]

364. Political Diaries, vol. 2, pp. 167, 231.

365. Political Diaries, vol. 2, p. 186.

366. Political Diaries, vol. 2, pp. 194-95. The British considered Mohammad Shafi`, the most grasping merchant of Bushehr. Idem, vol. 2, p. 259.

367. Political Diaries, vol. 2, pp. 215, 224.

368. Political Diaries, vol. 2, pp. 223, 230.

369. Political Diaries, vol. 2, pp. 231, 240, 247.

On 17 July 1907, Sheikh Mohammad the Imam Jom`eh died of dysentery; his condition had been systematically neglected by his factotum Sheikh Mohammad. Only on the last day was a doctor sent for. He was the head of the Akhbaris and at one time had 1,000 followers, but many were driven away by his factotum's bad behavior. His son-in law Sheikh Mohammad `Ali was expected to be confirmed as the next Imam Jom`eh.[370]

On 26 July 1907, a meeting was held at the *Chahar Borj* where Haji `Abdol-Rasul, Haji Sayyed Mohammad Reza, Haji Mohammad Shafi`, Haji Mohammad `Ali Dehdashti, Sayyed `Abdol-Reza and Mirza `Ali Kazeruni were nominated as supervisors of the local council. Also, the governor announced his resignation. He asked for a testimony that he had oppressed nobody and had taken no money from anyone. People were glad that he left, because they had complained about his incompetence to Tehran. Indeed, Sa`id al-Saltaneh was unfit for his task and could not even keep order in Bushehr, let alone take care of the rest of his tasks. Insecurity in and around Bushehr had increased over the last few months due to the governor's incapability. Nevertheless, during the short time that he was governor, he managed to cause many headaches due to his decision to open the Shif route between Borazjan and Bushehr. It was believed he did so after having received a sum from the Khan of Angali, although traffic via this alternative route failed to take off. Many merchants suspected that Tehran had sent him to weaken the reform movement, in which he was successful by playing on the enmity and jealousy of the merchants. Before leaving Bushehr, the governor made it known that all civil pensions had been abolished, military pensions were reduced and his own salary of 7,000 was reduced to 1,000 *tumans*/year. However, the abolishment of the revenue assignments (*teyul*), as many other instructions from Tehran, remained a dead letter, because the governor lacked the power to implement them. He left on 20 January 1908 to Tehran and was robbed of all his goods and horses en route to Shiraz via Liravi. One year earlier, on his departure, Daryabegi had said that he expected to be back, and so he was. For Daryabegi was Sa`id al-Saltaneh's successor and he appointed the *kalantar* to be in charge of the town and the *kadkhoda* of the suburbs until his arrival. Sayyed Morteza Ahrami and Sayyed Javad protested against Daryabegi's return.[371]

On 1 August 1907, an informal meeting of the 12 principal merchants took an oath to work together to establish a local council. This committee called itself *anjoman-e ettehadiyeh* and actively tried to organize the election. They distributed voting papers to eligible voters, wich had to be filled out and returned before 21 August 1907. This was the first attempt to have a real election. It was expected that it would be successful if the process was completed before Daryabegi's arrival. Haji `Abdol-Rasul posted a notice that if elected he would not serve, which was a mere attempt to placate the governor. However, the merchants themselves unintentionally torpedoed the election. During a meeting of merchants to resolve the *hammal-bashi* problem voices were raised and one participant called Haji `Abdol-Rasul a "turkey-cock." He left immediately and went to Sadr al-Eslam who issued a statement that the election in the absence of the governor

370. Political Diaries, vol. 2, p. 269. Sheikh Mohammad fled, but later tried to return to Bushehr with the support of tribal chiefs, whom he had 'bought.' Idem, vol. 3, pp. 423, 467, 491. 504.

371. Political Diaries, vol. 2, pp. 259, 276-77, 285, 459; Administration Report 1907-1908, p. 7; Administration Report 1908, p. 7; Sa`adat 1390, p. 158 (Sa`id al-Saltaneh's most memorable deed was to take four cannons that had been stored in the Customs since 1901 and erect them in front of Government House).

was illegal. This statement reflected the sentiments of most of the olama, who were afraid of losing influence. Therefore, they opposed the election for the council in the absence of the governor. They argued that when Daryabegi returned the process could be started again. The merchants then posted a notice to the walls of the coffee-house stating that they had tried to collaborate with the olama to establish a local council, but that one of them dissented. Rather than cause agitation they, therefore, abandoned their effort. This event showed the olama's hostility to the council, which they feared would encroach upon their judicial monopoly.[372]

Daryabegi arrived on 23 August 1907. He was accompanied by a special official (*ma'mur*), tasked with revenue collection and its remittance to Tehran. Therefore, Daryabegi reintroduced illegal taxes, because they were included in his revenue contract. The petty trader, the butchers and a few drapers closed their shops out of protest against the continued exactions by the *kalantar*. They re-opened their shops, except the butchers, when threatened by the governor with punishment. On 26 August the five main butchers took refuge in Sadr al-Eslam's house. The *kalantar* then took 50 of their sheep and killed them. However, Sadr al-Eslam declared the meat to be unlawful. The next day, Daryabegi promised to suspend the *kalantar*'s exaction for one month, during which period they had to arrange that the Minister of Finance would eliminate the charge from the governor's revenue contract.[373]

On 26 August 1907, Daryabegi gave the 'supervisors' of the election permission to proceed. The voting cards in Haji `Abdol-Rasul's office were to be counted on 13 September in the Masjed-e Now, when the president of the local council would be elected. The election supervisors complained to the *Majles* about Haji `Abdol-Rasul's reactionary behavior, with whom they quarreled. However, the counting of votes did not take place as very few voting cards were filled out. On 16 September Daryabegi received a telegram from the *Majles* that the local council should consist of six not 12 members. He then convened a meeting of olama and chief merchants and explained that the system had to be changed. Sayyed Mohammad Reza protested against this and his rival Haji `Abdol-Rasul counter-protested, which led to an acrimonious exchange and the meeting broke up. Daryabegi arranged for a reconciliation, but each party complained about the other in telegrams to the *Majles*. In reply, the *Majles* stated that the election must be by social class. Because Daryabegi and the supervisors were at odds with each other nothing happened for a while. On 6 October Sayyed Morteza Ahrami sent a telegram to the *Majles* claiming the right to be election supervisor, because he was one of the first and hardest supporter of 'liberty.' On 2 October Haji Sayyed Ja`far Shirazi on behalf of the *Majles* sent a telegram to Bushehr that (i) elections by *afrad* (individuals) was presently harmful; (ii) election by *afrad* harmed the interests of the olama; (iii) Bushehr had to sent speedily two pious and capable deputies to Tehran.[374]

Daryabegi complained bitterly that local governors were prevented from settling disputes and suppressing agitation, because people would cry *zolm* or 'injustice' and the *Majles* would put a stop to any action he wanted to take. "He further stated that the people

372. Political Diaries, vol. 2, pp. 285, 294, 303; Martin 2000, p. 194. Turkey-cock or *buqlamun*, also means, 'chameleon,' and hence metaphorically is used to indicate changeability. Here the term clearly was used as a pejorative.

373. Political Diaries, vol. 2, pp. 310, 320.

374. Political Diaries, vol. 2, pp. 321, 331, 341, 352, 364, 374.

even here in Bushire understood the word 'liberty' and 'institution' to mean an opportunity for acting as they liked, and for displaying their own jealousies."[375] In November 1907, Daryabegi made a show of refusing to accept bribes by publicly returning money and presents offered to him. In the first part of November he made an effort to constitute a local council. During the festival (*eyd*) after Ramazan, when merchants called on him for congratulations he used the occasion to induce them to do so. On 10 November he published a statement in which he outlined all his efforts to get a council formed and how and who worked against him. Therefore, he was forced to take the initiative himself and force its constitution and fixed the following timetable for specific groups to meet and elect their representative:

Monday, 11 November: Guilds and traders
Tuesday, 12 November: Gentry and landowners
Wednesday, 13 November: Sailors and dealers in ships' stores
Thursday, 14 November: The great merchants
Friday, 15 November: The olama

Daryabegi also warned that non-attendance meant the loss of the right to vote in the future according to the Constitution. The result of the various meetings was:

Artisans: Mirza `Ali Kazeruni
Gentry: Haji Sayyed Mohammad Reza Kazeruni
Landowners: Sheikh Naser Khan
Sailors and ships chandlers: `Abdol-Reza b. Mohammad Qambar
Olama and *Rowzehkhvans*: Sheikh `Ali Dashti

Sadr al-Eslam raised an objection against merging olama with *rowzeh-khvans* as this was "not proper." The formal inauguration of the local council took place on 22 November 1907 in the presence of the governor, the principal merchants and the elected members, accompanied by music, at a house rented for its use, over which the national flag was flown. The rent of the house (144 *tumans*/year) and the wages of its servants (180 *tumans*/year) were paid by the council members.[376]

On 9 December 1907, Zayer Gholam Hoseyn, a Tangestani village chief (*kadkhoda*), came to complain to the local council that the Khan of Tangestan had forced him to pay more than his normal taxes. He was accompanied by 20 *tofangchis*, who, when they heard one of the council members say 'take him' (*begir*), thought that their chief was being arrested. They surrounded the building and aimed their rifles at the council. The Zayer had to climb on the roof to assure them that there was no problem and he was safe. On 13 December the council met to elect a deputy for Tehran, which, as usual, did not happen.[377]

---

375. Political Diaries, vol. 2, p. 419.
376. Political Diaries, vol. 2, pp. 428-29, 440, 465.
377. Political Diaries, vol. 2, pp. 464-65.

Local reaction to dissolution of the *Majles*

When on 17 December 1907, the news that Mohammad `Ali Shah had dissolved the *Majles* became known in Bushehr, it caused little uproar. A meeting of the local council was convened and a telegram was sent that the people of Bushehr were prepared to support the *Majles* and sacrifice their lives. On 20 December another meeting was held, which decided to send telegrams to councils in other towns as well as one to the shah informing him that Bushehr would only obey his commands when he supported the *Majles*. Daryabegi approved of the council's messages, but suggested to send even a stronger worded telegram than the Tabriz council had sent to Tehran. Despite the turmoil in the rest of Persia after the abrogation of the Constitution Bushehr remained quiet. According to the British Resident, that was because, "the Bushiri of course regards his town as distinct from Persia and all the current generation wants is some reasonably form of government under which he can pursue his business avocations undisturbed." The fact that the local council was formed two years later than elsewhere in Persia was indicative that there was limited interest in the subject. Moreover, once the local council had been formed it did not inspire great confidence as it was presided over by "a disreputable trader named Mirza `Ali, [and] it interfered with every matter, great and small." Cases were even more difficult to resolve than previously and the average Bushehri got tired of the assembly "and of the busybodies composing it." And when it was abolished after the coup d'état, people experienced it as a relief not even with apathy as in Shiraz.[378] In fact, there was disillusionment with the reform movement among the merchant class. The chief merchant of Bushehr publicly stated in the local council: "I wanted a liberal Government, but now I see that it is a failure for two reasons: firstly, it has brought disrespect on myself and on other merchants, whereas formerly I was respected by all. Now every low class man in the town is free to lampoon me; secondly, this form of government has been in existence two years and it has only become a cause of insecurity for our trade and of ruination of commerce."[379]

Therefore, it was not surprising that by the beginning of 1908, a *Majles* deputy from Bushehr was still not present in Tehran. This again led to some local acrimony and the holding of an election for this deputy in February 1908. Although a new council had been chosen, a *Majles* deputy from Bushehr still was not present in Tehran. There was continued polarization, even within likeminded groups such as olama and merchants. During Daryabegi's absence at Bandar Abbas, some 30 Bushehris (apart from the German Mirza, men of no importance) formed an *anjoman-e safa'i* (Purity council) and asked for recruits. On his return Daryabegi scolded his deputy for allowing this and promised to suppress the group. He did so, because when he had been away he had formed a corps of volunteers at Bandar Abbas and Lengeh and probably wanted to have the initiative to do the same in Bushehr. The *anjoman-e safa'i* complained to the council that the vessels of the Customs Department were more expensively operated than necessary. The local assembly decided to ask for comments from the Department and further suggested that it hire Indian rather than Baghdadi engineers. The *anjoman* further demanded more transparency with regard to the revenue situation and the government departments, while it championed

---

378. Administration Report 1908, p. 2.

379. Political Diaries, vol. 2, pp. 471-72, 477; Administration Report 1907-1908, p. 12; Administration Report 1905-1906, p. 23.

the cause of the local garrison, whose soldiers had not been paid and were maltreated. The latter sought asylum and then they were paid. On 27 December the merchants also met and decided to form a third *anjoman*. On 6 January 1908, some 30 merchants formed the *anjoman-e tejarat* to promote trade. To make clear that this commercial council was composed of common people, and therefore, of no importance, Mirza Gholam Hoseyn Kazeruni, Sayyed Mohammad Reza and other leading merchants telegraphed the Minister of Commerce that the *anjoman* had nothing to do with them. In mid-January 1908, the mullahs formed a fourth *anjoman* called *anjoman-e Showkat-e Eslam* (council for the glory of Islam). However, the Imam Jom`eh and Sayyed Javad did not join. This new *anjoman* decided to hold a first meeting on 30 January and that none of the members would attest documents without the knowledge of the other members, while all sums received for attestation would be accounted for to the anjoman. In short, its aim was to safeguard the prerogatives of the olama in all legal matters. It further wanted that the rules of the market inspector (*hisbah*) be applied. Therefore, it ordered the *kalantar* to examine weights in the bazaar and to report those who used false weights. It also intended to levy one-fifth (*khoms*) from the income of merchants and others as dues to their religious guides, i.e. themselves. The various new *anjomans* decided not allow employees of foreign consulates to join them, while the foreign consulates decided to prohibit their employees to join such organizations. To create even more confusion around 20 March a fifth, the *anjoman-e akhavi* was formed. Its objectives were not known, but its members were mostly from Behbahani quarter. Finally, in mid April 1908, an *anjoman-e `edalat*, the sixth one, was formed, which was mainly composed of fraudulent debtors and their friends.[380]

Not to be outdone by the creation of these various interest groups, which might steal his thunder, in mid-January 1908, Sayyed Morteza Ahrami sent a telegram to the *Majles* complaining that the Bushehr council was not active and many complaints were not dealt with. Also, that Sheikh `Ali Dashti was incompetent and therefore, a new representative of the olama needed to be chosen. On 7 March 1908, Sayyed Morteza Ahrami and Sayyed Javad sent a telegram to Tehran complaining that Mas`ud Soltan, the *kargozar* favored the British at the expense of Persians.[381]

The various *anjomans* also wanted to be heard and made more noise than the local council. In January 1908, the *anjoman-e tejarat* made a concrete proposal to the *Majles* to pay off the Russian debt. It suggested that Persia's population amounted to some 15 million, of which 2.5 million were wealthy. If this wealthy part of the population would each pay 1 *tuman*/month for 12 months this would yield 30 million *tumans*, which was enough to pay off the Russian debt and allow Persia to begin with a clean sheet. The *Majles* replied that it liked the idea, but this was not the time to do it. It its turn, the *anjoman-e safa'i* sent letters to the *Majles* asking, as a citizen's right to know, that the governor and the head of the Customs Department submit documents so that their management of revenues and expenditures might be controlled. It also accused the local council of being too timid, which did not reply, but complained to the governor. The governor sent his deputy to the *anjoman* apologizing for the council's attitude and offered 500 *qrans* for the *anjoman*'s expenses, which it declined. The Customs Department informed the council that it was unable to provide it with the information asked for. On 8 February 1908,

---

380. Political Diaries, vol. 2, p. 477; vol. 3, pp. 18, 30, 41, 51-52, 86, 109, 120, 146; Martin 2000, pp. 194-98. On the *hisbah*, see Floor 1971b and Idem 1985.

381. Political Diaries, vol. 3, pp. 30, 101.

the *anjoman-e safa'i* published a letter asking the governor to form a so-called *edareh-ye nazmiyeh* or to allow it to ask the *Majles* to allow it do it. The governor replied that they should wait till *Nowruz*, when he would know whether he would still be governor.[382]

Having been rebuffed by the governor and the Customs Department for asking for their financial statements the council sent a telegram to Tehran. The Minister of Finance replied that this was none of their business and that they should ask the *Majles* for that information. One week later he informed the council that it could ask the governor. However, when they did so the governor refused, claiming to have no such orders from Tehran.[383] Undaunted by its relative lack of success the *anjoman-e safa'i* wanted to open a tannery to which end it created a company and sought a capital of 5,000 *tumans* with 500 shares; 4,400 allegedly had already been subscribed.[384] At that time anonymous leaflets were distributed stating that a secret society had been formed aimed at removing tyrants. It was believed that these were written by the *anjoman-e safa'i*. One week later the threat was repeated, stating that if a member tried to impede the functioning of the council, he would be dealt with. The text also mentioned that the secret society had 27 members.[385]

Because of all the acrimony, slander, threats, lack of any hope of making difference, or just for financial reasons, some council members resigned. Sheikh `Ali Dashti resigned from the council as his promised remuneration was not paid. Daryabegi offered him 1,000 *qrans* if he stayed. The representative of the gentry Naser Khan Chahkutahi also resigned. In the beginning of May 1908, Sayyed Mohammad Reza, representative of the gentry, made it known that was not willing to bear the expenses of the council's upkeep and resigned. Haji `Abdol-Rasul, a leading merchant and Sheikh Naser, resigned as well. The first two were the most influential members. Haji Mohammad Ja`far and Sheikh `Abdol-Nabi (Fakhr al-Eslam) were elected to replace the two who resigned; Sheikh Naser was urged to stay and accepted.[386]

Sayyed Morteza Ahrami was very active and gained in influence, also through his links with some of the more radical-leaning *anjomans*. For example, when on 7 March 1908, the governor bastinadoed and imprisoned the *hammal-bashi* who had spoken ill of him in the council, it was Sayyed Morteza Ahrami who interceded and not only arranged for his release, but also that he was given a shawl as a present (*khel`at*). Furthermore, at the suggestion of the *anjoman-e safa'i* the council chose Mirza `Ali Kazeruni, the representative of the artisans and Sayyed Morteza's henchman, as its president. When on 17 March 1908, the mullahs met in council Sayyed Morteza Ahrami argued for sending Tangestanis to help the olama of Shiraz.[387] In mid-April 1908, nationalist fervor increased, so that members of the *anjoman-e ettehadiyeh* enlisted as national volunteers and were drilled by Shoja` al-Mamalek. At the beginning of May, the *anjoman-e safa'i* members also began taking drill lessons. Mirza Hoseyn of the German consulate presented 20 so-called uniforms made of grey shirting to the volunteer members of the *anjoman-e safa'i*.[388]

---

382. Political Diaries, vol. 3, pp. 59, 67.
383. Political Diaries, vol. 3, pp. 66, 75.
384. Political Diaries, vol. 3, p. 153.
385. Political Diaries, vol. 3, p. 59.
386. Political Diaries, vol. 3, pp. 41-42, 51, 166.
387. Political Diaries, vol. 3, pp. 100, 120-21.
388. Political Diaries, vol. 3, pp. 146, 158, 172.

A great many people believed that Daryabegi was in secret trying to undermine the council; he visited the *anjomans*, encouraging them to critically follow its activities. The local council informed the various *anjomans* that they had no official standing and therefore, should not communicate directly with the government. However, they ignored this, the more so since the governor encouraged them to have direct contact, which lend credence to those who believed that Daryabegi was undermining the council.[389]

The Shah sent a telegram saying that although a constitutional monarch he could not accept the agitation by ill-intended people. He instructed the governor to deal with disturbers of the peace. This was followed by telegrams from various cities stating that the shah's promises could not be trusted. Around 10 June 1908, some petty merchants asked Sayyed Morteza Ahrami to head a demonstration in support of the *Majles*; they also intended to make the IBP and Customs stop working. Supported by Mirza `Ali Kazeruni, president of the council and Sayyed Baqer they occupied the council room and incited people to close their shops. The shops in the bazaar remained closed until 20 June, when people had enough. At first the governor did not act, but on 18 June he harangued the demonstrators pointing out that this action did not help the *Majles*. If they really wanted to help they had to collect money and send it. The rowdies frightened the merchants and traders who wanted to open their shops. The agitators received financial support from a collection held in town to which the German dragoman (10 *tuman*) and the broker of Wonckhaus (5 *tumans*) contributed.[390]

In mid-June 1908, Daryabegi hired a large number of *tofangchis* to guard the suburbs. After the bombardment of the *Majles* on 23 June, Daryabegi convened the local council on 25 June and told its members that he had orders to dissolve it and asked its members not to hold any meeting. Apart from the president nobody objected; the other members told the president to accept reality and overruled him. The bazaars which had been closed off and on since 14 June re-opened on 25 June and remained open; the town remained quiet. The news of Mohammad `Ali Shah's coup d'etat was received in Bushehr without much concern. At Daryabegi's request the local *anjomans* were also discontinued. On 29 June, Daryabegi received orders to watch the council members closely; its president did not leave his house.[391] The governor informed people that henceforth he would hear civil cases himself.[392]

In mid-August 1908, Mohammad `Ali Shah asked Daryabegi to sent 20,000 *tumans*; he replied that he had already paid last year's revenue and could not collect this amount. One week later the shah telegraphed him again for an advance of the current year's revenue and this time the governor sent the money via Arbab Jamshid's agent, but he asked for a written assurance that the amount would be refunded if he was recalled before year's end. By the end of the month he had not received such assurance, while there was talk that he would be replaced. In fact, having been unable to pay another larger sum, Daryabegi was replaced on 8 September, when Mo`azzez al-Dowleh telegraphed Shoja` al-Mamalek, the artillery officer to take charge of the town on his behalf. On 10 September 1908, Daryabegi received a telegram questioning why he had handed over government. He

389. Political Diaries, vol. 3, pp. 51-52, 172.
390. Political Diaries, vol. 3, pp. 192-93, 200.
391. Political Diaries, vol. 3, pp. 205-06, 210.
392. Political Diaries, vol. 3, p. 222.

Sayyed Morteza Ahrami

then went to the *Chahar Borj* with many *tofangchis*, but Shoja` al-Mamalek also had many musketeers. After some shooting it was agreed that he would leave after dark to save face. Daryabegi was helped with 3,500 *tumans* from Sheikh Hoseyn of Chahkutah so that he was able to send the full demanded amount to Tehran and secure his post. This meant that the governor had to favor the Ahmadi route. However, on 14 September he was dismissed after all and left via Mohammareh to Tehran. Shoja` al-Mamalek took charge of the government again on behalf of Mo`azzez al-Dowleh. On 11 October 1908 the latter arrived in Bushehr.[393]

Mohammad `Ali Shah's coup d'etat caused disturbances throughout the country. Copies of the olama of Najaf's telegram denouncing the Shah's coup d'etat were posted in several streets in Bushehr, as well as a copy of a cartoon from *Punch*, showing the Shah's closing of the *Majles*. On 6 November 1908, a placard was posted in the bazaar and coffee

393. Political Diaries, vol. 3, pp. 258, 262-63, 269, 275, 280, 301.

shop asking people to contribute money for the revolutionaries of Tabriz and to refuse paying taxes. It was removed and taken to the governor.[394] In Bushehr, there was no one in authority to take matters in hand. Daryabegi was replaced in October 1908 by the amiable and opium-smoking Mo`azzez al-Dowleh, who was as incapable as his brother Asaf al-Dowleh, the incapable governor-general of Fars. When he was in Bushehr he made not "the least attempt to govern." The *sowars* hired by the local government to guard the suburbs were not paid since the new governor's arrival. They threatened to leave if they were not paid. Mo`azzez al-Dowleh arrived in October 1908 and after one month left to Chabahar where he remained the rest of the year. Therefore, to conduct any business in his absence was difficult, which for the British in particular meant the settlement of commercial claims.[395] On 1 January 1909, 150 soldiers arrived under Mirza Ahmad Khan as the new garrison. He had to collect the revenue from Dashti and Dashtestan whose Khans refused to pay following the orders from the olama of Kerbela, and thus, they returned empty-handed. However, after much pressure Zayer Khedr paid 300 out of the 2,000 *tumans* due.[396]

The existing local power vacuum demanded to be filled and the man who felt that he should heed the call was the Tangestani mullah Sayyed Morteza Ahrami, who had been active in Bushehr politics since 1906. Who was this Sayyed, who had come out of nowhere and had acquired an increasingly influential role? Sayyed Morteza, a native of Ahram (hence his sobriquet Ahrami), was about 42 years old at that time. He was a newcomer, who had studied 8 years in Shiraz and thereafter for some time in Najaf. He returned in 1900 to Ahram, where he established himself with the title of Mofattesh al-Olama. Here he acquired influence among the Tangestanis, on whose support he totally depended, and after some time he settled in Bushehr. Because of his contacts with government officials in Bushehr and Tehran he rose in people's estimation. His chief advisor at that time was Mashhadi `Ali Ahrami, the *farrash-bashi* of the French Consulate.[397]

Tangestanis occupy Bushehr

In engineering the uprising of March 1909, Sayyed Morteza Ahrami, was partly inspired by the activities of Sayyed `Abdol-Hoseyn Lari and partly by the exhortations of olama of Najaf, who, according to the British Resident, "realized when it was too late that they had misplaced their confidence."[398] Sayyed `Abdol-Hoseyn Lari led an Islamic movement in Lar, but after he had been expelled from Lar in 1907 by Zell al-Soltan, he had been living off the land, i.e., loot taken from the lands and properties of his enemies, in particular Qavam al-Molk. With the fall of Mohammad `Ali Shah, the succession by his minor son Ahmad Shah, and the establishment of a powerless regency government he

394. Political Diaries, vol. 3, pp. 320, 324.

395. Administration Report 1907-1908, p. 7; Administration Report 1908, p. 7; Political Diaries, vol. 3, p. 395; Sa`adat 1390, pp. 158-60.

396. Political Diaries, vol. 3, p. 414.

397. Political Diaries, vol. 1, pp. 469-70.

398. Administration Report 1909, p. 11. This was not entirely true. In mid-April 1908, Mohammad Kazem Khorasani had criticized the local council for its constant bickering and differences and exhorted its members to unite to support the Constitution and "keeping the public peace." However, when Sayyed Morteza Ahrami was sent to Najaf, he proposed to send him back to Bushehr, which the local council, including some local mullahs, strongly opposed. Political Diaries, vol. 3, pp. 576, 705, 721, 762.

saw an opportunity to make a come-back. As of January 1909, Sayyed `Abdol-Hoseyn Lari tried to kindle the revolutionary spirits of the people of the Garmsir by a mixed message of religious exhortation and the promise of non-payment of taxes. Via a network of agents Sayyed `Abdol-Hoseyn Lari sought to mobilize support for his cause. One these agents was Sayyed Asadollah Esfahani, *pish-namaz* of Jahrom, who arrived from Kerbela in Bushehr. He immediately tried to create trouble for the Customs Department, because its revenues were the main source of income for Mohammad `Ali Shah. However, there was not much support for his call to action and on 19 February 1909 he left via Lengeh to Lar. He allegedly carried letters from the Khans of Dashti and Dashtestan to Sayyed `Abdol-Hoseyn as well as a letter from the president of the former local council who offered to establish a new one if the Sayyed wanted this. The cold shoulder treatment to the Sayyed's agent was partly due to the fact that during an earlier visit he was suspected of being a Babi. What was also worrisome was the news that Sayyed Asadollah convened several meetings in which he agitated against the Customs.[399] Given these developments is was no surprise that in early February 1909, Tehran telegraphed (probably at the suggestion of the Customs Department) that the governor had urgently to return to Bushehr "to maintain more order in the Gulf." It was expected that he would be recalled, the more so since Daryabegi informed friends that he would become governor again after Nowruz.[400]

Although the Bushehris were not willing to follow Sayyed Asadollah Esfahani, he certainly inspired Sayyed Morteza Ahrami. In fact, in the first week of February 1909, the latter considered organizing an uprising but he abandoned the idea lacking the necessary funds.[401] This failure to act apparently was reported to Sayyed `Abdol-Hoseyn Lari, who was said to have scolded Sayyed Morteza Ahrami for having kept quiet instead of opposing the shah. He then allegedly contacted Zayer Khedr to send Tangestanis to Bushehr to create disturbances. The British Resident urged the deputy-governor to be on his guard. The *kargozar* told Sayyed Morteza Ahrami that any such action only would invite foreigners to interfere, which seemed to have a salutary effect, be it a temporary one. The rumors of an uprising were strong enough that the Russian Consul-General contacted the British Resident as to whether their offices should be moved, but the deputy-governor said he had taken precautionary measures. Both the Rishahr *kadkhoda*, a Tangestani, and Zayer Khedr had given assurances that the Tangestanis would cause no trouble.[402]

Sayyed `Abdol-Hoseyn Lari wrote another letter to Sayyed Morteza stating that he had ordered the people of Lengeh and Bandar Abbas to expel the Belgian Customs officials and instead replace them with a national Persian Customs Department. He added that Bushehris, led by Sayyed Morteza, should be trailblazers so that others would follow their example. He also wrote a victory letter (*fathnameh*) to the Khans of Dashti and Dashtestan ordering them not to pay their taxes.[403]

Around 12 March 1909, Sayyed Morteza Ahrami received a telegram from the Kerbela and Najaf olama ordering that no customs revenues should be paid to the Belgian

---

399. Political Diaries, vol. 3, pp. 441, 467, 476; Sarvestani 1383, p. 148; see also Sayyed Morteza Ahrami's letter attacking Qavam al-Molk and Daryabegi and the request from some people in Lengeh to have Sayyed Morteza come to their aid. Ranjbar 1389, pp. 91-93.

400. Political Diaries, vol. 3, pp. 455, 467.

401. Political Diaries, vol. 3, p. 467.

402. Political Diaries, vol. 3, p. 485, for another version of this rumor, see Idem p. 492.

403. Political Diaries, vol. 3, p. 492.

officials and to expell them. Similar messages were sent to the leading merchants. The latter didn't know what to do; they didn't want to ignore the olama, but at the same time their business depended on foreign credit and the relations with foreign merchants. Sayyed Morteza Ahrami suggested that they clear their goods through customs but pay the duties into the IBP, stating that it should not be paid to the Shah or his officials. This was not realistic and to gain time they telegraphed the olama in Kerbela asking whether the messages were genuine.[404]

Sayyed `Abdol-Hoseyn Lari continued to incite local mullahs in the Gulf Ports to rouse the people to drive out the Belgian Customs agents and take control of the customs receipts. His call to action and arms had success in Bushehr, where his message about the customs receipts appealed to the Tangestani followers of Sayyed Morteza Ahrami, who gave their activities a sheen of religious legitimacy. Their foray into Bushehr was made even more attractive by the governor's absence in Mekran and the knowledge that the garrison of 200 Isfahani *tofangchis* would not oppose them. In short, Sayyed Morteza Ahrami had an easy task when taking over Bushehr.[405]

The first sign that an uprising was in the making came around 20 March 1909, when the Persian telegraph chief made it known that Sayyed Morteza Ahrami had received a telegraphic letter of credit for 1,000 *tumans* from Sayyed `Abdol-Hoseyn's agent in Bandar Abbas to overthrow the regime in Bushehr and take control of the Customs.[406] This news seemed to have some basis in fact, because Sayyed Morteza Ahrami started gathering *tofangchis* and making other preparations for a takeover. He only waited for the mourning months (23 January to 23 March 1909) to be over. On 22 March 1909, ostensibly to support the nationalist cause, Sayyed Morteza Ahrami with a large number of armed Ahrami and other villagers[407] took control of Bushehr. On that same day, the *Mir Panj* or garrison commander convened the officials, mullahs and merchants to discuss the situation. During this meeting Sayyed Morteza showed orders from the olama of Kerbela forbidding the payment of taxes to the shah. One mullah asked whether the orders were genuine, but he was told to shut up. Sayyed Morteza Ahrami with 300 *tofangchis* nearby told the meeting that he would kill anyone who disagreed with him. He asked officials to join his movement, but they resigned, being afraid of their life and property. After the meeting Sayyed Morteza Ahrami accompanied by some mullahs and merchants went to *Chahar Borj* where he raised the constitutional flag[408] and had a 21 salute fired. The victors sent the following telegram to Najaf: "city taken; assembly opened; customs taken; government fled, nation victor." On 24 March the Sayyed sent a letter to the consuls announcing that he taken over the government on behalf of the Nation. Further, that many officials had resigned and that he had assumed their functions. Finally, that he had taken steps to keep order and safety for foreigners. Tehran reacted immediately by awarding the Sayyed

404. Political Diaries, vol. 3, p. 504.

405. Sa`adat 1390, p. 161 has 400 soldiers.

406. Political Diaries, vol. 3, p. 515.

407. Sa`adat 1390, p. 162 (Ra'is `Ali Delvar 70 men; Zayer Khedr Khan 120 men; Sheikh Hoseyn Khan Chahkutahi 60 men; Ahmad Khan, son of Heydar Khan 30 men; and Hasan Bakhshu 30 men, or a total of 310 men).

408. In the Fifth Amendment to the Constitution of 1906, the lion and sun motif in the flag of Iran was described as a passant lion that holds a saber in its paw and with the sun in its background. A decree dated September 4, 1910 specified the exact details of the logo, including the lion's tail ("like an italic S"), the position and the size of the lion, his paw, the sword, and the sun.

with the title Nezam al-Olama and the news that Daryabegi had been reappointed governor. The Sayyed replied that he refused the title and did not recognize the government in Tehran until the *Majles* was restored. Mo`in al-Tojjar telegraphed the Sayyed to be moderate and above all not to rebel against the shah. He telegraphed, Mullah Hoseyn, the Ottoman vice-consul and his friend, urging him to pacify the Sayyed and give him information.

On 23 March 1909, Mostafa Navvab arrived at the Customs House on behalf of the Sayyed and demanded an immediate payment of 1,000 *tumans*. Mr. Zwinne refused, although the Customs House was occupied by Tangestanis. The next day the Sayyed opened negotiation with Zwinne asking him to continue in his function on behalf of the Nationalists. Zwinne was willing to accept on condition that the receipts would be paid into the IBP or a respectable merchant until matters were resolved. The Sayyed refused this, but in the afternoon he ordered the customs staff to return to duty on pain of losing their house and property. Zwinne advised them to comply; Moses Khan was appointed acting director, against his wishes, but he was left no choice. The occupation of the Customs House worried the British as its revenues were security for the £300,000 loan to Persia and its monthly 30,000 *tumans* revenues were pledged to the IBP to pay the interest on advances and overdrafts to the Shah and his ministers. The British consul, who was only allowed to have informal contacts with the Nationalists, contacted them and explained the situation and expressed the hope that like in the north, where Nationalist leaders continued to process Russian claims, they would do likewise with British claims in Bushehr. However, despite specific orders from Najaf and Tehran that British claims were in order and must be respected Sayyed Morteza Ahrami used the Customs revenues as spoils to distribute among his *tofangchis*. He broke open the Customs safe and divided about 20,000 *tumans*. The Customs were open for business on 25 March and 3,000 *tumans* were collected, which were paid to Haji Mirza Gholam Hoseyn Kazeruni to hold for the Sayyed, who thus became the unwilling banker of the Nationalists.[409]

Mo`azzez al-Dowleh, the governor of Bushehr, returned from Mekran on 25 March 1909. He had no idea what had happened meanwhile in Bushehr, because when he set foot on the wall he was immediately arrested and placed in a private house at Sayyed Morteza Ahrami's orders. This was said to be done for his own sake, as well as to ensure his brother's good behavior (Asaf al-Dowleh, the governor-general of Fars). Because he did not trust the Sayyed, Mo`azzez al-Dowleh sought asylum in the British Residency a few days later. He stayed there until the Sayyed pledged that he was allowed to leave to Shiraz, which he did; later that year he died in Tehran. On 26 March, Ahmad Khan Tangestani, son of Heydar Khan and Zayer Hoseyn Bakshu arrived with some 300 *tofangchis*, making a total of 1,000 riflemen. As the new arrivals had a blood feud with Zayer Khedr, fights were expected to break out among them. The Khan of Borazjan offered to send 1,000 *tofangchis*, while Heydar Khan of Rig refused to give any help, being opposed to the the Nationalists.[410]

---

409. Administration Report 1909, pp. 10-12; Political Diaries, vol. 3, pp. 522-23; FO 248/96, Telegram Cox, 29-30/03/1909; FO 248/96, "National Movement" Cox 31/03/1909; Faramarzi 1390, pp. 30-33 (with picture of Sayyed Morteza); Bashiri 1367, vol. 2, p. 116; Vothuqi 1375, pp. 137-38. For the situation in Lengeh and Bandar Abbas, see Floor 2010 and Idem 2011 a.

410. Administration Report 1909, p. 8; Sa`adat 1390, p. 166; Political Diaries, vol. 3, pp. 523-24; FO 248/96, "National Movement" Cox 31/03/1909.

On 29 March Sayyed Morteza Ahrami wrote to the British Resident stating that: "one of the first duties of national party is to preserve the undoubted interests of [the] British Government and nation." He proposed to set aside 500 *tumans* daily of the Customs revenues to pay for the daily expenses of the *tofangchis* and to entrust the remainder to trustworthy Persian merchants to be selected by both sides for a period of three months, during which their differences on the issue of the Customs revenues might be settled. However, the British wanted the money to be paid into the IBP. Also, they did not have much faith in the Sayyed. He called himself the President of the Nationalists, but he had been unable to induce people to work with him or to form an *anjoman*. Cox described him as "a half educated fanatic mullah who merely controls the situation owing to the fact that he is a native of [the] immediate hinterland and can at any time call in a mob of Tangistani riflemen as he had done in the present case. ... Persian public whether nationalist or otherwise have no confidence in bona fides or personal integrity of Seyyid." Therefore, Cox replied to the Sayyed's letter that he considered it an opening to serious and friendly negotiations.[411]

Meanwhile, Sayyed Morteza Ahrami tried to govern Bushehr. He was supported by Aqa Mostafa Navvab, "a petty local merchant of evil reputation who is a claimant for British protection, but whom the Residency refuses to recognize" and Mirza `Ali Kazeruni, "also a petty merchant of shady character, indebted to British and other merchants for some 13,000 tomans." It was also believed that he was covertly supported by Mirza Hoseyn, dragoman of the German consulate. As the Sayyed was unschooled in financial, administrative and other essential matters, these three acted as his advisors and collaborators. As soon as it became known that Sayyed Morteza Ahrami had distributed the customs receipts among his *tofangchis*, many trouble seekers from the entire countryside (Tangestan, Dashti) came to Bushehr, some at the Sayyed's request, others on their own accord. Sayyed Morteza Ahrami claimed he had 3,000 men for which he needed to draw on the customs receipts for their daily wages, despite opposition from members of the local assembly. His force was estimated to be 1,000 and never more than 1,500. That number of armed peasants constituted a threat to public safety of Bushehr. They soon acted on their own and the Sayyed then claimed it was not his responsibility. However, there was no other authority to maintain order and guarantee safety of life and property. The population was on guard on top of their roofs, "firing promiscuously into the air or over the roofs of their houses." Gangs of *tofangchis* were looking for loot and booty, but between many of them there was a blood feud, which they sometimes tried to settle in Bushehr. As a result, there were constant troubles. Fearing for people's safety the British Resident ordered *HMS Fox* to come to Bushehr from Bandar Abbas. On 2 April it arrived in the roads where it remained. Meanwhile, things were getting out of hand, while the number of *tofangchis* grew.[412]

The merchants were not impressed with the Sayyed's governance and did not want to share any responsibility. However, when a small group among them noticed that there were various groups among the *tofangchis* who were hostile to each other they tried to induce the Sayyed to change his behavior or to find himself in opposition. On Friday 2 April 1909, he agreed to have that day's receipts paid into the IBP in the joint name of

---

411. FO 249/960, Telegram Resident Cox to Tehran, 28 March 1909.
412. Administration Report 1909, p. 12; FO 248/96, "National Movement" Cox 06/04/1909.

three respected merchants. On 3 April they tried to convince the Sayyed to submit an accounting of the money received so far, but he evaded doing so. Meanwhile, his lieutenants, Mostafa Navvab and Mirza `Ali appeared to be deserting to the opposition, while some sections of the *tofangchis* had already deserted him. Therefore, on 4 April he informed the Resident that he had resigned and was no longer responsible for law and order.[413]

Despite his resignation, the Sayyed did not allow Mirza Ahmad Khan, the nominal Nationalist governor to assume his function. The local committee also allowed him to resume control on his terms. They met on 6 April 1909 and it was decided that the Sayyed would receive a salary of 300 *tumans*/month and the *tofangchis* 2 *qrans* per day. The committee also decided not to ask an accounting of the 18,000 *tumans* already received, which, ostensibly was for payment of the *tofangchis*. On 7 April the Resident met with the three merchants on the committee in whose name the Customs receipts were now being paid. They told the Resident they could not do anything, in fact they were terrified and asked for British protection. The Sayyed had decreed that the *tofangchis* be paid daily out of the Customs receipts. However, on 7 April the receipts were insufficient and the *tofangchis* were unwilling to wait till the next day. On 8 April, they ran into town and looted the food bazaar before sunset and during that night stole many merchandise and piece goods. This caused a panic and the closure of the bazaar. On that same day, the British Resident sent messages to the members of the local committee, protesting against the violence and looting and warning that this might have consequences if not corrected. When no reply was given the Resident warned the committee that unless it took action he would have to put in their place troops to protect British subjects and other foreigners. Finally, the Sayyed, the merchants and Mirza Ahmad Khan replied, admitting that they were not responsible for maintaining law and order in the town; moreover, they could not control the *tofangchis* and even asked the British Resident for help to induce them to leave. "The town was by this time in a state of panic."[414]

In the afternoon of 8 April the consuls met. The IBP manager informed the meeting later that the three merchants in whose name the Customs receipts were paid had withdrawn 2,500 *tumans* under threat by the Sayyed. They also told him that henceforth they had nothing to do with the Nationalists committee or the customs money.[415] On 9 April 1909, the Russian, German and Turkish representatives met with the British Resident to urge him to take action to provide security; almost the entire British mercantile community did the same. Thus, Sa`adat, a local contemporary historian, wrongly claimed that only the imperialist powers were behind this, for it is clear that other countries with no political interest in Persia were very worried by the lack of security in Bushehr. The British Resident did not want to land troops and therefore, in the evening of 9 April gave Sayyed Morteza Ahrami an ultimatum, "warning him that if the tufangchis were not cleared of the Island by 5 P.M. next evening, men and guns would be landed to provide security for British and foreign subjects." Some *tofangchis* left that night, "but only to lurk on the island;" they quarreled among themselves and preyed on the inhabitants of the suburbs, where many Europeans lived. On the morning of 10 April there was an altercation on the road used by European merchants going to town and returning home; one was killed another wounded and a blood feud was started, thus a group of 120 men discussed taking retaliatory action. Sayyed Morteza stated he was not responsible for

413. Political Diaries, vol. 3, p. 535.

414. Political Diaries, vol. 3, pp. 551-52; Administration Report 1909, p. 12.

415. Political Diaries, vol. 3, p. 552; FO 248/96, "Local News Abstract" Cox 12/04/1909.

the security of the town, which was still full of *tofangchis*. The bazaars remained closed, while people did not sleep, being afraid. At 4 p.m. the Resident published a proclamation that blue-jackets would be landed, because there was no authority and there was an imminent threat to people's life and property, and that the troops would withdraw as soon as normalcy returned.

NOTICE

To whom it may concern

It has not been hidden from any one that for several days past a very large number of tofangchis, variously estimated at from 800 to 2,000, have been present in the town; it is also plain that for the last four days these tofangchis have not been under any control; they have raided the bazaar and committed many robberies.

The persons who introduced these tofangchis have shown themselves unable to keep them in hand and they have become an imminent danger to the lives and properties of British and foreign subjets and to the peacable community at large.

The 24 hours are now on the point of expiring and there are still a large number of the tofangchis in the town and others waiting in suburbs on the island.

If they are not all out by 5 o'clock, men will be landed.

But all are informed plainly that this measure has been forced upon the British Government by the absence of any resposible authority able to control these tofangchis or guarantee the safety of the persons of British and foreign subjects. They are landed solely for this purpose, and will be withdrawn as soon as security is restored.

Source: Political Diaries, vol. 3, pp. 553-54.

No response came to the proclamation and thus at 5 p.m. of 10 April 1909, 100 men landed with four Maxim guns. Fifty were stationed at the Residency south of the town and the other 50 lodged in the Customs premises next door to the IBP and the Wonkhaus office. The landing party restored order to a great extent. The British Resident offered sepoy guards to foreign representatives if they so desired. The Russian Consul-General had his Cossacks, but asked for a guard for Mr. Mishtolt, the agent of the Russian Navigation Company. Four men were sent to the French vice-consulate, which normally had a guard of Persian soldiers, and 10 men were sent to Wonckhaus at Listermann's request. Not only was it close to the Customs, but it had in storage a quantity of kerosene and piece goods that also might attract looters. These were withdrawn the next day in consultation with Listermann as the guards of the Customs premises would take care of the Wonckhaus office.[416]

416. Political Diaries, vol. 3, pp. 552-53; Administration Report 1909, pp. 12-13; Bashiri 1367, vol. 2, pp. 115-17; FO 248/96, "Local News Abstract" Cox 12/04/1909.

After the landing of the British, force Sayyed Morteza came to the Residency to protest. He maintained that he was responsible for maintenance of law and order and therefore, he needed a large force of *tofangchis* as well as to stop the Daryabegi from arriving. He also assured that the life and property of foreigners would be protected. The Resident pointed out that during the last two weeks the Sayyed had been unable to do exactly that or to interest any respectable Bushehri to cooperate with him to form a local council. He had already stated his inability to control the *tofangchis* and had said that he was not responsible for their activities. Moreover, 20,000 *tumans* Customs receipts had been misspent and wasted and goods had been stolen. Given the level of insecurity there was no choice but to interfere and keep order until a viable local authority was able to maintain law and order.[417] Sayyed Morteza Ahrami felt isolated, because he realized that he had invited the *tofangchis* and that due to his mismanagement of local affairs much money had disappeared from the Customs, the bazaar had been looted, insecurity reigned in town, all because of the presence and misbehavior of the *tofangchis*, which had led to the landing of the British force and he feared that he was going to be blamed. On 11 April 1909, therefore, he drew up an *esteshhad-nameh* (testimony) stating that the *tofangchis* had only been in Bushehr to protect the Constitution and not for any personal gain or to riot. Sayyed Mohammad `Ali (Sadr al-Eslam's son-in-law) and Sheikh al-Hokama (a physician) took the document to the olama who had to sign first, after which they had to take it to the merchants. However, nobody was willing to sign the document.[418]

From 10 April to 10 May 1909, Bushehr looked peaceful due to the 100 men landing party. Many *tofangchis* left and their chiefs sent letters to the British Resident stating that they had come to support the Nationalist cause and found that is leaders were only lining their own pockets. Given this reality and the British proclamation it had convinced them to withdraw and return home. The town's people were encouraged and started to partially open shops, but the community leaders, of whom Sayyed Morteza Ahrami was the most disturbing element, continued to intrigue and quarrel. He still kept 200 to 300 *tofangchis* with him, who caused much fear in the town. Every night there was shooting from the roofs, while the bazaars remained closed. The Persian commercial community was not strong enough to oppose him and was not willing to work with him, "as long as he refused to clear his character by rendering an account of Customs receipts, appropriated by him and his confederates and by sending away the gang of tufangchis which surrounded him." On 13 April all the chief inhabitants, both Nationalist and royalist, stated that as long as the Sayyed remained in town it would be impossible to restore order.

On 14 April 1909, the British Resident sent a message to the local council stating that given the presence of the *tofangchis*, the bazaars remained closed and normal life was at a standstill, while certain ill-disposed persons intended to induce more *tofangchis* to come to town. Given this situation he even heard that the population intended to seek refuge at the British Residency. Therefore, the Resident warned the local council that, if it did not take speedy and effective action, he would be forced to take steps to prevent more *tofangchis* to enter the town. On 15 April, Mirza Ahmad Khan, the nominal Nationalist governor, issued a notice that there was no further need for precautionary shooting at night, because strong patrols of Persian soldiers would maintain security in the town.

---

417. Political Diaries, vol. 3, p. 573.
418. Political Diaries, vol. 3, p. 553; FO 248/96, "Local News Abstract" Cox 12/04/1909.

Sayyed Morteza Ahrami wrote to the Resident that he had sent most *tofangchis* away and only kept a few for his personal needs. He had done his best to defend the Constitution, while his opponents were now inviting Sheikh Hoseyn of Chahkutah to take control. He was in blood feud with the Tangestanis and the Angalis, thus, creating a recipe for further disorder. If that happened it was not his responsibility. However, during that time he did his utmost to induce the *tofangchis* to return and re-assert his control.

In view of Sayyed Morteza's activities the Resident published a second notice on 15 April, 1909. He reiterated the reasons for the landing of the British force and its beneficial effect. However, certain ill-disposed persons were engaged in recalling the *tofangchis*, which would result in unrest, danger and insecurity. Therefore, a patrol would be placed outside the town to prevent any armed men entering the town. The *Amir Panj* immediately reacted and wrote to the Resident that this was unnecessary as he would guarantee the security of the city. The next day he sent a field-gun and a guard of Chahkutahi *tofangchis* at Moqam (where the road from the interior entered the island) and placed pickets on the plain. Therefore, the Resident considered withdrawing his own patrols, if this security screen proved to be effective. On 16 April a leaflet was distributed bemoaning the British occupation of Bushehr and exhorted people to jihad, to expel the British. On that same day, Sayyed Morteza Ahrami sent a letter to the Resident in which he stated that "he now realised the philanthropic aims of the British Government, and in order to enlighten others, he deemed it advisable to issue a suitable notification! In the latter document he informed the public that it was now quite evident that the British Government had found it unavoidable to land troops and in doing so, had no animus against the popular cause or intention of departing from their avowed policy of non-intervention."

It was clear the Sayyed was getting desperate, as he had little or local support and he was thinking about how to escape unscathed from the mess he had created. Also, a chief mullah in Tehran sent him a telegram stating that it was contrary to the Nationalist interest to interfere with the rights of foreigners. Therefore, he should heed the wishes of the British government, especially with regards to the Customs receipts. At the same time telegrams arrived from the olama of Najaf stating that their orders were genuine and another telegram expressing their annoyance with the differences that had broken out among the people of Bushehr, who had to unite against the despotic rule of the Shah.

Attempts to reestablish the local council were also underway. Sayyed Morteza Ahrami offered to become a member and give an accounting of the Customs receipts, but his offer was refused. In an about turn, on 17 April 1909, Sayyed Morteza telegraphed the shah offering his loyal services. The latter replied by accepting and awarding him again with the title Nezam al-Olama. On the same day, Mirza Ahmad Khan wrote the Resident pointing out that the *Mir Panj* had engaged the services of Chahkutahi *tofangchis* who were in a blood feud with all other tribes. However, these other tribes needed to come to Bushehr for business. Therefore, he asked the Resident to make Sheikh Hoseyn to withdraw his men in five days. However, given that security was well maintained the Resident saw no reason to act.[419]

The self-constituted local council met on 24 April 1909. Seventeen persons were present among whom was the *Mir Panj*. Several letters were discussed that urged the local council to resolve local issues and restore order, so that the British had no reason

---

419. Political Diaries, vol. 3, pp. 573-77; FO 248/96, "Local News Abstract" Cox 26/04/1909.

to stay. However, the council reached no conclusion. Sayyed Morteza Ahrami continued to gather *tofangchi*s from wherever he found them, so that he had about 80. On 27 April 1909, the soldiers of the Chahar Mahal regiment took refuge (*bast*) under the Residency flagstaff, because for the last year their wages were not paid. On 28 April, the Resident sent the soldiers to the local council to plead their case, but without result. The next day, angry about this result, the soldiers tried to attack the *Mir Panj* twice. Sayyed Morteza Ahrami was also present; he was pressed to give an accounting of the Customs money, about which he was very vague. He asked for a regular salary, in which case he would retain only 20 *tofangchi*s and dismiss the rest. After the meeting the *kargozar* with three of the most influential members of the local council visited the Resident to discuss the maintenance of security and the functioning of the Customs. The Resident gave them advice as well as a draft unsigned note of steps that they might wish to take.

It was only on 30 April that the local council discussed the Resident's note, which suggested that (i) they had to assume responsibility for law and order; (ii) they should appoint a person in charge of actually maintaining order; and (iii) they should draw up a budget, detailing necessary expenses and what should be paid out of the Customs receipts and what from the *kalantar*'s revenues, who farmed the city's taxes. The local council was unable to take any decision, beyond deciding to keep Sheikh Hoseyn Chahkutahi to maintain security. He was allowed to keep 400 instead of 250 *tofangchi*s, otherwise he threatened to leave. Sheikh Hoseyn feared an attack from his Angali and Tangestani enemies. At that time, the *kalantar* paid 55 *tumans*/day for the *tofangchi*s, but the council wanted 110 *tumans* from the Customs receipts. Mirza Hoseyn, the German dragoman continued to make trouble and encouraging the Sayyed; as they were neighbors it was easy to contact him unobserved.

On 1 May 1909, three sayyeds and merchants on behalf of the local council visited Sayyed Morteza Ahrami and tried to induce him to account for the monies received from the Customs and to dismiss his *tofangchi*s. Sayyed Morteza Ahrami said that he would dismiss his guards if the Resident gave assurances through the German consul that he would withdraw the landing party in three days. When this reply was reported to the local council, the *Mir Panj* said that now it was clear the Sayyed Morteza Ahrami was acting under outside influence and clearly he took his cue from the German consul. The delegation also brought a written reply in which the Sayyed accused the council of intriguing against him and of arranging that the British occupied Bushehr. He made it clear that he would continue to oppose them. Some members were upset, but Sheikh Hoseyn Chahkutahi, who was present, then said that the Sayyed had no power and his words were but empty threats. After much discussion, rather than itself taking responsibility, the local council telegraphed Najaf about the Sayyed and asked for instructions.[420]

On 2 May 1909, because the Persian soldiers were still under the Residency's flag, the local council pressed the *Mir Panj* to pay the men a considerable amount. However, the compromise proposed was not accepted by all soldiers and so the deal fell through. However, the hold-outs relented later and on 4 May they were paid in groups of 10 and they left the Residency having received assurance that there would be no retaliation. The local council was unable to write a budget because the merchants were afraid to put their signature under it being afraid that they would be personally responsible for payments.

---

420. Political Diaries, vol. 3, pp. 588-89, 597; FO 248/96, "Local News Abstract" Cox 26/04/1909; FO 248/96, "Bushire News" Cox 01/05/1909.

Ra`is `Ali Delvari (standing, hands clasped in the center) with his men.

Therefore, it was difficult to get funds for their expenses, but the Resident approved payment of certain arrears and the payments of the guards against the Customs receipts.[421]

Daryabegi governor again - end of Tangestani occupation

One of Sayyed Morteza's objectives was: "to hold the place against the Darya Begi, who had been dispatched from Tehran as the only person likely to be able to handle the situation." The Sayyed claimed that the rest of the community was against him and would not allow Daryabegi to enter the town on behalf of the hated Shah. However, his ambitions were shelved when on 4 May 1909, Sheikh `Abdol-Qasem Kazeruni, who had been sent by the Sayyed to Najaf returned to Bushehr. He brought orders from Najaf stating that Daryabegi had given assurances to protect the Constitution and that they, therefore, approved his appointment. If Daryabegi would have arrived shortly thereafter, the situation might have been quickly corrected, or so the Resident believed, but he was held up by the impassibility of the Tigris and he reached Bushehr only on 10 May, accompanied by Sayyed Asadollah on behalf of the olama of Najaf, and was well received by everybody. He gave assurances that he would maintain law and order and the Resident withdrew his troops and the *HMS Fox* and *HMS Sphinx*, that came on 27 April, left on 20 May.[422]

Daryabegi made it clear that Sayyed Morteza would have to repay the Customs monies and that nobody would be allowed to have a personal guard of *tofangchis*. On 10 May 1909, Sayyed Asadollah sent a message to Sayyed Morteza Ahrami, who paid him a visit the next day. He was came accompanied by his *tofangchis* who patrolled the streets, while he was inside. Sheikh Hoseyn and the *kalantar* visited Sayyed Morteza Ahrami on

421. Political Diaries, vol. 3, pp. 598-99.

422. Administration Report 1909, pp. 12-14; Political Diaries, vol. 3, p. 551-53 (Sayyed Asadollah is here called `Abdollah, but in later reports his name appears as Asadollah); Sa`adat 1390, pp. 160-66; on the dragoman of the German consulate, see also Nura'i 1385, p. 121.

behalf of Daryabegi asking him to dismiss his *tofangchis* and account for the Customs monies; he refused both demands. He asked Daryabegi to come, which he did on 13 May. In reaction he dismissed some *tofangchis*, but replaced them with others. Sayyed Asadollah said in the local council that it was clear that Sayyed Morteza Ahrami was under the influence of the "Germani," meaning the German dragoman. On 14 May, Ra'is `Ali Delvari, a Tangestani chief, who had started the looting of Bushehr, came to visit Sayyed Morteza Ahrami. Sheikh Hoseyn complained to the Daryabegi, who sent a strong message to the Sayyed; as a result, Ra'is `Ali left that same evening. Daryabegi wanted to make an expedition into Tangestan to punish its people for the looting of Bushehr and to prevent that they them making more trouble. He asked the local council to support his proposal. On 15 May the local council received a petition asking that the Daryabegi be allowed to punish the Tangestanis. The local council dutifully asked the governor to do so.[423]

However, Tehran did not reply to the governor's telegram so he had to wait. On 18 May 1909, the local council met, but did no react to a letter from Sayyed Morteza Ahrami in which he demanded (i) to be permitted to keep 20 *tofangchis* for his protection; and (ii) the delivery to him of four persons for punishment as enemies of the Constitution. On that same day, after Daryabegi had given assurances that he would take all necessary measures to maintain law and order, the Resident released 2,000 *tumans* from the Customs receipts for current expenses, withdrew the landing party and *HMS Fox* left for Masqat. The Resident also published a Notice announcing the withdrawal of the British troops, the reasons why, and an invitation to all inhabitants to try to avoid a recurrence of lawlessness. Both the Resident and the Russian Consul-General jointly urged the local council to bring about a reconciliation between the shah and the people. The local council wired Tehran about Sayyed Morteza Ahrami's continued efforts to recruit *tofangchis*, while on 23 May 1909, following a closed door meeting in the house of Sayyed Asadollah, the Najaf representative, the local council sent telegrams to various persons (Najaf olama, nationalist leaders) denouncing Sayyed Morteza Ahrami.[424]

To Hajaj Islam, Nejef

Seyed Murteza, took possession of the Customs and took 21,000 cash, 178 rifles, 17 revolvers, 22,000 cartridges. His tofangchis plundered the place. The place was in a disturbed contition. Foreigners' property plundered. English Consul brought soldiers. After some time Derya Begi arrived and gave a letter of assurances. The soldiers were withdrawn. Sayed Ahremi has got 100 tofangchis in town. He daily invites the Tangistanis to come to town. On the arrival of Tangistanis again at the place the soldiers will be landed again. Then they will never be withdrawn. Seyed Ahremi is ready to shed blood and get the intervention of foreigners. The people are quiet till they hear your decision. You have to check this and the sooner the better, so that the dignity of Islam should not be lost.

Anjumani Vilayat, Bushire.

Source: Political Diaries, vol. 3, p. 618; for the Persian text, see Ranjbar 1389, p. 93.

423. Political Diaries, vol. 3, pp. 611-12.

424. Political Diaries, vol. 3, pp. 617-18.

On 24 May 1909, news arrived that a large number of Tangestanis had gathered at the village of Gurak, across the Mashilah, intending to attack Bushehr. Sayyed Asadollah and Daryabegi went to see Sayyed Morteza Ahrami, whom they blamed for this amassing of armed men and ordered him to put a stop to it. He replied that it only showed that the *tofangchis* could enter Bushehr at any time they wanted in spite of Daryabegi and others. However, he had already written to them to disperse and withdraw. Daryabegi was unable to get orders from Tehran to expel Sayyed Morteza Ahrami. He was frustrated about this and suggested to the Resident that the British and Russian Legations might be able to help in this regard. Both the Resident and the Russian Consul-General spoke to Daryabegi the next day and wired their Legations what was discussed. After meeting with the German dragoman on 25 May, Sayyed Asadollah became less hostile toward Sayyed Morteza Ahrami suggesting to leading members of the local council that it would be better to come to an agreement with him. The self-constituted local council told Daryabegi that it wanted to dissolve itself and that elections should be held to form a new one. Sayyed Asadollah's change of mind was also evident during a meeting of the local council on 28 May (without the representatives of the merchants), urging the council to make friends with Sayyed Morteza Ahrami, a 180 percent *volte face* of his previous position when he had denounced him. That same day Sayyed Morteza Ahrami, frightened by Daryabegi having landed a gun from the *Persepolis*, sent a letter to the Tangestani chiefs to return to their homes and copied this letter to Daryabegi.[425]

On 1 June 1909, the local council discussed the arrangement for a new election. Also, the Daryabegi received orders to dismiss all regular troops and only employ local men in their stead. However, dismissing them was impossible as they were owed back-pay, for which he had no money. He further received separate instructions to take action against Sayyed Morteza Ahrami, to whom he immediately suggested to make a pilgrimage to Najaf. Meanwhile, Sayyed Morteza Ahrami was quietly moving all his ill-gotten gains to Ahram. On 3 June 1909, a notice was published by the committee of supervisors (*nozzar*) for the election of the local council. The supervisors were: Sayyed Mohammad `Ali (mullah), Sayyed `Abdollah (mullah), Sayyed `Abdollah (physician), Haji Mirza Gholam Hoseyn (merchant), Haji Reza Behbahani (merchant), and Sheikh Mohammad Hoseyn (headmaster of the school). The notice stated that blank voting papers would be handed out by the committee from 4 to 19 June, except on Sundays, Thursdays, and Fridays from 9 a.m. until sundown. Eligibility for voters and candidates was the same as for the previous council. The local council was to be known as *anjoman-e eyalati* instead of *anjoman-e velayati* with 12 instead of 6 members. The doubling of the membership was to ensure that the mullahs who were members of the current local council could retain their seat, otherwise they would have protested. The votes would be received on 18 and 19 June and the supervisors were located at the Malek al-Tojjar's house, where the then local council also met.

Sayyed Morteza Ahrami immediately reacted by writing to Daryabegi that this election was illegal and that he had to chose the future members of the local council. Daryabegi became very angry and told the messenger that the Sayyed had to stop making a nuisance of himself else he would expel him from Bushehr. On 5 June 1909, Sayyed Morteza Ahrami posted a notice outside his house with his ideas how the members of

425. Political Diaries, vol. 3, pp. 629-30.

the new local council should be chosen. To ensure that the notice was not torn down he had placed a *tofangchi* near it. Daryabegi wrote to Ra'is `Ali Delvari to no longer support Sayyed Morteza Ahrami and not to endanger himself. He himself had dismissed 100 of Sheikh Hoseyn's *tofangchis* and would further reduce that number and therefore, suggested that Ra'is `Ali should do the same. Whether in reaction to this friendly advice or not, but in the night of 5 to 6 June, Ra'is `Ali Delvari with 250 armed men came to the Mashilah two hours before sunrise intending to march to Bushehr. Sheikh Hoseyn's brother who was on guard duty wanted to prevent him from doing so, but Daryabegi had given explicit orders to avoid fighting. Therefore, he informed his brother, while Ra'is `Ali moved to Sangi. Sheikh Hoseyn's *tofangchis* took up position at the road to resist him and placed a gun in the middle of the road. Allegedly another 200 or so Tangestanis were also expected to come by sea, reason why Daryabegi had the gunboats patrol the sea with orders to fire on any boats with armed men suspected coming from Delvar. On 6 June 1909, the Delvari *tofangchis* were forced to flee with the loss of five killed and several wounded. To the governor and others it was clear that Ra'is `Ali had come to Bushehr at Sayyed Morteza Ahrami's invitation, who denied this. Therefore, Daryabegi convened a meeting of merchants and notables at the *Chahar Borj* to decide what to do with the Sayyed. It was decided to take strong measures. Daryabegi ordered him to leave Bushehr with the *Persepolis* within four hours, else force would be used. The Sayyed accepted the official order, but wanted assurances concerning his safety. Two days later Daryabegi again sent the same order to the Sayyed. He refused, even at the urging of Sayyed Asadollah, and supported by some 70 men remained holed up in his house. His *tofangchis* occupied 3-4 neighboring houses and awaited events. After 2 p.m., Daryabegi sent soldiers and *tofangchis* with two guns from the *Persepolis* under the *Mir Panj* to attack the Sayyed. There was much firing without doing any great damage, but at 5 p.m. a breach was made in the Sayyed's house, through which the *Mir Panj* and the soldiers entered, while the defenders fled or surrendered. They found that the Sayyed had flown; by chance during a search for him the soldiers found him dressed as a Tangestani boatman, after a small boy had pointed him out to them. He was trying to leave town, but then went to the Ottoman consulate, which was surrounded by *tofangchis* so he tried to get into the British Residency. However, the gates were closed and he was arrested at the flagstaff and taken to and confined in the *Chahar Borj*. Meanwhile, the soldiers and the town's rabble looted the Sayyed's house. In the morning of 8 June 1909, the Sayyed was taken to the *Persepolis*. One of his henchman, Mirza Gholam Hoseyn took refuge in the Armenian church, but was handed over to Daryabegi. On Daryabegi's side five men were killed and on the Sayyed's side also five men. In total eleven persons, including the Sayyed and his *monshi* were arrested and imprisoned. About 200 rifles, a large quantity of ammunition and a large store of provisions and water were found in the Sayyed's house indicating that he had prepared for a long siege. On 9 June the local council met and sent telegrams with the news and commending Daryabegi's action. That same day Daryabegi told the soldiers and gunners that he had orders to dismiss them, but in view of their brave behavior he had asked Tehran to allow them to stay. At the same time, Daryabegi was collecting *tofangchis* from Rig to launch an expedition into Tangestan. He also sent a telegram to Najaf asking what should be done with Sayyed Morteza to which on 14 June a reply came stating that he should be punished and expelled.

Zayer Khedr, who had been assisting Daryabegi, left Bushehr on 10 June to defend his village and Chahkutah against an imminent attack by Ra'is `Ali Delvari and Gholam

Hoseyn and Hasan Bakhshu, two Tangestani Khans. Zayer Khedr was able to encircle the other force and Sheikh Hoseyn Chahkutahi was expected to attack from the Bushehr side. Pressed on all sides the two other Khans abandoned Ra'is `Ali and joined Zayer Khedr, although Hasan Bakhshu later killed one of Zayer Khedr's followers. Ra'is `Ali had dug in behind a trench at Ameri on the seaside and offered the following terms: the Sayyed should be allowed to return to his house and live there; four men should be handed over to him to be killed for the four that had died on his side, and the Sayyed's house should be rebuilt and his plundered goods be restored based on a list to be provided by the Sayyed. If these terms were not accepted he would attack Bushehr, "and pay no attention to the foreigners or natives." In reaction, Daryabegi reinforced his defense force with *tofangchis* from Rishahr and put up Sayyed Morteza Ahrami's house for sale.[426] Meanwhile the government in Tehran pressed Daryabegi to remit the revenues, but he had no funds to even to pay the two month's arrears of the soldiers.[427]

On 13 June 1909, the *Persepolis* returned from Rig with 300 *tofangchis*. On 14 June there was supposed to have been an election, but there was little enthusiasm, the more so since the candidates, according to the British Resident, were shady characters who did not inspire respect. On 15 June the local council met to discuss to plan for its elected replacement. Voting for the local council took place on 18 and 19 June, but few voters were showing up. On 20 June the result was made known:

> Mullahs: Sayyed Morteza, Sadr al-Eslam, Sayyed `Abdollah Behbahani, Sayyed Mohammad `Ali, Fakhr al-Eslam, Sayyed `Abdol-Reza Hakim, and Sheikh `Ali Dashti.
>
> Merchants: Haji `Abdol-Rasul Ra'is al-Tojjar, Haji Sayyed Mohammad Reza, Haji Mirza Gholam Hoseyn Kazeruni, Haji Reza Behbahani, and Haji Mohammad `Ali Dehdashti.[428]

On 20 June 1909, the newly elected local council met. Daryabegi asked it what to do with Sayyed Morteza Ahrami and suggested to send him to Rig in custody or to Najaf. It was decided to send him to Najaf. The governor did not like this and telegraphed Tehran pointing out the downside of doing so, but he received no reply. On 26 June the local council elected Sayyed `Abdol-Reza Hakim as president and Haji `Abdol-Rasul Ra'is al-Tojjar as vice-president.

The past events were a lesson in irony. Daryabegi was welcomed by the same people who wanted to be rid of him only a few months earlier, but who now hoped that he would restore Bushehr to normalcy, which he did with some success. In the same vein, the same people who had supported Sayyed Morteza Ahrami now attacked him and wanted to expel him. However, not everybody was happy with Daryabegi's return and

---

426. Political Diaries, vol. 3, pp. 639-41, 646-48, 653-55; Administration Report 1909, pp. 8, 14; Sa`adat 1390, pp. 166-68; Faramarzi 1390, pp. 34-36; Ranjbar 1389, pp. 93-97 (there also was a perceived threat of an attack by the forces of Sayyed Abu'l-Hasan Lari); Mashayekhi 1391, pp. 117-18 (Sayyed Morteza claimed that goods to a value of 20,000 *tumans* had been taken from his and his neighbor's house). If true, one wonders how he had obtained so much money.

427. Political Diaries, vol. 3, p. 641.

428. Political Diaries, vol. 3, pp. 653-54.

Ra'is `Ali Delvari, for example, was still camped outside Bushehr ready to make life difficult for the newly arrived governor. To forestall this, Daryabegi marched with an armed force to the place where Ra'is `Ali was holed up. On 23 June 1909, Daryabegi moved to Moqam with 300 infantry and 3 guns, 250 *tofangchis* under Ahmad Khan of Rig and 250 *tofangchis* under Sheikh Hoseyn Chahkutahi. Zayer Khedr joined him later with 250 *tofangchis*. Daryabegi sent an ultimatum to Ra'is `Ali demanding that he hand over Delvar to Zayer Khedr and he and Hasan Bakhshu to refund all monies and goods that they had plundered in Bushehr. On 26 June Zayer Khedr took Ahram. His opponents withdrew to Ambarek, where later they were attacked by Daryabegi's force. Ra'is `Ali and Hasan Bakhshu and their men fled and took to the hills, abandoning their villages. Daryabegi further burnt down Hasan Bakhshu's village of Ambarek and, as punishment, cut down many date trees with a value of 2,000 *tumans*,. However, on 5 July 1909, Ra'is `Ali reoccupied Delvar. On his return, Daryabegi withdrew funds from the Customs to pay for this short campaign [429] On 7 July Sayyed Morteza Ahrami was sent on a mail steamer to Basra to go to Najaf. In Najaf, he wrote several letters to Akhund Mohammad Kazem Khorasani and the *Majles* giving his version of events in Bushehr, defending his actions, complaining about Daryabegi's behavior toward him, the destruction and looting of his house and about his expulsion.[430]

On 4 July 1909, the local council wrote to the British Resident that it wanted to take charge of the Customs, "paying the receipts into the bank, the interest on the British loans being paid, and the balance retained here instead of being remitted to Tehran." The Resident replied it would be better to wait for the results of discussions in Tehran. On 15 July the *kargozar* informed the Residency that the local council actually wished that no money would be sent to Tehran; it was either prepared to pay 30,000 *tumans*/month to cover the interest on the outstanding loans with the rest to be used for local government, or else to put the net balance in the bank. This was reported to the British legation in Tehran.

The local council of Isfahan asked for financial support, but Sadr al-Eslam strongly opposed this, because he would never agree to send money to the Bakhtiyaris, who wished to dethrone the shah. The members of the local council were less than enthusiast about their work; "several are frankly disgusted with the whole thing." On 17 July 1909, the local council held a meeting to announce the abdication of Mohammad `Ali Shah and the accession of Ahmad Shah. At the same time they expressed their anger with Daryabegi about the subscription to the nationalist cause. The local council further decided to meet daily, except Fridays. On 21 July Daryabegi announced three days of holidays to celebrate the accession of Ahmad Shah. The bazaars were closed, there were some illuminations and fireworks. The biggest *tamasha* or show was arranged by the German dragoman and his friends (all supporters of Sayyed Morteza) who erected a *pandal* on the sea front and gave a splendid entertainment with iced drinks, illumination etc on 23 July.

In response to telegrams from Najaf received on 12 July, that preached *jihad* against the Russians, Sayyed Asadollah and others gave stirring speeches and 30,000 *qrans* were collected of which 12,000 were sent to Isfahan. On 11 August 1909 it was decided to

429. Political Diaries, vol. 3, pp. 662-63, 671, 679-80.

430. Administration Report 1909, p. 14; Political Diaries, vol. 3, pp. 679; Mashayekhi 1391, pp. 111-18; Ranjbar 1389, pp. 99-106.

remit the balance, about 1,000 *tumans*, to Isfahan.[431] During September the local council did hardly anything beyond sending telegrams to Tehran informing the government that Sayyed `Abdol-Hoseyn Lari was a good Constitutionalist and was innocent of the accusations made by Sunnis. All these telegrams were written and paid for by his agent Haji `Ali Lari. Relations between Daryabegi and the prime political local mover, Sayyed Asadollah, became so bad that the Sayyed withdrew to his house and refused to do any further business.[432]

By October 1909, despite being urged by Tehran, the local council still had not elected a delegate to the *Majles*. The Minister of Interior also informed the local council that the appellation *eyalati* was wrong, it should be *velayati* and only have six members. As a result, preparations were made for new elections. The deputy-governor tried to arrange the registration of votes, but did not make any progress due to intrigues by interested parties. In November 1909, the new local council was elected, including Mirza `Ali Kazeruni, whose election was protested immediately and therefore, the deputy-governor dissolved the local council to await the return of Daryabegi to decide what to do. In early December 1909, a letter from Daryabegi in Jask was received asking the members not to resign. Consequently, the local council resumed its meeting, but Ra'is al-Tojjar and two major merchants did not want to attend the meetings.[433]

The Russian vice-consul Kadloubovsky, who had been very helpful during the Sayyed Morteza Ahrami troubles, left to Shiraz when the troubles were over. En route his caravan was attacked at Kazerun. His chief, Consul-General Passek tried to return to Bushehr, but on 25 November, his caravan came under attack near Khan-e Zenyan and he returned to Shiraz. The German consul Listemann left on leave of 20 April 1910, and was replaced by Wassmuss, "a young man without previous experience of Persia or its language." According to the British Resident, he was taken advantage of by his dragoman, an intriguer who fed him distorted information on local matters to make life difficult for the British at a time when the safety of all foreigners depended on the policy of the British Residency. The dragoman of the German consulate, without instruction of his chief, was in contact with Sayyed Morteza Ahrami, "and assisted him with advice and drafts of letters, when in correspondence with the Residency." The Resident hinted Wassmuss should not to rely on his dragoman, but he said he had faith in his subordinate and was sure that he was not involved in the local intrigues. The dragoman also advised him concerning the quarrels with the *kargozar*. After Sayyed Morteza Ahrami was ousted the problem did not reoccur.[434]

Mirza Ahmad Khan Daryabegi remained governor despite attempts to oust him and the virulent attacks in the Indian (i.e. the Persian newspaper *Habl al-Matin*) and the Persian press. In March 1910, he was reappointed on condition of accepting a schedule of taxes amounting to 94,000 *tumans* and an annual salary of 6,000 *tumans*. From March until mid-June he was absent from Bushehr collecting taxes in the other parts of his governorate.[435] The situation in Bushehr was still bad. Daryabegi had been forced to exit

---

431. Political Diaries, vol. 3, pp. 679, 704.
432. Political Diaries, vol. 3, p. 721.
433. Political Diaries, vol. 3, pp. 739, 762, 780-81.
434. Administration Report 1909, p. 9.
435. Administration Report 1910, pp. 11-12; Political Diaries vol. 4, p. 93; Ranjbar 1389, p. 103.

the political stage rather ignominously 2-3 times in the last few years. Tehran believed he was the man to bring normalcy to Bushehr after the Sayyed Morteza Ahrami troubles, but he found that under the new regime his problems only increased. He had no troops to enforce his authority or to collect taxes. The uncontrolled press was vitriolic in its misinformation and accusations, resulting in constant telegrams from ministers or the *Majles* in Tehran, who were ignorant of the local situation. Under these circumstances it was a wonder that there were individuals who were willing to accept the job of governor.[436] It was not helpful either that Sayyed Morteza Ahrami wrote to the *Majles* denouncing Daryabegi's allegedly oppressive administration, an accusation that was shortly thereafter supported by a letter from Akhund Khorasani, who asked for the Sayyed's return and the repair of his house. Although he did not want the Sayyed to return, Daryabegi nevertheless acted as if he was not the main obstacle to such an event. In reply to the pressure from Tehran he replied that the Sayyed's return was not an easy matter as it would be opposed by the British.[437] Also, in March 1910, it was reported that during a visit to Najaf, Daryabegi's *mostowfi*, Mirza Mehdi Khan, had invited Sayyed Morteza Ahrami to return. However, Mohammad Kazem Khorasani told him that the Sayyed would not leave "until arrangements were made for payment to him of an allowance for which he (the Mujtahid) had made an application to the central authorities."[438] In April 1910, Mohammad Kazem Khorasan wrote Ra'is al-Tojjar that he considered Sayyed Morteza an innocent and wronged man and asked him to agitate with other merchants to bring down Daryabegi, the Sayyed's nemesis.[439] In July 1910, Daryabegi started repairing Sayyed Morteza's house, which was in response to a repeated request by Akhund Khorasani and pressure from Tehran.[440]

Daryabegi had not much success with the local *anjoman* either. In January 1910, the local *anjoman* met twice per week. However, several of its members spent most of the first six months of 1910 intriguing against one another, in particular the followers of Mirza Hoseyn, the former dragoman of the German consulate. He declared that he had cut his ties with the Consulate and got himself elected at the beginning of the year as one of the two candidates slotted for the Gulf Ports to the *Majles*. The other one was Mirza `Ali Kazeruni, a disreputable petty merchant and a fraudulent bankrupt. After their election Mirza `Ali Kazeruni and Mirza Hoseyn fell out and accused each other of all kinds of chicanerie. The former accused the latter of still being in German service, which led Wassmuss to complain to the governor, who ordered the two not to use the German consul's name in their quarrels. Therefore, many residents, including the governor, considered asking Tehran to have their election cancelled. In March 1910, Mirza Hoseyn and Sayyed Asadollah were told by the *anjoman* that, according to the rules, they were no longer members as they had not attended the last 10 meetings. Both were also denounced as having used illegal methods to get elected and were not sent to Tehran. One month later, Sayyed `Abdollah Behbahani, the *anjoman*'s chairman resigned, so that it only had three members instead of the legal six. Mirza Hoseyn then became dragoman of German

436. Administration Report 1910, p. 3.
437. Mashayekhi 1391, pp. 119-23; Ranjbar 1389, pp. 102-08.
438. Political Diaries vol. 4, p. 65; Ranjbar 1389, p. 107.
439. Political Diaries vol. 4, p. 93.
440. Political Diaries vol. 4, p. 139; Mashayekhi 1391, pp. 124-25; Ranjbar 1389, p. 108.

consulate again.[441] From the relative safety of that function he continued to scheme. When Haji Mohammad Hasan, a political rival, was appointed agent of Wonckhaus this led to a quarrel with Mirza Hoseyn. They accused each other of organizing the Sayyed Morteza's disturbances, intriguing against the British Residency, etc. It also became clear that part of the property of Mo`azzez al-Dowleh, the former governor was held by the *kalantar*. The *anjoman* asked the deputy-governor to collect these goods, but it was given the cold shoulder. When in March 1910, Tehran accused Daryabegi that he was remiss in maintaining law and order in the Gulf Ports, he told the *anjoman* that he would resign unless it supported him. As a result, Agha `Ali, one of his flunkies and Agha Mostafa sent telegrams to Tehran denouncing the suggested dismissal.[442] Because the *anjoman* was under-strength, at instructions from Tehran, in April 1910 preparations were made to hold elections to replace the three departed members. The two ousted members protested their ouster and declared the elections irregular.[443] Things became even worse when one month later the Imam Jom`eh left to Najaf, so that the *anjoman* had only two members. The deputy-governor then ordered that it should hold no further meetings. However, Mirza `Ali Kazeruni, a member, asked to Tehran for instructions to hold new elections. By June 1910, only one member, a fraudulent bankrupt, of the *anjoman* remained; none of his colleagues further attended. Daryabegi tried to revive the *anjoman* after his return. With great difficulty Daryabegi was able to pay the arrears in ration money to the artillerists, but then the infantry claimed 7 months' pay. Tehran told him to pay the men with the help of the *anjoman*, which no longer existed. Therefore, in July, Daryabegi tried to revive it. He reconciled Mirza `Ali Kazeruni and Mirza Hoseyn with Fakhr al-Eslam and tried to induce Sayyed `Abdollah Behbahani, the ex-president to return to the *anjoman*.[444] This did not happen, because in August there were elections for the municipal council (*anjoman-e baladiyeh*), so that, as a result, the old *anjoman* was abolished without any local protest and without Tehran knowing about.[445] However, all local councils were officially abolished in November by circular telegram from Tehran to all governors, which entrusted "Governors with powers to inflict punishments on their own authority."[446] Nevertheless, there was still great confusion about the status of the local council, when in December 1910, three telegrams arrived for the *anjoman*. The telegraph chief offered them to two former members who refused to receive them. He then asked the governor what to do. Because Daryabegi did not want Tehran to know that the *anjoman* no longer existed, he convened a meeting of merchants where the telegrams were opened and read.[447]

441. Administration Report 1910, p. 13; Political Diaries vol. 4, pp. 10, 65. At the insistence of the mullahs of Tehran and Resht, no *Nowruz* festivities were held in 1910, although it fell right after the mourning months of Moharram and Safar, 1328(13 January to 13 March 1910), to protest against the presence of Russian troops in the North. Administration Report 1910, p. 16; see also Political Diaries vol. 4, p. 48-49. *Nowruz* fell on 21 March 1910 or 9 Rabi` I 1328, which is the day of *`Eyd-e-Shuja'* or *`Eyd-e-Zahra*, which marks the end of the two-month mourning period (*`azadari*).

442. Political Diaries vol. 4, pp. 10, 49. For "a note on the history and character of Mirza Husein," 6 June 1911, see FO 248/1024.

443. Political Diaries vol. 4, p. 65.

444. Political Diaries vol. 4, p. 139.

445. Administration Report 1910, p. 13; Political Diaries vol. 4, pp. 93, 117.

446. Administration Report 1911, p. 13.

447. Political Diaries vol. 4, p. 296.

Even during his four-months' absence the problems in Bushehr followed Daryabegi. In May 1910, the captains of the artillery men took refuge in the Customs House to protest non-payment of their wages and wired Tehran. From Bandar Abbas, Daryabegi sent two drafts of 500 *qrans*, but the drawee refused to pay.[448] On 19 June, 1910, after an absence of four months in Bandar Abbas and Lengeh, Daryabegi returned. He made a deal with the artillerists, who then left their sanctuary. The locally hired police were not paid for two months, but were paid by the *kalantar* out of the tolls levied on muleteers coming to Bushehr.[449] Another potential headache for Daryabegi was the reappearance of the local newspaper *Mozaffari* in Bushehr in May 1910. In April its editor met with the deputy-governor, the *kargozar* and Sayyed Asadollah and received permission to restart publishing on condition of submitting his text to the local authorities. The British Residency was upset when he published an article criticizing the use of European officers in quarantine and medical institutions and it asked the deputy-governor to be a stricter censor in the future.[450]

During the period of his four months' absence from Bushehr, *Amir Panj* Ahmad Khan, who was deputy-governor and commander of the Persian regiment at Bushehr, officiated. However, he was not a strong administrator, although he was well educated and an English speaker. He had a disagreement with Daryabegi after the latter's return and was dismissed. Daryabegi first replaced him with Sheikh Naser Chahkutahi Shoja` al-Mamalek (commander of the *tupchis*) and then with Mirza `Abdol-Reza, son of one of Malek al-Tojjar's slaves, all of whom were incompetent, acording to the British. The *Amir Panj* left Bushehr with his regiment mid-August 1910.[451]

Just after his return to Bushehr, there appeared an attack on Daryabegi in the Tehran newpaper *Majles* (nr. 122 of 4 June 1910) as being too friendly to the British and of being corrupt. The British Resident believed that the article had been written by Sayyed Asadollah Qarakhani, the self-styled representative of the Najaf olama, who in 1909 had accompanied Daryabegi to Bushehr, but now had become his enemy. One month later, the *Majles* newspaper (nr. 132 of 4 July) retracted the accusation against Daryabegi and asked for a commision of enquiry, saying that the author of the article was an upstanding person, who was ready to prove the veracity of his statement.[452] Although his opponents branded Daryabegi as a corrupt reactionary he nevertheless tried to introduce new institutions that were favored by the Nationalists. He intented to establish modern judicial, municipal and police institutions in Bushehr. However, he was informed by Tehran that it would send qualified persons to head these institutions. Nevertheles, Daryabegi hired 10 policemen and appointed two merchants to act as Commercial Assessors of the new proposed court.[453] He further reiterated his proposal to disband the existing understrength garrisons of the Gulf Ports and instead hiring local men (500 infantry; 150 artillery, 100 sovars). He offered to pay for these himself, provided that he only had to pay the same revenues as in 1900.[454] Although this proposal was clearly advantageous to Daryabegi, it

448. Political Diaries vol. 4, p. 93.
449. Political Diaries vol. 4, p. 117.
450. Political Diaries vol. 4, p. 94.
451. Administration Report 1910, pp. 11-12; Political Diaries vol. 4, pp. 93, 268.
452. Political Diaries vol. 4, pp. 118, 168.
453. Political Diaries vol. 4, pp. 9-10.
454. Political Diaries vol. 4, p. 9.

Zayer Khezr Khan Tangestani

had the potential to resolve a structural problem, viz. that of non-payment of the soldiers. It was also an immediate one, because on 17 August 1910 the soldiers took refuge at the British Residency for not being paid for 7 months and their clothes money for 3 years. Their commanding officer said he could do nothing and Tehran had given him an unsatisfactory reply. While discussions were underway with the deputy-governor the soldiers said Tehran had wired them that they were allowed to leave, which they would do after they received their money.[455]

455. Political Diaries vol. 4, p. 166.

Bushehr Threatened by Tangestanis

Several times during 1910 an invasion of Tangestani and other *tofangchi*s was feared, as in April 1909. In May 1910, Ra'is `Ali Delvari was imprisoned by the *kargozar* after a complaint of the French consul about the financial claim by a French arms dealer in Masqat. He released him on 1 June after Haji Mohammad Hoseyn Dehdashti gave security and his relatives had threatened to molest the *kargozar* unless he was freed.[456] However, the main reason for this fear in town was the feud between Sheikh Hoseyn Chahkutahi and his brothers, "the latter claiming that the villages of Abu Tawil, Tul-i-Ashki and Kanar Abadi should be given to them to live in, and the former declining to do so." He was backed by Daryabegi, the brothers by Zayer Khedr, the chief of Tangestan, who had a feud with Sheikh Hoseyn, because he had supported Heydar Khan, whom he had driven from his land. At a certain moment Sheikh Hoseyn killed one of his brothers, Sheikh `Ali in cold blood and on 26 July the other brother, Sheikh Mohammad attacked the village of Choghadak supported by Zayer Khedr. On 9 August 1910, Daryabegi led 150 men and two cannons to suppress the trouble. There was some fighting on a daily basis and firing could be heard in Bushehr. Allegedly, Sowlet al-Dowleh intervened on behalf of Zayer Khedr and was said to have instructed Moghith al-Dowleh (deputy-governor of Dashti and Dashtestan and Nezam al-Saltaneh's agent) to arrange for Daryabegi to return to Bushehr. Whatever the truth, Daryabegi and Zayer Khedr made peace, which was good for them but not for Sheikh Hoseyn, who, abandoned by his friends, had to accede to all the demands of his brothers. In October 1910, he gave them the three villages and he was left only with Ahmadi. The result was that Zayer Khedr and his Tangestanis were unchallenged in the district around Bushehr, while the reason for Daryabegi's sortie had not been resolved. Daryabegi returned to Bushehr on 9 August and then went to Bandar Abbas. Immediately thereafter, Zayer Khedr demanded payment of 2,000 *tuman*s from the *kalantar* of Bushehr and Zayer Haji, Sheikh Hoseyn's agent, as a fine for the assistance given to the latter. He threatened to come and take the money by force if it would not be paid. People in Bushehr took the threat seriously and measures were taken to meet this challenge at Daryabegi's telegraphic instructions. Arrangements were made with the chief of Rig to send reinforcements. On learning this Zayer Khedr claimed he never had any hostile intentions towards Bushehr. In fact, he had been offered the office of *kalantar* of Bushehr by Sowlat al-Dowleh the Qashqa'i tribal leader, but he had declined.[457] Apparently, Sowlat al-Dowleh had intimated that he had been offered or had an interest in the governorship of Bushehr. At that time there were about 100 Tangestanis wandering around Bushehr, while the *kadkhoda* was a Tangestani and if a Tangestani also had become *kalantar*, Bushehr would have been under their control, which would have been an undesirable situation.

The third time a possible attack was feared was when the Customs Department was exerting itself to prevent smuggling. In reaction, a number of Customs *modir*s were killed. However, this was apparently not sufficient, for the Dashti Khans gathered at Ahram, Zayer Ahmad's home base and announced their intention to jointly attack and sack Bushehr.

---

456. Political Diaries vol. 4, p. 118.

457. However, in November 1910, when `Abdol-Rasul was afraid that Zayer Khedr intended to replace him as *kalantar* he secured support of Sowlat al-Dowleh, the Qashqa'i chief. Political Diaries vol. 4, p. 268.

Nezam al-Saltaneh with Russian officers visiting their ship

Daryabegi was worried enough that on 23 November 1910, he moved 6 km out of Bushehr with 80 men and one cannon. He had contact with Zayer Khedr who assured him no such attack was planned and he then withdrew to Bushehr on 27 November. He induced Zayer Khedr to come to Bushehr and to discuss matters with the director of Customs. During his stay there it was alleged that he and Daryabegi made a secret pact together to resist Sowlat al-Dowleh should he have any hostile intentions towards Daryabegi or Zayer Khedr.[458]

On 17 October 1910, the British sent a note to the government in Tehran containing an ultimatum to restore order on the Bushehr-Isfahan road, otherwise Great Britain would insist on the formation of a Persian force under British officers that would do so. This note hardly provoked any reaction in Bushehr. Only Mirza `Ali Kazeruni wrote a telegram that was signed by some of the olama, merchants and others and sent it to Shiraz asking their compatriots to urge Sowlat al-Dowleh not to give any cause for foreign intervention and preserve the peace. On 29 December, Sowlat al-Dowleh arrived in Bushehr, which worried Daryabegi very much as Tehran had assured him that the chieftain would not cross the borders of Fars. He was accompanied by 300-400 tribesmen and nearly every Khan of local importance from around Bushehr with his followers joined him. There were some 1,200 tribesmen on the island at one time. The reason for this 'gathering of the clans' was the expected arrival of Nezam al-Saltaneh, the recently appointed governor-general of Fars, who did not arrive until early January and left on 29 January 1911. En route to

458. Administration Report 1910, pp. 14-15; Sa`adat 1390, pp. 172-73, 176-77; Political Diaries vol. 4, pp. 140, 167-68, 204, 228-29, 268-70, 297, 329.

Shiraz, Nezam al-Saltaneh made a swift incursion into Tangestan to punish Zayer Khedr, but Daryabegi sent his own troops to protect the chief. Because the British Resident was concerned about the growing numbers of tribesmen and consequently petty acts of pilfering and trespass, he visited both Sowlet al-Dowleh and Daryabegi and gave them a friendly warning. In the past such large numbers of tribesmen on the island had resulted in lawlessness and danger for Europeans. Therefore, he warned them, at the first sign of that, troops would be landed as in 1909. Both interlocutors gave assurances and told him not to worry, all was well and in hand. Nevertheless, several robberies took places in homes of members of the Residency staff. Because there were no reports of robberies in homes of other Europeans, it was believed these were engineered by enemies of Daryabegi to discredit his administration and bring him down. Because of that the Resident preferred to arrange matters locally with Daryabegi rather than involve Tehran. Daryabegi had guards placed as well as patrols during the night and gradually paid the compensation demanded. An attack by *Habl al-Matin* on this arrangement led to further credence that his enemies were all behind it, the more so since there were no further incidents.[459]

Movaqqar al-Dowleh becomes governor

Again in March 1911, there was again unrest in Bushehr's hinterland (Ahmadi, Chahkutah), allegedly caused by Nezam al-Saltaneh. When one of his deputy-governors, Amir al-Molk of Dashti moved towards Bushehr, Daryabegi became so afraid that he informed the Residency of his intention to take refuge. The *kadkhoda* of Rishahr posted several small groups of *tofangchis* in the suburbs to defend the town. The Residency assured Daryabegi that it was unlikely that an attack would take place.[460] On 8 April 1911, almost without warning, Mirza `Ali Mohammad Movaqqar al-Dowleh, of Bushehri origin, arrived from Shiraz and replaced Daryabegi. The Residency advised Daryabegi to accept the change without opposition. However, he had no faith in his successor's intentions (who reportedly was accompanied by Amir al-Molk of Dashti) or in those of the central government. Because most of his servants had left out of fear of an attack on his house, Daryabegi felt he needed protection and therefore, he took refuge in the home of the First Assistant Resident, Captain Birdwood and left the next day by steamer to the Shatt al-Arab en route to Tehran. As *kargozar*, Movaqqar al-Dowleh had functioned effectively and while he was a friend of Qavam al-Molk, he was a bitter opponent of Sowlat al-Dowleh. He was on friendly terms with the British Resident, but "he was known to be a person of violent likes and dislikes." Despite their good relations, the British did not welcome his appointment at this time, due to the prominent part he had played in the Qavam-Sowlet feud and his enmity towards the latter and Nezam al-Saltaneh, which implied that Bushehr might be drawn into the torrid political intrigues of Shiraz. Also, he seemed to owe his appointment to Mo`in al-Tojjar and thus it was doubted whether he could pursue an independent policy. Meanwhile, in the early parts of 1911, Nezam al-Saltaneh tried to recover revenue arrears. As a result, the whole countryside was in uproar. His encounters with several Khans were unsuccessful and it left some of them, such as Zayer Khedr and

---

459. Administration Report 1910, pp. 15-16; Sa`adat 1390, pp. 180-82, 188-89; Political Diaries vol. 4, p. 297-98.

460. Political Diaries vol. 4, p. 353.

Jamal Khan of Dashti, stronger than before, reinforced by Tehran's failure to replace Nezam al-Saltaneh quickly with a successor after his dismissal in October 1911.[461]

On 31 July 1911, Movaqqar al-Dowleh convened the notables and informed them that Tehran had approved the construction of two forts at the village of Tangak, 11 km from the town on the way to the Mashilah. He further proposed to build a water reservoir there, for which he tried to collect money from local merchants. Neither project was realized, although he built a small tower (see below).[462] One month earlier, Movaqqar al-Dowleh had banned soldiers from engaging in petty trade. They then demanded to be compensated for lost income; the governor then paid them and they went to their barracks. In November 1911, however, he stopped paying the soldiers, until he received orders from Tehran.[463] Consequently, on 2 December, 340 soldiers and 20 NCOs took refuge in the British Residency saying they had not been paid for 14 months; they left on 19 December after the governor paid them 7,000 *tumans*. However, there were continued payment problems with the soldiers in early 1912, which were only temporarily resolved by a partial payment in April of that year.[464]

In 1911, because of the Russian occupation of much of Azerbaijan (including Tabriz) and its advance towards Tehran (stopping at Qazvin) there was an anti-foreign mood in the country and there were calls to defend the country against the infidels. Several chiefs (Dashtestan, Dashti, Tangestan) declared they were ready to do so and with their own funds as the government had none. A call by mullahs in Bushehr to boycot British goods was declined by the merchants as it was impossible and because the British had taken no action in Persia and therefore, the mullahs dropped the issue.[465] In January 1912, there was a continuation of anti-foreign agitation, but it had no effect in Bushehr, due the indifference of the merchant class. There was some preaching by low-ranking clergy (Sheikh Abu'l-Karim Kazeruni, Majd al-Zakerin Shirazi and Mullah Esma`il) bristling to make a name for themselves, against Persians in the service of foreigners, but none were molested. Also, two days before his death Akhund Kazem Khorasani wrote a letter stating there was no ground for anti-British hostilities. Later the olama from Tehran sent similar messages as did the Persian government. The movement had more success in the hinterland where Sayyed Morteza Ahrami made overtures to various chiefs to repeat his 1909 adventure. Some 240 men joined him amongst whom was Ra'is `Ali Delvari. In March 1912, he also engaged in various talks between local chiefs about reconciliation between them. However, despite much talk and posturing no action materialized.[466]

When Daryabegi was governor he had opposed the Sayyed's return. In fact, when in March 1911, news arrived that Sayyed Morteza would come from Basra by steamer to Bushehr, Daryabegi asked the British Resident to help and stop him from landing anywhere on Persian soil. In response the Resident wrote a letter to steamer's capitain, but the Sayyed was not on board.[467] However, after Daryabegi's departure Sayyed Morteza

---

461. Administration Report 1911, pp. 11-12, 14; Sa`adat 1390, pp. 190-91; Political Diaries vol. 4, pp. 365, 435.

462. Political Diaries vol. 4, p. 421.

463. Political Diaries vol. 4, pp. 408, 461.

464. Political Diaries vol. 4, pp. 473, 524, 541, 553.

465. Political Diaries vol. 4, pp. 473-75.

466. Political Diaries vol. 4, pp. 494-95, 524.

467. Political Diaries vol. 4, p. 352; Ranjbar 1389, pp. 113-17.

saw his chance and in May 1911 he arrived in Delvar. Although Movaqqar al-Dowleh had no previous history with Sayyed Morteza he took steps to prevent him from coming to Bushehr.[468] He must have left again, because the British reported that on 22 October 1913, Sayyed Morteza Ahrami returned to Bushehr from Kerbela and went to Dashti; he returned to Bushehr on 7 December where for the time being he lived quietly and did not want to attract attention to himself.[469] However, the Sayyed would continue to play a minor role in local tribal feuds, disturbances and intrigues, sometimes even hinting at a craving to play a more important political role (see below).

Towards the end of 1912, there were signs that Daryabegi tried to make things difficult for Movaqqar al-Dowleh so that he might return as governor to Busher. He tried to enlist the support of the director of Customs and Mo`in al-Tojjar, who was intriguing in Tehran. The latter had supported Movaqqar al-Dowleh's appointment but found him insufficiently supporting his interests. Also, the Swedish Gendarmerie officers, who arrived in Bushehr in November 1912, had a strong bias against Movaqqar al-Dowleh, because one of Daryabegi's old retainers was attached to them. When Mokhber al-Saltaneh, governor-general of Fars, appointed Daryabegi commander of the military forces of Fars, Movaqqar al-Dowleh became very concerned when Daryabegi was in nearby Borazjan. This force was paid for by the British government, which in 1912 had decided to make available £2,000-3,000 to Mokhber al-Saltaneh to shore up his administration and to create a viable military force. Some money had already been advanced to pay some of the arrears of the troops.[470]

Movaqqar al-Dowleh was forced to levy illegal taxes as the Belgian officials did not pay him. One of the results was a reduced respect for him from the petty Sheikhs and Khans within his governorate. This was because the Belgian Finance officials by stopping payment of the governor's wages or threatening to do so, "spared no pains to convince all and sundry that they and not the local Government were the supreme authority in the district." Meanwhile, Bushehr's hinterland was greatly disturbed, and until December 1912, Dashti and Dashtestan were without a governor; no revenue was collected, although rival chiefs launched plunder expeditions and rival factions were settling feuds in the old-time fashion. Traffic on the road to Shiraz was often interrupted or caravans were forced to take little used tracks to avoid areas of conflict. It was popularly believed that if the 260 British Indian troops had not landed on 30 December 1911, Zayer Khedr's tribesmen certainly would have entered Bushehr and arrested the *kalantar* `Abdol-Reza. A squadron of the Central India Horse remained in Bushehr the whole year; they were housed in buildings erected by Malek al-Tojjar in Rishahr.[471]

---

468. Political Diaries vol. 4, p. 380; Ranjbar 1379, p. 118. In early October 1911, the governor banned Sayyed Morteza Ahrami, who wanted to go to Mecca, from passing through Bushehr. He then collected *tofangchis* to go to Ahram to try and reconcile Zayer Khedr with Bahador al-Soltan's relatives. In mid-August a fight took place between Sheikh Hoseyn Chahkutahi, supported by his cousin Bahador al-Soltan, chief of Ahram and Zayer Khedr, in which the chief of Ahram was killed. FO 248/1033, Bushire News ... ending 15 October 1911 (no. 56 of 1911); Idem, Bushire News ... ending 27 August 1911 (no. 51 of 1911).

469. Administration Report 1913, p. 9.

470. Administration Report 1912, pp. 13-14; Political Diaries, vol. 4, pp. 616, 641; vol. 5, p. 8. Later it was decided to make available £100,000 per year, of which not more than £8,000 per month might be spent. Government of Great Britain 1914, p. 63 (nr. 152).

471. Administration Report 1912, pp. 16-17, 19, 26; Political Diaries, vol. 4, pp. 567-68, 589-90, 600-01.

After the killing of Mme Constant on 8 March 1913, the foreign consuls were very upset and met with the British Resident to discuss measures to ensure order and safety. Cox offered guards to those who had no consular guards. Also, the headquarters of the Jask regiment was transferred to Bushehr, based on the argument that if the British did not do it, some other power might send troops to protect foreigners. However, the British-Indian troops were under strength and hardly enough to protect its own depot at Bushehr and provide guards for foreign residents. In 1913, the force had a strength of 200 men under four British officers. The governor at the end of the year intimated that this force was unwelcome, but this was ignored. There were again some disorders in April by Tangestanis, when Zayer Khedr besieged Choghadak, a village belonging to the Khan of Ahmadi. It was considered to send in the British-Indian troops, but before that was decided, the Tangestanis had been repelled and returned to Ahram.[472]

However, a more serious incident took place on 12 June 1913, as part of a punitive operation against Tangestan. The operation was the result of a case of piracy by Tangestanis against a Dubai pearling boat in 1911, for which no compensation was offered or paid. Therefore, the Resident and the government of India agreed to launch a punitive expedition "to exact reparation." The planned operation aimed to seize all vessels lying on the Tangestan coast from Delvar to that of Karri. The impounded vessels would either be taken to Bushehr or beached at Khark. If no payment was made, the vessels would be burnt or sold. Prior to the operation the governor of the Gulf Ports was informed and invited to participate. However, he declined, pointing out that Tangestan was not under his jurisdiction and so the British decided to go ahead alone. On 12 June, the commander of the British Persian Gulf flotilla sent two armed cutters and a steamboat to bring in ten dhows lying off the village of Omari. Some 40 men fired on the cutters when these were at 500 m off-shore; the cutters replied by firing their Maxim gun and returned after the dhows were hauled up. The naval commander then sent a boat to demand the surrender of the men who had fired and in response the messenger-boat was fired upon as well. Therefore, he decided to bombard the village on 14 June and land a party of 250 men to take action against the village and tow the dhows away. Because Omari was within firing range towards nightfall on 14 June, at noon on 15 June all ships opened fire. After the second bombardment a landing party took the dhows, but they were fired upon and suffered one dead and five wounded. After the party landed the villagers, who suffered 30 wounded, fled. The village was seriously damaged and 15 dhows were scuttled, because they were too far onto the beach to haul away. An envoy from Delvar was told to pay compensation, if not then Delvar (2 km in-land) would be bombarded on 19 June and all dhows on the coast would be destroyed. On 22 June, after shelling Delvar, a landing party of 450 men took the village and destroyed it. During the demolition a large party of some 350 men fired upon the British troops, but they were driven back and disappeared. The landing party returned to the ships at the end of the day without suffering any casualties. On 24 June 1913, a party landed at Khur Khorweir and launched five dhows. On 2 July, the Resident informed the British Minister at Tehran that as far as he was concerned the punitive operation against Tangestan was ended. Twenty vessels were destroyed and 11 were held under guard at Khark for ransom. The Minister informed

472. Administration Report 1913, pp. 7, 15, 30; Political Diaries vol. 5, p. 10. In July 1913, there 400 Rajputs in Bushehr, not counting the Residency guard, guards at private houses and guards at Khark. http://www.qdl.qa/en/archive/81055/vdc_100023576861.0x000032.

the Persian government and urged it to make funds available to the governor of Bushehr so that he might impose the government's authority over the area, although it formally fell under Fars.[473]

Despite all this, the Bushehris and even to some extent the British seem to have had a positive appreciation of Movaqqar al-Dowleh, certainly the reformist part of the population. He was an enlightened man who took the welfare of Bushehr to heart. He established new government offices such as that of justice (*adliyeh*), taxes (*maliyeh*), police (*nazmiyeh*), transportation (*naqliyeh*) and the municipality (*baladiyeh*) (see chapter four). He further built a small tower outside the town, where people coming from outside had to place their arms, before entering Bushehr. He also started collecting taxes from newly made orchards in the town's environs and stopped taxing those that had fallen into disuse and did not transfer the gate duties (annually more than 18,000 *tumans*) to Tehran, which was very popular locally.[474] However, in 1913 the British observed that Movaqqar al-Dowleh's attitude towards them was "somewhat supine of late." He allegedly had pro-German sentiments like the Persian public in general, which was anti-Russian, suspicious of Britain and therefore pro-German. If need be, the governor could also be forceful. When the *kalantar* Mashhadi `Abdol-Rasul was arrested in 1912 this led to disturbances. Therefore, in early 1913, the governor forced him to sign a promissory note for 45,000 *qrans* payable on demand and on 16 January released him at the intercession of Sheikh `Ali Dashti and on security of Mirza Mohammad Kazeruni. His successor as *kalantar*, `Abdol-Reza Khan was not entirely satisfactory, but the best available. He also nominally performed the function of police chief.[475]

After the ouster of Mohammad `Ali Shah in 1909 with the help of Bakhtiyari forces, the Bakhtiyari tribal leadership acquired much political clout and influence. Apart from participating in various Cabinets as ministers and getting governorships, they started to throw their weight around. One of the Bakhtiyari chiefs, Amir Mojahed, the governor of Behbahan had extracted about 100,000 *tumans* there, without paying a penny to Tehran for tax arrears. He also wanted to plunder the coastal ports of Liravi and Delam and demanded the revenue of the past two years plus that of 1913. Since 1840, Liravi had been merged with Behbahan, but in 1887 its port Delam was put under the Gulf Ports. Before or in 1900, the district was granted to Sa`id al-Saltaneh, "a quondam Governor of the Gulf Ports." He paid 2,000 *tumans* in taxes to Tehran and farmed the district to the Liravi Khans for 6,500 *tumans* net. The Khans paid it regularly to the Imperial Bank of Persia (IBP) at the suggestion of their relative of Hayat Da'ud. Revenue had been paid up to March 1912, when Amir Mojahed came to Behbahan. Sheikh Khaz`al had urged the Khans to pay their respects and when then they did, they were fleeced by Amir Mohjahed, who demanded an IOU for the revenue of 1911-13. After a British protest, Tehran ordered Amir Mojahed not to interfere with Liravi. However, he made such threatening moves that the Khans of Shabankareh, Angali and Chahkutah wrote to Heydar Khan of Hayat Da'ud saying that they were ready to send men to help the Khans of Liravi and Hayat Da'ud against Amir Mojahed. The Residency, not wishing any further disturbances, suggested that it would be best to place Liravi under the Gulf Ports, the more so as in the

473. Government of Great Britain 1914, pp. 93 (nr. 225), 110 (nr. 246), 112 (nr. 253), 113 (nr. 255), 115 (nr. 259, 261), 116 (nr. 262), 122 (nr. 274), 127-28 (nrs. 288-89).

474. Sa`adat 1390, p. 191; Administration Report 1913, p. 13.

475. Administration Report 1913, pp. 6, 13.

past it had been part of the district of Bushehr under the Al Mazkur. Moreover, all the Khans involved recognized the Khan of Hayat Dau'd as their chief. Finally, the district was a private fief paying its revenue via the IBP. In July 1913, it was rumored that the fief holder, Sa`id al-Saltaneh wanted more revenue, if not he would sell or lease his fief to the Bakhtiyari Khans. The Residency suggested that Tehran buy Liravi back for the original price that Sa`id al-Saltaneh had paid for it. In October 1913, the Bakhtiyaris once again made demands for revenue and the Residency once again urged its purchase and its transfer under the Gulf Ports.[476] In February 1914, Sa`id al-Saltaneh mortgaged the district with the IBP for an advance of 20,000 *tumans* repayable in semi-annual installments of 2,500 *tumans*. The Liravi Khans punctually paid the two installments plus the tax revenue to the IBP in Bushehr rather than to the owner. Despite this, in May 1914, the Belgian Finance Agent in Bushehr ordered the Khans to pay the revenue to him; at the same time it appeared that Mornard, the Treasurer-General in Tehran, had made a secret deal with Salar-e Mo`azzem, the Bakhtiyari governor of Behbahan to have him levy the taxes from Liravi and pay it to Bushehr. In August 1914, the Bakhtiyaris pressed the owner to sell Liravi and in September it was learnt that the Bakhtiyaris had him pay a higher rent. However, the British Minister warned the Bakhtiyaris to stay away from Liravi.[477] The Khans of Liravi were upset, because the owner, Sa`id al-Saltaneh, returned from Europe and wanted to sell the district to the Sheikh of Mohammerah, which Agha Khan and Heydar Khan, the chiefs of Liravi, strongly opposed, but the plan fell through. Agha Khan owed money, due to locust and other problems, and therefore, had a cash-flow problem. However, he was able to pay his arrears, which set at ease the minds of Agha Khan and Heyder Khan, because a sale to powerful political bigwigs like Sheikh Khaz`al and Qavam al-Molk, would have meant higher rents, which they had the power to enforce.[478]

Bushehr under the Pax Britannica

Whereas in 1914 Bushehr's umland was relatively quiet, this changed in early 1915. After the outbreak of World War I on 28 July 1914, the German consulate started to intrigue with Ra'is `Ali and other chiefs as early as September 1914 and the results showed in 1915. Wassmuss had been acting consul in Bushehr until July 1914 when he left to Europe on leave. He returned in January 1915 in Shushter leading a mission (Linders, Bohnstorff, some Persians and 3-4 Indians) to foment trouble in the region against Great Britain (in Persia, Afghanistan, NW Frontier). He preached *jihad* and distributed large sums to influential men and mullahs. En route to Bushehr, Wassmuss's party was arrested, but he escaped. On 9 March 1915, Consul Listemann and the Wonckhaus agent Eisenhutt were arrested on suspicion of inciting the Tangestanis. Papers found in the German Consulate provided evidence of a widespread plot organized by Kardoff, the German charge d'affaires, to attack all British representatives and communities in the spring of 1915. Movaqqar al-Dowleh and many others were rightly upset by the arrest and the subsequent deportation of the Germans given Persia's neutrality. Wassmuss used the arrest as a lever to incite the tribes in Bushehr's environs, who did not need much

476. Administration Report 1913, pp. 31-32.
477. Administration Report 1914, p. 10.
478. Administration Report 1920, p. 5; Administration Report 1921, p. 3.

Wassmuss with Tangestanis

prodding. Ghazanfar al-Saltaneh of Borazjan formed an alliance of Khans consisting of himself, Sheikh Hoseyn of Chahkutah, Ra'is `Ali of Delvar and Zayer Khedr of Ahram against the British. All these chiefs had much resented British interference with their smuggling as well as their predatory activities on the trade road to Shiraz and now saw their chance to gain much real as well as political coin by continuing with their pillaging and freebooting activities under the guise of defenders of the constitution and the nation. They threatened to attack Bushehr and wrote insulting letters to the governor and the acting Resident. Heydar Khan of Hayat Da'ud, who had become unpopular with the Democrats and pro-Germans by arresting the Wassmuss party, took advantage of an old feud between Shabankareh and Borazjun by making an alliance with the former. The alliance was joined by the Khans of Liravi and Rudhilleh. Ahmad Khan of Angali did not join but remained friendly.[479]

On 23 March 1915, Wassmuss arrived in Shiraz and announced that he was the German consul. By distributing funds he aimed to induce Mokhber al-Saltaneh, the

479. Political Diaries, vol. 6, p. 25; Faramarzi 1390, pp. 125-26 does not consider these alliances the result of pre-existing enmity, hostilities and feuds, as described above (see also Appendices III, IV and V), but as chosing the side of the British against the freedom fighters (*mojahedin*); see also Ya Hoseyni 1382, nrs. 29, 32. In December 1914, both Ghazanfar al-Saltaneh and `Ali Delvari wrote to the Persian government offering help to defend Persia's honor and neutrality and large amounts of money (20,000 *tumans*), whereas prior to that time they had been reluctant and delinquent tax payers. One month later, the former wrote a long article justifying his decade long non-payment of taxes. Ya Hoseyni 1382, pp. 42, 44-45, 51-55 (nrs. 6, 8, 13). However, despite the promise of money, they never paid one penny to defend the nation's honor, despite a plea from the governor-general of Fars for funds, Idem 1382 nr. 62. For articles concerning protests against the arrest of the Germans, see Idem 1382, nrs. 20, 22, 24-28, 32, 40.

governor-general and the gendarmes to support his aims and activities. Mokhber al-Saltaneh established close contact with Ghazanfar al-Saltaneh and the Gendarmerie officers at Borazjan and Kazerun, which became centers of pro-German intrigue. All the successive commanders of the Gendarmerie in Fars, Major Pravitz, Captains Pousette, Oertengren and Angmann were very ready to help Wassmuss. In May 1915, Ghazanfar al-Saltaneh incited and supported Agha Khan, a nephew of the Khan of Shabankareh to rebel. The latter asked and received help from Rig and Rudhilleh and there were skirmishes during the hot season, which cost old Esma`il Khan of Shabankareh a good sum of money. The British liked this development as it prevented Ghazanfar al-Saltaneh's men from joining Sheikh Hoseyn and Zayer Khedr attacking Bushehr. Therefore, the British occasionally gave the friendly Sheikhs presents of arms and ammunition.

On the night of 5-6 May 1915, the governor received information that Haji `Ali, Zayer of Tangak was smuggling arms for the hostile Khans and tried to arrest him. However, he and his men defended their village against the governor's men. The governor asked the British Residency for support, which sent a few men and, as a result, the village was taken and Haji `Ali, who was wounded, took refuge at the Imamzadeh. He remained there until lack of water forced him to surrender to the governor, who imprisoned him. Because the hostile Khans were felt to be a growing threat, it was decided to occupy a strategic point in Tangak and two other villages overlooking the Mashileh. A support line was started that guarded the approach to the island on the east "and runs across the Island about half a mile South of the Sabzabad Residency."

In that same month, Wassmuss came to Ahram, later joined by Bohnstorff, and began recruiting men and giving presents to Sheikh Hoseyn and Zayer Khedr, chiefs with whom he consorted most. At his urging, the chiefs increased their force to a few hundred at Choghadak and Gurak. In mid-June 1915 Wassmuss again visited Ra'is `Ali at Delvar. The latter then talked to Dashti chiefs who were pro-German. This had the desired result as almost 200 Dashti *tofangchis* came to Delvar or Shamshiri. Zayer Khedr had further talks with Sheikh Hoseyn, and the two met Ghazanfar al-Saltaneh at `Isavand. Wassmuss further visited Gurak and Chahkutah and allegedly paid Sheikh Hoseyn 12,500 *tumans* and a similar sum to Zayer Khedr. He urged them, and they agreed, to take immediate action, while he also was said to have paid £50 to Sayyed Morteza Ahrami to support his cause. The latter urged them not to take immediate action but to make adequate preparations. This they did by placing their irregular troops on military footing.[480] The people of Bushehr were afraid of a Tangestani attack, the more so when frightened villagers came into town with their belongings or buried them as well as because of warning messages from relatives in the district. This fear was borne out when on 6 July Zayer Khedr and Sheikh Hoseyn sent an 'ultimatum' to government officials announcing that they were ready to attack the town. However, they would not damage the property of Persian and foreign civilian subjects, because they only wanted to drive out the British troops and obtain the return of the deported Germans. On 12 July 1915, there was news that a party

480. For some of Ra'is `Ali Delvari's motives, see Adamiyat 1349, p. 98-100. Sheikh Hoseyn Chahkutahi and Zayer Khedr allegedly each received £2,000 (12,500 *tumans*) and Sayyed Morteza Ahrami £50. FO 248/1103, Confidential News Summary for the month of June 1915; Idem, Bushire Diary ending 3rd July 1915; Appendix IX. Whether the money helped or not, a fact is that they needed money as is clear from the fact that in March 1916 Sayyed Morteza Ahrami, who then lived in Gurak, co-signed a letter addressed to various anti-British groups in Shiraz asking for financial support to buy arms to attack the British in Bushehr. Mashayekhi 1391, pp. 141-42.

of some 200 Tangestanis and Dashtis led by Ra'is `Ali had crossed the Kuzi wadi, about one mile south of Sabzabad. A party of British-Indian troops went there and ran into a well concealed enemy party; two British officers were killed as was one sepoy, while two were wounded. During the fight, *HMS Lawrence* launched some shells, which the British believed forced a party of 500 men led by Zayer Khedr and Sheikh Hoseyn that was about to cross the Mashileh to return. They had intended to simultaneously attack the outpost there on the east. As a result of this "outrage, combined with the general anti-British attitude of the Persian Government and people," London decided to occupy Bushehr until (i) steps were taken to punish the Khans who had committed the outrage; (ii) indemnities were paid for the two officers (£5,000 each) and men (£500 for the killed and £100 for the wounded); (iii) the German and Austrian agents fomenting trouble in Persia were arrested and expelled; and (iv) Mokhber al-Saltaneh was removed as governor-general of Fars (with the understanding that he would be replaced by Qavam al-Molk who would have the right to appoint the governor of the Gulf Ports). Because the Persian government failed to give the required satisfaction and to protect British interests, lives and property, the British occupied the port on 8 August 1915. By 5 a. m., the town was under the control of the British forces. The gendarmerie put up some resistance, but were ordered by the governor to lay down their arms and march to Shiraz. The British troops occupied all government buildings, including the Post and Telegraph, and the German and Turkish consulates. Anti-British persons were rounded up and arrested, while Persian gunboats were seized and used by the British. Apart from hoisting the British flag and imposing martial law, the British also immediately issued stamps with the overprint 'Bushire under British occupation.' Lt. Col. Lane, the officer commanding the troops, became military governor and deputy-resident civil administrator, while some Persian officials were dismissed. Movaqqar al-Dowleh was sent to Bombay one week later where he remained in retirement. [481]

On 9 August 1915, the British published a statement justifying the occupation of Bushehr.

---

481. Administration Report 1915, pp. 2-5; Political Diaries, vol. 6, pp. 63-64, 79 (the German Legation ordered Wassmuss to return to Tehran; the British forwarded this telegram to the Khan of Borazjan to be passed on to Wassmuss and the Khans who supported him), 81-82 (with details about the Shabankareh-Borazjan conflict), 129; Ya Hoseyni 1382, nos. 75, 78; Faramarzi 1390, pp. 40-58 (with letters exchanged between Sheikh Hoseyn Chakutahi and British officials about the arrest of the German officals); Mokhber al-Saltaneh 1344, p. 270. The British offered to pay rent for their use of the *Azerbaijan* and the *Mozaffari*, which was accepted by Tehran. Nura'i 1385, pp. 205-07, 210; for detailed accounting of the rent which was paid via IBP to the DG Finance (Mornard) in Tehran, see Nura'i 1385, p. 208.

British Occupation Stamps

PROCLAMATION

The Government of His Britannic Majesty has issued instructions that His Majesty's forces now at Bushire shall immediately occupy the town and Island, assume administration of Bushire and take control of the Customs House.

This action has been taken by His Majesty's Government, owing to the conviction which has been unwillingly forced upon them, that the Persian Government can no longer maintain order in Bushire and the neighbourhood, a conviction which has received fresh confirmation from the recent regrettable attack by tribesmen on Bushire in which two British officers were killed and three sepoys killed and wounded.

The situation is thus one which cannot be tolerated by His Majesty's Governmen who have therefore been compelled to take such measures as may be considered necessary in their own interests and will continue to occupy Bushire until such time as the Persian Government undertake to exact full reparation from the guilty parties for the recent attack and to comply with the other demands of the British Government.

No hostile action will be taken against the officials and people of Bushire unless they themselves take hostile measures.

In compliance with the orders of the exalted [British Government] the people of the Island of Bushire and all concerned should therefore take note that from this day I have taken over all Government of Bushire on behalf of the British Government.

A.P. Trevor, Major
Civil Administrator of Bushire.

Source: FO 371/2434, no. 1459.

It had been the intention to shell Delvar, but *HMS Juno* only arrived on 5 August 1915 and its crew was indisposed and thus the shelling was postponed. On 9 August *HMS Juno*, *Paramys*, *Dalhousie*, and *Lawrence* went to the area opposite Delvar, but the weather was bad and a landing impossible. This finally happened on 13 August, but not before the targeted population was given advance notice of the bombardment.

> TO RAIS ALI AND THE INHABITANTS OF DILWAR
>
> Whereas acting in concert with other khans hostile to the British Government, Rais Ali of Dilwar and certain of his followers and some of the people of Dashti invaded the Island of Bushire with hostile intention to the British Residency, and shot two British officers and wounded three sepoys out on patrol passing near-by and subsequently attacked the British outposts; the said Rais Ali is hereby informed that his village will be bombarded and the Towers and houses and a portion of the date gardens destroyed on the 10th of August 1915 as a partial retribution for the offence.
>
> By order of the High British Government
> A.P. Trevor, Major
> Civil Administrator of Bushire.
>
> Source: FO 371/2434, no. 1466.

As a result of the military operation, the fort was blown up and "considerable punishment was inflicted on Rais `Ali and his tribesmen." Casualties on the British side were one British and one native officer, 7 marines and seamen and five sepoys killed and one naval officer, 24 seamen and 176 sepoys wounded. The force returned to Bushehr on 16 August.[482] Thereafter, Bushehr became involved in a little war of its own, due to the rebellion of the tribal chiefs of the districts along the trade route to Shiraz and their attacks on Bushehr. Because the hostile country extended to within 16 km (10 miles) of the port, all traffic inland by this route and access to Bushehr was prohibited from July 1915 till March 1916. Transshipments via other ports were also affected. By September 1915, German emissaries had so much control over Isfahan that British subjects left the city, which led to a suspension of trade with Bushehr. German intrigues, supported by the Swedish officers of the gendarmerie, led to the removal of the British colony from Shiraz in November 1915 and the transfer of the male part to Qal`eh-ye Kalat near Ahram; the women were sent to Bushehr. The hostile Khans demanded (i) the return of all German and Persian prisoners; (ii) return of sequestered funds belonging to Sheikh Hoseyn and Ghazanfar al-Saltaneh; and (iii) the departure of British troops, except for 16 men, presumably the normal consular guard. If accepted, the Khans promised to remain on friendly terms with

---

482. Administration Report 1915, p. 5; Political Diaries, vol. 6, pp. 144-45; Faramarzi 1390, pp. 67-68; Moberly 1987, pp. 98-101.

Khalu Hoseyn Bordekhuni

Parade of the transfer of authority to Daryabegi in October 1915

the British. In December 1915, serious fighting broke out in Shiraz and the rebels were able to oust the acting governor-general of Fars. Also, the branches of the IBP fell into the hands of the Germans and the British prohibited money transactions with those places.[483]

When the British restored the administration of Bushehr to the Persian government Daryabegi was appointed and replaced the British military governor on 16 October 1915, during an official ceremony with a military band, speeches, and the hoisting of the Persian

483. Trade Report 1915-16, pp. 1-2; Political Diaries, vol. 6, pp. 156-57; Moberly 1987, pp. 124-25, 138-38; Faramarzi 1390, pp. 92-95; O'Connor 1930, pp. 231-40.

Ahram Fort

flag.[484] Since Daryabegi had taken over as governor of Bushehr he had been frustrated by an unresponsive government in Tehran, his balancing act to retain good relations with the hostile Khans so as to maintain his reputation as a Nationalist, his worry about the permanency of his position as well as about his family, which was in Shiraz and out of contact, and the lack of funds to function as governor. Not only did not he receive any appreciation or payment, but neither did the other local government officials nor *tofangchi*s that he hired to protect the town. His state of mind usually oscillated between despair, resignation and wanting to resign to optimism when he received some rare good news. In fact, without loans from the Residency his administration would have fallen apart. The hostile Khans considered him to be in league with the British and therefore, despicable. On 5 January 1916, some 100 *tofangchi*s and cavalry crossed the Mashileh to waylay a British cavalry patrol, but not finding it the raiding party returned. However, the mood among the besiegers of Bushehr had changed somewhat, now they expected being attacked by the besieged. Every evening they moved into trenches dug about one km in front of their most advanced camp. There also was discontent among the Tangestani *tofangchi*s with their chiefs.[485] During the second and third week of August 1916 tribesmen made many nightly raids. The first was done prior to the occupation to a house behind the outpost line that was used as a signaling station. Later until 20 August raids were carried out against the houses of Messrs. Gray Paul, the IBP, Messrs. Dixon, and the assistant Superintendent of Telegraphs. Nobody was injured or captured. The British advised Europeans who lived scattered about the island to take up residence in the town or sleep in the telegraph building near army HQ. After the attack on the telegraph building, where the women spent the night, most of them left Bushehr. On the night of 16 August, the Russian Consulate was attacked and on 19 August the British Residence at Sabzabad. The party involved in this attack suffered some wounded, who could not retreat and were found in the wadis near Zanganeh at the eastern end of the island. A British force sent to dislodge the attackers failed in its objective and they withdrew under cover of darkness.

Brig. General Brooking took over as commanding officer on 24 August 1916 and as military governor on 26 August. During that time another raid was made on the town and an outpost led by Ra'is `Ali Delvari himself who was killed, which was a great loss for the hostile chiefs and a benefit to the British as he had been the most active and determined of them. On 9 September a force of more than 500 tribesmen was discovered in the wadis at Zanganeh; they were attacked and "driven out at the point of the bayonet." Retreating over the Mashileh they were hit by machinegun fire and a cavalry charge; the enemy was believed to have suffered more than 100 casualties; 40 dead were found at Zanganeh, who were buried at the Imamzadeh. The British, who lost one British officer, two seamen, two native officers and 25 Indian sepoys, nevertheless stated that "this affair gave the tribesmen a severe lesson and they did not give much trouble for some time thereafter." Brig.

---

484. Sa`adat 1390, p. 211 (the British had refused Abu'l-Qasem Shirazi Nasir al-Molk II as governor); Moberly 1987, pp. 56-57, 67, 73, 87, 98. Movaqqar al-Dowleh wrote a scathing article in January 1915, exposing the lies and innuendos in a sensational newspaper article by a nationalist about the situation in Bushehr. Ya Hoseyni 1382, pp.62-68 (nr.16; see also nrs. 59, 61, 65). In October 1915, the government of Persia first appointed Nasir al-Molk as governor of Bushehr, but he resigned. Then Mas`ud al-Soltan was appointed, but finally Daryabegi was selected and appointed. Idem 1382, nrs. 178, 184, 197, 202, 208-09 (the British first did not allow Daryabegi to enter Bushehr), 211, 218-19, 228 (hoisting the flag), 237, 464 (in mid-1916 he began collecting taxes). Ya Hoseyni 1382, nrs. 75, 78; Faramarzi 1390, pp. 66-67, 96 (Daryabegi British tool)

485. Political Diaries, vol. 6, pp. 143, 155, 169, 185-86.

From left to right: `Abdol-Reza Khan, chief of police and Sayyed Mohammad Doktor, secretary to Wassmuss.

Brooking was replaced by Brig. Edwardes on 13 September. Brooking had appointed two assistant military governors, one for the town and one for the outside. There was no problem in town, the population was "very quiet and orderly." The customs, finance, police, and postal departments continued to work under their own officials except that the *kalantar* ("head of the Town Administration and Police") `Abdol-Reza was removed and replaced by Haji Yusef. The Persian telegraph was closed, because the lines had been cut long before the occupation. There were occasional raids by sniping parties on outposts. On 9 December 1915, a rather larger attack took place of about 100 men who came to the cavalry camp at Rishahr and fired at it; another party fired at the British Residence at Sabzabad; only one sowar was killed and one horse wounded. [486] To provide better protection, the British troops occupied a line of 9.6 km of outposts stretching from the North coast along the east side of the peninsula to a point of about 2.8 km E.S.E. of the British Residency and then turning westward to the sea. To the east there was a good visibility and shooting range, but to the south the land was uneven, traversed with many wadis and crags situated to the east of the peninsula.[487]

---

486. Administration Report 1915, pp. 6, 9 (*HMS June* plus two smaller craft remained at Bushehr); Faramarzi 1390, pp. 70-90 (with more details); Ya Hoseyni 1382, nr. 70. In March 1916, the British naval authorities detained the two Customs launches, see IOR, P 1431/1916 (10 March 1916); Sa`adat 1390, pp. 204-10.

487. Government of India 1924, p. 92; Mahrad 1978, p. 91; Ya Hoseyni 1382, nrs. 94, 96, 100, 102, 104, 110-11, 113. For the composition of the Bushehr garrison, see Administration Report 1917 p. 1.

During the first quarter of 1916, the hostile Khans basically ceased hostilities, apart from some potshots at the British outposts and even those ceased after April. Zayer Ahmad held the male members of the British colony in Shiraz prisoner at Ahram, while the British had 15 to 20 prisoners who were captured at Zanganeh on 9 September 1915, including Khalu Hoseyn, a Dashti Khan and Zayer Hoseyn, a nephew of Zayer Khedr. Mid-April 1916, the Khans sent a letter offering to hand over the prisoners on condition that they would receive a pardon for their crimes, which was refused. The more so, because they did not want to give up Major O'Connor, the British consul in Shiraz. During the early part of 1916, it was contemplated to launch a punitive raid to bring about the liberation of the prisoners at Ahram. During March and April, the Mashileh was too wet to allow passage of guns, but by 27 April the soil was sufficiently hardened. A reconnaissance was done; the enemy fired and their trenches and the towers in Choghadak villages were destroyed. This made the Khans fearful and Ghazanfar al-Saltaneh induced Fath al-Molk, who held Shiraz, "to send a telegram saying how loyal and friendly Ghazanfar was and also got Soulet himself to write to the Daryabegi in the same strain. Ghazanfar himself wrote declaring that he had disarmed the 30 Gendarmes at Borasjun." However, it was decided that a raid would do more bad than good and might endanger the lives of the prisoners.

Although the British prisoners in Ahram were well-treated, Mr. Pettigrew, one of the prisoners, died on 27 April in Ahram due to angina pectoris. Another prisoner, Dr. Azzopardy was released due to illness on 30 June 1916. The closure of the trade road had a negative impact on the rebellious Khans, who became anxious about their situation, the more so, since militarily they were significantly weakened. Wassmuss had financial problems and therefore "his influence had entirely gone. In fact, at Ahram there was a strong feeling against him" and in May 1916 shots were fired at him. The British in Bushehr made plans to have the prisoners escape; maps were made, routes described and secretly sent, Dashti Khans were ready to take them in as soon as they entered their territory, but finally the plan was rejected as being too risky. At last, in July 1916 negotiations started with the Khans, but a pardon was not on the table. Mr. Christmas fell ill and he was exchanged for two prisoners; he arrived on 2 August in Bushehr. Finally, an exchange of prisoners was agreed upon. Khalu Hoseyn and the captured Tangestanis for Major O'Connor and the other British prisoners. Furthermore, monies belonging to Sheikh Hoseyn were returned and tea confiscated at Bahrain, which Zayer Khedr claimed to own, was to be returned. Lastly, it was agreed to reopen the route across the Mashileh via Ahmadi to Borazjan. On 10 August 1916, the exchange took place; Zayer Hoseyn was not present, because due to a mistake he had been sent to Bombay. This problem was solved by O'Connor remaining with the Khans until Zayer Hoseyn returned, which he did on 20 August and O'Connor was released. Tangestani tribesmen, except for known dangerous characters, were allowed to enter Bushehr. The Shiraz road was open and trade went up and down. However, this stopped when on 17 December 1916 Naser-e Divan occupied the gendarmerie barracks in Kazerun. The road was closed immediately and trade was suspended. Naser-e Divan, who was in collusion with the hostile chiefs, asked them for reinforcements. As a result, the hinterland was disturbed again, only the center had moved from Borazjan to Kazerun.[488]

---

488. Administration Report 1916 pp. 3-4; Political Diaries, vol. 6, pp. 198-99, 225, 237-38; Moberly 1987, pp. 160-61, 178-79, 204; Ya Hoseyni 1382, nrs. 466-68; O'Connor 1930, pp. 240-49. For the correspondence between the Tangestani chiefs and the British concerning the hostages, see Faramarzi 1390, pp. 106-22. For a short bio of Khalu Hoseyn Dashti or Bordekhuni, see Hamidi 1380, p. 278. On Naser-e Divan, see Floor 2011 b.

In October 1916, the removal of the German emissaries and influence from Fars and the establishment of a strong governor in Shiraz, who was supported by the recently created *South Persian Rifles* under Percy Sykes, combined with strong policing of the Shiraz-Isfahan road led to heavy forwarding of goods to unload stocks. Those who profited most were the muleteers and tribal chiefs who collected more illegal duties than ever from passing caravans.[489] Consequently, there were clashes between the blackmailers on the road. In accordance with the agreement of the chiefs, they avoided any conflict with the British, so that the British had no justification to deal with the abuses on the road. On the coastal plain hostilities continued between Sheikh Hoseyn of Chahkutah, supported by Zayer Khedr and less so by Ghazanfar al-Saltaneh, and Ahmad Khan of Angali, but there was no real change in the line-up of the various feuding parties. Similarly, the fighting between Ghazanfar al-Saltaneh and Shabankareh continued. Zayer Khedr had his own problems being challenged by a combination of Tangestani chiefs in May and June 1917. Trade continued, be it sometimes via devious paths, and there were improvements to 1916, in spite of the bad harvest and high prices for goods. Wassmuss still had his HQ in Ahram; he visited Ahmadi shortly in March 1917 and Khaviz in the summer. In April, Messrs. Dettmar, Oertel and Bruggmann joined him, who had lodged with Sowlat al-Dowleh and then went to Ahram via Khormuj, the residence of Jamal Khan of Dashti. Dettmar died in August in Khaviz and on 18 September 1917 Bruggmann was arrested close to Bushehr, while trying to leave the country. On 23 or 25 May 1918, Wassmuss, Oertel and 13 others left Ahram, Sayyed Mohammad Doktor, Wassmuss's secretary and medical adviser had left earlier to Behbahan with his family.[490]

The Post World War I Years

In September 1918, a British Strike Force moved to Shiraz to relieve that town from an attack by hostile tribesmen and bring the trade road under control by removing all rebellious chiefs. As a result of these military operations, a light railway was laid between Bushehr and Borazan, about 65 km and a considerable portion of the Bushehr-Shiraz road was made passable for motor traffic. By the end of 1918 the roads were safe and trade traffic boomed.[491] There were eight aero-planes in Bushehr, which supported the troops and carried out bombing raids. Begin 1919, supported by Indian troops and aero-planes, Daryabegi attacked Zayer Khedr's positions and drove him out of Khaviz and Hasan Khan's *tofangchis*, a British nominee and Zayer Khedr's nephew, was placed there and held the Khaviz-Ahram valley at the end of 1919. However, beyond Khaviz nothing was achieved. At that time the deputy Resident with a large escort accompanied Zayer `Abdollah, the former head of the Customs House *tofangchis* and a Dashti, whom Daryabegi had appointed chief of Dashti. The aged Jamal Khan was captured in Khormuj and Zayer `Abdollah installed in his place. He maintained himself there with the support of Faqih Zeyn al-Din, a kinsman, with 300 *tofangchis* and was able to pay the taxes for the

489. Report 1916-17, p. 2.

490. Administration Report 1917 p. 3; Political Diaries, vol. 6, pp. 334-35, 378, 404, 418, 422, 432; Moberly 1987,pp. 240, 261. For a photo of Sayyed Mohammad Doktor with `Abdol-Reza Khan, the chief of police, see Roknzadeh 1352, p. 128.

491. Report 1918-19, pp. 1-2; Political Diaries, vol. 6, p. 417; Moberly 1987, pp. 320, 346-47, 355, 374-78; Faramarzi 1390, pp. 128-50. For more details, see Floor 2011 b, pp. 169-71.

Khormuj valley north of the Mund River. He could not bring to order the other Dashti Khans. These were not openly hostile, but helped the rebel Khans with *tofangchis* and refused to meet with Daryabegi.[492] During the entire war period, Daryabegi remained governor and his "experience and local knowledge, combined with his steady attitude of friendliness, were valuable assets to British interests." He was now officially known as Ahmad Khan Sardar Daryabegi and carried out his function as governor of the Gulf Ports not only in Bushehr, but also in other parts of his jurisdiction such as in Lengeh. During these missions, Soleyman Mirza, the Chief of the Finance Department acted as deputy governor.[493] Because of his pro-British attitude, Daryabegi felt that the British owed him more than a medal. In January 1919, Consul Bill reported that "Darya Begi has several times indicated that his object in life is to retire on a British Govt. pension."[494] I have not been able to ascertain whether Daryabegi actually received a British pension.

Meanwhile, Sheikh Hoseyn and Zayer Khedr continued with their petty raids, but on 28 April 1919, Zayer Khedr made a mistake. He occupied the village of Baghak and the railway 11 km from Choghadak. When news arrived at Bushehr, a force was sent immediately during the night and arrived early in the morning at Baghak, which it surrounded. Of the 40 men, eight were killed and 24 made prisoner; Zayer Khedr had left the village before the attack, but it stopped his activities for some time. A short while later, Ghazanfar al-Saltaneh was captured by Agha Khan in Faryab, but he was allowed to escape. However, later he was again arrested and imprisoned for a while before being allowed to return on certain conditions.[495]

In June 1919, Asaf al-Molk arrived in Bushehr and took over from Daryabegi as deputy-governor for Dashti, Tangestan and Dashtestan. He took up residence in Borazjan and toured the surrounding area accompanied by a SPR escort. Sheikh Hoseyn and Zayer Khedr were tired of their circumstances and wrote to Asaf al-Molk that they wished to come to terms. They were given safe conducts and met Asaf al-Molk and Capt. Fraser at Samal. Sheikh Hoseyn and Zayer Khedr only would accept reinstatement of their previous positions, would not listen but only wanted to dictate. Negotiations were broken off and the situation remained as it was. Asaf al-Molk also wanted to meet the Dashti Khans at Khormuj during his tour, but only two showed up (Khalu Hoseyn of Dayyer and Ahmad Khan of Lawar), the others refused to come and submit. It was too hot to take military action which was deferred. When the cold season started, the military commanders did not want to move and it was decided that Asaf al-Molk would have to go to Khormuj to induce the Dashti Khans to talk and thus cut off their support from the rebel Khans. The Dashti Khans had intimated that they refused to submit to Zayer `Abdollah, because he was socially an inferior, a refugee and not even a Khan, but they were willing to submit to Asaf al-Molk. To make this possible, Daryabegi transferred Zayer `Abdollah as deputy governor of Lengeh. However, by the end of 1919 the Dashti Khans still had not met with Asaf al-Molk. In August 1919, Sheikh Hoseyn and Zayer Khedr had been told their case would be reviewed. As nothing happened they started raiding again after three

492. Administration Report 1919, pp. 3, 6; Political Diaries, vol. 6, pp. 443, 445, 451, 456.

493. Administration Report 1916 p. 2; Administration Report 1917 p. 1; Administration Report 1918, p. 1; Administration Report 1919, p. 2; Faramarzi 1390, p. 150-62.

494. FO 248/1229, Telegram Bushire to Legation Tehran, 11/01/1919.

495. Administration Report 1919, pp. 3-4; Political Diaries, vol. 6, pp. 467-68; Faramarzi 1390, p. 167-70; Floor 2011 b, p. 171; FO 248/1229, Report Bushire Field Force, 28/11/1919.

Ahmad Shah in Bushehr

months. When a few Zayer Khedr's followers raided Baghak with the intention to shoot the headman, they only wounded him. Then Hasan Khan came with more men from

Ahram and was wounded; he was taken to Bushehr hospital, his thigh had been shattered and there was gangrene, but he refused amputation and died on 8 December 1919.[496]

Sheikh Hoseyn and Zayer Khedr remained defiant; the Dashti Khans met with Asaf al-Molk at Khormuj and promised to obey, but when he asked them to fight, the chiefs refused. Asaf al-Molk then arrested three of them, Hoseyn Khan, `Abdol-Humeyd and Karim Khan, through treachery. Their followers started fighting with Asaf al-Molk's *tofangchis*, who were supported occasionally by RAF bombings at Asaf al-Molk's request. Plans were made for a joint operation of the SPR and the Bushehr force to capture or expel the rebel Khans from Tangestan. However, the detailed plan was shelved as the British government prohibited any action which resulted in spending more money or making more military commitments, since it had been decided to evacuate the force in spring. Thus, there were only the occasional bombings. In fact, in April-May 1920, the remainder of the Strike Force left Bushehr. Only a small force remained behind, which was rotated annually.

There were reports that Asaf al-Molk treated his prisoners badly to induce the population of Dashti to come and make terms with him, which they refused to do with him. The British then convinced Asaf al-Molk to hand them over to the military authorities for detention. The invitation to the sayyeds and other leading men of Dashti to come and discuss terms for the release of the Khans provided they promised to pay their taxes had no result and after one month the Khans were handed over to Asaf al-Molk. The arrival of the Shah and the resignation of Asaf al-Molk was the moment to end this unsatisfactory situation. The Khans were released by royal clemency and sent to Dashti. Later those of Dashti were told to choose their own *zabet* and Hoseyn Khan, who was chosen, was appointed by Salar Nosrat, who succeeded Asaf al-Molk. Salar Nosrat turned out Mohammad Khan from Ahram, but as he did this only to get money he was reappointed at the insistence of the Residency.

On 18 May 1920, Ahmad Shah arrived in Bushehr by sea and from there went to Mohammerah. He was welcomed by Farmanfarma, who had come by tractor from Borazjan on 14 May, as well as by the population at large.[497] In July 1920, Sheikh Hoseyn tried and failed to capture Chahkutah. Daryabegi wanted to attack him but could not raise *tofangchis* from the local Khans and therefore, asked help of regular troops. The SPR sent a force from Kazerun. On the night of 21-22 July 1920, a force of 100 infantry, 50 cavalry and one Austrian gun attacked. Sheikh Hoseyn, one of his sons and 20 others were killed and many were wounded; the SPR suffered 13 casualties of which were five dead. Soon thereafter Zayer Khedr wrote Daryabegi that he would come to Ahram to settle his affairs and would obey his orders. He sent two of his sons to Bushehr as hostages. However, this was not followed up when Daryabegi was dismissed. Zayer Khedr, who had remained quietly at Khaviz, then came to Ahram which he occupied. Mohammad Khan left the fort with a few man as garrison and came to Bushehr to ask for help. He was told to return else he would lose the Residency's support. Zayer Khedr did make a move to take the fort. Mohammad Khan did not return, so that Salar Nosrat was sent to Ahram to put his own agent in the fort so that neither Zayer Khedr nor Mohammad

---

496. Administration Report 1919, pp. 3-4; Political Diaries, vol. 6, p. 475, 477-78. These negotiations are not mentioned by Faramarzi 1390. For a description of Khormuj, see Hamidi 1380, pp. 290-91.

497. Political Diaries, vol. 6, p. 589.

Khan could occupy it. Matters remained thus till the end of 1920. By that time Movaqqar al-Dowleh still had not arrived and it appeared that Zayer Khedr was the only possible candidate for the post of *zabet*.[498]

Mirza Sir Ahmad Khan Daryabegi, who received a honorary KCIE on 1 January 1920, remained governor until 20 September 1920. He left a few days later and had the telegraph chief officiate, awaiting his successor Movaqqar al-Dowleh, whose brother Mas`ud al-Soltan arrived on 23 November 1920 to take over as acting governor.[499] In the Bushehr elections at the end of December 1920 five candidates competed for two seats in the *Majles*. Mirza `Ali Kazeruni had the most votes, more than half. He was Wassmuss's right hand during the war. Mirza Mahmud Behbahani was the second man chosen, but was disqualified as being under age and then Sheikh `Abdol Karim Shirazi, "a man of no note" was chosen.[500] Movaqqar al-Dowleh never came to Bushehr and his brother Mas`ud al-Soltan acted until mid-March 1921, when he was confirmed as governor, because his brother became Minister of Public Works in Ziya al-Din's cabinet. In August 1921, Mas`ud al-Soltan was informed that he was to be replaced by Moshar al-Dowleh and thus he left shortly thereafter, handing over authority to Sayyed Hoseyn, the chief of the Municipality. Moshar al-Dowleh arrived on 2 October 1921. According to the Resident, he was "a better educated and more civilized person than is customary to find in this appointment, having spent several years in Paris and visited England." Moshar al-Dowleh remained in office until 30 September 1922. The *kargozar*, Yamin al-Mamalek, officiated as governor until the end of the year and then was confirmed as governor.[501]

In 1921, although relatively free of the atmosphere of Tehran, the anti-British or better the anti-foreign feeling was more openly expressed in Bushehr. Otherwise the Bushehris had little interest in what happened in the rest of the country, e.g., the coup d'etat of February 1921 did not excite anyone in town. However, the proposed new municipal taxes did. Hoseyn Khan, *zabet* of Delam oppressed the people and a large number of leading personalities came to Bushehr to see the governor to ask for his dismissal. They also wired Tehran, which in July ordered the governor to dismiss him. Heydar Khan was given the first opportunity to remove him and replace him with somebody else, but he refused, though he disapproved of him. He feared that the person appointed by the governor Bushehr would be hostile to him and make trouble. Tehran was adamant and threatened to send the *Persepolis* and remove Hoseyn Khan by force. At the suggestion of the Residency, then in August, Heydar Khan temporarily appointed one of his own men, who was later replaced by Qoli Khan.[502]

The deputy governorship of Dashti and Dashtestan was vacant for most of the year, but towards end of 1922 Jalil al-Saltaneh was appointed. Otherwise there was little change in the tribal situation. Ghazanfar al-Saltaneh remained in Borazjan. Although he was still intriguing, outwardly he behaved as promised to the Residency when he was allowed to return to Borazjan in 1921. He actively interfered with the situation in Shabankareh,

498. Administration Report 1920, pp. 2-3; Political Diaries, vol. 6, pp. 493, 542, 650, 657, 672; Faramarzi 1390, pp. 168-70, 174-80.

499. Administration Report 1920, p. 1; KCIE means 'Knight Commander of the Order of Indian Empire.'

500. Administration Report 1920, pp. 1, 5-6; Political Diaries, vol. 6, p. 689.

501. Administration Report 1921, p. 1; Trade Report 1921-22, p. 1; Administration Report 1922, pp. 1-2; Political Diaries, vol. 6, p. 766.

502. Administration Report 1921, p. 6; Political Diaries, vol. 6, pp. 704, 722, 738-39, 749.

where there was some lackluster fighting between Sohrab Khan, the *zabet* and his relative Agha Khan, who defended the right of Jahangir Khan, Sohrab Khan's younger brother. A force from Borazjan tried to divide Shabankareh between Sohrab Khan and Jahangir Khan and there was some fighting. Finally, the governor-general resolved the dispute by declaring that Sohrab Khan was the *zabet*. Dashti was unsettled throughout the year. Hoseyn Khan the nominal *zabet* was ignored by the other Khans and no revenue was collected. This was not for lack of funds, because some smuggling took place, as usual, via its small ports. In Tangestan, Zayer Khedr remained a troublemaker and opposed the authorities. He refused to pay his taxes to the deputy governor of Dashti and Dashtestan, occupied a village in Dashti, encouraged the levying of *rahdari* at a village on the trade road and was feared to have intentions to take Choghadak. Nevertheless, he was given the title of Amir Afkham by Tehran. Of the Bushehr Khans, Sheikh Hoseyn of Chahkutah was the most troublesome, until his death in 1920 fighting the SPR, according to the British.[503] They considered him almost as big an intriguer as Ghazanfar al-Saltaneh, because he involved himself in many different affairs in the adjacent districts. During the hot season he had a tomb (*gombad*) erected near the Imamzadeh close to Sabzabad (the location of the Resident's house, who lived there year round) intending to transfer his father's remains there. He was induced not to do so, including by the Sayyeds of the Imamzadeh, but he clearly wanted to make his father into a martyr. Sheikh Mohammad received the title of Sardar Ashja from Tehran and a robe of honor from Reza Khan. There was some desultory fighting between Sheikh Mohammad and his neighbor the Khan of Angali, who had a standing feud. Apart from this, Agha Khan kept the district of Bushehr quiet.

The district of Hayat Da'ud was in good order as usual; Heydar Khan paid his taxes regularly and gave no trouble. Liravi and Rudhilleh, which were managed by his relatives were also in good order. Nevertheless, Heydar Khan was attacked by Tehran and Reza Khan, the Minister of Defense. A few members of the *Majles* such as Mirza `Ali Kazeruni also instigated attacks against Heydar Khan. Moreover, Moshar al-Dowleh, the governor of Bushehr was not a friend of his. This was partly because he was friendly with the British, partly due to jealousy about the benefits he received from the APOC and the pearling at Khark. Another source of trouble for Heydar Khan was the Bakhtiyari governor of Behbahan, Ziya al-Saltaneh, who still wanted to interfere with Liravi.[504]

Bushehr under Central Government Administration

After World War I Persia seemed to be a country that was up for grabs; its central government had little or no authority and the various regions were controlled by petty chiefs and warlords. There was a situation of *moluk-e tavayef*, i.e. small and large carved out fiefdoms run by local 'kings'. This situation was satirized in the satirical journal *Mullah Naser al-Din* that provided a description of the United States of Persia, which consisted of: the Soltanate of Maku, the Tabriz kingdom, the Caliphate of Gilan, the Emirate of Astarabad, the Khanate of Tehran, the Empire of Qom, etc."

503. For another view, see Faramarzi 1390, which has a picture of the tomb on p. 178.

504. Administration Report 1922, pp. 6-7; Political Diaries, vol. 6, p. 766; vol. 7, p. 7 (the Governor of the Gulf Ports tried to have Ghazanfar al-Saltaneh removed from Borazjan), 74, 106, 125, 174 (Hoseyn Khan finally was buried in the mausoleum on 17 April 1923). For a picture of the mausoleum, see Hamidi 1380, p. 240.

For the first time in a century, Great Britain did not have to deal with a rival foreign power to control Persia, because that is what what it wanted to do. Lord Curzon was the most outspoken proponent of this policy in the British Cabinet. However, not everybody in the Britsh government agreed with this approach, while many politicians in Persia did not either. The *Majles* rejected the 1919 Anglo-Persian Agreement, which basically would have turned the country into a British protectorate. After this rejection, the British government withdrew its troops (except from Bushehr), preferring that a strong local government would take over Persia; of course, one guided by Great Britain. Such a configuration it considered to be a sufficient buffer against the Soviet 'threat.' Therefore, Great Britain welcomed the coup d'état of February 1921, which it may have helped bringing about. However, the British had not expected that Reza Khan, who was an unknown quantity, would play an increasingly important role. His success on the battlefield in northern Persia (against Mirza Kuchek Khan, Pesiyan, Simko) bolstered his influence and the British began to see him as the better alternative to civilian leaders, who so far had only disappointed them. To consolidate his position in Tehran, Reza Khan had to bring the south under his control, which brought him into direct confrontation with British interests. Great Britain had to choose. It supported Sheikh Khaz`al and other coastal Sheikhs in their bid for quasi-autonomy, but finally chose Reza Khan's centralizing policy. This choice was facilitated by the fact that Reza Khan's military rule did not seem to have the corruptive practices of the old, tried and failed civilian rule. Given the decision not to get militarily involved in Persia, Great Britain believed that a clearly successful leader such as Reza Khan offered the best protection for its interests in the region, in particular the protection of India. The latter was key, for Great Britain had no interest in Persia per se, but only in its role as a buffer between India and those who wanted to challenge Britain's role there. Therefore, it acquiesced in Reza Khan's anti-British measures as long as these did not weaken the protection of India. The controlling hand of Reza Khan and his supporters was felt in all areas of government. His executive arm, the new modern army, immediately made quite a difference in terms of safety on the roads. Moreover, in Bushehr (as in many other places) the military overrode civil authority. The governor became a mere figure-head, while various attempts were made to transfer municipal and other funds to the central treasury at Tehran.[505]

In 1922, the control of the central government increased over Bushehr, in particular that of the Ministry of War, which instructed the Finance Department to transfer all revenues from indirect taxes to the military. The road guards were replaced by the military, who had the real authority and not the governors. In early March 1922, governor Moshar al-Dowleh was informed, as were all governors throughout the country, that his salary was reduced to 500 *tumans*/month plus 100 *tumans* for his secretary and 10 *tumans* for his servant, while he could no longer employ *tofangchis* and *sovars*. Nominally there the governor had 75 *tofangchis*, although only 62 actually served, and their wages, as those of the police, were in arrears. Moreover, in early 1922, there were no funds to pay local government officials. After an imminent riot by the *tofangchis* on 3 May 1922 was diffused by the governor, Tehran released funds to pay them.[506] In September 1922, a force of 160

505. Trade Report 1923-34, p. 1; Political Diaries vol. 7, p. 125.

506. Political Diaries vol. 7, pp. 32, 44-45. See also, Willem Floor, "The Coup-d'Etat That Had To Happen," *Motale`at-e Tarikhi. Zamimeh-ye Majalleh-ye Daneshkadeh-ye Adabiyat va `Olum-e Ensani* (Daneshkadeh-ye Ferdowsi), 9-10 (1384/2006), pp. 11-28. For the possible British role in the 1921 coup d'etat, see Yann Richard, "Le coup d'etat de 1921 et ses sources historiques," *Studia Iranica* 38 (2009), pp. 69-103.

men under *Yavar* Mohammad `Ali Mirza arrived. When Reza Khan visited Bushehr in November 1922 the significance of this move became very clear as he stated that the troops were the local representatives of the chief authority in Persia. He made it clear by word and deed that Tehran was serious to govern Bushehr and the tribes. When dealing with the tribal Khans Reza Khan ignored the governor, whose position he weakened by placing the police under the garrison commander. Most importantly for the British was Reza Khan's anti-British bias that guided his actions. On arrival, he talked about the British troops and stated that they would soon depart, because the Persian army could ensure security in the south. The British disagreed with this assessment. According to the British Resident, the troubles in Dashti and Dashtestan still required the presence of British troops, the more so since the Persian troops were of insufficient strength to deal with them. Reza Khan caused real dismay when he arrested Allah Karam Khan, son of Heydar Khan CIE of Rig, who had come to Bushehr to pay his respects to the shah. He had done so at the urging of his father, because of alleged lack of respect in his behavior toward Reza Khan. Given Heydar Khan's position and his friendly relations with the British, his arrest was locally seen as a challenge to the British position in the Persian Gulf. Despite the British Legation's intercession, Allah Karam remained in military detention. Meanwhile, attacks were also made on the position of Heydar Khan whose right to Hayat Da'ud and Khark was questioned and whose fiscal obligations Tehran tried to increase despite existing *farmans*. Reza Khan knew what he was doing. He demanded: (i) an immediate assessment of Hayat Da'ud, (ii) that Heydar Khan would obey the Persian government (which he had always done) and (iii) that he would accept Persian troops in his territory. He further ordered the garrison commander to hand Choghadak to Sheikh Mohammad, "son of the late enemy of ours, who had been killed during the rebellion." Finally, to make sure that his message was understood, he gave robes of honor to the sons of Sheikh Hoseyn of Chahkutah.

Agha Khan remained *kalantar* of Daleki until the fall of 1922 when he sought refuge in Bushehr, after having learnt that the governor-general of Fars had been bribed to replace him with Yadollah, Fathollah's cousin. Tehran had assured the Residency that the governor-general had been instructed not to evict Agha Khan without the consent of his landlord, Nezam al-Saltaneh. However, the garrison commander, at the orders of the military authorities of Fars, installed Yadollah. Reza Khan later promised to re-install Agha Khan, but the garrison commander refused to take action claiming contrary orders from the Ministry.[507]

These events and the overbearing personality of the *Sepahsalar* overshadowed the arrival of Ahmad Shah on his return from Europe on 29 November 1922.[508] There was no contest as to who made the greater impression, given the difference in behavior between

507. Administration Report 1922, pp. 6-7; Political Diaries vol. 7, pp. 18 (the Persian government was upset that Heydar Khan had made an agreement with the APOC on 6 October 1921, granting it drilling rights at Ganaveh, which the Persian government rightly considered an unlawful action), 125, 149, 158 (Allah Karam Khan was released on 25 January 1923). The Nationalists had already expressed their enmity toward the Khan of Rig in 1915, mentioning his (pearl) revenues as well as that he paid his taxes, be it not enough according to the nationalist author. These same authors never aimed similar accusations against the rebellious and tax dodging chiefs of Dashti, Dashtestan and Tangestan, see Ya Hoseyni 1382, nr. 35.

508. Administration Report 1922, pp. 4-5.

Ahmad Shah and Reza Khan during their arrival in Bushehr. In fact, Ahmad Shah made not such a good impression, despite efforts to make him welcome.

> The Officer Commanding the Port borrowed a launch from the British trading company Mespers. Flying a gigantic Persian flag, he put-putted out the ten miles to the anchorage to greet the Shah. The Commander felt that a royal salute should be fired in His Persian Majesty's honor, but he had no cannon. So he drew his revolver with a fine flourish and started shooting in the air just as the Shah got halfway down the ladder. Ahmad Shah thought it was an attempted assassination and scampered like a frightened squirrel back into the security of the *Varsova*. 'It took a bit of persuasion to get him off the ship after that,' Captain Fitzherbert told us.[509]

When Ahmad Shah finally made it safely to terra firma; he stayed three days in Bushehr. To welcome him, the main streets and the sea front were decorated in his honor and were illuminated at night. He left by car on 2 December 1922 to Shiraz where he arrived on 4 December.[510] Reza Khan's visit to Bushehr was more and very significant.

> It sent a violent jar through the whole frame work of administration in the South. It was well stage managed; all the circumstances attending it were calculated to impress the people with the fact that the Sipah Salar was introducing a new era for the Persian Government. The announcement '*l'etat c'est moi*' seemed in his case to be authentic; and his actions and evident power flattered the national self-esteem. But it was not only British prestige in the South which suffered. The authority of the local Civil Government and the semi-independence of the tribal Chiefs received shrewd blows.

Reza Khan clearly identified the power of the central government with military power. The British were concerned how their lower prestige on the Persian side would play out on the other side of the Persian Gulf. They also were concerned, whether Reza Khan would be able to deliver and overcome the political, administrative and geographical difficulties. In particular, the British considered his undermining of the local authorities and tribal chiefs a dangerous experiment.[511] They further believed that "Provided Reza Khan survives long enough to train some of his officers to carry on his work, and provided that the revenue of the country prove equal to the strain in usual times when there are no arrears to supplement them, it seems probable that Persia will get to her feet. The year has been a successful one for the Prime Minister."[512] Of one thing there was no doubt in 1923, Reza Khan was the absolute ruler of Persia, "whilst towards the end of it he became *de jure* as well as *de facto* head of the Government."[513]

509. Hall 1947, p. 194.
510. Administration Report 1922, pp. 4-5.
511. Administration Report 1922, p. 8.
512. Administration Report 1923, p. 4.
513. Administration Report 1923, p. 1.

Towards the end of 1922 Reza Khan began to turn the country into a military administration and as a result, the governors-general and governors were mere figure heads; the army commanders acted independently and interfered in administrative matters without even consulting the governor. Also, the new government was able to settle all tax arrears of tribal chiefs and others in the south. The deal with the Bakhtiyari Khans included the permission to claim 14 years of arrears from Liravi! The Residency learnt later about and protested vehemently. At the end of 1923 troops were sent to Dashti and Dashtestan to collect revenue arrears from the Khans.[514]

The new policy making the military the authoritative power in Persia became very clear in Bushehr after Reza Khan's visit in December 1922. It was evident to everybody in Bushehr that the arrest of Heydar Khan's son was on the orders of Reza Khan; the governor was powerless in this matter and all orders went to the military commander. The police force also remained under the military despite the governor's protests that he needed some enforcement agency to be taken seriously. Again, the Persian Customs boats *Persepolis* and *Mozaffar* were put under military control. To subdue the tribes and make Great Britain withdraw its troops, the Persian military were reinforced. In early 1923 a force of 100 men arrived. Furthermore, the *Amniyeh tofangchi*s on the trade road were dismissed and the security of the road transferred to the military. Local forces were reinforced and detachments were sent to outlying places.

Yamin al-Mamalek, who had been acting governor since 30 September 1922, was confirmed as governor on 30 January 1923. He then issued a manifesto justifying his past conduct and outlining a policy of independence in the future. However, his weakness for money "exceeded even the limits sanctioned by custom in Bushire." When he failed to bring a about speedy punishment of those guilty in a grisly murder there was public outrage, because it suspected him of wanting "to screw as much as he could out of all concerned before submitting the case to Tehran." He also lost public confidence. When in June 1923, in broad daylight, a number of extraordinary murders were committed "by a man, who, despairing of getting justice in a money suit, took the law into his own hands and proceeded to kill his debtor, a mullah and his family and two vakils." This led to general public outcry and the demand for the governor's recall. The telegraph office was besieged and occupied for two weeks by crowds who refused to leave until the governor was dismissed. Yamin al-Mamalek was insulted and even given physical ill-treatment in the street, but he remained calm and showed courage. He was recalled on 4 June 1923.[515]

During the governor's absence, the telegraph chief and later the deputy-governor Dabir al-Homayun officiated. As of 29 July 1923, Nasr al-Dowleh was governor. The Resident described him as "a youngish man of little or no experience of civil administration, his previous service having been mostly military." He was clearly a less forceful personality than his predecessor, moreover, he was beholden to various local groups, from whom he accepted money, which seriously handicapped the little maneuverability and authority that he had. For he had very little of it, because the real power was in the hands of the military, and the little that was left in the hands of the Finance Department. He did not even have a police force and thus was a mere figurehead.[516] Nasr al-Dowleh

514. Administration Report 1923, pp. 1-2.
515. Administration Report 1923, pp. 1-2, 5, 7.
516. Administration Report 1923, p. 5; Political Diaries vol. 7, p. 181.

was governor until 28 May 1924; he was summoned to Tehran having been accused of taking bribes relating to the Liravi affair. The *kargozar* Mo`azzad al-Soltan acted as interim governor, until the arrival of Veqar al-Molk on 22 June 1924. The Resident described him as friendly, but "handicapped by lack of driving power and lack of wealth, and by the fact that the military are the real power in the land." Therefore, he was active in the municipality and tried to improve local security.[517] There was one advantage to the military taking control in that they were able to collect large arrears from the tribal Khans in the south. However, their increased power, authority and access to money also exposed that the "vaunted honesty and disinterestedness of the military, so much insisted upon by Army Headquarters at Tehran, are a sham."[518]

The anti-British feeling, which surged in December 1922 abated thereafter. The reference to the need for British troops to leave and the arrest of Allah Karam Khan were such signals, but after the Khan had been released at the end of January 1923 little of it remained. There was an attempt to rouse anti-British sentiments by putting up of placards allegedly written by Allah Karam Khan intimating that if he would not have been released the British would have freed him. However, the military took the placards down and Allah Karam Khan stated publicly that he had nothing to do with them. The tomb of Sheikh Hoseyn of Chahkutah and the dome (*gonbad*) at Sabzabad which his son intended to become an anti-British monument, also failed to achieve its objective. Zayer Khedr's death[519] did not lead to anti-British sentiments, although the Shiraz press was very venomous on that occasion. The fact that Britain remained aloof from local political life also gave these forces no opportunity of which to take advantage. This was clear when Sheikh Heydar of Hayat Da'ud came to Bushehr mid-summer 1923 to make peace with the Persian government and get it off his back. He did so because he was still being pressed for a revenue re-assessment and full submission to the government. The Resident reported to Tehran and Reza Khan gave assurances that no action would be taken against Heydar Khan without informing the British. In spite of this, the Finance Controller, "apparently on his own responsibility," went to Khark with four Cossacks to assess the revenues realized by pearling there. Heydar Khan was prepared for this and had an armed force on the island that prevented the party from landing. This could not, of course, be overlooked even if the Finance Agent was in the wrong. Reza Khan regarded it as an insult to his army and gave orders that if Heydar Khan did not agree immediately to the demand a military expedition would be sent to subdue him. The newly arrived governor, Nosrat al-Dowleh, to avoid an armed conflict invited Heydar Khan to Bushehr to make peace, a move supported by the British. He was given assurances and was well treated during his one week stay and when he left he gave "a guarantee of loyalty." He was apparently satisfied with the results of his discussions, although the Finance Department had not changed its demands or tune. The matter of to whom the pearl revenues belonged had

517. Administration Report 1924, p. 5.

518. Administration Report 1924, p. 1.

519. O'Connor 1930, p. 246 described his jailer as "totally uneducated and ignorant, and vain-glorious and boastful to an almost insane extent. This was party due, no doubt, to flattery from Wassmuss and messages which were supposed to have arrived for him from the Kaiser and from the Amir of Afghanistan, etc., telling him what a fine fellow he was, and so on. . ... But apart from this he was naturally a vain, unstable creature, and there were days when he would emerge from the inner recesses of his fort and stalk about the courtyard, brandishing a long spear and telling everybody what a fine fellow he was."

not even been discussed. The British Resident made it clear to Heydar Khan that given the changed circumstances, Great Britain would no longer maintain friendly relations with the tribal leaders to the exclusion of local Persian authorities and he was strongly urged to accept the new reality.

One result of this visit was the inclusion of Hayat Da'ud, Rig and Liravi among the districts that nominated the candidates for election to the new *Majles*. Voting papers were distributed and it was even thought that out of 13,000 votes permitted for Bushehr for its two candidates that Heydar Khan would get enough to have his nominee elected. But after a lot of intrigue Mirza `Ali Kazeruni in Tehran and Ahmad Akhgar of Shiraz were elected. The former was an ex-*Majles* deputy and known for his anti-British attitude. Therefore, the British never forgot in their correspondence to note that he had been forced to leave Bushehr as a fraudulent bad debtor and forger. Akhgar had no relationship with Bushehr at all and was also believed to be strongly anti-British. His election was due to the fact that Dashti and Dashtstan, which formed a large part of the electoral district of Bushehr, was under the administrative control and influence of the governor-general of Fars. Therefore, the voting for Bushehr was controlled in Shiraz, not in Bushehr. As soon as the results were made known, bribes were handed out and strings pulled to upset the election of Akhgar, which the partisans of Nezam al-Saltaneh's son (who was next on the list) claimed to have been illegal. An official was appointed to investigate, money changed hands, but the result remained unchanged.

The expulsion of the *mojtahed*s by the British from Iraq in mid-summer had little impact in Bushehr; on 10 August 1923, the bazaars were closed only one instead of three days as ordered by the olama, for this action was not welcomed by the trades' people. At the end of September 1923, Haji Sheikh Mehdi al-Khalesi, the chief deportee, arrived at Bushehr en route to Tehran. He was given a reception on a very modest scale, but surprisingly aroused no interest among the people of Bushehr and there were no anti-British demonstrations. The merchants were not interested and hardly contributed for the expenditures for his entertainment. The *mojtahed*, who barely spoke Persian, kept very quiet and did nothing to foment anti-British sentiments.[520]

The call for a Republic and the Khuzestan rebellion did not arouse one iota of interest among the population of Bushehr. Only the more influential Khans gave signs of a vague anxiety. The military tried to get the people behind the idea of a Republic, but the merchants were totally uninterested.[521] It was a good thing too that the Bushehris showed no interest, because Reza Khan abandoned his quest for it at *Nowruz* 1925. He resigned, but was immediately reinstated and so nothing changed. On 25 November 1924, Reza Khan arrived in Bushehr en route to Mohammerah to deal with Sheikh Khaz`al's rebellion. He only stayed one day, because on 26 November he left for Delam. With the defeat of Sheikh Khaz`al the Khans of the Garmsir had to give up all hope that they might regain their independence. When Heydar Khan of Hayat Da'ud asked the Resident what he should do the British Resident told him "to show that he was a loyal subject."[522] This was certainly a piece of advice better given to the Tangestani Khans, who were not inclined to change their ways. Although a convert to Islam, Mr. Roberts, an employee of

520. Administration Report 1923, pp. 8-9; Political Diaries vol. 7, pp. 184 (Nasr al-Dowleh arrived on 29 July 1923), 188, 192, 196-97.

521. Administration Report 1924, p. 6; Political Diaries vol. 7, p. 223.

522. Administration Report 1924, pp. 6-7.

the Military Works in Bushehr, was wounded in his house. It was found that the attackers had been sent by Mohammad `Ali, son of Zayer Khedr to kill an important European to make trouble for the government. Mohammad `Ali was arrested and kept in military detention until August, when the government paid 600 *tumans* in compensation.[523]

Bushehr under the Pahlavis

The Reza Shah period

That the military remained in charge was clear from the opening of the first girl's school in Bushehr in February 1925, despite opposition from the olama. Also, that the military took over the Municipality in September, when there were differences between the latter and the revenue authorities. Although the public did not like it, in October the garrison commander took control of all municipal matters. The takeover had positive results, such as the widening of the streets, allotting sites for the markets, regulating prices for foodstuffs, and insisting that public baths and shops were kept clean. The tribesmen in the port's environs were unhappy with the strong government, the more so since conscription was feared. In October 1925, Ahmad Shah returned from a trip to Europe to avoid the end of his reign. Reza Khan drummed up support through the military. As a result, the notables sent sympathetic messages to the nationalist, i.e. anti-Qajar party in Tabriz. In reality nobody outside official circles in Bushehr cared and nobody was interested either in the bread riots in Tehran. Bushehr elected four deputies to the *Majles* that had to decide the future of the dynasty. The election was rigged, but nobody was interested to make a fuss about it. The change of dynasty had no impact on Bushehr, people were apathetic. Likewise, the general public was not celebrating when Reza Khan was enthroned on 15 December 1925. In that same month, a district committee was formed of local heads of departments to make the government function better. However, neither the director of Customs nor the garrison commander were present, which made this attempt at decentralization an empty gesture.[524]

Reza Khan Atabegi Veqar al-Molk was governor until his death on 17 September 1925. He was friendly to the British, but not popular with the Persians, "as he was a weak man and had no money of his own to spend." However, had brought the police again under the governor's control and reduced the dependence of the civil administration on the military. After his death his assistant Mohammad Karim Khan Vaziri officiated. On 13 October 1925, his successor Mirza Ja`far Khan Khvajeh-Nuri Movaffaq al-Dowleh arrived. He was well connected, because he was the uncle of the governor-general of Fars. The Resident described him as "a friendly, amiable man, but of no great strength of character, and he left no mark on Bushire." That would have been difficult, because he left already on 26 June 1926. As usual the *kargozar* acted as governor pro-tem. His successor, Ahmad Khan Nikpay Mofakhkham al-Molk arrived on 19 November 1926. It was a change of fresh air, because he was an able man who stood up to the military.

523. Administration Report 1925, pp. 9, 13.
524. Administration Report 1925, pp. 8-9.

In 1908, he had already served in Bushehr as *Mir Panj* (garrison commander) and "had a reputation of being the one honest man in Persia." However, in his next post in Isfahan, he succumbed to temptation and amassed much wealth.[525]

In March 1926, with the departure of the detachments of the 1/16 Punjab Regiment there were no longer any British soldiers left, as the regiment was not replaced. On 24-26 April 1926, Reza Shah's coronation was celebrated; the town was festively decorated and illuminated, but there was not much enthusiasm for it, although people appreciated the holiday. Shortly thereafter, the Shah reduced the role of the military in the civil administration throughout the country. This was possible, because the military had squashed all relevant opposition, their man was the ruler of the country, and therefore, the Shah opted for a less overt military role. Elections of the 6th *Majles* were held in Bushehr with the usual "jobbery and corruption." Sheikh `Ali Dashti and Nezam al-Saltaneh were elected, respectively, editor of Tehran newspaper *Shafaq-e Sorkh* and the son of the former governor-general of Fars, who was "a local absentee landlord of little importance."[526]

In June 1927, Mirza Ahmad Khan Nikpay was recalled to Tehran. He left on 22 June 1927. His deputy Mirza Mehdi Khan Nashaki officiated until the arrival of the new governor Mirza Gholam `Ali Khan Fotuhi Mo'in al-Molk, CVO on 21 September 1927. He had been private secretary to Ahmad Shah, had been to Europe with him and spoke French and some English. He was friendly, pleasant, but a weak individual. He was not happy in Bushehr, because the department heads ignored him and he felt powerless to do something about it. In 1927, Reza Shah's coronation was celebrated on 25 April with receptions, a parade, an official evening dinner followed by fireworks, but there little enthusiasm for the event in town, and celebrations were on a lesser scale than in 1925. The feud between Tangestanis and Chahkutahis, despite efforts by the military to mediate continued in 1927, with some attacks and casualties on both sides. In September 1927, the sons of the late Sheikh Hoseyn murdered their uncle Sheikh `Abdollah, with whom they had a long-standing hostile relationship, because they suspected him of conspiring with the Tangestanis. `Abdollah Khan's son was also killed. In November 1927, Sayyed Morteza Ahrami arranged a truce between Chakutahis and Tangestanis.[527] This is the last time that there is a report on the Sayyed's activities. In Gurak, where he had established himself as *mojtahed*, he played a traditional role in local politics.[528] Only in February 1927, there is a report intimating that he saw a larger political role for himself, because at that time he claimed to have received a copy of letter addressed to the olama in Najaf, sent by the chief *mojtahed* of Lucknow, exhorting them to take action against Ibn Sa`ud and promising funds to finance such action. Sayyed Morteza allegedly forwarded this letter to the shah, threatening to raise forces himself if the shah took no action against the Wahhabis.[529] Sayyed Morteza died on 14 August 1937 in Bushehr, which town recently erected a statue in his memory and honor.[530]

---

525. Administration Report 1925, p. 6; Administration Report 1926, pp. 1-2 (Ahmad Khan spoke English and had been in Great Britain); Political Diaries vol. 7, p. 241.
526. Administration Report 1926, pp. 1, 3.
527. Administration Report 1927, pp. 1-3; Political Diaries vol. 7, p. 606. CVO is 'Commander of the Royal Victorian Order,' a British award given in recognition of distinguished personal service to the British sovereign.
528. Political Diaries vol. 7, p. 105.
529. Political Diaries vol. 7, pp. 467-68.
530. Political Diaries, vol. 12, p. 541. For a photo, see Mashayekhi 1391, p. 272.

Mirza Gholam `Ali Khan Fatuhi remained governor until 20 May 1928, when he left suddenly for Tehran. `Abdollah Khan Monajjami, the provincial director of Finance officiated from 26 May till 31 August, when Sardar-e Entesar Aqa Mozaffar Khan Aslam took over as governor. He was a high ranking former military officer and a former member of the Turco-Persian Frontier Mission in 1901. He spoke French, German, Arabic, Turkish and knew a little English and Russian. He came from Kermanshah where he had been governor. He was an easy-going, but a strong man. He took a great interest in municipal affairs and pushed reforms through vigorously. His brother, Doctor Amir Khan Aslam was the Shah's physician. On 25 November 1928, Reza Shah arrived from Mohammerah and left on 27 November. The recently imposed conscription and the new compulsory headgear were not popular and during shah's visit, "there was certainly a noticeable lack of enthusiastic display of loyalty." However, there was also a general lack of interest in politics, "may be due to a large strain of Arab than in Persia proper."[531] Although Reza Shah was feared, he was not popular and was criticized in private for being a dictator. The new dress rules, conscription and disarmament were bitterly resented and opposed by the tribesmen. This resulted in a revolt among the tribes in S. Persia in 1929, which kept the army very busy in putting it down. Apart from a little trouble at Borazjan, there was no rebellion in the Bushehr district. The Tangestanis were fighting among themselves once again. The governor feared that the fighting might spill over to Dashti and Dashtestan. Therefore, he and the garrison commander frequently visited the district. By the end of 1929, the rebellion was over and the government sent 2,000 troops to disarm the Tangestanis and Dashtis. Because poverty was growing among the people, this gave rise to some discontent with the regime.[532]

Sardar-e Entesar was an energetic, tactful and popular governor. He was a hard worker, but because the heads of the local government departments (military, police, finance, customs, and Justice) acted independently and received their orders from Tehran, he only had a limited area of responsibility. Like some of his predecessors he focused on municipal affairs. He widened some bazaars and improved the roads. His assistant Sadid al-Saltaneh Kebabi was called to Tehran and placed under arrest.[533] In 1930, Sardar Entesar was absent from Bushehr for 7½ months on leave and as member of Perso-Turkish Frontier Commission. He was instrumental in disarming some of the Dashti and Dashtestan tribesmen, which was completed by the end of March 1930. He was also able to nib in the bud Ghazanfar al-Saltaneh's rebellion, which threatened to become general, which action was much appreciated by Reza Shah. He further obtained approval for the improvement of the town, harbor, etc, but due to lack of funds none of these plans were implemented. Hoseyn `Ali Khan Shahruzi, the director of the PT, officiated from 12 May till 22 December. According to the British he was "a petty official, afraid to take the smallest responsibility and quite unsuited for the appointment of Governor." Also, he was

531. Administration Report 1928, pp. 2, 4, 7.

532. Administration Report 1929, p. 5. On 28 December 1928 (6 Dey 1307), the *Majles* approved the uniform dress law (*Qanun-e motahhed al-shekl namudan albeseh-ye atteba`-e Iran dar dakheleh-ye mamlekat*). Although the law did not define what constituted 'uniform dress,' men, because the law was only applicable to them, nevertheless were forced to wear Western-style clothes and the so-called Pahlavi cap, a kind of French kepi, available in beige and black. On this and subsequent new dress rules, see H. E. Chehabi, "Staging the Emperor's New Clothes: Dress-Codes and Nation-Building under Reza Shah," *Iranian Studies*, vol. 26/3-4 (1993), pp. 202-29.

533. Administration Report 1929, p. 2.

unpopular with the townsmen and tribesmen, because he showed a total lack of practical administrative ability. Mirza Esma`il Khan Amir Ebrahimi was assistant governor from 2 February until 24 March when he returned to Tehran. Mohammad Khan Zand replaced him. Sadid al-Saltaneh returned in September 1930 after 17 months of imprisonment. He was told it was all due to a misunderstanding and as recompense he was appointed deputy governor of Lengeh. Elections were held for the *Majles*, giving most of the votes to Sheikh `Ali Dashti and Haji Mohammad Reza Behbahani, as ordered by Tehran. Both the urban and the rural population of the governorate were unhappy with the social and economic situation. In particular, they did not like the conscription, disarmament, the new dress rules and the higher land revenue (60% increase). Merchants and traders also were unhappy, because the new foreign exchange law and the higher customs duties made importing almost impossible. As a result, the general discontent manifested itself in criticism of Reza Shah, whom the general public considered a usurper of the people's constitutional rights.[534]

On 9 February 1931, Sardar-e Entesar became governor-general of Fars in addition to his function as governor of the Gulf Ports. His assistant-governor Mohammad Khan Zand was in charge of Bushehr, an arrangement that did not work out. Sardar-e Entesar himself admitted that having two functions was too much work for one man. He was recalled on 20 July 1931, probably due to the military with whom he had clashed. His successor in Bushehr was `Ali Asghar Khan Taleqani who arrived on 26 July on which date the Gulf Ports were separated from Fars. Mostly, he had served in the Finance Department in the north and knew English, French, and Russian and the Resident considered him a "sensible and quiet fellow." Zand was still assistant-governor and most of the time dealt with matters concerning the municipality, "where he made certain improvements." The tribesmen in Bushehr's environs still resented the dress regulations, the conscription, the disarmament and trade restrictions.[535]

There still was not much cooperation between the civil and military authorities, in particular concerning security. This had unfortunate result, because whereas in 1930 the sons of Sheikh Hoseyn had supported the government against Ghazanfar al-Saltaneh, they rebelled in 1931, due to the tactless behavior of the military. In April 1931, Sheikh Nasir with 30 armed men occupied Choghadak some 25 km east of Bushehr and bastinadoed the headman who had leased the village from the government. By the end of 1931 most chiefs had been rounded up and sent to Tehran. The commander of the Kerman regiment when operating in Shibkuh, arrested 13 Arab chiefs and sent them to Tehran. This led to unrest and the Sheikh of Teben, Sheikh Mohammed b. Ahmad Khalfan who escaped arrest, mobilized the remaining Arabs. At the end of 1931 he was still in rebellion, despite 2,000 troops sent against him. He visited Bahrain and Hasa and wanted to go to Riyad, but the Emir of Hasa did not allow him to go beyond Hofuf. He returned to Teen and

534. Administration Report 1930, pp. 2-3,6; Political Diaries, vol. 9, pp. 3, 34, 239, 266. A visiting commission found Mirza Nasrollah Khan Hekmat, the deputy-governor of Borazjan guilty of taking bribes. He pleaded force majeure as his salary was only 40 *tumans* and he received no allowances for a clerk or a *farrash*, while he was expected to keep an establishment as governor. It did not help, for he was sent to Shiraz. Administration Report 1931, p. 3.

535. Administration Report 1931, pp. 3, 7.

attacked a Persian customs launch, killed an inspector and wounded an *Amniyeh* guard. "At a service held in memory of the deceased Inspector, Mulla Abdullah al Fazil, a blind preacher and 'Rozakhan' of Bushire made certain references to the services rendered by the late Colonel Muhammad Taqi Khan (supporter of Saiyid Zia-ud-Din and the late Khiyabani (a republican) both of whom were viewed by the present Shah as his rivals. The Mulla was promptly placed under arrest and deported."[536]

In 1932, Mirza `Ali Asghar Khan Taleqani made an effort to make a difference as governor by inducing the various government departments to work together instead of opposing each other. It was also a year with a complete crop failure and water shortage. He did everything to help the sufferers and was able to overcome Tehran's apathy by convincing the central government to exempt wheat and fodder imports from the trade monopoly restrictions. Given the lack of enthusiam for Tehran's policy mesasures, the people of Bushehr showed little enthusiasm when Tehran ordered that there should be rejoicing about the cancellation of the d'Arcy concession. On 3 December 1932, only a few shops were decorated and illuminated.[537] On 21 October 1934, Taleqani was summoned to Tehran. During his absence *Na'eb* `Abdollah Khan Minjal, the acting chief of police was governor pro tem. Zand, the assistant-governor officiated until 23 July and from 21 October `Abdol-Shakur Amin. The latter became honorary president of the municipality and the assistant of the new governor was Mohammad `Ali Mirza Rokni.[538]

Because of the disarmament there was little lawlessness in the district. Gholam `Ali Sabz, a renegade roadguard turned robber, who had been accepted back into the fold after having been very helpful with disarmament in the previous year, killed someone. He was rid off in time-honored manner. One of the leading men of Chakutah was induced to invite him to his house and then to shoot his guest in cold blood. Another gang in Chahkutah was gotten rid off in similar manner. The deputy governor was appointed in Bandar Rig as governor of Hayat Da'ud, Rudhilleh and Liravi and its chiefs, viz. Allah Karam Khan, `Ali Khan son of `Ali Khan, Mohammad Khan and Aqa Khan were ordered to go to Shiraz. The former complied, the other three tried to get permission to remain home.[539]

In February 1935, ballot papers were sent from Tehran. The governor instructed his officials to see to it that Haji Mohammad Reza Behbahani and Shokrollah Safavi, editor of Tehran newspaper *Kushesh*, were elected as *Majles* deputies and a few votes allowed for other candidates to make it seem democratic. The result was as ordered, Safavi received 20,793 votes, Behbahani 20,667 votes and two so-called competitors respectively, 1,144 and 347 votes.[540] In mid-June 1935, the law abolishing the Pahlavi cap and replacing it with the European brimmed hat was enforced in Bushehr by the police and local officials. The *Amniyeh* did the same in the countryside. Hatmakers had to make "only sun-helmets and caps, and merchants were given facilities to import sufficient quantities of sun-helmets and felt hats to meet local requirement." In a short, while a large variety of headgear was seen, "varying from the local made sun-helmet, casques, not unlike those worn by

---

536. Administration Report 1931, p. 8; Administration Report 1932, pp. 6, 8.
537. Administration Report 1932, pp. 3-4.
538. Administration Report 1934, p. 3.
539. Administration Report 1934, pp. 5-6.
540. Administration Report 1935, p. 8.

halberdiers in Mediaeval Europe,'gorblimey' caps and harlequin cricket caps." Any opposition was immediately suppressed. Sayyed Musavat of Borazjan who spoke against the reform was arrested and taken to Shiraz for trial and punishment. Schoolmistresses and girls were told to go without the veil. At year's end nobody wore the Pahlavi hat and schoolgirls went without their *chador*.[541]

Rokni remained governor until 23 July 1935. His assistant Amin was acting governor until 23 November, when Amanollah Ardalan became governor. He remained in office until 27 May 1936. His assistant Amin officiated from 28 May until 8 July, when the new governor Ahmad Sadri arrived. Amin remained assistant-governor until 30 September 1936. This was also the year that the law on unveiling was passed, which was implemented rigorously. The younger and good-looking women had no problem with the new law. Some of the husbands opposed it, allegedly on financial grounds. This made sense, because when women wore a *chador* there was little dress competition possible between women, however, without it 'fashion' had begun and to dress wives costs more. The government was aware of this problem and gave one month's pay of those of its employees whose monthly wage was less than 100 *tumans* to enable them to buy their womenfolk the necessary outfit. Of course, most people considered the 'unveiling' sacriligious and contrary to Islamic law. In 1936, the government further decided that women were not allowed to wear the traditional headband, while also turbans were not permited any longer either, apart from the Imam Jom`eh and three other leading mullahs.[542] The governor was assisted by Taqi Medhat until 21 March 1937, when he was replaced by Mohammad Karim Navvab. On 25 March 1937, Reza Shah and the crownprince were in Bushehr. The questions raised by the Shah mainly concerned the drop in population and the scheme to bring sweet water to Bushehr from Ab-e Shapur.[543] On 12 April 1938, Sadri was recalled. During his absence `Enayatollah Parvaneh, director of Finances officiated. On 26 April 1938, Hasan Farzaneh the new governor arrived; he remained in office until the end of May 1940. During his administration Bushehr's jurisdiction was reduced. The new governorate extended from Delam in the North to Kangan in the South and as far Borazjan in the interior and for administrative purposes it was placed under the governor-general of Fars. The new governor tried to improve his town. He raised the sea-front, planted trees on it to make it a pleasant walk. He also focused his interest on the bazaar and saw to it that shops were clean.[544] The outbreak of WWII was of no great interest to the people of Bushehr; only some merchants worried about the loss of markets and thus business. However, after Germany's initial victories people showed more interest in the course of the war, often from an individual point of interest. Of course, the annual celebration of the 1921 coup d'etat on 23 February was celebrated by parades by the garrison, boy scouts and school boys, with, finally, a march past the Shah's portrait.[545]

---

541. Administration Report 1935, p. 8.

542. Administration Report 1935, pp. 2-3; Administration Report 1936, pp. 2, 6; Political Diaries, vol. 11, pp. 551, 578, 754; vol. 12, pp. 8-10, 41-42, 66, 160.

543. Administration Report 1937, pp. 1-2. For the preparations of the visit and presents ordered to be given and a description of the visit itself, see Political Diaries, vol. 12, p. 372, 400-02.

544. Administration Report 1938, pp. 2, 6; Administration Report 1939, p. 2; Administration Report 1940, p. 2.

545. Political Diaries, vol. 14, pp. 5, 31, 121-22, 165. On the practice of showing the same respect to the Shah's portrait as to him in person, see Floor 2005 a.

THE MOHAMMAD REZA SHAH PERIOD

In 1941, the administration of the governorate became even less effective than previously by the frequent change of the governor, while corruption among government officials was rampant. Ironically, Mr. Khakpur, the person sent from Tehran to stamp out corruption in the Economics Department, was arrested himself for embezzlement and corruption. Mohammad Esma`il Navvab, the head of the Municipality was summoned to Tehran to answer allegations of corruption, while Capt. Esfandiyar, who had earned a reputation for "uniquely successful corruption" was appointed head of the Gendarmerie. The head of the military recruiting station was accused of corruption and, as result, dismissed and the station was closed. Governor Mir `Ali Zaher was in function from January till 14 August and from 6 to 18 September, while for the remaining period three different persons were acting governor. All of these developments did not contribute to good governance, although the appointment of the garrison commander Col. Malek Nasri on 16 September as acting governor worked better than the British had expected, because he considerably improved local bread distribution.[546]

On hearing the news from Tehran that allied troops had invaded Persia on 25 August 1941 people in Bushehr reacted calmly. A few days earlier, the garrison commander, Lt. Col. Malek Nasiri had posted some troops between the town and Halileh. However, they took no action against the British or any other foreign subjects or buildings. When one night a rumor spread that four British warships had arrived at Bushehr people in town showed some alarm. Immediately, troops were ordered to take up positions to resist any landing. However, once it was reported that the government in Tehran had surrendered on 29 August "even known pro-Axis enthusiasts changed their politics and became pro-British." After Reza Shah's abdication there was hope and optimism in Bushehr for a better future. However, this hope was soon doused; prices rose, bread became scarce due to the absence of rain and reduced sowing, while corruption among local officials rose, although their salaries had been doubled in many cases. Due to these developments, people wondered whether Persia would not have been better off after all under Reza Shah.[547] There was some revival of the local optimism, due to the demand for labor by the car assembly plant, which was short of workers.[548]

People's attitude toward Great Britain became somewhat positive, because they saw that its ships imported food into Persia, while the truck assembly plant provided employment. However, people were very dissatisfied with the governor's, conscription officers' and the Economic Department's corruption. Against the latter steps were taken to improve performance and people were dismissed.[549] In February 1943, Tehran announced that the Municipality, Police and Finance Departments had been placed directly under its control. This meant that the governor-general only controlled the governorate and the Foodstuffs Department of Bushehr. However, the latter also was placed under Tehran one month later.[550] Despite the shortages of food and high prices Bushehr's labor market was almost at full employment. When in May 1943, a British officer wanted to recruit 2,000

546. Administration Report 1941, pp. 3-4.
547. Political Diaries, vol. 14, pp. 494-95, 539; Administration Report 1941, pp. 8-10.
548. Administration Report 1942, p.10.
549. Political Diaries, vol. 15, pp. 94, 117; Administration Report 1941, p. 10.
550. Political Diaries, vol. 15, pp. 402, 435.

coolies to work in Khuzestan he only was able to hire 100 men. This was due to the fact that most local labor was employed in the reconstruction of the airfield, the loading and unloading of ships, and in the truck assembly plant.[551]

In February 1944, political life started to become more varied in Bushehr, because the `*Adalat* or Justice Party wanted to establish a sub-committee in Bushehr. To that end a meeting was held at the house of the brothers Mahmud and Ahmad Borazjani at Sangi. As a result, Ahmad Borazjani was appointed chairman and his brother as secretary; 30 persons were enrolled as party members. The party's aim was "democracy and the improvement of conditions in Persia."[552] In April 1944, the *Azadegan* Party was organized in Bushehr by Mr. Riyazi, but it was not known what its program was. Both parties made some propaganda by sending telegrams to Tehran and by writing articles in the local press. The `*Adalat* Party was the tool of `Ali Dashti, a Bushehri who was a *Majles* deputy for Tehran, and an enemy of the two *Majles* deputies for Bushehr (Khalil Dashti and Mr. Safavi).[553]

In January 1945, the governor-general of Fars, General Firuz, visited Bushehr. On that occasion the local *Khalij-e Fars* newspaper issued a supplementary edition asking his intervention as to the following problems that bedeviled the town's population:

> (i) Permission to distribute rationed cloth to the public after more than one year of non-issue;
>
> (ii) Arranging the distribution of the cigarettes that had arrived from Shiraz;
>
> (iii) Lifting of the embargo on transporting foodstuffs (ghee, fruits, potatoes, vegetables) from Shiraz to Bushehr;
>
> (iv) Supply of firewood and charcoal to Bushehr when there is a shortage;
>
> (v) Improving the supply and quality of flour as well as opening more bakeries to prevent over-crowding;
>
> (vi) Resolving the shortage of medicines in the Health Department; now people had to buy them on the black market at exorbitant prices;
>
> (vii) Increasing the budget of the Education Department and improving the way it operates.[554]

In February 1945 the *Tudeh* Party became somewhat active in Bushehr. Its local head, Ja`far Ahangari, was a blacksmith, but more influential members kept in the background. Many *Tudeh* leaflets found their way into town, probably via postal messengers from Shiraz. Articles reflecting *Tudeh* points of view appeared in the Shiraz newspapers *Sorush* and *Aqiyanus*. The British had articles published in the local press written by pro-British Persians. The Party appointed a newsagent in Bushehr to sell *Tudeh* pamphlets and papers. It was also said that pro-Russian sentiments were aired in the coffeehouses along

551. Political Diaries, vol. 15, p. 486.
552. Political Diaries, vol. 16, p. 27.
553. Political Diaries, vol. 16, pp. 75, 95-96.
554. Political Diaries, vol. 16, pp. 293-94.

Sa`adat School Band

the Bushehr-Shiraz road, which was believed to be the work of pro-*Tudeh* truck drivers. Mr. Mahallati of the `*Adalat* Party came to town to give a talk at the *Sa`adat* school. His talk did not mention Russia or Communism, although immediately thereafter *Tudeh* pamphlets were posted on the walls of houses and shops. The British Resident suspected that his main purpose was to collect money from officials by promising not to cause any trouble or to write bad things about them in the Shiraz press. *Tudeh* leaflets from Shiraz continued to be distributed in Bushehr, while a visiting Russian was spreading Russian propaganda in coffee-houses and contacting *Tudeh* members and workers.[555]

The Allied victory in Europe was enthusiastically celebrated in Bushehr. All government buildings and vehicles were decorated and beflagged. The shops in the bazaar were decorated with flags, carpets etc, while at night they were illuminated (*cheraghani*). Bazaaris also erected three triumphal arches and parties with music and dancing were given in the bazaars. Officials gave receptions, the schoolboys marched in town with their band and flags and ended their march by singing anthems at the British consulate. Local newspapers printed special issues, while the `Alavi printing-house published a colored commemorative leaflet.[556] The dropping of the A-bomb and the Final Victory was announced early in the morning of 13 August 1945 in Bushehr by a long blast of the *E`temadiyeh* Mill's siren. The surrender of Japan did not result in the same jubilation as in May, but people were relieved and hoping that normal life would return. Various receptions were held, while the APRRF fed the poor, despite the fact the harvest had been good, but prices did not drop.[557]

555. Political Diaries, vol. 16, pp. 323, 327, 329, 374-75.

556. Political Diaries, vol. 16, pp. 398, 401.

557. Political Diaries, vol. 16, pp. 472, 474; Administration Report 1945, pp. 2, 14-15.

The tribal revolt and occupation of Bushehr

The end of the war meant change for Persia, if only because the occupation forces were being withdrawn. It also was the last time that the waning star of Bushehr would appear in Persia's political firmament. This was not due to any hopeful change for the better in the town's socio-economic situation, but rather because of national politics. The political scene in post-war Persia saw a fight between several forces, each of which wanted to turn the country into a different direction. Most radical was the *Tudeh* Party that wanted to create a state based on the Soviet model. Moreover, with the establishment of the break-away Pishevari regime in Azerbaijan this Party could point out how things could become all over Persia. Opposing the leftists were various conservative groups on the right, some of which were anti-British as well as reformers, who wanted to take a middle road. Persia's new prime-minister since March 1946 was Qavam al-Saltaneh, an old veteran politician and wealthy landowner, who basically wanted to maintain the status quo, be it with a weakened shah. However, to do so he had to contend with these disparate political forces as well as with Russia and Great Britain, who wanted to continue to hold their influence over the country. Before he could tackle the internal problems he first had to come to an agreement with Russia, which he did in March 1946. As a result, Russia withdrew its troops and was offered an oil concession, which was counterbalanced by a similar offer to the Americans. Also, Qavam reached an agreement with the rebels in Azerbaijan to solve their differences. Finally, he pursued a friendly policy to the *Tudeh* Party by lifting restrictions imposed on it and cracking down on pro-British politicians and organizations.[558] As a result, the Shiraz Democratic Party formed a movement that later was called Fars National Movement, which demanded that the same rights given to Azerbaijan should also be granted to Fars.

These developments immediately had their impact on Bushehr. The elite in Bushehr and its hinterland were conservatives and so was most of its tradition-bound population. For example, in 1945, *Shorush* and *Aqeyanus*, two Shiraz newspapers had advocated the establishment of a branch of the *Tudeh* Party in Bushehr, but the strong anti-Russian feelings there prevented this.[559] Also, when Mr. Safavi, the local *Majles* deputy left town on 18 May 1945 he was called a traitor by Mr. Dashti, a communist and the director of the Bushehr Power Company. Mr. Safavi's supporters beat up Mr. Dashti and he escaped being thrown into the sea.[560] Therefore, the events in Azerbaijan (the establishment of a Soviet client state) greatly worried the people in Bushehr and in November 1945 many telegrams were sent to the shah and the *Majles* to express their loyalty.[561]

Nevertheless, *Tudeh* Party activities in Bushehr increased as they did in the rest of the country. In April 1946, *Tudeh* leaflets were found on the walls in town. These were brought by Jalil, the mailman and handed to the *Tudeh* agent, Mr. Sami of the Education Department. When people started to remove them *Yavar* Mohajer, chief of police and a *Tudeh* sympathizer, stopped them.[562] In May 1946 the *Tudeh* Party became more active in Bushehr. An article in the Shiraz newspaper *Shorush* accused the British consul of

558. Abrahamian 1982, pp. 225-30.
559. Administration Report 1945, p. 9.
560. Political Diaries, vol. 16, p. 400.
561. Political Diaries, vol. 16, p. 580.
562. Political Diaries, vol. 17, p. 83.

having exported wheat from Ganaveh not to Abadan but to foreign parts. Therefore, a bread shortage was in the offing. The same story was delivered in a speech by `Abdol-Rasul Parvizi. This story had an impact on Tehran. At orders from Tehran, the Finance Department sealed all grain storehouses in town. It offered to buy wheat, but at 260 *tumans*/ton nobody was willing to sell. This move caused an artificial shortage in town. The governor protested in Tehran against this decision, but without success. He also published an article in the Bushehr newspaper *Nur Afshan* denying the allegations in the *Shorush* article.[563] In May 1946, *Tudeh* activists from Shiraz organized a strike in the *E`temadiyeh* Mills and obtained "an exorbitant increase of wages, as well as demands calculated to give the Tudeh Party a large share in the control of the Mill." It was said that output had dropped by 35% and that the mill was operating at a loss. The workers demanded that the *Tudeh* agents submit an account of the money that was collected from them, because there was a rumor that the money had been remitted to the private account of *Tudeh* leader Parvizi. After this strike the *Tudeh* was able to induce dock workers to strike, demanding an increase of their daily wages from Rls. 25 to Rls. 70. The governor, after the departure of the *Tudeh* agents, who had to return to Shiraz to assist in strikes there, and when there was no ship in port, settled with the workers at a rate of Rls. 45/ per day.[564]

The sudden rise of the *Tudeh* Party's influence in Bushehr led in June 1946 to the formation of a Tribal Union and even to a tribal revolt in Fars (see below). A similar development, to check the influence of the *Tudeh* party, could be observed at the national level. In June 1946, Qavam al-Saltaneh announced that nation-wide elections would be held. His objective was to to break the *Tudeh* party's influence by offering a non-Communist reform agenda as well as to defeat royalist and pro-British candidates. Qavam then announced the formation of the Democratic Party, whose aim was to offer an alternative to the *Tudeh* Party to ensure that this Party would not win the elections. Qavam further announced a series of socio-economic reforms benefiting the urban labor class and the peasants. Finally he appointed four *Tudeh* ministers to his cabinet.[565] In July 1946, the Democratic Party was also formed in Bushehr, which led to the resignation of some *Tudeh* members. The governor, who supported this Party, unsuccessfully tried to induce the local merchants to join. The *Tudeh* Party continued to be active by organizing a strike at the *E`temadiyeh* Mills despite telegrams from Tehran declaring the strike illegal, because no prior notice had been given. Management did not seriously oppose these activities, because Mr. Agar was busy selling his shares. After a meeting he was induced to return as managing director.[566] When the Residency moved to Bahrain in August 1946, the *Tudeh* Party claimed that this was due to its efforts.[567]

Given Qavam al-Saltaneh's background (conservative, wealthy landowner) it is unlikely that he actually intended to realize these various proposed reforms. It may well be that he counted on a knee-jerk reaction from conservative forces, such as Naser Khan Qashqa'i, with whom he had very good relations. And indeed, these various activities

563. Political Diaries, vol. 17, pp. 108, 132.

564. Political Diaries, vol. 17, pp. 132-33.

565. Abrahamian 1982, pp. 231-37; Avery 1967, p. 396.

566. Political Diaries, vol. 17, p. 153-54. The leader of the Tudeh at Bushehr was Ali Qodsi, a petty merchant. Idem, vol. 17, p. 182.

567. Political Diaries, vol. 17, p. 209.

evoked strong feelings among the conservative elite, who felt that Qavam's cabinet was dominated by the *Tudeh* Party, if not had sold out to it. Therefore, one may well question Abrahamian's rather neutral discussion of this eposide, who wants us to believe that Qavam al-Saltaneh was surprised by the right's backlash. This backlash manifested itself by unrest in the army, pressure from Great Britain and a tribal revolt in the south.[568] It is only the latter that concerns us here, because it was the tribal intervention that launched Bushehr onto the national political scene.

Captain Pettigrew, the British consul in Bushehr only learnt about the intended formation of the Tribal Union towards the end of May 1946, when Fathollah Khan Hayat Da'udi told him about it. Fathollah Khan wanted to launch the Tribal Union, because he was concerned about the growing influence of the *Tudeh* Party and the decrease of the influence of local tribal leaders, which decrease was exarcebated by their internal conflicts. Its objective was to promote unity and settle disputes between the tribal chiefs as well as to oppose the *Tudeh* Party and to represent the tribes' common interests to the government. He asked whether the British government would favor the Tribal Union, and, because he knew that the Union might quickly disintegrate if its members were unable to settle their differences, he asked the British consul whether he would consider to arbitrate their disputes. The consul replied that the British government always welcomed action that would reduce quarrels and fights among the tribes, but given his position he could not assume the role of arbiter. The consul made it clear that the British government could not in any way support or sponsor the Union and he asked Fathollah Khan to make this very clear to the other Khans. The consul gave the same message to Mansur Khan of Shabankareh, whom he saw shortly thereafter. In the second half of June, Fathollah Khan informed the British consul at Bushehr that in principle all leading Khans had agreed to join the Union to which end they would have a meeting in late June to "record their final agreement." On 29 June 1946, Fathollah Khan gave the British consul a copy of the written final agreement (see Appendix X). At the same time, he told the consul that Naser Khan Qashqa'i, after having learnt about the formation of the Tribal Union, had expresed interest to join. At that time, the consul had not yet brought these developments to the notice of the governor of Busher, while he wired the British Legation that it was quite likely that "the British Government will be assumed to be in sympathy with the union-- if not accused of playing a more active part."[569]

In early July 1946, Fathollah Khan Hayat Da'udi was in Shiraz to negotiate with Naser Khan Qashqa'i to join the Tribal Union. He had moderate success, because Qavam al-Molk was absent and the Qashqai's refused to cooperate. In the Bushehr area it received strong support.[570] As a result, tribal leaders of the Fars ports met in secret in Dehkohneh near Shabankareh and agreed on the following program: (i). Demand the same rights as obtained by the Azerbaijan rebels; (ii). Resist if the government used armed force against them; (iii). Refuse to make conscripts available for military service; (iv). Control of the collection of the customs revenues; and (v). Elimination of all special parties and to fight the *Tudeh* Party. A second committee of the same tribal leaders met in the village of Chahar Rusta'i in Hayat Da'ud and sent their agreed upon points to Fahimi, the governor of Bushehr. Each Khan in his area of influence: (i). would maintain safety and law and

568. Abrahamian 1982, p. 235; Avery 1967, p. 396.
569. FO 248/1415, Consul to Legation, Tehran. 1 July 1946.
570. Political Diaries, vol. 17, p. 154.

order; (ii). would promote social and economic development in particular among peasants, farmers and merchants; iii). an attack on one of them would be resisted by all; (iv). in case of a disagreement between two of the undersigned the others would immediately call for a meeting to resolve this by majority vote; (v). in case decisions had to made a meeting would be called and decided by majority vote, while to maintain unity there would be bi-monthly meetings. Finally, in the interest of the country, the 12 undersigned were committed to let bygones be bygones and maintain complete unity. This statement was signed by: Sheikh Soleyman Nasuri, Ahmad Angali, Malek Mansur Shabankareh, `Ali Tangestani (Chah Piri), Gholam Razmi Dashti, `Ali and Amrollah Shabankareh, Ardashir Shabankareh, Khan `Ali Hayat Da'udi, Mohammad `Ali Liravi, Ne`matollah Hayat Da'udi, Ne`matollah Sowlati, Hajj Mohammad Beglerbegi, and Fathollah Hayat Da'udi. [571]

On 14 July 1946, the postmaster informed Fahimi, the governor of Bushehr that the Khans had met in Dehkohneh and agreed to jointly oppose any force used against them. On 17 July, Fahimi replied that without any documentary proof he could not react, because he did not know who had signed it. The postmaster replied that the Khans had met again this time in Choghadak and that after the meeting all had gone to Khormuj. On 19 July Fahimi replied that such a meeting was not against the country's interests. The next day the postmaster replied that such a meeting of the Khans in Dashti and Dashtestan, who all had serious conflicts, if not blood feuds with each other, was without precedent and that the authorities should take more interest in these meetings. He further reported to have been informed that the Khans had sworn unity on the Qoran and had ordered their peasants to buy arms. In the last week of July, Fahimi wrote that he did not lend credence to this report because the postmaster had not seen any purchase of guns. [572]

In the last week of August 1946, Fathollah Khan Hayat Da'udi met with Naser Khan Qashqa'i and later in Shiraz met with the British consul. On 14 September Fathollah Khan went to Ahram and met with the local Khans reporting that "the government agrees with our movement and even the English support us." During that meeting Fathollah Khan proposed to attack Bushehr and a fixed date was agreed upon. This implies that he apparently met with Pettigrew, the British consul, although there is no report of such a meeting. Pettigrew reported that on 14 September "it became widely known that some sort of revolt was likely." On 19 September, Pettigrew received information that the Khans gathered at Chaghodak and on that same day the telegraph lines were cut. The assistant governor (the governor was in Shiraz) had no notion of what was happening. When Pettigrew asked him about the expected disturbance, he "even replied that there was no trouble. He was unable to explain, and if fact displayed ignorance of, the unusual activity amongst the Gendarmerie and Military, who were moving about in a state of armed readiness."[573]

After 19 September 1946, all *Tudeh* activities in Bushehr stopped; some of its leaders fled town, probably due to the tribal revolt. This anti-*Tudeh* revolt all of sudden broke out on 20 September, although there had been signs that this was in the offing one week earlier.[574] On 20 September both forces moved into the gendarmerie barracks, opposite

---

571. Bushehri 1327, pp. 132-34. For short, very positive, biographies about some of these men, see Hamidi 1380, pp. 101-02, 153-60, 343-35, 406-09 (with photos).

572. Bushehri 1327, p. 134 (Fahimi was absent from Bushehr since 28 August).

573. Bushehri 1327, pp. 134-36; Political Diaries, vol. 17, p. 209.

574. Political Diaries, vol. 17, pp. 209-10.

the house of the consulate's physician. Unlike the governor, the garrison commander of Bushehr, Parviz Arasteh, was very much aware of what was going on in Ahram and therefore, he sent a message to the garrison in Khormuj. He instructed the commanding officer to withdraw into the fort, not to let the Khans invite him to avoid being taken hostage. Further, to make use of the enmity among the Razmi Khans and in particular with Zayer Hoseyn Jamali-nezhad, Zayer `Abd`Ali Mahmudi and `Abdollah Mozaffari so that they would not undertake any action. Also, to find out where the Khans stored their arms and to report this immediately. Moreover, to use the conflicts between Gholam Razmi and the other chiefs. Finally, to defend himself to the last bullet, to arm all men, to use the bullets effectively, and to store food and water for men and animals.[575]

Unfortunately, the message fell into the hands of Gholam Razmi. He informed the Khans that the military in Bushehr knew of their plans and that therefore, the attack should take place one week earlier, i.e. on 20 September 1946. On 16 September *Sargord* Arasteh informed the army commander in Kazerun that Ra'is Ali Tangestani intended to attack Bushgan, but it was also possible that this was in support of the activities of the Qashqa'i Khans, because trucks with riflemen of the various Khans had gone to Ahram. Therefore, he had placed the Bushehr garrison on the alert. On 18 September the commander of the Fars Division ordered the troops of Borazjan to Kazerun and those in Khormuj and Bardestan to move to Bushehr. Arasteh replied that this was impossible, because if the troops left the safety of the fort of Khormuj they would be attacked. He also suggested that the Borazjan troops might stay in which case he could take control of the fort there.[576]

Meanwhile, Gholam Razmi immediately marched to Khormuj and invited the unsuspecting commanding officer for talks and took him hostage. When the garrison's sergeant learnt about this he closed the gate and defended the fort against Gholam Razmi's attack; both sides suffered casualties. The siege lasted 9 days, until a soldier from Bushehr came with the news of the fall of Bushehr, and the garrison surrendered. Gholam Razmi seized the government sugar and cloth in the fort. On this news the Bardestan garrison, which was besieged by Gholam Karami and Gholam Hoseyn Dashti, also surrendered. Sheikh Soleyman Nasuri saw to it that no looting took place. `Ali Dayyeri also played a postive role in safeguarding the soldiers. The Nasuri brothers, who were chiefs of the Thalatheh ports (Dayyer, Taheri and `Asalu), did not participate in the Bushehr disturbance, but sent some of their riflemen to Halileh, near Bushehr, but then, having achieved nothing, they returned.[577]

On 18 September 1946, Malek Mansur Shabankareh and his brother Ardashir attacked Borazjan. The soldiers and gendarmes were about to leave for Kazerun when the riflemen arrived by truck. They first took all government buildings and then surrounded the fort. The sayyeds and notables asked Malek Mansur to desist but he refused. Ebrahim Ghazanfar, son of Ghazanfar al-Saltaneh gave refuge to the chief of police. More tribal levies came and in view of their small number the gendarmes fled after dark. All

575. Bushehri 1327, pp. 134-36; Political Diaries, vol. 17, p. 209.
576. Bushehri 1327, pp. 138-39.
577. Bushehri 1327, pp. 132-33, 140-41.

government sugar, cloth, and tobacco were seized, while the government archives were burnt. Similar action was undertaken in Liravi.[578]

On 20 September 1946, Arasteh reported by radio to General Razmara that he was under attack from that evening. He had food for 20 days, but water only for a few days and would defend his position till the last bullet. On 21 September all was quiet as the parties were negotiating. Arasteh also wrote a letter to Fathollah Hayat Da'udi and `Ali Tangestani advising them to desist and asking what their intentions were. They replied they wanted the surrender of all army and gendarmerie personnel. Arasteh in consultation with the government department heads decided to resist. In that meeting Arasteh also formulated a proposal for the leaders of the attackers, to wit: (i). that the Khans would not attack until a definite answer had come from HQ; (ii). that they put a few motor vessels at his disposal to evacuate all arms and government goods, and (iii). would wait until whatever was arranged for the Kazerun garrison would also apply to Bushehr. The Khans replied that the military had no other duty than the surrender of arms and of Bushehr and they gave Arasteh 24 hours to comply. When the delay had expired Arasteh asked for an extension, which was denied. In the afternoon of 21 September trucks with armed riflemen took the Bahmani guard post, plundered its stores and set fire to the building. Because the garrison had not more than 600 men, Arasteh gave orders to take up position at the Neydi barracks, which at 6 PM were surrounded by 800 tribal levies. When the fighting started some olama and notables went to Fathollah Hayat Da'udi and `Ali Tangestani to prevent bloodshed, but they refused to desist.

That same evening, via Pudar along the coast, a small group of rebels attacked Bushehr itself and occupied the Customs House without meeting any resistance. They then moved to the Municipality and seized Col. Safiri, its chief. They also ordered the police to hand over their arms. After having taken the town Fathollah Khan Hayat Da'udi and `Ali Tangestani took up quarters in the Municipality, while their levies saw to the maintenance of law and order. `Abdol-Hoseyn Baneh Gazi was appointed mayor. Fathollah Khan Hayat Da'udi became acting governor and all heads of government departments were replaced by tribesmen. The road to Shiraz was closed, while the telegraph stopped functioning, but there still was communication by cable and wireless. Fathollah Khan Hayat Da'udi informed the postmaster that he had to maintain communications with the other ports and that all postal traffic was under his censorship. He also took over the Bank-e Melli, where Fathollah Khan Hayat Da'udi seized more than Rls.6.5 million, owed to the State, representing the value of government wheat, sugar and tea. By wire, co-signed by the Imam Jom`eh (Hasem `Adnani) and two leading merchants (Ebrahim Khorma'i, `Abbas Mahmudiyan), he and `Ali Tangestani informed Qavam about this and asked him to accept their demands (basically, to abolish Reza Shah economic policy measures and not harm their children who were held as hostages). Qavam replied that he was busy reforming the country's affairs and that he was surprised that until now he had never heard any of their complaints. He pointed out that their behavior was at odds with their patriotic and peace loving intentions. Qavam further asured them that no hair of their children would be touched.[579]

578. Bushehri 1327, pp. 141-42.

579. Bushehri 1327, pp. 145-49; Political Diaries, vol. 17, pp. 209-10.

From midnight 20 September 1946 the fighting continued for five days. Thereafter, from 23 to 27 September, life was almost normal in Bushehr, except that there was senseless shooting from government forces at the British physician's house that the tribesmen had taken, which only endangered civilians. The houses near the barracks, amongst which the house of the British consulate's physician, Dr. Easy, was taken, which had plenty of water because of its large water tank. The house was plundered and ransacked. This was the only incident of plundering, because the tribesmen otherwise kept good discipline. Dr. Easy's house had been taken on 23 September, after he had been allowed to leave during a short truce. On 27 September, Dr. Easy was able to get some immediate necessities from his house. According to Bushehri, this visit, ostensibly to remove furniture, in reality was a visit by the British consul himself to hand over the house to the attackers.[580]

Driven by thirst on the night of 27 September (Bushehri has 28) the soldiers made a sortie to Dr. Easy house's where the besiegers lodged and took it; on both sides there were casualties. Therefore, a few olama and notables came to Arasteh telling him that continuing the fight was senseless as already some tribesmen had been killed and wounded and killing and wounding more people would make no difference. Also, there was no hope that he would receive any help and therefore, it would be best to put down his arms. Meanwhile, Fathollah Khan Hayat Da'udi sent a threatening letter to the besieged. During the talks Arasteh told his troops to stop firing, but because the attackers were only a few meters distance from the barracks he started firing again fearing an attack. He then sent a man to Fathollah Khan asking to withdraw his men, if not he would execute the negotiators inside the barracks, which had the desired result. Arasteh then let the mediators go. Fathollah Khan was furious about this and ordered his men to fiercely attack the barracks. Finally, the soldiers ran out of water; women who came to bring them water were told to go away by the besiegers and one was even shot by them. In a meeting with all the Khans, a few olama and notables and all heads of departments, Fathollah Khan said that they had come to claim people's rights. "I am willing to cease the fraternal killing, if you are willing to persuade Arasteh to lay down his arms and hand them to the leaders of the movement." The Khans were not willing to wait for further results from Tehran and made this known in town. They also freed all prisoners, which increased insecurity in the town. Arasteh explained his position in a notice to the public.[581]

Bushehri has a different chronology than the British consul, according to whom the government forces, having used up all their ammunition, surrendered in the night of 28 September. The troops had to leave all their arms and equipment in Dr. Easy's house and compound and were allowed to disperse. On 29 September a government airplane flew over Bushehr and dropped a notice from Razmara in which he expressed the hope that the soldiers would live up to the ideals of duty and courage. Also, that the houses near the gendarmerie barracks were going to be attacked and should be vacated. The airplane, after having dropped its leaflets, strafed the town with its guns and dropped some bombs, allegedly on tribal positions near the gendarmerie, which put fear into the tribesmen. However, according to the British consul the plane indeed carried out an air attack, but on Dr. Easy's house when consular staff were busy salvaging its contents and not "on tribesmen" as Tehran announced and Bushehri repeats. The doctor's car was hit, but no

580. Political Diaries, vol. 17, pp. 209-10.
581. Bushehri 1327, pp. 150-52.

other damage was inflicted. After the surrender of the military garrisons of Khormuj and Kazerun, respectively on 1 and 3 October, all fighting stopped.[582]

According to Bushehri, the air attack took place on 29 September, but the fighting only ended on 30 September 1946. On that day Arasteh decided to announce a pause in the fighting and sent Sehami, the commander of the gendarmerie to discuss a cessation of hostilities. After 4 hours a letter was brought from the Khans stating they were willing to do so. It was then decided that Arasteh himself would open discussions with the Khans. However, during the discussion the tribesmen suddenly attacked and overcame the thirsty troops and took the officers prisoner. Thus, after nine days of resistance the barracks fell. In Bushehr, the Khans seized 950 rifles, 3,000 bullets and 30 heavy and light machine-guns, although according to Pettigrew they had no longer ammunition. The Bushehr garrison suffered 9 dead and 11 wounded, but the tribesmen had suffered a higher, although unknown number of casualties. As a negotiating ploy, the Khans sent a telegram to Razmara stating that all soldiers were imprisoned and would be tried. Razmara replied angrily and accused them of treason and of selling out their country and that punishment would be their fate.[583] However, all soldiers in Bushehr and Khormuj who were captured after their surrender were released after a few days and taken by ship to Khorramshahr. Therefore, Abrahamian's report about the massacring of the garrisons in Bushehr and Kazerun is erroneous.[584]

During a meeting on 1 October 1946, with the merchants and notables of the town, Fathollah Khan told them that the Khans' armed resistance was not because of differences with the central government, but to be united in the demands of "our rights," i.e. the same rights that the government has granted those in Azerbaijan. During that meeting 27 of those present were elected to form a provincial council, while heads of departments also were appointed. The Khans also took charge of the archives of the government departments and destroyed those concerning conscription. Fathollah Hayat Da'udi and `Ali Tangestani used the cash they had taken from the Finance Department and Customs for their troops. In total Rls.3.5 million from the Bushehr Customs; Rls.51,500 from Ganaveh and Rls.218,000 from Delam and a cheque of Rls.782,000 from the IBP. Ilyas Girginpur gave more than Rls.2.5 million to Naser Khan Qashqa'i. Later the Khans also arrested some smugglers and some of the staff of the Customs House, who after being tortured, paid them a large sum. They also seized 58,577 bags of white and brown sugar, and the Khans delivered 6,373 bags of sugar to Ilyas Girginpur and Sharifi, the agents of the Qashqa'i brothers. Also, 4,750 bags of brown sugar were given to the Qashqa'i and Kazeruni tribesmen. The Khans also gave five bags of sugar as blood price to the heirs of each killed tribesman and two bags for each wounded man.[585] On 4 October, from Bushehr, one of the Qashqa'i leaders read an announcement on the radio, which set out some of the grievances of the tribal leaders.[586]

---

582. Political Diaries, vol. 17, pp. 209-10.
583. Bushehr 1328, pp. 154-56.
584. Abrahamian 1982, p. 235. Bushehri 1327, pp. 122, 164 and the British consul Pettigrew (Political Diaries, vol. 17, p. 210) make it clear that all soldiers were released and that, apart from those killed during the fighting, nobody else was killed.
585. Bushehri 1327, pp. 156-57.
586. FO 248/1469, Consul to Legation, 05/10/1946.

By 15 September 1946, the Qashqa'is had surrounded Shiraz and marched on Kazerun. On 20 September, Naser Khan Qashqa'i sent an ultimatum with nine demands to the government in Tehran, which had to be met by midnight of 23 September. General Zahedi, who had come to Shiraz on 19 September to take over command of the troops in Fars, contacted Naser Khan Qashqa'i and a committee was formed to discuss terms. On 3 October Kazerun fell to the Qashqa'is but their attack of Marvdasht failed. In reaction, Tehran sent troops from Abadeh to reinforce the Shiraz garrison, which on 5 October reached Shiraz.[587] Fathollah Khan Hayat Da'udi had gone to the Qashqa'i camp in early October, where he tried to boost Qashqa'i morale, which was dampened by the realization that they had to face the tanks and the planes of the army, when they attacked Shiraz, as was planned. Fathollah Khan told them that at Kazerun tribesmen had taken a tank with their bare hands, that machine gunning from the air was not as effective as they believed, and that bombs dropped by planes did not explode.[588]

Since 22 September 1946 discussions were held by the Qashqa'i and other tribal leaders with general Zahedi and Amir Homayun Bushehri. Both sides wanted to reach an agreement, because Zahedi and Bushehri wanted to avoid fighting with the tribes, while Naser Khan Qashqa'i, his brothers and his mother were ready and willing to compromise.[589] As a result, on 8 October a tentative agreement was reached. Tehran summoned Zahedi to discuss the various issues. Zahedi transferred command to Col. Hushmand, who, unlike the general, wanted to attack the Qashqa'is.[590] Fortunately, this did not happen, because on 18 October 1946, a final agreement was reached on a number of issues, amongst which:

i. Formation of a provincial council;
ii. Increase of Parliamentary representation for Fars;
iii. Credits for health and education;
iv. Government officials to be local men where possible;
v. General pardon for the tribes, and
vi. Fars National Movement to remain.[591]

Because of the tribal takeover, business in Bushehr was brought to a standstill, also because the *Bank-e Melli* had a very small cash balance. It was helped out by the IBP at Fathollah Khan's request. Transport to and from Shiraz became possible in mid-October, be it under tribal escort. Fathollah Khan spent almost all his time in Bushehr trying to

587. FO 248/1469, Diary of Events in Fars, July-August 1946. For the text of the announcement, see Appendix XI.

588. FO 248/1469. Telegram Consul Shiraz to Legation, 05.06/1946; Idem to Idem, 06/10/1946; Idem to Idem, 10/10/1946.

589. FO 248/1469, Telegram consul Shiraz to Legation Tehran, 24/09/1956; Idem to idem, 25/09/1946; Idem to idem, 27/09/1946. For a short bio of Amir Homayn Bushehri, the third son of Mo`in al-Tojjar, see Hamidi 1380, p. 169.

590. FO 248/1469. Telegram consul Shiraz to Legation Tehran. 09/10/1946.

591. FO 248/1469, telegram Consul Shiraz to Legation Tehran, 20/10/1946. For the text of Gen. Zahedi's proclamation of the agreement, published in the newspaper *Iran* 18/10/1946, see Appendix XII. As a result of this agreement, a Village Doctors Scool (*Amuzeshgah-e Ali-ye Behdari*) was established in Shiraz in October 1946. Zabih Ghorban. *Medical Education in Shiraz, A Personal Memoir*. N.p., 1989, p. 13.

Ra`is `Ali Tangestani

get the other tribal leaders not to act for personal gain but for the public benefit. As a result, tribal administration was better than had been the case the last few years, acording to Pettigrew. To the great satisfaction of the public the rationing of sugar and tea to the entire governorate, which had ceased for the last 7 months, was resumed. General Zahedi sent some officials to take over the civil administration and by the end of October, all but some 50 tribesmen had returned home, where they were needed for plowing their land.[592]

On 25 October 1946, the coastal Khans went to Borazjan to meet with Naser Khan Qashqa'i and together they entered Bushehr the next day. On 27 October a meeting was held in the governor's office where Naser Khan spoke to a group of notables about the development of Bushehr and the abolishment of the trade monopoly (which had been abolished in November 1945!). The Khans gave him Rls.950,000 from the Customs revenues. Because the wages of government workers had not been paid for months the British consul of Shiraz came to Bushehr to discuss this with Pettigrew after which he returned to Shiraz. Fathollah Khan Hayat Da'udi was invited to join Naser Khan Qashqa'i for talks in Shiraz; after a two days' stay he returned. In the governor's office he told a group of notables that General Zahedi, commander of the Southern Army and Amir Homayun Bushehri had stated that they were in complete agreement with the actions taken by the Khans. Zahedi would immediately issue rules for the election of the provincial council. Also that Bushehr would have a representative in the chief administrative committee of Fars. The current governor of Bushehr, Hoseyn Shabankareh was dismissed because he had opposed the objectives of the Khans and he had to transfer his duties to Mr. Rishahri. On 8 November 1946, *Sargord* Badi`pur and *Sarvans* Hamzeh and Rasepar in company of Mehrab, Naser Khan Qashqa'is agent came to Bushehr to arrange for the filling of the posts of mayor and gendarmerie commander. However, due to the Khans' lack of cooperation and other problems they returned to Shiraz. A few days later Fathollah Khan Hayat Da'udi went to Shiraz to arrange for the handover of the government arms and the matter of the government sugar. He then went to Dehkohneh to speak with Malek Mansur Khan and told him that the general amnesty only applied to the Qashqa'i brothers. In reaction to this news Malek Mansur mobilized his riflemen and immediately wanted to march again to Bushehr and retake it. When this was reported to the governor he quickly alerted Javad Bushehri, the governor-general in Shiraz. The latter wired Fathollah Khan Hayat Da'udi and Malek Mansur Shabankareh expressing the hope that he had been misinformed, but if not, he advised them to demobilize their troops and go to Bushehr and execute the agreed upon plan concerning the arms and sugar. The governor of Bushehr drew the governor-general's attention to the fact that Fathollah Khan Hayat Da'udi still had men in Bushehr, that the police and gendarmerie had none and that people felt unsafe and unsure about their situation. Meanwhile, General Hushmand Afshar the new commander of the Fars Division asked Tehran to confiscate all of Fathollah Khan Hayat Da'udi's property in Shiraz.[593]

Bushehr and the other ports were incommunicado for two months, because all communications were under the control of the Khans. Their propaganda was aired at fixed times by the APOC radio. Zahedi left Shiraz to discuss matters with Qavam al-Saltaneh and then remained in Tehran; he was replaced by *Sartip* Hushmand Afshar. However, Amir Homayun Bushehri working with the Qashqa'i brothers tried to change Afshar's

592. Political Diaries, vol. 17, pp. 229-30.
593. Bushehri 1327, pp. 160-64.

decision, which angered him. Therefore, he tried to have Tehran recall Homayun Bushehri. Contrarisewise, Naser Khan tried in Tehran to have Hushmand Afshar recalled and to replace him with an old friend of his. [594]

Fahimi, the governor of Bushehr, on his return on 22 November 1946 felt even more insecure and was even less effective than before. Mr. Qotb, chief of the Bushehr court and Mr. Ghafuri of the Customs Department also returned and took up their old posts. The Mayor, Hoseyn Shabankareh had continued to work with the approval of the tribal leaders, but later they wanted to him to leave, as noted above. Therefore he left, hoping to be reappointed. His assistant Mr. Rishahri took over, although the Municipal council was hardly functioning at all. Later, `Abdol-Hoseyn Baneh Gazi became the new head of the Municpality, according to Hamidi. Meanwhile, business was improving somewhat in Bushehr, all communications having been restored. The *Bank-e Melli* got a new manager (Mr. Billadi) and with funds made available by IBP was able to restart business. Discussions between local tribal leaders, led by Fathollah Khan Hayat Da'ud and Ra'is `Ali Tangestani, and a commission from Tehran were inconclusive, although it bolstered unity among the various tribal groups. However, agreement was reached on the return of the machine guns and the rifles seized by them to arm the gendarmerie. There was also agreement on the future of the police and gendarmerie, which would be recruited locally and bring their own arms. Finally, "it was understood that no Military forces will be stationed in Bushire." The commission was pleased with the fact that all sugar that the Khans had ordered Customs to deliver had been paid for. However, there was only optimism that Tehran would approve of the decision by the tribal leaders that part of the money (Rs 3.5 million) received for the distributed sugar had been paid to the tribal forces. Despite the imminent elections for the *Majles*, the provincial council and the municipal council there was hardly any political activity to mobilize voters. In fact, there was general apathy and disinterest in how and when the elections would be conducted and who would run for office. Moreover, the *Tudeh* Party was moribund, so that it looked like that winners would be appointed rather than elected.[595]

On 3 December 1946, the workers of the PT went on strike, because their wages had not been paid for months. At the insistence of Fathollah Khan the governor paid them immediately from the reserve funds of the Finance Department, which ended the strike. As he had expected and hoped, Hoseyn Shabankareh was reappointed as mayor, despite his bad reputation and having 'sold' contracts for road repair and the like. On 14 December the governor sent a notice to the tribal leaders from the governor-general (*ostandar*) stating:

> (i) that Husain Shabankareh was appointed Mayor of Bushire,
>
> (ii) that Gendarmes and police would be recruited locally from men producing their own arms,
>
> (iii) that the tribal leaders should refrain from interfering in the administration, except when assisting the Mayor,

---

594. Bushehri 1327, pp. 164-65.

595. Political Diaries, vol. 17, pp. 261-63 (the commission, led by the President of the High Court, Sarabandi arrived on 23 and left on 28 November 1946); Hamidi 1380, p. 162.

(iv) to return all Government property taken during the revolt,

(v) that elections would be held directly the police and Gendarmerie were re-established.

(vi) to stop armed men from coming into Bushire.

(vii) that the police and Gendarmerie posts at Borazjan, Ganaveh and Bandar Dilum would be re-opened.

On 25 December 1946, to everybody's surprise three military planes dropped leaflets over Bushehr. One of them said that elections would not be held until military posts were established and that would only happen once the tribesmen had returned the arms taken from the army. As a result, recruitment of Tangestanis for the police was stopped, because they said they had no private arms. Those arms that they had belonged to Ra'is `Ali Tangestani who would allow them to be used only if their officers were Tangestanis. In Bushehr itself 40 unarmed locals were recruited for the police. The British consul had little faith in their reliability in a fight. Fathollah Khan went to Shiraz to discuss the elections, but when he returned at the end of December it was still unknown when these would be held. In fact, there was a kind a resignnation that even when elections were held it was unlikely that these would be free elections. Nevertheless, Fathollah Khan advised the other Khans to cooperate with the government and return all arms. Although they also wanted to maintain their tribal union to better represent their interests vis a vis the government, it was clear that this union was on its way to dissolution as its members were joining (or were going to join) Qavam's Party.[596]

In January 1947 political life in Bushehr came alive again. The prime-minister's Democratic Party was chaired by Yusef Sami, the former local *Tudeh* leader. The tribal leaders were slowly returning arms taken from the army. They did so on purpose, because they did not want to deal with the military commander of Shiraz (there were as yet no army assets in the Bushehr governorate) and waited for the new governor-general to arrive. By the end of February only some 300 rifles and several machine guns had been returned.[597] In May 1947, a new 500 men garrison arrived as well as 80 gendarmes. There were also signs that tribal unity was coming apart. In the run-up to the election Fathollah Khan Hayat Da'udi supported Faramarzi, which caused `Ali Tangestani sleepless nights, as he feared a falling apart of the Khans. He appealed to the British consul (Galloway) "to cement the ranks for 'old times' sake, this to save `Ali Tangistani from delivering a greater number of arms than he wants to and most unkindest of all, from building a wall round the barracks to protect them from the savage attack of his own tribe."[598] However, it was to no avail, for in June 1947 the Khans of the Bushehr governorate (Fathollah Khan Hayat Da'udi, `Ali Tangestani, and Malek Mansur Khan of Shabankareh) agreed to contribute some Rls. 100,000 for the repair of the military barracks as well as to supply 1,000 tons of wheat and 500 tons of barley to the military depot.[599] Because the Khans had taken all tea and sugar from the Customs during the tribal revolt, the government made

596. Political Diaries, vol. 17, pp. 293-95.
597. Political Diaries, vol. 17, pp. 327, 352.
598. Political Diaries, vol. 17, p. 427.
599. Political Diaries, vol. 17, p. 451.

no further allotment of tea and sugar, until payment had taken place. The town suffered also in another way when in July the Lafka sands (at the eastern extremity of town) were flooded; water stood one meter deep, causing much damage and discomfort to the houses of Jabri `Aliabad inhabitants. The new governor went to Shiraz and returned with some promises such as: the construction of a new well-equipped hospital, a seawall to prevent flooding, and the reparation of the Customs jetty.[600]

In short, by the end of 1947, life in Bushehr was back to normal. The increasingly divided Khans, all of them war profiteers, had made their last stand and lost, but they made yet another bundle in the name of their 'subjects.' The latter continued to eke out a living, while the former, although weakened and curtailed in power, continued to do well. The result of the negotiations carried on between the government and the Qashqa'is, promising amnesty, were finally also applied to the Khans of the Bushehr governorate. As a result of the tumultuous year of 1946, the *Tudeh* Party had no further activities in Bushehr. The Tribal Union was ineffective due to increasing disagreements among the Khans, and was absorbed by Qavam's Democratic Party, which then had the political field to itself. Also, the army felt stronger and more confident, and, instead of giving in to demands by the Khans imposed increasingly more difficult demands on them. Consequently, whatever political gain the Tribal Union had gained in 1946 it had already lost by the end of that year.[601] How Bushehr overcame its further decline and how the Khans were brought to heel has to be the subject of another study.

600. Political Diaries, vol. 17, p. 473.
601. Administration Report 1946, p. 4.

4

Government and Civic Institutions

In this chapter the functioning of the various government institutions that existed in Bushehr are discussed. These institutions include those that existed from the beginning of the nineteenth century together with those that were newly created after Persia's constitutional revolution. Furthermore, the functioning of new local civic institutions is presented as well as a description of all the foreign consulates that at one time were found in Bushehr.

The Customs Department

During the Qajar period the manner of the Customs department organization changed. The first period was one where the Al Mazkur Sheikhs fixed the different levels of tariff per product category, levels that they could, and sometimes did, change unilaterally. Persian and non-Persian merchants were charged the same tariff schedule, although wealthy merchants were able to negotiate better terms. During the period that the Al Mazkur Sheikhs were temporarily replaced by Persian governors the same tariff regime applied. In 1768, the customs duties at Bushehr were said to be 8-9%, but in 1791, they were probably lower, when they were characterized as "very moderate." Malcolm qualified them as "trifling." Waring stated that import duties were about 5% plus one piece of chintz from every bale imported. In 1803, according to the English East-India Company (EIC) records, duties on sugar, cinnamon, iron, lead and rice were 4 to 5%. In the 1820s, according to Fraser the duty "though it varies in some instances, may be taken at 5 percent generally," and in 1836 it was said to be 4% on average.[1] However in 1816, according to Buckingham, there was not a single tariff at Bushehr.

> The customs duties are regulated by package and quality of the goods. Rice and sugar pay each half a rupee per bag; pepper, cassia, cloves, cardamoms, and other spices, six rupees per bag; camphor, two rupees per box; China ware, four rupees per chest; Mokha coffee, two rupees per bale; and sweetmeats, three rupees per package. The duties on Indian piece goods vary considerably, according to their quality, but average at about ten per cent.; and those on the European articles, of cloth, iron, steel, lead, and tin, at not more than five per cent. on their invoice price. The duties on the exports or returns are less: horses and money, which form the greatest portion of these returns, are both

1. Grummon 1985, pp. 275-76, 286; Waring 1973, p. 79; Fraser 1984, p. 213.

> exempt from duties of any kind, as well as old copper, and Persian carpets; dried fruits pay only one rupee per package, assafoetida, a rupee per jar; rose water, two rupees per case of several bottles; and Shiraz wine is free.[2]

Buckingham is borne out by a statement by the British Resident in Bushehr of the duties levied on imported goods in 1822/23, which were on average 3.07% (see Table 4.1).

4.1: Statement showing the estimated value of the imports in 1822/23 and the estimated amount of duty levied on the same at the Bushehr Custom House

Description of Goods	Value of Goods	Amount of duty as a percentage	Total Amount of Duties
	Bombay Rs		Bombay Rs
Indigo	22,71,200	1.37	31,115.44
Europe Piece Goods	8,20,500	9.07	74,419.35
Indian Piece Goods	1,41,200	5.78	8,161.36
Sugar	3,56,975	1.59	5,675.90
Sugar Candy	75,456	2.86	2,158.04
Tea	3,200	3.04	97.28
Shawls Cashmere	3,16,000	0.61	1,927.60
China Ware	31,000	5.44	1,686.40
Cardamums	16,100	2.72	437.92
Cassia or Cinnamon	38,100	4.57	1,741.17
Camphor	1,300	3.26	42.38
Lead	5,920	2.29	135.57
Glassware	46,550	0.78	363.09
Woollen Cloth	1,000	3.08	30.80
Sal ammoniac	42,100	0.71	298.91
Rice	41,580	1.14	474.01
Silks (China)	7,400	9.87	730.38
Lac	6,615	1.83	121.05
Jappan or Redwood	518	3.05	15.80
Pepper	25	3.14	0.78
Supposing the duty on the following to be the same as the average of the preceding			
China Root, Twist, Sundries, Pickle, Tobacco, Cotton and Miscellaneous	42,185	3.07	1,295.08
Total	42,64,924	3.07 average	1,30,919.31
Residency on the Persian Gulf Bushire 5 July 1836 J. Hennell, Asst. and Acting Resident	Errors accepted		

Source: NA, FO 248/75

2. Buckingham 1971, p. 354.

The level of the customs tariff was not so much of the problem as was the governor's arbitrary behavior in applying it. It happened that he took any merchandise for his own use or sale, and instead of paying for it he ran up a balance in favor of the owners to be liquidated by remitting them the duties on further imports, until the amount owed was made up. This had a negative influence on trade, of course. Buckingham provides an example of the effect of such behavior. At the time of his visit (1816), Sheikh `Abdol-Rasul, the governor was at war with some chiefs. He needed lead and it so happened that there was a ship in the roads that carried that product. However, its owner refused to land his cargo afraid that the governor would seize it and pay much later. He paid the captain the additional freight and went to Basra instead.[3]

In May 1836, the second period of the Customs system's reorganization began when the shah granted British merchants the same rights as Russian ones as per the 1828 Treaty of Turkomanchay. Although this new measure was welcomed in Bushehr, initially there were many questions that were raised by James Hennell, the British Resident, about the application of the new rule. This was quite understandable, because the local authorities in Bushehr had as yet not been informed of the shah's decree and Hennell himself had not a copy of the text of the Turkomanchay Treaty, which he asked to be sent to him. He further commented:

> Given the importance of the existing customs system I propose to defer implementation of the term of this new royal *farman* until I receive orders from Bombay on this issue. Also, does the *farman* only apply to British merchants residing in Bushire or to British merchants in general? Can the bona fide agents of British merchants in India also benefit from these new terms, supposing them to be Persian subjects and residing on Persian soil? If a general merchant, a Persian residing in Persian, becomes an agent of a British merchant in India can he also benefit from this new order for his employees? In the event of a British merchant or agent residing in Persia importing British goods and selling these to a Persian merchant are these goods also beneficiary under the new rule, in particular the levying of the local customs rates in the interior? The duty of 5% ad valorem is it to be levied on the invoice price or on the value of the place to where it is taken, and in case of disagreement of the value how is that solved? Is it proposed to carry out these new rules before the Persian government has taken the necessary steps to exempt British goods from *rahdari* and internal fees such as town duties? We may expect disputes with farmers of *rahdari* and town duties, who want to charge their fees, how are we going to resolve these?[4]

Soon all these questions were resolved, but what was significant was that thereafter British, and by extension European, merchants operated under a different customs tariff than Persian ones, who continued to pay duties according to an established schedule. Officially, Europeans only had to pay 5% ad valorem (in cash or kind), but in reality they often paid more. A European merchant received a pass or *javaz* after having paid customs duties, which exempted him from paying internal duties. However, when moving

3. Buckingham 1971, pp. 354-55.
4. NA, FO 248/85, Hennell to McNeill, 05/07/1836.

upcountry, local and city officials often refused to acknowledge the validity of the pass and levied internal duties, the most important of which was *rahdari* or road tax.[5]

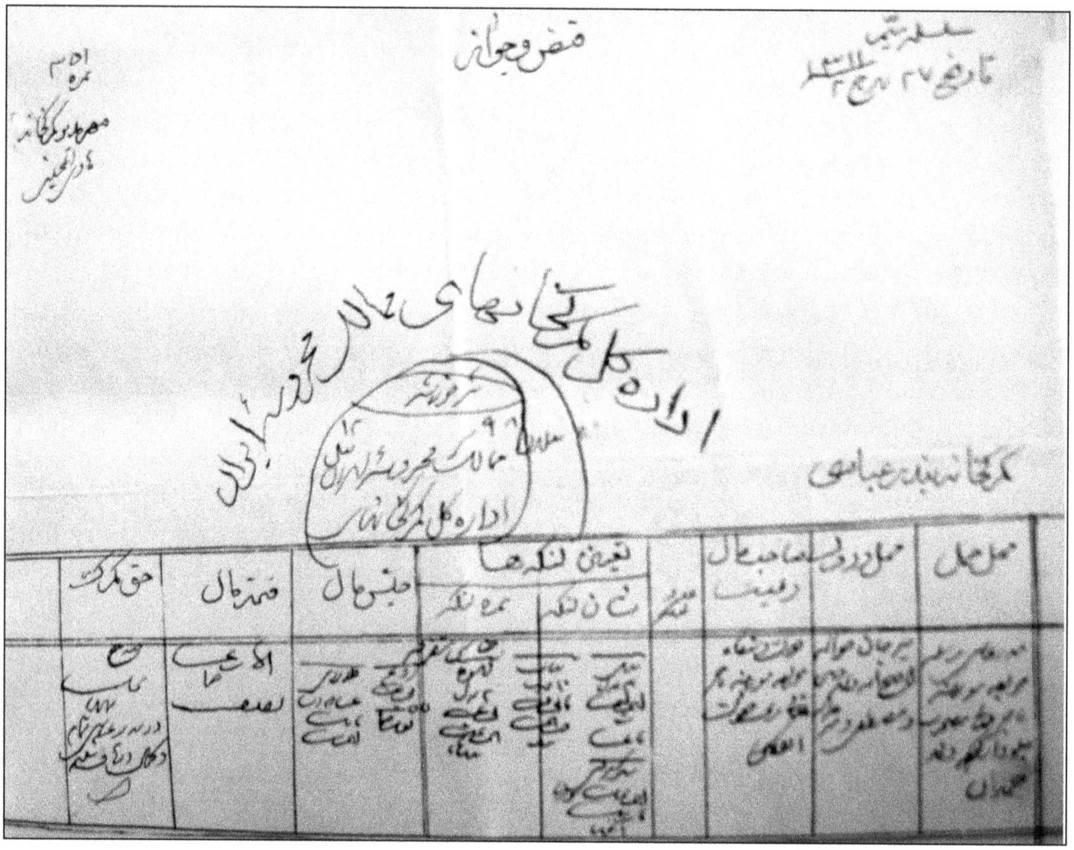

A *javaz* or proof of customs payment.

An additional change, be it a minor one, in the Customs organization took place after the definite ouster of the Al Mazkur Sheikhs in 1850. Thereafter, Tehran appointed rotating governors, who were outsiders and members of the Persian bureaucracy. This meant that these governors not only farmed their governorate, but, in addition, also the right to collect customs duties. This farming arrangement did not change the nature of the customs schedule itself, which remained the same with a highly differentiated level of tariffs per product category.[6] Sometimes, it also happened that the Minister of Trade acquired the lease of all customs houses of Persia, but then subleased the different jurisdictions to various operators. In 1873, the Bushehr customs were leased to an Isfahani for 32,000 *tumans*, who was not the governor. The Customs farmer used his own staff and the governor's officials did not interfere.[7] There was quite some turnover in Customs farmers. In 1878, the Customs were farmed by Naser al-Molk of Shiraz, although Haji

5. On the functioning of the customs system, see Floor 1998 b, pp. 373-400; see also, Saldanha 1986, vol. 7/2, pp. 170-75.
6. For a list of import and export duties at Bushehr in 1868, see Floor 1998 c; in 1873, see Administration Report 1873-74, pp. 51-53, and in 1881, see Administration Report 1881-82, pp. 48-51.
7. Administration 1873-74, pp. 14-15.

Ebrahim was his agent who took care of day-to-day operations.[8] In 1884, the customs were managed by the governor Mohammad Hoseyn Khan as agent of Amin al-Soltan.[9] In March 1885, Amin al-Soltan leased the customs of S. Persia to Malek al-Tojjar, the Bushehri commercial bigwig.[10] In 1890, governor Sa`d al-Molk sold the customs revenues for 91,000 *tuman* (£26,000) with 5,000 *tuman* (£1,400) for himself as gratuity (*pishkesh*). The farmer also made a profit, meaning that the total fiscal revenues of Bushehr were much larger.[11]

There were also problems other than the collection of more than the 5% duty. One problem was when in 1873, a British steamer had a fire while in the roads; it discharged its cargo, most of which was for Basra. The governor of Bushehr claimed one-third of the whole cargo as salvage as well as customs duties for the rest that was temporarily stored and re-shipped. The matter was referred to Tehran and the claim was denied.[12] In April 1884, the Customs farmer and prime-minister, Amin al-Soltan ordered his agent not to accept receipts for payment of grain export passed to foreign merchants or their agent delivered by governors of other ports. The governor-general of Fars told these governors to avoid giving such receipts. The British Minister in Tehran protested and the government of Persia gave orders to the governor-general of Fars to refund all monies collected over 5%. In August 1884 some were repaid, but there still remained problems with double payments of customs.[13]

A larger problem was that of the levying of transshipment duties and the disallowing of re-exportation of goods from Persian ports. For example, it happened that when several ships were lying in the roads that goods were transferred from one ship to another, which activity was liable to the payment of a duty. Likewise, when a merchant landed goods in Bushehr, or any other Persian port, but finding he could not sell them re-exported them to sell these goods in, for example, Basra, he had to pay export duties. Apparently demanding payment in these cases had not been customary until 1843. In that year, Messrs. Lynch & Co. landed goods at Bushehr for transshipment to Basra, as they were told by the owner of their chartered vessel that they could do so. However, the Customs Master or *shahbandar* refused to give his permission for re-shipment unless a fee was paid. Messrs. Lynch & Co. indignantly wrote to Kemball, the British Resident: "What is his authority to detain our goods, which is contrary to the treaty and the principle of the free port that is Bushehr. Both supercargo and captain of the Columbia have told us to transship our goods as they want to leave or we have to pay further demurrages. Any further detention will cause damage and other cost and for any loss we hold you responsible."[14] Kemball asked Sheikh Naser III about this practice, who told him it was the custom to levy 0.5% on goods transshipped in this port. Kemball also asked in town among the best informed people, who told him that a similar case had never before happened. Therefore, he decided submit the case to Sheil, the British Minister in Tehran and suggested to Mr. Lynch to give a bond pledging to pay 0.5% without waiting for the result of any appeal, if they

8. Administration Report 1878-79, p. 9.
9. Administration Report 1883-84, p. 8; Administration Report 1884-85, p. 8; Sa`adat 1390, p. 116.
10. Administration Report 1885-86, p. 8.
11. Curzon 1892, vol. 1, p. 235.
12. Administration 1873-74, p. 5.
13. Administration Report 1884-85, p. 8.
14. NA, FO 248/263, Messrs. Lynch & Co. to Kemball, 13/10/1843.

wanted to make one.[15] Lynch refused this option. He was told by local merchants that this was just a case of bribery by the governor. However, if Sheil ruled that it was legal then he would pay the 0.5%.[16] Although Kemball replied that Lynch had misunderstood him, the latter further wrote that "Prior to this, we had a similar shipment per Caroline and we did not pay a penny as it was transshipped from the ship into a buggalow. We could have done the same, but preferred to demand it as a right. The whole was carried out by native agents from which we benefit. You chose the Sheikh's side, because his claim is either just or not, and you demanded a bond thus siding with him."[17] The result was that Tehran decided that no transshipment fee had to be paid.

In Europe and India it was customary to charge only a small fee as transshipment duty, while the existence of so-called bonded warehouses obviated the charge of export duties. The lack of such warehouses was seen as a problem for some, but not all merchants. In 1868, the Dutch consul-general Richard Keun was able to obtain this right for the Netherlands. Under the terms of the proposed arrangement, goods could be re-exported from Bushehr on payment of 1% duty plus a fee for storage. However, the government of the Netherlands for various reasons was not interested in obtaining this right and did not ratify the proposed Treaty. Under the most-favored nation clause, other European states would have been able to avail themselves of this privilege. In 1874, the British regretted not having obtained this right and the Resident explictly mentioned in his annual report the need for a system of drawbacks.[18]

However, in February 1883, Col. Ross, the British Resident was not in favor of the introduction of bonded warehouses as proposed by the government of Persia.[19] Ross commented that the real objective of the Persian proposal was to give the Persian government some financial advantage rather than benefit the merchants. The reason was that the proposed rules implied that all landed goods had to be stored in government warehouses before these were transported inland, thus giving the government a reason to charge rent that was higher than normal. However, if the government just wanted to introduce a system for the bonding of goods, it would be cheaper for foreign merchants to use their own godowns, which, by treaty, they had the right to build, purchase or hire. Ross further added that if the government wanted to build a warehouse it should do so at the Customs house, which had insufficient capacity.[20] To get a reaction from the business community, Ross raised the issue of bonded warehouses with the Chambers of Commerce of Bombay and Karachi, which were in favor of their establishment. However, informed merchants in the Persian Gulf differed in opinion. They agreed that bonded warehouses were needed if trade was still only being carried on with sailing ships. However, with the establishment of regular trade with steam ships, Bushehr had lost its importance as an entrepot. In fact, there was hardly re-export from Bushehr any longer. However, French merchants disagreed and lamented the non-ratification of the abovementioned Dutch-Persian Treaty. Finally, the British authorities decided not to further pursue this issue, because re-export at Bushehr was insignificant and at other Persian ports no re-export

---

15. NA, FO 248/263, Kemball reply to Lynch, 13/10/1843.
16. NA, FO 248/263, Lynch to Kemball, 14/10/1843.
17. NA, FO 248/263, Kemball to Lynch 14/10/1843; Idem, Lynch to Kemball 16/10/1843.
18. Floor 1988 c; Administration 1873-74, p. 14.
19. NA, FO 248/402, Persian text of the rules re bonded warehouses.
20. NA, FO 248/402, Lt. Col. E.C. Ross to Thomson, 06/03/1883.

duty was levied.[21] A related problem occurred, when in 1891, the Customs farmer tried to collect ground rent on goods stored for more than 15 days. However, the merchants of Shiraz vehemently opposed this and he abandoned the plan.[22]

In particular because the British, but also other European, consuls complained about the collection of internal duties, the government in Tehran considered various alternative arrangements to resolve this problem. This discussion started seriously around 1871, when Mirza Hoseyn Khan, Moshir al-Dowleh proposed to levy one tariff for all merchants and suppress all inland duties. However, strong opposition by Persian merchants put an end to this. In 1882, Amin al-Soltan developed a proposal to reform the customs system, a proposal that included the establishment of bonded warehouses, discussed above. However, he abandoned his reform plan and after protests, made some minor upward adjustments to the duties. In 1895, the government made a proposal to levy 5% on the export of opium, but this was rejected by merchants in the south of Persia.[23]

National Customs Department

It is clear from the above that the discussion between merchants and the Persian authorities as well as the latter with the British government was slowly moving towards the establishment of a national Customs department directly under the central government rather than one where each jurisdiction was farmed out to the highest bidding individual. This constituted the third period in the organization of the Customs system. Uniform rates and more transparency did not sit well with customs farmers, who liked to haggle with major merchants over special lower rates and allow smuggling. Perhaps an even stronger development that drove the Customs department to a national one was the shah's need for money. His only major source of cash revenue was that of the customs receipts, which the government of Persia offered potential lenders as security for loans. On 17 May 1897, Amin al-Dowleh, the Prime-Minister (1896-98) signed a contract with the Imperial Bank of Persia (IBP) to receive 850,000 *qrans* monthly to pay government expenditures in exchange for receiving the customs revenues of Bushehr and Kermanshah. The IBP took control of the Bushehr Customs department, but withdrew in August of the year after the government of Persia repaid its loan. Thereafter, Daryabegi, the governor of the Gulf Ports farmed the customs of Bushehr, but this proved to be of short duration.[24] Because Mozaffar al-Din Shah (r. 1896-1907) needed money again, Amin al-Soltan, the new Prime-Minister was able to secure a loan from Russia in the fall of 1898, with the customs revenues of Northern Persia and the income of the fishing concession of the Caspian Sea as security. In March 1899, Amin al-Soltan placed the customs of Kermanshah and Azerbaijan under the management of Belgian officials to increase government revenues. In 1900, Amin al-Soltan was able to obtain a new Russian loan on security of all customs revenues, except those of Fars and the Gulf Ports. Because the customs revenues of Kermanshah and Azerbaijan had increased so much under Belgian

21. Floor 1988 c; Saldanha 1986, vol. 7/2, pp. 173-74.
22. Administration Report 1891-92, p. 10.
23. Floor 1998 b, pp. 392-93; Administration Report 1891-92, p. 11.
24. Saldanha 1986, vol. 7/2, p. 177; Sa`adat 1390, pp. 123-24.

management, Amin al-Soltan decided to place the entire national customs system under Belgian officials, which led to a 600% increase of total customs revenues in one year.[25]

As a result, as of 21 March 1900, the Customs Department of Bushehr came under the direct management of the central government. As state executives of the new system, Belgian officials took control of the Customs Department at Bushehr. "It is stated that they will not, at first, enhance the rate for native-owned goods, or interfere with vested interests, and if this is the case, the new arrangements may turn out satisfactory and increase the revenue of the Persian Government without exciting much opposition."[26] The man in charge as Director-General of the Customs of Fars was Mr. Simais who arrived in Bushehr at that time. It was intended to levy 5% ad valorem on all goods imported by Persian merchants instead of varying specific rates. As expected the merchants opposed this and refused to clear their goods from customs. For one month business was suspended. Therefore, because disturbances were expected, the government of Persia introduced a new tariff on a sliding scale that was more favorable to Persian merchants than the uniform 5% rate. The merchants also rejected this, but the government held firm and in the first week of August 1900 this new tariff was applied. Since then it was business as usual and the 5% rate was applied without a problem. Thus, as of that time, foreign and Persian merchants were treated in the same way as to the level of customs duties to be paid. Also, the Customs Department forcefully began to supervise arms traffic. To get better at this, the government of Persia intended to buy two gunboats to check smuggling. The first year of the Belgian administration yielded positive results. Simais confiscated more than 1,000 rifles and 200,000 rounds of ammo, while the government of Persia received higher revenues, viz. 3,947,000 *qrans* instead of 2,400,000 qrans or a 60% increase. On 30 November 1901, there was a 'spontaneous' demonstration of 200 women and children, who went to the homes of the olama to protest that a European was inspecting the homes of Moslems![27] The Belgian led Customs Department also tried to increase revenues by other means. When goods were transferred between ships the Customs charged 2.5% ad valorem. The British Legation protested, arguing that in accordance with treaty stipulations no other customs duties were allowed above the 5% rate, although agreeing that payment of a small fee would be acceptable. Joseph Naus, the Belgian official who was Minister of Customs, took the position that the Treaty of Turkomanchay did not grant any exemption of transit or transshipment fees in Persian ports. The British countered that although this was correct, the collection of the transit fee was contrary to 60 years of established practice as well as to instructions given by the government of Persia in the past. Finally, the British agreed to the payment of a transshipment fee of 1/8 *qran* per package levied on goods transferred within the harbor, and ¼ *qran* per package on goods landed and kept in bond and later re-exported within 20 days, although the Customs department might extend this period.[28]

---

25. Jones 1986, vol. 1, pp. 82-86; Sa`adat 1390, pp. 46-47.
26. Administration Report 1899-1900, p. 3.
27. Administration Report 1900-1901, p. 3; Sirjani 1361, p. 603; Sa`adat 1390, pp. 141-52 (with the texts of telegrams sent by protesting merchants), 151-52 (protest against Simais). See also Bérard 1910, p. 250. This was one of the least effective aspects of the Customs department. As of 1882, the Persian government had banned the import of arms and ammunition. This ban was repeated in July 1891 when it became clear that many arms were imported. Administration Report 1891-92, pp. 10, 19.
28. Administration Report 1901-1902, p. 2; Saldanha 1986, vol. 7/2, p. 178.

Meanwhile, the government of Persia was negotiating a new loan with both Russia and Great Britain, which would give either country more control over fiscal policy with regard to foreign trade. The Russians were more eager than the British, who wanted more certainty about the new scale of duties before taking a decision. Therefore, Great Britian asked Persia not to agree to any new loan before it would be able to submit its own proposal. However, the Mozaffar al-Din Shah was desperately in need of cash and Persian trade with Russia was more important than with Great Britain. The British, who thought that the issue of the new customs tariff was still open to negotiation proposed to send an expert to Tehran. However, in December 1901, London learnt that Persia on 9 November 1901 had already signed a Commercial Convention with Russia. Because the Turco-Persian treaties of 1823 and 1848, which provided an opening to other nations to claim most-favored status, formed the last obstacle for the formulation of a new Customs Treaty, in August 1902, unbeknownst to the British, Naus negotiated with the Ottomans a new treaty replacing all earlier treaties. The new Ottoman-Iranian treaty granted both countries most-favored nation status in customs matters. As a result, on 27 December 1902 Russia and Persia ratified the new Customs Convention, which on 14 February 1903 came into force.[29]

Apart from the fact that the new tariffs were disadvantageous to British and Indian imports, what Great Britain feared more than anything else was that as of then, the government of Persia could impose any level of customs rate on British and Indian goods. This fear was not groundless, because the only assured cash that the government of Persia could count on were the customs revenues. Therefore, increasing those revenues were in its interests, the more so, because this would make it easier to obtain new loans from Russia. If this would happen, Russia might demand the imposition of higher tariffs thus, further disadvantaging British interests. Great Britain, therefore, decided to accept the new Customs tariff as a fait accompli and induce Persia to sign a new treaty with Great Britain that was similar to the one signed with Russia. At least, in this way, tariffs could not be indiscriminately increased without British consent. Despite opposition by Naus, who did not want Persia to give up its right to unilaterally raise tariffs, the Prime-Minister agreed to this British proposal, which was signed in Tehran on 9 February 1904, four days prior to the Russo-Persian tariff taking effect.

Under the new tariff instead of a uniform 5% ad valorem duty on imports and exports, a schedule of specific duties by category of goods was imposed. Especially injurious to British interests was the imposition of a weight tariff on piece goods, because Indian cottons were heavier than those imported from Russia. As to British exports, grain, depending on the category, henceforth paid a tariff ranging from 3.5 to 20% and opium 8.5%, whereas export of dried fruit, almonds, and raw cotton, which were all exported to Russia, were exempted from export duties. The merchants protested against the new tariffs and wanted 3-months to sell goods in customs, but the government refused.[30] Under the new Customs Convention, the jurisdiction of the Bushehr Customs Department included the minor ports of Halileh, Delvar, Dayyer, Taheri, Kangan, `Asalu, Charak and

29. Entner 1965, pp. 53-55; Jones 1986, vol. 1, pp. 86-88; Saldanha 1986, vol. 7/2, p. 180.

30. Entner 1965, op. 68ff; Saldanha 1986, vol. 7/2, p.180-81; Administration Report 1902-1903, p. 2.

Nakhoda-bashi (Commander) of all customs vessels

the island of Kish. In December 1904, despite British opposition, a customs post was also established on the island of Khark.[31]

31. Saldanha 1986, vol. 7/2, pp. 182-83; Sadid al-Saltaneh 1371, pp. 55, 85-86. In 1904, the customs *modir* at Halileh was paid 15 *tumans* and his three *tofangchis* 18 *tumans* per months. The *modirs* at the other posts likely received the same pay.

These were not the only problems that the new Customs Convention created for Great Britain. British men-of-war customarily came to Bushehr to take on provisions. In March 1902, Mr. Golzad the British naval contractor complained to the British Resident that he had to pay a 10% on supplies that he sent to the *HMS Lawrence*, on which he already had paid 5% on import. Naus informed the British that the payment was not an export duty, but a "payment for exemption." After further correspondence, in March 1905 Naus informed the British that the Bushehr officials would continue to levy 10% on supplies of grains and livestock supplied to British government ships.[32]

From the very beginning of the Belgian administration, the government of Persia had expressed the intention to buy gun-boats to prevent smuggling. In December 1902 or January 1903 it bought the Belgian yacht *Selika*, which was renamed *Mozaffar*, to be used by the Customs Department. The vessel was armed with two guns and sailed with a crew of Persian sailors and initially was under Belgian officers. In September 1903 Persia wanted to buy more gun-boats and preferred those that could be constructed in Bombay to those offered from Europe. The government of India agreed to the construction of five steam launches at £3,000 each. At the request of Naus, the government of India waived the 25% levy that the Royal Indian Marine charged to foreign government's orders, hoping that in future Persia would look for British assistance in case of the development of its resources in the Persian Gulf.[33]

Up to September 1904, the Customs Department had operated with temporary regulations. However, in that month the long awaited Customs regulations were published, and to the dismay of many merchants, strictly applied. This was, of course, to be expected, because in the interpretation of the various rules, the individual directors of the different Customs Departments had a certain flexibility. Over time, having precedents, arguments, protests and the like their application would become less contested.[34]

One negative aspect of the new customs tariff was the delay experienced in clearing goods, because the bulk of imports, of which the most was British, paid duty by weight. There was as yet no clear transparent system concerning measurements, etc. and merchants were at the mercy of the customs officials. Small traders in particular were hit, due to the new petty expenses, stamps, and fees, which in case of big order were insignificant. Also, steamships ran on a tight schedule and did not allow their local agents much flexibility, which added to cost for consignees.[35]

Although by 1904, there was as yet no impact on British trade due to the new tariff, merchants were unhappy and the British Resident had his ups and downs with the Belgian customs officials. This remained a problem throughout the management of the Customs Department by Belgian officials. These had an unenviable task. They had been hired by the government of Persia to optimally manage the national Customs system with a view to maximize revenues. At the same time, Persia's major trading partners, Russia and Great Britain were engaged in serious competition to establish their political influence over Persia to the cost of the other. Whenever Belgian officials took decisions, even when

32. Saldanha 1986, vol. 7/2, pp. 185-86.
33. Saldanha 1986, vol. 7/2, pp. 186-87.
34. Administration Report 1904-1905, pp. 3-4. For an English version of these regulations, see DCR no. 646, Miscellaneous Series, London 1906.
35. Administration Report 1903-1904, p. 23; Administration Report 1904-1905, pp. 21-22.

they were the right ones, either the British or Russians would accuse them of being in the hands of the other power. A local customs director like the one in Bushehr could be overruled or pressured by Tehran, when Russia and Great Britain could, or at least, tried to enforce their point of view on the government of Persia. The situation became even more complicated after 1907, when with the establishment of the constitutional government in Persia, the Belgian officials also could be accused by nationalist politicians of favoring their own interests or that of either Russia and/or Great Britain. The position of the Belgians worsened after 1911, when Great Britain financially propped up the government of Persia. The British officials found it difficult to accept that they had no say about daily operations, when it was their money that paid for it. When after October 1917, Russia was no longer a threat to British interests in Persia it became even more difficult for Belgian officials to withstand British pressure, although to their credit it must be said that they did. In spite of all these pressures, the Belgian officials maintained that they only represented the interests of Persia and often strongly opposed outside pressure to give in to foreign demands. Of course, it is true that some individuals could get along with each other better than others, because of their character, as is clear from observations made by British officials about individual Belgian officials.[36]

Dambrain, who left on leave in May 1904, was replaced by E. Waffelaert until mid-February 1905. British relations were poor with Waffelaert, whom they considered troublesome; they further remarked that "The Belgian Administration is still intensely unpopular." The British were still smarting because of the new 1903 tariff, which was not of their own making and indeed was an impetus to smuggling. However, apart from lamenting that "Nothing is likely to cure this state of things, short of a return to an allround 5 per cent. duty," they had not much to contribute nor could they do anything about the new reality.[37] What hurt British *amour propre* was the enormous power of the Belgian director of Customs and the respect that he enjoyed with the Persian authorities. Dambrain, e.g., was greeted at Lengeh in April 1904 with a salute of 7 guns and other honors normally accorded to a Persian governor. Likewise, the governor of Bushehr, Daryabegi, whom nationalists decried as being pro-British, seemed to be totally under Belgian control, because they paid his salary.[38] No wonder the British officials were upset.

Fortunately, J. Heynssens, who was friendly and reasonable in his relations, according to the British, at first pursued the hard line of his predecessor. In particular, his insistence on art. 15 of the Customs treaty ("consignees have to declare goods in person; discrepancies between invoices and contents were fined") caused opposition and finally led to the refusal of Persian and European merchants to clear their goods. The Bushehr business community, Persian and European, had drawn up identical documents with their grievances for their consuls. The Persians even sent a telegram to the shah and PM and tried to mobilize their counterparts in Isfahan, Shiraz and Yazd. The result was congestion, given the small storage capacity of the Customs wharf, and orders were cancelled by importers and consignments sent elsewhere, so that trade came to a standstill in April and May. In June 1905, Tehran telegraphed Daryabegi to get Heynssens to relax the rules, which he

---

36. For a detailed discussion of the role of the Belgians in Persia and their efforts to remain true to Persia, their paymaster, see Destrée 1976 and Laureys 1996.

37. Administration Report 1903-1904, p. 2; Administration Report 1904-1905, p. 5; Administration Report 1905-1906, p. 3; Destree 1976, p. 95.

38. Saldanha 1986, vol. 7/2, p. 187; Administration Report 1904-1905, p. 3.

did, after instructions from Tehran. He promised to discuss the merchants' complaints, make changes where he could and ask Tehran what do when he could not. On 2 August 1905 Heynssens sent a memo responding in such a way that most grievances were taken care of. As a result, the merchants were not further interested in pursuing the remaining ones, even when reminded by their consuls. Having been treated with consideration, it took away all discontent. Nevertheless, the British Resident believed that Heynssens' approach towards Persian merchants and coastal traders was "too direct and inelastic to please them" and the Customs Department was still unpopular with the general public, who had the support of the mullahs. "Thus when in February 1906 the Director-General prohibited the landing of cargo from native coasting boats at private wharves as had previously been the custom, an appeal to the Uluma was at once made, and on this occasion the latter were able to induce the Director-General to cancel the order, on the boatmen agreeing to discharge their cargo in the presence of a customs official." In October 1905 the inland Customs Bureau at Daleki was abolished at the urging of the Residency.[39]

There were two things that the British Resident could not stop complaining about, one was smuggling and the other was the refrain that Persia should return to the 5% tariff. The latter, as pointed out above, was an unrealistic *fata morgana*, while the Customs department indeed did not have capacity to deal with the increased arms and other smuggling activities. Not only did it lack the means, but also in isolated places customs officials were at the mercy of the local population. In May 1905, in the small port of Karri (Tangestan) a customs official sent to investigate arms smuggling was flogged and expelled by the inhabitants, and the *Mozaffar* when sent there could do nothing given that the inhabitants were armed to the teeth. The Customs Department's enforcement capacity did not improve, even though four sea-going launches were delivered at the end of 1906, as they were not much used, because of lack of funds.[40] Also, according to the British, in the year thereafter, despite active smuggling the five Customs launches were not optimally used.[41] The British Resident was rather sanguine about arms smuggling, because these arms were bought locally and did not end up in the NW province and other place inconvenient for the British. "On his way to Shiraz by the now deserted Firozabad route the Resident learnt of several village depots in the hinterland for the distribution of arms, and the advantages or disadvantages of the latest patterns in vogue seemed to be almost the sole topic of interest among the peasants met with."[42]

---

39. Administration Report 1905-1906, p. 16; Political Diaries, vol. 1, pp. 76, 85, 90, 94, 104, 108. For the Persian text of the protest of the Persian merchants, dated 25 April 1905, that they submitted to Heynssen and the latter's reply, see Hamidi 1378, pp. 127-29. According to Administration Report 1904-1905, p. 5, M. Heynssens took over on 29 March. In June 1905, merchants protested against the import duty on dates and date juice (staple food). As a result, in December the rate was reduced from one *qran* to 10 cent *ad valorem*. Political Diaries, vol. 1, pp. 108, 239.

40. Administration Report 1905-1906, pp. 15-16; Administration Report 1906-1907, p. 12. In early February 1906, the Customs Department ordered all fishing boats to pass the Customs House for inspection. The fishermen protested to the Imam Jom`eh saying they went out a night fishing and returned after 3-4 hours and could not stay the whole night at Customs to check for smuggled goods. At the Imam Jom`eh's request the order was canceled. However, all other native craft had to land at Customs not at private wharfs as was the custom. After a protest, the mullahs induced the director of Customs to cancel the order, but agreed to the presence of customs officials at landing. Political Diaries, vol. 1, p. 281, 286.

41. Administration Report 1907-1908, p. 8.

42. Administration Report 1907-1908, p. 8.

Waffelaert replaced Heynssens just before end of the year. In his previous tenure he had shown himself to be anti-British and, according to the British Resident, followed the Russian Consul-General's lead, in particular in the case of quarantine and postal arrangements. Also, he was said to have received a Russian decoration. Therefore, Waffelaert had come to the conclusion that his posting in Kermanshah was due to his attitude towards the British. Therefore, during his absence he communicated to the British Resident that he would be more cooperative and friendly, if he would return to Bushehr. However, he only remained 6 months and left in September for Europe, because the government of Persia refused to renew his contract. The advent of the new constitutional government allegedly caused the Belgian administration to be less friendly to British interests. Because the nationalists were hostile towards Naus and his Belgian staff and consequently the position of the Belgian officials became more difficult over time. The new government, for example, ordered the Belgians, who often employed Iraqi Christian and Persian Armenian clerks, who generally were better educated and spoke French, to replace them with Persians. The latter were mainly recruited from the educated and nationalist class, which was hostile towards the Belgian staff and even worked against them. "Under the old regime, if they wanted a reasonably peaceful time the Belgian Directors found it profitable to cultivate either the Russians or ourselves, they now had rather to propitiate the parliamentary element and the Persian vernacular press, which otherwise lost no opportunity of making things uncomfortable for them." Also, the local *anjomans* interfered with all branches of government. Due to the country's desperate financial situation the Customs directors were pressed to produce more revenues, which meant applying the rules strictly, and not liberally or not at all where it was deemed unsuitable for the situation in Bushehr. As a result, the 'enmity' that existed prior to the 1903 Tariff was revived, now merchants not only had to cope with the insecurity of the road and the blackmail by road guards, but had to suffer the strict application as well as "the intricacies and catchpennies of the Customs Regulations." The result was indeed as expected, viz. Customs revenues did not go down, despite the insecurity on the trade road and problems of transporting goods to Shiraz.[43]

At the beginning of 1908, Leleux arrived as inspector-general, but he chose to reside at Mohammerah. Constant was acting director till May when he left on leave. M. Zwinne became acting director until Stas arrived and he remained in function till the end of December 1908, when Zwinne became *de facto* director. Stas left in the second week of January when his contract expired. Zwinne was a new arrival from Belgium, which made him "ultra punctilious in the enforcement of the letter of the law without due consideration of the particular circumstances of each case." For example, he employed special spies who went to the bazaars to find places where aniline dye was sold. On 25 December 1908 a quantity of the illegal dye was confiscated. Nevertheless, he weathered Sayyed Morteza's troublesome period with equanimity, despite being expelled from the Customs, and later he made a deal with the Sayyed returning to work "on certain constitutional conditions." (Chapter 3). On 27 April 1909, Leleux arrived, who took over from Zwinne. Because of the tense political situation at that time, the Resident asked Zwinne, whether Leleux had arrived at a written agreement with the *anjoman* concerning his

43. Administration Report 1907-1908, pp. 7-9; Saldanha 1986, vol. 7/2, p. 187.

assumption of the post, which was the case. Leleux was reasonable in his official dealings, or so the British opined.[44]

Leleux was replaced by Constant on 12 May 1910, who maintained friendly relations with the British. He had a serious problem to deal with, because the chiefs of Tangestan and Dashti opposed Customs' efforts to interdict smuggling, murdering the *modirs* in their area and threatening to attack Bushehr. The Customs Department asked Daryabegi to punish them, but the tribal levies that were willing to support him in Lengeh and Bandar Abbas refused to fight their Tangestani neighbors. The Customs posts in Dashti and Tangestan were then closed and all import and export from that area prohibited. Smuggling, a well organized business, still went on of course.[45] The Tangestani Customs guards under Zayer `Abdollah Khan, the *ra'is-e tofangchiyan gomroki* of Bushehr had no qualms collecting the taxes from the chiefs in Bushehr's hinterland (except from the Tangestani chiefs who asked for a delay) as well as from the *banader-e thalatheh*, where he went in the fall of 1910 with the *Persepolis*.[46] Despite very active smuggling, the Customs Department did not have the resources to curb it or protect its staff. In August at Shivu, the *modir* was killed by his *tofangchis*.[47]

Before 1900 the governor used to farm the Customs and Land Revenue from Tehran and the surplus was his income. After 1900, the governor had nothing to do with Customs, while for some time, the latter also collected land revenue from easy districts, the remainder was left to the governor. In compensation, the governor received a monthly payment, which formerly was 15,000 *tuman*, but in early 1912 was reduced to 11,200 *tuman*. Customs suspended this payment on 21 March 1912, claiming that the Imperial Bank of Persia (IBP) objected to it as being contrary to the 1911 loan agreement. When it was made clear to the IBP that the payments were made from land revenue and not from Customs, the IBP gave up its objection, but demanded that Customs and land revenue receipts were separately recorded and that Customs receipts could not be used, as had been done in the past, to make good the shortfall in other revenues; payment from Customs receipts were only to be used after the IBP's share had been paid. Payment was resumed in July only to be stopped again in September by Zwinne, while acting for Constant who was on leave. Outwardly, he was friendly with the governor, but Zwinne was upset by the governor's alleged improper attitude towards the Belgian-managed Finance Department as well as that his accounts for last year were irregular. Zwinne did not state these reasons to the governor or Residency, but he had done so in secret behind the governor's back back. In a telegram in October, Mornard, the Treasurer-General in Tehran, offended the governor, in which he characterized him as behaving like 'a rebel' and giving vague reasons for stopping payments. Zwinne, when asked for the reasons of the telegram, gave evasive replies. Shortly thereafter, he left for Bandar Abbas, when Constant returned in November. He took the same position as his predecessor but he disagreed with the manner in which Zwinne had dealt with the matter. Because he received no money, the governor used this as a pretext to levy taxes such as *kalantari*, `*alafi*, and others that amounted to road duties

44. Administration Report 1908, p. 7; Administration Report 1909, p. 9; Sa`adat 1390, p. 163 (Zwinne was replaced by Musa Khan, his chief clerk and interpreter); Political Diaries, vol. 3, p. 405.

45. Administration Report 1910, p. 13; Hamidi 1378, pp. 68, 174 (welcoming Constant as *Irandust*), 190-91 (with a report about the *modir* killed at Kangan); Sa`adat 1390, p. 176.

46. Nura'i 1385, p. 220; Hamidi 1378, p. 93.

47. Administration Report 1911, p. 13; Administration Report 1912, p. 15.

or *rahdari* and contrary to the Treaty. Further, when asked to take action, the governor claimed to be unable to do so as he had no funds. The non-payment of wages also reduced his standing with the petty chiefs, because the Belgian Finance Department explained this to everybody as clear proof that they and not the governor were the supreme authority in the district. At the end of the year, Constant wrote a memo showing the governor's improper keeping of accounts. The Resident told Constant to give Mornard and the governor a copy at the same time, for it allowed the governor to provide arguments against the allegations made, which were "a severe indictment of his financial" management.[48] The conflict between Constant and the governor continued into 1913, when finally with the help of the British Residency things were settled in a satisfactory manner. Beginning in 1913, Mokhber al-Saltaneh, the governor-general of Fars appointed Mas`ud al-Mamalek as governor or rather *ma'mur* of Dashti and Dashtestan. However, he was unable to collect the taxes. Therefore, in June 1913 the Shiraz Finance department suggested that it might be better if the governor of Bushehr would assume this function, as he was better placed to do something. Mokhber al-Saltaneh first opposed the idea, but then transferred the governorship of Dashti and Dashtestan to Movaqqar al-Salteneh. This pleased the British Residency, which further opposed Mokhber al-Saltaneh's wish to replace Movaqqar al-Salteneh by Daryabegi, his own man.[49]

Constant remained in Bushehr until end March 1913 when Zwinne took over. The reason for his departure was a sad one, because Mrs. Constant was killed on 8 March. She was buried the next day in the RC cemetery. Constant believed that he was attacked, because he was also the director of the Finance Department, a combination of functions that he had always opposed. The governor believed Sheikh Shahad, a man sacked by Constant from the Customs Department was behind it; despite much effort the man, who had fled, was never found. Another man was arrested as the possible perpetrator, but he was released at the end of the year as there was no evidence against him. The Belgians demanded a compensation of 1,250,000 francs which was paid.[50]

4.2: List of provincial directors of the Customs Department (1900-37)

Name	Duration	Observation	Source
H. Simais	21 March 1900 - ?	Died on leave in Belgium	Report 1900-1901, p. 3; Sa`adat 1390, p. 139
C. Dambrain	? January 1902 - May 1904		Destree 1976, p. 332; Administration Report 1904-1905, p. 5
E. Waffelaert	May 1904-28 February 1905		Administration Report 1904-1905, p. 5
J. Heynssens	29 February 1905-February 1907		Administration Report 1904-1905, p. 5

48. Administration Report 1912, pp. 16-17. By 1912, the Customs chief of Bushehr was in charge was in charge of (i) customs of the governorate; (ii) taxes; (iii) provincial post; (iv) provincial telegraph; and (v) supervision of trade in intestines. Political Diaries vol. 4, p. 589.

49. Administration Report 1913, pp. 13-14.

50. Administration Report 1913, p. 14; Sa`adat 1390, p. 193 (allegedly the murder was committed by one the family of the Khan of Borazjan and two other men, because he could no longer stand the abuse heaped on him by Constant); Government of Great Britain 1914, pp. 28-29 (nrs. 54-55).

Name	Duration	Observation	Source
E. Waffelaert	March 1907-September 1907		Administration Report 1907-1908, p. 8
A. Constant	September 1907-May 1908	Acting director	Administration Report 1908, p. 7
Zwinne *	May 1908-end December 1908	Acting director	Administration Report 1908, p. 7
A. Stass	End December 1908-10 January 1909		Administration Report 1908, p. 7
Zwinne	11 January 1909-27 April 1909	Acting director	Administration Report 1909, p. 9
L. Leleux	28 April 1909-12 May 1910		Administration Report 1909, p. 9
H. DeGraeve	13 May 1910- ? 1910	Asst. director	Administration Report 1910, p. 12-13
A. Constant	? 1910-end March 1913	Zwinne officiated from August-November 1912	Administration Report 1910, p. 12-13; Idem, 1912, p. 15; Idem 1913, p. 14
Zwinne	End March 1913- March 1914		Administration Report 1914, p. 7
H. Bourgeois	29 March 1914- April 1918		Administration Report 1914, p. 7; 1915, p. 3; 1916, p. 2; 1917, p. 1; 1918, p. 2
E. De Kerckheer	April 1918-?		Political Diaries, vol. 6, p. 427
A. Stas	?-4 May 1928		Administration Report 1928, p. 3
A. Hunin	4 May 1928-14 May 1928	Inspector-General of Customs acted as pro-tem	Administration Report 1928, p. 3
Vali Mohammad Mirza Nowban	14 May 1928-26 October 1928		Administration Report 1928, p. 3
Paul Wolters	27 October 1928-October 1930		Administration Report 1930, p. 4; Political Diaries, vol. 9, p. 74
A. Stas	October 1930-26 July 1931		Administration Report 1930, p. 4
-	27 July-11 September 1931	Temporary arrangements	Administration Report 1931, p. 5
Mirza Habibollah Khan Bahruzi	12 September 1931-23 June 1932	Acting director	Administration Report 1931, p. 5
L.B. Vandenrydt	23 June -17 October 1932		Administration Report 1932, p. 4
Mirza Lotfollah Khan Dowlatshahi	17 October 1932-6 August 1933		Administration Report 1932, p. 4
L.B. Vandenrydt	6 August -December 1933		Administration Report 1933, p. 3
LaFontaine	December 1933-May 1934		Administration Report 1933, p. 3

Name	Duration	Observation	Source
Mohammad Vali Mirza Nowban	18 May 1934-?		Administration Report 1934, p. 3
?	?		
Ahmad Zelli	August 1937-? January 1940		Administration Report 1937, p. 6; Political Diaries vol. 14, p. 3
LotfAli Dowlatshahi	?-end October 1945		Administration Report 1945, p. 8
Mohammad Ghaffari	End October 1945-?		Administration Report 1945, p. 8

* According to Destrée, A. Wagner is mentioned as being DG of the Customs department of Bushehr in December 1907 and possibly also in 1908, which is not borne out by the other available sources. Destrée 1976, pp. 184, 349.

On 29 March 1914, Bourgeois replaced Zwinne, who remained in function throughout the period of British occupation of Bushehr (see Table 4.2) and "because of the war [he] was steady in his desire to work with the British."[51] After the British occupation of Bushehr in August 1915, all government departments continued to work under their own officials. However, henceforth the receipts of the customs and finance departments were deposited in the IBP and a part was used for the administration of Bushehr. The balance was used to pay one or two claims and the indemnities for the soldiers killed or wounded.[52] This was not a major change with past practice. In 1910 the net proceeds of the Customs revenues of the Gulf Ports were also assigned to service the government's loan granted by the IBP in the amount of £1,250,000.[53] The proceeds from Customs duties on imports and exports at the Bushehr Customs-house developed as follows:

4.3: Customs Receipts (1809-1917; 1946-48)

Year	Bushehr Customs	Gulf Ports Customs	Source
1809	100,000 Rs		Kinneir 1971, p. 70
1820s	22,000 *tuman*		Sani` al-Dowleh 1294, vol. 1, p. 299
1850-51	22,000 *tuman*		Binning 1857, vol. 1, p. 151 (entire revenues, incl. Customs)
1862-63	15,000 *tuman*		Pelly 1865 a, p. 48
1873-74	32,000 *tuman*		Administration Report 1873-74, p. 14
1878	63,000 *tuman**		Sirjani 1361, p. 91
1881	60,000 *tuman*		Stack 1881, vol. 1, pp. 24-25
1884	80,000 *tuman**		Issawi 1971, pp. 84, 97-104

51. Administration Report 1914, p. 7; Administration Report 1915, pp. 2, 3 (Moses Khan or Mr. Kachaturian was personal assistant to the Director of the Customs department); Hamidi 1378, p. 79, 174, 224.
52. Administration Report 1915, pp. 6-7.
53. Trade Report 1910-11, p. 2.

Year	Bushehr Customs	Gulf Ports Customs	Source
1888-89	85,000 *tuman*		Administration Report 1888-89, p.35.
1890	91,000 *tuman*		Curzon 1892, vol. 1, p. 235 (this was the lease price, minus the profits)
1894-95	1,10,000 Rs		Administration Report 1894-95, p. 31
1896-97	1,10,000 Rs		Administration Report 1896-97, p. 23
	in £	in £	
1907-08	125,502	175,565	Trade Report 1911-12, p.
1908-09	88,833	123,462	Trade Report 1911-12, p.
1909-10	64,416	99,016	Trade Report 1911-12, p.
1910-11	-	97,776	Trade Report 1911-12, p.
1911-12	87,730	93,555	Trade Report 1911-12, p.
1912-13	89,303	75,567	Trade Report 1911-12, p.
1913-14	82,280	92,928	Trade Report 1913-14, p. 5
1914-15	99,246	64,033	Trade Report 1914-15, p. 3
1915-16	125,609	110,914	Trade Report 1915-16, p. 3.
1916-17	99,895	237,998	Trade Report 1916-17, p. 3
1917-18	112,827	409,751	Trade Report 1917-18, p. 3
	In Rupees		
1946	11.866.299, 15		NA, FO 371/15473
1947	16.635.488,05		NA, FO 371/15473
1948	6.641.015,30		NA, FO 371/15473

* = amount paid by the tax farmer
see similar table in *tumans* in Trade Report 1912-13, p. 15.

Despite the war, Customs revenues rose at the end of 1914 and were expected to continue to do so in 1915, because the "Russian railways are congested and Azerbaijan is disturbed so that Russian trade routes are closed." Increased imports of tea and other goods and customs also increased because there were no more imports via Baghdad and Russia, while in the first quarter, imports via Mohammerah were stopped due to disturbances there. The higher figures for 1915-16 are due to the duty on tea of which larger quantities were imported. The figures further show the growing importance of other ports after 1916 (see chapter 2).[54]

During WWI, the British naval blockade and occupation of Basra had reduced arms traffic to almost nothing.[55] However, with the reduced British presence in the Persian Gulf towards the end of WW I, arms smuggling was on the uptake, which yielded the Khans on the littoral considerable revenue.[56] Nevertheless, there was a change in the way arms

54. Administration Report 1914, p. 7; Administration Report 1915, pp. 2, 3; Hamidi 1378, pp. 79, 174, 224; Trade Report 1916-17, p. 3; see also, Sadid al-Saltaneh 1371, p. 49-50, 84-85.
55. Administration Report 1914, p. 4.
56. Administration Report 1917 p. 4; see also Sa`adat 1390, pp. 36-38.

smuggling was carried out. By 1921, it was found that arms traffic no longer occured with fully loaded dhows, but rather with a few rifles and ammo hidden among general cargo.[57] In 1921, the government of Persia issued new Customs Regulations, which was strongly opposed by merchants, who for a long time refused to clear their goods from the Customs in Bushehr. However, when they realized that the government was not going to give in the merchants gave up their opposition and accepted the new higher tariff.[58] The government imposed ban on cabotage of *qrans* in 1923, not only stifled intra-costal trade, but it also led to smuggling.[59] Although the government repealed this ban one year later, the imposition of a new tax on sugar and tea in May 1925 also resulted in smuggling. Because of the increased smuggling the government took additional steps to curb this. The Customs Department ordered the building of several new motor dhows, each of which was armed with a maxim gun to successfully seize armed smuggling vessels. However, instead of soldiers they placed policemen on board who didn't know how to operate a maxim gun. And thus, it happened that when a customs dhow wanted to inspect a boat and was met fire from old-fashioned rifles, the customs boat fled because nobody could operate the maxim![60]

Because in early 1928, smuggling continued unchecked and even increased, the military commander, accompanied by Hunin, the Inspector-General of the Customs Department and 50 men went to `Asalu with an armed dhow. The people of `Asalu opposed the landing of the Customs dhow and started firing at it killing the helmsman and therefore, the dhow returned to Bushehr. In reaction, the military posted a few guards at Delvar and `Asalu, but this had no significant impact on smuggling, because smuggled sugar and tea entered Bushehr in large quantities. According to the British Resident, "the Tangestani smugglers almost always escape when sighted." The new Autonomous Customs tariff of 10 May 1928 further depressed trade, because it increased customs on most goods.[61] However, the government had more success in curbing smuggling when it used Kazeruni *tofangchi*s, who, not being friendly with the smugglers, were willing to do their preventive job. However, outside Bushehr in the small villages, smuggling continued unchecked, due to the absence of any enforcement capacity. Ironically the absence of robberies in Bushehr's environs was ascribed to the profits gained with smuggling. Therefore, in 1929 there continued to be much smuggling, which activity was only dampened by the fall in the silver price and the approach of winter.[62]

In 1930, additional government measures such as the imposition of a 20% surcharge on the existing tariff was a powerful incentive for smugglers, because the potential profits were high. The c.i.f. price of a bag of sugar from Marseilles was 15 *s.*, while in December 1930, the wholesale price (incl. all taxes) amounted to 180 *qrans* equivalent at the bazaar rate to £1.15.0 (35 *s.*) or £3 at the government rate. To curb smuggling the government made it difficult to transport smuggled goods upcountry, which, indeed, led to a decrease

57. Administration Report 1921, p. 8.
58. Trade Report 1920-21, p. ii.
59. Administration Report 1923, p. 11.
60. Administration Report 1925, p. 8.
61. Administration Report 1928, pp. 4, 8. Under the 1928 Autonomous Customs Tariff Persia's right to increase her import tariffs were restricted until May 1936. After that date it was at liberty to fix different tariff rates, in negotiation with its trading partners. Simmonds 1930, p. 5.
62. Administration Report 1928, p. 9. Administration Report 1929, p. 6.

in the smuggling activity.[63] In 1931, the imposition of the 60% surcharge translated into an 80% tariff, which was music to the ears of smugglers. As a result, in July 1931, so much smuggled sugar was landed in Dashti ports that this caused a drop in sugar prices in Shiraz. Despite frequent encounters with smugglers, the Customs Department was unable to stop the flow of smuggled goods. Therefore, Tehran appointed L. B. Vanderrydt, a special inspector, who arrived on 7 December 1931. He was "an elderly man, newly hired, and quite inexperienced, and probably too old to learn," the British commented. Vanderrydt, announced after his arrival that he would end smuggling by attacking the root cause "providing the tribesmen and smugglers with the necessities of life!" He sent various proposals to Tehran, but he finally realized "that service under Persia was a peculiar and thankless task."[64] However, his task was not made easier, when in 1932 six naval vessels arrived from Italy as well as three preventive steamers and eight motor dhows for the Customs Department. However, they were all commandeered by the Navy, and thus, Vanderrydt had neither staff nor vessels to prevent smuggling. He made no inspection of the area in 1932. Therefore, he turned his attention to improve the Customs yard and buildings and the relaying of the Customs trolley lines.[65] This development had a negative impact on the Customs' preventive smuggling section, which worked in a half-hearted manner. The arrival of a military lieutenant, who took charge of the section mid-1933, brought a much needed improvement, in particular when he seized 1,500 bags of sugar and other goods. A subsidiary guard was formed under a military captain. "The idea was to enlist time served soldiers, hire gun men and enlist the sympathy of the Tangistanis, apparently on the principle of set a thief to catch a thief. The result seems to be that smugglers are sometimes caught unless they pay us some 60 Rials for a bag of sugar smuggled which sum is to be divided between the Guard and Customs Mudir (Manager)."[66]

Anti-smuggling activities were less vigorously pursued in 1933 than in the preceding years and Tehran took notice. In February 1934, a committee of seven inspectors arrived from Tehran and posted a note in the town that any complaints against officials would be investigated. In Tangestan the committee arrested 28 smugglers, customs officials and road guards on suspicion of involvement in smuggling. After further investigation 15 were discharged and the rest remained in military custody. Those found guilty were sentenced to imprisonment. Probably as a result of this commission, another one of 13 officials arrived on 13 May and started raiding houses and shops and searching trucks for contraband. At the Customs yard, luggage of travelers was rummaged and even mail bags were inspected. "The ruthless manner in which these searches were carried out caused intense resentment amongst all classes and culminated in one of the Inspectors being attacked and beaten by a mob of infuriated shopkeepers." This was reported to the authorities Tehran who ordered the commission to use normal methods. It continued its work till December, "when the system of separate and independent inspecting bodies was abolished by the Central Government." The commission also sent a circular to all departments warning its staff that abetting smuggling was punishable by the death penalty. This had little effect

63. Administration Report 1930, p. 9. The British considered Hunin "a sensible individual," but Wolters, the director was "universally unpopular, even with his own colleague Hunin." Political Diaries, vol. 9, pp.74-75.

64. Administration Report 1931, pp. 11-12; Administration Report 1932, p. 4.

65. Administration Report 1932, p. 4.

66. Administration Report 1933, p. 3.

and smuggling flourished. In fact, in June 1934, a band of Tangistanis smuggled sugar in broad daylight within a few miles of Bushehr and, although they were intercepted, they escaped. The total catch by Customs officials in 1934 was: 890 packages of sugar, tea, piece goods, etc, 5 dhows and 16 rifles.[67]

The year 1934 not only brought the two commissions of inspectors to Bushehr, but also a major change in the management of the Customs Department, in particular, it was the year when the government took over from the Belgian administrators. The change was not unexpected given the nationalist and Persianization policy that was favored by the government in Tehran. The first sign of change occurred on 18 May 1928, when Hunin, who had earlier replaced Stas as provincial director of the Customs Department, was replaced by Mohammad Vali Mirza Nowban, the first Persian director of the Bushehr Customs Department.[68] On 26 October 1929, Nowban was replaced by Paul Wolters, who "succeeded in making himself much disliked by the merchants and traders and even by his own Belgian colleagues." Although there were many complaints against him to Customs HQ and the *Majles* about him, no action was taken. He served as director of Customs at Bushehr from 1 January until October 1930, when A. Stas[69] replaced him until 26 July 1931, when he left to return to Belgium after 30 years of service in Persia. The British Resident commented: "Though personally quite pleasant he was afraid to take the smallest responsibility and was entirely in the hands of his subordinates." Until 11 September 1931, Mirza Habibollah Khan Bahruzi was acting director, when Paul Wolters replaced him; he came from Bandar Abbas, where merchants had also complained about him. He was Inspector-General for a few months, but in April 1932 a visiting commission found him and some other Customs officials guilty of taking bribes and they were sent to Tehran. Against Wolters no charges were pressed; he was allowed to leave Persia, but his contract was not renewed. Mirza Habibollah Khan Bahruzi took over again. According to the British Resident, he "was a most delightful official, always obliging as his involved regulations permitted." He tried to eradicate some of the malpractices of his subordinates and was so successful that one of them anonymously complained to Tehran. He then, of course, was accused of malpractices. This affected his health and he had to leave Bushehr on 23 June 1932 on medical advice. He handed over to L.B. Vanderrydt. On 17 October 1931, Mirza Lotfollah Khan Dowlatshahi took over from Vanderrydt.[70] Dowlatshahi remained until 6 August when Vanderydt replaced him. He in his turn was replaced as director at the of end of 1933 by La Fontaine. In early 1934, La Fontaine and Vanderrydt handed over their duties to two of their subordinates as their contracts had run out and were not renewed. On 18 May Mohammad Vali Mirza Nowban took over as director of customs.[71] In the same month, the Customs Department stopped using French for its records and henceforth these were only kept in Persian. The French typewriters were offered for sale.[72]

---

67. Administration Report 1934, p. 3.
68. Administration Report 1928, p. 3.
69. Administration Report 1929, p. 3 (Hunin remained inspector general till February 1929, when he left on leave and Wolters officiated for him until his return on 31 May, when Wolters left); Administration Report 1930, p. 4 (Hunin, inspector and head of the preventive department was transferred at the end of March 1930 and became inspector-general of the national customs department).
70. Administration Report 1931, p. 5; Administration Report 1932, p. 4.
71. Administration Report 1933, p. 3; Administration Report 1934, p. 3.
72. Political Diaries, vol. 11, p. 153.

In February 1935, the Finance and Customs Departments were merged on the orders of Davar, the Minister of Finance. Nowban was appointed provincial director of the joint Customs and Finances Department. Also, the separate independent inspection commissions in Bushehr were abolished. These changes made no difference to the smugglers who were active via the Tangestan, Dashti and Shibkuh ports and Lengeh. From there the smuggled goods were even transported as far as Tehran, while they flooded the market in towns closer to the coast. "They bought seized goods at the official auctions and utilizing the customs seals on their own smuggled goods, passing them off as Customs Preventive sale goods. The government had therefore to open a shop in each town for the sale of their seized goods." Moreover, when in mid-1935 the rupee exchange rate rose, smugglers exported silver to the Arabian coast where they only paid 290 rials per rupee a hundred as against 600-620 rials a hundred in Persia. In three encounters between Customs and *Amniyeh* with smugglers the latter beat the former, killing some guards and escaping with their caravan. Only in one case were smugglers arrested when they ran into conscripts, six were arrested and five officials who had abetted them were arrested and sent to Shiraz for trial and punishment.[73]

Given these developments, the government considered the Customs guards to have failed in their task to prevent smuggling and fired most of them. The remainder was merged with the *Amniyeh*, which was believed to be more disciplined and efficient. However, the exchange rates of foreign currency outside Persia were so attractive that gold jewelry, silver coins, and Persian banknotes were smuggled out to buy foreign exchange. Therefore, there was much Persian currency on the Arabian side, whose import back into Persia the government tried to prevent.[74] To stem the increased smuggling activity the *Majles* passed a law, which became effective in July 1936, that smugglers were to be tried by court-martial and those who resisted arrest were to be given the death penalty; those who surrendered would get lighter sentences. However, these harsh measures did not deter the smugglers. More successful, were the measures to beef up the *Amniyeh*'s capacity with regard to the smuggling of sugar in Bushehr and district, but not beyond it. Caravans of smugglers went via Farrashband and Firuzabad, and also via Larestan to the interior. The caravans were well protected and the smugglers invariably defeated the *Amniyeh* that had to withdraw with losses. By year's end the *Amniyeh* had lost 20 men and only in one instance had they been able to kill 9 smugglers and wounded two. In October 1936, because of their inefficiency and corruption, it was decided to remove the prevention of smuggling from the *Amniyeh* and give it to the military. In 1936, the authorities in total caught: 1438 packages, 6 dhows, 13 smugglers and 14,800 rials in banknotes.[75] Because the road guards and the Customs guards were even more unreliable than the frontier guards- their predecessors, the government transferred their task concerning the ports north and south of Bushehr to the navy. Bushehr itself remained the responsibility of the road guards, assisted by the police department.[76]

The Tariff Autonomy Treaty of 1928 expired on 10 May 1936. On 22 May the government introduced a new tariff, which was not mainly ad valorem as in the past, but mostly specific. Duties were levied in local currency instead of gold rials, which

---

73. Administration Report 1935, pp. 2-4.
74. Administration Report 1936, p. 3.
75. Administration Report 1936, pp. 4, 7.
76. Administration Report 1937, p. 2.

involved a surtax, fluctuating with exchange rates, eventually amounting to 160 percent. In general, the new tariff imposed higher duties on most imports, but smaller on mass consumer goods and necessities. In addition a road tax on gross weight was charged on most imports, in particular high luxury goods.[77] In August 1937, the new provincial director of Customs, Mr. Zelli established a rationalized system of marketing and storing cargo and the promulgation of new of landing charges tariffs. Other changes included the construction of a second electric crane and the extension of the wharves (Chapter 2). All this activity contradicted the prevailing opinion that Bushehr's situation was deteriorating, but at least not yet. The reason was that Bandar Shahpur still had problems of its own, one of which was that as yet it did not have proper port and railway facilities. In 1938, the Finance and Customs Departments were separated.[78] Due to continued smuggling of Japanese piece goods an official from Tehran came and took over the entire stock of the Company and retailed these at relatively low prices to local inhabitants. Also, quantities were sent to towns inland. This stopped smuggling but not of Japanese silk. Customs caught some smuggled goods, while 20 professional smugglers were deported to towns in the interior.[79] The policy of having government monopoly departments sell their goods at reasomable prices had a downward effect on the level of smuggling of these goods. However, the smuggling of all other goods (artificial silks, footware, perfumery, etc) continued.[80] The outbreak of WW II in 1939 brought smuggling to a halt, because there was a lack of supplies on the Arabian coast.[81] Also, the government firmly established its rule over the littoral and hinterland, while the allowances made in the past to local chiefs to reduce smuggling were no longer paid. As a result, by the late 1940s the smuggling was under control and there was a proper list of tariffs. There was, however, continued pilfering of goods from the steamers, while smuggling of foodstuffs (tea, sugar, wheat) increased during WWII.[82] Also, the period after the Allied invasion was a very difficult one for the Customs Department, because smuggling increased significantly. The coastal Dashti and Tangestani chiefs disarmed the hated gendarmerie, which meant that the Customs officials were unable to enforce their authority. The closing the the naval office in Bushehr also meant that naval ships could not intervene either. Consequently, throughout the war period smuggling remained a problem.[83]

The Bushehr office sent monthly accounts to the Central Customs Organization in Tehran as well as Customs receipts, minus operating costs. In 1947, the Customs Department in the Bushehr governorate had a staff of 63, (excluding the Customs guards who were involved in the prevention of smuggling) as follows:

1 director, responsible for the whole goverrnorate
2 assistant directors, mainly for Bushehr Port.
1 inspector of sub-offices in the governorate
60 clerks etc.

---

77. Gray 1938, pp. 1-2.
78. Administration Report 1937, p. 6; Administration Report 1938, p. 3.
79. Administration Report 1938, p. 3.
80. Administration Report 1938, p. 9.
81. Administration Report 1939, p. 7.
82. Political Diaries, vol. 15, pp. 190, 223, 226.
83. Administration Report 1941, p. 4.

The Bushehr governorate was divided into five Customs divisions, three of which were split into sub-divisions.

Ganaveh	Delvar	Lavar	Abukhak	Kangan
Bandar Rig	-	Bukkharg	-	`Asalu
Delam	-	Rostami	-	Taheri
Khark	-	Karib	-	Dayyer
Rudhilleh	-	-	-	Tombak

Each division and sub-division was headed by a Customs officer assisted by 4-6 armed guards. These were recruited from the Army and commanded by seconded Army officers. There were about 200 to 300 Customs guards, and armed like the Army and gendarmerie.

Apart from guarding the Customs posts they crewed the motor launches that patrolled the sea lanes. They also had trucks to make raids on coastal villages to reduce and discourage smuggling.[84]

The Kargozari

Another important central government official in Bushehr was the *kargozar*, the agent of the Ministry of Foreign Affairs, who was the "medium of communication between foreign officials and the higher local Persian authorities." More specifically, he had to settle any cases in dispute between foreign and Persian subjects in the so-called *kargozar* court, in collaboration with foreign consuls.[85] At least in 1908, but probably from the beginning of the official's presence in Bushehr, Armenians and Christians fell under the *kargozar*.[86]

The creation of the office of *kargozar* was the result of the implementation of the Treaty of Turkomanchay (1828), when a special office (*divan-e mohakemat-e kharejeh*) was created to deal with cases that arose between Persians and foreigners. The office of *kargozar*, which came into being in the late 1830s, was the successor of the secretary (*dabir*) of that office, although a fully developed *kargozari* was only established around 1880, according to Martin and Nouraei. However, there are several indications that show that the office of *kargozar* was already operational in the Persian Gulf and elsewhere in the 1850s, if not earlier.[87]

---

84. NA, FO 371/15473.
85. Administration 1873-74, p. 5; Trade Report 1920-21, p. 1; Heravi 1372, p. 138 (to stop foreigners from exporting antiquities from Persepolis). On this function in general, see Martin and Nouraei 2005.
86. Political Diaries, vol. 3, p. 101.
87. Martin and Nouraei 2005, who are wrong when they state that the office of *kargozar* came into being in the late 1860s. In a letter by consul Abbott in Resht to Alison, the British Minister in Tehran dated 18 June 1861, he writes that as of 1842 a *kargozar* had been appointed there to deal with the foreign consuls. Apparently this official had first been appointed by the local governor, for Abbott further notes that it was only in 1853 that this official was appointed for the first time by the Ministry of Foreign Affairs in Tehran. The letter contains interesting information about the functioning of the *kargozarate*. NA, FO 248/199, nr. 14, unfoliated.

Already in 1856, and possibly earlier, there was a *kargozar* for the port of Bushehr, Mirza Ahmad.[88] At the end of 1859, the government of Persia wrote a letter to the British Minister in Tehran in which it insisted that the British Resident in Bushehr had to take up all local matters with the *kargozar* of Bushehr.[89] There are further letters from the *kargozar* of Bushehr dating from 1862 and 1865, probably Mirza Ahmad, who in 1862 or 1863 was appointed as chief of the passport agents of the three ports (*omana-ye tazkereh-ye banader-e thalateh*) and was based in Bushehr.[90] Also, irrespective of their appellation, passport agents were charged to deal with claims by foreign subjects on Persians.[91] These passports officers, therefore, may be considered *kargozars*, only with a different title.[92] In fact, in one document it is explicitly stated that it was from the *kargozar* or the *amin-e tazkereh* of the ports of Fars.[93] Usually a large office such as that of Bushehr had a separate passport officer (*amin-e tazkereh*), who was needed even more when in February 1895 the government of Persia applied a stricter passport policy. Henceforth, foreigners without a duly vised passport by their governments were "required to have them vised by the passport clerks, as on other frontiers, upon payment of fixed fees."[94]

When in 1888, Bushehr became the residence of the governor of the Gulf Ports the *kargozar*'s jurisdiction likewise was extended as was his title, viz., *kargozar-e banader*. He had two deputies respectively in Bandar Abbas and Bandar-e Lengeh,[95] while his office was also referred to as the central office (*edareh-ye markazi*).[96] In 1917, the *kargozari* of Bushehr, after deducting wages of his deputy and the *amin-e tazkereh* had 474 *tumans* in other expenditures per month. All these expenditures were to be paid out of the rent of the government-owned vessels, the remainder to be sent to Tehran via Mirza Abu Taleb, the manager of the Islamic Company (*modir-e sharekat-e eslamiyeh*) in Tehran. However, the Customs Department said it was unable to make these payments, even if orders would arrive from Tehran to do so, because this was contrary to the text of the contract between the governments of Persia and Great Britain. The Ministry then asked the Customs Department to forthwith send a copy of the contract, which apparently it did not have

---

88. NA, FO 248/168, Daryabegi to Jones rec. 28/10/1856; Lorimer 1915, vol. 1, pp. 2077-78 mentions "the local Karguzar was one of the most important prisoners taken by the British at the capture of Bushire [in 1857]." For another early occurrence of the *kargozar*, see NA, FO 248/318, unfoliated (a number of letters in Persian to and from the *kargozar*).

89. Saldanha 1986, vol. 7/II, p. 1, who makes clear that the *kargozar* was still operational in Bushehr in 1859. See also, Habibi and Vothuqi 1387, pp. 211-12, doc. 49 (13/08/1859), doc. 51 (August 1859), 222-23, doc. 72 (25/10/1861), which describes his problems of getting paid. This restriction, i.e. limiting contacts between the consuls and the authorities to the *kargozar* was lifted in 1868. Saldanha 1986, vol. 7/2, p. 151.

90. Habibi and Vothuqi 1387, pp. 228-29, docs. 82-84; Habibi and Vothuqi 1387, p. 245, doc. 113 (06/04/1865); Sa`adat 1390, p. 44. The so-called *banader-e thalateh* were Taheri, Kangan, and `Asalu.

91. Habibi and Vothuqi 1387, p. 227, doc. 80 (06/06/1862).

92. It was in March 1857 that Persia for the first time established a system of passports. IO, R/15/1/173, Sheil to Hennell, 18/03/1857, f. 26. There was also a *monshi-ye mohamm va karpardaz* in Shiraz, charged, among other things, with affairs concerning foreigners in Bandar Abbas. Habibi and Vothuqi 1387, p. 220, doc. 67 (1860).

93. Habibi and Vothuqi 1387, p. 345, doc. 302 (26/11/1882)

94. Administration Report 1894-95, p. 10; these regulations were renewed in March 1900. Saldanha 1986, vol. 7/2, p. 160.

95. See Floor 2010 and Idem, 2011 a. For the office equipment requirements of the *kargozari* in Bandar Abbas, see Nura'i 1385, p. 264.

96. Nura'i 1385, p. 187.

or could not find.[97] Later Tehran asked the British government to agree to pay the money to the local Finance Department in Bushehr.[98]

There were many local civil suits and complaints between Persians and foreigners and to settle them was no easy matter and a long drawn-out process. These cases were mostly commercial issues, but also those concerning passports, nationality, inheritance and the like.[99] The experience with the performance of the *kargozar* was generally not a positive one, as far as the British were concerned. In July 1861, Capt. Jones summed up his opinion on the matter as follows:

> As to the efficiency of the kargozari, I don't think they should employ men such as have been sent so far. Not a single claim of ours has been attended to, much less settled; the old system of direct appeal to the governor at least brought some result, although not all that was desired. Without relevant education, no local experience, and little kmowledge on any subject and profoundly ignorant on what they should know, the advantage of their appointment is questionable. Added to ignorance, there is a desire for illicitly profit from their position, who then can trust him to mediate in international affairs. Their only interest is to create problems to benefit from it. Whatever it is, a passport, a document to be legalized, a complaint to be adjusted, goods embarked or a nuisance abated, the kargozar ensures that there will be delay or refusal just to test the level of price that he can get. If you don't bribe nothing gets done. Worse, he will engage in litigation on the other side. It is neither good for us nor for the Shah's government, in fact worse.[100]

Capt. Disbrowe, Jones's temporary successor held the same view, arguing that the *kargozars* "so far have been useless, I cannot quote one case of importance dealt by them and brought to a satisfactory solution."[101] This opinion would not change very much over time, although there were *kargozars* who were more diligent in processing and handling claims. But even when the *kargozar* was efficient and competent his decisisions were often undermined by the governor. A case in point was a complaint by a British protected person against a Persian subject. The *kargozar* ruled against the defendent, who ignored the ruling. The *kargozar* then intercepted a letter, which stated that the governor had told the defendent to ignore the *kargozar*'s ruling. In a public meeting the *kargozar* asked the governor whether this was true and why the defendant had not yet been punished for refusing to abide by his ruling. Both the *kargozar* and the British Residency lodged an official complaint, the more so since the governor had interfered in many other cases.[102]

---

97. Nura'i 1385, pp. 207, 209, 228-31.

98. Nura'i 1385, p. 237.

99. Nura'i 1385, pp. 25, 27, 30, 105, 191, 200, 203-04 (passport; nationality); Idem, 110-11, 116-17, 128, 201 (inheritance); Idem, 115 (deserting soldiers).

100. NA, FO 248/198, Jones to Alison, 19/07/1861.

101. NA, FO 248/206, Capt. Disbrowe, officiating Resident to Alison, 20/11/1862; Idem, Ahmad Khan to Disbrowe.

102. NA, FO 248/232, Lewis Pelly/ off Lengeh a/b Dalhousie to Ronald J. Thomson, charge d'affaires, 25/10/1869.

At the same time, it must be realized that the *kargozar* was always in a very delicate and difficult position. Even if a Persian debtor did not bribe the *kargozar*, he did not want to be known as the promoter of the foreigner's interests, and on the other hand because he did not want the consul to report unfavorably about him in Tehran, he steered a middle course, trying to get the creditor accept part payment of the debt.[103] If possible the problems were resolved locally, but if the *kargozar* disagreed with the Resident, "an appeal has to be made to the capital," and if need be the Legation was asked for support.[104] The outcome was determined by the amount of the claim (small claims were usually settled quickly) and whether the Persian or European side had appealed to patrons in Tehran. When political pressure was applied to get cases moving again that had been dragging on for months, if not years, this did not necessarily mean that a solution was nearer. For example, a claim of Messrs. Gray, Paul & Co against `Abdol-Nabi had dragged on for a long time. The governor refused to bring the case to closure because of lack of support from Tehran. When the British government put pressure on the government in Tehran it finally sent a special agent to Bushehr to arrive at a settlement. However, this did not have the desired result and a solution was as remote as before.[105] The special agent from Tehran, Mirza Musa Khan stayed 16 months in Bushehr living on the pocket of the debtor. As a result, according to the British, he mainly was concerned about `Abdol Nabi's interests. Another case was that of an Armenian, who allegedly had swindled an Englishman. In both case the perpetrators escaped from custody.[106] There was a rare felony case dealt with the *kargozar*. On 10 September 1924 at Ganaveh, a sub-assistant surgeon Sobhraj in the employ of the Anglo-Persian Oil Company (APOC) entered the bedroom at night where the wife of Haik Azizian, an Indo-European Telegraph Department (IETD) telegraph operator, was asleep. Mr. Azizian chased Sobhraj from his house and stabbed him with a knife. At the Resident's request the *kargozar* investigated the matter and decided not to take any action against Azizian as already he had been suspended for three months. Sobhraj was dismissed by the APOC.[107]

Therefore, it was not surprising that in 1901 the British Resident expressed the vain hope of the mercantile community that the setting up of the new Customs department might lead to the establishment of a regular court for the dispensation of justice. Because of the absence of such a court, and the obstruction engineered by the *kargozar* and other local authorities, it was very difficult to recover any claims from Persian subjects. The result was that cases were referred to Tehran, which involved endless delay before a settlement would be finally reached.[108]

---

103. Floor 1977, p. 71. The *kargozar* could imprison people. Nura'i 1385, p. 60.

104. Administration 1873-74, p. 5.

105. Administration Report 1880-81, pp. 9-10.

106. Administration Report 1881-82, p. 6. For a discussion of the functioning of the *kargozar*'s court, see Floor 1977, pp. 71–76 and Martin and Nouraei 2005. For examples of how claims of British subjects were dealt with, see Saldanha 1986, vol. 7/2, p. 127-47.

107. Administration Report 1924, p. 8.

108. Administration Report 1900-1901, p. 26.

4.4: List of *kargozar*s of Bushehr (1869-1927)

Name	Duration	Observations	Source
Mirza Ahmad	October 1856-?		FO 248/168, Daryabegi to Jones rec. 28 October 1856
Mirza Mehdi	?-1860		FO 248/189, Jones to Alison, 23 September 1860; FO 248/206, Jomadi I 1278
Mirza Syed Khalil	1861-62		FO 248/198, Jones to Alison, 5 April 1861
Mirza Ahmad	1862-?		Habibi and Vothuqi 1387, pp. 228-29, docs. 82-84
Mirza Mohammad Khan	January 1869 - ? 1878		Saldanha 1986, vol. 7/2, pp. 10, 151
Mirza `Ali Akbar Khan	Fall 1878-1881	Educated in Europe	Administration Report 1878-79, p. 9; De Rivoyrie 1883, p. 137; Sirjani 1361, p. 97
Haji Mirza `Abdollah Khan	1881-1883?	Previously *kargozar* in Bandar Abbas	Administration Report 1881-82, p. 6; Idem, 1882-83, p. 5
Mirza Mohammad Khan Mo`tamen al-Vezareh	? – November 1886	Previously *kargozar* in Shiraz	Administration Report 1886-87, p. 8, 11
Mirza `Abdol-Karim	November – December 1886	Pro-tem	Saldanha 1986, vol. 7/2, p. 10
Najaf Qoli Khan	December 1886-1889?		Administration Report 1886-87, p. 11; Idem, 1888-89, p. 11; Sirjani 1361, p. 361
Haji Mirza `Abdollah	?-June 1895 †	Also deputy governor	Administration Report 1895-96, p. 7
Mirza Mohammad `Ali	1895-?		Sadid al-Saltaneh 1362, p. 6.
Mirza Ahmad Khan	1899		Nura'i 1385, p. 1
Movaqqer al-Dowleh	March 1903?-May 1907		Administration Report 1902-1903, p. 2; Idem, 1903-04, p. 1; Idem 1907-1908, p. 10
Mirza Ahmad Khan Mas`ud al-Soltan	June 1907-December 1908	Acting for his brother Movaqqer al-Dowleh	Administration Report 1908, p. 7;
Ettela` al-Dowleh	February 1909-?		Administration Report 1909, p. 8

Name	Duration	Observations	Source
Mirza Gholam `Ali Khan As`ad al-Soltan	1910-October 1911		Administration Report 1910, p. 12; Idem 1911, p. 12
Mas`ud al-Soltan	October 1911-June 1915		Administration Report 1915, p. 2; Nura'i 1385, p. 11
Vacant	June 1915- ?	Vacant	Administration Report 1915, p. 2
Mo`azed al-Soltan	April – November 1919		Administration Report 1919, p. 1
Yamin al-Mamalek	December 1919-April 1923		Administration Report 1923, p. 6
Sadeq al-Molk	April-29 July 1923		Administration Report 1923, p. 6
Mo`azed al-Soltan	30 July 1923-4 November 1924		Administration Report 1923, p. 6
Mohammad Mirza `Ali Khan Montaser al-Molk	5 November 1924-26 November 1925		Administration Report 1924, p. 5; Idem, 1925, p. 6
Sadid al-Saltaneh	27 November 1925-?	Montaser al-Molk's assistant; officiated	Administration Report 1925, p. 6
Mohammad Mirza `Ali Khan Montaser al-Molk	?-22 July 1927	Office abolished	Administration Report 1927, p. 2

In the fall of 1878, Mirza `Ali Akbar Khan, who was educated in Europe, became *kargozar*. He replaced Mirza Mohammad Khan, who for many years held this function, but was removed for misconduct at the instigation of the British Resident.[109] However, when he became pro-tem governor of Bushehr in 1881, he was so obstructive to British interests that the latter also engineered his recall. His successor was Haji Mirza `Abdollah Khan, the *kargozar* of Bandar Abbas.[110] In February 1883, the governor of Bushehr departed and left Haji Mirza `Abdollah Khan, the *kargozar* in charge.[111] In 1886, Mirza Mohammad Khan Mo`tamen al-Vezareh the *kargozar* of Shiraz was appointed to Bushehr.[112] In November 1888, Mo`tamen al-Vezareh, because of problems with the Customs receipts, was given house arrest and deprived of food for two days. He was able to escape and took sanctuary with the British. After much correspondence he was allowed to leave for Tehran for the examination of his case. He was dismissed and succeeded by Najafqoli Khan, according to the British, "a person of no standing or of much experience," who held the post until March 1889.[113] He was then replaced by Haji Mirza `Abdollah, who remained in function for six years and during his last year also as deputy governor; he died in June 1895.[114] Mirza Mohammad `Ali succeeded him, although he remained in Tehran. He

109. Administration Report 1878-79, p. 9; Saldanha 1986, vol. 7/2, p. 10, 151.
110. Administration Report 1881-82, p. 6.
111. Administration Report 1882-83, p. 5.
112. Administration Report 1886-87, p. 8
113. Administration Report 1888-89, p. 11; Administration Report 1886-87, p. 11.
114. Administration Report 1895-96, p. 7.

delegated his responsibilities to his brother Ahmad Aqa, although in reality it was Haji Mirza Hoseyn Bank who did the actual work.[115]

Because by 1900, many claims of British firms had not been settled, Mozaffar al-Din Shah decided to send Hosam al-Vezareh as special commissioner to look into this matter; he arrived on 29 April 1901. However, as he had no authority to enforce his decisions, the local authorities did not support him and as a result his mission was a total failure.[116] Because of the lack of progress in settling claims the new *kargozar*, who arrived in 1901, was tasked to address this issue.[117] However, he was a total disappointment (to the British at least), because he did nothing to settle claims and this situation remained unchanged until 1905.[118] This lack of progress was mostly due to the political and financial situation of Persia. It was not very helpful either that Mirza `Ali Mohammad Movaqqer al-Dowleh, "an enlightened Shirazi with a European education," who held the function of *kargozar* during 1903-07, did so without any enthusiasm, and in fact against his will. Therefore, it was unsurprising that to placate the British, in 1905, Tehran once again promised to send a special commissioner (*ma'mur*), but he never went beyond Shiraz.[119] The failure to settle the outstanding claims, even of serious cases such as that of Dixon and Co. vs. Haji Nasir "for sums due on accepted bills" was not only costly for the British firm, but for trade as well. These higher transactions costs led to higher costs to the consumer, but also discouraged trade, because the Dixon and Co. case demonstrated that "the universal commercial principle providing that 'accepted bills must be met without question' cannot be regarded as an axiom of commerce in this country." Traders became more cautious in granting credit, because most trade was done on the basis of long-term credit.[120] Finally, in March 1906, Tehran instructed Movaqqar al-Molk to exert himself, which prodded him into action. As a result, the British submitted some 93 cases over the last 10 years (value Rls.2,73,480) for settlement. In two sessions 25 cases were discussed, but a settlement was still not forthcoming.[121] In May 1907, Movaqqer al-Dowleh departed from Bushehr and left his brother Mas`ud al-Soltan in his place as pro-tem. Like his brother, he was reasonable in his dealings, but the fact that Daryabegi, the governor was their bitter enemy limited their effectiveness.[122] Nevertheless, finally there was slow but an improving settlement of claims, because both the *kargozar* and Persian merchants were somewhat more cooperative.[123] Movaqqar al-Dowleh remained in Shiraz and his brother Mas`ud al-Soltan continued to act in his stead. He did so until June 1908 when he left to Shiraz.[124] His successor Ettela` al-Dowleh only came in February 1909. He tried to introduce

115. Sadid al-Saltaneh 1362, p. 6 (Both men were rich and had much property in Shiraz and Bandar Abbas. Their father was Aqa Mohammad Hasan, who was a nephew of the late Mirza `Abdollah Khan `Un al-Molk whose wealth they inherited in 1894. Their mother was the daughter of the late Mirza Abu'l-Qasem, of the Bab's family).

116. Administration Report 1900-1901, p. 3; Idem, 1901-1902, p. 2.

117. Administration Report 1902-1903, p. 2.

118. Trade Report 1903-1904, p. 2; Trade Report 1904-1905, p. 5.

119. Administration Report 1906-1907, p. 15; Administration Report 1907-1908, p. 7. End March 1904, Movaqqer al-Dowleh acted as pro-tem governor for a while. Idem, 1903-1904, p. 1.

120. Administration Report 1905-1906, p. 3.

121. Administration Report 1905-1906, p. 23.

122. Administration Report 1907-1908, p. 7.

123. Administration Report 1907-1908, p. 10.

124. Administration Report 1908, p. 7.

regular legal procedures for the hearing and deciding of claims and complaints submitted to him.[125] He had an unsavory record, although in his previous positions in Mohammerah and Baluchestan he had been friendly to British interests. However his last position was in Kerman and then he became a journalist publishing a newspaper called *Isfahan* until he received this appointment. The British Resident opined that "He is a person of extravagant habits and generally out of elbows, and was a good deal under obligation of the Residency for friendly help in the past or substantial recognition for co-operation rendered." He indeed delivered, because during 1909 he helped settle various British claims. However, he got into conflict with the German consul concerning a dispute involving Wonckhaus and three British firms. The British were satisfied with his handling, but the Germans were not. Also, because of a ceremonial matter, they tried to have him removed by contacting their Legation, but failed. However, he had bad relations with Daryabegi and he therefore, was transferred to Mohammerah.[126] His successor Mirza Gholam `Ali Khan As`ad al-Soltan was friendly, very cautious and timid in dealing with British cases.[127] He remained in office until October 1911, when he was replaced by Mas`ud al-Soltan, the younger brother of Movaqqar al-Dowleh, the governor of the Gulf Ports.[128] He was as pleasant in his relations as before, be it that in all matters he followed his brother's lead and therefore, he was appreciated by the community of foreign merchants.[129] If he was rather less active than desired in settling cases, this was rather due to excessive opium smoking than anti-British attitude.[130] Mas`ud al-Soltan remained *kargozar* till the British occupation on 8 August 1915, when he was relieved and allowed to leave for Mohammerah. When Bushehr was handed over to the Persian government on 16 October 1915 he was reappointed, but did not dare to return to Bushehr as his old enemy Daryabegi had become its governor.[131] As a result, the post of *kargozar* remained vacant in 1916.[132]

In April 1919, Mo`azed al-Soltan arrived as *kargozar*; he was not a success; he went revenue collecting in Dashti and the Baluk and stirred up trouble by making promises to the rebel Khans (Sheikh Hoseyn and Zayer Khedr), "the results of which have not yet disappeared." On his return he found that his papers had been tampered with and he then went to Mohammerah judging his position untenable. The new *kargozar* Yamin al-Mamalek arrived in December of that year,[133] but he resigned when Daryabegi, the governor of the Gulf Ports left his function.[134] However, Yamin al-Mamalek was asked to remain *kargozar*, which he did,[135] and he officiated both as governor and *kargozar* until April 1923, when Sadeq al-Molk, became acting *kargozar*, whom the British Resident

125. Political Diaries, vol. 3, p. 467.
126. Administration Report 1909, p. 8.
127. Administration Report 1910, p. 12.
128. Administration Report 1911, p. 12.
129. Administration Report 1913, p. 13.
130. Administration Report 1913, p. 6.
131. Administration Report 1915, p. 2.
132. Administration Report 1916, p. 2
133. Administration Report 1919, pp. 1-2. According to, Faramarzi 1390, p. 161-66, Mo`azed al-Soltan was banished by the British, because of his patriotic services rendered to Sheikh Hoseyn Chakutahi. In British sources no mention is made of this, while these usually make a point of it when an official is transferred because of British demands.
134. Administration Report 1920, p. 2.
135. Administration Report 1921, p. 1.

described as "a rather conceited and inexperienced young man from Tehran." The latter remained till 29 July, when he was succeeded by Mo`azza al-Soltan, who had held the post before. He remained the rest of the year. Mo`azza al-Soltan had been anti-British in the past but was more impartial with a friendly governor in place. According to the Resident, "He is a man of independence and strong character with whom our official relations have been on the whole satisfactory, though, in correspondence, he is given to intemperate and even uncivil language; and is far too ready to make a case out of the most trivial cases."[136] When the governor left on 28 May 1924, Mo`azza al-Soltan was acting governor until 22 June 1924, when the governor's successor arrived.[137]

Mo`azza al-Soltan remained *kargozar* until 4 November 1924. The Resident found that he had become more anti-British after the governor left, meaning that he had become difficult to deal with. Therefore, the British applied pressure in Tehran and as a result, he was replaced by Mohammad Mirza `Ali Khan Montaser al-Molk, OBE. The latter was pro-British, but could not show it, because he would fall foul of the military.[138] As expected, Montaser al-Molk was pleasant and helpful in his relations with the British. In November 1925 he was elected *Majles* deputy for Bushehr and left on 26 November. During his absence his assistant Sadid al-Saltaneh officiated, who likewise was helpful.[139] Mohammad Mirza `Ali Khan, returned in 1926 and continued to be agreeable and helpful. According to the British, he was popular with merchants, who wanted him to become governor. Their wish became reality for two months between June and August 1926, when he officiated for the governor when the latter was on leave.[140] The *kargozari* office was officially abolished per 7 July 1927 and a separate passport office was established to issue passports. Mohammad `Ali Khan Montaser al-Molk the last *kargozar* left for Tehran on 22 July 1927 and his assistant Sadid al-Saltaneh was appointed passport officer. All work that was the *kargozar*'s was transferred to the governor's office.[141] Sadid al-Saltaneh remained passport officer till 10 May 1928. He was appointed assistant governor of the Gulf Ports on 23 September 1928. Although, matters that in the past had been dealt with by the *kargozar*, thereafter, languished, because there were three governors in quick succession and they were not much interested in judicial affairs.[142]

The Finance Department

Until 1850 Al Mazkur Sheikhs were mostly in charge of Bushehr paying an annual agreed sum to the governor-general of Fars. The same was true when they were temporarily replaced by other governors. With the ouster of the Al Mazkur in 1850, the Bushehr jurisdiction was under a Persian governor and local officers of the shah. The Customs and tax revenues were either contracted for by the governor or accounted for in detail to the royal treasury.[143] In 1873, the governor of Bushehr collected the land revenue,

136. Administration Report 1923, p. 6.
137. Administration Report 1924, p. 5.
138. Administration Report 1924, p. 5.
139. Administration Report 1925, p. 6.
140. Administration Report 1926, p. 2 (Sadid al-Saltaneh continued to be his deputy).
141. Administration Report 1927, p. 2.
142. Administration Report 1928, p. 2.
143. Pelly 1865 a, p. 33. On fiscal issues during this period in general, see Floor 1998 b.

paying a fixed sum to Tehran. At that time, the Bushehr revenues were assessed at ca. Rs. 1,50,000; the local duties were levied at the city gate.[144] In 1851, according to Binning, "Taxation on cultivated land does not depend on the size or quality of land, but on the number of animals employed in tilling the soil." The poor peasants were oppressed and sometimes had to pay the tax on their animals twice in the same year. Moreover, they were subject to all kinds of exactions. Date plantations had to pay an annual amount per tree, about 0.5 *qran* or sometimes more, while "no remission is granted when trees die or are destroyed." When their number increased the tax was increased.[145]

This system remained in place until 1910, even before the Finance Ministry (*vezarat-e dara'i*) was created by the law of 12 June 1911 (22 Juza 1290). This meant that thereafter, financial matters were no longer the governor's bailiwick, but were under the entire control of the local agent of the national tax office (*edareh-ye maliyeh*). Its local branch was under the responsibility of the newly created post of financial agent (*ma'mur-e maliyeh*) of which over the years an increasing number were appointed to the various governorates. Given the importance of Bushehr as a revenue earner, it was one of the first governorates to receive such an agent, who arrived on 18 October 1910. He was appointed by the Minister of Finance, and was in charge of the collection and management of the governorate's revenues and as such, the agent was locally known as *ra'is* or *amin-e maliyeh*. The first agent appointed to Bushehr was Mahmud Khan, a former interpreter of the Imperial Bank of Persia (IBP) in Shiraz, from which post he had been dismissed. He had great difficulty to commence working, due to the lack of the governor's cooperation.[146] In October 1911, due to changes in the management of the country's finances with the appointment of a Treasurer-General, the post of *ra'is-e maliyeh* was abolished. In Bushehr, the salary of the *amin al-maliyeh* seems to have been distributed among the Customs staff, although no Persian was appointed to take care of his tasks, which in fact, were transferred to the provincial Director of Customs. However, in actual practice the Belgian official only collected revenues in those districts where it was easiest to collect taxes; tax collection in the others was the governor's task. As compensation for this task, the governor initially received 25,000 *tumans* per month, but later this amount was reduced to 11,200 *tumans*. However, several times this payment was stopped, as indicated above in the section on the Customs department. Because the governor had no income he began levying illegal taxes.[147] At the end December 1913, because the reach of the Belgian Finance officials was limited, the governor-general of Fars sent a recently created military force led by Col. Merrill to help collect the revenue of Dashti and Dashtestan (which were not yet officially transferred to Gulf Ports governor), but despite this costly operation only 13,000 *tumans* were collected out of 35,000 *tumans* that were due. Shortly thereafter, the ex-*kalantar* `Abdol-Reza collected some more arrears.[148]

---

144. Administration 1873-74, pp. 14-15. Octroi duty is a tax levied on certain goods brought into a city.

145. Binning 1857, vol. 1, pp. 150-51 (in 1850, the entire revenue of Bushehr, including customs was 22,000 *tumans*).

146. Hamidi 1378, pp. 18, 22; Administration Report 1910, p. 12; Political Diaries vol. 4, p. 228 (here he is called Mirza Mohammad Khan).

147. Administration Report 1912, pp. 15-16. According to Nura'i 1385, p. 90 (19 Moharram 1331), the Customs director was de facto the chief of the taxation department. According to Political Diaries vol. 4, p. 553, when `Abbas Khan, *ra'is-e maliyeh*, resigned in May 1912 the chief of the Customs Department had his deputy Moses Khan assume that function.

148. Administration Report 1913, p. 10.

In Tehran in 1915, agreement was reached about the bureaucratic arrangements of the administration of the country's finances and as a result, the finance department was separated from the customs department. This also had consequences for the various provinces, and on 5 May 1915, Soleyman Mirza became chief of the Finance department of Bushehr.[149] At that time the Bushehr revenues were as follows:

4.5: Bushehr tax revenues in *tumans* from 1302/1882 to 1333/1915

Location/Year	1302/1882	1325/1907	1329/1911	1333/1915
Chahkutah	800	2,200	800	1,300
Angali	900	5,500#		700
Rudhilleh	4,022	4,000	4,225	4,800
Ahmadi	700	700	700	800
Hayat Da'ud + Khark	1,796	4,500	1,795	4,800
Rishahr	850	800	850	850
Tull-e siyah + Choghadak	700	800	700	700
Zira	1,600	-	1,600	1,600
Deylam	2,000	-		2,000
Banader-e thalatheh*	4,800	-	3,000	4,800
Araq banderole in Bushehr	400	-	360	400
Jews and shirkeshan Bushehr	600	-	-	-
Dhabayeh Bushehr	-	-	-	500
Bushire gate	-	6,500		-
Bakers p.y.	-	-	640	-
Oil-mill p.y.	-	-	200	-
Dyers p.y.	-	-	72	-
Alcohol p.y.	-	-	620	-
Shops p.y.	-	-	400	-
Transport p.y.	-	-	3,000	-
Court fees	-	-	1,800	-
Municipal fees	-	-	600	-
Expected revenues	-	-	1,000	-
Cut in pensions	-	-	5,000	-
Total	19,168	25,000	27,363	23,250

Source: Sadid al-Saltaneh 1371, pp. 44-46, 116 (the totals have been corrected).

*Banadar-e thalatha = Kangan, Taheri, `Asalu

This also includes the revenues of Shif

149. Administration Report 1915, p. 3.

In August 1915 British troops landed in Bushehr (Chapter 3), which for the next three years remained under British military occupation. During the occupation, the Finance Department continued to work under its own officials.[150] However, the receipts were deposited in the IBP and a part was used to finance the local administration of Bushehr.[151] Soleyman Mirza remained Finance agent until his death on 19 October 1918; Mirza `Abbas Khan the departmental accountant was his temporary replacement.[152] The new Finance agent, Salar-e Mofakhkham arrived in September 1919, and on arrival announced that he intended to leave before the hot season.[153] Indeed, he left in March 1920 and was succeeded by Salar-e Nosrat, who in his turn was succeeded on 5 June 1920 by Mesrop Khan. The British Residency continued to supervise the local government's financial accounts, as it had already been financing it.[154] This was related to the rejection of the Anglo-Persian agreement in June 1920.[155]

In 1921-22, the *edareh-ye tahdid va dukhaniyat* in Bushehr was merged with the Finance department.[156] In 1923, the Finance Department, which was under Hakim al-Mamalek in Bushehr, initiated a major tax collection operation. With military support he collected the arrears from the Khan of Angali, from Salar-e Ashja (agent of Nezam al-Saltaneh, leaseholder of Dashti) and from some of the Sheikhs along the littoral. In the beginning of the year, the official in charge of 'indirect taxes' was ordered to collect these on behalf of the Finance department; later the collection of the 'indirect taxes' was merged with the Finance department and came under the Finance chief. These indirect taxes included the taxes on caravans leaving Bushehr, which formed the main source of income of the Municipality, using them for local works. This merger, therefore, caused consternation in Bushehr, because the municipality was afraid that all the money would be remitted to Tehran and that the municipality would be penniless. The governor organized protest meetings, but the order remained in force. However, the Finance department allocated all the municipal revenues to the municipality. The Finance department also tried to get obtain the receipts collected by Customs through a small fee on every package cleared, which was handed to the Education department and used to maintain three schools in Bushehr. People were furious, as this fee was a private voluntary initiative for the public good, and the bazaar was closed in protest. This time the Finance department relented.[157]

4.6: List of directors of the Finance Department (1910-1935)

Name	Duration	Observations	Source
Mahmud Khan	18 October 1910-October 1911		Administration Report 1910, p. 12; Idem 1912, p. 15

150. Administration Report 1915, p. 6.
151. Administration Report 1915, p. 7.
152. Administration Report 1918, p. 1.
153. Administration Report 1919, p. 2.
154. Administration Report 1920, p. 2.
155. See N.S. Fatemi, "Anglo-Persian Agreement of 1919," [iranica.com].
156. Vothuqi 1381, p. 48.
157. Administration Report 1923, p. 6.

Name	Duration	Observations	Source
Post of *ra'is-* or *amin-e maliyeh* unfilled	October 1911-5 May 1915	Customs Department is in charge of Finance Department	Administration Report 1912, p. 15
Soleyman Mirza	5 May 1915- 19 October 1918 †	Mirza `Abbas Khan officiating 19/10/1918 till September 1919	Administration Report 1915, p. 3; Idem 1918, p. 1
Salar-e Mofakhkham	September 1919-March 1920		Administration Report 1919, p. 2
Salar-e Nosrat	March -4 June 1920		Administration Report 1920, p. 2
Mesrop Khan	5 June 1920-?		Administration Report 1920, p. 2
Hakim al-Mamamlek	1923?-May 1926		Administration Report 1923, p. 6
Yahya Khan Qarakhanian	May 1926-October 1927		Administration Report 1926, p. 2
Mirza Hasan Khan Farzad Matin al-Soltan	October 1927-18 March 1928		Administration Report 1927, p. 2
`Abdollah Khan Monajjami	18 March 1928-15 May 1929		Administration Report 1928, p. 2
Mirza Hoseyn Khan Moshiri	15 May 1929-30 April 1930		Administration Report 1929, p. 2
Sayyed Ahmad Khan Ashrafi	1May – August 1930		Administration Report 1930, p. 3
Mirza Mehdi Khan Zahedi Moqavvam al-Molk	August 1930-17 May 1931		Administration Report 1930, p. 3
Hasan Khan Matin al-Soltan Farzad	17 May-15 July 1931		Administration Report 1931, p. 4
Mirza `Ezzatollah Khan Shoja`i	15 July 1931-		Administration Report 1931, p. 4
Mohammad Vali Mirza Nowban	February 1935-	Revenue and Customs Department merged	Administration Report 1935, p. 3
See Customs Department	- 1938	Revenue and Customs Department separated	Administration Report 1938, p. 3
-	March 1940-?	Economic Department separated from Finance Department	Administration Report 1940, p. 2
Dowlatshah	?-October 1945	Economic Department merged with Finance Department in 1941	Administration Report 1940, pp. 4-5; Administration Report 1942, p. 5
Mohammad Ghaffari	?-beginning October 1945		Administration Report 1945, p. 8
Behruz Kasma'i	Beginning October 1945-?		Administration Report 1945, p. 8

In October 1924, the land tax was increased by 35%.[158] Hakim al-Mamalek remained head of the Treasury department despite the fact that "His grasping habits made him universally disliked in Bushire." In municipal matters he opposed the military. In May 1925, new duties on tea and sugar were imposed to pay for road and railway development projects. As a result, smuggling increased significantly.[159] In May 1926, Hakim al-Mamalek was replaced as Finance Controller by Yahya Khan, an Armenian. The former allegedly had a deficit of 2,000 *tumans* in his accounts. In February 1926, Tehran imposed a compounded road tax on all imports and exports in lieu of all the petty taxes along the trade road that formerly were levied by municipalities, which was a heavy burden for Bushehr.[160] In October 1926, Mirza Yaya Khan was replaced by Mirza Hasan Khan Farzad Matin al-Soltan; the former was charged with having made payments without approval during Major Hall's visit in December 1926. Matin al-Soltan, educated in Great Britain, was friendly, but at the end of the year, it was rumored that Bushehr would be made independent of the Finance office in Shiraz and would deal directly with Tehran, and therefore, a more senior man would be appointed.[161] `Abdollah Khan Monajjami arrived on 18 March and replaced Matin al-Soltan. He was rather anti-British; "he is disliked by both Persian officials and non-officials on account of his boorishness, rough treatment, and the unnecessary hitches he raises in paying bills sanctioned by higher authorities." He was a protégé of Firuz Mirza, the Finance Minister.[162] As soon as Firuz Mirza was arrested his protégé Monajjami was summoned to Tehran to be questioned regarding embezzlement. He left on 15 May 1929. Vali Mohammad Mirza Bowban officiated for him, while his successor Mirza Hoseyn Khan Moshiri arrived on 20 September.[163] Hasan Khan Moshiri remained in charge until 30 April; Sayyed Ahmad Khan Ashrafi was acting director of the Finance Department from 1 April till August 1930, when the new director Mirza Mehdi Khan Zahedi Moqavvam al-Molk arrived. He held this post until 17 May 1931, when a commission found him guilty of corruption and embezzlement of 20,000 *tumans*. On 9 June 1931, he was sent to Tehran under military escort. Zahedi was succeeded by Hasan Khan Matin al-Soltan Farzad, who was replaced on 15 July by Mirza `Ezzatollah Khan Shoja`i.[164] Zahedi's fate apparently did not change the behavior of his subordinates, for on 8 September 1931 about 100 men from Dashti came to complain about the exactions by the Revenue Collector Mirza Hasan Khan, who was demanding a tax of 2 *qrans* per date tree. The governor sent the head of the Finance department and the deputy governor to investigate. As a result, the tax was reduced by 36% per tree.[165]

The Finance Department was responsible for: (i) the collection of direct and indirect taxes: (ii) acting as general accountant for all government departments, except for Customs:

---

158. Administration Report 1924, p. 6.
159. Administration Report 1925, p. 6.
160. Administration Report 1926, p. 2.
161. Administration Report 1927, p. 2.
162. Administration Report 1928, p. 2.
163. Administration Report 1929, p. 2.
164. Administration Report 1930, p. 3; Administration Report 1931, p. 4 (Farzad and his wife were attacked by robbers at Borazjan on 21 July 1931, who took all their belongings even the clothes they wore. Two suits of clothing were sent from Bushehr).
165. Administration Report 1931, p. 4.

and (iii) managing the Treasury. The taxes include income tax, taxes on crops, taxes on slaughtering, taxes on lotteries, and taxes on the production of alcohol. The Department was not involved with the budgeting process of other government departments. The latter sent their draft proposal to their line superiors in Tehran; once the budget was established it was next to impossible to obtain additional funds.

All those engaged in trade or business with an annual income of more than Rls. 12,000 year had to obtain a license from the Finance Department, which had to be renewed every year. Merchants had to keep books, which might be inspected any time by the Finance Department. Small traders did not have to keep books. Their annual income was estimated by an assessment committee chaired by the governor. Government officials with a salary above Rls.1,000/month had to pay income tax.[166] In 1939, "Merchants pay annually from 1 per cent to 4 per cent on their net profit; according to the amount; employees drawing over Rials 200 per mensem [month] pay from 2 ½ per cent to 3 per cent on their salary." Many shopkeepers and artisans who had asked exemption of income tax given their low income were told to pay at level of income estimated by revenue authorities, despite protests.[167] Before 1934, all crops and livestock were taxed and collected from the producers. Finance Department officials visited the rural areas at a certain time of the year to assess the crops. After the harvest they visited again and taxes were collected at the rate of 3% of the assessed value and collecxted from the landowner. As this system was open to fraud it was abolished in December 1934. Henceforth, crops were taxed when these were marketed in the towns or exported. The rate remained 3% but was levied on the price of the product, "and the basis is fixed with due consideration for freight and total quantity."[168] A Land Registration Department was opened in June 1938. There were many complaints by people that their property had been overvalued. However, appeals did not lead to any change; it was assumed because the government needed more revenues. In 1939, the Land registration office opened a branch in Rig where little progress was made. Registration fees depended on the assessed value of property. In 1940, land registration continued not only in Bushehr and Rig, but also in Borazjan. According to the British consul, the officals assessed properties at arbitrary value, assuaged by bribes. New branches were to be opened in Delam, Dayyer, Kangan and Taheri.[169]

In March 1940, the Finance Department was divided into the Finance Department and the Economic Department (*Edareh-ye Eqtesad*). In 1941, the two departments were merged and were placed under the head of the Finance Department. The purpose of the merger was to improve their performance and effectiveness. However, the Economic Department remained without a head and in 1942 worked under the orders of the Ministry of Foodstuffs, implying that the department had been separated from the Finance Department.[170] In 1942, the Land Registration Department was reopened, after its closure due to the Allied invasion. This was a potentially very useful activity, because rich people had started to invest in land and buildings. Therefore, property prices rose almost 3-fold

166. Administration Report 1939, pp. 3, 8.
167. Administration Report 1939, pp. 3, 8.
168. NA, FO 371/15473.
169. Administration Report 1938, pp. 3, 6; Administration Report 1939, p. 2; Administration Report 1940, p. 3.
170. Administration Report 1941, pp. 4-5; Administration Report 1942, p. 8.

compared with 1941. Outside town it was impossible for the Department to operate due to the prevailing insecurity.[171]

The Finance Department collected land revenue, income tax and indirect taxes, which as before were assessed arbitrarily and had no relation to profits. Bribery removed the pressure of discontent. The Economic Department had control over monopolies of tobacco, opium, sugar and tea, piecegoods, wheat, matches, and the skin, wool and cotton company [172] and the revenue from taxes on import and sale, which formed a large part of the government's budgeted revenues. The Economic Department of Bushehr only dealt with the sale of all locally produced monopoly goods and the sale of all monopoly goods. Producers have to sell these products, on pain of heavy penalties, to the Economic Department at prices fixed by the Central Finance Office in Tehran. These prices are always lower than market rates, which resulted in significant smuggling activity. Since the abdication of Reza Shah the rules concerning imports were somewhat relaxed. Merchants were allowed to import tea, sugar, and cotton piece goods provided they paid the monopoly tax and import duties. For sugar a special permit had to be obtained from the Mininstry of Finance, and importers of tea were obliged to buy a certain percentage of Persian tea. The latter was of inferior quality, but the government charged the same price as the higher rates of imported tea. The monopoly on the sale of local rice was abolished, but import of rice was only possible through obtaining a special license.[173] In September 1945, it was announced that all departments, except the military and gendarmerie, would henceforth be directly under Tehran instead of Shiraz.[174] On 27 February 1946, the Economic Department was merged with the Finance Department. Probably in connection with that change, the Finance Department for Bushehr, which, until then, had been a branch of that for Fars province, was placed directly under Tehran, after much local pressure on Tehran.[175]

The Municipality

As soon as the constitutional movement began in 1906, Bushehris participated fervently in the ensuing political debate. Interested parties created an *anjoman* or local council in which merchants such as the Malek al-Tojjar played an important role.[176] As soon as the law permitting the creation of a municipality was passed, Bushehris established such an organization. However, one of the problems that beset the new municipalities was that there were quite a few people who felt they were second to none, while most lacked the education and experience on how to cooperate and manage the welfare of a community. Because of personality battles the town was divided not along Party lines (because Parties

171. Administration Report 1942, p. 8.

172. Administration Report 1940, p. 2; Political Diaries, vol. 14, p. 55.

173. NA, FO 371/15471.

174. Political Diaries, vol. 16, p. 497. The Shiraz Finance Department had an American advisor since 1943, who made regular inspections of the Bushehr branch. In 1945, a new American financial advisor was appointed, John W. Phillips, an enormous improvement, because his predecessor was known to be corrupt. Administration Report 1945, p. 8.

175. Political Diaries, vol. 17, pp. 31 (Behruz Kasmai, the director of the Economic Department left in February 1946; he was replaced by Eskanderi, who was succeeded by Ahmad Showkat on 9 August 1946), 32.

176. *Revue du Monde Musulmane* 4 (1908), p. 162.

did not yet exist) but along that of individual interests. As a consequence, the results of the election were contested and accusations about irregularities were exchanged between various *primo dons*. It was only through arbitrage that the situation was finally resolved.[177]

Because the local council, the quasi-forerunner of the Municipal council, had been unable to develop any program of street cleaning and the collection of refuse by the donkey drivers, although it had discussed this at length, in May 1908 (see chapter 3), Daryabegi asked the *anjoman-e tejarat* to take charge of these tasks. The *anjoman-e tejarat* refused as it would bring it in disrepute with the population.[178] The governor then tried to establish a municipal council to take charge of the conservancy and the lighting of the town. He sent for representatives of the quarters and suburbs and intended to put a proposal to them.[179] However, it was three years later, after the passing of the Municipality Law of 20 June 1907 (*qanun-e baladiyeh*) establishing the rules for a Municipality that this new institution, the *anjoman-e baladiyeh* was formed. Elections for it were held in the first week of August 1910, organized and supervised by the governor. Twenty persons were elected and Sayyed Hoseyn Behbahani a.k.a. *Baladiyeh* was appointed chairman with a monthly salary of 700 *qrans* and Rokn al-Tojjar was the council's secretary. The council became active in January 1911 and met twice per week. One of its first actions was to order the mat-sheets and platforms in front of houses and shops to be removed as they were a hindrance, two baker shops were opened where bread was made with sweet water and sold cheaply; other bakers were ordered not to sell at higher prices. However, as control of prices was the *kalantar*'s responsibility, he refused to yield this task to the municipality. But none of these actions really were long-lived and the only result was some cleaning of the streets and a marked increase in the price of bread and meat. Furthermore, the council wanted to hold a census before levying a house-tax, while the sweeping of the streets, repairs of the bazaars and public roads, and street lighting were discussed. A beginning was made with the sweeping, paving and widening of the bazaar. The council further asked for a tender of 500 lamps for lighting the streets; it was willing to pay 250 *tumans*/month, which was to be financed via a 2-*qran* tax per bazaar shop. Payment was to be enforced by the police and in case of non-payment there had to be immediate distrain of goods, for which a receipt was to be given. Tehran wired the council that its tax on wheat, barley, and lime that it had initiated was prohibited.[180]

The council's strength and activities in municipal affairs varied over time; at one time there were only two members. Initially, the *anjoman* was not popular, because most of its members were noneties and its decisions resulted in the demand for funds, meaning new taxes.[181] Moreover, the law (art. 93) stated that the title of the head of the municipal council (*ra`is-e anjoman*) was the *kalantar* (this title was changed to *shahrdar* in the 1940s).

177. *Revue du Monde Musulmane* 10 (1910), pp. 585-86.

178. Political Diaries, vol. 3, p. 66.

179. Political Diaries, vol. 3, pp. 66, 179.

180. Political Diaries vol. 4, pp. 166, 329; Administration Report 1910, pp. 13-14. The newspaper *Habl al-Matin* had good hopes for the municipality, which was planning to clean up and pave the bazaar. Hamidi 1378, pp. 66, 70. The newspaper *Jonub* was very negative and wrote on 4 February 1911 that Bushehr had a municipality in name only, one that did not have executive powers. Idem 1378, pp. 18, 33; see also the newspaper *Mozaffari*, Idem 1378, pp. 178-79 (with a list of the names of the 18 members of the municipal council). For a photo of Rokn al-Tojjar, see Roknzadeh 1352, p. 96, for a photo and short bio of Sayyed Hoseyn, see Hamidi 1380, p. 150..

181. Political Diaries vol. 4, p. 203.

Furthermore, the council started levying octroi on goods coming into town, which brought them into conflict with the *kalantar*, who promptly used the revenues for his own use.[182] Both the title of the head of the municipal council and the levying of city taxes caused some problems, because the office of *kalantar* was already an existing position with tasks and revenues that reverted to the municipality. Under the traditional fiscal system local city gate and other octroi taxes were farmed. In the early nineteenth century, it was usually the *kalantar*, who farmed the collection of these taxes. The *kalantar*, variously referred to in European sources as market supervisor, chief of police, farmer of the local excise tax and mayor, indeed fulfilled all of these functions (see below), while he also was tasked with the control of the prices of life necessities as part of his overall responsibility to maintain law and order.[183] The exactions by the *kalantar* could be quite excessive such that in mid-May 1907, Bushehr's five butchers asked to be allowed to pay the expenses of Bushehr's deputy to the *Majles* on condition that they would be exempt from the exaction of the *kalantar*. Finding that the people were against him and the governor taking a larger share than before, the *kalantar* resigned, but not before having collected 2,736 *tumans* in six months time.[184] On 11 July 1907, the *kalantar* had a muleteer severely beaten who refused to pay the illegal gate-tax of 19 *shahis*, which the *kalantar* collected.[185] On 1 August 1907, the butchers closed their shops due to grievances about the *kalantar*, who had just given the concession for the animal skins they had slaughtered to a certain Reza-ye Pushti for 1,000 *tumans*/year, on condition that he would pay 8 *tumans* per 20 goatskins. As these skins were of good quality he would still make a good profit despite the low prices in Bombay. The other butchers felt left out; they reopened their shops after the *kargozar* had promised to look into the matter.[186] The same problem occurred in 1910, when Mashdi Abdol-Rasul, the *kalantar* acted arbitrarily in a dispute with the butchers, who then closed their shops.[187] In early January 1909, the *kalantar* began levying a small fee on goods passing the *Darvazeh* or the Bushehr Gate. He also claimed the monopoly of the sale of barley and hay for sale to muleteers at his own price.[188] In April 1910, Tehran accorded the *kalantar* the monopoly of all salt available in the bazaar. Henceforth it was to be sold under supervision of the governor at 16 *qrans* per Hashem *man* of 56.2 kg. Thus far the collection and sale of salt had been free, which was sold at 3-4 *qrans* per Hashem *man*. On 15 June, having received no reply from Tehran about what to do with the salt appropriated, the *kalantar* returned the salt to its owners thus ending the salt monopoly.[189]

The above shows that the revenues collected by the *kalantar* were significant and that the holder of the function could make a lot of money, not only for himself, but also for others. For example, in July 1908, there was much intrigue about who would get the post of *kalantar*. `Abdol-Rasul had been recently appointed, but the dragoman of the German consulate and others want to reinstate the former holder Haji Yusef. The latter only wanted

182. Political Diaries vol. 4, p. 166.
183. Hamidi 1378, pp. 70. 153.
184. Political Diaries, vol. 2, p. 186.
185. Political Diaries, vol. 2, p. 259. This tax was illegal, because all internal trade taxes had been abolished in the 1903 Customs Treaty with Russia and Great Britain. However, the revenues of this tax were still included in the governor's fiscal schedule and the Minister of Finance demanded its remittance.
186. Political Diaries, vol. 2, p. 285.
187. Political Diaries vol. 4, p. 203.
188. Political Diaries, vol. 3, pp. 423, 441.
189. Political Diaries vol. 4, pp. 66, 118.

to accept the post, if the Shif route would be reopened. Usually the *kalantari* was farmed for 15,000 *tumans*. `Abdol-Rasul was said to have paid 18,000 *tumans*, but the syndicate financing Yusef's bid was said to have offered 21,000 or even 23,000 *tumans* with the help of the Khan of Shif. The higher bid and the Khan's interest were due to the fact that Haji Yusef formerly levied 2 *qrans* per load of goods going via Shif, which route offered better opportunities for smuggling and higher revenues for the Khan of Shif.[190]

In September 1910, therefore, the *anjoman-e baladiyeh* asked the governor for a list of local taxes levied by him through the *kalantar*. Daryabegi refused saying that they were included in his tax schedule, which was none of their business. He suggested they ask Tehran; this upset the council so much that six of its members resigned. On Daryabegi's departure to Bandar Abbas the council wanted to discuss its involvement in local affairs with him, but he refused to receive them.[191] The municipal council remained active, because in October 1910, it informed all masons not to lay foundations for new homes without its permission.[192] Because of the lack of real authority and of funds to implements some of its program, by December 1910, the *anjoman-e baladiyeh* had only four instead of 20 members, "none of whom do any Municipal works."[193]

There were no funds to finance the activities that the municipality wanted to undertake. All funds had to be requested from Tehran, which, if money was available, it distributed such funds based on a proposed budget. These budgets, such as the one from Bushehr, displayed much of the same defects of the absolutist royal system that the revolution had claimed to displace.[194] "The net revenue from any other source is remitted to Tehran and not used for the province's needs at all. This has resulted in a growing dilapidated appearance of the town. The trusts or *vaqfs* also have fallen into a ruined state due to the poverty of the beneficiaries. Municipal leaders want to change this by introducing new taxes, but it is difficult to raise additional funds under current circumstances as well as to spend them judiciously and effectively."[195] This led to the decision of 12 February 1911 to tax alcohol consumption and collect these fees, while the Municipality also laid down rules applying to drinking alcohol and gambling in public, including for Moslems.[196] These taxes were not approved by Tehran. Others such as tax on horses, donkeys, carriages, etc., approved by Tehran in March 1911, were much resented locally by those who hawked wood, water, etc. for people's daily needs and donkey-owners, mainly water sellers and those who supplied the bazaar with its goods. In reaction they protested with some success by going on a strike. The municipal council was suspended in April 1911 after the troubles at the Turkish consulate (see below police section).[197]

190. Political Diaries, vol. 3, p. 238.
191. Political Diaries vol. 4, p. 203.
192. Political Diaries vol. 4, p. 228.
193. Political Diaries vol. 4, p. 296; in October 1910, an inspector of *Baladiyeh* was expected, but he did not arrive. Political Diaries vol. 4, p. 228.
194. *Revue du Monde Musulmane* 10 (1910), pp. 585-86.
195. Trade Report 1910-11, p. 1.
196. *Revue du Monde Musulmane* 14 (1911), p. 158. There was the occasional article in the press advocating the purchase of Moslem goods only and those made by non-Moslems only if there was no choice. However, the same paper (*Mozaffari*) shortly thereafter took exception to an anti-Jewish pogrom in Shiraz, of which many survivors fled to Bushehr, and wrote that this was a shame. *Revue du Monde Musulmane* 15 (1911), pp. 162, 555
197. Political Diaries vol. 4, pp. 352, 365-67, 380-81, 409.

On 1 July 1911, the governor reinstated the municipal council and its previous members were reappointed. It consisted of one president (*ra'is-e baladiyeh*), at that time Sayyed Hoseyn Behbahani, and three or four local members. Furthermore, the governor locally collected 203 *tumans* for municipal activities to which he himself contributed 50 *tumans*. Moreover, he ordered 300 lamps to be placed in the streets and to collect a monthly fee of 1 *qran* from each householder. The president of the municipal council suggested that the disliked new taxes should also be levied. The municipal council further asked the governor to lower the price of meat from 4 *qrans* to 3.6 *qrans* and to abolish illegal exactions from butchers, except 1 *qran* for each sheep/goat killed. He agreed, but the butchers ignored the price measure and sold meat at the old price. The governor allowed the municipal council to collect "a gate tax of 5 cents [*shahis*?] per transport mule, 3 cents [*shahis*]? per donkey entering the town." He also increased the tax on arak from 0.5 to 1 *qran*/bottle. In short, the council's activities were confined to the occasional street cleaning, paid for with the proceeds of 'illegal' taxes levied by the governor for this and other purposes.[198] Thus, in principle self-supporting, in 1913, the municipality started realizing various public works such as the rebuilding of the seawalls, construction of new roads and a beginning was made with public lighting of the town and the main road leading to the suburbs. Each night 180 lamps were lit inside the town and outside on the droschky road to the west as far as Mehtabi, where seven lamps were lit, but not when there was a moon. Because of public health concerns there was continued removal of garbage by donkeys, although these were in insufficient numbers. The municipality had a prison and employed some 40 policemen recently provided with uniforms, blue for winter and khaki with red facings for summer. Most importantly, the central administration accepted the principle that municipal taxes should be spent in the location that raised them.[199]

Prior to this time, the town's (i.e. not the municipality's) fiscal revenues were known as *kalantari*, for reasons discussed above. The name change of these revenues indicates that the *kalantar* had now been placed under the municipality. These revenues were collected from pack animals, prostitutes, opium addicts (*shireh-kesh*) etc., yielding an annual income of 18,000 *tumans*. From 1911, the collection of these taxes was discontinued, while other taxes were levied such as *tahdid-e taryak*, *navaqel*, *haqq-e tanzif*, *araq banderol*, and *araqkeshan* taxes.[200] Each month, one *qran* was collected for garbage removal per house, known as *haqq-e tanzif*. The opium dross (*sukhteh*) had to be sold to the municipality (*tahdid-e taryak*). Each *methqal* (4.6 g) 2 *shahis*, and each person cannot bring more than 16 *methqal* to the office. The revenues of the *tahdid-e taryak* belonged to the municipality and started in 1913 as of July/August. From each *methqal* 3 *shahis* was collected as banderole fee. Thus, one *man* of 9 `*abbasi* (3.7 kg) of opium yielded 11 *tumans* and 4,000 *qrans*. From all 10 coffee houses, except for Kaki and Bon Kul, the municipality received 2 *tumans* 15,000 *qrans* (*araqkeshan*). From each droschkeh the municipality collected 2 *tumans* per month (*navaqel*). Later when the number of cars (mainly Fords) increased in Bushehr as of the early 1920, the Muncipality levied a monthly duty of 5 *tumans* per car. Six donkeys and 8

---

198. Political Diaries vol. 4, p. 408; Administration Report 1912, p. 17; Nura'i 1385, p. 46. For a short biographical note of Sayyed Hoseyn Behbahani, see Hamidi 1378, p. 240.

199. Trade Report 1913-14, pp. 1, 6; Sadid al-Saltaneh 1371, p. 39, 44, 119; FO 248/1033. Political Diary July 1911, p. 13 (items 693-96).

200. Sadid al-Saltaneh 1371, p. 39; Sa`adat 1390, p. 39. For a more detailed list of taxes, see Hamidi 1378, pp. 70-72.

men were employed to clean the town, each were paid 30 *shahis* p.d.[201] In May 1913, the municipal council began collecting a tax of 1 *qran* per house except from those belonging to poor sayyeds and mullahs. It was estimated that 1,100 houses would be subject to this payment. Its revenues were to be used for street lighting.[202]

4.7: Revenues of the municipality of Bushehr around 1910 (in *tumans*/year)

From the kitchens (*ashpazha*) and sheep-head cooks (*kallehpazha*)	800
From the mills (*ʿassarkhaneh*) a.k.a. *kargah*	500
From Sif for storage (*haqq al-arz*) of merchandise	800
From Sif, fee on wheat and barley	400
From Sif fee on firewood and other items	250
From the Jews who make araq from dates	620
From the butchers	800
Total	4,170

Source: Sadid al-Saltaneh 1371, p. 44.

These revenues were farmed out and represent the situation before the new taxes mentioned above (*tahdid*, etc.) were introduced. These new revenues were not farmed out and, therefore, did not represent a fixed annual amount, and were in addition to the ones in Table 4.7.

4.8: Expenditures of the Bushehr municipality in 1913 (in *qrans*)

Category	Per Month	Per Year
Chief	500	6,000
Clerk	250	3,000
Clerk	150	1,800
Farrash	60	720
Guard at Shif	75	900
Street cleaning	700	8,400
Gate keeper	60	720
Cost lighting summer road, incl. lamps and wicks	500	6,000
Repair lamps	100	1,200
Stable granary for the municipal donkeys	20	240
Tea consumption	10	120
Granary for the muncipal office	50	600
Office expenditures	30	360
Various	100	1,200

201. Sadid al-Saltaneh 1371, pp. 39, 112; Trade Report 1923-24, p. 1.
202. Political Diaries, vol. 5, p. 123.

Category	Per Month	Per Year
Total	2,605	31,260

Source: Sadid al-Saltaneh 1371, p. 81.

Movaqqar al-Dowleh, who had begun the above program of public works in 1913, also wanted to tax foreigners to help continue the municipal work. After contacting London, British subjects were advised to pay the tax, on condition that they were allowed to refuse to pay if he or his successors used its revenue in a way that did not benefit British subjects, or that the funds were squandered or not used for the purpose indicated. The British government stipulated that any tax, other than allowed under the 1903 Convention, had to be for the use of public utility, "whereby British subjects benefit equally with others and does not involve any breach in the validity of that instrument." Another condition was that other foreign subjects also paid the tax. Probably due to this last condition the provincial controller of Finance informed the Residency that he had deferred the levying of this user fee until he received new orders.[203]

In 1920, Sayyed Hoseyn Siyadat, the chief of the Bushehr municipality worked hard for Bushehr's general welfare and made small improvements for the town and kept order. Still, Bushehr as a whole and especially its center remained a filthy place. The municipality's incidental efforts at cleaning the streets had little effect, while drainage remained non-existent and during the rains each street was a sewer conduit unto itself.[204] Nevertheless, the municipality did its best to improve the town. There was even an effort to repair the most important road leading to Bushehr, but permanent metalling was shelved due to lack of funds, and it was doubtful whether the soft stone and mud put down would last the winter. Because the number of motor cars in Bushehr increased there was a need of good roads. To that end the government levied a monthly tax of 5 *tumans* on every car for road maintenance. As a result, the main road towards Bushehr on the island was kept in fairly good repair; but no attempt was made to repair any other roads.[205] In September 1925, the Ministry of Finance considered the transfer of control over the Municipality and its revenues to the military. Despite strong local popular opposition, one month later, the garrison commander indeed took control over the Municipality and took steps to widen the streets, allocate sites for markets, regulate prices of foodstuffs and to promote cleanliness in shops and public baths. Apparently, by June 1926 the Municipality was again under civilian control. The government budgeted 100 *tumans*/month for the Municipality, which was further allowed to collect the vehicle tax and use its estimated monthly revenue of 400 *tumans*. It was reported that the funds were to be used for road repairs. Unfortunately, the budget was not yet approved and released. As a consequence, municipal affairs were in "a disgraceful condition" in September 1927, when Major Hall, the American financial advisor visited Bushehr. This state of affairs was brought to his notice and, as a result, the Fars Finance Department approved and allocated the Municipality's budget.[206]

---

203. Administration Report 1913, p. 9.

204. Trade Report 1920-21, p. 1; Trade Report 1920-21, pp. 1-2. For a short biography of Sayyed Hoseyn Siyadat, see Hamidi 1380, p. 150.

205. Trade Report 1921-22, p. 1; Trade Report 1923-24, p. 1.

206. Political Diaries vol. 7, pp. 305, 308, 372, 417.

However, for any other activity, in particular sanitary improvements, funds were lacking. Nevertheless, local officials maintained law and order and administration was working.[207]

Elections for the municipality were held in July 1930 and from 46 persons whose names were submitted to Tehran, 11 comparative nonentities were approved for the council. The new municipal council was chaired by the former president Sayyed Hoseyn Behbahani Siyadat, which decided on a budget of 24,000 *tumans* and proposed various taxes to raise that amount. Tehran rejected the budget and allowed the following taxes:

3% of the rent of property (in addition to ordinary tax).

1 *qran* per bottle on Persian liquors.

3 *qrans* per bottle of foreign liquors.

20-60 *qrans* per month on garages, restaurants and hotels.

15-50 *qrans* per month on electricity consumption and ice plants.

10% of the net income of cinemas and theaters.

1-10 *qrans* on the assessed value of houses worth 400 *tumans* each.

At the end of 1930 little progress was made in collecting these taxes due to people's poverty.[208]

With Sayyed Hoseyn Siyadat presiding over the municipality, the work on the widening and improving of streets decreased after the governor, Sar-e Entesar left to Shiraz. In July 1931, the Bushehr weekly, *Khalij-e Iran*, commented on the inactivity of the municipality, and submitted that persons with contagious diseases were allowed to sell goodstuffs in the bazaar, baths were not inspected, and no attention was paid to the roads. Woken up by this criticism, the municipality raised the tax on hotels to 60 *qrans* per month. Hotel keepers protested, went on strike and closed their hotels; two days later the rate was reduced to its normal level of 20 *qrans*. Between 23 March and 24 July 1931 the income of municipality was 27,203 *qrans* and there was a net balance of 3,000 *qrans*. "In the last quarter of the year the municipality decided to increase its income of Tomans 36,000 per annum by raising taxes. It increased the weighing tax as from the 15th October and in some items the increase was quintupled." In December 1931, it was decided to open two more avenues, one bisecting the town from East to West and the other from North to South. This required pulling down 60 houses and thus house-owners protested.[209]

In September 1932 elections were held for municipal council members (with a term of two years). Elected were Mirza Mehdi Timsar, Mirza `Abdol-Qasem Tavakkol (merchant), Sayyed Hoseyn Siyadat Behbahani (former council-president), Mirza Khalil Dashti, Aqa Sayyed Mohammad Siyadat (son of the ex-president), Haji Darvish Khoshabai

---

207. Administration Report 1928, p. 7.

208. Administration Report 1930, p. 4. The municipality had proposed a budget of 48,000 *tumans* to be funded from the *hammal-bashi* (24,000), tax on houses (12,000) and tax on boats (12,000). Political Diaries, vol. 9, pp. 239, 326 (for a new schedule of municipal taxes in November 1930). The deputy governor was honorary chair of municipality. Administration Report 1934, p. 4. In 1940, a tax of 1 rial per unit of electricity consumed was imposed as of April, which was collected through the suppliers of power. Administration Report 1940, p. 7.

209. Administration Report 1931, p. 5.

(trader), Mirza Ahmad Borazjani (trader), and Mirza `Abbas Salami (pleader). The last four were new members.[210]

The municipality's financial situation remained precarious in the years to come. It was difficult to collect taxes, because people were impoverished due to the drop in trade, while several traders moved to Shiraz, soon to be followed by many others. Nevertheless, the municipality continued to function quietly with a budget that over the years varied from 24,000 to 30,000 *tumans* per year, paid in monthly installments by the Finance Department. About one third (10,000 *tumans*) of this was spent on wages and some quarter (7,000 *tumans*) on repairs and improvements. The municipality employed 70 men to clean the streets. Since 1933, the municipality also funded a dispensary and its staff, and from 1936 a small asylum and a small center for lepers (see chapter one). In 1933 it paid 7,000 *tumans* extra for town improvements. The sources of income were octroi duties, taxes on houses, shops, liquors, tobacco, passages, etc. In the past these taxes were collected by the municipality, when revenue were claimed to have amounted to 4-5,000 *tumans* per month.[211]

As of 1934, the municipality received a monthly budget of 2,000 *tumans*. In April of that year, new taxes were levied: persons leaving by sea had to pay 8 rials in 1st class, 4 rials in 2nd class and 2 rials as deck passengers; persons leaving upcountry paid 4 rials p.p. in cars and 2 rials for trucks; the excise tax for spirits was raised to 1 rial. The money was to be used for an elementary school and to provide 10 beds for a ward for poor persons in the town infirmary. Given the financial situation, only 50 people were employed to keep the town clean.[212] Although as a visitor to the town in 1934 was much impressed with the governor's program of street cleaning, she rightly, be it rhetorically, raised the question: how can you keep the streets clean, when "as soon as the cleaner had passed than a women throws out a heap of broad-bean skins through her door and her children use the narrow alleys as lavatories?"[213] As a result, the town was still fairly smelly, and with only very few moderately decent roads.

In 1935, from 29 candidates voted for by the public the government selected 9 for the municipal city council, viz. Mohammad Hoseyn Talebi; `Ali Akbar Dewani; Mehdi Timsar; Sayyed `Abdol-Rasul Kazeruni; Sayyed Mohammad Siyadat; Sayyed Mohammad Tabataba'i; Yusef Okhuvat, editor of local weekly *Khalij-e Iran*; Ahmad Borazjani; and Mohammad Khorram. It functioned from 15 March when it had a deficit of 10,000 rials as people were too poor to pay their taxes. Leveling the town streets was therefore abandoned, but as mentioned previously, 50 persons were employed to clean streets and take care of the lighting and also 10-beds for poor and one local government school were financed. On the instruction from Tehran it provided 20 sofas for Hoseyniyehs to recite the Koran and say prayers for the benefit of the dead. These were formerly held in mosques for 1½ days, "but are now to be held for 2 hours only with the mourners sitting on sofas instead of squatting on the floor. No steps had been taken to implement this reform at year's end as the public considered it "unwarranted interference with a long-standing

---

210. Political Diaries, vol. 10, p. 126.

211. Administration Report 1931, p. 6; Administration Report 1932, p. 4; Administration Report 1933, p. 3-4.

212. Administration Report 1934, p. 4.

213. Merritt-Hawkes 1935, pp. 5-6.

sacred custom." The council received their monthly 20,000 rials very irregularly.[214] In 1936, this played havoc with the municipality's program to resume leveling streets due to its budget deficit. It nevertheless employed 70 people to clean streets and take care of the public lighting. Furthermore, the municipality maintained 10-beds for the infirmary, a local school, and "a small asylum for a few mentally ill persons and an isolated house for accommodating some 20 lepers" and it would continue to do so thereafter. Only in June 1936 did the council show interest in market prices and "fixed the price of mutton at Cts. 70 instead of Cts 80 previously." Its budget allotment of 25,000 rials a month is paid irregularly.[215] In that same year the Municipality employed a Russian engineer, who in February 1936 began taking measures in the town. He also marked many house; all this with the objective to make four streets that would run straight through the town. How and in which direction the streets would run was sill unknown.[216]

The only real road in Bushehr, i.e. to Sabzabad was under repair at the end of 1935. However, it was patch work executed by about 12 men with a hand-roller. Consequently, one year later the road was already shows signs of breaking up.[217] Although in 1937 the municipality received 2,600 rials monthly, which was an increase, it was not sufficient to do much about street repairs. It also raised money via subscription a total of £150 and bought land for a new cemetery outside the town. The old cemetery was turned into a Sport Club. To increase its monthly income foodstuffs were taxed, in some case as high as 10%. However, in July 1937 the municipality announced that Tehran had repealed the 3% house tax on private homes as well as a few octroi taxes of foodstuffs. Instead there was a new schedule of taxes which resulted in higher food prices by 5% to 10%. As a result, on 28 July the bakers went on strike, because they wanted to raise the price of bread from 2.15 rials to 3 rials/*man* of 2.9 kg. In reaction, the government took over the bakeries and sold bread at 2.4 rials/*man*. The governor of Bushehr also made an effort to beautify the port, when he had the seafront repaired and trees planted on it to make it a pleasant place to walk. He further saw to it that the bazaar and its shops were kept clean.[218] In 1938 the municipal council took the initiative to develop a five-year plan for the city. Among other things thing it intended to build and maintain "lazarette, to construct a public park and to improve road communications in the town. They have raised their budget to Rials 30,000 a month and are maintaining a sanitary staff of 70 persons. The Municipality's efforts to ensure a regular and sufficient supply of electricity and ice were successful." To pay for it all municipal taxes continued to be levied in addition to a 3% *ad valorem* for goods coming into the town, which were valued at the police post about 8 miles above Bushehr. This worked as follows: "One or two packages from the consignment are then taken by the Finance Department agent and held up at the post

214. Administration Report 1935, pp. 5-6; Political Diaries, vol. 11, p. 441.

215. Administration Report 1936, p. 5.

216. Political Diaries, vol. 12, p. 44.

217. Administration Report 1936, p. 10.

218. Administration Report 1937, pp. 3, 6; Political Diaries, vol. 12, p. 512. In April 1937, the following members were elected to the municipal council: Khalil Dashti (president), `Ali Golshani, Mehdi Kazeruni, Ahmad Borazjani, Mohammad Hoseyn Barakat, `Abbas Mohammadiyan, Yusef Okhuvvat (editor of the Bushehr weekly *Khalij-e Fars*), `Ali Bash Navid,and Sayyed Mohammad Tabataba'i. Political Diaries, vol. 12, pp. 406, 469-70. In November 1937, the municipality turned an old cemetery to the north east of the town into a public garden. To that end the graves were leveled. In March 1939, school children planted date-palm shrubs and sowed pastochio nut seeds. Political Diaries, vol. 12, p. 593; vol. 13, p. 287.

until the merchant concerned pays the tax levied and sends a lorry again to bring the remaining goods into town."[219] However, in 1939 the Minister of the Interior did not approve the municipal 5-year plan. Consequently, the municipal budget of 20,000 rials per month only sufficed to pay the 70 sanitation staff. These revenues were raised by the collection of a municipal tax 3% *ad valorem* on imports from the interior, 8% on house rents, 10 to 20 rials per month from shopkeepers. Nevertheless the municipal council was very active in trying to improve quality of bread and provide regular and adequate supply of ice in summer.[220]

On 16 May 1939, Mahmud Al Aqa was appointed *bakhshdar* of Bushehr and the town council (*shura-ye bakhsh*) consisted of: Slashir (sic; postmaster), Amir Divani (police office), Aurush (census officer), Dalili (local revenue chief), Haji Mohammad Barakat (merchant), Ahmad Borazjani (merchant) and Yusef Okhuvvat (editor *Khalij-e Fars*) as well as three officials representing the Customs House, the Law Courts and the Health department of Bushehr.[221] Despite the fact that in 1940, the municipality had an annual budget of 300,000 rials, there was little improvement in services. In October 1940, the head of the municipal council was even accused of accepting bribes. However, having shared some of those gains with the investigating tribunal the case was dropped by year's end.[222] Because of the worsening economic situation, the Municipality's revenues from local taxes and other sources dropped significantly. In June 1941, it was Rls. 80,000 or only two-thirds of its normal monthly expenditure. As it was doubted that Tehran would make up the difference the council decided to put up with the deficit for the time being.[223] As a result, the Municipality did not much, although its budget allocation was raised was Rls. 300,000 to Rls. 380,000. After many complaints, Mohammad Esma`il Navvab was finally replaced as head of Municipality by Sayyed Mohammad Siyadat, a local merchant.[224]

In August 1942, Mr. Kasmai became the new president of the municipality although he remained in Shiraz for the time being. When he finally came to Bushehr, he shortly thereafter became acting governor of Bushehr for one year. However, on 24 February 1943, Mr. Kasmai reassumed his post of president of the Municipality.[225] In April 1943 the street cleaners of the Municipality went on strike, stating their monthly wages of 18 *tumans* was inadequate given the prices of foodstuffs. One week later their wages were raised to 25 *tumans*. In that year the mayor was Mr. Pezeshki, who did not like it very much in Bushehr. He was replaced by Mr. Kasmai in August 1943, against which the governor protested, probably considering him too pro-British. In September 1944, Hoseyn Shabankareh replaced Kasmai as head of the Municipality. The governor opposed his appointment given his police record. Much money was allegedly spent on municipal projects, but there was no evidence of results on the ground and the municipality's

---

219. Administration Report 1938, pp. 3, 9. A lazarette is a hospital for those affected with contagious diseases.
220. Administration Report 1939, pp. 3, 8.
221. Political Diaries, vol. 13, p. 337.
222. Administration Report 1940, p. 3.
223. Political Diaries, vol. 14, p. 437.
224. Administration Report 1941, pp. 7-8.
225. Political Diaries, vol. 15, p. 225, 407; Administration Report 1942, p. 5.

affairs did not advance.[226] In 1945, the road from Bushehr to Sabzabad was bad again; only potholes were filled with earth in October, which was immediately washed away by the rain.[227]

By 1947, there were two municipalities in the governorate, i.e., Bushehr town and Borazjan. Every two years elections were held for the municipality, supervised by the *farmandar*. The latter had a list of interested and eligible candidates, and the people were asked to elect 27 candidates. From these 27 the governor or *farmandar* selected 9 for the municipal committee, whose choice was confirmed by the Ministry of Interior. Thereafter these 9 members elect a chairman. The Bushehr municipality had a permanent staff of 87, most street cleaners, i.e. 1 employee for every 68 inhabitants, as follows:

1 *shahdar* or executive officer
1 chief accountant
2 assistant accounts
3 chief revenue collectors
8 assistant revenue collectors
1 head clerk
2 assistant clerks
1 head of the sanitary department
2 assistants to the head of the sanitary department
1 inspector of roads, public buildings and lighting
1 municipal engineer
4 municipal inspectors ("the *shahdar*'s 'Gestapo'")
60 street cleaners.

The *shahdar* was appointed, on the governor's recommendation, by the Minister of Interior. His task was to supervise the staff, fix retail prices of perishable food stuffs (bread, meat, fruit, fish, vegetables, etc.). Also, he was responsible for sanitation, lighting, water supply, road and sea-wall repairs, maintenance of the playing fields, and assisting the Education department to enforce compulsory education. The funds to operate the municipality come from municipal taxes on goods made and consumed in the town. In 1947, these amounted to Rls. 4 million. As in the past, the municipality's activities were mainly focused on improving its roads, public buildings and the water supply system. Sanitation in the town was still primitive, but it was expected that this would improve when more water would be available from the new water project (Chapter 1).[228]

226. Political Diaries, vol. 15, pp. 485, 511, 565, 585; Political Diaries, vol. 16, p. 197; Administration Report 1946, p. 2 (Hoseyn Shabankareh was still mayor in 1946 and the only one paid out of Municipal funds).
227. Administration Report 1945, p. 10.
228. NA, FO 371/15473.

The Chamber of Commerce

A former Persian Minister of Commerce after numerous complaints to lift the ban of grain exports, lamented the fact that his government could not get an unbiased advice on such requests from a Chamber of Commerce composed of Persian and European merchants in the various part of the country. In December 1908, in reaction to this, representatives of British firms in Bushehr decided to form the Bushehr British Chamber of Commerce to promote their common interests. It immediately asked the British Resident to push for action to suprress the lawlessness of the road to Shiraz. They met regularly except during the summer months. In 1921, it was still active.[229]

Persian merchants in Bushehr were also discussing the establishment of a Chamber of Commerce with a view to better organize trade in imitation of foreign models. As a result, in December 1909, they established a Chamber of Commerce; both Chambers complained about the management of the Customs House and the uncivil behavior of its subordinate staff. There was also the occasional article in the press advocating the purchase of Moslem goods and those made by non-Moslems only if there was no other choice.[230] In April 1910, the Persian Chamber of Commerce protested against the new rule banning the export of aniline dyed carpets, claiming that this was contary to free trade. On 5 July 1910, the governor informed its members that he had orders to search houses that contained arms and ammunition.[231]

Although in September 1911, the Persian Chamber of Commerce still existed,[232] it apparently was dissolved thereafter, because in 1920 it was reported that for the first time a Chamber of Commerce was established. However, it must have been again dissolved, because in June 1923 it was reported that "a new Chamber of Commerce has replaced the old one. It has not, however, the full support of the Bushire merchants and will probably give place to a freshly constituted one." There still was not a new Chamber in May 1924, when the *kargozar* tried to establish a new Chamber with himself as president. One month later he was successful; five members were elected and the *kargozar* had to apppoint five other members to be selected from among merchants and government employees. Initially the Chamber had six members, but as of about the mid-1940s it had 12, who were elected every two years. Only those actively engaged in a business in Bushehr could join and all registered merchants were qualified to vote. After the election a president was chosen. Initially, it was a quasi extension of local government. After the Monopoly Law was passed "The main duty of this Chamber is to apportion the right of importation to the traders the Bushire portion of the tea and sugar goods." This portion was determined by Tehran. It appears that the Chamber was dissolved in 1930, because on 16 November 1931 the governor called a meeting of merchants announcing that Tehran wanted to establish a Chamber of Commerce at Bushehr and those convened had to select 27 merchants, of whom 9 were chosen to form the Chamber. In 1933, at the suggestion of Tehran, the

---

229. DCR 4397 (Bushire, 1908-09), p. 10; Administration Report 1921, p. 6; Political Diaries, vol. 3, p. 383.
230. Political Diaries, vol. 3, p. 781; *Revue du Monde Musulmane* 15 (1911), pp. 162.
231. Political Diaries vol. 4, pp. 65, 450.
232. Political Diaries vol. 4, p. 140.

Chamber of Commerce passed a resolution to boycott trade with Russia.[233] The governor of Bushehr also tried to use it to promote all kinds of commercial projects. In 1936, the governor at first wanted to start a kind a shipping company with motorized dhows to keep the cargo trade between Persian ports in local hands. When it became clear that motor dhows were inadequate for this purpose, the Chamber gave up this idea. When the Chamber declined to go along, the governor wanted it to form a Steam Navigation Company. At the first meeting merchants offered to invest 1,550,000 rials (£15,500). Its other activity was to form a Company for the sale of motor vehicles.[234] In 1935, the Chamber of Commerce had formed two companies and considered creating a third one for running motor dhows to keep trade between the ports in the hands of locals, but abandoned the idea when found that the dhows were useless for this purpose.[235]

At the end of 1940, the Chamber of Commerce was reorganized; it severed its connection with the governorate and consisted of six merchants. Although it remained under the supervision of the governor it was no longer part of the local government and it dealt directly with the Ministry of Commerce. In 1947, its staff consisted of a clerk and a typist. The operating costs of the Chamber were financed by a tax of 1% of the income tax paid by merchants. The tax was collected by the Finance Department and paid into the Chamber's bank account. In 1947, its president was Abbas Mohammadian. Its main function was to inform the Ministry of Commerce of trade developments; to fix landing charges; if possible settle commercial disputes between merchants; to answer trade questions from abroad, to keep all merchants informed of new government regulations, and to inform the governor when merchants have problems with the transportation of goods.[236]

The Modern Banks

In 1889 a branch of the Oriental Bank Corporation was opened in Bushehr, while the *Imperial Bank of Persia* (IBP) bought out this bank and established itself at Bushehr the following year.[237] Having the monopoly of modern banking in Bushehr the IBP did good business, which lasted until it had to face competition and a changed political and economic climate.[238] However, this was not without hitches. In 1897, "A small native banking establishment, conducted entirely by Persian merchants, and with a capital of £20,000 in shares, opened that year under the style of Bushehr Trading Company." The IBP strongly protested against this activity, branding it as an infringement of its concession.[239] However, the flooding of the market with *bijaks* or notes made 'payable to bearer' was caused by the problems with Persian currency, in particular the existence of a large number of bad coins. The Bushehr Trading Company collected many good qrans

233. Political Diaries vol. 7, pp. 182, 235, 241; Administration Report 1933, p. 3. The Chamber of Commerce continued to supervise the distribution of sugar and tea quota to local merchants. Administration Report 1934, p. 3. For the names of members of the Chamber of Commerce in 1930, see Political Diaries, vol. 9, p. 4. For the 1931 reconstitution of the Chamber, see Idem, vol. 9, p. 613.

234. Administration Report 1936, pp. 4-5.

235. Administration Report 1935, p. 5; Political Diaries, vol. 13, p. 357 (members of the Chamber).

236. NA, FO 371/15473; Administration Report 1921, p. 6; Administration Report 1933, p. 3; Administration Report 1936, pp. 4-5; Administration Report 1940, p. 8.

237. Administration Report 1889-90, p. 29; Administration Report 1890-91, p. 18.

238. On the IBP's performance in Persia, see Jones 1986.

239. Administration Report 1897-98, p. 18.

and sent them upcountry, paying their local bills with their own *bijaks*, mostly to small traders, who could not refuse to accept them. European firms dealing with Persians also had no choice but to accept them or otherwise receive payment in bad *qrans*. However, they had great difficulty getting rid of them. Also, it was doubted whether the Bushehr

Imperial Bank of Persia

Trading Comp would be able to redeem all the *bijaks* it has issued. Fortunately, for the mercantile community, as a result of the IBP's protest, the government of Persia declared *bijaks* illegal as of 1 June 1899.[240] As a result, of this decree the *bijaks* totally disappeared from the market by 1900, a development also made possible by newly minted good qrans that were avalable in larger quantities than before. Also, the availability of nickel coins to relieve the pressure on the scarcity of copper coins eased that problem.[241] Thereafter, the IBP was the only player left in the field of modern banking until 30 years later when the *Bank-e Melli* opened a branch.

As part of the enthusiasm that followed the grant of a constitution in 1906, some reformers proposed to form a national bank. In Bushehr, like elsewhere in Persia, this idea was received with great enthusiasm. Merchants outdid one another in promises of contribution to its establishment, but by March 1907 its popularity had waned in Bushehr and nothing came of it.[242] More lasting was the creation of the *Bank-e Melli* , which was established by the *Majles* in 1927. On 17 February 1929, it opened for business in Bushehr. The Bushehr branch was staffed by two Germans and a small staff of local

240. Administration Report 1898-99, pp. 7, 32
241. Administration Report 1900-01, p. 32.
242. Administration Report 1906-1907, p. 12.

clerks. At first it started cut-throat competition with the IBP, but later in the year it was less active. Despite its established position, the IBP felt the competition, because Bushehr was such a small community, but its deposits remained as high as ever. Moreover, the IBP had doubts whether the new bank was profitable, but as long as the government paid all salaries of the *Bank-e Melli* staff, its management had one worry less.[243] Because both banks suffered from *Bank-e Melli*'s low rate policy, in early 1930 the IBP and *Bank-e Melli* agreed to jointly set rates of discount to end their competition of offering uneconomic rates that only benefited merchants! The IBP director was busy not because of the market, but due "to the inadequacy and inefficiency of his staff." Fortunately for the IBP, most merchants continued to bank with it, because they felt it to be safer, being not a government organization.[244] However, there must have been official pressure to change their banks, because in 1931 the majority of Bushehr merchants had an account with the *Bank-e Melli*, which provided the same service as the IBP, and moreover, had the advantage that it was favored with all official transactions. The foreign exchange law tended to deprive banks of overseas business. Under the new Persian-Russian Commercial Treaty, all sugar imports were placed under the *Bank-e Melli*. However, in December 1939, the monopoly was transferred from the *Bank-e Melli* to the Finance Department.[245]

4.9: List of directors of the Bushehr IBP branch (1930-40)

Name	Period
Macrae	?-16 April 1931
E.S. Matheson	16 April 1931-?
Mr. Evans	?1933-6 April 1934
W.I.R. Bulfields	7 April 1934-May 1935
J.K. Millar	May 1935-9 March 1937
L.C. Cartwright	10 March-6 September 1937
V.H. Glendenning	7 September - 31 December 1937
R.N.O. Ross	1 January-23 May 1938
J. Donaldson	24 May-25 December 1938
M. Tagg	26 December 1938- 40?

Source: Administration Report 1933, p. 2; Idem 1934, p. 2; Idem 1935, p. 3; Idem 1936, p. 2; 1937, p. 2; Idem 1938, p. 2; Idem 1939, p. 2; Idem 1940, p. 2; Political Diaries, vol. 9, p. 479.

In 1932, the two competing banks were joined by a third one, the Russian bank, which was opened with much fanfare and an interest rate of 3% to 4% on current accounts were offered. Because the Russians had a trade monopoly, in accordance with the Persian-Soviet Trade Agreement of January 1931, some merchants opened an account, "but very soon realized the emptiness of the Bank as a Bank." Thereafter, Persian merchants began a boycott of Russian goods, maybe incited by the Persian government.[246] The IBP kept the confidence of the Bushehri merchants despite the *Bank-e Melli*'s competition. The

243. Administration Report 1929, p. 7; see Jones 1986, vol. 1, p. 218 for the IBP's assessment of the *Bank-e Melli*.
244. Administration Report 1930, p. 10. There also was a measure of cooperation at the national level, see Jones 1986, vol. 1, p. 225.
245. Administration Report 1931, p. 12; Administration Report 1939, p. 8; Jones 1986, vo. 1, p. 218.
246. Administration Report 1932, p. 2.

Russian bank was a bank in name only, "all its funds were kept in the strong rooms of the National Bank."[247] In 1932, the *Bank-e Melli* had a successful year and extended its business to the detriment of the IBP. Persians were less afraid of government scrutiny of their accounts if they banked with *Bank-e Melli*, although they were still apprehensive that their funds might be claimed to fund government projects. The Russian bank offered 1% on current account, 3% on deposit accounts and 5% on deposits for three years. Furthermore, it intimated that only merchants with a current account at the bank would be allowed to do business with the Russian Trading Company. A number of small traders opened accounts, but only one or two of the important traders did. "The absence of bankrupcies is an indication of conservation of resources rather than of a healthy business climate; merchants are said to be living on capital rather than trading with it and use every opportunity to accumulate funds abroad."[248] The IBP and the *Bank-e Melli* continued to do business and vie for a client base that was dwindling, even though the business and the business climate grew less attractive.[249] At the end of 1939 importers were helped by the "removal of the ban on the purchase of foreign exchange except at official rates." However, since the ban had never been effectively applied its demise was of marginal importance, although now banks could be asked to find sellers of foreign exchange.[250] In March 1942, there was a shortage of small coins. This may have been due to the fact that the *Bank-e Melli* did tranfer enough cash to places where it was more in demand; some people such as drivers earned three times more but did not deposit their money in the bank, and the presence of British and Russian troops.[251]

The Judiciary

Although there were no regular, i.e. permanent, courts in Bushehr town, in actual practice there was a dual judicial system of ad-hoc religious or *shari'a* courts presided over by *qadis* and ad-hoc secular or *`orf* courts administered by secular government officials. In the rural areas of the Bushehr governorate, where some 90% of the population lived, village and tribal leadership as well as landowners applied mostly customary law.[252] Islamic law was applied in case of marriage and divorce, but often inheritance rules still followed customary rules in rural areas. In Bushehr town, the practice was that (i) misdemeanors were taken care of by local institutions such as the chiefs of the extended families, chiefs of the city quarters and of the guilds applying customary law; (ii) felony cases were in general dealt with by the secular authorities such as the police chief (*darugheh*) and the governor applying customary law. The latter usually issued sentences by executive order without basing himself on any law. The bastinado was carried out in front of the *Chahar Borj*, which was also used as a prison;[253] (iii) torts were either dealt with by the secular or the religious judiciary, the latter in particular if it concerned matters of family law; (iv) civil disputes were mostly dealt with by the religious judiciary applying Islamic law,

247. Administration Report 1932, p. 3.
248. Administration Report 1932, p. 8.
249. Jones 1986, vol. 1, pp. 235ff.
250. Administration Report 1939, p. 5.
251. Political Diaries, vol. 15, p. 64.
252. Pelly 1865 a, p. 42; Lorimer 1915, vol. 2, p. 1789; Administration Report 1880-81, p. 25 n. ("Large landowners and persons of rank usually claim and exercise the privilege of punishing their tenants and retainers, and a 'Zanjirkhana' (chain-room) is often attached to the establishment.")
253. Lorimer 1915, vol. 2, p. 348; Nura'i 1385, p. 3.

and (v) cases involving both Persian and foreign subjects were referred to the *kargozar*. Although there were exceptions to this categorization, in general it held true.[254]

Unfortunately, not much known is about the practice of the judiciary.[255] The limited data suggest that cases could and were influenced by bribery, influence peddling and political pressure. The governor's ad-hoc court usually was swift to do justice, using corporal punishment and torture, but the governor also had to take political realities into account. In late June 1842 an attempt was made to set fire to a bungalow belonging to Haji Mohammad `Ali Safi's, a boat under the British flag at anchor in the roads. This was a serious crime, because if the fire had been set, other boats, house and bazaar might have been burnt as well. Sheikh Naser, the governor, gave the bastinado to one of the followers of the *darugheh* (Esma'il Beg) suspecting him of the crime. Under the torture he said it was his master who was the instigator out of resentment against the private owner of the vessel. The perpetrators were in prison, but Esma`il Beg, the *darugheh* on hearing this fled to asylum with Sheikh Hasan, the chief qadi. Sheikh Naser did not dare to broach the asylum and Sheikh Hasan would not deliver the man for punishment. The British Residency's treasurer, Essai, was surprised that the *darugheh* had been given asylum given that much loss of life and property might have occurred, and he was not the only one. Therefore, Sheikh Salman, the qadi's nephew told the people: "why does a Moslem vessel have a British flag? Sheikh Hasan will not give him up to Naser or to be taken from the country." Essai, therefore, thought that the qazi had put Esma`il Beg up to this.[256] In case of theft it also happened that the governor would force the village headman to provide compensation for the stolen goods, if the theft had occurred in or near the village.[257]

The ad-hoc religious courts were basically the home of a few Islamic scholars who acted as qadi, often the leading person among them was recognized as the chief qadi.[258] This was, for example the case with Sheikh Hasan Bushehri,[259] of whom it was known that he was not averse to financial gain. The person to whom Captain Wilson, the British Resident owed money having died in 1828, he asked the chief qadi which person was entitled to receive payment. The qadi replied: "that he soon could decide that point, but wished to know in the first place, whether the captain would prefer to pay one person rather than the other." Despite this openness to bribery, this man was regarded as one of the most upright magistrates in the area.[260] This experience may have led Mignan, who was in Bushehr in 1830, to report that: "Justice is a marketable commodity; he who has the heaviest purse secures from the kazi the most favourable decision, and a rich man, although his hands may have been steeped in the blood of his own parent, can, by bribery,

254. On the issue of the judiciary in general, see Floor 1983 a, pp. 113-147; Administration Report 1880-81, pp. 24-25. On the *kargozar*'s court, see above.

255. For two case studies, see Floor 1983 b, Martin 2008.

256. NA, FO 248/108, J. Edwards/Bushire to Robertson/Khark, 27/06/1842; NA, FO 248/108, Essai Johannes treasurer/Bushire to Robertson/Khark, 24/06/1842.

257. Hamidi 1378, pp. 123-24.

258. Nura'i 1385, pp. 2, 60, 62 (*mahkamheh-ye shar`*); Sadid al-Saltaneh 1362, p. 9 (*mahkameh-ye Imam Jom`eh*).

259. Sheikh Hasan Bushehri was a member of a well-known Shiite family of Bahraini `olama, the Al `Osfur. He was the second son of Sheikh Hoseyn b. Mohammad, who was qadi and Imam Jom`eh of Bahrain. After his father's death, who was succeeded in his functions by his eldest son, Sheikh Hasan went to Bushehr in 1805, where he was active as qadi and Imam Jom`eh of that port city; he died in 1845. Oshkuri 1369, vol. 2, p. 73; Afshar Sistani 1369, vol. 2, pp. 558-59.

260. Anonymous 1830, p. 3.

especape with impunity."[261] In 1877, according to the Dutch consul Richard Keun, the *mojtahed* of Bushehr, Sheikh Ahdali was too old and feeble to be occupied with judicial matters and therefore, left these to his son-in-law Sheikh Mohammad, who sold 'justice.' Part of the bribe was paid immediately, the remainder when a favorable verdict was issued. Likewise, witnesses were suborned or bought as were the authorities.[262]

Political clout also influenced the outcome of court cases. Having made a debtor pay his creditor, the prince-governor called the latter and told him in open court that if it had not been for him he would never have received any payment. Therefore, it was only just that he also should reap some benefit. The prince-governor then returned half the sum to him and kept the other half.[263] Things had not changed some 40 years later when Haji Mohammad Garik complained that Humad b. Shehab, a merchant connected with the British Residency, refused to pay his debt and return a house belonging to him. The latter submitted that he needed time till his partner Mohammad `Ali returned, in which case he would be able prove his right. Although the law allowed this delay Haji Mohammad Garik said in court that the governor would not allow this. According to the British Resident, it was clear that Humad b. Shehab's opponent was not the claimant, but Nasir al-Molk, the all powerful governor, who just had it in for all those who were connected with the British Residency.[264]

In 1864, Naser al-Din Shah ordered that, once per month, so-called justice boxes (*sanduq-e `edalat*) be placed in public squares of the major towns of Persia. People could drop in their petitions and the boxes were only to be opened in the shah's presence. Not much is known about its effect, although the practice seems to have fallen into abeyance. But again in February 1874, Naser al-Din Shah issued a decree that justice boxes should be placed in the public square of the larger towns. The objective remained the same, i.e. petitions from all classes could be sent directly to shah. It is not known whether such a box was placed in Bushehr in 1864, but ten years later it certainly was. Perhaps based on the disappointing result of the first attempt, or due to general lack of confidence in higher authorities, people in Bushehr were not enthused about this measure. In fact, no petitions seem to have been dropped in the box in Bushehr,[265] however, when the shah's order "to abolish the octoi duty on fruit and vegetables at Bushire,"[266] this was much more popular. One reason for the lack of impact of the justice-boxes may have been the fact that governors "ordered a watch to be kept on those boxes; the bastinado was freely administered to any indiscrete person dropping in a petition."[267] Despite the public's muted response, the custom seems to have intermittently survived in later years. However, it did not have an impact on the way justice was sought and done in Persia.[268]

---

261. Mignan 1839, vol. 2, p. 141.

262. NA, 2.05.38 (new 1370-1386), Keun to van der Does, 19/01/1877 plus appended letters to Zinoviev and Schimanovsky.

263. Anonymous 1830, pp. 2-3.

264. NA, FO 248/263, `Abdol Mohammad 2nd *monshi* to uncovenanted ass. resident, 17 Shavval 1286 - 20/01/1870; Idem, Mirza Mohammad Khan, FO Agent to uncovenanted ass. resident 21 Shavval 1286 -24/01/1870; Idem, uncovenanted ass. resident to Mirza Mohammad Khan, FO Agent, 21 Shavval 1286 - 24/01/1870.

265. Ettehadiyeh 1989, pp. 51-61.

266. Administration Report 1874-75, p. 5.

267. Curzon 1892, vol. 1, p. 465.

268. Schneider 2006, p. 37.

The Shah's proclamation of 1888 concerning his subject's rights and liberties was made public in Bushehr like in the rest of the country. It did not have any impact on how government officials dealt with the people of Bushehr, despite the British Resident's guarded optimistic observations, when he wrote: "The effects of this measure are not yet palpable, but, owing chiefly to increased intercourse with Europeans and interchange of ideas with them, there is gradual amelioration of the conditions of the people in progress, and the Royal Proclamation is a sign of the times at all events, and may yet bear fruit."[269] However, the reality on the ground and the fact that neither this Resident nor his successors or anyone else ever referred to the Proclamation again is telling in and by itself.

After the constitution had been granted by the shah, people expected the establishment of modern courts given the discussions in Tehran. Moreover, people knew that because of the constitution proper procedures had to be followed (investigation, determination of guilt), before somebody could be punished or sentenced to prison. The political turmoil not only had its impact on secular institutions. In April 1907, the *shari`a* courts no longer were respected by the people and the chief mullahs, Imam Jom`eh, and Sadr al-Eslam who operated these courts were reviled and cursed by the people.[270] In early December 1908, the deputy governor received instructions from Tehran to form an *`Adliyeh* instead of the former town council. It was his intention to hold a meeting with representatives of the population to select its members. However, because of all the local political troubles this did not happen (see chapter 3). Once these troubles were over, in August 1909, Sayyed Asadollah Najafi suggested that the local council should establish a small court of justice to settle cases. However, due to petty jealousies between the local council and the governor nothing came of it. It took another year, before the deputy-governor established this temporary court with the approval of the olama and merchants. This temporary court heard a number of cases ranging from theft to property disputes.[271] Already in January 1910, Daryabegi had wanted to establish a modern court, but he was told to wait until Tehran had sent instructions and staff to implement such an institution. Nevertheless, Daryabegi appointed two merchants to act as Commercial Assessors of the new proposed court. In October 1910, an inspector of Justice was expected, who does not seem to have come.[272] In 1911, the judicial reforms of Moshir al-Dowleh led to the establishment of five classes of secular law courts (*adliyeh* courts), to wit: the supreme court of cassation (*tamiz*), the court of appeals (*estinaf*), the court of first instance (*ebteda'i*), the criminal court (*jaza'i*), and the petty court (*solhiyeh*), which decided civil suits up to 250 *tumans*.[273] As there was a dearth of qualified personnel, initially only in a few major cities were the new law courts established. One of these cities was Bushehr, where the governor established an *anjoman-e `adliyeh* or Judicial Committee "for the disposal of civil cases, court-fees being met by an advance payment of 10 per cent. on the amount of the claim."[274] Apparently, the new court was suspended in 1911, because in 1912 we learn that it was re-established by the governor "to inquire into civil

269. Lorimer 1915, vol. 1, p. 2053.

270. Political Diaries, vol. 2, p. 157.

271. Hamidi 1378, pp. 152-53, 160-61, 207-08; Political Diaries, vol. 2, p. 157; vol. 3, pp. 368 (06/12/1908), 704, 720.

272. Political Diaries vol. 4, pp. 10, 228.

273. For a discussion of how the judicial system worked during the Qajar period see Floor 1983 a and b.

274. Administration Report 1911, p. 13. The mullahs declared Fazal, the man selected to head the *`adliyeh*, to be unfit to serve, because he did not have a certificate issued by them qualifying him for that function. FO 248/1033, Political Diary for October 1911, no. 948.

cases and those for which he has no time himself; a 10% fee is charged. All monies paid to the `*adliyeh* serve to pay its members, a measure that initially worked out well."[275] Also, the new court had made a real impact, because in September 1913, a meeting of the leading olama of Bushehr "declared that the prestige of the clergy had suffered considerably of late by the institution of the Adliyeh Court." Some of them even stated that the court was contrary to the *shari`a*, that the olama should not recognize its decisions and sent a protest telegram to Tehran.[276]

4.10: Expenditures of the `*adliyeh* court in 1913 (in *qrans*)

Category	Per Month	Per Year
Chief	600	7,200
Clerk	200	2,400
Clerk	120	1,440
Farrash 2 men at 60 p.m.	120	1,440
Granary	100	1,200
Office expenditures	110	1,320
Total	1,250	15,000

Source: Sadid al-Saltaneh 1371, p. 81.

The `*adliyeh* court was a court of the first instance, which dealt with most criminal cases and all civil and customs cases. But cases such as first degree murder or forgery, which were subject to the death penalty and those cases subject to imprisonment of more than three years had to be referred to the higher court in Shiraz, after a preliminary hearing in the Bushehr court. The proceedings of the new court sometimes clashed with the traditional religious court. For example, in 1913 a dispute about the payment of debt did not result in a definite decision by the `*adliyeh* court. The court considered that the plaintiff did not have sufficient evidence and reliable witnesses to be able to award his claim. Therefore, the plaintiff took his case to the court of the Imam Jom'eh, who decided in his favor applying other standards, which move did not resolve the case, of course.[277] In mid-1915 the *ra'is-e `adliyeh* was so corrupt that the people of Bushehr called his office *zolmiyeh* or that of 'injustice.'[278]

It seems that after 1918 or thereabouts the `*adliyeh* court had been closed for a number of years, because in 1927 it is reported that the `*adliyeh* court was again re-established, but people in Bushehr had no confidence in it whatsoever. In fact, by that time the `*adliyeh* courts throughout Persia were referred to as *zolmiyeh* or courts of injustice, in popular parlance. Therefore, it was no surprise that all civil cases continued to be taken to the religious courts.[279] In early January 1928, Sheikh Mohammad Hadi Saduqi was appointed

---

275. Administration Report 1912, p. 17; see also Nura'i 1385, pp. 42, 63.
276. Political Diaries, vol. 5, pp. 256, 290, 388.
277. Nura'i 1385, pp. 122, 125-26.
278. Political Diaries, vol. 6, p. 64.
279. NA, FO 416/80, Haworth (Bushire) to Clive, 09/05/1927, f. 123; Floor 1983 a, p. 132; Administration Report 1927, p. 2.

ra'is-e `adliyeh of Bushehr where he arrived on 13 February. He opened the court of 1st instance with a ceremony on 18 February 1928. Sheikh Mohammad Hadi Saduqi was removed after complaints against him in early November 1928. He had a "sordid reputation as an opium eater and bribe taker." He told a friend that the appointment had cost him 900 *tumans* and therefore, he had to recuperate that investment. He was soon replaced by Mirza Ne`matollah Khan Ashti, a more junior man.[280] Mirza Ne`matollah Khan Ashti remained in Bushehr till July 1929, when he left on leave; on his return he became the public prosecutor. The post of chief judge of the *`adliyeh* court remained vacant till 23 November 1929 when Mohammad `Ali Pishva assumed charge of the courts.[281] Mohammad `Ali Pishva only remained until the end of March 1930, when he left to Tehran to discuss his salary and that of prosecutor Ashti as earlier requests had not been successful. He returned 3½ months later having obtained a raise of 250 *tumans* and for Ashti of 200 *tumans*.[282] Mohammad `Ali Khan Pishva remained *ra'is-e `adliyeh* until 30 July 1931, when he resigned because his salary was not raised. This was a loss for Bushehr, because Pishva had an excellent reputation as a judge, while his successor, Mirza Mehdi Khan Shari`atmadari was known to take even the smallest bribe.[283] In November 1940, the court at Bushehr was downgraded from a court of the first instance to one of small cases. Merchants were unhappy, because this meant that for all cases involving more than Rls. 5,000 they had to go to Shiraz for settlement. In July 1943 it was recommended that Bushehr should have again a Court of the First Instance, but it was only in September 1944 that its status was raised to that of a District Court.[284] In September 1945 Bushehr was separated from Fars and came directly under Tehran. This had an immediate positive effect on the petty court (*dadgah-e bakhsh*). Until then every decision had to be submitted to Shiraz, but as of that change only to the court of the first instance (*dadgah-e shahrestan*), which could decide any case presented to it.[285]

No major administrative or jurisdictional change came to this situation during the the two following decades. In 1947, the staff of the court at Bushehr consisted of: 1 chief judge, 1 judge, 2 public prosecutors, and 1 magistrate. This court still heard most criminal cases and all civil and customs cases. Occasionally, an official of the Judicial Department, who was authorized to try smuggling cases, held court in the Customs building. However, there was a significant change in the way the judicial system operated after 1941. During Reza Shah's reign (1925-1941), arbitrary arrests, house searches, imprisonment for a long period without trial, and concentration camps for political prisoners were rife. However, this was a thing of the past after his abdication in 1941. Henceforth, only after a judge had signed a warrant could the police or gendarmerie arrest somebody. Nevertheless, there still was room for much improvement. Although the laws enacted by the *Majles* were comprehensive the judiciary was still too much an instrument of the executive. In outlying areas summary justice still existed, despite tours made by the chief judge of the court of the first instance. Lawyers seldom appeared in court to defend criminals, because

280. Administration Report 1928, p. 3.
281. Administration Report 1929, p. 3.
282. Administration Report 1930, p. 4.
283. Administration Report 1931, p. 4.
284. Political Diaries, vol. 14, p. 236; vol. 15, p. 541; vol. 16, p. 201. Mr. Falsafi, a judge of the Bushehr court was replaced in June 1946 by Abdol-Aziz Qotb. Political Diaries, vol. 17, p. 131.
285. Administration Report 1945, pp. 7, 9-10.

(i) the evidence was often condemning, and (ii) it was bad for one's reputation.[286] In short, the rule of law was still not an entirely objective blind instrument.

The Police

The overall responsibility of maintaining law and order in Bushehr was the governor's task. Apparently, Sheikh `Abdol-Rasul was a hands-on governor, because Mignan reported that was "a shrewd and clever man, and a good *practical* magistrate. He often visits the coffe-houses incognito, and few robberies are ever committed without detection.[287] However, in practice, the governor delegated this task to the *kalantar* ("head of the Town Administration and Police") and *kadkhoda*, the former for Bushehr town and the latter for its suburbs. Also, there was a *darugheh*, who in 1842 was accused of having organized the burning of a buggalow that sailed under the British flag. All three offcials were supported by a staff of so-called *gazmeh*, *shagerds* or *tofangchis*.[288] Their presence must have been rather low-key, because around 1880 a French traveler commented that there was no police at all in Bushehr.[289]

In 1910, the *kalantar* was Mashhadi `Abdol-Rasul, who was hostile to the British Residency that had complained a few times about him. The *kadkhoda* was Zayer `Ali Tangestani, except for July, when Daryabegi reinstated Qaid Mohammad Ja`far, a former *kadkhoda*. This appointment was opposed by Zayer `Ali's supporters who were afraid that their smuggling activities would be less successful and lucrative. Ra'is `Ali Delvari and other Tangestani chiefs came to Imamzadeh near Sabzabad residency and asked the Resident to intervene, so that neither person, but a third party be appointed. They had a blood feud with the Qaid and wanted to avoid trouble. The latter brought the matter to the notice of the governor, who on 11 July sent his deputy, Sheikh Naser Khan Chakutahi. As a result all came to see Daryabegi, who canceled Qaid's appointment and was forced to appoint a Tangestani, his deputy's son, Sheikh Seyf Chakutahi, otherwise he risked an invasion of Tangestani *tofangchis* as in 1909 and he had no troops. The Tangestanis were happy as they saw Sheikh Seyf as a supporter of Zayer `Ali, who later on was appointed as *kadkhoda*.[290]

In 1910, the provincial *anjoman* discussed the establishment of a modern police force (*pulis*) to replace the old system with the *darugheh*, *gazmeh*, and *shagerd*, who were all on the take. Among the 30 police officers employed at that time, there was not one who was capable of proper speaking or writing a report.[291] After Bushehr had established a munici-

286. NA, FO 371/15473. There was a *ra'is-e ta'minat* (head of the security department) in Bushehr, at least since 1927. Political Diaries vol. 7, p. 525.

287. Mignan 1839, vol. 2, pp. 141-42.

288. On these and other police officials and their organization, see Floor 1971 a; Idem, 1971 b; Idem, 1973; Sa`adat 1390, pp. 54, 250.

289. de Rivoyre 1883, p. 135.

290. Nura'i 1385, p. 7; Administration Report 1910, p. 12; Political Diaries vol. 4, p. 139; NA, FO 240/108, J. Edwards/Bushire to Robertson/Khark, 27/06/1842; Idem, Essai Johannes treasurer/Bushire to Robertson/Khark, 24/06/1842. The *darugheh* was given asylum by Sheikh Hasan, the chief qazi despite the fact other boats, houses and bazaar might have been burnt as well. The British suspected that the qazi was the real instigator of the fire. On the functions of the *kalantar*, *darugeh*, and *kadkhoda* in Qajar Persia, see Floor 1971 a, Idem, 1971 b, and Idem 1973.

291. Nura'i 1385, p. 7; Administration Report 1910, p. 14.

pality, the government in Tehran sent `Abdollah Khan E`tezad-e Hazrat as police chief (*ra'is-e nazmiyeh*). He arrived on 19 December 1910 and started his work in January 1911. From the very beginning, he spent his time wrangling with the governor and the *kalantar*, who told him that they had no funds for him. Tehran also announced the dispatch of an Inspector of Justice and an Inspector of Municipality, but they did not arrive. All of them would have been an unnecessary and useless charge on the city's revenue.[292] Despite this negative reaction, the new police chief took control over the local 30 man strong police. However, he had great difficulty finding funds to pay his men and, therefore, considered levying a tax on opium and arrack. The police chief ordered drunks to be arrested, he posted men at Jewish shops to collect the 0.5 *qran* tax per bottle sold. Furthermore, he asked the governor to place soldiers instead of policemen at the consulates and add these policemen to his force. Moreover, he asked to be allowed to hire more men, including *sovar*s and *tofangchi*s to patrol the suburbs which were under the *kadkhoda*. The *kalantar* and *kadkhoda*, of course, disliked this new official, fearing to lose their job and therefore, their perquisites, such as the levying of *rahdari* and other unnamed fees (*naqliyeh*) from the muleteers.[293]

This was indeed what happened. The *ra'is-e nazmiyeh* having no funds started levying a tax on alcohol and opium, and assisted the municipal council in levying other imposts such as a fee on horses and donkeys. The water carriers incited by the *kalantar* complained to the governor, who offered no help. In the night of 13 February 1911, a bullet was fired through the house of the British Residency's *monshi* and the following night an armed policeman was caught climbing the wall of the Turkish consulate. The British believed that these incidents were aimed to embroil one party with the foreigners. The most serious result was the killing of a gunner by the deputy police chief, who himself was then killed. This happened because the gunners, who tried to make a living as petty traders, tried to convince shopkeepers to close their shops protesting the new taxes. In April 1911, to put an end to this, the deputy-governor went to the bazaar, and remonstrated with them. This led to an altercation in the bazaar. According the British, Mostafa Khan, the deputy chief of police "was insulted by one of the gunners, who then drew his revolver and killed him on the spot." According to the newspaper *Jonub*, this incident happened after the police had fired shots in the air to disperse the crowd, and either on purpose or by accident one gunner was killed. Mostafa Khan, the alleged killer fled pursued by the other gunners. He wanted to take *bast* or sanctuary in the Residency, but found the gates closed and then went to the Turkish consulate, where only one police officer was present as a caretaker. A mob forcibly entered the Consulate and shot the deputy chief and dragged his body through the streets. The police officer who had tried to save the deputy-chief was mortally wounded as was one of the crowd, a *komach-forush*. According to the newspaper *Jonub*, `Abdol-Rasul, the *kalantar* was the instigator of the entire incident. The Ottoman consul, Nabil Ziya Beg, huffed and puffed about the violation of the Consulate

---

292. Administration Report 1910, p. 12; Political Diaries vol. 4, pp. 296 (here he is called Mirza Mo`azed al-Mellat, *ra'is-e nazmiyeh*), 328. According to the newspaper *Jonub* `Abdollah Khan took control over the police department on 13 January 1911. Hamidi 1378, pp. 19, 22, 70, 79, 197.

293. Administration Report 1910, p. 14; Political Diaries vol. 4, p. 329; Nura'i 1385, p. 7; Hamidi 1378, pp. 31, 203 (text of the announcement of the new taxes by the municipality). The *kalantari*'s expenditures amounted to 21,780 *qrans* in 1911 for the chief (12,000), his deputy (2,400), bazaar lighting (1,200), reception cost (1,200), rent for *majles* (600) wages for 3 bazaar guards (1,260) and stipend for the goaler or *zanjirbash* (720). Sadid al-Saltaneh 1371, p. 80.

Haji Yusef, Chief of Police

and demanded that his government supply him with a guard. Although initially he was accompanied by a guard wherever he went, a permanent guard was not made available, because the Persian government apologized and paid 1,500 *tumans* demanded to the family of the police officer. In reaction to these events, in April 1911, the governor abolished the post of *kadkhoda* and in July 1911 he abolished the function of *kalantar*. Thus, Mashhadi `Abdol-Rasul was out of a job, for which in March 1911, he had paid 16,000 *tumans*. All this meant that the experiment with the *ra'is-e nazmiyeh* was not a success and only created problems for the governor, and as a result, the unpopular position of *ra'is-e nazmiyeh* was abolished.[294]

In May 1911, for a while, the new deputy-governor acted as police chief, but later that month he appointed as such Mirza Mahmud, the former deputy-governor of Lengeh.[295] The governor had abolished the post of *kalantar*, which yielded 15,000 *tumans*, because it was not included in his tax schedule and thus, the function and its taxes were illegal. However, in June 1912, being short of funds, the governor re-established the *kalantari* taxes to raise funds for a mission to Bandar Abbas.[296] Therefore, Mashhadi `Abdol-Rasul was reinstated as *kalantar* and as chief of police and remained in these functions until the beginning of November 1912, when the governor had him arrested. The British were happy, because they considered him a rascal who was hostile to British interests and always tried to obstruct them. Also, they believed that he was in league with the arms smugglers. These included Zayer Khedr, who, on 22 November 1912, put pressure on the governor to demand the *kalantar's* dismissal by closing the road between Ahmadi and Bushehr. He also redirected caravans via the prohibited routes of Ahram and Shif, thus benefiting Zayer Khedr and his friend Ahmad Khan of Angali. This also caused a problem for the British because a caravan for the British Indian troops (Central India Horse) could not leave on 25 November 1912. The governor suggested that the Residency use the troops to open the road, but before a reply from Tehran was received, the road was opened because of intervention of Sayyed Morteza Ahrami, who, after having prodded them to action, convinced the malcontents to do so to avoid eventual confrontation with Indian troops.[297]

Despite these activities the governor remained adamant and, after `Abdol-Reza had returned from deportation to Jask in January 1913, he re-appointed him as *kalantar* (and possibly also as *kadkhoda*), who by now had a force of 40 *tofangchis*, paid for out of illegal taxes levied on transport animals entering the city.[298] `Abdol-Reza remained *kalantar* and chief of police (*edareh-ye nazmiyeh*) until British occupation of Bushehr in 1915.[299] After the occupation, the police continued to work under their own officials except that the *kalantar* `Abdol-Reza was removed and replaced by Haji Yusof. The latter remained *kalantar* in the years thereafter.[300]

---

294. Administration Report 1911, pp. 13-14; Hamidi 1378, pp. 26-27, 31-33, 219-20; Political Diaries vol. 4, pp. 340-41, 352.

295. Political Diaries vol. 4, p. 380.

296. Political Diaries vol. 4, pp. 408, 567.

297. Administration Report 1912, pp. 14-15; Political Diaries vol. 4, pp. 625-27 (Abdol-Rasul had held this function for 10 successive years), 641.

298. Administration Report 1912, p. 17; Administration Report 1913, p. 6; Political Diaries vol. 5, pp. 9, 32. In 1912, the *kalantar* dealt with cases of theft and disorder as well as with a case of the accidental firing at a house during the hunt. Nura'i 1385, pp. 22, 39, 45, 47-48, 91.

299. Administration Report 1915, p. 2; Nura'i 1385, p. 168. In 1913, the chief of police earned 3,000 *qrans* per year and his 25 policemen at 70 *qrans* per month cost 21,000 *qrans* per year. Sadid al-Saltaneh 1371, p. 81.

300. Administration Report 1915, p. 6; Administration Report 1916 p. 2. For a photo of Abdol-Reza and Hajj Yusof, see Roknzadeh 1352, pp. 128, 141.

4.11: List of chiefs of police of Bushehr (1910-1931)

Name	Duration	Observations	Source
Mashhadi `Abdol-Rasul	1900- 19 December 1910	*Kalantar*	Administration Report 1910, p. 12
`Abdollah Khan E`tezad-e Hazrat	19 December 1910-April 1911	Chief of police	Administration Report 1910, p. 12; Idem, 1911, p. 14
Mirza Mahmud	May-August 1911	Chief of police	Political Diaries vol. 4, p. 380
Mashhadi `Abdol-Rasul	August 1911-November 1912	*Kalantar* and chief of police	Administration Report 1912, p. 15
Abdol-Reza	November 1912-August 1915	*Kalantar* and chief of police	Administration Report 1912, p. 17; Idem 1913, p. 6; Idem, 1915, p. 2
Haji Yusof	August 1915-?	*Kalantar* and chief of police	Administration Report 1915, p. 6; Idem, 1916, p. 2
Yavar Mostafa Khan Albruz	?1925 - 6 April 1928		Administration Report 1925, p. 6; Idem, 1928, p. 3
Yavar Hasan `Ali Khan Bayat*	15 April-September 1928		Administration Report 1928, p. 3
Ali Naqi Khan Sarim Nezam	September- 25 November 1928	Officiated	Administration Report 1928, p. 3
Yavar Hasan Qoli Khan Bayat*	25 November 1928- 28 April 1930		Administration Report 1930, p. 3
Yavar Gholam Hoseyn Behzadi	28 April 1930-24 February 1931		Administration Report 1930, p. 3; Idem, 1931, p. 4
Soltan Gholam Hoseyn Daneshpur	24 February 1931 -		Administration Report 1931, p. 4
Major `AliReza Jahanara	- d. 19 August 1941	Commissioner of police	Political Diaries, vol. 14, p. 491
Major Khahpur	19 August -14 November 1941	Idem	Political Diaries, vol. 14, p. 491
Captain `Abdollah Mujab	14 November 1941-May 1942	Idem	Political Diaries, vol. 14, p. 557; Administration Report 1942, p. 6
Lt. Avar	May 1942-September 1942	Chief of police (was notoriously corrupt)	Political Diaries, vol. 15, p. 287
Lt. Qahramani	September-October 1942	Officiating	Political Diaries, vol. 15, p. 287
Col. Qa'em Jahed	October 1942- †October 1943; temporarily replaced by Rasadban Ghaffari	Idem (was army officer)	Political Diaries, vol. 15, p. 287; Administration Report 1942, p. 6; Administration Report 1943, p. 9

Name	Duration	Observations	Source
Sarbahr Massoumi	?-3 August 1945		Administration Report 1945, p. 8
Yavar Mohajer	3 August 1945-June 1946	Kameli acting chief	Administration Report 1945, p. 8; Political Diaries vol. 17, p. 131
Pasyar Safiri	7 July - 14 December 1946		Political Diaries vol. 17, p. 153
Sarbahr Dej Bakhsh	15 December 1946-?		Political Diaries vol. 17, p. 293

* This is the same person, but his name is slightly different in 1928 from the one given in 1930, probably due to a reading/printing error.

It is not known for how long Haji Yusof remained in office and who replaced him thereafter. It is quite likely that he continued to serve as *kalantar* until the end of the British occupation. In February 1925, the *kadkhoda* and his *tofangchis*, who were responsible for the protection of Bushehr's suburbs, where the European colony and wealthy Bushehris lived, were replaced by the military, "who are naturally more reliable."[301] Shortly thereafter reference is made again to the function of police chief, because it is reported that on 20 March 1925, the *ra'is-e qoshun* or the officer commanding the troops of the local garrison and *Yavar* Mostafa Khan Albruz, the *ra'is-e nazmiyeh* quarreled. Because the people sided with the former, reluctantly, the governor had to suspend the police chief.[302] On 6 April 1928, the reinstated *Yavar* Mostafa Khan Albruz was sent under arrest to Ahvaz to answer questions about his involvement in corruption. He returned on 13th and left for Tehran on the 15th April, when he was replaced by *Yavar* Hasan `Ali Khan Bayat who was recalled to Tehran in September. During his absence `Ali Naqi Khan Sarim Nezam officiated. *Yavar* Hasan `Ali Khan Bayat retook his position in Bushehr from 25 November 1928.[303] *Yavar* Hasan Qoli Khan Bayat remained police chief till 28 April 1930, when he was replaced by *Yavar* Gholam Hoseyn Behzadi. The British considered Bayat to be a capable officer, who kept his men in order, but found that his successor was less efficient. As of July 1929, the police force was "clad in a new uniform of light blue Persian cloth with a hat that appears to be a copy of a French soldier's helmet." The force was very active enforcing the new dress regulation, in particular the wearing of the Pahlavi hat after Nowruz.[304] *Yavar* Gholam Hoseyn Khan Behzadi remained police chief till 24 February 1931 when he was replaced by *Soltan* Gholam Hoseyn Daneshpur. Mohammad Khan Jazib, who was notoriously corrupt, remained in charge of the Security Department till mid-January 1931, when Mirza `Abbas Uriyan relieved him. It is not known, whether these changes in personnel was aimed at improving management, but this seems to have been one of the department's problems, because on 5 September 1931, 10 policemen took sanctuary (*bast*) in the Imamzadeh outside town protesting the harsh treatment by their superior. They were given assurances by the police chief, but only moved when the deputy-governor showed up and gave the assurances of their safety. The British

301. Administration Report 1925, p. 8.
302. Administration Report 1925, p. 6.
303. Administration Report 1928, p. 3.
304. Administration Report 1929, p. 2; Administration Report 1930, p. 3; Political Diaries, vol. 9, p. 75.

commented that "the custom of bast, so common in the past, was dying out and this was the first time since many years."[305] In 1934, there even was one traffic officer.[306]

In 1931 the jurisdiction of the Bushehr police department was changed. Initially, this jurisdiction reflected that of the governor of the Gulf Ports and therefore, extended from Bandar Delam to Lengeh. However, in the first half of 1931 this jurisdiction was reduced to the area from Bandar-e Delam on one side and to Borazjan on the other. Henceforth Lengeh and Henjam were placed under the police department of Bandar Abbas.[307] In September 1942, the police were placed under Shiraz, instead of directly under Tehran.[308] The year 1942 was a difficult one for the police because after the departure of Major Mujad, *Rasadban* (Lt.) Avar temporarily replaced him. He was utterly corrupt, because he wanted to make most of the limited time available to him, which led to an enormous increase in smuggling and pilfering. The British Resident urged Tehran to replace Avar, and thus *Pasyar* (Col.) Jahed, a old Army officer was appointed, who restored discipline among the police.[309] By the late 1940s, the jurisdiction of the police of the Bushehr governorate was limited to a few urban areas, as follows:

4.12: Police jurisdiction in the 1940s

Area	Officers/*kalantar*	Men
Bushehr	4	50
Ganaveh	1 lieutenant	20
Bandar-e Rig	1 "	20
Bandar-e Delam	1 "	20
Borazjan	1 captain	20
Total strength	8	130

After the tribal uprising of September-October 1946, the recruitment for and composition of the police and gendarmerie was changed. On 15 December 1946, a new young police chief *Sarbahr* Dej Bakhsh and *Sarvar* Hamzehpur chief of gendarmerie arrived to start a new chapter in policing.[310]

All the police officers in the sub-districts were still under the police chief of Bushehr (*ra'is-e shahrbani*), who held the rank of captain (*sarvan*). He was assisted by two 1st lieutenants and one 3rd lieutenant. There was a plains clothes section for criminal investigation and a passport section. The local police chiefs were referred to as *kalantar*; in case of crimes

305. Administration Report 1931, p. 4. A number of thefts occurred in Bushehr in March 1933 of which Bida thieves, who were "known as 'the bleating thieves' (for they first bleated like sheep in the vicinity of the houses they wanted to visit," were accused. They had pitched their tents at Gurak village, 11 km s.e. of town. Political Diaries, vol. 10, p. 238.

306. Merritt-Hawkes 1935, p. 5. In 1930 the chief of the Police Departments of the Gulf Ports established police stations in Ganaveh, Rig, Delam, Borazjan, Minab, Henjam, Qeshm and Jask. As of February 1930, the Bushehr police were instead of being administratively under the chief in Khuzestan directly under Tehran. Political Diaries, vol. 9, p. 4.

307. Administration Report 1931, p. 4.

308. Political Diaries, vol. 15, p. 261.

309. Administration Report 1942, p. 6.

310. Political Diaries, vol. 17, p. 293.

they investigated the matter and sent their findings to the local court. The police force was also in charge of the Bushehr prison that had a capacity for 50 prisoners. Only those who completed their military service were hired as policemen; this was a popular occupation, because of its side-benefits. The police were armed with the same rifles as the military.[311]

The Gendarmery

With the breakdown of central government authority and power in the early twentieth century, the latent violence in the area above Bushehr manifested itself and focused on two objectives. First, get control over the routes of commercial traffic to be able to tax it; and second, prevent old enemies from doing the same. Given the lucrative nature of taxing trade, the traditional feuds acquired an additional financial nature and became more and more accentuated. As a result, mini-wars between various local chiefs were fought and many people, on both sides, were killed, just to control more stretches of road. After 1907, following the partition of Persia into British and Russian zones of influence, the levying of illegal imposts of trade caravans passing from Bushehr to Shiraz and beyond, and even raiding and plundering those caravans, was justified by its perpetrators as harming British interests. There is no doubt that some British firms suffered damage, but tens of thousands of Persians, who were the buyers and/or sellers of those goods or who transported them were the ones who paid the real price. Often, they lost their goods and animals, while consumers were confronted with ever higher prices. They, therefore, were less appreciative of this enforced contribution to 'the anti-British effort,' which only benefited a number of local chiefs, now hailed as anti-imperialism fighters. However, the latter were engaged in the same plunder and looting business that they had been in before they found out that they were nationalists and that robbing caravans was the proper nationalist thing to do.[312]

Although in the nineteenth century the major trade route between Bushehr and Shiraz had never been totally secure, generally, forceful governors of Fars were able to control the local chiefs, whose districts were adjacent to this route and thus ensure safety on the road. Partly by the stick (military action) and partly by the carrot (local chiefs supplied *rahdars* or road guard and received part of their income) governors of Fars were able to reduce robberies and attacks on caravans. However, between 1905 and 1918, when Persia had a central government that became weaker and more irrelevant by the day, local chiefs saw an opportunity to earn additional funds. Apart from a weak and incapacitated government, another incentive for these chiefs was that the collection of *rahdari* had been ruled illegal and thus, one of their sources of income was rapidly drying up. At the same time, the government of Persia still included the amount of the now illegal taxes in the revenues to be paid by local governors and chiefs. To provide themselves with additional income, these chiefs imposed and levied illegal fees on travelers and caravans passing through their territory, and fought with other chiefs for control of larger segments of the trade route.[313]

As a result, during the period between 1908 and 1911 there were a total of 64 attacks on caravans, which resulted in a loss of some 1 million *qrans* to merchants.[314] The endemic

---

311. NA, FO 371/15473.
312. See, e.g., *Jonub* 1371, year 1, 20 Ramazan 1329 (14/09/1911), p. 3.
313. Floor 2011 b, pp. 130ff, 190-92.
314. Government of Great Britain 1912, pp. 92-94.

feuding between competing chiefs as well as the raiding and robbing not only had its impact on the route trade took, but also on its volume. Trade via the Bushehr-Shiraz route declined from 1907 due to fighting between the Arab, Lor, and Qashqa'i tribes and among the chiefs of Kazerun, Daleki, Borazjan, and other places along the route. Because of the resulting insecurity, goods could not be shipped for months. The road problem was not made easier by the continuous high turnover of governor-generals of Fars. What made matters worse, was that the local khans along the trade route acted totally independent from the governor-general of Fars. Their constant fighting caused the road to be unsafe or entirely blocked for months, while they also exacted illegal imposts. Moreover, because of ill-treatment by the 'road guards' many muleteers refused to travel the trade route causing a shortage of transport capacity and thus higher rates.

In mid-1911 the major trade road became unsafe again due to troubles in Shiraz. Trade came to a total standstill, for although the road was open, goods could not be distributed from the market towns, due to anarchy in their hinterland. In October and November 1911, the Bushehr -Shiraz road was partially and then entirely closed. When it was opened again, robberies immediately took place. The situation of the road was so bad that in October 1910 the British warned Tehran that "unless order was restored within three months," they would themselves police the Bushehr-Isfahan road, hinting that a 1,200 local force under British officers would do that. The announcement of the formation of a Swedish-officered gendarmerie by the government of Persia in September 1911 gave Tehran some respite.

On 8 December 1912, two Swedish officers, Major Brandel and Captain Nystrom arrived in Bushehr to start recruiting; the governor had already brought together a number of recruits some time earlier. The Swedish officers were viewed with some suspicion because Daryabegi was Mokhber al-Saltaneh's (governor-general of Fars) army commander, while they were accompanied by three of his old Bushehr cronies, which led to unpleasantness between them and Movaqqar al-Dowleh, the then governor. They believed that the latter as friend of Qavam al-Molk was hostile to the Gendarmerie and any action taken by the governor, such as the arrest of the *kalantar*, was viewed with suspicion. Matters did not improve due to the arrival of a certain Mohammad Reza Veneziani, an Italian Jew and a convert to Islam, who would act as interpreter, and of Montaser al-Molk, commander of a detachment of the Malayer regiment. The latter had caused problems in Isfahan and it was made clear that he intended to make the governor's position untenable. The British Resident was afraid that the inexperienced Swedes would be drawn into the various local intrigues and hoped they would be guided by his advice.[315] By March 1913, Major Brandel had enlisted 200 men from the districts around Bushehr with whom he established control over the Bushehr-Shiraz road. However, there were problems with the gendaremrie force. According to the British, "The Persian officers are their great weakness; once away from their Swedish officers they are all apt to relapse into brigandage and rapine." This indicated that there was a problem with discipline, resulting in harsh repressive punitive methods. As a result, by March 1913, Major Brandel was left with 30-40 men that had originally come down with him from the north, because 168 gendarmes, Tangestanis, had resigned en masse after two of them had been stripped naked and flogged for some offense. This was not only a problem for Brandel, but also for

315. Administration Report 1912, pp. 26-27. Bushehris referred to gendarmes as *jandar*. Hamdidi 1380, p. 221.

the British, because in the south everybody believed that the gendarmerie was a British instrument and consequently, all its mistakes were blamed on the British.[316] Therefore, Cox, the British Resident, was very upset when he learnt that on 17 April 1913 Major Brandel, without having consulted anyone, intended to raid Borazjan and had asked the Khan of Ahmadi, an enemy of the Khan of Borazjan, to join forces with him. Given the political repercussion of seeing the gendarmerie taking sides Cox was able to convince Brandel to drop this plan.[317]

Because the levying of *rahdari* was suppressed and because the Fars governor paid the local Khans a subsidy to refrain from doing so, Shiraz proposed that the gendarmerie be replaced on the lower end of the Bushehr road by guards of the local Khans. The Residency approved the proposal and so did Tehran, but the problem was where would the money come from. The districts of Dashti and Dashtestan did not yield enough revenue and the governor of Bushehr lacked the force to do something about as was clear in 1913. The revenue of the Gulf Ports also did not yield enough surplus.[318] Therefore, the gendarmerie continued with its task and was quite effective in bringing security to the trade road in 1914, according to the British. "Rahdari had ceased, caravans and travelers have passed practically unmolested and credit must be given to the Gendarmerie for having brought about, for the moment, this satisfactory state of affairs."[319]

The national gendarmerie fell apart when it sided with anti-British nationalists and changed from an instrument of law and order into the military arm of a political movement. When in November 1915, a nationalist group in Shiraz took over the city and arrested all British citizens including the British consul, this action was taken with the support of the local gendarmerie. When Shiraz was retaken by Qavam al-Molk in April 1916, with the help of some dissenting gendarmes, the Fars gendarmerie ceased to be an effective force. Percy Sykes, who commanded the British-officered South Persian Rifles (SPR), took Shiraz in the fall of 1916, where he incorporated the remaining Fars Gendarmerie into the SPR.[320] After the Shiraz event the government of Persia dismissed most Swedish officers and only four remained. At the insistence of Russia the weakened Gendarmerie was renamed *Amniyeh* in the spring of 1916.[321]

After the British strike force had established security on the trade route in 1918, the SPR took over its role, after the British troops had withdrawn. For as long as the SPR guarded the roads there were hardly any robberies, but this changed when it was disbanded in 1921 and replaced by *tofangchi*s in the employ of provincial government. Because they were not paid regularly, it was feared that fleecing, oppressing and even robbing would resume. Some robberies were already reported and *rahdari* was levied on the lower part of the road. Also, the road was not being maintained and repaired and some parts were hardly passable for wheeled traffic.[322] The 160 SPR guards were replaced by 23 road guards and seven *sovar*s, whose number was insufficient; this led to robberies. Therefore, in March

316. Administration Report 1913, pp. 3-4, 22.
317. Administration Report 1913, p. 22.
318. Administration Report 1913, p. 32; Administration Report 1914, p. 10. For details, see Floor 2011 b, pp. 171-72.
319. Administration Report 1914, p. 9; Cronin 1996, p. 111; Hamidi 1378, pp. 93, 96.
320. On these events, see Floor 2011 b, pp. 163-70.
321. Ineichen 2002, p. 156.
322. See Floor 2011 b, p. 170.

1922, Reza Khan, the Minister of War then increased the number of guards to 130 on this road.[323] Reza Khan himself came to Bushehr in December 1922, but after his departure from Bushehr the levying of illegal taxes began again on the trade road; merchants protested, but were told to lodge their complaints in Shiraz. However, they knew that the governor-general was unable to take action against the levying or punish the Khans and thus, they did not even bother to do so. By the end of the year some repairs were made to the road in connection with the shah's arrival; the shah still had to walk considerable distances. But this did not mean that the road was passable.[324] Illegal taxes continued to be levied such as *navaqel* or municipal transportation taxes at 2 points on the road from all vehicles and animals, as well as *rahdari*, *`alafi*, etc.[325] There were improvements in 1923 when the *Amniyeh* under the energetic *Yavar* Malekzadeh, supported by Cossacks of the regular army, was able to curb the levying of illegal imposts. Guard posts of 4-5 men were established at intervals of 6-12 km and regulations were published stating that the force only took responsibility for stolen goods, when this occurred at these guarded halting stations. Indeed, the *Amniyeh* paid compensation for certain goods stolen or robbed, by imposing fines on villages near the site of the robberies. However, things fell apart in 1924, when the irregularly paid *Amniyeh* road guards were no longer employed, as they were only a little better than robbers. The entire mercantile and muleteer community was pleased, although here and there fees like *`alafi*, *rahdari*, etc. were still collected. However, this was a temporary military intervention, because in subsequent years the *Amniyeh* guards were guarding the road again.[326]

In 1926, there were attacks again on the trade road and in the hinterland, while there were also local disturbances between Angali and Shabankareh as well as between `Asalu, Galledar, Kangan and Gavbandi, which unsettled the tribes. The Tangestanis sent a group of soldiers back, who had come to arrest suspects on an attack in Bushehr.[327] Early in April 1927, Fathollah Beg and Heydar Beg and followers at Daleki began collecting illegal fees from muleteers and wounded two *Amniyeh* guards. On 17 April a combined force from Bushehr and Shiraz drove them into the hills. In June 1927, Fathollah Beg was said to have submitted himself to the commander at Borazjan and was made *kalantar* of Daleki. Heydar Beg and his men stayed in the hills.[328] Although the *Amniyeh* was reorganized on the trade road, it still was not efficient and security was only restored by the military force sent in November 1929.[329]

At the end of 1930, the *Amniyeh* 's strength was increased to 500. Moreover, all men were engaged locally at 6 *tumans*/month with a daily allowance of 2 *qrans*. They were paid regularly for 2 months when suddenly their wages were reduced to 5 *tumans*. Some guards started to beg and this became known. The *yavar* was arrested and dismissed from service. The *Amniyeh* officer at Ahram was also taken to Tehran for bribery and maltreatment

323. Administration Report 1922, p. 3; *Fars*, year 3, nr. 41, pp. 6-7, 13 (Shawwal 1337/1919).
324. Administration Report 1922, p. 5.
325. Administration Report 1923, p. 10; for details see p. 21.
326. Administration Report 1923, pp. 1, 7, 10, 15-16, 2; Idem, 1925, p. 14; Motahharizadeh 1383, pp. 182, 185-87 (docs. 121, 124, 127, 130).
327. Administration Report 1926, p. 4.
328. Administration Report 1927, p. 2.
329. Administration Report 1929, p. 4.

accusations.[330] Lt. `Ali Asghar was commanding officer of the *Amniyeh* till 26 September 1931, when he was replaced by *Yavar* Abu Torab Majd, who had served with the SPR.[331] In June 1931 the *Amniyeh* HQ and barracks were moved from Bushehr to Bahmani village, next to the telegraph office and housed in a commodious building known as Malek's house that was rented.[332] Despite the *Amniyeh*'s increased strength and performance, in 1932 there were monthly attacks on motor vehicles on the trade road. Some 15 *Amniyeh* guards and passengers were killed. During the famine of 1932, highwaymen warned lorry drivers to carry foodstuff but no *Amniyeh* guards, thus they would be safe as only the food would be taken. In the second half of the year security on the road improved, but during tribal migrations hold-ups still occurred, and a band of Chahkutahi tribesmen was still at large to make occasional attacks.[333] In the years thereafter, traveling on the trade road was safe, but off road there were bandits raiding villages and caravans and fighting with the *Amniyeh*.[334] In March 1939, the *Amniyeh* was incorporated into the military, which intended to improve the quality and effectiveness of this rural police service.[335] When in November 1940, the sub-governorships of Ahram, Khormuj and Kangan were abolished to save cost this caused security problems. Their duties were carried out by subordinates of the governor of Bushehr, who engaged in imposing exactions, which "raised the natural feeling of hostility among the tribes towards the authorities and there were serious classes between tribesmen and police and road guards. In December, 26 road guards were killed."[336]

The gendarmerie's task was to protect the roads and internal security. Therefore, it had jurisdiction over all rural areas except the tribal ones. They were a unit of 200 men, split into 6 platoons spread over the governorate in Bushehr, Ganaveh, Delam, Borazjan, Ahram and Kangan. The commanding officer in Bushehr was a major assisted by three captains. The platoons were supposed to be led by officers, but due to their shortage this was not possible; all officers, in fact, were army personnel. Recruitment for the gendarmerie was more popular than the police as it offered more opportunity for kick-backs (e.g. from smugglers). The gendarmerie was hated and feared by the rural population, because of its repressive behavior. Until they were merged with the military in 1945 or thereabouts, they fell under the Minister of the Interior. Due to the merger their number decreased from 200 to 50 in the governorate. This number formed a mobile armed police "to assist the Administration and Court in enforcing decrees and executing warrants." The move was welcomed by the rural population, as the Army did not have, as yet, the same reputation for extortion and repression.[337]

---

330. Administration Report 1930, p. 5.
331. Administration Report 1931, p. 3.
332. Administration Report 1931, p. 6.
333. Administration Report 1932, pp. 6, 9.
334. Administration Report 1936, p. 6.
335. Political Diaries, vol. 13, p. 285.
336. Administration Report 1940, p. 4.
337. NA, FO 371/15473. In 1945, the post of gendarmerie commander was held by *Sargord* Begleri, *Sargord* Badipur and *Sarvan* Sahami, who was also in charge at year's end. Administration Report 1945, p. 8.

The Army

Under the Al Mazkur Sheikhs, the defense of Bushehr was assured by local levies that the Sheikhs could call upon. These were mostly from the surrounding areas and in particular the Demukh Arabs who lived at Chahkutah. The Sheikh's militia served without pay. "They find their own arms and consist of working men attached to different trades, for we discovered the dyer by the black hue of his hands, the tinker by the smut on his face, the tailor by the shreds that adhered to him from his shipboard."[338] In 1816, according to Buckingham, the Sheikh of Bushehr had no standing troops and depending on his needs he called up sufficient men. The forces available to the governor varied with the period of the year and ranged from 100 to 1,000. These were mostly horsemen supplied by local chiefs, "without discipline or uniformity of dress, and furnishing their own arms and accoutrements at their own caprice."[339] The manner of mobilizing the Sheikh's levies was rather interesting.

> He mounted two large braziers of Pillau on a camel, and sent it to parade round the country. The rough pace of the animal put the ladles in motion, so that they struck the sides of the vessels at marked intervals, and produced a most sonorous clang. As it traversed Dashtistan, it collected the mob of every district; everyone had tasted the Arab hospitality of the sheikh, and every one crowded round the ancient standard of their chief, till his camel returned to him surrounded by a force sufficient to repel the threatened encroachments. In every new emergency the camel was again sent forth, and all was quiet again.[340]

In this way he could raise at least 6,000 men. Depending on the political situation the Al Mazkur Sheikhs could also directly appeal to Tangestani chiefs, if these were not threatening Bushehr itself.

Due to the conflict with Great Britain and the retreat of the British Residency to Khark, the shah had sent some regular troops to Bushehr, whom its governor, Sheikh Naser was supposed to pay. By 1841, the pay of the soldiers was in arrears, which led to an altercation. Sheikh Naser's Arab levies fired on the troops of which three were seriously wounded. In view of this, the commander of the regular troops withdrew his men from the town and wrote to Shiraz. Sheikh Naser tried to induce him to return and to forget about the whole affair. However, he was not willing to pay the large sum that the commander of the troops was asking.[341]

However, all this changed after the fall of the Al Mazkur 'dynasty' as the hereditary governors of Bushehr, because the central government placed a permanent garrison of about 300-400 soldiers (*sarbaz*) and an artillery section (*tup-khaneh*) with at least two

---

338. Morier 1812, p. 25; Ouseley 1819-23, vol. 1, p. 255.
339. Buckingham 1971, p. 351.
340. Morier 1812, p. 18; Sani` al-Dowleh 1294, vol. 1, p. 300.
341. NA, FO 248/99, Hennell to Sheil, 24/07/1841.

canons. The garrison was regularly relieved, usually after one year or so in the fall.[342] The relevance of the permanent garrison increased in policitical importance after the British attack on and occupation of Bushehr in 1856. After the British had returned control of the port to the Persian authorities, they again placed a permanent garrison in the town to defend it against any foreign (read, British) attack. In 1861, the garrison consisted of 600 men, who wore red jackets.[343]

The soldiers probably were housed in former sepoy barracks built by the British,[344] which were a virtual death trap. On 4 March 1874, at the request of the governor, the British Residency surgeon Waters together with the *hakim-bashi* and the commanding officer made a medical inspection of the barracks. The reason for this inspection was that of the 700 soldiers who had arrived in Bushehr in April 1873 some 300 had died since then due to intermittent fever.

> At the time of inspection 200 men were fit for service and were lined up, while I inspected their quarters. Each apartment has a space of about 1600 cubic feet, is badly ventilated, destitute of all comfort. In each, apart from some, one 2-9 persons were suffering from fever, supervened in many cases by dysentery. Many of the sick were prostrate and beyond recovery and were not cared for re medical care, food and clothing. In some rooms the evacuation from the sick and dead were sickening. At night some 25 men are huddled-the sick, dying and healthy together- in there despite the fact that there is not more than 130 square feet space. The commander would like to move the regiment to Kazeroon or Shiraz, this is advisable, but also the sick need to be moved from the contaminated atmosphere in which they lay. I was assured that care would be given to the sick and that none would be left behind if they marched away. In short, 200 men were unaffected, another 100 are throughout town, and 160 invalids; the latter in a state of squalor, dirt and misery that is indescribable. They are terribly overcrowded, badly fed, their bodies only partially covered and that with rags. The vicinity of the barracks is interspersed with ordure. The regiment must move to ensure that the living survive, but also for the town, as the barracks with its dysentery outbreak may contaminate the city.[345]

Although the British asked the Persian authorities to take appropriate action not much was actually done to improve the situation.

In 1878, an Azerbaijani regiment was based in Bushehr. The "most frequent active employment of the soldiers is operating against the peasantry to enforce payment of

---

342. NA, FO 248/150, Capt. Kemball, Resident to Sheil, 18/08/1852; Idem, Capt. Kemball, Resident to W.J. Thomson, charge d'affaires 15/09/1853 (relief force arrived on 8 September); Idem, Kemball to Thomson 15/12/1854 (On 21 November, a relief force of 400 infantry plus a detachment of artillery arrived); Heravi 1372, p. 72.

343. Brugsch 1863, vol. 2, p. 244.

344. Shepherd 1857, p. 131. NA, FO 248/146, Mirza Hasan Ali Khan, governor Bushehr to Mirza Ahmad *monshi* Residency, 12/09/1851 received; NA, FO 248/150, Capt. Kemball, Resident to Sheil, 18/08/1852.

345. NA, FO 248/300, Dr. Waters to Pelly, 04/03/1874; Idem, Pelly to Thomson, 04/03/1874.

revenues."[346] Their uniform was "a sort of blouse of blue cotton," and a head-dress of black sheepskin. However, they looked more as soldiers than they probably were given the condition of their arms. According to Geary, "They seemed half-drilled, and were very slouching and careless in all their movements. The arms of the guard, piled up in front of the tumbled-down barracks, were in a very bad order. The bayonets were covered with rust; and had apparently never been cleaned since the time that they were distributed to the men. I need not say that there were no breech-loaders. Some field-pieces were to be seen in a shed; they were quite uncared for, covered with the dirt of the last march."[347] Not only were these arms badly maintained they also were ineffective. They were described as being, "A row of old iron cannon of European manufacture, mostly ship guns, mounted on rickety carriages of very primitive construction." Moreover, it was more dangerous to stand behind them than in front of them.[348] This state of affairs did not change in the decades thereafter. In 1880, the port's garrison consisted of two companies of infantry and one battery of artillery. The infantry was still slovenly with old rusty percussion muskets. The artillery amounted to eight bronze field guns in a similar state of uncleanness. The garrison also had four mortars under cover in the barracks.[349] Ten years later the same situation existed. The garrison then consisted of 300-400 infantry and 50-60 gunners with some old and decrepit cannons lying near the governor's residence.[350] By 1900 the number of soldiers had further dwindled. The governor was supposed to have one batallion of regular soldiers and 50 artillery men, but he only had 200 infantry and 20 gunners plus a few mounted irregulars as a personal guard. Its artillery consisted of six breech-loading mule guns, and 25 muzzle-loading guns, but these were practically useless. As elsewhere in Persia, soldiers seldom received their pay and therefore, worked as laborers, barbers, etc.[351] The non-payment of wages sometimes led to demonstrations by the soldiers, such as in July 1897, when the garrison took sanctuary (*bast*) under the British Residency flagstaff and asked British help to get their pay that had not been paid for five months. An arrangement was made and the soldiers returned.[352] Following the establishment of a constitutional monarchy in 1906, like elsewhere in Persia, a local assembly was convened in Bushehr. However, the soldiers as usual were not paid. Although there was supposed to be a garrison of 400 there were perhaps only 100 in town. When in January 1908 the soldiers believed that their officers had received their pay and that they did not receive anything they took sanctuary (*bast*) with the local council and appealed to it. The officers told the council that indeed the soldiers were each owed 170 *qrans*, but they had not received any funds from Tehran. When the council established that this was true it telegraphed Tehran about the problem. The soldiers left the sanctuary, but in April 1908 they were ordered to return to their home in Chahar Mahall (Isfahan). It was further

---

346. Administration Report 1878-79, p. 30. Until June 1877, the Saravandi regiment was stationed in Bushehr. Sirjani 1361, p. 73.

347. Geary 1878, vol. 1, pp. 82-83.

348. Fogg 1885, p. 173.

349. Stack 1882, vol. 1, p. 26. In 1881, the Malayer regiment was garrisoned in Bushehr. Sirjani 1361, p. 164.

350. Curzon 1892, vol. 1, pp. 232-3.

351. Lorimer 1915, vol. 2, pp. 348. The military also had an arsenal near the town gate, which measured 1,086 square *zar*. Because it as well as the military stables were dilapidated the governor wanted to sell them. Hamidi 1378, pp. 18-19

352. Administration Report 1897-98, p. 6; the same happened in 1907, see Martin 2000, p. 198.

announced that henceforth the wages of all soldiers, officers, and government officials would be paid in the presence of the local council. This made much sense if the council had any money, which it did not, and thus, this regulation also remained a dead letter.[353]

Some enthusiasts even saw the need to organize a local militia to defend Bushehr, despite the presence of the local garrison. Forty guild members were trained by the captain of the *Persepolis* with sticks, because they had no arms. The governor gave the group the name of *Mojahedin fi sabil ollah* (fighters on the path of God), but despite this lofty name, many people were unhappy with this group; the government in Tehran likewise made its displeasure known. When the various *anjomans* dissolved in June 1908, the local militia also came to its end. In 1910, the town's garrison still consisted of 200 soldiers and about 20 artillery men.[354] What was new was that since 1885 the governor had the 600 ton gunboat *Persepolis* at his disposal (see below).

In January 1910 the governor formally had 500 infantry, 150 artillery men and 100 *sovars*, i.e. Tehran paid for that number of men. However, less than half were recruited and those that were, did little military services, mostly earning a living in the bazaar as a petty merchant or trade. The infantry, which had been recruited in Isfahan, had not been paid for seven months nor given their clothing allowance for three years. Thus, they took sanctuary in the British Residency. When negotiations were going on the soldiers announced that they had received a telegram that gave them permission to leave Bushehr pending settlement of their claim. They then left with the *Amir Panj*, their commander, in mid-August 1910. The artillerymen were not paid either and took sanctuary in the Customs House; the Daryabegi reached a compromise with them.[355]

The garrison remained in its dysfunctional state. The regiment that left in August 1910 due to non-payment of wages was only replaced in May 1911 by 300 soldiers under one officer. Their wages were already considerably in arrears and in Bushehr payment remained irregular, if paid at all. The governor barred them from making a living through petty trading as was usual for Persian soldiers. The result was that in early December 1910, 340 soldiers and 20 NCOs took *bast* under the British Residency flagstaff, because they had not been paid for 14 months. The governor was directly approached and grudgingly gave 7,000 *tumans* to the soldiers who left some 14 days later. Because the amount did not cover their claim, they next sat in the Turkish consulate, while also bothering the British Residency. On 30 May 1911, gunners arrived to relieve the previous detachment, but they were not happy with their situation and by September seven had departed. At the end of April 1911, 50 *sowars* arrived from Shiraz for duty, but they were not paid either and joined the soldiers in their *bast*.[356] As a result, there was no garrison in Bushehr thereafter. The only force at the governor's disposal was the 30 *tofangchis* of the police force. There still was one 8 cm and one 7 cm gun. In the absence of a garrison, the governor, if he

---

353. Political Diaries, vol. 3, pp. 41, 142.

354. Martin 2000, p. 186; Trade Report 1910-11, pp. 1-2. However, in December 1909, the local *anjoman* assessed the stength of the local garrison and found that there were 19 officers and 195 soldiers and about 20 gunners, while there should have been 400 infantry and 100 artillery. Political Diaries, vol. 3, p. 781.

355. Administration Report 1910, p. 14; Trade Report 1910-11, pp. 1-2; Hamidi 1378, p. 74.

356. Administration Report 1911, p. 14; see also Nura'i 1385, p. 29; Hamidi 1378, p. 165; Sa`adat 1390, p. 27.

needed soldiers used levies from Dashtestan.[357] Because in April 1911 it was expected that new troops would arrive, the problem was raised where to billet them, because there were no livable barracks, but no good solution was found apart from repairing the old Shekeri caravanserai 3 km outside of town.[358] The artillery squad (*tupchis*) used to number 26 men and 3 officers. The men were paid 30 *qrans*/month each and the officers respectively 90, 120 and 200 *qrans*/month. In April 1913, the governor in consulation with the director of Customs decided to reduce this number to 18 men at 60 qrans each under two petty officers (each 150 *qrans*) and one senior officer (at 250 *qrans*). The men were banned from engaging in petty trade.[359] As of 1914, the local garrison was paid by the Customs Department. The commanding officer received 950 *qrans* and the petty officers 120 *qrans* each. When the latter complained about their pay they were told they could resign, which they opted not to do. The Customs department supplied the Bulwardi soldiers with new rifles in exchange for their old ones.[360]

From August 1915 until 1925, the British-Indian regiment quartered in Bushehr provided security to the town. The British force consisted of 6 battalions of Indian infantry, a cavalry squadron and a mountain battery with crews, which were quartered in Bushehr, Rishahr and other places and required the takeover of most private houses in Rishahr.[361]

Modern Army Garrison

It was only in 1922 that once again regular Persian troops were stationed in Bushehr. However, neither in numbers nor in equipment were they as adequate to replace the British-Indian troops, the last of which departed in 1925. The troops in Bushehr were regularly inspected. *Sarhang* Seyfollah Khan from Shiraz stayed one month in the spring of 1923, and Mohammad Taqi Khan, the commander of the Shiraz Brigade came to inspect them in the fall of that year. As a result, discipline and moral of the troops seemed good. They were punctually paid, took themselves seriously and were taken seriously by others. The arrival of the modern army changed the situation locally and people perceived it that way. A small unit was sent to Delvar ostensibly to check smuggling, but in fact it served only to announce that the army intended to make its presence felt in future. It certainly had success of keeping the road safe, which benefited trade and people felt optimistic as they had not felt for a long time. The presence of the troops also had a tranquilizing effect on the hinterland. When Zayer Khedr Khan and his younger son were murdered in April 1923, there was no outbreak of violence and civil war as would have happened before. Immediately 100 men were sent from Bushehr to keep order and if possible arrest the killer. After one month they returned having kept things quiet in Tangestan. In November 1923 a force of about 600 infantry with four machine guns, 100 cavalry and 30 artillerists with two mountain guns arrived from Shiraz to begin collecting arrears in Dashti and Dashtestan, and possibly start disarming the tribes. Heavy rains in December prevented

357. Sadid al-Saltaneh 1371, p. 37; Administration Report 1912, p. 17; Hamidi 1378, p. 196 (even the two guns had been taken away at the orders from Shiraz).

358. Hamidi 1378, p. 228.

359. Political Diaries, vol. 5, p. 95.

360. Political Diaries, vol. 5, p. 389.

361. Mahrad 1979, p. 89

them from doing the latter. However, the chiefs paid two years arrears or 23,000 *tumans*. The troops returned mid-January 1924 and returned to Borazjan, leaving some 150 as a garrison at Khormuj, which later was withdrawn. As a result of this action, the power of the local Khans received a significant blow. In fact, a Khan's position depended on whether he did the Army's bidding or not. When Ghazanfar al-Saltaneh, the *zabet* of Borazjan, refused to pay higher taxes (10,000 instead of 6,000 *tumans*) he was immediately replaced by his nephew, Ata Khan. He, together with Sheikh Mohammad of Chahkutah was able to raise the required amount of money. As the Army needed more revenues for the swelling military, other Khans, when faced with the same choice, had no option but to comply and pay, even if this could result in their ruin. This policy pursued by the Military Command aimed to break up of the tribal system, which as a side effect also eliminated "what little there remains of British influence upon tribal affairs in the Bushire Hinterland."[362]

In January 1924, a ship with airplanes, parts and ammunition, accompanied by four French pilots, arrived at Bushehr. Because the weight of the goods road transport was considered too problematic it was decided to assemble the planes at Bushehr and fly them to Tehran, to which end a hangar was constructed close to the airfield. After a first failure due to engin trouble, finally one plane left on 1 March for Shiraz and a second one two weeks later.[363] Because of the military presence in the south, there was nothing like the tribal feuds and fights that marked the area in the past; the Khans had all been reduced to neutrality and insignificance. Only Sheikh Mohammad of Chahkutah seemed to have an 'in' with the military and as a result was the leading personality among the Khans. It was due to him that Akhgar was elected to the *Majles* against the wishes of Bushehr community and its officials.[364] This was but one of the many items that indicated that the army interfered with the civil administration of the country. According to the British Resident, the situation was worse, because "The vaunted honesty and disinterestedness of the military, so much insisted upon by Army Headquarters at Tehran, are a sham."[365] One of the aspects of the army interference in local affairs was the manner in which it recuited labor, temporary or for longer periods, particularly for road construction. The US vice-consul in Bushehr reported that in 1924, "troops scoured the city, seizing everybody with democratic justice, -tribal visitors, domestic servants and respectable merchants. Although a good profit was realized from the seizure of wealthier merchants, others were forced to labor under the hot sun for a bit of bread and water daily. Foreign business houses sent searchers to rescue their employees, and officials demanded the release of their servants. All who could do so escaped from the town, or found concealment in harems. The nomads, whose tents are pitched outside the city, took refuge in this consulate."[366]

In 1925, the army's chief of staff during his visit of Bushehr relieved *na'eb-sarhang* `Ali Asghar Khan of his command as *ra'is-e qoshun* and replaced him with *na'eb-sarhang* Mohammad Qoli Khan Asad (Sardar Bahador), who was educated in Great Britain, a

---

362. Administration Report 1923, p. 7; Administration Report 1924, p. 6; Political Diaries vol. 7, pp. 56 (the first local military commander of the new Persian army was *Yavar* `Abdol-Hoseyn Khan Qazvini, who was anti-British and suspected of having Bolshevik sympathies), 66-67.

363. Political Diaries vol. 7, pp. 213, 218, 223 (on 23 February 1924, there was a short strike by the French mission due to non-payment of their wages; they also complained that the planes were not new, but reconditioned ones).

364. Administration Report 1923, p. 11.

365. Administration Report 1924, p. 1.

366. Cronin 1997, p. 209.

pleasant fellow, and a brother of Sardar Asad Bakhtiyari. He investigated several cases of corruption and interference in civil matters. Two officers of the Dashti force were also relieved because of charges of extortion and blackmail. The former was reduced to *Yavar*; the other two were also suitably punished.[367] Due to a general outcry against excessive militarism, orders were given to return to the civil administration and the military governors of Delam, Dashti and Dashtestan were replaced by civilians.[368] Sardar Bahador remained garrison commander in 1926. "He distinguished himself by exacting heavy bribes from our old friend Haider Khan," in all 7,000 *tumans*. In June he arrested Heydar Khan's son, Allah Karam Khan on charge of having interfered with a telegraphic communication. The military court found him innocent.[369]

4.13: Estimated distribution of troops in the Bushehr Area (1923-28)

	1 Aug 1923	31 Dec 1923	31 Dec 1924	Dec 1925	Dec 1926	Dec 1927	Dec 1928
Bushehr	100	100	130	260	186	274	100
Borazjan	100	100	50	60	240	11	5
Behbahan	80-100	80-100	2,500*	300	110	-	n.a.
Delvar	10	10	3	3	8	-	n.a.
Lengeh	-	60	50	25	21	-	30
Dashti	-	400	30	50	...	-	n.a.
Delam	-	15	400*	15	3	-	n.a.
Choghadak	-	-	-	-	-	9	-
Daleki	-	-	-	-	-	11	20
Lawar	-	-	-	-	-	-	20
Shin	-	-	-	-	-	-	25
`Asalu	-	-	-	-	-	-	20

Source: Administration Report 1923; Administration Report 1924, p. 6; Administration Report 1925, p. 7; Administration Report 1926, p. 3; Administration Report 1927, p. 3; Administration Report 1928, p. 4.

* The higher number in this year is due to the Khuzestan campaign to suppress Sheikh Khaz`al's rebellion.

Na'eb-sarhang Mohammad Qoli Khan Asad was temporarily replaced by *Soltan* Esma`il Khan and left on 13 July. His successor on 22 August was *Yavar* Mohammad `Ali Mirza from Shiraz, who in turn was replaced in November by *Yavar* Amanollah Khan from Shiraz.[370] The latter was commanding officer till 19 August 1928, when he was relieved by *Yavar* Mohammad Taqi Khan Arab, who was in the SPR, and knew a little English.[371] He remained in function till 15 June 1929, when from 10 July 1929 onwards *Yavar* Qasem Khan Vajdani took over. He served until 24 May 1930. There after *Na`eb-sarhang* `Azimi

367. Administration Report 1925, p. 7.
368. Administration Report 1926, p. 2.
369. Administration Report 1926, p. 2.
370. Administration Report 1927, p. 2.
371. Administration Report 1928, p. 2.

commanded from 24 May till 30 June 1930 and then *Yavar* Mahmud Khan Parvin from 30 June till the end year. "He proved a source of trouble to his colleagues in reporting them to Tehran against them."[372] It would seem that the army in Bushehr was rather relaxed in the way its officers executed their daily tasks. In 1934, Mrs. Merritt-Hawkes observed that "Many officers, all unshaven, were sitting on the wooden benches covered with carpets, most of them eating sunflower and other seeds and spitting the shells out in a very untidy manner. ... Soldiers came to the tea-houses to ask their officers to sign reports, and several were instructed to do up the buttons of their coats or trousers. The number of quite decent Persians who go about with their trousers undone is astounding."[373]

Early in 1928, the garrison commander received the go-ahead to sell the military barracks, which were filthy and very unhealthy, and move the garrison to the village of Bahmani. However, as there were no good bids he could not move as there was no money to build new barracks.[374] The troops then moved to the large barracks at Bahmani that were once used by the British army of occupation. The army also maintained training establishments for army and *Amniyeh* recruits at Bushehr.[375] In 1936, the military bought land outside town to construct barracks large enough to accommodate a regiment. They commandeered all available labor, including those that were constructing the new textile mill, as well as building materials, so that not only the Bushehris in general were inconvenienced, but in particular Mr. Agar, who could not complete his factory nor could the Persian Wireless Telegraph Authorities complete their wireless set station. At the end of 1938, when the Bushehr garrison numbered 8,000 men, the barracks were almost complete and local garrison occupied them.[376]

4.14: Size of the Bushehr garrison (1933-40)

Year	Number	Source/Observations
1933	1,850	Administration Report 1934, p. 4
1934	1,800	Administration Report 1934, p. 4
1935	600	Administration Report 1935, p. 6
1936	600	Administration Report 1936, p. 5
1937	600	Administration Report 1937, p. 4
1938	8,000	Administration Report 1938, p. 4
1940	5,000	Administration Report 1940, p. 3; three companies of infantry and one MG detachment

In March 1939, the *Amniyeh* was merged with the Bushehr garrison. At that time, Bushehr recruits had to serve 8 months in the barracks and 16 months as road guards. At the end of 1940, some road guards were replaced by army recruits; in Bushehr 160 of them were used as such. This was done in the hope that the soldiers would be more

372. Administration Report 1929, p. 2; Administration Report 1930, p. 3; Administration Report 1931, p. 3.
373. Merritt-Hawkes 1935, p. 8.
374. Administration Report 1928, p. 4.
375. Administration Report 1932, p. 5.
376. Administration Report 1936, p. 5; Administration Report 1937, p. 4; Administration Report 1938, p. 4.

accommodating to peasants, whose complaints about road guards had grown very bitter. However, these hopes "were unfulfilled and peasants tired of complaints killed road guards whenever they were alone."[377]

At the time of Allied invasion of Persia in August 1941, Bushehr's army garrison consisted of three infantry companies and one MG section with 3 maxim guns. After Reza Shah's abdication, its strength was reduced by desertion, sp that by the end of 1941 it strength may have been 300 men in all. Until July 1941 some 800 recruits were sent to Shiraz for training, but thereafter no more recruits were selected, while no reinforcements were sent from Shiraz. In October 1941, Capt. Trabarsi, the garrison commander was arrested for corruption and replaced by Capt. Yusef Nuri.[378] In 1943, *Sargord* Nuri was replaced due to his interference with tribal matters for his own and the Khan's interests, and replaced by *Sargord* Bozorg Omid.[379]

4.15: List of the Bushehr garrison commanders (1924-1940)

Name	Duration	Observations	Source
Yavar `Ali Asghar Khan	?1924-1925		Admin Report 1924, p. 8
Na'eb-sarhang Mohammad Qoli Khan Asad (Sardar Bahador)	1925-13 July 1927	brother of Sardar Asad Bakhtiyari	Admin Report 1925, p. 7; Idem, 1927, p. 2
Soltan Esma`il Khan	13 July-22 August 1927	Pro tem	Admin Report 1927, p. 2
Yavar Mohammad `Ali Mirza	22 August-November 1927		Admin Report 1927, p. 2
Yavar Amanollah Khan	November 1927-19 August 1028		Admin Report 1927, p. 2; Idem, 1928, p. 2
Yavar Mohammad Taqi Khan Arab	19 August 1928-10 June 1929		Admin Report 1928, p. 2; Idem, 1929, p. 2
Yavar Qasem Khan Vajdani	10 July 1929- 24 May 1930		Admin Report 1929, p. 2; Idem 1930, p. 3
*Na`eb-sarhang* `Azimi	24 May-30 June 1930		Admin Report 1930, p. 3
Yavar Mahmud Khan Parvin	30 June 1930-	Lt. Mazaheri acting from mid June-24 August 1931	Admin Report 1930, p. 3; Idem, 1931, p. 3
Major Niknam	?-23 March 1936		Admin Report 1936, p. 5
Major Qotbi	23 March		Admin Report 1936, p. 5
Major Niknam	?- September 1937		Admin 1937, p. 4
Major Jalayer	September 1937-July 1938		Admin 1937, p. 4

377. Administration Report 1939, p. 3; Administration Report 1940, p. 3-4.

378. Administration Report 1941, p. 8.

379. Administration Report 1943, p. 10.

Name	Duration	Observations	Source
Lt. Col. Karimi	July 1938-22 February 1939		Admin 1938, p. 4; Idem, 1939, p. 3
Captain Yusof Nuri	22 February 1939- mid 1940		Admin 1939, p. 3
Captain Tabarsi	July 1940-October 1941		Admin 1940, p. 4; Political Diaries, vol. 14, p. 164
Captain Yusof Nuri	October 1941- ? 1943		Administration Report 1941, pp. 8; Administration Report 1943, p.10.
Sargord Bozorg Omid	? 1943		Administration Report 1943, p.10
Sargord Pakravan	?1944- 10 April 1945		Administration Report 1945, p. 8
Sargord Arasteh	10 April 1945-May 1947		Administration Report 1945, p. 8
Sargord Namju	13 May 1947-		Political Diaries, vol. 17, p. 427

The army suffered a major setback when it surrendered to tribal forces in October 1946, as a result of which no army units or gendarmerie were present in Bushehr after that date. Although the conflict was the tribes was resolved, it was only in February 1947, that *Sargord* Arasteh returned charged with the responsibility of collecting his defeated army. On 13 May 1947, the new Bushehr garrison of about 500 men arrived under *Sargord* Namju. Reception in town was lukewarm, although there some flags were shown and two sheep were killed.[380] By 1947, the garrison of the governorate consisted of an understrength *gerdan* or battalion of about 600 men (normally some 800 men) of mostly conscripts. Only the officers and NCO's above the rank of lance-corporal (*sar-jowqeh*) were professional career soldiers. It included a signal section, but the only artillery it had were two 12-pounders, mainly used for firing salutes. It further had four 3-ton trucks, two jeeps and 3-4 motor cycles. The battalion was usually commanded by a major, and 1st lieutenants being company commanders. The bulk of these troops were stationed in Bushehr, with small garrisons of one platoon-strength in Borazjan and Khormuj. These were regularly recycled. The Bushehr garrison was part of a brigade, which had its HQ at Kazerun. In contrast to the 1920s, in case of need for military intervention, the governor informed the provincial governor (*ostandar*). He then made the decision to use military force and orders were issued by the HQ of the Fars Division in Shiraz. Only in case of an emergency could the governor in consultation with the local commander decide to use military force.

The number of troops varied per season. During the hot season most conscripts were being trained in the Kazerun area. However, care was taken that always some 200 men remained in Bushehr, equal to three bare-bone rifle companies and one machine gun company, with three 0.5 machine guns of Czech make. The soldiers were armed with Czech modern rifles, which were kept in fair condition. However, ammunition was

380. Political Diaries, vol. 17, pp. 351, 375, 427.

in short supply, so that during training conscripts never actually fired a gun. The rest of the equipment was not in good condition. The troops were housed in barracks at the junction of the Bushehr-Shiraz and Bushehr-Bahmani roads. These were built in 1937 and later in 1947 surrounded by a strong wall with turrets. The costs were met by a fine imposed by the government on the people of Dashtestan and Tangestan after a pacification operation in July 1947.[381]

Disarmament Campaign

As soon as Reza Khan became Minister of Defense his aim was to bring the country under the control of the central government. One way of doing that was to make unruly elements pay taxes as well as to disarm them. It would seem that a first attempt to do so was considered in 1923. At the end of that year a force of about 600 infantry with four machine guns, 100 cavalry and 30 artillery men with two mountain guns arrived from Shiraz to begin collecting revenue in Dashti and Dashtestan, and possibly start disarming the tribes. Heavy rains in December prevented them from doing this.[382] Because Reza Khan was occupied up north, the centralizing of power and subduing the tribes was spasmodic in the south; no force was used to disarm tribes, nevertheless, in 1925, 10,000 rifles were handed in.[383] Early in 1924, Tehran again sent orders to disarm the people of the districts of Dashti and Hayat Da'ud, but Mirza Taqi Khan, the head of the Cossacks advised not to do so and the order was withdrawn. The Khan of Dashti promising to pay half of the arrears, which led to the withdrawal of the troops, only a few pickets remained behind. In May 1924, a force was sent to Dashti to collect 12,000 *tumans*. The Khan of Rig paid 6,000 *tumans* and promised to pay another 6,000 over the next 6 years.[384] During July-September 1925 attempts were made to disarm the country around Bushehr; some 1,000 old rifles and 10,000 cartridges were collected from the Khans of Hayat Da'ud, Rudhilleh and Angali, but it is certain that the tribesmen kept their best weapons. In Dashti, Dashtestan and Tangestan the tribesmen refused to hand over arms; as the *ra'is-e qoshun* did not have enough troops he let it go.[385]

In October 1926 disarming operations started in Dashti and Dashestan. *Na'eb-sarhang* Atapur with 240 men went to Borazjan, and in December *Na`eb-sarhang* Mohammad Qoli Khan with 50 more men and two machine guns followed. The divisional chief of staff came down from Shiraz with a large force. A force of 250 soldiers was stationed in Dashti as of December 1926, but the Khans were still hesitating to hand over arms and had only paid 1,000 *tumans* so far. A larger force under the chief staff of 400 men plus Qashqa'i levies went to the hinterland of Taheri.[386] In March 1927, it was said that the chief of staff of the Fars division had arranged for the surrender of 600 rifles with the Dashti chiefs in exchange for the licensing of the remaining rifles and the payment of 2-years tax arrears. He also claimed to have collected 2,000 rifles from districts through

381. NA, FO 371/15473.
382. Administration Report 1923, p. 7
383. Administration Report 1925, p. 1.
384. Administration Report 1924, p. 6.
385. Administration Report 1925, p. 8.
386. Administration Report 1926, pp. 3, 10.

which he had marched. According to the Resident, he appeared to have achieved little, however, and the rifles were all old ones.[387]

In November 1929, 1,500 of the Naderi regiment with guns and two armored cars arrived in the district commanded by *Sarhang* Ahmad Khan Mo'ini to disarm the population of Dashti, Dashtestan and Tangestan. In December, 400 more troops arrived to reinforce the Bushehr garrison that grew to about 760 men. By the end of December the Expedition Force had collected 2,000 rifles from Borazjan and Tangestan. Half of Tangestan and Dashti remained to be done. The Dashtis, who could field 8,000 men, were preparing to resist, but no further action was undertaken.[388] The disarming campaign took place again from December 1929 to March 1930 and allegedly 9,000 rifles were collected in Dashti and Dashtestan, though in reality probably much less. When the Naderi regiment marched past Bushehr it was welcomed by the population with shouts of 'Long Live the Shah'.[389]

The disarmament campaign continued. In March-April 1931, the Kerman regiment collected 1,200 rifles in Shibkuh and then came to Dashti where 341 rifles were collected; later the military collected 100 rifles and two machine guns, which the tribesmen had captured from the military in the previous year. Assisted by Reza Qoli, the Khan of Ziyarat, the military disarmed most men in Dashti and Dashtestan. In Baluk (Dashti) Sheikh `Abdol-Rasul, the son of the late Sheikh Hoseyn of Chahkutah tried avoiding the surrender of his arms and was summoned to Bushehr. His *nakhoda* was flogged until he revealed where 80 rifles were hidden in the Sheikh's house, the latter was sent to Tehran. Ra'is Asad, a rebel, captured Baghak in September, but he was chased away. On 21 September 1931, he killed an *Amniyeh* guard and wounded another after which he occupied Khaviz and expelled all Shirazis, "who were preparing lime-juice for export." He surrendered in October after several encounters with the military. In October an *Amniyeh* detachment was besieged in Oli village and was only allowed to leave after intercession of Sayyed Bahmiyar by promising to stop disarming people. In November 1931, 800 soldiers arrived at Borazjan to operate in Dashti and Tangestan. They were able to collect 900 mostly old rifles in Dashti. During the last week of December 1931 a group of rebels holding out in Dashti's inaccessible hills attacked the military and killed about 40 of them.[390] Although the disarmament campaign continued, it met with little success, but according to a recent order, a smuggler could be shot on sight or if captured executed. Therefore, few were ever caught with arms.[391] In 1933, the disarmament drive continued; more than 400 rifles were confiscated. As a result, the Bushehr hinterland was mostly quiet, although the beginning of the census led to a few attacks in Dashti and Tangestan and one or two people were killed. In 1934, 300 rifles were collected without any problem.[392]

In 1935, due to the ongoing disarmament, many bandits fled into the mountains, some refusing to disarm, while others fled to escape punishment for their misdeeds. They raided villages and caravans, some people were killed and they took away herds

---

387. Administration Report 1927, p. 2.
388. Administration Report 1929, p. 4.
389. Administration Report 1930, p. 5; Administration Report 1930, 6; Political Diaries, vol. 9, pp. 3, 34, 74, 108.
390. Administration Report 1931, p. 6.
391. Administration Report 1932, p. 6.
392. Administration Report 1933, pp. 4-5; Administration Report 1934, p. 5.

and grain. Haji Mohammad of Abada (a Tangestan village) was one of the conspicuous bandits. To reduce tension the military allowed one hundred of them to return to Dashti and Tangestan, with safe-passage, on condition that they disarmed. Haji Mohammad was killed, while his son and brother were killed by some men in October 1935. Others were decoyed by their enemies into their villages and killed at the instigation of the military. At year's end, only Gholam Hoseyn Karam of Tangestan and `Abdol-Hoseyn of Kaki (90 km south of Bushehr) were still at large and they raided a village or grain caravan going from one village to another.[393]

The disarmament campaign continued in 1936. "On mere suspicion of their being in possession of arms, the peasants were flogged, heavily find and imprisoned." Therefore 50 Tangestanis came to Bushehr to complain about the military authorities and their methods. However, the military did not change their behavior and on the least suspicion, flogged peasants to get information on where guns were hidden. This method did not work well, because in 1937 only 80 rifles and some ammunition were confiscated and in 1938 a mere 100 rifles and 2,000 cartridges. In 1938, there were still outlaws in the mountains despite despite their decimation by the military and the removal of all tribal chiefs.[394] Therefore, one may well raise the question whether the disarmament campaign had yielded the desired result. According to the British, there was little result to show for it. In fact, it was believed that in Tangestan more rifles were captured by Tangestanis from road guards than vice versa. Also, the Dashti chief `Ali Esma`il caused many problems and with his 300 man force, he several times bested government troops sent against him. Finally diplomacy was tried, but even here he bested the officials, for although he had to surrender 50 old rifles he seems to have captured more than 50 from troops sent against him.[395] The campaign languished during the 1940-46 period due to the insecurity in Dashti and Tangestan, which the army was not able to suppress until the 1950s.

Compulsory conscription

In April 1923, the *Majles* abolished the old recruitment system and adopted a new law imposing universal and compulsory conscription for young men to serve in the military (*qanun-e khedmat-e nezami-ye ejbari*). The conscription law ordered universal military service for 2 years for all males of 21. Exempt were married men or sole breadwinners, also university educated men, while those who had completed secondary school only had to serve one year. Although adopted in 1923, the law was only put into effect in November 1926 due to strong opposition by the olama against the very concept of conscription.[396] The law was amended in 1931 stipulating that University trained men also had to serve, be it for one year only and those with secondary school education for 1.5 years. In addition, conscripts might be called up for refresher training within the next ten years after completion of their military service. Apart from bribery to get exemption, not every man was called when he was 21 and sometimes this might happen some five

393. Administration Report 1935, p. 7.

394. Administration Report 1936, p. 6; Administration Report 1937, p. 4; Administration Report 1938, pp. 4-5.

395. Administration Report 1940, p. 4.

396. Floor 1998 b, pp. 365-66.

years later. This was, of course, very convenient for men in the mid- or late twenties, who were starting a career.[397]

The olama still had not given up their opposition, because in 1927, the olama of Isfahan and Shiraz sent telegram to their colleagues in Bushehr requesting them to close the bazaars in protest against conscription; they complied, be it with no result.[398] The recruitment was carried out by a special military commission in cooperation with the civil administration, which was established in Bushehr. Usually, the conscripts were trained with the Bushehr battalion and only served in Fars.[399] On 28 January 1928, *Na'eb-sarhang* Ahmad Khan Akhgar arrived in Bushehr to open a recruiting depot for compulsory military service. The newly opened Census Department of Bushehr had been working to prepare lists of eligible men and youths of 21-24. These were called up and those medically fit were inspected by the conscription board consisting of the governor as president, and/or his assistant as President of the Municipality, Dr. Bahrami or his assistant (a few years later by a military and a local doctor) and about half a dozen leading citizens. About 40% of the youths were found unfit and 40% were granted exemption (e.g. they were breadwinners), and a few of the fit ones were actually recruited. Bribes were given to be exempted. This was reported and a doctor was summoned to Tehran. Conscription was unpopular and leading citizens sent telegrams to Tehran asking exemption from army service and to be used instead for the Navy. Tempers ran so high that the governor feared the occurrence of demonstrations like those that had taken place in Shiraz.[400] Given the outcry against compulsory recruitment and the outbreak of the Qashqa'i rebellion, Tehran sent orders to close the recruiting depot in Bushehr on 17 March 1929. As a result, the recruiting officer returned to Shiraz.[401]

However, as soon as the tribal revolt had been put down, Tehran sent *Yavar* Khanlar Khan Afshar as recruiting officer to Bushehr. He arrived at the end of October 1930 and one month later announced the recruiting depot opening. As noted above, concomitant with the start of the conscription drive was the establishment of the census department (*sejell-e ahval*), "the chief use of which is in connection with compulsory military service." In 1929, Aqa-ye Mofazzal was in charge of that office,[402] who was replaced by `Abdol-Majid Khan in December 1929.[403] Dr. Bahrami refused to join the recruiting committee that consisted of the governor or his assistant, the commander or his assistant, the recruiting officer, the president of the municipality, civil and military physicians, the local judge, the director of revenue, the chief of police and four leading merchants. Lists with the names of 18,000 men in the age group of 21-24 years were posted. Some 200 men were exempted as breadwinners, many others fled. Only 57 were recruited and taken for training to the barracks, while 76 who volunteered for the navy were exempted from military service. In spite of the low number recruited, conscription remained unpopular

397. NA, FO 371/15473

398. Administration Report 1927, p. 3.

399. NA, FO 371/15473.

400. Administration Report 1928, p. 3.

401. Administration Report 1929, p. 4.

402. Administration Report 1929, p. 3. The police also collected population data, be it mainly on migration. Administration Report 1934, p. 4.

403. Administration Report 1930, p. 4.

and efforts were made to exempt the youths of the Gulf Ports.[404] `Abdol-Majid Khan Farrokhi (the only Sunni official) remained chief of the census department till 20 July 1931, when he was replaced by Qavami. The former was "a man of literary tastes and his good treatment was appreciated by the people."[405] The recruiting office was closed on 9 July 1931, when *Yavar* Khanlar Khan left for Tehran. The recruitment process in Bushehr had shown that its young men were "notoriously unhealthy." Consequently, many exemptions were given due to ill-health and in many cases the exemptions were justified. However, quite a few were obtained through bribery, while there were also some desertions.[406] In January 1932, the recruitment office was reopened, and new examinations took place. About 60% of the youths were exempted due to bad health and other reasons.[407] In 1933, census operations were started at Dashti and Ahram and Khark. Its purpose was not to implement a normal census but to determine how many young men were available for military service. It was, therefore, no surprise that as of 1935 branches of the recruitment bureau were also opened in the district. The beginning of the census was not without incidents because there were a few attacks in Dashti and Tangestan and 1-2 people were killed.[408] The conscription office was opened in August 1934. The census was continued in Bushehr and its sub-ports in June 1934 by undertaking a house-to-house inspection. Although the manner of the census looked as if the authorities were very strict, in fact they were less rigorous in determining eligibility for conscription than before. Many exemptions were announced, but even so nobody was recruited as the barracks were full. Occasionally groups of 50 men were taken when similar groups left the barracks after having completed their 2-year service. In December 1934 the conscription bureau moved to the Naval Bureau to see that those constripted from coastal towns served in the navy.[409] In 1935 the conscription bureau was reopened, but this time also with branches in the district. The conscription committee examined the exemption documents and sent 300 men to Khorramshahr to serve in the Navy, of whom 50 were sent back as being unfit for service.[410] In 1936, the conscription bureau selected 400 men, 200 of which were sent to Khorramshahr to serve in the Navy and 200 were sent to the barracks in Bushehr.[411] In 1937, "The recruiting bureau re-opened with its usual members, the Governor as President, a Doctor from the Military Department, and one from the Persian Naval Department, the Imam-i-Jumah, two local merchants, and the Head of the Police Department. Branches were also re-opened in the districts." In total, 1,212 youths were selected of which 370 were sent to Khorramshahr to join the navy, the rest were sent to the barracks at Bushehr.[412] In 1938, the Recruting office was much stricter than ever before in its selection of recruits. Few exemptions were allowed, while 1,950 men were recruited, 500 went to Shiraz, 180 to Khorramshahr to serve in the Navy, and the remainder was sent to the local barracks in Bushehr.[413] In 1939, the

404. Administration Report 1930, p.5
405. Administration Report 1931, p. 5; Administration Report 1930, p. 4(He was also a poet).
406. Administration Report 1931, p. 6.
407. Administration Report 1932, p. 5.
408. Administration Report 1933, pp. 3, 5.
409. Administration Report 1934, pp. 3-4.
410. Administration Report 1935, p. 6.
411. Administration Report 1936, p. 5.
412. Administration Report 1937, pp. 3-4.
413. Administration Report 1938, p. 4.

recruiting office was strict again; it selected 1,820 conscripts, of which 420 were sent to Shiraz, the rest to the barracks in Bushehr. Moreover, some 450 old conscripts were called up for a refresher course of one month. For the first time an effort was made to distinguish between educated and uneducated recruits. The trend was to send educated men for training to Shiraz.[414] In 1940, the same strict policy was applied. As many as 1,500 recruits were selected, most of whom were sent to Shiraz. Also, old recruits were called up for a refresher course.[415] This system continued to be applied thereafter, be it with less success (less recruits were available from insecure areas) and more corruption.

The Navy

In 1865, Naser al-Din Shah wanted to acquire a number of naval vessels to exercise better control over Persia's coastal waters. He intended to crew the vessels with Arab and Indian sailors under British officers. However, Great Britain opposed the plan, because it believed that the Shah's real objective was to occupy Bahrain. Although rebuffed, the Shah did not give up and sent somebody to Europe who allegedly bought a sail ship, which was expected to arrive in Bushehr in the fall of 1868. However, the purchase may never have taken place, because no such vessel arrived in Bushehr, and thus, the dream of creating a Persian navy evaporated.[416]

To increase customs revenues, it was suggested to Naser al-Din Shah that this might be achieved by firm control over the ports with the help of naval ships. Therefore, in 1883 the Shah decided to buy each year a naval vessel and thus, slowly build a flotilla that would be able to achieve the desired objective. The tender for the first two ships was won by a German firm; the cost was £32,000. As a result, as of 1885, Persia had the beginnings of a navy in the guise of the German-built 600 ton gunboat *Persepolis* and a smaller (36 tons) riverboat, the *Susa*, which was sent to Mohammerah. The ship arrived in May 1885 with a German crew. Thereafter, it was commanded by four German officers and 40 Arab sailors, and everything on board was neat and well maintained. Its armament consisted of four 7.5 Krupp guns and two old Gardner machine guns.[417] Later, the German officers were replaced by Persians.[418] Initially, the vessel seems not have been used at all, because in 1890 Harry de Windt commented, "she has never moved since her arrival. Her bottom is now covered with coral and shells, her screw hard and fast, while the four steel Krupp guns which she mounts are rusty and useless."[419] The reasons for the vessel's neglect were an inexperienced local crew, absence of docking facilities, and lack of funds to pay for its costly upkeep; the customs farmers were not interested in paying for the vessel's use and maintenance, because they wanted to increase their revenues by preventing smuggling. Therefore, the governors of Bushehr started to use the *Persepolis* as a means of coercion

414. Administration Report 1939, p. 3.

415. Administration Report 1940, p. 3.

416. Habibi and Vothuqi 1387, pp. 283-84, doc. 173 (24 March 1868).

417. Lorimer 348, 1465; Gordon 1906, p. 266; Hamidi 1378, pp. 111-13, 121-22 (details about purchased cannons). It was a 600 tons screw steamer with 5 small breech-loading guns; its speed was 10 knots. *The Naval Annual* 1900, p. 295. In 1918, it was repaired at Bombay. IOR/L/PS/11/134, P. 1166/1918. Locally, the vessel was called *Pachampelis*. Hamidi 1380, pp. 184, 188.

418. Hamidi 1378, pp. 113, 163, 240-41.

419. De Windt 1891, pp. 218-19 (its purchase price was £30,000); Sadid al-Saltaneh 1371, p. 37.

First Iranian captain of the Persepolis

enforce their rule. In January 1903, the government of Persia reverted to its previous policy, when it bought the Belgian yacht *Selika* to be used by the Customs Department, which was renamed *Mozaffar* (see above). In 1906, four sea-going launches built at the Royal Indian Marine Dockyard were delivered to the government of Persia, which were to be used by the Customs department to interdict smuggling, in particular arms smuggling. However, "owing to the general chaos and dearth of funds, little use has as yet been made of them."[420] Thus, the Customs Department managed the naval ships *Persepolis* and *Mozaffar* plus the five Customs launches bought in Bombay in 1906. These measured 22 meters and 5.5 meters wide, drawing 2.1 meters of water, with a speed of 9 knots, but by 1920 only 6 knots. Their purchase price was 60,000 rupees or 21,000 *tumans* each. Their names were: *Gilan*, *Tehran*, *Khorasan*, *Azerbaijan*, and *Mazandaran*. In about 1918, the *Tehran* was sold, while the *Khorasan* was out service.[421] By 1922, the *Persepolis* only had a skeleteton crew, who, because they were not paid, sold the ship's fittings to make ends meet. "The denuned hulks could not be budged."[422]

Although Bushehr was Persia's first naval base, where at the end of the nineteenth century the first Persian gun-boats were stationed, the modern navy that came into being during the reign of Reza Shah Pahlavi was no longer based at Bushehr. Naval HQ were at Mohammerah/Khorramshahr, where in 1931 the new 17.6 meters long launch *Chalchilla* bought from Germany at 20,000 *tumans* was taken after it arrived at Bushehr under its own steam coming from Port Said. Captains Ebrahim and Salem Pio had gone there to collect it. On 31 August 1931, the *Chalchila* left Bushehr for Mohammerah. In September 1931, 58 conscripts from Bushehr and a larger number from Mohammerah

420. Administration Report 1906-07, p. 12.
421. Sadid al-Saltaneh 1342, p. 647; Sa`adat 1390, p. 28.
422. Hall 1947, p. 194.

An Iranian warship

were sent to Italy for training to serve in the Persian navy. It was reported that about 250 Persian officers and men were in Italy. In that year, two sloops and four patrol boats were launched at Palermo for Persia in the presence of the crown prince and the Court Minister Teymurtash. The vessels were expected to arrive in Persia in the fall of 1932 with a mission of 15 Italian officers on board.[423] The Persian sailors did not want to serve voluntarily in the navy. Therefore, they did not re-enlist when their compulsory period had expired. This despite the fact that they received 15 *tumans* per month, as well as food and clothing, whereas army conscripts were only paid 7.5 rials per month. However, at the beginning of 1933 naval pay was three months overdue.[424]

The purchase of the naval vessels in Italy had two objectives. First, Reza Shah wanted to establish Persian control over the littoral and have a Persian presence in the Persian Gulf as an expression of its sovereignty and of self-assertion vis-a-vis Great Britain. Secondly, given the new economic policy with state monopolies for the import and trade of a range of products (see above), there was a need to prevent smuggling of both the goods concerned as well as arms. Failure to do so might reduce the impact of the government's objectives, the more so since the coast between Bushehr and Lengeh was the favorite landing area of the smugglers.[425]

On 29 October 1932, the ships ordered from Italy arrived at Bushehr, to wit: two sloops of 950 tons, called *Babr* (Tiger) and *Palang* (Panther) and 4 coastal boats of 320 tons, called *Shahbaz* (Falcon), *Shahrokh* (Condor), *Karkas* (Vulture) and *Simorgh* (Phoenix).

423. Administration Report 1930, p. 5; Administration Report 1931, p. 7.
424. Administration Report 1933, p. 5.
425. Burrell 1972, p. 185f.

They were in time for the arrival of Reza Shah on 3 November 1932. The Italian officers were disappointed as Persia was completely different from what they had been told. They accompanied Reza Shah to Mohammerah, where they depended on the Anglo-Persian Oil Company for material comforts such as food and drinks. The new vessels made patrols up and down the coast a few times, singly and in a flotilla. Soon after their arrival all Customs vessels were made over to the Navy HQ at Mohammerah. The naval preventive campaign hurt the smugglers, who strongly complained about the naval operations.[426]

With the availability of the new ships, the naval office at Bushehr under Major Gholam `Ali Khan Bayandor continued cruising along the coast, capturing sailing boats and reducing smuggling. The crews of the sail boats were armed and invariably put up a strong defense. In 1933, the *Karkas* was the only vessel that had not captured a smuggling dhow. To make up for this lack of success, when it moored at Bushehr, its crew searched many houses, which greatly upset the local authorities, who complained to Tehran. Another incident in that same year was when Capt. Pishva was summoned to Tehran, because one of the smugglers said that the Captain had taken money from him. Nevertheless, the new naval vessels had considerable success in the prevention of smuggling (see Table 4.16).[427] Because of his successful campaign against smugglers, which he continued, Bayandor was promoted to Lt. Colonel. He remained in office at least until 1940, when he was promoted to Rear-Admiral. In 1934, a total of 12 dhows were taken, of which several were burnt, while others were used for naval purposes. In addition, the *Shahrokh* captured the rebel Sheikh Mohammad b. Ahmad Khalfan of Teben.[428] The *Babr* and *Palang* went to dry-dock in Bombay in January 1935 and returned in March 1935.[429] However, as of 1936, Persian ships went to the dry dock in Khorramshahr.[430] In May 1935, the *Palang* went to Basidu and Henjam and in each a small naval post of 12 men under a petty officer was established.[431]

The Persian naval presence and its activities in the Persian Gulf led to problems with the British Admirality. Persia wanted to have the right to search both Persian and Arab vessels, just like the British Navy, which the British Admiralty and the government of India were loath to grant. Despite diplomatic maneuvering the two sides failed to reach an agreement, but fortunately incidents were small in number.[432]

4.16: Results of naval anti-smuggling activities 1933-1938

Ship/year	1933	1934	1935	1936	1937	1938
Babr	1 dhow	3 dhows/1320 packs	Dry dock	5 dhows/ empty	2 dhows/600 packs	-

426. Administration Report 1932, p. 5.
427. Administration Report 1933, p. 5.
428. Administration Report 1934, p. 6; Administration Report 1940, p. 4.
429. Administration Report 1934, p. 6; Administration Report 1935, p. 6.
430. Administration Report 1936, p. 6.
431. Administration Report 1935, p. 6.
432. Burrell 1972, pp. 185-87.

Ship/year	1933	1934	1935	1936	1937	1938
Shahrokh	2 dhows	2 dhows/90 packs	Dry dock	3 dhows/171 packs + crew of 2 dhows	-	2 dhows/500 packs
Shahbaz	2 dhows	3 dhows/600 packs	7 dhows/605 packs	-	-	-
Palang	6 dhows	1 dhows/500 packs	1dhow/ goods/cash; 10 boxes tea, 20 bags sugar, cash	-	-	5 dhows/800 packs
Karkas	-	3 dhows/440 packs	-	-	1 dhow/500 packs	-
Simorgh	2 dhows	-	-	-	-	-
Niru, a tug	-	-	-	-	-	4 dhows/350 packs

Source: Administration Report 1933, p. 5; Administration Report 1934, p. 6; Administration Report 1935, p. 6; Administration Report 1936, p. 6; Administration Report 1937, p. 4; Administration Report 1938, p. 4.

The Bushehr naval office continued the suppression of smuggling. Gunboats came regularly to Bushehr, while in 1940, efforts were made to register all local sailing craft.[433] The naval office was closed in December 1941 and management of the port was handed to the Customs Department.[434] In 1947, as a sign of Bushehr's reduced economic importance as well as a reduction in smuggling activities, only a lieutenant was in charge of Bushehr's naval office. This officer was responsible for all port installations, recording arrival and departure of all vessels, maintenance of the lighthouse and for local naval recruitment.[435]

The Telegraph

In 1863, the Indo-European Telegraph Department (IETD) started operations in Persia, following the Anglo-Persian agreement of 6 February 1863.[436] As a result, a telegraph cable (connecting Jask-Bushehr) had been laid in a channel north of Henjam, where from 1869 to 1881 there had been an IETD station.[437] Initially, the IETD telegraph station and offices were at Rishahr, but in 1876 these were moved to Bahmani, at 5 km

433. Administration Report 1936, p. 6; Administration Report 1940, p. 4.
434. Administration Report 1941, pp. 9.
435. NA, FO 371/15473.
436. On the establishment of the telegraph, its difficulties, operation, network and development, see Rubin 1999; Lorimer 1915, vol. 2, pp. 2404-38; Goldsmid 1874.
437. Lorimer 1915, vol. 2, p. 2419. In 1872, linking Henjam with Bandar Abbas had been discussed, but the Persian side could not make up its mind whether it wanted the telegraph connection. Habibi and Vothuqi 1387, p. 329, doc. 261 (01/02/1873)

A drawing of the Indo-European Telegraph building

from Bushehr, where the IETD rented five bungalows belonging to the heirs of Haji `Ali Akbar Haji Abu'l-Qasem. It was a series of six fine buildings, with a club-room, garden, and lawn-tennis court. Just below it the wires ran into the sea.[438] By 1920, the IETD employed some 15 staff.[439] A wireless telegraphy was not yet installed, although this started in 1914. There was a temporary one at Rishahr, but it had some troubles with the transmitting station. Despite the novelty, "messages have been sent on behalf of local Persian authorities without exciting remark." It was expected that the new ships of the British-Indian Steam Navigation Company were to be fitted with wireless telegraphy.[440]

Also, since the 1880s or thereabouts, there was a Persian telegraph station in Bushehr, which was connected with the larger Persian system. This was for national communications and operated separately from the IETD. Persian telegraph officials were present both in Bushehr and Rishahr.[441] After the British occupation of Bushehr in August 1915, the Persian telegraph was closed, because the lines had been cut long before the occupation.[442]

Because of the growing importance of the wireless and the introduction of the telephone, the telegraph lost ground and finally only occupied a peripheral role.[443] The IETD ceased to exist on 1 March 1931; all landlines were handed over to the government of Persia and the cable stations at Bushehr, Henjam, Jask and Chahbahar to the Imperial and International Communications Ltd (IICC). "Thus ended a 60 year old control of telegraphs in Persia linking up India with Europe." The reason was the availability of more modern forms of communications, greatly reducing volume of traffic, growing losses for the IETD and the Indo-European Telegraph Company. Mr. Homanufir took over the IETD department stores in Bushehr.[444] In 1932, the government of Persia complained about British flags at IICC telegraph stations and the same held for British consulates, if

438. Sadid al-Saltaneh 1371, p. 37; Curzon 1892, vol. 1, p. 236; Stack 1882, vol. 1, p. 27; Sa`adat 1390, pp. 44-45. The IETD staff was housed "in two large buildings, one rented from John Avict at 150 rupees per month, and the other rented from Muhammad Tuki at 300 qiran (125 rupees) per month." Rubin 1999, p. 316.

439. Government of India 1924, p. 49.

440. Administration Report 1913, p. 3; Administration Report 1914, p. 11.

441. Mahrad 1978, p. 90; Sa`adat 1390, p. 45. About the Persian telegraph system, see Soli Shahvar, "Telegraph. i. First telegraph lines in Persia." iranica.com.

442. Administration Report 1915, p. 6.

443. Rubin 1999, pp. 531-32.

444. Administration Report 1931, p. 3.

Indo-European Telegraph building

these were flying flags from a fixed flagstaff. Tehran only allowed flags from poles above the consular building. In February 1932, Tehran sent orders that flagstaffs planted in the ground should not be used anymore after 22 February, with which the British Residency complied. The main mast was left to carry the beacon (red and white lights), which was used by steamers entering the inner anchorage. The IICC flagstaffs were all dismantled.[445] In 1934, the IICC changed its name to Cable and Wireless Ltd.[446] The change in name did not result in a profitable business. There was not much traffic, so that the expenses in Bushehr, Jask and Chahbahar were more than income. Also in the year thereafter Cable and Wireless Ltd continued to lose money.[447] A wireless set at 1.2 km northeast of Rishahr Point was replaced in 1934 by a short-wave emitter, which was expected to be replaced when the Bushehr wireless would be operational. In 1937 the wireless station was opened to be taken over in December from Messrs Cable and Wireless Ltd.[448] In 1937, the wireless equipment and telephone exchange belonging to the British government were handed over to Persia.[449] In 1942, the post, telegraph and transport were frequently intterupted by brigands. In September 1943, the British censor closed down the Persian wireless. All wireless traffic from and to Bushehr was handled by Cable & Wireless Ltd. On 25 September 1945, the Persian wireless station was reopened, which was the occasion of an official ceremony.[450]

---

445. Administration Report 1932, p. 3.
446. Administration Report 1934, p. 2.
447. Administration Report 1935, p. 3; Administration Report 1936, p. 2.
448. Mahrad 1970, p. 90; Administration Report 1937, p. 6.
449. Administration Report 1937, p. 6.
450. Political Diaries, vol. 15, p. 858; vol. 16, p. 497; Administration Report 1942, p. 10 (the censor had arrived in 1942, but at the end of that year he only dealt with telegrams); Administration Report 1945, p. 11.

Since May 1905, there was a telephone connection between the British town office and the Sabzabad Residency although the government of Persia had not been asked for its approval. It had given permission in 1891 for a telegraphic connection that was never realized and that was considered to be sufficient.[451] In the second half of 1913, Haji Rahmatollah Khan came from the Telephone Company in Tehran to Bushehr; in total 36 telephone connections were installed in the town and 6 outside town. Bushehr and Rishahr were also linked by telephone.[452] In 1925, there were 52 telephone subscribers in Bushehr who paid 20 *qrans* per month, which fee was increased for length of a wire above 1,500 meters.[453] In 1947, there were 136 lines. However, the system was not very good; calls farther away than 9 km were almost impossible and to get a telephone connection was only possible with the greatest of difficulty.[454]

The Mail

British-Indian post offices and savings banks had operated in the Persian Gulf since 1864 in Bushehr as well as in other Persian ports at a later date. Their establishment occurred with the acquiescence of the government of Persia, for no formal agreement was concluded as to their operation. The entire operation was at the cost of the government of India, which also subsidized the mail steamers that carried the mail, although Persians also benefitted from their service.[455]

Following the establishment of a Persian postal system in 1877, the government of Persia established a weekly postal service between Tehran and Bushehr. The mail messengers or *qaseds* stopped at the main places en route and it was expected that trade would benefit from this new service.[456] Also, arrangements were agreed as to how the interchange of the two mail systems (Persian and British-Indian) was to function. The postal service worked quite well; moreover, its rates were moderate. From Bushehr, "letters weighing somewhat over a tola can be sent to Shiraz for a penny; and letters of half an ounce go to all parts of Europe for two pence and a half."[457] The first Persian postmaster of Bushehr was a certain Zeytun, who was originally from Jolfa.[458] Although initially the Persian mail worked fine, soon thereafter it did not as indicated by the many complaints.[459] Apart from complaints about the quality of the service there also was the problem of lost mail due to attacks on the mail transport between Bushehr and Shiraz. In 1897 the government even sent a force to deal with the issue as well as that of several robberies, but without success.[460] In 1895, to enhance the level and interlinkage of postal service, the government of Persia

451. Saldanha 1986, vol. 7/2, p. 85.
452. Sadid al-Saltaneh 1371, pp. 97-98 (with a list of the numbers, subscribers and fees); Mahrad 1978, p. 91.
453. Hadow 1925, p. 32.
454. Robert 1948, p. 26; NA, FO 371/15473
455. Saldanha 1908, vol. 7, "Précis of the Affairs of the Persian Coast and Islands," p. 189; Lorimer 1915, vol. 1, p. 15; vol. 2, pp. 2445-46, 2452-54.
456. Administration Report 1876-77, p. 5; Sa`adat 1390, p. 44.
457. Administration Report 1877-78, p. 8; for postal tariffs see Idem, p. 20.
458. Later Zeytun taught English, while in 1896 he was a clerk in the office of Da'ud Sasan; because of his wit people called him *Sheytan* or 'devil.' Sadid al-Saltaneh 1362, p. 6.
459. Administration Report 1878-79, p. 11; Administration Report 1878-791879-80, p. 7.
460. Administration Report 1897-98, p. 6; Mail attacked en route. Administration Report 1899-1900, p. 1.

Postal conference in Bushehr in 1922. Sitting from the right: Major Henri Lou, representative of the Indian post; Mr. Meritor, head of the Iranian post; Yamin al-Mamalek, kargozar and chairman of the conference; Col. Trevor, British Resident; Mirza Hoseyn Shahruzi Fakhim al-Dowleh, head of the Banader provincial post. Standing from the right: Captain Owzhir, head of the Iraqi post; Mr. Terrie, chief- inspector of the Banader post; Sir Arnold Wilson; Mirza Masih Khan Arjomand, head of the Arabistan [Khuzestan] post.

established a postal service between Bushehr and Arabistan.[461] In 1895-96, the post master was Asadollah Khan. By August 1896 he was nine months in function. His salary was 25 *tumans* per month.[462] At that time, the mail arrived every Thursday in Bushehr and left on Sunday, although this might differ somewhat depending on the week.[463]

In June 1900, an informal agreement was made with the new Customs department that all mail to or from British officials, both civil and military, was exempted from customs control. Although later the customs officials wanted to cancel this privilege, the Resident was able to convince them to leave matters as they were.[464] However, in 1901 the service of the British-Indian postal office between towns in Persia was discontinued, when the Belgian administration of the postal system rightly objected to this practice.[465] Henceforth, the British-Indian post office received local letters for foreign countries when franked with Indian stamps; from up-country it received a sealed bag with letters for abroad.

461. Administration Report 1895-96, p. 8.

462. He was a British subject, because his father, who was from Shiraz, migrated to India where he was born in Bangalore. As a youth he returned to Persia and joined the Post ministry. "Because he does not know people's rules and customs they complain about him." Sadid al-Saltaneh 1362, p. 5.

463. Sadid al-Saltaneh 1362, pp. 7-8.

464. Saldanha 1908, vol. 7, "Précis of the Affairs of the Persian Coast and Islands," p. 189.

465. Lorimer 1915, vol. 2, p. 2457.

Local letters for foreign countries were not dealt with by the Persian post office.[466] It may have been because of this conflict that from 1902 until 1907 the mail came under the Customs department.[467] As of 9 April 1905 the Customs officials began levying customs from British staff not covered by the Customs regulations.[468] Also, in 1905, there were discussions between the governments of Persia and Great Britain about the Persian complaint that British post offices in the Persian Gulf had a privileged position, because they did not necessarily conform to international rules.[469]

After the British occupation of Bushehr in August 1915, the postal department continued to work under its own officials.[470] In 1921 the government of Persia demanded that all British post offices in the Persian Gulf and Khuzestan be closed or transferred to the Persian postal department by 1 January 1922. The British were not happy about this, because they had no confidence in the efficiency, reliability and range of services that the Persian postal department could supply. Subsequent negotiations culminated in a Postal Conference held between Great Britain, Persia and Iraq in Bushehr from 5 to 9 December 1922. During this conference it was decided to hand over the Indian Post Office to the Persian postal authorities on 14 April 1923. The British doubted that the Persian post could maintain quality of service given its lack of experience compared with 60 years of that of the Indian Postal Department. This was apparent from the beginning as service was not optimal; stamps were insufficient, delay in delivery of parcels, and "the rupee money order and V.P.P. system has almost ceased to exist." The British blamed this on the lack of commitment of Persian postal officials, despite the hard work of M. Chauviaux, Inspector General of Posts in the south. However, it was not only lack of a proper work ethic, but because the staff was also inexperienced, suffering from ill-health, and were irregularly paid. Furthermore, "inelastic financing arrangements due to the system of Treasury administration" imposed by the Americans, caused a congestion of parcels for upcountry in Bushehr. There were some 7 tons of parcels waiting, but the contractor refused to process them as the government owed him 1,500 *tumans*. The local government had no funds and Tehran refused to make funds available. Finally the Inspector General made an advance from his own pocket which eased the situation somewhat.[471] In short, the start-up problem was partly due to arrears in payment of the postal contractor and partly due to the ban on export of specie which held up the working of the Money Order Service, but it gradually improved.[472]

---

466. Saldanha 1908, vol. 7, "Précis of the Affairs of the Persian Coast and Islands," p. 194.

467. Sadid al-Saltaneh 1342, p. 648.

468. Saldanha 1908, vol. 8, "Précis on International Rivalry," p. 82; Saldanha 1908, vol. 7, "Precis of the Affairs of the Persian Coast and Islands," pp. 192-93; Lorimer 1915, vol. 2, pp. 2457-58. According to Sadid al-Saltaneh 1342, p. 648, the mail in Bandar Abbas was under the Customs department as of 1902 until 1907.

469. Administration Report 1905-1906, p. 18; Saldanha 1986, vol. 7/2, p.189-94.

470. Administration Report 1915, p. 6.

471. Administration Report 1923, p. 11; see also p. 22 (Shiraz and elsewhere). As of 1922, the government of Persia was assisted by a number of American financial advisers, who are the Americans referred in the quote, see Millspaugh 1973.

472. Trade Report 1923-24, pp. 1-2; Administration Report 1921, pp. 7-8; Administration Report 1922, p. 5. The value payable post (V.P.P.), a system still offered by the Indian postal service, is designed to meet the requirements of persons who wish to pay for articles sent to them at the time of receipt of the articles or of the bills or railway receipts relating to them, and also to meet the requirements of traders and others who wish to recover, through the agency of the Post Office the value of article supplied by them.

Under Chauviaux's management there was a great improvement, and efficiency was much higher. However, he left on 22 October 1924 and was replaced as director by a Persian, Arjmand, who was a poor substitute. As a result, there were still important delays in the delivery of packages. This situation did not change for the better either in 1925, because Arjmand "is not very competent and his subordinates go their own ways with results as might be expected."[473] In 1925, the situation changed for the better as the old contractor `Ali Asghar Khan Davani *Qased-bashi* was rehired, who delivered excellent results. The mail was regularly carried by relays of mules at four points on the 190 miles journey and reached Shiraz in 3.5 days, even during winter.[474] In March 1925, for the first time mail was sent by air from Bushehr to Tehran.[475] As of 1926 there existed a motor postal service between Borazjan and Bushehr that functioned well most of the year and continued to do so in the years thereafter. Beyond Borazjan the mail continued to be transported by mules. Moreover, Arjmand, went on leave in August 1926 and was replaced by Haydar Khan Brahman, whom the British considered to be an improvement. The latter was replaced by Mirza Hoseyn Khan Shahruzi on 8 December 1927, which was not an improvement.[476] Shahruzi remained postal director until October 1928, when the Post and Telegraph Departments were merged and he became its new director. Mirza Sehhatpur, the telegraph chief became deputy director of P&T.[477] In September 1928, the P&T announced that it had established a link with European International Air Services via Russia, and that the P&T would accept postal matters for foreign countries (see Airlines section). Overall postal arrangement also improved. Shahruzi continued as director of P&T until December 1930, when he left on leave. His deputy Haji Khan Sehhatpur was acting director until 15 July 1931, when he was relieved by Mirza Ahmad Khan Farzanegan, who unlike Shahruzi was a courteous man. In July 1930, Tehran ordered the opening of a school in Bushehr for the training of signalers and postal clerks. However, this idea was abandoned due to climate reasons and thereafter training took place in Tehran.[478] In February 1940, a censor was stationed in Bushehr, in fact right at the door of the post office. He read all addresses on the enveloppes and his "principal duty would appear to keep a check on the number of complaints sent direct to His Majesty."[479]

In the years thereafter P&T and other communications functioned fine. In fact, in 1947, according to the British consul, the post, telegraph and radio were surprisingly good taking into account the poverty of the governorate. The P&T Department kept one or two staff in the Customs building to deal with parcel-post from steamers. By then there were post offices in Bushehr, Khormuj, Ahram, Delvar, Dayyer, Kangan, Taheri, Ganaveh, Bandar Delam and Bandar Rig. The last three were linked by telegraph to Bushehr and

473. Administration Report 1924, p. 7; Administration Report 1925, p. 9.

474. Administration Report 1925, p. 19.

475. The enveloppe of the first postal flight from Tehran to Bushehr is listed as Muller #13; American Air Mail Catalog Pioneer #4, canceled March 20, 1925, franked with Persia #687 vertical pair. The enveloppe of the second postal flight from Tehran to Bushehr is listed as Muller #21; canceled April 20, 1928, franked with Persia #s 727, C2 and C4. (both enveloppes were for sale on ebay in March 2015).

476. Administration Report 1926, p. 4; Administration Report 1927, p. 5; Administration Report 1928, p. 9.

477. Administration Report 1928, p. 3. Some subordinates complained that Shahruzi was a Bahai. Administration Report 1929, p. 3.

478. Administration Report 1928, p. 5; Administration Report 1929, p. 6; Administration Report 1930, pp. 4, 10. The Post office was next to the British Residence in town. Mahrad 1978, p. 90

479. Political Diaries, vol. 14, p. 33.

there was a radio link between Bushehr, Taheri, Kangan and Khormuj. The Bushehr station was installed in 1938; the transmitters were of medium medium and high frequeny power (M/F and H/F). Mail from the branch offices was cleared twice a week and land mail from Bushehr to Shiraz three times. Air mail was irregular as this depended on the weather, and seasonal hajj diversions to Mecca, etc.[480]

The Airlines

The first airplanes that came to Bushehr were those in support of the British strike force that in September 1917 moved from Bushehr to Shiraz to secure the trade route between the two towns. In 1919, there were a total of eight airplanes in Bushehr, who supported the British troops and carried out bombing raids. Thanks to the British military, the town had an aerodrome of 1,000 x 1,000 yards as well as a workshop for repairs and maintenance.[481] Furthermore, the Persian military had designated the roadstead of Bushehr as a landing site for sea planes.[482] The aerodrome was situated about 4 km or a 40 minute walk southeast of the town and was equipped with a hangar. Towards the seaside it was abutted by the German consulate building a few hundred meters away, which had stood empty since 1915, and next to it was a small Arab fishing village, probably Mahmudabad. To the northwest of the hangar were three buildings belonging to Imperial Airways, one of which most likely served as a rest-house.[483] The hangar was built at the aerodrome in 1924. This was at the time of Reza Khan's visit to Bushehr. On that occasion free flights were given to local notables in February and one plane flew to Shiraz in March.[484] Occasionally, the airfield was used by British, Italian (stopovers) and Persian military planes or by Junkers military support flight missions.[485] The crews of the Junkers Airmail Service flights stayed in the empty former German consulate during their stops and to that end they brought field beds, bedding, cooking utensils, tinned food, petroleum lamps and the like.[486] In May 1934, the Persian government bought the former German consulate building for use as a quarantine station for air passengers.[487]

As of 1920, the town was visited by a variety of private aviators on their way to or from India, or participating in one or another air race that were popular at that time.[488]

480. NA, FO 371/15471; Administration Report 1933, p. 9.

481. Administration Report 1919, p. 6; Administration Report 1921, p. 7; Böhme 1977, p. 251; FO 248/1229, Report Bushire Field Force, 28/11/1919 (an aerodrome was also built at Kazerun and Khormuj).

482. Mahrad 1970, p. 90.

483. Böhme 1977, pp. 243-44, 250; Government of Great Britain 1945, p. 504. Ebtehaj 1932, p. 184 mentions this rest-house, but does not report where in Bushire. It is very likely, however, that this was at the airfield.

484. Administration Report 1924, p. 6.

485. In February 1924, Brig. Gen. Amanollah Mirza, chief of staff, returned from Europe. He left several airplanes, Citroën cars and war material in Bushehr, but it was impossible to bring this equipment up-country due to their weight and lack of a carrosable road. Two planes were flown to Shiraz by French pilots, but both were damaged. Administration Report 1923, p. 20. For the military missions flown for the government of Persia by Junkers, see Böhme 1977.

486. Böhme 1977, pp. 244, 248-49, 252; Administration Report 1930, p. 2.

487. Political Diaries, vol. 11, p. 153.

488. Administration Report 1920, p. 6.

Photo of German consulate with village

Oddly enough no planes visited Bushehr in 1921, but in the following years until 1940, there was the usual sequence of official and private planes.[489]

A new chapter in Persian aviation history began on 21 April 1928, when Junkers Weekly Airmail Service started its regular service between Bushehr and Tehran. It was then possible to travel from London to Bushehr via Berlin, Moscow, Baku and Tehran, although a faster service had yet to be developed. Throughout the existence of this service Junkers maintained a regular and very efficient service. The German company maintained this air service under a concession from the government of Persia. This concession had been agreed upon in 1925 for a period of five years for flights between Tehran-Enzeli, Tehran-Bushehr, and Tehran-Kuratu. In addition, Junkers agreed to transport the Persian mail, and it was allowed to keep the postal surtax. The government of Persia provided a subsidy of 15 *qrans* per flight km for a period of 18 months. It was only in April 1927 that the first Junkers plane, which had been specially built to transport mail, landed in Tehran.[490] The Junker Company made use of ordinary single engine, metal mono-planes, and to keep cost down with little or no ground staff. The German planes carried both passenger and cargo. In the beginning the plane left Tehran on Friday arriving at Bushehr 6 hours later and returned the following morning. As this did not allow government and consular officials in Bushehr much time to write replies to Tehran Junkers changed its schedule on 18 October 1928. Henceforth, the plane arrived on Thursday and left the following Sunday. On Fridays and Saturdays the plane made special trips to Mohammerah and Bandar Abbas. This schedule also complemented that of the sea-mail. "As the fast up mail

---

489. Administration Report 1921, p. 7; Administration Report 1926, p. 3 (3 private British planes, 2 Danish and 1 Spanish plane passed through); Administration Report 1927, p. 4; Idem 1928, pp. 5-7 (list of planes landed); Idem, 1937, p. 9.

490. Mahrad 1978, pp. 142-44. For a discussion of other activities of Junkers in Persia, see Idem, pp. 134-44,350-58; see also Böhme 1977.

The Bushehr airfield with small plane

steamer arrives at Bushire on Wednesday and the down mail on Sunday, the new timings are especially convenient for overseas travelers." On the trip to Tehran, the planes stopped at Shiraz after 1¼ hours and Isfahan after 3½ hours. The British Resident commented that Junkers "have established a great name for regularity, civility and safety in Bushire, and they are deservedly popular."[491] By 1928, it was possible to travel from London to Bushehr via Berlin, Moscow, Baku and Tehran, in five days for a ticket price of £50 per person.[492] In 1929, Junkers operated two flights per week. Moreover, as of March 1929 it used newer and larger planes capable of carrying a load of two-thirds of a ton plus seven passengers. This higher load allowed it to transport cargo such as opium and silver bullion to Bushehr.[493] Although Junkers had a perfect record in maintaining a regular and efficient service, it had to reduce its schedule to one flight per week in May 1931.[494] This was an indication that there were financial problems, which were confirmed by the fact that the promised freight plane service by Junkers did not materialize.[495] The financial problems were not resolved, because the government of Persia refused "to make good their running losses in Persia at a time when the parent Company (in Germany) got into financial difficulty." As the Junker's concession ran till the end of February the last Junkers plane left

---

491. Administration Report 1928, p. 5; Administration Report 1929, p. 7. The six two-man crews that serviced this route in 1930 were: K.B. Kindermann-Clausmann; Stams-Wendt; Jüterbogk-Otzen; Maringer-Schweitzer; Kudriavzeff-Boguslowsky (Russians); and Mosbacher-Katzke. Böhme 1977, p. 252.

492. Administration Report 1928, p. 5; Lingeman 1928, p. 27.

493. Administration Report 1929, pp. 4, 7. For two Junkers flyers with its time table and tariff schedule (for freight and cargo), see Mahrad 1979, pp. 138-39. The wealthy merchant Golshan was the local Junkers agent in Bushehr. Böhme 1977, p. 252.

494. Administration Report 1930, p. 10; Administration Report 1931, p. 7; Administration Report 1931, p. 11.

495. Administration Report 1931, p. 12. For a discussion of Junkers' pre-existing financial problems, see Mahrad 1978, pp. 148-51.

Bushehr on 26 March 1932. In this way Persia lost an efficient economic air service that it found impossible to replace during the next decade.[496]

Persia might have been connected to the burgeoning airline traffic already in 1925, because in that year Persia and Great Britian concluded an airplane agreement that accorded Great Britain certain landing sites. However, the *Majles* refused to ratify the agreement, thus forcing Imperial Airways Ltd to shelve its planned service between London and India as it needed landing sites in the Persian Gulf. Finally both parties concluded a new three-year agreement on 1 January 1929 that allowed Imperial Airways to land and take off from Jask and Bushehr. The government of Persia committed itself to properly equip the airfields for operational use. Therefore, Imperial Airways was not allowed to erect any buildings.[497] In March 1929, Imperial Airways began a service between Great Britain and India, for on 23 March the 'City of Baghdad' arrived from Basra at Bushehr.

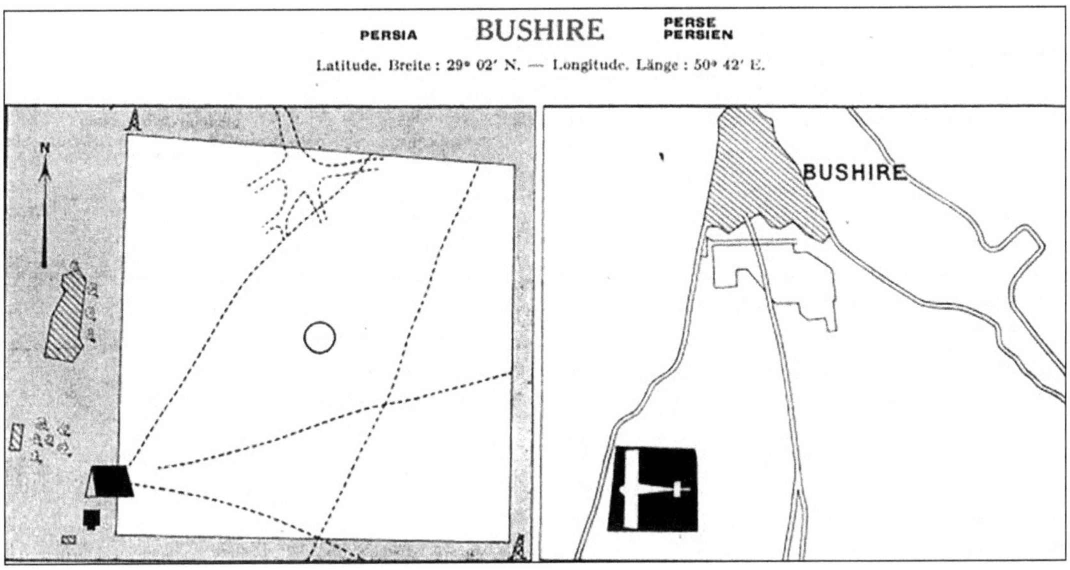

Map of location of Bushehr airfield

Locally it meant that there was a service with Bushehr-Karachi-Basra and Baghdad once per week. Thereafter, Imperial Airways maintained a regular mail services, although its planes were often behind schedule.[498] In 1931, Imperial Airways maintained a weekly mail service between Great Britain and India with moderate punctuality. In wintertime the eastbound machines were usually late. In that year there also were many private British planes that refueled at Bushehr.[499] In 1932, due to diplomatic problems between Great Britain and Persia, Imperial Airways' concession was only extended by six months until

496. Administration Report 1932, p. 6; Mahrad 1997, p. 151. The following information was clear dated and wrong. "Junkers planes fly between Bushire and Tehran. Also connections with Bombay and London, via Baghdad with Imperial Airways. Ebtehaj 1932, p. 184.

497. Mahrad 1979, pp. 144-48. It is unclear who built the Imperial Airways buildings adjacent to the airfield (see above).

498. Administration Report 1929, pp. 4 (on 5 September the 'City of Jerusalem' crashed at Jask when landing at night; one passenger and one Imperial Airways employee burnt to death, "the others escaped with injuries."), 6.

499. Administration Report 1931, p. 7.

1 October 1932. Prior to that date, Imperial Airways had already started to use airfields on the Arabian coast where it transferred its operations and it did not return to Bushehr.[500]

The loss of the Junkers airmail service and the connection with Imperial Airways was partially compensated by the airmail linkages that other European air carriers provided. In 1928 and 1929, KLM carried out a number trial flights to Indonesia, which only carried mail.[501] In 1930, KLM made further trial flights via Bushehr, while the French Air Union joined the other two European carriers in using Bushehr by starting a service to Indo-China in December of that year, when its first plane passed through.[502] In 1931, Air Orient maintained a fortnightly service between Paris-Saigon, although at a very irregular schedule. KLM maintained a weekly service between Amsterdam-Batavia (now Jakarta).[503] The KLM planes functioned with clockwork regularity. According to the British Resident, "Their organization, execution, and machines were all excellent." As of March 1932, Air Orient also started a weekly service. Both Companies were somewhat hampered by a new Persian regulation that stipulated that after 1 October 1932 each plane required a special permit to land, which caused delays, of course.[504] The problems with the regulations apparently were ironed out, because in 1933 KLM's weekly service continued to perform without mishap. The same could not be said about Air France's weekly service, because "they do not fly up to the daily schedule as do the Dutch machines."[505] Air France, a company formed in October 1933 through the merging of five French air carriers including Air Union and Air Orient, operated nine planes per month. KLM flew twice per week to and from Europe and in 1932 it intended to have four planes per week on the Amsterdam-Batavia route.[506] Air France continued with a weekly schedule, but as of 12 June 1935, KLM started a bi-weekly service (see Table 4.17) On 17 July 1935, KLM suffered a serious accident. One of their planes caught fire while taking off; it was destroyed with its mail, but its 4-man crew and 6 passengers escaped without severe injury. They all left on 19 July in a relief plane.[507]

4.17: KLM flight schedule between Amsterdam and Batavia (Jakarta)

Route	Hours
From Amsterdam to Batavia, Friday	6.25 am
From Batavia to Amsterdam, Saturday	3.30 pm
From Amsterdam to Batavia, Monday	6.45 am
From Batavia to Amsterdam, Tuesday	3.00 pm

Source: Administration Report 1935, p. 7.

500. Administration Report 1932, p. 6.
501. Administration Report 1928, pp. 5-7 (9 military and private British, 1 Swiss, and 2 private German planes passed through); Administration Report 1929, pp. 6-7.
502. Administration Report 1930, p. 10.
503. Administration Report 1931, p. 7 (many private British planes landed for refueling).
504. Administration Report 1932, p. 6.
505. Administration Report 1933, pp. 4-5 (24 private British and one Finnish plane made a stopover).
506. Administration Report 1934, p. 10 (37 private British planes made a stopover).
507. Administration Report 1935, p. 7 (21 private British aviators made a stopover in Bushehr).

Air France maintained its weekly schedule via Bushehr, but after October 1936 KLM skipped Bushehr as a regular stop and flew directly from Basra to Jask. Occasionally KLM planes still landed at Bushehr for refueling or to pick up previously booked passengers. This happened 40 times in 1938 and 33 times in 1939.[508] The Air France weekly schedule remained unchanged in 1937. Because KLM had been the sole airmail carrier, this change in schedule also meant that henceforth Air France carried the mail.[509] However, due to neglect of the airfield, which consisted of soft sandy soil, planes experienced landing problems during the rainy season. In November-December 1938 the airfield was water-logged and several times planes were unable to land for a total of 20 days. The mail was dropped but could not be picked up.[510] The same problem was encountered in 1939, when during November-December the airfield was water-logged for 25 days, but the mail was dropped.[511] In May 1940, because of the German conquest of most of Western Europe, Air France discontinued its service in June 1940, while KLM ceased to call from July 1940.[512] After World War II, these Companies used Bahrain instead.[513]

Because of the discontinuation of Junkers Air Service in 1932 the government of Persia was keen to start its own domestic air carrier[514] and perhaps in this context Tehran sent a wireless transmitting set to Bushehr in May 1935 to be erected at the airfield for use by passing planes. However, the wireless was still not operational by year's end.[515] It was finally installed by a French engineer in June 1936, but the KLM engineer found it dangerously situated for landing planes. He protested and the set was moved 2.5 km from the airfield. In November 1936, two Persian engineers started to make the wireless set operational with masts etc.[516] In the first half of 1937 the wireless station became operational. The naval authorities had erected a beacon for aerial and maritime navigation, but there was something amiss with the installation as "the light has rarely been seen." A similar flashing light beacon was installed at Kish.[517] During the 1938-1940 period, the beacon on the airfield still was not regularly operated.[518] The government radio station with a small meteorological station was transferred to the government of Persia by the Government of Pakistan in 1947.[519]

The installation of the wireless in Bushehr set may not have had anything to do with the plans for a domestic air carrier, but on 5 July 1936, the arrival of captain Dowlatshahi, a Persian aviation officer, left no doubt about this intention. He started to level the landing ground to make it suitable for Persian planes. It was said that from 21 March 1937, they would carry mail between Tehran-Isfahan-Shiraz-Bushehr. In expectation of this event,

---

508. Administration Report 1936, p. 6 (37 private British aviators made a stopover in Bushehr); Administration Report 1937, p. 4 (23 private British aviators made a stopover in Bushehr); Administration Report 1938, p. 4 (10 private British aviators made a stopover in Bushehr); Administration Report 1939, p. 3 (5 private British aviators made a stopover in Bushehr).
509. Administration Report 1937, p. 8; Mahrad 1978, p. 90.
510. Administration Report 1938, pp. 8-9; Böhme 1977, p. 244.
511. Administration Report 1939, p. 3.
512. Administration Report 1940, p. 4 (8 AIOC planes made a stopover in Bushehr).
513. NA, FO 371/15473.
514. Mahrad 1979, p. 153.
515. Administration Report 1935, p. 5.
516. Administration Report 1936, p. 4.
517. Administration Report 1937, pp. 3-4, 6.
518. Administration Report 1938, pp. 4, 6; Administration Report 1939, p. 3.
519. NA, FO 371/15473.

the post office sold airmail stamps. In August 1936, two planes arrived, each with an officer and a mechanic to inspect the landing ground and then returned to Tehran. The weekly, *Khalij-e Iran* announced that the airmail service would start soon, but by the end of the year it had not yet started.[520] Whether this was related to the plans to start a domestic airmail service is not clear, but in August 1939, the acting governor of Bushehr invited leading merchants to make a contribution to the newly formed *Civil Aviation Club of Iran*. Only 50,000 rials were collected. As this was considered insufficient the Bushehr authorities continued to try and find more funds, by asking almost every man, woman and child. Finally, 140,000 rials were sent to Tehran, which was much impressed by this munificence.[521]

In 1941, only AIOC planes landed in Bushehr in 1941. The airfield was improved by the British, so that by 1943 it had three runways; two of 1600 m and one of 1200 m. The approaches to the field were also eased by the leveling of a hill. Also, at `Asalu an air strip was built, which was further extended in 1945.[522] In June 1944, *Iran Tour* announced that it would begin a passenger service on the Tehran-Isfahan-Shiraz-Bushehr route as of 28 June. The first plane landed on 3 July and a second one on 8 July. There was only room for three passengers in the plane.[523] During the war, the RAF maintained the airfield of Bushehr. The airfield remained in adequate condition, but after heavy rains on 13-14 January 1945 with hail stones of 5 cm diameter, it became temporarily unserviceable.[524] The *Iran Tour* service did not last long, for in April 1945 it was reported that the same company would begin a trial air service between Tehran and Bushehr via Shiraz and Isfahan on 20 April. The regular service began on 5 May, including airmail. The planes had room for four passengers.[525] In 1945, the landing strip at `Asalu was extended as proposed by the British consulate.[526]

In May 1946 a second airline, *Sharekat-e Iran* (an American company), opened service to Bushehr at lower rates than *Iran Tour*. In July it was so popular that there were too many passenger for the plane on two occasions. In August air service was spotty, and *Sharekat-e Iran* stopped operating at the end of the month.[527] In November 1946, there was one flight of a new company, *Iran Airways*, but it then ceased operations temporarily. In January 1947 no plane came at all to Bushehr, because the airfield in Shiraz was in bad repair.[528] In February 1947, a new airline "Transcontinental and Western Air Inc,' began a daily service between Abadan-Bushehr-Shiraz. The planes had room for two passengers; the pilots were American. From then onwards *Iranian Airways* arrived regularly every Wednesday returning that same day to Shiraz, while there was a daily service with Abadan. In July, *Iranian Airways* arrived regularly every Wednesday returning that same day to Shiraz.[529]

520. Administration Report 1936, p. 4.

521. Administration Report 1939, p. 4; Political Diaries, vol. 13, p. 438 ("even the poorer classes were not exempted.")

522. Administration Report 1941, pp. 9; Administration Report 1943, p. 11; Administration Report 1945, p. 11.

523. Political Diaries, vol. 16, p. 126 (with price list), 148.

524. Political Diaries, vol. 16, p. 292; Administration Report 1945, p. 11.

525. Political Diaries, vol. 16, p. 378 (with price list); vol. 17, p. 32; Administration Report 1945, p. 11.

526. Administration Report 1945, p. 11

527. Political Diaries, vol. 17, pp. 132, 153, 182.

528. Political Diaries, vol. 17, pp. 262, 327.

529. Political Diaries, vol. 17, pp. 352, 375, 473.

The Bushehr airfield 1955

By 1947, there were two air fields in the governorate, one at Bushehr and a smaller one at Ganaveh. The one at Bushehr had a surface of a mixture of sand and gravel with three runways; N/W-S/E 1,800 m; N/E-S/W 1,200 m; N-S (approx) 1,800 m. Therefore, the surface was rough and "is liberally sprinkled with small loose pebbles." It had a windsack, and white boundary markers. There was a hangar with room for 3 small planes, and a small building for Customs officials, finally a store for fuel and fire-fighting equipment. The field was used mainly by Dakotas belonging to *Iranian Airways* and by small Club aircraft that operated an air-mail service down the Persian Gulf.

The airfield at Ganaveh, about 30 miles north-west of Bushehr had one single runway of a natural surface of 1,000 m (N/W-S/E direction). It was only suitable for small aircraft, and it did not have a windsack. Both air fields were under military supervision, to which end a small detachment of frontier guards was stationed there. Their task was to report to Tehran arrivals and departures of foreign planes. The maintenance of the air fields was the responsibility of the Ministry of Roads, but the local government in actual fact was charged to keep the runways in serviceable condition.[530]

Representatives of Foreign Governments

In Bushehr, as in other Persian Gulf ports various countries were represented by consular officers, either to promote trade, to show the flag, or for other reasons. Those countries that did not have a consulate in Bushehr sometimes sent a trade or other representative for short visits, which also included calls on other ports. In various publications there is some confusion, however, which and how many countries had a consulate in Bushehr. For example, Stevens writes that "Ten foreign consulates were once established there,

530. NA, FO 371/15473.

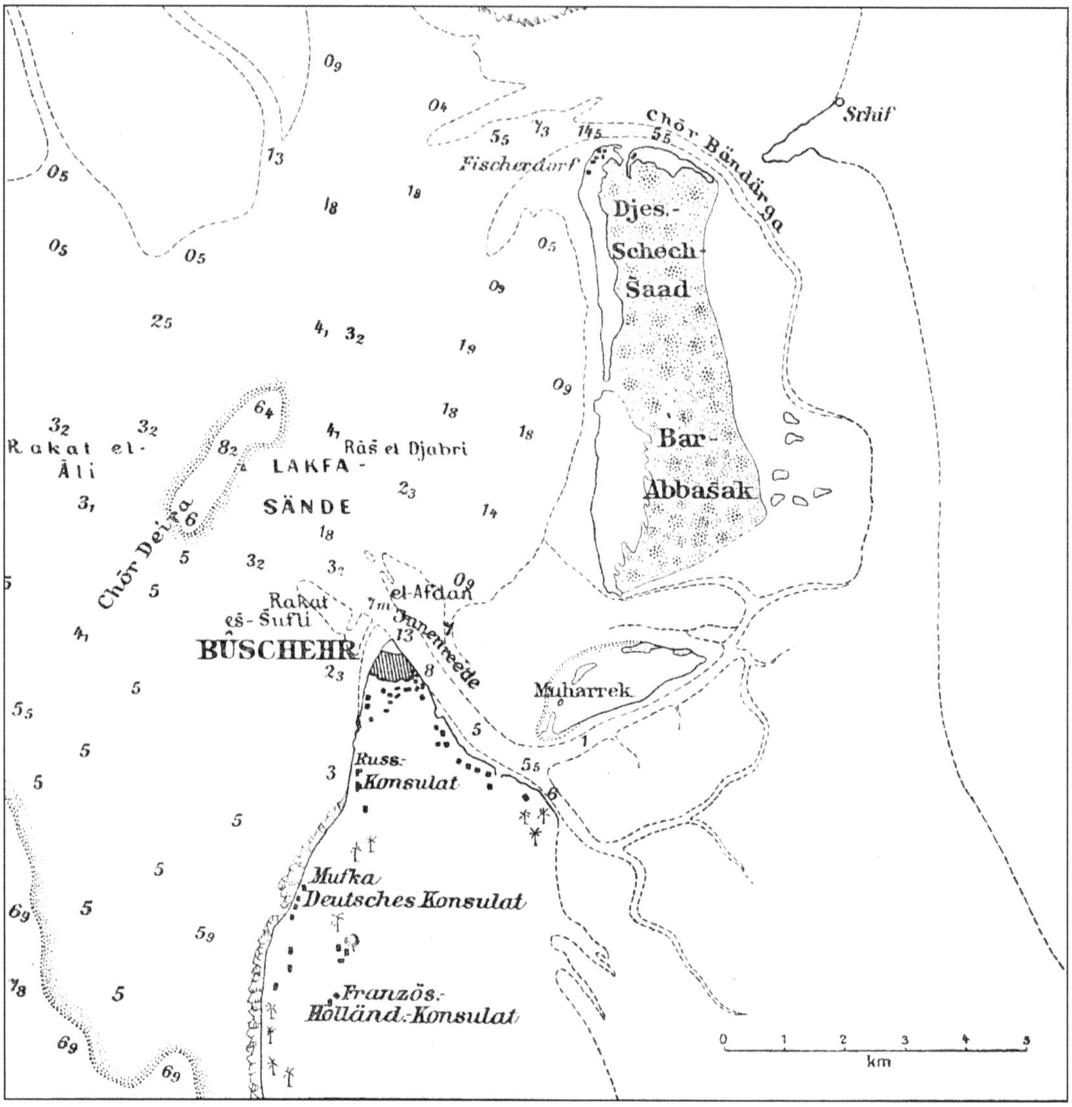

Map of Bushehr (1910)

in 1957 there was one foreign resident, a Russian maid servant.[531] As is clear from what follows there never were ten consulates in Bushehr, although there were sometimes ten countries represented by a consul (Table 4.18). Another author mentions that there was an Italian consulate in Bushehr in 1916, but there was not.[532] Sadid al-Saltaneh, who should have known better and probably confused Norway with Sweden, wrote that the latter country had a consular representative in Bushehr, which it did not.[533] The countries that were represented are listed in order of the starting date of their representation in Bushehr (see Table 4.18).

531. Stevens 1962, p. 284.

532. Cursetjee 2001, p. 114.

533. Sadid al-Saltaneh 1371, p. 37.

4.18: List of countries with consular representation in Bushehr and their timeframe

1. Great Britain	1822-1946
2. The Netherlands	1868-1934
3. The Ottoman Empire	?-1915
4. France	1889-1934
5. Germany	1897-1915
6. Russia	1901-1935
7. Norway	189?-1940
8. Italy	1915- (1924)
9. USA	1884-1896; 1924-1925
10. Greece	?-1934
11. Iraq	1932-1936
12. Estonia	1933-1936

Great Britain

Since 1763, there was a British commercial Resident in Bushehr. He was not a representative of the British or Indian government, but of the East India Company (EIC). Between 1769 and 1775 there was no EIC Resident as relations had been broken off with Persia. Relations were re-established in 1775, but soon thereafter the EIC wanted to withdraw from the Persian Gulf as it only incurred growing losses. However, because of the war with France, which still had possessions in India, the EIC wanted to ensure rapid communications with Europe via the Persian Gulf. To that end one agent remained stationed in Basra and one in Bushehr; otherwise the post was of no importance. This is also indicated by the fact that Bombay appointed a Persian as Resident between 1798 and 1803. When Mr. Hankey Smith resigned as Resident in 1811 the Bombay government decided that as of 29 March 1811, the Political Residency at Bushehr was abolished and reduced to its former nature that of a "*Commercial Residency only*," tasked with the protection of British trade and shipping and British subjects engaged in either, because the British government was henceforth taking charge of all political matters." However, as it was thought necessary to maintain a representative at that post for the preservation of the East India Company's political privileges inclusive the right to hoist the British flag and for the eventual purpose of making occasional purchases of the products of Persia, Mr. Bruce was ordered to remain in temporary charge of the station."[534] However, in December 1822, due to the naval operations to prevent maritime violence by the Arab coastal population the function of Political Resident at Bushehr was restored.

Until April 1835 the Resident was accredited at the court of the governor-general of Fars. However, as of that date Bombay decided that the Resident should no longer have regular contacts with Shiraz and also that all local grievances and complaints, except for issues of a piratical nature and those affecting the lives and property of British subjects, had to be addressed directly to the British Minister in Tehran instead of as previously submitted to the governor-general of Fars for redress. The new rule was strictly adhered to,

534. Saldanha 1986, vol. 2, p. 82; Lorimer 1915, vol. 1, p. 1948.

even though the governor-general of Fars was offended. Therefore, the Resident received permission to ask Shiraz for the redress of minor issues, also to relieve the British Minister in Tehran of too much trouble.[535]

The British Resident, like other European consuls, was commonly termed *balyuz*.[536] Until 1858, the Resident was an employee of the East India Company (EIC) and after that he fell under the Government of India. However, as Consul-General, a function the Resident also held, he was under the Foreign Office, which caused many complications.[537] The main task of the Resident was the suppression of piracy and the promotion of peace among the coastal chiefs, while at the same time absolutely refraining from "all interference in the intestine [internal] quarrels of the different Chiefs, as well as from affording protection to persons obnoxious to Government, provided such interdiction did not comprise the high name, honour and generosity of the British nation."[538]

For a number of years, the British Resident as consul-general also acted as consul for France, Norway, the Netherlands, Italy, Greece and Estonia. In most cases this function was but a sinecure involving no real work, apart from some official correspondence. This varied from notifying the authorities about his appointment as consul for these countries, as well as corresponding if the Persians had questions about it, to writing obligatory notifications. For example, representing the Dutch meant sending official letters on official holidays such as the shah's birthday.[539]

The British Residency, because of it being an agency of the EIC, was referred to as *Sarkar*. At the turn of the nineteenth century there were two buildings, which in Bushehr were called *Kuti*. One was the old factory of Residency, which was situated within the town walls. It was "a large straggling building near the sea side; the left wing is breaking down."[540] In 1821, Fraser described the building as follows: "The British factory was a native building, the apartments of which, chiefly opening to a court-yard, were for the most part small, comfortless, and ill-aired. A house had at one time been built, at some distance from the town, in a situation to command the only good water near it, and the fresh sea breeze, but the jealousy of the Persian government was awakened, and an order was sent from court to have it destroyed."[541] At that time it was decided to occupy a new factory, which was situated about 3 km from Bushehr, at the eastern end of the town.[542] A piece of land, on which some local huts were standing, was rented from Sheikhs Rahmah and Naser for 100 rupees per month. The huts were repaired or converted into servants' houses and store rooms, and a new Residency building was constructed. The Residence had a gate, then a large court, in the center of which was the Residency itself, "a large square building of two stories: surrounding it are irregular ranges of outhouses, containing

535. NA, FO 248/85, Hennell/Camp near Bushire to Willoughby/Secr. Bombay Govt, 07/08/1837; Idem, Persian letter from prince Shiraz to Hennell, n.d..

536. Binning 1857, vol. 1, p. 139; Sadid al-Saltaneh 1371, p. 85. The term *balyuz* via *bailo* probably comes from the Latin word *baiulus* which originally meant 'porter'. In the Ottoman Empire *bailo* was the title of the Venetian resident or consul, who oversaw his community of compatriots and had to promote his country's trade; later it was used for all other European consuls.

537. On the Residency system, see Onley 2007, pp. 14-29.

538. Saldanha 1986, vol. 2, p. 172.

539. Nura'i 1385, p. 173 (in 1914),

540. Morier 1812, p. 57.

541. Fraser, Narrative, p. 55.

542. Morier 1812, p. 58; Alexander 2000, p. 93; Stack 1881, vol. 1, p. 27.

rooms for visitors, stables, &c."[543] In 1828, it was described as follows: "The Residency is a large and convenient building, surrounded by a wall, is situated at the southern extremity of the town, close to the beach, and is guarded by a detachment of the Bombay marine batallion, commanded by a native subaltern."[544] After the events of 1827 (see above) lines for the guards adjoining the Residency were built as an alternative to the proposal to build a fort like new residency, but the Resident, Capt. Wilson pointed out that the government of Persia would view such a move with great suspicion.[545]

When in 1850, the Al Mazkur dynasty of Bushehr was permanently ousted from Bushehr and replaced by a Persian governor appointed by Tehran, the British government had to sort out to whom it owed the monthly rent (see below). It finally decided to buy the Residency ground piece-meal from the heirs of the original owners.

> The Residency building originally belonged to Sheikh Rahmah and Sheikh Naser grandsons of the head of the Mazkur family. Sheikh Rahmah's moiety has descended to his great-grandson of the same name and he therefore gets half of the monthly rent. Sheikh Naser by will left half of his share to the mother of the present Sheikh Hoseyn; she being dead he as her only surviving child gets one-quarter of the rent. The other half was divided among 9 parts, 2 of which went to each of his 3 sons. Sheikh Abdol-Rasul, Sheikh Derwish and the present Sheikh Abdollah, and one 1 part to each of his 3 daughters, viz. Fatemeh Bibi, Kotchick and Mariam. The present Sheikh Naser inherits the 2 parts of his father the late Abdol-Rasul and one part from his uncle Darvish. The other part belonging to the latter has descended to Sheikh Rahim, the son of his sister Fatimeh, who also inherits the part originally belonging to his mother Bibi Kotchik- is still alive and draws her own portion. Mariam is dead but her 2 daughters draw her share. Sheikh Abdollah is living and draws his 2 parts.

The monthly rent of 209 Mohammad Shah is rupees is divided as follows:

Sheikh Rahmah one half or 18/3610450

Sheikh Hoseyn one quarter or 9/365225

Sheikh Naser 2/361160

Sheikh Rahim 2/361160

Sheikh Abdollah 2/361160

Bibi Kotchik 2/361160

Sub-Total 20315

543. Alexander 2000, p. 93 similar description in Binning, who added that a flagstaff was erected towards the sea. Binning 1857, vol. 1, p. 142.

544. Kempthorne 1835, p. 284; in 1840, a similar description by Ellis 1866, p. 96, who adds "about one mile from the town landing place; ... and a small barrack; the whole surrounded by a wall or rampart varying from ten to twenty-five feet high, and generally with a parapet and loop-holes, with large double gates to the interior."; Lorimer 1915, vol. 1, p. 2103 (1850 description); Hamidi 1380, pp. 525-27.

545. Saldanha 1986, vol. 7/2, p. 83.

British consulate building

2 daughters of Bibi Mariam1/36580

Total 20895

Thus Sheikh Naser is legally entitled to only 2/36 part of the Residency and rent.[546]

However, the heirs did not sell their land and thus, the ground on which the Residency was built remained in the hands of Persian subjects.[547]

Additions were made to the Residency, as a result of which, by the 1870 it was "a large pile of buildings, with a great deal of court below, and great deal of staircase and veranda above. On one of the flat roofs is a structure which is common to all the superior houses of Bushire - a room built like a cage, with poles and laths, in which the hot nights of summer are passed. The town lies behind the resident's house. In front, about fifty yards from the gate, there is a sea-side terrace, a quarter-deck, as it were, belonging to

546. NA, FO 248/146 (undated).

547. See Appendix XIII 1A & 1B

the Residency, but open to all comers; and below this the waters of the Gulf ripple."[548] The British also had a ball-room in town where parties and dances took place. It was a two-storey building near the *Amiriyeh* and locally it was known as *beleyrom*.[549] In August 1946, the British Residency was moved from Bushehr to Bahrain. Thereafter, the buildings were occupied by the Persian Ministry of Justice.[550]

During the greater part of the nineteenth century, the staff of the Residency at Bushehr consisted of 1 Resident, 1 assistant Resident, 1 assistant surgeon, 1 accountant, 1 clerk, 1 treasurer, 1 *shroff*, 1 Persian and 1 Arabic *monshi*, as well as agents at Sharjah, Bahrain, Lengeh and Shiraz. Later some additional staff was added. To maintain British influence in the Persian Gulf and protect its interests better consular officials were appointed for (i) the Karun and Arabistan (consul as of 1890), (ii) Bandar Abbas (vice-consul as of 1900), and Lengeh (vice-consul as of 1910).[551] In addition, the Residency had an Indian guard unit for protective and ceremonial purposes. In the first decades of the nineteenth century, "The Resident's guard is composed of sepoys, who, by the regulations, should be changed every five years, but they are permitted to remain till they become so lax in discipline as scarcely to deserve the name of soldiers. The guard is mustered at sun-set, when they mostly appear in their shirts and night-caps, and the sentries walk about without their muskets."[552] In 1856, the Indian guard consisted of 1 *subadar*, 2 *havildars*, 2 *naicks*, 1 drummer, 1 fifer, 30 privates.[553]

In the 1870s the British journalist Geary remarked that "The Persians always regarded the Residency at Bushire with great and not altogether unnatural jealousy."[554] This was partly due to national pride, i.e. the desire to exercise sovereignty over one's own territory and resources. Partly it was due to the inability to do so, due to the lack of means, political will, and actual Persian presence, let alone control over the Persian Gulf littoral. The fact that towards the end of the nineteenth century, the British considered the Persian Gulf as 'a British Lake' and that the British Resident in Bushehr was considered, even by the British themselves, as the "Governor General of the Gulf," was an understandable source of resentment, of course. These sentiments of jealousy, resentment, envy, and rancor were a major factor in the daily relations between Persian officials in Bushehr and the British Residency, as is clear from Chapter 3. Therefore, when Persia under Reza Shah wanted to assert control over the Persian Gulf, this was opposed by the old guard of British policy makers, in particular in the India Office. The view of the Foreign Office to treat Persia on terms of equality only gained ground slowly, as the India Office believed that the Pahlavi regime would not be of long duration. Although Persia did not ask for

548. Arnold 1877, p. 406; Hamidi 1380, pp. 525-37; see also De Windt 1891, p. 218 who further mentions 2 or 3 "lawn-tennis courts, and a broad stone walk almost overhanging the waves, a favourite rendezvous for Europeans in the cool of the evening." See also, Bradley 1910, p. 39; Lorimer 1915, vol. 2, p. 342. The changes to the Residency were sometimes challenged by the Persian authorities. FO 248/232, Report Residency *Monshi* 18/10/1890; see also Appendix XIII 1C.

549. For further details and a photo, see Hamidi 1380, pp. 150-51.

550. Burrell 1972, p. 165; Stevens 1979, p. 285.

551. Saldanha 1986, vol. 7/2, pp. 69-73 (also their remuneration). For photos of two *monshi*s of the Residency, see Roknzadeh 1352, p. 76.

552. Morier 1812, p. 58.

553. Saldanha 1986, vol. 7/2, pp. 72, 79-82 with further details. In 1851, the Resident had a guard of 36 Indian sepoys. Binning 1857, vol. 1, p. 142; see also Lorimer 1915, vol. 1, pp. 2104, 2145.

554. Geary 1878, vol. 1, p. 56.

British residency Sabzabad

the closure of the British Residency, Timurtash, the Minister of Court let it be known that its continued existence was a regrettable reminder of the past. Although the British government finally agreed to the Residency's removal, it insisted that the Resident was recognized as Inspecting Consul-General. This was unacceptable to Persia, because this would have meant regular visits by British warships to its ports. The final removal of the Residency from Bushehr to Bahrain in May 1946 put an end to this matter, but not to other outstanding Persian Gulf related issues between Persia and Great Britain.[555] Great Britain maintained its consulate at Bushehr until July 1947, when with its closure the last foreign representative left the town and closed this long chapter in its history.

4.19: List of British Residents at Bushehr (1763-1946)

Name	Duration	Observations	Source
Benjamin Jarvis*	1763		Saldanha vol. 1, p. 457
William Bowyear*	1766 †		Saldanha vol. 1, p. 457
James Morley*	1768-69		Saldanha vol. 1, p. 457
	1769-75	Post abolished	
John Beaumont*	1775-80		Saldanha vol. 1, p. 457
Edward Galley*	1780 – ca. 1789		Saldanha vol. 1, p. 457
Charles Watkins*	About 1789-1792		Saldanha vol. 1, p. 457
Nicholas Hankey Smith*	October 1795 - September 1798		Saldanha vol. 1, p. 457

555. For a good discussion, see Burrel 1972.

Name	Duration	Observations	Source
Mehdi `Ali Khan*	September 1798 - January 1803		Saldanha vol. 1, p. 457; Idem vol. 2, p. 76
	January - April 1803	Post vacant	
Jonatham H. Lovett*	April 1803-February 1804		Saldanha vol. 2, p. 76
Samual Manesty*	February -August 1804	Self-appointed acting	Saldanha vol. 2, p. 77
Lt. William Bruce*	August 1804-1807		Saldanha vol. 2, p. 77
Nicholas Hankey Smith	1807- July 1808		Saldanha vol. 2, p. 78
Captain Charles Pasley*	July -September 1808	acting	Saldanha vol. 2, p. 78
Lt. William Bruce*	September - end 1808	acting	Saldanha vol. 2, p. 78
Surgeon Andrew Jukes*	December 1808-May 1809	In charge	Onley 2007, p. 261
Lt. William Bruce*	May 1809-	acting	Onley 2007, p. 261
Stephen Babington*	April 1810	In charge	Onley 2007, p. 261
Nicholas Hankey Smith	September-October 1810		Saldanha vol. 2, p. 81-2
Lt. William Bruce*	October 1810-November 1822	Lt. Robert Taylor Oct.-Nov. 1810 acting; asst. Surgeon James Orton in charge Aug. 1813-April 1814; James Dow in charge Nov. 1819-Jan. 1820 and June 1820; asst. surgeon John Todd in charge Jan.-March 1822	Saldanha vol. 2, p. 81-82, 148, 310; Onley 2007, p. 261
Lt. John McLeod	November 1822-September 1823 †		Saldanha vol. 2, pp. 148, 310
Capt. Henry Hardy	Sept-Nov. 1823		Onley 2007, p. 263
Col. Ephraim J. Stannus	November 1823- February 1827		Saldanha vol. 2, p. 253, 310
Capt. D. Wilson	June 1827 ?	Lt. Hennell in charge March 1831	Saldanha vol. 2, p. 253, 310; Onley 2007, p. 263
Dr. McNeill	?-November 1831		Saldanha vol. 2, p. 310
David A. Blane	November 1831-June 1834	Capt. S. Hennell, acting June 1834	Saldanha vol. 2, pp. 264, 309-10; Onley 2007, p. 263
Surgeon Thomas MacKenzie	July 1835-	In charge	Onley 2007, p. 263
Maj. James Morrison	Oct. 1835-Oct. 1837		Onley 2007, p. 263
Surgeon Thomas MacKenzie	Oct. 1837-May 1838	In charge	Onley 2007, p. 263
Capt. Samuel Hennell	May 1838 - 26 November 1841	Officiating till June 1838; thereafter Resident	Onley 2007, p. 263
Col. Henry D. Robertson	26 November 1841- April 1843	Officiating ; Lt. Arnold B. Kemball April-Dec. 1843 officiating	Onley 2007, p. 263

Name	Duration	Observations	Source
Capt. Samuel Hennell	April 1843 -April 1852	Maj 1845; Lt. Col. 1850	Saldanha vol. 2, p. 318; Surgeon Thomas MacKenzie
Capt. A.B. Kemball	April 1852- July 1855		Saldanha vol. 2, p. 318
	July - Oct. 1855	Post vacant	Onley 2007, p. 263
Capt. Felix Jones	Oct. 1855 – 27 February 1857 and from October 1857- December 1862	During the British occupation of Bushehr there was no Resident; officiating till Oct. 1857	Saldanha 1986, vol. 7/2, pp. 51, 67, 87; Onley 2007, p. 263
Capt. Herbert F. Disbrowe	April - November 1862	Officiating	Onley 2007, p. 263
Col. Lewis Pelly	December 1862 - October 1872	First as Major and acting Resident until Nov. 1862, then officiating until April 1864	Saldanha 1986, vol. 7/2, p. 150; Onley 2007, p. 263
Lt. Col. E.C. Ross	October 1872 - 11 April 1876	Maj; Lt. Col. in 1875; acting	Administration Report 1876-77, p. 6; Onley 2007, p. 263
Lt. Col. W.F. Prideaux	11 April 1876-August 1877	Acting	Administration Report 1876-77, p. 6; Idem, 1877-78, p. 7; Onley 2007, p. 263
Major Charles Grant	August – November 1877	Officiating	Administration Report 1877-78, p. 7; Onley 2007, p. 263
Lt. Col. E.C. Ross	November 1877 - 28 March 1885		Administration Report 1877-78, p. 7; Idem, 1885-86, p. 9
Lt. Col. S. B. Miles	29 March 1885 - 30 October 1886	Acting	Administration Report 1885-86, p. 9; Idem, 1886-87, p. 5
Col. E.C. Ross	30 October 1886 - 29 March 1891		Administration Report 1886-87, p. 5; Idem, 1890-91, p. 5
Major Adelbert C. Talbot	29 March 1891 - 28 May 1893	Officiating until Sept. 1891	Administration Report 1890-91, p. 5; Idem, 1893-94, p. 15; Onley 2007, p. 263
Capt. Stuart H. Godfrey	28 May - 6 June 1893	Officiating	Administration Report 1893-94, p. 15
Major J. Hayes Sadler	7 June - 21 July 1893	Officiating	Administration Report 1893-94, p. 15
James A. Crawford	21 July - 19 December 1893	Officiating	Administration Report 1893-94, p. 15
Major J. Hayes Sadler	19 December 1893 - 5 January 1894	Officiating	Administration Report 1893-94, p. 15
Col. Frederick A. Wilson	5 January 1894 - 10 June 1897		Administration Report 1893-94, p. 15

Name	Duration	Observations	Source
Lt. Col. Malcolm J. Meade	10 June 1897 - 7 April 1900	Officiating until March 1898	Administration Report 1897-98, p. 12
Maj. C. A. Kemball	7 April 1900 – 25 April 1904	Acting; Lt. Col. in 1901	Administration Report 1900-01, p. 6; Onley 2007, p. 263
Major Percy Z. Cox	25 April 1904 – 8 December 1913	Officiating until Oct. 1905; Lt. Col. in 1909 - Maj. Arthur P. Trevor in charge August 1909-March 1910	Administration Report 1913, p. 12; Onley 2007, p. 263
John G. Lorimer	8 December 1913 – 8 February 1914 †		Administration Report 1913, p. 12; Idem, 1914, p. 5
Capt. L. Birdwood	8 February – 8 March 1914	Officiating	Administration Report 1914, p. 5; Onley 2007, p. 263
Major Stuart G. Knox	8 March – 1 November 1914	In charge; deputy Resident - Maj. Arthur Trevor April 1915-Dec. 1917 deputy - John Hugo H. Bill, deputy Dec. 1917-Sept. 1919 - Maj. Cecil H. Gabriel deputy Sept--Nov. 1919 - Lt. Col. Arthur P. Trevor deputy Nov. 1919-Oct. 1920	Administration Report 1914, p. 5; Onley 2007, p. 263
Lt. Col. Percy Z. Cox	1 November 1914 – 5 October 1920		Administration Report 1914, p. 5
Lt. Col. Arnold Wilson	5 October – 1 November 1920	Officiating	Administration Report 1920, p. 1
Lt. Col. Arthur P. Trevor	1 November 1920 – 14 April 1924	Lt. Col. Stuart G. Knox acting April-Oct. 1923	Administration Report 1920, p. 1; Onley 2007, p. 263
Lt. Col. F.B. Prideaux	14 April 1924-	Lt. Col. Charles G. Crosthwaite officiating 2 June- 2 October 1925	Administration Report 1924, p. 4
Lt. Col. Lionel Berkley H. Haworth	1927 – 2 November 1928		Administration Report 1927, p. 1; Idem, 1928, p. 1
Frederick William Johnstone	2 November 1928 – 28 April 1929		Administration Report 1928, p. 1;
Lt. Col. Cyril C.J. Barrett	29 April – 8 November 1929		Administration Report 1929, p. 1
Lt. Col. Hugh V. Biscoe	9 November 1929 – 16 July 1932	Lt. Col. T.C. Fowle officiating 30 May-31 October 1931	Administration Report 1929, p. 1; Idem, 1931, p. 1

Name	Duration	Observations	Source
Lt. Col. Trenchard C. Fowle	16 July 1932 – 31 August 1939	Lt. Col. Gordon Loch officiating 11/04 to 11/05 and 20/07 to 19/10/1933 and 11/07 – 19/10/1934 and 28/07 to 16/10/1935 and 25/07 to 19/10/1936; O.K. Faroe from 18/08 to 22/11/1937; Hugh Weightman 02/08 to 27/09/1938	Administration Report 1932, p. 1; Idem 1933, p. 1; Idem, 1934, p. 1; Idem, 1935, p. 1; Idem, 1936, p. 1; Idem, 1937, p. 1; Idem, 1939, p. 1; Onley 2007, p. 266
Lt. Col. C. Geoffrey Prior	1 September 1939 - August 1946	Lt. Col. W. Rupert Hay officiating in October 1941-Sept. 1942; Lt. Col. Arnold C. Galloway officiating May-Nov. 1945	Administration Report 1939, p. 1; Idem, 1940, p. 1; Onley 2007, p. 267
Lt. Col. W. Rupert Hay	May 1946		Onley 2007, p. 267

* Commercial Resident; those without * are Political Resident.

For information on some individual Residents, see Judith Phillips Stanton, *The Collected Letters of Charlotte Smith*. Bloomington, Indiana UP, 2003, p. 779; Dennis Wright, *The English among the Persians*, London, 1977; Saldanha 1986, vol. 2, chapters XII and XIV, pp. 75-79, 82-89.

The Netherlands

The Dutch consulate in Bushehr was established in 1868 at the suggestion of Dr. Johan Schlimmer, a Dutch physician teaching at the *Dar al-Fonun* in Tehran and a royal physician, in response to the requests of Dutch shippers who complained about the high incidence of theft and pilfering during unloading of their ships and the absence of any effective mechanism for redress from the Persian authorities after they had lodged a complaint. The first consul was Richard Charles Keun, a member of a Dutch family that had resided for many generations in Smyrna. He was fluent in Arabic, Turkish and Persian and was well versed in the region's culture. He remained in Bushehr until 1878, when he went on leave.[556] He built a residence that he called *Holandarabad*, which was south of Bushehr in the village of Hofreh.[557] In October 1884, Keun returned after a few years of absence.[558] He left on leave in 1886 and returned in February 1887.[559] In 1888, the Dutch government decided to withdraw its consulate from Bushehr, but after pressure

556. Floor 1988 c; Idem 2013 a, pp. 257-58; Administration Report 1873-74, p. 5. In 1870, the Dutch naval vessel *de Curaçao* visited Bushehr, about which "some inhabitants of Bushehr," sent a letter to the *Javabode* of 1 October 1870, no. 231, in which they described the friendly and welcoming reception by the Bushehr populace of crew and vessel and referred to the old ties that existed between the port and the Dutch.

557. Sadid al-Saltaneh 1371, p. 51; Mahrad 1979, p. 89.

558. Administration Report 1884-85, p. 8.

559. Administration Report 1886-87, p. 9.

Holandarabad

from A. Hotz, the head of *Hotz & Zonen*, the major Dutch import and export firm in Persia, this decision was cancelled.[560]

Keun's most notable achievement in Bushehr was the construction of his residence, but otherwise, beyond promoting Dutch trade and getting into conflict with local business interests, his record was rather thin. When Keun left he was replaced by W. Groeneweg, the local representative of *Hotz & Sons*.[561] Apparently, the Dutch government considered the use of local agents of *Hotz & Sons* a more attractive financial solution to the consular problem in Bushehr, because in 1897, Groeneweg was replaced as consul by H. C. van der Zee, who was his successor as agent of *Hotz & Sons*.[562] When Moesman replaced H. C. van der Zee in the latter function he likewise assumed the duties as acting Dutch consul, until about mid-1902, when *Hotz & Sons* bankruptcy meant that he no longer had a function and left Persia.[563]

4.20: List of Dutch consuls in Bushehr (1868-1902)

Name	Duration
R.C. Keun	1868-1889
W. Groeneweg	1889-1897
H.C. van der Zee	1897-1899
Moesman	1899-1902

Source: Administration Report 1884-85, p. 8; Idem, 1886-87, p. 9; Idem, 1889-90, p. 9; Idem, 1897-98, p. 6; Idem, 1899-1900, p. 7; Idem, 1902-1903, p. 7

560. Administration Report 1888-89, p. 12; NA, 2.05.38 (old B 149, inv. 1 = new 1370-1386), Hotz to Hannema, 06/11/1888; Hannema to Hotz, 22/11/1888. Keun was appointed as Consul-general in Tehran.
561. Administration Report 1889-90, p. 9; Floor 1988 c.
562. Administration Report 1897-98, p. 6.
563. Administration Report 1899-1900, p. 7; Administration Report 1901-02, p. 4; Administration Report 1900-1901, p. 6 (Moesman went 4 months on leave); Administration Report 1902-1903, p. 7.

۸ ۴۴ ۴

بوشهر

(مسرت و تبریک)

بحمد الله و المنه در این یکساله حکمرانی جناب ... سالار معظم دام اقباله العالی خیلی با اهالی خوش گذشت خاصه بضعفا و فقرای اجتماعات در خصوص بستن سدّ که بی اندازه راحت و متشکرند امسال بکلی از سرقت و ناامنی در خاک ناد را سیمی بود هر کجا سرکشی و خودسری بود از باس سطوت حکومت پاید امن و اطاعت کشیده بجای خود نشستند و در این آخر هم گرفتاری زایر خضر تنکستانی مزید آسایش عمومی و هنیت اهل و خارج گردید عموم اهالی آسوده خاطر و فارغ البال بدعاگوئی دولت ابد مدت و استدامت حکومت جناب معظم له اشتغال ورزند —

این ایام هم تلگراف مبارک حضرت اشرف ... اتابک اعظم دامت شوکته العالی در صدور فرمان همایونی و ابقای حکومت سال جدید معظم له و اعطای یکقبضه شمشیر مرصع از درجه اول باشی و سرافرازی جناب معظم له باعث مسرت قلوب عموم اهالی از خودی و بیگانه گردید —

اجزاء اداره مظفری عن صمیم القلب بعرض تبریک پرداخته ازدیاد عمر و علو اقبال و دوام حکمرانی این حکمران معارف پرور را از درگاه الهی مسئلت دارند —

نیز تلگرافیکه از حضرت اجل ... نظام السلطنه بحکومت جلیله رسید حامل خلعت جناب مجیر السلطنه برادر والا گهر جناب ... سالار معظم حکمران کل بنادر خلیج فارس دام اقباله العالی میباشند که عما قریب وارد خواهند شد —

جناب وحید الملک نایب الحکومه بندر لنگه و عباسی با میل دوشنبه ۲۵ ذیقعده موقتاً وارد بوشهر شدند و لیکن از معلوم بهمین زودی بمعاودت بمرکز حکمرانی خود خواهند نمود —

تاریخ ۱۴ ذیقعده اعلان تعرفه جدید گمرکی از اداره گمرکات منتشر شد چون قبل از وقت در خصوص تجار و اهالی اطلاعی نرسیده بود و هریک از تجار دارای مال التجاره موجوده در گمرکخانه و اموال التجاره آمدنی که تازه خواسته اند بوده و میباشند پس از اطلاع تشکیل مجلس مشاوره نموده آراء شان براین قرار گرفت که مهلتی بخواهند صورت عریضه نوشته توسط اداره گمرکات بطهران مخابره و استدعای ۳ ماه مهلت نمودند باجابت نرسید پس از آن یکماه و تا عید نوروز مهلت خواستند نیز باجابت نرسید فعلاً تجار محترم از تصرف مال التجاره وارده از گمرکخانه مطابق تعرفه جدید امتناع دارند ولی مال التجاره صادره که از عشور معاف است هر روزه مرخص و حمل و نقل مینمایند و نیز اغلب تجار محترم تلگرافات منع خرید و حمل مال التجاره به بمبئی و لندن مخابره نموده اند (و محقق با مضرات هم نخواهد ماند —)

تجارتخانه (هاتس و پسر تاجران و لندنی) که سالهاست در اکثر نقاط ایران خصوص بوشهر مفتوح بود این ایام مسدود شد (خودکشی رئیس بزرگ آنها در لندن از چندی قبل در افواه بود) (مستر موسمن) رئیس فصل بوشهر هم عشر اول ذیقعده با جهاز روسی به بندر لنگه مسافرت و با یکل ۲۵ ذیقعده مراجعت کرد روز جمعه ۲۹ ذیقعده جناب ادسینکو جنرال قونسول دولت فخیمه روسیه آفیس مزبور را مسدود و مهر و لاک نمودند تا بعد چه شود و محقق شود که کسر آنها چه مبلغ است —

حرکت بجای کربلائی شکر الله حمالباشی نسبت بجناب شیر الغاب ... علم البند

Mozaffar paper with article re Hotz bankruptcy

As of 1902 until 1911, Dutch interests were represented by France. In that last year the French consulate was temporarily closed.[564] Therefore, as of 1911, the British consul-general at Bushehr looked after Dutch interests. When in 1912 a new French vice-consul was nominated to Bushehr the Dutch Minister in Tehran told the British Legation there that it considered the British not the French should take care of Dutch interests in Bushehr. This position was probably prompted by the fact that it would take until September 1913 before a new French vice-consul arrived in Bushehr.[565] Therefore, the British consul-general continued to represent Dutch interests until early 1924. This change was due to the fact that Dutch interests in Persia in general were henceforth represented by the USA. G. G. Fuller US vice-consul arrived on 1 April 1924 in Bushehr. He left on 7 September 1924 to Tehran, and the rest of the year the US consulate was closed and thus nobody took care of Dutch interests.[566] The Dutch consulate remained closed until the arrival of Fuller in Bushehr and was closed again with his departure.[567] As the US had withdrawn its consulate from Bushehr the Dutch consulate remained closed until 6 October 1926, when the acting French consul assumed this charge,[568] because the USA no longer took care of Dutch relations. Thereafter France represented Dutch interests until 31 July 1934, when it closed its consulate in Bushehr on 1 Augustus 1934. This also meant that thereafter there was no consular representation of Dutch interests in Bushehr.[569]

Ottoman Turkey

It is not known from when the Ottomans had a consul or *shahbandar* as he was traditionally known in Persia,[570] but already in 1873 the British report the presence of an Ottoman consul in Bushehr.[571] During the 1890s, Ottoman consuls were no longer present in Bushehr, because for many years Turkish interests were looked after by a local Persian subject, Mullah Hoseyn. It was only at the end of 1909 that the Porte sent Nebil Ziya Bey, a professional consul, who came with his family. He had never been to the East and did not like it there.[572] In 1910, the Turkish consul called upon his nationals to take military service in Baghdad; the persons most affected were Baghdad Christians employed by the Customs Department.[573] Nabil Zia Bey served until September 1911 when Aguiah Bey succeeded him.[574] Aguiah Bey left on 11 July and was replaced by Nejed Bey on 21 December 1913.[575] Nejed Bey remained in function until 3 July 1913 when he committed suicide. Mullah Hoseyn, a local Persian subject and the Turkish dragoman

564. Administration Report 1911, p. 11.
565. Administration Report 1912, p. 13.
566. Administration Report 1924, p. 5.
567. Administration Report 1925, p. 5.
568. Administration Report 1926, p. 1.
569. Administration Report 1934, p. 2; Administration Report 1935, p. 2.
570. Sadid al-Saltaneh 1371, p. 111.
571. Administration Report 1873-74, p. 5.
572. Administration Report 1909, p. 10.
573. Administration Report 1910, p. 18.
574. Administration Report 1911, p. 11.
575. Administration Report 1913, p. 12.

Ottoman consulate

officiated thereafter.[576] When in 1914 he wanted to have two armed guards at the building, exactly south of the British Residency, outside the town, the *kargozar* informed him that the *shahbandari-ye Othmani* was not allowed to do so.[577] The dragoman Mirza Hoseyn remained in charge of the Ottoman consulate until August 1915 when British troops occupied Bushehr and removed the Turkish flag.[578] This was the end of Ottoman consular presence in Bushehr. The dragoman never tried to reopen it and it remained closed.[579]

4.23: List of Ottoman consuls in Bushehr (1909-1914)

Name	Duration
Ahmed Hamdi Bey	September 1909-18 November 1909
Mullah Hoseyn caretaker	? - end 1909
Nebil Ziya Bey	End 1909 – September 1911
Aguiah Bey	September 1911 – 11 July 1913
Nejed Bey	21 December 1913 – 3 July 1914
Mullah Hoseyn Turkish dragoman officiated	3 July 1914 – August 1915
Closed permanently	8 August 1915

576. Administration Report 1913, p. 6.
577. Nura'i 1385, p. 70; Mahrad 1979, p. 89.
578. Administration Report 1915, p. 2.
579. Administration Report 1916 p. 1; Administration Report 1924, p. 5.

Source: Administration Report 1909, p. 10; Idem, 1911, p. 11; Idem, 1913, p. 12; Idem, 1914, p. 6; Idem, 1915, p. 2; Political Diaries, vol. 3, p. 763.

France

In the 1880s, trade via Bushehr started to become of greater interest to France when the market share of its sugar started to increase. To show French interests as well as its flag, a French man-of-war visited Bushehr in 1886.[580] It was only in 1888 that France opened a vice-consulate in Bushehr with the arrival of its vice-consul in Basra, Mr. Piat on 5 March 1889. He only stayed for one year, and as of 5 March 1890 the dragoman Haji Mirza Hoseyn took care of French interests until June 1897.[581] On 8 January 1893, Mr. Guès, the clerk of the Mombay consulate, was appointed vice-consul at Bushehr. He arrived in Bushehr in April and he stayed there until 11 May 1894. On 15 October 1894, Mr. Santi was appointed vice-consul in Bushehr, where he arrived on 14 March 1895. He proposed that the French sugar industry appoint an agent at Bushehr to promote their product. Santi left on 5 May 1896.[582] In June 1897, Mr. Ferrand arrived as the French vice-consul; he remained till the end of October and was succeeded by Mr. Bryois who arrived in February 1898.[583] M. Bryois, the French vice-consul left in August 1899. During his absence the dragoman Mirza Hoseyn officiated.[584] To house the French vice-consul, the French government bought *Holandarabad* the elegant villa built by the first Dutch consul in Bushehr in Joffareh or Hafrah.[585] As of 6 August 1901, Mr. Chaloin assumed the task as French vice-consul in Bushehr.[586] On 5 July 1905, Chaloin left on leave and during his absence the consular dragoman Mirza `Ali Reza Khan Motarjem al-Saltaneh officiated.[587] In mid-1907 Chaloin returned after a two years' absence.[588] He remained in office until November 1909, when he was removed "for certain irregularities." After his departure Great Britain took care of the French interests in Bushehr.[589]

4.21: List of French consuls in Bushehr (1889-1934)

Name	Duration
Mr. Piat	1888-1889
Dragoman Haji Mirza Hoseyn officiated	1889-June 1897
Mr. Ferrand	June – October 1897
Mr. Bryois	October 1897-August 1900
Dragoman Haji Mirza Hoseyn officiated	August 1900-6 August 1901

580. Administration Report 1886-87, p. 9.
581. Administration Report 1889-90, p. 9.
582. Vadala 2536, p. 167.
583. Administration Report 1897-98, p. 6.
584. Administration Report 1899-1900, p. 7; Administration Report 1900-1901, p. 6.
585. De Vilmorin 1895, p. 346; Vadala 2536, p. 167; Wagenvoort 1926, p. 82.
586. Administration Report 1901-1902, p. 4.
587. Administration Report 1905-1906, p. 27.
588. Administration Report 1907-1908, p. 20.
589. Administration Report 1909, p. 9.

Name	Duration
Mr. Chaloin	6 August 1901-5 July 1905
Mirza `Ali Reza Khan Motarjem al-Saltaneh officiated	5 July 1905
Mr. Chaloin	Mid-1907 – November 1908
British consul-general officiates	November 1908-17 January 1910
Mr. L. Heritte	17 January 1910- April 1911
British consul-general officiates	April 1911-16 September 1913
Mr. Ramire-Pie Maxime Vadala	16 September 1913-March 1919
Haji Mirza Hoseyn officiating	March- December 1919
British consul-general officiates	December 1919- beginning 1921
Mr. U. Sudreau	Beginning 1921 - end October 1921
British consul-general officiates	End October 1921-
Mr. U. Sudreau	23 November 1920- 192?
Mr. Lidin	Beginning 1924 – 21 June 1924
Closed temporarily	21 June - end 1924
Mr. U. Sudreau	?end 1924 – 10 June 1925
Fr. Bernard, a RC priest officiated	10 June – 4 November 1925
Commandant Trenga	4 November 1925 – end 1927
Mr. Louis Lucas	Beginning 1928 – 22 March 1930
Mr. G. Cassin	22 March 1930- 31 July 1934
Caretaker – closed permanently	1 August 1934- 1940

Source: Administration Report 1888-89, p. 12; Idem, 1889-90, p. 9; Idem, 1897-98, p. 6; Idem, 1899-1900, p. 7; Idem, 1901-1902, p. 4; Idem, 1905-1906, p. 27; Idem, 1907-1908, p. 20; Idem, 1908 or 1909, p. 9; Idem, 1910, p. 11; Idem, 1911, p. 11; Idem, 1913, p. 6; Idem, 1919, p. 1; Idem, 1921, p. 1; Idem, 1924, p. 5; Idem, 1925, p. 5; Idem, 1927, p. 1; Idem, 1928, p. 1; Idem, 1930, p. 2; Idem, 1934, p. 2; Idem, 1940, p. 1; Political Diaries, vol. 6, p. 682; Vadala 2536, pp. 166-69.

On 17 January 1910, L. Heritte arrived in Bushehr as the French vice-consul.[590] In April 1911, Heritte left on sick leave, and once again the British consul-general took charge of French interest and continued to do so until 16 September 1913, when Ramire-Pie Maxime Vadala arrived and took over the responsibility as French vice-consul.[591] Valada left in March 1919 and was succeeded by Haji Mirza Hoseyn as acting vice-consul, who left on sick leave in December. After that date the French vice-consulate was entrusted to the British consul-general until the arrival of U. Sudreau in early 1921. However, he only remained until the end of October 1921, when again Great Britain assumed French consular tasks.[592] Sudreau returned to Bushehr in 1923 and was French vice-consul until early 1924, when he was replaced by Lidin until 21 June 1924, when the consulate was closed.[593] Sudreau returned to Bushehr in early 1925, but went on leave on 10 June. Fr. Bernard, a Roman-Catholic priest officiated until 4 November, when he was replaced

590. Administration Report 1910, p. 11.
591. Administration Report 1911, p. 11; Administration Report 1923, p. 6. According to Vadala 2536, p. 168, he was appointed on 17 February 1914 and he arrived in Bushehr in September 1914.
592. Administration Report 1919, p. 1; Administration Report 1921, p. 1; Administration Report 1922, p. 1.
593. Administration Report 1924, p. 5.

French consulate

by Commandant Trenga, who remained in office until the end of 1927.[594] In 1928 Louis Lucas replaced Trenga and remained in function until 22 March 1930,[595] when George Cassin succeeded him. At that time the market share of French sugar in Persia was under downward pressure and therefore, the French charge d'affaires and commercial attaché came from Tehran to Bushehr to find out why French trade had decreased and how its prospects were in view of Persian restrictions of foreign trade. How important this was to France is indicated by the fact that Mr. Rebel, IG of St. Louis Sugar Comp. Marseilles was in Bushehr in April 1930 to study its market conditions so as to learn how to beat Russian sugar competition.[596] In 1931 Cassin's consular jurisdiction was extended to include Kerman, Shiraz and Mohammerah. He further spent four months in Shiraz returning on 28 October 1931 to Bushehr.[597] Given the declining prospects of French sugar imports, Cassin was vice-consul until 31 July, when he closed the consulate on 1 August 1934.[598] Thereafter the French consulate remained closed; there was only one caretaker to look after the building for the time being and it was vacant thereafter.[599]

594. Administration Report 1925, p. 5; Administration Report 1926, p. 1; Administration Report 1927, p. 1.
595. Administration Report 1928, p. 1; Administration Report 1929, p. 2; Administration Report 1930, p. 2.
596. Administration Report 1930, pp. 1-2.
597. Administration Report 1931, p. 2.
598. Administration Report 1934, p. 2; IOR/L/15/6/148.
599. Administration Report 1935, p. 2; Administration Report 1936, p. 1; Administration Report 1940, p. 1; IOR/L/15/6/149.

Germany

As is clear from Table 4.22 the German consulate was opened in Bushehr in November 1897.[600] This probably happened in connection with the fact that in 1896, R. W. Wonckhaus established a business in Lengeh. By 1905, the mother-of-pearl shell trade was entirely in his hands. Not only was it a German company that exported these shells, but most were exported to Hamburg (Germany).[601] Officially the German official held the rank of vice-consul and it was only raised to rank of consul toward the end of 1911.[602] When Robert Hauck left on leave in June 1899 he was replaced by Reinhardt, who went on leave in April 1900 and was temporarily replaced by Roesler. He returned in March 1901 and was replaced by von Mutius in March 1902. The latter held the office until May 1905, when Listemann became the longest serving German consul in Bushehr. He left one year later to serve at the embassy in Tehran and he was not replaced. He returned in April 1910 and remained in Bushehr until May 1913 when he left for a short mission. He was temporarily replaced by Wassmuss until July 1913.[603] According to the British, Listemann was correct to them, friendly with the Russian consul-general, but at daggers drawn with the French physician and the Belgian Customs director and with part of the British commercial community over personal matters.[604] Further, he had friendly contacts with anti-British tribal chiefs who were blocking traffic on the road to Shiraz.[605] On 9 March 1915 the British arrested Helmut Listemann and deported him to India. He was accused of espionage and of instigating various groups to engage in anti-British activities.[606] Thereafter, the German consulate remained closed. In May 1934, the Persian government bought the former German consulate building, which locally was known as Emarat-e Jermani, although the German referred to it as Alamanabad.[607]

4.22: List of German consuls in Bushehr (1997-1915)

Name	Duration
Dr. Robert Hauck	November 1897- June 1899
Dr. Reinhardt	June 1899-24 April 1900
Roesler	24 April 1900-March 1901
Dr. Reinhardt	March 1901-end March 1902
Von Mutius	End March 1902-8 May 1905
Helmut Listemann	8 May 1905-March 1906
Vacant	March 1906-1 April 1910

600. Administration Report 1897-98, p. 6. According to Ballantine 1879, p. 59 there was a German consul in Bushehr in 1875, but he probably meant the Dutch consul.
601. See Floor 2010, pp. 84-85.
602. Administration Report 1911, p. 11.
603. Administration Report 1913, p. 12.
604. Administration Report 1912, p. 29.
605. Von Tzschirner-Tzschirne 1918, p. 159.
606. Administration Report 1915, p. 2.
607. Political Diaries, vol. 11, p. 153; Hamidi 1380, p. 48 (with a description of the building and particulars about its consntruction).

The German consulate

Name	Duration
Helmut Listemann	1 April 1910-19 May 1913
Wassmuss, pro tem	19 May 1913-8 July 1913
Helmut Listemann	8 July 1913-9 March 1915
German consulate closed permanently	

Source: Administration Report 1897-98, p. 6; Idem, 1899-1900, p. 7; Idem, 1900-1901, p. 6; Idem, 1902-1903, p. 6; Idem, 1905-1906, p. 26; Idem, 1906-1907, p. 16; Idem, 1910, p. 11; Idem, 1913, pp. 6, 12; Idem, 1915, p. 2.

During 1928-1930 German interests in Bushehr were unofficially taken care of by Wassmuss. The reason was that he had started farming in Choghadak and Ahmadi in 1925, where he had imported some modern agricultural machinery. However, he had no success and lost money.[608] Despite the financial reversal, Wassmuss kept his farm going. In 1926, he had a good harvest, but 1927 would be critical for him.[609] Although Wassmuss continued farming in 1928 he made no profit. "During the winter months he supplements his earnings by hauling our motor lorries, which get stuck in the Mashileh mud, with his Fordson tractor: he charges 20 Tomans per lorry."[610] At that time, he told Hall, the American financial advisor in Persian government service: "I once resolved that I would

608. Administration Report 1925, pp. 9, 24; see also Hall 1947, pp. 321-23.

609. Administration Report 1926, p. 4.

610. Administration Report 1928, p. 9.

Wassmuss farm at Choghadak

Aerial view of Wassmuss farm at Choghadak

drive the British forces out of South Persia to the very last unit. Well I did, though not quite in the way I had expected. In those wagons and tractors I drove the last of their wartime equipment across the Mashileh- to be loaded onto boats in Bushire-and they paid me for doing it!"[611] It may have been for this reason that he started to unofficially take care of German interests in Bushehr.[612] In 1929, it was rumored that Wassmuss, still farming without profit, wanted to sell and move out.[613] Wassmuss did suspend his farming at Choghadak and in mid-1930 he went to Tehran.[614] Part of his lack of success was due to Sheikh Naser of Ahmadi and his followers, who secretly intrigued against Wassmuss, ravaged his fields, and stopped his irrigation water at critical growing times.[615] In 1930, Wassmuss was sued by the sons of Sheikh Hoseyn Khan of Chahkutah for 11,881 *tumans* for promissory notes given to them in 1915. Wassmuss did not have money and was not allowed to leave Bushehr and his "property in the German Consulate [was] attached to the Law Court." His appeal failed and he then appealed to High Court in Tehran, going to Tehran to attend his case. Meanwhile, the German consulate, which was south of town, was occupied by pilots and mechanics of Junkers airways.[616] During the first half year of 1931 Wassmuss's appeal to the High Court went in his favor; his property was released. However, his heart was broken by his former friends' perfidy and he returned to Germany.

611. Hall 1947, p. 324.
612. Administration Report 1928, p. 2; Administration Report 1929, p. 2.
613. Administration Report 1929, p. 7.
614. Administration Report 1930, p. 10.
615. Hall 1947, pp. 322-23.
616. Administration Report 1930, p. 2; Mahrad 1979, p. 89; Faramarzi 1390, pp.59-62 (with facsimile of handwritten IOU by Wassmuss for 16,666 *tumans*); for more details about Wassmuss's agricultural project, see Mikusch, pp. 305-32.

On 29 December 1931 aged about 52 he died suddenly in Berlin.[617] After Junkers Airways stopped coming to Bushehr (1932), the only German presence in Bushehr was the office of the *Deutsche Dampfschifffahrts-Gesellschaft Hansa*, which as of 1940 remained in charge of a Persian clerk.[618]

Russia

Although Russia's commercial and political influence did not reach as far as the Persian littoral, nevertheless in 1901, to throw its weight around, it opened a consulate-general in Bushehr as well as a consulate in Bandar Abbas. This step had been preceded with visits by various Russian diplomats, military officers, and scientists who all submitted their reports which led to the establishment of a Russian consular representation as well as the initiation of the Odessa steamship line (see above). In spring 1887, Vonblumor of the Russian Cossacks came to Bushehr.[619]

The Russian consulate-general was established on 17 September 1901, when M. Ovseenko arrived in Bushehr.[620] He left at the end of July 1903 and was succeeded by Passek,[621] who was replaced by Andre Miller in May 1906.[622] Andre Miller was replaced by Kaloubovsky in November 1908.[623] Apparently Passek was appointed again to Bushehr in 1910, but he remained in Shiraz. He only returned to Bushehr on 1 October 1910 and two weeks later returned to Russia. Kaloubovsky then became acting consul-general.[624] Kaloubovsky remained in that function until April 1911, when Dmitrieff arrived as the new consul-general.[625] He was less than one year as consul-general when he committed suicide on 10 March 1913. Thereafter, Loiko officiated until the arrival of Belayew on 17 August 1913. When he left on 6 November he was replaced by Loiko as acting consul-general.[626] When Loiko departed on 5 May 1919 the Russian consulate-general was closed.[627]

4.24: List of Russian consuls-general in Bushehr (1901-1924)

Name	Duration
Ovseenko	17 September 1901-end July 1903
Passek	End July 1903-May 1906

617. Administration Report 1931, p. 2; Hall 1947, p. 324. The Dutch also mention the presence of the Ottoman *shahbandar* in the 1870s.
618. Administration Report 1940, p. 1.
619. Administration Report 1887-88, p. 12, see also p. 13; in general, se Saldanha 1986, vol. 7/2, pp. 1-5.
620. Administration Report 1901-1902, p. 4.
621. Administration Report 1903-1904, p. 5.
622. Administration Report 1906-1907, p. 15.
623. Administration Report 1908, p. 7. For the expenditure of the Russian consulate and its staff, see Sadid al-Saltaneh 1371, p. 111.
624. Administration Report 1910, p. 11.
625. Administration Report 1911, p. 11.
626. Administration Report 1913, p. 12.
627. Administration Report 1918, p. 1.

Russian consulate

Name	Duration
Andre Miller	May 1906-November 1908
Kadloubovsky	November 1908-
Passek	? – October 1910
Kadloubovsky acting	October 1910-April 1911
Dmitrieff	April 1911-10 March 1913
Loiko officiated	10 March 1913- 17 August 1913
Belayew	17 August – 6 November 1913
Loiko	6 November 1913 – 5 May 1919
Closed	5 May 1919 - 8 April 1923
Lindin	8 April 1923 -1924
Closed	1925-1940

Source: Administration Report 1901-1902, p. 4; Idem 1903-1904, p. 5; Idem, 1906-1907, p. 15; Idem, 1908, p. 7; Idem, 1910, p. 11; Idem, 1911, p. 11; Idem, 1913, p. 12; Idem, 1918, p. 1; Idem, 1925, p. 5; Political Diaries vol. 7, p. 174.

It was only in 1923 when the government of Soviet Russia appointed Lidin as consul-general in Bushehr. He was "a quiet young man, and has been on the whole discreet." The British did not know much about his activities. Apart from a get-to-know visit, he paid no other visits to the British Residency during the entire year and he did not call on the French consul at all. The British did not know either whether Lidin was engaged in secret activities, although outwardly his activities didn't seem to be very successful. The Soviet consul tried to form a Communist Party and to start a democratic newspaper; both attempts failed, probably due to lack of funds. Also, he was unable to form a pro-Russian group among local businessmen and officials.[628] Whether due to lack of prospects and/or lack of funds, the Soviet consulate-general was closed in 1925, except from 30 November to 9 December and from 16 to 25 December when Walden, the consul-general for Fars visited Bushehr.[629] In the following years the Soviet consulate-general remained closed, except when there was a visitor from up-country. Between 19 and 24 October 1926, `Abdol-Samad Khan, assistant to the consul-general of Fars, was sent to study the possibility of exporting locally grown cotton to Russia.[630] `Abdol-Samad Khan was again in Bushehr in August-September 1927 to oversee repairs to the consulate building. Moreover, Mirza Esma`il visited twice as a reporter of the consul-general Fars.[631] In June 1928, the Soviet consul-general made a short visit to "attend the opening ceremony of the Soviet firm named 'The Russian Traders for the East.'" However, the consulate remained closed. The firm also acted as news agents for the consul-general in Shiraz.[632] In September 1929, Batmanoff visited Bushehr for one week. 'The Russian Traders for the East' occupied the consulate henceforth.[633] Batmanoff visited Bushehr three times to meet with *Sharq* Company' steamers that brought cargo to Bushehr, but the consulate remained closed, although the Russian traders occupied the building.[634]

As of 1931, the Russian consulate was occupied by the Soviet Eastern Trading. Polycarpe Ananief, the consul-general of Fars was in Bushehr during 4 -19 April 1931. It was the first time that the consul-general called on the British Resident since the renewal of diplomatic relations between Great Britain and the Soviet Union. He again visited in October and introduced Alexander Simikoff, the manager of the Soviet Eastern Trading. He unsuccessfully protested against the police ban on illuminating a red star at night on their flag. He returned to Shiraz 16 October. On 7 November 1931, the Soviet Eastern Trading company celebrated Soviet National Day. It gave a reception in the consulate, which was attended by about 50 merchants, but no officials. Simikoff announced that just then a treaty had been signed between their two countries strengthening the friendly relations.[635] The Eastern Trading company continued to occupy the consulate, while the consul-general stayed there during his visits.[636] In June 1933, the Soviet Union closed its trading company in Bushehr. Only one Soviet ship came to the Persian Gulf that year, which was refused to unload its cargo in Bushehr and went to Mohammerah.[637] In 1934, a Russian Armenian clerk remained in charge of Russian Trading concern, which seemed to have done no business at all that year.[638] He left in November 1935 to Resht, leaving a caretaker in charge of the consulate.[639] The Armenian clerk returned from Resht in October 1936 and took charge of Russian Trading company, although he did

628. Administration Report 1923, p. 9.
629. Administration Report 1925, p. 5.
630. Administration Report 1926, p. 1.
631. Administration Report 1927, p. 1.
632. Administration Report 1928, p. 2.
633. Administration Report 1929, p. 2.
634. Administration Report 1930, p. 2.
635. Administration Report 1931, p. 2.
636. Administration Report 1932, p. 2.
637. Administration Report 1933, p. 2.
638. Administration Report 1934, p. 2.
639. Administration Report 1935, p. 2.

no business.[640] In the years thereafter, the Soviet consulate building was vacant. It was a nice building with two towers and surrounded by a wall, 1.2 km south of the British one in Bushehr.[641] On 9 September 1940, Paul Andrevich Serbekov, legation secretary with Alexandre Antipov, Russian trade representative came to Bushehr for one day.[642] Later the Russian consulate was reopened, but the man in charge, Alexander Beljaev, committed suicide on 4 January 1942 "as a result of a somewhat sordid intrigue with the Swiss wife of the Persian Medical Officer of Health."[643] On 24 February 1942, a Russian mission arrived in Bushehr consisting of M. Zoren, head accompanied by M. Sharapoff (Soviet Foreign Trade Department) and Ms Rymena as English interpreter. Also there was Comrade Chorostoshevsky.[644] However, this did not result in the re-opening of the Russian consulate.

Norway

It is not clear why Norway was represented in Bushehr as there were no trade relations with Persia. Probably, it was the result of Norwegian vessels occasionally calling on Bushehr (chapter two). However, those visits were so infrequent such that in 1909 the British consul-general in Bushehr, who represented Norwegian interests commented: "The grounds for the Norwegian consulate are spurious, it is a sinecure."[645] I have not been able to determine when Norwegian representation started. In 1910, the German consul Listemann took over the Norwegian vice-consulate from Mr. Krumpeter of Wonkchaus & Co on 27 April 1910, which means that it already existed prior to that year.[646] The German consul apparently transferred this task, because in August 1911 A.H. Wright, the Manager of the Bushehr branch of the Imperial Bank of Persia took over the charge of the Norwegian vice-consulate from the agent ofWonckhaus & Co.[647] Mr. Wright continued in this task until 22 April 1913, when his successor F. H. C. Gibbs assumed that responsibility.[648] Mr. Gibbs was vice-consul of Norway until 28 February 1914, when his successor W. F. Manson took over.[649] Manson in his turn transferred the vice-consulate to his replacement whose name I have been unable to trace. In 1919, the then branch manager of the IBP, C. A. Gardner was the Norwegian vice-consul and he held that function until 13 May 1921, when his successor A. A. Slesser took over. He transferred this task to the British consul-general on 25 August 1921.[650] For the remaining period of this study that is until 1940, the latter would represent Norwegian interests in

640. Administration Report 1936, p. 2.

641. Mahrad 1979, p. 89.

642. Administration Report 1940, p. 1.

643. Political Diaries, vol. 15, p. 4; Administration Report 1942, p. 6 (On 6 [sic] January he either shot himself or he was shot by his wife, because of the Swiss wife).

644. Political Diaries, vol. 15, pp. 35, 63.

645. Administration Report 1909, p. 10.

646. Administration Report 1910, p. 11.

647. Administration Report 1911, p. 11.

648. Administration Report 1913, p. 12.

649. Administration Report 1914, p. 5; Idem, 1915, p. 2.

650. Administration Report 1919, p. 1; Idem, 1921, p. 1.

Bushehr.[651] Despite the sinecure, sometimes the British consul-general had more work than normal such as when he was appointed vice-consul of Norway in 1927, but the official papers had not yet arrived.[652] In 1930 and 1931 the government of Persia did not want to recognize the British consul-general as Norwegian vice-consul. It argued that this person should be a Norwegian national. The problem was finally resolved in June 1931 after correspondence between the Persian and Norwegian governments.[653]

ITALY

Although in December 1887 an Italian vessel visited Bushehr,[654] there were hardly any trade relations between Persia and Italy. In the papers of the Persian *kargozar*, it is explicitly stated that in 1915 there was no Italian representation in Bushehr.[655] However, on 2 July 1914, Dr. Marobbio arrived in Bushehr to represent Italian interests. He left shortly thereafter and Italian interests were then represented by Capt. W.G. Neale of the British Residency.[656] In the following year the British consul-general took charge of the Italian representation, but after 1915 there is no longer mention of this.[657] In 1924, the British reported that the Italian consulate was closed. The next Italianate event happened in February 1938, when an Italian warship made a courtesy visit. This visit may have been in connection with the Italian Lloyd Triestinio Company, which since 1935 operated an irregular service of cargo vessels to Bushehr (chapter two).[658]

USA

Although the USA had diplomatic relations with Persia since 1884 it had no trade relations of importance with the country.[659] For unknown reasons the US decided to open a vice-consulate in Bushehr. The first consular agent as of 1884, was Tigranes G. Malcolm.[660] From 31 October until 25 November 1886, during a leg of its voyage around the world, the American frigate *USS Brooklyn* visited Bushehr. The Captain and several of his officers visited Shiraz and Persepolis, where they were friendly received and entertained.[661] Tigranes Malcolm was dismissed from his post in 1896, after he had reported

651. Administration Report 1922, p. 1; Idem, 1923-1940, pp. 1-2.
652. Administration Report 1927, p. 1.
653. Administration Report 1930, p. 2; Idem, 1931, p. 2; see further, IOR/L/PS/12/3661.
654. Administration Report 1887-88, p. 12.
655. Nura'i 1385, p. 204.
656. Administration Report 1914, p. 6
657. Administration Report 1915, p. 2.
658. Administration Report 1924, p. 5; Administration Report 1938, p. 2.
659. Yeselson 1956, p. 62. In August 1860, the American bark *Storm King* under Capt. Charles Millet arrived at Bushehr from Boston with a cargo of American sheetings and shirtings and returned with a cargo of dates. However, there was regular trade with the USA and Masqat. Malcolm 1887, p. 272.
660. Yeselson 1956, p. 30. According to Sadid al-Saltaneh, the Armenian Tegran Malcolm was one of the first category merchants of Bushehr; his forebears came from Isfahan to Bushehr. His brother Arsham was his partner in trade; they traded mostly in arms. They served the British and therefore, enjoyed their protection. Zell al-Soltan liked them very much and invested much in Bushehr in property and new buildings. Around 1910 Tegran became blind. Sadid al-Saltaneh 1362, p. 6.
661. US Government 1887, p. 23; Administration Report 1886-87, p. 9; Sirjani 1361, p. 277.

that his life was threatened by unruly mobs and that the *kargozar* had prevented the erection of a flagstaff at the US consulate. However, it appeared that he had never been threatened and only had been involved in intrigue, using his status as a British citizen, a Persian subject and American vice-consul as a shield to further his dealings in guns and wheat.[662] On 1 April 1924, G.G. Fuller US the vice-consul arrived in Bushehr, opened a vice-consulate and left on 7 September to Tehran. This visit probably was in connection with the visit of the *USS Trenton* in August to transport the remains of Major Imbrie. For the rest of the year 1924 the consulate remained closed.[663] It remained closed until 10 August 1925, when G.G. Fuller returned from Tehran. He left Bushehr again on 29 September 1925. It was expected that it would not be opened again, which was borne out by its permanent closure.[664]

Various other countries

Also, there were some countries represented in Bushehr that, except for Iraq, had no relations with Persia at all. In 1934, the British consul-general represented Greek interests, Estonian interests from 1933 until 1936, and Iraq from 1933 until February 1936.[665]

In addition to the abovementioned countries there were the occasional officials from other countries that came to Bushehr. Most remarkable, of course, was the arrival of the Japanese commercial mission, which arrived in the summer of 1880. At the same time, a Japanese warship visited the port.[666] It took some time before Japanese products would finally enter the Persian market in considerable quantities. When that happened, the Japanese minister in Tehran visited Bushehr twice, once in 1931 (Akio Kasama) and the second time in 1933 (M. F. Okamado). In that last year, a Japanese commercial traveler came to Bushehr to solicit orders.[667]

Although Austria had trade relations with Persia it was not represented in Bushehr, but the Austrian Lloyd line once sent a vessel in October 1887 and in 1888 one of its steamers *Calypso* sailed between Basra and Bushehr. These visits were related to Austrian interest at that time to have a better maritime connection between Triest-Suez-Aden-Mohammareh-Ahvaz.[668] Moreover, in 1897, 1899 and 1900 an occasional Austrian vessel called on Bushehr (chapter two), but this did not lead to any commercial follow-up.

---

662. Yeselson 1956, pp. 47-48. The US vice-consul John Tyler considered him to be a "sharp,pushing man of business."
663. Administration Report 1924, pp. 1, 5.
664. Administration Report 1925, p. 5.
665. Administration Report 1933, p. 2; Idem, 1934, p. 2; Idem, 1935, p. 2; Idem, 1936, p. 2. Greek representation may have to do with the fact that occasionally Greek steamships called on Bushehr, see Appendix VII.
666. Administration Report 1880-81, p. 10. For a report of this mission, see Yoshida 1373.
667. Administration Report 1931, p. 2; Administration Report 1933, p. 2; see Kazama 1380.
668. Administration Report 1887-88, p. 12; Slaby 1982, pp. 199-200.

Afterword

Bushehr was a typical Persian Gulf port, but had none of the characterstics of the so-called colonial port cities. I.e. it was and remained a small compact town, with mud and coraline-built houses, date huts, narrow winding streets, and unsanitary conditions and did not develop into a multi-cultural major port where different cultures and diverse environments met and interacted and through which people and ideas flowed. By the mid-nineteenth century, Bushehr changed from a port of call to a port of transit, a caravan terminus for the interior. It continued to maintain its predominant position between 1797 and 1917, although competition from three other ports (Bandar Abbas, Mohammareh and Basra) for the position of gateway to Southern Persia increasingly threatened this position. There were several reasons why Bushehr won the competition with the other ports. These included its active and prosperous commercial community and their close relationship with merchants in Shiraz and Isfahan. Its function as a distribution center for southern Persia and it was the seat of government for the Persian Gulf Ports, while the customs farmer, *kargozar*, and many foreign consuls and merchants also settled there, which further enhanced its central position on the littoral. Thus, the prosperity of Bushehr depended largely on the up-country markets, security of the roads, administrative function, and a positive business climate. However, when the central government favored the development of ports and road infrastructure of Khuzestan Bushehr could not complete and slowly, but surely was reduced to a minor port.

Although Bushehr's volume of trade increased significantly during the 19th century relatively speaking its trade was not very important reflecting the small size of Persia's economy. To put the trade of Bushehr in some perspective it is instructive to read Col. Pelly's characterization of it. In 1866 he wrote: "And it is probable that a year's traffic, along a well-frequented Persian road, might be stowed away in the shipping of an average London yard. The imaginative mind of Persia attributes to this, her almost sole sea-port, an incomparable commerce."[1]

The political rule of Bushehr may be divided into three distinctive periods. The first one was that of Arab rule by the Al Mazkur. Given their interest to maintain their quasi-autonomy and Arab character they had to keep control over the governorate. This was their strength and weakness. It was their strength for as long as they were able to galvanize the support of the Arabs and other ethnic groups of the Garmsir. However, it was also their weakness, because their hereditary claim meant that they were an easy prey for financial demands of the governor-general of Fars. A governor appointed by the central government could walk away from the post, if demands became to onerous, as indeed happened. However, this was not a choice for the Al Mazkur, who were used as a milkcow. This meant that they had to raise funds by imposing on their people and

1. Pelly 1865 a, pp. 48-49.

the merchants. This meant that the various petty chiefs in Bushehr's hinterland allowed themselves to be used by Shiraz against the Al Mazkur in its game of cat-and-mouse to milk the Sheikhs of Bushehr. It required the Al Mazkur instead of being the *primus inter pares* to be just one of the players, thus increasingly losing influence and getting involved in blood feuds. It further meant that merchants found their burden too onerous and much trade moved to other parts. This weakened the Al Mazkur, both militarily and financially, which finally led to their downfall.

With the demise of the Al Mazkur in 1850, the rotating Persian governors proved less of a target for oppressive governors-general of Fars. Moreover, increased trade in the Persian Gulf in general and Bushehr in particular made it also easier to satisfy everybody's interests. Instead of local intrigue, fights, and drama the period after 1850 is a rather pedestrian one. Grain embargos, commercial claims and the like dominate the correspondence of this period. The only thing in common with the pre-1850 period was the occasional offense given, or perceived to be given, to either British or Persian pride and the knee-jerk demand for satisfaction. But even these events diminished towards the end of the nineteenth century, due to growing influence of Great Britain and a weakened national and local government.

The third period begins with the Constitutional movement; during this period the governor's authority was diminished due to a weak central government, while it ended with the strongly centralizing state under the Pahlavi shahs, when governors shared authority with bureaucratic institutions that depended directly from Tehran. Although an unknown minor cleric, Sayyed Morteza Ahrami, with the help of tribal Tangestani forces took control over Bushehr for a few months in 1909, during which time they caused more harm than good (plundering the city before abandoning it), there was little popular interest or support for the Constitutional movement in Bushehr despite the activities of some loquacious and outspoken nationalists. The notables, in particular the merchant and religious class, were not greatly interested, and, as a result, the local *anjoman* was and remained a weak institution that was more of interest to those who wanted to advance their politcal career than to the local population and their immediate problems. In fact, governors such as Daryabegi and Movaqqar al-Dowleh did more to advance modern institutions and ideas in Bushehr than most of the self-appointed defenders of the people and religion. Even the occupation of Bushehr in August 1915 by the British did not provoke any popular outrage or opposition. What opposition there was came mainly from outside, from the tribal forces in Dashti, Dashtestan, and Tangestan, and, apart from some skirmishes with British forces in 1915, their opposition was insignificant.

It was only as of the 1920s, under the strong, nationalistic and centralizing Pahlavi regime that governors had more authority, be it as executor of policies and activities that had been decided upon in Tehran. Since around 1911, the governor's traditional fiscal, judicial and law enforcement tasks were delegated to separate branches of national administrative institutions. However, over time the governor acquired more say in these matters as local coordinator and chief-executor of the national government's policies. Also, in the economic area, governors tried to boost the flagging commercial prospects of their port, be it with little success. This was mainly due to the fact that those policies and investments that harmed Bushehr's position were taken at the national level, on which local governors had little influence.

The same apathy and disinterest of the Bushehri population in political matters, such as the Constitutional movement, was noticeable both before and after WW I; neither the coup d'etat (1921), the drive for a Republic (1924), nor the change of dynasty (1925) evoked any emotive reaction among the population. Such lack of interest was understandable, because Bushehr, in particular after WW I, entered a period of economic decline. People were not able to make ends meet and therefore, had more important problems to worry about than electing an *anjoman*, a deputy for the *Majles*, or worry about political issues that they neither understood nor would improve their life. As a consequence, they left for other parts of the Gulf, in particular to the new and growing ports of Khorramshahr and Abadan, so that between 1920 and 1940 Bushehr lost about 70% of its population. As a result, the merchant class lost a major part of their local clientele. Moreover, it also lost business opportunities at the regional and national level. First, due to the continued decline of Bushehr as a port, its decreasing population and, second, after 1930, due to the state monopolies of various consumer goods, which made normal trade almost impossible and basically hamstrung the business community. The WW II years did not bring much improvement in this situation, so that after the war Bushehr was but a small, insignificant, and sleepy port.

Appendix I.

List of governors of Bushehr and its district (1789-1947)

Name	Period	Observations	Source
Sheikh Naser II	1789- May 1807		See chapter 3
Sheikh `Abdol-Rasul b. Naser II	June 1807		See chapter 3
Mohammad Nabi Khan	September 1807-1811		See chapter 3
Mohammad Ja`far Khan	1811-March 1813		See chapter 3
Mehdiqoli Khan Qajar	March 1813-November 1814		
Sheikh `Abdol-Rasul b. Naser II	November 1814-February 1832	Sheikh Mohammad b. Naser II, interim 1815; Mirza Hasan Khan pro tem. Aug. 1815; Anushirvan Mirza till October 1815	See chapter 3
Sheikh Ahmad	November 1826 – February 1827	Usurper	See chapter 3
Noshirvan Mirza	February – June 1827	Pro tem	See chapter 3
Naser III b. `Abdol-Rasul	February – June 1832		See chapter 3
Rezaqoli Mirza	June 1832- Novermber 1834		See chapter 3
Mirza `Ali Khan	November 1834-March 1835		See chapter 3
Naser III b. `Abdol-Rasul	March 1835-May 1838		See chapter 3
Mirza Mohammad Reza	1-7 November 1837		See chapter 3
Mirza `Abbas	May - 8 December 1838		See chapter 3
Mirza Asadollah	8 December 1838 June 1839		See chapter 3
Mirza Mohammad Hoseyn	8 June - 26 August 1839		See chapter 3
Sheykh Hoseyn Al Mazkur	26 August 1839-February 1840	Self-appointed acting governor	See chapter 3
Naser III b. `Abdol-Rasul	August 1839-October 1850	Sheikh `Abdollah Al Mazkur, acting 05/ 1840 to 02/1841; 08/42 to 09/1845; Sheikh Hoseyn Saleh, acting 01 to 09/1849	See chapter 3

Name	Period	Observations	Source
Mohammad `Ali Khan Nazem al-Molk	10 to 12?/1849	Mirza Mehdi Khan deputy	See chapter 3
Mirza `Ali Khan, son of Qavam al-Molk	September 1850-1856		Busse 1972, p. 295; Sa`adat 1390, p. 48
British occupation	9 December 1856 until 29 October 1857		NA, FO 248/183, Felix Jones to Ahmad Khan 25 February 1858
Ahmad Khan Nava'i	1857-58		Sa`adat 1390, p. 48
Hasan Khan Qarachadaghi Azerbaijani	1858-59	Dashti, Dashtestan and Bush	Busse 1972, p. 340
Soleyman Mirza	1859-60	Idem	Busse 1972, p. 343; Sa`adat 1390, p. 48
Mehr `Ali Khan	1860-61	Idem	Busse 1972, p. 345
Mirza Ahmad Khan `Amid al-Molk	1862-65	Idem	Busse 1972, p. 347; Transactions BGS, vol. XVII (1865), p. 172
Asadollah Mirza	1865-1868	Idem	Busse 1972, p. 352
Naser al-Molk	1868-1873	Idem	Busse 1972, p. 364
Asadollah Mirza	1873-75		Administration Report 1873-74, p. 5; Sa`adat 1390, p. 48
`Abdol-Hoseyn Khan Sartip	1875-76	Idem	Busse 1972, p. 384; Administration Report 1875-76, p. 4; Sa`adat 1390, p. 48
Hoseyn Qoli Khan Sa`d al-Molk	Until 11 May 1876	Idem	Administration Report 1875-76, p. 4
Abdar-bashi governor-general of Fars; then Malek al-Tojjar	11/05 till 27/06/1876 30/06 till August 1876	Kerbela'i `Evaz, officiated for Malek al-Tojjar	Saldanha 1986, vol. 7/2, p. 5
Ehtesham al-Dowleh	August 1876 till March 1878	Haji Mirza Esma`il Vazir as deputy for Ehtesham al-Dowleh, the nominal governor	Administration Report 1876-77, p. 4; Busse 1972, p. 388; Saldanha 1986, vol. 7/2, p. 5; Sa`adat 1390, p. 48
Haji Mohammad Baqer Khan	March 1878 until 12/09/1881		Busse 1972, p. 397, 399; Administration Report 1880-81, p. 10; Saldanha 1986, vol. 7/2, p. 5; Sa`adat 1390, p. 49
Mirza Mohammad Mostowfi-ye Nezam Mo`tamed al-Soltan	1881-82	Mirza `Ali Akbar acting; Mirza `Abdollah Khan acting	Busse 1972, p. 417; Sa`adat 1390, p. 49; Administration Report 1881-82, p. 6;
Nasir al-Molk	1882-83	Mirza `Abdollah Khan acting as of February 1883	Buss 419; Administration Report 1882-83, p. 5
Mirza Mohammad Hoseyn Khan, Mo'taman al-Molk	1883- June 1885	Abu'l-Fath Khan his son-in-law acted as of January 1884	Administration Report 1883-84, p. 8; Saldanha 1986, vol. 7/2, p. 5; Administration Report 1885-86, p. 7
Nowzar Mirza	June 1885	Appointment cancelled	Administration Report 1885-86, p. 7
Haji Mohammad Mehdi Malek al-Tojjar	June 1885-May 1886		Administration Report 1885-86, p. 7; Sa`adat 1390, p. 49
Haji Fath `Ali Khan	June 1886		Administration Report 1886-87, p. 9; Saldanha 1986, vol. 7/2, p. 5

Name	Period	Observations	Source
Nowzar Mirza	February – October 1887	resigned October 1887, but was persuaded to stay	Administration Report 1887-88, p. 10; Sa`adat 1390, p. 49; Saldanha 1986, vol. 7/2, p. 5; Administration Report 1887-88, p. 11
Mohammad Hasan Khan Sa`d al-Molk	November 1887-March 1891	Heydarqoli Khan deputy, March 1888-?	Administration Report 1887-88, p. 11; Sa`adat 1390, p. 49
Nezam al-Saltaneh	March 1891-September 1892	Idem	Administration Report 1891-92, p. 9; Sa`adat 1390, p. 49
Rezaqoli Khan, his nephew	September 1892-March 1893	Deputy governor for his uncle	Administration Report 1892-93, p. 12
Mohammad Hasan Khan Sa`d al-Molk	March 1893-March 1894	Second time	Administration Report 1892-93, p. 12; Sa`adat 1390, p. 49
Mohammad Reza Khan Qavam al-Molk	March 1894-7 March 1895		Report 1893-94, p. 10; Administration Report 1895-96, p. 6-7; Sa`adat 1390, p. 49
Haji Mirza `Abdollah	7 March 1895 -November 1896	Deputy-governor	Administration Report 1895-96, p. 7
Hosam al-Saltaneh	December 1896-March 1897		Administration Report 1896-97, p. 10 Sa`adat 1390, p. 49
Eqtedar al-Soltan	March-September 1897		Administration Report 1897-98, p. 6
Amir Panj, garrison commander	September 1897-?	Deputy-governor	Administration Report 1897-98, p. 6
Mojir al-Saltaneh	October 1897; annulled		Administration Report 1897-98, p. 6
Qavam al-Molk, son E`temad al-Soltan officiating	November 1879-February 1898		Administration Report 1897-98, p. 6; Saldanha 1986, vol. 7/2, p. 5
Malek al-Tojjar	February-March 1898	Deputy-governor	Administration Report 1897-98, p. 6
`Emad e Nezam	March 1898	Servant Farmanfarma, governor-general of Fars	Administration Report 1897-98, p. 6
Sa`id al-Soltan	April 1898	Idem	Administration Report 1898-99, p. 6
Mozaffar-e Nezam	May 1898	Idem	Administration Report 1898-99, p. 6
Mo`ezz al-Mamalek	June – September 1898	Idem; nephew of Sa`d al-Molk and Nezam al-Saltaneh	Administration Report 1898-99, p. 6
Ahmad Khan Daryabegi	September 1898 – April 1901		Administration Report 1898-99, p. 6; Sa`adat 1390, p. 49
Salar-e Mo`azzam, nephew of Nezam al-Saltaneh	August 1901-March 1904		Administration Report 1901-1902, p. 1; Sa`adat 1390, p. 49
Ahmad Khan Daryabegi	March 1904-December 1907	Second time	Report 1903-1904, p. 1; Sa`adat 1390, p. 49
Haji Sa`id al-Saltaneh	January 1907		Administration Report 1906-1907, p. 11; Sa`adat 1390, p. 49

Name	Period	Observations	Source
Ahmad Khan Daryabegi	August 1907-October 1908	Third time	Administration Report 1907-1908, p. 7; Sa`adat 1390, p. 49
Mo`azzez al-Dowleh, brother of Asaf al-Dowleh, governor-general of Fars	October 1908- March 1909		Administration Report 1908, p.7; Sa`adat 1390, p. 49
Ahmad Khan Daryabegi	May 1909-8 April 1911	Fourth time	Administration Report 1909, p. 8
Mirza `Ali Mohammad Movaqqar al-Dowleh	8 April 1911-8 August 1915		Administration Report 1911, p. 12; Sa`adat 1390, p. 49
Lt. Col. Lane	8 -26 August 1915	Military governor	Administration Report 1915
Brig. General Brooking	28 August-13 September 1915	Military governor	Administration Report 1915, p. 6
Brig. General Edwardes	13 September 1915-16 October 1915	Military governor	Administration Report 1915, p. 6
Ahmad Khan Daryabegi	16 October 1915-23 November 1920	Fifth time	Administration Report 1916 p. 2; Sa`adat 1390, p. 49
Movaqqar al-Dowleh	23 November 1920-October 1921		Administration Report 1920, p. 1
Moshar al-Dowleh	October 1921-30 September 1922		Administration Report 1921, p. 1
Yamin al-Mamalek	October 1922 (deputy) 30 January 1923- 4 June 1923		Administration Report 1922, p. 1
Dabir al-Homayun	5 June 1922-29 July 1922	Pro tem	Administration Report 1923, p. 5
Nasr al-Dowleh	29 July 1922-28 may 1924		Administration Report 1923, p. 5
Mo`azzad al-Soltan	28 May 1924-22 June 1924	Pro tem	Administration Report 1924, p. 5
Reza Khan Atabegi Veqar al-Molk	22 June 1924-17 September 1925		Administration Report 1924, p. 5
Mohammad Karim Khan Vaziri	17 September-13 October 1925	Pro tem	Administration Report 1925, p. 6
Mirza Ja`far Khan Khvajeh-Nuri Movaffaq al-Dowleh	13 October 1925-22 June 1926		Administration Report 1925, p. 6
Kargozar (Montaser al-Molk)	22 June – 19 November 1926	Pro tem	Administration Report 1926, p. 2; Political Diaries, vol. 7, p. 417
Ahmad Khan Nikpey Mofakhkham al-Molk	19 November 1926 – 22 June 1927		Administration Report 1926, p. 2
Mirza Mehdi Khan Nashaki	22 June – 21 September 1927	Pro tem	Administration Report 1927, p. 2
Mirza Gholam `Ali Khan Fotuhi Mo`in al-Molk	21 September 1927 – 20 May 1928		Administration Report 1927, p. 2
`Abdollah Khan Monajjemi	20 May – 31 August 1928	Pro tem	Administration Report 1928, p. 2
Sardar-e Entesar Aqa Mozaffar Khan Aslam	31 August 1928 - 9 February 1931		Administration Report 1928, p. 2
Hoseyn `Ali Khan Shahruzi	21 May-21 December	Pro tem	Administration Report 1930, p. 3

Name	Period	Observations	Source
Mirza Esma`il Khan Amir Ebrahimi	2 February till 24 March	Assistant governor and pro tem	Administration Report 1930, p. 3
Mohammad Khan Zand	9 February – 26 July 1931	Assistant governor and pro tem	Administration Report 1931, p. 3
`Ali Asghar Khan Taleqani	26 July 1931 – 21 October 1933		Administration Report 1931, p. 3
`Abdollah Khan Minjal	21 October – 31 December 1933	Pro tem	Administration Report 1933, p. 3.
Mohammad `Ali Mirza Rokni	January 1934 – 23 July 1935		Administration Report 1934, p. 3.
`Abdol-Shakur Amin	23 July – 23 November 1935	Assistant governor and pro tem	Administration Report 1935, p. 3
Amanollah Ardalan	23 November 1935 – 27 May 1936		Administration Report 1935, p. 3
`Abdol-Shakur Amin	28 May till 8 July 1936	Assistant governor and pro tem	Administration Report 1936, p. 2
Ahmad Sadri	9 July 1936- 12 April 1938		Administration Report 1936, p. 2
`Enayatollah Parvaneh	12 – 26 April 1938	Pro tem	Administration Report 1938, p. 2
Hasan Farzaneh	26 April 1938- 31 May 1940		Administration Report 1938, p. 2
Mahmud Al-e Aqa	1 June - 10 September 1940	Assistant governor and pro tem	Administration Report 1940, p. 2
Hasan Farzaneh	11 -24 September 1940		Administration Report 1940, p. 2
Mahmud Al-e Aqa	25 September- 24 November 1940	Assistant governor and pro tem	Administration Report 1940, p. 2
Mir `Ali Zahir Homayun	25 September 1940-14 August 1941	Mohammad Esma`il Navvab pro tem	Administration Report 1940, p. 2; Political Diaries, vol. 14, p. 491
Sarhang Malek Nasiri	15 September 1941-15 November 1941	Military governor	Political Diaries, vol. 14, pp. 511, 557-78
Captain `Abdollah Mujab	15 November 1941-12 January 1942	Pro tem; police commissioner	Political Diaries, vol. 15, p. 3
Mir `Ali Zahir	12 January 1942- † 6 August 1942	Mr. Kasmai pro tem as of 18 September 1942-?	Political Diaries, vol. 15, p. 3, 221, 261, 287
Mr. Abasalti	Until 4 October 1942	Pro tem	Political Diaries, vol. 15, p. 287
Mr. Kasmai	4 October 1942- 16 February 1943	Acting governor; Pasyar Jahed, chief of police pro tem 16-24/02/1943	Political Diaries, vol. 15, p. 407
Mehdi Hesabi	24 February 1943-29 April 1946	Acting Lotfollah Dowlatshahi, chief of Customs 19/07-30/10/45	Political Diaries, vol. 15, p. 407, vol. 17, p. 81; Administration Report 1945, p. 8
Reza Fahimi	29 April 1946-10 July 1947	Fathollah Khan, acting governor 22/09-15/10/46; Mr. Navvab, acting 15/10-24/11/14	Political Diaries, vol. 17, pp. 81, 209, 230, 261, 473
Amir Arfa` Qavami	10 July 1947- ?		Political Diaries, vol. 17, pp. 427, 473

Appendix II

Memorandum on the system of cultivating the date palm in the vicinity of Bushire, with some information connected with its growth, produce, price, &c., &c., by Mr. J. C. Edwards, 2nd Assistant Resident.

Offshoots which spout around the foot of the female tree are procured from Busreh, Kateef or Bahrein, and transplanted to wherever the cultivator may desire to have a date grove. These offshoots may be produced of all sizes, but the smaller ones-say one foot high- are preferred, as the chances of injury from transplanting are less than to those of a larger size. After being transplanted they require to be eaten daily for two or three years. The soil in which they are planted should be soft, and the base of the plant surrounded with manure. The manure used in these parts for this purpose is horse-dung mixed with earth, and allowed to decompose for a year before being used.

Where water is very plentiful these offshoots are known to have sprung up rapidly and borne fruit within four or five years. But where water is scarce, and the soil hard, ten or twelve years elapse before any signs of fruit are visible.

Opinions differ in regard to the rearing of date trees from seed. Some aver that the trees thus reared never come to perfection; others say they do and bear fruit, but are generally weak and never satisfactory. It has also been suggested that if the date seed be planted with the fruit it would germinate sooner and thrive better than if the seed were sown alone. But all agree that the offshoots are best, inasmuch as they take less time to grow, and are by far more strong and productive than the trees reared from seed. These offshoots "are extremely hardy, and may remain for eight or ten weeks exposed without injury. Their average weight is about six pounds."

The date tree first shows its blossom in February; these sprout around the heart of the tree in strong covers very much resembling swords scabbards in shape. They split about March and show a bunch of blossoms milky white in color. The cultivator has now to decide what number of bunches he should leave on the tree, and withdraws the superabundance. The number of bunch blossoms on each tree varies from 12 to 24, but it is seldom that more than 12 are allowed to remain for fruit.

At this period also the cultivator has to impregnate the blossoms of the femake tree by joining thereto some portion of the blossom of the male tree. This is done by simply depositing a sprig or two from the male into a bunch of female blossom and lightly binding it up with a sprig. The male tree is distinguishable by its blossom, which is of a reddish tinge, while that of the female is milky white. The blossom of the male tree is only used for impregnating and does not turn into fruit. It is averred that in places where the date palm grows thick together, the wind scatters the pollen of the male blossom, and that the female trees thus become impregnated with it, saving the cultivator further trouble on his head.

When through neglect or oversight the female tree fails to be impregnated, it is asserted that the fruit it bears does not become to perfection, is seedless and insipid.

The blossom of the date tree is known in Persian by the name of Tarah (طاره), the process of impregnating Budadan (بو دادن), the male tree Nar (نر), and female Madah (ماده).

About May the fruit begins to form, and from this time to September, when the fruit is perfectly ripe, the tree sheds the superabundance, which is used as food by the proprietor or those he employs to watch his property. At this period the fruit is known as Khumal (خمال), and is green in color.

In June and July the fruit is known as Kharek (خارك), and is either red or yellow in color. It is now fit to be eaten, and where marts are close, such quantities as are saleable are cut down for the purpose.

In August the date becomes soft and juicy; it is known as Ratab (رطب), and sold in the bazaars as food, but it is not yet in a fit state for preservation, as if kept for two or three days it would turn sour.

In September the date is known as Khurma (خرما). It is now in a fit state for preservation. After being taken off the tree it is gathered into a tank or trough and exposed to the air and sun, where it throws off its extra juice and sufficiently hardens to allow of its being packed up in baskets an prepared for exportation.

The juice is gathered and stowed in skins or jars; it is called Dushab (دوشاب), and is used by the poorer classes in lieu of sugar.

The juice is also used in preserving dates in jars, this is done by mixing these with sesame seed, ginger powder, and the kernels of walnuts. This preserve is called Khurma-Shirah (خرما شيره), and is much prized both for use in the Persian Gulf and for exportation.

There is a species of a date called Kharak Bereymi (خارك بريمى) which does not ripen beyond the Kharak stage. The mode of preserving this has been to boil it well with water, and then to expose it to the sun and air till hardened. If well packed and preserved from damp, this will keep for some time, but if kept in air-tight tins, might keep for an indefinite period in a dry climate, this is called Kharek-i-pukhtah (خارك پخته)

Another species, the Zahidi (زاهدى), does not ripen beyond the Ratab stage. In fact, it ceases to progress between the Kharak and ratab, and is left to remain on the tree till hardened by the sun and atmosphere. It is then cut down and packed in baskets. This species is not much used for food, as it finds a more profitable mart in India where it is much sought after by distillers of arrack.

There are more than a hundred varieties of date known by different names which it would not be easy to enumerate or describe, nor would there be much utility in doing so, for they would only be understood by the natives of these parts, to whom it is a matter of great consequence, to know the name of the date they purchase, as prices are invariably regulated thereby. As an example, I marginally enumerate the species of dates received as samples from the Chief of Dashtee, which may be said to comprise about all the varieties found in this plain, but in Bahrein, Kuteef, El Hasa, and Busreh there are a great many more kinds, all distinguishable by separate appellations.

Khareh-i Khaneyzi	خارك خنيزى
Kabkab	كبكاب
Kandi	قندي
Shakar	شكر
Kantar	قنطار
Hallow	حلو
Maktub	مكتوب
Khush-Kharek	خوش خارك

Shekh Ali	شیخ عالی
Sherunu	شرونو
Kharu	خارو
Juzi	جوزي
Chehal-Gazal	چهل گزل
Khatu-Shahabi	خاتو شهابی
Nirini	نیرینی
Shahuni	شاهونی
Kaidi	قایدی
Sisi	سیسی
Rash	رش
Kharek-Katu	خارك كتو

Prices of dates vary in the ratio of 1 to 4.

The best description comes from El Hasa known as Khelas (خلاص). These are packed in skins of 70 to 120 lbs., and this year may be priced at the average rate of 15 krans per 124 lbs.

The next in quality is the Kharek-pukhteh (خارك پخته) from Busreh, valued at about 12 krans per 124 lbs.

The Hallow (حلو) from Busreh claims attention next, and is seldom sufficient for the demand. Value ranges from 6 to 7 krans per basket of about 140 lbs.

The Zahidi (زاهدي) is about the same price as the Hallow (حلو) and is procurable at Busreh.

The Samerun (سعمرون) from Busreh, is very common, and commands between 4 and 5 krans per basket of 140 lbs.

These prices would only stand good for this year, as each year the price is regulated, *first*, by the quantity forthcoming, *secondly*, by the demand, and *thirdly*, by the craft available for export.

The date palm is a source of great help to the poor. They feed on its droppings from May to September, and keep the produce as food for the next seven months; the branches supply them with fuel and material for hutting, the fruit branches when divested of fruit are used as brooms, and the leaf turned into rope or matting, the stem cut up and used in house-building.

The date tree is called	Nakhl	نخل
The stem when cut up	Jadu	جدوع
The branches	Gurz	گرز
The lower part of the branches	Tapul	طاپول
Used as ful or floats for fishing nets.		
The leaf	Pish	پیش

Toddy is not extracted from the date tree, as the people of these parts have not yet acquired a taste for this liquor. But the experiment has been made, and good toddy can be extracted therefrom at the cost of the fruit.

(Sd.) J.C. Edwards

Uncovtd. Assistant Resident, Persian Gulf

P.S. - In the spring of each year it is necessary to take away the offshoots that sprout round each tree, as these prevent the parent tree from thriving.

Source: Administration Report 1877-78, pp. 43-46.

Appendix III

Chahkutah and Tul-i-Siah

With Chahkutah and its surrounding villages is now included Ahmedi, which was formerly a separate entity owned by the family, of which the Telegraph ghulams, Mullah Abdullah and Agha Muhammad Quli, are now the representatives, Agha Mustapha Bahmiar of Chogadak and Tul-i-Siah being a near relation. Shaikh Hussein of Chahkutah ejected them many years ago, but has had a hard struggle to retain Ahmedi the importance of which arises from its position as the first stage on the caravan route. Tul-i-Siah and Choghadak occupy a vague position: Shaikh Hussein Khan of Chah-kutah considers himself the suzerain, but Agha Haidar, the Zabit of Chogadak, and his brothers pay revenue independently to the Governor of the Gulf Ports, and similarly collect road exactions at Chogadak. Agha Haidar has, however, always assisted Shaikh Hussein in his quarrels, and looks to him for support. The Zabit of Tul-i-Siah also claims the villages of Ali Changi and Gurak on the borders of Tangistan, but these are now managed by the ruler of Tangistan.

The boundaries of Chahkutah and Chogadak are on the:

North-West: Between Husseinaki and Hassandum in Angali.

North: Between Husseinaki and Isawand in Borazjun, between Isawand in Borazjun and Ab-i-Tawil; between Tul-Ashki and Bulferiz in Tangistan.

East: Between Chahkutah and Samal in Tangistan.

South: Chahkutah and Chah-i-Pir in Tangistan; between Chogadak and Buneh-Giz and Gurak in Tangistan.

West: The district extends into the Mashilleh between Chogadak and the mainland of Bushire.

The following villages may be considered as part of the district:

Chahkutah	Tul-Ashki
Ahmedi	Konarabadi
Husseinaki	Chogadak
Dawaireh	Tul-i-Siah
Ab-i-Tawil	

The maliyat of Chahkutah is 1,500, of Ahmedi 700 tomans: that of Chogadak and Tul-i-Siah 750: the Khan's revenue is derived from taxation of cultivated land, and also from rahdari and alafi from caravans passing Ahmedi. Chahkutah and the nearest villages have been for generations in this family, which boasts of Arab descent. The present ruler, Shaikh Hussein, has been constantly at war during the past few years. His brothers Sheikh Ali Mohammed and Abdullah united to force him to share their father's villages with them: and they were for years in sanctuary in Borazjun and Angali.

Sheikh Ali was killed in a quarrel by Shaikh Hussain in 1911: Shaikhs Mohammed and Abdullah raised a revolt in 1911 and were joined by Zair Khidar of Tangistan and Ahmed Khan of Angali. During some sharp fighting the elder brother was killed and Shaikh Abdullah, wounded took 'bast' in the town Residency with about 80 of the Zangineh tribe, inhabitants of Chahkutah. Later they went back, and Shaikh Abdullah was given the village of Ab-i-Tawil by Shaikh Husseim; but blood-feud and enmity still prevails between the brothers. Shaikh Hussein was for many years a close ally of Darya Begi, and introduced Zair Khidar, then an unimportant Kedkhuda of Tangistan, to his favour. In 1909 Darya Begi, accompanied by Shaikh Hussein in an expedition against Zair Khidar and again in 1910, but then the Governor of the Gulf Ports made friendship with the Tangistani chief and authorised him to attack Shaikh Hussein in support of the latter's brothers. Much fighting ensued, but Nizam-us-Soltaneh on his way to Shiraz took up the cudgels for Shaikh Hussein, sent Qashgais under Amir-ul-Mulk to assist Shaikh Hussein, and the Tangistanis and Angalis were beaten off. Shaikh Hussein manifested his enmity against Dary Begi by threatening to capture him in Bushire, in consequence of which Darya Begi after his dismissal took 'bast' with the Residency. Muwaqqar-ud Douleh, when appointed Governor, at first supported Shaikh Hussein, then turned against him and favoured Zair Khidar. Shaikh Hussein was openely defiant to the Governor as long as Nizam-us-Soltaneh was in power, and since then has been invoking the Residency's support to prevent the Governor from taking his revenge. In 1911 he contracted with Nizam-us-Soltaneh to be answerable for the revenue of Ahram, Khawiz and Tangistan for the sum of 46,000 tomans for a period of 6 years by arrangement with the Tangistani Khans, protegés of Nizam-us-Soltaneh. In October 1911 these were however turned out of Tangistan by an uprising on the part of Zair Khidar, who besieged some of the Khans with one of Shaikh Hussein's sons and men in the fort of Qalat.

The outstanding feature of Chahkutah politics is blood enmity with Angali on the one hand, and Zair Khidar of Tangistan on the other, and insubordination as regards the present Governor of Bushire. Possession of Ahmedi, which has often been threatened, is the most important factor for the Shaikh, because of the large revenue derived from exactions from muleteers. He is also desirous of obtaining a hold on the northern part of Tangistan. He always professes very friendly feelings towards the Residency, but is a great arms-dealer and importer, like most headmen in a position to participate in the traffic.

The ruling family tree is on the next page:

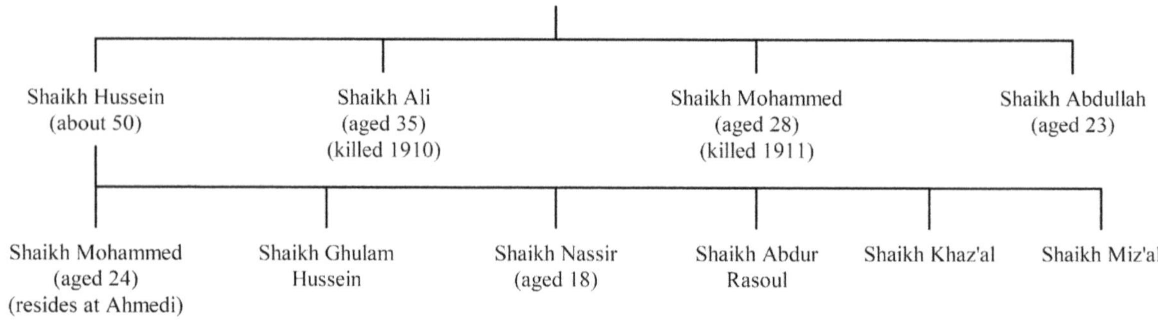

Chogadak and Tul-i-Siah had till 1912 been ruled by Agha Mustapha Bahmiyar.

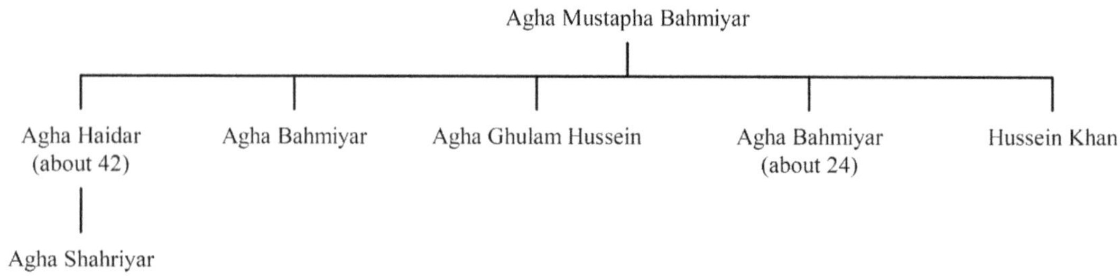

Agha Haidar lives at Chogadak with the younger Bahmiyar and Hussein Khan, his half-brothers.

Agha Ghulam Hussein and the elder Bahmiyar live at Tul-i-Siah, 360 tomans are remitted from the revenue annually on condition of provision for guarding the route.

Appendix II, Administration Report for 1911; see also Hamidi 1380, pp. 238-41.

Appendix IV

Tangistan

Tangistan, as at present composed, includes localities formerly separate entities such as Samal and Ahram, and the Khawiz valley. The last named is the only portion in the mountains, and outside the coast plain; the Tangistani chiefs, its purchasers, have brought it under Tangistan proper. The present boundaties of the district are on the -

West: the mashilleh from neaer the caravan route to its end, then along the sea-coast to Karri.

South: from this point to the hills begind (which separate it from inland Dashti) and northwards along the crest of these hills to a gulley flowing out past Kullul, a little to the north; south of Bagh-i-Abi to the mountains north of the Kuh-i-Bairami.

North: from the Mashilleh, south of the caravan road, south of Chogadak, north of Alichangi, then east of Chahkutah, and north-westwards till it meets the Borazjan border; west of Bulferiz and gandumriz; then turning eastwards north of Gulungun, along alow range of hills till it reraches the Tang-i-Haft Mulla.

East: southwards along the range of coast mountains, past the Kuh-i-Dukhtar to the entrance of the Tang-i-Wahush, then long the range to east of the Khawiz valley, south of Modahu and Ashi.

A low range of hills separates the villges on the sea coast from the rest of Tangistan. The villages of Tangistan are:

Sea-coast	Inland valley	In the Khawiz valley	In Northern Tangistan
Pakushi	Baghak	Banjun	Bulferiz
Tangistan	Tukhmari	Khawiz	Gandumriz
Gargur	Shamshiri	Gishi	Gulangun
Goinak	Qala Mangali	Yakh	Samal
Khashm-i-Saadat	Khiari	Modahu	Abad
Qaleh-i-Taqi	Ambarak	Ashi	Chah-i-Pir
Nargiszar	Shuraki	-	Mohmed Ahmedi
Dilwar	Samail Ali	-	Konar-ei-Baye
Baraki group	Ma Taheri	-	Konar-i-Abadi
Gahi, Bashi	Qaleh Qalat	-	Alichangi

Sea-coast	Inland valley	In the Khawiz valley	In Northern Tangistan
Bulkhair	Bagh-i-Abi	-	Buneh Giz
Rustami	Ahram	-	Ali Gurgi
`Umari	Dumiredu	-	Gurak
Bunju	Gulaki	-	-
Karri	Tumb-i-Seh	-	-
Salimabadeh	-	-	-
Khabidu	-	-	-
Khwahir	-	-	-
Madumari	-	-	-
Makri	-	-	-
Shahabi	-	-	-
Vakanku	-	-	-

Ahram, the Khawiz Valley and Samal are properties of Nizam-us-Soltaneh, (being farmed for about 6,400 tomans in 1911); but the grant was made by the Government in Tehran irrespective of the rights of ownership possessed by the Khans of Tangistan themselves in the date gardens of Ahram. The maliyat of the rest of Tangistan is 2,500 tomans.

At the time of the British War of 1856, when the Tangistanis put up a brief resistance, their district was in the undivided control of Baghir Khan. For much longer, however, they had been notorious for their inroads into Bushire, the outskirts of the town and the island being from time to time raided by them. After Baghir Khan's death the district got gradually out of the control of its own chiefs. For a time the famous Mohammed Khan of Dashti ruled it, subsequently Hassan Khan, son of Baghir Khan. Haidar Khan, a nephew of the above, was kept prisoner at Shiraz for many years previous to 1890. Afters his return he and his cousin Ali Khan ruled alternately, but weakly and badly; and several Kedkhudas made themselves practically independent, including a certain Kedkhuda of Baghak, Hali Mohammed Ali. Maliyat was not paid, and the Khans, in bad odour with the people, were finally driven out through the Darya Begi's championship of Zair Khidar, son of the above Kedkhuda of Baghak. This man originally agreed to act as Kalantar of the district under the Khans, and got together the maliyat, and finally dispossessed the Khans. From 1905 onwards, Zair Khidar and the various Kedkhudas remained each supreme in his own village or surroundings, the most notable being Hassan Bakshu in Ambarak, Ghulam Hussein Haji Khidar in Shuraki, Reis Ali in Dilwar. The Khawiz valley and Ahram were farmed by Zair Khidar, who amassed money but was very lenient.

In 1911 Nizam-us-Soltaneh rejected Zair Khidar's overtures, having with him in his suite some of the younger Tangistani Khans. Zair Khidar was attacked by a force of the Nizam, beaten back to the hills, and his village Shemshiri destroyed. Sharp fighting ensued, in which some of the kedkhudas, like Hassan Bakshu, took the part of the Khans. Baghir Khan, Bahadur-us-Soltaneh was killed, but old Haidar Khan went back to Ahram with the other Khans on Nizam-us-Soltaneh's behalf. They remained in power as long as Nizam was Governor-General, but in October Zair Khidar attacked them in the fort of Qalat, and, as their supporters melted away, they were forced to fly the district. Muwaqqer-ud-Douleh, the new Governor [of Bushehr], put Zair Khidar in charge of all Tangistan, and they maintain friendly relations. The other Kedkhudas are by no means subordinate to Zair Khidar, though Zair Khidar can raise the most men. Reis Ali of Dilwar has become rich, and therefore of some importance, through successful smuggling.

The number of tufangchis in Tangistan is altogether perhaps 1,000, but there are so many blood feuds and enmities that more than 300 would most unlikely be found together. At the time of Seyyid Murteza's introduction of the Tangistanis into Bushire in 1909, 1,000 men were said to have been collected, but the number was really much less, and they were attracted by the prospect of loot.

The family of the Khans of Tangistan is:

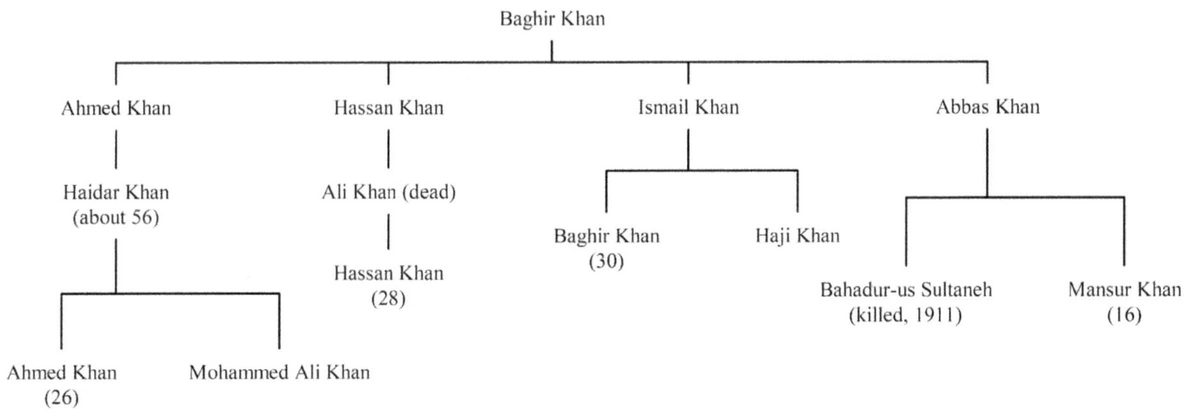

Zair Khidar's residence is at Shamshiri, his fort at Qalat near Ahram.

Appendix II, Administration Report for 1911.

Notes by Mr. H. G. Chick, commercial adviser to the Political Rwsidency in the Persian Gulf, upom various districts of Fars and of the Gulf Ports.[1]

1. For a photo of Mr. Chick, see Roknzadeh 1352, p. 150.

Appendix V

Hayat Daoud and Rudhilleh

The district of Rudhilleh was until 15 years ago entirely separate from Hayat Daoud, and then belonged to a certain Mohammed Khan; its present connection occurs from the fact that its resident Khans since then have been members of the Hayat Daoud family, who defeated and drove out the last owners. The present chief of Hayat Daoud lived during his father's life-time, for some years at Mohmedi in charge of the district; after his succession the third brother, Hussein Quli Khan, took over charge. As the family's interests are much bound up, and all pay allegiance to the eldest brother at Bandar Rig, the districts are taken together.

Hayat Daoud is about 33 miles long by 27 wide. It is bounded on the:

West: by the sea from the Kuh-i-Bang hills as far as the outflow of the Sir-i-Bidu to the sea;

South: by the Sur-i-Bidu, to its rise in the Mohur-i-Hayat Daoud behind Chaharrustai, separating Hayat Daoud first from the Rudhilleh district, afterwards from Shabancara;

East: Hayat Daoud territory extends 15 miles into the mountains from the coast range, and marches with Kashkuli country; but it has no villages in the hills, which are only used for pasturage;

North: from the middle of the Kuh-i-Bang hills, north of the village of Bang, across from the narrow valley to their east, and north of the village of Shul to the coast range, then across the mountains for some 15 miles.

In the political territory of Hayat Daoud are also (i) the port and village of Bunder Dilam with about 1 mile square each side of it, and (ii) the islands of Kharg and Khargu, about 25 miles from the mainland of Rudhilleh.

The geographical district of Rudhilleh is some 21 miles long from near Shief to Bidu, and 19 miles wide from the sea to near Kureband. It is bounded on the:

West: by the sea from the outflow of the Shir-i-Bidu to some 5 miles north-west of Shief, which is in Angali.

North: it is separated from the district of Shabancara by a line running north from the Rudhilleh river between the villages of Manun in Rudhilleh and Mukaberi in Shabancara as far as the Sur of Bidun near Anjiru; south of the Rudhilleh river the boundary with Angali is between Kurraband and Zerdaki in Angali, and then runs south to within a few miles of Shief.

In 1904, during the Governorship of the Gulf Ports by the present Nizam-us-Soltaneh, the introduction of Customs posts along the ports of the district led to difficulties with the Khans, who had previously managed their own Customs. This difficulty was settled by the Khans agreeing to the establishment of a Customs post at Bandar Rig, and at Bandar Dilam, and the levy of duties under the new Tariff; but in return for the remission of nearly all the maliyat (revenue) at which the districts were assessed. The balance still paid amounts to 18,000 tomans for Hayat Daoud; 4,020 tomans for Rudhilleh.

Recently in 1910 an arrangement was come to between the Provincial Customs and the Khans by which the latter agreed to the establishment of a post near the mouth of the Rudhilleh river, and the Customs to pay the Khans 1,000 per annum; one-third of this goes to the son of the chief Khan of Bandar Rig, one-third to the son of Mohammed Khan, the brother who resides at Chaharrustai, one-third to the son of Hussein Quli Khan at Rudhilleh.

A Customs post has also been opened at Genaweh, a small port between Bandar Rig and Kuh-i-Bang.

The revenue of the Khans is drawn from taxation of land under cultivation, and from tithes of all produce exported from the districts, also from date gardens and other sources. One of the most important villages is Shul between the Kih-i-Bang mountains and the coast range, and on the borders of Lirawi.

The ruling family would appear to be a branch of that ruling in the time of Mir Mohanna, the pirate in 1760, when Bandar Rig was a more influential port than Bushire; but their rise and extension of power dates only from the past two generations.

Khan Ali Khan, who died about 15 years ago, was continually in trouble with the Governor of the Gulf Ports, and in consequence of his turbulence and arrears his two eldest sons Haidar Khan and Mohammed Khan were, in their boyhood, brought up in Bushire, as hostages for their father's conduct. Khan Ali Khan was constantly fighting, and generally victorious over, Haji Hassan Khan of Lirawi, the district immediately north of Kuh-i-Bang.

After his death his sons divided their spheres of influence as follows:

> Haidar Khan took Bandar Rig
>
> Hussein Quli Khan took the district of Rudhilleh.
>
> Mohammed Khan took Chaharrustai and acts as commander of the forces of the district,
>
> Further, after the death of Murad Khan, brother of Khan Ali, the ports of Bandar Dilam and Genaweh were by family arrangement entrusted to his son, Hussein Khan, and the latter's sons.

The strength of the district and Khans lies however in the unity of control, for all are obedient to the eldest brother, Haidar Khan, whose word is law in the district, and outside also. Their wealth, and successful business in smuggling, has perhaps added to their power in former years.

Moreover by his sister's marriage to Agha Khan, the third son of Haji Hassan Khan of Lirawi, and other marriage ties, besides the lessons of several defeats, Haidar Khan had acquired a ruling voice in the policy of the Khans of Lirawi and their district. Lirawi today is practically part and parcel with Hayat Daoud.

Haidar Khan, who is *not* a fighting Khan, wields great influence by his sagacity and powerful position over the Khans of Shabancara and Angali as well, while he enjoys cordial relations with the Kashkuli Khans, his neighbours across the mountains.

The Khans for many years have been almost independent of the Cental and Provincial Governments; the Governor of the Gulf Ports never meddles with the districts, nor sends soldiers or officials there, and it would be beyond his power at present time to dismiss or change the Khans. Their relations with British officials and traders have been very friendly for some years.

The districts of Hayat Daoud and Rudhilleh have for many years enjoyed the greatest transquility; in the greater part of the district a rifle cannot be fired without the consent of the Khan. Their tufangchis must however exceed 1,000 in number.

The principal villages are:

Of Hayat Daoud (about 26 in all)		Rudhilleh (about 15)
Bandar Rig	Cham Shahab	Mohmedi
Genaweh	Chah-i-Bardi	Mainun
Chaharrustai	Kullar	Kureband
Bidu	`Arash	Muziri
Muhammed Salehi	Cheharburj	Khasham Hamud
Kuhak	Mal-i-Mahmid	Cham-i-Halqeh
Allahyari	Yezdpushan	Guwabin
Bang	Farakhwari	Qaleh Sarhan
Bahmiari	Ghishawi	Qaleh Sukhteh
Puzegah	Gav-i-Sefid	Askeri
Abbasi	Jezireh	Rustami
Gomarun	-	Feraki
-	-	Haji Ali
-	-	Khasham Ahmed

Appendix VI

VI.1: Most important import commodities 1873-1923 (in Rupees; from 1904 in £)

Year	Cotton goods	Thread - twist	Indigo	Metals	Spices	Sugar	Tea	Wool-en goods	Specie	Total
1873	18,08,000	79,500	5,20,750	1,49,400	98,640	6,29,000	48,000	52,000	6,17,405	46,02,925
1874	15,25,000	62,400	4,02,400	1,44,900	66,150	6,28,800	36,000	21,000	1,25,000	35,97,700
1875	20,67,800	1,72,000	7,38,600	4,27,875	45,800	7,98,650	1,06,750	1,20,050	76,800	51,58,823
1876	20,94,000	70,000	2,16,000	4,69,600	1,19,500	7,04,875	27,850	1,41,400	1,80,000	45,96,999
1877	4,74,000	77,000	3,50,000	3,91,300	1,32,000	10,69,700	14,000	76,000	1,40,000	83,67,115
1878	30,00,000	55,000	4,80,000	4,92,300	1,04,000	9,40,000	50,000	84,000	12,10,000	73,95,560
1879	87,40,000	2,40,000	10,16,000	5,22,000	44,300	8,18,500	1,00,000	67,500	64,90,000	1,87,76,900
1880	70,37,500	47,000	8,40,000	21,08,500	1,87,000	20,70,000	1,60,000	4,75,000	19,15,000	1,68,66,050
1881	20,60,000	4,000	3,90,000	12,80,100	1,03,500	11,41,500	2,60,000	1,62,500	4,33,000	70,33,800
1882	51,15,500	37,500	2,80,000	21,07,200	1,06,200	6,84,200	2,08,000	1,31,200	4,48,000	1,01,88,980
1883	70,62,500	1,41,000	4,47,700	25,41,700	1,33,100	13,13,000	2,15,950	2,14,700	2,32,000	1,37,39,200
1884	49,66,000	40,000	1,84,500	9,95,300	1,31,820	17,14,370	2,24,400	2,35,000	1,07,650	1,00,97,500
1885	51,22,320	59,600	6,67,600	9,03,200	1,58,000	12,28,880	2,81,460	2,78,570	55,420	99,62,170
1886	37,60,900	26,920	5,38,400	5,88,070	1,33,980	12,41,450	1,34,640	4,10,670	2,11,570	82,73,230
1887	46,46,900	32,250	5,19,300	7,41,580	1,31,380	6,37,320	2,48,450	2,78,120	1,30,200	87,15,680
1888	47,14,950	1,04,400	3,84,900	3,46,900	1,06,290	5,10,750	2,11,050	2,61,120	3,25,670	81,35,360
1889	61,51,200	1,15,900	7,31,500	11,78,970	1,37,910	11,27,740	3,77,930	2,58,270	23,160	1,16,03,570
1890	95,66,200	1,17,150	5,96,250	15,81,800	1,45,200	17,98,570	4,26,510	5,11,410	1,03,120	1,65,48,710
1891	1,13,12,000	1,03,950	3,96,500	19,14,000	1,89,920	7,08,960	9,53,400	2,54,010	1,61,350	1,72,80,870
1892	1,00,63,530	1,17,150	5,19,500	8,76,140	2,19,040	22,02,790	7,94,710	77,310	1,03,120	1,64,58,850
1893	76,66,430	1,13,400	7,63,150	11,19,010	2,13,950	24,58,110	12,27,590	4,13,450	2,08,340	1,56,97,950
1894	1,06,73,320	2,48,140	9,51,830	6,80,090	1,93,160	13,70,600	13,44,020	4,23,150	3,43,900	1,83,51,110
1895	1,13,97,600	2,49,400	6,89,300	2,74,370	63,500	8,75,930	7,62,720	2,84,620	5,81,610	1,83,04,490
1896	61,59,000	1,31,280	3,88,470	5,02,275	40,910	12,11,973	7,32,975	1,49,644	4,73,531	1,34,01080
1897	1,08,57,560	80,000	4,23,060	4,05,450	75,640	11,89,790	5,40,900	1,82,730	4,52,860	1,83,25,270
1898	60, 91, 470	71,400	4,94,520	6,81,350	97,730	11,19,540	8,43,200	2,18,020	9,66,660	1,34,95,390

Year	Cotton goods	Thread - twist	Indigo	Metals	Spices	Sugar	Tea	Wool-en goods	Specie	Total
1899	56,08,380	1,44,690	2,98,380	10,35,540	1,79,525	13,14,245	9,59,205	40,195	12,97,665	1,37,47,920
1900	74,27,470	1,52,200	5,35,750	8,45,540	1,48,929	23,88,019	9,58,945	3,35,503	28,77,654	1,98,45,947
1901	1,12,65,475	1,77,200	3,33,790	5,71,005	1,90,201	21,35,564	2,44,72,172	2,34,900	43,01,661	2,44,72,172
1902	63,30,585	2,10,600	93,870	5,11,279	1,18,966	26,85,474	21,77,816	1,14,850	25,36,505	1,65,09,101
1903	301,500	17,182	18,786	213,610	14,485	86,318	62,119	26,740	33,703	870,803
1904	312,611	21,920	27,181	112,794	9,939	197,988	59,172	16,322	101,598	889,825
1905	306,671	17,645	21,164	21,165	8,259	126,810	64,489	19,292	63,390	761,932
1906	364,039	13,585	16,657	22,881	11,407	178,802	56,376	27,498	8,659	863,842
1907	526,847	26,930	30,500	33,494	13541	118,087	79,582	26,808	69,095	1,052,043
1908	396,788	20,600	13,028	34,210	12,200	96,679	69,645	14,225	23,187	793,465
1909	280,051	19,197	19,974	22,570	7,709	136,036	38,609	10,726	82,349	717,091
1910	301,080	15,601	5,576	24,811	3,219	127,933	31,963	13,677	55,778	675,614
1911	460,434	17,885	5,844	22,534	7,416	142,973	36,722	11,027	89,710	932,531
1912	520,308	13,118	4,117	10,389	7,172	194,434	26,287	15,873	38,066	951,720
1913	320,559	16,174	4,575	29,249	8,909	221,612	23,738	8,066	26,261	825,767
1914	262,958	16,349	1,290	26,383	17,505	145,437	70,171	8,634	10,559	669,339
1915	280,472	24,243	40	9,961	24,908	77,874	264,540	4,161	6,844	777,317
1916	453,485	55,031	15,818	15,364	13,946	288,799	62,438	32,276	103,655	1,299,562
1917	861,537	47,296	27,741	15,106	31,598	691,556	145,501	81,518	51,676	2,439,179
1918	1,118,547	57,545	37,891	13,427	45,629	572,126	576,159	95,948	9,553	2,946,450
1919	1,067,927	129,583	9,480	108,726	15,342	603,374	212,360	57,661	15,711	2,723,357
1920	677,287	59,896	21,021	34,362	12,581	565,336	188,748	113,785	9,679	2,462,797
1921	632,245	25,548	23,240	16,306	8,352	386,510	46,512	16,707	?	1,526,594
1922	695,740	33,553	26,739	9,125	12,420	189,035	114,512	1,320	?	1,382,961
1923	851,376	38,840	32,299	25,610	23,422	509,711	132,931	2,634	?	2,011,772

Source: Administration Report 1873-1905; Political Report 1906-1923.
Because the export data of some countries have not been listed the column of total trade is greater than the sum of the other entries in that same year.
in Rupees; from 1904 in £.

VI.2: Imports into Bushehr during 1873-1923 (in Rupees; after 1905 in £)

Year/ Country	Great Britain	Other W. Europe	Persian ports	India	Arabian Coast Bahrain	Kuwait, Basra, Baghdad	Muscat	Java	China	Total in Rupees
1873	7,57,780	-	1,98,782	23,58,064	52,734	5,05,092	27,469	6,88,600	-	46,02,925
1874	5,55,500	-	1,82,520	20,22,310	51,200	1,10,540	17,380	6,43,850	-	35,97,700
1875	15,78,150	-	1,42,830	28,74,660	25,660	81,800	11,380	4,29,975	-	51,58,825
1876	17,55,660	-	2,33,280	18,14,699	64,470	2,33,280	14,110	5,31,000	-	45,96,999
1877	7,00,300	-	2,00,925	16,77,240	47,040	58,530	26,280	6,39,600	-	33,67,115
1878	20,82,500	-	6,92,600	34,40,000	7,200	4,01,900	34,000	6,31,000	-	73,95,600
1879	72,26,500	-	5,61,100	1,02,94,350	63,500	79,600	5,650	5,08,800	-	1,87,76,900
1880	62,16,100	-	2,17,700	82,72,150	2,00,600	4,19,900	34,900	13,82,200	33,000	1,68,66,050
1881	22,49,000	2,51,000	5,31,600	25,73,500	36,300	1,23,600	23,300	9,43,000	2,66,500	70,33,800
1882	54,45,000	3,46,500	4,16,100	38,19,150	30,630	3,81,680	41,620	2,00,000	3,26,800	1,01,88,980
1883	63,69,300		4,44,000	54,39,800	32,650	2,53,300	44,650	3,50,000		1,37,39,200
1884	43,54,500		2,43,740	39,81,890	23,100	1,32,600	22,070	2,66,000		1,00,97,950
1885	48,96,160	4,79,400	74,730	42,04,440	23,300	28,750	32,940	1,50,000	35,350	99,62,170
1886	37,91,820	3,66,300	-	-	29,350	1,30,230	64,700	-	33,330	82,73,230
1887	42,61,490	3,51,290	-	-	38,080	34,230	83,140	-	1,27,210	1,16,03,570
1888	42,87,700	1,560	-	35,38,750	12,600	42,210	50,080	-	1,23,420	80,68,310
1889	60,75,990	4,78,810	-	48,05,280	10,850	28,400	56,330	-	98,190	1,15,65,770
1890	86,92,300	8,14,240	-	56,88,270	11,720	54,990	54,680	-	-	1,64,87,800
1891	1,19,35,765	3,18,610	-	46,03,485	29,530	20,510	21,265	-	1,97,800	1,71,43,390
1892	90,19,820	10,70,530	-	59,48,070	19,340	1,28,250	22,800	-	1,03,780	1,63,86,310
1893	77,39,380	12,32,750	-	62,44,260	29,150	1,30,050	19,170	-	99,670	1,55,31,970
1894	96,13,960	9,21,830	-	69,91,000	12,670	1,75,990	23,980	-	2,28,550	1,80,64,430
1895	1,22,35,000	6,08,560	-	44,64,140	5,730	4,14,500	16,000	-	1,44,870	1,79,78,760
1896	66,99,647	17,19,752	2,52,429	39,03,138	-	4,42,867	1,54,235	-	65,355	1,34,01,080
1897	1,23,82,080	9,77,280	4,39,820	33,36,110	-	4,13,110	1,79,500	-	1,75,200	1,83,25,270
1898	64,26,200	8,23,010	14,78,430	36,88,360	1,37,400	5,74,960	58,690	-	2,19,570	1,34,95,390
1899	66,28,830	11,28,327	19,91,820	33,72,900	20,025	3,61,995	54,045	-	2,02,425	1,37,47,920
1900	1,07,31,547	22,97,215	18,97,652	41,63,122	25,350	2,87,766	71,961	-	2,62,516	1,98,45,947
1901	1,34,98,202	25,26,766	18,34,054	47,72,206	1,17,885	12,20,247	36,862	-	2,50,889	2,44,72,172
1902	83,70,733	40,16,158	6,22,979	39,25,511	53,050	5,53,566	37,714	-	4,12,643	1,65,09,101
1903	69,74,434	9,16,255	6,15,851	47,59,784	36,293	4,58,745	36,946	-	7,11,214	1,42,55,457
1904	389,323	198,388	-	204,009	2,116	19,590	475	7,870	20,299	889,825
1905	322,167	127,182	-	176,255	6,299	51,517	1,057	9,696	13,396	761,932
1906	332,942	201,698	-	263,540	3,702	11,799	1,443	19,931	9,899	863,842
1907	572,113	62,123	-	355,166	3,210	32,870	2,915	6,874	1,630	1,052,043

Year/ Country	Great Britain	Other W. Europe	Persian ports	India	Arabian Coast Bahrain	Kuwait, Basra, Baghdad	Muscat	Java	China	Total in Rupees
1908	377,769	82,793	-	294,930	1,903	21,275	1,677	2,470	1,898	793,465
1909	203,769	117,647	-	362,902	2,688	11,113	26	443	4,611	717,091
1910	283,797	114,509	-	243,021	3,282	9,322	644	10,150	2,425	675,614
1911	415,772	143,594	-	292,879	4,201	32,911	850	20,095	6,669	932,531
1912	453,653	197,212	-	218,838	2,964	35,186	1,112	10,963	9,514	951,720
1913	252,651	244,486	-	265,436	2,286	32,262	706	10,790	7,471	825,767
1914	193,704	107,893	-	334,817	11,889	7,608	2,005	1,703	2,408	669,339
1915	75,333	3,706	-	668,570	-	7,364	-	8,038	814	777,317
1916	208,298	246	-	1,036,818	-	17,147	-	3,963	-	1,299,562
1917	122,080	393	-	2,258,305	-	18,592	-	-	-	2,439,179
1918	479,749	25,310	-	2,280,968	11,884	13,309	-	54,199	43,659	2,946,450
1919	719,012	54,947	-	1,284,840	10,720	61,205	13,657	21,908	143,652	2,723,357
1920	692,636	135,375	-	1,077,286	10,158	28,625	892	174,205	40,753	2,462,797
1921	362,395	141,397	-	776,894	6,735	10,422	2,293	113,236	37,264	1,526,594
1922	498,451	193,541	-	536,315	2,394	3,447	-	56,380	11,590	1,382,961
1923	596,235	369,594	-	776,330	6,659	8,822	248	78,223	25,120	2,011,772

Source: Administration Report 1873-1905; Political Report 1906-1923.
Because the export data of some countries have not been listed the column of total trade is greater than the sum of the other entries in that same year.
in Rupees; from 1904 in £.

VI.3: Principal export commodities 1873-1923 (in Rupees and as of 1904 in £)

Year	Animals	Raw cotton	Fruits + veg.	Opium	Silk raw	Wool	Woolens	Specie	Total
1873	1,35,00	1,85,600	99,299	12,57,520	1,73,880	28,000	1,24,000	10,53,396	39,20,729
1874	92,000	82,750	52,470	14,52,800	1,25,400	22,500	96,400	4,46,000	30,91,775
1875	75,000	1,59,600	32,730	7,90,500	89,500	40,500	19,600	2,89,500	18,62,230
1876	1,21,600	30,518	1,79,700	20,57,000	2,00,000	16,600	1,46,530	19,30,000	60,04,806
1877	64,800	13,83,370	1,25,620	33,46,000	1,20,000	18,000	33,700	7,30,000	77,35,640
1878	6,11,000	17,00,000	36,800	51,00,000	1,50,000	9,000	32,000	10,80,000	1,37,41,300
1879	79,250	6,20,000	22,800	51,52,200	2,30,000	33,500	27,500	16,50,000	80,94,900
1880	2,50,000	9,05,000	1,30,700	62,12,000	1,63,000	90,000	60,800	13,50,500	1,00,17,850
1881	16,000	2,83,000	71,050	57,45,000	3,28,500	50,000	55,000	2,65,000	79,83,800
1882	60,000	2,92,500	76,200	36,55,000	2,76,500	55,000	74,700	20,62,500	65,66,220
1883	78,050	3,35,000	1,86,150	33,68,200	3,45,300	4,800	3,93,000	8,82,000	73,72,300
1884	54,150	7,87,500	1,24,550	33,06,000	1,42,900	14,850	1,96,800	5,64,720	67,34,570
1885	96,400	9,32,800	1,52,700	42,53,000	86,870	14,760	1,39,800	3,88,250	74,45,170
1886	58,900	2,26,250	1,38,340	42,43,000	1,19,560	19,700	4,19,700	5,98,860	71,89,990

Year	Animals	Raw cotton	Fruits + veg.	Opium	Silk raw	Wool	Wool-ens	Specie	Total
1887	54,900	10,09,200	1,81,490	29,39,500	1,70,200	41,760	2,00,400	4,29,860	62,49,550
1888	60,300	6,13,340	1,79,000	22,00,000	1,07,010	1,27,320	2,20,800	3,63,320	59,64,680
1889	26,550	11,60,750	2,39,300	33,86,000	43,810	1,42,680	3,08,750	5,06,470	81,51,620
1890	54,100	15,99,720	2,48,690	48,05,000	31,150	64,400	1,43,120	9,55,200	95,49,670
1891	51,950	7,76,870	4,45,770	47,22,000	1,57,750	2,03,720	1,59,150	7,01,200	93,51,690
1892	73,050	6,97,000	4,28,120	54,17,500	91,550	97,950	2,83,370	9,44,860	1,00,93,910
1893	72,000	3,14,190	1,27,770	33,46,000	4,25,050	72,450	11,87,230	8,18,240	84,81,940
1894	70,800	1,74,610	2,05,250	45,62,290	82,100	2,94,220	14,18,070	12,54,850	1,01,13,050
1895	60,300	22,070	3,00,860	33,06,200	78,600	1,74,990	19,25,900	4,49,160	95,18,880
1896	44,370	68,115	1,86,793	37,70,479	96,237	1,94,616	4,53,898	7,72,327	74,85,289
1897	4,800	17,604	60,124	31,10,520	80,000	3,73,575	3,60,340	5,80,732	62,80,526
1898	11,700	7,650	2,58,040	33,68,120	47,450	2,34,750	5,23,570	3,06,860	68,27,550
1899	61,290	54,575	2,83,030	45,87,000	67,635	71,150	4,87,810	4,67,220	79,40,220
1900	25,280	3,51,800	7,38,614	51,57,900	61,300	37,952	8,89,176	11,12,885	1,06,55,066
1901	25,500	53,970	3,60,630	45,87,000	67,635	71,100	4,86,810	4,67,220	86,04,732
1902	6,300	1,01,622	3,98,260	26,28,400	9,400	31,672	2,60,110	1,99,542	52,23,025
1903	4,333	4,216	16,546	178,032	-	1,128	42,317	17,922	366,666
1904	8,645	11,704	32,741	199,136	-	4,542	31,431	31,436	454,981
1905	6,560	11,741	53,276	124,156	-	2,817	70,450	60,572	469,941
1906	4,120	13,872	55,415	157,777	-	8,159	63,414	45,542	598,421
1907	2,332	7,936	32,216	238,405	-	3,732	36,826	24,042	497,990
1908	1,117	4,122	22,681	196,044	-	10,875	39,070	31,809	432,596
1909	2,489	8,858	45,702	117,320	-	5,993	63,948	4,118	400,892
1910	4,279	5,430	36,241	53,732	-	4,898	55,329	25,210	348,950
1911	1,561	7,807	54,046	246,036	-	4,747	62,032	8,941	669,020
1912	319	4,034	47,828	293,861	-	3,794	78,949	20,625	637,091
1913	265	2,219	51,106	295,687	-	5,152	64,588	17,732	601,765
1914	55	228	31,556	454,093	-	5,136	27,024	79,337	719,171
1915	305	308	17,919	347,498	-	14,791	51,151	49,458	583,056
1916	195	236	12,697	236,338	-	56,847	18,093	103,655	443,434
1917	420	4,153	24,361	622,188	-	11,490	12,244	51,676	820,951
1918	300	18,018	27,783	189,039	-	1,098	24,675	2,929	395,150
1919	400	25,656	51,107	337,340	-	5,907	128,169	20,546	917,655
1920	35	12,751	39,173	498,405	-	672	144,630	-	898,571
1921	-	773	62,666	285,389	-	-	151,868	-	680.097
1922	17	8,195	81,033	664,340	-	768	119,775	-	1,079,780
1923	-	36,998	69,657	1,246,433	-	1,339	160,460	-	2,057,078

Source: Administration Report 1873-1905; Political Report 1906-1923.
Because the export data of some countries have not been listed the column of total trade is greater than the sum of the other entries in that same year. in Rupees; from 1904 in £.

VI.4: Exports from Bushehr 1873-1923 (in Rupees and as of 1904 in £)

Year Country	Great Britain	Persian ports	India	Arabian Coast and Bahrain	Turkey and Turkish Arabia	Muscat	Java	China	Red Sea	Total
1873	3,18,307	3,52,377	13,03,245	2,67,297	4,98,409	5,297	60,434	9,75,920	1,38,567	39,20,729
1874	4,66,400	2,43,790	6,83,240	2,03,695	1,42,730	13,700	1,48,150	9,86,400	1,48,150	30,91,775
1875	2,90,800	1,82,100	5,14,980	1,33,500	1,82,100	6,300	68,500	5,67,000	24,400	18,62,230
1876	6,61,700	4,06,350	23,59,890	3,31,300	1,63,018	-	1,25,300	16,52,000	2,98,848	60,04,806
1877	7,70,320	2,39,400	30,31,830	1,18,070	5,02,820	-	30,12,700	Incl Java	60,500	77,35,640
1878	10,82,000	1,58,000	63,78,000	4,38,400	1,58,000	12,000	16,000	50,00,000	43,000	1,37,41,300
1879	2,29,700	3,150	22,64,200	3,14,550	2,02,500	2,650	30,000	50,00,000	36,100	80,94,900
1880	9,49,000	14,500	22,98,200	4,67,700	4,72,500	50,250	43,500	54,66,000	1,95,400	1,00,17,850
1881	5,20,500	95,000	9,72,400	1,11,200	1,08,200	58,800	1,55,200	57,27,000	1,16,800	79,83,800
1882	12,29,800	1,39,950	14,64,500	93,720	6,13,350	72,100	-	27,35,000	1,49,400	65,66,220
1883	17,13,600	1,19,250	16,84,600	85,850	4,95,200	65,550	-	25,68,600	2,73,850	73,72,300
1884	9,93,300	76,090	18,55,290	55,240	3,62,780	65,250	-	27,97,000	3,44,620	67,34,570
1885	6,75,390	1,18,150	18,27,430	25,930	2,58,060	44,270	-	38,07,000	6,54,080	74,45,170
1886	11,79,620	-	16,36,000	77,630-	3,91,700	35,030	-	32,47,000	3,10,400	71,89,990
1887	13,30,810	-	21,65,170	76,960	3,45,510	52,990	-	17,72,000	2,57,890	59,64,680
1888	7,69,130	-	19,56,290	52,550	5,19,000	36,450	-	20,61,000		57,60,350
1889	12,28,360	-	24,55,720	52,060	4,94,080	45,920	-	32,87,000		78,25,490
1890	9,46,570	-	29,15,810	58,450	5,44,310	19,150	-	44,84,000	3,40,160	93,60,460
1891	18,01,920	-	23,98,860	36,700	6,19,870	33,740	-	41,22,000	2,61,950	93,51,690
1892	11,30,510	-	21,00,370	92,140	10,82,450	13,830	-	49,21,310		93,51,690
1893	27,19,770	-	23,62,660	1,14,880	3,12,720	13,020	-	29,19,000		80,22,730
1894	17,54,370	-	18,76,660	1,45,100	11,32,620	25,870	-	41,16,490		95,35,580
1895	28,22,290	-	12,39,190	1,02,690	7,35,200	62,310	-	31,68,480		89,41,360
1896	18,14,018	3,56,165	12,99,928	1,41,956	3,85,742	2,10,321	-	27,26,664		74,85,289
1897	15,49,723	2,28,195	12,12,768	63,188	1,17,801	1,92,113	-	25,83,360		62,80,526
1898	18,470,540	86,900	11,60,380	-	1,81,420	20,660	-	28,25,770		68,27,550
1899	11,74,620	1,49,700	14,29,095	1,935	2,56,410	60,540	-	43,39,005	43,39,005	79,40,220
1900	23,27,602	1,29,264	20,39,612	-	3,22,313	16,327	-	47,02,500	47,02,500	1,06,55,066
1901	16,52,689	4,06,034	13,57,986	1,38,332	3,37,412	14,695	-	39,76,836	39,76,836	86,04,732
1902	13,57,898	2,09,644	12,78,125	22,164	2,07,719	14,260	-	17,95,430	2,07,719	52,23,025
1903	7,73,540	1,81,503	13,78,976	61,913	3,85,916	45,741	75	27,89,600	4,15,377	64,55,630
1904	72,527	-	122,911	8,429	27,819	436		184,760	242	454,981
1905	92,615	-	152,617	14,064	40,704	1,101	1,469	104,982	13,867	469,941
1906	174,563	-	151,251	12,604	43,818	1,601	3,035	110,075	104	598,421
1907	245,794	-	84,007	9,429	41,323	2,659	4,724	47,191	15,013	497,990

Year Country	Great Britain	Persian ports	India	Arabian Coast and Bahrain	Turkey and Turkish Arabia	Muscat	Java	China	Red Sea	Total
1908	143,558	-	94,851	5,757	40,496	612	-	107,744	1,818	432,596
1909	127,064	-	98,390	14,379	36,619	2,024	-	69,266	9,680	400,892
1910	115,107	-	98,046	15,917	33,871	1,268	-	29,078	1,734	348,950
1911	275,435	-	89,877	11,970	39,657	304	6,000	119,104	1,366	669,020
1912	277,320	-	122,439	16,086	48,794	746	37,454	63,127	1,612	637,091
1913	96,969	-	99,464	18,758	30,192	760	248,885	21,056	4,641	601,765
1914	361,055	-	147,302	10,445	40,785	2,221	35,658	24,978	672	719,171
1915	285,125	-	137,292	6,131	47,788	136	-	21,709	-	583,056
1916	158,635	-	109,724	-	10,865	-	-	18,625	68	443,434
1917	284,588	-	153,450	-	13,170	-	-	69,050	-	820,951
1918	27,658	-	112,398	3,937	48,061	-	-	38,774	-	395,150
1919	60,997	-	400,311	42,064	37,822	-	-	178,117	-	917,655
1920	89,087	-	245,009	12,839	24,266	-	-	376,651	-	898,571
1921	68,527	-	195,016	3,291	9,747	1,742	-	284,512	-	680.097
1922	88,120	-	216,688	19,998	5,680	-	-	141,000	-	1,079,780
1923	154,958	-	370,748	43,464	7,992	685	-	243,484	476	2,057,078

Source: Administration Report 1873-1905; Political Report 1906-1923.
Because the export data of some countries have not been listed the column of total trade is greater than the sum of the other entries in that same year.
in Rupees; from 1904 in £.

Appendix VII

VII.1 A: Average number of vessels that entered Bushehr (1873-1880). In the following tables the first figure in each cell indicates the number of vessels and the second figure the total tonnage of ships having been cleared.

Where from	1873	1874	1875	1876	1877	1878	1879	1880
UK *	2 -1,500	4 - 2,400	3 - 1,500	1 - 500	-	1-400	1-340	1-646
Java*	4 - 1,800	5 - 1,750	4 - 1,600	1 - 336	5 -2,585	2-1,080	4-2,060	4-2,364
Mauritius*	1 - 400	1 - 400	1 - 450	-	5 - 1,650	2-700	-	-
Mail steamer	26 - 26,000	36- 36,000	53 - 37,100	47 - 37,600	52 - 55,952	52-49,400	65-46,670	65-52,130
Merchants' steamers	8 - 10,000	15 - 17,550	8 - 8,000	10 - 10,000	15 - 12,990	13-11,050	16-9,600	18-11,466
Other steamers	-	-	-	-	28- 24,500	22-21,560	16-14,000	8-8,624
Turkey/ pilgrim steamers	2 - 1,000	2 - 1,000	3 - 3,000	5 - 5,000	6 - 5,160	3 -2,580	4-3,640	7-7,805
India	21 -2,100	19 - 2,280	15 - 1,500	22 - 2,400	22 - 2,090	19-2,300	24-2,990	19-2,120
Zanzibar	2-140	5 - 600	6 - 630	5 - 450	8 -600	5-375	6-480	8-640
Arab coast	17-540	38 - 1,140	39 - 975	40 - 1,200	52 - 1,560	56-1,680	65-910	50-750
Persian coast	100 -3,000	85 - 2,975	90 - 2,880	95 - 3,325	100 - 3,500	180-6,300	40-680	80-1,200
Masqat	11 -550	6 - 450	5 - 393	5 - 500	8 - 800	9-855	16-480	22-660
Kuwait/Basra	63- 2,835	57 - 2,850	55 - 2,915	60 - 4,800	55 - 4,400	50-3,750	120-5,400	150-7,500

Source: Administration 1873-74, p. 19; Administration 1874-75, p. 10; Administration 1875-76, p. 45; Administration 1877-78, p. 89; Administration 1878-79, p. 110; Administration 1879-80, p. 90; Administration 1880-81, p. 105.
* = Square-rigged; merchant's steamers owned by Persian and/or Bombay merchants

VII.1 A: Average number of vessels that entered Bushehr (1881-1885)

Where from	1881	1882	1883	1884	1885
India *	-	-	3-1,500	2-750	1-483
Java*	7-3,766	1-464	4-2,000	2-864	1-503
Mauritius*	-	-	-	-	-
Mail steamer	128-92,880	128- 99,312	129-109,820	125-109,216	126-119,640
Merchants' steamers	34-24,140	28-18,872	37-25,480	42-27,893	36-21,360
French steamers	-	24-22,080	26-26,100	28-31,760	12-12,240

Where from	1881	1882	1883	1884	1885
Other steamers	17-16,255	21-21,420	45-47,037	23-25,872	50-61,000
Turkey/pilgrim steamers	5-5,195	10-10,210	6-5,850	8-8,444	-
India	28-1,680	8-680	3-270	5-300	6-325
Zanzibar	6-360	4-300	4-260	3-180	6-270
Arab coast	85-2,125	120-3,600	70-1,050	90-1,350	150-2,846
Persian coast	190-4,750	250-6,250	100-1,500	112-1,905	100-1,680
Masqat	30-1,800	60-2,100	12-360	14-350	30-875
Kuwait/Basra	250-10,000	100-4,000	90-4,050	120-3,600	44-1,890
Red Sea	10-500	2-300	-	-	4-210
Total steam			250-218,837	226-215,226	111-103,821
Sailing			279-7,490	340-8,096	172-5,034
Total			529-226,327	566-223,323	283-111,154

Source: Administration 1881-82, p. 45; Administration 1882-83, p. 59; Administration 1883-84, p. 67; Administration 1884-85, p. 61; Administration 1885-86, p. 45;
* = Square-rigged; merchant's steamers owned by Persian and/or Bombay merchants
Mail steamer = BISNC +Persian Gulf SN; French = Mesnier & Co.

V.II2 A: Number of vessels that cleared Bushehr, by nationality (1886-1895)

Nationality	1886	1887	1888	1889	1890	1891	1892	1893	1894	1895	1896
British*	-	30-1,500	32-1,861	37-1,761	31-3,008	28-2,240	25-3,000	30-2,400	35-6,800	30-2,400	22-1,760
British	107-95,11	94-87,861	100-91,894	110-209,984	110-106,396	142-145,801	126-131,590	107-114,533	111-129,638	132-170,434	104-124,477
French	4-5,310	2-2,682	-	-	-	-	-	-	2-1,000	-	3-3,273
Norwegian		-	-	-	-	-	-	-	6-7,203	1-994	-
Dutch		-	-	-	-	-	-	-	-	1-696	-
German	-	-	-	-	-	-	-	-	-	3-3,193	1-1,926
Persian*	166-3,970	150-6,000	49-1,225	42-1,470	30-2,700	30 2,100	119-4,940	115-7,475	150-6,000	135-5,400	100-4,600
Others*	69-1,920	20-690	-	-	-	-	-		-	-	-
Others	-	-	-	-	-	-	-	2-2,264	-	-	-
Turkish*	-	15-300	6-330	55-990	15-1,050	8-840	40-2,800	35-1,500	40-6,400	35-1,750	45-2,250
Turkish	-	-	-	1-2,800	-	-	-	2-2,769	6-7,203	1-1,389	3-1,389
Masqat-	-	7-700	7-700	12-960	7-630	10-800	8-1,200	15-2,250	60-6,000	17-1,700	&25-2,250
Arab	-	-	41-1,965	13-605	7-280	-	30-1,500	25-1,250	30-1,600	35-1,400	40-1,600
Bahrain	-	-	-	-	-	8-480	-	-	-	-	-
Total steam	111-100,821	96-90,543	100-91,894	111-112,784	110-106,396	142-145,801	127-132,390	111-119,566	121-140,509	138-176,706	111-131,065
Sailing	235-5,890	222-9,100	135-5,881	159-5,786	90-7,668	84-6,100	222-13,440	220-15,475	315-26,800	252-12,650	232-12,460
Total	348-106,711	318-99,543	235-97,775	270-118,570	200-114,064	226-151,901	349-145,830	331-135,041	436-167,309	390-189,356	343-143,526

Source: Administration 1886-87, p. 27; Administration 1887-88, p. 37; Administration 1888-89, p. 32; Administration 1889-90, p. 33; Administration 1890-91, p. 21; Administration 1891-92, p. 24; Administration 1892-93, p. 29; Administration 1893-94, p. 29; Administration 1894-95, p. 30; Administration 1895-96, p. 26; Administration 1896-97, p. 22
* = sailing vessels; & = carried French flags.

VII.2 A: Number of vessels that cleared Bushehr, by nationality (1897-1907)

Nationality	1897	1898	1899	1900	1901	1902	1903	1904	1905	1906	1907
British*	18-1,420	15-1,800	50-5,000	40-4,000	25-1,250	112-11,350	84-8,800	95-8,890	12-900	2-229	3-208
British	90-96,703	76-83,230	101-118,928	111-132,787	109-125,760	95-104,500	74-81,400	64-70,400	153-192,563	157-221,333	175-229,224
French	2-3,273	-	-	-	-	6-480*	4-320*	8-640*	-	-	-
Norwegian	-	1-1,202	1-1,203	-	-	-	-	-	-	-	1-1,138
Dutch	-	-	-	-	-	-	-	-	-	-	-
German	-	-	-	-	-	-	-	-	-	8-14,588	13-22,874
Austrian	1-835	-	2-3,107	1-1,500	-	-	-	-	-	-	-
Russia	-	-	-	-	3-4,513	2-2,200	3-3,300	2-2,200	5-5,715	5-6,819	4-7,623
Persian*	130-3,900	160-3,600	200-8,000	60-2,400	80-3,200	95-4,085	120-5,040	80-3,360	400-10,000	204-3,778	156-4,488
Others*	-	-	-	-	-	-	-	-	-	-	-
Others	-	-	-	-	-	-	-	-	-	-	-
Turkish*	50-2,500	75-3,750	60-4,200	90-5,400	50-2,000	49-3,960	37-4,250	41-3,500	60-2,400	54-1,611	19-461
Turkish	1-1,1215	1-1,389	2-2,778	1-1,277	-	-	-	-	-	1-1,138	-
Masqat-	20-2,000	5-650	12-1,440	8-1,200	10-800	40-1,600	25-1,000	30-1,200	10-700	-	-
Arab	35-1,125	42-1,610	80-4,000	60-2,400	80-3,200	85-2,400	125-3,750	100-3,000	680-212,538	463-251,813	373-264,909
Bahrain	-	-	-	-	-	-	-	-			
Total steam	94-100,453	78-85,822	106-126,016	113-135,564	112-130,273	97-106,700	77-84,700	66-72,600	158-198,278	172-245,238	192-259,730
sailimg	253-10,945	297-11,410	402-22,640	448-25,500	515-16,000	387-23,875	395-23,160	354-20,590	522-15,260	291-6,575	181-5,179
total	347-111,398	375-97,232	508-148,676	561-161,064	627-146,273	484-130,575	472-107,860	420-93,190	680-212,536	463-264,909	373-264,909

Source: Administration 1898-99, p. 52-53; Administration 1901-02, p. 33; Administration 1904-05, p. 49; DCR 4179, p. 59;
* = sailing vessels; & carried French flags.

VII.2 A: Number of vessels that cleared Bushehr, by nationality (1908-1918)

Nationality	1908	1909	1910	1911	1912	1913	1914	1915	1916	1917	1918
British*	-	-	-	-	-	-	-	1-68	-	-	-
British	174-216,607	163-209,135	165-228,978	146-274,444	147-279,353	161-253,114	138-225,655	125-195,250	96-135,515	75-117,738	59-96,728
French	-	-	-	-	1-2,500	-	-	-	-	-	-
Norwegian	-	-	-	-	=	-	-	-	-	2-2,132	1
Swedish	-	-	-	-	-	-	-	1-2,120	1	3	2
Dutch	-	-	-	-	-	-	-	-	-	-	-
German	12-21,156	10-18,266	11-24,425	12-36,349	12-33,649	23-60,515	6-16,745	-	-	-	-
Austrian	-	-	-	-	-	-	-	-	-	-	-
Russia	4-7,376	4,7888	4-7,632	5-8,441	5-8,963	7-9,276	1-1,780	-	-	-	-
Japan	-	-	-	-	-	-	-	-	11-16,775	10-13,407	11
Persian*	207-6,478	486-12,669	308-7,853	485-11,646	382-8,721	281-6,982	445-12,427	319-7,507	286-6,466	410-8,951	n.a.

Nationality	1908	1909	1910	1911	1912	1913	1914	1915	1916	1917	1918
Turkish*	29-875	108-3,242	92-2,924	64-2,089	133-3,518	112-3,242	166-5,256	-	-	-	-
Turkish	-	-	-	-	-	-	-	-	-	-	-
Masqat-	-	-	-	-	-	-	-	-	-	-	-
Arab	1-49	-	-	-	-	-	-	205-5,109	117-3,893	208-6,290	n.a.
Bahrain	-	-	-	-	-	-	-	-	-	-	-
Total steamers	190-245,139	178-235,703	180-261,035	200-319,234	201-325,665	192-325,495	139-244,180	126-197,370	108-152,290	92-133,343	73-96,728
Total sailing vessels	237-7,402	594-15,911	400-10,777	*549-13,735	*515-12,239	*393-10,224	*611-17,683	*525-12,682	*403-10,349	*618-15,241	n.a.
Total	427-252,541	772-251,614	580-271,812								

Source: Report 1910-11, p. 41; Report 1911-12, p. 47; Report 1912-13, p. 50; Report 1914-14, p. 39; Report 1914-15, pp. 44-45; Report 1915-16, p. 36; Report 1917-18, p. 31; Report 1918-19, p. 25;
* = sailing vessels;

Nationality	1919	1920	1921	1922	1923	1913	1914	1915	1916	1917	1918
British*	-	-	-								
British	102-292,306	154-345,900	177-395,589	156-324,767	164-622,915						
French	-	-	-	-	-						
Norwegian	1-4,779	3-5,521	-	-	-						
Dutch	-	-	-	-	-						
German	-	-	-	-	-						
Austrian	-	-	-	-	-						
Russia	-	-	-	-	-						
Japan	-	-	-	3	3						
China	1-2,080	5-6,538	2-2,460	2	2						
Persian*	n.a.										
Others*											
Others											
Turkish*											
Turkish											
Masqat-											
Arab											
Bahrain											
Total	104-299,165	162-345,900	177-298	161-324,767	169-622,915						

Source: Report 1919-20, p. 34; Report 1920-21, p. 38; Report 1921-22, p. 42; Reeport 1922-23, p. 59; Report 1923-24, p. 75;
* = sailing vessels;

VII.2 A: Number of vessels that cleared Bushehr, by nationality (1928-1940)

Nationality/ year	1928	1929	1930	1931	1935	1936	1937	1938	1939	1940
British	n.a.	n.a.	n.a.	n.a.	n.a.	n.a.	227	182	151	113
German	n.a.	n.a.	n.a.	n.a.	n.a.	n.a.	37	n.a.	34	-
Russian	3	5	8	9	n.a.	n.a.	4	-	-	-
USA	-	-	-	3	n.a.	n.a.	4	1	3	10
Japan	-	-	-	-	n.a.	n.a.	16	n.a.	23	20
Italy	-	-	-	-	n.a.	n.a.	1	-	5	7
Netherlands		-	-	-	-	n.a.	2	1	3	10
Norway	-	-	-	-	-	-	-	1	-	-
Greece	-	-	-	-	-	1	-	1	-	-
Egypt	-	-	-	-	-	-	-	-	-	1

Source: Administration Report 1928, p. 8-9; Administration Report 1929, p. 6-7; Administration Report 1930, p. 8, 10; Administration Report 1931, pp. 10, 12; Administration Report 1934, p. 9; Administration Report 1935, p. 11; Administration Report 1936, p. 9; Administration Report 1937, p. 8-9; Administration Report 1938, p. 7-8, 10; Administration Report 1939, p. 5-6, 9-10; Administration Report 1940, p. 5-6, 9.

Appendix VIII.

Circular to British subjects, and firms in Bushire. "Bushire Hospital."

No doubt all are aware that for some years past certain of the inhabitants of Bushire have been desirous of seeing a proper hospital erected at Bushire. Some 3 or 4 years ago, under the auspices of the late Government of the Ports it was agreed by all Persian merchants that the sum of one shahi per package should be collected through the Director of Customs on all Persian imports at this port. The sum thus collected was placed in a special account at the Bank and now amounts to Rs.15,000.

The project hung fire on account of the events of 1915-16 in Bushire and neighbourhood, but has now been revived: and it is desired to proceed to construction as soon as the estimated cost of building, etc., has been subscribed or is in other ways forthcoming.

On the other hand the Residency Surgeon has long been dissatisfied with the present building, rented by the Government of India, which though well situated is in an extremely dilapidated condition and entirely unsuitable for use as a hospital. It is obvious to all who reside at or visit Bushire that proper hospital accommodation is necessary. Apart from the large number of poor people coming daily to the present Free Dispensary for treatment, patients requiring operations or careful nursing come in from a region 200 miles in radius, which is without a single European practioner. Every now and then Europeans are brought ashore seriously ill, and despit the absence of any real hospital provision more than one Britisher owes his life to what accomodation there is. The need for better accommodation is likely to be accentuated with the development of trade, etc., in the Gulf.

What is desired by the Residency Surgeon consists of a small tiled operating theater, bathrooms, special rooms for women patients, for eye and ear cases, for sceptic cases, separate rooms for better class and paying patients, for Europeans, besides wards for men: to be furnished with beds and hospital bedding: and additional supply of instruments and fittings: and a trained (lady) nurse, 2 regular male ward nurses (Persian), and additional compounder, sweeper, etc.

The purchase of the present site, the erection of the building sketched by the Residency Surgeon, and provisions of beds, fittings, etc., is estimated to cost at least Rs.20,000, possibly 25,000 *Tumans*. The monthly salaries of the additional staff are estimated at 200 *Tumans*, and the Persian merchants are willing that the one shahi collection on imported packages should provide this recurring expenditure.

Towards the initial expenditure about Rs. 15,000 is already in the Bank and in a meeting of some 20 Persian merchants at the Government house on the 20th instant some 4,700 *Tumans* were subscribed: and I have allotted the sum of £780 towards this charitable object.

A telegram has been sent by His Excellency the Governor to Muin-ut-Tujjar in Tehran asking him to make a free grant of the present dispensary and site.

The hospital, it is agreed, shall be under the medical charge of the Residency Surgeon and his present staff. - I now issue this appeal for personal subscriptions from British subjects and others in Bushire before asking financial assistance from the Government of India, in the same way as local subscriptions were raised 8 years ago in Muscat for the Muscat hospital and the Government of India contributed towards the balance of the cost.

(Sd.) A. P. Trevor
Major
Deputy Political Resident, Persian Gulf

March 21, 1917

Source: IOR/L/PS/11/182.

Appendix IX

Proclamation by Sheikh Hoseyn of Chahkutah (early July 1915).

In the name of God the , the Compassionate, the Merciful.

Fundamental military rules which have been made in accordance with the exigencies of these parts.

Firstly. A respected German has arrived in these frontiers of Persia, and was insulted and robbed and has now made complaints.

Secondly. The English attacked Tangak where they committed murders and robberies and different outrages in these parts. Under these circumstances defence has become incumbent and we are ready to fight by the grace of the Imam of the age.

Secondly, everyone prompted by Muhammadan zeal and adherence to his tribe assists the jehad, he will be of the victorious party; and every one who joins for the sake of greed and riches, it will have no result or benefit for him.

Thirdly. Without the bill and the signature of the Commander-In-Chief, the Treasurer is not authorized to pay a dinar to anyone.

Fourthly. The nation of Dashti are two parties, who are under the authority of Rais Abdul Hasan and Faqih Zain-ud-Din, provided the two individuals should also give assurance that the tufangchis of Dasti [sic], from Kullul to Dayyir are under their authority and command, and that they will be responsible for their control; of else if any of the Chiefs be present and there be any of the chiefs of the other tribe present and the Chief of the latter absent, they should give assurances to the Chief present so that the latter may give assurances to the Commander-in Chief.

Fifthly. At the time of the commencement of war at places on the border, which are in danger and joined to the sea, as well as Nusainaki and Ahmadi, and Shief, military guards should protect them and make watch.

Sixthly. A suitable party fit for fighting will be selected for the maintenance of order in the army, to be under the order of the Commander-in-Chief. Any of the troops, who may disobey or create disorder, he will be fined, imprisoned or killed according to his fault. If the Zabit of Tangistan himself creates disorder and his imprisonment is impossible, he should be punished by rifle fire as is due.

Seventhly. The German Consul [Wassmuss], who is present, should give a list of the sums spent by him ever since his arrival at this place for the expenses of the military people and as presents to the chiefs, with the exception of the men of learning, and it should be signed by the Proof of Islam [Sayyed Morteza Ahrami] at Ahram, so that afterwards the Chiefs of this place may not be liable to calumny.

Eighthly. Shaikh Husain Khan and Zair Khidar Khan have decided to bear their own expenses and those of their own staffs. They have further undertaken to contribute 80,000 *Tumans* to the respected German Consul as an assistance, in case of necessity.

Ninthly. The salaries of the men, presents to the servants, fines and the booties will be managed by the Commander-in-Chief and if any one without order infringes this, he will be held respsonsible.

Tenthly. It has been decided that each company of 20 men should have one head, and that each five companies should be under one chief, on condition that wherever they may be stationed, the men should present themselves every evening before the officer.

Eleventhly. Wherever the forces become victorious, the prisoners captured should be first disarmed. After giving up their arms they should be kindly treated, and the property and life of impartial non-combatants should not be molested.

Twelftthly. Which is the number of the twelve Imams this is concluded. The forces which arrive at, pass through or are stationed at a town or village, should treat the people in such a way that it should be only good, and they should not inflict loss, and have consideration for them and not molest them. If they have any requisitions as regards provisions, they should make them in a kind and considerate manner, otherwise they will be punished by the Commander-in-Chief.

Dated Sha`ban 1333, July 1915.

signed Shaikh Hussein Chakutahi

Source: FO 248/1103

Appendix X

Text agreement coastal Khans

English translation by British Residency staff.

In view of the fact that security, welfare of the peasants and peace in the country always depends upon unity and sincerity among the public, the following persons therefore assembled on the first of Tirmah 1325 (22nd June 1946) in the village of Chehar-Rustai, Hiat Daud: -

> Shaikh Sulaiman Nasuri and brothers and cousins, Ahmad Khan Angali, Malik Mansur Shabankareh, Rais Ali Tangistani, Rais Ghulam Razmi, Ali Khan Shabankareh, Khan Ali Khan Hiat Daudi, Mohammad Ali Khan Liravi, Namatullah Khan Hiat Daudi, Namatullah Khan Sowlati, Haji Mohammad Baiglar-bagi, Fathullah Khan Hiat Daudi,

being chiefs and Khans and Shaikhs of Banader-i-Slas, Dashti and Tangistan area, Rudhilleh, Daliki and Isvand, and made a complete compromise for all previous offenses which was among some of the party and created a powerful unity among all the existing chiefs with real sincerity and unionship and the following five articles of their policy were adopted by the majority of votes and taken oaths (by Quran) for the loyalty in oberving the conditions of their policy for ever.

1. All the above Shaikhs, Khans, chiefs of the areas guaranteed to maintain peace and security in their areas more than before and to ensure to avoid slighest insecurity or irregularity in their area and to pursue this objective with all their powers.

2. The above chiefs guaranteed to cause real safety and welfare to all concerned in their areas and to take action with regards to the improvement in education, hygiene and economic affairs, and any other activity which may be useful to the public should be taken with their best efforts in order to enable all classes of peasants such as agriculturalists, cultivators and dealers to carry out their business with great freedom and assurance.

3. The signatories of this guarantee have taken severe undertaking to assemble in case of any danger which may occur for one or two of the party and to take strong measure with sacrificing their property and life to restore peace to such party who has suffered.

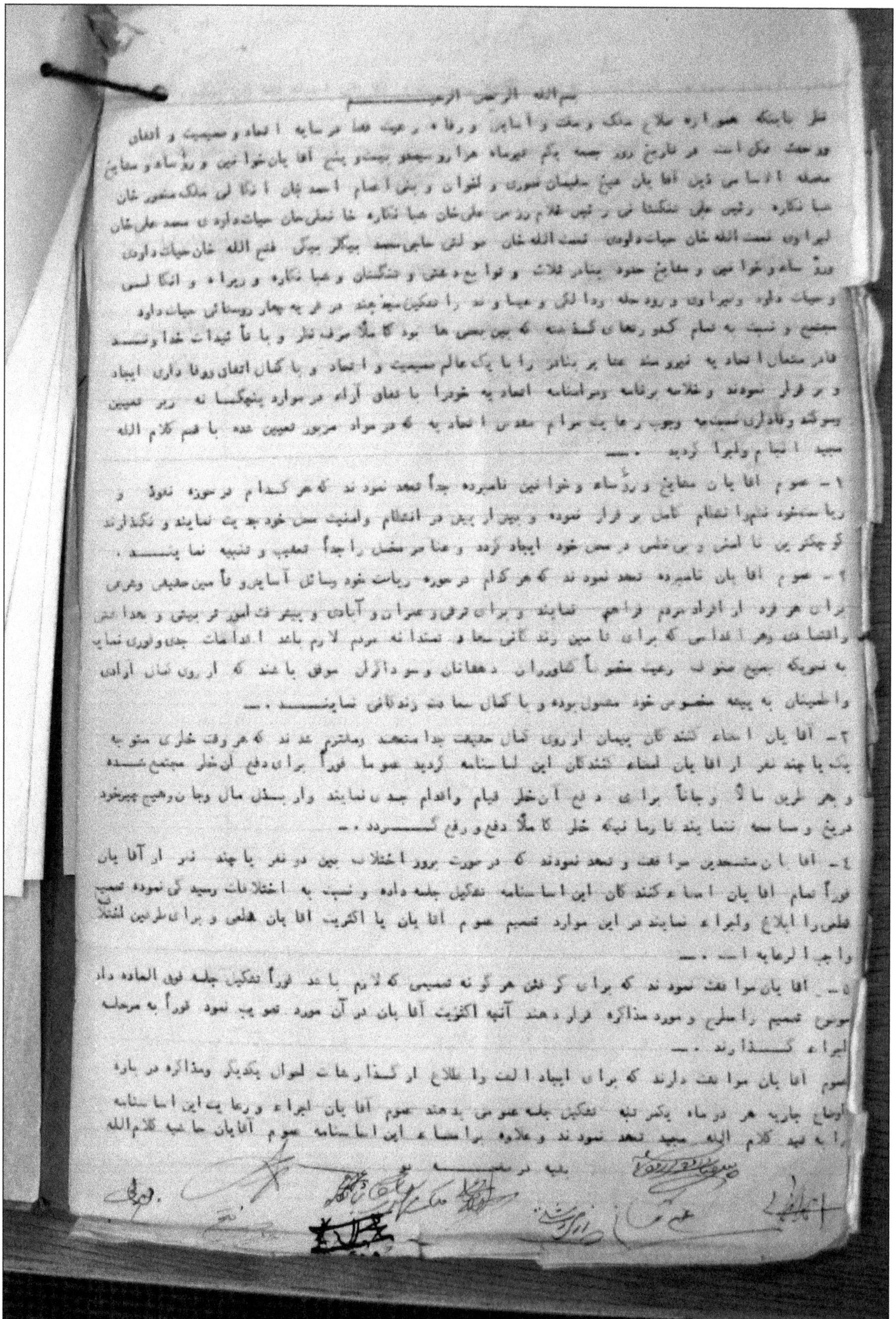

بسم الله الرحمن الرحیم

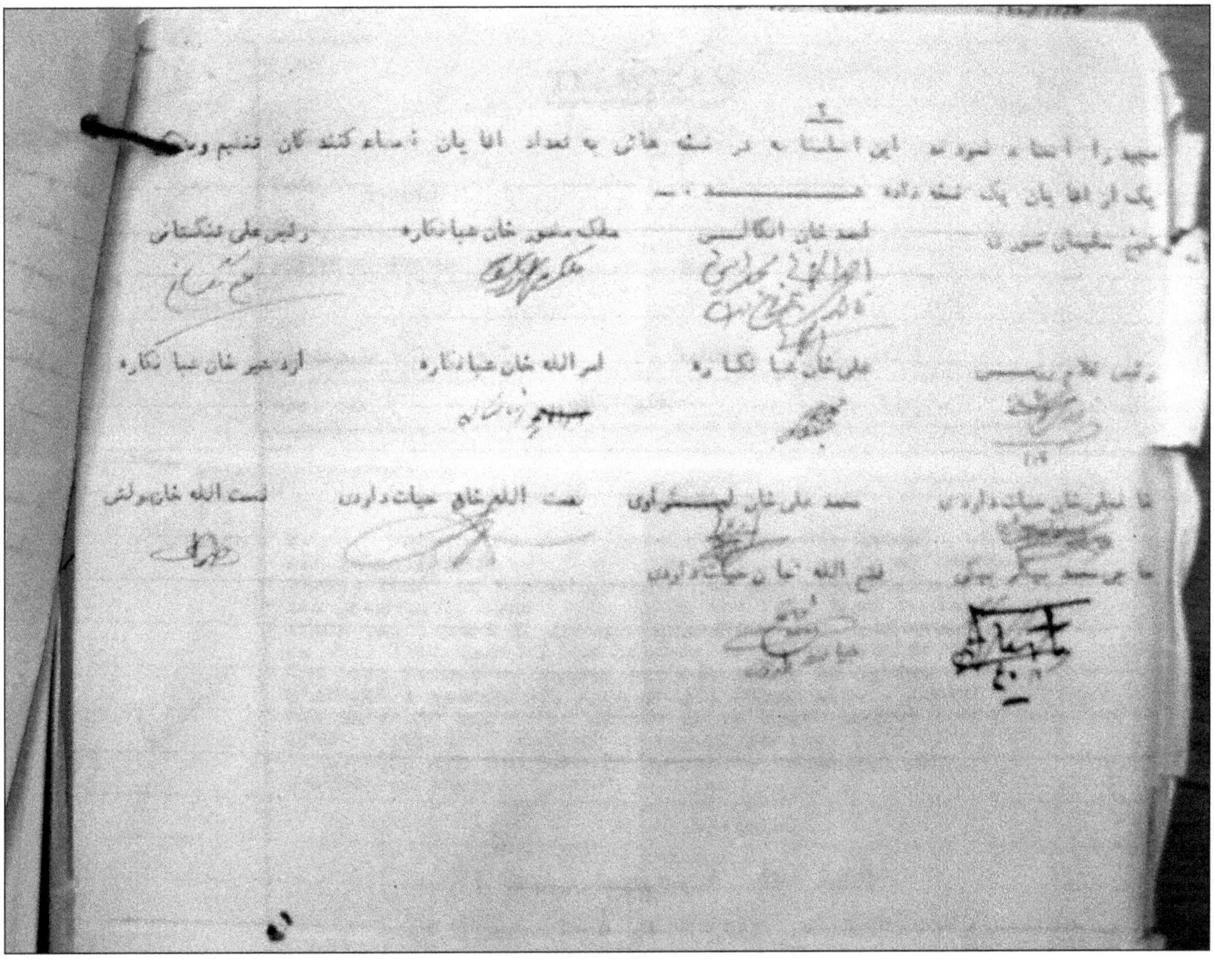

4. In case of any dispute between the two parties or among parties the signatories have undertaken to hold a meeting and to take decision in settlement of that dispute. Any decision taken by all or by majority of votes would be final and the parties involved should obey same.

5. The above chiefs have come to an agreement that if it is found necessary, to hold a meeting immediately and the subject to be discussed completely for decision. Any decision accepted by the majority should at once be carried out.

In order to acquaint themselves with the occurrence and informations, the above signatories agree to hold supplemetary meeting once every two months. All the signatories have taken oath in respect of performing the contents of this agreement and in addition to signing this document, they have signed the margin of the Quran. Sufficient copies of this agreement has been made out for each member concerned.

Signed by 14 [sic; 12] chiefs as mentioned above.

Source: FO230/1450

Appendix XI

Text of the broadcast by one of the Qashqai leaders from Bushire over the Cable and Wireless Limited Radio taken down by the Anglo-Iranian Oil Company Monitoring Services on 4 October 1946.

In view of the fact that injustice and cruelty on the part of the dictator Pahlavi was imposed on the Iranian Nation and especially on the tribesmen of Fars during the last 20 years which policy was also followed by the Cabinet of the present Prime Minister Qawam us Saltaneh in enforcing his dictatorship and his unreasonable orders, the inhabitants of Fars, its tribesmen and all the chiefs made a complete union and movement without interference of any foreigner and demanded their rights from the Central Government and requested provincial autonomy. The tribes of Qashaqai, Mamasani, Arab, Boir Ahmadis of Central Fars province, and the tribes of Hayat Dawood, Dashti, Tangistan and Dashtistan belonging to southern Fars (Persian Gulf area) joined brotherly hands and on the night of the 20th September surrounded the towns of Shiraz, Bushire, Kazerun, Burazjan, Khurmuj, Jahrum, Lari and Fasa. The military garrison at Bushire surrendered themselves with their arms on the noon of 28th September to Fathullah Hayat Dawoodi and Rais Ali Tangistani the leaders of the national force. On Thursday the 3rd October the Persian military garrison at Kazerun surrendered to Khosrow Khan Qashqai and Husain Quli Khan Rustom the leaders of the national force at Kazerun. There has so far been no clash between the Persian Force and Qashqai at Shiraz but the Persian force at the above town is strongly being surrounded. The inhabitants of Shiraz have appealed to the Central Government through the Government commission which came to Shiraz some time ago but no solution has [been] reached yet.

The servants of foreigners who have the brand of treachery on their foreheads, in order to please their masters, wish to mix this national movement with foreign interference but fact[s] can never be hidden. The Farsis are hereby inviting correspondents of all newspapers in this world to travel to the area where this movement has occurred and be assured that all the leaders hold themselves responsible for such traveller visiting the area and to inspect all the military barracks and to expose to the world if they see any slight interference of any foreigner in these affairs. Muzaffar Firuz the traitor of his Home and a worshipper of foreigners whose uncle's crimes in the affairs of Azerbaijan are prominent it being obvious that they caused the revolution in Azerbaijan through the clear assistance of foreigners, through the open help of those foreigners and by foreign weapons is calling such crime as democratic movement but he is calling this holy Fars movement which is merely for the salvation of Iran and protection of religion and national integrity, as a foreign intrigue.

While this piper of Teheran is deceiving the simple and good-believers of Fars by means of tricky telegrams he sends the aeroplanes belonging to the shameless Pahlevi force above the towns of Fars to inform the inhabitants by means of leaflets saying they intend bombing the houses and towns and shelling unprotected houses in the villages where a few innocent children, women and cattle have been killed. The warriors of Fars who have always shown their bravery on dangerous occasions did not care for this cowardly injustice and they will not sit quiet until they obtain their rights.

Source: FO 248/1469.

Appendix XII

Text of the Proclamation issued by Maj-Gen Zahidi about the agreement reached between the Government and the National Movement in Fars,

(Text taken from the newspaper 'Iran' of 18 October, 1946)

To the Directory Body of the Fars Movement.

From the first day when the Movement in Fars began and I was charged by His Highness the Prime Minister to assume charge of the Ustan and together with His Excellency Amir Humayun, special representative of the Prime Minister, watched with interest the development of the Fars Movement, both M. Humayun and myself became familiar with the intentions of those taking part in the Movement; we found, contrary to rumour, that those gentlemen started this Movement with the object of obtaining those rights which are essential to the social existence of a civilised people, while at the same time duly considered complete national unity and the defence of Iran's independence. We reported by telegraph to the Prime Minister and we then received instructions to proceed to Tehran to submit further details. We did so and gave to His Highness a report on the grievances of the people in Fars and those taking part in the Movement, both tribes people and townsmen. We hereby bring to the notcie of our dear brothers of Fars the agreement of His Highness on the following points:-

1. His Highness Qavam-us-Saltaneh has always paid and will always pay attention to the full enforcement of the Fundamental Law.
2. The Provincial Council for Fars will be formed by order of His Highness the Prime Minister.
3. With the opening of the 15th Legislative Term of the Majlis the necessary Bills will be tabled to provide for an increase in the number of Deputies from Fars.
4. The linking of railways to the Province of Fars will be put into practice at the first possible opportunity.
5. The asphalting of roads in Fars is part of the Government's programme and the necessary action will be taken to see that it is carried out.

6. Sufficient funds have been allotted to be spent on health and educational problems in Fars.

7. With regard to economic affairs, the Fars representatives are at present in the Capital and the practical result of their deliberations will shortly be announced.

8. In connection with the amendment of existing Laws, a Commission has been appointed to draft the necessary Bills and to get them ready for submission to the 15th Legislative Term of the Majlis.

9. Regarding the election of officials from among the inhabiants of Fars, instructions have been given for such action to be taken as fast as possible.

10. As some of the townsmen, tribesmen and others may have acted against the Laws and Regulations in the name of the Movement and contrary to the intentions and instructions of the Leaders of the Movement, His Highness Qavam-us-Saltaneh, the Prime Minister, has granted amnesty to such people as from the present date.

11. The National Movement in Fars will, while based on the principle of patriotism and the protection of the independence and integrity of the country, continues to enjoy the personal support of His Highness Qavam-us-Saltaneh, the Prime Minister.

In conclusion we think it necessary to point out that in the course of the interview we have recently had with His Excellency Muhammad Nasir Qashqai,we informed him of the above points to which he agreed in good faith. It was agreed that on Wednesday evening the 24 Mihr 1325 (16th October, 1946) all the tribesmen who were around Shiraz should return to their homes. We therefore expect that the Directory Body of the Movement who have succeeded in securing agreement and whose legitimate requests have been accepted by His Highness Qavam-us-Saltaneh, the Prime Minister, will show their steadfast patriotism and will inform all the inhabitants of Fars and especially those of Shiraz so that relying on the special favours of His Highness the Prime Minister they may resume their labours in peace of mind.

Dated 23 Mihr 1325 (15th October, 1946)
Signed Maj-Gen Zahidi
O/C the Forces of the South, and

Javad Bushiri
Special Representative of His Highness the Prime Minister.

Source: FO 248/1469.

Appendix XIII

Facsimiles of Persian letters

1a. Correspondence concerning the ownership of the British Residency building.

Because in Persia there neither existed a cadaster nor an official office for the registration of property deeds and other legal documents this situation gave rise to often spurious claims and challenges to real estate in the possession of long-time owners. Such cases could become costly to such property owners and made them liable to blackmail, the more so if powerful officials supported such claims. One such case concerned a claim to the British Residency building that once was owned by their heirs of the last Al Mazkur Sheikh. After the building was sold to another owner one heir nevertheless laid a claim to the building 32 years after the sale, because a statute of limitations does not exist in Shiite law. This and similar cases showed the need for judicial and legal reform as well as for the creation of a cadaster and the official registration of all official documents.

Copy of a Memorandum
From Persian Foreign Office
To the British Legation
Dated 14th April 1890.

It appears from a memorial submitted by Fatimah Soltan Bibi Sheikh Hoosain from Bushire to the Foreign Office that according to a deed of musalahah bearing the seals of the 'olemas of Bushire, she has a case against Aga Mohamed Raheem for half of the Residency building, and that the said Aga Mohamed Raheem having become connected with the Residency, has taken forcible possession of the complainant's rights. That the Residency without any grounds protect and support him, and also that the said Aga Mohamed Raheem does not consent to appear before a shara` or any other tribunal.

For this reason the Foreign Office requests the Legation that strict orders may be despatched as readily as possible to the British Resident, requiring him to abstain from supporting Aga Mohamed Raheem in view to his being induced to appear with the complainant before any sara` which may be acceptable to both parties, so that the case may be settled according to the evidence in possession of the parties.
translated by J.P. Sequiera.

1B. Memorandum

Fatimah bint Shaikh Hoosain

Claim to share of Residence building sold by her father to Haji Abdun [sic] Nabi

In July 1871 Shaikh Husain sold a share of Residency to Haji Abdul Nabi Safar and passed a deed.

In 1873 Shaikh Husain died. The rent for said share of Residency was paid to Haji Abdul Nabi (confidential news agent of British Residency) until his death in 1884, after which it was paid to his son Agha Mahomed Raheem (who succeeded his father personally & as confidential news agent).

In November 1889 Fatimah, daughter of Shaikh Husain produced a document purporing to be a 'musalihah' or deed of settlement (or compromise) dated A.H. 1255 or A.D. 1839 by which Shaikh Husain transferred his land, houses in Bushire and without to his wife.

The daughter claims on this deed on ground that the case to Haji Abdul Nabi was null and void her father having some 32 years previous to the sale transferred his property to his wife. The wife was living at the time of the sale to Haji Abdul Nabi and must have been aware of it.

It appears that Shaikh Husain has sold most of his property in similar manner without any protest from the wife (if the plea were admitted it would effect a great many tanures [sic] in and near Bushire which have held good for two generations).

Fatimah daughter of Shaikh Husain is a descendant of the former Shaikhs of Bushire and claims most of Bushire and suburbs as ancestral property, and has been in the habit of preferring claims similar to the present one, and by aid of certain influences has succeeded in extorting money by such means.

A Persian princess the Badr-ed-Dowlah is related by marriage to Fatimah, which accounts for certain attention being paid to her statements at the capital. One Mirza Khani assistant foreign office agent at Bishire assists the lady in her enterprises.

As the whole affair appeared to me preposterous and by no means a case for any court, I consulted the Saad-ul-Mulk, governor of Bushire, who at once assured me he knew all about Fatimah's practices and would undertake to quash the present attempt at imposition.

The foreign office agent (karguzar) of Bushire continued to press the matter apparently under orders from Kowam-id-Dowlah. I have replied that I had referred to the governor and had promised to explain the matter to His Highness the Amin-us-Soltan.

I understand His Excellency the Nizam-es-Soltaneh did write on the subject. This was in March. I have not heard myself any further from the governor who is absent, but in April H.E. during my absence forwarded a telegram from Kowam-ud-Dowlah to himself to effect that: "Fatimah Khanum claimed portion of the Residency from Agha Mahomed Raheem on legal documents and that it is said that Mahomed Raheem on account of his connection with the Consulate retains forcible possession (N.B.) of the property and does not obey that shara. That if he is a Persian subject what right has the consulate to potect him. Communication has been made to the British Legation. Order both parties appear in a law court. &ca.

Bushire 7th May 1890.

[signed] E.C. Ross.

2. Government protests against higher wall of Residency

The Persian authorities were very sensitive as to possible infringement of their sovereignty by foreigners. This even extended to changes in buildings such as the one in which the British Residency was located. Over the course of a century this building underwent change through renovation, extension, and/or reconstruction. Sometimes the legitimacy of such changes were questioned by the authorities in Tehran. This also might happen in case of such minor changes in the building that the local governor did not even bother the British Resident with the complaint, but dealt with it himself.

Report by Agha Mulla Ahmed, Residency Moonshi.

Dated 18th October 1890.

During the course of conversation His Excellency the Saad-ul-Mulk said that: he has received a telegram from Tehran to the effect that: "the Residency building has been pulled down, and the new building has been made very high and extended to the extent of 5 'zara' in the street." His Excellency has without corresponding with the Resident on the subject sent a direct reply saying that there was a foundation stay (سکوی) of old in front of the Residency and this is included in the building, but the roads have not been made narrow by this, and the new construction has not affected the public traffic. But the building is made high in order to get in ventilation during the summer. The ground of the Residency building belongs to Bushire subjects and it is taken on hire. It does not belong to the British government. This was talked on during the conversation but His Excellency did not say that this may not be communicated to the Resident. But as it was necessary to acquaint the Resident of this, I have submitted it for his information.

3. Petition of the horse merchants of Bushehr to Haji Aghasi, Prime Minister (September 1844)

In 1837, Farhad Mirza, governor-general of Fas, allowed the export of horses to India only after payment of 2 *tumans* tax per horse in Shiraz. Horses bought in the littoral paid less. In 1840, a man from the collector of horse duties came down from Shiraz to Bushehr to count the horses. If there were more horses than in the document that showed how many had left Shiraz, and thus without paying duty there, then he demanded that the Shiraz duty be paid on those horses, i.e. horses from Dashtestan and elsewhere had to pay the higher fixed Shiraz fee. The horse dealers therefore, petitioned the prime minister "to order to ban this innovation and that the old rule be re-established." The following pages:

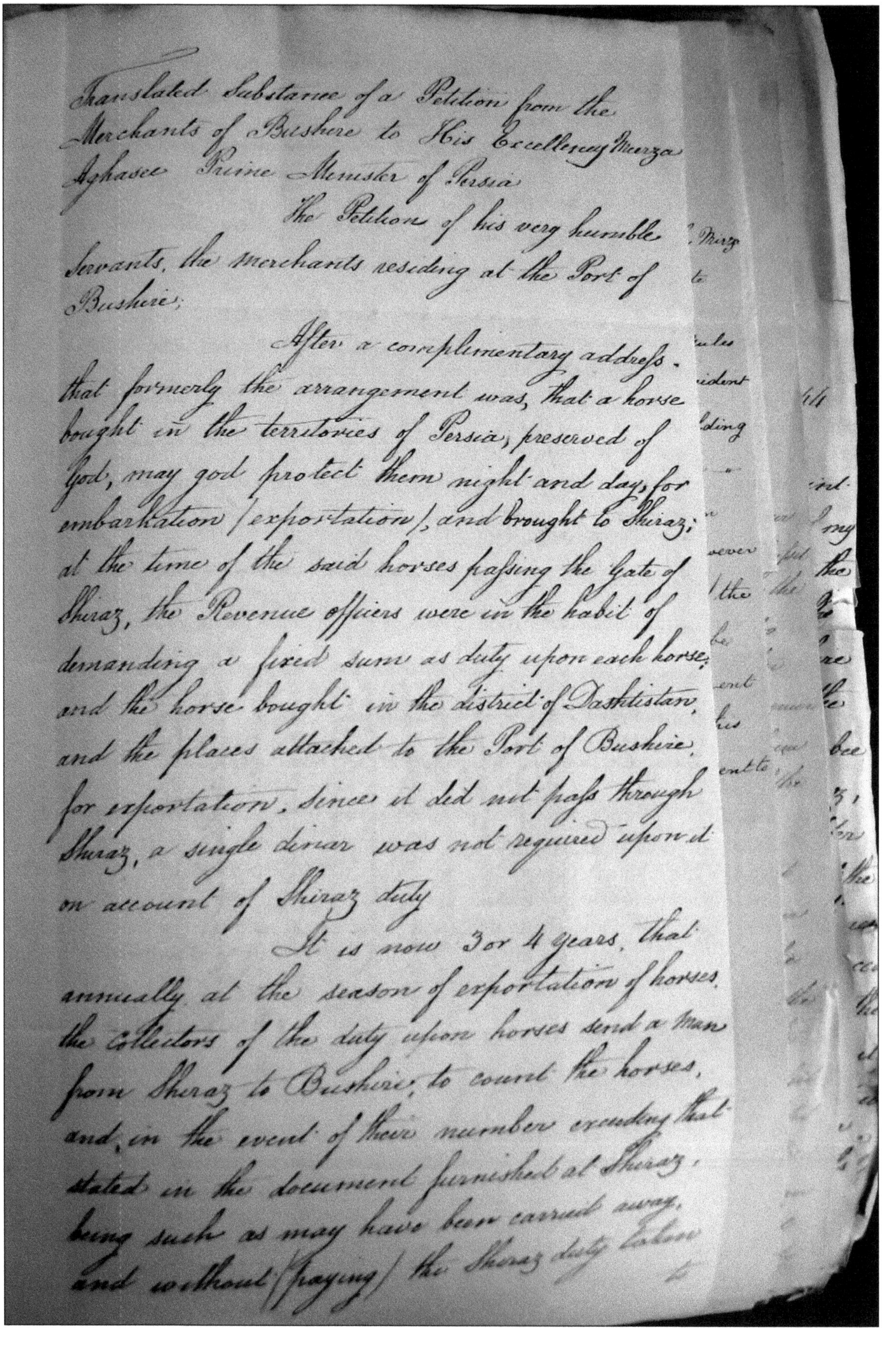
Translated Substance of a Petition from the Merchants of Bushire to His Excellency Merza Aghasee Prime Minister of Persia

The Petition of his very humble Servants, the merchants residing at the Port of Bushire;

After a complimentary address. that formerly the arrangement was, that a horse bought in the territories of Persia, preserved of God, may god protect them night and day, for embarkation (exportation), and brought to Shiraz; at the time of the said horses passing the Gate of Shiraz, the Revenue officers were in the habit of demanding a fixed sum as duty upon each horse; and the horse bought in the district of Dashtistan, and the places attached to the Port of Bushire, for exportation, since it did not pass through Shiraz, a single dinar was not required upon it on account of Shiraz duty

It is now 3 or 4 years, that annually at the season of exportation of horses, the Collectors of the duty upon horses send a man from Shiraz to Bushire, to count the horses, and, in the event of their number exceeding that stated in the document furnished at Shiraz, being such as may have been carried away, and without (paying) the Shiraz duty Taken [illegible] to Bushire, to receive the Shiraz duty upon the horses so carried away - At the present time, in the course of this proceeding, they also demand the fixed Shiraz duty upon horses that have come to Bushire from the district of Dashtistan and the Environs, unconnected with Shiraz, and upon which previous to this a single dinar on account of the Shiraz duty was never levied; Upon this point too they are very pressing - This proceeding is an innova-tion, and it is evident and manifest that His Excellency etc etc in the fulness of his favor for the subject and unbounded and wide spreading justice will not consent to this fresh innovation, that it should obtain and be established in this everlasting and ever enduring state. Our prayer from his boundless favor is, that through His Excellency's etc etc kind and compassionate aid, a fate bearing etc etc firman may be obtained from the Durbar of His Majesty etc etc the King, that the Collectors of Shiraz Customs upon horses, shall not levy the Shiraz duty upon horses coming to Bushire from Dashtistan and the neighbourhood; that this innovation shall be abandoned and the old arrangement have force, in order that the minds of these poor servants be relieved and set at rest and they will ever pray for the prosperity etc etc

of

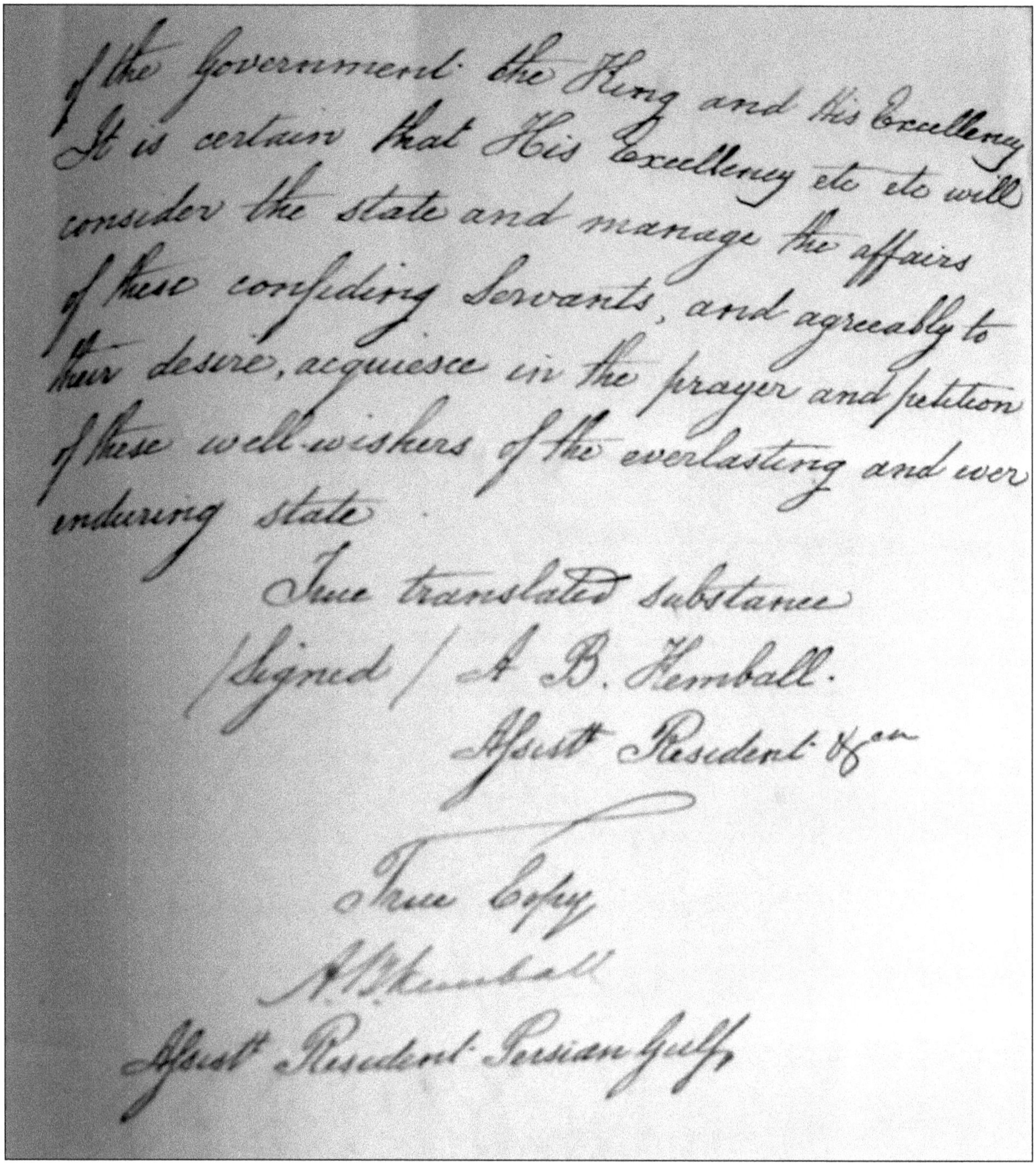

of the Government the King and His Excellency
It is certain that His Excellency etc etc will
consider the state and manage the affairs
of these confiding Servants, and agreeably to
their desire, acquiesce in the prayer and petition
of these well-wishers of the everlasting and ever
enduring state.

True translated substance
(Signed) A. B. Kemball.
Assist Resident &ca

True Copy
A. B. Kemball
Assist Resident Persian Gulf

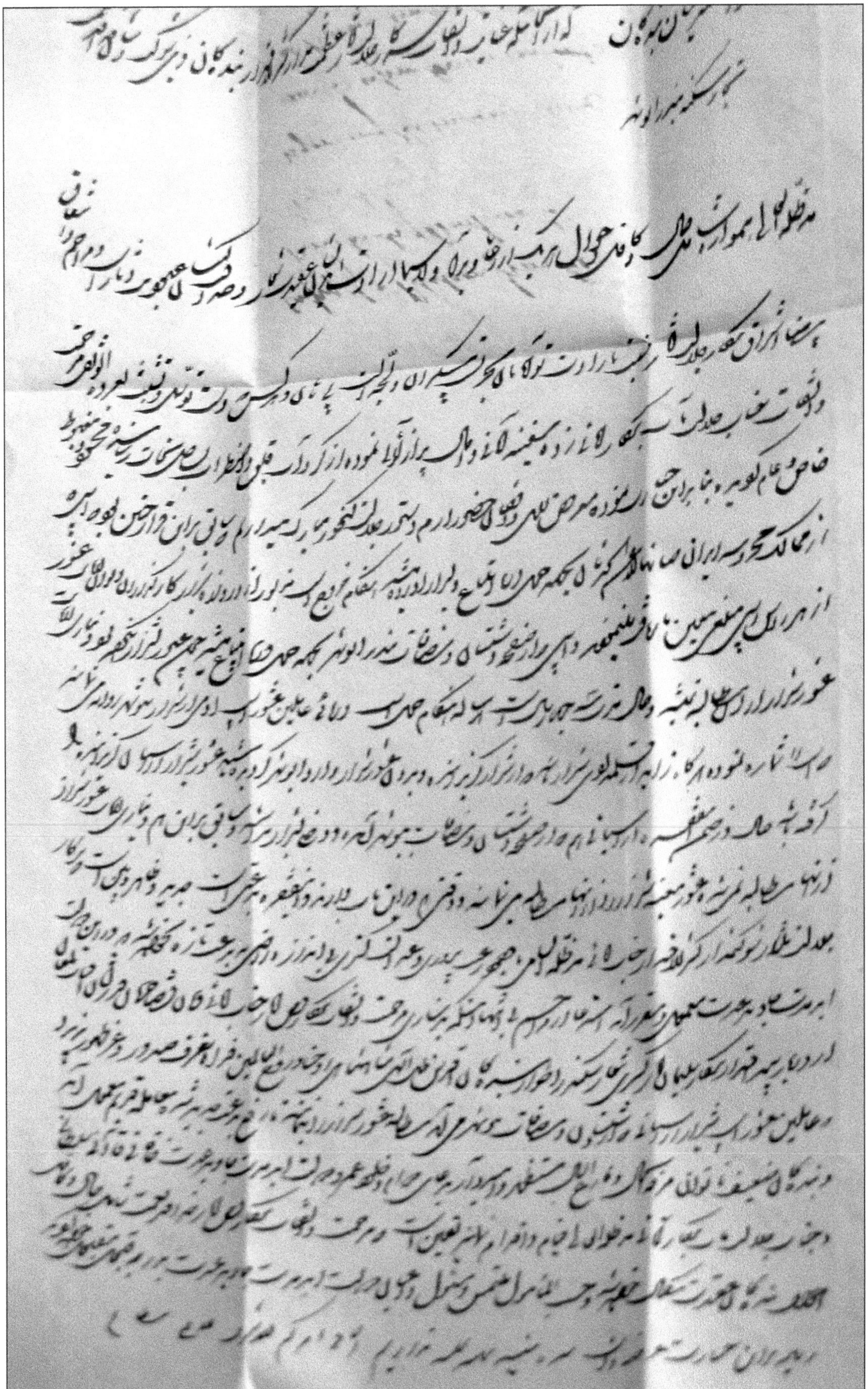

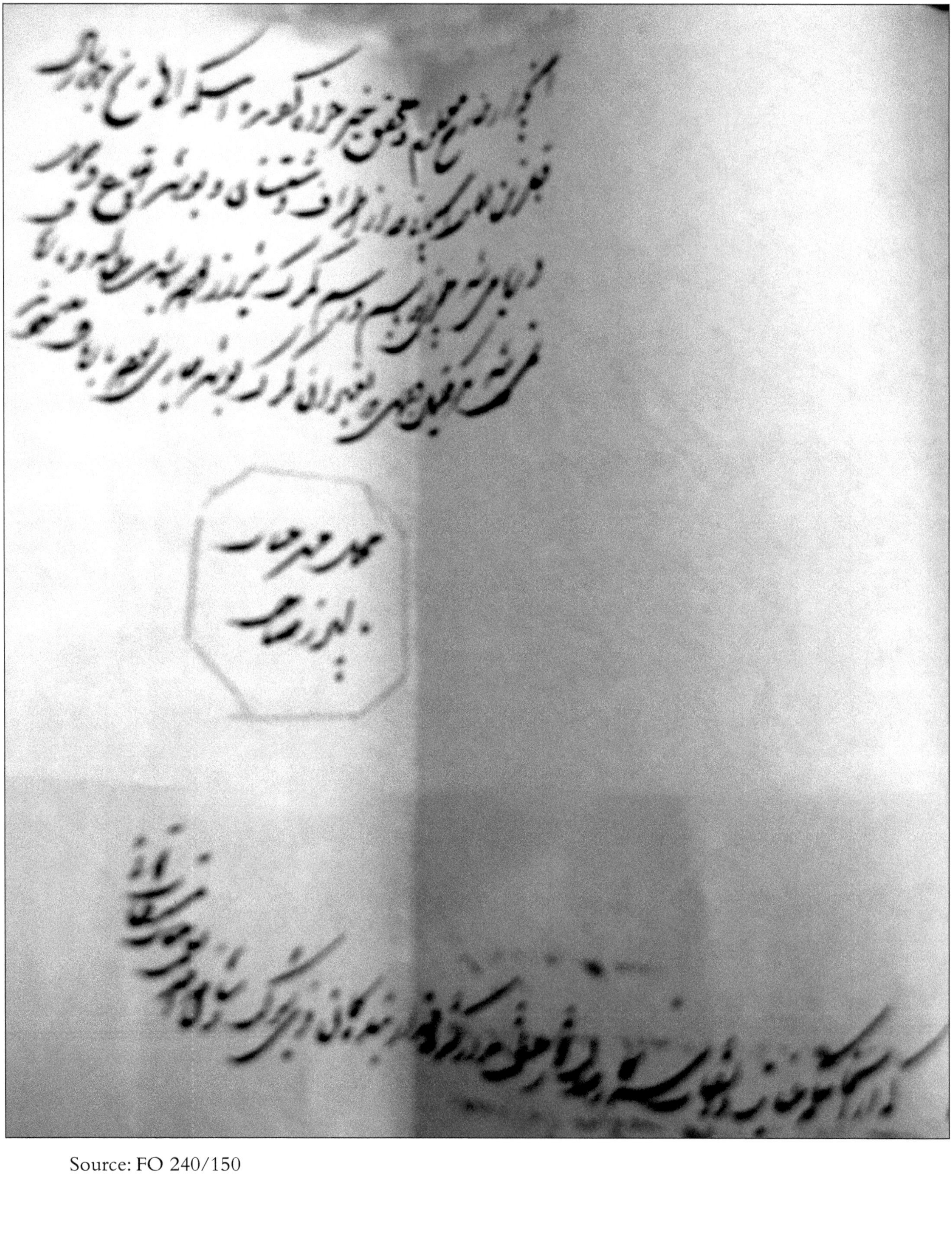

Source: FO 240/150

4. Text of the *Eshteshhad-nameh* concerning the horse and mule tax, September 1844.

To support the horse dealers' petition they organized the issuance of a testimony (*esteshhad-nameh*) from leading merchants of Bushehr, who stated that "it has never been the rule to demand the Shiraz tax from merchants, Persian and British, exporting horses," except once when Farhad Mirza was acting governor. Facsimiles of the pages follow:

Source: FO 240/150

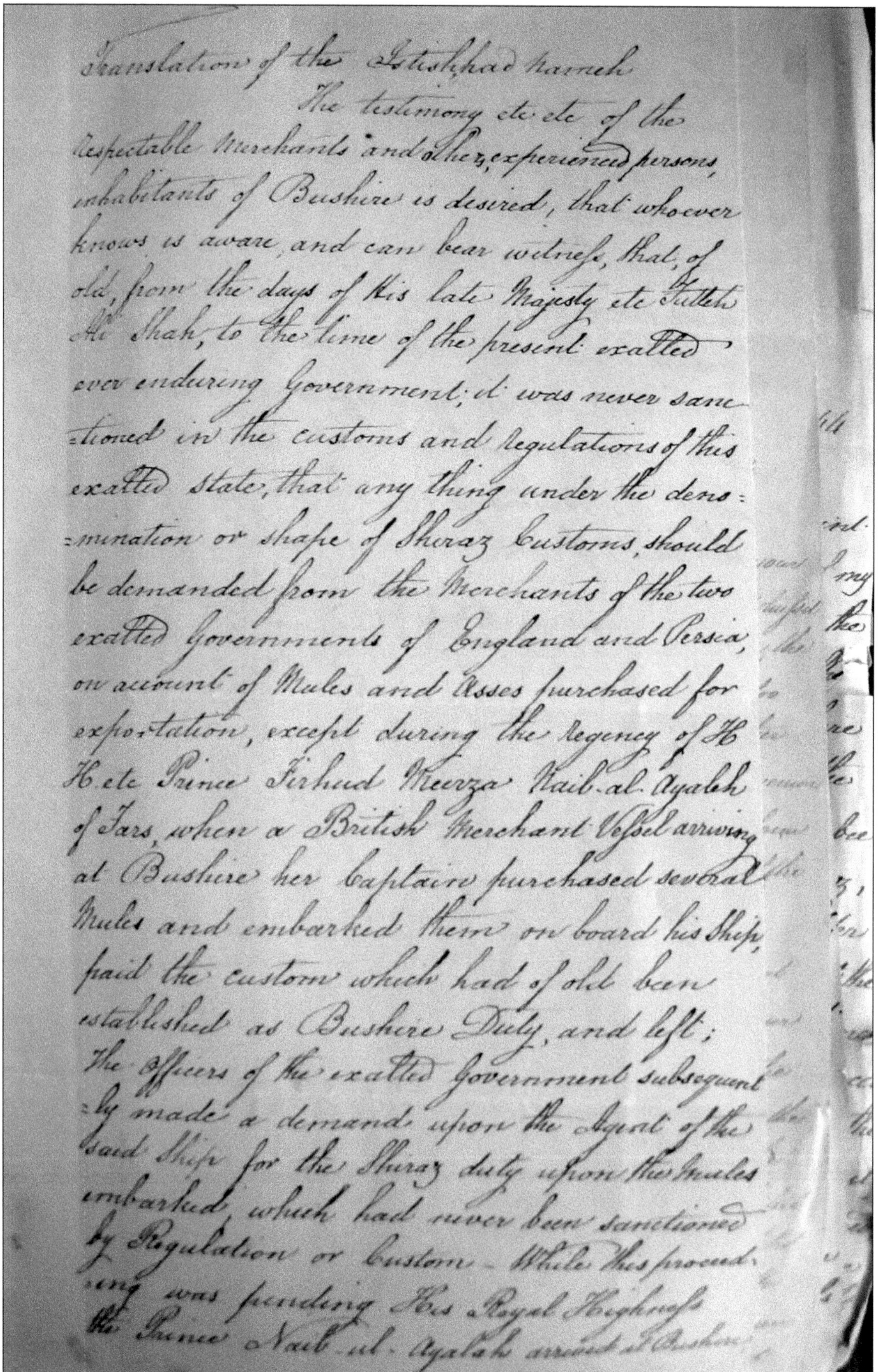

Translation of the Istishhad nameh
The testimony etc etc of the
respectable Merchants and other experienced persons,
inhabitants of Bushire is desired, that whoever
knows is aware, and can bear witness, that, of
old, from the days of His late Majesty etc Futteh
Ali Shah, to the time of the present exalted
ever enduring Government, it was never sanc-
-tioned in the customs and regulations of this
exalted state, that any thing under the deno-
-mination or shape of Sheraz Customs, should
be demanded from the Merchants of the two
exalted Governments of England and Persia,
on account of Mules and Asses purchased for
exportation, except during the regency of H
H etc Prince Firhad Meerza Naib al Ayaleh
of Fars, when a British Merchant Vessel arriving
at Bushire her Captain purchased several
Mules and embarked them on board his Ship,
paid the custom which had of old been
established as Bushire Duty, and left;
the Officers of the exalted Government subsequent
-ly made a demand upon the Agent of the
said Ship for the Shiraz duty upon the Mules
embarked, which had never been sanctioned
by Regulation or Custom – While this proceed-
-ing was pending His Royal Highness
the Prince Naib ul Ayaleh arrived at Bushire

on its being explained in his August presence that this was an innovation, and had never been established in practice by the Exalted Government; he ordered and decided that the demand on this head should be relinquished, and would not consent to the entertainment of an innovation, and the establishment of a custom which had never before prevailed;

will, it is desired and requested, according to his own knowledge and cognizance, attach his testimony in the Margin, that at the time of need this may serve as evidence.

True translation

(Signed) A B Kemball.

Asst. Resident &c.

True translation

A B Kemball

Asst. Resident Persian Gulf

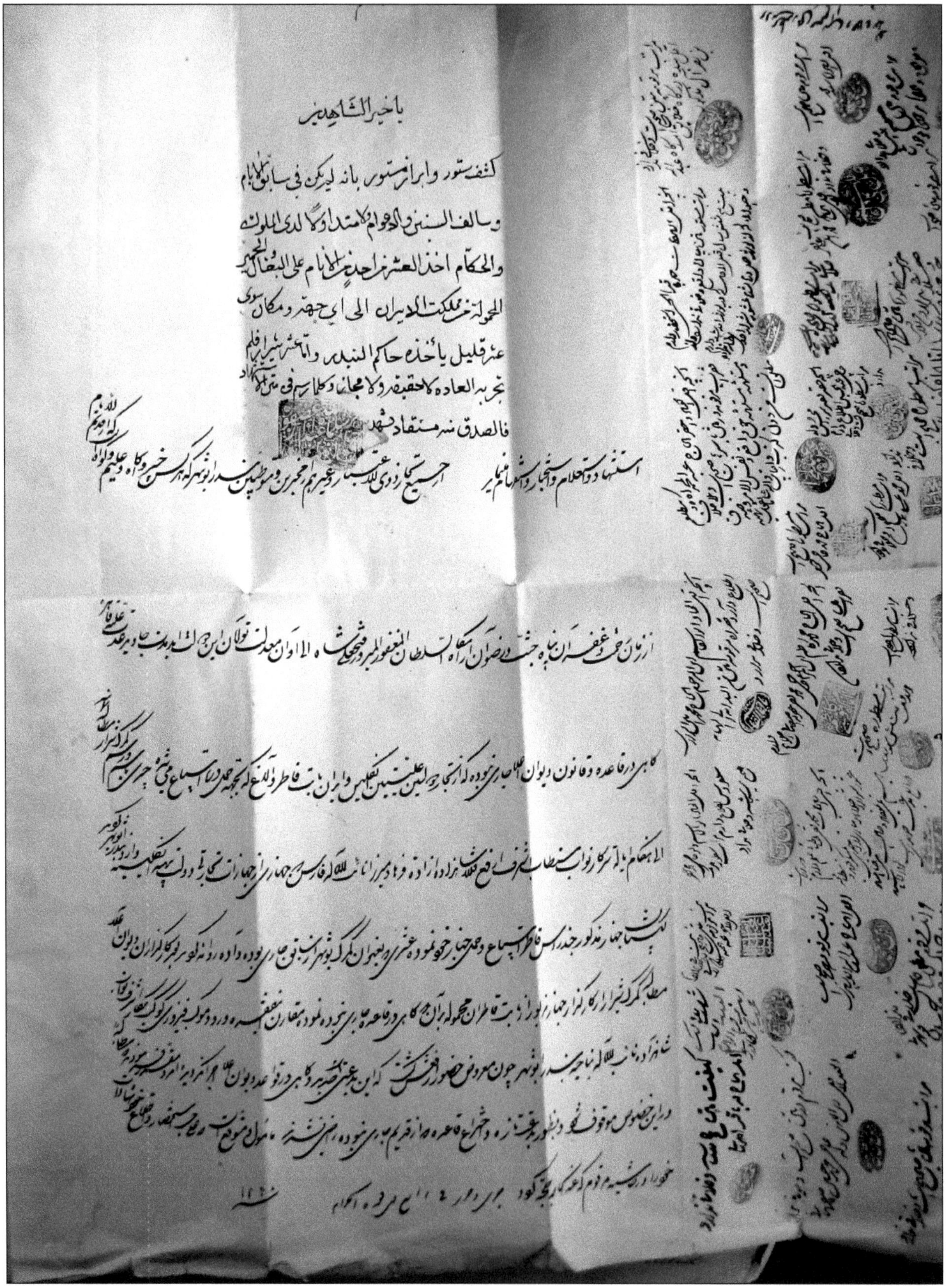

باخير الشاهدين

كشف ستور واظهار مستور باند لم يكن في سابق الايام

وسالف السنين والاعوام لامتداد ولا لدى الملوك

والحكام اخذ العشر من احد من الانام على البغال الحمير

الحمولة من مملكت الايران الى اي جهة ومكان سوى

عن قليل يأخذه حاكم البندر

5. National Sanitary Commission authorizes British physician to take steps to contain the outbreak of the plague. Tehran 23 October 1896.

Decision of the National Sanitary Commission that British quarantine officer was the best placed to take action to prevent outbreak of contagious diseases. It also discussed various steps that should be taken.

Source: Nationaal Archief , Legatie Perzië, Inv. 16.

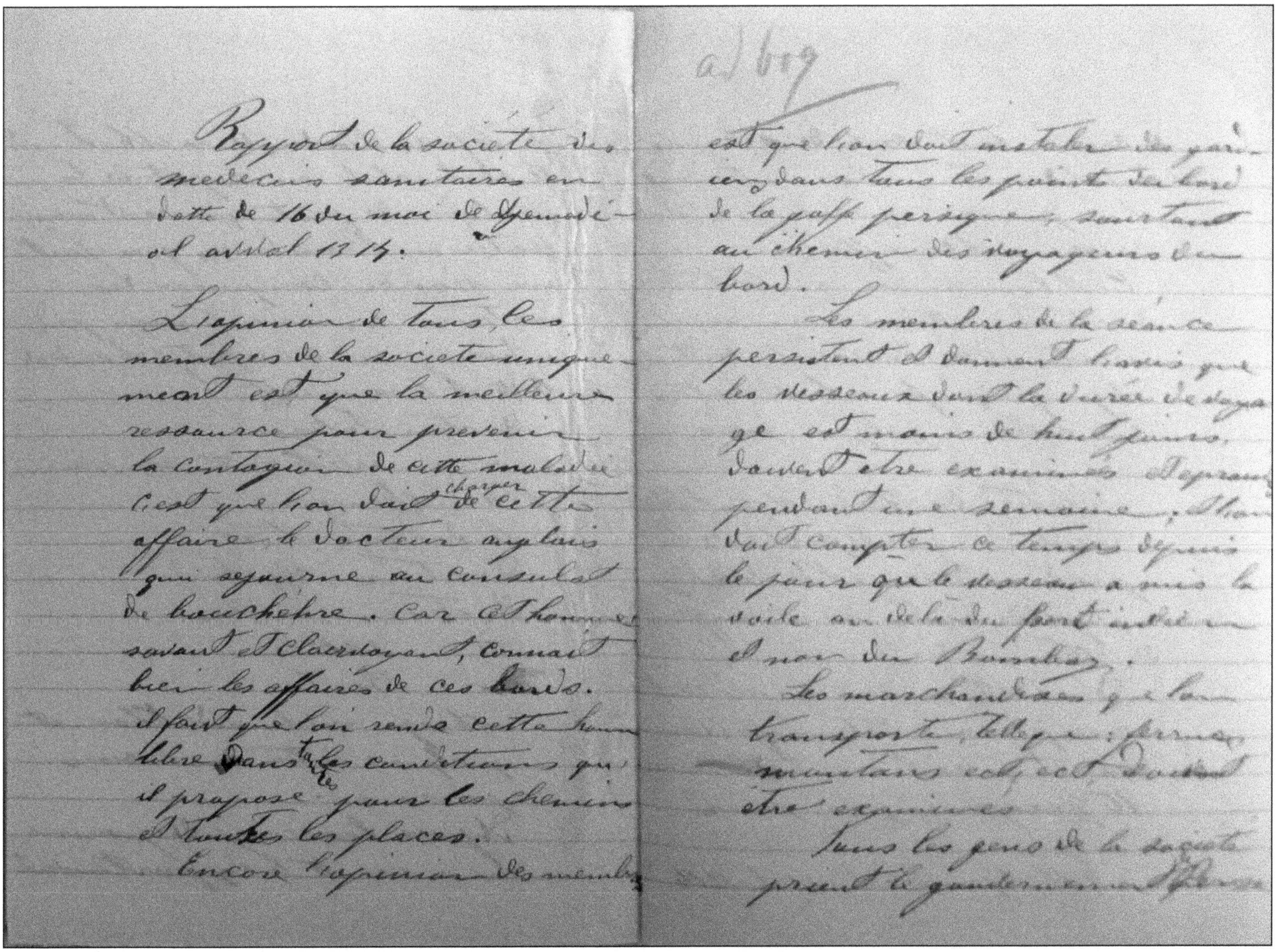

Rapport de la société des medecins sanitaires en datte de 16 du moi de djemadi-ol avval 1314.

L'opinion de tous les membres de la société uniquement est que la meilleure ressource pour prevenir la contagion de cette maladie c'est que l'on doit charger de cette affaire le docteur anglais qui sejourne au consulat de Bouchehre. Car cet homme savant et clairvoyant, connait bien les affaires de ces bords. Il faut que l'on rende cette homme libre dans toutes les conditions qu'il propose pour les chemins et toutes les places.

Encore l'opinion des membres

ad 609

est que l'on doit installer des gardes dans tous les points du bord de la golfe persique, surtout au chemin des voyageurs du bord.

Les membres de la séance persistent et donnent l'avis que les vesseaux dont la durée de voyage est moins de huit jours, doivent etre examinés et quarantés pendant une semaine, et l'on doit compter ce temps depuis le jour que le vesseau a mis la voile au dela du port indien et nom du Bombay.

Les marchandises que l'on transporte, telles que : fermes, mentans etc etc doivent etre examinées.

Tous les gens de la société prient le gouvernement Perse

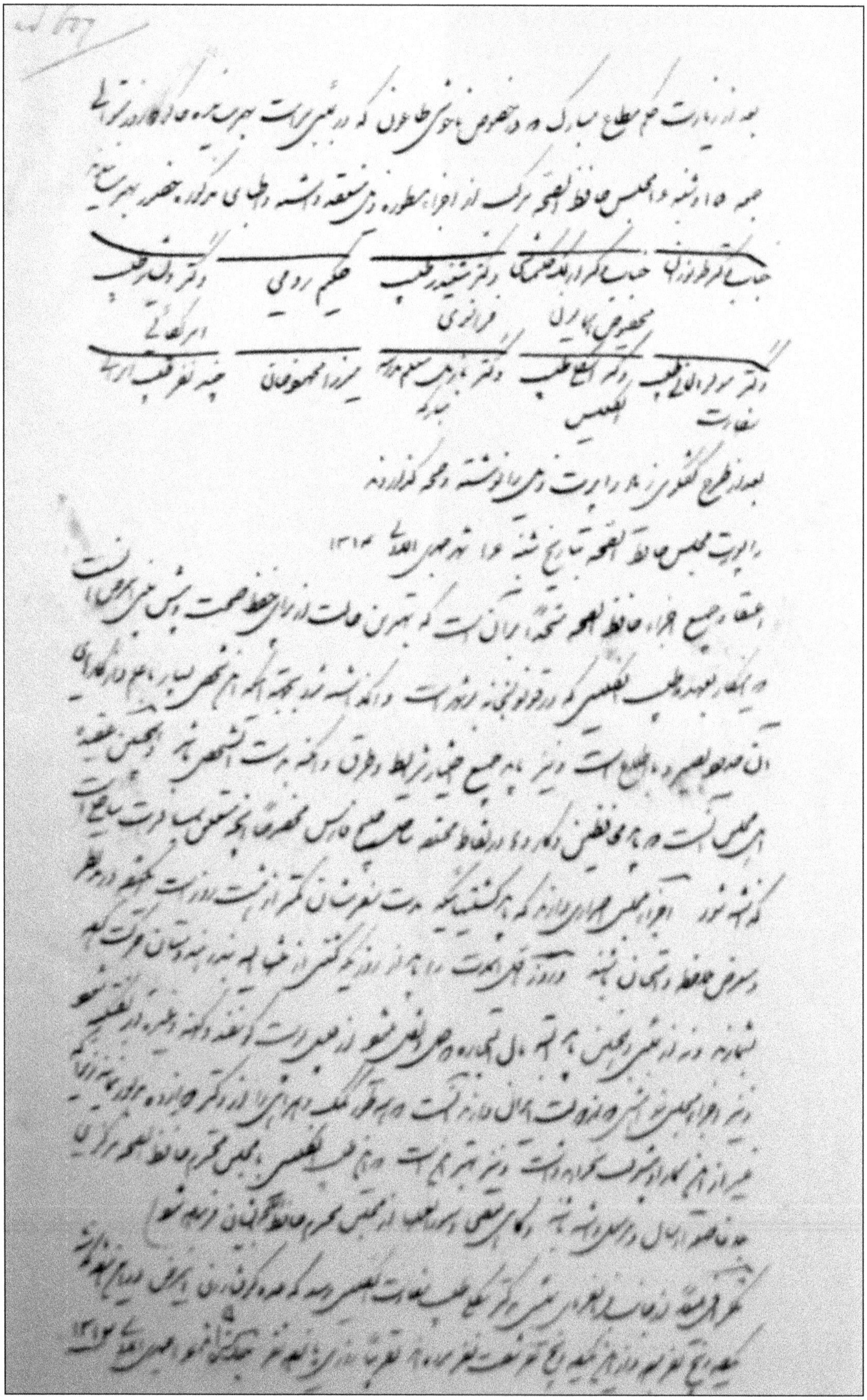

de donner toute sorte de secours
à cet docteur, car autrement
il ne pourra réaliser ces
dessains et ces affaires.
C'est bon aussi que cet
docteur ait une communication
directe avec la societe centrale
et que quelquefois la societe
lui envoie quelques avis

Notre docteur vient de
recevoir une depeche de la
part du gouvernement de Bombay,
au sujet de nombre des gens affectés
de cette maladie:
Dans cette semaine passée de cent
cinq personnes étaient affectées,
soixante en sont mortes, environ
15 ~~personnes~~ par jour.

le 16 Djumadi al awal 1314

6. Imposition of Harbor Duties

In August 1853, Mirza Reza, the *vaqaye`-negar* all of a sudden imposed harbor duties or an anchorage fee. The Persian consul in Bombay, where such a tax was levied, had suggested its application as a means to increase revenues for the Shah. Not only the British opposed this new tax, but so did local owners of vessels as well as the governor, be it each for different reasons. The British opposed it because it was in contravention of treaty obligations. The governor was against it, because he was not involved in the scheme. The owners of vessels, especially those sailing to India, opposed the tax, because in Indian ports, where a similar tax was collected, this was done to pay for harbor improvements such as buoys, light-houses, etc., improvements that were totally lacking in Bushehr. Therefore, some of them protested against the new fee.

6a. Protest of the British Resident

Protest against appointment of agent for the collection of freight of British vessels (February 1837). Protest by Haji Adam *nakhoda* against payment of anchorage fees (August 1853) below and in the pages that follow, in English and Persian.

Source: FO 248/150

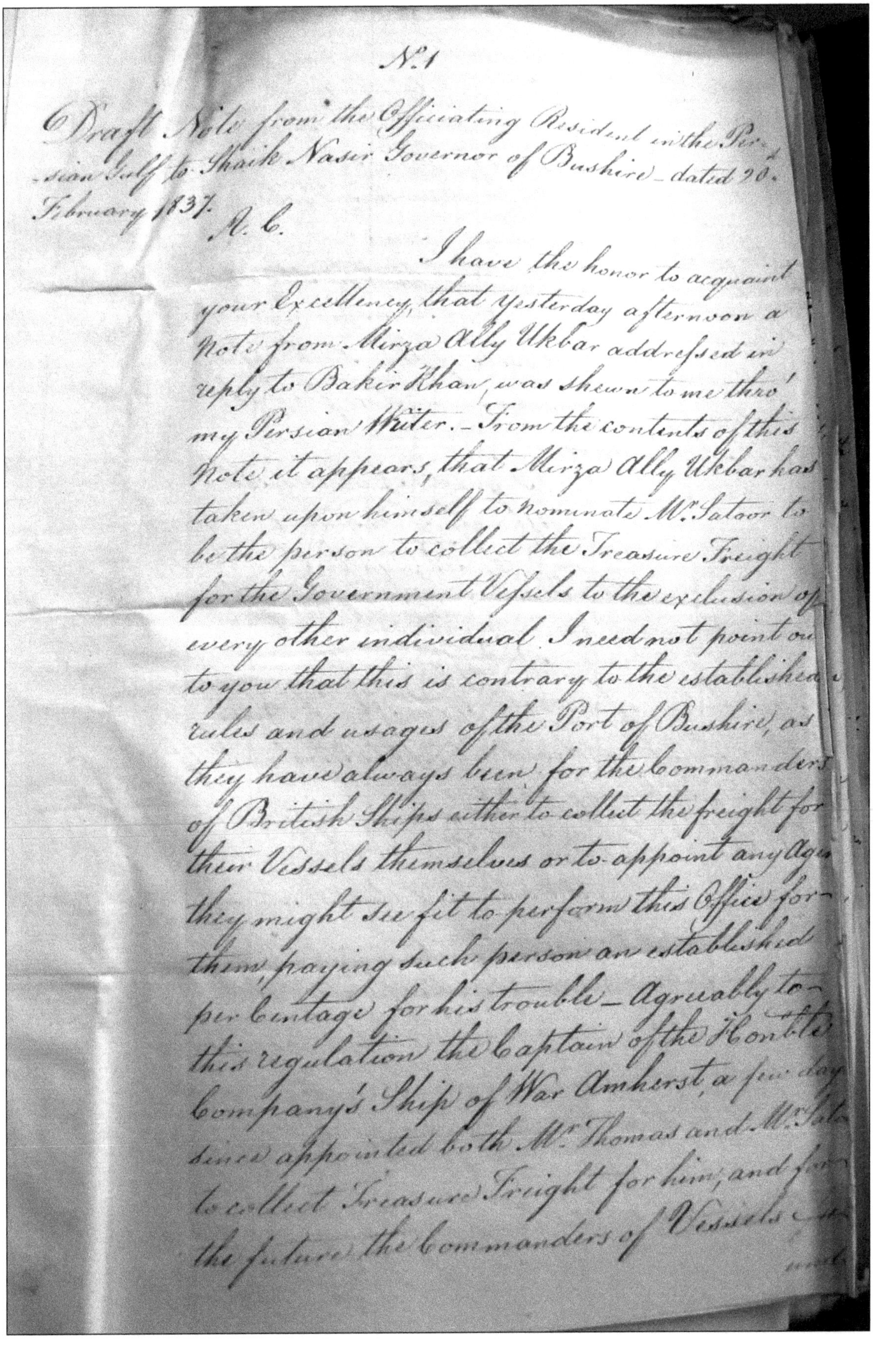

No. 1

Draft Note from the Officiating Resident in the Persian Gulf to Shaik Nasir Governor of Bushire – dated 20th February 1837.

A. C.

I have the honor to acquaint your Excellency, that yesterday afternoon a Note from Mirza Ally Ukbar addressed in reply to Baker Khan, was shewn to me thro' my Persian Writer. – From the contents of this Note it appears, that Mirza Ally Ukbar has taken upon himself to nominate Mr. Sataor to be the person to collect the Treasure Freight for the Government Vessels to the exclusion of every other individual. I need not point out to you that this is contrary to the established rules and usages of the Port of Bushire, as they have always been for the Commanders of British Ships either to collect the freight for their Vessels themselves or to appoint any Agent they might see fit to perform this Office for them, paying such person an established per Centage for his trouble – Agreeably to this regulation the Captain of the Hon'ble Company's Ship of War Amherst, a few days since appointed both Mr. Thomas and Mr. Sataor to collect Treasure Freight for him; and for the future the Commanders of Vessels and

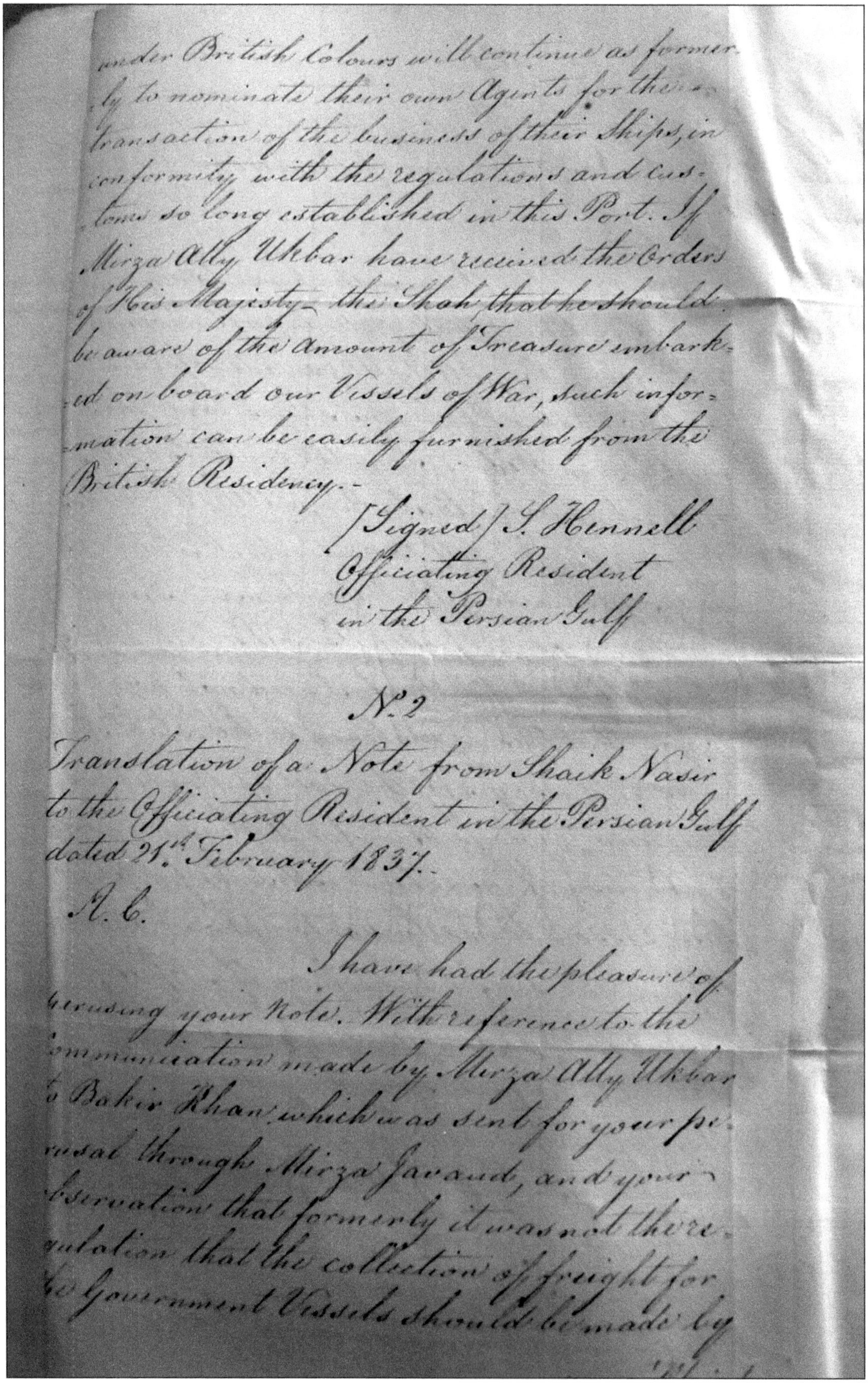

under British Colours will continue as former-
ly to nominate their own Agents for the
transaction of the business of their Ships, in
conformity with the regulations and cus-
toms so long established in this Port. If
Mirza Ally Ukbar have received the Orders
of His Majesty the Shah, that he should
be aware of the Amount of Treasure embark-
ed on board our Vessels of War, such infor-
mation can be easily furnished from the
British Residency.-

[Signed] S. Hennell
Officiating Resident
in the Persian Gulf

No. 2

Translation of a Note from Shaik Nasir
to the Officiating Resident in the Persian Gulf
dated 21st February 1837.

A. C.

I have had the pleasure of
perusing your Note. With reference to the
communication made by Mirza Ally Ukbar
to Bakir Khan which was sent for your pe-
rusal through Mirza Javaud, and your
observation that formerly it was not the re-
gulation that the collection of freight for
the Government Vessels should be made by

+Mr. Satoor

+Khojah Mal ollah alone, I beg to inform you that I have communicated most fully with Mirza Ally Ukbar the Wakaya Nigar to the + effect, that before the present time it was not established that the Exports and Imports of this place should be ascertained. In reply the Mirza intimates that this was certainly not the case formerly, but that he has received the Orders of His Majesty the Shah that not a single deenar, or particle of Merchandize, is to be embarked without his knowledge, agreeably to the Royal Furman which he holds. The fact is as he states. The arrangement made by him with the Merchants was, that the collection of the freight for the Ships should rest with Khojah Mal-ollah he being considered a perfectly honest and trustworthy person not only in this but in all other places, and who to the present time has never committed any fault — +Khojah Abraham however, has been to blame and the reason he was sent for was, lest the Merchants should deny (their having sent freight). This arrangement is still in force. + Upon my bringing that part of your note, where you say that any information the Wakaya Nigar might wish for could be got from the Residency, to the notice of

+It will be observed that the Shaik avoids the subject of the infraction of the established regulations of the Port, but would make it appear as if an objection had been made to the Imports and Exports of the place being ascertained an insinuation which is quite unfounded.

+ Mr. Thomas

+ The only observation made was that he could be furnished from the Residency with the amount of Treasure shipped on board the Vessels of the

of that personage he replied by saying refer
to the Royal Firman and let the Orders there-
in set forth be acted upon. he further Stat-
ed that he had had no instructions to re-
ceive his information from the Residency.
that although the two States were as one, yet
that it was necessary that a Servant Should
act according to the Orders of his Superior;
that he was directed to ascertain according
to rule and Custom the Exports and Imports
both of Money and Merchandize and to
make a monthly report of the same to His
Majesty the Shah. He concluded by saying
that if any one besides Mal Ollah interferes
in the collection of freight for Ships confusion
will arise and the Resident will not allow
that the affairs of the Government should be
disordered. - I beg to assure you that as far
as I can learn Merza Ally Ukbar has no
other desire than that the business of the dee-
wan should be duly arranged. If any one
wishes to make the affair doubtful be assured
that he is wrong. as there is no other object
than the one above specified. -

True Translation

(Signed) S. Hennell
Officiating Resident Pa

True Copies

6B. Protest of Haji Adam

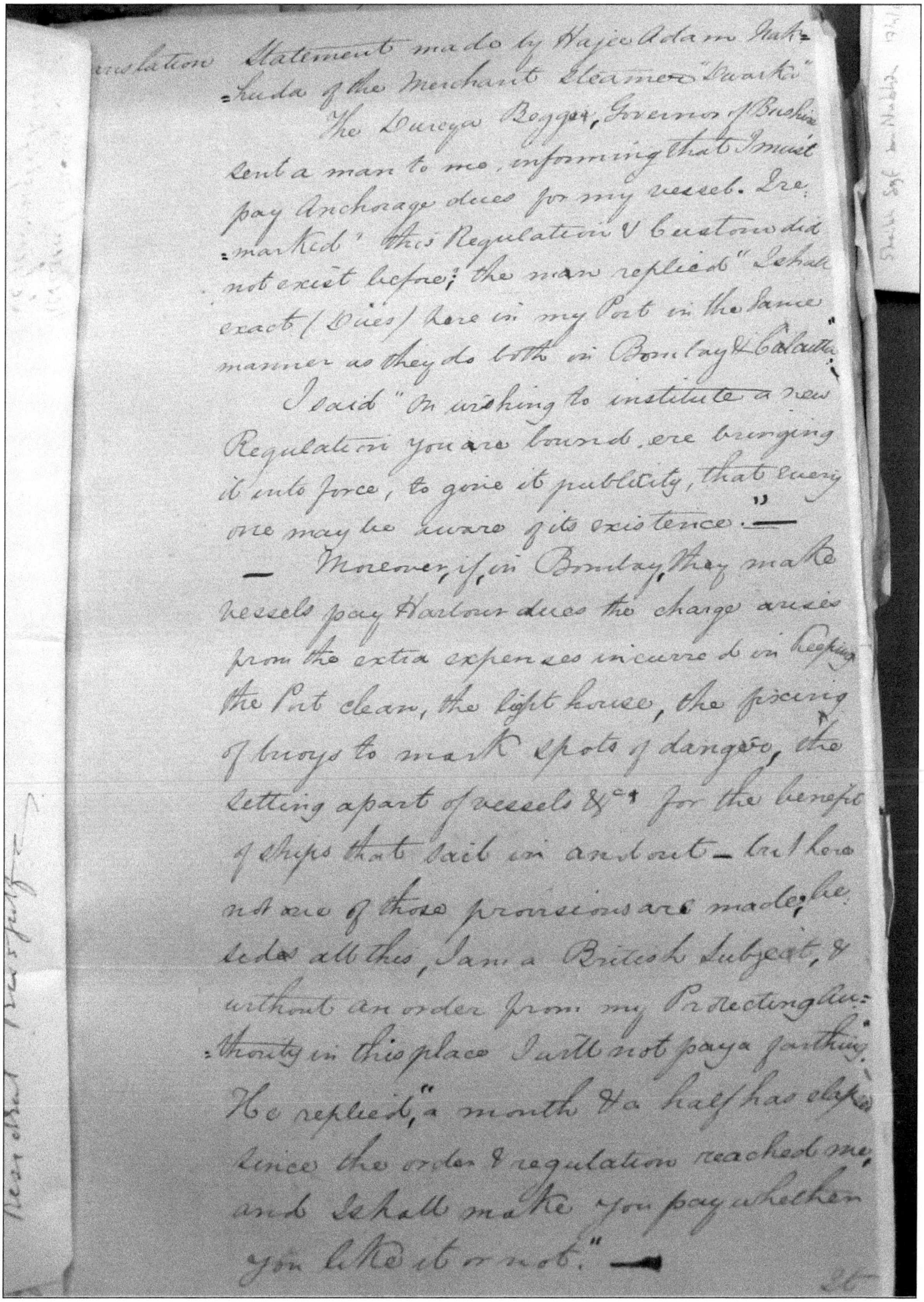

Translation Statement made by Hajee Adam Nak-
-huda of the Merchant Steamer "Dwarka"

The Dureya Beggee, Governor of Bushire sent a man to me, informing that I must pay Anchorage dues for my vessel. I re-marked "this Regulation & Custom did not exist before; the man replied "I shall exact (Dues) here in my Port in the same manner as they do both in Bombay & Calcutta"

I said "On wishing to institute a new Regulation you are bound, ere bringing it into force, to give it publicity, that every one may be aware of its existence." —

— Moreover, if, in Bombay, they make vessels pay Harbour dues the charge arises from the extra expenses incurred in keeping the Port clean, the light house, the fixing of buoys to mark spots of danger, the setting apart of vessels &c. for the benefit of ships that sail in and out — but here not one of those provisions are made; besides all this, I am a British Subject, & without an order from my Protecting Authority in this place I will not pay a farthing." He replied, "a month & a half has elapsed since the order & regulation reached me, and I shall make you pay whether you like it or not." —

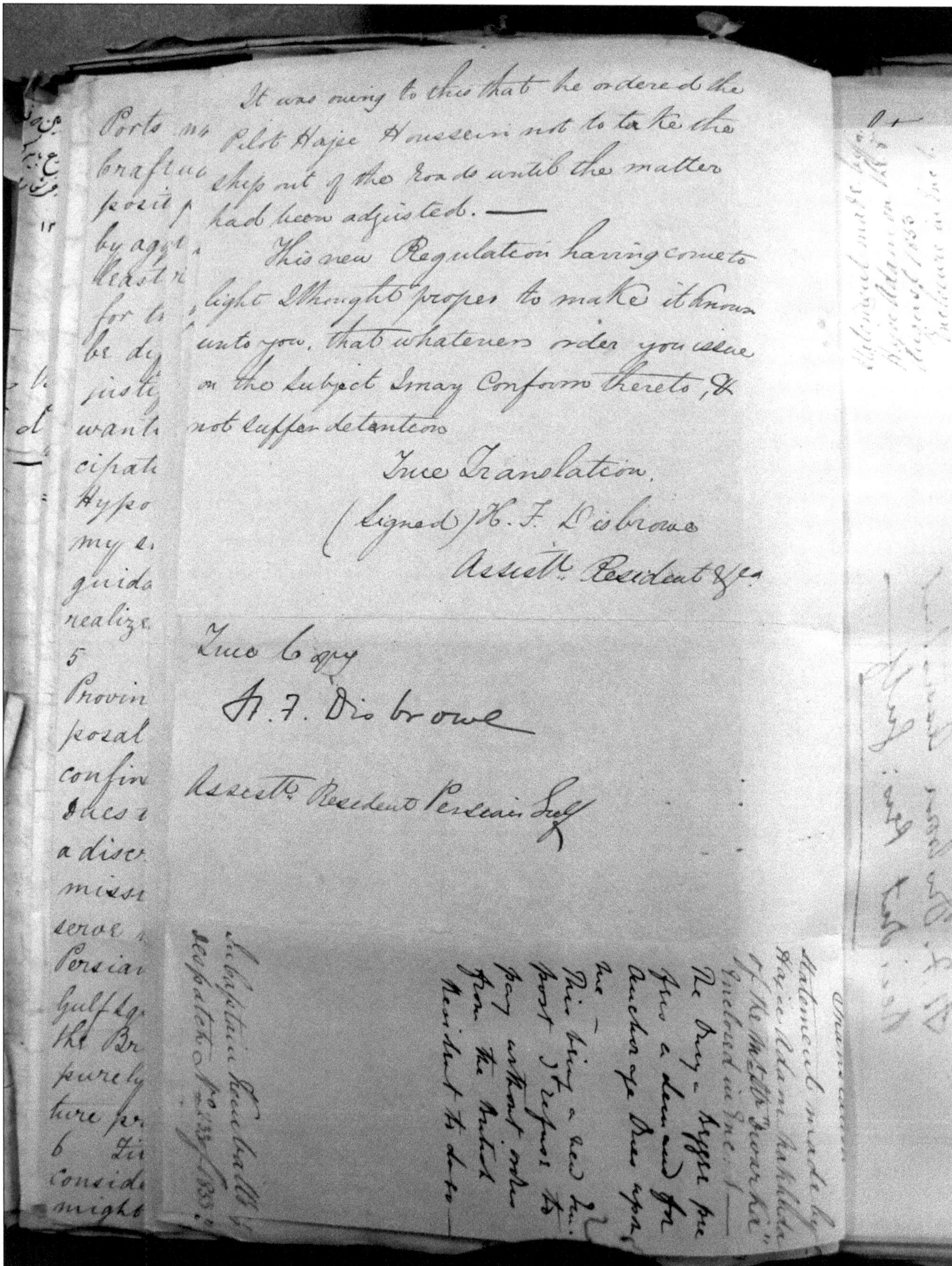

It was owing to this that he ordered the Pilot Hajee Housein not to take the ship out of the roads until the matter had been adjusted. —

This new Regulation having come to light I thought proper to make it known unto you, that whatever order you issue on the subject I may conform thereto, & not suffer detention

True Translation.
(Signed) H. F. Disbrowe
Assistt. Resident &c.

True Copy
H. F. Disbrowe
Assistt. Resident Persian Gulf

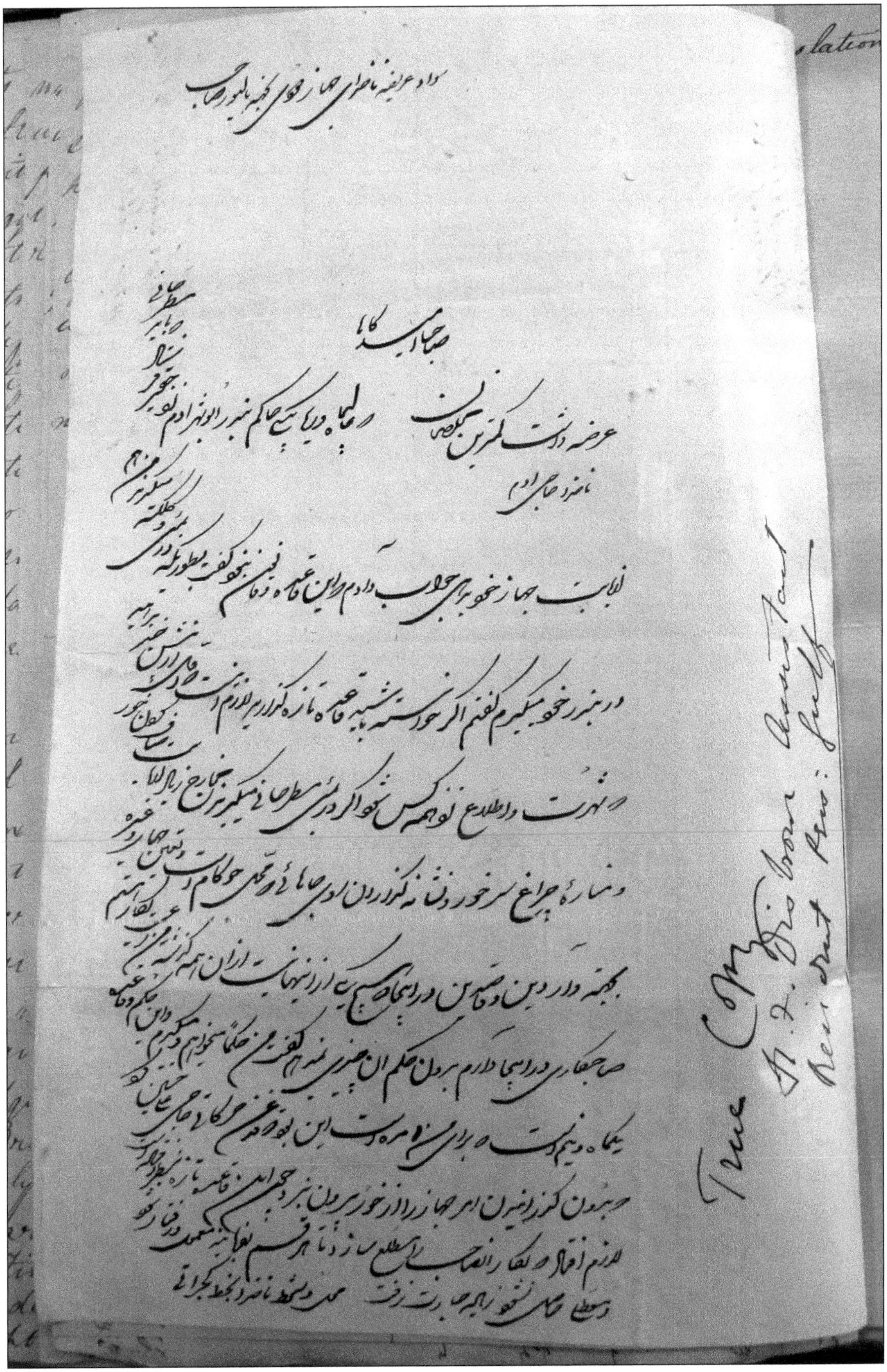
True Copy
Resident Pers: Gulf

7. The importance of proper address or a lesson in etiquette.

Correspondence concerning the proper address of British and Persian officials.

When on 18 November 1857, Ahmad Khan Daryabegi arrived in Bushehr he behaved rather haughty toward the British Resident, Felix Jones. The latter wrote: "He expected more personal attention which I did not consider safe to do. According to custom, the governor brings the first visit to the Resident and I deemed it humiliating under the present circumstances to deviate from custom. The more since I knew that Ahmad Khan aimed to depreciate British influence in the Gulf. His ungraciousness to send the lowest civil official he could find to take over the town from me was indicative of his designs despite his honeyed words in his and the Shiraz authorities' letters. The evasive character of his reply when I raised this with him confirmed for me that this was premeditated. I therefore took shelter in my higher position as Resident, and as guest of the Persian Government. The Residents have never considered anyone superior to themselves other than the prince governor of Fars. The governors of the seaports have only jurisdiction of their port and environs and the Resident also over the independent maritime tribes in Arabia and Oman (to whom he is HBG's representative) and the entire seaboard of Persia. Ahmad Khan has no authority 20 miles beyond his city so an appeal to him has no use, although he is Lord of the Sea and wants moreover homage in his district as he were at court. Therefore, I consider it a farce when the Persian Prime Minister wrote re Ahmad Khan that he has authority over the islands and Bandar Abbas in the Gulf. I think the PM aims to depreciate British authority in the Gulf. I therefore have decided not to submit to anything that smells of degradation in particular at present period. Therefore, until I hear different from you I will not have contacts with the governor on matters concerning the Gulf unless they concern his district, but, if necessary and as before, address the prince governor of Fars. Otherwise I see a loss of old established prestige and sacrifice of interests that will be to our detriment in Persia, Arabia and India. If Persian govt wants to promote its trade interests it should cooperate with British officers to whom these interests are confided in this quarter. FO 248/168, Cmdr Felix Jones to C.A. Murray envoy-extraordinary 26 November 1857.

Although in April 1858 matters seemed to have been resolved between the two parties only three months later another problem of perceived disrespect raised its head that gave rise to interesting correspondence, as shown in the appended documents.

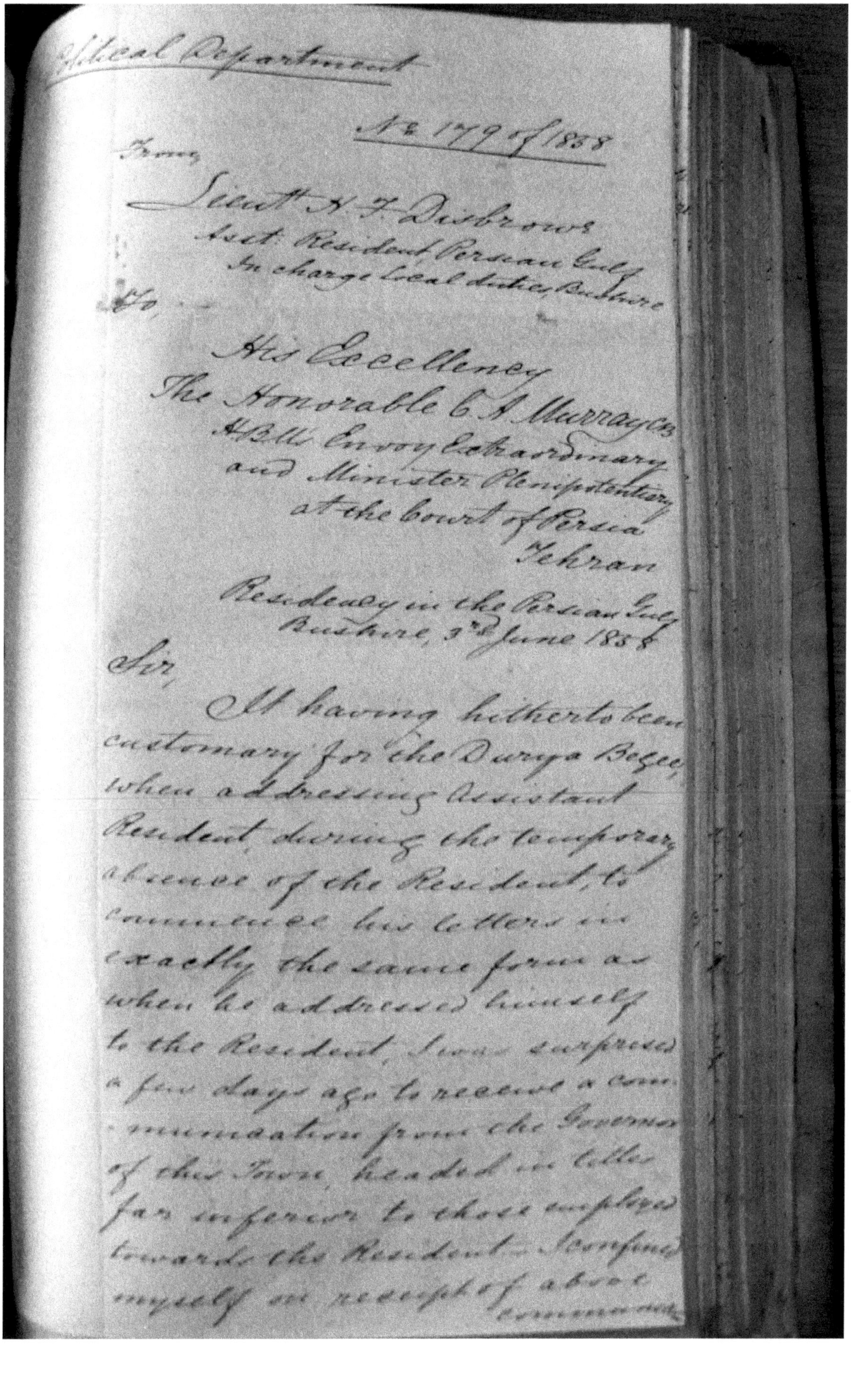

Political Department

No 179 of 1858

From

Lieut H. F. Disbrowe
Asst. Resident Persian Gulf
In charge local duties, Bushire

To

His Excellency
The Honorable C. A. Murray CB
H.B.M's Envoy Extraordinary
and Minister Plenipotentiary
at the Court of Persia
Tehran

Residency in the Persian Gulf
Bushire, 3rd June 1858

Sir,

It having hitherto been customary for the Durya Begee, when addressing Assistant Resident, during the temporary absence of the Resident, to commence his letters in exactly the same form as when he addressed himself to the Resident, I was surprised a few days ago to receive a communication from the Governor of this Town, headed in titles far inferior to those employed towards the Resident – I confined myself on receipt of above communica-

communication, to pointing
out to the Governor the irregu-
-larity of the course he had
pursued, and to requesting
him in future to address me
in same style as it had been
his custom to address Residents.
To this I received no reply.—

2. It is not my desire
to trouble Your Excellency with
more details than appear ne-
-cessary to enable Your Ex-
-cellency to pronounce just
judgement in my behalf.— I
may, however, be permitted to
remark, that the titles conferred
upon me by the Governor are
inferior to those conferred by
the Political Resident at Bushire
upon the British native Agent
at Sheeraz. This surely is a
glaring irregularity.— I may
likewise point out to Your Ex-
-cellency that the Prince Govr
of Fars has honored me with
verbatim the same form of
address as he has honored
the Resident when addressing
him.—

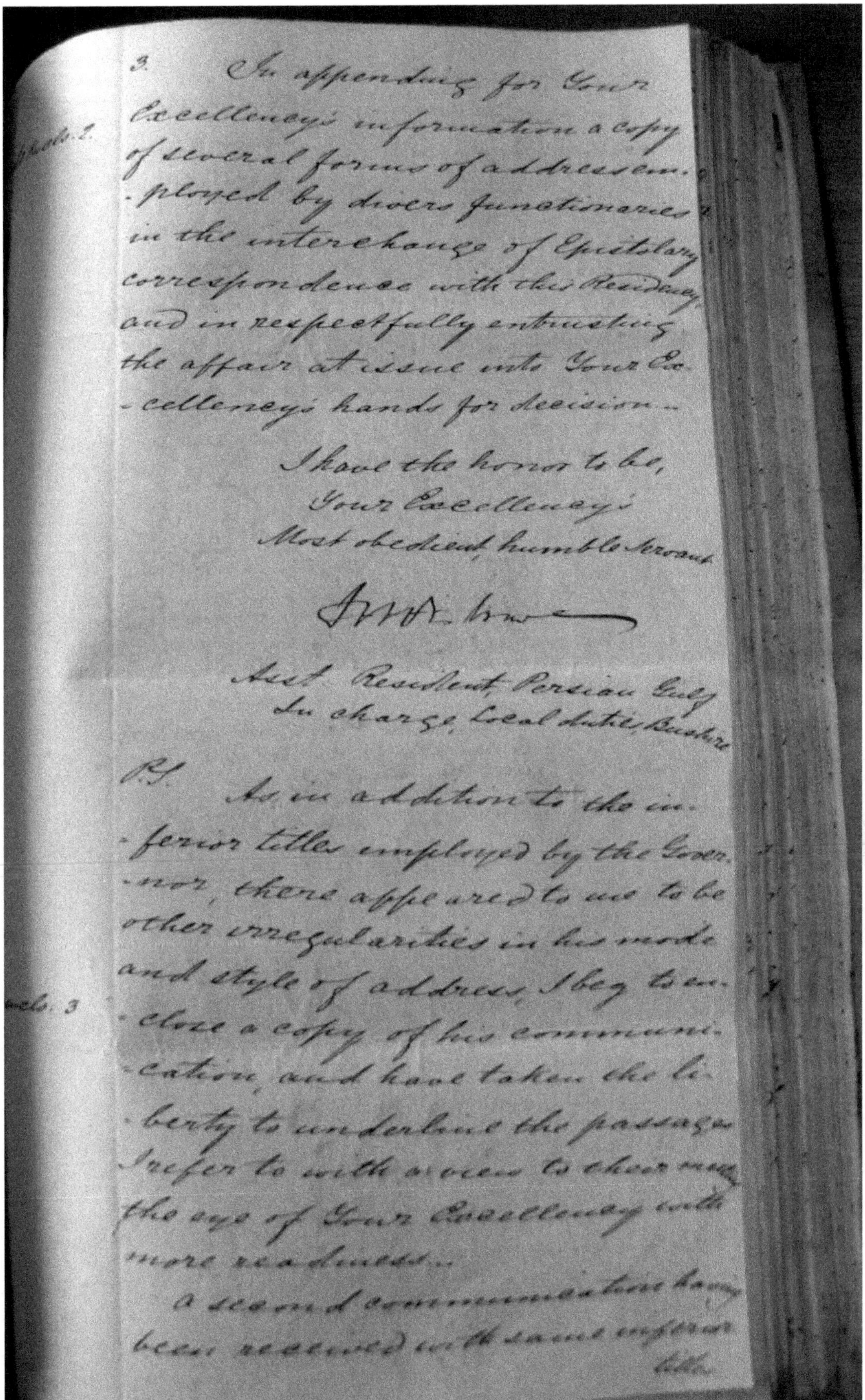

3. In appending for Your Excellency's information a copy of several forms of address employed by divers functionaries in the interchange of Epistolary correspondence with this Residency and in respectfully entrusting the affair at issue into Your Excellency's hands for decision.

Enclo. 2

I have the honor to be,
Your Excellency's
Most obedient, humble Servant

[illegible]

Asst. Resident, Persian Gulf
In charge, Local duties, Bushire

P.S. As, in addition to the inferior titles employed by the Governor, there appeared to me to be other irregularities in his mode and style of address, I beg to enclose a copy of his communication, and have taken the liberty to underline the passages I refer to with a view to their meeting the eye of Your Excellency with more readiness.

Enclo. 3

A second communication having been received with same inferior title

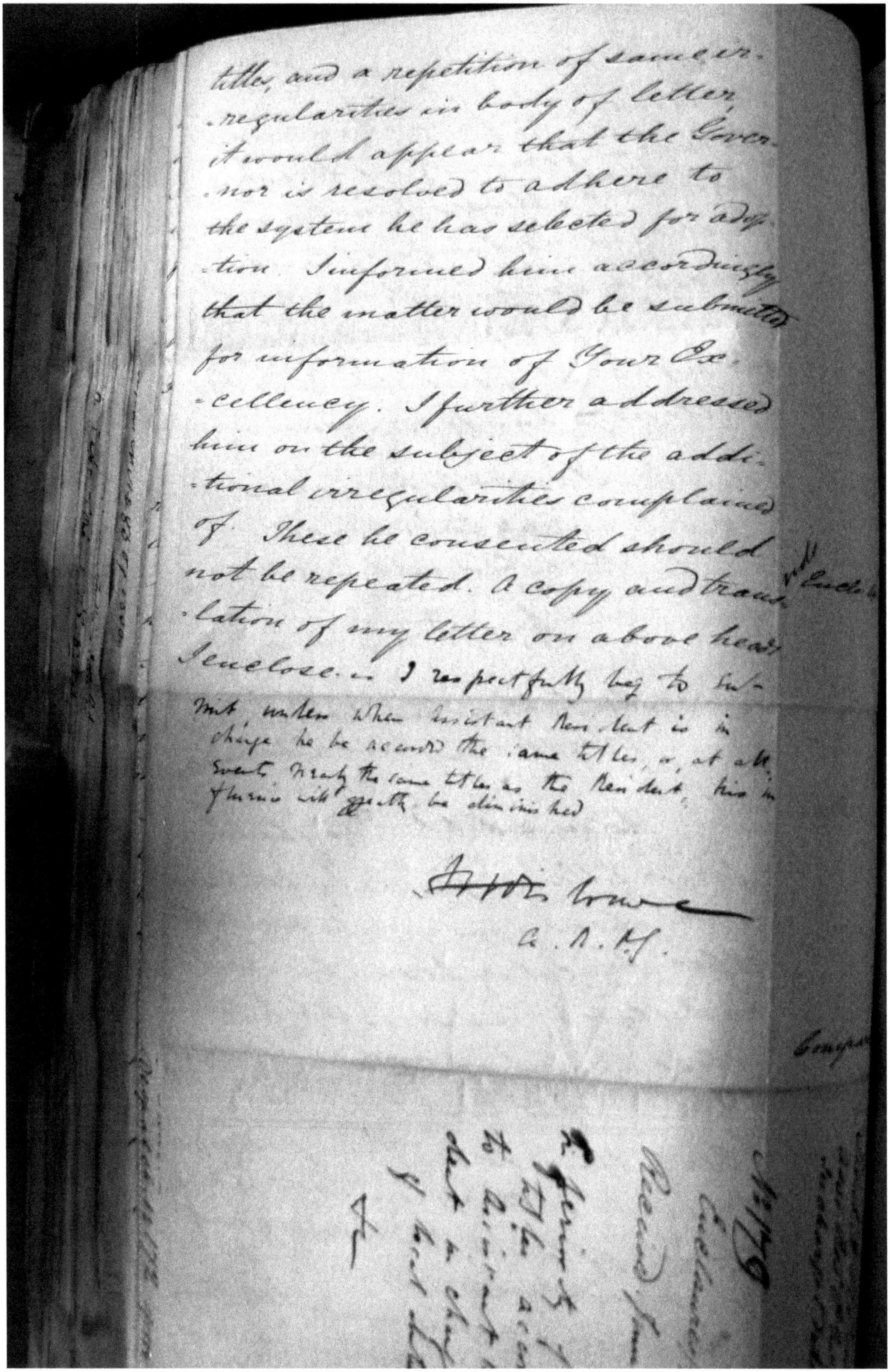
titles, and a repetition of same ir-
-regularities in body of letter,
it would appear that the Gover-
-nor is resolved to adhere to
the system he has selected for adop-
-tion. I informed him accordingly
that the matter would be submitted
for information of Your Ex-
-cellency. I further addressed
him on the subject of the addi-
-tional irregularities complained
of. These he consented should
not be repeated. A copy and trans-
-lation of my letter on above head
I enclose. — I respectfully beg to sub-
mit unless when Assistant Resident is in
charge he be accorded the same titles, or, at all
events nearly the same titles as the Resident, his in-
fluence will greatly be diminished

[illegible] Lowe
A. R. P. G.

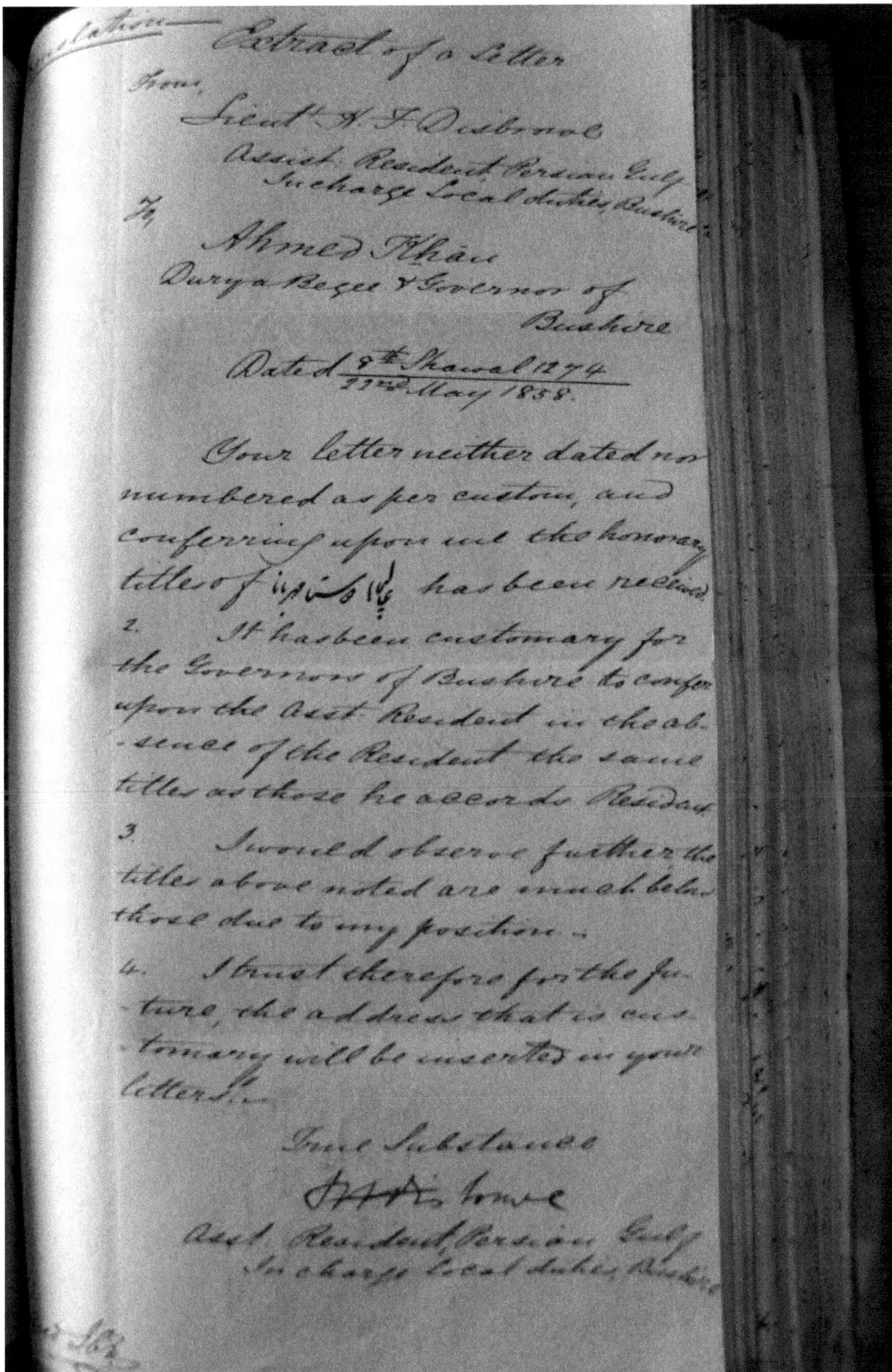
Translation—

Extract of a Letter

From,

Lieut. H. F. Disbrowe

Assist. Resident Persian Gulf
In charge Local duties, Bushire

To,

Ahmed Khan

Durya Begee & Governor of
Bushire

Dated 8th Shawal 1274
23rd May 1858.

Your letter neither dated nor numbered as per custom, and conferring upon me the honorary titles of [illegible] has been received.

2. It has been customary for the Governors of Bushire to confer upon the Asst. Resident in the absence of the Resident the same titles as those he accords Resident.

3. I would observe further the titles above noted are much below those due to my position.

4. I trust therefore for the future, the address that is customary will be inserted in your letters.

True Substance

H. F. Disbrowe

Asst. Resident, Persian Gulf
In charge Local duties, Bushire

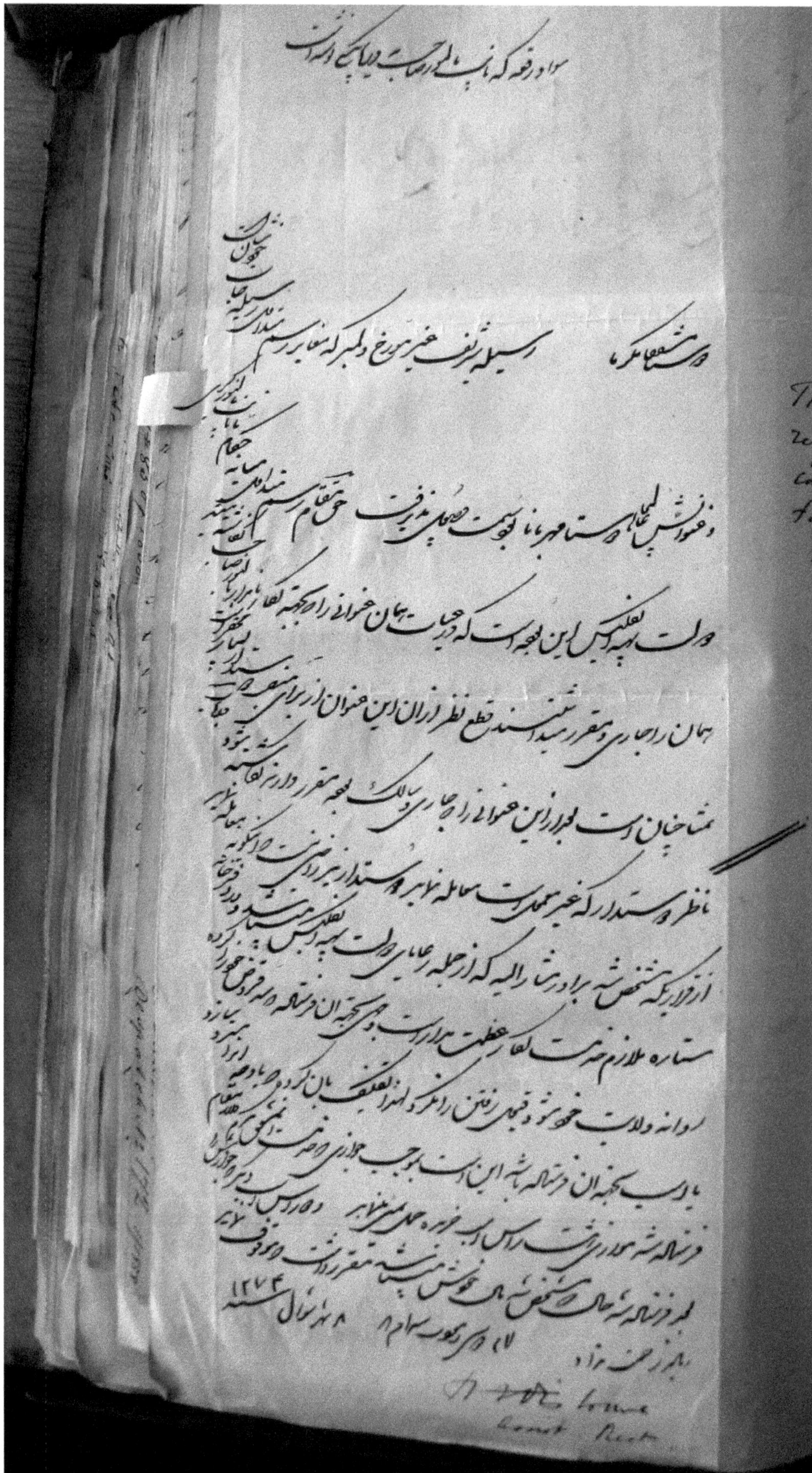

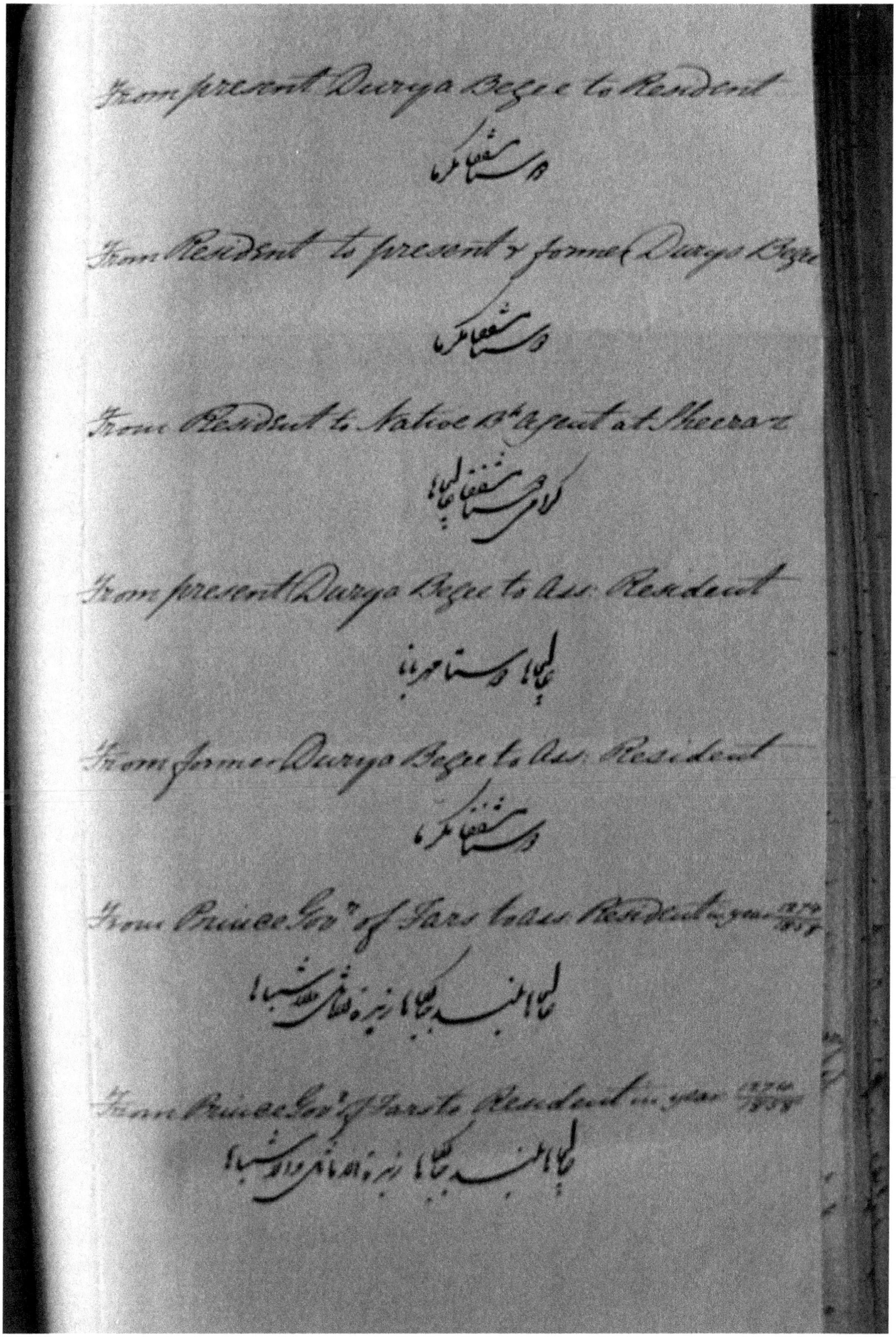
From present Darya Beggee to Resident
From Resident to present & former Darya Beggee
From Resident to Native Br. Agent at Sheeraz
From present Darya Beggee to Ass. Resident
From former Darya Beggee to Ass. Resident
From Prince Gov.r of Fars to Ass. Resident in year 1274/1858
From Prince Gov.r of Fars to Resident in year 1274/1858

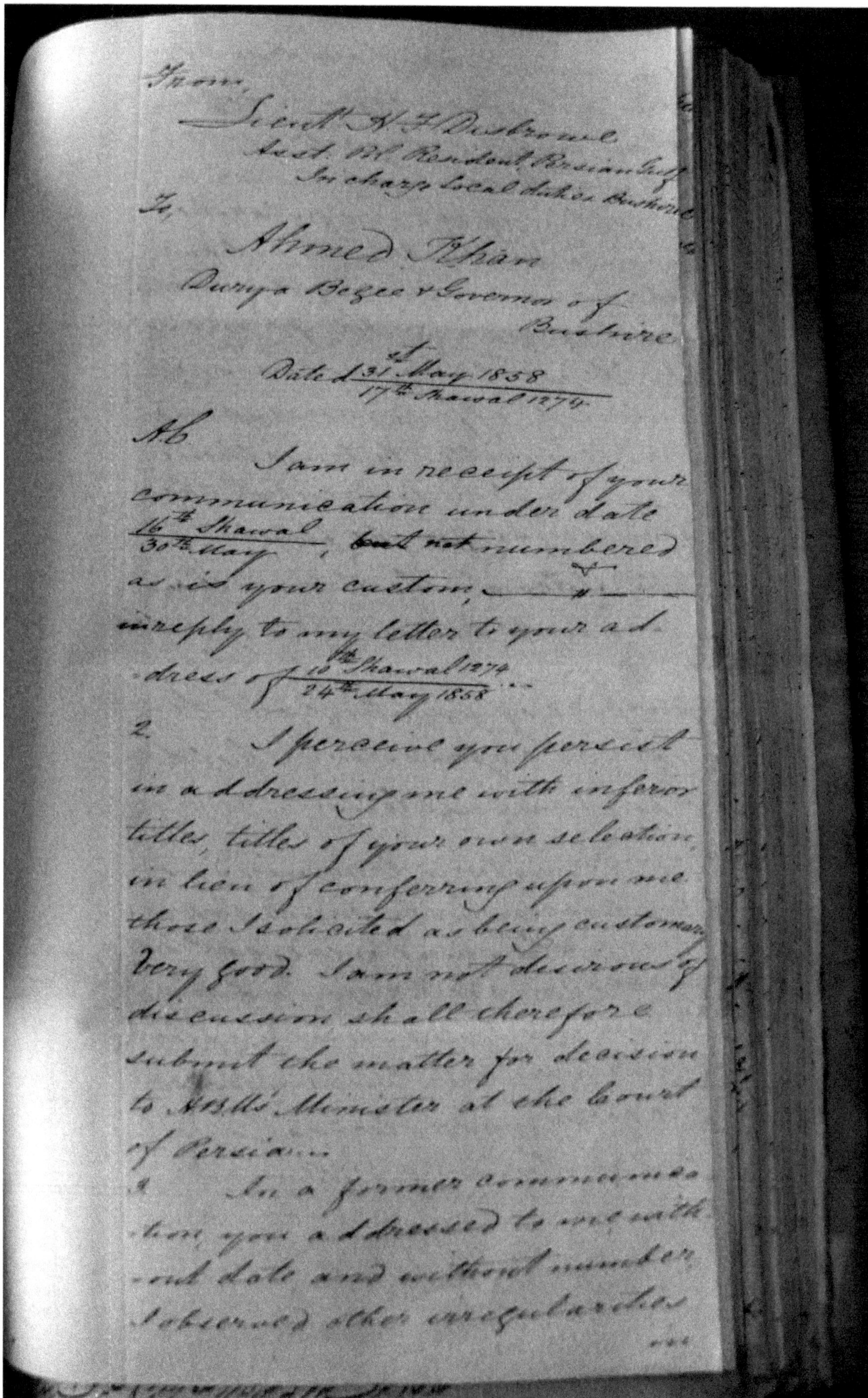

From,
Lieut. H. F. Disbrowe
Asst. Pol. Resident Persian Gulf
In charge local duties Bushire

To,
Ahmed Khan
Durya Begee & Governor of
Bushire

Dated 31st May 1858 / 17th Shawal 1274

A.C.

I am in receipt of your communication under date 16th Shawal / 30th May, ~~but~~ not numbered as is your custom, & in reply to my letter to your address of 10th Shawal 1274 / 24th May 1858.

2. I perceive you persist in addressing me with inferior titles, titles of your own selection, in lieu of conferring upon me those I solicited as being customary. Very good. I am not desirous of discussion, shall therefore submit the matter for decision to H.B.M's Minister at the Court of Persia.

3. In a former communication, you addressed to me without date and without number. I observed other irregularities ...

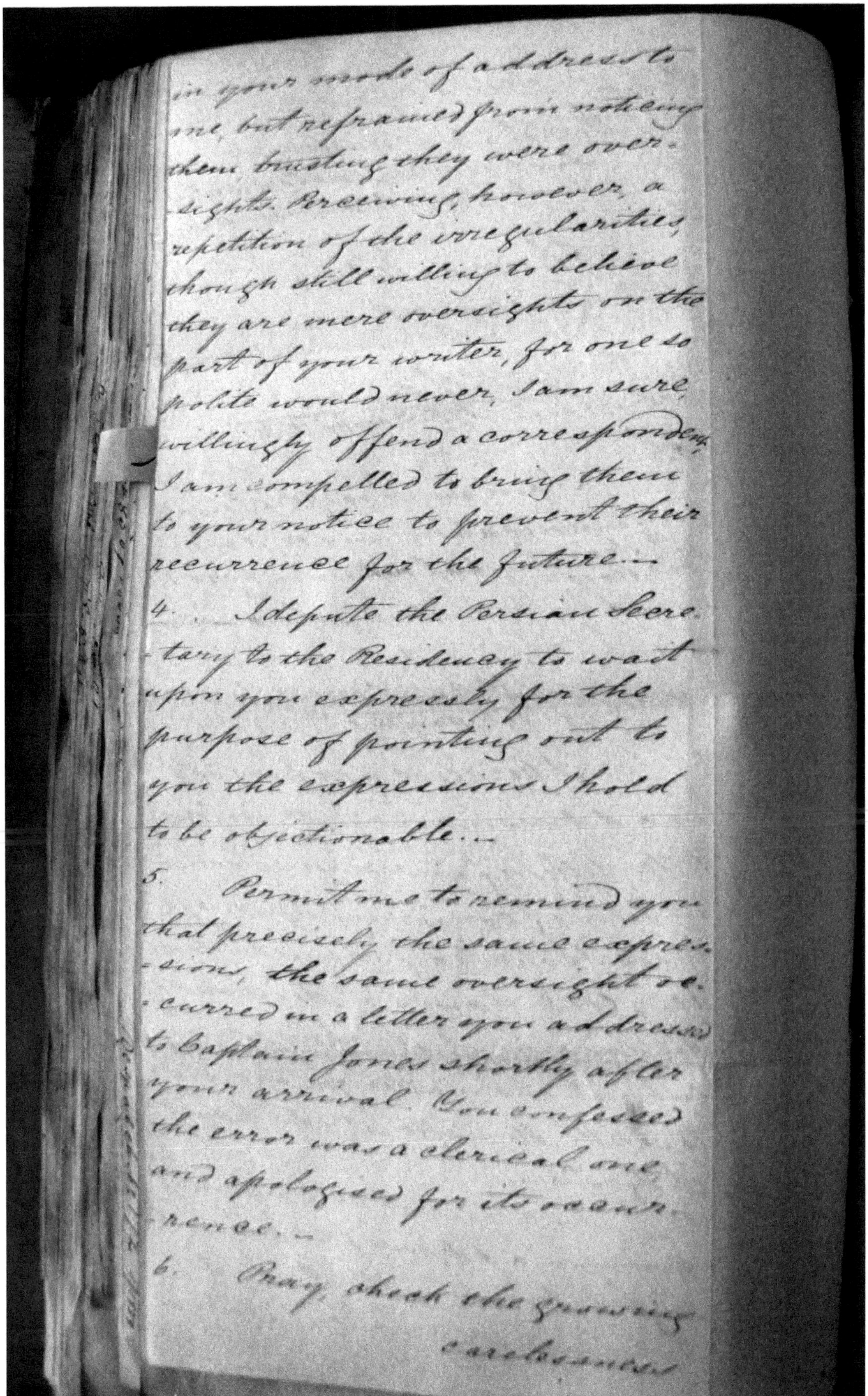

in your mode of address to
me, but refrained from noticing
them trusting they were over-
sights. Perceiving, however, a
repetition of the irregularities,
though still willing to believe
they are mere oversights on the
part of your writer, for one so
polite would never, I am sure,
willingly offend a correspondent,
I am compelled to bring them
to your notice to prevent their
recurrence for the future.—

4. I depute the Persian Secre-
-tary to the Residency to wait
upon you expressly for the
purpose of pointing out to
you the expressions I hold
to be objectionable.—

5. Permit me to remind you
that precisely the same expres-
-sions, the same oversight oc-
-curred in a letter you addressed
to Captain Jones shortly after
your arrival. You confessed
the error was a clerical one
and apologised for its occur-
-rence.—

6. Pray, check the growing
carelessness

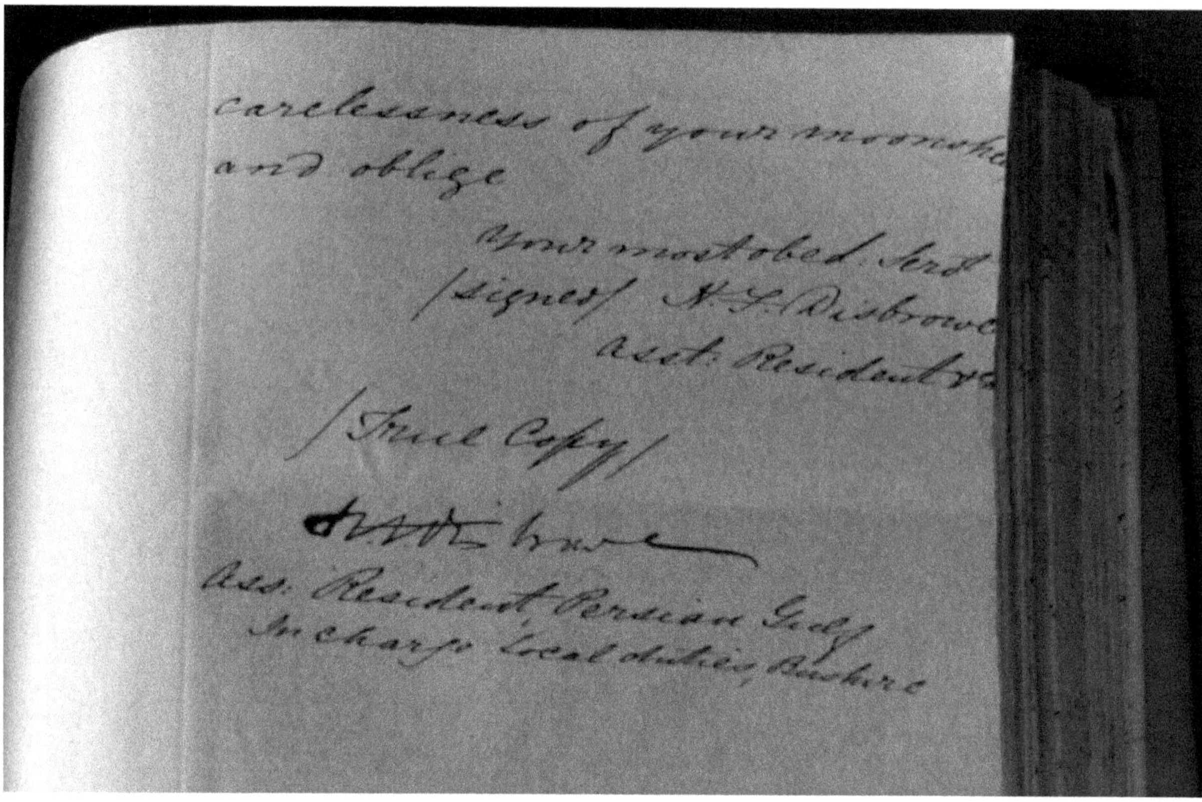
carelessness of your moonshe
and oblige

Your most obed. Servt
(signed) H. L. Disbrowe
Asst. Resident &c

(True Copy)

[illegible]
Ass. Resident, Persian Gulf
In charge Local duties, Bushire

Source: FO 248/168

Bibliography

Archives.

National Archives (Kew Gardens, London).

FO 60/24, 25, 114, 463, 658.

FO 78/241.

FO 248/38, 52, 76, 85, 99, 108, 129, 146, 150, 157, 168, 176, 183, 189, 198, 199, 206, 229, 232, 263, 271, 281, 290, 300, 318, 329, 402, 412, 424, 448, 484, 544, 567, 960, 961, 1024, 1229, 1415, 1450, 1469.

FO 371/15473, 40222.

FO 416/80.

IOR or India Office Records (British Library, London).

L/PS/11/182

L/PS/12/86

R/15/1/43, 61, 78, 117, 147, 154, 173

R/15/2/1

V/24/2639

Nationaal Archief (the Hague, the Netherlands).

VOC 1295, 1329, 2254

Books and Articles

`Abbasi, Mohammad Reza and Badi`i, Parviz eds. 1372/1993. *Gozareshha-ye owza`-ye siyasi, ejtema`i-ye viilayat-e `ahd-e naseri*. Tehran: Sazman-e Asnad-e Melli.

Abrahamian, Ervand 1982. *Iran Between Two Revolutions*. Princeton; Princeton UP.

Adamiyat, Mohammad Hoseyn Roknzadeh 1349/1970. *Fars va jang-e beyn al-mellal*. Tehran: Eqbal.

Administration Report = *Administration Report on the Persian Gulf Political Residency for the year (1873 to 1940)* in Government of India. *The Persian Gulf Administration Reports 1873-1947*, 10 vols., Gerrards Cross, Archives Editions, 1986.

Ael 1931. *Po Persii i Mesopotamii*. Leningrad: Ogiz.

Afkhami, Amir Arsalan 2003. "Health in Persia iii: Qajar Period." *Encyclopedia Iranica*, vol. XII, Fasc. 1, pp. 104-111.

Afshar Sistani, Iraj 1369/1990. *Negahi beh Bushehr*. 2 vols. Tehran.

Amanat, Abbas 1983. *Cities & Trade: Consul Abbott on the Economy and Society of Persia 1847-1866*. London: Ithaca press.

___, 1997. *Pivot of the Universe. Nasir al-Din Shah Qajar and the Persian Monarchy, 1831-1896*. Berkeley: University of Californa Press.

Amin, Abdul Amir 1967. *British Interests in the Persian Gulf* Leiden: Brill.

Anonymous 1801, "Directions for Sailing up the Gulf of Persia and to Bassora," in: Joseph Huddart ed., *The Oriental Navigator, Or, New Directions for Sailing to and from the East Indies, China, New Holland*. London, pp. 170-78.

___1828, "Voyage from Muscat to Bushire in the Persian Gulf," *The Oriental Herald*, vol. 19, pp. 136-44.

___ 1830, "Persian Sketches," *The Atheneaum: an original literally miscellany*, Glasgow, 1830, pp.1-11.

___ 1832, "Asiatic Intelligence - Bushire," *Asiatic Journal*, vol. 10 (January-April), p. 34.

___ 1832-1833, *American Railroad Journal*, New York, vol. 1, part I (July-January), p. 797.

___1838, "Communication of Asiatic Intelligence- Persia," *The Asiatic Journal and Monthly Miscellany*, vol. 27 (Sept-Dec.), p. 220.

___ 1865, "A brief account of the province of Fars," *Bombay Geographical Society* XVII, pp. 175-85.

Ansari, Nowshin 1363/1984. "Ketabkhanehha-ye Iran az Ta'sis-e Dar al-Fonun ta Enqelab-e Mashrutiyat," *Ayandeh* 10-11, pp. 667-79.

AP = Accounts and Papers, Government of Great Britain, Parliamentary Papers.

AP 30 (1862) LVIII, Report [on the trade of Persia] by Mr. Eastwick, secretary of the Legation, pp. 68-75.

AP 30-31 (1864) LXI, Remarks by Mr. Consul-General Abbott on the Trade of Tabreez for the Year ending 20th March, 1863," pp. 199-201.

AP 25-26 (1866) LIV, LV, Report by Mr. Consul-General Abbott on the Trade and Commerce of Tabreez for the Year 1865," pp. 474-76.

AP 29 (1867-68) LXVIII, Report by Mr. Consul-General Abbott on the Trade and Commerce of Tabreez for the Year 1866,"

AP 32 (1867-68) LXVIII, Report by Mr. Consul-General Keith Abbott on the Trade and Commerce of Tabreez for the Year 1866," pp. 59-63. ??

AP 34 (1866) LXXII, Report [on the trade of Persia] by Mr. W.J. Dickson, secretary of the Legation,"

AP 29 (1866) LXVIII, Report by acting consul Henry H. Ongley on the Trade and Commerce of Ghilan for the Year 1866."

AP 29 (1867-68) LXVIII, Report by Mr. Consul-General Abbott on the Trade and Commerce for the Year 1867," pp. 499-502.

AP 29 (1871) LXV, Report by Mr. Consul-General Jones on the Trade and Commerce of Azerbijan for the Year 1870," pp. 960-61.

AP 23 (1872) LVIII, Report by Mr. Consul-General Jones on the Trade and Commerce of Tabreez for the Year 1872," pp. 1189-92.

AP 27 (1873) LXV, Report by Mr. Consul-General Jones on the State of Trade in the Province of Azerbijan for the Year 1872," pp. 968-69.

AP 30 (1878) LXXV, Report by Mr. Consul-General Jones on the Trade and Commerce of Tabreez for the Year 1877-8," pp. 1696-98.

AP 37 (1887) LXXXV or DCR 69, Report for the Year 1885 on the Trade of Tabreez by Mr. Consul-General Abbott," pp. 1-3.

AP 39 (1895) XCIX or DCR 1569, Report on the Trade of the Province of Azerbaijan for the Year 1894-95 by Cecil G. Wood," pp. 1-5.

Arnold, A. 1877. *Through Persia by Caravan*. New York.

Bader, Ralph H. 1919. "Persia. Teheran." *Supplements to Commerce Reports, Annual Series*, no. 57a, 4 December. Washington DC: US Government, Department of Commerce.

Ballantine, Henry 1879. *Midnight Marches Through Persia*. Boston-New York.

Bagoz, Ilhan 2007. "Rain making ceremonies in Persia," *Iranian Studies* 40/3, pp. 385-404.

Bashiri, Ahmad ed. 1367/1988. *Ketab-e Naranji. Gozareshha-ye siyasi-ye vezarat-e kharejeh-ye rusiyeh-ye tzari dar bareh-ye enqelab-e mashruteh-ye Persia* 3 vols. Tehran: Nur.

Basu, D. ed. 1985. *The Rise and Growth of the Colonial Port Cities in Asia*, Berkeley, CA.

Bélanger, Charles 1838. *Voyage aux Indes-Orientales pedant les années 1825 a 1829* 2 vols. Paris: Arthus Bertrand.

Benjamin, Israel Joseph. 1859. *Eight Years in Asia and Africa from 1846-1855*. Hanover.

Beth Hillel, David. *The Travels of Rabbi David D'Beth Hillel; from Jerusalem, through Arabia, Koordistan, part of Persia and India*. London, 1832.

Bharier, Julian 1972. "The Growth of Towns and Villages in Persia 1900-1966," *Middle Eastern Studies* 8/1, pp. 51-61.

Bird, J. 1971. *Seaports and sea terminals*. London.

Binning, R.B. M. *A Journal of Two Years' Travel in Persia, Ceylon, etc.* 2 vols. London, 1857.

Böhme, Adolf 1977. *Wir flogen für Iran*. Steinebach-Wörthsee: Walter Zuerl.

Bonine, M.E. 1980. *Yazd and its Hinterland: A Central Place System of Dominance in the Central Iranian Plateau*. Marburg/Lahn.

Braunagel, W. 1925. *Autofahrten in Persien*. Neustadt a/d Haardt.

Brittlebank, William 1873. *Persia during the famine: a narrative of the east and of the journey out and home*. London: Basil Montague Pickering.

Broeze, F. ed. 1989. *Brides of the Sea; Port Cities of Asia from the 16th-20th Centuries*. Honolulu.

Brucks, Captain George Barnes. 1990. "Memoir Descriptive of the navigation of the Gulf of Persia," in Andrew S. Cook ed. *Survey of the Shores and Islands of the Persian Gulf 1820-1829*. 5 vols. Gerards Cross, vol. 1, pp. 123-226.

Brugsch, Heinrich. 1863. *Die Reise der K.K. Gesandtschaft nach Persien 1861-1862*, 2 vols. Berlin: J.C. Hinrichs.

Buckingham, J.S. 1971. *Travels in Assyria, Media, and Persia*. Westmead.

Burrell, R.M. 1972. "Britain, Iran and the Persian Gulf: some aspects of the situation in the 1920s and 1930," in Derek Hopwood ed. *The Arabian Peninsula: society and politics*. London: Allen & Unwin, pp. 160-88.

Burton, Richard Francis 1885-88. "The Terminal Essay, section D," appended to vol. 10 of *The Book of The Thousand Nights and a Night*. 10 vols. London.

Bushehri, Esma`il Nurzadeh 1327/1948. *Asrar-e Nahzat-e Jonub*. Tehran: Tabash.

Busse, Heribert translator 1972. *History of Persia under Qajar Rule*. New York: Columbia UP.

Chirikov, E. I. *Putvoj zhurnal russkogo komissara-posrednika po turetsko-persidskomu razgranicheniyu* (St. Petersburg, 1875) translated into Persian by Abkar Masihi as *Siyahatnameh-ye Mosyu Cherikof*. ed. Ali Asghar `Umran (Tehran, 1358/1979) and partly into English as "Extracts from the Diary of Y. I. Tchirikof," in Schofield, Richard. ed., 12 vols. *Iran-Iraq Border*, vol. 2, pp. 327-471.

Collins, E. Treacher 1896. *In the Kingdom of the Shah*. London: T. Fisher Unwin.

Connolly, A. 1834. *Journey to the north of India overland from England*. 2 vols. London

Cronin, Stephanie 1997. *The Army and the Creation of the Pahlavi State in Iran, 1910-1926*, London: Routledge.

____, 2007. *Tribal Politics in Iran. Rural conflict and the new state, 1921-1941*. London: Routledge.

Cursetjee, C.M. 1918. *A Voyage in the Gulf. The Land of the Date*. San Jose.

Curzon, G. N. 1892. *Persia and the Persian Question*, 2 vols., London.

Davies, Charles E. 1997. *The Blood-Red Flag. An Investigation into Qasimi Piracy 1797-1820*. Exeter.

DCR or Diplomatic and Consular Reports, Government of Great Britain:

DCR 113, Report by Mr. Herbert on the Trade and Industries of Persia AP 85 (1887).

DCR 646, Persian Customs Regulations. (London, 1906). Miscellaneous Series.

DCR 1376, Report for the Years 1892-93 and 1893-94 on the Trade, &c. of the Consular District of Ispahan. Report of a Journey made to Yazd, Kerman, and Shiraz, and on the Trade &c. of the Consular District of Ispahan by J.R. Preece (London 1894).

DCR 1662, Report on the Trade and Commerce of Ispahan and Yezd for the Year 1894-95 by Preece (London 1896).

DCR 2346, Report for the Year 1898 on the Trade and Commerce of the Persian Gulf by Col. M. J. Meade (London, 1899),

DCR 3951 Report for the year 1906-07 on the trade and commerce of Bushire by vice-consul H.G. Chick (London, 1908).

Dehqani, Hoseyn 1389/2010. *Tarikh-e Te'ater dar Bushehr*. Tehran: A'ineh-ye Ketab.

Den Tex, N. J. 1971. "Onze Handel in de Perzische Golf en de Roode Zee," *De Economist* 1, pp. 1-41.

De Panisse, Comte 1867. *La Russie, la Perse, l'Inde. Souvenirs de voyage 1865-1866*. Paris: Jouaust.

Destrée, Annette. 1976. *Les fonctionnaires belges au service de la Perse 1898-1915*. Leiden: Brill.

Dieulafoy, Jane. 1888. *A Suse. Journal des fouilles 1884-1886*. Paris: Hachette & Cie.

Douglas, J.A. 1923. "The Bushire-Shiraz Road," *Journal of the Royal Central Asia Society* 10/2, pp. 104-22.

Driessen, H. 2005. "Mediterranean Port Cities: Cosmopolitanism Reconsidered," *History and Anthroplogy*, 16 (1), pp. 129-141.

Dubeux, Louis 1841. *La Perse*. Paris.

Dupré, A. 1819. *Voyage en Perse fait dans les années 1807, 1808, 1809*. 2 vols. Paris: J.G. Dentu.

Ebtehaj, G.H. 1932. *Guide Book on Persia*. Tehran.

Ehlers, E. 1971. "Die Städte des südkaspischen Küstentieflandes," *Die Erde* 102/1, pp. 6-33.

___ 1975, "Die Stadt Bam und ihr Oasen-Umland/Zentral Iran", *Erdkunde, Archiv für wissenschaftliche Geographie* 29/1, pp. 38-452.

___ 1992, "Capitals and Spatial Organization in Iran: Esfahan, Shiraz, Tehran", in Adle, Chahryar and Hourcade, Bernard eds. *Téhéran Capital bicentenaire*, Paris: IFRI, pp. 155-72.

Elgood, Cyril 1951. *A Medical History of Persia*. Cambridge: Cambridge UP.

Ellis, Lady. 1866. *Memoirs and services of the late Lieutenant-General Sir S.B. Ellis, K.C.B., Royal Marines, from his own memoranda*. London: Saunders, Otley, and Co.

English, Barbara. 1971. *The war for a Persian lady*. Boston.

Entner, Marvin L. 1965. *Russo-Persian Commercial Relations, 1828-1914* Gainsville, Fl.

Eqtedari, Ahmad. 1348. *Athar-e Shahrha-ye Bastani: savahel va jazayer-e Khalij-e Fars va Darya-ye `Oman*. Tehran.

Esfahani, Mirza Nasrollah. "Gozaresh-e Safar-e Ma'muriyati – Bandar `Abbas 1298-1299," in Iraj Afshar, *Daftar-e Tarikh. Majmu`eh-ye Asnad va Manabe`-ye Tarikhi*. Tehran: Bonyad-e Mowqufat-e Doktor Mahmud Afshar, pp. 431-86.

E`temad al-Saltaneh, Mohammad Hoseyn Khan 1363/1984. *Tarikh-e Montazzam-e Naseri*. 3 vols. ed. Mohammad esma`il Rezvani. Tehran: Donya-ye Ketab.

___, *Dorar al-Tijan fi Tarikh-e Bani-ye Ashkan* 1308/1890. 3 vols. Tehran: lithograph.

Ettehadiyeh, Ma`sumeh 1989. "The Council for the Investigation of Grievances: A Case Study of Nineteenth Century Irnaian Social History," *Iranian Studies* 22, pp. 51-61.

Ettehadiyeh, Mansureh and Rudi, Sa`id eds. 1385/2006. *Dar Mahzar-e Sheykh Fazl Allah Nuri: Asnad-e Hoquqi-ye 'Ahd-e Naseri*. Tehran: Nashr-e Tarikh-e Iran.

Faramarzi, Ahmad 1379/2000. "Banader va jazayer-e khalij-e Fars," in eds. Iraj Afshar and Karim Esfahaniyan. *Pazhuheshha-ye Iranshenasi. Namvareh-ye doctor Mahmud Afshar*, vol. 12. Tehran: Bonyad-e Mahmud Afshar, pp. 576-696.

___, 1390/2011. *Sheikh Hoseyn Khan Chahkutahi*. ed. Qasem Ya Hoseyni. Bushehr: Daneshnameh-ye Ostan-e Bushehr,.

Farashbandi, `Ali Morad 2535/1976. *Khandan-e Tangestani*. Tehran: Gahr.

___, 1359/1980. *Tarikhcheh-ye Hezb-e Demokrat-e Fars*. Tehran: Eslami.

Fasa'i, Haji Mirza Hasan Hoseyni. 1378/1999. *Farsnameh-ye Naseri*. 2 vols. ed. Manuchehr Rastgar Fasa'i. Tehran: Amir Kabir.

Floor, Willem. 1971 a. "The office of kalantar in Qajar Persia," *Journal of the Economic and Social History of the Orient, Journal of the Economic and Social History of the Orient*, vol. 14, pp. 253-68.

___, 1971 b. "The market police in Qajar Persia, the office of darughah-yi bazar and muhtasib," *Die Welt des Islams*, vol. 13, pp. 212-29.

___, 1973. "The police in Qajar Iran," *ZDMG*, vol. 123, pp. 293-315.

___, 1979. "A description of the Persian Gulf and its inhabitants in 1756," *Persica* 8, pp. 163-85.

___, 1982. "Bathhouses," *Encyclopedia Iranica*, accessible at www.iranica.com.

___, 1983 a. "Changes and Developments in the judicial system of Qajar Iran," in: *Qajar Iran*, E. Bosworth & C. Hillenbrand eds. Edinburgh: Edinburgh UP, pp. 113-147.

___, 1983 b. "Hotz versus Muhammad Shafi`: a case study in commercial litigation in Qajar Iran," *IJMES*, vol. 15 (1983), pp. 185-209.

___ 1985a. "A Description of Masqat and Oman anno 1673/1084 H," *Moyen Orient & Océan Indien*, vol. 2, pp. 1-69.

___ 1985b. "The office of muhtasib in Iran," *Iranian Studies*, vol. 18, pp. 53-74.

___, 1998a. *The Afghan Occupation of Iran*. Paris: Etudes Iraniennes.

___, 1998b. *A Fiscal History of Iran in the Safavid and Qajar Periods 1500-1925*. New York: Bibliotheca Persica.

___ 1988 c. "Le droit d'entreposage dans Qajar Iran," *Studia Iranica* 13 (1988), pp. 59-77 and 179-182.

___, 1999. *The Persian Textile Industry in historical perspective, 1500-1925*. Paris: L'Harmattan.
___, 2000. *The Economy of Safavid Persia*. Wiesbaden: Reichert.
___, 2003 a. *Agriculture in Qajar Iran*. Washington DC: MAGE.
___, 2003 b. *Traditional Crafts in Qajar Iran (1800-1925)*. Costa Mesa: MAZDA.
___, 2004 a. *Public Health in Qajar Iran*. Washington DC: MAGE.
___, 2004 b. "Tea Consumption and Importation in Qajar Iran," *Studia Iranica* 33, pp. 47-111.
___, 2004 c. "Borazjan in the 19th century," *IRAN* 41, pp. 179-200.
___, 2005 a. *Wall Paintings and other figurative mural art in Qajar Iran*. Costa Mesa: MAZDA
___, 2005 b. *The History of Theater in Iran*. Washington DC: MAGE.
___, 2006a. *The Persian Gulf 1500-1730. The Political Economy of Five Port Cities*. Washington DC.
___, 2006 b. "The importation of indigo into Qajar Iran," *Studia Iranica* 35/2 (2006), pp. 237-259.
___, 2007 a. *The Persian Gulf. The Rise of the Gulf Arabs. The Politics of trade on the northern Persian littoral 1730-1792*. Washington DC.
___, 2007 b. "Dutch wholesalers and retailers in Qajar Persia, 1815-1914," *Studia Iranica* 36/2, pp. 185-226.
___, 2008. "Weights and Measures in Qajar Iran" *Studia Iranica* 37/1, pp. 57-115.
___, 2009 a. *Textile Imports into Qajar Iran. Russia versus Great Britain. The Battle for Market Domination*. Costa Mesa: MAZDA.
___, 2009 b. *Labor and Industry in Iran, 1850-1941*. Washington DC: MAGE.
___, 2009 c. *Guilds, Merchants, and Ulama in nineteenth century Iran*. Washington DC: MAGE.
___, 2010. *The Rise and Fall of Bandar-e Lengeh. The Distribution Center for the Arabian Coast, 1750-1930*. Washington DC: MAGE.
___, 2011 a. *Bandar Abbas, The Natural Trade Gateway to Southeast Iran*. Washington DC: MAGE.
___, 2011 b. *The Persian Gulf. Links with the Hinterland*. Washington DC: MAGE.
___, 2014 a. *The Hula Arabs of the Shibkuh Coast of Iran*. Washington DC: MAGE.
___, 2014 b. *Masqat, city, society and trade*. Washington DC: MAGE.
___, 2015 a. *The History of Bread in Iran*. Washington DC: MAGE.
___, 2015 b. "The Practice of Cursing in Iran," *ZDMG* 165, pp. 155-84.
Floyer, Ernest Ayscoghe. 1882. *The Unexplored Baluchistan*. London.
Fogg, Wm. Percy. 1875. *The Land of Arabian Nights*. Chicago.
Forester, Colonel. 1929. *Economic Conditions in the Persian Gulf* April 1929, Department of Overseas Trade. London.
Fotuvvat, Mehdi 1383/2004. *Ruyaruyi-ye Baqer Khan Tangestani ba lashkar-kashiha-ye englis beh Bushehr*. Bushehr.
Francklin, William 1790. *Observations made on a Tour from Bengal to Persia in the Years 1786-7*. London.
Fraser, J.B. 1826. *Travels and Adventures in the Persian Provinces and the Southern Banks of the Caspian Sea*. London.
___ 1984, *Narrative of a Journey into Khorasan in the Years 1821 & 1822*. New Delhi.
Gamble, F.H. 1935. *Economic Conditions in the Persian Gulf* October 1934, Department of Overseas Trade. London: HMSO
Geary, Gratan 1878. *Through Asiatic Turkey. Narrative of a Journey from Bombay to the Bosporus*. 2 vols. London: Sampson Low, Marston, Searle & Rivington.
Gilbar, Gad G. 1976. "Demographic Developments in late Qajar Persia," *Asian and African Studies* 11, pp. 125-56.
___ 1978, "Persian Agiculture in the late Qajar period, 1860-1906: some economic and social aspects," *Asian and African Studies* 12/3, pp. 312-65.
Gleadowe-Newcomen, A.H. 1906. *Report on the British-Indian commercial mission to south-eastern Persia during 1904-1905*. Calcutta.
Gordon, T.E. 1906. *A varied life; a record of military and civil service, of sport and of travels in India, Central Asia and Persia, 1849-1902*. London: John Murray.
Government of France 1914, *Rapport Commerciaux des agents diplomatiques et consulaires de France* – no. 1079 Perse.

Gouvernement Imperiale de la Perse, 1913a. *Le Fars. La question des Tribus. Situation Politique Generale. Routes du Sud. La reforme administrative*. Tehran.

___, 1913b. "Reformes Administatives," *RMM* 22, pp. 85-150 and *RMM* 23, pp. 1-108.

Government of Bombay, 1856. *Selections from the records of the Bombay Government No. XXIV-* New Series. Bombay. [reprint Cambridge: Oleander Press, 1985]

Government of Great Britain, 1841. *Correspondance relating to Persia*. London: HMSO.

___, 1910. Persia No. 1 (1910). *Further Correspondance respecting the Affairs of Persia*. London: HMSO.

___, 1911. Persia No.1 (1911) *Further Correspondance respecting the Affairs of Persia*. London: HMSO.

___, 1912. Persia No. 5 (1912). *Further Correspondance respecting the Affairs of Persia*. London: HMSO.

___, 1913. Persia No. 1 (1913). *Further Correspondance respecting the Affairs of Persia*. London: HMSO.

___, 1914. Persia no. 1 (1914). *Further Correspondance respecting the Affairs of Persia*. London: HMSO.

___, 1945. *Persia. Geographical Handbook Series*. Naval Intelligence Division. London.

Government of India, *Annual Report* on the Administration of the Persian Gulf Residency for the year 1875-76; 1888-89; 1889-90 in *The Persian Gulf Administration Report 1873-1947*. 10 vols. Gerrards Cross: Archive Editions, 1986.

Government of India, *Report on the Trade of Bushire* 1910-11, 1911-12, 1912-13, 1913-14, in *The Persian Gulf Trade Reports 1905-1940* (Bushire) 2 vols. Gerards Cross: Archive Editions. 1987.

Government of India 1924. *Military Report on Persia* 4 vols. Simla, n.p. (vol. 4, part 2, Fars, Gulf Ports, Yazd and Laristan).

Gray, F. A. G. *Report on the Economic and Commercial Conditions in Iran during 1937*. London, 1938.

Grummon, Stephen R. 1985. *The Rise and Fall of the Arab Shaykhdom of Bushire: 1750-1850*. unpublished dissertation Johns Hopkins University.

Habibi, Hasan and Vothuqi, Mohammad Baqer 1387/2008. *Barrasi-ye tarikhi-ye siyasi va ejtema`i-ye asnad-e Bandar `Abbas*. Tehran: Bonyad-e Iranshenasi.

Hamidi, Sayyed Ja'far1360/1981. *Nahzat-e Abu Sa'id Ganaveh'i*. Tehran.

___ 1380/2001. *Farhangnameh-ye Bushehr*. Tehran: Vezarat-e Ershad.

Hoare, J.N. 1937. *Something New in Iran*. London: CMS.

Höltzer, Ernst 2535/1976. *Persien vor 113 Jahren* ed. Mohammad Assemi. Tehran: Vezarat-e Farhang va Honar.

Hoseyni, Sayyed Abu'l-Hasan 1391/2012. *`Olama-ye Al `Osfur az Bahrayn ta Bushehr*. Bushehr: Daneshnameh-ye ostan-e Bushehr.

Hurewitz, J.C. ed. 1957. *Diplomacy in the Near and Middle East*. 2 vols. New York.

Issawi, Charles. 1971. *The Economic History of Iran*. Chicago: Chicago UP.

___, 1971. "The Tabriz-Tabzon Trade, 1830-1900: rise and decline of a route," *International Journal of Middle East Studies*, 1/1/, pp. 18-27.

Jaubert, P. Am. 1821. *Voyage en Armenie et la Perse*. Paris: Pélicier-Nepveu.

Jonub, Ruznameh-ye 1371/1992. eds. Kheyr al-Nesa (Badr) Tangestani and Ahmad Tangestani. Tehran: `Ali Reza Tangestani.

Kanin, Abdol-Hoseyn 1391/2012. *Joghrafiya-ye Ostan-e Bushehr*. Tehran: Ayineh-ye Ketab.

Kazama, Agu'i 1380/2001. *Safarnameh-ye Kazama. Safarnameh va Khaterat-e Agi'u Kazama nakhostin vazir-e mokhtar-e Zhapon dar Iran (1308 ta 1311 khorshidi)*. Hashem Rajabzadeh tr. Tehran.

Kazeruni, Mohammad Ebrahim. 1367/1988. *Sharh-e Banader va Jazayer-e Khalij-e Fars*. ed. Manuchehr Setudeh. Tehran.

Kempthorne, Lt. G.B. 1835. "Notes made on a survey along the eastern shores of the Persian Gulf in 1828," pp. 263-85.

Keyhan, Mas`ud. 1310/1931. *Joghrafiya-e Mofassal-e Iran* 3 vols. Tehran.

Kinneir, John MacDonald. 1813. *A geographical memoir of the Persian empire*. London: J. Murray.

Küss, Walther 1911. *Handelsratgeber für Persien*. Berlin: n.p.

Landor, A. Henry Savage. 1903. *Across Coveted Lands*. New York.

Lindberg, K. 1955. Voyage dans le sud de l'Iran. Lund: Gleerup

Lorimer, J. G. 1908-15. *Gazetteer of the Persian Gulf, Oman, and Central Arabia*, 2 vols., Calcutta.

MacGregor, C. M. 1879. *Narrative of a Journey through the province of Khorassan* 2 vols. London: Wm. Allen & Co.

MacLean, H. W. 1904. *Report on the Conditions and Prospects of British Trade in Persia*. London: HMSO.

Mahdavi, Asghar and Afshar, Iraj 1389/2001, Afshar, Iraj and Mahdavi, Asghar. eds. *Yazd dar Asnad-e Amin al-Zarb* (Tehran: Farhang-e Iran Zamin, Tehran.

Mahdavi, Mo`ezz al-Din 1342/1963. *Akharin Ma'muriyat*. Tehran: n.p.

Mahrad, Ahmad 1978. *Iran am Vorabend des II. Weltkrieges*. Osnabrück: Eigenverlag.

___, 1979. *Die deutsch-persischen Beziehungen von 1918-1933*. Frankfurt: Peter Lang.

Mafi, Hoseyn Qoli Khan Nezam al-Saltaneh. 1361. *Khaterat va Asnad-e Hoseyn Qoli Khan Nezam al-Saltaneh Mafi*. eds. Ma`sumeh Nezam-Mafi et al. 2 vols. Tehran: Nashr-e Tarikh.

Mahrad, Ahmad 1978. *Iran am Vorabend des II. Weltkrieges: eine Matierialsammlung deutscher, britischer, und sowjetischer Geheimberichten*. Osnabrück: n.p.

___ 1979. *Die deutsch-persischen Beziehngen von 1918-1933*. Bern-Frankfurt: Peter Lang.

Malcolm, T.G. 1887." Resources and Trade of Bushire 7 August 1886," *Reports from the Consuls of the United States* 68, p. 273

Markovits, Claude 2000. *The Global World of Indian Merchants 1750-1947. Traders of Sind from Bokhara to Panama*. Cambridhe: Cambridge UP.

Martin, Bradford G. 1959. *German Persian Diplomatic Relations 1873-1912*. The Hague: Mouton.

Martin, Vanessa and Nouraei, Morteza. 2005. "The Role of the *Karguzar* in the Foreign Relations of State and Society of Iran from the mid-nineteenth century to 1921. Part I: Diplomatic Relations," *Journal of the Royal Asiatic Society* XV/3, pp. 261-77.

Martin,Vannesa 2000. *Iran between Islamic nationalism and secularism: the Constitutional Revoilution of 1906*. London: I.B. Tauris.

___, 2008. "Murder in Bushehr in 1844:the case of Bibi Asilu," *IRAN*, vol. 46, pp. 285-92.

Mashayekhi, Abdol-Karim 1377/1998. *Madraseh-ye Sa`adat-e Bushehr az chand Zaviyeh*. Bushehr: Markaz-e Bushehr-Shenasi.

___, 1382/2003. *`Isaviyan dar Bushehr*. Bushehr.

___, 1391/2012. *Sayyed Morteza Mojtahed-e Ahrami va Mashrutiyat-e Jonub-e Iran (Asnad va Madarek)*. Bushehr: Daneshnameh-ye Ostan-e Bushehr.

Matthee, Rudi; Floor, Willem; and Clawson, Patrick 2013. *The Monetary History of Iran, 1500-1925*. London: I.B. Tauris.

___, 1390/2011. Bandar Bushehr. Pishgam-e madrasehsazi-ye jonub-e Iran. Tehran: Mo'ssaseh-ye Tarikh-e Mo`aser-e Iran

___, 1394/2015. Yad-e Abu Shahr (`aksha-ye qadim-e Bushehr). Bushehr: Bonyad-e Iranshenasi.

Milburn, William 1813. *Oriental Commerce*. 2 vols. London: Black, Parry, and Co.

Millspaugh, Arthur Chester 1973. *The American Task In Persia*. New York: Arno Press.

Ministerie van Buitenlandsche Zaken (the Netherlands), *Consulaire Verslagen en Berichten* no. 48 (25 November 1896).

Mo'azzeni, Hamid 1389/2010. *Sinema dae Bushehr*. Bushehr: Shoru`.

Moberley F.J. 1987. *Operations in Persia, 1914-1919*. London: HMSO.

Mohammadi, Abu'l-Hasan (translator) 1361/1982. *Qesas: tarjomeh-ye ketabi az Masalik al-afham, ta`lif-e Shahid-e Thani, va Sharayi` al-ahkam, ta`lif-e Mohaqqeq Helli*. Tehran: Nashr-e Daneshgahi.

Monteith, William 1857. Notes on the Routes from Bushire to Shiraz, etc., Journal of the Royal Geographical Society 26, pp.108-119.

Mountstuart Elphinstone, 1998. *An Account of the Kingdom of Caubul* (London, 1815] New Delhi: Munshiram Manoharl.

Murphey, Rhoads 1989. "On the Evolution of the Port City," in Broeze, F. ed., *Brides of the Sea: Port Cities of Asia from the 16th-20th Centuries*, University of Hawaii Press, Honolulu, pp. 223-245.

Naofumi, Abe n.d. "Who Acknowledges His Rights. Prelude to the 'modernization' of the Judicial System in Mid-Nineteenth Century Iran as Seen in Persian Legal Documents," [http://utcp.c.u-tokyo.ac.jp/publications/pdf/UTCPBooklet17_03_Abe.pdf].

Nas, Peter J.M. 2005. "Port Cities," *IAES Newsletter* 37, p. 32.

Nateq, Homa 1368/1990. *Iran dar Rahyabi-ye Farhangi 1834-1848*. Paris.

Nezam-Mafi, Ma`sumeh; Mansureh Ettehadiyeh (Nezam Mafi); Sa`vandiyan, Sirus and Ram Pisheh, Hamid eds. 1361/1982. *Khaterat va Asnad-e Hoseyn Qoli Khan Nezam al-Saltaneh Mafi.* 3 parts in 2 vols. Tehran: Tarikh-e Iran.

Nezam al-Saltaneh Mafi 1391. *Asnad va Mokatebat-e Reza Qoli Khan (Salar-e Mo`azzam) Nezam al-Saltaneh Mafi (1321 q/1903 m).* ed. Khadijeh Nezam-Mafi. 2 vols. Tehran: Tarikh.

Norden, Hermann. Under Persian Skies. Philadelphia 1928?

Nura'i, Morteza. 1385/2006. *Asnad-e Kargozari-ye Bushehr.* Tehran: Mo'assaseh-ye Motala`at-e Tarikh-e Mo`aser-e Iran.

O'Connor, Frederick 1931. *On the frontier and beyond* (London: John Murray).

O'Connor, J. E. 1884/85. Review of the Trade of British India for 1878/79-1883/84 India Office, PAP vol. Lviii,

Olivier, G-A. 1807. *Voyage dans l'empire Ottomane, l'Egypte, et la Perse*, 6 vols. Paris.

Oppenheim, M. Freiherr von. 1900. *Vom Mittelmeer zum Persischen Golf*, vol. 2, Berlin. D. Reimer.

Oshkuri, Hasan Yusefi 1369/1990. "Al-e `Osfur," *Da'ereh al-Ma`aref Bozorg Eslami*, Tehran.

Ouseley, William 1819-23. *Travels in various countries of the East; more particularly Persia.* 3 vols. London: Rodwell and Martin.

Pelly, L. 1864. "A visit to the port of Lingah, the island of Kishm, and the port of Bunder Abbass," *Proceedings of the Royal Geographical Society* 8, pp. 251-58.

___, 1865 a. "Remarks on the Tribes, Trade, and Resources around the shore line of the Persian Gulf," *Bombay Geographical Society* XVII, pp. 32-112.

___, 1865 b. "Remarks on a recent Journey from Bushire to Shirauz," *Bombay Geographical Society* XVII, pp. 141-57.

Perry, John R. 1979. *Karim Khan Zand, A History of Iran 1747-1779.* Chicago: Chicago UP.

Pfeiffer, Ida 1852. *A Woman's Journey Around the World.* London.

Pirzadeh, Haji 1343/1964. *Safarnameh-ye* [...]. Ed. Hafez Farmanfarma'iyan. 2 vols. Tehran: Daneshgah.

Plaisted, Bartholomew. 1757. *A Journal from Calcutta in Bengal, by Sea, to Busserah.* London.

Polak, J. E. 1862. "Beitrag zu den agrarischen Verhältnissen in Persien", *Mittheilungen der K.-K. Geogr. Gesellschaft* VI, pp. 107-43.

Political Diaries = *Political Diaries of the Persian Gulf* 1904-1947, 17 vols. n.p. Archive Editions, 1990.

Pottinger, H. 1816. *Travels in Baluchistan and Sind.* London.

Qa'em-Maqami, Jahangir 1340/1961. *Bahreyn va Masa'el-e Khalij-e Fars.* Tehran: Tahuri.

Al-Qasimi, S. M. 1986. *The Myth of Arab Piracy in the Gulf.* London: Croom Helm.

Ragette, Friedrich 2003. *Traditional Domestic Architecture of the Arab Region.* Sharjah: American University.

Ranjbar, Mohammad `Ali ed. 1389/2010. *Fars az mashrutiyat ta jang-e jahani-ye avval.* Tehran: Sazman-e Asnad.

Reza'i, Omid ed. 1387/2000. *Asnad-e Mahkameh-ye Sayyed Sadeq Tabataba`i (Sangelaji).* Tehran.

Rich, Claudius James 1839. *Narrative of a Journey to the site of Babylon in 1811 ... with Narrative of a Journey to Persepolis.* London.

Rishahri, Abdol-Hoseyn Ahmadi 1382/2003. *Sangestan. `Aqayed va rosim-e `ammeh-ye mardom-e Bushehr.* 2 vols. Tehran.

Risso, Patricia 1986. *Oman & Muscat, an early modern history.* New York: St. Martin's Press.

Rivoyre, Denis de. 1883. *Obock, Mascate, Bouchire, Bassorah.* Paris: E. Plon & Cie.

Roknzadeh-Adamiyat, Mohammad Hoseyn 1352/1973. *Deliran-e Tangestani.* Tehran: Eqbal (7th ed.)

Rusta'i, Mohsen 1382/2003. *Tarikh-e Tebb va Tebabat dar Iran (az `ahd-e Qajariyan ta payan-e `asr-e Reza Shah).* 2 vols. Tehran: Sazman-e Asnad va Ketabkhaneh-ye Melli.

Sa`adat, Mohammad Hoseyn 1390/1912. *Tarikh-e Bushehr.* eds. Abdol-Rasul Kheyrandish and Emadol-Din Sheikh al-Hokamayi/ Tehran: Mirath-e Maktub.

Sadid al-Saltaneh, Mohammad `Ali Khan. 1342/1963. *Bandar `Abbas va Khalij-e Fars* ed. Ahmad Eqtedari. Tehran.

___, 1362/1983. *Safarnameh-ye Sadid al-Saltaneh.* ed. Ahmad Eqtedari. Tehran: Behnashr.

___, 1370/1991. *Tarikh-e Masqat va `Oman, Bahrain va Qatar.* ed. by Ahmad Eqtedari. Tehran: Donya-ye Ketab.

___, 1371/1992. *Sarzaminha-ye shomali-ye peyramun-e khalij-e Fars va darya-ye `Oman dar sad sal-e pish 1324-1332 h.q.* ed. Ahmad Eqtedari. Tehran: Jahan-e Mo`aser.

___, 1381/2002. *Seyd-e Marvarid. Al-Manas fi ahval ghavas al-ghavas*. ed. Ahmad Eqtedari. Tehran.

Sa`edi, Gholam Hoseyn 1345/1966. *Ahl-e Hava*. Tehran: Daneshgah.

Safiri, Felurida 1364/1985. *Pulis-e Jonub-e Iran. Es. Pi. Ar.* Translated by Mansureh Ettehadiyeh and Mansureh Ja`fari Fesharaki. Tehran: Tarikh-e Iran.

Saldanha, J.A. 1986. *The Persian Gulf Précis* 8 vols. Gerrards Cross.

Sani` al-Dowleh, Mohammad Hasan Khan 1294/1877. *Mer'at al-Boldan-e Naseri*. 4 vols. Tehran, litho.

Sargent, John 1820, *Memoir of the Rev. Henry Martin*, 2 parts. Boston: Samuel T. Armstrong.

Sarvestani, Mas`ud Shafi`i 1383/2004. *Fars der enqelab-e mashrutiyat*. Shiraz: Bonyad-e Fars-shenasi.

Sayebani, Ahmad 1368/1989. "Badgirha-ye Bandar `Abbas," *Ayandeh* 15/10-12, pp. 868-69.

Sayyah, Hajj 1346/1967. *Khaterat-e Hajj Sayyah ya Dowreh-ye Khowf va Vahshat*. eds. Hamid Sayyah and Seyfollah Golfar. Tehran: Ibn Sina.

Schacht, J. 1987. "Kisas," EI[1] (2nd ed.) IV, pp. 1038-40.

Schneider, Manfred. *Beiträge zur Wirtschaftsstruktur und Wirtschaftsentwicklung Persiens 1850-1900* (Stuttgart: Franz Steiner, 1990).

Schneider, Irene 2002: "Muhammad Baqir Shafti (1180-1260/1766-1844) und die Isfahaner Gerichtsbarkeit," *Der Islam* 70, pp. 252-72.

___, 2006. *The Petitioning System in Iran*. Wiesbaden: Harrassowitz.

Seton, David 1995. *The Journals of David Seton in the Gulf 1800-1809*. ed. Soltan Muhammad al-Qasimi. Exeter: University of Exeter Press.

Shiraz, Ibn `Abd el-Kerim `Ali Reza von 1888, *Das Tarikh-i Zendije*. Ernst Beer (ed.), Leiden: Brill.

Simmonds, S. *Economic Conditions in Iran (Persia)*. London, 1935.

Sirjani, Sa`idi. 1361/1982. *Vaqaye`-ye Ettefaqiyeh. Gozareshha-ye khafiyeh-nevisan-e englisi*. Tehran.

Slaby, Helmut 1982. *Bindenschild und Sonnenlöwe*. Graz.

Stack, Edward. 1882. *Six Months in Persia*. 2 vols. New York: G.P. Putnam's Sons.

Stevens, Roger. 1979. *The Land of the Sophy*. New York.

Stirling, Edward 1991. *The Journals of Edward Stirling in Persia and Afghanistan 1828-1829* ed. Jonathan L. Lee. Naples: Instituto Universitario Orientale.

Stocqueler, J. H. *Fifteen Months' Pilgrimage through untrodden tracts of Khuzistan and Persia*. 2 vols. London: Saunders & Otley.

Sykes, P.M. 1902. *Ten Thousand Miles in Persia*. New York: Charles Scriber's Sons.

___, 1969. *The History of Persia*. 2 vols. London: Routledge and Kegan Paul.

The Naval Annual 1900. ed. Thomas Brassey: Portsmouth: Griffin & Co.

Todd, F.H. 1937. *Report on Economic and Commercial Conditions in the Persian Gulf* 1936, Department of Overseas Trade. London: HMSO.

Tuson, P. 1979. *The records of the British Residency and Agencies in the Persian Gulf*, London, 1979.

Tyan, E. 1965: "Diya," EI[2], II, pp. 340-43.

US Government 1887 *Report of the Secretary of the Navy ... the Two Houses of Congress*. Washington: GPO.

Vadala, R. 2536/1977. *Le Golfe Persique* translated into Persian by Shafi` Javadi as *Khalij-e Fars dar `asr-e este`mar*. Tehran.

Vail Motter, T. H. 1952. *The Middle East Theater. The Persian Corridor and aid to Russia*. Department of the Army: Washington DC.

Vilmorin, A. Lacoin de. 1895. *De Paris a Bombay par la Perse*. Paris.

Vosuqi, Mohammad Baqer 1375/1996. *Larestan va jonbesh-e mashrutiyat*. Qom: Farhang-e Hamsayeh.

Vosuqi, Mohammad Baqer ed. 1381/2002. *Tahavollat-e siyasi-ye safahat-e jonubi-ye Iran. Majmu`eh-ye gozareshha-ye kargozaran-e banader va jazayer-e maskun-e khalij-e Fars*. Tehran: Markaz-e Asnad va Tarikh-e Diplumasi.

Wagenvoort, M. 1926. *Karavaanreis door Zuid-Perzie*. Santpoort.

Wellsted, James Raymond 1840. *Travels to the City of the Caliphs, along the shore of the Persian Gulf*. 2 vols. London: H. Colburn.

Whitelock, Lt. 1838. "Descriptive Sketch of the Islands and Coast situated at the Entrance of the Persian Gulf," *JRGS* VIII, pp. 170-84.

Wigham, H.J. 1903. *The Persian Problem*. New York.

Wilson, A.T. 1928. *The Persian Gulf*. Oxford.

Wirth, Eugen 1976. *Der Orientteppich und Europa*. Erlangen: Fränkische Geographische Gesellschaft.

Wolf, Joseph 1861. *Travels and Adventures*, London: Saunders & Otley.

Wright, Denis 2001. *The English amongst the Persians*. London: IB Tauris.

Ya Hoseyni, `Esmat al-Sadat 1387/2008 a. Torshi, Shirini va Nanha-ye Bushehr. Tehran: Tolu`-e Danesh

___, 1387/2008 b. Ghazaha-ye Mahalli-ye Bushehr. Tehran: Tolu`-e Danesh.

Ya Hoseyni, Sayyed Qasem ed. 1382/2003. *Asnad-e matbu`ati-ye jonbesh-e moqavemat-e jonub-e Iran 1333-1334 q*. Bushehr.

___, 1387/2009. *Zohur va soqut-e khandan-e Tangestani*. Tehran.

___, 1390/2011. *Tarikh-e Chap va Chapkhaneh dar Bandar Bushehr*. Bushehr: Zamzamha-ye Rowshan.

___, 1393/2014. *Ruznameh-ye Mozaffari-ye Bushehr. Vazi`at-e zanan pish az mashruteh*. Tehran: Shirazeh.

___, Yeroushalmi, David 2009. *The Jews of Iran in the Nineteenth Century*. Leiden: Brill.

Yoshida, Masaharu 1373/1994. *Safarnameh-ye Yushida Masaharu: nakhostin ferestadeh-ye Zhapon deh Iran-e dowreh-ye Qajar 1297-1298 hejri qamari*, tr. Hasem Rajabzadeh, Mashhad.

Index

B

C

M

S

T

U

V

W

Y

Z

OTHER MAGE TITLES BY WILLEM FLOOR

THE PERSIAN GULF SERIES

A Political and Economic History of 5 Port Cities, 1500–1750

The Rise of the Gulf Arabs, The Politics of Trade on the Persian Littoral, 1747–1792

The Rise and Fall of Bandar-e Lengeh, The Distribution Center for the Arabian Coast, 1750–1930

Bandar Abbas: The Natural Trade Gateway of Southeast Iran

Links with the Hinterland: Bushehr, Borazjan, Kazerun, Banu Ka'b, & Bandar Abbas

The Hula Arabs of the Shibkuh Coast of Iran

Muscat – City, Society and Trade

IRANIAN HISTORY

Agriculture in Qajar Iran

Public Health in Qajar Iran

The History of Theater in Iran

A Social History of Sexual Relations in Iran

Guilds, Merchants, and Ulama in Nineteenth-Century Iran

Labor & Industry in Iran 1850 -1941

The Rise and Fall of Nader Shah: Dutch East India Company Reports 1730-1747

Games Persians Play: A History of Games and Pastimes in Iran from Hide-and-Seek to Hunting

ANNOTATED TRANSLATIONS

A Man of Two Worlds: Pedros Bedik in Iran, 1670–1675
Pedros Bedik
translated with Colette Ouahes from the Latin

Astrakhan Anno 1770
Samuel Gottlieb Gmelin

Travels Through Northern Persia 1770–1774
Samuel Gottlieb Gmelin

Titles and Emoluments in Safavid Iran: A Third Manual of Safavid Administration
Mirza Naqi Nasiri

IN COLLABORATION WITH HASAN JAVADI

The Heavenly Rose-Garden: A History of Shirvan & Daghestan
Abbas Qoli Aqa Bakikhanov

Travels in Iran and the Caucasus, 1652 and 1655
Evliya Chelebi

www.ingramcontent.com/pod-product-compliance
Ingram Content Group UK Ltd.
Pitfield, Milton Keynes, MK11 3LW, UK
UKHW050954270726
473659UK00006B/34

9 781933 82386